THE AUTHORIZED B...

'Moore's great gift is his abi... p... again ... To understand what ... p... ministership and afterwards, it re... ...ant to understa... ...ho she was: Moore's Thatcher will now be the definitive account' Anne Applebaum, *Daily Telegraph*

'Thrilling ... few authorized biographies are as searching and candid. If, like many of us, you are one of Thatcher's children, and think you know it already, you would be wrong. This is a biography full of revelations' Robert McCrum, *Observer*, Books of the Year

'A triumph. Moore admires his subject, but he is not afraid of her or unwilling to address her failings' Michael White, *Observer*

'Sparkles with insight, drama and wit ... it's a triumph which all future Thatcher biographies will be measured against – and found wanting' John Preston, *Daily Mail*

'Outstanding. Not only is he the first biographer to have had unrestricted access to her personal papers and every surviving private letter written by her, he also approaches each historical event with which she was involved as an opportunity to understand better her personality, beliefs, fears and prejudices' Sir Malcolm Rifkind, *Scotsman*

'He has succeeded in revealing a figure who remains solitary even at moments of triumph, when the world seems at her feet. Her contradictions and complications are explained beautifully ... Anyone looking for the truth about her times will find this a treasure trove ... riveting' James Naughtie, *The Tablet*

'An exceptional political biography with dozens of incidental pleasures ... it is full of Dickensian walk-on parts and deliciously redolent of its period' Philip Hensher, *Spectator*, Books of the Year

'He has spoken to practically everyone who ever had anything to do with her, and interweaves their recollections skilfully to bring out wider themes. He has also been given access to private diaries which bring immediacy to the narrative ... Above all, in this first volume, he has the young Margaret's letters to her elder sister Muriel ... a goldmine ... leaves the reader repeatedly awestruck ... More than just biography, this is excellent history ... a tremendous achievement' John Campbell, *Independent*

'A masterful account of how she came, she saw and she conquered'
Economist, Books of the Year

'For anyone who is seriously interested in Margaret Thatcher
or the political history of Great Britain in the quarter of a century
after her entry into politics, Moore's book is essential reading ... an
immensely impressive achievement and takes its place among
the great political biographies of the 19th and 20th centuries'
Philip Ziegler, *Spectator*

'One of the fascinations of this biography is the way Charles Moore
searches for the underlying personality of Margaret Thatcher,
whom he admires but cannot fully relate to. Good biographies, and
this is an exceptionally good one, tell us things we did not know
about the life of their subject' David Owen, *New Statesman*

'His biography will be the fullest, most objective and best
[biography], not only of Mrs Thatcher, but of any modern politician'
Daniel Johnson, *Standpoint*

'Masterful ... a work of gripping narrative intensity ... Charles
Moore's authorized biography is the source to which debaters
on all sides will apply again and again for facts, insights and
interpretation' David Frum, *Prospect*

'A life's work of research and interviewing ... Moore offers us enough
new material to offer a fresh, even vulnerable person behind the
mythology ... elegant and vivid' Jane Merrick, *Independent on Sunday*

ABOUT THE AUTHOR

Charles Moore was born in 1956 and educated at Eton and Trinity
College, Cambridge, where he read History. He joined the staff of the
Daily Telegraph in 1979, the year Margaret Thatcher came to power,
and as a political columnist in the 1980s he covered several years of
Mrs Thatcher's first and second governments. From 1984 to 1990 he was
Editor of the *Spectator*; from 1992 to 1995 Editor of the *Sunday Telegraph*;
and from 1995 to 2003 Editor of the *Daily Telegraph*, for which he is still
a regular columnist. He lives in Sussex with his wife, Caroline, and they
have grown-up twins. This is his first book. The second and concluding
volume of Moore's authorized biography of Margaret Thatcher, *Herself
Alone*, will be published in 2015.

CHARLES MOORE

Margaret Thatcher

The Authorized Biography
Volume One: Not For Turning

PENGUIN BOOKS

PENGUIN BOOKS

Published by the Penguin Group
Penguin Books Ltd, 80 Strand, London WC2R ORL, England
Penguin Group (USA) Inc., 375 Hudson Street, New York, New York 10014, USA
Penguin Group (Canada), 90 Eglinton Avenue East, Suite 700, Toronto, Ontario, Canada M4P 2Y3
(a division of Pearson Penguin Canada Inc.)
Penguin Ireland, 25 St Stephen's Green, Dublin 2, Ireland (a division of Penguin Books Ltd)
Penguin Group (Australia), 707 Collins Street, Melbourne, Victoria 3008, Australia
(a division of Pearson Australia Group Pty Ltd)
Penguin Books India Pvt Ltd, 11 Community Centre, Panchsheel Park, New Delhi – 110 017, India
Penguin Group (NZ), 67 Apollo Drive, Rosedale, Auckland 0632, New Zealand
(a division of Pearson New Zealand Ltd)
Penguin Books (South Africa) (Pty) Ltd, Block D, Rosebank Office Park,
181 Jan Smuts Avenue, Parktown North, Gauteng 2193, South Africa

Penguin Books Ltd, Registered Offices: 80 Strand, London WC2R ORL, England

www.penguin.com

First published in Great Britain by Allen Lane 2013
Published in Penguin Books 2014
001

Typeset by Jouve (UK), Milton Keynes
Printed in Great Britain by Clays Ltd, St Ives plc

A CIP catalogue record for this book is available from the British Library

ISBN: 978-0-140-27956-6

www.greenpenguin.co.uk

To my father, Richard Moore,
and my mother, Ann,
my first history teachers

and in memory of
Peter Utley and Shirley Letwin

Contents

PART THREE
Power, 1979–1982

I belong to the middle class, and to the strongest part of it . . .
H. Hensley Henson, *Retrospect of an Unimportant Life*, vol. i

Preface

At his trial, Socrates famously said that 'the unexamined life is not worth living'. He had not, of course, met Margaret Thatcher. From childhood, through the whole of her life until the infirmities of old age prevented her, Mrs Thatcher worked without cease. For her, work had a semi-religious significance, and it was the only way of life she knew. Even after she had left politics, she would always say 'There's so much to do!' She hated the fact that she no longer had the chance to do it.

Such people do not look back. Even as they act, they do not pause to observe how they are acting. They focus always on their goals, and have a horror of wasting time. Almost the only sense in which Margaret Thatcher examined her own life was to criticize her conduct on a particular occasion – such-and-such a speech had not been good enough, she had not prepared herself properly for such-and-such a meeting. She did this out of a puritanical desire for self-improvement, to make sure that she performed better next time. She hardly ever sat down to reflect upon the past. It is true that, when she became the leader of the Conservative Party, she ransacked her memory for the small-town stories and paternal precepts which were the foundations of her beliefs, but she did so in order to advance her cause, not in any spirit of autobiographical inquiry. Much of her astonishing energy derived from this lack of detachment: if she had spent time looking back, she would have had less time to press forward. Just by watching Mrs Thatcher in action, noting what the novelist Alan Hollinghurst (in *The Line of Beauty*) called her 'gracious scuttle', her hurrying gait as she moved from meeting to meeting, you could see that hers was a life with no space for self-examination.

Once she had left office in November 1990, however, Lady Thatcher (as she then became) was forced to think about her own story. Publishers were knocking on her door, clamouring for her memoirs. She did not really want to write them, because she always disliked personal disclosure. Indeed, she had no real idea how to set about such a task. She was utterly unlike, for example, Winston Churchill, for whom the books he wrote about what he had done were almost as important as the deeds themselves. But, furious at the way she had been forced from office, she did want to set out the accomplishments of her eleven and a half years as prime minister. She wanted to produce a book which vindicated her beliefs. Her publishers, of course, were more interested in her intimate memories and juicy revelations, so it was a mighty task for her loyal and able team of literary assistants to square this circle. Members of the team recall how difficult it was to persuade Lady Thatcher to come up with the telling anecdotes, personal touches and clear narrative on which good memoirs depend. She found it hard to concentrate on the past, and she disliked the whole idea of revealing anything which had taken place privately. And although her memoirs were written well before the decline in her mental powers which became apparent by the end of the twentieth century, she was not naturally accurate in the account she gave of her own life. Her memory, so amazingly retentive when it came to mastering the facts and figures of government, failed when asked to pin down the details of her own history. She had been too busy living it to have recorded it in her own mind. The two volumes of memoirs which emerged, *The Downing Street Years* and *The Path to Power*, were highly professional accounts. They skilfully replicated on the printed page the tartness which Mrs Thatcher often used in oral expression but which tended to desert her when she wrote things down formally. They coaxed out of her much more than she would ever have produced if she had worked alone. They represented her thoughts and attitudes authentically. But they could never quite overcome the problem that they were the autobiography of someone who did not think autobiographically.

Once the memoirs were out of the way, the question arose of what should happen to the Thatcher papers – the huge number of records accumulated over her political career. Although offered a very large sum of money by an American university, Lady Thatcher declined it, and gave an undertaking to the then Cabinet Secretary, Sir Robin Butler, that her papers would not be disposed of without her first offering them to the nation. Given that her own university, Oxford, had refused her an honorary degree when she was prime minister, she turned instead to Cambridge. In 1997, with the agreement of her family, she offered the papers, on permanent loan, to Churchill College, which has the best archive of modern British political documents. Once this was accomplished, her advisers then raised the matter of a biography. After some discussion, Lady Thatcher reached the view that, since her biography would undoubtedly be written, it would be best not to stand aside from the process, but to choose an author who, in her judgment, could be trusted with paper that had not yet been seen by the public and with the testimony from colleagues and family which the public had not yet heard. In 1997, the choice fell upon me. My impression was that I was chosen mainly for two reasons. As an editor, political journalist and commentator who had followed the period closely, I knew the dramatis personae. And, although my writing had generally been sympathetic to Mrs Thatcher, I was never part of her 'gang'.

The arrangement that Lady Thatcher offered me was that I would have full access to herself, for interview, and to her papers. She would assist all my requests for interviews with others, including access to members of her family. Her writ also extended beyond Britain's shores, particularly across the Atlantic, where numerous friends, acquaintances and former officials agreed to share memories, diaries and documents, many of which had never before seen the light of day. As a result of her support for the book, the then Cabinet Secretary, Sir Richard Wilson, gave permission for all existing and former civil servants to speak freely to me about the Thatcher years, and allowed me to inspect government papers, held back from public view under the thirty-year rule. The permission to study government paper was granted on the understanding that all quotations from them used in my manuscript should be submitted to the relevant departments before publication to make sure that they did not compromise national security. A few minor changes were made, but nothing of substantial importance to the book was removed. The book is not an official history, and so the Cabinet Office had no remit (and no inclination) to influence or suppress any of its views. It is described as the 'authorized' biography, because Mrs Thatcher asked me to write it, but our agreement also stipulated that Lady Thatcher was not permitted to read my manuscript and the book could not appear in her lifetime. This was partly to spare her, in old age, any controversy which might result from publication, but mainly to reassure readers that she had not been able to exert any control over what was said. It was helpful to some of the people I interviewed to know that she would never read what they told me. I was paid not by Lady Thatcher, but by my publishers, Penguin.

It is fair to say that, when Lady Thatcher and I first discussed the project in 1997, she regarded it with the same lack of interest which she usually showed in her own past. Always keen to stick to whatever she had undertaken to do, she granted me several lengthy interviews, and was invariably co-operative. In later years, as her memory declined and long, formal interviews became impossible, she would join me for friendly lunches at which I would extract small nuggets of information from our chats. But what was extraordinary, when one compares it with the way male politicians so often pick over the tiny details of their past achievements, was that she never once urged me to take a particular line, or even inquired what I intended to say about anything. Like all remarkable leaders, she had a great egotism. She always believed that she, and she alone, had rescued Britain from its post-1945 years of semi-socialist decline. She believed that the '-ism' which derived from her married name would make a permanent difference to the story of human freedom. But she was not at all touchy, or even anxious, about what history might say about her.

This put her biographer in an unusual position. Most biographers working on a living subject have to deal with his or her intrusion, over-enthusiasm or hostility. It is difficult for them not to write in their subject's shadow. I kept expecting to come under hers, but I never did. This gave me enormous freedom. On the other hand, Lady Thatcher's lack of aptitude for this sort of work could make her a frustrating source. She could rarely advise me on whom I should talk to about X or where I might find Y. (Luckily, many of those close to her could.) She had turned the key in the lock for me, but seldom seemed to know what was in the room beyond. And when I interviewed her, she found it hard to understand that historical inquiry is not the same as political combat. Her tendency, when asked a question about her past – what her father's political views had been, say, or whom she had known best at Oxford – was to rush from the particular to the general. On one occasion, I asked her a question about her mother's occupations. She replied that her mother had been a good seamstress and 'she did wonderful voluntary work. And that's the thing about the women of Britain – they do wonderful voluntary work – not like French women,' and before I could stop her, she had made her escape from an uncongenial private subject to the area of political generalization which she preferred. Often, when all I wanted was a simple piece of information, I would find myself treated to a disquisition on some great matter like the rule of law, unintentionally provoked by a chance word. Sometimes, when her blood was up, Lady Thatcher would decide to ignore altogether the fact that I was her biographer and would treat me as if I were one of those television interviewers, such as Robin Day, with whom she had jousted over the years. 'You only say that because you're a socialist!' she might shout when she felt in a tight corner, though (as she well knew) I was never a socialist in my life. She had a way, as Alan Clark once noted, of 'jumping the rails' in conversation. This was fascinating to experience, but not easy for the historian.

For most of her career, Margaret Thatcher showed the same lack of interest in her own papers as in her life story. She was one of those tidy people who get a positive pleasure from throwing things away. She saw it as one of the housewifely virtues of which she was proud. Before any general election, she made a point of clearing her desk in case she did not return to it. Whenever she moved house or office, which was fairly often, she threw away great piles of documents. She kept almost nothing from her childhood, and allowed a large number of family papers to be destroyed after her father died in 1970. Very little was retained from Oxford, or from early married life. As well as being uninterested in her own records, Mrs Thatcher was naturally secretive and guarded. She did not believe that others had a right to know about her life outside the public sphere. When, in the course of this work, I discovered more than 150 letters that Margaret had written to her sister Muriel between the end of the 1930s and the beginning of the 1960s, I learnt much more about her private life than had previously been revealed by all the other sources put together. She did keep some press cuttings of her early speeches, but tended to throw away things which she considered more personal. By her own account, she did not see the point of keeping many political papers while she was a young MP, or even when she was secretary of state for education, because 'I just didn't think I was going to be important.' It was only when she stood for the party leadership in November 1974, winning it in February 1975, that she began to keep serious political files. This is attributable more to the fact that she had more people around to organize such things than to any interest of her own in keeping records.

Nor was Mrs Thatcher like those Victorian leaders who wrote voluminous diaries and recorded their thoughts in incessant letters to one another. She never kept a diary. She dashed off enormous numbers of letters (very rarely fully dated), often in her own hand, and with a warmth and charm which delighted the recipients, but these rarely revealed her thoughts in detail. Much more often, they were a few words of thanks, condolence or sympathy. They sometimes contained casual remarks which shed an interesting light on her views, but they almost never set out her reasoning on public questions at any length, or analysed her colleagues closely. She was interested in both these things, but felt safer expressing herself orally. Very occasionally, she put aside time to write her own private account of some important matter. The most striking of these, discussed in this volume, is her account of the Falklands War, which she wrote a year after the Argentine invasion. But, on the whole, the press of business and the fear of leaks reined in any desire she might have had to commit herself on paper. By far the most revealing written records of her political views are the notes she scribbled, as prime minister, on the vast volume of paper which poured across her desk. These were immediate reactions, to be picked up and interpreted by her private secretaries, normally seen by them alone. They are full of her urgent, often angry style, punctuated more by exclamation marks than by full stops, and emphasized by heavy underlining. She wrote hardly any memos herself.

So Mrs Thatcher's biographer finds himself examining a life unexamined by the person who lived it. To me, this makes the work more fascinating. In her story of constant activity, one tries to discern the great themes – the nature of her ambition, the foundations of her beliefs, the development of her political skills, her attitude to love, marriage and family, and her methods of rising and surviving as a woman in a world almost completely controlled by men. The fact that she was the first and only woman leader of a British political party made everything different. It is for this reason that I refer to her, throughout her public career, as 'Mrs Thatcher': that is what people called her, and the word 'Mrs' was very important in their minds. The attitudes of colleagues, rivals and voters towards her – and her approach to them – were radically affected by her sex. Her handbag became the sceptre of her rule. She hardly analysed any of this at all, but she lived it out, often in situations of high drama. My task is to tell this exciting story, and to try to explain – as she never did or wanted to or could – what lies behind it.

There is so much to tell that the biography requires two volumes. I decided that the obvious break which she made in her autobiography – her victory in the general election of 1979 – would be the wrong one. It would make volume two, which would have to contain the whole of her crowded time as prime minister, unnecessarily dense. The break comes, instead, with her victory in the Falklands War in 1982. This was the decisive experience which made her leadership unquestioned within her party. Because of it, she reached her zenith. It provides the natural, climactic moment with which to end the first half of her story.

Readers will see that, once Mrs Thatcher becomes prime minister, there is no easy way to organize the narrative. This is always a problem with the lives of people acting simultaneously in different fields. In many ways, it is preferable to try to tell the story purely chronologically. In politics, as in life, one thing leads to another. It is also valuable, in rendering the life of a prime minister, to show how disparate events cut across one another – a terrorist attack, a bad by-election and a run on the pound may happen all on the same day, and the occupant of 10 Downing Street must deal with all of them at once. In general, I have followed this method. But there are times when a particular subject is so intense, and so separated from the ordinary run of other events, that it has to be treated in a separate chapter. In this volume, I have treated Northern Ireland, the Cold War and the Falklands in this way.

I am also conscious, in writing volume one, that volume two will follow. There are some themes which, though already present in the period covered in the first volume, became more important later. To avoid duplication, therefore, I have given rather little space in volume one to privatization and to Mrs Thatcher's dealings with intelligence. Both of these will be discussed more fully in volume two. The same applies to what might be called the myth of Margaret Thatcher. She became a hate-figure to the left, a heroine to the right, and a leader of immense prestige abroad, particularly in the United States and Eastern Europe. This, too, will be dealt with more fully in the second volume.

Although I have spent my career in journalism, following politics closely, I must admit that I often find political biography dull. The amount of detail can seem disproportionate to the rather moderate interest of the character whose life is related. In the life of Margaret Thatcher, the amount of detail is huge, but the interest of the character does not fail. In the reaction to her death, it has intensified. She is someone about whom it is almost impossible to be neutral. People are fascinated, appalled, delighted by her. Many think she saved Britain, many that she destroyed it. The only thing that unites them is their interest. As she passes from current controversy into history, this interest is undimmed. Mrs Thatcher is becoming a national archetype round whom argument will forever swirl, like Henry VIII, or Elizabeth I, or Nelson, or Winston Churchill. And because of her sex, her beliefs and her character, she is also a global archetype – a leader against whom all others are measured: for some, a cautionary tale, for others, a lodestar.

Acknowledgements

First, I must thank the late Lady Thatcher for giving me the opportunity to write this book. The offer to be her authorized biographer came as a complete surprise, but it was an honour which I could not refuse. She was as good as her word in providing me the complete access, in so many forms – including interviews and the sight of all her papers – which she had promised.

From her offer, help from all other members of her family flowed. I talked extensively to the late Sir Denis Thatcher. Sir Mark Thatcher and Carol Thatcher have both been interviewed for the book and have kindly helped me with information whenever asked.

Lady Thatcher's elder sister (her only sibling), Mrs Muriel Cullen, had never spoken publicly before, beyond one brief press interview many years ago. We met for two substantial conversations before she died. In addition, and with assistance from her son Andrew, she allowed me to read the large and previously completely unknown collection of letters which Margaret wrote to her as a young woman. From the way the letters were piled in old cases and bags in the attic, I formed the impression that no one had re-read them since Muriel first received them. This collection is a treasure trove which gives a unique account of the private life of Margaret Roberts. I was further helped by talk with Mrs Cullen's daughter Jane Mayes, who also furnished me with family photographs. At all times, the Cullen family have shown me great kindness. I particularly appreciate it, because they are people who dislike publicity. Andrew Cullen would much rather be working on his farm. After so much time amid the clashing egos of Westminster, I found this very sympathetic.

Lady Thatcher always managed to command the loyalty of able and efficient personal staff, and they have been immeasurably valuable to me. I think particularly of Mrs Cynthia Crawford, the legendary 'Crawfie', who was rarely far from her boss's side for more than thirty years, Mark Worthington, her long-standing private secretary, Gilly Penrose, until recently her personal assistant, and Kate Sawyer, one of the wonderful carers who made so much difference to her declining years. Julian Seymour, the director of Lady Thatcher's private office, has been the best possible friend I could have had in my endeavours – decisive, funny, resourceful and, when needed, irascible. It was Julian who first conveyed the idea of the biography to me, and it is he who has stuck with me and it from the first.

It was one thing, however, for Lady Thatcher to have the idea, and quite another for me to turn it into something that could be published. For this to happen I depended first on my wise agent, Gillon Aitken, who has looked after me ever since, and then on Penguin, who accepted it. The man who commissioned it there was Andrew Rosenheim, who took a big punt at a time when Margaret Thatcher was much more out of fashion than she is now. The man who succeeded him was and is Stuart Proffitt, the greatest, best educated and most honourable editor in British publishing. Stuart has proved an admirable midwife after a much more than elephantine pregnancy.

There are two main, enormous collections of Thatcher papers. Her personal and political papers are deposited with the Churchill College Archives Centre, Cambridge, which has created a dedicated Thatcher archive to house them. It may give a sense of their scale to consider that, if I lived to be a hundred, and did no other work, I would still not be able to read everything that is there. I am most grateful to Dr Allen Packwood, the director of the Churchill archives, and, above all, to the Thatcher archivist, Andrew Riley. Andrew is one of the two people in the world who know the most about Margaret Thatcher, and his thoroughness, efficiency, good humour and active interest in his subject are beyond praise. This work would have been impossible without him. I should also like to thank his right-hand archivist, Sophie Bridges, and all his staff.

The other person who knows the most about Lady Thatcher is not me, but Christopher Collins. He is the editor of www.margaretthatcher.org, the Margaret Thatcher Foundation website. This pioneering enterprise collates and publishes online everything that she ever said in public, much that she said in private and relevant documents from all over the world. It revolutionizes the study of contemporary history, and will soon be copied everywhere. Nothing is too much for Dr Collins, except the tendency of others to throw away Thatcher papers. To them, he is unforgiving. For me, he is the fount of knowledge.

The government papers, of course, are also vast in scope. Most of those covered in this volume have now been released to the National Archives at Kew. I studied the great bulk of them, however, before they were released, in Whitehall, under the sympathetic protection of Tessa Sterling, Head of Official Histories at the Cabinet Office, and Sally Falk, Deputy Head. Sally, in particular, has been my constant guide for nine years. Neither has lost her patience, even when we all had to move from Admiralty Arch to the new home in the Treasury. I must also salute Chris Grindall, now retired, who brought me up so many files from the distant bunkers beneath. I have greatly profited from working in close proximity to various official historians, including Sir Stephen Wall, Ian Beesley, Gill Bennett and Rodney Lowe. I am also grateful for the wisdom of Patrick Salmon.

The cooperation of the Cabinet Office was offered to me, at Lady Thatcher's request, by the then Cabinet Secretary Sir Richard Wilson, now Lord Wilson of Dinton, who helpfully decided that I should be given the rights of an official (i.e. government) historian, though I am not one. This privilege has continued under his successors, Lord Turnbull, Lord O'Donnell and Sir Jeremy Heywood. Successive prime ministers – Tony Blair, Gordon Brown and David Cameron – have been warmly interested in the project. I should also like to thank Doug King, and other members of the Royal Household for their courteous cooperation.

The archive material about Lady Thatcher in the United States is astonishingly rich. Her relationship with America really was special, and the documentation is huge. Here the bulk of the grinding daily work is not mine, but that of my Director of US Research, Daniel Collings, the most accurate, intelligent and tenacious scholar I have ever worked with, who has laboured for more than eight years in the presidential libraries and other archives. He has also taken on the lion's share of the US interviews, talking to, for this volume alone, almost eighty top American policymakers and a healthy slice of the British foreign policy establishment. My thanks to Anthony Seldon for pointing Daniel my way.

For primary source material on the American side, I owe a great debt to the libraries of Presidents Ford, Carter, Reagan and Bush Sr. Over the years, Daniel and I have filed requests for many thousands of documents, using the Freedom of Information Act and Mandatory Review process. Many of these have borne fruit, and the results lie within these pages. Our guides throughout have been the libraries' hardworking archivists, for whom we have the greatest admiration. We would like to pay particular tribute to the unfailingly helpful and all-knowing Shelly Williams at the Ronald Reagan Library in Simi Valley, California. Keith Shuler at the Jimmy Carter Library in Atlanta, Georgia and Robert Holzweiss at the George H. W. Bush Library in College Station, Texas, also deserve extra special thanks.

My research has benefitted from Freedom of Information Act requests filed directly with the FBI, CIA, the Department of Defense and the State Department. Of these the last has been by far the most productive and I thank all the staff there, especially Lorraine Hartmann, who has overseen repeated appeals with patience and true dedication.

I wish to express my gratitude to the staff at numerous libraries and archives across the United States, including the United Nations, the IMF, the English-Speaking Union, the Library of Congress, the US National Archives, the National Security Archive at George Washington University, the Hoover Institution at Stanford University, the Widener Library at Harvard University, the Mudd Library at Princeton University and the Lauinger Library at Georgetown University.

In the United States, so many former office holders and officials have been extremely generous with their time. I am deeply grateful to all of them. For this volume in particular I learnt a great deal from Zbigniew Brzezinski (who also kindly shared excerpts from his private diary), Richard Allen, Bud McFarlane and George Shultz, all of whom witnessed my subject with their respective presidents at close quarters. As ever, Henry Kissinger provided a unique perspective, particularly on Margaret Thatcher's early experiences in the US. Edward Streator and the late Jim Rentschler also proved deep mines of previously unknown information and gave willingly of their time (and, in the latter's case, his private documents) on multiple occasions. I remain in their debt. Peter Robinson generously shared insights, papers and even his own manuscript on Margaret Thatcher and President Reagan, all of which were of great value to me. From the academic world I would like to thank Professor Douglas Brinkley at Rice University for his help with President Reagan's diaries and Professor Giles Scott-Smith at Leiden University, who generously shared his research into Margaret Thatcher's 1967 visit to the United States.

Other institutions consulted include: the Conservative Party Archive at the Bodleian Library, Oxford; the Archives Nationales in Paris; Somerville College, Oxford (Pauline Adams); Elizabeth Boardman at Brasenose College, Oxford (vital in tracking down Tony Bray); Kesteven and Grantham Girls School; the *Grantham Journal*; and the archive of the English Speaking Union. Professor Sir David Butler, with Professor Denis Kavanagh, has built up a unique record of contemporary interviews about British elections, at Nuffield College, Oxford. It has been invaluable for this book, and David Butler has helped me enthusiastically and generously. I am also, as a long-standing member, always in the debt of the London Library.

Several people have shown me private papers – diaries, letters, etc. – and pictures never before seen. I must particularly thank Marigold Webb, for letting me study the gripping diary of her father, Airey Neave; Sir John Hoskyns, parts of whose diaries have already been published, but whose unpublished bits, now revealed, are even more telling; Megan Reece, for her father's unpublished manuscript; Lord Luce for his, about the Falklands; the late Lord Deedes, my former Editor and for so long my counsellor on Thatcher matters, for various glimpses of his archive; Lady Antonia Fraser, for snippets of her diary; Lady Colnbrook, for private sight of her diaries; Lords Renwick and Hannay for manuscript memoirs; Peter Cropper for his private papers; Sir Malcolm Rifkind for notes from the 1970s; Dame Mary Morrison for photographs and other material; the Mclaren family for pictures of Robert Henderson; Tony Bray for pictures of himself; Mrs Shirley Ellis for photographs of the young Margaret and her in Grantham; Sir Adam Ridley, for his admirably full political papers; Lord Vinson of Roddam Dene for materials about the Centre for Policy Studies; Lady Ryder for notes kept on journeys with Mrs Thatcher; and Mrs Ann Gold for letters of her brother, Edward Boyle.

This book is the first of two volumes, and so not all those who have already helped me feature here prominently or, in quite a few cases, at all. Two vital witnesses, for example – President George H. W. Bush and Lord Powell of Bayswater – are almost invisible in volume one, although, in the case of Charles Powell, everything I write has benefitted from his conversation over many years. I hope that anyone who feels he or she should have been mentioned in these acknowledgments will tell me, but will also feel comforted by the fact that volume two offers me the chance to correct errors and omissions.

The following have kindly given interviews for this volume. Many of them have never spoken before: David Aaron; Sir Antony Acland; Kenneth Adelman; Jonathan Aitken; Andrew Alexander; Richard Allen; Martin Anderson; Charles Anson; Lord Armstrong of Ilminster; Dr John Ashworth; Jacques Attali; Sean Aylward; James Baker; Lord Baker of Dorking; John Banks; Ralph Baxter; Lord Bell; the late Lord Belstead; the late Sir Kenneth Berrill; the late Lord Biffen; Dennis Blair; the late Lord Blaker; Haden Blatch; Michael Blumenthal; Professor Eric Bolton; Sir Clive Bossom; Richard and Veronique Bowdler-Raynar; Sir Rodric Braithwaite; Field Marshall Lord Bramall; Tony Bray; Sheila Browne; the late Lord

Brightman, and Lady Brightman; Lord Brittan of Spennithorne; William Brock; Sir Nigel Broomfield; Dr Harold Brown; Dr Zbigniew Brzezinski; Lord Burns; Richard Burt; President George H W Bush; Professor Sir David Butler; Sir Michael Butler; the late Sir Adam Butler; Lord Butler of Brockwell; the late John Carbaugh; Frank Carlucci; Lord Carrington; Sir Bryan Cartledge; Dr John Casey; Anthony Chamier; Sir John Chilcot; John Clare; Judge William Clark; Sir John Coles; Lady Colnbrook; Robert Conquest; Lord Cope of Berkeley; the late Sir Percy Cradock; Mrs Cynthia Crawford; Chester Crocker; Peter Cropper; the late Lord Cuckney of Millbank; Andrew Cullen; Mrs Muriel Cullen; President Valery Giscard d'Estaing; Ken Dam; John Dauth; Jonathan Davidson; Charles De Chassiron; Timothy Deal; Mrs Jean Dean; the late Michael Deaver; the late Lord Deedes; Professor David Dilks; Lord Dobbs; Lord Donoughue of Ashton; Noel Dorr; Sir Edward Du Cann; Kenneth Duberstein; Andrew Duguid; the late Lawrence Eagleburger; Sir Michael Edwardes; Mrs Shirley Ellis; Sir Brian Fall; Lord Fellowes; Edwin Feulner; Roger Fontaine; Roy Fox; the late Milton Friedman; Robert Funseth; Tessa Gaisman; John Gerson; Sir Martin Gilbert; the late Lord Gilmour of Craigmillar; Dermot Gleeson; David Gompert; Sir David Goodall; Sir Philip Goodhart; Oleg Gordievsky; The Earl of Gowrie; Mrs Patricia Greenough; Alan Greenspan; Lord Griffiths of Fforestfach; the late Mrs Mary Grylls; Lord Deben; Richard Haass; Sir Douglas Hague; the late Alexander Haig; Joan Hall; Peter Hannaford; Lord Hannay of Chiswick; Paul Hare; the late Lord Harris of High Cross; Professor Pauline Harrison; Philip Havers QC; John Hedger; Mrs Madeline Hellaby; the late Mrs Josie Henderson; the late Sir Nicholas Henderson; Lord Heseltine; Sir William Heseltine; Charles Hill; James Hooley; Robert Hormats; Sir John Hoskyns; Derek Howe; Lady Howe of Idlicote; Lord Howe of Aberavon; Lord Howell of Guildford; the late Lord Hunt of Tanworth; Robert Hunter; Lord Hurd of Westwell; Sir Robin Ibbs; the late Fred Iklé; Sir Bernard Ingham; Bobby Ray Inman; John Izbicki; Michael James; Peter Jay; Lord Jenkin of Roding; the late Sir Michael Jenkins; Paul Johnson; the late Frank Johnson; Lord Jopling; Lord Kerr of Kinlochard; Michael and Rachel Kinchin-Smith; Lord Kingsdown; Bob Kingston; the late Jeane Kirkpatrick; Dr Henry Kissinger; Sir Timothy Kitson; the late Lord Laing of Dunphail; Tony Lake; Lord Lamont of Lerwick; Sir Tim Lankester; Gib Lanpher; Lord Lawson of Blaby; the late Sir Frederick Lawton; the late Admiral Sir Henry Leach; John Lehman; Paddi Lilley; Josephine Louis; Lord Luce; Brian MacArthur; Sir Murdo Maclean; Sir Christopher Mallaby; the late Lord Marsh of Mannington; Mrs Jane Mayes; Lord Mayhew of Twysden; Lord McAlpine of West

Green; Romilly, Lady McAlpine; Robert McFarlane; Edwin Meese; Sir Christopher Meyer; Sir Peter Middleton; Vice-President Walter Mondale; the late Sir Fergus Montgomery; Lord Moore of Lower Marsh; Richard Moose; Gwen Morgan; the late Max Morris; Bob Morris; the late Sir Charles Morrison; the Hon Sara Morrison; Robert Moss; Tony Motley; the late Dermot Nally; David Nicholson; Thomas Niles; Dr Edward Norman; Sir John Nott; Sean O'Callaghan; John O'Sullivan; Sir David Omand; Sir Michael Oppenheimer; Stanley Orman; Mrs Amy Ormond; Lord Owen; the late Henry Owen; Sir Michael Pakenham; the late Sir Michael Palliser; Lord Parkinson of Carnforth; Matthew Parris; the late Miss Jane Parsons; Sir Michael Partridge; Lord Patten; Lord Patten of Barnes; Sir Geoffrey Pattie; Michael Pattison; Gordon Pepper; Judy, Lady Percival; Richard Perle; Colin Peterson; Derek and Tessa Phillips; Richard Pipes; John Poindexter; Amanda Ponsonby; Michael Portillo; Lord Powell of Bayswater; General Colin Powell; Charles Price; the late Clive Priestley; Lord Prior; the late Stephen Probyn; the late Sir Michael Quinlan; the late Sir Timothy Raison; Nancy Reagan; the late Sir Gordon Reece; Thomas Reed; the late Lord Rees; the late Lord Rees-Mogg; Lord Renton of Mount Harry; the late Jim Rentschler; Lord Renwick of Clifton; William Rickett; Sir Adam Ridley; Sir Malcolm Rifkind; Mrs Betty Robbins; Roger Robinson; Peter Robinson; David Rockefeller; General Sir Michael Rose; Donald Rumsfeld; the late Lord Runcie; Lady Ryder of Wensum; Lord Ryder of Wensum; Lord Saatchi; Nick Sanders; Dr James Schlesinger; Sir Michael Scholar; Brent Scowcroft; Raymond Seitz; Sir Nigel Sheinwald; Rob Shepherd; the late Sir Alfred Sherman; George Shultz; the late Lord Simon of Glaisdale; Jeremy Sinclair; Fred Silvester (by correspondence); Walt Slocombe; Miss Lorna Smith (by correspondence); Geoffrey Smith; Sir John Sparrow; Mrs Betty Spice; the late Beryl Sprinkel; Sir John Stanley; Sir Kenneth Stowe; Norman Strauss; Edward Streator; Barry Strevens; Nick Stuart; William Taft IV; Sir Teddy Taylor; Lord Tebbit; Carol Thatcher; the late Sir Denis Thatcher; the late Lady Thatcher; Sir Mark Thatcher; Pamela Thomas; Harvey Thomas; Sir Derek Thomas; Lord Thomas of Swynnerton; Major-General Julian Thompson; James Thomson; the late John Tiplady; Ken Tisdell; Gregory Treverton; Lord Turnbull; Hubert Vedrine; Paul Volcker; Sir John Ure; Sir Robert Wade-Gery; Lady Wakeham; Lord Waldegrave of North Hill; Brian Walden; the late Lord Walker of Worcester; Sir Stephen Wall; the late Dr Kenneth Wallace; the late Sir Alan Walters; Sherry Warner; Sir Douglas Wass; the late Lord Weatherill; Marigold Webb; Simon Webley; Shirley and Alan Wells; Sir John Weston; Sir Clive Whitmore; the late Mrs Margaret Wickstead; Philip Wilcox; David Willetts; the late Dr Richard Wirthlin; Paul Wolfowitz; Lord Wolfson; June Wood; Mrs Rita Wright; Lord Wright of Richmond; the late Sir Oliver Wright; Lord Young of Graffham; Dov Zakheim.

A number of others were interviewed on the condition that they remain anonymous. For their help I am deeply grateful.

Scores more have helped in other ways:

– at Penguin Books, Richard Duguid and Rebecca Lee (editorial managers), Peter James (copy-editing), Christopher Phipps and Marian Aird (indexing), Stephen Ryan and Michael Page (proofreading), Ruth Pinkney, Taryn Jones and Rita Matos (production), Jim Stoddart (art direction), Lisa Simmonds and Claire Mason (design), Donald Futers (assistant to Stuart Proffitt) and particularly Isabelle de Cat and Cecilia Mackay (picture research);

– all those who have helped with research. Of these, after Daniel Collings, the one who has put in the most hours is Dr David Shiels, an expert on Northern Ireland. I also, in the early days, employed Matthew Slater and later, from time to time, Peter Snowdon. Jo Dutton tracked down for me Margaret's schoolgirl French penfriend (unfortunately deceased before discovered). This band of 'irregulars' produced excellent and vital work but, as the only person with security clearance for the government papers, I did the great bulk of the British research unaided. I must also thank my sister-in-law, Lucy Coventry, who brought precision to the whole text, and especially to the complicated task of the endnotes;

– while I was still editing the *Daily Telegraph*, I had virtually no time, but I did have a wonderful secretary in Frances Banks and the best driver in the world, Keith Lake. Both of them eased my Thatcher burden greatly. Nowadays, I am assisted at the *Daily Telegraph* by Pat Ventre. It is not her job to help with this book, but her constant support is a great comfort.

The person who has held the project together throughout is Virginia Utley, who was originally my secretary in the 1980s. From maintaining and updating all my contacts, to processing my manuscripts, to keeping order amongst evolving versions of the text, Virginia has proved as invaluable as ever. Her late father, T. E. 'Peter' Utley, is one of the dedicatees of this book. Peter Utley helped form me at the *Daily Telegraph* more than thirty years ago and gave me, with his subtle historical sense, my first understanding of the Thatcher phenomenon.

In all those years, I have always worked for the *Daily Telegraph* or the *Spectator*, or both, and I have covered the story of my subject from that vantage point. Mainly via these two publications, I learnt about the politics, culture and history of the Thatcher era from Bill Deedes, Colin Welch,

Alexander Chancellor, George Jones, Sarah Sands, Andrew Gimson and many more. I have had innumerable conversations – both 'grave and gay', as people used to say – with Ferdy Mount, Dean Godson, Nicholas Garland, who sees it all with an artist's eye, and my dear friend Frank Johnson, who died before his time. All that talk informs this book. I must also thank my proprietor for most of my time as an editor, Conrad Black. He appointed me to two of my three main jobs, and kindly allowed me to take on the Thatcher contract despite my editorship of his main paper.

My thanks are also due to the present owners and management of the *Daily Telegraph*. Sir David and Sir Frederick Barclay, and Sir David's son, Aidan, have always been enthusiastic about my study of the woman they all admire. So have the chief executive, Murdoch MacLennan, my editor, Tony Gallagher, and the deputy editor, Ben Brogan. They showed this by serializing the book. I am also grateful to Richard Preston, Chris Deerin and Robert Colvile. All have been supportive throughout, even when Thatcherizing has threatened to get in the way of daily work. So has Fraser Nelson, the editor of the *Spectator*.

As well as formal interviews, conversation about my subject with political practitioners who are also friends has been of immense value. Many of these conversations took place before I knew I would be writing this book, but are no less helpful for that. I think particularly of William Waldegrave, the late Nick Budgen, Robert Salisbury, Frank Field, Norman Tebbit, Peter Carrington, Alistair McAlpine, Richard Ryder and the late Alan Clark. (The last was undoubtedly unreliable, but often brilliantly perceptive.)

Sir Martin Gilbert and Andrew Roberts, at my request, kindly advised me how to write a political biography.

I have also talked often and informally to people who knew the private Margaret Thatcher for many years, notably Caroline Ryder, Amanda Ponsonby, Romilly McAlpine, Cynthia Crawford and Carla Powell. Unstructured chat with such friends has helped me understand Mrs Thatcher, the woman.

Coming from a journalistic background, I knew much less about the civil service than about politics. It has been fascinating to talk to so many public servants of the Thatcher era. Because they are trained to take notes, they tend to have more accurate memories than politicians, who are forever rushing. The best witnesses to Mrs Thatcher's working life were often her private secretaries, to most of whom I have spoken. In the period covered by this volume, I am particularly grateful to Sir Bryan Cartledge, Sir John Coles, Sir Michael Scholar and Sir Clive Whitmore for the time they gave me and the thought they put into it. I must also mention the former Cabinet Secretary, Lord Armstrong of Ilminster, whose precise mind and memory remain completely undimmed and whose supply of perceptive insights and anecdotes seems never to dry up. His successor, Lord Butler of Brockwell, has been equally helpful, chiefly with the second volume. Alan Petty has helped guide me towards the less visible parts of government.

In my Thatcher travels, I have been sustained by much hospitality. I am particularly grateful to Richard and Veronique Bowdler-Raynar, who invited me to stay at Schloss Freudenberg – almost the only place Mrs Thatcher would consent to visit for a holiday; Philip and Isabella Naylor-Leyland, at Milton, scene of the great Falklands rally; Charles and Carla Powell in the Campania; Romilly McAlpine in Venice; and Julian and Diana Seymour at Restharrow.

Richard and Kate Ehrman tolerantly kept a bed for me whenever I visited Oxford to consult archives or interview the retired civil servants who so often end up being Heads of Houses there. Richard and Kate also read and commented on my manuscript with great care, as did Noel Malcolm, Fellow of All Souls, Harold James, Professor of History and International Affairs at Princeton (all the material dealing with the economy), Andrew Riley, Archivist of the Thatcher Papers, my father, Richard Moore, and my father-in-law, Ralph Baxter. Kate Ehrman's additional kindness was to hold my hand whenever I attempted to speak, read or listen to the French language.

Over many years, my most frequent talks about my subject have been with the Ehrmans, with Oliver and Isabel Letwin, and with Owen and Rose Paterson. In all these cases, the context has been friendships going back for more than 30 years. This is the best sort of talk, and I can never thank them enough. Oliver's late mother, Shirley, is a dedicatee of this book.

My special thanks should go to Tommy, my hunter who jumps everything, and to Diana Grissell, MFH, who directs his care. They have been essential to my sanity.

Finally, I must thank my family, especially my sister, Charlotte, and my brother, Rowan. As far as I know, no Moore of my line, apart from me, has ever supported Margaret Thatcher. In many ways, this has been a good place for her biographer to start: in studying my subject I have enjoyed what feels like a forbidden pleasure. Besides, without my parents, Richard Moore and Ann Moore, I might never have learnt the fascination of history. This book is dedicated to them.

Our twins, Kate and William, were seven when this project began, and now they are adults. Except for the incident when Will lost the entire manuscript when playing, without permission, on my computer, they have been models of good behaviour and good fun. Because they were born in the last year of Mrs Thatcher's premiership, they give me a perspective which someone like me, who first voted in 1979, would otherwise lack. My wife Caroline has been consistently loving and tolerant as I have spent so much time, for so long, with 'the other woman'. I am more grateful to her than I can say.

List of Illustrations

PART ONE

The approach, 1925–1959

I

Grantham

'Mahogany and child'

Phoebe Stephenson took her granddaughter Muriel Roberts upstairs. Through the bedroom door came the cry of a newborn baby. 'Can you hear something?' Phoebe asked the four-year-old Muriel. 'I said "no",' Muriel recalled more than seventy years later. 'I *could* hear something but I wouldn't say so.'[1] With this lack of fanfare, on 13 October 1925, the future Margaret Thatcher came into the world.

She was born Margaret Hilda Roberts, in the house of her parents Alfred Roberts and his wife Beatrice Stephenson – 1 North Parade, Grantham, Lincolnshire. They lived above the shop, a grocery that Alfred Roberts had bought in 1919. Muriel was Margaret's only sister. The Robertses had no sons.

The son of a bootmaker from Ringstead in Northamptonshire, Alfred Roberts had left school at the age of thirteen because of the need to make a living, but he longed for education, and acquired it by voracious reading and study. He had risen through the retail trade, having, early in life, been an assistant in the tuck shop at Oundle School. He was a local preacher (what Anglicans would call a lay preacher) in the Methodist Church, and a few notes for his sermons survive. In these, the only trace of his lack of formal education is the occasional misspelling – 'attemp', 'waisting your time', 'beleif', 'desease'.[2] The hand is elegant and the expression clear and fluent.

On one page of an old schoolbook, in notes for a sermon delivered after the Second World War,[3] Alfred Roberts reflects on 'The neglected length of mahogany counter' and what might be made of it: 'what a thing of beauty it became when the craftsman contributed all his skill of polishing. But the beauty was there, just waiting to be revealed.' On the same page, Roberts offers another example:

> The neglected child, ragged, dirty, unattractive, removed from the squalor of a home and parents who showed her no love or care, to foster parents who brought love, care and affection into its life. What a transformation.

The child was gloriously beautiful, a most lovable disposition, and infectious cheerfulness. These things were there all the time but only when someone made their full contribution did they become part of human experience.

When Alfred Roberts's younger child had made her 'full contribution' to her country, she re-read these notes, in preparation for her memoirs, and linked the two stories. On a yellow Post-it note stuck to the page, she wrote 'Mahogany and child'.

The mahogany counter with which Margaret grew up and across which she sometimes served customers was always beautifully polished. 'If you get it from Roberts's . . . you get – THE BEST' boasted an advertisement in the *Grantham Almanack* in 1925, and those who remembered the grocer's shop said that the boast was justified. Although North Parade is beyond the end of Grantham High Street, better-off families from the centre of town would make the extra journey for the extra quality. Mary Wallace, for example, whose father was the leading dentist in the town, and who was almost the only other Grantham girl of Margaret's generation to go to Oxford, remembered her mother doing so.[4] Margaret herself lovingly recalled: 'Behind the counter there were three rows of splendid mahogany spice drawers with sparkling brass handles, and on top of these stood large, black, lacquered tea canisters . . . In a cool back room . . . hung sides of bacon which had to be boned and cut up for slicing. Wonderful aromas of spices, coffee and smoked hams would waft through the house.'[5] Mary Robinson, who worked as an assistant in the shop, remembered that it had 'better biscuits' – a key quality indicator at that time – than Roberts's commercial and political rival, the Co-op.[6]

The shop stood on a corner between the richer and poorer districts of the town, and served both of them. As well as being a high-class provision merchant, Roberts's was also a post office, and therefore served the clients of the early welfare state. Poverty and bourgeois comfort lived close to one another, and Margaret used to walk past the labour exchange on her way to Kesteven and Grantham Girls' School, although by the time she entered KGGS in 1936 unemployment in Grantham had halved from its peak of 2,300 in 1933. Seventy years later, she remembered a widow in black entering the shop with two small children: 'She asked if she could have three small oranges for the price of two because she had to be so careful.'[7] She explained, 'Life was not something we did not know about. We were right in it.'[8]

The Robertses saw it as their duty to help in a small and discreet way where they found distress. Every Thursday afternoon, which was early closing day for the shop, Beatrice Roberts would have a 'big bake'. Two

or three of the loaves would go out to 'people we knew' who were on hard times. The act of charity had to be obscured before it could be accepted: Margaret would hand over a loaf saying, 'Mother's had a big bake and she wondered whether you would like this. It is home-made, and it's better than bought ... You had to be very careful. People ... are very proud.'[9]*
According to Muriel, fellow Methodists regarded Roberts as almost a soft touch: 'If they wanted money, "Oh, Alf will give us some." We hadn't got it but we gave it.'[10] But, like the man in the song, Alfred Roberts did well by doing good. The shop prospered. He added the premises of 2, 3 and 4 North Parade to those of No. 1 with which he had started, and not long before Margaret's birth he opened a second shop in Huntingtower Road, about a mile away towards the station. It was opposite this that Margaret attended her first school, Huntingtower Road County Elementary School. Roberts never became rich, and when he died in 1970 he left little more than his modest house and a few pieces of furniture: of the chattels, his famous daughter took only two chairs.[11] But he established a secure and respected business, which gave him the base from which to serve the town as a councillor, a Rotarian and a Methodist.

The base was quite austere. The house had no garden, no hot water, and an outside lavatory. After the war, during which Roberts's reliability and efficiency as a grocer had allowed him to increase his wealth in the era of rationing when these qualities were at a premium, Roberts could afford to buy a separate house, with a garden, at No. 19 in the same street. It was called Allerton, named, as suburban houses of that date often were, after an aristocratic seat, in this case that of the Stourton family in Yorkshire. But, all the time that Margaret was living exclusively at home, home was 1 North Parade. She was proud of the business and intensely proud of her father, but she could early see the limitations of where she lived. In 1985, she told Miriam Stoppard: 'Home really was very small and we had no mod cons and I remember having a dream that the one thing I really wanted was to live in a nice house, you know, a house with more things than we had.'[12]

Home was strict as well as small. It was dominated by work, and by religion. The shop was open until 9 p.m. on a Saturday and 8 p.m. on a Friday. Monday was washing day, and Tuesday ironing.[13] Because of the demands of the shop, Margaret 'never went on holiday with Mum and Dad',[14] and because of the prevailing atmosphere of constant work, she

---

* This was a traditional form of charity. In George Eliot's *Silas Marner*, Dolly Winthrop, the wheelwright's wife, brings poor Marner some lard-cakes, imprinted with the initials of Jesus, giving the excuse that she has had a baking the day before and that the cakes are more than she needs.

never daydreamed or was idle. As her daughter Carol put it, 'She never experienced nothingness.'[15] Sunday was a day of almost continuous religious activity. Alfred Roberts's preaching circuit was centred on Finkin Street Methodist Church, a handsome building in the middle of the town. The family attended Sunday services there, and sometimes at the much closer chapel in Brownlow Street. There was Sunday school at 10 o'clock, morning service at 11 o'clock, afternoon Sunday school after lunch and another church service in the early evening. For almost half the Sundays in the year, her father was out for part of the day preaching in surrounding villages. His role often meant that he brought visiting speakers home, and on more than one occasion these speakers, from far-flung regions where Methodism was spreading, were black, an extreme rarity in Grantham at that time.[16] It seems to have been meeting Methodist missionaries from India that inspired Margaret with her ambition, curious in someone little more than a child, to join the Indian Civil Service. After listening to them, she remembered, 'I wanted to be an Indian civil servant, because I thought that India was a remarkable place and I would love to be a part, a cog in the wheel, of this great empire. And I think my father said to me at one stage, "I'm not sure if it'll be part of the British Empire by that time."'[17] Margaret appreciated and even enjoyed many aspects of Methodism. She loved the 'powerful combination' of the teaching of John Wesley and the hymns of his brother Charles.[18] She participated fully in the musical life, as did her parents (she was a mezzo-soprano, her mother a contralto and her father a bass; both she and her mother played the piano, and when she was eighteen she learnt the organ). In her memoirs, she notes that she first learnt to play on a piano which was inscribed with the name of the maker John Roberts, her great-uncle, who also made church organs.[19]* And she also enjoyed the conversation on public questions which tended to take place in the parlour of the shop when Methodists repaired there after the evening service on Sunday.[20] 'Father taught me to like what he called "discussion",' she recalled.[21] Although she attended the Church of England in later life, appearing in her last years every Sunday at the services in the Royal Hospital, Chelsea, Margaret Thatcher never repudiated the Methodism of her childhood, with its reverence for truth-telling, hard work and putting into practice the teaching of Scripture. Her father's sermon notes

---

* This tradition of music mattered to the Roberts family. After he retired from his business, Alfred Roberts stayed with a friend and helped him repair the organ at Marston church. He wrote to Muriel about it: 'It's strange that I should be doing this sort of work following in the footsteps of the Roberts family' (27 April 1961). When his widow, Cissie (Margaret's stepmother), moved out of Allerton in 1982 she offered Margaret the piano.

are full of precepts and expressions which one almost can hear her own lips speaking: 'There is no promise of ease for the faithful servant of the Cross,' 'God wants no faint hearts for His ambassadors,' even 'We must avoid the principle of a Denominational Closed Shop.'[22] 'We were Methodist and Methodist means method,' Margaret told one biographer.[23] She always loved method.

She also studied her father's speaking technique. 'Have something to say. Say it as clearly as you can. That is the only secret of style,' he wrote in his sermon notes,[24] quoting Matthew Arnold, and she never diverged from this view. She watched him reworking the ideas of the Gospel: 'he always found a new way of putting the message ... There aren't any new messages. There aren't any new sins. But you have to find a way of putting it which is in keeping with the times.'[25] She admired his methods, but also observed with a critical eye. Speaking of him in the present tense thirty years after his death, she said: 'He's not very demonstrative. He's very thoughtful ... Sometimes I'd say, "Pa, that was your sermon voice, your sermonizing voice" and then it would be a bit lighter. If you're giving a message from the Old or New Testament you're conscious of a responsibility ... If you're giving a message which is your beliefs you are also conscious of a responsibility but you're not necessarily interpreting your Maker but doing yourself.'[26]

Margaret was always very restrained in any criticism of her upbringing. She permitted herself only a few guarded remarks. She said that the family's religious life set them 'a little bit apart ... from one's fellows' and that church 'can be slightly overdone'. 'You must never be like the parable of the Pharisees [Luke 18:9–14] ... because you just really know how you fall short of the ideal.'[27] She indicated how much she enjoyed visiting her schoolfriend Jean Farmer, whose father was a builder at Fulbeck, 10 miles outside Grantham, where the atmosphere was freer and more joyful. When staying there, she told one biographer, 'they all went to tennis together. They all went to dances together. They would all do far more of those things – out with other people where there was laughter and fun!'[28] Jean Farmer in turn remembered a serious atmosphere in the Roberts household, with Alfred Roberts as 'one who didn't unbend'. She was 'a bit in awe of him'.[29]

Margaret's elder sister, Muriel, however, was harsher about the girls' religious upbringing. 'It was all church, church, church,' she said. 'We had an uncle every Christmas who sent us religious books. Oh God how we hated it. You weren't allowed to play games. That really is bigoted, isn't it?'[30] Roberts's grocery stood immediately opposite the Roman Catholic church of the town and Alfred Roberts had friendly relations with Father Leo Arendzen, the popular parish priest. But when Father Arendzen one day invited him over to see the pictures in the church, Roberts refused, saying, 'No, no, no. I'll never put my foot inside a Catholic church.'[31] Later, when Margaret was the young candidate in Dartford, her parents worried that one of her friends was a Catholic, and that she might fall under her influence, though in fact the woman in question was a 'slave to Margaret' and not the other way round.[32]* Such attitudes were not at all uncommon at that time, and there is other evidence that Alfred Roberts was quite broad-minded about religious affiliation. Margaret's schoolfriend Margaret Goodrich, for example, recalled that his friendship with her father, an Anglican clergyman, was notable for its interdenominational warmth.[33] But it seems fair to say that the Robertses, being serious about all such things, made their daughters feel them more than would have been the case in most families. When Margaret came to have children of her own, Beatrice Roberts protested when she learnt that they were taken to the Church of England rather than to Methodist services.[34]† In the minds of the Roberts girls, the blame for restriction and narrowness fell on their mother, not their father. It has been written that Margaret was Daddy's girl, and that Muriel was closer to her mother. According to Muriel, this was not so, or rather the closeness to the father was true of both girls, not only of Margaret. Throughout his later years, particularly as a widower, Alfred Roberts kept up a closer correspondence with Muriel than with Margaret (this was partly a matter of time, because of Margaret's busy career, but then matters of time are often matters of something else as well): 'I think, if anything, I was closer to him than she was. It was always to me, even in later life if there was any trouble, that he came.'[35] In fact, Roberts's surviving letters (which are all post-war) show love for both his daughters, though sprinkled with small reproaches to Margaret for not paying him quite enough attention. And it is certain that in everything he did he tried to advance his girls. In the middle of the war, he went to Canon Goodrich, seeking help to prepare Margaret for the general paper in her university entrance. 'My great wish', he told Goodrich, 'is to get Margaret into Oxford. I wonder if you could coach her.'[36] This was not the action of a paterfamilias who wished to keep his daughter tied to hearth and home. 'He wanted me to have what he hadn't had,' his daughter recalled.[37]

---

* Margaret herself recalled being envious of Catholic girls because of the ribbons they wore for First Communion. In her childhood, she said, a Methodist girl caught wearing ribbons would be told, 'First step to Rome!' (Correspondence with John O'Sullivan.)

† Margaret was always very vague about the sacramental aspect of religion. When the present author asked her, at the baptism of Oliver Letwin's twins (to one of whom she stood godmother), about the baptism of her own twins, she said perplexingly, 'Oh well, they were christened, but they didn't have the water.'

In Muriel's view, Beatrice Roberts was 'a bigoted Methodist . . . Margaret and I weren't close to her . . . We just didn't click with her.' As a result, Muriel believed, Margaret grew apart from her mother as quickly as she could: 'Mother didn't exist in Margaret's mind.' Margaret always expressed herself more charitably and tactfully on the subject, but without much enthusiasm. Famously describing herself in *Who's Who* as '*d* of late Alfred Roberts', with no mention of her mother, she tended to speak of Beatrice, if at all, in a subsidiary role. Asked by Miriam Stoppard, 'What example did your mother set you, as opposed to your father?' Margaret Thatcher replied: 'Oh Mummy backed up Daddy in everything as far as you do what is right.' She explained her role by recourse to the Bible, or rather, the Bible as reworked by her beloved Rudyard Kipling in his poem which Mrs Thatcher referred to as 'The Mary and the Martha' (its actual title is 'The Sons of Martha'): 'Mary was the one who listened at the feet of Jesus and always was interested in what was going on and Martha was the one who always went, "Now is there enough to eat?" "Do you want fresh clothes?" "Would you like to lie down?" This was my mother . . . I still retain it.'[38]

It is telling that Margaret retained the Kipling version, because it is highly complimentary to the Sons of Martha (it is a pity that he had nothing to say about the Daughters of Martha). The Sons of Martha are the people in life who make sure that God's work is actually done:

> They do not preach that their God will rouse them a little before the nuts
>   work loose.
> They do not teach that His Pity allows them to drop their job when they
>   dam'-well choose.

Rather do they see things through to the end without pretension:

> Not as a ladder from earth to Heaven, not as a witness to any creed,
> But simple service simply given to his own kind in their common need.

There is nothing that Margaret Thatcher admired more than 'simple service simply given', and she believed that that was what her mother contributed.

But she did not like it much at the time. The letters she wrote to Muriel in the 1940s mention their mother often, but almost always in passing and usually in connection with some prohibition. In the summer of 1944, she asked Muriel: 'Do you think the person who makes the handbags could make me one in maroon leather like your blue one. I have decided that maroon would be the best colour for my wardrobe as I am having that pinky dress made up . . . I haven't told Mummy or Daddy about this as I am sure that Mummy at any rate would think it very extravagant.'[39] In the same year, during the long vacation after her first summer at Oxford, she indicates a sense that she has become intellectually more sophisticated than her mother. She went with Beatrice to see *Now, Voyager*: 'I have never liked Bette Davis but nevertheless I thought she was simply marvellous in that film.' Mrs Roberts, though, did not like it so much: 'I think she would have preferred it to end happily ever after sort of style.'[40] Perhaps it is not surprising that Beatrice Roberts had her reservations, since the film concerns a daughter's defiance which so shocks her overbearing mother that she dies of a heart attack. 'I loved her dearly, but after I was fifteen we had nothing more to say to each other.' Before the age of twenty, Margaret was leaving her mother behind.

It would be a mistake, though, to think that the mother's influence was ever expunged from her daughter's character. Jean Farmer, the closest friend of her youth, thinks that 'Margaret probably absorbed more from her mother than she realizes – she was a hard worker, ran her house really well and helped in the shop.'[41] Margaret Thatcher was herself always more a Martha than a Mary: she loved domestic labour, finding it therapeutic to cook, to sew, to decorate her house and to clean. She was an enthusiastic home-maker. It was sad and touching, in her old age, for staff to find her, lost for something proper to do, clearing out and relining drawers which were already spotlessly tidy.[42]

Beatrice Stephenson, the daughter of a cloakroom attendant at Grantham station, had been a professional seamstress before she met Alfred Roberts through the Methodist Church and married him in 1917, and she taught her daughters the finer points of sewing and how to adapt existing material for new uses. Margaret followed closely her mother's precept, 'Never leave the house looking untidy,'[43] and when Margaret Thatcher was bringing up her own children in the 1950s she did not forget her practical lessons. One contemporary at the Bar remembered Mark and Carol wearing duffel coats lined with their old nursery curtains.[44] In the more than 150 letters from her to Muriel that survive, clothes (quite often illustrated by rough drawings) are a far more common subject of discussion than politics, and in her eighth decade Margaret could still remember minute details about what she had worn as a child. Thus she described the dress that her mother had made her for the Christmas party of the League of Pity (now the NSPCC): 'It was of soft pink satin: eight or nine rows of smocking in pale blue and below, pink and blue ribbons, with a flat bow at the back ...'* Nor did Margaret forget the more general example

---

* It is also true, however, that Margaret was a little embarrassed that she and Muriel always wore the outfits that their mother had designed for them. It made her self-conscious 'that our things were different from others' (Patricia Murray, *Margaret Thatcher*, W. H. Allen, 1980, p. 22).

behind these domestic accomplishments. Throughout her life, including at the zenith of her power, she liked to remember human need – for food, or comfort, or praise, or consolation, though not, unless heavily prompted, for sleep. The unanimous testimony of Margaret Thatcher's personal staff is that she noticed their small needs and took personal pleasure in satisfying them. Indeed, her fussing round people was her favoured way of showing affection and concern: she loved to be practical, to feel that she had helped in a tangible way. She might leave her husband each morning to go and run the country, but not before she had cooked his breakfast. All this was the legacy of Beatrice Roberts.

What bothered Margaret in later life, though, was a sense of guilt. She felt that she had been unappreciative of her mother, and, unlike with her father, whom she believed to be the greatest positive influence in her life, found it difficult to light on the right words in public to convey her belated appreciation. In the end, she said simply: 'I don't think I thanked my mother enough, because you don't realize . . .'[45]

What did others think of the Robertses? Alfred Roberts made a strong impression. He was 6 foot 2 inches tall, with piercing blue eyes and wiry blond hair that turned white quite young. The prevailing view in the town was favourable. To the young Margaret Goodrich, he was 'a dignified, unusual sort of chap'.[46] Rita Hind, another fellow pupil of Margaret Roberts at KGGS, remembered that 'whenever his name was mentioned, it was mentioned with great reverence.'[47] Another schoolfriend, Shirley Walsh, described Roberts as 'a delightful man'.[48] According to Nellie Towers, a fellow Methodist, the town librarian told her that Roberts was 'the most well-read man in Grantham'.[49] Roberts was chairman of the library committee, and one of his daughter's most often repeated memories is of going with him to the library every Saturday to borrow a serious book for him and a light novel for her mother.[50] Mary Robinson, also a fellow Methodist, was employed by Roberts in the shop to help her after her father's death. This was an act of kindness on his part which he compounded by paying her five shillings per week more than had been agreed.[51]

There are opposing views, though they are harder to find. Kenneth Wallace, son of the Roberts's dentist, was fond of Margaret and used to invite her round to listen to his collection of classical records – Sibelius, Beethoven. He thought her friendly and a 'good conversationalist' but he found her background 'very limited', and guessed (a surmise which is confirmed in her own correspondence with Muriel) that 'she enjoyed the company of a more cultured family than her own'. He found Roberts unnecessarily strict about allowing young men into the house (not that he was ever Margaret's boyfriend) and thought his manner 'patronizing'.[52] His sister, Mary, found Roberts 'rather forbidding' and the speeches (which, as a local worthy and governor, he sometimes made at the school) almost unendurable: 'They said nothing whatsoever – he would just point his finger at us and proclaim "And what I say is true."'[53] Both of them give countenance to the theory, also supported by Nellie Towers, that Alfred Roberts had an eye for other women. Kenneth Wallace's wife used to say, 'I wouldn't trust that man an inch. If he had half a chance, he'd have his hand up my skirt.'[54] And Mary Wallace says he 'touched women in a way completely uncalled for'.[55]*

As for Beatrice Roberts, referred to by some as 'Bee' and others as 'Beaty', only rather distant and external impressions seem to survive. Kenneth Wallace considered that there was 'more to her than met the eye ... she encouraged Margaret to get out and about. She appeared a little hen-bird, but she had quite a lot of steel.'[56] But on the whole Grantham regarded Mrs Roberts as shy, retiring, quiet and plain. Born in 1888, Beatrice was nearly four years older than her husband, and by the 1930s had no pretensions to good looks, style or display. 'She was completely under old Roberts's thumb,' said Mary Wallace. 'She was just there to do things for them. I got the impression that Margaret felt that too.' Madeline Edwards, who later became joint head girl of KGGS with Margaret Roberts, remembers Mrs Roberts as 'a small woman. Had a bun. She always looked slightly worried [sic].'[57] Nellie Towers said that Beatrice Roberts was always 'very prim and proper'; 'she kept the children beautifully clothed with the little tailored coats, but in her own dress she kept no decorations about her, she was all

---

* Much excitement was caused in Grantham by the appearance – and then the suppression – in 1937 of a novel called *Rotten Borough*, by Julian Pine, the pseudonym for Oliver Anderson, the son of the vicar of Harlaxton, a neighbouring village. It is a spirited but nevertheless embarrassingly bad burlesque of English provincial life, with thinly veiled caricatures of local characters, including Lord and Lady Brownlow, the local grandees. In one incident in the book, the new paper in the borough, the *Weekly Probe*, exposes the conduct of a man named Tompkins, whom it calls 'the Naughty Councillor'. The Naughty Councillor ensures that the High Street is lit by gas rather than electricity because he has shares in the gas company. He insists that the new lights be 'erected smack outside' his own grocer's shop 'on the Ground that it was situated at a very Dangerous Corner and would save a lot of lives, but really he thought it would sell a Lot of Hams, for He was a Grocer in a Big Way of Business'. One evening, says the *Probe*, Tompkins 'thought he would have a Bit of Fun with one of the Young ladies who served behind the counter' but is unluckily noticed doing so by passers-by, because he failed, in his haste, to draw the blind and is illuminated by the lights that he had himself installed. Tompkins then 'hanged Himself with a pair of Woolworth's braces in a Public Convenience'. It is widely believed, including by one witness who knew the author of *Rotten Borough* well (private information), that Tompkins was modelled on Alfred Roberts who, as well as being a grocer, with a shop on a busy corner, was involved in the running of the municipal gas company. There is, however, no proof, and there was certainly never any public scandal about Roberts.

very plain.' Developing the theory of the Robertses' marital unhappiness, Nellie Towers declared: 'I see where the fault was. It was Beaty that was cold.'[58] Jean Farmer saw Mrs Roberts as 'anxious to do her best for her girls' and also emphasized the pains she took in making up their clothes so well, including their school uniform. Like so many, she was struck by the huge amount of effort the Robertses put into everything, and the care they took with the results: 'Her parents had to work hard for their money and they valued every penny.'[59] All surviving impressions of Beatrice Roberts, even those from her daughters, are somehow exterior ones, as if no one really knew her.

The Grantham in which Alfred Roberts became an increasingly important figure was a modestly successful market town which shared the economic hardships of the 1920s and early 1930s and the definite recovery of the mid-1930s. In 1919, there were 19,700 people in the Grantham Municipal Borough; by 1938, there were 20,600. The parliamentary constituency had nearly 50,000 voters and so extended into the surrounding villages. The agricultural interest was still dominant, with factories in the town producing agricultural machinery. The Belvoir Hunt, the foxhound pack of the Duke of Rutland, always met in Grantham on Boxing Day. Roberts would take his daughters along. He was a keen supporter of foxhunting for the unusual reason that without it foxes would steal babies from prams.[60] The young Margaret enjoyed her rural walks out of the bowl in which Grantham sits to pick roseships on Hall's Hill, and she particularly delighted in visiting friends like Jean Farmer, or the elegant rectory of Canon Harold Goodrich, incumbent of Corby Glen and father of her schoolfriend Margaret, but she and her family were really town mice. Although closely linked to the country, the town was by now large enough to have a distinctly urban character. In an early letter about a game of tennis in Grantham, Margaret disparages her unchosen partner as a 'yokel':[61] it was always towns, preferably cities, which allured her.

The most powerful local man – and the biggest landowner – was Lord Brownlow, whose Cust family had long been seated at Belton, just outside Grantham. He was so close a friend of the Prince of Wales that he was criticized for his association with him after his abdication as King Edward VIII in 1936. The young Margaret made a good impression on the Custs. According to her sister Muriel, Caroline Cust, Lord Brownlow's daughter, used to 'rave' about Margaret. A photograph reprinted in Lady Thatcher's memoirs[62] shows her at a Baptist Christmas party smiling brightly out beside the young and elegant Lady Brownlow. Although it was often said that the grocer's daughter was somehow antagonistic to the traditional Tory aristocracy, this was not really so (although a few of them reacted snob-bishly to her). The Brownlows were only the first of several grandees who looked favourably on her and whom she, in turn, admired. When she became prime minister, Mrs Thatcher arranged with the then Lord Brown-low to borrow silver from Belton, by this time owned by the National Trust, to improve the cutlery at Downing Street. She also borrowed a green enamel box, painted with views of Grantham, which had been presented to Lord Brownlow when he had completed his year of office as mayor of the borough.[63]*

It was the approach of war that brought strong economic growth to Grantham. The town benefited from its position on the main road and rail links between London, the north-east and Scotland – the opening sen-tence of Margaret Thatcher's memoirs is: 'My first distinct memory is of traffic'[64] – and it increased its industrial base. Between 1932 and 1943, rateable value (the basis of the calculation for property taxes) rose by 60 per cent, which was very helpful to Alfred Roberts in his capacity as chair-man of the borough's finance committee. From 1934, new factories were being built in Grantham at the rate of about one a year. There was a good deal of engineering, the firm of Ruston and Hornsby, for example, which built engines. Aveling-Barford made steamrollers and tractors, and in 1938 the munitions company B.M.A.R. Co. opened a factory, run by Denis Kendall at the then astonishing salary of £10,000 per annum. Kendall, a glamorous, not to say flash, figure, drove a motorbike and had liaisons with prominent local women. In 1942, standing as an independent, he won the first wartime parliamentary by-election to turn out the National Gov-ernment candidate (a Conservative), campaigning as a 'production man' critical of the 'gang' round Winston Churchill, though not of Churchill himself. During the war, Kendall displaced Lord Brownlow as the leading figure in the town, certainly in terms of local press coverage, and in the 1945 general election he was re-elected to Parliament, defeating the Con-

---

* There was a popular theory in circulation that Margaret Thatcher had Cust blood. The story was that Margaret's grandmother Phoebe Stephenson had been a maid at Belton (even this fact has never been established). She was seduced, the theory goes on, by Harry Cust, a famous womanizer and, in all probability, the true father of Lady Diana Cooper. Her maiden name was Crust – almost Cust – and her granddaughter supposedly had 'Cust eyes'. Caroline Cust, now the Hon. Mrs Caroline Partridge, told the present author that she believed in the theory, though in her view Cust was Margaret's father, not her grandfather. This is impossible, since Harry Cust died eight years before Margaret was born. There is no evidence for the theory and its details don't add up, as shown by John Campbell in his biography *Margaret Thatcher* (2 vols, Jonathan Cape, 2000, 2003, vol. i: *The Grocer's Daughter*). It was widely believed, how-ever, in grand Tory circles. When the present biographer put the theory to Margaret Thatcher, she answered, with a certain pride: 'Blue eyes aren't the preserve of the aristocracy.'

servative candidate by more than 15,000 votes. By 1939, full employment
had returned to Grantham. Working shifts had to be staggered to avoid
the traffic jams caused by the myriad bicycles.

War also brought the armed services to Grantham in large numbers.
There were four RAF bases locally, including the RAF College at Cran-
well.* Margaret's letters to Muriel about dances in the area during the war
always mention the hordes of flight lieutenants eager for a dance. Grantham
provided the national headquarters for Bomber Command (Margaret Roberts's dentist, Mr Wallace, also treated 'Bomber' Harris); and from October
1943 there was a large USAAF presence in the town. Denis Kendall
exploited the resentments to which the American influx gave rise. US
servicemen were paid five times more than British ones, and were accused
of immorality with local girls. Kendall complained that they were allowed
to rent the Guildhall for entertainment when the same privilege had been
refused to British servicemen. In Parliament, he caused a storm by alleging
that Americans were accosting girls in the street. The accusation was
promptly rejected by Lord Brownlow and by the Chief Constable. But it
is certainly the case that the town became a place much fuller of young
men and girls seeking one another. According to Terry Bradley, after the
war a Labour councillor and opponent of Alfred Roberts, the High Street
was known to have a 'five bob side', where officers picked up girls, and a
'half a crown side' for the other ranks.[65] It was in response to the problems
of war that Roberts was prepared to unbend his Sabbatarian principles,
defying his fellow Methodists by voting in favour of the Sunday opening
of cinemas for the troops, because he believed that it was better for them
to have entertainment than to have nothing. His daughter cited this as
evidence of his pragmatism and independence of mind.[66]

Alfred Roberts began his career in local politics well before the war. He
was first elected in the St Wulfram Ward, where he sat as an Independent
Ratepayer from 1927. Although Margaret was always slightly evasive on
the point, Muriel was quite definite that their father was originally a Liberal
in politics,[67] but Roberts was also a strong supporter of the convention
dominant at the time that national party allegiance should be kept out of
local government, and he maintained this throughout his career, so much so
that when he died in 1970 the local press could only speculate on his political affiliations. In the fluid politics of the early 1930s, Roberts became a
supporter of the Conservative-dominated National Government – the coalition designed to deal with the slump, headed by the formerly Labour Prime

* The wartime atmosphere at these bases is best captured in Terence Rattigan's 1942 play *Flare
Path*, which is set near one of them.

Minister Ramsay MacDonald – seeing himself as without clear party allegiance. In his address as president of Grantham Rotary Club in July 1936
he described himself as 'like a good many people, often hopelessly and utterly
in the wilderness in the political world, sometimes believing in one party,
sometimes in another as others had been doing these last few years. There
was a feeling that one could not look to any particular party or creed for
the salvation of men and ridding them of fear.'[68] When Margaret was chosen
as prospective parliamentary candidate for Dartford in 1949, her father
broke the habit of a lifetime by speaking at a party political meeting, in her
support. In justifying his position, he told the meeting that the Conservative
Party now stood for 'very much the same things as the Liberal Party did in
his younger days' (see Chapter 5). Margaret offered her own explanation
for his views in her memoirs: 'Like many other business people he had . . .
been left behind by the Liberal Party's acceptance of collectivism.'[69]

Before and during the war, ideology did not intrude very much into the
work of the council. In economic questions, for example, the only significant
split occurred in early 1935 when a slum-clearance scheme was proposed
which would knock down 106 houses and accommodate 415 people. The
council divided over whether or not this should be done by a direct labour
force, Alfred Roberts opposing. Roberts quickly attained, and then held for
more than twenty years, the chairmanship of the finance and rating committee on the council. The *Grantham Journal* called him 'Grantham's
Chancellor of the Exchequer'.* He was the efficient and careful guardian of
the council's budget, not an ideologue or a campaigning politician.

But since Labour was the only party which defied the convention about
political identification on the council, it is fair to say that, for Roberts,
Labour was always his political opponent. The Chamber of Trade, with
whose support he was first elected, existed in opposition to the Labour
Party, and to the associated Co-operative movement. And in the 1935 general election Roberts decided to throw his growing influence in the town
behind the Conservative candidate, Sir Victor Warrender,† despite the fact
that many of his fellow Methodists had supported the Peace Ballot which
ended in that year.‡

---

* Before she became Conservative Party leader, Mrs Thatcher always said that her highest
ambition was to be the first woman Chancellor of the Exchequer. She regarded any political
job to do with money as more 'real' than any dealing with what she sometimes called 'the welfare thing'. She may have derived this view from her father.
† Victor Warrender (1899–1993), educated Eton; Conservative MP for Grantham, 1923–42;
government whip, and holder of minor ministerial posts; created Lord Bruntisfield, 1942.
‡ The Peace Ballot, organized in 1935 by the League of Nations Union to seek support for its
international peacemaking in the face of rearmament, has been curiously misrepresented by

It was this that gave Margaret her first taste of politics. She helped fold Warrender's election addresses into envelopes, and on polling day she acted as a runner, taking information about who had voted from the tellers at the polling station to the Conservative Committee Rooms so that they could make sure that their canvass turned out to vote.[70] Margaret Thatcher was never quite sure exactly what generated her early and enthusiastic allegiance to the Tories: 'I don't know why I was so staunchly Conservative. I think it was the idea of my father that you can get on somehow.'[71] But she immediately took to Warrender: 'I'll tell you what struck me. He had a presence, a natural presence. He had an overcoat on. It was a good overcoat. Good, not flashy. He was rather a handsome man. When he spoke, you listened.' She felt pleased 'to be treated on an equal level by an unequal . . . He understood that personality attracted votes.'[72] As so often in her dealings in later life, she was susceptible to good-looking men, to elegant clothes, to what used to be called an air of breeding.*

In forming his views on the international scene, Alfred Roberts probably gleaned more from Rotary than from any political party. Rotary was, and is, a worldwide movement. It grew in popularity between the wars, having been founded in the United States at the beginning of the twentieth century. Grantham Rotary got its charter in 1931, and Roberts was a founder member. In 1935 he became its annual president. With its motto of 'Service above Self', Rotary was a thoroughly worthy organization, composed largely of business-men and dedicated to social improvement and charitable endeavour. The records of its meetings, as detailed in the *Grantham Journal*, show a slightly comical list of improving subjects chosen for the club's lectures – 'modern psychology', a talk on road rollers (which were locally manufactured) and the history of tithes and rent charges. The organization's approach to politics was deliberately uncomplicated. It called for people to sink their political differ-ences in the wider public interest, and this applied, too, on the international scene, where a sentiment of reconciliation was much stronger than one of confrontation with Hitler. Margaret Thatcher said that her family first realized that there was something wrong with Hitler 'when we heard that he had sup-pressed Rotary'.[73] She saw the wider world through Rotarian eyes.

---

history. It is true that most of those taking part supported peaceful negotiation, but 6.8 million voted that the use of force against aggression was justified, as compared with 2.4 million who said that it was not.

* The two corresponded in warm terms in the 1970s and early 1980s, and when Mrs Thatcher was prime minister, she often stayed at Schloss Freudenberg near Zug in Switzerland, the home of Lady Glover. One man to whom she made a pilgrimage at his family's home in Gstaad was the by then extremely old Victor Warrender. A witness says that their meeting was emotional and touching: Mrs Thatcher thanked him for being the foundation of her political ambition. (Interview with Richard Bowdler-Raynar.)

As the chairman of Grantham Rotary's international service committee, Alfred Roberts organized visiting speakers. Because of this, and his voracious reading, he was probably as well informed as any other member about world affairs. Both Margaret and Muriel remembered that he was given favourable pamphlets about Hitler by his fellow Rotarian and local GP, Dr Jauch, whom they believed to be a German;* but that Roberts had been unconvinced. Despite her respect for Dr Jauch as a doctor, Mrs Thatcher remembered him as a 'very cold man'.[74] What is clear, though, is that Roberts's Rotarianism, and perhaps his Methodism as well, made him sympathetic to appeasement, particularly as embodied by Neville Chamberlain, the Prime Minister since 1937, and about as perfectly Rotarian a figure as ever reached 10 Downing Street.

As the speaker at the annual dinner of Grantham Rotary on 26 January 1939, Roberts reminded his audience of Rotary's clear rule of avoiding politics and not recommending 'forms of government'. 'They [that is, Rotary] took no sides as to whether there should be a dictatorship, monarchy or republic,' said the report of his speech. Nor did they enter into controversy about 'world personalities, either in attack or defence', but they did have principles of 'justice, truth and liberty' which drove them to say that 'weak nations have sacred rights too, and that they must be respected'. Since Rotarians were animated by these principles, said Roberts, 'It did not matter to them whether people were strongly armed or whether they were almost unarmed. They had seen, quite recently, what one man could do, armed only with a neatly-rolled umbrella, with his mind made up and his will intent on peace. (Applause.)'[75] Roberts was referring to Chamberlain's agreement with Hitler, signed in Munich in October of the previous year and later to became notorious. It is fair to say that, in speaking as he did, Roberts was expressing a sentiment shared by probably three-quarters of the British population. 'Appeasement' was not then a dirty word, but one used by the appeasers themselves; they believed that peace could be preserved by talking. Those, like Winston Churchill, who disagreed were attacked as warmongers. Roberts's views were the conventional ones. At the same dinner, various speakers worried about the banning of Rotary in Germany and Italy, which they attributed to the international character of the organization, but they stuck to the view that Rotary's concept of 'fellowship' offered the best 'pathway to peace' in an increasingly threatening climate.[76]

Margaret Thatcher, of course, became famous for her dislike of appeasing dictators (she compared Western weakness towards Saddam Hussein in 1990 with that shown to Hitler, for example)[77] and for her admiration

---

* Dr Jauch was actually of Swiss parentage.

of Churchill. For this reason, perhaps, she did not like directly to admit that her father had been a supporter of Chamberlain, but approached the subject rather more obliquely. Chamberlain, she later insisted, 'was a very honourable man ... I often thought he knew that in 1938 he must gain time to get us ready. I believe he gained more in that last year than Hitler ... it may be that we owe Chamberlain a great debt of gratitude for his judgment for what happened during those years. And it brought Winston forward that much more.'[78] She said that honourable men try to find honour in other, foreign governments: 'perhaps it has been one of the faults of British politicians that we look at other politicians through slightly rose-tinted spectacles thinking they are as we are.'[79]

Once war came in September 1939, however, any hesitations were put on one side, and Alfred Roberts became a more and more important figure in Grantham as the town responded to the crisis. He was one of three councillors appointed, when war began, to the emergency committee which exercised the powers of the full council, becoming its vice-chairman in 1942, and he threw himself into numerous war-related activities. He had been involved in the council's original ARP (Air Raid Precautions) plans in 1938, and during the war he played a leading part in Civil Defence and became chief raid welfare officer, dealing with questions like the rehousing and care of those who had been bombed. In 1940, he set up a British Restaurant – part of a national scheme for places providing basic food where workers could eat without using up their ration allowances – first for munitions workers in Bridge End Road, and later a second restaurant at the school room attached to the Finkin Street Methodist Church where he preached. He was prominent in the National Savings Movement, whose Local Savings Committees encouraged thrift and helped finance the war effort. All this work was not only worthy but genuinely demanding when combined with running his two shops. In 1940, Roberts was offered the mayoralty of Grantham, but had to refuse owing to lack of time. In February 1943, he was made an alderman, a form of unelected councillor now abolished outside the City of London, appointed by the council itself as a mark of respect and local distinction. Roberts, aged fifty at that time, was probably the youngest Grantham man ever to be chosen for the office. The circumstances in which he lost it, more than ten years later, were to make a profound impression upon his daughter. Just after the war ended, Roberts was again offered, and this time accepted, the mayoralty. From the beginning of the war until her departure for Oxford in October 1943, with Muriel absent in Birmingham for her training as a physiotherapy nurse, Margaret was in effect an only child at home. She witnessed at close quarters the endless labour and public spiritedness of her father, a life which, because of war, shrank the sphere of private pleasures even smaller. Duty, work, patriotism – and the sense of an enemy – dominated.

Even as he drafted his speech about peace and war to Grantham Rotary, Alfred Roberts was preparing to put his Rotarian principles to a practical test. It was the custom at KGGS that many of the girls had foreign pen-friends: Margaret had a French girl called Cilette Pasquier* from the Savoie, but Muriel had an Austrian one called Edith Mühlbauer. Edith was Jewish, and at some point her parents, suffering persecution after Hitler's *Anschluss* of Austria in March of the previous year, wrote to Roberts asking if he would take Edith in so that she could escape the Nazis. He agreed, and arranged with fellow Rotarians that she should stay with several families in turn. The correspondence between Roberts and Edith's parents does not survive, but on 21 January 1939 Edith herself wrote from Vienna to Roberts saying that the permit for the visa to England which followed his invitation had arrived. Typing neatly, in uncertain English, she thanked him for his help – 'I will never in my whole live forgett it you' – and went on to ask practical questions about reaching the Roberts family: 'Have I to take the train from London to Grantham† or the ship?'[80] In fact, the bureaucracy of permitted escape took some time, and on 23 March Edith wrote again, saying there was yet more delay, but that she should be allowed out of Austria within a few weeks: 'First of all let me thank you for your kind letter and enclosed photograph. I am ever so glad that you helped me and that there are various other people which want to help me too, and take me into their nice homes. I really hope to be happy there.'[81]

Unfortunately, generous though the Robertses were, Edith was not terribly happy with them. Hints of the problem surface in the memories of Margaret and Muriel. 'We didn't have a proper bathroom in those days,' said Margaret; 'she was used to better things.'[82] Muriel said Edith was a 'nice girl', but also that 'she had a wonderful wardrobe . . . and I think that they were well breeched in Austria.' As if to protect her from possible threat, Edith's Jewishness was not mentioned, but it seems also to have contributed to the provincial Robertses' sense that she was rather apart from them.[83] Edith didn't like the Robertses' Sunday-afternoon walk into the fields beyond Grantham: 'She said, "It'll ruin my shoes."'[84]

---

* Lady Thatcher mistakenly refers to her as Colette in her memoirs. She was known as Cilette, but her baptismal name was Cécile. Cilette Pasquier was to marry Franck Sérusclat, a Socialist Senator for the Rhône region from 1977 to 1999. She and Margaret never met, and she died in 1982, apparently without knowing that her former penfriend had become the British prime minister.
† Grantham is land-locked.

What seems to have happened is that Alfred Roberts was shocked by Edith's sophistication, her smart appearance and her tendency, at that time thought extremely dangerous in teenage girls, to wear make-up. In the slightly acid words of Madeline Edwards, whose family also accommodated her, Edith was 'a very grown-up seventeen-year-old'.[85] She would sit at the window of her bedroom in North Parade looking out on to the street and making Roberts feel, according to one of her contemporaries, that 'it was like Amsterdam'.[86] Edith told Mary Wallace that she found 1 North Parade a 'repressive household'.[87] She was 'patently unhappy' there.[88] This produced a major row between Roberts and his fellow Rotarian, Mr Wallace, the dentist. The two men started shouting at one another and Wallace told Roberts: 'You asked this girl over, and you're not looking after her properly and she's very unhappy.'[89] This version is implicitly confirmed by Muriel Cullen, who says that 'Daddy refused to accept responsibility too much and went round to all Rotarians in turn persuading them to have Edith ... I sometimes think he regretted having got her over.'[90]

Certainly Edith did not stay in North Parade for long. She arrived some time in April, and by 16 May is writing to Muriel from the house of Madeline Edwards in Welby Gardens. She apologizes for not having replied earlier to Muriel's letter, but explains that she has already moved house twice before reaching the Edwardses: 'it seems to me as if I am a gipsy.' So she probably lived at North Parade for no more than a fortnight. The fact that she writes warmly to Muriel (mentioning Muriel's sister whom she germanicizes as 'Margit') shows that relations were not broken, and her letter states that 'I often go for a walk to see your dear father Mr Roberts, and ask if there are today any letters for me.' She was clearly grateful to the Robertses for helping her, and said so again when tracked down by journalists in old age, living in Brazil to which she and her family shortly afterwards escaped. But the experiment did not really work, and she finally came to rest in Grantham in the larger and more sophisticated home of the Wallaces, with whom she stayed for the best part of a year.

The story of Edith shows Alfred Roberts in an interesting light – a well-intentioned man, determined to live by his principles, genuinely kind, but also stern and forbidding. Perhaps it was easier to admire him than to live with him. Margaret, several years younger than Edith, did not know her well, but she was shocked above all by one feature she related of her life in Vienna: 'She said that Jewish women were being made to scrub the streets.'[91]

2

Scholarship girl

'You're thwarting my ambition'

In Margaret's earliest known letter,[1] of which only one sheet survives, she analysed her exams. She had just sat School Certificate (the rough equivalent of the GCSE), in the summer of 1941, and found the pace intense – 'As you can imagine this mean't [sic] a terrific amount of swotting.' The biggest problem was presented by geography. The first paper, based on work with the Ordnance Survey map, was not too bad, but 'the other paper on the British Isles and one continent was very disappointing. For one continent we did America and the questions on it were not at all bad, but out of the three on the British Isles there was only one we could touch.' All of them involved a fairly detailed knowledge of Scotland and Ireland and their towns. 'Unfortunately we had not touched island [sic] and had had precisely two lessons on Scotland . . . However we managed to survive it and went home to dinner hoping for a decent biology paper in the afternoon.' Even at the age of fifteen, the map of her future political sympathies is laid out. England and America understood, Scotland little studied, Ireland *terra incognita* and Continental Europe not even mentioned.

Margaret's sister had just taken her own exams in Birmingham. 'CONGRATULATIONS ON YOUR SPLENDID EXAM RESULTS I think everyone in the town knows about them by this time,' Margaret inserted at the top of the letter. Confident that the subject of her own School Certificate is overwhelmingly fascinating to Muriel, she wrote, 'I will send you the papers as soon as I can, but first I want Mr Marks to see them.' Harold Marks was a master at the King's School, the boys' grammar school in Grantham, for whom she had great respect. Her father had arranged for Marks to act as Margaret's occasional private tutor. It is striking that she should immediately have sought validation and advice from outside her school: there were, of course, no men at KGGS.

In the event, Margaret need not have worried. She got a credit in geography. In her second letter, written to Muriel on 20 September 1941,[2] she tabulates her full results. She got distinctions (the top grade) in chemistry, arithmetic and algebra, and credits in all other subjects with the exception of life drawing, in which she managed only a lowly pass. Having charted these, she lists the results of her fellow pupils. Although she does not make the point from the information she sets out, it is clear from the data that none of the other girls mentioned managed three distinctions. Indeed, eleven out of forty failed. This led to a parting of the ways, with some girls staying in a lower form to retake and others, such as Margaret, setting their sights on university.

With the ready nostalgia of the very young, Margaret laments the changes: 'Life in 6 Lower is not half as nice as life in form Va. Our crowd have broken up of course and several have left ... There is not the form spirit that there used to be ... we used to cling together ... but now ... so many of the old links are missing, there is nothing to hold us together.' The fall in numbers was astonishing. In V Lower, Margaret recorded, there had been fifty-three girls.[3] After Christmas 1941, there would be only four – Margaret, Madeline Edwards, Jean Farmer and Lorna Smith, who was new. Many girls had left due to the plentiful availability of jobs during the war. Margaret's old companions, Joan Orchard and Pat Maidens, had been held down a year; of her intimates, only Jean Farmer survived in the same class. Margaret and Jean were also the only remaining scientists. Always sensitive to possible condescension, Margaret considered the Sixth Form (the year above her) 'rather superior', though expressing pleasure that Margaret Goodrich (see previous chapter) had been made head girl, since 'she is one of the decent ones.'

To mark the last jolly time before school began once more, Margaret went to the pictures:

> ... Jean came in, and Joan came down [from her parents' house on a hill outside Grantham], then we all went to the State [one of Grantham's cinemas] in the afternoon and stayed tea, as a last splash before we started school. We saw *This England* with Constance Cummings, Emlyn Williams, and John Clements. We enjoyed it, although it was a historical film, for the greater part. With it was *Romance of the Rio Grande* with Caesar [sic] Romero and Patricia Morrison. For tea we had <u>salmon</u> salad. We happened to strike a lucky day for there was also jam and chocolate biscuits.*

---

* To attend both films on the bill was an act of minor defiance against the wishes of Mr and Mrs Roberts. They thought that their girls should go only to those films properly chosen on their merits, rather than watching whatever happened to be on. (See Margaret Thatcher, *The Path to Power*, HarperCollins, 1995, p. 14.)

On returning to school, Margaret was not greatly impressed with all of the teaching staff: 'The new games mistress is not as young as we have been used to having. Her name is Miss Dales, and she looks about 30. The history mistress is very disappointing. She is quite middle-aged and very dowdy in dress.' And as for Miss Amor, the geography teacher who had also been her form mistress, she had now, in her new role of vice-head, grown 'too big for her boots', so much so that 'she would not come and take stock cupboard at all on Friday.' Margaret reserved a specially tart comment for the headmistress, Miss Gillies, about her handling of the exam results: 'There was no message of congratulation (or sympathy) from the Head, just a blunt "Pass" or "Fail".'

She set her shoulder to the wheel of work, however, and shared her thoughts about the future with her sister:

When going into VI Lower you need not necessarily decide what career you are going to take up except that it would be helpful in choosing subjects ... Daddy does not like the idea of medical at all, but I am taking Biology, Chemistry and Maths main with French subsid. The next idea on the list is to go to University, and take a science degree then sit for a Civil Service exam for posts abroad. A degree is necessary for this for a woman. Of course I shan't be able to go to University at all unless I get a scholarship.

In the whole letter, there is no direct mention of the war, though at the time Germany was invading Russia and Britain was almost the sole champion of the free world, the United States not having yet entered the conflict. The historical moment in which Margaret was living impinges only indirectly and in small ways – the emphasis on the rare availability of salmon salad, a passing mention of the fact that the evacuated Camden School for Girls was sharing KGGS's facilities, the increasing age of the teaching staff. The war, which was to play so important a part in forming her beliefs and her idea of her country, was treated by her at the time only as a backdrop against which the life of school was played out.

Already, in her first words that posterity has left us, the fifteen-year-old Margaret Roberts shows herself clear, confident, ambitious, diligent, clever and slightly acidulous.

What was her education, and how did it form her? At her primary school in Huntingtower Road, Margaret did well. The story has often been told, in slightly differing versions, about the prize she won at the age of nine.*

* Russell Lewis, in his *Margaret Thatcher* (Routledge & Kegan Paul, 1975), says the prize was for poetry recital at the local eisteddfod, the festival of Welsh origin which was popular in

When the head congratulated her on her luck, Margaret retorted, 'I wasn't lucky. I deserved it.' The tale is sometimes taken to indicate big-headedness or arrogance, but more likely it shows the young Margaret's literal-mindedness.* She had not been lucky; she *had* deserved it, so she felt bound to say so. To say anything else would be to cast doubt on the entire judging process.

The first surviving motion picture – a short and jerky cine film – of Margaret Roberts dates from 1935. In that year, Grantham celebrated its centenary as a borough, and she paraded, with her school, to help form the word 'GRANTHAM' out of human bodies. In the film, the nine-year-old Margaret Roberts can be discerned preparing to do so: 'appropriately enough, I was part of the "M".'[4]

In the following year, Margaret won a scholarship to Kesteven and Grantham Girls' School. KGGS, as it is and was always known, was the best school in the area that a girl could attend. Founded in 1910, it was a fee-paying girls' grammar school, but with about a quarter of the girls attending exempt from fees. Scholarship girls entered after an equivalent of the later universal eleven-plus exam; fee-paying girls could enter from a much younger age. When Margaret arrived in September 1936, there were about 330 girls in the school, including Muriel, who was not a scholarship girl. Because of its high reputation, KGGS drew on families from quite far outside Grantham, as well as from the town itself. The social background of the pupils varied from the prosperous or highly educated (top managers in the engineering firms, the Anglican clergy) to daughters of poor families who had got in on their wits. In the financial scale, the Robertses probably stood slightly below the middle of the school; in the social, because of Alfred's growing role in the town, rather higher.

Despite her scholarship, Margaret went straight into the B Stream. This did not reflect any academic defect on her part, but simply the fact that an unusually large number of scholarship girls had been admitted in that year, and not all could be accommodated in the A Stream. The effect of this was to foster the slight but definite sense of separation from most of her peers that many felt Margaret showed. It also threw her together with Jean Farmer, the

---

Grantham at that time. Nellie Towers, in her interview for *Maggie: The First Lady* (Brook Lapping Productions for ITV and PBS, 2003), says she was being congratulated for this and for winning the church music festival piano solo prize. It is possible that the story conflates more than one occasion.

* Literal-mindedness was a quality that Margaret Thatcher observed in herself. In her memoirs, she says, 'I was perplexed by the metaphorical element of phrases like "Look before you leap". I thought it would be far better to say "Look before you cross" ...' (Thatcher, *The Path to Power*, p. 17).

builder's daughter from Fulbeck. Jean, too, was a scholarship girl, the only other one in the B Stream, and because of this, she said, 'we were a pair'[5] for the two years before they graduated to the A Stream, and, indeed, until Margaret went to Oxford and Jean to teacher training college in 1943. Jean was an easygoing, popular girl, known, in the parlance of the time, as a 'scream',[6] and it was she and her family that first gave Margaret the sense that life could be more fun than it was in North Parade. It was in response to Margaret's demand that she be allowed Sundays as free and jolly as those of the Farmers that Alfred Roberts produced his famous response: 'Margaret, never do things just because other people do them. Make up your own mind what you are going to do and persuade people to go your way.'[7] Margaret both kicked against such injunctions and imbibed them respectfully. She resented what her father taught, but generally believed that he was right.

Jean Farmer liked Margaret without reservation. She describes her as 'a very pleasant, happy, fun-loving girl', not at all under stress and even 'happy-go-lucky'. She was a 'slightly plump' girl who was 'polite, hardworking and joined in everything'. The two of them 'never had a cross word', and Jean was irritated in later years by the criticisms of Margaret which she felt were unfair, such as not having a sense of humour or being too imperious: 'I didn't find her at all bossy . . . she was exceptionally nice.' The two spent the odd weekend at one another's parents' houses, and the Farmers once took Margaret with them for a weekend in Skegness – a modest outing by modern standards, but quite a thing for the girls at the time. They were also excited by an expedition they made to Stamford Boys School to see *The Barber of Seville* performed in French ('though we couldn't understand a thing they said'). Jean did not regard Margaret as a genius, but she did note her 'marvellous powers of concentration' and one of her most famous characteristics as prime minister: 'she didn't need as much sleep as we did.'[8] Jean's parents were particularly fond of Margaret too, and it was Jean's father, Jack, who chaired the Conservative Party meeting in Fulbeck in the general election campaign of 1945 at which Margaret did the warm-up for the Tory candidate. This was one of the first public speeches that she had made.* The Farmers kept up with Margaret, writing to congratulate her on her public successes. In March 1974, following the Tory defeat in the general election the previous month, Margaret, who had seen Jean again while opening a comprehensive in

---

* Lady Thatcher told the present author that she spoke in public in the Grantham by-election of 1942, but this does not appear to be the case: it seems unlikely, since she would have been only sixteen.

Formby where she now lived, wrote back: 'It was good to see Jean when I opened a school. She looks marvellous. I think we have both "worn" very well!'* She went on, 'It seems a long time since I was "home" in Lincolnshire. In some ways, I think they were happier and fuller days than those I live now. The days in London are and always will be very busy – but there is not the warmth and the friendship of the small town and village.'⁹ In reality, Margaret probably did not like Grantham excessively, and was certainly keen to get away from it, but she admired the values that she learnt there. And there is no doubt that she felt a real affection for the Farmers and the spontaneity of their village life.†

Jean Farmer was not alone in thoroughly liking Margaret. Another friend was Shirley Walsh (now Ellis), a pretty girl on whose doorstep in Avenue Road Margaret chose to arrive every morning ('she was always early')¹⁰ so that they could walk to school together across the River Witham. It was Margaret who informed her, on one of these spring mornings in 1940, that invading German forces had parachuted into Holland. And it was Margaret and Shirley, when they were a bit older, who would work together at Toc H, the mission for servicemen, on a Saturday serving in the forces canteen. In Shirley Ellis's view, Margaret 'was never disdainful of her schoolfriends or peers' and showed a good sense of humour – 'She didn't instigate, but she joined in': she had 'no dislikeable characteristics'. Evidence of humour – the slightly dry wit which Margaret exhibited in later years – can also be found in her correspondence with Muriel. Writing about a bus trip back from a hockey match, she describes how the vehicle was so crowded that the girls had to sit on sacks of potatoes 'which by the time we arrived at North Witham were just about cooked and mashed'.¹¹

And although all her contemporaries attest to a seriousness in Margaret which made her different from the others, she took part in all the normal interests and activities of a teenage girl of that period. She enjoyed tennis, and played hockey well enough (at centre half) to be in the school team. More striking, and more apparently at odds with her upbringing, was a strong interest in glamour, both in films and in fashion. Almost every letter to Muriel mentions the latest films to hit Grantham. In the letter in which she mentions going to the *This England* double bill with Jean and Joan, she discusses five other films. *Bittersweet* and *Pimpernel Smith* are coming soon,

---

* Note that Mrs Thatcher praises her own looks as well as Jean's. She never found it easy to hand out unreserved compliments to other women.

† Jean Farmer herself, though always much less ambitious than Margaret, declared, 'I wasn't terribly impressed with Grantham. It didn't have a lot to offer' (interview with Mrs Jean Dean).

she says,* but she has just been to see *Rebecca*, which she thinks 'one of the best I have ever seen, with a well-concealed plot'.[12] She also went with her mother to *Love on the Dole*, she wrote, a film about unemployed Lancastrian cotton workers between the wars, 'the spectral army of three million lost men', unusual in the wartime period for addressing social problems of this kind. It was not to Margaret's taste: 'I can't say I enjoyed it, although it was a good film.' In the following month, a Deanna Durbin season at Grantham continued: 'I went to *Nice Girl* with Jean and Joan. I thought it was rotten.'[13] Films in Grantham were made more acceptable in the eyes of Margaret's parents by the fact that one cinema, the Picture House, was owned by the Campbells, customers and respected neighbours of Roberts in nearby, rather grand Welby Gardens. J. A. Campbell was a fellow Rotarian of Alfred Roberts. Their daughter, Judy, who lived there with her parents in the 1930s, was a very beautiful woman, and became a well-known actress and the first to popularize the song 'A Nightingale Sang in Berkeley Square'.† Margaret knew Judy a little, and greatly admired her. She also had a partiality for the films of Ginger Rogers, which led Jim Allen, Grantham's leading local historian of Margaret Thatcher, to ask her in old age if she liked Rogers because of her portrayal of a woman succeeding in a man's world in *Kitty Foyle*. 'No, it wasn't,' replied Lady Thatcher. 'I always wished I could have danced like her.'[14]

By Margaret's own account, the 'biggest excitement of my early years' was her only pre-war trip to London, at the age of twelve. She went to stay with Methodist friends of the family, the Revd Mr Skinner and his wife – the minister who was much later to marry her and Denis. The Skinners took her to the obvious London sights, including Parliament and Downing Street, and St Paul's Cathedral ('where John Wesley prayed on the morning of his conversion').[15] 'But the high point was my first visit to the Catford Theatre in Lewisham where we saw Sigmund Romberg's famous musical *The Desert Song*. For three hours I lived in another world, swept away as was the heroine by the daring Red Shadow – so much so that I bought the score and played it at home, perhaps too often.' Rather touchingly, she

---

* In her memoirs, Lady Thatcher says that her 'views on the French Revolution were gloriously confirmed by Leslie Howard and lovely Merle Oberon in *The Scarlet Pimpernel*' (Thatcher, *The Path to Power*, p. 14). This may be so, but the film came out in 1934, at a time when Margaret was a little young for it. It seems more likely that she is remembering *Pimpernel Smith*, also starring Leslie Howard, which updates the story of the Scarlet Pimpernel and places it in war-torn Europe.

† Judy Campbell, who died in 2004, was also the mother of Jane Birkin, equally famous for a very different sort of love-song, 'Je t'aime . . . moi non plus', in the late 1960s. Jane's daughter, Charlotte Gainsbourg, starred in the painfully explicit film *Antichrist* early in the twenty-first century.

writes of the trip that the Skinners' 'kindness had given me a glimpse of, in Talleyrand's words, "*la douceur de la vie*"'. For all her subsequent fame, she seldom had time throughout her life to savour this indefinable quality, but when she did, she loved it. She also thrived on the excitement of places that mattered. London traffic and crowds 'seemed to generate a sort of electricity', even the soot of the buildings lent a 'dark, imposing magnificence which constantly reminded me that I was at the centre of the world'. Except in political allegiance, the centre was always where she wanted to be.

Apart from films, the other way to bring glamour to unexciting Grantham was through clothes. Margaret would never have wanted to be trendy, even if the word had existed at the time, but she constantly sought elegance and quality in what she wore. It was a time, because of the war and later the post-war rationing, as well as her parents' careful budgeting, when these were not easily attained. Her correspondence with Muriel includes a constant series of requests for bits of material or nylons or buttons and so on, and a detailed discussion of fashion and beauty, of where it is possible to obtain the right things, and at what price. On 30 July 1944, a few days after the abortive Bomb Plot by German officers against Hitler, she writes to Muriel that, going to Lincoln with Jean, she had 'hoped to do a bit of shopping with odds and bobs thinking that tomorrow was August 1st and we should be able to use the new coupons, but now of course I have discovered that it will only be July 31st, and so I shan't be able to do much as I have only one coupon left.' Nevertheless, she went the previous day to Chambers in Grantham 'and bought two underwear sets that I am very pleased with. I got a white Kayser set and a pink rather dainty set of some other make. I also got pink uplift bras . . .' She then chose 'a Vogue pattern for a frock. I think there will be just sufficient material over to make a small berry [sic: she meant beret] shaped hat of the kind that are in fashion now. If that man can make me a handbag, it should be a nice set when it is finished.'[16] For her birthday in 1941, her father gave Margaret a pound so that she could buy a powder bowl, 'telling me to bring back the change'.[17] She found a nice but plain one for 10 shillings (50p) ('just ordinary glass with a little gold paint round the top'). 'There's one I should very much have liked,' she goes on. 'It was green, very large and cut glass. The only objectionable thing about it was its price – 32/6.'[18]

Margaret always exhibited a practical approach to things, whether to price or to friendship. Lorna Smith, who came into the school in September 1941, remembered her as 'quiet, hard-working, poised, calm and self-confident. Some people found her slightly irritating, and even rather conceited, but I fear there was an element of envy there! For myself, I found her pleasant and helpful, for which, as a new girl at the school, I was immensely grateful.' To Lorna, Margaret displayed the rather brisk, mothering sort of kindness which, in later life, she always showed to those who worked closely with her: 'one bitterly cold winter's morning I had to cycle to Grantham, with no breakfast, to have a nerve removed at the dentist's. Staggering out of the surgery, some time later, I ran straight into Margaret, who was shopping. She took one look at my ashen face, and steered me to Catlin's Café for a restorative hot drink. She will not remember her kind deed, but I have never forgotten it.'[19] What marked Margaret out, though, was her sense of purpose. As Shirley Ellis put it, 'She always stood out because teenage girls don't know where they're going. She did.'

And this purposefulness was accompanied by a fondness for simple moral precepts that never left her. It was a custom for schoolgirls in the 1930s to keep autograph books. These were not so much, as in future generations, to obtain the signatures of famous people as to collect the signatures of friends and the little improving remarks or quotations which they might want to inscribe. On 23 March 1937, the eleven-year-old Margaret Roberts wrote in Madeline Edwards's autograph book:

> Tis easy enough to be pleasant,
> When life goes by with a song.
> But the one worth while
> Is the one that can smile
> When everything goes dead wrong.

Rita Hind (later Wright), another schoolfriend, kept the inscription of fifteen-year-old Margaret Roberts on 22 June 1941 (the day, as it happens, when the world received the news of Hitler's invasion of Russia): 'A little thing is a little thing, but faithfulness in little things, is a great thing.' Shirley Ellis's autograph book did not survive, but she remembered what Margaret wrote in it in 1939: 'Smile a while and when you smile another smiles and then there's miles and miles of smiles.'

Precepts, once learnt, had also to be proclaimed. Margaret's Methodist upbringing and her father's example made it natural for someone of her interests to want to speak in public, unusual though this was for a woman at that time. It was many years, however, before she started to make speeches of her own. Her first public performances were recitations, and she favoured such poetry – well-known passages of Longfellow, Tennyson, Whitman or Kipling – as made its moral meaning plain and expressed it with grandeur and force. It was partly for these exercises that she began the first of several stints of elocution lessons which were to punctuate her career. According to Connie Pitchford, a KGGS contemporary, Margaret suffered from 'a slight lisp and had trouble pronouncing her Rs'. In 1936, she and Connie had elocution lessons together.[20] From these, not from any later, political attempt to improve her social standing, springs the cut-glass voice for which Margaret was later to be criticized. In those days, all elocution teachers tried to enforce a very precise, carefully enunciated version of received pronunciation, and for Margaret, who was already competing in declamation competitions, it would not have been possible to win without eliminating all traces (which seem anyway to have been slight) of a Lincolnshire accent. Later, her carefully modulated tones used to irritate many of her contemporaries at Somerville, Oxford, who considered them 'artificial'.[21] So in a sense they were, but the purpose of the artifice was more purity of diction than climbing up the greasy political or social pole. Margaret herself understood that artificiality was frowned upon: her lessons had taught her the importance of avoiding exaggeration and melodrama: 'you were taught not to over-express. To over-express is to undermine your meaning because it becomes artificial.'[22]

The lessons produced results. In 1937, Margaret won the silver medal at the Grantham eisteddfod for her recitation of John Drinkwater's 'Moonlit Apples' and Walter De La Mare's 'The Travellers'. In 1939, Shirley Ellis remembers sharing a prize with her for declaiming Tennyson's 'Ulysses'. And Margaret, though by no means a literary girl, was someone easily stirred to passion by the high sentiments and noble expressions of poetry. 'I loved language and rhythm,' she recalled,[23] and she appreciated poets, such as John Masefield or Henry Newbolt, who indulged this love. 'Kipling was our hero, with the breadth of his writing,' she said,[24] and throughout her life she always had some quotation from him – 'A truth that's told with bad intent /Beats all the lies you can invent,' for example – readily retrievable from her memory (although this quotation is misattributed by her – the lines are by William Blake). One may speculate that Kipling, as well as the Methodist missionaries, excited the idea of India in her imagination. She loved what were then the 'obvious' anthologies of English poetry, such as Palgrave's *Golden Treasury* and Quiller-Couch's edition of the *Oxford Book of English Verse*. To her first serious boyfriend, she gave a copy of Palgrave. To the man whom, before Denis, she most nearly married, she sent the complete works of Shakespeare. Neither choice shows any originality of literary taste, but her reverence and affection for great writing were genuine. She extended these feelings, above all, to the Authorized Version of the Bible, singling out Isaiah, the Gospels and the Acts of the Apostles: 'There is no greater English literature.'[25] Her choice of Acts is slightly unusual, and worth noting – it is the most important book in the Scriptures about the propagation of a message to the world. And to the end of her life she retained the words of scores of the classic English hymns in her mind. At Denis's funeral in July 2003, when her anguish and mental confusion were such that she was not sure whether it was her husband's or her father's coffin in front of her, she was seen to sing all the hymns, word-perfect, without looking at the service sheet.*

This is how Lorna Smith, arriving as a shy new girl in September 1941, remembers the Lower Sixth at KGGS:

> Our combined sixth Forms shared a form-room, furnished with a desk and two long tables, at which we sat facing each other. The more senior girls usually sat opposite me, so I was able to contemplate the stars in my new firmament.
>
> There was Margaret Goodrich ('Margie'), clever, kind and attractive, well turned-out, and with her bright burnished red hair tied in a neat bow. She was inclined to be Miss Gillies' 'pet', but it did not spoil her.
>
> Her younger sister, Joan Goodrich ('Joanie') might be at the table, too. She was also clever, but very quiet and hardly ever spoke. She had a very pale complexion, and her hair was black, and sleek as a starling.
>
> Then there was Madeline Edwards, with her long Titian mane, proud of her Welsh origins, strong of character, a natural leader, and immensely gifted. She excelled in almost everything, especially in the arts and music.
>
> . . . and sometimes Margaret Roberts was there, too, when she was not 'swotting' in the chemistry lab, where she could usually be found.
>
> Not as striking, perhaps, as the girls already described, and with rather 'mousey' hair (like mine!), she nevertheless had even features, a clear complexion, intelligent grey-blue eyes, a very good figure and legs, and a sharp intellect. She radiated quiet confidence.

Lorna shared history revision with Margaret, which included a weekly session on 'Current Events'.

> After one of these classes . . . we were lolling about in our form-room, gossip-ing, and thinking about our futures. Margaret said she was going to be a scientist, but she was also interested, like her father, in politics, and would perhaps try for Parliament one day. 'Imagine – an MP!' I said, admiringly. 'Perhaps you could <u>even</u> be Prime Minister!' She waved away the idea, but she was looking both dreamy and purposeful. Since then I have heard her disclaim all such ambitions, but that is a clear memory.†

---

* The present author witnessed this.

† Margaret Goodrich has said, and Mrs Thatcher has confirmed in slightly different form (see Patricia Murray, *Margaret Thatcher*, W. H. Allen, 1980, p. 38), that her first moment of real-ization that she wanted to be an MP was at Margaret Goodrich's twenty-first birthday party

Discussion of politics, though, was a rarity at KGGS. There was plenty of talk, of course, about the progress of the war, but this concerned Britain's military fortunes, not the conflict's political rights and wrongs. Reflecting the parents of the girls, the school's prevailing allegiance was vaguely Conservative, but those girls who enjoyed debate were more likely to centre on religious questions than political ones. 'I think our faith mattered more,' said Rita Hind.[26]* The girls were very idealistic, she said: it was 'a very moral period', with no girls known to have boyfriends while at school. 'There were more important things to do than boys,' Margaret remembered.[27] It was a time of aspiration, and of a love of education. 'We didn't see the emptiness that would follow the war,' said Rita Hind. It was this high-minded atmosphere which Margaret drank in, and cherished: 'I'm quite sure she wanted to keep alive the spirit of the Thirties or revive it.'[28] No one remembered Margaret debating political issues at this time, though all remembered her interest in the subject. Indeed, there is scarcely a single instance, in all her surviving correspondence from the 1940s, of Margaret expressing a political view on any subject. Her political involvement is clear, but all her mentions of it refer to organization, meetings, speeches and so on, not to the substance of policy or ideas.

In the context of what she calls the school's 'strong religious bias, led by our high-principled Head' (Miss Gillies), Lorna Smith remembered many schoolgirl discussions about faith, not least a surreal conversation with Margaret on an afternoon walk from school into Grantham just before Christmas in 1942. 'She remarked that, really, she didn't think she could believe in angels. "Oh, why?" I asked, wondering what Ald. Roberts would think. "Well," she replied, "I have worked it out scientifically that in order to fly, an angel would need a six-foot-long breastbone to bear the weight of its wings."' Lorna added, perhaps superfluously, '. . . Margaret could be very earnest at times.'[29]

There was something else that Margaret worked out scientifically, with alarming results. In the spring of 1943, the post-exam celebrations resulted in ink being spilt on the 'precious parquet floor of our form-room'.[30] For Lorna Smith, this was a second offence.

---

on 22 December 1944, when she assented to the proposition put to her by another girl that she wanted a political career. In fact, as Lorna Smith's story indicates, the idea was floating considerably earlier.

* Almost all the former KGGS girls interviewed for this book continued to maintain an active religious life, all of them Christian except for Madeline Hellaby (née Edwards), who converted from Unitarianism to the Bah'ai faith.

Knowing that soap-and-water was useless, what was to be done? Surely, this time we would be expelled. Then someone thought of our star scientist – Margaret Roberts would know what would remove the now-spreading black stain. Her remedy was that it should be sprinkled with bleaching-powder and then have hydrochloric acid poured on (stolen from the lab.). I scrubbed away furiously, and sure enough, the boards began to recover. But the next moment I was almost overcome by the fumes and had to rush out-of-doors, quite blue in the face – no one knew that the lethal mixture would give off chlorine gas. Our violent coughing and splutterings alerted the staff, who were too genuinely concerned about us to be angry at the mess. Indeed, the next day, there was surprisingly little retribution; I suspect that Margaret had quietly been to Miss Gillies and owned up to her near-fatal advice. (My lungs have not been the same since.)

As well as being religious, the school was competitive, at least in its higher academic echelons, and no one more so than Margaret. Rita Hind remembered that she, Margaret and Madeline Edwards used to vie for the top places, and that, in doing so, Margaret displayed more determination than she did natural talent: 'Most things with Maggie were learnt or contrived.'[31]* Even the good-natured Lorna Smith found Margaret's pride in her academic attainments rather tiresome: 'I recall [in July 1942] being slightly "miffed" when Margaret told me afterwards, and rather boastfully, that our form-mistress had said that all our geography results were extremely disappointing – except hers.'[32] Her faults, in the eyes of her contemporaries, concerned her tendency to come top, to be right and to rub it in. And it is noticeable that the ones who most resented her tended to be those who were themselves stars in the school firmament. Both Madeline Edwards and Margaret Goodrich recalled her irritating tendency to ask the first, well-informed question of any visiting speaker, even when she was a little girl in the fourth form ('We'd look at one another and say, "She's at it again,"' said Madeline Edwards); and Margaret Goodrich remembers, at her own twenty-first birthday party in December 1944, a friend turning on Margaret Roberts and saying, 'If you don't stop bossing us, I shall stamp on your foot.'[33] The less competitive girls, such as Lorna, Jean and Shirley, found Margaret less oppressive.

Once in the sixth form, Margaret became a prefect, and she seems to

* Mrs Wright is unique in referring to Margaret as 'Maggie' in her interview. There is no evidence that anyone, apart from President Reagan, who knew her ever called her this at any stage of her life, though it became the name preferred by tabloid headline writers. When asked about her names, Lady Thatcher replied, 'I don't like them, especially the Hilda: it has an ugly hard sound. But I would rather be Hilda than "Maggie"' (interview with Lady Thatcher).

have taken to her duties with the energy, dedication and slight exasperation at the weaknesses of others which were to mark her later career. In December 1941, she writes to Muriel about the preparations for a charity Fun Fair at the school. The decision was made to run the thing in forms, with each form getting up two competitions. 'I happen to have form IV Lower A who are rather young,' writes Margaret, and there was:

> a lot of extra work as posters had to be made to draw people's attention to the fact that they simply MUST go to room seven . . . Well, you know I am no artist so I got two of my form to promise to do some posters for Thursday morning. On Thursday they both came to me and said they were sorry but . . . On Thursday evening I had to sit down and do them myself . . . The youngsters are very enthusiastic but not very ready to do a lot.

Her competition raised 30 shillings and her stall £10 – 'an excellent result'.[34]*

Margaret was not considered an intellectual genius, but she was right at the top of the class, and consistently got good reports and good results. As early as Christmas 1936 she is recorded as having 'worked steadily and well throughout the term. She has definite ability, and her cheeriness makes her a very pleasant member of her form. Her behaviour is excellent.'[35] Even after promotion to the A Stream, Margaret continued to come top every year except one, in which she came second, and reports commended her for virtues like 'care and thoroughness'. Words like 'very satisfactory', 'thoughtful and helpful' and 'keenly interested' abound. Her 'power of sustained interest' was noted. When Margaret applied to Oxford, Miss Gillies, who, as we shall see, had a scratchy relationship with her pupil, nevertheless noted, in her reference, that 'she is a very logical thinker' and 'has a very clear mind'.[36] Miss Gillies's final report had a touch of coolness in its praise: 'Margaret is ambitious and deserves to do well. She has shown herself capable of a very thorough mastery of facts and is, I consider, now ready for the experience of wider scholarship which a University education can offer.'

Margaret accepted and admired the ethos of KGGS. Although, as education secretary from 1970 to 1974, she found herself landed with the task of permitting the closure of grammar schools if local authorities demanded it, and thus closed more than anyone in her position before or since, the process made her miserable. She loved grammar schools, which she regarded as the ladder of opportunity for able children from unprivileged

---

* Margaret Thatcher only rarely dated her handwritten letters exactly. They most commonly say just the day – for example, 'Tuesday' or 'Sunday evening' – or nothing at all.

families. When she visited KGGS in 1986 to open the Roberts Hall in memory of her father, who had been, for almost forty years, first a governor and then chairman of the Governors, she declared: 'I would not have been in No. 10 but for this school.'[37] And, after an earlier visit, as leader of the Opposition in 1977, she wrote, in her letter of thanks to the then head-mistress, 'For me, the school's motto has always been particularly true.'[38] The motto is *Veras hinc ducere voces* – 'To lead true voices from here' (a quotation from Horace's *Ars Poetica*) – and it is fair to say that, despite all the evasions that politics requires, Margaret Thatcher was always excep-tionally concerned to tell the truth as she saw it. When she accepted a peerage, she took her title from her school, not from her town, becoming Baroness Thatcher of Kesteven. Replying to a letter of congratulation from Shirley Ellis, she said: 'I am glad our KGGS friends like the title.'[39]

It is probably the case, however, that Margaret's relationship with her school, as with Grantham itself, was slightly more ambiguous than she would have allowed. Local feeling that she could have done more to use her fame to promote the school's interests may perhaps be discounted – she did keep well in touch with the school and she did, after all, have other things to do – but what is more significant is the conflict Margaret encoun-tered as a pupil when she decided to try for Oxford to read chemistry, a subject in which she was particularly strong, and whose teacher, Miss Kay, she greatly respected.

It related to the character of the headmistress. When Margaret first arrived at KGGS, the headmistress was Miss Gladys Williams, who had held her position from the founding of the school in 1910. Margaret loved Miss Williams: she was always much influenced in her feelings about women (and, indeed, about men) by their manners, appearance and demeanour, and Miss Williams impressed her for these reasons.* Her 'quiet authority . . . dominated everything', she records in her memoirs. 'I greatly admired the special outfits Miss Williams used to wear on important days . . . when she appeared in beautiful silk, softly tailored, looking supremely elegant.' With this elegance, though, she combined another vir-tue high in Margaret's pantheon: 'she was very practical. The advice to us was never to buy a low-quality silk when the same amount of money would purchase a very good-quality cotton . . . The rule was always to go for

---

* Most of the young Margaret's harshest comments are reserved for those who make nothing of their appearance and exhibit sourness or slatternliness. In a letter to Muriel written in December 1941, she describes the school's hockey-team visit to a match in Melton: 'Their gym mistress was an awful old irritable thing. She had a spotty complexion, lank, greasy hair – eton-cropped, wore glasses and dowdy clothes. She found fault with everything possible and actually coached her own side while refereeing.'

quality within your own income.'[40] Despite proving to be the most successful career woman in the whole of British history, Mrs Thatcher liked the display of lady-like qualities and traditionally female accomplishments. She notes approvingly that Miss Williams made all girls 'however academic' take domestic science for four years,[41] and she records without complaint, though she herself studied the subject, that Miss Williams had in her day discouraged maths in the sixth form, because it was considered so difficult for the girls.[42] Jean Farmer had similar impressions of Miss Williams as 'a tiny person, beautifully dressed, looks could quell, not a hair out of place'.[43] So did Rita Hind, who found her 'elegant, stately and white-haired . . . her expectations were high. She was compassionate but distant.'[44]

In 1939, Miss Williams retired. Her successor, Miss Dorothy Gillies, was very different. More of a scholar than Miss Williams, she also had much more of a temper. 'She was a fiery Scot,' said Rita Hind,[45] and she once threw her shoe at someone. Madeline Edwards remembers her hurling books and shouting at the girls, 'You're all suet puddings.' Even the official school history implies some abrasions, saying that Miss Gillies was 'misunderstood' and comparing her with Goldsmith's village schoolmaster: '"If severe in aught, the love he bore to learning was at fault. Yet he was kind . . ."'[46] It should be remembered, as a huge extenuation of Miss Gillies's conduct that, unlike Miss Williams, she had to deal with the difficulties of a school in wartime. These included the facts that Camden School for Girls was evacuated to the KGGS premises for five terms until late 1941, forcing all the KGGS classes to take place in the morning only, and that the right staff were scarce. Worse, there was always the prospect of bombing. Grantham suffered twenty-one raids between September 1940 and October 1942, and in that final and most severe attack thirty-two people were killed. No one at the school was hurt in raids, but the tennis courts were all dug up to build air-raid shelters, and the burden of disruption and of responsibility that war put upon the headmistress was heavy indeed.

Perhaps because Miss Gillies was not Miss Williams, she and Margaret did not get on. Margaret considered her ungracious. Miss Gillies thought that Margaret needed taking down a peg. Their main disagreement concerned Margaret's application for Oxford. By the time of School Certificate, Margaret expected to go to university, though she recognized that she might not be able to afford to do so without a scholarship. With her customary care, she began to make plans, choosing science as her likely university subject because 'Science was the way of the future.'[47] She declared to Muriel that she would drop maths because 'I couldn't get on with Grumpy Grin [Miss Grindley, the maths teacher]: her explanations were as clear as mud.'

Again, she consulted Mr Marks, and followed his suggestion of switching to geography. She buckled down also to biology ('I never dreamt there was so much inside a worm before. One of the toughest jobs is to find the ovary . . .') and announced, 'I have decided to take Latin to help with Biology, and also because you must have it for entrance to most universities.'[48]

It is not true, then, as some biographers have asserted, that Miss Gillies, who was herself a classicist, forbade Margaret to learn Latin at the school. Her studies continued to go well and in 1942, before she had taken Higher Certificate (the equivalent of the modern A Level), she was offered places at Nottingham University, the nearest university to Grantham, and Bedford College, London. But the idea of Oxford grew in the minds of Margaret and her father, and was resisted by Miss Gillies along with the extra Latin teaching required, allegedly provoking Margaret to say, 'You're thwarting my ambition.'[49] According to Muriel, Margaret told Miss Gillies that she wanted to go to Oxford and Miss Gillies said: '"I'm afraid you can't. You haven't got Latin." She said, "I'll get it," and so she went to the Latin master of the boys' school* and she got her Latin [meaning her Latin School Certificate] in a year and she got in.'[50] Margaret never forgot what she considered to have been Miss Gillies's obstruction, though she does record that the head lent her Latin textbooks, including one written by her father.[51] In later years, she paid fulsome tribute to Miss Williams and none to Miss Gillies. Most KGGS old girls of that era remember the occasion in 1960 when Margaret, returning for the school's speech day as a newly elected MP and the guest of honour, actually corrected Miss Gillies on the Latin she had used in her introduction. Lorna Smith wrote, 'The audience was overcome with embarrassment; it was well known that the Head had taught Margaret every Latin word she knew!'[52] This was far from the case, but Margaret's rudeness is still remarkable.

Part of the problem that worried Miss Gillies was haste. Margaret eventually took her Oxford entrance when she was only seventeen, hoping to go up the following autumn, almost exactly on her eighteenth birthday in 1943. This hurry was not solely the result of Margaret's drive and ambition: there was a special wartime reason for it. All girls not already in further education by the time they were eighteen were liable for call-up to the services, and so most of them, anxious to get on with their education, made sure they got in early. Women did not take part in combat, and, it seems, there was no stigma of draft-dodging against girls in this situation.[53]

---

* It has also been suggested that Margaret was given Latin lessons by Fr Leo Arendzen, the Robertses' neighbour and the local Roman Catholic parish priest. (Letter from Canon A. P. Dolan.)

Indeed, the Grantham dentist's daughter Mary Wallace was proud of the precedent she established by persuading Oxford to take her in the Hilary (summer) term of 1943 solely so that she could avoid call-up.[54] The Grantham grocer's daughter, however, was a little more uneasy. 'I felt a little bit guilty,' she recalled, 'but that's the way my birthday came up.'[55] If, as Miss Gillies had suggested, Margaret had waited for another year, she would probably have been forced to serve.

This is very nearly what happened. Part of the problem about the Latin was the need to mug it up so fast, and there were other weaknesses, too, which Margaret needed to remedy. Although her science was strong, her wider education was considered less assured, and it was for this reason that her father went to Canon Goodrich* and got him to coach her for the Oxford general paper. When she did sit the scholarship for Somerville College, Oxford, she narrowly failed to achieve it. Instead, she was offered an ordinary place for the autumn of 1944, which involved returning to KGGS for an extra year to avoid the call-up that would follow her eighteenth birthday on 13 October 1943. This she did, but still facing the probability that her arrival at Oxford would be further delayed by the call-up, or that her degree would be shortened to two years so that she could do National Service afterwards.

The Michaelmas term at KGGS began that year in August because of the need for a longer break in October to help with the wartime potato harvest. For the first time in its history, the school had two head girls – Madeline Edwards and Margaret Roberts, polar opposites in interests and style, but each having a forceful personality. It is alleged by some of Margaret's contemporaries that she was given the post through the influence of her father as chairman of the Governors, but this is anachronistic: Alfred Roberts did not become chairman until after the war. Madeline and Margaret were the only obvious candidates. Indeed, they were the only two remaining girls who had taken their Higher Certificates. It is not clear why both were offered the post: perhaps it was considered invidious to appoint one and exclude the other.

In any event, Margaret's first taste of supreme authority did not last long. Three weeks into the school term, a girl who had a Somerville place dropped out and the college offered an immediate place to Margaret. She accepted, and vaulted suddenly into another world.

* See Chapter 1.

3

Love and war at Oxford

'Is it marble, Margaret?'

Margaret was apprehensive about Oxford. She had never been away from home for more than a few days before, and wartime made the separation greater. The gulf between Grantham and Oxford, however, was more one of milieu than of distance. She was the first woman in her family to go to university, and the first of either sex to go to Oxford. The only people she knew there were Mary Wallace and Margaret Goodrich, neither of whom was at her college, and both of whom came from a more educated social background. She consulted them.

Mary Wallace, who remembered that Margaret's entry to Oxford 'created quite a stir' in Grantham, received Margaret in her parents' house in the High Street in September 1943, where she found her 'very earnest'. 'She was very keen to do the right thing,' and, as so often in her later career, expressed this in an anxiety about 'what sort of clothes to wear'.[1] In Margaret Goodrich's view, 'Oxford was a big jump for her, not for us [that is, her sister Joan and herself] because the clergy had a certain status.' She recorded that when she and her father first visited Margaret in her rooms in Somerville, they found her lonely and disconsolate, toasting a teacake by a fire that was rationed to one scuttle of coal per week.[2] Margaret herself admitted that she felt 'shy and ill-at-ease'.[3] She sometimes walked alone round Christ Church Meadows and into Addison's Walk in Magdalen. In doing so, she felt she was fulfilling C. S. Lewis's injunction in *Christian Behaviour* (1944) to set aside time for solitary thought,[4] but one may guess that her isolation was not entirely voluntary.

One of Margaret's problems was money. Without a scholarship, she had to depend on what her father could manage and on what various small college bursaries could provide. In those days, it was possible to have most of your fees paid if you promised, on going down, to become a teacher, but this Margaret refused to do, believing that it was a vocation she did not have.[5] While her parents did their best, sending small sums and cakes baked by her mother that made the teas in her room well above average, she was always short. She recalled that it was only after she had taught at a Grantham school during the Long Vacation at the end of her first year that she could afford to buy that most basic tool of Oxford life, a bicycle.[6] It would be quite wrong to give the impression that most of the undergraduates were terribly rich, or that Margaret was terribly poor; and besides, the rigours of war reduced the social differences that had prevailed in the 1930s. But lack of funds did contribute to Margaret's sense of adversity that had to be overcome daily, and also to the impression which she created among her contemporaries. Their memories of her at Oxford often include the idea that her appearance was 'brown', both in hair and clothes, and somehow in personality:[7] Rachel Willink, one of the only two women before Margaret to become president of OUCA, the Oxford University Conservative Association, and daughter of a wartime Conservative minister, remembered her as 'quiet, rather mousey', 'rather a brown girl', someone who 'hadn't got the style' to 'make up' for her background. In after years, she said, people who had known Margaret at Oxford found it 'a thing out of nature' that 'that rather humourless mouse' had been so astonishingly successful.[8] According to Mary Wallace, who was also an officer of OUCA, Margaret was 'merely tolerated' by the grandees of the Tory club as 'someone who could be relied on to do the donkey work'.[9] To them she was a 'slogger', without star quality.

No letters from Margaret survive from her first year at Oxford, but in the fairly numerous ones she wrote, almost all to Muriel, in her next three years clothes and the difficulty of affording them provide the main subject. Brownness recurs: 'the rust-coloured material . . . will fit in with the brown side of my wardrobe,' she wrote in an undated letter sent after returning early to Oxford, in order to do fire-watching, before her second year in September 1944. She takes advantage of the journey from Grantham via London to pay her first ever visit to Bond Street, 'though I didn't tell Mummy so', and buys brown court shoes called Debutante Lanette to match her brown handbag at Marshall and Snelgrove. 'Also I had in mind to get a nigger brown [this was a standard name for a haberdashery colour of the time, not a racist phrase of Margaret's invention] fairly plain frock' in order to have 'a completely brown-fawn rig-out'.

She found one. A problem, however, arose: 'It looked absolutely stunning and I was thrilled to bits with it. I was just about to say I'd take it when I suddenly remembered that I hadn't asked the price . . . after all this was the <u>inexpensive</u> gown floor wasn't it? Much to my open-mouthed dismay, the assistant said it was £20 . . .' Luckily, Margaret was able to find, among woollens, what she described, breathless for lack of punctuation, as 'a fairly plain little frock with a peter pan collar two little pockets on the bodice and two to match on the skirt' for £3 16s. Even this price was high for Margaret, but the 'elderly' assistant then did a hard sell: 'she saw that I was a little surprised and said that it was superb value for money [always the way to Margaret's heart] and it was not necessarily how much you paid for a frock that counted which I could quite believe after trying on the "inexpensive gowns".' The bargain-hunter was persuaded, as she excitedly recounts: 'Well to cut a long story short I bought the frock and I'm sure that it is one of the most worthwhile purchases I've ever made. I'll try to smuggle it home next time to show you without Mummy seeing . . . I shall be well set up for frocks then for any and every occasion.'[10]

Margaret was self-conscious, too, about her weight. When the present author once asked her what she thought of her own looks as a young woman, she answered, 'Oh, I never thought I was good-looking. I thought I was slightly overweight.'[11] In those days, it was by no means as unfashionable as it is today for a woman to be quite plump, but, in another part of the letter quoted above, Margaret, with scientist's humour, expresses her anxiety: '. . . I still weigh about 10st 4lbs . . . The slight decrease in volume doesn't seem to have made much difference to the mass . . . Can you recommend . . . anything from the medical point of view for reduction of the area of the seat and control of the tummy muscles – oh and also reduction and uplift of bust?'[12] At one point her weight reached 10 stone 10 pounds, quite a lot for a twenty-year-old girl of 5 foot 5 inches.*

But if Margaret might be disparaged as a slightly podgy, frumpy person, someone beneath notice, by some in Oxford's grander circles, she faced almost the opposite problem within her own college. According to Betty Spice, who, with Margaret, was one of only three girls in her year in the college reading chemistry, the tables in hall at Somerville were divided into three columns, and these tended, in practice, to represent different groups within the college. The tables nearest the high table seated the 'more exotic types', foreigners, Jews, Nina Mabey (the future novelist Nina Bawden) and articulate girls who read PPE (philosophy, politics and economics). The tables at the other end were the haunts of the public school girls. Those in the middle belonged to the grammar school products, many from back-

---

* Her anxiety about her weight was to persist. In October 1974, Mrs Thatcher told the BBC's *Any Questions?*: 'Oh, I've tried to lose weight . . . If I didn't, I'd just get enormous. I lose half a stone every year and promptly put it back on . . . but I do think people should look after their weight. You know, one Labour politician in Parliament said to me, "If politicians can't have enough self-discipline over what they eat, how can you expect them to have enough self-discipline over their political lives?"' (Christopher Collins, ed., *Complete Public Statements of Margaret Thatcher 1945–90 on CD-ROM*, Oxford University Press, 1998/2000).

grounds similar to Margaret's own. It was natural to them to accommodate Margaret, therefore, and they did so, but without great enthusiasm on their part or, possibly, on hers.* Her voice was part of the trouble. 'When she talked, she was not natural,' Betty Spice remembered.[13] She was 'pretty, in a baby-doll sort of way', but 'You couldn't get close to her. She didn't want us because we were only grammar school girls. She was interested in making her way with people who would help her.' Another exact contemporary, Jean Southerst, also noted her speech and appearance: 'Her voice, elocution-trained, was regarded as affected, and her preoccupation with her appearance caused amusement. She went to the most expensive hairdresser in Oxford (Andreas) and spent days during the vac. combing the West End for suitable dresses.'† Margaret's first elocution lessons had been to improve a mild speech impediment and help her declaim in public. According to Joan Parker, a pupil at KGGS, slightly younger than Margaret, the girls would have whole-class elocution lessons in which Lincolnshire vowels were erased so that the girls no longer said 'moostard' or 'coostard'.[14] Amy Wootten, who read maths in the same year and sat at Margaret's table in hall, denied that Margaret was at all 'snooty', but said that she was 'not outgoing': she was 'never in a position where she owed anyone anything'.[15] Mary Mallinson, who shared digs in Walton Street with Margaret in her last year, noted her as someone who was always 'unobtrusively neat and well-groomed' and not easy to know.[16] Pauline Cowan, who shared digs with Margaret in Richmond Road, the previous year, 1945–6, says that Margaret was 'not socially climbing' but, rather, 'diffident': 'I never felt of her as obviously very happy.'[17]

In fact, matters were not as bad as this might suggest. Margaret won respect. Even Betty Spice records that she was 'an honest person',[18] and that she quite enjoyed being teased about possible boyfriends at meals in hall ('She would blush from the neck upwards'). Pamela Rhodes thought her 'very mature for her years',[19] and Jean Southerst, a fellow Methodist, recalled that 'her room in college was always open for pleasant evenings for gossip, poetry reading (I owe her much for that) and partaking of the excellent coffee and cakes etc., which, as a grocer's daughter, made her a very popular hostess!'[20] She impressed as someone who would do what she promised and who 'had a clear idea of what she wanted to attain'.[21]

---

* This difficulty in 'placing' Margaret recurred when she returned to Somerville for its centenary dinner in 1979. According to Amy Wootten, no one knew with which group of alumnae she would be seated.

† Betty Spice believed that Margaret's voice was as it was because 'Daddy had made her have elocution lessons before she came up.' This is not the case, as explained in Chapter 2.

And Margaret happily took part in the jollifications of fellow female students. At the end of her third-year exams, she wrote to Muriel that she had been with friends to see the film *Quiet Wedding*: 'It's an absolute scream. I laughed more than I have for months, I wish you'd seen it. On Tuesday night we went to see *Passage to Marseilles*, with Humphrey Bogart . . . It wasn't a bad film but it wasn't outstanding either. We enjoyed it because we were celebrating. Did I tell you that seven of the men failed?'[22]

The sort of qualities which Margaret displayed were not of the type to endear her to the typical student mind, which values spontaneity over carefulness. Here is Mary Mallinson recalling an incident at the very end of their time at Oxford, the Sunday before Finals in the Walton Street digs with their fellow lodger, Mary Foss.*

Margaret was up to her eyes . . . Mary Foss and I had had an easier year, but Mary was in a panic because she had spent a lot of time in social activities during the year and suddenly realised how much she hadn't done. We were each in our rooms, Mary downstairs and Margaret and I on the first floor, when there was a loud thump. Margaret and I rushed downstairs and found Mary flat out in a faint on the floor. We did what we could then went back upstairs to get on with our revision. When the same thing had happened for the 4th time, Margaret looked at me and said that we couldn't spend all day rushing up and downstairs. She realised that it was a form of hysteria. Having agreed that on no occasion had Mary suffered any injury, she suggested that next time we just left her. She wasn't being unkind. She was being realistic and practical. She had so much work to do and just could not afford the time . . .[23]

Of the four women's colleges at Oxford, Somerville was the most austere. There was a joke current at the time about the different reaction of girls at the different colleges to a friend who said she had just met a young man. The woman from Lady Margaret Hall said: 'Who are his parents?' The one from St Hilda's said, 'What games does he play?' The one from Somerville said, 'What is he reading?' and the woman from St Hugh's said, 'Where is he?'[24]

The prevailing expectation among the undergraduates of her college

---

* Mary Foss converted to Roman Catholicism in rather dramatic circumstances. A Primitive Methodist from Cornwall, she fell in love at Oxford with an undergraduate called David Balhatchet, who was a Catholic. She converted to Catholicism and married him. Mary's mother had a heart attack as a result of her daughter's conversion and refused to attend the wedding. (Mrs Balhatchet died some years ago. The author has the above information from Mrs Mary Williamson.) The story of Mary may have contributed to Beatrice Roberts's fear of Roman Catholic influences on Margaret (see Chapter 5).

was of work which involved educational or public service. There was little thought of business or money or glamour, or a political career. Life was serious and the privilege of a woman's education at a great university had to be repaid. Margaret herself believed devoutly in worthiness and public service, but she applied these beliefs during her career in a way which many Somervillians did not like and with a success of which some, perhaps, were jealous. There was some resentment that, of all the girls who went to Somerville, it had to be she who became world famous. She exhibited what many considered a sort of smug perfection. Betty Spice said, 'We're not proud of Margaret. We found it a bit galling that she became prime minister, and that she married Denis and got his money and then had the twins in one go.'[25] At the fiftieth anniversary of Margaret's year's matriculation – 1993 – Somerville laid on a dinner, with drinks in the college's new Margaret Thatcher Suite. Seeing the bust of the ex-Prime Minister there, one of her contemporaries went up and covered it with a windcheater, to widespread amusement.[26] Something similar applies to many of Somerville's dons, particularly those under the influence of Janet Vaughan, the Principal of Somerville from 1945, and one of those progressives who regard being a Conservative as a sort of mental defect. 'She stood out,' she told a pair of biographers. 'Somerville had always been a radical establishment and there weren't many Conservatives about then . . . she was so set as steel as a Conservative . . . We used to entertain a good deal at weekends, but she didn't get invited. She had nothing to contribute, you see.'[27] Pauline Cowan remembers dining at Somerville high table shortly after Margaret became prime minister in 1979. 'We're all wearing black,' the dons told her.[28] It could be argued that Margaret's career exemplified the tradition of radicalism which Janet Vaughan invoked: her youthful Conservatism certainly showed a determination not to conform. The truth is that most of her Somerville contemporaries did not know her terribly well, and were not strongly attracted by what they did know.

For her part, Mrs Thatcher always spoke warmly of Somerville, even including Janet Vaughan – 'a remarkable person',[29] whose subsequent scientific work she followed with interest. If she noticed any hostility, she did not mention it, let alone reciprocate. She maintained her admiration for the college system – 'A college is a college, thank goodness'[30] – and although she was deeply hurt by Oxford University's vote to refuse her an honorary degree when she was prime minister, she never directed any of the same feeling towards her college. Partly because of her warm respect for Daphne Park, Principal of Somerville from 1980 to 1989,* she maintained an interest in

* Daphne Park (1921–2010), educated Rosa Bassett School and Somerville College, Oxford;

the place throughout her years as prime minister. But it is also true that she kept no close friends from Somerville days.

In a letter to Muriel of 19 April 1945 (less than two weeks before the death of Hitler, but the war is not mentioned), Margaret describes returning to the college slightly earlier than her fellows (probably to take part in a short electioneering course organized by OUCA). She went into dinner after arriving and 'to my dismay' found herself:

> in solitary state, alone in that immense hall except for the maid to wait on me. The dons have dinner in their private dining room during the vac. so there was no question of their company thank goodness. I had a marvellous dinner. First there was some lovely creamy soup and then some very tender lean beef, together with roast potatoes, caulyflower [sic], and white sauce provided the main course. Finally there was some lemon jelly with lemon flavoured meringue on top.

After dinner, she couldn't find a porter, so she hauled her own trunk to the bottom of her staircase, but finding it too heavy, unpacked it in the quad and 'carried my things up in armfulls [sic]'. 'I then began to unpack the contents of my room to alleviate its bareness a little,' but by half-past eleven she was exhausted and went to bed.[31] This is not the letter of someone who hates her college, nor yet the letter of someone who is wholly happy there.

Part of Margaret's relative isolation at Somerville derives from the fact that she was a scientist. As a chemist, she was one of only five women in her year in the entire university. Long hours in the labs, and at lectures which, unlike those in the arts, were more or less compulsory, kept her away from much of the society of her fellow Somervillians. Although she worked hard, Margaret did not particularly enjoy life in the lab: 'I was much more interested in the theory than in the practical work.'[32] She was fortunate, though, that, in Dorothy Hodgkin, Somerville had one of the most distinguished chemists in the world. Mrs Hodgkin, who later won the Nobel Prize for chemistry, was famous for her crystallographic analysis of the structure of molecules, and later discovered important information about the structure of penicillin. Penicillin, the first antibiotic, had been discovered in 1928, but its pioneering trials had taken place much later, in Oxford, two years before Margaret went up: it was what would now be called the cutting edge of science at that time. According to Margaret's fellow chemist Betty

---

leading figure in the Secret Intelligence Service; Principal of Somerville College, Oxford, 1980–89; created Baroness Park of Monmouth, 1990.

Spice, Dorothy Hodgkin was a 'brilliant chemist, but an awful tutor', whose tutorials used to trickle away into complete silence,[33] and Pauline Cowan, while not going so far, agreed that she was bad at teaching first-year students.[34] Margaret, however, felt an enormous respect for Mrs Hodgkin. Perhaps because of this, she elected, for Part II chemistry, to work with Mrs Hodgkin in person. Most Oxford undergraduate courses were and are three years long. It was possible for chemists to obtain an unclassified degree after their exams at the end of three years, but the full, classified BSc with honours was awarded only to those who stayed on a further year for research, culminating in a thesis which was 'viva-ed' (discussed at interview). This is what Margaret chose to do, under the supervision of Dorothy Hodgkin.

'I must say I was very pleased with her for this,' Professor Hodgkin wrote to a scientific colleague in 1988. 'I tended to encourage my Somerville chemists to spread their wings if they wanted to go off into other fields ... I was sent from America and Moscow several gramicidin, antibacterial peptides, which are still providing difficult problems for X Ray analysis ... Gerhard Schmidt [a Jewish refugee scientist] started working on the simplest, gramicidin S from Moscow ... Margaret helped him with growing heavy atoms containing crystals but all proved too complex to solve.' (Indeed, it took over forty years more to solve some of them.) 'The measurements they did were eventually useful.'[35]

How good a scientist was she? She certainly had a serious interest in the subject – one which she would deploy in future years. She liked to point out that she was the first prime minister with a science degree, rather than boasting that she was the first woman prime minister. After going down, she went back to Oxford to call in on old friends in the crystallography department, and she records, in letters to Muriel written during and shortly after Oxford, the pleasure of meeting famous scientists like Linus Pauling and Max Perutz, and of visiting Cambridge to meet fellow crystallographers. She worked hard at it, too, winning two college prizes in her first two years, experiencing many an essay crisis and demonstrating the ability, so famous in later life, to study late into the night. When she took her exams at the end of her third year, she had to sit some of them in the sanatorium. Margaret told friends that she was ill at the time, but there is some evidence that she was suffering more from nervous exhaustion brought on by overwork.[36] At the end of her fourth year, she was awarded a respectable second-class degree. Janet Vaughan, a scientist but not a chemist, said disparagingly of Margaret: 'She was a perfectly adequate chemist. I mean nobody thought anything of her.'[37] But her judgment may have been coloured by the strong political antagonism she felt towards Margaret in later years. Professor Hodgkin, who also differed politically from Margaret,* but knew her and liked her better, was fairer: 'I came to rate her as good. One could always rely on her producing a sensible, well-read essay and yet there was something that some people had that she hadn't quite got.'[38]

Margaret herself would not have disagreed with her tutor's view. Speaking in praise of Dorothy Hodgkin in later life, she referred to a conversation with Max Perutz in which, she said, he told her that, in science, 'reason and maths can get you so far, but you need inspiration on top.' There is 'a fascinating link', she went on, 'between art and science'.[39] Dorothy Hodgkin, she believed, had that inspiration, that artistic, imaginative gift. It is not something she would ever have claimed for herself. Indeed, for all her astonishing self-confidence in some areas, Margaret never boasted of an intellectual mastery that she did not possess: at Oxford, she met many people who were her intellectual superiors, and she had no trouble recognizing this and deferring to them.

It was true, too, as Dorothy Hodgkin also said, that 'she was not absolutely devoted' to chemistry,[40] that, as Betty Spice put it, 'her heart wasn't in it'.[41] While at Oxford, she developed a growing interest in the law. In her memoirs, she records that her father, as mayor of Grantham in 1945-6, sat automatically on the magistrates' bench. She would go along with him, during vacations, to the Quarter Sessions, at which an experienced lawyer would be in the chair as recorder: 'On one such occasion my father and I lunched with him, a King's Counsel called Norman Winning ... At one point I blurted out: "I wish I could be a lawyer; but all I know about is chemistry and I can't change what I'm reading at Oxford now." '[42] Winning said he had read physics at Cambridge but had then stayed on to do a second degree, in law. She replied that she could not afford to do this, so Winning explained that the other way ('very hard work') was to get a job in or near London, join an Inn of Court and study for the Bar in the evenings. In her memoirs, Mrs Thatcher sets all this in the context of her later life – 'And this in 1950 is precisely what I had done'[43] – but it is important to note that the bent towards law was already so strong at Oxford as to tempt her away from chemistry, and to remember that, in 1945-6, she had no clear prospect of being able to do what Winning suggested. When she

---

* Dorothy Hodgkin was a member of the anti-nuclear Pugwash group of scientists considered by many to have been extremely credulous in their attitude to the Soviet Union. She used to write to Mrs Thatcher from time to time to put the case against cruise missiles and warn her not to listen too much to Soviet dissidents. Mrs Thatcher remained affectionate towards her, but thought her views naive. Having received her at Chequers in 1983, she said to her fellow guest and at that time Principal of Somerville, Daphne Park, 'Is it possible to educate Dorothy a bit more on the issue of Russia?' [interview with Lady Park of Monmouth]

started applying for jobs before leaving Oxford, one of the considerations which governed her choice was the possibility of combining the job with legal studies. Writing to Muriel in the early summer of 1947, she describes interviews for a job at ICI's Billingham plant near Stockton. She likes the idea of the work, but says that it is six hours from London which 'would be an awful disadvantage for the Bar Exams'.[44] Although she began reading for the Bar before her marriage in 1951, the certainty that she could afford to start a legal career came only with the financial security that Denis Thatcher brought her.

In later years, Margaret Thatcher discerned a pattern in her youthful interests: 'As a Methodist in Grantham, I learnt the laws of God. When I read chemistry at Oxford, I learnt the laws of science, which derive from the laws of God, and when I studied for the Bar, I learnt the laws of man.'[45] This was an honest enough résumé of her reverent interest in the splendour of certain types of knowledge. Her belief in the rule of law as the foundation of politics was one of the strongest and most often repeated in her creed. But her account probably underplays the extent to which she saw all her main occupations, the law not the least, as instrumental to her pursuit of a political career. Thus at Oxford she remained an active Methodist, even going on the preaching circuit, where her sermons were reported as 'most impressive'.[46] She was a keen member of the Bach Choir. She was a conscientious and interested chemist, but her obsession, her dream, was politics. 'I had a passion for history,' she said fifty years later, 'and a passion for politics. Politics is living history.'[47] She was probably projecting on to the past an interest in history which she did not exhibit much at the time, but it is true that she had already conceived a passion for politics. She joined OUCA as soon as she went up to Oxford, and threw herself into its activities. Hers was not, at this stage, a strong engagement with political ideas and beliefs, nor yet the undergraduate love of politicking. It was simply a determination, entered into without apparent self-examination, to engage in political life, re-energize political organization, and to do it as well as she possibly could.

Although the war provided the subject of constant and consuming interest for undergraduate conversation, it had the curious effect of making Oxford less actively political than at many other periods, notably the 1930s. This was partly because so many men were away in the forces. The Oxford Union, the centre of university political debate, allowed only men to take part in debates.* It was also because the overriding need to win the war

---

* Even when she was president of OUCA, Margaret could only attend Union debates in the gallery, and then only if she were given guest tickets by a member.

produced, if not agreement about post-war politics, at least a determination not to quarrel. As Margaret Thatcher said, when talking fifty years later about the wartime political atmosphere at Somerville, 'You couldn't but be patriotic in wartime because so much was at stake.'[48] Contemporaries remember that, although the progress of the war was constantly discussed in casual mealtime conversations, controversial issues were not. According to Amy Wootten, typical Somerville table talk would move between war news to its small consequences – 'They've got bananas in a shop in the High' – to the ordinary gossip of the day. Most undergraduates were quite religious, and, as at KGGS, it was more likely God than Soviet Communism or economic policy that they, including Margaret, could be found debating.[49] Political awareness was quite low. Amy Wootten, in fact, was under the misapprehension that Margaret was a Liberal, just because her two fellow chemists were.[50]

This absence of political controversy characterizes Margaret's correspondence with her sister throughout her time at Oxford. Admittedly, Muriel was not a highly political person, but it is still striking that Margaret's letters to her contain scarcely a single expression of political views and next to nothing about current political events. Politics, when it occurs, is presented as an activity requiring a great deal of work but also opening up social opportunities and giving pleasure. It is something to be done, not something to be debated. Only one witness can recall having an actual political argument with Margaret at Oxford. Pauline Cowan remembered that Margaret was the very first person she met at Somerville and that Margaret's first act had been to try to recruit her for OUCA which, considering herself a Communist, she refused. Pauline shared digs with Margaret in Richmond Road in 1945–6, and recalled the 'rather unpleasant breakfasts' cooked by the landlady consisting of dishes like hot pilchards with mashed potato. She and Margaret had at least one argument over breakfast about the structure of post-war society and how egalitarian it should be. She cannot remember much of what was said, but she collected the sense that 'Margaret disapproved as well as disagreed.'[51] This argument was exceptional, though. Even Mary Wallace, who knew Margaret from Grantham and was active in OUCA, has no memory of her ever expressing any political views.[52]

Conservatism at Oxford towards the end of the war, although it had a surprisingly large number of recruits, was not spoiling for a fight. It did not, for instance, warn of the dangers of too uncritical an association with Stalin or cry out in protest at the growth of the welfare state. When working on her memoirs in the 1990s, Margaret struggled to recall her views at the time. On Anglo-Soviet friendship, she said, 'We never felt right about it. This unbelievably cruel man got to be called "Uncle Joe" because of wartime propaganda.'[53] She also recalled reading Friedrich von Hayek's *The Road to Serfdom*, which was published in 1944.[54] But there is a sense that these memories are dredged up rather than strongly felt, and Margaret herself admitted that 'I cannot claim that I fully grasped the implications of Hayek's little masterpiece at the time.'[55] 'The times were political,' she declared of her Oxford period in 1994; 'how on earth had war happened again?',[56] but there is no evidence that this was the subject which she and her fellow youthful Tories discussed much. Indeed, there is a curious, cosy feeling about student political discussion at that time, as if people believed, somehow or other, that everything was going to be all right.

The fact was that, in common with almost all her fellow Conservatives at the end of the war, Margaret had a fairly strong belief in the capacity of Whitehall men and ideas to run the country in a humane and orderly way. She admired the White Paper on Full Employment, closely and directly influenced by Keynes, which appeared in 1944, and she credited 'Winston', as she always in later life referred to Churchill,* with wisdom in creating the Ministry for Reconstruction and Development. Administrative thinkers like Oliver Franks† at the Ministry of Supply, who subsequently served her well in his inquiry into the Falklands War, commanded her confidence, as did Sir William Beveridge for his report on Social Security in 1942 and R. A. Butler for his Education Act of 1944.[57] She liked the fact that the wartime economy was 'an economy with a purpose' which gave almost everyone a job.[58] She said that she didn't feel she was a 'right-wing Tory' at the time: 'Fairness is a big streak in the British character,' a streak which was satisfied by rationing.[59] To the extent that her Toryism at this stage went beyond an instinctive loyalty to the non-unionized classes of society, its chief characteristics were a sense that collectivism threatened both freedom and economic success, and a romantic imperialism which saw the British Empire as ensuring civilized values, even in its process of decline. Indeed, these two things combined in her perception. She said that what she wanted was 'a freer society, which produced a large part of the power

---

* Mrs Thatcher was often criticized for referring to Churchill thus, as if she were presuming acquaintance with the great man. It seems more likely that she was repeating the usage of fellow Young Conservatives, rather as the equivalents, in her time, would call her 'Maggie', without pretending that they knew her.

† Oliver Franks (1905–92), educated Bristol Grammar School and Queen's College, Oxford; philosopher at Oxford and Glasgow Universities, 1927–45; Permanent Secretary, Ministry of Supply, 1945–6; Provost of Queen's College, Oxford, 1946–8; Ambassador to the United States, 1948–52; chairman, Lloyds Bank, 1954–62; Provost of Worcester College, Oxford, 1962–76; chairman, Falkland Islands Review Committee, 1982; knighted, 1946; created Lord Franks, 1962; Order of Merit, 1977.

that made Britain great'.[60] She was also struck with the idea that Utopias were dangerous. Although a scientist, she recalled that she was always suspicious of those who tried to apply the scientific method to politics: 'you get Utopian government.'[61] In 1944, she saw the film of J. B. Priestley's play *They Came to a City*, and derived from it the idea that 'You can't get a solution that ignores human nature.'[62]

The end of the war in Europe in May 1945 and the general election in July hardened politics up. Margaret took part in the campaign – mostly, since it was held on 5 July,* in Grantham rather than Oxford. In those days, the mainstay of election campaigns was the public meeting, and it fell to Margaret to act as the warm-up speaker for the Conservative candidate, Squadron Leader Worth, as he toured the villages surrounding Grantham night after night. She remembered these occasions quite self-critically: 'I wasn't terribly good at keeping going. My training had been scientific. Therefore I spoke in short sentences . . . machine-gun style,'[63] but her readiness to do so showed precocious courage. She already had some experience of speaking, having talked that spring, for example, to the Grantham Rotary Ladies on 'A Day in the Life of an Oxford Undergraduate' and having put on a performance at OUCA of which she boasted to Muriel: 'I gave my paper on Agricultural Policy which was a staggering success.'[64] But as she was a woman and someone who, aged nineteen, was still not old enough to vote,† when she spoke she was bound to attract local attention.

One meeting, at Sleaford on 25 June 1945, was extensively reported by the *Sleaford Gazette* ('Rousing Meeting at Mart'). Margaret, warming up for the candidate for his sixth meeting of the day, was described as 'the very youthful Miss M. H. Roberts, daughter of Alderman A. Roberts of Grantham'. She struck out at once into world affairs, and how prosperity could not return to this Britain 'until we had helped to put the other European countries onto a wholesome footing', by re-establishing trade. She spoke of Germany: 'Miss Roberts said that once in her lifetime, twice in many people's time, and three times in the lives of some people, Germany had plunged the world into war. Germany must be disarmed and brought to justice. She did not mean that they should be deprived of everything, but just punishment must be meted out.' The formulation about the frequency with which Germany had caused war is almost uncannily similar to that repeatedly used by Lady

---

* Because of the need to collect votes from servicemen abroad, the result was not declared until 26 July.

† The voting age, at that time, was twenty-one.

Thatcher in the 1990s, although sometimes the word 'Germany' was replaced with 'Continental Europe'.

Much of her Sleaford speech was in praise of Winston Churchill – the country 'must see that they do not lose the only remaining man who had the world's confidence' – and it was in this context that Margaret Roberts uttered an apparently surprising view about the Soviet Union: 'The Socialists said that we did not want to make friends with Russia but Mr Churchill and Mr Eden had gone to Russia and had worked unsparingly for co-operation with Russia.' She saw Britain as a great power that should play an equal part in discussions with America and the Soviet Union.

And she dwelt on the theme which, at that time, most fired her imagination: 'Miss Roberts was very fervent in her determination to stand by the Empire. It was the most important community of peoples the world has ever known. It was so bound with loyalty that it brought people half way across the world to help each other in times of stress. The Empire must never be liquidated.'[65]

There is something laughable, perhaps, about the thought of the nineteen-year-old alderman's daughter laying down the law for the world in this way, but also something astonishing and impressive. It and other speeches made by Margaret during the campaign caused Liz Barrington, an old nursing friend of Muriel, to write to her a couple of weeks later:

> I must say I was overjoyed to hear of her marvellous effort at election speaking. You have a very clever sister – and no wonder you thought it wiser to remain unheard when you went home! You – above all people!! I wonder where she will eventually end up? Maybe I shall be able to say, 'Oh yes I have the pleasure of knowing that young lady' in days to come . . . not forgetting her sister who will I am still certain find the footlights in some way or another. Don't laugh, I mean it.*

Liz adds: 'Like yourself I did not wish to vote Labour or Tory.'[66] Was it this that Muriel chose to 'remain unheard' in the Roberts household?

Clement Attlee's Labour Party was swept to office by a landslide. In Grantham, Denis Kendall, the flamboyant Independent, held his seat against the Tory challenge. Margaret attended the count in Sleaford and then went to the Picture House in Grantham to watch the results come through on the screen.[67] They shocked her. Sixty years later, Margaret said that the loss of Winston Churchill was 'really quite shattering',[68] but she

---

* Muriel never did hit the footlights. She married a farmer, Willie Cullen, of whom more later, but one of the pleasant surprises of writing this book has been discovering in Muriel a character perhaps even more formidable than her famous sister.

also came to see in it the natural high point of the process of collectivism which, from 1979, she tried to reverse.[69] At the time, however, it seemed to her against nature and it ended her experience, until then continuous in her entire political memory, of Tory dominance. As it was to do even more markedly in 1974, defeat galvanized her.

The Oxford to which she returned in October 1945 was changed in atmosphere – by the atom bombs and subsequent allied victory in the Far East, by the Labour election victory, and by the return or first arrival of undergraduates who had fought. Although Margaret had been quite close to the war in Grantham, which was bombed more than most places, she was rather unusual in that none of her immediate family served. Meeting men who had done so excited her. She had returned to what she called 'a more mature Oxford' which benefited from being 'more cross-generational'.[70] By this time an officer in OUCA, she joined its policy sub-committee with Stanley Moss, an undergraduate who returned injured from the war, and Michael Kinchin-Smith, who subsequently married Rachel Willink. Their report, produced that term, was ambitious in its scope. The first part, grandly entitled 'The Basis of Conservatism', was drafted by Moss; the second, 'The Role of the Conservative Party Today', was written by Margaret and by Kinchin-Smith,[71] but the three put their signatures to the whole.

Moss's section is windy and sometimes obscure, and none of the pamphlet is scintillating, in either manner or matter, but there are notes to be found of what later became the Thatcher tunes: 'the individual is more important than the system,' 'Individual enterprise is the mainspring of all progress,' 'there is no empirical evidence at all for the existence . . . of the mystic community, state or nation that figures in all systems opposed to this principle, such as the Nazi.' It is also oppositional in tone, much more so than would have been the case during the war. While saying that the party should eschew factionalism, it demands 'strong and vocal' criticism wherever the government exceeds its electoral mandate, and declares that threats to liberty should be opposed by 'every possible weapon of resistance and without thought of compromise'. The toughest comments refer to the Conservative Party itself: 'It is suggested that this general election marks a turning point in the political development of the country equivalent to the election of the Reform Parliament of 1831 and that a reorientation of conservatism within the framework of the 20th century state such as that carried out by Peel will be necessary if the party is to avoid annihilation.' The party needs to be 'much clearer than in the past as to what its basic principles are'; it needs 'house-cleaning'; it should have a proper research department (which, thanks to R. A. Butler, it duly got). The section labelled 'Policy' begins:

Conservative policy has come to mean in the eyes of the public little more than a series of administrative solutions to particular problems, correlated in certain fields by a few unreasoning prejudices and the selfish interests of the monied classes. If this extremely damaging view is to be refuted it is essential that the relation between overall policy and the various solutions be shown and that the latter be demonstrably free from any suspicion of compromise between national and sectional interests. Where Labour and Conservative are in general agreement, it must be proved that the resultant policy is a conservative policy, derived from conservative and not socialist principles if these clash.[72]

Re-reading the pamphlet fifty years later for her memoirs, Lady Thatcher jibbed at a few passages, such as a section which appears to propose a redistribution of wealth, attributing them to the other authors, and particularly at a comically self-important passage on the nature of leadership: 'In an organisation such as OUCA, relying on voluntary effort, perhaps the ideal is a position parallel to that of Roosevelt as President of the United States, following public opinion while at the same time moulding and keeping slightly ahead of it.' That self-contradiction of leading and following at the same time, she declared, was not her style.[73] But in general she accepted that these had been her thoughts at the time. They were scarcely revolutionary ideas, but they did represent a fiercer, more rebellious and more socially mobile Conservatism than had expressed itself in wartime. It was a Conservatism which could not assume its right to rule, and knew that it had to fight for its existence.

In the following March, Margaret was an Oxford representative at the conference of the Federation of University Conservative and Unionist Associations (FUCUA was the unhappy acronym) at the Waldorf Hotel in London. Both she and Kinchin-Smith spoke in favour of a resolution, which she moved, 'demanding that oft-repeated resolutions' for more working-class officers and candidates 'be implemented forthwith'.[74] At a conference at Swinton College, the country house in Yorkshire reserved at that time for weekend gatherings for intelligent young Tories to discuss ideas, Margaret remembered getting into an argument with those of her fellows – more left-wing and better born – who wanted a redistribution of wealth. '"How would this work"', she recalled asking sharply, '"in relation to large country estates?" Answer came there none.'[75] In October 1946, the same month in which she became president of OUCA, Margaret went for the first time as a representative to the party conference in Blackpool. By the standards of Tory conferences at that time, the mood from the floor was rebellious. The rank and file attacked the leadership for not putting forward clear Tory policies and beliefs. She was 'entranced', she wrote.[76] This is perhaps the only recorded occasion when anyone has used that word about a Conservative conference, and yet it is probably an apt one in Margaret's case. She identified with the feelings of the body of the Tory hall, and felt liberated and uplifted by them. Such identification would one day help make her leadership so secure for so long when more senior figures in the party hoped to undermine her. In 1946, those senior figures felt a little beleaguered. 'I had the sense', wrote Margaret, 'that the Party leadership – with the notable exception of the Party Leader [Churchill] – had arrived at Blackpool prepared to reconcile itself and Conservatism to the permanence of socialism in Britain . . . This was decidedly not what the rank and file wanted to hear . . . My instincts were with the rank and file, though I had not yet fully digested the strong intellectual case against collectivism . . .'[77]

It should not be thought, however, that Margaret's meritocratic, 'rank and file' political beliefs went so far as to exclude her from the Oxford Tory mainstream. Serious though the young Margaret Roberts was about everything, including her politics, no one should imagine that she had no interest in pleasure, elegance and the sphere of society into which she had not been born. However genuine her political convictions, she also saw OUCA as a form of social advancement, the opening of the door upon a more civilized world. She might, in the words of William Rees-Mogg, another Oxford (slightly younger) contemporary and a future editor of *The Times*, have been a 'narrow-gauge' Conservative,[78] but she saw OUCA as widening her, and raising her up.

One of the chief embodiments of the world to which she aspired was Edward Boyle.* Neither handsome nor self-confident, Boyle was nevertheless a very appealing figure to Margaret. An Etonian at Christ Church who had already inherited a baronetcy, he was a man of intellectual refinement and gentle good manners who immediately captured her respect in a way that no one else managed until, years later, she met another kindly baronet, Keith Joseph. Boyle was generally seen as a future Conservative prime minister by his fellow undergraduates and was 'brilliant in a way you couldn't quite fathom'.[79] He was also vague, known for shaving and then forgetting to wash the white remains of shaving soap off his face.[80] Boyle,

---

* Edward Boyle (1923–81), 3rd baronet, educated Eton and Christ Church, Oxford; President of the Oxford Union, 1948; Conservative MP for Handsworth, 1950–70; resigned as junior minister over Suez, 1956; Minister of Education, 1962–4; Vice-Chancellor, Leeds University, 1970–81; created Lord Boyle of Handsworth, 1970.

who was to become minister of education under Harold Macmillan, later moved to the extreme left of the Conservative Party, but in the 1940s was closer in politics to Margaret. His influence over her was anyway not so much ideological as moral. She considered that he had 'a great mind. He never had a mean or trifling thought.'[81] And, as so often in her feelings about people, this admiration for his mind and character was linked with an attraction towards his physical surroundings. She vividly remembered, from Oxford times, Boyle's mother's 'fabulous flat in Portman Square' with its 'treasures', some of them Chinese: 'To me it was a different world. I'd never been in a flat like it.' She also remembered in the 1960s, when she and Denis were renting a cottage in Kent, visiting Edward Boyle at his family's house, Ockham in Sussex, and being given 'the best wine'. Boyle fell on hard times towards the end of his life: 'Edward wouldn't have known about money: it was just there.'[82] She did not share his form of unworldliness, but she loved him for it, and for his lack of snobbery towards her.*

There was no one else quite like Boyle in OUCA, but to those of the upper class who were friendly towards her she felt a particular affection. The Earl of Dalkeith,† another Christ Church man later to become a Conservative MP and, after that, Duke of Buccleuch, was one such. When he was an officer of OUCA in 1947, he called together the better off among the OUCA committee and said, 'Look here, we've got somebody here who's our hardest worker. She pedals off to Morris Cowley [the motor works] when Edward Boyle couldn't even cross the road. She's going to be prime minister one day, but she hasn't got any money, so let's get up a Special Fund for her.'[83] Dalkeith asked for £25 each, but could not remember, nearly sixty years later, whether it was raised or what, precisely, it was for.‡ He recalled that Margaret was 'completely unchippy; so nice'. History does not record Margaret's attitude to the gift, but she described Johnny Dalkeith as 'rather a marvellous person'.[84]

---

* Their rapport was maintained to the end, despite deep political differences. When Edward Boyle was dying of cancer in 1981, he called on Mrs Thatcher at No. 10 to say goodbye. They talked alone.

† (Walter) John Montagu Douglas Scott, 9th Duke of Buccleuch (1923–2007), educated Eton and Christ Church, Oxford; served RNVR, 1939–45; Conservative MP (as Earl of Dalkeith) for Edinburgh North, 1960–73.

‡ One friend of Dalkeith who remembers being asked for the money says that it was to buy Margaret a bicycle. Lady Thatcher told the present author that she thought this was probably correct. If so, she is possibly mistaken in her memoirs in saying that she bought a bicycle herself in her second year. If Dalkeith was right that she 'pedalled off' to Cowley before she received her present, whose bicycle did she ride? It also seems highly unlikely that, in those pre-inflationary days, even the grandest undergraduates could have subscribed £25 each.

It is clear from Margaret's letters to Muriel what pleasure she derived from her OUCA friendships and what prestige she believed she had acquired by her OUCA work. Writing to her on OUCA paper in October 1946, she thanks Muriel for the twenty-first-birthday present she sent her and asks if she can borrow her pearls and her black dinner frock because she has to go to two OUCA dinners in quick succession. She also explains that she has written to thank Mrs Nidds, a Grantham neighbour, for her present: 'The reason it was such a large package was that there was an OUCA card in, and I thought she might like it for show.'[85] In May of the following year, when Muriel's birthday is approaching, she writes to tell her sister that she has found her '<u>sheer</u> silk stockings – fully fashioned . . . (<u>not</u> black market)' plus 'a bottle of "Great Expectations", the one created specially for Valerie Hobson'.* She also mentions that she went to Cambridge for a Conservative (Balfour Club) dinner, after which 'at about midnight – we unmoored a punt and went on the river. (I did not wear my black velvet frock thank goodness.)'[86]

In January 1947, Margaret wrote to Muriel explaining that she was attending an OUCA dinner for L. S. Amery, the leading Churchillian, and another for Lord Woolton, the Chairman of the Conservative Party: 'This in addition to the annual dinner'.[87] 'My black velvet frock looks positively opulent! The skirt is cut on the cross so it hangs beautifully.' The rush of dinners leads her to ask Muriel for the loan of her black and gold evening dress. It is clear, too, that OUCA produces more informal pleasures. 'Neil and Roger', she writes, 'have been round to tea etc. several times. Two evenings we have been out "on the razzle" and have had the most hilarious time.'

'Roger' was Roger Gray, from the Queen's College, a handsome war veteran who had just become president of the Oxford Union and, as such, was probably the best-known undergraduate in the university. Margaret mentions that, because of his 'arduous duties', she will probably see less of him this term. 'Neil' was Neil Findlay, from Worcester College, unpolitical, but a great friend and wartime comrade of Roger Gray and, like him, fond of parties and drinking.†

Both men appealed more to Margaret than she did to them. Roger, appar-

---

* Valerie Hobson: famous actress, and later the wronged wife of John Profumo, Minister of War under Harold Macmillan.

† Roger Gray, who died in the 1990s, went on to a career at the Bar where he ended up as a recorder of the Crown Court. Friends believed that his undoubted brilliance was dimmed by his heavy drinking. Findlay became an executive in the paper industry. Neil's son Max became an internet legend in 2011 when film of his dog Fenton chasing deer went viral as 'Jesus Christ in Richmond Park'.

ently, 'found her rather hard work' and sometimes, after a few drinks, would poke her chest and say, 'Is it marble, Margaret?'[88] It was not. Margaret was smitten with Neil, a fact of which he was half aware. According to Neil, Margaret felt attracted towards people with a greater social presence than her own, and they didn't always respond. He felt a little sorry for her.[89]

At the time of Margaret's crush on Neil, which probably began in late 1946, only little hints emerge in her surviving letters to Muriel. 'Bumped into Neil only once this term – that was in the Grocer's,' she wrote in May 1947,[90] but a later letter shows what she had felt. After becoming the candidate for Dartford in early 1949, Margaret moved to lodgings there. From these she wrote to Muriel describing a recent chance meeting: 'When I went to Canterbury a week last Sunday for the political weekend school, I saw Neil Findlay with his new wife at the station on the way back. I don't think they saw [me] for Neil is very short-sighted and I didn't go up to them. His wife is a smart woman but she looked a Jewess.* She was dark with a fair complexion and the typical long nose. I was standing with Doric Bossom (son of A. Bossom† MP for Maidstone): and Ian Harvey, candidate for East Harrow,‡ and was glad that if he saw me, I wasn't too badly off for male company. I didn't feel one single twinge when I saw him. Strange how shallow infatuation is.'[91]

For all its jauntiness, the letter reveals some anxiety on Margaret's part at being at a disadvantage in relation to Neil Findlay, and at being seen alone when he is with another woman. She spoke the truth when she said that the wound had healed. In the 1950s, the Findlays found themselves living in Swan Court, Chelsea, the same block of flats as the Thatchers, and were on good terms with them.[92] But it is clear that at Oxford she was susceptible to men she thought glamorous, and feared being disregarded by them. She saw OUCA as her best way of overcoming any handicap. Writing to Muriel in May 1947 to discuss her sister's forthcoming visit to Oxford (her last before Margaret went down), she explains their social plans. She has asked Edward Boyle to get them tickets for a Union debate,

---

* This is one of a couple of occasions on which Margaret seems to be expressing the mild, unthinking anti-Semitism which was common at that time. These views did not survive her contact with Finchley.

† Sir Alfred Bossom Bt (1881–1965), educated Charterhouse and Royal Academy of Arts; Conservative MP for Maidstone, 1931–59; created Baron Bossom, 1960. Sir Alfred was one of Margaret's earliest patrons. It was from his house in Carlton Gardens that she and Denis went away after their wedding.

‡ Ian Harvey, by 1958 a junior Foreign Office minister, was forced to leave politics after being caught performing a homosexual act with a Guardsman in St James's Park.

and there is a possibility, no more, of their being asked to the President's farewell party afterwards. 'Edward also asked us to lunch one day – if he remembers,' she goes on, and she also hopes to 'wangle a meeting with Roger and/or Neil'. The problem, though, is that 'OUCA activities for the term finish with a garden party tomorrow and I'm otherwise powerless to ask them round. I'll just have to rely on their dropping in which they do on very rare occasions.'[93] Despite four successful years at the university, she was still in a position of traditional, womanly weakness.

Besides, she was still smarting from the loss of an earlier, more serious love.

It seems highly unlikely that Margaret ever had any boyfriends in Grantham. All those who knew her then, including her sister, believe there was none. There is no doubt, however, that Margaret was a carefully dressed young woman whom many considered attractive, and who noticed and enjoyed the attentions of others. People remember her rosy cheeks and elegant legs. Kenneth Wallace, of Grantham, was pleased with her fluent and intelligent conversation.[94] As she started to go to parties in Grantham towards the end of the war men, often servicemen, asked her to dance, and some pressed their suit quite strongly. In August 1944, at the end of her first year in Oxford, she joined the local tennis club in Grantham (she complained that she had 'schorched [sic]' her tennis dress with her iron) and went to its dance there. Before long '. . . I had settled down with a Flight-Lieutenant aged about 40!!!! Or rather he had settled down with me.'[95] At the turn of the year, she went to a dance in Corby, near Grantham:

> To my horror I recognised one of them – the bald one – as the Flight-Lieutenant whom I spent most of the evening with at the tennis dance in the summer. My heart sank when I saw him walking across the floor to ask me for the first dance . . . Fortunately, one of his friends stuck to me like a limpet. He was a lovely dancer so I didn't mind terribly. He was, I gather, a rather famous football referee for he had done at any rate one if not more cup finals. He was unfortunately rather difficult to get rid of. He wanted me to go to the pictures with him. I told him instantly that I was going back to Oxford for an electioneering course for a week . . . He eventually departed having given me his telephone no. name and all further particulars and telling me to ring him up when I got back. I shan't of course because I don't want to go around with a man of his age,* and when I vaguely mentioned the fact at home Daddy said, 'No, of course not!' in a very final tone.[96]

---

* Yet all but one of the men who were to attract Margaret's serious interest were considerably older than she.

Margaret then spent the rest of the evening with a thirty-year-old pilot who had done several operational flights over Germany. What she did not mention when keeping her suitor at arm's length – though she refers to it elsewhere in the same letter to Muriel – was that she already had a boyfriend.

The only previously known specific evidence of a particular man at this stage in Margaret Roberts's life comes from Margaret Goodrich's previously mentioned account (see Chapter 2) of what she believed to be Margaret's first declaration that she wanted to be an MP. Margaret Goodrich celebrated her twenty-first birthday with a small party in the rectory at Corby Glen on 22 December 1944, and Margaret Roberts went to the party, sharing a bed in the overcrowded house with Sheila Browne, much later to become chief inspector of schools during the Thatcher premiership. Both Margarets have recorded, in rather different versions,* that they sat round in the kitchen discussing their ambitions, and Margaret Roberts publicly recognized her own. According to Margaret Goodrich, her mother asked Margaret, and she said, as if she had thought of it before, 'I want to become an MP.'[97] In fact, as we have seen, she had already indicated her political ambitions to others, but what Margaret Goodrich also remembered was that Margaret had arrived clutching a carnation which 'seemed very precious to her' and had, she said, been given her by an Oxford boyfriend. She was concerned for its welfare, so Mrs Goodrich put it in a vase with water and an aspirin.[98] The name of the boyfriend was Tony Bray.

Tony was an army cadet, who had arrived in Oxford in October 1944, attached to Brasenose College, but, due to the exigencies of wartime, had been accommodated in the buildings of Christ Church. He was pursuing a special six-month course, devised to combine military training with lectures on the 'general sciences'. Educated at Brighton College, a minor public school in the south-east, Tony was from a solidly bourgeois background, and before joining up had already been an articled clerk to a solicitor. He was short and not particularly good-looking, but, by his own account sixty years later, 'not half bad as a dancer'.[99] Born in 1926, he was a little younger than Margaret.

The two had met through OUCA, probably at the association's coffee discussions at the Randolph Hotel, some time that autumn of 1944. Margaret seemed to Tony 'very thoughtful and a very good conversationalist. That's probably what interested me. She was good at general subjects.' He

---

* In *The Path to Power* (HarperCollins, 1995) Lady Thatcher incorrectly dates the occasion as being 'Shortly before my university days came to an end'.

was also impressed with her enthusiasm for politics – 'That was something very unusual. Not many girls were like that' – and, like Tony, she was 'a genuine, old-fashioned Conservative'. He was also taken with her appearance: 'She was a plump, attractive girl in a well-built way. That wasn't ill thought of,' and she had 'elegant, dark hair' ('I'd have told her I didn't like blondes if she had become blonde then'). She 'dressed elegantly, though not in a top stylish way'. He felt also that she had 'a degree of loneliness' which was part of 'the reason we got on'.[100]

At that time, it was unusual for couples to go around as 'an item', and Margaret and Tony did not do so. None of their university friends from that time remembered the one knowing the other. But, at tea in one another's rooms, where she proved herself a 'good housekeeper' with her cooking of crumpets, they quickly became close. He found her serious, and 'a bit bluestocking', but he liked the fact that she read a great deal and loved music. She took him to the Matthew Passion in which, as a member of the Bach Choir, she was performing. Tony respected her because 'she held her thoughts very sincerely'. At roughly the same time as he gave her the carnation – Christmas 1944 – she gave him Palgrave's *Golden Treasury* which he kept beside him every day until he lost it in a house move forty years later. It was his impression from the way Margaret kissed that she had had no boyfriend before, but she showed a delight in physical intimacy. They followed the rules of those days, however, and never slept together.

As he got to know Margaret better, Tony, whose parents were quite well off, noticed the 'great strain it was to finance her time at university'; she was 'not ashamed of her background' but exhibited 'a degree of reticence' about it. He detected that she was 'very determined to make good', but, with pleasure and surprise, he also noticed something else: 'She was a person who, though not apparently sociable, enjoyed socializing ... she astonished herself how much she could relax and be relaxed.' They had fun together.[101]

This pleasure, and the heightened sense of life's possibilities that comes through first love, can be found in Margaret's letters to Muriel. Her descriptions, normally rather tart or matter of fact, take on a different tone. On 25 March 1945, back in Grantham for the Easter vacation, Margaret wrote with details of every dance she had been to. Wartime had stopped the traditional full-scale Commem balls in the summer, but the approach of victory permitted a rash of college and other dances in March. Margaret went to five. The first, and best, was the Randolph Ball at the Randolph Hotel: 'We had a marvellous time ... Tony hired a car and we drove out to Abingdon to the country Inn "Crown and Thistle". I managed to borrow a glorious royal blue velvet cloak which match [sic] the blue frock perfectly.' Tony presented her with a spray of eight carnations 'sent for me from London so with the front part of my hair piled up on top Jean and Mary said I looked simply smashing. I felt absolutely on top of the world as we walked through the lounge at the Crown and Thistle and everyone looked up and stared.' In the manner of the wartime deprived, Margaret went on to describe, in detail, what they ate and drank: 'We went into the bar and had gin and grapefruit and then to the dining room for dinner. We had some lovely thick creamy soup followed by pidgeon [sic] and then a chocolate sweet. With it we had Moussec to drink. Moussec in case you don't know is a sparkling champagne.'*

When they reached the Randolph at a quarter to nine, 'Things were in full swing . . . The ballroom was marvellously decorated and all the lighting was done with huge coloured lamps operating from the balcony. The floor was simply packed so from the point of view of dancing it wasn't terrifically marvellous. The Duchess of Marlborough arrived soon after we did and seemed very nice. The refreshments were lovely. Altogether it was the best and biggest ball I've ever been to.'[102] Asked about it sixty years later, Tony remembered buying the carnations from Moyses Stevens. When reminded of Margaret's blue dress, he suddenly broke down in tears and said: 'It was a very special evening.'[103]

The next day was Somerville's dance, for which Margaret wore the same thing ('The flowers were still fresh'): 'There were two other Conservative couples there . . . so we teamed up and had a thoroughly gay evening.' The following week, there was Worcester College – 'We had a thoroughly hilarious time'; then Wadham – 'a bit of a bear-fight'; and finally, Merton, for which Margaret wore 'my green crepe frock'.[104]

Once term had ended, Tony whisked her off for a day in London which included coffee at Fullers in Regent Street, lunch at the Dorchester ('It is not the acme of hotels it is reported to be'), a matinée performance of Strauss's *A Night in Venice* at the Cambridge Theatre and finally a tea dance at the Piccadilly Hotel before Margaret got the train to Grantham and Tony returned to Oxford. For her, who had seen so little of the pleasures of the world, it was heady stuff.

It also, in her mind, betokened something quite serious, although Margaret seldom directly described her feelings to her sister. In the same letter to Muriel, she writes: 'Preparations are going ahead fast and furiously for next weekend. I do hope everything will be all right.'[105] Tony was coming to stay with her parents above the shop. This would not have happened if she had seen her relationship with Tony as some passing fancy; and her

* Actually it is an ersatz champagne.

parents, themselves serious-minded, unused to guests and protective of their daughters where men were concerned, would have regarded this as a potentially very significant occasion.

Such thoughts seem to have crossed Tony's mind, and to have worried him a little. In old age, he recalled that he and Margaret never discussed marriage, and that he, with his legal training, was very wary of doing so because of the threat, still lingering from Victorian times, of an action for breach of promise.[106] He thought of their relationship at that time as that of 'just a boy and girl who thoroughly enjoyed each other's company', which was hardly surprising, since he was only eighteen, but Margaret, perhaps, thought it meant rather more.

In any event, the visit to Grantham was 'all right', but not much better than that. Tony found Alfred Roberts 'slightly austere' and 'totally correct', a good, chapel-going man; Beatrice was 'very proper' and 'motherly'. The shop struck him as 'a very modest business establishment'. Tony and the Roberts family all attended the Methodist church together. It was not a riotous weekend.

It also marked a moment of parting. Tony's six-month course at Oxford had come to an end and his full military training began in April, very shortly before the end of the war in Europe. He went to Bovington Camp in Dorset. As early as 19 April, the day before Hitler's grim birthday celebrations in the Berlin bunker, Margaret wrote to Muriel* that a routine has been established in their communication: 'I usually have a letter on Tuesday morning ... He says there are all sorts of weird men there but fortunately the platoon he is in is composed entirely of Oxford cadets.' Tony, she said, had to work the whole time: 'On Saturday they are theoretically free from 2 o'clock but in practice there is so much to be done that this could hardly be called free time. Sunday they are again supposedly free but last Sunday Tony was peeling potatoes most of the morning!!'[107] The war in Europe ended on 8 May 1945.

After a month at Bovington, Tony went on to another training camp and continued to move from one establishment to another, including a return to Bovington, until he was posted to Germany in the following year after being commissioned in the Royal Inniskilling Dragoon Guards. He sent Margaret a photograph of himself in military uniform, which he inscribed to her. But at some time in the course of the ensuing year Tony's replies to Margaret's letters began to peter out and eventually stopped altogether. After writing some letters reproaching Tony for his silence, Margaret became so distressed that she wrote to Tony's mother, whom she

---

* This is the same letter as that in which she described her solitary dinner in Somerville.

had never met, to ask what had happened to him.[108] The answer was, nothing very much. It was simply, though his mother naturally did not say this, that Tony had decided that the relationship should be allowed to 'fizzle out'.[109]

To Margaret's sister Muriel, there was a clear explanation. Tony, she believed, was snobbish, and had decided that Margaret was not from a good enough family for him.[110] Tony, not surprisingly, saw things differently. He agreed that Margaret's background did make him uneasy, but not, he said, because of its relatively modest circumstances. What worried him was its austere seriousness. He wanted fun, and he found it. At his second stay at Bovington, he formed a relationship with a Dorset girl called Prudence whom he describes as 'vivacious, outgoing and attractive'. Once posted, he found that he 'was living in a fairly glamorous world in Germany – a cavalry regiment, green trousers, all the rest of it.' Aged barely twenty, he was not looking for commitment.[111]

What of Margaret herself? When asked by the present author, she replied with the understandable untruth that she had had no boyfriends before Denis, and when later asked specifically about Tony she acknowledged the circumstances described above but would not be drawn into any detail. As we shall see, there was more to come in the story of Tony Bray. But this occurred only after she had gone down from Oxford. In her last two years at the university, therefore, she had an absent and eventually an ex-boyfriend who was refusing to communicate with her. When Tony faded away, in her final year she formed her unrequited crush on Neil Findlay. She was successful at Oxford, getting a good second-class degree, rising to the top of Conservative politics there and making the contacts that would stand her in good stead in her career. But when she went out into the world of work in the summer of 1947, she was, as she had been when she first arrived at the university, fundamentally alone.

4

Essex girl

*'What a pity such a charming girl should be
lost to politics!'*

In the late summer of 1947, Margaret began her first job. She worked as
a research chemist at BX Plastics in Manningtree, Essex. 'Plastics', she
recalled, 'was one of the things of the future,'[1] but there is little evidence
that she was much interested. She records in her memoirs that she had been
expecting to work as personal assistant to the research and development
director. When it turned out that she would have to put on her white coat
and work in a lab, rather than with people, she was not pleased.[2] She saw
the job as necessary, no more. It paid her £350 a year (£400 was the rate
for the equivalent male employee), which was enough to live on, but not
to save from; and it was close enough to London to keep in touch with
politics and to contemplate reading for the Bar while she waited for the
slow business of submitting the thesis and being interviewed for her BSc
at Oxford, a process that was not complete until the winter of 1948. She
had no intention of staying in Essex for long.

Settled in digs in Colchester and travelling out to Manningtree in the company bus every morning, Margaret felt that life, compared with Oxford, was
rather dull. 'The wear and tear on clothes of all kinds is terrific in industry,'
she complained to Muriel. 'By the way, HAVE MY SHOES COME BACK
FROM UDALL's YET? I've asked in every blessed letter I've written home
[where Muriel was now living with their parents] but not a word about them
have I received in reply.' At her lodgings, 168 Maldon Road, the home of a
young widow with two children called Enid Macaulay, she tried to look on
the bright side: 'Mercifully one is not too lonely in the evenings as there are
other people in the digs too.' She went occasionally to the 'flicks' (her word)
with a fellow lodger, Teddy West, but he '<u>doesn't dance</u>',[3] and he soon
developed a girlfriend who, Margaret reported Mrs Macaulay as saying, was
'as common as muck – thoroughly tarty, but she's got hold of him and is
trying to rush the affair as soon as possible . . . Apparently she's not a fashion
artist at all but traces flower designs for scarves etc. from designs drawn by

someone else.'⁴ Margaret's indignation suggests that she found Teddy West quite attractive.

The lack of money was a constant preoccupation. The rent, which began at two guineas (£2.10) per week, soon went up to £2 10s (£2.50), which Margaret found 'more than a little worrying'.⁵ Every small excursion or purchase had to be carefully weighed:

> Not going to Oxford this weekend, I decided to buy a really nice undie-set to go under my turquoise chiffon blouse. I got a very nice one, scalloped all round the top and round the pants and with some open broderie anglaise on it. It is a very pale turquoise colour and cost £5-5-0.* I'll not have to spend anything else for the rest of the month! ... Oxford will have to wait until next month. Anyway a nice undie-set is essential to go away with.⁶

Because she could not afford a perm, she changed her hairstyle – 'am now wearing it in a big doughnut bun at the back – as it doesn't need any curl worn that way.'⁷ When she wrote to her father asking for money for a tweed suit, she sent it to the shop in North Parade rather than to her parents' new house there, so that the request would not be seen by her less indulgent mother.⁸ But she also wrote to Muriel with financial advice born of her current difficulties:

> if you're trying to scrape together a 'nest egg', do you think it's wise to have a very expensive holiday? I know that sounds a bit like the parents, but I'm getting awfully money minded these days and realising how nice it would be to feel one's bank balance was somewhere between £30 and £50 if one <u>needed</u> to buy anything or go anywhere in particular.⁹

One victim of Margaret's shortage of money was her own mother, who almost always appears in the correspondence as a faintly disapproving and embarrassing figure: 'I shan't be able to afford a birthday present for Mummy so shall just send a card.'¹⁰

In this rather pinched world, it was politics, as in the past, that provided Margaret with acceptance and excitement: 'If Methodists aren't very friendly, Conservatives are. Someone learned of my being here in Colchester and the word has gone round like wildfire. Every meeting I step into I'm greeted with "It's Miss Roberts isn't it?"'¹¹ A little later, she wrote: 'I still don't like the work very much but the politics and social life are beginning to go with a swing which compensates for a lot.'¹² One of the first

---

* It is worth noting how much more expensive such items were in those days. The modern equivalent would cost less than £60. The five guineas Margaret paid represented about £150 in today's money.

people she met through the Conservatives was Brian Harrison, a Cambridge graduate 'with a small estate of 1500 acres'[13] in Essex and further family lands in Australia. Harrison, whom she had first encountered at a Conservative graduates' conference earlier in the year, was a veteran of the war in the Far East and a leading light in the 39–45 Group, an organization of Essex Tories with war experience. With her taste for older, soldierly men, Margaret warmed to the tall, sporting, kindly Harrison and to his group, and attended their meetings. Harrison, who was to become Conservative MP for Maldon in 1955, remembered Margaret with affection as 'an attractive girl ... very very clued up', good company and a good dancer. She was 'ambitious', he said, 'but intelligent enough to hide it'.[14] He was also chairman of the Colchester Young Conservatives, and into this organization Margaret threw herself. In early October 1947, she took part in their Brains Trust on the economic crisis ('The Socialists were all of the intellectual type and quite nice'),[15] and soon she was one of their regular speakers warming up the soapbox at St Botolph's Corner, Colchester, every Saturday night for 'Cub' Alport,* the Tory candidate, whom Harrison considered 'pompous' and Margaret also disliked.†

By the next spring, Margaret had become a leading figure among the Colchester Tories. In April 1948, she told Muriel, 'I have been doing quite a lot of speaking lately and have begun to talk completely without notes.'[16] In a postscript written on 11 May, she describes a weekend political school at Colchester. As is generally the case in her letters when writing about politics, she does not mention what was discussed. Something else engrossed her attention:

> the competition for the best dressed woman there being fiercely contested by Jean Murphy and I [sic] ... I turned up in my black two-piece and black hat on Saturday – she wasn't wearing a hat that day – but on Sunday she turned out in a floral dress, fox fur and straw boater with strands of veiling tied under the chin – I didn't like the hat myself and definitely thought it too much with a fur. I was wearing my blue frock and hat and wine coat and accessories. I think I won the day both days.[17]

---

* Cuthbert ('Cub') Alport (1912–98), educated Haileybury and Pembroke College, Cambridge; served war of 1939–45; director, Conservative Political Centre, 1945–50; Conservative MP for Colchester, 1950–61; Minister of State, Commonwealth Relations Office, 1959–61; British High Commissioner in Federation of Rhodesia and Nyasaland, 1961–3; created Lord Alport, 1961.

† 'For heaven's sake tell Willie [Cullen, Muriel's husband] not to mention my name to Alport. I don't like the man and didn't get on frightfully well with him in Colchester' (letter to Muriel, 28 Feb. 1951). When Margaret Thatcher was prime minister, Alport so disliked her policies that he resigned the Conservative whip in the House of Lords.

It has often been said that Margaret Roberts was much too serious a young woman to consider the social aspects of life among the Conservatives. Nothing could be further from the truth, serious though she was: she saw the Tories as her social theatre. She went to the Derby with them ('don't tell parents!') and to the Boat Race, performed for them and dressed up for them. When she wore her black two-piece for the first time in Colchester, she wrote that 'The only chance I get to wear my best black clothes these days is at Conservative meetings of some sort!' The two-piece 'caused quite a stir in the digs and complimentary comments came from all sides except Mr West, who said not a word, to my annoyance!'[18]

In April 1948, Margaret went to a grand dinner in the House of Commons given by Alan Lennox-Boyd, later to become colonial secretary.* As the only woman present, she sat next to the host: 'I wore my pale blue frock and hat, wine shoes, handbag and gloves and short new musquash jacket. The ensemble looked very nice indeed.' After 'a marvellous dinner with all the appropriate wines', she went for drinks at Edward Boyle's flat, with a couple of other guests, until two in the morning. The next day she paid her first ever visit to Knightsbridge, inspected the new Roosevelt memorial and saw a film about the life of Roosevelt.[19] Back in Colchester, she addressed a discussion group on the British Empire. The audience was 'very interested and didn't fidget from start to finish and I was speaking about an hour.' She gave a talk to the Young Conservatives on 'Science in the Modern World' and she also took part in a Brains Trust of several rising Conservatives including 'Brig. Powell (the Conservative Central Office authority on housing)', her first recorded encounter with Enoch Powell,† the man who, many believe, cleared the intellectual path for what came to be called Thatcherism.[20] Life was opening up. 'I shall be awfully sorry when the time comes to leave Colchester,' she wrote.[21]

There was another reason for Margaret's improved self-esteem. On 17 February 1948, she wrote to Muriel to describe 'the most marvellous weekend in Oxford', which included a sherry party at the Union, a visit to old crystallography colleagues, an OUCA dinner and drinks at Lord

---

* Alan Lennox-Boyd (1904–83), educated Sherborne and Christ Church, Oxford; Conservative MP for Mid-Beds, 1931–60; Secretary of State for the Colonies, 1954–9; created Viscount Boyd of Merton, 1960; chaired mission to Rhodesia sent by Mrs Thatcher 1979. His son, Mark, was to be PPS to Mrs Thatcher, 1988–90.

† J. Enoch Powell (1912–98), educated King Edward's, Birmingham and Trinity College, Cambridge; Conservative MP for Wolverhampton South West, 1950–February 1974; Ulster Unionist MP for Down South, October 1974–87; Secretary of State for Health, 1960–63.

Tweedsmuir's manor house* out of town. But the real purport of the letter was kept to the end:

> Nor is that all. When I opened one of the letters that Daddy had forwarded to me, the one with the typewritten envelope [to avoid identification by the Robertses?] and postmark 'Oxford' in it was contained a letter from Tony Bray!!!! The letter was very weird and sentimental 'For three years I have not been able to write to you due to circumstances beyond my control . . .' and so on in that strain. He has apparently just been demobbed and returned to Oxford last week. It's as well I didn't run into him unawares. I shall write back and tell him to let sleeping dogs lie. Don't tell parents about this. All told it has been quite an eventful weekend! I shall go up again just as soon as I can afford it.[22]

Tony had returned from military service in Germany and was now doing a full honours degree at his old college in Oxford. He had had his fun, and was now missing Margaret. His letter had been, he said fifty-six years later, sincere: 'I would have meant it. I was serious. I wasn't just being gallant.'[23] Despite what she had written to him about letting sleeping dogs lie, Margaret took up his invitation to meet – which he had renewed in a further letter – though not with unseemly haste. She told Muriel that she would see him in Oxford 'more to let him see how I've changed than to see him!' On 18 May 1948, she confided in Muriel an account which she had not given in her regular letter to her parents, for rather sly reasons, as she herself explained:

> Have written account of Oxford weekend in Ma and Pa's letter. Bits left out or not made clear are
>
> 1. That I was staying with the Mandelbergs [Oxford Conservative friends]. I thought Pop might think I had a very expensive weekend at a hotel and maybe stump up . . .
>
> 2. That I met Tony Bray again once or twice over the weekend. I went to have a late tea with him at 5 o'clock on Friday evening and we drifted on from there to see School for Scandal at the New Theatre and dinner at the Randolph.† He is more grown up now than formerly although his appearance has changed but little. Strangely enough I found him extremely easy to get on with. There was no embarrassment whatsoever. I was wearing my

---

* The house, Elsfield, was the estate of Tweedsmuir's father, the novelist John Buchan.
† In suggesting an almost casual meeting with Tony, Margaret forgets her own letter to Muriel a week earlier which told her of the plan: 'I'm seeing Tony for dinner and theatre on Friday evening. Plan to wear musquash and pale blue frock. If I can possibly afford it I want Andreas to perm my hair' (letter to Muriel, 11 May 1948).

pale blue frock for theatre – which is rather lovely. We scarcely referred to our past 'association' except indirectly by discussing what had happened since we last met. He, I gather, has had a damn good time on the continent – especially in Brussels [where he went on leave]. The only direct reference I had of times past was when he said quite steadily – 'you only realise what you had when you've lost it – and you know what I'm referring to.' However I ignored the remark and conversation rapidly picked up and flowed on.

Affecting an insouciance that she clearly did not feel, Margaret continues:

For want of something else to do, I went on the river with him in a punt on Saturday afternoon. There I had a full-blooded apology – which I must in all fairness say sounded very sincere, that said he felt when he went in the army he was expecting to go to the far East for 3 years at least [the war had still been on in Japan] and that he couldn't 'ask me to hang on' all that time, but he didn't want to kill the feeling between us by writing and saying let's finish. He now realised that his very inaction must have killed anything there was between us and that in any case it was quite apallingly [sic] rude not to have written. He determined to write the moment he came out of the Army but couldn't explain on paper all he felt. Hence the 'circumstances beyond my control'. Having said this apology, he in a very poised and mature fashion steered the conversation into lighter vein once again. I did not comment on the apology – he assured me he had not been infatuated with anyone else (I, of course, didn't mention Prudence). It all sounded to me as if it were partly true and partly false.

There was one more meeting with Tony that weekend:

I lunched with him again on Monday and we parted. No mention was made of any future arrangements for which I was truly thankful – for it just wouldn't have been 'on' for me, although I quite enjoyed seeing him again for a short time – it satisfied my curiosity – but he's a weird-looking chap to cart around the place!

By the way, he didn't know I had been President of OUCA – I didn't tell him until the last lunch when it arose naturally out of the conversation, – and he was immensely impressed. I also told him about the speakers' competition [a Young Conservatives' contest which Margaret had won] which impressed him still more.

Altogether I must say I enjoyed the weekend enormously. For two pins I would have said to hell with BX I'm staying up for another week. The weather was glorious from start to finish. Things couldn't have been more perfect than they were.[24]

Margaret did not maintain her resolve about making no future 'arrange-ments'. She had another letter from Tony in July and followed it up. Once again, she wrote to Muriel explaining that what she had said in her letter to her parents had been untruthful:

> In point of fact I was not meeting a 'crowd of old college cronies' in London yesterday, but Tony. He had written to say if I was ever in London to let him know – so I thought we might have quite an evening out yesterday – and we did. He came up from Southwick [the Sussex village where his parents lived] specially for the day (!). He met me off the train at King's X at 2.45 . . . After I had titivated we went along to Fullers in Regent St to have tea.

The couple went on to see *Carissima* at the Palace, where they had 'abso-lutely dead central seats' in the stalls.

> I was wearing my blue frock and little blue hat, little fur jacket with all wine accessories. And I forgot to mention he presented me with a spray of pink roses! Actually, my outfit looked extremely nice and I saw several people turn to look at it. During the interval we went and had gin and vermouth in the bar . . . Tony had booked dinner for nine o'clock at Kettner's – quite a fashionable West End restaurant.

The dinner, after more gin and vermouth, was 'wonderful'. 'I really enjoyed the evening very much – though I wouldn't dream of re-striking up the association with Tony . . . PPS. I don't want a job in a sales organisation – they're awful jobs. If you see any more adverts though let me know.'[25]

In some form at least, the association continued. In early December 1948, Margaret went to Oxford and told Muriel, 'I saw Tony twice during the weekend [the weekend in which she finally sat her viva for her BSc] . . . I did theatre and dinner with him on Saturday evening . . . and went to tea on Sunday.'[26] In January 1949, she wrote, 'I had a letter from Tony on Sat-urday asking me how I was etc but suggesting that we spend another day in town together sometime. An offer which I shall probably accept when I get a free Saturday.'[27] The next month 'I had a valentine from Tony! Quite a funny one, with a letter asking when I shall be visiting Oxford again.'[28]

After that, there are no further surviving mentions of Tony Bray in Margaret's correspondence. This is not surprising, perhaps, since he had once again shown interest in another woman. According to his account early in the twenty-first century, the relationship with Margaret had, indeed, rekindled in 1948, but late in the winter of 1949 he took a girl-friend skiing in Austria, telling Margaret that he was going for winter sports, but not mentioning the woman. Although he was fond of Margaret, he said, he realized that she was embarking on a serious political career and she was 'so determined to make her own way'. He believed that 'A woman should be a woman' and his idea of a woman did not include a full career. The renewed relationship with Margaret came to an end in 1949, and in June of the following year Tony Bray became engaged to the woman who remained his wife until her death more than fifty years later. He telephoned Margaret to inform her of the event and received 'polite congratulations: she didn't wax lyrical.'[29] He did not invite her to his wedding – 'It would have been the kiss of death.'[30]

For her part, Margaret, probably more excited by Tony than she would explicitly admit, even to Muriel, did not want to be hurt again.* In the winter of 1948, she wrote to Muriel, who by this time had a boyfriend called Ken,† and gave her sister some advice: 'I should definitely not give Ken anything for Christmas – he can give you something if he likes, that's different.' But she also expresses some self-doubt: 'I don't know that your "male" problem is the same as mine – you seem infinitely more successful with them than I do with his Colchester counterpart!'[31] The 'Colchester counterpart' is obviously a generic type of man that Margaret feels she cannot find, but was also, it seems likely, a man called David Papillon, a leading Young Conservative in Colchester, an able young solicitor and businessman, much liked and admired in the town. Margaret records her excitement when Papillon sent her a Christmas card or asked her to a party. He also travelled by train with her to the party conference in Llandudno in 1948 which put her decisively on the way to her political career. Margaret considered him smart, charming and powerful, and was 'rather cross' when her fellow lodger, Kay Stokes, turned up to his New Year party in a 'chiffon blouse exactly the same colour as my turquoise one'.[32] He was also unattainable because, unknown to Margaret, he was homosexual.[33] Throughout her life she remained innocent about such things. In any event, her letter to Muriel shows her looking for other men while Tony Bray was still on the scene, and feeling a little wistful about not really finding them. As is visible in her frequent references to how other people turned to look at her if she wore something striking, she depended heavily on the approval

---

* When asked about Tony Bray in 2004, Lady Thatcher said she remembered the royal-blue cloak she had worn to their dinner before the Randolph Ball. When reminded that Tony had got back in touch with her on returning from the army, regretting his neglect of her while in the army, she said, using words echoing his apology to her in Oxford, 'It's no good thinking over the chances you missed,' and would not be drawn further on the subject. (Interview with Lady Thatcher.)

† 'How nice to find an immaculate man!' Margaret had exclaimed to her sister when Ken first came on the scene in the summer (letter to Muriel, 22 Sept. 1948).

and attention of others for her self-confidence. This confidence continued to grow as her career prospered, and, as we shall see, 1949 proved to be the year when her success really began, but in the winter of 1948 she still felt a little frail.

There is one curious footnote to the story of Tony Bray and Margaret Thatcher. In 1973, Tony, who had pursued a career as a stockbroker, was engaged in a detailed study of the housing market. It was his job to forecast the development of house-building to see how the share prices of construction companies might move. In doing so, he formed the view that it would be logical to let sitting tenants buy their council houses, freeing up the receipts to build more housing. He worked up a paper on this and in 1974 sent it to Edward Heath,* by this time, following the Conservative defeat at the election in February, the Leader of the Opposition. He mentioned to Heath that he had known Margaret Thatcher at Oxford and so Heath, who by this time had made her shadow environment spokesman and therefore responsible for this area of policy, suggested that Bray talk to her. Margaret invited him to the Central Lobby of the House of Commons. The two had not met or spoken since 1950. Tony noticed a change in her manner over the quarter of a century: 'She was more the grande dame, aware of her own presence, a little bit condescending'; she made only the most glancing acknowledgment of their old acquaintance and got straight down to the policy, towards which she was very receptive. A lunch to discuss the policy more fully was planned, to be held at Tony's stockbroking firm, but when it eventually took place Tony found himself excluded from the occasion of which he was himself the architect. He does not know why, but blames colleagues, not Margaret.[34] He never saw her again.

Many people in the 1970s were toying with market-based solutions to the problem of council houses and the idea was current in Tory circles, so it would be an exaggeration to say that Mrs Thatcher was introduced to what turned out to be one of her most successful policies by her first boyfriend, but it has a grain of truth.

Tony Bray had been right to detect a hardening of Margaret's seriousness about a political career. Her opportunity came with the Conservative Party

---

* Edward Heath (1916–2005), educated Chatham House School, Ramsgate and Balliol College, Oxford; served war of 1939–45 (mentioned in despatches); Conservative MP for Bexley, 1950–74; for Bexley, Sidcup, 1974–83; for Old Bexley and Sidcup, 1983–2001; Government Chief Whip, 1955–9; Minister of Labour, 1959–60; Lord Privy Seal, 1960–63; President of the Board of Trade, 1963–4; Leader of the Conservative Party, 1965–75; Prime Minister, 1970–74; captain, Britain's Admiral's Cup team, 1971, 1979; Knight of the Garter, 1992.

conference in Llandudno in early October 1948. Margaret was to go, as a representative not of Colchester but of the Oxford Conservative Graduates' Association. She looked forward to the conference keenly and wanted to dress appropriately. She went shopping in London and visited Bourne and Hollingsworth and Peter Robinson: 'I decided I couldn't possibly go to Llandudno with the "communal" coat [this seems to have been a garment which the two sisters shared] as the only top-coat I had . . . so I drew some savings certificates out and bought a fine light-weight black wool swagger. It's of a rather distinctive design,' she wrote to Muriel,[35] and sketched a picture of it for her ('I've drawn it rather stunted'). The coat cost £9 11s 6d. As so often, Margaret added, '(Don't mention new coat to parents).'

As she prepared for the conference, Margaret had no clear thought that it would produce any development in her career. In August, indeed, although she also applied for new jobs in London, she had sent off an application to the Colonial Office in pursuit of her childhood ambition of working abroad as a civil servant in the Empire, sought referees and also put her name on the Overseas Scientific and Technical Register.[36] Such appointments would have kept her out of politics. And when she did reach Llandudno, she found the conference more disappointing than the one at Blackpool which had so excited her (see Chapter 3). 'The level of speaking was very low,' she told Muriel,[37] a view which may perhaps have been connected with the fact that, to her disappointment, she was not asked to speak for the motion which her association had submitted, calling for the retention of the special parliamentary seats for the universities and the City of London which Labour was pledged to abolish.

What did happen, though, is that the twenty-three-year-old Margaret fell in with an old Oxford mentor and friend, John Grant, a director of Blackwell's the booksellers, and a man she looked up to: 'I always enjoy talking with him. He's quite the most mentally mature person of his age (34) that I know.' At Llandudno, she had dinner with him on the Wednesday, and lunch and dinner with him on the Friday. On this last occasion, 'we had a long discussion over personal and political affairs and a job for me. We went on talking until 2.30 am.'[38] She discussed with Grant, among other things, the fact that she had no money to be a parliamentary candidate and that, because of this, she had not even tried to get on the party's central list of approved candidates.[39]

John Grant was the man who that week gave Margaret the introduction which was to launch her political career. According to Margaret's published account, at some point on the Friday Grant happened to be sitting next to John Miller, a builder who was the chairman of Dartford Conservative Association. Dartford, a Kent town by the Thames on the eastern fringes of London, was a strong Labour seat. Miller told Grant that the association was looking for a candidate because their existing one, a Major Grubb, had withdrawn. Grant immediately recommended Margaret Roberts to Miller. Miller objected that 'Dartford is a real industrial stronghold. I don't think a woman would do at all,'[40] but agreed that he and his wife Phee and their association's Women's Chairman should lunch with Grant and Margaret on Llandudno pier the next day (in that era, the party conference did not end until Saturday afternoon). The lunch took place and Margaret made a very favourable impression. Nothing definite seems to have emerged from it at the time. Indeed, in her full description of the conference in her letter to Muriel, Margaret makes no mention of the meeting with the Dartford dignitaries. But before the end of the year it had borne fruit.

Dartford invited Margaret to a preliminary interview in London on 30 December 1948. She got through to the final selection in Dartford, and on 31 January 1949 at the Royal Bull and Victoria Hotel was chosen, defeating the four men on the shortlist. Ken Tisdell, a Young Conservative who was present at the selection, said that she was 'streets ahead of anyone else'.[41] Living in the only constituency in the area where the Labour majority was safe, Dartford Conservatives were looking for a fighter and were prepared to take risks. For them, it was a positive advantage that Margaret was a woman, and a young woman at that. The Young Conservatives, in particular, identified with her, and felt that she expressed their hopes and fears.[42] 'They wanted to choose someone different,' said Lady Thatcher five decades later, 'someone with the chance of attracting attention.'[43]

Although selection of a candidate without the prior approval of the party list was somewhat unusual, Conservative Central Office sensibly did nothing to impede Margaret's progress. Instead, it sought to put an enthusiastic stamp on Dartford's choice. On the very day after her selection, Margaret saw Beryl Cook, the party's area agent (whom she quickly came to love and refer to as 'Auntie Beryl'). Miss Cook reported at once to Central Office, 'I was tremendously impressed and think that she is a winner.'[44] She also saw Marjorie Maxse, the party's Women's Chairman. Miss Maxse also gave Central Office an enthusiastic account. She described Margaret as 'very attractive-looking with a quiet efficiency which should stand her in good stead'. She noted that her 'platform knowledge and speaking ability were far above those of the other candidates'. 'She wants', added Miss Maxse, 'a salary of £500 a year and would like a job in some big chemical firm like the [sic] ICI . . . She is particularly keen on Empire subjects as well as ordinary bread-and-butter politics.'[45]

To complete the formal process for her adoption, Margaret supplied Central Office with five references. The least informative and most proforma was from Alport. The rest glowed. They came from her friend John Grant, from the admired David Papillon in Colchester, from Susan Brace, a neighbour in Grantham and the sister of the future Conservative MP Sir John Tilney,* and from Lord Balfour of Inchrye, a former air minister. 'A grand young candidate,' wrote Balfour laconically. 'Speaks well. Good-looking. Keen, knows her subjects. Watch and encourage.'[46] John Grant declared that Margaret 'more than anyone else ... was responsible for the resurgence of OUCA after the war, despite the fact that she is considerably younger than the men she was leading'. His 'despite' might better have been replaced with 'because of', since it was precisely with older men that Margaret could lead most successfully. Grant added that Margaret 'gets on well with men (without resorting to the more obvious feminine arts!) and appears to be able to avoid unpopularity with her fellow women'. The fullest reference came from Mrs Brace:

> I cannot exactly say how long I have known her, but certainly since she was a child. She took a surprising interest in politics even then, and I was astonished at her grasp of affairs and her facility in communicating her views ... For some years I served on the local Town Council with her father, who is exceptionally intelligent and able. Altogether her 'background' is that of 'public service' at its best, coupled with a very superior intellect and the anxiety to work hard for principles in which she believes.

*

For Margaret, her selection for Dartford was an even greater moment than her entry into Oxford. It revealed to her the extent of her political talents, threw her into the combat she always enjoyed and set her on the course of her life. It led to her marriage, and it made her intensely happy. In old age, she was not someone who necessarily enjoyed reminiscence, but memories of Dartford would always cause her eyes to light up. More immediately, Dartford also helped to get her out of something of a rut. The autumn and winter of 1948 in Colchester had not been particularly successful. She was still worried about money and unable to find a job which would take her to London. In late summer, she ran into trouble in her digs. In January, Mrs Macaulay had moved house to 17 Oxford Road, and Margaret, with characteristic domestic enthusiasm, had helped her clean,

---

* John Tilney (1907–94), educated Eton and Magdalen College, Oxford; Conservative MP for Liverpool Wavertree, 1950–February 1974; knighted 1973. Margaret Thatcher met Tilney when they were both aspiring parliamentary candidates and admired him. He was friendly to her throughout, becoming a particularly strong supporter in the 1970s. His wife, Guinevere, advised Mrs Thatcher on clothes in the early years of her premiership.

paint and distemper the new house. But in the course of the year, relations had deteriorated: 'it happened like this,' Margaret wrote to Muriel:

> the children have been getting very cheeky lately . . . If ever we dared to speak sharply to them, she [Mrs Macaulay] ticked <u>us</u> off and not the children. Last Sunday, however, Hayward-Smith [another lodger] did complain, and she lost her temper thoroughly, went off at the deep end and told him to go on Saturday . . . She asked in a belligerent tone if we [Margaret and Kay Stokes] had any complaints to make about the children, and we mentioned a couple of things – she was furious, told us that her children were as well-behaved as any in Colchester and if we thought that – then Hayward-Smith was going and the same thing applied to us as well.[47]

With a certain eagerness to take Mrs Macaulay at her word, fed up with 'atmospheres' in the house and being taken for granted about doing the washing up, Margaret and Kay decided to move, and said so to Mrs Macaulay, who became overwrought. 'She broke down, said she had a £50 overdraft at the bank and that she had had two miserable years ever since her husband died and had tried to do the best for the children . . .' Margaret's reaction was very characteristic: 'we felt really sorry for her. However it didn't blind us to the fact that if she had a fifty pound overdraft it is <u>her own</u> fault as she has no idea how to spend money.'[48] Margaret and Kay took matters into their own hands and moved to 19 Lexden Road, temporary lodgings, in search of a place of their own to rent. There Margaret could give her own entertainments, but they were not always successful. On one occasion she invited a local Young Conservative round for supper to 'discuss Christianity and Conservatism', but 'he turned out to be a bit of a bore. He's rather inclined to talk as if he's in the pulpit half-the-time, and he's very self-righteous. He does the right thing because it's the right thing to do – not because he spontaneously wants to do it. He didn't go until 2 o'clock and I was very bored with him by then.'[49] Despite her own strict moral standards, Margaret already evinced a preference for rather more raffish men. She and Kay fell in with actors at the local rep and went with them to a party with dancing to 'a darned good radiogram'. 'To our amazement when we arrived Mrs Macaulay was there . . . I think she was considerably shaken to see us, – especially with such debonair looking men and obviously the envy of the whole party.' Mrs Macaulay looked 'rather tarty – not so much in dress as in behaviour and of course her figure doesn't help.'[50] By Christmas, she and Kay had found a flat of their own at 42 Cambridge Road, which Margaret was keenly decorating: 'I have got half-a-yard of peach material – almost an exact match to the set Mummy gave me, and have made a deep frill . . . It looks lovely – most expensive in fact.'[51]

But the unsuccessful job hunt continued and Margaret began to resent Kay for nosiness: 'I hate anyone knowing half of my private affairs . . . In many ways she is an intensely jealous person and will try and belittle anything I do.'[52]

But it was hard for anyone to belittle Margaret's achievement in being selected for Dartford aged twenty-three. She leapt at the chance, and her thoughts turned, as so often, to clothes. Two weeks after her selection, she wrote to Muriel: 'I'm going down to Dartford this week-end to stay with the Millers. Hope Mummy will get my housecoat done as soon as possible though I know she is very busy but if I am going down to stay with various officials in the constituency I shall have to look nice from skin outwards and from head to heel the whole 24 hours. There are some quite nice utility nightdresses around at 20–25/- [shillings] . . .' Margaret had gone out and 'bought a very cheap wine hat which I took all the tawdry trimmings off and put one big grey pom-pom in their place'.[53] She noted eagerly all the reactions to her Dartford selection, especially one:

> I haven't seen David Papillon since the Dartford news came out but messages go back and forth through Kay. I gather he is saying . . . what a pity such a charming girl should be lost to politics! She'll find it very heavy-going, wonder if she'll stay the course. The what a pity such a charming girl lost to politics – such an unnatural life, should have stayed at home, sentiments have been re-echoed and in a way, I suppose they are complimentary.[54]

Margaret liked to bank such praise, but if she herself felt any of the qualms about a political career for a woman that so many voiced, she never recorded them.

Instead, she looked forward to her adoption meeting, the occasion when, having been selected, she was formally proclaimed as the candidate. Then, as now, adoption meetings were foregone conclusions. Their purpose was to assemble a large crowd and present the prospective candidate to the association, the constituency and the press. Margaret's was called for 28 February 1949 at Electricity House, Erith. She went home to Grantham the weekend before to prepare herself, her wardrobe and her speech. The only new thing she could afford for the meeting was a black hat.[55] She had a new haircut but not, to avoid expense, a perm: 'I think I'd better start in the constituency with a hair-style now rather than change it in a few weeks.' And she expressed anxiety of a happy, almost childlike kind about the meeting: 'I hope everything goes well. I know they are going to give me a bouquet at the end.'[56]

Shortly before the great day, however, another significant event, unrelated to Dartford, took place. 'On Monday evening,' Margaret wrote to

Muriel, 'I went to dinner with a Scotch farmer who has a place around these parts. He came to the 39–45 group and introduced himself to me. He's quite a keen Conservative worker in the Dovercourt area where his farm is.' At the 39–45 Group party, the man asked Margaret if she would speak at one of their village meetings. 'A few days later he turned up at Lawford Place [the offices of BX Plastics] and asked to see me! Excuse – he wanted to let me know about a debate that had been arranged. I still said I didn't know my plans. Then a day later he 'phoned and asked me to go out to dinner with him – when could I go, any night would suit him . . .' He got his way:

> Eventually I said yes and we dined at the George. He's about 35 and has a kind of naïveté that only Scotsman [sic] can have. I expected to be bored to tears but in fact he was really rather sweet with quite a sense of humour. He practically presented his credentials to me. His farm is worth £25,000, he has 3000 £1 shares of ICI now standing at 47/-, a thousand of something else, five hundred of this and that and so on and so forth. And he paid surtax last year. And being a Scotman [sic] he left a ninepenny tip for the waiter. I could have fallen through the floor. That's how people with money keep it! He's had a new Rover on order for three years. He bought a refrigerator a few months ago. He's having two new sheds built at a cost of £900. All this – over dinner!

Her suitor was pressing:

> He drove me home in his present rather old car – and got quite ardent on the way! I said I couldn't possibly fix another definite date so he's going to 'phone me! The funniest part is that although I have been introduced to him twice, I can never catch his name and still don't know it! His people are farmers . . . He speaks with a frightfully Scotch accent. I'm afraid he's going to be an awful nuisance. But I'd rather like to see his farm as a matter of curiosity. I gather the farmhouse is three hundred years old. From what I can make out two of his sisters live with him.[57]

Before Margaret had found out the name of her Scottish farmer, Dartford had welcomed its new Conservative candidate. Four hundred people appeared at the electricity showrooms, and only one member opposed the adoption of Miss Roberts. According to the *Erith Observer*, the chairman, John Miller, revealed, perhaps rather tactlessly, that four prominent local businessmen had been sounded out for the candidacy and had declined. He praised Margaret, saying that she 'was sincere about her faith and was brilliant'. Then Margaret herself spoke. 'She stressed', says the paper, 'that Imperial Preference [free trade within the Empire, and tariffs outside it] was still the cornerstone of Conservatism.' She said that during the war 'members of the Empire . . . came across the world to fight for the Mother Country,' so now was the time to 'fight the economic war' with the help of our imperial allies. There was no advocacy of the free trade of which, in theory at least, she was later to become an advocate. In sticking up for Imperial Preference, Margaret was taking a rather old-fashioned Tory position which descended from Joe Chamberlain through Neville Chamberlain. She was identifying with pre-war bourgeois right-wing views in a way that showed independence from the attitudes of the current party leadership. She also declared, as she was so often to do in later years, that 'The Government should do what any good housewife would do if money was short – look at their accounts and see what was wrong.'[58] Then her father, who had travelled from Grantham for the occasion, spoke. He told the audience that 'by tradition his family were Liberal, but the Conservative Party today stood for very much the same things as the Liberal Party did in his young days.' A Young Conservative was quoted as saying that they were all 'terribly bucked' that a young person had been selected.[59]

The success of the meeting is attested to by all surviving people who attended it. Margaret's enthusiasm, knowledge and panache made an overwhelmingly favourable impression. She knew that she had done well. She wrote to Muriel to describe the scene, though making no mention of their father's speech. 'It was a thrilling affair,' she wrote. 'People who had come to be very critical were all won over by the end of the evening. They gave me a lovely bouquet of pink carnations, blue irises, blue grape hyacinths and prunus blossom.' 'When the meeting was over,' she continued,

> I went back and had drinks with the people I had been dining with,* Mr and Mrs Soward. He is a director of a small paint company in the constituency. A co-director of his, a Major Thatcher,† who has a flat in London (age about 36, plenty of money) was also dining with them and he drove me back to town at midnight. As one would expect he is a perfect gentleman. Not a very attractive creature – very reserved but quite nice. He's not very fond of meeting 'people' – he says he doesn't get on with them awfully well. We arrived back at Liverpool St at about 1 am and packed me into the milk train which left at 3.40. Altogether it was a thrilling evening.[60]

Before closing, Margaret reverted to lesser subjects, asking, via her sister, for more help from her seamstress mother: 'if she is going to do the panties

---

* In her memoirs, Lady Thatcher misremembers this event, stating that the dinner was after the meeting.
† It is not clear whether Alfred Roberts accompanied his daughter to the drinks. There is no evidence that he met Denis on this occasion.

I would like them in the style we did the parachute ones – cut on the cross from a small yoke, but don't bother her if she is very tired.'

The 'small paint company' of which Stanley Soward was a director was called the Atlas Preservative Company, and Denis Thatcher was its general manager. Atlas was his family business, making paints, wood preservers, deck cleaners and industrial chemicals at the factory in Erith. After a successful wartime career as a staff officer, Denis had very much wanted to stay on in the army, which he loved, but a promise to his father to come and look after the firm had called him back. As an old boy of a minor public school (Mill Hill), a former officer mentioned in despatches, and the man in charge of his own prosperous firm, Denis was socially a cut above Margaret. He was also quite active in the Dartford Conservative Association. Indeed, he was one of the four local businessmen whom John Miller had approached to be the parliamentary candidate. Denis had refused the offer,[61] confident that he did not want a political career. If he had accepted, he would presumably never have met Margaret and there would not have been a prime minister called Mrs Thatcher. Even before he met her, he had made way for her.

According to Denis, his friend and colleague Soward had invited him for the night of the adoption meeting with the words 'Come to dinner: I want you to meet a very pretty girl,' without saying who she was. When Denis arrived, he said to himself, 'Good God, it's the candidate!' He thought Margaret was 'a nice-looking young woman, a bit overweight'.[62] His chance to get to know her better came because of the transport arrangements of those days, and because Margaret could neither drive nor afford a car. At that time, there was no Dartford Tunnel under the Thames and, of course, no M25 motorway, so the journey from Dartford to Colchester, today about an hour's drive, involved either crossing the Thames by ferry or driving right back into central London to get a train (or driving right out again). Because Denis lived in London, reverse-commuting to Dartford, it was easier for him to drive her to Liverpool Street. As her letter to Muriel reveals, Margaret is mistaken in her memoirs when she says that Denis got her to the station at midnight. It was 1 a.m. Did he then stay talking to her for the full two hours forty minutes before the milk train left? If he did (as her phrase 'packed me into the milk train' suggests), it would explain how she had formed what was, for her, an unusually full first impression of the man. If not, and he had left her in a waiting room in the cold February small hours, would she have described him as a 'perfect gentleman'?

Back in Colchester, her romance, if that is the right word, was developing. In the same letter in which she described her Dartford adoption, Margaret told Muriel: 'My Scottie farmer met me off the train' and took her to *A Lady from Edinburgh* at the Ipswich rep and then for dinner at the Great White Horse. 'I thoroughly enjoyed the evening, but I'm afraid he's got it rather badly.' She now knew his identity: 'His name, by the way, is William Cullen, and he lives at Foulton Hall (!) Ramsay near Dovercourt.'[63] She invited Muriel to come down to Colchester to meet him. Her motives for doing so were interesting. Four days earlier, she had written to Muriel: 'Went to the flicks yesterday with my farmer friend and got him all primed up to meet you sometime. I showed him the snapshot of you and I [sic] together – and he said he could scarcely tell the difference so I should think we could easily substitute me for you. When can you come down for a weekend?'[64] She seemed at one and the same time to be searching for a husband for herself and for her sister, and to be thinking of the man who was chasing her in the latter role.

5

Dartford and romance

'I think we are both getting very fond of one another'

Dartford was not what Tories call their natural territory. It was a heavily industrial seat with cement works, engineering companies, defence firms like Vickers Armstrong with big factories, industries connected with river traffic, and a strong trade union presence. There were areas of the constituency, such as Temple Hill, where it was considered inadvisable for a Conservative canvasser to go unaccompanied. Much of Erith was 'red-hot Red'. One Young Conservative woman of the period remembered canvassing a house where the occupier, a Labour voter, insisted on receiving her while sitting on his outside lavatory.[1] Political meetings were liable to heckling and disruption. A substantial minority of Dartford residents commuted to London for clerical and managerial jobs, and on the fringes of the constituency were a few farms and the more prosperous suburbia in which Conservatives traditionally thrive. But this was a Labour place in what, after the electoral victory of 1945, were, both in percentage of the vote and in spirit of the age, the most Labour years of the century. In Dartford, the Labour majority of 20,000 was unassailable.

The young Margaret Roberts, however, set out cheerfully to assail it. Although she was probably genuine in the admiration she professed in later years for moderate socialists in that era ('They were fighting for the underdog'),[2] she was utterly convinced that Labour policies could not work. In this she was closer to the party grass-roots than to the patrician leadership of the party which, after 1945, was in a rather defeatist frame of mind. In particular, she was close to small business and to the aspirations of young lower-middle-class people like herself born with no great advantages. They worried that the tax, controls and nationalization which had been such features of the Labour government would deny them the opportunities which they had hoped would open up with the end of the war. As the general election of 1950 approached, their anxieties were strong. They, and she, were ready for the fight with Labour – always referred to as 'the Socialists'. There were many such young people in Dartford in 1949, and

Margaret's arrival as candidate recruited them in ever greater numbers. The membership of the whole association rose from 2,300 shortly after she was first adopted to 3,160 shortly before she left in 1951. Nowadays such high figures would not be found in the safest Conservative seats in the country, but even for the time they were remarkable. Several hundred of the members were Young Conservatives, at that time an enormously strong national organization with good local roots, much more tribal and social than directly political. Many of these Dartford YCs formed lifelong bonds that survived into the twenty-first century, and virtually all of them identified with and admired Margaret. These people – bank clerks and bank managers, solicitors' secretaries, a man who worked in his family firework-making business, a woman who was PA to a big local builder – saw in their smartly dressed, polite and keen young candidate a slightly grander or idealized version of themselves.

Although they regarded her as 'upper-class educationally',[3] which they respected, they also considered Margaret their own: 'She was one of us in a way.'[4] 'She got us all going again,' said one, and all were struck by her 'perfect manners' and the fact that she was 'very grateful for what we did'. This was in contrast to some other Tory candidates, notably Edward Heath, who already sat for the neighbouring seat of Bexley, and who, though himself young and of similar social origins to Margaret, treated the Young Conservatives who worked for him (some of whom would cross the border from Dartford when called) as 'the lowest of the low: we were kids to him.'[5] Margaret was 'plump, smart, pretty, loved hats, lovely skin'; she 'always looked right', and yet had her feet on the ground and 'always knew the price of everything', there was 'no side to her at all'. They also noticed and admired the fight she had in her – 'I was amazed how brave she was' – and her obvious sincerity: 'whatever she said she really meant it.'[6] Pat Luker, who worked very closely with Margaret in the second of her two Dartford campaigns in 1951, probably summed up her appeal most eloquently when she said, 'I think she was really, truly English. Everything was for the good of the country, the English people. We wanted everything English to be good.'[7] Note that the word 'English' rather than 'British' is used. Although always Unionist in theory, Margaret Thatcher saw her country through a very English prism.

Margaret quickly got to grips with the constituency. She found that it was quite badly run, the agent being inefficient. Although, as candidate, she was not responsible for such matters, she brought enough pressure to bear after the 1950 election to make sure that he was replaced.[8] The treasurer, she complained to Muriel, 'hasn't produced any audited accounts in years'.[9] She was luckier in her Labour opponent. The sitting Member,

Norman Dodds, was a man whose politics, in later life at least, she respected – 'a really sound Labour chap'.[10] He believed, she said, in greater social cohesion rather than hard-left socialism.[11] At the time, Dodds made the mistake of underestimating her and perhaps patronizing her because of her sex. Their first meeting took place at a dance given by the chairman of Crayford Urban District Council. Margaret described it:

> Dodds was very nice to me personally but I am told at one of his meetings he had been flaying me right and left and saying some very harsh things. The introduction itself was most amusing. We were dragged out into the middle of the ballroom and quite a ceremony was made of the whole affair. I wore my black velvet frock with long white gloves, pearls, and long drop pearl ear-rings. Mr Dodds said he was very sorry I was an opponent! He then publicly asked me for the next dance and the M.C. said what did I request. I said a Tango. They said which one. I said 'Jealousy'! We danced the whole dance – the only couple on the floor – no one else joined us.

The press took pictures and asked for reactions: 'I said "we were in tune when dancing" and Mr Dodds said "in perfect harmony". I imagine the report will make front page news next week!'[12] It did.[13]

Earlier in the month, Dodds had engaged Margaret in a long and complicated correspondence in the *Dartford Chronicle* about the Labour government's Direction of Labour Order in which, as always, she had driven into the argument with a bulldozer of facts. In the course of this, he had unwisely invited her to have a public debate with him, and she seized the opportunity. The debate took place in late November and Margaret distinguished herself by her detailed attacks on the Labour government's policy of bulk-buying for rationing, for its disastrous groundnuts scheme in West Africa, and for the recent devaluation, in which the currency had moved from a fixed rate of 4 US dollars to the pound to 2 dollars and 80 cents. She called for a new policy by which 'the pound can look the dollar in the face and not in the bootlaces'.[14] Conservatives who attended remembered this meeting as one where she really proved her mettle and her knowledge. At one point, Dodds responded disbelievingly, 'if you've got the figures'. She had.[15] The strong tone of Margaret's adoption speech continued as she started to campaign in the constituency. She emphasized, in relation to the Communist revolution in China, what she called 'the division of the world into two camps'.[16] At home, she called for a recovery of personal responsibility: 'In wartime there was a slogan "It all depends on me." People seem to have forgotten that, and they think it depends on the other person.'[17] And she offered women what would nowadays be called empowerment – the idea that they knew better than their masters: 'Don't be scared of the high language of economists and Cabinet ministers, but think of politics at our own household level.'[18] Women had particular gifts in public affairs, which they should use: 'Women have a special bent as technicians in human relationships, and we have come to understand the human aspect of our problems.'[19]

It is equally true, though less noticed, that Margaret seemed to accept the consensus of the day about what later came to be called the welfare state. Speaking to the Conservative Association's annual general meeting a month after her adoption, she went into great detail about the Beveridge report of 1942 which led to the creation of the National Health Service and modern social security. Misleadingly she credited the Conservative domination of the wartime coalition with these ideas, and did not try to question them. She preferred to point out that 'They are no use if the country goes bankrupt' and that they were no substitute for arranging these matters for oneself: 'Miss Roberts stressed that the security a family could have by saving its own money, buying its own house and investing, was far better than the ordinary security one would get from any national scheme.'[20] Neither at the beginning of her career nor when she was prime minister, did Margaret Thatcher ever reject the wartime foundations of the welfare state, whether in health, social policy or education. In this, she was less radical than her critics or some of her admirers supposed. Her concern was to focus more on abuse of the system, on bureaucracy and union militancy, and on the growth of what later came to be called the dependency culture, rather than on the system itself. Similarly, Margaret's dislike of too many government controls, though real and strong, did not take her, at this time, to the full free-market view that they should all go. 'There is a whispering – in fact, a shouting campaign in operation,' she complained, '– that if the Tories get back they will take off all the controls, but this is untrue. It was the Tories who introduced the finest food rationing system during the war.'[21] In saying this, she was drawing a contrast with post-war rationing, which had actually got more severe, and seemed to be going on for ever. She shared the growing dislike of what Winston Churchill disparaged as 'Queuetopia', but her experience as the daughter of a wartime grocer gave her faith in the powers of national emergency organization as well as in the efficacy of markets.

Perhaps the candidate's strongest appeal, and it was one made much stronger by her youth and sex, was a stirring call for effort, success and a recovery of national greatness. Writing an article in the local press, she declared that 'Women are intensely patriotic, and the loss of Britain's prestige under the present Government weighs heavily on their minds.'[22] Perhaps Margaret was simply projecting her own feelings on to the whole of her sex, but if so, it was a projection to which many responded enthusiastically. In particular, she galvanized the Young Conservatives. When they saw a Conservative government back in power, she told the YCs excitedly, 'they and all Young Conservatives up and down the country would be able to say with Keats, "Bliss was it in that dawn to be alive, but to be young was very heaven."'[23] The true author of those famous lines was in fact Wordsworth, not Keats, and he was speaking about the French Revolution, but the unlikely application of them to the YCs was all Margaret's.

Margaret's Dartford candidacy required a rearrangement of her life. She had to get out of Colchester and earn more money. She achieved both by securing a job, with the help of the Tory Party chairman, Lord Woolton, as a research chemist at J. Lyons and Co., the food company, in Hammersmith: 'hats and nice accessories are the order of the day so I'm told – even for laboratory work,' she complained to Muriel, thinking of the extra expense.[24] As with the job at Manningtree, Margaret showed very little interest in it, and certainly no career ambition. She was concentrating more and more on politics, and thinking of the Bar as a profession. But, as with everything she did, she was conscientious and put her work to use. Before long, she was talking to the Dartford Rotary Ladies Day about food research into dried eggs and the like – 'Another recent problem concerned sandwiches which were to be eaten at 20,000ft in the air,' read part of a surreal report in the local paper.[25] By July, she was lodging at Galley Hill, Darenth Road, Dartford, the home of Mrs Lilian Edwards, a former mayoress of Dartford. She got up at six to walk to Dartford station, took the 7.10 train to London and returned on the 6.08 to an evening's political work in the constituency.[26] The expense was worrying, and the burden of work would have crushed many a spirit, but for Margaret the whole thing was exhilarating, not least the clothes: 'Mrs Prole [a milliner in Colchester] has made me a smaller black velvet hat with a white ostrich feather on it and it looks very charming. Not so dressy as the green cock feathers – much more a hat for any occasion.'[27] To have dinner with Sir Alfred Bossom, the benign old Member for Maidstone, soon to prove one of Margaret's kindest patrons, she had to borrow Muriel's white blouse.[28]

There remained the matter of 'Scottie'. Back in Colchester, Willie Cullen took Margaret to the Caledonian Ball at the town hall. Margaret reported to Muriel: 'I was something of a curiosity as he usually takes his sister! I think I set some tongues wagging. Someone came up to Bill while I was standing with him and said "You'll be getting married next!" He [Willie Cullen], by the way, is 34.' He also took her to the 'flicks': 'He is awfully sweet; I am getting quite fond of him, and a very welcome relaxation. And he brought me a pair of nylons on Saturday that his sister had managed to procure up in Scotland! Also he never takes me out without producing a box of chocolates with some sweets!'[29] But Margaret was strengthening her idea of herself as matchmaker, having heard that Muriel had more or less broken with her fading suitor: 'Glad to hear you are trotting round with persons other than the august Ken. Hope it shakes him up a bit,' and again urged Muriel to Colchester: 'You had better come down here some other weekend to meet the current boyfriend. By the way, he will never become your brother-in-law though I have high hopes that he may be mine one day!'[30] On 8 April, only a few weeks after the relationship had begun, Margaret had Muriel to stay in Colchester and introduced her to Willie Cullen.

The flirtation continued, perhaps a merry diversion for Margaret, perhaps more serious for Willie. Willie kept a diary for the year 1949, mainly a terse, bald record of agricultural doings. His entry for 25 April is typical in tone, but unusually eventful: 'Carting dung to bottom of lane. Attended Mistley Court with Fred re tractor. Fined £8-15-0 for 9 charges [he had driven his tractor on steel wheels on the public road, and had been arrested]. 6 women hoeing potatoes. Met Margaret at 5.30 B.X. [Plastics]. We went to Flatford, a splendid evening.' In the following day's entry, Margaret inserted the time of their next meeting in her own hand. She also inscribed her Colchester address in the front of the diary, with two kisses, and occasionally interpolated her own account of an event in Willie's pages. On 18 March, she wrote: 'We went to the Caledonian Ball and had a lovely time. Wore black velvet frock, pearls and long drop earrings. MHR.' When Willie won the huge sum of £69 7s 6d on two horses called Squanderbug and Scorned at Newmarket ('SAW PRINCESS ELIZABETH, AND SHE SAW ME!' Margaret wrote of her first sight of the woman whose eighth prime minister she would eventually become), he took Margaret to lunch in Colchester that weekend to celebrate. They went to Jacklin's, a well-known local restaurant, before an afternoon together in the cinema watching Bob Hope in *Paleface*. The whole 'farming fraternity' was present in the restaurant: 'All heads were turned towards us as those facing the door sounded the alarm! There was a stunned silence for a couple of seconds followed by a sudden outburst. They all turned round to look and then chattered about us for the whole of the rest of the meal! One of them – Bill Strang – the biggest tease of the lot, tore up some silver cigarette paper into small pieces and threw it all over William as he (Bill) walked out past our table!'[31] When he took her to the cinema to see *Bad Lord Byron*, two of the farmers and their wives were there, and the same thing happened again: 'Being Scotch,* of course they had to turn round and see who else was there. They spotted us before we spotted them; they then proceeded to make so many wild signs and so much noise that we soon saw who they were!'[32]

Willie persevered, giving Margaret 'frightfully expensive' Crêpe de Chine scent and visited her 'every other day with butter, eggs and grapes etc.'[33] when she was ill in May. The record of one of his presents, particularly well suited to the recipient, survives, thanks to the camera. Margaret wrote to Muriel to describe it: '. . . William has given me a very nice black-calf handbag. It's not an awfully expensive one as my conscience wouldn't let me do that – but I chose a very nice one at £7-3s. We had my initials put on as well and it looks awfully nice . . . I quite loftily say it's not "very expensive" – it's about twice as much as you or I would pay. But compared to some of the others (£15–£20) it's quite reasonable. I'll have to hang on to William for a while longer now!'[34] Margaret drew a picture of the bag for Muriel, and one can see exactly how well it suited its owner from a press photograph of the two of them at a Dartford fête. There is an almost humorous heartlessness of youth in all of this, a Margaret who plays with men and enjoys it. In the very same letter, she mentions another date. She was going to the North Kent Rotary Ball, she said, 'with a chap called Denis Thatcher (34)† who is managing director of the Atlas paint works in Erith . . . He's all right – but is most unpopular with his men. He's far too belligerent in dealing with them and they naturally don't like it.'[35]

Willie Cullen introduced Margaret to his family. In May, she was received for dinner at Foulton Hall, his farm near Harwich where his sister Agnes kept house ('the perfectly natural hostess', said Margaret). She enjoyed the dinner, but it made an interesting impression upon her:

> The wives were typical wives – they know of domestic matters and nothing else. I stayed with the men after supper talking about many other things and when William suggested that maybe we ought to 'join the ladies' David [Macaulay, a local farmer] said in rather contemptuous fashion 'Why, – they don't talk politics or anything else in there.' And that's how they regard their wives. And indeed when we did join the ladies for half-an-hour or so much later, conversation flagged entirely.[36]

---

* Willie Cullen was part of a colony of Scottish farmers who had come down to Essex together before and during the war to escape the poor state of agriculture in Scotland; they retained a strong collective identity.
† Margaret appears to have forgotten she mentioned Denis to Muriel a few weeks before.

What is visible here is not only Margaret's lifelong preference for male company, but a sort of presentiment of what marriage to Willie Cullen would involve. Socially, she had begun to feel part of a more cosmopolitan sphere. And she knew that, both by temperament and by intellect, she could not be happy as a farmer's wife. When she next visited Foulton, she reported that 'the sitting-room looks smaller in daylight.'[37] The initial meeting which Margaret had set up must have been successful, however, because Muriel came down again to see Willie and, with Margaret, to meet his mother too. Margaret wrote to explain that old Mrs Cullen was nervous because she was 'afraid her English isn't good enough or something'. She therefore gave her sister very particular instructions about what to wear: 'I expect you'll have your high-wayman coat on, but don't come too exotic underneath. We must be as nice as possible to make Mrs Cullen feel at her ease. Why she should be apprehensive I don't know because she is an excellent farmer.'[38] Perhaps because the Roberts sisters avoided being 'exotic underneath', the meeting seems to have been a success, and Willie liked Muriel more and more, as was intended. Indeed, he seemed to fit in with Margaret's master-plan slightly more readily than was pleasing to her. 'I had a shock yesterday,' she wrote to Muriel from Dartford in July, 'when I had a letter from William to say that he was travelling up to Glasgow by car to fetch his mother down while the harvest is on and would probably call at Allerton [the house in North Parade which the Robertses bought after the war].' Muriel, of course, was at home with her parents, and Margaret was not. 'Hope Mummy is looking reasonably respectable,' she went on. 'Do let me know their reactions. I hope to goodness he doesn't give Daddy the impression of being a prospective son-in-law, it would scare Pop out of his wits at the moment. Anyway, I can't see it ever coming off.'[39]

The visit took place, and was repeated on Willie's return journey south. Muriel gave her sister a full report. Margaret replied:

> I was most amused to hear the other side of the story of the 'Bill'* visit. He told me he could have stayed much longer! . . . Daddy's only comment to me was 'He seems a sensible sort of chap . . . whoever you want to marry it will be all right by me, my dear.' So I was very glad you gave details of actual comments. I shan't marry Bill for though very fond of him I am not in love with him and a marriage between us would falter after 2 or 3 months. We have completely different outlooks, and quite different sorts of friends. While I get on all right with his, he would feel out of water with mine.[40]

---

* William Cullen was most commonly called Bill by Margaret at this time. He came generally to be known as Willie.

What Margaret was saying, with a rather mature delicacy, was that her ambitions in life were higher than anything that the hard-working plain Scottish farmer could satisfy. She was surely right.* She hurried home to see Muriel, complaining that she was so busy that she would 'probably arrive looking like the wreck of the *Hesperus*'.[41]

In the course of the autumn and winter of 1949, the relationship between Margaret and Willie Cullen continued to cool and that between him and Muriel warmed. Margaret had earlier told Muriel that her Dartford role meant 'There is very little time for "private life" down here. And even if there were time one wouldn't be allowed to be seen around in Dartford with anyone in particular.'[42] After the summer, it was widely believed that Attlee, the Prime Minister, would call an election quickly, and Margaret threw herself into the preparations, unhappily convinced that her association was not yet ready for the fight. In the course of her campaigning, however, she met a man who interested her. Scribbling to Muriel in pencil in the early autumn, she said that she was feeling the strain of the campaign without getting any thinner, but she had had a brief respite: 'I went up to the Southern Hospital for the afternoon and evening with the medical superintendent ... He's a most unusual chap and like a number of his profession still a bachelor. He's over 40, so he'd do quite nicely for you! He said I was to 'phone whenever I felt fed up with politics, but of course I shan't.'[43] 'William says he hasn't heard from you yet,' she chided in the same letter. 'Do write to him as quickly as possible.' She added that she had teased Willie, who had her to stay at Foulton Hall just before her twenty-fourth birthday in October, with her new-found friend: 'I told him that I went up to the Southern Hospital with a doctor who impressed me very much – and he wrote back and said I was giving him a hint to get out.' And she referred again to Denis Thatcher, reminding her sister that 'He was the one who drove me back to town on the night of my adoption meeting and whose works I later went round.' Denis was taking her to dinner and the theatre that night, she added, and had invited her to the Paint Federation Ball at the end of November.[44] This letter is notable for referring to three of only four men (Tony Bray being the other) who were ever important in the affairs of Margaret's heart. There will be more of the bachelor doctor at the Southern Hospital later. Margaret was toying with the idea of choosing between them all. When she finally came to choose,

---

* Muriel and Willie's younger son, Andrew Cullen, made a comparable analysis of the situation, when interviewed in 2004: 'Margaret probably realised my Dad wasn't going to up sticks from here [Foulton]' and so she did not want to marry him.

she would do so with the utmost seriousness, but she was not above enjoying the game on the way.

What exactly happened in the next two months is partially obscure, and the participants interviewed by the present author – the two Roberts sisters – did not want to shed much light on it. But, one way or another, Willie Cullen did 'take the hint to get out' or rather, to change partners. The process of being gently dumped by Margaret and pushed towards Muriel instead must have been a complicated one. It seemed to involve a good deal of negotiation, but with no apparent falling out between the sisters. Willie Cullen recorded in his diary what was probably his last meeting with Margaret alone: he took her to see *The Third Man* in London on 27 October 1949. On 16 December he arrived to stay at the Robertses' house in Grantham for the weekend and took Muriel out to the Golf Club Dance. Margaret was not present. Early in January 1950, writing from 63 Knole Road, the address of her new Dartford landlords, local Conservatives called Mr and Mrs Ray Woollcott, Margaret kept Muriel fully informed of the course of the break-up: 'I have written to William in the vein I told you. He wrote a letter to me – much warmer in tone than his others and the two must have crossed in the post ... We are meeting in London on Saturday afternoon to talk over the various aspects of "we three" and it will then be broken off between he and I [sic], for good and all.' It was better for them to meet, she wrote, perhaps anticipating a slight unease on Muriel's part, because 'it would be easier, for when we meet again in a different relationship such as we were sketching out over Xmas, if we parted in the flesh – not by letter – as friends. Hope you approve.'[45] In fact, the meeting did not take place. In a postscript, Margaret writes that Willie had rung her to cancel the meeting because 'he has a party on in Colchester'. Instead, they discussed matters over the telephone. 'I told him from henceforth that I would "in law" only be taking a sisterly interest in future. He seemed quite satisfied and is quite pleased with "future prospects".'[46]

Once 'we three' were rearranged, Margaret was keen to get everything settled. Willie Cullen went up to the Robertses in Grantham at the end of January, and Margaret wrote to Muriel beforehand urging her on: 'I do hope it comes off and I see no reason for the pessimism you showed in a former letter.'[47] It did come off. A formal, typed letter, the first such that survives, was sent to Muriel by Margaret from her Conservative Committee Rooms on 2 February 1950, where she was campaigning in the general election which Attlee had called, slightly earlier than he needed to, for 23 February. She detailed where Willie would stay for his visit to Dartford (the Bull) and where Muriel would be billeted (at Knole Road). Behind this was the fact that Willie and Muriel were engaged. On 14 February, St Valentine's Day, only a week before polling day, Margaret wrote another formal letter, again typed by a secretary, which said, without comment, 'I saw your engagement in the *Telegraph* this morning.' It added instructions for the couple's visit, 'You, Daddy and I shall be dining with Lord Dudley Gordon on Tuesday night. Bring something decent to wear. You will be coming to the Count with me on Thursday night, so bring a smart hat.' In her own hand, however, and presumably written so that no assistant would see it, Margaret added a PS: 'So glad the announcement is in today's *Telegraph*, one feels it gives the stamp of finality to the whole affair. Gather you're having diamonds in your ring, a plum coloured corduroy suit to go away in and a blue gown for the ceremony . . . The campaign goes fairly well – we are having packed meetings.'[48]

A minor family row ensued about the announcement in the *Daily Telegraph*. Alfred Roberts had placed the notice and described himself in it as 'Ald.', short for Alderman. Muriel was upset by this, and continued to be so more than fifty years later, feeling that it turned her wedding into a municipal announcement.[49] Margaret concurred, perhaps for the slightly different reason that local government titles are not grand enough to parade on social occasions. 'I agree with you that it was quite wrong. I raised my eyebrows at the time.'[50] The mistake was not repeated in the invitation to the wedding itself. As soon as the election was out of the way, Margaret, who was to be the only bridesmaid at the wedding in April, threw herself into its every detail. Muriel must have a headdress with a veil 'otherwise folks won't know bride from bridesmaid. I'll just have a little draped cap.' She made suggestions about flowers, gloves and the importance of not having silver shoes because they would look 'a bit back-streetish',[51] and drew a sketch of the frock, of her own design, which she proposed to wear. She also instructed Muriel on how to take her fiancé in hand – 'Was disgusted to read the way he turned up for the weekend. See that he takes the right clothes to Paris [where they went on honeymoon]' – and told Muriel to buck up: 'Don't worry about pre-wedding jitters.'[52] On no account, she said, must Muriel allow Willie's sister, Agnes, to go on living with them after their marriage.* All Margaret's interventions were well meant, and it is clear that she always had what she considered Muriel's best interests at heart, but her sister would not have been human if she did not sometimes

* She did not, but returned to Scotland where she never married and maintained a consistently unfriendly relationship with Muriel for the rest of her life, while remaining very fond of her brother. When Miss Cullen was asked what Willie most liked to discuss in their weekly telephone conversations over the years, she said, 'Ooh, his shares!' (interview with Miss Agnes Cullen).

feel irritated to be told what to do, almost to have had her marriage arranged, by an unmarried woman four years her junior. Unfortunately, none of Muriel's letters to Margaret survives, but we know that she did sometimes feel some irritation with the orders issuing from Dartford.[53] Her marriage to Willie Cullen proved long and successful (he died in 1998), but the way it was plotted was probably slightly galling. As Andrew Cullen, one of Muriel and Willie's two sons, said: 'Dad did hold a soft spot for Auntie Margaret.'[54] In old age, Muriel described her relationship with her sister with characteristic briskness: 'She [Margaret] says, "I consider my sister my best friend." All she means by that is that I told her what I thought.'[55] Muriel's daughter, Jane, believed that the relationship between the two sisters was, on the whole, good, but said: 'The Robertses are not very good at feelings. They deal with facts and reality.'[56]

Although Margaret never really had any intention of marrying Willie Cullen, what probably precipitated the break was the arrival on the scene of the medical superintendent from the Southern Hospital. The doctor in question was called Robert Henderson. Already forty-seven when Margaret first met him (and therefore just over twice her age), he had enjoyed a distinguished medical career. He was a blacksmith's son from Clatt in Aberdeenshire who left school early and was apprenticed to a local garage. One of his former teachers, however, who noticed his talent, persuaded his father that he could become a doctor, and he entered medical school in Aberdeen. In that city's hospital in the 1930s, Henderson devised his own version of a tank respirator he had seen in America for the treatment of patients who could not breathe. In 1933, his 'iron lung', as the device came to be widely known, saved the life of a ten-year-old boy with polio. During the war, the machine was manufactured and distributed to hospitals throughout Britain and the Empire. It became famous and saved many lives. In 1940, Henderson was appointed medical superintendent of the Southern Hospital in Dartford, which had 1,700 beds and admitted, at the time of the Blitz, more patients than any other hospital in England. It was in this post that Margaret first met him, some time in the summer of 1949. Because the navy used 500 of the beds there, and Henderson excelled in the treatment of submariners who, in those days, often contracted tuberculosis, he was made a surgeon captain RNVR, entitled to wear the uniform. In 1947, he was given the CBE for his services to medicine. He was greatly admired for his work in this enormous and hard-pressed hospital. A thin, drily amusing man, he loved roses and country life, a good party and especially a good Bloody Mary.[57] Physically, he resembled Denis Thatcher, although he was shorter and considered to be better looking. He was also 'a very good dancer'.[58] He was canny with money – '£100 would go for ever'[59] – and a supporter, though not actively involved, of the Conservatives. He liked women. In 1949, he was still unmarried.

In Margaret's letters to Muriel, Robert Henderson is the only boyfriend who is invariably referred to with respect, sometimes even with tenderness. The 'most unusual chap' whom she got to know in the summer became a much closer companion as the year waned. In the letter which describes her parting with Willie Cullen, Margaret makes it clear that Robert was, as she most certainly would not have put it, 'there for her': 'In the evening I met Robert on the Dartford station. We had apparently travelled down by the same train. He had to go back for a nurses' dinner but afterwards he came up to Knole Road and picked me up and we went for a drink. He said he thought I looked flat and miserable and I ought to go out for a little while on my first night back. Wasn't it sweet of him?' She was self-mockingly nervous, however, of her chances with him. He had spent Christmas, she said, with a rich family 'who own half the farms in Essex' and had 'five daughters of marriageable age . . . The prospects don't look very hopeful do they!?'[60] Later in January 1950, she wrote that 'Robert and I are seeing very little of one another at the moment as there is a little thing called the general election in sight,' but in the same letter, resumed a bit later, she says that she has been to a 'wonderful party' ('All Scotch', meaning the people, not the drink) with Robert, given by a friend of his who was 'consultant epidemiologist to the Royal family'. The couple got back to Dartford at three in the morning on a Saturday. And on the Sunday afternoon he drove her round the Weald of Kent and then gave her dinner at the hospital. 'I think we are both getting very fond of one another,' she added, '– in fact more than that. I hope so.'[61]

The entertainments became more glamorous and more intimate. In the postscript she wrote to Muriel on the typed letter about her sister's engagement, Margaret added,

> By the way after Polling day Robert and I are dining and dancing at the Berkeley . . . My new white frock is simply lovely and I've every intention of wearing it on that night in spite of the fact that it was mean't [sic] for the Divisional Ball. Hope you won't mind my going out then. On Saturday I'm going down to Eastbourne for the weekend. Robert is coming to join me on the Sunday staying overnight and he will drive me back on the Monday. Needless to say I'm looking forward to it tremendously.[62]

This was perhaps as near as Margaret ever came to enjoying a naughty weekend.

It is notable that no one surviving from Conservative politics in Dartford at that time has any memory of any connection between Margaret and Dr Robert Henderson. True to her intense dislike of other people knowing about her private life, she mentioned him to no one in Dartford, although she is remembered visiting the Southern Hospital with him to speak to the staff there.[63] Yet their relationship deepened, and was to continue almost until she left Dartford for good.

In her election address for the general election of 23 February 1950, Margaret Roberts spoke in her own distinctive voice. The 'first task' of a new Conservative government, she said, would be 'setting the finances of the nation in order', and she grounded her thoughts in the commonsense terms of the practical woman. Of nationalization, she wrote, 'To the housewife it conjures up a picture of a grate full of dust, ash and clinker that won't burn.' She praised the 'small shopkeepers' – 'I believe firmly that such men and women are part of the strength and backbone of England' – reaffirmed her support for Imperial Preference and declared that 'A separate house for every family is our aim.' And she made a promise about herself, which, more than most politicians' promises, was to prove true: if elected, 'I should carry out my task to the utmost of my ability, allowing myself no rest until the duties which fell to my lot were complete.'[64]

In a newspaper article the previous week, Margaret was even more explicit in offering her own vision of Britain and the crisis it faced under socialism. She set out four main themes – 'Britain amongst the Nations', 'Britain's Economic Independence', 'Nationalisation or Private Enterprise' and 'Frustration or Freedom'. She argued that Britain's reputation in the world had fallen low under Labour from its great height in 1945, that it had failed to join in resisting Communism and that 'The world needs her.' Discussing the American Lend–Lease programme which kept the nation afloat during the war, Margaret compared the United States with a friendly neighbour helping the man next door who had fallen on hard times and now dismayed by his failure to recover. Socialist profligacy was the problem. Far from paying off his debt, the neighbour 'is having to sell one or two pieces of his wife's gold jewellery to pay the grocer's bill'. This, referring to the sale of gold reserves to buy food, was what might be called a pre-echo of Harold Macmillan's famous attack on Mrs Thatcher over privatization for 'selling the family silver'. Margaret then challenged the voters: 'Are YOU going to let this proud island race, who at one time would never accept charity, drift on from crisis to crisis . . . ? Or do you believe in sound finance . . . ?' Quoting 'a young unknown engineer from one of the Dominions',* who had written to her asking what had happened to the

---

* This was the name for nations such as Australia, Canada and New Zealand, which came later to be referred to as 'the white Commonwealth' and, later still, as 'the old Commonwealth'.

sturdy British love of freedom, she made her own passionate plea: 'It was not a Government that built up the skill and craft of this country – the woollen goods, the beautiful china, and the precision engineering, which have made their way into the markets of the world. It was private individuals who patiently persevered, building up their businesses bit by bit.' The British spirit had to be rediscovered: 'Do you want it to perish for a soul-less Socialist system, or to live to recreate a glorious Britain? YOU WILL DECIDE.'[65] In the whole of her career, Margaret Thatcher was to diverge very little from the substance and the tone of this article. It is, perhaps, the first clear text of Thatcherism. As with Thatcherism when fully formed, the emotional force behind the piece is not a doctrine about economic liberty – strong though that is – but a romantic belief in the greatness, and a sad lament at the decline, of her country.

With such powerful beliefs, and a precocious confidence in her powers of expressing them, Margaret Roberts fought the campaign with gusto. And she was happy to put herself and her background centre-stage. She had heard, she told a public meeting on 7 February, that some people thought 'she came from a moneyed family; that was not so. She had to work for her living as a food chemist and had been in the habit of leaving Dartford on the 7.15am train and returning at 7pm to do her political work.'[66] Nor did she think her extreme youth a problem: 'William Pitt was Prime Minister of England [sic] when he was 24. Mr Anthony Eden went into Parliament at my age and has represented the same division ever since.'[67] Believing that the candidate should be immediately identifiable by the way she looked, she invested in a hat from Bourne and Hollingsworth with a black and white ribbon, to which she added a 'bit of blue inside the bow' and alternated two suits.[68] She threw herself into the campaign, speaking outside factory gates to the all-male workers in defiance of trade union officials, and addressing huge public meetings night after night – 'heckling suited me a treat'. She went everywhere in the constituency except for pubs, believing that it 'wouldn't do' for a woman.[69]* The campaign went extremely well, but Margaret gave it almost more than she had. Speaking more than forty years later, she said, 'I have never felt so tired in any election since.'[70] The result declared, late at night on 23 February 1950, was:

Norman Dodds (Labour)	38,128
Miss M. H. Roberts (Conservative)	24,490
A. H. Giles (Liberal)	5,011
Labour majority	13,638

* Lady Thatcher told the present author that, for this reason, she had never been into a pub alone in her entire life.

Margaret had knocked 6,000 off Dodds's majority, doing much better than the average Tory candidate, without, of course, coming near to beating him. Nationally, Labour clung on to power by an overall majority of six, which made a second election quite soon highly probable. The party was still 2.6 per cent ahead of the Conservatives in its share of the popular vote, but it lost seats disproportionately because there was a strong swing of 6 per cent to the Tories in London and the Home Counties, compared to a national one of only 2.4 per cent. This was known as 'the revolt of the suburbs', a phrase which well expresses Margaret's own attitude. Margaret allowed her supporters no time for rest. 'You sign on for next time tomorrow morning,' she told them in her speech after the count at Dartford Grammar School.[71] A few days later, Dartford Conservative Association held a party to celebrate the first anniversary of Margaret's adoption and presented her with a 16-foot scroll containing the names of 991 active supporters. 'Dartford', she assured them, 'will certainly have first refusal of my services as a candidate in the next election.'[72] They did not refuse. In fact, however, Margaret did secretly consider an alternative. South Hammersmith Conservatives, fighting a Labour seat with a smaller majority than that at Dartford, approached her. She confided this to Muriel and explained that 'their 2,000 adverse majority is even more solid than Dartford's 13,000. I don't feel it would be worth changing under those circumstances.'[73] Her devotion to Dartford was qualified by the strength of her ambition.

With her second candidacy assured, Margaret immediately set about making complementary arrangements for her life. She began driving lessons, began looking for a flat in London and – the flat being part of the career plan – began reading for the Bar. Her first point of contact in the law was David Renton,* the Conservative MP for Huntingdonshire, to whom she was introduced through his family connection with Dartford. He remembered her visiting him in his chambers in March 1950: 'In sailed a good-looking woman, twenty-four, mouse-coloured hair, plainly dressed, with no jewellery. She took everything in.'[74] She asked his advice and he recommended his own Lincoln's Inn, and offered to sponsor her. Even Margaret quailed slightly under the amount of labour involved in reading for the Bar. 'My goodness there's a lot of work to be done and it will come terribly expensive,' she wrote to Muriel some time in the summer,[75] but

---

* David Renton (1908–2007), educated Oundle and University College, Oxford; Conservative MP for Huntingdonshire, 1945–79; QC, 1954; Minister of State, Home Office, 1961–2; created Lord Renton, 1979.

she enrolled and, in August, was admitted to Lincoln's Inn. Always impressed by tradition, she was delighted with the receipts she received: 'magnificent-looking things done on beautiful paper and perfectly printed'.[76] Following the rule that, to qualify, students should eat dinners in their chosen Inn of Court, Margaret had her first in October. She wrote to Muriel, curiously nervous, 'Tonight I am dining at Lincoln's Inn for the first time . . . It's hard doing anything new for the first time.'[77]

The relationship with Robert Henderson continued, although it began to show some signs of difficulty. 'I go out with him most weekends and one night during the week,' she told Muriel in March. 'But whether it will ever come to anything I very much doubt for he thinks the difference between our ages very great.'[78] He, for his part, was somewhat circumspect about introducing Margaret to his friends: she described him as having 'reverted to form in seeing little of me while he has visitors'.[79] In May 1950, she complained, 'Robert I have scarcely seen recently.'[80] He mattered as much to her as before, though. She arranged for him to meet Willie Cullen, something she would not have done if she had not expected the relationship to last, and she reported happily: 'I gather they got on like a house on fire . . .' She was worried about Robert's health: 'he has a very bad duodenum and if he eats anything which disagrees with him he feels wretched for days.'[81] In June, he was operated on: 'I might be allowed to go in for ten minutes . . . They are removing part of the tummy and duodenum and severing the jugular vein. It is a bigger job than Robert thought. He was feeling a little depressed when I went down to see him last night.'[82] The operation went well, but required a long convalescence. He went to stay for some of the time with his sister in Aberdeen. When he returned 'looking a lot better and feeling very fit', she resumed her Sunday-night visits to him at the Southern Hospital 'as usual'.[83] It is unlikely that these visits ever involved Margaret staying overnight. There is no evidence that their relationship was ever physically consummated.

Knowing Robert meant, among other things, finding out more about the medical and nursing professions and how they had been affected by the introduction of the National Health Service by the Labour government in 1948. As well as her weekly visits to the Southern Hospital for Sunday dinner with Robert, Margaret also met more nurses and doctors. In the mid-summer of 1950, she went to the West Hill Hospital Nurses Reunion, an event which provoked something near an outburst to Muriel: 'It was quite a nice afternoon but my goodness how I should hate the sort of life they lead. The various members (lay-members) of the Hospital Management Committee were strutting about and I looked at some of them and thought "Our New Masters".' Although never opposed to the principle of care free at the point of use to all patients which the NHS enshrined, Margaret believed strongly that the way it was introduced worked against the freedom of individual hospitals and submitted doctors and nurses to unnecessary and overcentralized control, some of it exercised through the new management committees. With the coming of the NHS, Robert gradually surrendered some of the mastery of the huge Southern Hospital that he had possessed. Margaret watched this happening, and did not like it.

Since Robert lived in Dartford, it might be thought odd that his girlfriend was looking so hard to leave the place and find a flat in London. But in fact his presence in her life did have something to do with Margaret's attempts to move. With her fierce dislike of people knowing her inner thoughts and her private life, she had grown to resent her landlords, the Woollcotts. They were a well-meaning couple but, with no children of their own, they seem to have lavished on Margaret an attention which she found oppressive. Discussing Muriel's wedding pictures, and how a Dartford friend and helper, Mary Rohan, had offered to tint them, she adds, without punctuation: 'The Woollcotts curse them are also most anxious to see them and I expect we shall hear the usual childish drip when they do.' In the same letter, she reports a warning from Mary Rohan that the Woollcotts have been complaining about Margaret's secretiveness, and expresses her annoyance: 'You know how I hate everyone knowing my own affairs. Robert refuses to come in now, and as often as not I go to the end of the road and meet him at the traffic lights.'[84] It seems both touching and absurd that a forty-eight-year-old man felt it better to meet his girlfriend at the traffic lights rather than brave her landlady. Margaret obviously longed for a more grown-up solution.

But the search for a flat in town was hard. She found something promising, but, at 4 guineas a week, decided it was too expensive.[85] Possibilities of flat-sharing were canvassed without result. There were also the Rent Acts to be considered, which made unfurnished flats more attractive because they were rent-controlled. For a short period in June, Margaret took a tiny flat in Westminster Palace Gardens to look about her in London. She enjoyed the experience: 'I have loved the short stay in the London flat. It isn't nearly so strenuous as travelling up from Dartford daily and its [sic] nice not to be questioned by an enquiring landlord and landlady.' From it, she sallied forth to be the youth speaker offering a vote of thanks to Winston Churchill at a party rally at the Albert Hall on 7 June 1950, the only time she was to meet the great wartime Prime Minister: 'The Winston meeting went off quite well. I was absolutely terrified of the enormous audience but got through all right. Everyone was very flattering about it.' There is no record or memory of the private words that she and Churchill exchanged or of what she said in her vote of thanks. She also went to the Royal Tournament with Denis Thatcher, who was still, despite Robert, somewhere in the background, inviting her out for the odd treat and dinner.[86]

Life in the flatlet also sharpened Margaret's views about wealth and politics. 'The woman whose flat my flatlet is sublet from is Beauty Editor of *Modern Woman*. She lets off the upper storey. The other girl is or was secretary to Audrey Withers – editor of *Vogue* – I gather Audrey Withers is a terrifically strong socialist. It's a funny world, isn't it. I go down to Dartford 2 or 3 times a week.'[87] The expression 'It's a funny old world' would become one of Margaret Thatcher's better-known quotations after she commented thus to her Cabinet on the day she resigned as prime minister.

The search for a flat lasted into the following year. In February 1951, Margaret had been unsuccessfully negotiating with Morris Wheeler, a business bigwig in the Dartford Conservative Association. He owned several properties in London, but she had rejected his offer of a flat in Belgrave Road because it was in 'appalling condition', and he didn't want her to have his flat in St George's Square Mews 'as even he realised that it wasn't a very nice area'. 'I think Daddy will be relieved,' Margaret commented to Muriel, '– he was quite worried about its being in the heart of Pimlico!' She looked further afield: 'On Saturday I went to Dulwich at lunchtime. It is a terrible place – one is rather apt to think of it as being quite pukkha [sic] as there is a big public school there, but in fact the area outside there is bad.'[88]*

In the end, Margaret settled for the supposed horrors of Pimlico and 101 St George's Square Mews, moving in May 1951. She was joyful. Part of her pleasure came from the sense that she was at last living in the middle of things: 'It was a great thrill to come to London. In Grantham it was like swimming in a very small pool: you keep bumping into the sides.'[89] 'I said goodbye to the Woollcotts who of course were very nice at the last moment,' she wrote tartly to Muriel,[90] and then described in several letters and enormous detail the decorative and domestic arrangements, exercising her will and energy upon all who came in contact with her. She went to an electrician 'to have the iron fixed up with a flex and the electric ring mended. The electricians said they couldn't possibly do the flex before Tuesday so I told them to give me the parts and I would do it. They looked somewhat

---

* Margaret had clearly forgotten this earlier impression when house-hunting while prime minister. In 1985, she and Denis bought disastrously in Dulwich a house which proved completely unsuitable for her retirement.

stunned and tried to put me off by saying was I sure the iron was alright. I said firmly "Yes" and marched out of the shop with the plugs. I told the driver [taxi? removal van?] and he said oh I'll do it for you. He then discovered that they had given me a broken power plug so I marched very firmly back to the shop with it. I shan't go there again.'[91]

By this time, Muriel had given birth to her first child, Morton, and Margaret includes brief and brisk references to the baby in her correspondence – 'Glad to hear junior is progressing all right',[92] 'So glad to hear that you are home again and that the infant is making good progress. Hope the vomiting soon clears up'[93] – but she quickly returns to the subject of her own home-making, lamenting the absence of a bath, explaining how she is putting down the old pink lino from home, complaining that the sideboard has woodworm ('It only goes to show how careful one should be before buying').[94] Declaring that 'I will have to come up and see you soon,' Margaret does not suggest any desire to see the new-born baby, or her sister who had been quite ill after the birth, but rather that her reason for coming is 'I am practically out of eggs and they are my main diet at the moment – scrambled eggs on toast!'[95] In the same month, Margaret managed to pass her driving test, which her father had arranged for her to take in Grantham. Because she had two outstanding driving lessons paid for at the moment of passing, she went ahead and had them all the same,[96] showing a virtually inhuman determination to get value for money. At Lyons, unlike at BX Plastics, she had to work on Saturday mornings. Even she, so clearly enjoying herself in London, felt a little overwhelmed by the amount of work she faced: 'I have so much to do that I don't know where to turn next.'[97]

Her extreme busyness made others tired too. Writing to his elder daughter in January of the same year, Alfred Roberts inquired rather wistfully, 'Have you heard from Margaret recently? She isn't too good at correspondence. But I'm afraid it is the result of doing so much in other ways.'[98] When Margaret found her flat in supposedly dangerous Pimlico, her father did a great deal to help with finding furniture and passing on the old car which he had originally bought for Muriel. He felt rather unthanked for his efforts, depending on Muriel for news about whether he had given pleasure: 'It's good to know she is satisfied with what we got her for the flat for it has been no easy matter.'[99] Muriel also took the view that Margaret did not always notice the efforts and sacrifices her parents made for her as she tried to rise in the world.[100]

Later in the summer, Roberts's resentment of Margaret's supposed ingratitude began to connect in his mind with a rather different anxiety. He formed the view that Margaret's Dartford friend, Mary Rohan, was exercising a malign religious influence upon her. 'I have been very worried about Margaret these last few days,' he wrote to Muriel, 'about her always having Mary with her wherever she goes, and wondering if Mary was doing a lot of Catholic propaganda with Margaret. In fact I haven't been sleeping at nights although I haven't mentioned the reason to Mummy.' 'I have written to Margaret about it,' he went on, 'again unknown to Mummy, as I should be grieved beyond measure if the R/Cs got hold of Margaret. She would no longer be free, and they might cause untold family misery.' Roberts clearly saw any Romish tendencies as a form of filial betrayal:

> As you know, I have left you both free in regard to religion, as a parent must and does who trusts his children, but R/C is Spiritual Totalitarianism with all its damning intolerance for others. Margaret has been very hard at times and apparently ungrateful for all I've done, altho that hasn't & wouldn't stop me from doing all I could for either of you. But truthfully it has kept me poor, and I was beginning to rejoice that she would soon be well established & independant [sic] when she had got through the law business. Now comes this worry, and I had to know how things stand so I have written and am hoping & praying for the best. This is in confidence to you my dear, for I can open my heart to you.[101]

Margaret's reply to the letter Roberts wrote her, if ever it existed, does not survive, but she did remember her father's worries, attributing them to both parents: 'They would have thought becoming a Roman Catholic meant giving up one's freedom.'[102] There is no evidence that Roberts was justified in his anxieties. Margaret did not share her father's hostility to the Roman Catholic Church, and she became increasingly sympathetic to it in later life, but her strong Christianity was never of a Catholic or sacramental or even of a churchy kind. Neither in 1951, nor later, was she about to 'pope'. As for the idea that her sister could be 'influenced' by Mary Rohan, Muriel was clear: 'I just wrote back and said, "Don't be silly. It would take more than Mary or anyone else to influence Margaret."' Besides, Mary was 'a slave to Margaret'.[103]

One of Margaret's chief motives in getting and beautifying the flat was to impress Robert Henderson. He was quite often away from the hospital, getting free holidays on cruises as a 'doctor at sea' and she clearly feared that women on these voyages would prove more eligible than she. With amused horror, she described his wardrobe for a trip to Madeira. His maid, she told Muriel, had put out 'amongst other things 58 pairs of socks and 21 shirts!!! Robert has stacks and stacks of clothes. If rationing came in it wouldn't bother him at all.'[104] As soon as she got the flat, she was determined to entertain him royally. True, she also invited 'Dennis [sic]

Thatcher . . . for a drink and we then went out to dinner and along to the Festival of Britain,' but in the same letter she describes the more elaborate treatment she had given Robert: 'Tonight Robert is coming up and we are going out for dinner. Last time he came I cooked a slap-up dinner, four courses just to show him! But I can't rise to that every time.'[105] She valued his opinion: 'Robert came to the flat on Thursday evening last and was quite impressed with the sitting-room as it is looking at present.'[106]

The last surviving references to Robert Henderson in Margaret's correspondence date from May 1951. After that, nothing more is heard of him or Margaret's attitude to him until a letter, dated 25 September 1951, which Alfred Roberts sent to Muriel. It is worth quoting at length. Having first announced that Beatrice Roberts is going into hospital ('you will know what it is for'),* Roberts continues:

Next, which will be more surprising, Margaret and Dennis [sic] Thatcher are becoming engaged, although it will not be announced until after the election [Attlee had called a general election for 25 October], probably the Tuesday after in The Times, and likely to be married first week in December. This means she will not take up her new job [she had been offered a post in a trade association] but will go on with the Law job until qualified. As I told you, I met Dennis on the Sunday I left you and heard from Margaret that he had asked her to marry him and that she was considering it but wanted to see me first. I don't know if you have met him at Dartford but he is the Managing Director of Atlas Paints Ltd, factory at Erith. He has been taking Margaret about the place to various functions for almost two years but his proposal was unexpected. The Robert business upset Margaret very much but that will pass. Dennis has had an unfortunate experience. He was married during the war, but after only about five weekends' leave spent with his wife she left him. She is now Lady Hicks,† it appears the title did the damage. I told Margaret she could disregard this as he was in no way at fault and actually he is an exceedingly nice fellow also of course <u>very</u> comfortably situated financially. They both came down on Sunday for the day as he wanted to see Mummy and to get our consent.

Alfred Roberts went on to say that the wedding would be in London and 'Mummy and I will be the only ones from Grantham I expect.' Of Denis he added, 'He runs a 1948 Jaguar and also a Triumph, but is wanting to get a Jaguar Mark V . . .'[107]

---

* This may have been the first appearance of the cancer which was to kill Mrs Roberts nine years later, or it may be a reference to a gynaecological problem.
† Actually she was Lady Hickman.

What had happened? If one compares her references to the two men in her letters, it is clear that Margaret felt more tender towards Robert than towards Denis. Indeed, almost all her mentions of Denis are either neutral or mildly unflattering. She told Muriel, for example, after going to the play *His Excellency* with Denis, 'I can't say I really ever enjoy going out for the evening with him. He has not got a very prepossessing personality.'[108] With Robert, she took trouble. Although he seems to have destroyed all their correspondence, for the rest of his life Robert kept a couple of presents that Margaret had given him – the complete works of Shakespeare inscribed 'To Robert with love and Best wishes Margaret' and *Birds and Men*, a book by the radical environmentalist E. M. (Max) Nicholson inscribed 'to Robert with best wishes from Margaret April 1951' (his birthday was on 7 April). He also preserved, still in its envelope addressed in her hand, a large, mounted photograph of herself that Margaret sent him. Robert wrote on the envelope 'Margaret Roberts' and then, in a box, the word 'Thatcher'. Robert Henderson died in 1999 aged ninety-seven without ever having said much more than a few words on the subject, so far as is known, to friends, press or Josie, the widow he eventually married in 1960. But he was angered by a book, called *Five at 10* by Diana Farr, which appeared in 1985 and which discussed the lives of the spouses of five prime ministers. Passages about Denis's engagement to Margaret made reference to her friendship with Robert and suggested that there had been a competition between the two men for her hand. Robert told the *Daily Express*, 'I never ever courted Margaret or proposed to her. It's all ridiculous ... We were never romantically involved.'[109] But although it is almost certainly true that Robert never proposed to Margaret, they undoubtedly were romantically involved.

According to Josie Henderson, her husband liked to say that 'Denis had more money and more future and from then on, he [Robert] didn't stand a chance ... He understood that Denis was a much better catch.'[110] This cannot be the whole story, however, since it does not explain the fact that the two men ran in parallel for two years of Margaret's life with Denis, who met her before Robert, coming second in the race until the late summer of 1951. There is not the slightest hint in any letter of Margaret's that she is serious about Denis, while she explicitly states that she is so about Robert. In the opinion of Muriel Cullen, the problem between Margaret and Robert was simply the age gap of twenty-four years. For this reason, she said, Margaret did not let the relationship blossom into marriage.[111] Lady Thatcher herself confirmed this view. When asked about Robert Henderson by the present author, she said, 'He was a Scot, a very good doctor, but he was much older.' At the suggestion that Robert had perhaps hoped that she would be the future Mrs Henderson, she replied: 'I wouldn't disagree with that, but he was so much older.'[112] If the decision was as cut and dried as that, however, why did Alfred Roberts think that his daughter had been 'upset very much' by it?

On the other hand, it seems highly unlikely that Robert and Margaret parted on poor terms. Unlike with Tony Bray, she maintained friendly, though not close, relations with him. Not long after the birth of her twins, Carol and Mark, she wrote to Muriel about where she should have the infant Mark circumcised, an operation that was quite common among non-Jewish people at that time on grounds of hygiene: 'I don't like the idea of having it done on the Health service in London as you don't know who is going to do it but it costs £15–£20 to have it done privately! I am writing to Robert to ask who does it at the Southern Hospital under the health service because I know Mark would be wonderfully looked after there.'[113] It is not known whether the Southern Hospital did, in the end, carry out the operation, but the fact that Margaret was prepared to put her son's manhood almost literally in the hands of her former boyfriend suggests a high level of trust. When, in the 1960s, the Thatchers lived partly in Lamberhurst, they were fairly close neighbours of the Hendersons in Brenchley and had Robert and Josie over for drinks once or twice.[114] When informed, rather belatedly, of Robert's death, Lady Thatcher wrote to his widow in condolence, apologizing for the fact that she could not attend his memorial service because of a visit to the United States. Her words, though apparently slightly formulaic, gather more meaning when one knows the history behind them: 'Robert was a wonderful man and I know how deeply you will miss him. During his life he gave so much to others. He was one of those rare people of whom it can be said "they made a difference".'[115]

What of Denis Thatcher? Having suffered deeply in the collapse of his first marriage, and not being a man to act impulsively, he did not rush into anything. There is no evidence that he fell suddenly in love with Margaret Roberts. Rather, his admiration for the pretty, intelligent and spirited girl he had met on the night of her adoption meeting slowly grew. The first person who told him he should marry Margaret was an industry colleague, Tony Colley, chairman of the National Paint Federation dinner, to which Denis took her. Colley looked at Margaret, leant across to Denis and said, 'That's the one.' But he did not decide to propose to her until he went on a bachelor holiday in France with an old schoolfriend, Kent Green, in the late summer of 1951. Denis, who was 'rather bored with not too bright ladies', recognized Margaret as someone with a powerful mind and character 'different from any other young woman I'd ever met in my life'. He liked her ability to recite poetry.* 'Let's have a go,' he said to himself, and when he returned from the holiday, he did, proposing to her after dinner in his flat.[116]† Perhaps the key difference between Denis and Robert, from Mrs Thatcher's point of view, was that Denis asked her to marry him, and Robert did not. She feared that Robert might cast her aside and saw that Denis's offer pre-empted this. Speaking of not marrying Robert, she said, 'and then Denis came along. It is no good regretting what might have been.'[117]

She did not say yes or no at once. As Denis put it nearly fifty years later, 'She didn't leap at it.'[118] Denis's proposal was a surprise, as her father's letter on the subject to Muriel makes clear, and came at a time when her feelings about Robert Henderson were probably not fully resolved. She admired Denis as the ex-soldier, 'obviously someone who had known authority',[119] and was pleased to have someone who shared her political interests and views, and, to be blunt, someone who had a good job and could afford a good flat in Chelsea. He was a passport to the Home Counties respectability that she sought. She liked and lent on his knowledge of business and money. She recognized him as her social superior with 'a certain style and dash' including his penchant for fast cars.[120] She was bored by sport – he was a very serious rugby referee – but perfectly happy with his enthusiasm for it, and had no objection to his fondness for all-male jollifica-tion with what he called his 'chums' from the sporting and business worlds. She is probably not telling the truth when she recalls that he had a strong interest in opera which she appreciated.[121] She went away and pondered his offer: 'Things last better that way.'[122] She seems to have intuited, if not actu-ally discussed with Denis, the fact that he would accept her political ambitions, which was 'exceptional for a man of that generation'.[123] She could see that his financial and moral support would allow her to qualify for the Bar. She was worried by the fact of his divorce, but also believed him when he said that 'he really meant it this time'.[124] She wanted the security of marriage and children: she liked the age difference of eleven years. She accepted him.

The couple drove up to Grantham to see the Robertses. As they passed the Victorian town hall, which Denis considered 'the ugliest thing you've

---

* 'Denis was never a great reader,' says John Campbell in his biography of Mrs Thatcher (*Margaret Thatcher*, 2 vols, Jonathan Cape, 2000, 2003, vol. i: *The Grocer's Daughter*, p. 86), but this is not the case. Denis Thatcher has often been misrepresented as unintelligent. As well as being shrewd, he was a serious amateur student of history, particularly military history.

† It is doubtful whether Denis ever knew much about Margaret's relationship with Robert Henderson. He told the present author, though he might just have been being discreet, 'I never heard of a serious boyfriend.'

ever seen in your puff', he said to Margaret, 'sarcastically', '"Bet your old man's proud of that." She said, "Actually Father likes it very much." I said to myself, "Watch it, Thatcher!"'[125] The meeting was amicable. Denis found Margaret's parents to be 'sweet people', with 'old man Roberts' 'very quiet spoken and well read', but a bit 'straitlaced', and Mrs Roberts 'very quiet, very typical of a wife'. The conversation was, Denis remembered, 'A bit sticky. Eventually Margaret says, "Father, Denis does like a drink." Very long faces, long hunt through the house; finally blow dust off bottle of sherry.'[126] Arrangements for the wedding were made, the parties agreeing, perhaps because of Denis's divorce, that it should take place not in Grantham but in Wesley's Chapel in London which, according to Denis, a 'middle-stump' Anglican, the Robertses regarded as 'halfway to Rome'. Relations between Denis and Margaret's parents were to go on as they began – correct but never close. He felt that, although they had always done their best, Margaret had not had 'all that happy a childhood': 'It was work, work, work, all her life.'[127] Among other things, Denis provided what might be called a pleasure principle that her upbringing had almost entirely lacked. He too was a hard worker, but he enjoyed life, and he would help her enjoy it.

In the extremely short term, however, Denis's proposal presented Margaret with a problem. She did not want it known until the general election of 1951 was out of the way. Despite the universal popularity of marriage in those days, an engagement would not have been seen as an electoral advantage,* since wedlock generally signalled an end to a woman's career. Besides, an additional reason for secrecy lay in Denis's divorce, then a far more controversial issue than today. As Alfred Roberts had said in his letter to Muriel, Denis's marriage, contracted in wartime, had collapsed in his absence in the army through no fault of his own. The couple had married in 1942, but had quickly been separated by the demands of his military service. When he was demobbed in 1946, he found that his marriage was effectively over. His wife, also called Margaret (née Kempson), had taken up with a baronet called Sir Howard Hickman. She and Denis divorced in 1948. Interviewed about it by Denis's daughter Carol in the 1990s, the first Mrs Thatcher blamed herself: 'it was entirely my fault, and I regret it a lot ... The war was a strange time ... You grabbed happiness while you could.'[128]

Rather as Margaret probably had more romantic feelings about Robert

---

* It was also feared that there might be suggestions, by a few, that Margaret's marriage to a 'rich', older man was evidence of social climbing (interview with Patricia Greenough).

Henderson than she did about Denis, so Denis probably felt more passionately for the first Margaret (always known as Margot) than he did for the second. Asking Carol about her visit to Margot in old age, Denis inquired, 'rather misty-eyed', 'Is she still incredibly beautiful?'[129] He had fallen in love with the first Margaret suddenly, and so walked slowly, cautiously into a calmer, more longer-lasting love with the second. His hurt at the collapse of his first marriage caused him to avoid talking about it, a decision with which his second wife was naturally happy. 'I never met her,' she later recalled, 'and we never used to mention it. It was a typical wartime marriage.'[130] But it was not, of course, a matter indifferent to her. When Mrs Thatcher left 10 Downing Street in 1990, the Queen asked her if there was any honour she sought. She replied that she would like one for Denis (her own honours were to come in later years): she wanted him to become a baronet. Part of the motive for this was to ensure a hereditary honour for her son Mark, much of it was a simple act of gratitude to Denis, but it seems possible that the choice of a baronetcy may have been a form of polite revenge for the injury he had received long ago, or perhaps a backhanded acknowledgment of the way in which her husband had become free to marry her. Lady Hickman died in 1996. When this happened, Lady Thatcher confided to her long-standing assistant, Cynthia Crawford, 'Crawfie, I shall always be only the second Mrs Thatcher.'[131] She became, however, the first Lady Thatcher.

Anyway, for the course of the campaign for the general election of 25 October 1951, the engagement was concealed. Denis would appear in his Jaguar and help his secret fiancée canvass. On 15 October, he chaired Margaret's public meeting at a primary school in Belvedere, declaring: 'She has unlimited beauty, brains and charm, three qualities which we can do with in the House of Commons.'[132] Patricia Luker, a young secretary who was appointed Margaret's 'follower' for the campaign, and accompanied her every evening, remembered that Denis got very upset whenever Margaret was heckled and had to be restrained by her and others from intervening. She was impressed by Denis's loyalty, but surprised that Margaret had accepted him: 'I thought what a funny man for her to want to marry. He didn't have an awful lot of conversation.'[133] All the office was sworn to secrecy and the secret held, although at one point a man from the *Daily Mirror* (Margaret attracted national newspaper interest as a woman, and the youngest parliamentary candidate) came into the Conservative office, having got wind of it. He was sent away without a story. The news was eventually put out to the press on the eve of poll, a decision which was not Margaret's. In later years, she believed it had been done by Beryl Cook to attract some last-minute votes.[134] This irritated her.

*

Between the elections of 1950 and 1951, Margaret consistently grew in stature as a candidate and as a rising figure in the Conservative Party. As at Oxford, she made herself available for what others would not. Clive Bossom,* the son of Margaret's patron Sir Alfred and himself the Conservative candidate for Faversham in Kent at the time, remembered that she would always agree to weekend speaking engagements at places beyond her constituency, and that her speaking ability was high.[135] W. F. Deedes,† also a Kent candidate (at Ashford) in 1951, noted the impact Margaret always made at the Conservative Prospective Parliamentary Candidates' Association meetings. 'Once she opened her mouth the rest of us began to look rather second-rate,' he said, and indeed her knowledge and eloquence were a source of some irritation to her fellow candidates.[136] Through the association, she met present and future leading lights of the party, notably the Colditz hero Airey Neave,‡ whose support in the leadership battle in 1975 would ensure her victory. 'David Maxwell Fyffe [sic]§ came to address us [at the association],' she told Muriel. 'As usual he was brilliant in his analysis of the situation – His bearing is superb.'[137]

Margaret started to become part of a Tory social network – at that time still dominated by the well-off, the ex-military and the landed Etonians – which, more than might have been expected, she enjoyed. At the beginning of each new parliamentary session in November, Alfred Bossom, who felt that 'MPs' wives had a raw deal,' would give a huge party for the Tory clans at 5 Carlton Gardens, his grand London house, erecting a special tent with wooden walls running out from house to garden. Up from his castle in Kent came tapestries and even suits of armour for the occasion. The guests wore black tie and, after being briefed on the contents of the Queen's Speech by the Prime Minister at dinner at No. 10, the Cabinet would go on to Bossom's party, dressed in white tie. Although only a candidate rather than a Member of Parliament, Margaret received invitations

* Clive Bossom (1918–), educated Eton; Conservative MP for Leominster, 1959–74; succeeded father as baronet, 1965.
† William Deedes (1913–2007), educated Harrow; Conservative MP for Ashford, 1950–74; Minister without Portfolio, 1962–4; editor, *Daily Telegraph*, 1974–86; created Lord Deedes, 1986.
‡ Airey Neave MC, DSO, (1916–79), educated Eton and Merton College, Oxford; prisoner of war, 1940–42; first British officer to escape from Colditz and make a successful 'home run'; Conservative MP for Abingdon, 1953–79; head of Mrs Thatcher's private office and Shadow Secretary of State for Northern Ireland; assassinated by Irish National Liberation Army, March 1979.
§ David Maxwell Fyfe (1900–1967), educated George Watson's College, Edinburgh and Balliol College, Oxford; Home Secretary, 1951–4; created 1st Earl of Kilmuir, 1954; Lord Chancellor, 1954–62.

to this famous annual event, and was treated with kindness by Alfred Bossom. When he heard that she and Denis were to be married in London, he immediately offered his house for the reception.[138] Margaret was very happy to make use of such connections, and frequently did so in search of better jobs. 'When Parliament assembles again,' she wrote to Muriel from her newly rented flat about her renewed search for the right employment, 'I'll take up all the offers of "Come and have dinner with me" that I've had from various members and see what I can do in that direction.'[139]

Between the two elections, the tone of politics changed. The Korean War, which began in June 1950, brought home the reality of the Communist threat and raised the spectre of a wider war. Communism was an issue on which Margaret knew where she stood. In a letter to Muriel unusual for the extent to which it discusses the content of politics, she described a meeting of the United Nations Association in Dartford at which she spoke with her Labour opponent, Dodds, and several others, including Lord and Lady Strabolgi: 'Lord and Lady Strabolgi – Red as you make them – were the main speakers ... The other three were very leftist. By the time they had finished you would have thought Communist countries a demi-paradise and that Britain must disarm. I gave them 10 minutes of what I thought about their views! As a result Dodds wouldn't speak to me afterwards and Lord and Lady S. went off without speaking as well. Several people congratulated me, so I wasn't bothered.'[140] In a speech in Dartford two months later, she warned that the 'Communist menace ... might break out in other places',[141] and two months after that she declared: 'If Germany were to become another Korea tonight, every one of us would shake in our shoes.' 'The only thing that allowed Britain time to negotiate', she added, 'was her atomic superiority.'[142]* And the subject was the theme of her New Year message in the *Dartford Chronicle*: 'we must firstly *believe* in the Western way of life and serve it steadfastly. Secondly we must build up our fighting strength to be prepared to defend our ideals, for aggressive nations understand only the threat of force.'[143] The idea of Britain as a strong nation alone and brave had religious echoes in Margaret's mind, deriving from the biblical idea of the righteous remnant. At the Dartford Free Church Federal Council annual meeting, she chose the text from Genesis in which Abraham pleads with God to spare the righteous from the destruction of Sodom and Gomorrah – 'Peradventure ten shall be found there.' Margaret pointed out that 'Had those ten righteous men been found they could have saved the cities from destruction,' and that in the New Testament it was

---

* Britain, under the Attlee government, had decided to develop a nuclear bomb. However, it did not test a device until 1952.

twelve righteous men – the Apostles – who saved the world. She then applied the text to our age. 'In their own lifetime,' the *Dartford Chronicle* reported her as saying, 'it depended on the few men of the Battle of Britain to save civilisation from immediate doom.'[144] Throughout her career, the story of 1940 was the myth (by which is not meant untruth) which most dominated her imagination.

Unable to maintain his party's tiny majority in Parliament, and suffering from divisions between left and right which had provoked the future Prime Minister Harold Wilson* and the left-wing orator Aneurin Bevan to resign from the government in protest over the imposition of charges for false teeth and spectacles, Clement Attlee called a general election for 25 October 1951. As earlier agreed, Margaret stood in Dartford for the second time. In the election campaign itself, the issue of Communism and the threat to peace was still running strongly. At her adoption meeting, Margaret told her audience, who first sat down together to listen to Winston Churchill's party political broadcast on the radio, that the 'most serious aspect of the situation was the Socialist insistence that the Conservatives were warmongers'. This charge was repeatedly levelled by the front page of the Labour-supporting *Daily Mirror*, which ran the headline 'Whose finger on the trigger?', suggesting that Churchill's was more trigger-happy than Attlee's. 'If we can co-operate on matters of defence,' Margaret went on, 'through the Empire and the United States, and so to greater things, we can defend the world on a world basis.'[145] These words contained the germ of her later developed belief that the 'English-speaking peoples' alone could ensure freedom and security. Her election address contained a similar call to arms: 'Britain . . . must be strong, strong in arms, and strong in faith in her own way of life. The greatest hope for peace lies in friendship and co-operation with the United States of America.'

The woman who argued for strength was exhibiting it in her own patch. Although she remained as popular as ever in the constituency, it was clear that her power did not rest in her charm alone, but also in her steel. Early in what turned out to be the election year of 1951, Margaret discovered that her friend and association chairman John Miller had invited the socialist mayors of Dartford, Erith and Crayford to the association's annual ball. She was beside herself, and described her reaction to Muriel:

> I was absolutely furious – they all actively campaign against us and personally against me at election time, and it happens to be my Anniversary Ball. I

---

* Harold Wilson (1916–95), educated Wirral Grammar School, Bebington, Cheshire and Jesus College, Oxford; Prime Minister 1964–70, 1974–6; created Lord Wilson of Rievaulx, 1983.

flew to the phone and asked John who had invited them ... John said he
had invited them on the grounds that they were above politics. I was very
cross indeed ... I told him it was an insult to me and highly discourteous
not to have let me see the list before it went out. John told me that I was
being very <u>awkward</u>, that he hadn't been able to get me on the 'phone. I said
there was such a thing as a 2½d stamp ...[146]

Fraternizing with the enemy was something that Margaret never enjoyed.
She recalls in her memoirs how much she and her fellow Tories took heart
from Aneurin Bevan's jibe that they were 'lower than vermin', forming a
Vermin Club of those who won new recruits for the party.[147]

The campaign itself was hard fought and boisterous. In those days,
election controversy was not permitted on BBC Radio, or on television
(which few possessed), except in the controlled and stilted form of party
political broadcasts. So elections were fought in the newspapers and, much
more than today, in each constituency. Election meetings, in large places
and small, were often packed. Margaret fought with all her vigour. One
meeting, at Crayford town hall, shortly before polling day, got out of hand.
While Margaret was speaking elsewhere, the warm-up was being given by
Melford Stevenson KC, later to become famous as the most outspoken
conservative judge on the bench. He seems to have warmed them up too
thoroughly, for by the time Margaret arrived the chairman of the meeting
told her that he had just sent for the police. 'For God's sake don't do that,'
said Margaret. 'Leave it to me.'[148] She succeeded. The *Dartford Chronicle*
recorded that 'For the first nine minutes of her speech – during which time
she dealt with Conservative policy with regard to peace – there was not
one comment from the body of the hall . . .'[149] This time, she had a straight
fight with Dodds, with no Liberal candidate. The result was:

Norman Dodds (Labour)	40,094
Miss M. H. Roberts (Conservative)	27,760
Labour majority	12,334

She had cut Dodds's majority by a further 1,300. In the country as a
whole, Labour actually got more votes than the Conservatives and more
than in 1950, but the votes stacked up too heavily in safe Labour areas,
allowing the Conservatives to gain more seats. The Tories also had a 4 per
cent lead over Labour with women voters, a reward for their emphasis on
the problems of consumption and rationing. Under Churchill, they returned
to power for the first time since the war, with an overall majority of seventeen, but Margaret Roberts went off to get married.

6

Marriage, the law and Finchley

'The necessary fervour'

The first surviving letter from Mrs Thatcher, rather than Margaret Roberts, dates from the middle of February 1952, two months after her marriage to Denis. Writing from 112 Swan Court, Chelsea Manor Street, London, Denis's sixth-floor bachelor flat, Margaret informs her sister Muriel that the couple's planned first cocktail party together is postponed because of the death of King George VI on 6 February. Although perfectly content in tone, the letter is certainly not ecstatic. It is practical, and its main theme, as so often for people in London even well into the 1950s, is shortage. There is an 'egg famine' in town, she declares, and she wants to buy some eggs from Muriel and Willie's farm 'on a strictly business basis'. She has also been in search of clothes: 'I've got the turquoise set from Peter Jones but the only pleated waist slips they have are in that rather violent pink.' She is starting a law course with Gibson and Weldon ('*the* law tutors') – ten weeks, for three days a week – but only in the criminal law: 'Roman law I realise I can cram on my own.'[1] Another aspect of the mourning for the late King was the cancellation of the rugby international, which Denis would otherwise have attended. Margaret's substitute activity was probably less to her husband's taste: she took Denis off to hear her speak at a dedication service in Camden Town of the Methodist chapel run by Mr Skinner, the kindly minister with whom she had stayed on her sole pre-war visit to London. The next day they attended Sunday service at Wesley's Chapel in the City Road to hear Mr Spivey, the minister, who, with Mr Skinner, had married them there.

The wedding had taken place on 13 December 1951. The bride remembered it as 'a cold and foggy December day'.[2] As befitted the weather – and perhaps her slightly uneasy status as a woman marrying a divorced man – she did not wear white, but a velvet dress of sapphire blue, modelled on the black velvet dress she had cherished at Oxford, and a striking hat, in the manner of Gainsborough's portrait of Georgiana, Duchess of Devonshire, clinging to the back of her head with ostrich feathers cascading down the right-hand side. The photograph shows a sparkling, happy and pretty young woman, with a bridegroom who looks – and was – older and more shy. The couple were married to the strains of 'Immortal, invisible' and 'Lead us, heavenly Father, lead us'. The words of the latter hymn were to prove prophetic as the marriage successfully carried the couple for more than half a century 'o'er the world's tempestuous sea'. About fifty people attended, and the reception was held at Alfred Bossom's great house in Carlton Gardens. The best man was Kent Green, with whom Denis had spent his last holiday as a bachelor. Denis failed to make a speech. Forty years later, he told his daughter that (oddly in view of the fact that he had been married before) 'I didn't know I was meant to'.[3] Perhaps he was already observing the rule which, in later life, he made firm, that he would never make a speech 'in front of Her'.

The Thatchers spent their wedding night in the Savoy Hotel in London – 'a wonderful hotel', Margaret wrote to Muriel. '. . . You just press a bell and a valet or maid or waiter appears.'[4] Then they flew to Estoril in Portugal by flying boat. Thence, after a few days, to Madeira, and another Savoy Hotel, where they spent Christmas: 'Some of the people with us are very nice but some are rather "tatty" tourists: Jews and novo [sic] riche. Talking of Jews – one of the directors of J. Lyons, a Gluckstein, is with us. He and his wife are very nice.'[5] In her memoirs, Mrs Thatcher did not recall much lotus-eating. Nor did Denis: 'We stayed in the capital, Funchal,' he told Carol, 'and did a sort of economic survey: we went and looked at people making lace and other things and went and toured the Madeira Wine Company.'[6] But at the time Mrs Thatcher entered happily into the pleasures of the place. On Christmas Eve, she sent a postcard to Muriel: 'Funchal really goes gay at Christmas . . . We change for dinner every night and dine and dance either here or at Reids hotel . . . You can get pure silk shirts made to measure for £3 each & nylon socks for 15/- a pair so it is indeed a paradise for men buying clothes.'[7] The weather was too bad for the return journey to involve a flight to mainland Portugal, and they crossed by boat with Mrs Thatcher very sea-sick. They returned to England via Paris, where Denis had business to transact.

Mrs Thatcher enjoyed her newly married life. She had improved social status, a husband she liked and respected, and a comfortable mansion-block flat which she set about redecorating with her customary domestic energy. Writing to Muriel on 28 January 1952, she excitedly described the whirl of events – the annual dinner of the Inns of Court Conservative Association where Anthony Eden, Foreign Secretary in the new government, 'seems a new man since he came back to office', parties, meetings. 'The days simply fly past.'[8] In her memoirs, she waxes lyrical about this period, especially for young married people like herself: 'The 1950s were ... the reawakening of normal happy life after the trials of war-time and the petty indignities of post-war austerity.' Echoing Wordsworth as she had in Dartford, she said that to be in her situation at that time was 'very heaven'.[9] But there was to be no slackening of pace, no exile from the great world to the kitchen. The death of the King gave her the opportunity to set out her views of what the new reign should bring for her sex and generation. In an article entitled 'Wake up, women' in the *Sunday Graphic*, Mrs Thatcher announced, 'If as many earnestly pray, the accession of Elizabeth II can help to remove the last shreds of prejudice against women aspiring to the highest places, then a new era for women will indeed be at hand.' She advocated the combining of marriage and a career for more women, and regretted that 'The term "career woman" has unfortunately come to imply in many minds a "hard" woman devoid of all feminine characteristics.' She traced this prejudice: 'Far too often, I regret to say it comes from our own sex.' In her view, though, 'The idea that the family suffers is ... quite mistaken'; a career meant 'a wife can be a much better companion at home.' She praised various current women role models, including Janet Vaughan from Somerville, and asked 'Why not a woman Chancellor – or Foreign Secretary?', though judiciously stopping short of calling for a woman prime minister. Using a technique to subvert the opposite sex at which, in later life, she became very practised, Mrs Thatcher added: 'And if they [women] made mistakes, they would not be the first to do so in those jobs!'[10]

When she had left Dartford after the general election of 1951, Margaret Roberts had said, 'I shall not be contesting this division again, but I have no intention of leaving politics,' and this was no more than the truth. In the letter to Muriel quoted above, she refers to coming on to stay with the Cullens after a political conference in Maidstone. At the beginning of April 1952, Alfred Roberts wrote to his elder daughter: 'We had a letter from Margaret ... obviously scrawled in great haste for it appears that, if anything, she is busier now than before marriage ... I hope she isn't chasing Denis about too much after his being so poorly.'[11] And he mentioned that she was to speak at a Regional Savings Conference in Nottingham. It was also at this time that Mrs Thatcher had what was to be her only experience of being married to a political candidate. In the Kent County Council elections of April 1952, Denis was persuaded to stand as a Ratepayer, a label that tended to be used by Conservatives in areas where national parties were thought inappropriate for local government. He lost without, it seems, investing much emotional or physical energy in the contest, and without canvassing. As Mrs Thatcher put it succinctly in a letter to Muriel: 'Denis went the way of all the others who were fighting bad seats in the County Council elections but he wasn't too disappointed.'[12]* But although, as we shall see shortly, politics never vanished from her mind, Mrs Thatcher's immediate career preoccupation was with the law.

Her first law exams took place on 12 and 14 May 1952, and she was called to the Bar on 9 February 1954, but in between came motherhood. Her baby was expected on 29 September 1953, but early in August Mrs Thatcher, who had experienced quite a difficult and exhausting pregnancy, suffered labour pains and went into Queen Charlotte's Hospital in London on 14 August. The next day the doctors told her, which she had not previously suspected, that she was carrying twins, and that they were on their way. They were born by Caesarean section then and there, a girl, Carol Jane,† and a boy, Mark. Each weighed 4 pounds. Denis did not attend the birth (at that time, hospitals did not permit fathers to be present). He did not even know it was happening, since he was watching the England v Australia Test match at the Oval.‡ When he got home from the Oval, he found a message from the hospital telling him to come at once.

According to Carol, Denis's reaction to the first sight of his children was to exclaim: 'My God, they look like rabbits. Put them back.'[13] And there is no doubt that he was not immediately attracted by babies. In the 1990s, when staying with friends where the Thatchers were fellow guests, the present author's wife, also a parent of twins, sought to engage Denis on the subject. What had been his first thought, she asked him, on the discovery that he had two babies? 'I just wished the little buggers had been drowned at birth,' was his reply. Although Mrs Thatcher would never have thought, let alone spoken, in such terms, she was not someone who settled to the task of dealing with infants as if this was her vocation in life. She was pleased to have twins, but more because it meant that she need not

---

* In *Below the Parapet: The Biography of Denis Thatcher* (HarperCollins, 1996), p. 58, Carol Thatcher records that Denis's candidacy had been 'a few years before'. This seems to be erroneous.

† It took some time to agree on Carol's name. When she came out of hospital more than a month later because of her low weight and an infection, Margaret still wrote of her to Muriel as 'the little girl twin'.

‡ In *Margaret Thatcher* (2 vols, Jonathan Cape, 2000, 2003, vol. i: *The Grocer's Daughter*), John Campbell questions whether it could really be true that the birth took place without Denis knowing, and suspects the story of being 'romantic embroidery', but this ignores the fact that telephoning the hospital was not then the easy matter that it later became, and that, as Mrs Thatcher explained in her letter to John Hare (see p. 119), she did not know she was bearing twins until the day – Saturday – that they were born. At a time when fathers were completely excluded from the process of birth, it seems perfectly possible that the operation went ahead without anyone hunting for Denis.

get pregnant again than because of a wild enthusiasm for motherhood. 'Neither of my parents', wrote Carol, 'could be described as being natural or comfortable with young children.'[14]* Besides, as we shall see later, Mrs Thatcher had been planning her career on the expectation of one child or, at least, one at a time. Twins altered the case. As she lay in her hospital bed, she worked out how. By her own account, she was almost frightened by the emotional impact of the birth, the miracle of life sharpened by the perils of prematurity – 'Oddly enough, the very depth of the relief and happiness at having brought Mark and Carol into the world made me uneasy' – and she realized that she must keep the idea of a career constantly before her eyes: 'I needed a career because, quite simply, that was the sort of person I was.'[15] She decided, despite her new burden, to go ahead and sit her Bar finals on 1 December. She also received a letter from John Hare, the party vice-chairman in charge of candidates, congratulating her on the birth and asking her if, in the circumstances, she wanted her name withdrawn from the candidates' list.[16] Mrs Thatcher confirmed that she did, but not in a way that suggested any permanent turning from the political path: 'we had no idea there were two of them,' she wrote on 2 September, 'until the day they were born . . . I think I had better not consider a candidature for at least six months. The household needs considerable reorganisation and a reliable nurse must be found before I can feel free to pursue such other activities with the necessary fervour.'[17]

At Swan Court, an Austrian nurse, Gerda, was duly engaged for the first few weeks, and she was followed by Barbara, a nanny from Kent who stayed for five years. Nanny Barbara was often quoted as saying that when the Thatchers left the house in the morning for work, 'He was very good at remembering to wave up to the nursery window [from which the twins were watching] . . . whereas Mrs Thatcher, whose mind was already on the job, would forget.' The full context of the quotation, however, makes clear that it was Denis who was detached from the care of the children whereas Margaret was not: 'Mr Thatcher left parenting to Mrs Thatcher and me.'[18] Just after the twins came home for the first time, Denis was briefly away,

* Mrs Thatcher was always kind to children, however. When she was secretary of state for education, civil servants noted that she was much better than her predecessor at paying enthusiastic attention to pupils during school visits. But, perhaps because of the seriousness and literal-mindedness which she recognized in herself, she never seemed quite to get the hang of children's behaviour. At one lunch party in the country in the 1990s, two young sons of one of the guests ran outside to play and came and tapped on the window of the dining room. They then stuck out their tongues and shoved their thumbs into their ears and wiggled their fingers derisively. Lady Thatcher very sportingly wiggled back, but then turned to the present author and said, 'What a funny gesture. I wonder what it means.' It seemed strange that she could have been a mother without ever finding out.

and there was a gap in domestic help. 'We have several outstanding bits of entertaining to do,' Margaret told Muriel, 'but as I shall be on my own all day and all night doing 3-hourly feeds throughout the 24 hours with 2 bairns that will have to wait. Fortunately I am now very fit.'[19] The sixth-floor flat had only three bedrooms and was quite ill-suited to young children. When the twins were three, Denis solved this by renting the flat next door so that 'I could slam the door on all three of them.'[20]

Driven and career-oriented though she was, Mrs Thatcher was definitely a concerned and conscientious mother. Her letters to Muriel, which become more sporadic and brief in the 1950s, show a woman attentive, in a slightly uninquiring and practical way, to the needs of her children. When they were five months old, she wrote a busy, post-Christmas letter, thanking her sister for their romper suits to which she herself had added smart little white collars. Mark, she said, had a 'tummy bug' which she dealt with – 'I slept in the nursery as I should have been about all night and probably have woken Denis, so it seemed to me more sensible to let Nanny have a decent night's sleep.' The bug caused a laundry problem because 'We have always operated with the minimum number of vests (7 between them).' She also mentioned the problem of Mark's circumcision, and the fact that Denis's South African cousins, the Pellatts, were staying. The Thatchers took them out to dinner: 'my goodness – do they eat! Hors d'oeuvre and soup and entrée and cheese! Denis and I had the usual 3 courses only but in spite of that the Bill was £7-15s! We shan't take them out again in a hurry!'[21] A year later, she congratulated Muriel on the birth of her daughter ('the fact that it was a girl [Muriel's first two children had been boys] seemed to make it all worth-while'). The twins, she said, were 'in the pink' and had just had '2 little friends round': 'Having made all the cakes and scones the night before I left Nannie to get on with it. With three nannies I should only have cramped their style.' Dealing literally with the small change of life, she tells Muriel that she has just bought a 'knockabout' dinner and tea service, Royal Doulton 'Coppice', and paid the bill of £16 10s out of sixpences she had saved up in a jar.[22]

Although it was not in Mrs Thatcher's nature to subject her children or indeed the rest of her life to close emotional analysis, the correspondence discloses vignettes of character, small judgments scarcely considered as they are made, yet still significant. 'Mark and Carol had a bit of set-to,' she wrote, 'which resulted in Mark being pierced on his arm by a gardening fork'* and requiring a tetanus injection.[23] 'Mark can ride a fairy cycle and is very anxious to have one,' she told Muriel in the same month, but the

---

* In childhood, as later, the Thatcher twins competed against one another. Mark remembered Carol being annoyed that there was a Sussex village called Mark Cross, but no village bearing

price of £12 was high and 'we'd have to get two and that would be too much of an item this year'.[24] At Christmas 1957, however, her son was satisfied with his Christmas present: 'Mark liked his particularly because it had bullets in it.' Later, Carol does piano and dancing lessons, but without much success: 'I don't think she has very much music in her – she has no sense of pitch. She can't sing in tune with the notes at all.'[25] 'Carol's school', she wrote on 18 November 1963, 'is much better run than Mark's but one usually finds that girls' schools are more highly organised.'[26] Earlier, when Carol began a new school in September 1960, her mother noted, 'She gets very strung up about new things although she doesn't say much.' In the same letter, mentioning the fact that Abbey Evans, Barbara's replacement as nanny, is away for six weeks helping a former employer move house, Mrs Thatcher, by this time an MP, addresses the problem: 'It will be very difficult but I shall have to try to get more time off. I don't want to upset the children by having a new person in for a short time.'[27] And when the twins first go to school, together, Mrs Thatcher notes: 'They seem to be enjoying school but doing a tremendous amount of painting there.'[28] The 'but' in that sentence is characteristic.

Busy lives require endless arranging, and a great deal of Mrs Thatcher's mental energy was consumed in what, in our generation, is called juggling. This was particularly apparent in relation to holidays, a phenomenon which the Thatchers regarded as occasionally necessary, but unpleasant, like going to the dentist. There were searches for hotels at the seaside, and for arrangements which would allow the parents to delegate some of what was seen as the burden of looking after the children all the time. On one occasion, this provoked something close to a row between Barbara and Mrs Thatcher, as the latter explained to Muriel:

> Her nose is rather out-of-joint again this week because she came back and said that one of the Nannies' employers had offered to take a house at the seaside for a month for nannie and the two children if she could get another nannie with charges to go half-shares. I said that after my experience last year I certainly wasn't prepared to take the children away to a hotel while she was away and she could have them for a fortnight while we were away. That didn't suit her, she said she'd had enough of hotels! She sulked for about 2 days![29]

By Carol's account, it was Nanny Barbara who took Mark and her on their first ever holiday, to Broadstairs.[30] Later, the Thatchers took to visiting

---

her name. For his part, Mark was annoyed that people sang carols, but not 'marks'. (Interview with Sir Mark Thatcher.)

Seaview, Isle of Wight, *en famille*, a holiday which they had to cut short to get back for the election campaign of 1959 which returned Mrs Thatcher to the House of Commons for the first time. When she was prime minister, she was famous for her dislike of taking a break and her readiness to come back to work early on the excuse of a crisis. At work or at leisure, time management dominated. 'I have forgotten our Easter egg arrangements,' she wrote to Muriel from the House of Commons early in her career there, '– shall I get mine an egg from you and you get yours an egg from me? This is so much simpler than risking their getting smashed in the post.'[31]

The truth is that Mrs Thatcher was frightened of boredom and what she called 'vegetating'. House-proud and fond of her family though she was, she associated the danger of ennui with the life of a housewife. In Carol's view, 'She would have hated being a housewife.'[32] In an article for the Young Conservatives' monthly paper *Onward*, written when the twins were still babies, Margaret was eloquent on the effect of having the twins: 'As well as being exhausted, however, I felt nothing more than a drudge.' The way to cure this, in her view, was through careful planning: 'I quickly found that as well as being a housewife it is possible to put in eight hours' work a day besides.' This was actually good for the children, she claimed, because 'When looking after them without a break, it is sometimes difficult not to get a little impatient and very easy only to give part of one's attention to their incessant demands.' 'Homework', Carol recalled, 'was her middle name.'[33] The mother's absence was fine, Margaret argued, because 'If she has a powerful and dominant personality her personal influence is there the whole time and the children's upbringing follows the lines which she directs.'[34] This is thinly veiled autobiography. Mrs Thatcher was worried, too, that glamour and excitement would slip away. 'We don't seem to have any "functions" in the offing,' she complained to Muriel in the summer before the twins' second birthday. 'They seem to get fewer and fewer as time goes by and now I only wear evening dress about four times a year. Not that I am bothered – an evening out is an expensive item.'[35] Interviewed on the verge of her first election for Finchley in 1959, she told the *Evening News* that 'I should vegetate if I were left at the kitchen sink all day. The twins are at school and in any case I have a full-time nanny … I don't think the family suffers at all through my political ambitions.' In old age, she came to recognize that this was a fiction, and she worried that the family had suffered far too much, but the fiction had been a necessary one, for Margaret Thatcher knew perfectly well that she *had* to have an all-consuming career, come what may.* She did her best to mitigate its

---

* Denis Thatcher was also, in later life, afflicted by a sense of guilt about the way the twins

damaging side-effects, but she could never contemplate abandoning it. 'I have no right to complain,' Carol remembered. 'But I don't think our childhood was a very important part of her life, to be honest.'[36]

Another effect of Margaret's marriage to Denis was a growing separation, though never an estrangement, from her sister Muriel and from her parents. This was partly a matter of geography, but more, perhaps, one of class. Denis was a town mouse, a public schoolboy and very comfortably off. Willie Cullen was a Scottish farmer through and through, and though he looked after his money well, he did not have the opportunity or desire to cut a dash with it. In the early days, Denis would occasionally play golf with Willie in Colchester, but the Cullens resented what they took to be his condescending tone: 'How are things down on the farm then?' he would ask, to their irritation,[37] and this resentment grew in later years, when they came to regard Mark as big-headed through his mother's success and Denis as 'moving in circles with people who have more money than he has'.[38] Quite often Margaret would visit Foulton unaccompanied by Denis. 'As kids,' Carol recalled, 'we thought that was great' – the farm was large and ran down to the sea, giving opportunities for adventure.[39] The Cullens always excepted Margaret herself from any charge of snobbery and condescension, and were critical only of the fact that she always put her political work before anything else. She kept in reasonably close touch, meeting Muriel monthly for lunch in London, and even writing to her, as late as the early 1960s, when Mrs Thatcher had become a junior minister, to suggest that they jointly visit the Queen's dietician to lose weight: 'I need half a stone off and we could therefore go together . . .'[40] She was friendly, honest and trusting, if not effusive, in her letters to her sister, but it is also clear – it was implicit in her decision not to marry Willie Cullen – that she was conscious of a social gulf between herself and her sister's family, a gulf which, as we shall see later, put her father more on Muriel's side of the fence than on hers. This tension expressed itself over a trivial matter. When Muriel gave birth to her daughter in January 1955, the Cullens considered naming her Agnes after Willie's unmarried sister who had been expelled from the house after their marriage. This idea was probably not one that appealed as much to Muriel as it did to Willie anyway; to Margaret it was anathema. She weighed in: 'You used to like "Penelope" and "Nicola" – have either of those come up for consideration? For heaven's sake let <u>one</u>

---

were brought up. He told the present author that he should have spent more time with them when they were young. Business frequently took him abroad for almost the whole of the summer. He delegated a good deal of the twins' upbringing to their nanny, Abbey. 'Teach the children some manners,' he instructed her (interview with Carol Thatcher).

of your children have an English name as England is the country of William's <u>choice</u> as distinct from that of his birth.'[41] The truth is that one rarely finds a good word for the Celtic parts of the British Isles in the life of Margaret Thatcher, although two of her boyfriends were Scots. In January 1954, the Thatchers went on what she called 'the annual pilgrimage to Twickenham' for the England v Wales game. 'Personally,' Margaret told her sister, 'I never enjoy the Welsh game very much as the Welsh don't know how to win or how to lose.'[42] Luckily for Mrs Thatcher's feelings, Muriel and Willie settled on plain, English Jane as the name for their daughter.

But Mrs Thatcher was now moving into a world which was more that of Penelope or Nicola, a combination of professional Chelsea and semi-suburban, highly Conservative Kent. Her life in London, while certainly not grand or fashionable, had some pretensions to elegance. The Thatchers would get good tickets to shows, opera, films – *Madame Butterfly*, *The King and I* ('you realise of course that it is a true story'), *Quadrille*, Olivier's *Richard III* ('absolutely first-class') – and buy good-quality furniture and clothes, though always very careful about price. She bought a summer coat from Peter Jones, for example, which, because it had been worn by a mannequin, was reduced from 12 guineas to 79s 6d (£3 97.5 pence).[43] They gave plenty of cocktail parties and buffet suppers and, of course, attended Conservative balls ('Mrs Anthony Eden received us. Really she is a most colourless personality').[44]* Occasionally they danced at the Colony Club in Berkeley Square.[45] It was more Denis's world than the one she had been brought up in, and she was very keen to be a part of it. One Saturday, because Denis was refereeing rugby at the military academy at Sandhurst, Margaret joined him, and was much struck with what she saw: 'I had no idea it was such a wonderful place – the grounds are enormous but what impressed me most was the young chaps who go there. Saturday afternoon was naturally off-duty time but we didn't see so much as even one person slouching. They held themselves as if in military uniform and went about their business in a most impressive way. They were an intelligent bunch of kids too.'[46]

Pursuing their haut-bourgeois dream, and driven out of Chelsea by the Tory government's ending of rent control and the needs of the twins for more space, the Thatchers moved, before Christmas 1957, to Farnborough in Kent. The house was called Dormers, and stood in a suburban cul-de-sac. They were nearly gazumped, and had to pay £6,600. Carol and Mark 'adored' the place, she describing it as 'a magical childhood home in a long

---

* This is a very typical Mrs Thatcher judgment of another woman. In fact, Clarissa Eden was well known for her beauty, intelligence and strong character.

avenue of detached houses and generous gardens'.[47] Immediately after they had bought Dormers, Mrs Thatcher threw herself into 'the problems of the bathrooms and sanitary arrangements. However, I expect we shall get it spick and span in time.' The conveyancing and stamp duty cost £245; 'That's before we start.'[48] When they got there, they did not like it at first. On New Year's Eve 1957, she wrote to Muriel: 'It seems a very tight community here. "Foreigners" are definitely not made welcome. So far, the only glimpse of either of our neighbours has been when one of them scowled at us when Denis parked the car for a few seconds opposite the greengrocer's van when I was asking the delivery man to call! Our next-door neighbour had to slow down his car to get through the gap! We miss Chelsea very much but after 6 years it would be surprising if we settled down in a fortnight.'[49] In fact, the house, though convenient for Denis's work in Dartford, proved awkward for Mrs Thatcher's commuting to the Inns of Court, let alone for her political life later, but it did give the twins their nearest approximation to a permanent home with which they could fall in love. Margaret herself literally put down roots: she 'became manic about gardening' and grew 'dahlias the size of dinner-plates', while Denis became a keen mower, declaring daisies 'public-enemy number one'.[50] For Margaret, it was a long way, on the whole a pleasantly long way, from life above the grocer's shop in Grantham.

By the time of the move to Farnborough, Mrs Thatcher was a practising barrister. Having passed her Bar finals on 1 December 1953, she consulted John Senter QC, a leading light in Conservative legal circles and a well-known tax lawyer. He encouraged her, but said that she should first get a grounding in the criminal law. On Senter's recommendation, she obtained pupillage with Fred Lawton (later, as Sir Fred, an Appeal Court judge),* one of the most remarkable and most liked lawyers of his generation, whose extensive common-law practice offered her experience in civil as well as criminal cases. Also in Lawton's chambers was Airey Neave and, a little later, Robin Day,† who was to become the best-known television political interviewer of his time. When Mrs Thatcher was called to the Bar in February 1954, her name appeared in the alphabetical list between that of Dick Taverne, later a Labour MP whose defection from the party made

---

* Frederick Lawton (1911–2001), educated Battersea Grammar School and Corpus Christi College, Cambridge; criminal advocate; QC, 1957; High Court judge, 1961; Lord Justice of Appeal, 1972; knighted, 1961.
† Robin Day (1920–2000), educated Bembridge School and St Edmund Hall, Oxford; President of Oxford Union, 1950; barrister; joined BBC, 1955; newsreader, ITN, 1955; presenter of BBC *Panorama*, *World at One* etc.; chairman, BBC *Question Time*, 1979–89; knighted 1981.

him the trailblazer for the Social Democrats, and Jeremy Thorpe, later the Leader of the Liberal Party. The fee for pupillage was £50 for six months, plus five guineas for the clerk. 'As I am costing Denis that much,' Mrs Thatcher wrote to Muriel, 'I shall just have to go about in rags when my present clothes drop off me!'[51]

Pupillage was hard to obtain because of the continuing shortage of rooms as a result of war damage, and doubly hard for a woman because of prejudice. The entry form for would-be barristers at Lincoln's Inn always used the male pronoun, so Mrs Thatcher had to insert 'she' and 'her' by hand. Barristers' clerks, in particular, tended to oppose women because they thought they would earn them less money. Married women were thought particularly unlucrative. When Mrs Thatcher was finally established in chambers her clerk was heard to say, 'I wish I could put Miss in front of her name instead of Mrs: she'd get more work.'[52] But Fred Lawton had already had two women pupils whom he had forced his clerk to accept. He had a policy of taking only one pupil at a time, each for a year, so the relationship was close: 'before very long,' he said of Mrs Thatcher, 'I came to appreciate that she was the best pupil I had ever had . . . She was diligent, quick on the uptake . . . She had a feeling for the law . . . And it's equally clear that she was fascinated by the human aspects of the kind of work I did.'[53]* When the two met again at a party when she was prime minister, Mrs Thatcher 'propelled me into a corner' and started talking about a murder case in which Lawton had been involved when she was a pupil. Thirty years later, she remembered every detail of it.[54] Lawton was always impressed by her ability to apply whatever knowledge she had acquired, noting in particular a case concerning a breach of warranty on the sale of chemicals in which she deployed her scientific background ruthlessly to cross-examine, pre-trial, all the chemical experts. He considered that, if she had stayed in the law, she would have been a highly successful QC, 'but I don't think she would have been the first woman Law Lord, because she hadn't got that depth of mental capacity that you have to have if you're a Law Lord.' Her only shortcoming as Lawton's pupil was that she never established a good relationship with the clerk, Stanley Hopkins. He came to Lawton and said: 'I wish you'd tell that pupil of yours that I'm not the chambers boy who carries books.'[55] Hopkins had never been friendly to the idea of women pupils. According to Lawton, however, 'a rather randy Welshman' in the chambers was friendly to the idea for the wrong reasons. He made a pass at her: 'I gather she dealt with it very firmly.'[56]

---

* Mrs Thatcher liked even the most trivial cases. 'I had to go to Cambridge Assizes last Friday,' she wrote to Muriel in May 1955, 'and thoroughly enjoyed it. It was a case about onion seeds!'

Mrs Thatcher perfected in her legal work the accuracy and meticulousness which she was to display in her career as a minister. When she became a Cabinet minister, she wrote to Lawton to tell him that it was the training she had received from him that made her redraft letters from civil servants, to their fury.[57] But her feeling about the law went deeper than that. In conversation at her zenith and in her retirement, the phrases 'the rule of law' and 'not just liberty, but law-based liberty' probably came up more often than any other. She saw the law, even more than democracy, as the shibboleth that distinguished free from unfree societies.[58] And in Mrs Thatcher's mind, the rule of law had found better expression in Britain than almost anywhere else. 'I was increasingly fascinated', she wrote, 'by the mysterious and cumulative process by which the courts of England had laid the foundation for English freedom.'[59] She admired A.V. Dicey's *The Law of the Constitution* with its emphasis on the sovereignty of Parliament, and her views on these matters contributed over the years to her growing suspicion of the claims of the European Union. Her period at the Bar was almost the last in which such opinions were unquestioned within the legal profession. Fred Lawton put it thus: 'we all grew up I'm afraid with the jingoistic attitude that British law is best. It was something with which you never argued.' In his view, the English lawyer of that time had 'an astonishingly narrow intellectual training'. The English law was fundamentally different from the Continental in that, on the Continent, 'all laws take into account human rights' whereas English law 'took the view that you took into account the rights of individuals'. On the Continent, rights existed only when proclaimed by law. In Britain, they existed automatically, without government fiat, unless the law abridged them. According to the English law, said Lawton, 'a statute is to be construed by the words used in it and by nothing else . . . The Continental view is that statutes . . . are to be construed according to the purpose for which they were passed . . . Well, this was all foreign, strange to us in the 1950s.'[60] It remained foreign to Mrs Thatcher for the whole of her life. She saw such wide-ranging law as a usurpation of the work of politicians, and its universal claims as contrary to national independence.

It is doubtful, however, strongly though she absorbed such doctrines, whether Mrs Thatcher gave a great deal of thought to them at the time. She was an ambitious, busy and in a sense conventional young woman, not an intellectual, and she needed to work out how to make the law, at least for the time being, a good career. Towards the end of her twelve months, she came to Fred Lawton and told him, as he remembered it: 'There is nothing I would like more than to stay in these chambers and do the kind of work you do. But as a young married woman with young children I just could not lead the life you lead. I couldn't sit in a room and have the clerk come in at 4.30 and tell me that I was first in the list at Norwich the next morning at 10.30, he'd booked me a room at the Royal Hotel and there was a train which I could catch at Liverpool Street at 6. That's just not on for a married woman.' She went on, said Lawton, 'I shall have to find some other side of the law where I don't have to lead that kind of life.'[61] Influenced by John Senter, she chose tax.

Tax meant doing pupillage in Chancery, and so she moved to the chambers of John, later Lord, Brightman.* It was probably at this point that Denis made one of his very few recorded interventions in his wife's career plans. One night he came home and found her poring over papers concerned with accountancy. She explained that she thought a qualification in accountancy would be necessary for understanding tax law. Denis was firm: he knew about accountancy, and if she needed help about it, he would give it. She would be crazy to embark on yet another arduous branch of study.[62] As she generally did in areas which she recognized as his province, Mrs Thatcher accepted her husband's advice, and by the beginning of 1955 she was appearing in revenue cases before the Special Commissioners, with some trepidation: 'Revenue is really most intricate and I sometimes despair of ever having a comprehensive grasp of it.'[63] Her work also included company law, land law and trust law.

As usual, there was resistance to a woman. Mrs Thatcher was John Brightman's first ever female pupil. It would have made sense for her to use the room of Norman Daynes, an elderly QC who was very seldom present, but he had declared, 'Brightman, on no account is a woman ever going to sit in my room,' so she sat with Brightman in his own room, and he would ask his clients if they minded her sitting in on the conversation.[64] According to Lady Brightman, who considered Mrs Thatcher 'an attractive and charming woman', this arrangement gave rise to jokes: 'My husband's colleagues teased me about her looks.'[65] As was to prove so important in her political career, Mrs Thatcher benefited, in a sense, from the rarity of women, particularly attractive women, at the Bar. Without the slightest hint of impropriety, she nevertheless made it clear that she sought and enjoyed the company of clever, older men. The Bar consisted of little else, and many of them responded enthusiastically. On one occasion at about this time, Melford Stevenson, who had spoken for her at the uproarious election meeting in Dartford and was later to become a famously fierce

---

* John Brightman (1911–2006), educated Marlborough and St John's College, Cambridge; tax lawyer; judge of Chancery Division, 1970; judge of Industrial Relations Court, 1971; Lord of Appeal, 1982.

judge, brought Mrs Thatcher home for dinner with his wife without warning. Stevenson's son, John, dated his mother's lifelong hostility to her from this moment.[66]

After her stint with Brightman, Mrs Thatcher became a pupil of John Senter, her original patron, and here too she did well. But, for reasons that have never been quite clear, Senter decided to contract his chambers and so did not offer Mrs Thatcher the seat in chambers that comes after pupillage which he had earlier promised her. According to Peter Rowland, a fellow barrister at the time, Senter was 'a very strange man'; he was 'very unfair' to Mrs Thatcher and, in being so, went 'very much against the wishes of other members of chambers'. Mrs Thatcher made no public complaint but 'I knew from the occasional look that appeared on her face that she was extremely disappointed.'[67] In the view of Pamela Thomas (see below), Senter would not stand up against his clerk.[68] In any event, Mrs Thatcher had to look elsewhere for a seat in chambers. She ended up in those of C. A. J. Bonner at 5 New Square, Lincoln's Inn. But she practised only for a few months before her political career intervened.

As Mrs Thatcher well knew from the beginning, the Bar was a good entrée to politics, and many barristers were politically engaged. She joined the Inns of Court Conservative and Unionist Association, whose secretary, Pamela Thomas, got her on to its tax committee. Other Conservative barristers at that time included Patrick Jenkin,* later one of her Cabinet ministers, Tony Barber,† later Edward Heath's Chancellor of the Exchequer, and Geoffrey Howe,‡ her eventual nemesis. Pamela Thomas, who used to talk politics over coffee with her almost every day at the Bar, said that Mrs Thatcher was slightly right of centre in the party at that time, and that she was much distressed (as she confirms in her memoirs) by the collapse of the Suez adventure, when Britain, France and Israel attacked President Nasser's Egypt in 1956 after Nasser had seized the Suez Canal: 'She felt

---

* Patrick Jenkin (1926–), educated Clifton and Jesus College, Cambridge; Conservative MP for Wanstead and Woodford, 1964–87; Minister for Energy, 1974; Secretary of State for Social Services, 1979–81; for Industry, 1981–3; for the Environment, 1983–5; created Lord Jenkin of Roding, 1987.

† Anthony Barber (1920–2005), educated Retford Grammar School and Oriel College, Oxford; Conservative MP for Doncaster, 1951–64; for Altrincham and Sale, 1965–74; Chancellor of the Exchequer, 1970–74; created Lord Barber, 1974; chairman, Standard Chartered Bank, 1974–87.

‡ Geoffrey Howe (1926–), educated Winchester and Trinity Hall, Cambridge; Conservative MP for Bebington, 1964–6; for Reigate, 1970–74; for Surrey East, February 1974–92; Solicitor-General, 1970–72; Chancellor of the Exchequer, 1979–83; Foreign Secretary, 1983–9; Lord President of the Council and Deputy Prime Minister, 1989–90; created Lord Howe of Aberavon, 1992.

Eden* had been let down by others'[69] and she was perplexed and saddened by the fact that her old friend Edward Boyle opposed Suez, and resigned from the government over the issue. In her memoirs, she identified Nasser's political (though not military) victory in Suez as the cause of a great deal of the ensuing trouble in the Middle East: 'the bills were still coming in when I left office.' And she noted two other vital lessons of the debacle. The first was that it marked the moment when 'the British political class . . . went from believing that Britain could do anything to an almost neurotic belief that Britain could do nothing.' The second arose from the fact that the United States had not supported the Suez adventure, permitting a run on the pound which forced Eden to withdraw: Britain, she learnt, should never again get on the wrong side of America in any great enterprise.[70] In domestic matters, too, her views as a young barrister foreshadowed those in later life. Patrick Jenkin said that she already exhibited the toughness over economic policy for which she was later famous, rejecting the idea of co-partnership in the steel industry with the words: 'No, it must be a proper private sector business.'[71] She was a 'tip-top lawyer', said Pamela Thomas, but her political ambitions were clear – she wanted to be Chancellor of the Exchequer, the least 'female', perhaps, of all political jobs.[72]

Politics never really went away. On 12 June 1952, Mrs Thatcher's patron and admirer Beryl Cook wrote a memo to John Hare at Conservative Central Office. Miss Cook, the Home Counties and south-east area agent, recorded: 'Mrs Thatcher came to see me yesterday. To quote her own words – "It's no use; I must face it: I don't like being left out of the political stream."' She added: 'Mrs Thatcher tells me that her husband is quite in agreement with her views and would do all he could to back her if she did get a seat . . . I know myself that she can do this [nurse a seat] because now that she is married to a man who is comfortably off she will not have the financial worries she had while she was at Dartford.' 'Politics', said Miss Cook, 'is in her blood.'[73] A week later, Hare recorded a 'Note of interview' with Mrs Thatcher at Central Office: 'Miss Beryl Cook describes her as the best woman candidate she had ever known. I would also agree, as . . . she struck me as being a woman of immense personality and charm with a brain quite clearly above the average. I did my best to warn her of the

---

* Mrs Thatcher admired Eden much more than most post-Suez commentators. She saw him, because of his record in the 1930s, as 'the man who wanted to stand up against the foreign dictators'; she was also deeply impressed by the fact that Eden, who had fought in the First World War, would make a point of filling up his car from petrol stations run by ex-servicemen from his regiment. (Correspondence with Professor David Dilks.)

horrors of life in the House of Commons especially in so far as this life affects the home. Nothing I said deterred her. She would like her name to go forward for Canterbury . . .' Hare added that he would recommend her for any marginal or safe seat within a 30-mile radius of London.[74] Mrs Thatcher was unsuccessful at Canterbury, which is more than 50 miles from London, but it is interesting that her ambition was such that she was prepared to go well outside the 30-mile radius recommended by Hare.

Since there was never, truly, a point when Mrs Thatcher laid aside political ambition, though there was, as we shall see, one occasion when she claimed to be doing so, there may be no need to explain the timing of this attempted return to the fray. But it did coincide with an important incident in the political career of her father – its abrupt end.

Alfred Roberts had been made an alderman of Grantham in 1943. At that time, party politics did not dominate the local government of the town, but after the council elections of 1950 the Labour Party controlled Grantham Council. After the elections of 1952, Labour, with further gains, decided that it was dissatisfied with the equal Labour and non-Labour representation on the aldermanic bench (aldermen were chosen by the council rather than directly elected). The principle that Labour was entitled to more aldermen than its rivals was not disputed, but trouble arose because two of the three aldermen retiring were Labour and therefore, if the party was to gain an aldermanic majority, it would have to kick someone out. Because Alfred Roberts's term, which he wanted renewed, happened to end at that moment, he was the Labour Party's chosen victim. This provoked outcry. Aldermen had never been removed for party political reasons in Grantham before, and Roberts, because of the respect in which he was held, was considered a particularly unsuitable victim. A sermon in Grantham's parish church of St Wulfram's hurled anathemas against the evils of party politics, and even Denis Kendall, now no longer the town's MP but a member of the council, supported his former adversary and described the removal of Roberts as a 'mucky trick'.

According to Muriel Cullen, 'Daddy was expecting it. Mother wasn't'; he was upset, however, 'because he really loved Grantham'.[75] Certainly Alfred Roberts was prepared to make a drama of the occasion. Candidates stood fully robed as the aldermanic results were declared. When Roberts was voted off, he said, 'It is now almost nine years since I took up these robes in honour, and now I trust in honour I lay them down,'[76] and as he spoke, he pulled off his robes and laid them on the table in front of him. A fuller description was given in the *Grantham Journal* in Roberts's obituary in 1970; 'He stood, took off his robe, looked longingly at it as he laid it on the aldermanic bench, and then said with tremendous emotion and so quietly it was almost inaudible: "No medals. No honours, but an inward sense of satisfaction. May God bless Grantham forever." [77]*

The incident had a profound effect on Roberts's younger daughter. In what was probably the most revealing television interview she ever gave, with Miriam Stoppard in 1985,[78] Mrs Thatcher described her father being 'turned off that council' and said it was 'such a tragedy'. As she spoke of it, tears came into her eyes, and she had to pause for a moment. It was as if she had a premonition of the ingratitude which, she later believed, allowed her to be displaced from the Conservative leadership in 1990. As she put it, confusedly yet revealingly, to Jim Allen, Grantham's local historian, when he interviewed her after she left office: 'I thought my father's example there was so wonderful. So hurtful but so wonderful, and so dignified. But he was overwhelmed with letters, as I was. I didn't forget.'[79] It may not be too fanciful to see some of the impetus for Mrs Thatcher's attempted re-entry into politics in her father's downfall. His departure meant that, for the first time in her memory, he had no part in public life. Roberts left the aldermanic bench in May 1952, and Mrs Thatcher reapplied to Conservative Central Office in June.

In fact, as shown above, the arrival of the twins prevented Mrs Thatcher from going forward in politics quite as fast as she had hoped, but did nothing to quench 'the necessary fervour'. It seems likely that she had dropped the idea of standing in the coming general election because of her duties as a mother, but when the seat of Orpington became vacant because of the death of Sir Waldron Smithers, the sitting Conservative, it seemed too good a chance for Mrs Thatcher to miss. Orpington was close to Dartford, but much more Conservative, the heartland of the Tory suburban Kent to which marriage to Denis had introduced her. She telephoned Conservative Central Office to express her interest in December 1954, and was encouraged by John Hare.[80] Mrs Thatcher was shortlisted, but defeated by Donald Sumner, the chairman of the local party association. This rejection brought her closer than ever, before or since, to departing the political scene. Writing to Hare on 3 January 1955, Mrs Thatcher told him that she wanted to pursue tax and estate duty at the Bar. Orpington had been 'the only political temptation left for the next 10 years' because she had 'long had an affinity for it', but now that the temptation had been removed she wished to have her name withdrawn from the candidates' list.[81] Hare wrote back, urging her to reconsider if a winnable seat came up, but she replied

---

* The paper possesses a photograph of Roberts removing the robes. It has been asserted that cameras were not permitted to witness the occasion. If so, it is interesting that Roberts was willing to restage it for their benefit.

that she had 'quite made up my mind to pursue law to the exclusion of politics' and would not consider any offers before the coming election, though she was happy to make herself available as a speaker.[82] The ten years' self-denial, however, turned out to be thirteen months. On 28 February 1956, Mrs Thatcher wrote to Donald Kaberry, the new vice-chairman of the party responsible for candidates, and asked to come and see him. Once again, she used the word 'temptation' – the 'temptation to return to active politics'. She told Kaberry that her study of tax and company law had only made her more interested in a parliamentary career: it had turned her attention to 'the body which is responsible for the legislation about which I have come to hold strong views'.[83] Kaberry agreed to see her and got her to fill in the necessary form to become a candidate once again. Mrs Thatcher returned it with a note. 'When I come to write it all down on one sheet of paper,' she lamented, 'I seem to have done very little in the last 30 years.'[84] Few would have agreed, but, in any event, the second thirty years would overcompensate for any slacking in the first.

In the course of the following year, Mrs Thatcher tried for several seats. She declined to be considered for City of London and Westminster, telling Kaberry that she lacked the necessary distinction for such a seat, while at the same time putting herself forward for South Kensington.[85] She applied, unsuccessfully, for Beckenham and for Hemel Hempstead, and she flogged round the speaking circuit. 'I spoke at a women's afternoon meeting in North Kensington on Tuesday,' she wrote to Muriel while in the process of buying their new house in Farnborough. 'It went very well indeed – but what is the use of it's [sic] going well in a bad constituency?'[86] Her best chance seemed to be at Maidstone, where her benefactor Alfred Bossom was stepping down. Here, in March 1958, she made it on to the shortlist of three, her main rival being John Wells, ex-Eton, Oxford and submarine service during the war. Although the president of the local association reported to Central Office very favourably of the woman candidate with a 'tendency to the right of centre' ('A fine brain – great "appeal" – This lady should surely be in Parliament soon'), the report from the area agent makes it clear why she lost the selection to Wells:

> Mrs Thatcher spoke next, and went straight into politics, leaving only a very short time at the end of her talk for her tactics in nursing the seat. She was asked about her ability to cope as a Member, having in mind the fact that she had a husband and a small family, and I do not think her reply did her a lot of good. She spoke of having an excellent nanny and that as a Member she would have the mornings free (quite ignoring the fact that Members have committees in the mornings). She also spoke of having the weekends free,

and made no reference to spending time in Maidstone at the weekends.* She did say she would have to give up the Bar.[87]

It was all very discouraging. On her merits, Mrs Thatcher seemed to do well every time, only to lose because of her sex. And then came Finchley.

In March 1958, the elderly and somewhat inactive Member, Sir John Crowder, announced his retirement from Finchley, in suburban north London, at the next election. Mrs Thatcher put in her name, and was shortlisted, receiving the largest number of votes. But she did not allow herself to express high hopes. Writing to Muriel on 3 July, eleven days before the final selection, she began her letter with other matters. Denis, she said, had had to engage in the unpleasant sacking of the long-standing works superintendent because 'he just doesn't pull with the team,' and now he was in Africa (Entebbe, Uganda) on a big business trip. She worried about him: 'As Denis usually loses about 10 lbs on one of these trips, I hope he won't look too thin when he returns.' Then she mentioned the contest: 'Once again I have been shortlisted for a "safe" constituency. This time it is Finchley, which has a Conservative majority of 12,000. Three of us are on the final list† and we have to go down on Monday evening 14th July for the final selection. I expect the usual prejudice against women will prevail and that I shall probably come the inevitable "close second".'[88]

On the night, the 'usual prejudice' was certainly present. Even Derek Phillips, who, as the Young Conservative representative at the final selection, might have been expected to favour innovation, said to himself, 'If there's a lady, I shan't be voting for that lady.'[89] And John Tiplady, a postman who many years later became chairman of the Finchley Association, went along with his wife, who said she would never vote for a woman.[90] There were some, particularly women, who stuck by that view. Many, however, including Phillips and Tiplady, were won over. As Mrs Thatcher rather flirtatiously wrote to Donald Kaberry afterwards, '. . . I wore the outfit you said I was to wear the night I was finally selected,'[91] the 'black coat dress with brown trim' and small black hat[92] which she had been wearing when she called on him in April. John Tiplady noted her 'striking appearance' which he contrasted favourably with that of her rival, Thomas Langton, a local man and holder

---

* Mrs Thatcher consistently avoided making any commitment to having to live in any constituency which might select her. There was a limit to what could be imposed on Denis and the twins.

† In fact, it turned out to be a shortlist of four. One candidate, the war hero C. M. Woodhouse, had dropped out between rounds because he had been selected for Oxford, and so the executive committee, rather than allowing the contest to be between only two, inserted the next two candidates down. If anything, this made Mrs Thatcher's task easier, since two of the four were known to be slightly below par.

of the Military Cross, whom he remembered as a 'one-legged brigadier'. A director of the Gestetner copying company whispered to Tiplady, 'We're looking at a future Prime Minister of England.'[93] Derek Phillips thought she looked 'very smart', and was 'very much a true Conservative'. She seemed to have the 'more modern outlook' that they were looking for.[94] The absence of Mrs Thatcher's husband, still on business in Africa, made a notable contrast with the presence of the wives of the three men, but not one that necessarily harmed Margaret. There was something exciting about this good-looking, well-dressed thirty-two-year-old woman all alone and speaking with such force. In the first round, she came top, with Langton only one vote behind her. In the play-off between the two of them, she won by forty-six votes to forty-three. That, at least, was the declared result. But Bertie Blatch, the constituency Chairman responsible for counting the votes, told his son Haden that night: 'She didn't actually win. The man did, but I thought, "He's got a silver spoon in his mouth. He'll get another seat. So I 'lost' two of his votes and gave them to her.'[95] So Mrs Thatcher probably (unknowingly) won her way to Parliament through fraud. The absent, uncontactable Denis learnt of her victory by chance: 'I'd had a lot to drink and I staggered aboard the plane. I had to change in Kano in Nigeria and on the seat was the *Evening Standard* of the night before. I . . . turned over a couple of pages and there was this tiny little paragraph announcing that Margaret Thatcher had been adopted as Conservative candidate for Finchley. I've always said that it was bloody lucky that I was away because it was a close-run thing and if they'd taken one look at me they would have said, "We don't want this pair."'[96] The *Standard* headline which Denis saw said 'Tories Choose Beauty'.[97]

It was customary for the association's executive to endorse the chosen candidate unanimously, but in Mrs Thatcher's case it did not. A few, unreconciled to the idea of a woman, held out against her. The deputy area agent, Miss Harris, who had earlier predicted that a woman would not be selected, reported Mrs Thatcher's victory to Central Office and added that 'Unfortunately there were a handful who refused to give a unanimous vote at the end.'[98] This opposition, though now tiny, survived even Mrs Thatcher's triumphant adoption meeting on 31 July. A knot of five, whom Lady Thatcher was to describe as 'one woman and her little coterie',[99] refused to vote for her adoption.[100] In her letter to Kaberry, Mrs Thatcher wrote: 'I am learning the hard way that an anti-woman prejudice among certain Association members can persist after a successful adoption meeting.'[101]

The adoption meeting was Mrs Thatcher's first chance to present herself, via the press, to the voters of Finchley. She more than succeeded. 'The Conservatives of Finchley and Friern Barnet', declared the *Finchley Press*, which, being owned by the Conservative chairman, Bertie Blatch, knew which side its bread was buttered, 'have armed themselves with a new weapon – a clever woman.' 'Clad in restrained black and gold and with a small black hat' (the same outfit as at the selection?), the new candidate had given a 'clear-cut appraisal of the Middle East situation, weighed up Russia's propagandist moves with the skill of a housewife measuring the ingredients in a familiar recipe, pinpointed Nasser as the fly in the mixing bowl . . . no one could accuse her of throwing her womanhood at the audience.' The paper said, erroneously, but capturing the prevailing mood, that 'If any had come to oppose – they went away converted.'[102] The *Finchley Times* reported Mrs Thatcher's attack on the 'despotism' of the trade unions: 'A man', she said, 'should have the right *Not* to strike if he does not wish to. We must regulate trade unions and protect the individual worker.'[103] The paper carried more explanation of her position on the Middle East: 'In the Iraki [sic] revolt the people who were brutally murdered were Arabs. In any discussion on the Middle East we must take into consideration the State of Israel, because we were mainly responsible for its existence.'[104] The reason that the Middle East bulked larger in Finchley than in most British electoral contests was that the constituency had a substantial Jewish vote. At the time of Mrs Thatcher's selection, the Liberals had benefited from a row about attempts to block the admission of Jews to Finchley Golf Club, which insisted on prospective members stating their religious affiliation. This was thought to reflect badly on some Conservatives. And there was some anti-Semitic feeling in the association at the time. The outgoing MP, Sir John Crowder, is supposed to have complained that Conservative Central Office was trying to impose a choice on the constituency between 'a bloody Jew and a bloody woman'.* According to John Tiplady, the meeting which selected Margaret Thatcher was held on a Friday night so that orthodox Jews would be unable to attend.[105] This is not in fact the case – the meeting took place on a Monday – but Tiplady remembered it thus, suggesting that some sort of ill feeling did, indeed, exist. Not long after she had been adopted, Mrs Thatcher sought to mend the fences. Writing to Central Office on 17 September 1958, she discussed the problem:

> For reasons with which I need not bother you, the Jewish faith have allied
> themselves to Liberalism and at the last local election won five seats from
> the Conservatives on our council. We are now finding great difficulty in
> making headway in these areas, particularly in Hampstead Garden Suburb.

* See Dennis Walters, *Not Always with the Pack*, Constable, 1989, pp. 102–3. But note that in fact the 'bloody Jew' mentioned, Peter Goldman, was not shortlisted for Finchley. He was to be the unlucky victim of the Liberal by-election triumph in Orpington in 1962.

As Finchley has had a Liberal MP in the past we are naturally apprehensive and are now making great efforts to further the Conservative cause. I fear the division [that is, the constituency] as a whole has not been very dynamic in the past.[106]

Although the Jewish population was probably not the 25 per cent of the Finchley vote which Mrs Thatcher mentioned in the same letter, being in fact a fifth or less, it was nevertheless highly significant, indeed essential, for any candidate requiring the support of the middle classes. Through her Finchley experience, Mrs Thatcher conceived a strong admiration for Jewish values. Jews, she later declared, are 'one of the most scholarly races', and 'They also are the people of the Old Testament: how can you believe in the New unless you believe in the Old?'[107] She was attracted, too, by their very active sense of community – 'My, they were good citizens' – which expressed itself in 'not just talking, but doing and giving'. And she liked their entrepreneurial virtues, seeing Jews as 'natural traders' who managed 'positively to get on by their own efforts'.[108] During her premiership, she was often closer to Jewish religious leaders, notably the Chief Rabbi, Immanuel Jakobovits, whom she ennobled, than to Christian ones. But in her early days in Finchley she looked on Jewish matters in a more matter-of-fact way: she needed Jewish votes and she thought the Tories were sacrificing them unnecessarily. As we shall see, although her relationship with the Jewish community was fundamentally harmonious and productive, Mrs Thatcher did sometimes find Finchley Jews irritating. What is clear, however, is that she approached them without the prejudices which existed in some sections of her party, and they responded warmly. Helped, as she records in her memoirs,[109] by Ted Heath, who was then Chief Whip, Mrs Thatcher drafted in senior Conservative MPs to speak on her behalf. Notable among these was Sir Keith Joseph,* later her greatest political ally, MP for Leeds North East, and the most important Jewish Conservative of his generation. He came to speak for Mrs Thatcher in Finchley in February 1959.

Anyone can see, in retrospect, that Mrs Thatcher was certain to hold Finchley for the Conservatives at the next election, whenever it came. This moderately prosperous, petit-bourgeois, owner-occupied, suburban constituency was a safe Tory seat, and ideally suited for its chosen candidate. Although the phrase was not used at the time, Mrs Thatcher was upwardly

---

* Keith Joseph (1918–94), 2nd baronet; educated Harrow and Magdalen College, Oxford; Conservative MP for Leeds North East, 1956–87; Secretary of State for Social Services, 1970–74; for Industry, 1979–81; for Education and Science, 1981–6; founder and chairman, Centre for Policy Studies, 1974–9 (director, 1991–4); created Lord Joseph, 1987.

mobile, and so was Finchley. Besides, the political wind had been blowing in the party's favour. Harold Macmillan had replaced Eden as prime minister in January 1957 and set his course on expansionary policies. The era of post-war austerity was well and truly over, replaced by what, when it returned in the 1980s, was disparaged (by the conservative commentator Peregrine Worsthorne*) as 'bourgeois triumphalism'. David Kynaston, the social historian of post-war Britain, cites an advertisement for New Zealand butter which appeared in *Woman* magazine in the first week of 1957, as capturing the spirit of the age. 'Good food and plenty of it, full employment, well furnished homes – today's generation knows what Good Living really means!' ran the text, before praising the 'natural golden colour' of the butter.[110] Although Macmillan himself, born in the nineteenth century, seemed a rather old-fashioned, Edwardian figure, and even played up to this image, he was adroit at managing the politics of prosperity. It was he who, as housing minister, had made and fulfilled his party's pledge before the 1951 election, to build 300,000 houses a year. It was Macmillan who, on 20 July 1957, made a famous speech in which he declared: 'Indeed let us be frank about it – most of our people have never had it so good. Go around the country, go to the industrial towns, go to the farms, and you will see a state of prosperity such as we have never had in my lifetime – nor, indeed, in the history of this country.' It was true. The average real pay for industrial workers had risen by 20 per cent since the Tory victory in 1951. Earlier in the same year, Macmillan had written to an official at Central Office: 'I am always hearing about the Middle Classes. What is it they really want? Can you put it down on a sheet of notepaper, and I will see whether we can give it to them.'[111] As the general election of 1959 approached, he seemed to have found the answer.

In the very same 'never had it so good' speech, Macmillan himself had raised the question, 'Is it too good to last? . . . can prices be steadied while at the same time we maintain full employment in an expanding economy?' In the next decade, this question would come to dominate politics, but, in the late 1950s, people tended to think that it could be postponed. In January 1958, Macmillan's Treasury team, led by the Chancellor, Peter Thorneycroft,† and including Enoch Powell, had resigned in protest at the government's reluctance to hold back public spending adequately (the

* Worsthorne, Peregrine: 1923-   ; educ. Stowe, Peterhouse, Cambridge. Deputy editor, *Sunday Telegraph*, 1961-76; Associate Editor, 1976-86; Editor, 1986-89; Editor, Comment Section, 1989-91. knighted, 1991.
† Peter Thorneycroft (1909-94), educated Eton and Royal Military Academy, Woolwich; MP for Stafford, 1938-45; for Monmouth, 1945-66; Chancellor of the Exchequer 1957-58; created Lord Thorneycroft, 1967; Chairman of the Conservative Party, 1975-81.

disputed sum was a mere £50 million), saying that profligacy would lead
to inflation. Macmillan dismissed the resignations as 'little local difficulties', and more or less got away with it. The resignations much later came
to be seen as harbingers of monetarism, and were much admired by Thatcherites, but at the time they did not achieve their purpose. As the 1959
election drew near, the headline rate of inflation remained below 3 per cent.
Macmillan's political approach to public spending seemed to be vindicated.

In the budget of 1959, the Chancellor cut the standard rate of income tax
from 8s 6d (42.5 pence) to 7s 9d (38.5 pence) and reduced purchase tax and
the duty on beer. In September of that year, Macmillan called an early and
quick election, for 8 October. The manifesto asked, 'Do you want to go ahead
on the lines which have brought prosperity at home?' and 'Do you want
your present leaders to represent you?', questions which represented confidence or complacency, according to taste. 'Life's Better Under the
Conservatives', was the slogan, and so, in an immediate and directly material sense, it was. In later years, Mrs Thatcher looked back critically. In 1979,
she told Macmillan's official biographer, Alistair Horne, that 'I think part of
our post-1959 problems arose from an extremely over-generous Budget in
1959.'[112] But at the time she was mainly content to go with the political flow.

One of Mrs Thatcher's best political gifts, born of a rather surprising
lack of self-confidence and a female conscientiousness, was never to take
anything for granted. If her party risked complacency, she did not. She
campaigned ferociously hard. At the annual general meeting of the Finchley Conservatives on 23 March 1959, the chairman, Bertie Blatch, praised
her for the fact that she had fulfilled 130 requests to speak since her adoption less than eight months earlier.[113] Compared with her first campaign
at Dartford, Mrs Thatcher was more circumspect in advancing her personal
views, and she was happy enough to join in her party's boasting about its
ever-growing spending, but she nevertheless put down a few markers for
what would later be called Thatcherism. Speaking at a public meeting in
Friern Barnet on 3 April 1959, she addressed herself to the anxiety that,
despite the increase in material prosperity, there seemed to be little moral
advance. 'If one desires above all to build a responsible society of responsible citizens,' she asked, 'how can Parliament bring it about?' To the small
extent that it could, firm standards and the pursuit of excellence were the
keys. She told her audience that she supported the use of the birch for those
crimes of violence committed 'for the sheer love of brutality'. She was also
tackled on the emerging question of comprehensive schools. While saying
that some comprehensives might turn out to be very good, Mrs Thatcher
made it clear where her sympathies lay: 'We never believe in throwing out
what tradition and experience have proved to be very good indeed, and

replacing this by something as yet in the experimental stage.'[114] At her election adoption meeting on 21 September, she emphasized the simple verity which was so often to stand her in such good stead: 'The whole of our future at home and abroad depends on our having a solvent society,'[115] a doctrine to which Macmillan paid only formal obeisance. There is nothing, however, to suggest anything dangerously unorthodox in the views of the thirty-three-year-old parliamentary candidate. Although to the right of her party's leader, she endorsed the middle-way, unideological expansionism of the 'never had it so good' era. Her election address for the poll which Macmillan had called for 8 October categorized the main issues as 'Your Home . . . Your Job . . . Your Children . . . Your Defence . . . Your Vote', and offered a conventional mixture of security, prosperity and high spending. The respect in which the candidate for Finchley stood out was not ideological: it was because she was already a bit of a star – through her sex, her looks, her dynamism and her air of being, true blue though she was, something new for the Tory Party, a persuasive meritocrat. 'The business of the working class is on its way out,' she told an interviewer in the *Evening News* during the campaign. 'After all, aren't I working class? I work jolly hard, I can tell you.'[116] And somehow she induced the (female) interviewer to declare, 'she is, without question, an absolute honey.'[117]

At the count, rigid with nerves, Mrs Thatcher heard that she had increased the Conservative majority from 12,825 to 16,260, winning well over half of the votes cast. The result was:

Mrs Margaret Thatcher (Conservative)	29,697
Eric Deakins (Labour)	13,437
Ivan Spence (Liberal)	12,260
Conservative majority	16,260

The national result – a Conservative majority of 107 – was the party's best since the war. Margaret Thatcher reached Parliament at a peak in her party's fortunes from which it could only decline.

PART TWO

Parliament, 1959–1979

7

Member, minister

'She's trouble. What can we do to keep her busy?'

The new Member of Parliament who walked up the steps of the House of Commons with her characteristically short, brisk stride gave every air of outward confidence. The first person to greet her was her secretary, Paddi Victor Smith. The two had not met before. Miss Victor Smith was already the secretary for another Conservative MP, Frederic Bennett, and had applied for the additional work with Mrs Thatcher in order to earn extra money. She had gained the job without an interview. When she met Mrs Thatcher at the Members' entrance, she thought at once that she was 'very pretty, well groomed'; she felt 'surprised right from the start at how together she was'.[1] This impression of neatness and competence never went away. When, later, she visited Margaret at Dormers, Paddi Victor Smith noted that 'all her clothes were beautifully hung in plastic bags' and that she seemed to possess early prototypes of the freezer bags that are common today.[2]

Yet Mrs Thatcher probably felt less poised than she looked. Despite her electoral success and the security provided by her marriage, she remained an outsider. Although loyal to her family, she also found her lower-middle-class roots a little embarrassing. A few days after the 1959 election, she wrote to Muriel, thanking her for the congratulatory talcum powder that her sister had sent her, and complaining that she had 350 letters and 75 telegrams to answer. She was so busy, she said, that her lack of a housekeeper was becoming 'a major worry'. On election night, she added, her father's brother, Harold Roberts, had suddenly appeared: 'Would you believe it Uncle Harold turned up on election day. Visited two committee rooms, got himself into the count and then, as he hadn't arranged any transport back, I had to take him on to a party with me before driving him back to town.'[3]

Writing to Muriel three days later, the girls' father explained what had happened more fully, after remarking, rather sadly: 'We, so far, have only received a short letter from Margaret, but she says she is completely inundated with correspondence. We realise that so exercise patience.' Uncle

Harold, apparently, had decided, 'without previous indication to anyone, to go up to Finchley for the day'. There he found his niece, and 'attached himself to her for the rest of the night', going to the count and celebration party and then 'needing to be taken to St Pancras station at 4.30 am'. 'It has upset me very much,' Alfred went on, 'for much as I cling to Harold for he is a good man, obviously in every way he would be out of his element and become a responsibility to Margaret and Denis to look after which to their credit they certainly did.' Alfred Roberts had taken the matter in hand, he said: 'as kindly and reasonably as possible I have told him he mustn't obtrude.' He had also had cause to write to his sister, Frances Garland, whose husband Charlie had presented himself at the Thatchers' house without warning on a recent occasion: 'Frances has written a nasty letter in reply, but I will put up with that if it saves Margaret and Denis future trouble. Why do they want to cash in on Margaret's success in this pushing way.'[4]

Harold Roberts was a kindly man, and close to Alfred, but he was also considerably less successful than his brother. He lived all his life in Raunds, the Northamptonshire village in which the seven Roberts children were brought up, and worked for a shoe-making company. His unannounced presence on Margaret's great day was awkward, a scene reminiscent of Pip's reunion, when adult, with his simple brother-in-law Joe Gargery, in Dickens's *Great Expectations*. Being a conscientious woman, Mrs Thatcher looked after Harold that night, but being also an upwardly mobile one, she devoutly wished he wasn't there.

In the House of Commons, Mrs Thatcher's social origins do not seem to have been much held against her, even though the Conservative Party of that time was far more aristocratic, and probably more snobbish, than it is today. She had become, by marriage and, as it were, by adoption, part of the affluent middle class of suburban Kent (there was never any question of her living in Finchley). As such, she was one of many in the post-war Tory Party, and she did not, at this stage, make much of her Grantham grocer's-shop roots. Her class was not conspicuous. Her sex, however, was more of an issue. It did not mean that she was obviously ill used. If anything, the problem was rather the opposite. The courtesy shown to women Members had the effect of cocooning them in a cosy irrelevance. One of only twelve women Conservative MPs, and considerably the most attractive of them, Mrs Thatcher found herself treated with a studied politesse which she liked, but which, she perfectly well understood, was intended to restrict the scope of her political career. To this day, the unwritten conventions of the House request that a Member who is a Queen's Counsel is referred to as 'learned', that a former regular officer is 'gallant', and so on. When Mrs Thatcher entered the

House, they also indicated that a speech by a woman Member be described as 'charming', even when it clearly had not been. Margaret undoubtedly possessed and deployed charm, but the word did no justice to her abilities or to her ambition. She complained, in after years, that women MPs in the 1950s and 1960s were always shunted into what she rather vaguely referred to as 'the welfare thing'.[5] This was to be her fate for some time, but she was determined to escape it eventually, which helps to explain why she had studied tax law at the Bar and why her ultimate ambition was to be Chancellor of the Exchequer. In these early days, Mrs Thatcher was often called upon by newspapers or broadcasters looking for a 'woman' angle on political life. In her first appearance on BBC Radio's *Any Questions?*, in January 1960, she had to answer questions about the working week for wives ('it's not the hours you put in, it's what you put into the hours that counts') and to give advice on looking for a husband ('look for a husband who is kind. I think it is quite a rare virtue in men').[6] In the same month, a London paper asked her for tips on getting children to save ('My six-year-old twins always managed to get the coins out of their money boxes or to break them open. So each now has a savings box which cannot possibly be opened by anybody but the banking authorities').[7]

The new Member for Finchley was not part of any gang, or club, and never had any taste for trying to form a rival one with members of her own sex. Like most MPs at that time, Mrs Thatcher had no office of her own in Parliament. Unlike most, she did not find her way to the Smoking Room or other drinking haunts. Indeed, throughout the whole of her political career, she never once went into the Smoking Room unaccompanied, just as she never entered a pub alone.[8] There was a Lady Members' Room where she did a good deal of her work. Her secretary shared a room just off Westminster Hall with several others, and Mrs Thatcher therefore met their employers, notably her future deputy Willie Whitelaw,* quite often.† But she spent only functional time in that room, dictating letters. There were no telephones there, and if a call came through, ushers would summon the person called to answer the phone in a special booth. Nor was it a place for meetings. Financially, everything was on a shoestring: there was nothing remotely resembling the generous expenses which caused such a scandal in

---

* William Whitelaw (1918–99), educated Winchester and Trinity College, Cambridge; served in Scots Guards, 1939–46, awarded the Military Cross; Conservative MP for Penrith and the Border, 1955–83; Secretary of State for Northern Ireland, 1972–3; Secretary of State for Employment, 1973–4; Deputy Leader of Conservative Party, 1975–9; Home Secretary and Deputy Prime Minister, 1979–83; created Viscount Whitelaw, 1983; Leader of the House of Lords and Lord President of the Council, 1983–8.

† Betty Boothroyd, who was to become the first woman Speaker of the Commons, worked in the same office at that time, as secretary to a Labour MP, Geoffrey de Freitas.

2009. Members had to buy their own postage stamps and they paid their secretaries directly themselves. Mrs Thatcher paid Paddi Victor Smith 13 guineas per week, which was over the going rate, out of her annual salary of £1,250, in order to secure her exclusive services: 'She was a fairly exacting boss. She paid quite well, and expected a good day's work.'[9] Sometimes she would take Paddi with her to the hairdresser and dictate to her while under the dryer.

Hard work, as always, was Mrs Thatcher's sovereign remedy for every difficulty, and, by chance, the opportunity for a serious tranche of it arose almost at once. In the ballot, drawn by lot, for Private Members' Bills, always held at the beginning of the parliamentary session, she came second. These Bills were (and are) devices allowing legislation to be introduced from the back benches, and represented an opportunity for Members to make a name for themselves. Her place in the ballot ensured that her Bill would receive the requisite parliamentary time. It also meant that her maiden speech in the House, unlike almost all the others, would be substantive and legislative. From the very beginning, she was serious.

Mrs Thatcher herself records that she had some difficulty over her choice of subject for the Bill, and then over the Bill itself.[10] As she was as new a Member as it was possible to be, she was at first attracted to a Bill which was already sitting on the stocks about appeals in contempt-of-court cases. But after doing some initial drafting work on it she was warned off it by the Attorney-General as being too complicated for a Private Member's Bill (it is not the case, as she asserts in her memoirs, that she refused the whips' invitation to take on the Bill on the grounds that it was too dry). Next she considered a Bill which would restrict the rights of the union closed shop, a subject already dear to her heart. From this, though, she was also dissuaded by the authorities, who said that it would be impossible to legislate in the middle of the complicated court case on the subject then in progress. Eventually, Mrs Thatcher picked on something completely different. She chose the question of the admission of the press to the meetings of local government.

This issue was not plucked out of the air. It had become the subject of political controversy over the past year when several Labour councils had voted to exclude the press from some of their proceedings. In Liverpool, because a local paper had produced a blackleg edition during a print strike, the council used the device of 'resolving itself into committee'. By doing this, it could evade the existing 1908 law insisting that the press be admitted to meetings of the full council, and vote the journalists of the strike-breaking newspaper out of the chamber. In Nottingham, near enough to Grantham to come to Mrs Thatcher's personal attention, she witnessed a comparable example of what she described as 'socialist connivance with trade union power'.[11] The Conservative manifesto for the 1959 election had declared, 'We mean to make quite sure that the press have proper facilities for reporting the proceedings of local authorities.' It was in her zeal to fulfil this pledge that Margaret took it up as the subject of her Bill.

Her inner motive in choosing this subject has provoked controversy. According to one biographer, John Campbell, the explanation must be psychological, almost Freudian. He thinks the Bill was an attack on Margaret's father, most likely 'a . . . reaction against Alfred himself and the repression of her childhood'. Although there is no surviving evidence about Alfred's reaction to the Bill, Campbell thinks that 'most probably' Alfred Roberts would have regarded it 'as a clumsy interference with the right of local authorities to conduct their own affairs'.[12] Campbell also sees the Bill as presaging her anger, when prime minister, against the independence of local government: 'like the ratecapping legislation of the 1980s, her 1960 Bill was a general measure directed at all councils in order to control the abuses of the few.' 'There is', he complains, 'no recognition whatsoever of the positive value of local government.'

This analysis is not convincing. In bringing forward her Bill, Mrs Thatcher was not introducing a new principle of interference in local affairs, or trying to restrict the powers of councils to do their business, but strengthening the existing law of 1908 whose effectiveness had been weakened by the Local Government Act of 1933. As for her father and his influence, it seems unlikely that a measure of this sort, clearly directed against abuse, rather than against the principles of local government, should have upset him.* The 'first purpose' of the Bill, she said in her maiden speech, was to make sure that the public knew how their money was being spent, a principle with which Alfred Roberts would not have quarrelled. It is more probable that Mrs Thatcher found the subject matter approachable because she was the alderman's daughter, and therefore had good, if second-hand, knowledge of how local government worked. Besides, the people she intended to attack with her Bill were chiefly the sort who had deprived Alfred Roberts of his alderman's robes.

It was a political motive, the dislike of trade union power and its

---

* In an article called 'Local Government' in *Conservative Oxford* in October 1949, writing as the new Dartford parliamentary candidate, Margaret Roberts had argued that Labour was damaging local government by grabbing powers from it, leading to a 'loss of local responsibility' and making it less attractive to good people. It seems likely that the expulsion of Alderman Roberts would have confirmed this view, rather than turning her against local government *per se*.

municipal alliance with socialism, which galvanized Mrs Thatcher. When
the Bill was debated in standing committee, Charles Pannell, Labour
Mayor of Dartford when Margaret had been candidate there, now Member
for Leeds West and her friendly parliamentary 'pair',* put the classic
socialist view about blacklegs: 'To me with 40 years' trade unionism behind
me, the act of going to work when other men are on strike is one of the
depths of sin.'[13] Margaret profoundly believed the precise opposite, and
from the first sought ways of breaking that aspect of union power.

There may also have been an element of political calculation concerning
her own backyard. The greatest threat to Margaret Thatcher in Finchley
at this time came from the Liberal Party. Even though they finished a little
behind the Labour candidate in the general election of 1959, the Liberals
greatly increased their vote in that election and provided the growing political energy against which she had to fight. Ever since the golf-club row
of 1956, the Liberals in Finchley had been led by a pair of Jewish councillors elected in 1957. They eloquently argued that the borough was being
governed by a secretive and self-serving collection of Tories, sometimes in
unholy alliance with Labour; by 1958 there were seven Liberal councillors
elected. Admission to council meetings was one of the issues at stake here
since Liberals accused the Tories of deciding everything in 'secret' committee meetings from which the press were excluded and then presenting only
faits accomplis to the full council. There was a good deal of truth in the
Liberal attack, and the local Conservatives responded to it too dismissively.
In January 1958, a Conservative councillor in Finchley had defected to the
Liberals over this issue. It did no harm for Finchley's new Member of Parliament to put herself on the side of openness, and thus head off Liberal
attack. It also helped in her long campaign to recover Jewish support.
Much later, she was rewarded by the defection of one of the leading Jew-
ish Liberal councillors to the Tory ranks.†

If Mrs Thatcher expected plain sailing, however, she was quickly disabused. Although her Bill seemed to accord with Tory policy, the government
did not really like it very much. As early as 11 November 1959, Mrs
Thatcher received a letter from Sir Jocelyn Simon, the Solicitor-General,
warning of trouble ahead from the local government lobby. He was well
disposed to Mrs Thatcher, having been impressed by her contributions at

---

* 'Pairing' is the device by which members of opposing parties arrange, for mutual convenience,
to be absent from the same divisions, cancelling out each other's vote. It is approved by the
whips. A standing committee considers public Bills rather than policy subjects in general, and
is part of the legislative process. Bills go 'into committee' after second reading, which is the
chief occasion for debate of legislation by the whole House.
† For a discussion of all this, see *New Outlook*, August 1963.

the Inns of Court Conservative Association, and her habit at its dinners of making sure that she sat close to the guest speaker – evidence, he considered, of a laudable ambition.[14] Now he suggested, silkily: 'All this makes it particularly important that you should work in as close touch with Henry Brooke [the Minister for Housing and Local Government] as possible and, I should advise, defer to his views throughout. No doubt he will be a little embarrassed at having one of his programme Bills taken up by a Private Member; but he is a very nice fellow and perfectly sound on this issue and, I am sure, will give you his help provided you play perfectly fair with him.'[15] Simon added a point which would surely not have escaped the already publicity-conscious young MP: 'I am sorry that you were disappointed in your earlier projects, but you have certainly in the end got a Bill which will, with all the difficulties, give you a wonderful parliamentary experience and will certainly endear you to the Press!'

The fact was that the government was in a bit of a muddle. On 9 December, Henry Brooke* minuted the Cabinet Home Affairs Committee: 'Mrs Thatcher's Bill, coming at this moment, presents us with something of a problem. In our election manifesto we declared our intention of making quite sure that the press should have proper facilities for reporting the proceedings of local authorities. I drafted those words myself, and it is a pledge which we must honour.' The trouble was that Mrs Thatcher's Bill was 'wrong' to offer 'such wide-ranging rights to the press'.[16] There was a nervousness, though this was not spelt out, that law in this field might prove too heavy-handed, and stir up unnecessary conflict between local and central government. The government really preferred a code of conduct to legislation. The solution, agreed at the committee's meeting two days later, was that 'the appropriate course seemed to be to prepare and hand to Mrs Thatcher a Bill which the government could accept.' There was a danger that she might introduce a measure 'far from acceptable to the Government', and therefore 'she should be provided with a Bill only on the clear understanding that she would reject amendments which had not been agreed with the Government'.[17] This, more or less, is what happened. Three days later, Brooke contacted Mrs Thatcher and promised to arrange the services of Parliamentary Counsel in the drafting of the Bill so long as it was 'clearly understood between us that, if the Bill were presented on these lines, you would resist amendments to it which had not been agreed with me or my colleagues'.[18]

This understanding was reached in theory, but was, in reality, more of a misunderstanding. In a memo of 7 January 1960, a Ministry of Housing

---

* Henry Brooke's son, Peter, was to serve in Mrs Thatcher's Cabinet from 1988.

and Local Government official, C. J. Pearce, reported on an exhausting session with Mrs Thatcher and the parliamentary draftsman, John Fiennes. The new Member was being demanding:

> Mrs Thatcher wanted the Bill strengthened in ways which seemed to indicate that she was expecting a much more drastic Bill than we have had in mind. Some of her remarks suggested, moreover, that she would not put much conviction into opposing amendments which in her view would strengthen the Bill ... Mrs Thatcher ... is obsessed with the minority of the councils who might act irresponsibly, whereas we have had in mind the great majority of local authorities whose relations with the press are basically satisfactory. I could not help thinking that it was a pity ... that a Bill of such importance to local authorities should be in the hands of a Private Member whose knowledge of local government is limited, and who clearly holds a low opinion of local authorities, their members and officials.[19]*

Tension rose. On 11 January Mrs Thatcher wrote to Keith Joseph, the junior minister at the Ministry, saying that she was 'somewhat disappointed with the present attempts to deal with a penalty clause'; she was also unhappy that the Bill was not permitted to extend the same rules beyond councils to what, twenty years later, became known as quangos (quasi-autonomous non-governmental organizations). Dame Evelyn Sharp, the Ministry's Permanent Secretary, who was later to become famous through her appearances in Richard Crossman's Diaries, became alarmed. Mrs Thatcher, she said, 'seems to be going back on the clear understanding which I thought we had reached with her'. Dame Evelyn told Brooke that 'if she writes to me I would propose to remind her in no uncertain terms of what passed between us.'[20] In this tussle between civil servants who essentially wanted the Bill to achieve very little, and Mrs Thatcher, who wanted it to do what it purported to do, one can see, in miniature, the character of a thousand future disagreements between her and officials. On 11 January, Henry Brooke appended a shrewd little handwritten note to Dame Evelyn's memo. Mrs Thatcher's technique, he wrote, 'is to say she must have much more than she really expects to get!' Brooke pursued a serpentine course of supporting the Bill and distancing himself from it at the same time.

Margaret Thatcher rose for the first time in the House of Commons on 5 February 1960, and moved the second reading of her Bill. W. F. Deedes,

---

* Fiennes was even more anguished by the idea that the author of the Bill should have a serious say in its drafting. He argued unsuccessfully that she should not attend the relevant drafting meeting with Commons officials: 'I am not sure that it would be a good thing for Mrs Thatcher to do so. She probably has very little idea of the point at issue ... and if she treats them as she treated us, she may well put their backs up. This is not a thing you can say to her.'

the Member for Ashford, who was sitting just behind her, noticed that she had turned herself out particularly well for the occasion. With a certain male vagueness, he remembered her wearing 'a patterned gown. The dominant note was chestnut.' He noted also how economically she used her notes – 'a model of how to use notes in the House of Commons': her speech was learnt pretty well by heart and delivered with great self-confidence. The speech's success is indicated by Deedes's erroneous memory that it was only seven minutes long:[21] it was actually twenty-seven minutes.* Because she was legislating, Mrs Thatcher explained at once, she would dispense with the usual formalities of a maiden speech, which required that the speech be uncontroversial and make frequent reference to the joys of the constituency: '. . . I know that the constituency of Finchley which I have the honour to represent would not wish me to do other than come straight to the point.' The 'point' was the same, she said, as the purpose of the original 1908 Bill of 'guarding the rights of members of the public by enabling the fullest information to be obtained for them in regard to the actions of their representatives upon local authorities'. She emphasized what large sums local authorities spent (£1,400 million a year in England and Wales), and declared that 'the first purpose in admitting the Press is that we may know how those moneys are being spent.' The second, related basis of the Bill, and here she quoted from Sir Oliver Franks's report on Tribunals of Inquiry, was that 'Publicity is the greatest and most effective check against any arbitrary action.'

Private Members' Bills were, by convention, debated on a Friday, and it was therefore not unusual for the House to be thinly attended for them as MPs returned to their constituencies for the weekend. With her customary thoroughness, though, Mrs Thatcher had written individually to 250 of her backbench Conservative colleagues ('I have always believed in the impact of a personal, handwritten letter – even from someone you barely know')[22] asking them to attend and vote. Many did. Her Bill was carried overwhelmingly, by 152 votes to 39. And although some of the House's favourable reaction to her speech was formulaic – the convention that a new Member be heard politely and praised afterwards – it is clear that she had won genuine admiration. Barbara Castle,† who was to become, after

* At this time, Deedes led a double life, also writing (pseudonymously) for the Peterborough column of the *Daily Telegraph*. There, the following day, he described the speech as being 'of frontbench quality'.
† Barbara Castle (1910–2002), educated Bradford Girls' Grammar School and St Hugh's College, Oxford; Labour MP for Blackburn, 1945–79; Minister of Transport, 1965–8; Secretary of State for Employment and Productivity, 1968–70; for Social Services, 1974–6; created Baroness Castle of Blackburn, 1990.

Mrs Thatcher, the most important woman politician in British history, was enthusiastic from her left-wing point of view: 'it is always the progressive movements which are supporters of publicity.' 'It is conservatism', she added, 'which always needs secrecy to survive, and not Socialism.' Charlie Pannell, who opposed the Bill, nevertheless praised Mrs Thatcher's 'rather beautiful maiden speech'.* W. F. Deedes, winding up in support, congratulated Mrs Thatcher on 'her courage in laying hands on such a Bill'. As for representatives of the government, they were ready in their praise, if cautious in their endorsement. Henry Brooke said that Mrs Thatcher's 'fluency' had achieved the unusual feat of making a parliamentary reputation on a Friday: 'no words of mine can be too high praise for the brilliance of the speech.' He stood at a distance from the Bill, however, suggesting that it was a 'labyrinth' for a private Member, that he preferred a code of conduct to law and that the Bill might fail.[23] As so often in the key moments of her early political career, her husband was not there to see it: Denis was on a business trip to the Middle East.

The immediate result of the speech was a new rash of press attention. 'Fame and Margaret Thatcher made friends yesterday,' said the *Sunday Dispatch* (though really it had been the day before), and the paper manoeuvred her into betraying her ambition even as she disclaimed it: 'I couldn't even consider a Cabinet post until my twins are older.'[24] Later in the month, she was writing in the *Evening News*, however, under the headline 'I SAY A WIFE CAN DO TWO JOBS.'[25] And a few days later, she told the *Daily Express* 'What my daughter must learn in the next nine years'. Margaret wanted Carol to go to university: 'I don't want Carol to be taught too many practical subjects in her last years at school, but to learn academic subjects – yes, to slog away.' She wanted her to learn 'the domestic arts' too, but much of non-academic education could come from home, however wearing the process: 'Teaching manners and the social graces to a child of six and a half gives rise to alternate hope and despair. The nagging seems endless . . .'† Girls should do their best to look good, she thought, because 'a girl's appearance is very important for her self-confidence,' and if Carol wouldn't listen to her mother on the subject of make-up, she would 'send her to a teenage beauty centre'.

Margaret's hopes for her son and daughter were not very different, she told the paper. She wanted both to have a good education and a worthwhile

---

* There is probably a sexist joke (or gallant compliment) hiding in the phrase, with the words 'rather beautiful' governing the word 'maiden' rather than the word 'speech'.

† She was always, even when Carol was grown up, inclined to worry about her daughter's appearance, manners and deportment.

career. 'If money were short,' she went on, revealing her absolute assumption that her children would have a private education, 'and I had to choose between educating my son or my daughter, I would choose entirely on merit. (Except that my husband would probably insist that Mark went to his old school.)'* But she added that a boy can regulate the course of his life via his career more than a girl because 'To her there is one great unknown factor – marriage.' She considered the range of possibilities about her little daughter's marriage – being a young mother or an old mother, being married to someone who is 'a public figure' – but did not envisage the idea that her daughter would not marry at all.[26]†

Back in Parliament, Mrs Thatcher's Bill wended a tortuous way through committee. The Bill would have been better framed as legislation for the protection of the public, including the press, rather than a question of press privileges alone. It was duly amended to do this, and became the Public Bodies (Admission to Meetings) Bill after overcoming a filibuster in committee by the Bill's Labour opponents. She was able to make this change, however, only with a grant of government time, which put her more than ever at its mercy. The Bill was duly weakened the longer it was debated. Mrs Thatcher failed to get it applied to all committees with delegated powers, and a House of Lords amendment took all police authorities out of it. Keith Joseph complimented her on her 'cogent, charming, lucid and composed manner' but also said that the measure was 'not ideally suited for a first venture into legislation'.[27] The Bill became law at the end of October. It probably did not make a vast difference to the conduct of council business, but it founded Margaret Thatcher's parliamentary reputation, and gave her and officials the first of the hundreds of bruising encounters which were later to become famous. On the BBC's *Any Questions?* that November, Mrs Thatcher gave two answers born, perhaps, from her recent experience. On the abuse of politics, she said, 'I loathe this modern tendency to try to find a form of words that takes the meaning out of anything that you may say.' When asked about what form her eccentricity might take if she had any, she showed some self-awareness: 'I think the form would take extreme bad temper, sacking everyone through inefficiency and doing everything myself. And it would probably be done a great deal better and a great deal quicker, but I should be miserable as a result.'[28]

'I see according to the Press that Margaret was one of the only three women MPs who voted in favour of "birching",' Alfred Roberts wrote to Muriel

* In the event, this did not happen. Denis had been to Mill Hill; Mark went to Harrow.
† At the time of writing, Carol was not married.

in April 1961, 'but don't suppose voting against the Government will help her much in the party.'[29] Mrs Thatcher had taken part in the standing committee debates on the Criminal Justice Bill. In February, maintaining the view she had put forward as a Finchley candidate, she spoke in support of an amendment from a fellow backbencher, Sir Thomas Moore, which would have restored the corporal punishment for young offenders which Labour had abolished in 1948. She argued that 'the true purpose of punishment' should be 'the protection of the community' and that this protection was now inadequate because the purpose had been ignored by 'our desire for the humanitarian reform of offenders'. She did not believe that rehabilitation always worked: 'Some cases which come before the courts concern persons who are so hardened, vicious and amoral that a much more curative element is needed in the sentence.' This was true of 'the new young type of criminal, who uses violence not for the purpose of robbery, but for the sake of violence, and who takes a pleasure in inflicting violence'. 'I do not agree', said Mrs Thatcher, 'that crime is a symptom of mental disease,' and she went on to argue that, by saying that it was, 'we encourage in him [the criminal] a feeling of self-justification' which meant that 'we may completely blot out all feeling of guilt or shame.' She did not like corporal punishment, she said, but it was 'the only alternative readily available to beat the crime wave in the coming years'.[30]

Alfred Roberts was almost certainly wrong in thinking that his daughter's stand would do her harm in the party. Corporal punishment, at that time, was a touchstone issue among Conservatives, and those in favour of it were popular with the rank and file. In her speech, indeed, Mrs Thatcher was conscious of the opposite problem from that which her father feared, and was at pains to ward it off: 'I do not in any way seek either publicity or promotion by way of rebellion, but I do not think that can stop one from holding sincere views in this matter when I consider that it is necessary.'[31] This slightly odd formulation (what are the occasions when she would *not* have considered it necessary to hold sincere views?) was uttered at a time when party feeling was running quite strongly against the government on this issue. In the vote to which her father's letter refers, Mrs Thatcher was one of sixty-nine rebels, and at the Conservative Women's Conference in the same month, the liberal Home Secretary R. A. Butler was given a hard time about it. It is quite possible, indeed, since the whips sought always to balance opinion, that her promotion to ministerial rank was hastened by this signal that she stood slightly on the right of the party and was prepared to say so. This was the only occasion in her entire parliamentary career when Margaret Thatcher voted against the line of her own party.

The Alfred Roberts who had written to Muriel on the subject was a changed man. In the summer of the previous year, the health of his wife Beatrice had started to give more anxiety. In August 1960, he thanked Muriel for having had them both to stay: 'we are glad to have been able to come down to you and Margaret for the holiday ... for time is getting on with us now.' 'I hope Margaret will be able to relax for a few days now,' he added.[32] The following month, he wrote and described his wife's poor nights, noting too that Mark was just off to boarding school aged seven, and that Margaret had just had central heating installed.[33] At the end of the month, he told his elder daughter that 'Mummy is having another rest in bed today' but that the doctor 'says she's getting better and nothing to worry about'.[34] By the time of his next surviving letter, written on 16 December that year, Beatrice had died.

There is no mention of her mother's death or illness in any of Mrs Thatcher's correspondence (though what survives is certainly incomplete). In an undated letter written roughly in mid-September, she describes to Muriel the problems with the central heating and the hot water, Carol's anxieties about her new school and the difficulty of managing while the family nanny was away. She says nothing about her parents. There is also no record of her seeing her mother after August 1960, though the fact cannot be established for certain since her engagement diaries for that period do not survive.* The only sign of strain, though there could easily have been other causes, such as the burden of parliamentary work, was that Mrs Thatcher fainted in the House of Commons on 24 November. Throughout her career, she was inclined to faint, because of low blood pressure. The *Yorkshire Post*, the only paper to have reported the incident, attributed her minor collapse to overwork.

Beatrice Roberts died in Grantham on 7 December 1960. The family sent out a printed card thanking people for their condolences, in the names of Alfred, Muriel and Margaret. The day before, the *Liverpool Daily Post* published a chirpy piece by Margaret about how to combine family and political work. The woman in politics, she wrote, 'must have a complete fascination for the subject', something which, like being musical or mathematical, is innate, not learnt; 'charm is not enough!' she declared, a woman must also have 'courage and conviction, for without these qualities the

---

* One invalid who did receive a surprise visit from Margaret was her former boyfriend Willie Cullen, now Muriel's husband, who was in hospital in London with lung problems ('I have finished *The Cruel Sea*, the first book I've read since I left school'). 'What a surprise!' he wrote. 'I had your Margaret come in with a bunch of crysants – they cheer up the room ... Margaret looked well, and I told her I don't know how she gets through all the work.' (Cullen to Muriel Cullen, 9 November 1960.)

others are hollow and useless'. At half-term, she added, the children always come to Westminster 'and their greatest joy is to climb Big Ben'.[35] The article reads strangely in the (unmentioned) context of her mother's final illness.

Margaret and Denis invited the widowed Alfred Roberts to come and stay for his first Christmas on his own. From Dormers, he wrote to Muriel 'so that you may know that I am getting on all right'. 'Of course I miss Mummy,' he went on, 'and more so as every one is busy on their different jobs and engagements.' At Dormers, 'it seems lonely for a large part of the day.'[36] On 3 January 1961, still staying with Margaret, Alfred wrote to Muriel to announce his arrival at her house in a week's time. The twins were having friends to tea, he said, 'so I shall come up to my room to escape the din.' That night, he was going to the cinema in Bromley with Denis and Margaret – 'it is one of the very few nights they have free.' Margaret's version of the stay, written to Muriel after Christmas, betrayed growing impatience: 'Re Pop* – he is <u>determined</u> to stay with us both as long as possible. He told Abi† that he dreads the thought of going home. At the moment it is most difficult here as Mark and Carol are sleeping together and both disturb one another a great deal. Added to that Pop tends to wake them both when he goes to the toilet about 5–5.30 a.m. He is eating the most enormous meals and doing absolutely nothing.' With the return of Parliament, Margaret felt that she must move her father on: 'I shall <u>have</u> to shunt Pop off on Saturday 14th Jan . . . Will this be all right with you?' And she recommended that her sister set a clear time for their father's eventual return to Grantham, 'Otherwise he will just hang on and on and not take any hints.'[37]

After he returned from Essex to Grantham, the widowed Alfred Roberts wrote a series of bleak letters to his elder daughter. Not for the first time, he felt sorry for himself, and a little neglected by his younger daughter. 'I am trying to get myself adjusted to the new circumstances which isn't easy, but things are improving,' he wrote on 21 February. 'If I can get through the next four or five weeks I shall have got over the worst part . . . I don't suppose, by the look of things, I shall get any letter from Margaret again this week.' In fact, he was mistaken, but not much comforted, for he wrote again on 1 March, 'Have had a short letter from Margaret, but no enquiries as to how I am getting on . . . She seems frantically busy of course.' He

---

* Margaret's familiar address of her father varied. In later life, she would always refer to him as 'Father', but when he was alive he was very occasionally 'Pop', quite often 'Father', but mostly 'Daddy'. He was never 'Dad'.

† The spelling of Abbey's abbreviated nickname was not consistent within the family.

also mentioned that he had made a new will: 'You and Margaret are Executor and Trustees and also the estate will be divided between you. Any little gratuities to anyone else you will decide.' On 24 March he describes learning how to iron his own shirts and says, 'at the moment I am not feeling quite so lonely.' And on 19 April he wrote to thank Muriel for a birthday present: 'It is good of you to remember me like this. Unfortunately Margaret forgot but expect her mind was all on the Budget that day.' Transferring some of his sense of neglect to others he adds, 'I hope Margaret will remember to arrange for the boys [Muriel's sons] to visit the House of Commons – it will be just too bad if she doesn't do anything about it for it would be such an outing for them.' Perhaps Muriel reminded Margaret about their father's birthday, for a week or so later, Alfred informed her 'Margaret wrote to apologise for forgetting my birthday and has asked me to let her know what to send.'[38]

It would be wrong to say that Mrs Thatcher was undutiful in her behaviour to her father. There were other occasions on which she had him to stay, solving the twins' space problem – and perhaps her own irritation at his presence – by putting him in a local hotel; and in June she, Denis and Mark took him to the Test match.[39] The fact that he noticed a week when no letter from her arrives shows that, in most weeks, she did write. In these months, no letters from Margaret to Alfred survive, but one or two slightly later ones do. These show the busy daughter relating, in friendly though not intimate terms, the latest doings of herself and her family. At the beginning of September 1961 she tells him that she has taken the children to Camber Sands on the Sussex coast and that they have been burgled at Dormers ('I was disturbed [by the sound of their entry] but told myself not to be so silly and that I was imagining things'), losing their jars of sixpences, the twins' birthday money and jodhpur boots.[40] In midsummer of the following year, Margaret tells her father that she has just had a 'most interesting morning' presiding over an international symposium on the rehabilitation of the disabled, that she has a new agent in Finchley ('he talks rather a lot'), and that she has been to Ascot races (a contrast with her visit to the Derby a dozen years earlier which she had concealed from Alfred). She proudly boasts that she has been with Denis to a Buckingham Palace cocktail party. 'The Queen,' she writes with a touch of unconscious self-application, 'has a much stronger personality than most people realise and she is certainly <u>not</u> overshadowed by the Duke of Edinburgh.'[41] But what the whole correspondence – father to elder daughter, Margaret to Muriel, younger daughter to father – suggests is a woman so busy and so keen to get on that her family roots do not interest her very much and her family problems do not engage her imagination. Carol confirmed this, recalling that there was no sense of a Roberts clan, or of a strong influence of her grandfather in her childhood. Her mother 'did not yo-yo up and down to Grantham'.[42] In April 1962, after his birthday, Alfred Roberts wrote to Muriel as in the previous year to thank her for her presents. He mentions that he is going to stay with Margaret the following week, but says to Muriel: 'It is your affection that helps me to stand up against the awful loneliness that sometimes hits me.'[43] It seems unlikely that he wrote a letter of comparable warmth to Margaret at this time, or received one from her. Quite soon, Alfred Roberts married Cissie Hubbard, the widow of a local farmer, and his loneliness therefore ceased to be a problem for his daughters.

Exactly a year earlier, Margaret had given a revealing interview to God-frey Winn, one of the most famous feature journalists of the age, in the *Daily Express*. Winn took the Queen's imminent birthday (21 April) as the cue for his interview, and wrote: 'The woman opposite me on the sofa could not have been born and brought up in any other country except ours. With the Queen she shares not only a birthday year [in fact, she was born in the year before the Queen], but possesses the same flawless, cold-water, utterly English complexion.'[44] He said that he registered Mrs Thatcher – although of course he knew her background – not as a Grantham grocer's daughter but 'as someone from an upper-middle-class background whose husband enjoyed taking her with him to shoot in Scotland'. It is reasonable to assume that Mrs Thatcher had desired this effect (though Denis did not shoot), and had deliberately moved herself a long way from the mahogany counter in North Parade. This context, perhaps, helps to explain her remarkably frank comment to Winn about the mother who had died only a few months earlier: 'I loved my mother dearly but after I was 15 we had nothing more to say to each other. It wasn't her fault. She was weighed down by the home, always being in the home.' There can be no doubt of her desire to escape some of her background, particularly that part which, had she stayed in Grantham, would have circumscribed her because of her sex. To her father, even as she forgot to send him a birthday present, she paid tribute. 'He made me read widely,' she told Winn, 'and for that I owe him everything.'[45]

On 9 October 1961, Margaret Thatcher was offered her first government post by the Prime Minister, Harold Macmillan. With C. M. Woodhouse, who took up a post at Aviation, she was the first of the new intake to be promoted. In his diary's only explicit mention of the future prime minister, Macmillan wrote: 'Mrs Thatcher, a clever young woman MP, and Monty

Woodhouse are the newcomers.'[46]* Mrs Thatcher was also the youngest woman ever to have been made a minister, and the first with a young family at the time of appointment. Her job was parliamentary under-secretary at the Ministry of Pensions and National Insurance. Her salary was £3,250 a year. As had become usual in these important junctures of her life, Denis was away – on an export tour of Africa – when the offer was made. She told the papers that she had not dared cable him with the news before it was made public, so he learnt about it after everyone else.[47]

One newspaper said that 'She was dressed like any other housewife up to town for the day. A cossack hat in coney fur covered most of her fair hair which is just going grey at the temples. She was wearing a green wool jersey dress and a fine two-row necklace of pearls gleamed at her throat.'[48] When Mrs Thatcher saw the Prime Minister on appointment, however, she was, by her own account, smarter still. She wore 'my best outfit, this time, sapphire blue'.[49] And the party took full propaganda advantage of her arrival by putting her on the platform at the party conference in Brighton on the potentially unlucky Friday 13 October, her thirty-sixth birthday. She emerged, she recalled, 'from a royal blue car and wearing a royal blue dress and hat'.[50]

None of this sartorial excitement meant that her job was considered important, or that the party leadership had grand plans for Mrs Thatcher. Her very junior post was one of the few which were, in effect, reserved for women, partly because much of the work concerned pensions for widows. When Patricia Hornsby-Smith had resigned at the end of August, Mrs Thatcher was given strong hints that the job would soon be hers. In her memoirs, Mrs Thatcher records that Macmillan 'characteristically' advised her not to turn up to her new office before eleven o'clock the following morning, adding that she should then 'look around and come away. I shouldn't stay too long.'[51] She does not pick up that his suggestion probably reflected his low opinion of the job he had offered her. Women MPs at that time always ended up with 'the welfare thing'; 'you took a woman in, but you gave her welfare,' Mrs Thatcher recalled, 'either a welfare or education or social services job.'[52] The MPNI post did not interest many men, certainly not the men who aspired to run the Conservative Party. It was an unpolitical job, heavy on detail. Mrs Thatcher summed up its nature in an interview with ITN three days after her appointment: '. . . I think it

---

* Macmillan had been less impressed with Mrs Thatcher when she was first elected: 'The trouble is that none of the women MPs have a real brain' he wrote in late October 1959. 'I can think of none (at present) who could be a Minister' (Peter Catterall (ed), *The Macmillan Diaries*, vol. ii, p. 257).

offers scope both for the human side, which is helping people who are in need of help and also on the financial side and seeing that the scheme is sound.' The job concerned the nuts and bolts of the welfare state. Few people thought this mattered much at the time. Despite her preference for a man's job, especially an economic one, Margaret Thatcher gradually learnt that it did. It taught her how welfare worked, and did not work, and why government spent so much money.

When Mrs Thatcher arrived at the Ministry's office in John Adam Street for the first time, she found her minister, John Boyd-Carpenter,* waiting for her at the front door. Always susceptible to gestures of gallantry, she was impressed. So was Boyd-Carpenter by her. At first he had assumed that her appointment was what would now be called tokenism, or, as he put it, 'just one of Macmillan's gimmicks', but 'I soon found how wrong I had been to harbour such doubts. With her quick trained barrister's brain she mastered quickly the intricacies of National Insurance. And despite the fact that to the male eye she always looked as if she had spent the morning with the coiffeur and the afternoon with the couturier, she worked long and productive hours in the ministry.'[53] That same male eye had, in fact, spotted her talent from the very beginning, but had also been suspicious of it. On her arrival at the Ministry, she had also met the Permanent Secretary, Sir Eric Bowyer, a famously stern Glaswegian. Like Boyd-Carpenter, he immediately granted to Mrs Thatcher a privilege he gave to no other junior minister, probably in deference to her sex. He called on her in her office rather than demanding that she come to him, and always maintained this habit. After they had met her, the two men conferred. What did Bowyer think of her, Boyd-Carpenter wondered? 'She's very able. She will go a long way,' said the Permanent Secretary. The minister nodded grim agreement: 'She's trouble. What can we do to keep her busy?'[54] Mrs Thatcher was invited to make a study of the role of women in the benefits and National Insurance system. Her paper on the subject has not survived. But, according to Michael Partridge, at that time the private secretary to Bowyer, it was an impressive piece of work which foreshadowed the equalizing of the employment, pension and taxation rights of women which Mrs Thatcher was to put into practice in the 1980s.[55] It says something about the attitudes of the time that such a study was considered a dead-end thing to do.

Mrs Thatcher's day-to-day duties, however, concerned detail, not policy.

* John Boyd-Carpenter (1908–98), educated Stowe and Balliol College, Oxford; Conservative MP for Kingston-upon-Thames, 1945–72; Minister of Transport, 1954–5; of Pensions and National Insurance, 1955–62; Chief Secretary to the Treasury, 1962–4; created Baron Boyd-Carpenter, 1972.

The annual reports of the Ministry combine highly technical accounts of changes in the mechanisms of delivery of benefits with occasional specific anecdotes designed to show touches of humanity:

> A pensioner with a double amputation mentioned when attending an Artificial Limb and Appliance Centre that he was in difficulties about buying a pony for his firewood business; the Welfare Officer approached BLESMA (British Limbless Ex-Servicemen's Association) and Queen Mary's (Roehampton) Samaritan Fund, who together contributed a substantial sum for a dapple grey pony.[56]

Mrs Thatcher's first ministerial outing in the House of Commons finds her, among other things, arguing about what constitutes an injury in the course of employment ('Let us take the case of a worker who is going home to lunch when he stops to watch a cricket match and is hit by a cricket ball').[57] In the following week, she clashed with Barbara Castle about whether the 'guardian's allowance' could be used to subsidize voluntary organizations. And she defended – though, according to her memoirs, this was against her private view – the operation of the 'earnings rule' which capped the amount of money which widows could earn when receiving a state pension,[58] displaying a virtuoso knowledge of the detail involved.

Two reactions to the new young minister were noticeable on the part of Mrs Thatcher's parliamentary opponents. The first was what would now be considered a sexist appreciation of her charms. Willie Hamilton, for example, later famous as an anti-monarchist, said during a debate in the Commons, 'We appreciate the honourable Lady's statistics, but we do not like her figures – in the plural.'[59] She seems to have been happy to play up to this banter. In another debate, again on the subject of the cost of abolishing the earnings rule, Mrs Thatcher declared, perhaps by accident, 'I have got a really red-hot figure.' When several Members shouted, 'Hear, hear,' she came back: 'I am very glad that I am not wearing a red dress today. To continue, I have a bang up-to-the-minute figure.'[60] The other reaction was a respect for her debating abilities which shaded into exasperation at her lawyerly tendency to argue a case cleverly through the detail without apparent human feeling. Sydney Silverman, the leading opponent of capital punishment, said of her arguments over a group of women known as 'ten shilling widows', whose husbands had died before 1948: 'The honourable Lady has made a case . . . It is rather an administrative, bureaucratic, actuarial case – some people would call it a third-class insurance company case – but it satisfies her and I am not complaining.'[61] Another Labour MP, John Mendelson, summed up her way of presenting her case (against a Labour motion complaining that benefits had not kept up with inflation) in terms which set the pattern for attacks in the future: 'My impression at the end of the honourable Lady's speech was that all she had given us was a purely academic performance. It was remarkable that she was capable of making a long speech on the tragic position of many of our old people without making any reference whatsoever to her real experience of how they live.'[62] The notion of Margaret Thatcher's heartlessness was born.

In reply to such attacks, Mrs Thatcher was generally polite, but never conceded any ground, sometimes fighting back fiercely. 'The honourable Member will forgive me if occasionally I say "Nonsense" to him,' she told a frequent adversary, Douglas Houghton. 'I am sure he will take it in the right spirit. Nevertheless, I meant it.'[63] On the famous Night of the Long Knives, 13 July 1962, when Harold Macmillan tried to restore direction to his government by replacing seven out of the twenty-one members of his Cabinet, Mrs Thatcher found herself at the despatch box with a sore throat and without a minister because Boyd-Carpenter had just been promoted. She was full of spirit, however, joking that she would refer hostile comments from the Opposition to her minister 'when I have one', and fiercely attacking Michael Foot,* later to be the least successful Labour leader whom she faced, in the debate on the increased rate of National Assistance, as social security was then known. Foot was a 'master of the twist', she said (the dance of that name was just then fashionable), and she sounded a warning, implicitly critical of the policies of the government of which she was a part, that 'Government expenditure . . . over the last three years has been taking an increasing proportion of the gross national product. Honourable Members on this side of the House will not take too happily to that.' Foot's demands for more spending would make things far, far worse, she said: 'If we were to take the advice of eminent economists, coupled with the advice of the honourable Member for Ebbw Vale [Foot], we should have a riot and we would have no Army to quell it.'[64] Boyd-Carpenter noted that, as well as her capacity to extract 'the crucial issue' from 'a huge file bristling with National Insurance technicalities', Mrs Thatcher also showed something more important still. 'I first noted the courage when on the floor of the House of Commons she not only stood up to Richard Crossman† but, for all his formidable intellectual qualities,

---

* Michael Foot (1913–2010), educated Leighton Park School, Reading and Wadham College, Oxford; Labour MP for Plymouth Devonport, 1945–55; for Ebbw Vale, 1960–83; for Blaenau Gwent, 1983–92; Secretary of State for Employment, 1974–6; Leader of the House of Commons, 1976–9; Leader of the Opposition, 1980–83.

† Richard Crossman (1907–74), educated Winchester and New College, Oxford; MP for Coventry East, 1945–74; Minister for Housing and Local Government, 1964–6; Leader of the House of Commons, 1966–8; Secretary of State for Health and Social Security, 1968–70. A

scored off him again and again by the quick and adroit use of facts and figures.'[65] Crossman himself respected her: 'She is rather a pal of mine, I got on very well with her when she was at Pensions ... She is tough, able and competent ...'[66]

To understand how Mrs Thatcher saw her job and, indeed, how the entire welfare state was constructed, one must study three famous pieces of reform, begun in the Second World War, which dominated political thinking at the time and were accepted to a remarkable degree by the main parties. These were R. A. Butler's Education Act of 1944, which developed the split system of grammar school and secondary modern; the 1944 White Paper on Employment Policy, heavily influenced by Keynes, which for the first time made it the government's responsibility to manage the economy in order to maintain 'a high and stable level of employment' (soon interpreted as full employment); and the report by the economist William Beveridge, produced for Churchill's wartime coalition in November 1942, on Social and Allied Services. In the course of her career, Margaret Thatcher was to wrestle unhappily with the first and break almost completely – though she carried it everywhere with her in her handbag – with the second. With the third, however, she never parted company. Beveridge contained what she regarded as a sensible, though in some respects flawed, blueprint for the welfare state. Much less radical in this area than most of her critics supposed, she tried, both as a junior minister and when she came to run the country, to apply Beveridge's principles to the circumstances which then prevailed. When she became parliamentary secretary at MPNI, 'The first step was to re-read the original Beveridge Report.'[67]

Beveridge, who, like Keynes, was a Liberal in politics, sought to provide greater security for British citizens in all the changes and chances of their lives. The state needed to help, he believed, with systems of provision which guarded against 'the interruption or destruction of earning power'. There should be special provision at times of birth, marriage and death. The great increase in longevity meant that there had to be proper pensions for all. His scheme was, he said, 'first and foremost, a plan for insurance – of giving in return for contributions benefits up to subsistence level, as of right and without means test, so that individuals may build freely upon it'. The main vehicle was National Insurance, paid through the worker's weekly 'stamp' from his own wages and the employer's contribution. Its benefits were paid

---

leading Labour intellectual and (later) editor of the *New Statesman*, Crossman caused great public controversy by the posthumous publication of his *Diaries of a Cabinet Minister*. The government of the day unsuccessfully opposed their publication.

out without regard to means. Recognizing that there would be times when people had run out of cover or not been able to contribute to National Insurance, Beveridge also devised National Assistance to answer this need. It was, naturally, means-tested. In addition, he argued that his plan could not work without the avoidance of mass unemployment (hence the drive for the 1944 White Paper), and without reasonable 'free' health care. 'Medical treatment covering all requirements', Beveridge wrote, 'will be provided for all citizens by a national health service organised under the health departments.' Out of this airy phrase, and meriting only a five-page 'assumption' in a 300-page report, one of the most important, difficult and expensive projects of any government ever – the National Health Service – was born.

In planning as he did, Beveridge had a strong, innocent belief in the benign power of the state, but it was certainly not his intention to take away from individuals the incentive to look after themselves and their families, nor from private companies the ability to provide insurance. 'The State in organising security', he wrote in his report, 'should not stifle incentive, opportunity, responsibility; in establishing a national minimum, it should leave room and encouragement for voluntary action by each individual to provide more than that minimum for himself and his family.' One of his main reasons for not means-testing National Insurance was to avoid appearing to penalize thrift. 'Management of one's income', he said, 'is an essential element of a citizen's freedom' and it was 'wrong in principle' for the state to take the burden off insurance: 'The insured person should not feel that income from idleness, however caused, can come from a bottomless purse.' Therefore, when someone did have to be given National Assistance, the 'provision of an income should be associated with treatment designed to bring the interruption of earnings to an end as soon as possible'.

This was easier said than done, to put it mildly. But successive British governments had set themselves the task of trying to do it, and Mrs Thatcher accepted the essential principles of Beveridge. In fact, more strenuously than most, she sought to apply the spirit of the report – that need be answered, but idleness discouraged and independence not crushed. 'The Beveridge Report never meant to oust the voluntary principle,' she said in later years,[68] and this was true. Partly through her Methodist background, she knew something about the rise of voluntary associations of self-help in the nineteenth century, of friendly societies and 'ragged schools', and she was strongly in favour of such community projects, seeing them as the collective embodiment of the principle of 'Do as you would be done by'.[69] But she also believed that the increasing mobility and mass urbanization of British society had meant that not everything could be done by local knowledge and co-operation. Beveridge, in her view, joined up the dots, or, to use a metaphor more common in the debate, provided a floor but not a ceiling. She was and remained in favour of a basic state pension, and she agreed with Beveridge's idea that National Insurance should be exactly that, rather than tax by another name. As for the social problems of welfare, 'The dependency culture', she remembered in the 1990s, 'was not thought of then.'[70] Her attitude to questions of welfare was never one of pure free-marketry or devil-take-the-hindmost. It was more old fashioned, more influenced by the war, surprisingly confident that government was fit for the task. She wanted the state to mobilize to help the unfortunate, and always believed that there was no full private substitute for this, but she always feared two things – that the 'shirkers' would tend to benefit at the expense of the workers, and that the cost, if not carefully controlled, would produce national ruin.*

Mrs Thatcher's job at MPNI was to help to make Beveridge work. She had to deal with 'the difficulties which flowed from the gap between Beveridge's original conception and the way in which the system – and with it public expectations – had developed'.[71] These included the effects of inflation, the low flat rate of the state pension, the punitive effect of the earnings rule and the inevitable clash between the demands of all for higher, non-means-tested benefits and of some for more money in response to particular need. The evidence of Mrs Thatcher's time at the Ministry of Pensions is that she was aware of these problems but that it was above her pay grade to try to solve them. One of the reasons that she so admired John Boyd-Carpenter† is that he had addressed some of the more difficult questions in the field since he took up the job in 1955, notably by allowing people with reasonable private pension provision to contract out of the state earnings-related pension scheme and receive a rebate from their NI contributions. But Boyd-Carpenter was promoted out of MPNI less than a year after Mrs Thatcher joined him, and neither of his successors, Niall Macpherson and Richard Wood, had the desire or the political clout to effect further reform. Besides, the government was in political decline from 1962 and so lacked collective will. Mrs Thatcher's response to these constrictions was to work extremely hard at precise tasks, always bearing in

---

* Although conservative in moral questions, Mrs Thatcher maintained throughout her career a dislike of laying down the law about marital and sexual behaviour, and using the tax and benefit system punitively in this context. This was apparent during her time at MPNI. Opening a home for unmarried mothers and babies in her constituency, she declared that 'It is our job to help and not to sit in judgment' (*Finchley Press*, 24 May 1963).

† She told the House of Commons on 31 October 1969 that Boyd-Carpenter had 'taught me most of what I know about politics'.

mind that the Ministry had already become the second largest-spending government department (after Defence), and that she had to control costs.

Mrs Thatcher spent three years in post, ending only with the general election of October 1964, and she would have liked to have been promoted before then. But she enjoyed the work, and looked back on it as a positive time in her life. She immediately discovered her natural appetite for administration, and found scope for her combative qualities. Unlike Tory grandees, she received an education in the engine-room of government rather than the officers' mess, which proved to be to her advantage. She admired the senior officials with whom she worked, and they admired her too, though, as Clive Bossom, her parliamentary private secretary (PPS)* in 1961, put it, 'they did not love her.' One night, Bossom was with her in the Ministry when she was contemplating a pile of letters presented for her signature. As she read them, she ripped each one at the top of the page. 'I'm not sending these off,' she said, 'they're double Dutch.' Bossom also heard the official's response, out of Mrs Thatcher's hearing: 'Bloody woman. Her job is to sign them, not read them.'[72]

The government machine in which Margaret Thatcher was a minor cog nearly derailed. As early as 1960, inflation and the growth of government spending stoked up the demand for higher wages which produced the 'pay pause' for public employees, the first shadow of the incomes policies which were to weaken government after government until 1979. Economic growth started to slow. In March 1962, the Liberals won an astonishing victory at the Orpington by-election, gaining the seat from the Conservatives with a majority of nearly 8,000. On 14 January 1963, General Charles de Gaulle, President of France, finally rejected the British application, painstakingly negotiated by Edward Heath, to join the European Economic Community or, as everyone then called it, the Common Market. And in June of the same year, John Profumo, Minister for War, had to resign after he was discovered to have lied to the House of Commons about his affair with Christine Keeler, a prostitute who was alleged to have been carrying on at the same time with the Soviet naval attaché. Then, as Harold Macmillan's government started to totter, Macmillan himself fell ill. Stricken with prostate problems, and wrongly advised by a temporary doctor that he could not make a full recovery, Macmillan dramatically resigned on 10 October 1963, just as his party's annual conference met in Blackpool.

---

* The parliamentary private secretary is an MP who is bag-carrier for a minister. His is not a ministerial job, and is unpaid, but is often the first rung on the ministerial ladder. Bossom was the son of Margaret's patron, Alfred.

In this sequence of events, Margaret Thatcher played virtually no part. Her public pronouncements were loyal. She supported Common Market entry, though without any of the high rhetoric of the Euro-enthusiast. For her, it was a matter of access to greater markets. 'To enter into commercial obligations and treaties is an exercise of sovereignty, not a derogation from it,' she told Finchley Conservatives,[73] and she saw the EEC, although it had no declared military aspirations at that time, as part of the defence of Western Europe, especially West Berlin, against Soviet Communism. Her tone on the subject was calm, almost detached. 'The end of the world has not come if we don't go into it, but it would be far better if we did,' she said at a local Finchley 'Any Questions?' in August 1962.[74] She defended the pay pause. As Macmillan came under attack for mishandling Profumo, she described him as 'a man of the highest integrity and honour [who] should not, therefore, suffer for someone whose standards were not as high as his own'.[75] Not even in private did she offer a sustained critique of the Macmillanite direction.

Nevertheless, it is possible to discern the emergence of a distinct set of views not wholly at one with the top of the government. In her only parliamentary speech on the floor of the House before she became a minister, apart from those promoting her own Bill, Mrs Thatcher entered an economic debate, calling for the separate taxation of working women and noting that the current means of controlling public expenditure were inadequate.[76] She tended to take a stand in favour of financial stringency and a refusal to give in to demands for more public spending: 'You would think you were not bringing up your child properly if you said "yes" to everything they asked for. What sort of government would that be?' she asked the Finchley Conservative Women.[77] And in the matter of trade unions, where most ministerial pronouncements were extremely cautious, she made it clear where she stood: 'We are approaching a time when trade union laws ought to be revised.'[78] She also made it clear that she trusted the Old (white) Commonwealth better than the New, and she defended, against considerable protest from Jewish constituents, the right of Sir Oswald Mosley, the fascist orator, to hold a rally in Trafalgar Square. 'If Mosley's meetings are banned,' she told Finchley Tories, 'it means any meeting which the Communists do not like could be banned.'[79] Sitting in a surgery waiting for the doctor to look at Mark's boils, she wrote, exasperated, to her father, 'The constituency correspondence continues unabated with every Jew in the area demanding more curbs on freedom of speech.'[80]

As for the leadership itself, her support for Harold Macmillan was not enthusiastic. In her memoirs, Mrs Thatcher says she was at odds with the Keynesian expansionism of 'Supermac'. This is probably true, if one speaks of underlying beliefs, but there is little evidence that such thoughts were strong in her mind at the time. Her greater concern seemed to be a sense that Macmillan was beginning to fail as a decisive leader, and perhaps a mild dislike of his rather patronizing manner towards her. He was the sort of person, she said many years later in reference to his handling of Profumo, 'who thought things could be dealt with quietly and smoothed over'.[81] She did not mean this as a compliment. In July 1963, she had a party of Finchley Conservative women to tea on the terrace of the House of Commons. While saying that Macmillan could, of course, continue as leader (to say anything else in public would have been treasonable), she dropped strong hints about her admiration for R. A. Butler, applauding his work in sorting out the problems of Rhodesia and Nyasaland (soon to go spectacularly wrong), and praising his 'wisdom of years of experience' and 'terrific capacity for work'.[82] In the same month, Macmillan's PPS, Knox Cunningham, included Mrs Thatcher on a list of four junior ministers who were 'not in full support'.[83] When the leadership crisis broke in October 1963, she initially favoured Butler as Macmillan's successor, preferring him to Quintin Hailsham. 'RAB really had been the think tank,' she recalled, referring to his encouragement of the Conservative Research Department after the war; 'it would have been wrong in a way not to support him ... he'd done so much.'[84]

But in the course of the chaotic party conference which followed Macmillan's announcement of his departure, it became clear that, while Hailsham had overplayed his hand, Butler had underplayed his. Under the system of selecting a Conservative leader that then prevailed, no one, not even Members of Parliament, had a vote. The leader 'emerged' from a process of consultation. Following his successful speech to the conference, and the confidence that he inspired as being trustworthy and disinterested, Lord Home, the Foreign Secretary, began to emerge. Assisted by the fact that Macmillan himself, always opposed to Butler, now had severe doubts about Hailsham, the candidate he had originally preferred, Home's supporters grew in strength and number. Like Hailsham, Home was a member of the House of Lords, from which it was no longer considered possible to lead the Conservative Party, but this was not an insuperable objection since the law had just changed to permit heirs to seats in the Lords to disclaim them.* When Mrs Thatcher saw the party whips on the Monday morning after the party conference, the day after her thirty-eighth birthday, she told

---

* This reform was the result of a campaign by Anthony Wedgwood Benn, later famous as Tony Benn, a Labour MP who was determined to avoid succeeding his father, Viscount Stansgate, in the Lords, and thus sacrificing his political career.

them that she preferred RAB, but 'I was then asked my view of Alec. "Is it constitutionally possible?" I asked. Assured that it was, I did not hesitate. I replied: "Then I am strongly in favour of Alec." '[85] Although it is certain that Mrs Thatcher's view made no difference to the matter, Macmillan did what she wanted, and advised the Queen to send for Home.

Mrs Thatcher had then, and retained, a very high regard for the man who, on ceasing to be the 14th Earl of Home, became known as Sir Alec Douglas-Home. She always referred to him as 'Alec', while never referring to Macmillan as 'Harold', and she respected his judgment, his thoughtfulness and his personal goodness. She believed that the long illness which had kept him out of the war had given him time to deepen his understanding: 'I think he read everything, thought about everything and, as he would start to speak to you, he would speak with a depth, speak not in party political terms, but in depth of the history of England . . . of the United Kingdom and of the Empire.'[86] His only defect in her eyes was his manifest unsuitability for the television age. He 'was an extremely nice person but . . . not one the populace could take to . . . Television isn't kind to some people, although no one ever inspired more loyalty than Alec Douglas-Home.'[87] And although she was disappointed not to be promoted by the new Prime Minister, she was genuinely pleased by his arrival. A month after Home became prime minister in October, she wrote to her father to describe a lunch he had recently given at No. 10 for all his ministers: 'I got two menus signed personally by Alec Douglas-Home for the twins. They were very thrilled with them. I feel certain we shall be happy under the new administration. Home is a much more approachable person than Harold Mac ever was.'[88] Home was, in a way, the sort of man she most liked – someone whose birth might cause him to look down on her, and yet didn't, her ideal of a gentleman. In later years, she reserved particular scorn for the press attacks on Home: 'inverted snobbery is the worst thing. If anyone could accept me, I could accept them.'[89]*

The means by which Home became Tory leader caused mockery and anger among the more radical Conservatives. In a famous article in the *Spectator* on 17 January 1964, the editor, Iain Macleod,† a Tory MP and

---

* Home was tolerant even of her faults. After she became leader in 1975, he would say, 'Undeniably, she is a bossy woman. It's sometimes necessary to stand up for yourself.' (Correspondence with Professor David Dilks.)

† Iain Macleod (1913–70), educated Fettes and Gonville and Caius College, Cambridge; Conservative MP for Enfield West, 1950–70; Minister of Health, 1952–5; of Labour and National Service, 1955–9; Secretary of State for the Colonies, 1959–61; Chancellor of the Duchy of Lancaster and Leader of the House of Commons, 1961–3; Chairman of the Conservative Party, 1961–3; editor of the *Spectator*, 1963–5; Chancellor of the Exchequer, June–July 1970.

former party chairman who had refused to serve under Home, attacked 'the magic circle' of Tory grandees who controlled the process of choosing the leader, an assault which led to a change in the rules of selection of the leader and in the class composition of the party in Parliament. Mrs Thatcher disagreed with Macleod. Although, by her own admission, 'very much on the outside of even the outer ring of the magic circle',[90] she saw nothing wrong in principle with its way of proceeding, believing that the important thing was to get the right man, not how you got him. She did admit that 'the magic circle no longer provided the legitimacy for the men who emerged,'[91] but she was not pleased at its passing. 'It worked,' was her simple view. As for Macleod's article: 'It seemed to me like treachery.'[92]

Douglas-Home's premiership came late in the Parliament, and lasted, in the event, for less than a year, so its chief purpose was to enable Conservative recovery in time for the general election. In this, Mrs Thatcher played an energetic, though not very important, part. She told the people of Whetstone Ward to 'forget that Alec Home is the 14th Earl' (a fact that was constantly used against him by his Labour opponent Harold Wilson) and to recognize him as 'a tremendous patriot' with a 'quite extraordinary ability to see the wood as well as the trees'.[93] She loyally supported the government's record, including measures, such as the establishment of the National Economic Development Council, the National Incomes Commission and selective government help to industry, which she was later to decry.[94] Although clearly on the free-enterprise side of the party, she approached this subject more as a practical-minded, class-based politician than as an economist or an ideologist. 'We should always be wary of socialist promises,' she told Finchley Conservative Women. 'They are usually made with private enterprise money. It is the people, we the middle classes, who will have to pay the penalty of socialism in increased taxes.'[95] When the government, led on the subject by Ted Heath, set out to abolish most of the remaining price controls known as Resale Price Maintenance, Mrs Thatcher supported it, not with the arguments of free-market theory, but with reference to her father's attitudes: 'When small shopkeepers write and say: "I'm afraid it will put us out of business," I can only say that my father would have said the same thing 10 years ago. But Resale Price Maintenance has virtually gone from the grocery trade, and opportunities for small shops have increased.'[96] The grocer's daughter believed in letting business get the rewards of hard work, and was always opposed to heavy state control, but she was much less adamantly anti-protectionist, and the influence of her wartime experience inclined her to think that the state could play a useful role in setting some priorities in the economy. Privately, she was highly critical of Heath's campaign against Resale Price Maintenance, because of its timing. 'Resale Price Maintenance lost us the election,' she said while preparing her memoirs thirty years later. 'It was right, but you don't do it in the last year. Every single little grocer was right against it.'[97] When she later came to overturn the post-war economic consensus she did so because she believed it had failed, not because she had never believed in it in the first place.

When the general election was called for 15 October 1964, the political scientists David Butler and Anthony King chose Finchley as one of the constituencies which they wished to cover in depth for their book about the election.[98] They did so in the belief, which turned out to be erroneous, that Finchley was going to be 'another Orpington', scene of a dramatic Liberal revival under the party's glamorous young candidate, John Pardoe.* The young Bernard Donoughue,† later senior policy adviser to Harold Wilson and James Callaghan at 10 Downing Street in the 1970s, was sent to cover the constituency. His report began with the words: 'Finchley is a sprawling suburb of North-west London whose most striking social characteristics are prosperity, femininity and intellect.' In the borough elections of 1962, the Liberals had swept the board in Finchley and taken three out of five wards in Friern Barnet, also part of Mrs Thatcher's constituency, but had fallen back in the Barnet borough council elections of May 1964. Donoughue described Mrs Thatcher as 'an attractive mother of twins' and 'formidable', with a high recognition factor and the ability to answer questions with 'a barrage of official statistics'. Following the Jewish vote, he noted that a survey of Jews shortly before the election had suggested proportions of six Labour to three Conservative to one Liberal, but that, in the eventual result, the effect of Mrs Thatcher's campaign was to alter the proportions in her party's favour to 2:2:1. Remembering the same campaign more than forty years later, Donoughue said that Mrs Thatcher had seemed 'very intelligent, rather narrow, a little bit nervous . . . a pushy, lower-middle-class businesswoman with a lot of energy and ability'. She presented herself as 'a scientist, barrister and mother of two'. Her face was 'very well made', 'almost Japanese' in its perfection of form: 'No one would have thought "I'm not sure if I can trust her."' He particularly remembered a wet night at a public meeting in a school. Mrs Thatcher 'came in like one

---

* John Pardoe (1934–), educated Sherborne and Corpus Christi College, Cambridge; Liberal MP for Cornwall North, 1966–79; unsuccessful candidate for Liberal leadership, 1976.
† Bernard Donoughue (1934–), educated Northampton Grammar School, Lincoln College and Nuffield College, Oxford; senior policy adviser to Prime Minister, 1974–9; created Lord Donoughue, 1985; Parliamentary Under-Secretary, Ministry of Agriculture, Fisheries and Food, 1997–9.

of the Valkyrie, rolled her raincoat up and tossed it over her shoulder to a man without looking at him.'[99] It was Donoughue's first sight of Denis.

The Conservative candidate fought a vigorous election, conventional enough in its treatment of the issues. 'Prosperity – with a purpose' said her election address, pre-echoing the 'prudence with a purpose' of a Labour chancellor more than thirty years later, and it boasted of how much the government was spending on educational expansion and building new public housing. Donoughue reported that she began the campaign on economic prosperity and ended it attacking nationalization and Labour's defence policies. In order of importance the issues were: housing/land, education/science, defence, and then immigration and trade unions. Labour and Conservative combined to ignore the Liberals where possible. In an interview in the *Daily Telegraph*, Mrs Thatcher paired with a Labour candidate, Joan Lestor, to talk about what women politicians should wear. On hats, she said: 'I enjoy them. But they must have a good line and I can't stand bits and bobs.' On party colour: 'I adore red, but of course I can only wear it at home or on holiday.'* On jewellery: 'I enjoy it, but it mustn't overwhelm the person or the occasion.' On wearing black, she took a position from which she later diverged: 'I used to love wearing black till I turned up at a dinner party in it and found every other woman in it too. It's been colour for me ever since.'[100]

In any event, Mrs Thatcher won. The result was:

Mrs Margaret Thatcher (Conservative)	24,591
John Pardoe (Liberal)	15,789
Albert Tomlinson (Labour)	12,408
Conservative majority	8,802

Mrs Thatcher's majority was nearly halved, and the Liberals did better than in most of the country and Labour worse. But it was no disaster. Pundits, in general, were surprised by how well the Tories fared in the national result. They lost office, but Harold Wilson formed the first Labour government for thirteen years with an overall majority of only four. Mrs Thatcher began her first experience of opposition.

---

* In later life she turned against red. 'Red is too sharp,' she told the present author. Hats, she added, 'complete the picture'.

8

Opposition, 1964–1970

'Running out of other people's money'

Mrs Thatcher had never really known defeat before. True, she had lost both her contests in Dartford in 1950 and 1951, but these were known to have been unwinnable, and she personally had performed very well. The Labour victory of 1964, though narrow and expected, was her first experience of a definite setback in her career – the loss of a job, of power, of the capacity to get things done. She minded this very much, on behalf both of herself and of her country. 'I hated opposition,' she recalled. 'I was not a natural attacker.'[1] This remark reveals a startling lack of self-knowledge, since attacking was one of the things that she did best. But her dislike of opposition was genuine enough. She chafed at the lack of real responsibility. Her own standing in the Conservative Party was secure, but it was scarcely restorative to her spirits to be made the shadow spokesman for the ministry – pensions – which she had previously helped to run. In her analysis of the reasons for the Tory defeat which she developed gradually through the 1960s, she would find the germ of the views which came to full flower ten years later.

But her immediate anxieties were more personal than political. Denis suffered a nervous breakdown. For too long, he had worked too hard. Basil Tuck, his partner in Atlas, remembered that he would often have a drink with Denis in the Black Prince in Bexley at the end of a punishing day, and Denis would not leave to drive home till half-past nine.[2] Now, approaching his fiftieth birthday, Denis had the nearest thing that a no-nonsense, unself-pitying man can get to a mid-life crisis:

> I was working like nobody's worked before ... I was probably drinking a bit too much anyway. What worried me was my mother, my sister and my old aunt who had a fair block of shares in Atlas: none of them had any real money other than that which they could draw out of the company. I was a bit scraped on the deal [that is, he did not have a large enough block of shares himself] ... It seemed to me that the whole depended on the life of one man.[3]

The doctor told him that he must rest completely, and in the autumn of 1964 Denis took a boat to South Africa and stayed there for more than two months. He returned much restored, and went straight off to ski in Lenzerheide in Switzerland, where the family joined him for Christmas and New Year. His time out convinced him that he must spread the load, and later in 1965 he sold his company to Castrol, who immediately employed him. Thus he obtained a capital sum, and a good job. In due course, a further takeover gave Denis a new and even better job, in Burmah Oil.

In later years, Denis would always deny that this crisis had anything to do with Margaret's political career. It is true that he was always scrupulous in supporting her efforts and not interfering with the way she ran her life (he did not inquire about or try to run her personal finances, for example, which, since he was much shrewder with money than she, was probably a pity), but Carol Thatcher records that friends believed that Margaret's absorption in her own career at this time left him feeling isolated.⁴ She believed that, as well as being 'genuinely knackered', 'he didn't like every aspect of being married to a politician.'⁵ He may even have contemplated divorce. Certainly he saw this as a moment of decision about how to lead his life: 'I think he had to make up his mind. That was it.'⁶ In retrospect, it can be seen that the Thatchers were a winning combination. But at the time they more likely saw themselves as a middle-aged, middle-class couple who were working far too hard to enjoy themselves and might not be going anywhere very dramatic in their careers. In Carol's judgment, Denis had not yet achieved a satisfactory role in relation to his wife's career: 'He came into his own later on.'⁷

The twins, who were by this time away at boarding school,* knew of nothing amiss. They were used to Denis's long absences on business trips. But Margaret, naturally, was upset, though communicating this indirectly. Denis remembered: 'She was very worried. She didn't show it, but I think she said it to one or two of her closer friends . . . I think she would say that was a period which she won't like to live through again.'⁸ The episode goes unmentioned in her memoirs, but she herself later recalled:

> Yes, an awful lot depended on him. His sister's marriage broke down after the war, and he had to look after her and his mother as well as us. Eventually, everything came out all right, but for a time your world is upside down. Denis worried because if things matter to you, you don't take them lightly.

---

* Mark was at Belmont, the prep school for Mill Hill, Denis's old school. Carol was at Queenswood in Hatfield. Eventually she went to St Paul's.

It was a very worrying time, but at least I had an income. You must take the doctor's advice on these things and he needed a complete rest. I am very glad to have come through it.[9]

Mrs Thatcher would not be drawn further on the subject, but it seems reasonable to surmise that, when Denis left for South Africa, she had no certainty that he would ever return to her. It was not just that he was exhausted and confused: it was also possible that their marriage would end. If that had happened, her world would, indeed, have been 'upside down'. She would have been alone, without her husband's support and affection, with two children, not enough money, and a career which, given the attitudes of that time, would certainly have suffered. When she said, 'I am very glad to have come through it,' she was implying that she might not have done so. It was the worst personal crisis of her married life.

Tiny hints of her anxiety can be detected in her public pronouncements in this period. In debates in the House of Commons, she more than once brought up her own example as someone who, if widowed under fifty, would not be able to collect her benefit.[10] She cited this almost in jest, as part of a general argument about widows' entitlements and as making the point that her own party did not yet agree with her in the matter, but it does not seem fanciful to find an undertone of anxiety. 'I am rather lonely on this side of the committee in this matter,' she told the House.[11] She was rather lonely at home too. When Denis returned, the strain she had borne caught up with her and, very uncharacteristically, she fell ill, going down with pneumonia. She was not well enough to attend Winston Churchill's lying-in-state at the end of January 1965, and had to watch his funeral on television at home.[12] She was able, however, to offer a tribute to the great man in the *Finchley Press*. As well as the conventional praises of the national hero, she added one or two more distinctive touches. She noted the 'bitter blow' that Churchill had suffered in being dismissed from office in 1945 as soon as he had secured victory in war. And she said how much she liked 'his refusal ... to adopt new-fangled pronunciations of places and names', and admired his 'veneration of great institutions' such as Parliament.[13] Critics who regard Mrs Thatcher as an anti-historical radical tend to ignore her romanticism about Britain's past and her High Toryism about any attacks on the bits of that Britain – Commons, Lords, monarchy, armed services, 'Winston' himself – which she most admired.

Denis's change of job, and the family's greater financial security, allowed the Thatchers to move house. With no work reason any longer for them to live in the suburbs, and with the twins at boarding schools, they sold Dormers and bought a flat, 34 Westminster Gardens, Marsham Street, one of the functional London mansion blocks favoured by MPs, at the beginning of 1966. This ended Margaret's wearisome journey from Farnborough to the Commons. But the Thatchers did not want to lose touch with Kent, and towards the end of the same year they moved into what Margaret misleadingly described as a 'cottage' in the country. It was, in fact, a large, comfortable, rather ugly 'stockbroker Tudor' house, handsomely situated above the village of Lamberhurst and, less happily, the A21. It was called The Mount. Although the twins never came to regard it as home, and eventually persuaded their parents to sell in favour of a house in central London, Margaret and Denis enjoyed The Mount. Denis later remembered their arrival, shortly before Christmas 1966: 'Woke up. Lovely morning. Sun shining. I said: "Come on, love. Let's go to church." Do you know, the vicar was anti-South Africa and anti-Rhodesia! Came out. Said "Thanks very much, padre." Never went back!'[14] Despite this ecclesiastical disappointment, Denis found other pleasures in Lamberhurst. The golf course was visible from the house, and its proximity, and the leisure afforded by the fact that he was no longer refereeing rugby, persuaded him to play the game seriously for the first time. He enjoyed the local pubs, and he and Margaret made new friendships and renewed others. Among those who lived near by and visited them were Margaret's Oxford friend Edward Boyle, the party's education spokesman, and Robert Henderson, her most serious love before her marriage. Another neighbour, the satirist, controversialist and late-in-life Christian Malcolm Muggeridge, first met the Thatchers in this period, and began to exercise some intellectual influence upon her.

Margaret pursued her strong interest in buying antiques. In the 1950s, one day in Richmond Park, she had lost a tie-pin with two sapphires mounted upon it, a present from Denis, and since then she had preferred spending money (though not much)* on furniture and, above all, porcelain, which she enjoyed displaying in the cabinets for which The Mount afforded room. 'I was after colour,'† she remembered, and she bought Crown Derby, Worcester and Coalport. She became quite a familiar sight in the bric-a-brac shops of Tunbridge Wells and Wadhurst and the converted chapel

---

* To the end of her days, she remembered her extravagance in paying £66 in the mid-1950s for a lacquered cabinet with mirrors. Long after her memory for the details of political events had faded, she remained minutely accurate about what she had collected, where she had bought it and what she had spent on it.

† Mrs Thatcher's taste in porcelain was always for what was bright and perfect. When she became secretary of state for education, the Victoria and Albert Museum (for which she was responsible) supplied her with an 1840s Spode dessert service in bright pink. She complained that the pieces looked very dirty and demanded that they be cleaned. In fact, the 'dirt' was black spotting from original firing difficulties which could not be removed. (Correspondence with Dame Rosalind Savill.)

selling antiques on the A21 at Whatlington. Her strong home-making instinct had greater rein than before, and she felt relief that the financial and marital worries of 1964 were past. In the Labour landslide of 1966, it was Denis's turn to comfort her, rather than the other way round. He bought her an eternity ring 'because I was down in the dumps', which she wore for the rest of her life.[15]

Although Alec Douglas-Home had led the Conservative Party to a more successful election result in 1964 than many had predicted, Iain Macleod's attack on the magic circle had hit home, and many Tory MPs did not believe that Home should lead them into the next general election unless it were a snap one called within months of the previous contest. In late June 1965, Harold Wilson announced that he would not seek a dissolution that year, and so the Conservatives felt they had time to effect the change. Moves were made privately to push Home out, and in late July he decided to step down without a fight. This greatly surprised and upset Mrs Thatcher, who had known nothing of the plotting. She complained to the whips, saying, by her own account, 'Why didn't you tell us? We would have supported him.'[16] She believed, mistakenly, that Home's wife, Elizabeth, 'just couldn't stand it any longer' and she was angry at what she thought was the press misrepresentation of Home and their obsession with what she called 'knickerbockers on the grouse moor'. She was grateful to Home for his kindness to her, and she perhaps intuited that she would experience less of this quality from a successor more or less from her own generation.

The candidates for the first balloted Conservative leadership election ever held were Reginald Maudling,* Edward Heath and Enoch Powell, none of them from the patrician background of the Macmillan–Home era. Of the three, Powell was to prove by far the greatest influence on Mrs Thatcher, but there is no evidence that she considered voting for him. Although respected for his intellectual brilliance and eloquence, Powell, who had once resigned from office and twice refused it, was already viewed as a maverick. The choice, in the view of Mrs Thatcher and most of the parliamentary party (the sole electorate under the new rules), was between Maudling and Heath. Mrs Thatcher knew both men because of constituency contiguity. Heath's seat at Bexley had been next door to her when she stood in Dartford, and Maudling sat for Barnet, which bordered Finchley.

---

* Reginald Maudling (1917–79), educated Merchant Taylors' and Merton College, Oxford; Conservative MP for Barnet, 1950–79; President of the Board of Trade, 1959–61; Colonial Secretary, 1961–2; Chancellor of the Exchequer, 1962–4; Home Secretary, 1970–72; Shadow Foreign Secretary, 1975–6.

Initially, for no discernible ideological or political reason, but simply because she found him the more charming, Mrs Thatcher preferred Reggie Maudling. He was not really her type, though, being fat, lazy* and, as he had shown as the Chancellor of the Exchequer at the end of the last Conservative government, a natural overspender. So it was not very difficult for Keith Joseph, already the senior Conservative to whom she was closest, to persuade her to change her mind. He told Mrs Thatcher that Ted Heath had 'a passion to get Britain right',[17] a phrase which she was dutifully to use about him in public for years afterwards. She followed Joseph's advice, and voted for Heath. Remembering the 1965 leadership election in her memoirs, Mrs Thatcher says that Heath had 'swallowed a good deal of the fashionable interpretation of what had gone wrong in the world between the wars'. He feared nationalism whereas she feared 'the appeasement of dictators'.[18] But this, though a largely correct analysis of the eventual difference between the two, played no part in Mrs Thatcher's attitude to Heath at this time. She instinctively disliked his gauche manners and his uneasiness with women, but she respected his political seriousness and she liked his father, a down-to-earth character from a lower-middle-class small-business background quite like her own.[19]† She weighed the candidates fairly dispassionately and decided, without overwhelming enthusiasm, that Heath was the best. After what, by modern standards, was an enviably short campaign of less than a week, Heath won by 150 votes to Maudling's 133; Powell received 15 votes. Mrs Thatcher was probably giving a true account when she wrote in the *Finchley Press*, shortly after it was all over: 'The decision was a difficult one to make for both are good. We are all now working hard and happily under Edward Heath. He will be a tough taskmaster, but will only drive others as hard as he drives himself.'[20]

The tough taskmaster's first assignment for the MP from Finchley was a shift from pensions to a post as shadow spokesman on housing and land. This move was made on 15 October, two days after her fortieth birthday and on the same day as her first platform speech to the party conference. She used this occasion to deliver a competent but cautious speech on the domestic subject which was eventually to cause her more bother than anything else – the rates, as local government property taxes were then called.

---

* Mrs Thatcher, who generally eschewed what she called 'personal remarks', put it more gently, even in private: 'Reggie had a first-class brain but he didn't bestir himself as much as he should have done' (The Thatcher Papers, Churchill College, Cambridge, THCR 4/4).
† She later felt that Ted Heath had abandoned his father's common sense in favour of a more pompous, clubby Tory milieu.

'It is very difficult', she said, unringingly, 'to find a method of reform which would result in less hardship than the system we already have.' She opposed wholesale change, a version of which, many years later with the community charge (the so-called poll tax), she was to embrace. She sensed that the party conference wanted more than she had given them.[21]

In the six years of opposition, Mrs Thatcher held six shadow posts. The first three were as a junior spokesman – for pensions, then housing and land, then Treasury affairs – the second three in the Shadow Cabinet – dealing with fuel and power, transport and finally education. Some of these she liked more than others, being rather bored by transport and excited by economic policy, but common characteristics are visible in all her different guises. The first is that she could absorb almost any amount of detail and argue it through late-night sittings in the House of Commons. At a time, much more markedly so than today, when a politician's reputation depended on performance in Parliament, Mrs Thatcher again and again impressed her fellow MPs with her combativeness and her industry. Even the mighty could be made to tremble. In a debate on the Rating Bill less than two months after she took up the housing portfolio, she pleased colleagues by exposing her clever and famous ministerial opponent Richard Crossman in his ignorance of what did and did not count as reckonable income.[22] She was not witty like Iain Macleod, or intellectually original like Enoch Powell; she was not yet a star, but she was a worker and a fighter in a party which was slightly short of both. Nothing she did in those years brought her into the innermost circles of the Conservative Party, but virtually everything she did improved her reputation. She was given the opportunity to stretch out beyond the subjects traditionally handed to women MPs in both main parties, and she took it eagerly. Even earlier than her Labour opponent, Barbara Castle, Mrs Thatcher broke out of the parliamentary female ghetto. When, for example, she savaged the government's Selective Employment Tax in parliamentary debate on 5 May 1966, an admittedly partial Iain Macleod declared that this was the only 'triumph' he could ever remember a woman scoring in the House of Commons.[23]

The second noticeable characteristic is that Mrs Thatcher took advantage of every brief she was given to pursue a common political theme. Strong though she was on the detail, most of the time she articulated a purpose beyond it. She could see the onrush of socialism and she set out to resist it without apology. It would not be true to say that she was developing a 'Thatcherite' ideology which consciously diverged from the policies of Edward Heath, but it is certainly the case that her temperamental aversion to retreat and compromise came to the fore. She thought that Britain had done very well for most of the years of Conservative government and was now faring miserably under socialism. In Parliament and in the constituencies, year after year, she untiringly preached a gospel of economic freedom and opposition to the creeping power of the state. In 1965, one finds her deploying what was to become a favourite phrase, to Reading Conservative Women: 'Every Labour government we have had has foundered on money and they have always succeeded in running out of other people's money.'[24] In her election address of 1966, she warned that a second Labour administration would 'increase the power of the State at the expense of the subject'. In 1968, she told the readers of the *News of the World* that 'When it comes to economising, housewives have to, because the Government won't.'[25] And in the following year she declared to the Motor Agents' Association annual dinner: 'I wish that we in this country were prepared to praise personal success and to make it worthwhile tax-wise . . . It is not where a person comes from that counts, but where he can get to.'[26] She said 'he', but by 1969 she had already got further than any Conservative woman in history.

Like most front-rank politicians, Mrs Thatcher wasted little emotional energy on ill feeling towards her political opponents. She liked Harold Wilson, for example, describing him as 'very wily but very kind'.[27] She was on good terms with the rabble-rousing left-wing MP Eric Heffer,* whose Christian sincerity she respected, and she greatly admired most of those former coalminers who often sat in the House for mining seats, especially James Griffiths from Llanelly. She always liked Labour MPs who stood up for what she called the 'underdog'. But her hatred for socialist doctrines was absolutely genuine, and it gave her the necessary energy to develop her views and advance them vigorously. Harold Wilson's first two administrations, which ran from 1964 to 1970, accepted almost uncritically the idea that the state could control what the left liked to call the commanding heights of the economy. George Brown, Wilson's defeated rival for the leadership, was put in charge of the Department of Economic Affairs, invented by Wilson to assail the traditional dominance of the Treasury. Brown duly produced a National Plan ('a blueprint for inflation' in Mrs Thatcher's eyes), which purported to predict and direct all the main areas of the British economy. One of the means for this direction, and the one which it fell to Mrs Thatcher, as shadow housing and land spokesman, to oppose, was the proposed Land Commission which would control the price of development land. She quickly spotted that the minister responsible,

---

* Eric Heffer (1922–91), educated Longmore Senior School, Hertford; joiner; Christian Socialist; Labour MP for Liverpool Walton, 1964–91; Shadow Cabinet, 1981; left-wing candidate for Labour leadership, 1983 (came third). Mrs Thatcher attended his memorial service.

Fred Willey, 'did not understand a thing' about his own legislation, and harried him mercilessly. Her hatred for arbitrary state power, her interest in the rule of law and her tenderness towards property owners all came together. She told Willey that his Bill and its proposed levy overrode individual rights 'to an extent which we never thought would be introduced by any government in peacetime' and she protested at the chancy application of the tax: 'It is impossible even for a valuer coupled with an accountant and coupled with a barrister to say what amount of levy would be chargeable.'[28]

In the middle of her campaign against the Land Commission, Mrs Thatcher was moved by Heath into the area which she had always most desired, economic affairs, though only as the deputy Treasury shadow. Her boss was Iain Macleod. She was not close to Macleod ideologically, but she admired his political and rhetorical skills and his readiness to close with the enemy: 'Iain was the best *politician* I ever remember . . . he always understood that politics is a question of alternatives.' 'He chose me to do the hard work,' she said, and she happily filled the gap left by his lack of interest in policy detail.[29] Only two weeks after taking up her post on 19 April 1966, Mrs Thatcher found herself debating Labour's proposed Selective Employment Tax in Parliament, up against Jack Diamond, the Chief Secretary to the Treasury. As its name suggests, SET was a payroll tax; it sought to take money from some industries, mainly services, and redistribute some of it to others, mainly manufacturers. Its motive was both to raise more revenue, because economic growth predictions were proving overoptimistic, and to attempt industrial management. Its process was astonishingly complicated, collecting, as Mrs Thatcher later worked out, £1,130 million and then handing back £890 million of it within industry.[30] 'What the Chancellor wants to do', she explained in her first debate on the subject, 'is to pay 7s. 6d. a week in respect of employees in manufacturing industry. Why cannot he just give the industries 7s. 6d. a week? . . . I really think that the right hon. Gentleman needs a woman at the Treasury. This is just sheer stupidity. If my chief had come to me and put up a cockeyed scheme like that, I should have asked him if he was feeling all right.'[31] Mrs Thatcher then seized the moment to launch into a general denunciation of the thinking behind the Bill: 'Personally, I dislike permanent subsidies and the premium paid back to industry will in fact be a permanent subsidy . . . Of course, the Chancellor will be very popular with inefficient industries, but I do not wish to be popular with inefficient industries. I would rather be popular with the efficient . . . The inefficient benefit from them [subsidies] because they keep them in business when they ought to go out of business.'[32] This way of talking was notably bold, strongly against the grain of the times.

All through the summer of 1966, Mrs Thatcher attacked. She used the voice of the plain-speaking housewife: 'So once more the married woman who goes to the butcher, grocer and dry cleaner and then, when she is finished and wishes for a little pleasure, to the hairdressers, will find that prices are going up.'[33] This was not mere populism. Mrs Thatcher was working to what would now be called an agenda, and it was a feminist one. She noted that the tax system discriminated against married women because it simply added their income to that of their husbands rather than taxing them separately, and the problems would be compounded by SET because it punished the service industries, in which women were dispro-portionately employed, and created the same tax liability for a part-time woman worker working nine hours per week as one working the full forty-two hours.[34] She also assaulted the system, since abolished, by which estate duty was charged to widows, and she supported an amendment to give tax relief on maintenance payments to divorced or deserted mothers: 'I do not know how any man can stand at that Dispatch Box and recognise that family allowances on a man attract earned income relief yet say in the same breath that a woman who looks after her children does not deserve earned income relief on maintenance payments. He must be a very curious creature indeed.'[35]

In one debate, Mrs Thatcher launched into another housewife analogy: 'It is as absurd to use the Standard Industrial Classification for the purpose of selective employment payments as it would be to use a clothes washing machine for washing up crockery,' she said. At which point, Jack Diamond rose to intervene. Mrs Thatcher: 'The right hon. Gentleman is not so good on clothes washing and dish washing machines as I am, so he had better sit down. But I will give way to him if he wants me to.' Poor Diamond stuttered: 'I am terrified. I was only about to make a simple point . . .'[36] Later in the year, she used a similar technique to ridicule the government's growing attempt to regulate the growth of prices and incomes. She took the example of prices for women's fashions: 'One cannot control the price of a garment which has a mini-skirt in July, but a skirt four inches below the knee in January. I doubt very much that the President of the Board of Trade [Douglas Jay] would even notice the difference.'[37]* Such aggressive, if almost flirtatious, rhetoric was deployed to drive forward an essentially radical approach to taxation, more radical than most commentators have noticed. Mrs Thatcher was saying not only that tax was too high (income tax had now reached a top rate of 19 shillings and 3 pence, there being 20 shillings in the pound – that is 96.25 per cent). She was also questioning

---

* She was wrong there. Jay was known to have a marked interest in short skirts.

the entire wisdom of those who tried to run the British economy. They were wrong, she argued, and people who had nothing to do with government were much more likely to be right. More radical still, she was saying that women, through work, motherhood and marriage, understood more about the effects of taxation and inflation than the men who inflicted both. By implication, she was challenging not only the Labour government but the established order of things in both parties.

It was part of her skill in charming her party that her male colleagues in Parliament mostly enjoyed her approach rather than being frightened of it. At the highest levels of the party, however, suspicions were aroused that the rise of Margaret Thatcher might represent some sort of threat to male peace and tranquillity. Jim Prior,* later to become her dissident secretary of state for employment, has recorded that Heath considered the question of promoting her to his Shadow Cabinet after Labour's landslide at the general election of March 1966. In a meeting between Heath and William Whitelaw, the Chief Whip, Prior, who was Heath's PPS at the time, recommended Mrs Thatcher for what, by his own account, they all regarded as the 'statutory woman' slot: 'There was a long silence. "Yes," he [Heath] said, "Willie agrees she's much the most able, but he says that once she's there we'll never be able to get rid of her. So we both think it's got to be Mervyn Pike."'[38]† From their own point of view, Heath and Whitelaw were right. In 1975, Mrs Thatcher would beat first one and then the other in the contest for the party leadership.

Although Mrs Thatcher, kept out of the Shadow Cabinet for the time being, naturally chafed at the 'statutory woman' role, she also understood how to take advantage of it. Press and public interest in a woman in politics was high; and BBC Radio's *Any Questions?*, then the most influential current affairs discussion programme, was always in search of a woman to enliven the panel, and could rely on Mrs Thatcher to do so. Through this and other media appearances, she began to establish a marked public persona, appearing on *Any Questions?* ten times between 1966 and 1970. In these appearances, she never missed an opportunity to speak up for her sex, often to the disparagement of the male. To a questioner who complained about the 1966 World Cup taking up too much attention, she answered that those thus distracted were mainly men and so 'the women can get on

---

* James Prior (1927–), educated Charterhouse and Pembroke College, Cambridge; Conservative MP for Lowestoft, 1959–83; for Waveney, 1983–7; Minister of Agriculture, 1970–72; Leader of the House of Commons, 1972–4; Shadow Employment Secretary, 1974–9; Secretary of State for Employment, 1979–81; for Northern Ireland, 1981–4; created Lord Prior, 1987.
† Mervyn Pike was a woman.

and do the job in their absence.'[39] Asked whether judging a woman's intelligence by her legs could be applied to a man (a typical question of the
programme in that period), she replied: 'I really only ever look at a man's
head to see whether he's intelligent, and so often the answer is that he's not,
that one doesn't to look any farther.'[40] She knew exactly how far to go in
referring questions about women and their advancement to herself. To a
question about equal pay for the sexes, she said that she wondered whether
equal opportunity would still be withheld: 'there is an awful tendency in
Britain to think of women as making excellent Number Twos, but not to
give them the top job.' Another panellist, the broadcaster Kenneth Allsop,
cut in to suggest the possibility of a woman prime minister. Mrs Thatcher:
'Well, I wasn't quite thinking at that level.'[41]

Mrs Thatcher was always careful not to let the 'woman' persona degen-
erate into the mere character-acting that has ruined many a career in
British public life. Money and economics, about which women were traditionally held to be ignorant, were her strong suits. Always well briefed,
she talked seriously and intelligently, if not always originally, on serious
subjects. The frequent accusation of humourlessness does not do justice to
her readiness of repartee, her flirtatiousness and her ability to act up, but
seriousness, in one of her background, was something of which to be
proud. In one edition of *Any Questions?* she found herself up against her
country neighbour Malcolm Muggeridge, then at the height of his powers
as a public contrarian. A questioner asked what the panel felt about being
imitated. Muggeridge, who, by the way, was highly imitable, replied that
all people were 'intrinsically ridiculous'. Mrs Thatcher: 'This is a ridiculous
answer.' Muggeridge: 'Why?' Mrs Thatcher: 'You don't regard yourself as
an intrinsically ridiculous person.' Muggeridge: 'I do. Why are you contradicting me?' Mrs Thatcher: 'Because over dinner you took yourself
extremely seriously.' Muggeridge: 'You don't imagine you're a serious
person.' Mrs Thatcher: 'Well, I do. You may not.'[42]

And when it came to the moral and social questions which were so hotly
argued through the 1960s Mrs Thatcher found her sex an advantage, giving her stronger, more practical ground, in any dispute. In all her views,
she liked to refer, both in private and in public, to the individual example
or experience which she found persuasive. Her support for the legalization
of abortion, for example, came from the suffering she had observed of a
severely handicapped child of Bertie Blatch, her constituency chairman in
Finchley. The boy, she remembered, had often asked his parents 'Why
me?',[43] and this led her to believe that abortion of those with severe genetic
defects was the kindest course. Her backing of the liberalization of the
laws against homosexual acts derived from her observation of cases which

she had seen as a barrister, which she considered a humiliating intrusion into privacy and a waste of court time.[44] On the other hand, her experience as a mother made her instinctively hostile to the permissive society presided over by the Home Secretary from 1964 to 1967, Roy Jenkins, whom she privately referred to as 'shaky jowls'. She supported Mary Whitehouse's condemnation of pornography, and said that the 'average woman' feared sexual licence and drugs for her children. In a radio argument with Paul Johnson,* then the left-wing editor of the *New Statesman* and later one of the most enthusiastic converts to the right, she declared that 'I ... fail to see anything civilised about allowing ... the sexual act to be shown on the stage in a theatre,' and she countered Johnson's exhortation to relax, let everything happen and then life would settle down: 'I think as a legislator you have to legislate to try to retain the good standards and the best things in your society.' If all people were religious and good, you wouldn't have to, she said, but they weren't.[45] It was a similarly dark view about the persistence of human wickedness which inclined her to maintain her support for the death penalty. As for divorce, she opposed the additional liberalization of the 1960s which allowed automatic divorce after five years' separation, on the grounds that it would make it too easy to desert a woman.

Only once in this period, at the Conservative Party conference in Brighton on 10 October 1969, did Mrs Thatcher agree to take a prominent party platform to put forward her views on women's questions. The subject was nothing to do with her Shadow Cabinet portfolio, which was transport, but the organizers wanted a leading woman to promote the new policy document *A Fair Share for the Fair Sex*, an embarrassing title about which she publicly complained. Her opening was typical: 'I think it was Socrates who said long, long ago that when woman is made equal to man she becomes his superior, and I would not dissent from anyone as wise as Socrates.' Then she teased a councillor who had spoken from the floor against female emancipation: 'He said that women get married and have children, but men do not. This must upset the statisticians somewhere.' She then attacked the idea that housewives should be paid for the work that they do, joking that 'The husband would very soon be bankrupt' and arguing that nothing should be done to disturb the wife's right to support. In a sentence which summed up so much of her attitude to life, she declared, 'Equity is a very much better principle than equality.'[46]

*

---

* Paul Johnson (1928–), editor of the *New Statesman*, 1965–70; author of innumerable works of history.

Harold Wilson called a second election for 31 March 1966 in order to improve his slender majority. He won a second term as Labour prime minister easily. His new majority was ninety-eight. Since there was a strong public mood to give Labour more time and a bigger mandate, little blame attached to Edward Heath, who had been leader for only eight months, although this was the worst defeat for his party for more than twenty years. At his party's conference that autumn, Heath put new heart into the troops. 'Ted Heath went over really big,' wrote Margaret to Muriel, 'and has quite suddenly turned out to be human again. I was at a cocktail party in his suite when he overheard someone wish me a happy birthday. To my amazement he stopped the party and made everyone drink a toast to me! Maybe the champagne had an effect on him too.'[47] This is the only recorded instance of personal warmth between the two in parallel political careers lasting half a century. Margaret's tone shows that, even then, it surprised her.

Mrs Thatcher's own election campaign in Finchley had gone well. She warned in her election address that Labour 'would increase the power of the State at the expense of the subject' and she made much of the unchecked power of the trade unions, saying that 'we could delay no longer' the review of trade union law which had not taken place for sixty years.[48] 'A dislike of being dictated to is one of the more fundamental British characteristics,' she wrote in the *Finchley Press*.[49] She tapped into the economic anxieties of her constituents: 'Inflation means cheating the thrifty out of part of their savings.'[50] And she did not forget to emphasize her housewife side, telling the feminist Jill Tweedie (of all people): 'I've got a housekeeper but I still do the cooking myself . . . rush in, peel the vegetables, put the roast in . . . all before I take off my hat.'[51]

The question of British entry into the European Economic Community was revived, both because it reflected Heath's genuine enthusiasm for the project and because he hoped to exploit Labour divisions on the subject. Mrs Thatcher spoke up too, thinking in the terms of making 'Europe' a world power which she was later to deride. 'Europe has become a cornerstone of our campaign,' she told an election meeting. 'You will be aware of Mr Heath's [earlier] efforts to get us into the Common Market. Many of the difficulties facing us then [1963] no longer exist . . . I believe together we could form a block with as much power as the USA or Russia.'[52] But even in this campaign there was a hint of suspicion underlying her Europeanism: 'I don't like the idea of a Europe without us there, directing and guiding its powers.'[53]

The Liberal vote, nationally and in Finchley, fell sharply, so that Mrs

Thatcher, though winning fewer votes than on the previous occasion, increased her majority by 662. The results were:

Mrs Margaret Thatcher (Conservative)	23,968
Mrs Yvonne Sieve (Labour)	14,504
F. Davis (Liberal)	13,070
Conservative majority	9,464

Although the Labour victory was huge, economic problems closed in upon Harold Wilson's government. Inflation, wage rises, high government spending, low government revenues and an unfavourable balance of payments bore down upon the administration, resulting, eventually, in the devaluation of the pound from its fixed rate of $2.80 to one of $2.40, on 18 November 1967.* Mrs Thatcher was moved from her shadow Treasury brief in the month before the final collapse, but from the 1966 election until then she had a ringside seat, and she used it effectively to heap obloquy on Labour's head. Three things particularly struck her about what she witnessed. The first was the way that economic and financial difficulty diminished the personal credit of political leaders. Harold Wilson, she believed, was exposed as a trickster: 'The Prime Minister's problem is that Britain's creditors now understand him perfectly,' she told the House of Commons on 26 July 1966. The lack of trust meant that no specific remedy could work its effect: 'They are not judging the measures themselves; they are judging the set of men, headed by the Prime Minister, who brought them into operation.'[54] Her deputy villain in this set was the Chancellor of the Exchequer, James Callaghan. If, to Mrs Thatcher, Wilson was devious, Callaghan was incompetent. SET was brought in, she asserted, because the Chancellor got his forecasts wrong.[55] 'You can't say he has lost command of the situation – he never had it.'[56] Invited to give a platform speech at the Conservative Party conference in Blackpool that October, she hinted criticism of past Tory governments, saying that the tax burden under them had been 'high enough in all honesty'. She then announced the results of her careful study of all post-war Budgets to show that three of the four highest-taxing Budgets ever had been introduced by Jim Callaghan. 'This chap Callaghan', she told the cheering audience, 'must go.'

Her second lesson was to find her anxiety for the rule of law, and for clarity and due form in law-making, confirmed. Alert to the drafting of Bills, she always noticed when a clause was obscure, or gave the authorities

---

* General de Gaulle rubbed salt in the wound by again refusing British entry to the EEC, nine days after devaluation.

arbitrary power, or covertly changed the purposes of a tax. She quickly spotted, for example, that SET would break the rule which as a minister she had overseen, that National Insurance should perform the purpose for which it was named; SET showed 'the unwisdom of using the National Insurance system as a means of raising general revenue'.[57] It also gave arbitrary powers to the Ministry of Labour to decide who would get a rebate and who a penalty. The introduction of wage freezes, she believed, was also unfair. It meant that employers could not keep faith with promises they had already made to employees, and so undermined the sanctity of contracts. Bargains freely made were nullified: 'It is the first step on the journey to coercion.'[58] As individual 'prices and incomes orders' were laid before Parliament, Mrs Thatcher could fasten on the absurdity of individual situations to illustrate her point. In January 1967, the Rockware Glass Company wanted to pay a promised increase to its thirty-four maintenance engineers in their extra payment for keeping the furnaces going continuously. Mrs Thatcher angrily scorned the bureaucratic idea that to permit such a case would have 'repercussions': where was the rule of law if workers and bosses could not make and stick by their own agreements?[59] Again and again, she criticized prices and incomes policy for its inequity: 'It used to be a civil offence to break a contract, now it can be a criminal offence to keep a bargain.'[60]

Her third and most important lesson from her period as Treasury shadow, but also from her entire experience of the six years of opposition, was about the state's role in the economy. She had always believed that nationalization, high taxes and government interference were bad. Now she saw the car-crash she had predicted happening before her eyes. The government, she felt, was little better than a robber: 'the Government dislike[s] the fruits of investment going to those who supply the money to invest.'[61] It did not see that profits were good, representing the successful common interest of labour and capital. She said that Callaghan's 'message to all who work is "If you make it, I'll take it"'.[62] And she was not frightened of standing on moral high ground about taxation: 'Members of the Government have talked about social justice. There are many ways in which one can be socially unjust. One of them is to take away too high a proportion of anyone's income.'[63] She argued that tax avoidance (as opposed to evasion) was perfectly justified, indeed essential when rates were high. Clashing with Eric Heffer, who accused her of complaining about the top rate of tax although it affected only a very few people, she was unabashed: 'The honourable Gentleman is quite right. We are concerned with a comparatively small group of people, I do not deny that, but I say that the future of people in industry depends tremendously on the small group of people who can create more wealth, and they are far more valuable to the ordinary working person than those of us who work here, including the honourable Gentleman, who cannot.'[64]

Her dislike of tax led her to develop the idea, later so important in her attitude to housing, that tax relief was a far, far better thing than cash subsidy. Subsidy, she wrote in the *Building Societies Gazette*, 'implies that all income is ultimately vested in the State', whereas relief 'rightly enables people to keep *more of their own money* with which to discharge their own responsibilities'.[65] She went further, arguing that, because tax was where the shoe pinched each citizen, revolts against it were the main engine for British liberty. She told the Conservative Party conference in Brighton in October 1967 that:

> freedom has been gained in this country – not by great abstract campaigns, but through the objections of ordinary men and women to having their money taken from them by the State. In the early days, people banded together and said to the then Government, 'You shall not take our money before you have redressed our grievances.' It was their money, their wealth, which was the source of their independence against the Government. This is crucial.[66]

*

On 10 October 1967, ten days before she spoke in this vein to the party conference, Edward Heath at last gave Mrs Thatcher the recognition he knew was due to her talent, and promoted her to the Shadow Cabinet, as shadow minister for fuel and power. She was up against a minister, Dick Marsh,* whom she knew from Dartford days, and whose charm, good looks and relatively right-wing views endeared him to her. It indicates something of where she stood in the political firmament that, earlier in the year, a *Sunday Times* 'Spot the Prime Minister' magazine feature about rising political talent had given Mrs Thatcher's odds as 1,000–1, whereas Marsh was favourite at 5–1.[67] Nevertheless, she was now well known, well respected, popular with the party rank and file, and sufficiently trusted by the leadership to be asked to tackle subjects that went beyond her shadow portfolio. This last point was particularly important to her, as she did not want to lose touch with the wider economic debate from which she had learnt so much. She entered the Shadow Cabinet without any access to the confidences of the leadership, nor any notable influence on its ideology, nor any clear independent power base. Yet it was also clear that she was formidable.

---

* Richard Marsh (1928–2011), educated Jennings School, Swindon, Woolwich Polytechnic and Ruskin College, Oxford; Labour MP for Greenwich, 1959–71; Minister of Power, 1966–8; of Transport, 1968–70; chairman, British Rail, 1971–6; created Lord Marsh, 1981.

At fuel and power, Mrs Thatcher became more closely acquainted with the constraints under which the Conservative Party operated at this time. Although it found it easy to attack extensions of state ownership, it was much more uncertain about what should be done with those industries which were already state owned and run. Nationalization was not unambiguously unpopular with voters, and the Conservatives laboured under the belief that most of the industries involved would be unsellable, a view which reflected the overall weakness of the private sector at that time and an underlying lack of confidence in the future of free markets. In the same party conference speech, therefore, in which Mrs Thatcher was so robust about tax, she was more circumspect about nationalization. Positioning herself as someone with 'deep philosophical reasons' for opposing nationalization, she then added a caution: 'we must accept that many people judge these things purely upon the practical results, so let us start adopting that approach.' Privatization (as it was not then called) did not at present offer ready answers because 'No one will buy a rotten enterprise.'

Already in the 1960s, coal was the most contentious of the matters in the fuel and power brief. It still employed the largest numbers of men – more than 300,000 – and great swathes of its production were uneconomic. It also held a special place in the aristocracy of labour, one which Tories respected and feared from what they hoped was a safe distance. Mrs Thatcher's first encounter with it in her new post, however, was in a narrower but deeply emotional context. In October 1966, a coal-slag heap at Aberfan in Wales had slipped, engulfing a school and killing 116 children and 28 adults. A year later, the House of Commons debated the report of the investigating tribunal. Aberfan was an issue too painful for normal political argument, but Mrs Thatcher was struck by some of the lessons that emerged. She said she was shocked that the chairman of the National Coal Board, Lord Robens, had not gone to the scene of the disaster at once. She noted that the NCB's director-general of production had been given a report about the state of the coal tips but had not read the material. 'I despise any organisation or person', she told the House, 'who attempts to pass the buck further down the line,' and she added that 'It is a jolly sight easier to exercise control in private industry.'[68]

When she appeared on *Any Questions?* in Wales the following month, Mrs Thatcher described the report as 'the most damning indictment of a management that I have ever read', and she took the occasion, in answer to a question from an Aberfan bereaved mother, to give her view of the future of coal: '. . . I don't think coal-mining as such is on the way out. I think it will be reduced in amount, the uneconomic pits will go', and then it would revive.[69] Later in the month, in the House of Commons, she elaborated her views. She argued that the production target of 200 million tons was too high and that 'The future policy is undoubtedly to plan for a contracting coal industry.' The Central Electricity Generating Board's preference for coal, enforced by government, was very expensive, she said, and would be made more so by the Coal Industry Bill. If public money was to be spent, it would be better used closing more pits and helping unemployed miners get new jobs. Although her main case was economic, she made a moral one as well. Three miners were killed each week at work and there was a high incidence of industrial disease: 'if one were given a choice one would not send a son down a pit. I would not do so . . .'* She renewed her criticisms of the NCB: 'While the numbers of miners in the industry are being run down, the number of people on the Board is being put up. If a private enterprise did that, all hon. Members opposite would have a fine old time debating against me.'[70] Always the housewife, Mrs Thatcher never forgot to consider the effect of government fuel and power policy on the consumer. Attacking Barbara Castle in Parliament about rising prices in general, she turned to the cost of electricity: 'My bill is up. It came with a nice little apologetic note, but that does not alter the fact that it is up by 15 per cent, 3s. in the pound. This was another increase which was not referred to the Prices and Incomes Board.'[71] Although she and Keith Joseph did fantasise in this period about splitting power-generating capacity into three as a prelude to privatization,[72] Mrs Thatcher and her party did not come up with a plan for coal, and had no inkling of how the pits would eventually provide the political battleground on which Ted Heath would founder and she – much later – would triumph. All that is notable about her approach at this time is that she rejected the mystical approach to coal which was still so pervasive in British political culture.

Now that she was in the Shadow Cabinet, Mrs Thatcher began to show the first signs of developing an overall, publicly argued political position of her own. Her first big opportunity to present this came with the invitation to deliver the Conservative Political Centre Lecture at the party conference in Blackpool in October 1968. The CPC Lecture was the most

---

* Mrs Thatcher's rhetoric was notable for the number of times she mentioned hopes or fears for her children, particularly her son. A poignant example from this period comes from her speech to the North Finchley and Whetstone British and Foreign Bible Society (see *Finchley Times*, 28 October 1966 (http://www.margaretthatcher.org/document/101296)). In it, she spoke of the extreme horror of the death or serious illness of one's child and mentioned Aberfan. She praised the beauty of the language of the Authorized Version of the Bible ('the most beautiful piece of language that exists') and said that one of her favourite passages in the Bible was David's lament for his dead son, Absalom. It is clear from the way she speaks that the passage hit home because it led her to imagine her feelings if her own son were to die.

prestigious fringe meeting of the conference. The person asked to give it was thus marked out as a coming man, so this was Heath's way of saying that Mrs Thatcher was a coming woman. Indeed, it was on the subject of women's rights that he invited her to speak, but she rejected this with something approaching scorn. 'Ted said would I do "women in politics",' she remembered. 'I thought that was much too dull.'[73] She boldly told the *Daily Mirror* at the time that she had refused the subject of women – 'They've been around since Eve, you know.'[74] She chose instead the all-embracing title 'What's wrong with politics?'

To understand Mrs Thatcher's resolute unfashionableness throughout her career it is worth noting what she was doing at any particular time and compare it with what was happening elsewhere. Thus, on the day of John F. Kennedy's assassination in 1963, she was opening a charity bazaar in her constituency and attending a Rotary Club dinner. In the summer of 1968, when the Western world was turning on, tuning in and dropping out, and the Soviet Union was invading Czechoslovakia, she was sitting at The Mount, Lamberhurst, studying the thirty or so works of Conservative political philosophy, including the writings of Karl Popper on the open society, which she had got out of the library in preparation for her lecture. This was her first effort at organized philosophizing, and, unlike her later productions, it was her own entirely unaided work.

Some have criticized Mrs Thatcher's CPC Lecture for being rather naive, even plodding. Certainly its use of extensive quotation has a clumsily autodidactic feel, and her enumeration, point by point, of the seven reasons why the public now distrusted politicians was an uncomfortable survival of her barristerial training. But the lecture is interesting all the same for setting out many of the main beliefs that animated her, most of which were to matter more and more as the years passed. She herself recognized the lecture's importance, both intellectually and politically. She delivered it in a gold brocade coat-dress which she had deliberately chosen to attract the greatest possible amount of attention.[75]

The lecture attributed the growing distrust of politicians to a mixture of factors as various as the disappearance of independent Members of Parliament, more instant news on television and an increasingly disrespectful society. Her remedies were more coherent. 'I believe', she said, 'that the great mistake of the last few years has been for the government to provide or to legislate for almost everything.' The Tories themselves had not been guiltless. In the early 1960s, 'the emphasis in politics shifted.' At about that time 'growth' became the key political word and the contest between the parties became too much about economics, not enough about people. Those who promised the most through governmental agency seemed the most attractive, and so Britain entered into the era of national plans and then prices and incomes policy to control inflation. Now, she went on, there were calls for more 'participation' by the voter, but this was no good if it meant participation in more government decisions, rather than 'making more of his own decisions'. The trend was so bad that on incomes policy Conservatives and Labour sounded 'almost indistinguishable'. Governments could not run prices or incomes: 'we have too little regard for the essential role of government which is control of the money supply and the management of demand.' Governments had been paying for expenditure by 'printing the money'. Enter, for the first time, Thatcher the monetarist. The whole idea of 'keeping down incomes' made little sense to her, she continued: 'There is nothing wrong with people wanting larger incomes,' but the 'condition precedent' was 'hard work'. If people could keep more of what they earned they could contribute more to the general good, Mrs Thatcher said, and she used an image of which she and her supporters in later years would never tire: 'The point is that the Good Samaritan had to have the money to help, otherwise he too would have had to pass by on the other side.'

She ended with a call to Conservatives. She said that it was a distinctive and admirable feature of the British parliamentary system that there was no automatic consensus. An 'alternative policy' was always on offer, rather than a futile 'attempt to satisfy people holding no particular views about anything'. She ended by sounding the trumpet for conviction politics while blowing her own at the same time. At a recent university meeting, she said, 'a young undergraduate came to me and said, "I had no idea there was such a clear alternative." He found the idea challenging and infinitely more effective than one in which everyone virtually expects their MP or the Government to solve their problems. The Conservative creed has never offered a life of ease without effort.' Here the voice of Alderman Roberts in the pulpit was coming through. 'Democracy is not for such people. Self-government is for those men and women who have learned to govern themselves'. 'No great party', Mrs Thatcher concluded, 'can survive except on the basis of firm beliefs about what it wants to do.'

While there was certainly nothing disloyal in anything Mrs Thatcher told her Blackpool audience, it was nevertheless quite an artful performance politically. Her speech tapped into a growing unease about Heath's approach, a questioning of the merely technocratic leadership which tried to minimize all ideological differences and failed to offer an alternative account of economics or, indeed, of the purpose of government itself. It marked the speaker out as a person of principle, and of combative conviction. It also positioned her carefully in the rows within the party over its most controversial figure, Enoch Powell.

Earlier in the year, Powell had finally broken with Heath. Always stiff-necked and solitary, always far more intellectually original than his colleagues, Powell had carved out an increasingly distinctive place in the Conservative Party. When the leadership had leant towards centrism and corporatism, Powell had produced eloquent attacks on the idea that industry and government could successfully improve the British economy by working hand in hand. He had developed, too, the doctrines of what came to be called monetarism and heaped scorn on the idea that prices and incomes policies could control inflation. A heretic on defence, on which he was the party's shadow minister, he had raised questions about the effectiveness of nuclear deterrence and had suggested that Britain should withdraw its military presence east of Suez. There had been rows between him and his fellow frontbenchers, and Powell felt that he was being sidelined in the Shadow Cabinet, but it was on none of these subjects that the great break came.

In Birmingham, on 20 April 1968, Powell spoke to the city's CPC in a speech that he chose not to clear with Heath in advance, and which appeared to break a Shadow Cabinet consensus on the subject reached ten days earlier. That subject was immigration. Powell quoted a constituent of his who had told him that he wanted to leave Britain because 'in this country in 15 or 20 years' time the black man will have the whip hand over the white man.' Using the Registrar-General's projections for the growth of the immigrant population and its descendants, he declared: 'We must be mad, literally mad, as a nation to be permitting the annual inflow of some 50,000 dependants ... It is like watching a nation busily engaged in heaping up its own funeral pyre.' He attacked the Labour government's coming Race Relations Bill as the means by which the immigrant community would be able to 'agitate and campaign against their fellow citizens', and he ended with his vision of the apocalypse: 'As I look ahead, I am filled with foreboding. Like the Roman, I seem to see "the River Tiber foaming with much blood".'

Margaret had always been an admirer of Enoch Powell, ever since first meeting him in Essex in the late 1940s. The two were not personally close, partly because Powell was awkward in the company of women, and did not approve of women in politics, but they were on friendly terms, the two couples dining together occasionally. Always an admirer of intellectual attainment, and surprisingly humble about what she considered her own lack of it, Mrs Thatcher was in awe of Powell's brain ('His intellect was second to none') and drawn to his arguments. In later years she said, 'Enoch got us on to the right argument about inflation.'[76] She had never been deeply interested in questions of immigration, although such views as she had expressed in public were in favour of tight control of numbers. She considered it an 'irony' that Powell himself had admitted many immigrants, when he had been minister of health, to work in British hospitals.[77] On the Sunday morning when Powell's speech was reported in the newspapers, Ted Heath rang round Shadow Cabinet colleagues to tell them that he proposed to sack Powell. By her account, Heath said to Mrs Thatcher: 'Enoch must go.' She replied, 'Ted, I wouldn't heighten what he said too much,' recommending that he leave time for things to cool down. But Heath replied: 'No, no. Most people think he must go.'[78] Go he did, never to return to the front bench.

It was never likely, of course, that such a stripling member of the Shadow Cabinet as Mrs Thatcher could have dissuaded Heath from his chosen course of action, and the evidence does not suggest that she tried particularly hard to do so. The moment was significant for her, nonetheless. She contrived, without any disloyalty, to make it clear in party circles that she was quite sympathetic to Powell and, when invited to criticize him in the ensuing months, rather than doing so she would simply say how much she hoped that he would put forward his views in party forums. In her CPC Lecture, she prayed in aid the name of Enoch Powell, but she did so to point out the limits of private provision. Hospitals, she argued, were something the state could provide and the citizen could not, and she quoted Powell's ten-year hospital plan as minister of health to that effect. This was a cunning way to link herself with the great rebel: the leadership could not complain, and yet the link had been made. As the general election of 1970 approached, Mrs Thatcher continued quietly to maintain the connection with Powell. On the second night of the Selsdon Park Conference to hammer out the party's pre-election programme, on 31 January 1970, instead of dining at Selsdon with the Shadow Cabinet she chose to attend part of a dinner of her Finchley association at which Powell was the guest of honour.[79] She later publicly defended the invitation to the rebellious Powell, on the grounds of freedom of speech and because he had spent his 'war years in distinguished service in the Forces'.[80] During the 1970 election campaign itself Powell made a series of speeches about the 'hidden enemy within' – the leftist agitators, including the future Labour Cabinet minister, Peter Hain, who were trying to stop the South African cricket tour in Britain because of their opposition to apartheid. When the Home Secretary, Callaghan, who had been moved to the post after the devaluation of 1967, finally decided to stop the tour, Powell denounced him, feverishly comparing the capitulation to the sinking of *Repulse* and *Prince of Wales* in 1941, for having 'surrendered the rule of law to buy off the demonstrators'. Heath's office privately described the speech as 'fascist'. The journalist Andrew Alexander, a close associate of Powell, happened to call on Mrs Thatcher at home on 13 June to discuss the election campaign. She asked him to come with a copy of the *Evening Standard* which reported the speech. She read it and then said to Alexander: 'I agree with every word of it.'[81] Powell's phrase 'the enemy within' was one that, when she became prime minister, she did not forget. Much later, she was to make it famous and controversial as her description of the extremist leadership of the National Union of Mineworkers.

Margaret Thatcher, the crypto-Powellite of the CPC Lecture, began to attract wider attention. She was seen as a respectable voice of the Tory right. In the spring of 1969 the *Daily Telegraph* published pieces by her, called 'Consensus – or choice?' and 'Participation – in what?'[82] By then the party's reluctant transport spokesman, Mrs Thatcher ranged over far wider issues. Developing her CPC themes, she launched into further criticism of the Tory record: 'we were not as successful in controlling public expend-iture as we might have been, we were slow to get on to trade union law reform, we left surtax* too high and estate duty at confiscatory levels.' She attacked the consensus which 'would be to do nothing' and argued for 'the Right-wing approach, which is to increase the private sector'. Her attack on the chatter about 'participation' was that, in practice, this meant yet more politics. She preferred solutions which kept people clear of politicians and state power; 'it is important that young couples purchase their own home as early as possible. The chances are that they will never then come to be dependent on the State.'

There is every reason to think that Mrs Thatcher was sincere in her beliefs. They were newly articulated, perhaps, but she had always privately held them. They also helped her career. The Powell effect had been to threaten a split between the rather centrist, consensual and sometimes *de haut en bas* party leadership and the rank and file, who wanted more clearly Conservative positions. Mrs Thatcher could offer the rank and file some comfort. Combative and right-wing, and, through her sex and back-ground, a figure from outside the establishment, she put fire in Tory bellies without any threat of disloyalty to Heath. It was therefore fitting and sym-bolic that, when, in October 1969, her old Oxford friend Edward Boyle, dispirited by what he saw as the rightward drift of the party under the pressure of Powellism, resigned as education spokesman to take up an academic career, Mrs Thatcher should succeed him.

Like most British people of her generation, except for those who had served in the forces, Margaret Thatcher had travelled abroad very little. She first

---

* Surtax was the high rate of income tax on the top earners.

visited Continental Europe on her honeymoon, and her subsequent visits had largely been confined to skiing holidays. She had never been to the United States, or outside Europe at all. Denis travelled extensively on business, particularly in Africa, but the demands of career and children never gave her the time to accompany him, even if she had wanted to. Political or government business had not taken her abroad. In the period of 1964–70, this changed. Her growing seniority, and the freedom offered by opposition, allowed her to travel more. In those years, her foreign trips included visits to Israel in June 1965, to Sweden in 1968, to the Soviet Union in 1969 and to the United States in February–March 1967 and March 1969.

Her eight-day trip to Israel, the natural result of Jewish connections in Finchley, made a strongly favourable impression upon her. She toured the whole of the country and admired the purposeful activity everywhere. 'They don't pay people for being idle in Israel,' she reported,[83] rather implying that, nearer home, they did. And her Christian sensibility was moved by seeing the sights that Jesus would have seen: 'I stood on the shores of the Sea of Galilee.'[84] She reinforced her uncomplicated belief that Israel was a good country which wanted peace with its neighbours: 'Israel holds out the hand of friendship to all who will accept.'[85]

By far her longest and most important visits, however, were to America. The first, the more significant, lasted for nearly six weeks, the second for a month. Her first trip was on the State Department's International Visitor Program, a large-scale scheme, which exists to this day, to give prominent non-US citizens an extended opportunity to get to know the country. The programme paid all travel expenses and a per-diem living allowance of $25. Mrs Thatcher had been nominated for it by William J. Galloway, first secretary and political officer at the US Embassy in London, whose job was to cover British politics, particularly the Conservative Party. He noted her 'very strong will', her 'high standards of ethics and morals' and her rising political star.[86] In August 1966, when Mrs Thatcher was shadow Treasury spokesman, Galloway drew up a list of matters that he understood she wished to pursue on her trip, which she approved. Her main interests were listed as financial and economic matters, social security, insurance, industry and women's organizations. She expressed a particular wish to meet 'some women members of the Congress' and to 'gain impressions of the political atmosphere in various parts of the United States'.[87]*

---

* In a later draft, Galloway also reported that Mrs Thatcher would like to meet John Kenneth Galbraith, the guru of liberal economics, who had just delivered the BBC's Reith Lectures. This desire was not to be fulfilled.

Mrs Thatcher left London on 20 February 1967. The original plan had been for Denis to accompany her. Denis was always interested in America but, in the end, he decided that he could not afford to be away from his business for such a length of time. So Mrs Thatcher travelled alone. Her trip began, as was customary, in Washington DC. As was also customary, given the political orientation of the State Department, she was steered towards people to the left of her own views. She rushed through innumerable meetings in the capital. She met Senator Joseph Clark, a liberal Democrat who attacked President Johnson's record in Vietnam, and Margaret Chase Smith, the first ever woman to be elected to both the House of Representatives and the Senate. Her most prominent interlocutor was to have been Walt Rostow, then President Johnson's National Security Advisor, but Rostow passed her on to his deputy, Francis Bator, at the last minute.[88] To Rostow, Mrs Thatcher was an Opposition MP, who was not yet even a member of the Shadow Cabinet. Understandably, he decided his time was better spent elsewhere. No record survives of the content of her meetings. But according to John Campbell's biography, her meeting with senior officials of the International Monetary Fund showed that 'she did not always know how to behave' on such occasions: 'A senior [British] Treasury official serving in Washington was horrified by the way she lectured the Director of the IMF, Pierre-Paul Schweitzer – a languid, cigarette-smoking French intellectual of the type she had probably never encountered before – on subjects he knew far more about than she did – and altogether behaved "like a bull in a china shop".'[89]*

In fact, as she went round the country, Mrs Thatcher appears to have known perfectly well 'how to behave'. One of her hosts wrote to an official at the US Embassy in London to say that she was 'undoubtedly one of the most delightful and competent visitors we have had. She has charmed and impressed local sponsors from coast to coast.'[90] She visited the Du Pont chemical factory in Wilmington, Delaware, and was impressed by Palm Beach, Florida, when staying in Delray near by. She then headed north to Atlanta, where she was struck by the progress in civil rights for blacks, and

---

* Campbell notes his source for this story as 'private information', but since the only British Treasury official present at the lunch with Schweitzer was Douglas Wass, it seems reasonable to assume that the 'information' was his. Wass was permanent secretary at the Treasury when Mrs Thatcher first came into office in 1979, and was believed to have taken an equally dim view of her economic policy. When the present author interviewed him, he was less critical of her handling of Schweitzer. She had only a 'superficial knowledge' of the procedures of the IMF, but this was neither surprising nor discreditable. The cynical, worldly-wise Frenchman was simply 'the antithesis of her'. (Interview with Sir Douglas Wass.)

by the white mayor who told her 'I have no time to hate.'* In Houston, the NASA manned-spacecraft centre, with its wealth of cutting-edge technology, enthused her more than anything else in the entire trip. She was shown round by John Hodges, a former constituent of hers, now lost to the 'Brain Drain' which, she believed, Labour's tax policies had created. From Houston, she flew to San Francisco, sending a card to her sister Muriel saying that 'This is the most beautiful of them all.' Shocked to hear that most visitors just wanted to see the hippies, she went out to the redwood forests and was shown round a school, where she found the American children 'very, very articulate', and the Kaiser Foundation Hospital. In Los Angeles, she visited the NBC Color City, where she witnessed what she called the 'genuine artificiality' of the first colour-television studio in the world. She went also to the Strategic Air Command at Omaha, Nebraska, which prompted her to reflect that 'American casualness is misleading. There is nothing casual about their science and technology'. In Chicago, she saw the grain-trading market known as the Pit. Then she flew east, meeting the great economist Paul Samuelson, who was working on the control of inflation, at MIT. Thence to Montclair, New Jersey, which was twinned with Finchley, and finally to New York City, whence she flew to Albany for the day to meet the state Governor, Nelson Rockefeller, who was later to become Gerald Ford's vice-president.[91] Mrs Thatcher's sponsors' reports for San Francisco and New York survive. The former found her 'an extremely charming person, was very enthusiastic about her visit to the Bay Area'. The latter said that the people she met 'could hardly bear to part with her'.[92]

As she travelled, Mrs Thatcher gave speeches and interviews, of which a few were reported. The *Houston Post*, with a byline from the 'Women's staff', began: 'A gracious lady member of British Parliament pulled on velvet gloves when quizzed Wednesday about English trade with North Vietnam.' Mrs Thatcher defended this trade. Someone at the Houston press conference asked if the Common Market would bring ruin to Britain. '"Nothing will bring ruin to Great Britain," Mrs Thatcher replied briskly. "The Common Market is political as well as economic . . . if we went in for political reasons – the concept of a united Europe or prolonged peace – I believe we should."' She said that sterling's weakness was caused by excessive public spending, but the *Houston Post* described her as one 'who approves of the Keynes theory of economics because "we've found none better"'.[93] Almost nothing in her programme, or in her published thoughts, indicated much of the political figure that she would become.

---

* The mayor, Ivan Allen Jr, was echoing Atlanta's self-adopted mantra as the city 'too busy to hate'. Atlanta was one of the earliest US cities to develop an affluent and influential black middle (and upper) class, which drove integration deeper and faster than elsewhere.

Mrs Thatcher's own feelings about her visit were uncomplicatedly positive. Despite her fairly prominent position in British politics, she behaved
essentially like an energetic tourist rather than a politician dealing with
professional counterparts. Indeed, it is notable that Heath felt that he could
afford her absence for so long, and that he appears not to have charged
her with any political tasks. She was slightly dismayed at first. Grace Belt,
who managed her trip in New York, reported that when Mrs Thatcher
arrived in Washington she 'was perturbed not to have known in advance
what hotel she was staying in, had not realized that we would not have
planned her evenings and did not know that the second day would fall on
a holiday . . . I gather she felt pretty lonely during that time.'[94] She also had
not expected Washington would be hot and had to rush out and buy a
couple of summer dresses.[95] But, apart from this, she loved virtually every
moment of her trip. She was receptive and charming, and was charmed
and well received in return. She enjoyed American courtesy, American
warmth and American technology, business know-how and political culture. Her reactions contain little depth, plenty of clichés; nothing about
them suggests that she was looking for anything very specific in the way
of politics, ideas or contacts. Essentially, she approached the country with
the innocent optimism of the first-time visitor, and was not disappointed.
In her memoirs she wrote, 'The excitement which I felt has never really
subsided.'[96] This was the simple truth. She loved America, felt at ease there
and wanted to go back.

But she certainly took back political lessons from her trip. From that
time on, her speeches began to draw on American examples, often contrasting them favourably with the situation in Britain. Within months of
her return, she spoke, on different occasions, about the joys of America's
simple tax forms for low earners,[97] of its methods for reviving the coal
industry[98] and, in her CPC Lecture, of its concern to protect personal
privacy from government computers. Above all, she noticed the contrast
between a society with bearable tax rates and free markets, and the alternative: 'The maximum rate of tax on personal incomes in the United
Kingdom is 91.25 per cent . . . and for a married couple with two small
children it starts at an income of £18,900. The same marginal rate in the
United States . . . is 60 per cent, and it does not start until an income of
£77,000.'[99]

Her next visit to the US took place at the request of the English Speaking Union (ESU), a non-political association dedicated to strengthening
links among English-speaking people around the world, who invited Mrs
Thatcher to deliver a series of lectures. Ted Heath was reluctant to spare
her from the political fray at home in the course of 1968, so the trip even-

tually took place in March 1969, which meant that she missed the conference on the first draft of the party's manifesto for the next general election. Before she set out, she had to clear up a few troublesome logistics. The first problem was financial. 'Mrs Thatcher is not in the least grasping,' a London-based ESU official minuted her US colleague, 'but I gather from her secretary, (in Confidence) that the last time she visited the United States on a Leader Grant, she had occasionally to walk from A to B as she had not been provided with any money, or the wherewithall [sic] to take any form of transport, and in some cases her hotel bill was not taken care of. I have naturally assured the secretary that Mrs Thatcher will be very well looked after.'[100] A second issue concerned her preferred form of address: '. . . Mrs Thatcher has asked me to say . . . that as a member of parliament in her own right, she likes to be described as Mrs Margaret Thatcher MP although she is not a widow. She noticed that Mrs D. Thatcher had been put on the itinerary . . . Perhaps in all future communications to your branches you could tell them this.'[101] Mrs Thatcher toured America once more. She had two setpiece speeches for the ESU, delivered on several occasions across the nation. One, called 'Challenge to Democracy', appears to have recapitulated some of the themes of her CPC Lecture. The other, 'Preparing for the future: Britain and America', 'explains the special relationship between our two countries in the past and its relevance to the future. It discusses the tendency towards nationalism and separatism in the nations of the world, and its significance in the coming years. Bearing in mind the inability of each nation to impress its theories on others, each pursues its own ends. What can we do as nations to solve these problems?'[102] It is a pity that neither speech survives. All we know about them is the ecstatic reaction they or, perhaps more likely, Mrs Thatcher's personality engendered: 'She came, She saw, She conquered!' wrote the secretary of the ESU's central Florida branch to HQ in New York, making the nomenclatural mistake in her excitement, 'which, of course, can only mean one person – the stunning Mrs Dennis [sic] Thatcher . . . There were 150 members and guests present, and each and every one was charmed not only by the speaker's good looks but her very brilliant talk.'[103]

When she paid her first visit to the Soviet Union in 1969, therefore, Mrs Thatcher had a clear standard of superpower comparison. She travelled with her fellow Conservative MP, Paul Channon,* later a minister in her

---

* Paul Channon (1935–2007), educated Eton and Christ Church, Oxford; son of Sir Henry 'Chips' Channon, MP and political diarist; Conservative MP for Southend West, 1959–97; Minister for the Arts, 1981–3; Secretary of State for Trade and Industry, 1986–7; for Transport, 1987–9; created Lord Kelvedon, 1997.

Cabinet, and his wife Ingrid. Although an official guest, as opposition transport spokesman, of the Soviet government, she took a tip from a colleague and paid her own fare to make herself less beholden to her hosts. She visited the Kremlin, where she said that when her hosts asked her if NATO had not become irrelevant, she replied 'Certainly not.' She went to Moscow University and to GUM, the huge Moscow department store with 'pathetically little in it'.[104] She had lunch at the Soviet Academy of Sciences and demanded to see inside churches, which were purged of all religion. In Moscow, her interpreter showed her a sculpture of a man beating a sword into a ploughshare. 'That's communism,' he told her. 'It's not, you know,' she replied. 'It's the Bible.'* She travelled by train from Moscow to Leningrad (as St Petersburg was then called). There she was shown the docks, and a housing block where she noted that the people ate communally and there was little scope for family life. Even her taste for dry facts was exhausted by the 'endless statistics of production' recited by her hosts. Visiting one of the palaces on the edge of the city, she fell into conversation with an attendant. She asked him where his family was. 'In America.' 'Wouldn't they like to come back?' 'Oh, no, no, no.' As she boarded the plane for home, she remembered thinking to herself, 'Oh, the relief!'

When Heath made Mrs Thatcher his shadow education minister on 21 October 1969, he was pitching her into an area where Conservative principles seemed to conflict with what many real live Conservatives actually wanted. The difficulty lay in the comprehensivization of secondary schools, which was by then happening fast. This was the process which abolished selection at the age of eleven, and got rid of the 1944 division between grammar schools, attended by the more intellectually able, and secondary moderns, which educated the less academic majority. It was natural for Conservatives to favour the continued existence of the grammar schools. They represented excellence, they benefited from the exercise of parental choice, and they were the best ladder of advancement ever devised for bright children from poor backgrounds. Both Mrs Thatcher and Heath himself were classic products of the grammar school meritocracy. 'People like me', Mrs Thatcher remembered in the 1990s, 'had to have access to grammar schools so that we could compete with people like Shirley Williams.'[105]† But two great difficulties presented themselves.

---

* This story is told slightly differently in Lady Thatcher's memoirs, though the variations are not important. She was often imprecise in her memories of incidents, long before she suffered a loss of memory, due to small strokes, in the late 1990s.

† Shirley Williams (1930–), educated at eight schools in UK and USA and Somerville College,

The first was that state education at that time was largely out of the hands of the central government. Under the provisions of R. A. Butler's 1944 Education Act, which was esteemed by all parties, local education authorities, chosen from local government, decided on the provision of schools, and teachers decreed what went on in them. The arrangement was known as 'a national service locally delivered'. The role of Whitehall was an arm's-length one of paying for new school building and negotiating and paying – via grants to the local authorities – the salaries of teachers. This distance from schools themselves was treasured, and no one seriously attempted to overthrow it. As early as the 1950s, the comprehensive ideal had gained ground, and the very first comprehensive experiment, in 1957, was conducted by Leicestershire County Council, which was Conservative controlled. The Labour Party developed a fiercely ideological commitment to comprehensives, and translated this into central government pressure, but even without this the trend to comprehensivization was considered unstoppable. By the time Mrs Thatcher took up her position, almost a quarter of children were already in comprehensives, and all but about 30 of the 163 education authorities had submitted plans to comprehensivize. No central government, therefore, had the power to reverse this without new legislation and a battle with local government. Besides, the great majority of the local education authorities were Conservative controlled.

The other problem for the Conservatives was numerical. Just under a fifth of all children attended grammar schools. The parents of those who did not were much less satisfied, and much more likely to favour a system which was heralded as giving a chance to all. The big objection to grammar schools was the notion that children could be 'branded a failure' at the age of eleven. This fear of failing, Mrs Thatcher remembered in old age, was 'the fever that gripped education'.[106] Many Conservative voters had children who had failed or, they expected, would fail the eleven-plus, the examination which, as its name suggests, determined entry to secondary school at that age. For every Tory desperate to preserve the grammar school system, there might well be one desperate to get rid of it. In June 1966, for example, the Shadow Cabinet discussed an NOP poll which showed 65 per cent of the public in favour of comprehensives, and Conservative voters split exactly in half on the issue.[107]

The consequent mental paralysis afflicting the Conservative Party on

Oxford; Labour MP for Hitchin, 1964–74; for Hertford and Stevenage, February 1974–9; Secretary of State for Prices, 1974–6; for Education, 1976–9. Member of 'Gang of Four' which founded SDP; elected SDP MP for Crosby in by-election, 1981; lost seat, 1983; created Baroness Williams of Crosby, 1983.

the subject had, by the time Mrs Thatcher arrived on the scene, achieved the status of a policy. In a paper which he submitted to the Shadow Cabinet, Edward Boyle said that the issue was about 'the separation of children by ability at the age of 11'. 'Far more Tories than we always realise have been genuinely worried about the implications of 11-plus selection for their children.' In particular, parents feared their children being shunted away from the path that could lead them to university. Boyle went on to argue that 'The important thing is to ensure that this *institutional* change does not entail the sacrifice of the *traditions of learning and intellectual discipline* long associated with these schools [that is, grammar schools].'[108]* This was to prove easier said than done.

The policy therefore concentrated on resisting the 'rapid and universal imposition' of comprehensives by central government, a line which had some resonance because, in the controversial Circulars 10/65 and 10/66 which gave central government instructions to education authorities, Labour education ministers had attempted to put more pressure on local authorities to go comprehensive.† Under Circular 10/66, grants for new school building were tied to the progress of a council's schemes for comprehensives. The Tory fight became more a defence of the independence of local government, therefore, than a stand on the quality of education. The buzz phrase for what the Conservatives did not like was 'botched-up schemes'. Ideas of parental choice, such as vouchers, were formally considered only to be rejected. The party felt happier with the simple statistics which showed that whereas there had been 7 million children of school age in 1964, there would be 9.1 million in 1974. The task that politicians most wanted to talk about was spending more money on more buildings, more teachers and – a Labour promise which they had postponed and the Conservatives had adopted – the raising of the school-leaving age to sixteen.

Of Mrs Thatcher's own views on the subject, there was never any doubt. As early as 1965, she had told her Finchley Association's annual general

---

* As so often in Tory politics, there was a class issue lurking in all this. Old Etonians, like Boyle, tended to feel rather guilty about the question and therefore to side with the progressives. Mrs Thatcher, though she retained her liking for Boyle, observed this sharply: 'The trouble with Edward is that he has never got over coming from a good home and having a good education' (Correspondence with Professor David Dilks). Grammar school pupils were more robust. It is interesting to find the left-wing Peter Walker, Heath's blue-eyed boy and later an opponent of Mrs Thatcher, criticizing 'the degree of acceptance ... of the comprehensive formula' in the Shadow Cabinet (Conservative Party Archive, LCC 1/2/13, 15 July 1968). Walker was a grammar school boy.

† Circulars were important, because they were the Secretary of State's only method of urging a national policy upon all the local authorities.

meeting that she was 'very concerned indeed about the Government's intention to reorganise secondary education on comprehensive lines'.[109] 'I am a firm believer in grammar schools,' she told Friern Barnet Young Conservatives. 'For many years now they have been the ladder from the bottom to the top . . . I note that the leaders of both Conservative and Labour parties, as well as the new chairman of the Conservative Party [Anthony Barber], all went to grammar schools.'[110] But, by the time she took up her post, a general election was expected within the year. There was no time to rethink a subject in which, the Conservatives believed, they had simply to maintain their historic lead over Labour. The Conservative Research Department's review of education policy, produced a week after she arrived, put the matter rather complacently: 'Tory image on education still very good so that a more positive and distinctive programme may not be required.'[111] Besides, Heath evinced no interest in education.

So Mrs Thatcher decided to be the loyal executant of the existing policy, while adopting a somewhat different tone to that of her predecessor, Sir Edward Boyle. It was not a question, she told the press on her appointment, of comprehensives 'versus' grammars: what she was against was 'imposing' comprehensives.[112] She told the Commons that the Conservatives had always been 'forward-looking' on education – with the Butler Act, the expansion of universities, the improvement of primary schools – and she did not seek confrontation: 'the true relationship between Government and local authorities is that of partnership of both and not dictatorship by one.'[113] This partnership was to give her (and the local authorities) little joy in years to come. As for the teachers themselves, she felt quite kindly towards them. When they went on strike in London in November 1969, she condemned them in public, but in private she saw them as victims of the prices and incomes policy. She told the Shadow Cabinet that 'it was difficult not to sympathise with their case.'[114] Her slightly precarious stance was eased by the fact that the government tried to press ahead with comprehensives, this time by legislation compelling their introduction. By a great stroke of luck, while the Bill was in committee, two Labour MPs failed to attend for a crucial vote on 14 April 1970. The government was defeated, and the imminent election meant that there was no time to get the Bill back on track. In this atmosphere of government ideological zeal mixed with incompetence, Mrs Thatcher had the chance to promote her criticisms of the comprehensive ideal without actually having to turn against the whole process. She pushed the cause of the existing 'direct grant' schools, which were outside local authority control, emphasized problems of size and geography with many comprehensives, and spoke encouragingly to those local authorities which did not want to go comprehensive.

She could assault Labour's absolutism in the matter, and also its motives: 'As I listen to our educational debates, I think that the Labour Party must hate the middle class, because every time the worst they can say about a school . . . is that a large proportion of the middle class get through there.'[115]

On 10 February 1970, Alfred Roberts died, aged seventy-seven, shortly after listening to his daughter's appearance on BBC Radio's women's discussion programme *Petticoat Line*,* an interview she had recorded several days earlier. He had been ill for some time with emphysema, which had led to weakness in his heart. He also suffered from a cataract which could not be operated on because of his heart condition. In his last months he felt sorrowful and neglected, complaining, of his public work for Grantham, 'it is surprising how quickly it is all forgotten.'[116] He also lamented that 'I never hear anything from Margaret either by letter or by phone.'[117] Margaret did visit him in his last illness, and was much impressed by the number of friends and neighbours who came and cared for him ('How remarkable to finish up your life with so many genuine friends').[118] Carol remembered Margaret dropping in on her dying father when on the way to Scotland, and being 'very tearful' about the state of his health,[119] but her mother was not with him when he died. She was in London, receiving a delegation from the anti-comprehensive group the National Education Association ('She impressed us far more than Sir Edward Boyle ever managed to').[120] Two days later, she spoke in the Commons debate on the second reading of the ill-fated Education Bill. Alfred's funeral took place in Grantham on 16 February. According to Margaret's sister, Muriel Cullen, Margaret did not attend it. 'When we went to my father's funeral,' she recalled, 'of course she didn't go, did she? She'd got something on.'[121]

It would seem extraordinarily and untypically undutiful of Margaret not to have attended, and in fact she did go to the funeral. Her two engagement diaries of the period have her down for a meeting of the OECD (Organization for Economic Co-operation and Development) in Paris that day, but in both versions a line is run through the Paris entries, and through the whole day, though no mention is made of the funeral. The *Grantham Journal* also recorded her presence. In further conversation, Muriel remembered that Cissie Hubbard, the local farmer's widow whom Alfred Roberts had married after Beatrice's death, had arranged for his will to be read just before the funeral, which Mrs Cullen thought 'odd'. At this Victorian scene, Mrs Cullen remembered, Cissie invited Muriel and Margaret to pick any

---

* The title says much about attitudes of the time.

bits of furniture, antiques and pictures that they wanted. Margaret simply said: 'I want something that was my mother's.' Muriel was more forceful, saying, by her own account, 'I'll have that and I'll have that . . .' Afterwards, 'Margaret told me off. She said, "You were a bit blunt, weren't you?"'[122] It seems impossible, then, that Margaret would have gone to Grantham for the reading of the will and then failed to attend the funeral service immediately afterwards. The correct explanation is that she attended the church service, but not the ensuing cremation. The cremation was organized by Cissie, who upset Muriel by telling her that 'Family are going' and then adding, 'I suppose you're family.'[123] Margaret might have wanted no part in this. It is more probable, though, that, far from home, she took the train back to London in order – as her diaries indicate happened – to keep her appointments for the following day. It was typical of Margaret's attitude to her father when he was alive to behave correctly but perfunctorily, sometimes with a touch of impatience. In later years, perhaps feeling some guilt about this, she celebrated his influence and his memory more and more. In 1970, she was in too much of a hurry.*

From the beginning of 1970, the Conservatives felt they should be ready for a general election. Conscious that the party's policies still lacked final form, Ted Heath called a two-day conference of the Shadow Cabinet at the Selsdon Park Hotel in Croydon, beginning on 30 January. The conference became famous, though its fame was unjustified. Seeking to portray his opponents as right wing, Harold Wilson invented a figure called 'Selsdon Man' who, he claimed, had emerged from the conference as the hard-hatted, free-market, devil-take-the-hindmost spirit of Heath's Toryism. In speaking as he did, Wilson probably did the Conservatives a favour by portraying them as more distinctive, more aggressive and more united round a set of beliefs than they actually were. In his memoirs, Heath himself says, 'I can think of no major new departure which emerged from Selsdon Park.'[124] He rejects, with justification, the subsequent belief on the Tory right that Selsdon had raised the standard of what later became Thatcherism.

Heath does claim, however, that Mrs Thatcher talked 'a good deal of

---

* On 18 October 1970 Mrs Thatcher attended a memorial service at Finkin Street Church in Grantham at which a lectern was dedicated in memory of Alfred Roberts, half the cost being subscribed by the congregation and half by the Rotary Club. At the ceremony, according to Muriel Cullen, her sister complained to her: 'They don't know how to treat a Cabinet minister, do they?' Muriel replied, 'This service isn't for you.'

the interests of the middle class at Selsdon'.[125] The minutes, which are in a sort of abbreviated verbatim, provide little evidence of this. What they do indicate is that she brought into play her practical, female knowledge. When it was proposed that family allowances be paid only to the needy, she warned of the stigma that would be attached to collecting them from the Post Office in such circumstances. And when it was suggested that they be paid through the tax system rather than through direct handout, she said that if the allowance went to the husband and not the wife, 'it ceases to be a *family* allowance.'[126]

Most of her interventions, however, concerned her own area. She warned against singling out teachers for a battle over public sector productivity. Forbidden by Heath from any general discussion of education policy – he said that the party had already 'got our education policy' – she engaged in only one set-to with him and colleagues. It concerned the proposal for an independent university, favoured by free-marketeers and those worried by the trends in higher education, led by Max Beloff, an academic and Oxford contemporary of Heath's. The minutes show Mrs Thatcher asking, 'Can I make a speech giving it a fair wind?' Worried about the cost, Heath fights shy of this, and adds:

> Always said there is nothing to stop them doing it, put their own money in it, keep educational standards – but don't want it to come to State for money to keep it going. Never commit myself to saying whether independent schools are better than state ones or not ... As soon as one says one welcomes this, they say what practical form does your welcome take?

SIR KEITH JOSEPH: Only Royal Charters.

EDWARD HEATH: No.

MRS THATCHER: Can't get finance until they are sure they will get Royal Charter.

GEOFFREY RIPPON: Thatcher University Limited.

MRS THATCHER: That is the Open University [invented by Harold Wilson] for which we are refusing money ...

EDWARD HEATH: ... If you like to say they have right to set up independent university and if they reach standard, Privy Council will approve.

ANTHONY BARBER: Suggest we welcome it 'at no cost to the State'.

EDWARD HEATH: So unrealistic.

MRS THATCHER: If I can do it in a speech – they are desperately anxious to get a Royal Charter.

EDWARD HEATH: Not committing myself to a Royal Charter. Wouldn't trust Max Beloff for a minute [Beloff came from the left and at this time was

1. 'I just owe almost everything to my father': Margaret with her father, Alfred Roberts, c. 1927.

2. Beatrice Stephenson as a young woman. 'After I was fifteen we had nothing more to say to each other', Margaret remembered sorrowfully.

3. Margaret in the class of 1934 at Huntingtower Road County Elementary School in Grantham, aged nine.

4. The family grocery shop, North Parade, Grantham. 'If you get it from Roberts's … you get – THE BEST'.

5. The girls who matriculated at Somerville College, Oxford, in 1943. Margaret Roberts is third from left, back row.

6. Tony Bray, Margaret's first love, outside the Radcliffe Camera, Oxford. He was an undergraduate at Brasenose College. 'He's a weird-looking chap to cart around the place,' she wrote to her sister Muriel.

7. The wedding breakfast of Margaret's schoolfriend Shirley Ellis (*née* Walsh) in Grantham in 1947. Margaret sits on the further table to the right, in a distinctive little hat.

8. Tony Bray in the uniform of the 5th Royal Inniskilling Dragoon Guards, probably in 1946: 'a cavalry regiment, green trousers, all the rest of it'.

9. Anti-socialist siren: Margaret Roberts, the new Conservative candidate, plays the piano to voters in the Bull Inn, Dartford, 1949.

10. Margaret the scientist, working for J. Lyons, the food company. This picture was published at the beginning of the 1950 general election campaign: she was the youngest candidate for any party.

GENERAL ELECTION 1950
POLLING DAY: THURSDAY, FEBRUARY 23rd
DARTFORD DIVISION OF KENT

MARGARET

ROBERTS

the
CONSERVATIVE CANDIDATE

11. Margaret's first ever election address in Dartford, 1950. She cut the Labour majority by 6,000.

12. Looking up to Lord Woolton, the Conservative Party Chairman, at a briefing for the 1951 general election campaign at Church House, Westminster. Her rapport with older, powerful men is already evident.

13. The bridesmaid at her sister Muriel's wedding in April 1950. Muriel married Margaret's former boyfriend, William Cullen. Alfred Roberts is in the middle, Beatrice Roberts on the right.

14. Robert Henderson outside BuckinghamPalace after being invested with the CBE in 1947 for his services to medicine. 'I think we are both getting very fond of each other,' Margaret wrote, '– in fact more than that.' On the left is his younger sister, Ada.

15. The power of the handbag. Margaret Roberts, as candidate, queues for the autograph of the actress Patricia Dainton at a Dartford fête in 1951. The bag with her initials on it was given to her by Willie Cullen.

I forgot to tell you that William has given me a very nice black-calf handbag: It's not an awfully expensive one as my conscience wouldn't let me do that — but I chose a very nice one at £7-3. We had my initials put on as well and it looks awfully nice. It's a flat one with a clasp — see sketch — in a plain calf. I am very pleased with it indeed. Of course I quite loftily say it's not

initials on little flap.

'very expensive' — it's about twice as much as you or I would pay. But compared to some of the others (£15 - £20) it's quite reasonable. I'll have to hang on with William for a while longer now!

I should like as many trunks as possible as I have so much to pack up. I haven't heard any further news about digs yet.

Love
Margaret

16. The story of the bag: Margaret tells Muriel why she will 'have to hang on with William for a while longer now!'

had drinks with the people I had been
dining with, a Mr. + Mrs. Soward. He is
a director of a small paint company in the
constituency. A co-director of his, a
Major Thatcher, who has a flat in London,
(age about 36 plenty of money) was also
dining with them and he drove one back
to town at about midnight. As one would
expect he is a polished gentleman. Not
a frightfully attractive creature - very
reserved but quite nice. He is not very
fond of meeting "people" - he says he doesn't
get on with them awfully well. We
arrived back at Liverpool Street at
about 1 a.m. and packed one into the
milk train, which left at 3.40. Altogether
it was quite a thrilling evening.
    It took me about two days
to get over it but I eventually slept

17. 'Not a frightfully attractive creature' – Margaret gives Muriel her impression of
first meeting Denis, 'a Major Thatcher ... (age about 36, plenty of money)', after the
night of 28 February 1949.

18. Denis and Margaret after their engagement, which was concealed from Dartford voters in the 1951 general election.

19. Margaret and Denis cut the cake at their wedding reception at 5 Carlton Gardens, the house of Sir Alfred Bossom, 13 December 1951. Her hat was modelled on that of Georgiana, Duchess of Devonshire, in Gainsborough's portrait.

20. Married love: Denis fastens his wife's necklace at Dormers, Farnborough, Kent, where they moved just before Christmas 1957.

21. The twins: Mark and Carol
were born 14 August 1953. Denis,
who was watching cricket at the
Oval, did not know his wife had
been expecting twins until they had
been born.

22. Waving them away: Mark and
Carol leave Dormers for school, 1959.
Mrs Thatcher is not taking them to
school herself.

23. Gardening at Dormers,
but not dressed for the part.
Mrs Thatcher liked her flowers
bright but orderly.

24. At home with Mark and Carol, 1961.
There are few records of her relaxing
with her children.

in the Liberal Party, moving fast to the right]. Already got too many universities.[127]

On the greater issues, most notably how to handle the questions of prices and incomes, Selsdon did not resolve matters. But, thanks to Wilson's free publicity, the conference looked quite good, and the Conservatives stood high in the polls.

By May, this lead had reversed, and on 22 May 1970 Harold Wilson seized the chance to call a general election for 18 June. The Conservative manifesto, *A Better Tomorrow*, emphasized practicality. Launching it, Heath invoked 'modern techniques' and promised to change 'the whole style of government'. He made very little of what was to prove his most important single achievement – Britain's plan to enter the EEC. In the launch press conference, there was no question about education. The manifesto section on the subject began with the words 'In education above all the problem of resources is crucial,' and promised more spending on primary school buildings, the expansion of nursery schools and the raising of the school leaving age to sixteen. On the vexed matter of comprehensives, the manifesto supported the freedom of local education authorities to decide, but ventured that 'in most cases the age of 11 is too early to make final decisions which might affect a child's whole future'. It added, however, that comprehensivization 'on rigid lines is contrary to local democracy and contrary to the best interests of the children'. In short, it tried to have it both ways.

Mrs Thatcher was lined up to appear in party political broadcasts for the election, but after a pilot in which she was considered to have performed badly, being too stiff and unnatural,[128] she was withdrawn from the front line. She spent most of the campaign, which she expected the Conservatives to lose, in Finchley, focusing on economic woes, law and order, and – coding her criticism of mass immigration – conserving 'our British character'.[129] The choice for the British people, she said in a letter issued to the press on 1 June, was between 'two essentially different ways of life', one in which the state grabbed more and more power and the other in which 'the role of the State is to help people discharge their own responsibilities'. Mrs Thatcher's main foray outside the constituency was to Scarborough, to address the conference of the National Association of Head Teachers on 25 May. Still an ingénue in media matters, she failed to deliver a key part of her text because of the lateness of the hour, and was verbally roughed up by journalists who insisted on being allowed to report it all the same.[130] It proved to be the most controversial passage: 'There are those who wish only to read the comic strip and the headline, whose problems, stemming sometimes from home backgrounds, cannot be over-come, however dedicated the teacher . . .'* Labour tried to make something of this in the campaign, claiming that she was writing off a third of children as ineducable. It made little impact. To the confusion of the opinion polls, the Conservatives won the election with an overall majority of thirty-one. The Finchley result was as follows:

Mrs Margaret Thatcher (Conservative)	25,480
Michael Freeman (Labour)	14,295
G. Mitchell (Liberal)	7,614
Conservative majority	11,185

Both Mrs Thatcher's vote and her majority were up. Hearing late that night on the car radio that the Conservatives were winning, the Thatchers, who were driving to Lamberhurst, turned round, and went to the *Daily Telegraph* party at the Savoy.[131]

---

* John Izbicki, then education correspondent of the *Daily Telegraph*, found Mrs Thatcher almost tearful in her ballgown after the press assault on her for nearly depriving them of their story. He danced with her at the NAHT Ball, and then took her out along the promenade by the Grand Hotel to admire the sea lit by the moonlight. He was struck with her charms. According to his colleague, Brian MacArthur, then education correspondent of *The Times*, Izbicki said: 'Do you know, if I'd made a pass, I'm sure I would have been successful.' Charming though John Izbicki was, it is hard to believe that he was right.

9

Milksnatcher

'The Most Unpopular Woman in Britain'

Margaret Thatcher duly entered the Cabinet for the first time, as Edward Heath's secretary of state for education and science, accepting the appointment on 20 June 1970. Although she often referred to the fact that she was a scientist, she made very little of the fact that she had, briefly, been a teacher. She had not much enjoyed the experience.

She had found herself in the role because of the war. In a reorganization of the academic year to allow Lincolnshire pupils more time to help with the potato harvest in the autumn, the county's schools resumed for the Michaelmas term in the middle of August, after a break of only two weeks. In 1944 this allowed Margaret, whose long vacation from Oxford began in early June, to earn money and help the war effort by teaching at Grantham's Central School for Boys, which was short of staff, for nearly two months of the summer term, and then, until she returned to Oxford early for fire-watching duties there, for three weeks of the following term. Still aged only eighteen, she taught science, but also maths, and, under protest, other things too. 'School has not gone down any too well this past week,' she wrote to Muriel. 'We are working terrifically hard and I have no free periods at all. Also the marking is heavy. I have a set of <u>English essays</u> to mark this weekend as well as some algebra and physics and I've never seen such appalling tripe in all my life.'[1] She also had to take the boys for swimming lessons at the Grantham baths: 'We don't go in with them during the lessons, but stay on the bank and try to teach them by yelling at them what they are doing wrong. I don't think it is a very satisfactory method personally, but still I don't think I'd like to appear in front of them in a bathing costume with my present figure.'[2]

In addition to her formal duties, Margaret also took on the personal coaching of David, a would-be naval cadet, who needed cramming for his maths exams. 'I'm afraid he's not a very smart kid at all,' she told Muriel. 'He is alright while I am sitting over him watching everything that he does but the moment I leave him to his own devices everything begins to go wrong.'[3] Later she complained, '. . . I cannot make up for his lack of intel-ligence,'[4] and she did not 'hold out much hope for him because while he has improved a great deal since I have had him, – he still doesn't know his tables properly and nothing I can do for him can ever make up for that. I think teaching him has been the hardest earned £2-2s I've ever had or hope to have in my life.' She went on, 'I was relieved to have finished teaching on Friday evening. It was like being released to freedom once more.'[5] The school, however, was enthusiastic: 'Mr Thorpe [the headmaster] was awfully nice the last day and thanked me . . . all in front of the school who clapped wildly for what seemed like ages. ' She added, untruthfully, 'I was quite glad when the ceremony was over.' Margaret was happily conscious of having caused some excitement in the place: 'It has been quite a novelty for them to be taught by an Oxford undergraduate and I heard quite a deal of the "Oxford accent" being talked behind my back.'[6] Gerald Nick-lem, a pupil at the school, remembered Margaret appreciatively as 'an English rose' who had 'a lovely skin and hair attractively done, so we boys thought it a great treat to have this young lady teaching us.'[7]

No doubt it was wise of Mrs Thatcher not to dwell in later life on her experience as a teacher, though she did mention it if asked. Such a short stint at such a young age would never have stood comparison with the work of people who had given their life to the profession. But those few weeks were nevertheless of some importance to her. They gave her a certain respect for the hardships that teachers endure and reinforced her belief in the importance of making sure that children learn things properly. They also confirmed the feeling, which had earlier driven her to refuse the chance of the full bursary at Oxford that went with the promise to teach later, that she lacked the pedagogical vocation. To the observer of her reactions, her stint as a teacher provides evidence of (to put it kindly) her gift for leadership or (to put it unkindly) her bossiness. It is an early example of her belief, later so familiar to Cabinet colleagues, that people, particularly men, never did anything very well unless you stood over them while they did it. Mrs Thatcher always approached education with an odd mixture of feelings – a solemn conviction that it was overwhelmingly important for civilization and for the individual, combined with a certain impatience. Carol remembered that Mrs Thatcher, who was generally quite indulgent as a mother, did get 'very upset if we had bad reports from school'. She would upbraid her children strongly if this happened: 'I'd twigged before the Russians that she was the Iron Lady.'[8]

The Department of Education and Science did not stand high in the peck-ing order of Whitehall. First in Curzon Street, Mayfair, and then, in the latter part of Mrs Thatcher's term of office, south of the river in the aston-ishingly ugly new tower of Elizabeth House near Waterloo, it was geographically separated from the centre of power. Although Mrs Thatcher remembered the 'splendid old quarters' in Curzon Street with affection, the condition of their entrance was so squalid and the doormen so surly that officials used to arrange to meet visitors in the street outside and escort them quickly through, so they would not have to endure the horrors of the lobby for too long.[9] Many of the DES officials, including the Permanent Secretary, Sir William Pile, who came from the Home Office to take over in the month that Mrs Thatcher arrived in the job, would have preferred to be in other government departments. In part, this reflected the cultural assumption that education was a 'woman's subject', not worthy of the full attention of men whose job it was to rule.* More, it arose from the fact that education was organized in such a way that the Department had very little power. Pile's predecessor, Sir Herbert Andrew, described its work as 'like steering a boat with a rubber tiller'. According to one official's par-donable exaggeration, the Department 'ran only the V&A, Apsley House [the London home of the 1st Duke of Wellington, now a museum] and the Science Museum directly',[10] and even the arts and museums, for which Mrs Thatcher found herself nominally responsible, were handled by a separate minister, Lord Eccles, and on an 'arm's length principle'. Virtually every-thing in education was delegated, or mediated, universities receiving their money via the University Grants Committee and schools through local education authorities. These local authorities received an automatic central government grant worth 75 per cent of their spending.

In parliamentary answers to Education Questions throughout her time in office, Mrs Thatcher's most common reply begins with the words: 'I have no direct control . . .' The idea that central government should inter-vene directly in the curriculum, or even to ensure the quality of teachers, was seen as an affront to local and professional autonomy. The only aspect of the content of teaching prescribed by law, and therefore the responsi-bility of the Secretary of State, was religious education, and even here the task was delegated to experts and churches. The Department produced money – for school building and for teachers' salaries in particular – but not ideas. Mrs Thatcher was later to claim that she protested about this.

---

* Mrs Thatcher's predecessor, Edward Boyle, summed up the status of the education secretary in an interview given in 1971, when she held the post: 'You're quite right if you think of the people since the war who have been most associated with Education. It isn't a department which has enhanced one's career in politics' (*The Politics of Education: Edward Boyle and Anthony Crosland in Conversation with Maurice Kogan*, Penguin, 1971, p. 100.)

She remembered that she had said to Pile when she arrived: 'I'm worried about the *content* in schools, rather than the structure.'[11] It is true that there were a few occasions, especially towards the end of her time at the Department, when she mentioned this problem in speeches and interviews. In Cabinet, she sometimes complained of the automaticity of grants to local authorities. But there is no evidence that she made a serious attempt to change the balance of power. Indeed, her most immediately controversial policy – her scrapping of the Labour Circulars 10/65 and 10/66 which tried to force comprehensivization – took its stand on the principle of local independence. She never said that she was opposed to comprehensives in principle: instead she argued that good existing schools should be defended and that parents and local authorities should be able to make decisions for themselves, rather than be compelled to change.

Mrs Thatcher withdrew the Labour Circulars at once, telling her officials on her first working day (Monday 22 June 1970) that she would do so, and making the public announcement on 30 June. For this speed she was criticized. Wilma Hart, the Department's deputy secretary and *éminence grise*, tried to dissuade her from introducing a 'blanket policy'.[12] Unions and local authorities complained of the lack of consultation. Worse, from Mrs Thatcher's point of view, 10 Downing Street indicated displeasure at her failure to discuss the matter in Cabinet first.[13] Her very readiness to act was taken as a danger signal by those around Ted Heath, an example of the 'instant government' which he deplored. In his introductory remarks at his very first Cabinet meeting on 23 June, Heath urged ministers, 'Don't be rushed into hasty decisions of policy':[14] Mrs Thatcher had just rushed into one the day before. John Hedger, one of her private secretaries, remembered a conversation with a No. 10 counterpart at the time: 'God, this woman is really right wing.'[15] The feeling was that she was getting above herself. In her own view, however, Mrs Thatcher was simply doing what she had promised. The withdrawal of the Circulars had been in the election manifesto, and she regarded the election, she told the Commons when introducing her Circular, as 'the biggest consultation of all'. There was no need for legislation to effect their withdrawal. Therefore it should happen at once. In retrospect, she felt let down by the Department in the matter. No one told her, she complained, that to withdraw one Circular, you had to issue a replacement, so she hurriedly drafted one herself.[16]

In reality, the issuing of Circular 10/70, as her new policy was called, was more the signal of a change of tone than a reform of huge importance. It was not able, and it was not even intended, to stop the flow of new comprehensives in its tracks. 'We shall ... expect plans to be based on educational considerations rather than on the comprehensive principle,' she told the *Daily Telegraph*,[17] but, regardless of the principle, the comprehensive practice was so far advanced that not much could be done to stop it. On the day when Mrs Thatcher took office, there were 1,137 comprehensive schools in England and Wales, and hundreds of comprehensive schemes were pending. When she left it in March 1974, she had approved 3,286 comprehensive schemes and rejected only 326; she had saved ninety-four grammar schools. As she pursued her policy, Mrs Thatcher accepted the trend of the age, telling *The Times* that non-selective education was coming 'with increasing speed'.[18] She developed the argument that the Butler Act of 1944 had provided for a 'comprehensive' education service – the word appears in the Act – but that this did not necessarily mean that all schools had to take the same, comprehensive (that is, non-selective) form: comprehensiveness could be offered across an area, and was better if it included parental choice of types of school.[19] When she addressed her party's conference that autumn, she did not take her stand on the virtues of grammar schools, let alone the vices of comprehensives. Instead she spoke about the value of a 'variety of choice' and she did not make the theme the centrepiece of her speech, preferring to emphasize the building of new primary schools. All that 10/70 ensured was that no local authority was compelled to go comprehensive. It did not give Mrs Thatcher new powers to shape education: indeed, she made much of repudiating the very idea. Her sole legal power over whether an old school closed or a new one opened derived from Section 13 of the Butler Act itself. Early in her time in office, she continued her predecessors' habit of considering local education authority schemes for school reorganization as a whole, but from April 1971 she desisted. Always careful to follow a legally precise position, she decided to concentrate on the only thing which Section 13 provided for – the fate of individual schools. When her Labour shadow, Ted Short, complained that this way of proceeding could make 'nonsense of the whole area scheme',[20] she did not disagree with him, but insisted that she must perform her statutory duties.

There were successes. Mrs Thatcher prevented the compulsory comprehensivization of Birmingham which was already in train when she arrived in office, and after Labour took control of Birmingham Council in 1972 she was able to back the strong feeling in favour of many of the grammar schools in the city, saving nearly half of them. In general, however, the policy did not really please enough people enough. Particularly awkward were those areas controlled by Conservatives which wanted to go comprehensive. 'Look at who fought me,' she would lament in later years.[21] One of these was true-blue Surrey where, according to Short, she had organized an unsuccessful 'tennis court plot' at a 'secret' meeting with grammar school supporters in a tennis club to prevent comprehensives, which her own party had foiled. When she addressed the National Union of Teachers conference in Blackpool in April 1972, Mrs Thatcher found herself in the piquant situation of facing a boycott led by Surrey teachers, followed by a walk-out of about a hundred militant teachers during her speech. The left-wing union executive, resenting the discourtesy, led a standing ovation to her from the platform.[22]

Worse still was the problem in her own constituency, caused because Barnet Council wished to go comprehensive. In June 1971, Mrs Thatcher vetoed the part of Barnet's 'Plan C' which linked Woodhouse Grammar with Friern Barnet County School, and also forbade Whitefield School, Cricklewood, to go comprehensive, on the grounds of a split site and, in the latter case, the unsuitability of accommodation. Earlier in the year, she had already stopped other Barnet 'Plan C' schemes, although a consultation organized by the council had produced 86 per cent support for 'Plan C' from 28,000 replies. The normally loyal *Finchley Press* reported the local teachers as 'staggered' and quoted attacks on Mrs Thatcher by a prominent and usually friendly Conservative councillor, Vic Usher, who was chairman of the council's education committee. Usher expressed his 'tremendous disappointment'[23] and complained that an unrepresentative group had won the battle for 'Mrs Thatcher's ear'. There tended, in Conservative areas, to be a split between the education committees of councils, whose members saw things more from an overall organizational point of view and therefore wanted the tidiness of wholesale comprehensivization, and the Tory rank and file, many of whom worried greatly about educational standards and felt strongly about particular schools.*

Perhaps the least satisfied customer of the policy was Mrs Thatcher herself. Even she found the details of so many plans exhausting to deal with and, through overconscientiousness and anxiety about political consequences, lingered too long over many of them.[24] And although she genuinely believed that it was a bad idea that central government should decree the nature of every school in the country, she had little practical faith in the capacity of the only other source of power available at the time, the local authorities, to make the right decisions. 'She really hated it,' one senior official remembered. 'She chafed against her own policy that local

---

* Mrs Thatcher's sympathy with Tory grass-root sentiment brought some rather snobbish criticism on her head. Christopher Price, a Labour MP with an interest in education, wrote in the *New Statesman* (6 July 1973) that these rank and file 'are the bourgeois tradesmen like her father, who would not dream of touching a comprehensive with a bargepole. They use the local grammar school if their offspring are coachable into it, and turn to Miss Pringle's Academy for Young Ladies if they're not.'

authorities were free.'[25] This was noticed. *The Times Educational Supplement*, which was the voice of the educational establishment and Mrs Thatcher's opponent throughout, complained that she continued 'to hide behind the autonomy of the local authorities ... when it suits her, but as soon as they use their autonomy in a way she does not like, out comes the big stick.'[26] As for other policy solutions, she lacked the official support, the intellectual preparation and the political clout to produce any of her own. She rejected voucher schemes providing for real parental choice, on the grounds that their effects would be unmanageable. She warmly supported the existing direct grant schools, which mixed central government bursaries with fee-paying, but she did not dare to extend their number beyond the 176 schools already operating. In essence, she found herself presiding over a vast change of educational structure whose underlying egalitarian principles she did not support, but which she was powerless to reverse.

This sense of frustration was fed by a sense of isolation. At the DES, she did not feel among friends. In her memoirs, she describes the prevailing atmosphere there as 'self-righteously socialist'.[27] One of her first complaints on arriving at the Department was that she had seen lots of Marxist books for sale in Dillons, the London University bookshop. The officials' puzzlement at how to react to a matter which had nothing to do with them was interpreted by Mrs Thatcher as a sort of complicity in the act.[28]* After she had had Bill Pile and his wife to lunch at her home in Lamberhurst, she was irritated not to receive a thank-you letter from Pile's left-wing wife. Irritated, but not surprised: 'What do you expect,' she complained to an official. 'She's Communist Party. She's CP.'[29] On 12 September 1970, Ted Heath was called away at the last minute by the Palestinian hijacking crisis involving Leila Khaled, and Mrs Thatcher had to substitute for him as the speaker for the centenary dinner of the National Union of Teachers at Guildhall. She professed herself shocked by what she saw that night of the crony relationship between her officials and the NUT. 'It's a closed world,' she remembered thinking. 'I saw how closely some of our top civil servants were in with the NUT.'[30] This particularly worried her because of Communist influence in the NUT, a subject which she later raised in the Cabinet.

Mrs Thatcher's directly political accusations against her Department

---

* Oddly enough, Mrs Thatcher was quite a frequent customer of a left-wing bookshop at this time. Collett's, the avowedly Communist bookstore, also sold Chinese pottery, which she collected. The Education Secretary could therefore be seen inspecting the top floor where the pots were displayed (THCR 4/4).

were somewhat unfair. One of the officials she most roundly attacked for his politics was, in private life, a member of the Conservative Party.[31] On the other hand, Toby Weaver, standard-bearer for the advancement of polytechnics and one of the few whom Mrs Thatcher greatly admired, was a declared socialist, but he was redeemed in her eyes by his equally unconcealed Christianity. There was certainly not a pro-Labour atmosphere at the Department. Officials had found Ted Short, Mrs Thatcher's predecessor, pedantic, prickly and slow witted. They rejoiced to have a minister who was more intelligent and determined, ready in the despatch of business and much less inclined to stand on ceremony. 'You came out from a conversation with her feeling that you'd had three very hard sets of tennis,' said Nick Stuart.[32] Most liked her 'generous personality', which was attentive to personal troubles, gave parties to thank people for doing well and treated juniors as well as seniors attentively.[33] Many admired her charms as a woman; some, according to John Hedger, were even 'bowled over'.

There was, nevertheless, what might be called a cultural gap, some of which may have related to her sex. Pile, who always rather looked down on Mrs Thatcher and, according to a fellow senior official, 'never missed a chance to slag her off behind her back',[34] decided that 'it didn't look right' that the word 'hairdresser' should appear in her departmental diary, and so the coiffeur's name was substituted.[35] And it was not only the fact that she was a woman, but such a carefully turned out, utterly Tory woman at that. John Banks, private secretary at the beginning of her time in office, found her 'difficult to relate to' because of her 'mannerized [sic] style of talking to civil servants'. It struck officials, partly with amusement and partly with irritation, that Mrs Thatcher had never for a second considered sending her own children to state schools. (The twins were by this time sixth-formers. Carol was at St Paul's and Mark was at Harrow. Carol found it particularly difficult that her mother was education secretary while she was being educated.)[36] One day, Mrs Thatcher and Banks were driving past Pimlico Comprehensive in London, then a new and famous school. He said that he might send his son there. 'Oh John,' said Mrs Thatcher, 'you couldn't think of sending your child to that glasshouse.'[37] On a trip to Cambridge, she gave John Hedger a long talk about the importance of choosing the right house at a school for one's son. He found this noteworthy because she assumed (a) that one's son would go to a private school, (b) that he would board and (c) that there was no need to mention one's daughter. As Hedger put it, 'The department respected her enormously, but were bothered by her prejudices.'[38] In her turn, Mrs Thatcher was irritated by the opposite prejudices among her officials. One of her first acts on coming into office was to question the work of the Department's

Consultative Committee on Research into Comprehensive Education. An official minuted smoothly: 'I do not think that the Secretary of State need feel concerned about the completion of the research programme. It is not a propaganda exercise but a professional research programme conducted by a reputable research organisation.' Less than a week in the job, Mrs Thatcher scribbled at the bottom of the minute: 'This is one of the most disappointing and frustrating documents I have read. Not a penny after Dec. 1971.'[39] She remembered calling in a chief inspector of schools (she was not sure which) and saying to him: 'You're absolutely against grammar schools. They're being made to feel guilty but they're doing well ... They need a bit of praise from people like you,'[40] and she accused public-school educated men like Banks (Eton) and Nick Stuart (Harrow) of acting out of feelings of guilt induced by their privilege.[41] It is probably wrong to claim that the Department's officials were dedicated to building an egalitarian New Jerusalem. It would be nearer the mark to say that they shared the attitudes of the post-war settlement in education, and were resistant to change, especially from a woman, new to the Cabinet and from outside their own tribe, whose own ideas on the subject, while markedly different from their own, were not fully formed.* This slightly edgy relationship with her own Department helps to explain the fiasco which made her a household name for the first time and came quite close to aborting her political career.

One of the first actions of Edward Heath's new government was to inaugurate a review of all public spending. Mrs Thatcher immediately applied herself to this with the literal-mindedness in which, contrary to widespread belief, there always lurked an element of deliberate self-parody. Lord Belstead,† her most junior minister in the Department, attended the meeting in the DES when she announced her plan to issue Circular 10/70. 'Off you go to your rooms,' she said as she ended. Belstead made his way to the tobacco-stained office of the Permanent Secretary to discuss something. Then he heard a voice behind him, the distinctive tones of his new boss, directed at Pile: 'The PM says we must take extreme care with spending,

---

* At this time, a series of education 'Black Papers', published by academics, teachers and writers, including Kingsley Amis, who were worried about the trends in progressive education, caused a great stir. Mrs Thatcher was sympathetic to the Black Papers, and always gave their authors a friendly hearing, but there is little evidence that she tried to apply much of their thought to her action in government. The prevailing orthodoxy was strong in the opposite direction, and she did not feel ready to defy it.

† Lord Belstead (1932–2005), educated Eton and Christ Church, Oxford; born John Ganzoni, succeeded father as Lord Belstead, 1958; Leader of the House of Lords, 1988–90.

so therefore there will be no redecoration here without permission from
me.'[42] Pile gave his opinion of this style of leadership in later years: 'She is
the only person I know who I don't think I ever heard say, "I wonder
whether . . ." . . . she never delegated anything.'[43]

But Mrs Thatcher did fight her Department's corner. At a time when
school rolls were rising and almost the only power she had was her ability
to spend, she was determined to increase the DES budget. Her tactic for
doing so was to accept short-term cuts in exchange for long-term growth,
and cuts in non-educational aspects of her budget in favour of increases
in truly educational spending. The Treasury's attention focused on removing the subsidy for school meals in two stages and abolishing the
long-standing provision of free milk for health reasons to all primary
school pupils for their morning break. (In an earlier economy measure, the
previous Labour government had abolished the milk for secondary school
pupils.) The Chief Secretary to the Treasury, Maurice Macmillan, wrote to
Mrs Thatcher about this on 31 July 1970,[44] calculating that the saving on
the milk would be £9.5 million in 1971–2 and £14.4 million in 1972–3.
He added that the change would involve legislation. While happy enough
with the general drift, Mrs Thatcher immediately made it clear that she
would not accept complete withdrawal because it 'would be too drastic a
step and would arouse more public antagonism than the saving justifies'.
She proposed instead that milk still be issued to children up to the age of
seven,[45] and she suggested that the savings made should be redirected into
the 1972–3 and 1973–4 primary school rebuilding programme which was
her most trumpeted measure. When Macmillan demurred, pleading that
he was not getting enough cuts elsewhere, she replied: '. . . I am bound to
withdraw my acceptance of your original proposals for savings . . . I simply
cannot accept that education should be treated more harshly because you
have been disappointed in your expectations from other quarters.'[46] This
forced the issue to discussion in Cabinet, and on 29 September Mrs
Thatcher told the Cabinet that she had reached agreement to retain school
milk for infants, as she had insisted all along. When the Chancellor of the
Exchequer, Anthony Barber (who had taken up the post when Iain Macleod
died suddenly little more than a month after the election), announced his
public spending package at the end of October, Mrs Thatcher was judged
to have handled matters well. In addition to the promise to increase spending on primary school buildings, she had contrived to save the Open
University, an invention of Harold Wilson's which most Tories disliked but
which she believed would be 'a means of getting good teaching on television' and extend educational opportunity.[47] At a Cabinet meeting at the
end of July, she had successfully fought for the Open University against

most of the Cabinet, arguing that 'We can't make education our first sacrifice,' although Heath complained that the OU was 'not a university at
all'.[48] This saving of the Open University, in defiance of her seniors, was a
considerable achievement for an entirely untried Cabinet minister. When
the outcome of the spending exercise emerged in the autumn, even the
Guardian spoke of 'a remarkably light raid on the education budget'.[49]

Problems, however, began to grow. According to witnesses present at
the relevant early meetings in which the Department had agreed in principle to reducing free milk, no one had raised the political dangers (though
the correspondence referred to above shows that Mrs Thatcher herself had
some idea of them). These now became more apparent because of the
necessity for legislation (also not raised within the Department, but pointed
out by the Treasury – see above) to implement the cuts and to permit
authorities to sell milk to children who had previously received it free. The
original hope was that the milk cuts would be contained – one might
almost say concealed – in wider legislation led by Keith Joseph's Department of Health and Social Security about dental and prescription charges.
DES officials believed that this would 'cushion the political criticism'.[50]
However, the government managers rejected the plan because of lack of
time, and the DES had to forge ahead alone. By May 1971 it became clear
that opposition had grown. Education authorities and the Labour Opposition sought a power in the Bill for those authorities that wished to continue
to supply the milk free. Short wrote mischievously to Mrs Thatcher, 'you
have said on many occasions that you want local authorities to have more
freedom. Here is a chance to give them some.'[51] The 'freedom' was not
something that Mrs Thatcher could grant, since it would have been central
government that had to pay for it. But some Conservative backbenchers
started to say the same thing, if more politely. By the parliamentary debate
on the second reading on 14 June 1971, Short had worked up enough
excitement to be able to call the legislation 'mean, squalid and unworthy
of a great country ... typical of the philosophy of this astounding, pre-
Disraeli Government'.[52] Nutrition experts, social workers, the NUT, the
Child Poverty Action Group all pitched in against Mrs Thatcher. Here was
a subject on which everyone could easily have an opinion and where the
case for the cut, however reasonable, could never seem attractive.* The *Sun*

---

* Perhaps the only people who, for the most part, did not share the outrage were the children
themselves. The bottles of milk supplied at elevenses were unpopular with pupils partly because
few schools had the necessary refrigeration in those days and the milk, delivered early and
often sitting for hours in crates beside radiators, was warm and semi-separated. The present
author's generation felt liberated from the age of compulsory milk.

asked, 'Is Mrs Thatcher human?'[53] Several local authorities defied the regulations and continued to issue milk free to their pupils. At the Labour Party conference that September, a floor speaker coined the phrase 'Mrs Thatcher, milksnatcher', and it quickly became the only thing that most of the public knew about her.

All this fuss was peculiarly painful to Mrs Thatcher. It was her first experience of being hated for her public work, and it cut her to the quick that people should think that she – a mother – could be indifferent to the health and happiness of children. She felt the great unfairness of the whole thing and she realized, to her mortification, that she had allowed the press to develop a public character for her which was unattractive and damaging to her career. The signs of this problem had been visible as soon as she came into office. The education press corps, like the DES itself, were predominantly unsympathetic to her political attitudes,* and an informal gathering for them in the summer of 1970 had been, according to a later piece in the *Observer*, 'a disaster' because she had appeared not to understand a number of questions put to her on ordinary matters of policy.[54] Another early sign of the caricature that was building was a BBC *Panorama* documentary which appeared on 23 July 1970. The programme included a perceptive contribution by Shirley Williams which noted Mrs Thatcher's 'combination of high intelligence with the fact that she stands really rather on the right . . . and as such has become something of a heroine figure in the Conservative Party'. But the main purpose of the programme was to depict Mrs Thatcher as an aggressively middle-class Tory woman, able, but fundamentally unsympathetic and in favour of privilege. The camera began with the Education Secretary having her hair done. It continued with a subsequently famous sequence of the Thatchers at The Mount in which Margaret ferociously pruned roses while Denis charged up and down the 2 acres of grass with an enormous lawn-mower. Another sequence showed Mrs Thatcher in the chemistry class of a London comprehensive school in which pupils were learning about sulphur in food-making. Mrs Thatcher chips in with the children: 'Particularly on breakfast spoons you know, the spoons you use for boiled eggs. You dip in and, if they're silver, they go brown and Mother has to clean them. So these days we tend to use stainless steel, don't we?' Few, if any, of the pupils would have seen any silver at home. This was wonderful propaganda for the left. Mrs Thatcher thought the programme was 'a wretched little film'.[55] It helped to set a media and therefore a public mood which was against her. On 14

---

* Mrs Thatcher herself believed that only her admirer John Izbicki, of the *Daily Telegraph*, would give her a fair hearing.

May 1971 her speech establishing Liverpool Polytechnic was cut short by protests, including cries of 'School milk!' There were many more such scenes. Protesting students used to wait for her train at station platforms and charge up and bang on her window, an experience which made her dislike of trains terminal. Officials remembered her being actually frightened, and were touched by this symptom of human frailty.[56]* By November, the *Sun* marked her down as 'The Most Unpopular Woman in Britain'.[57]

The attacks produced an uncharacteristic self-pity. In an interview in the *Guardian*, she burst out, 'Why, why? Why are you doing it?',[58] and she earned a rebuke from the *Daily Mail* columnist Jean Rook – 'Show some spunk, Margaret. Remember flaming Barbara Castle when she came back at critics like a blow-lamp'[59] – advice which she took to heart. In some interviews about this difficult time, Mrs Thatcher liked to say how it had been worse for Denis, who had to bear all the attacks without being able to answer back. But really it was she, not he, who found the whole thing almost unbearable. It was Denis, forcing her to decide whether she was tough enough for this sort of thing, who brought her through it.[60] What also drove her on was the conviction that the policy was, in essence, right: 'The idea that most people couldn't pay a small amount for their children's milk was to me utterly ridiculous ... And it showed up those who were using it not really about school milk, but to try to get me out of Education.'[61] In later years, Mrs Thatcher gained a reputation for physical and psychological stamina, but though her determination was always present, the toughness had to be acquired by bitter experience. People who knew her in the 1970s often remarked how tired she seemed, and how upset by attack. 'Milk' was her first really big test, and she did not pass it easily. Indeed, once the milksnatcher row was all over, Ted Heath, unbeknownst to her, even raised the idea with colleagues that he should sack her. The chief whip, Francis Pym, told him that he could not dismiss the only woman in his Cabinet. Heath dropped the notion.[62]

The last straw came just before Christmas 1971. A DES official caught up with the fact that the Department had put out its milk Circular incorrectly, suggesting that local authorities could remit the charge 'in suitable

---

* One of the threats made to Mrs Thatcher was nastier still. A man approached her at a meeting and said that he was from the Angry Brigade, a minor terrorist grouping of the period, and she would be blown up in twenty minutes. He was lying, but she had to start thinking about the threat of terrorism for the first time. From the period of the milk dispute, and for the rest of her life, she was subject to the attention of extremists and mobs of protesters. This probably did her more political good than harm, but it was a heavy personal burden for her and her family to have to bear. In February 1972, she raised the matter in Cabinet, asking if government ministers were insured against terrorist attack (Cabinet Secretary's notebooks).

circumstances'. If this had been true, the whole purpose of the Bill could have been nullified. Pile wrote almost abjectly to Mrs Thatcher on 23 December, informing her of the error: 'I want to apologise unreservedly for this mistake which should never have happened. It adds a further embarrassment in an area which is already causing you much trouble.' Mrs Thatcher agreed to issue a correction at once and added that 'No. 10 ought to be informed.'[63] She was so angry with Pile that at the office Christmas party to which she had brought him a present she turned and whispered to an official: 'Put that Christmas present away. I cannot give it to him now.'[64] Perhaps because of the Christmas break, however, the correction of the Circular went out without publicity, and at this point the defiance of the milk edict rather mysteriously melted away. By 9 January 1972 Britain was embroiled in the first of the Heath government's miners' strikes and the media had lost interest in milk.

It was at this point that Ted Heath, showing a concern for which Mrs Thatcher always remained grateful, took matters in hand. Given that she had attracted so much bad publicity over milk for so small a financial saving, and that her public image was poor, she was in a vulnerable position. Heath could have decided to sack her, and had indeed given serious consideration to doing so. Instead he backed her. On 12 January he had her, Pile and other senior officials to Chequers to effect a reconciliation between them – Heath later recalled that she had been agitating to get Pile moved to another department[65] – and to plan a new direction for her tenure of the post. Heath had been impressed by Mrs Thatcher's tenacity, culminating in her victory in Cabinet over funds for school building in June 1971, in getting more money for her department. The deal, in essence, was to take the heat out of education, and to put money into it. The milk row had shown that the educational establishment was lining up against Mrs Thatcher. So had a smaller, but also bitter and eventually humiliating, dispute in which she had urged reform of the system by which subscriptions to the National Union of Students were automatically made from students' grants regardless of their wishes. Left-wing students had barracked her all over the country about the matter, led by the future Labour Foreign Secretary and Lord Chancellor Jack Straw, who was then president of the National Union of Students; and, in a period when confrontation was dreaded, she had received no backing from vice-chancellors for her attempt to abolish this government-funded closed shop. With the exception of Keith Joseph, Cabinet ministers had been lukewarm in her support when they discussed it in Cabinet in August 1971, fearing a needlessly bloody political battle. On 10 January 1972 she announced postponement of the question for a year. As for the question of comprehensives, the minutes of the

Chequers meeting show agreement that 'If the procedure for local objections was allowed to influence policy ... the Government might get the
worst of both worlds.'[66] From now on, she would concentrate instead on
those areas on which people could agree – more primary schools (on which
she had already made a good start), further education, more polytechnics,
raising the school leaving age, an expansion of nursery education and a
White Paper to set out the bright future.[67]

Following the Chequers meeting, Heath praised Mrs Thatcher in the
House of Commons. She used this, and her private knowledge of his support, for what is nowadays called a relaunch. A spate of press interviews
in January and February presented her as someone who had learnt from
her ordeal and bounced back. She emphasized her ordinariness: 'Whenever
I go over a school the teachers always say to me, "You're not at all how
we expected."'[68] To the journalist Lynda Lee Potter, with a touching glim-
mering of self-awareness, she said, 'The strange thing is, people *do* resent
it when you know the answers.'[69] 'I'm afraid I'll be remembered for milk,'
she told the *Liverpool Daily Post*. 'But I'd like to be remembered as the
Minister who actually, actually did raise the school leaving age instead of
just talking about it,' and she added, 'I must confess the record really is
pretty impressive. I think the Prime Minister thinks so too.'[70] The school
leaving age was raised from fifteen to sixteen with effect from September
1973. By May 1972 she was dropping hints about the expansion of nursery
schools. She was effective in her fight with the Treasury – officials remembered that 'it was almost literally true that Tony Barber [the Chancellor of
the Exchequer] walked backwards when he saw her coming'[71] – and at the
party conference at Blackpool in October she was able to trail her coming
'programme for the systematic expansion of nursery education'.

As a political tactic, Mrs Thatcher's readiness to shut up and spend
worked well. Ted Heath, increasingly beleaguered with economic and
industrial problems, was happy to have quiet on the schools front. The
educational interest groups were placated, and it became known that Mrs
Thatcher was persistent in arguing the case for better pay for teachers in
Cabinet. Max Morris, a Communist who became vice-president of the
NUT in 1972, and a pioneer thinker in the comprehensivist movement in
the 1930s, remembered Mrs Thatcher as 'very expeditious and businesslike'
and, despite her dislike of comprehensives, 'very pragmatic'. He was pleased
that she avoided confrontation with the union over the report into teacher
training which she had commissioned from Lord James of Rusholme, the
former high master of Manchester Grammar School, who delivered it in
January 1972. In later years, she expressed dissatisfaction with the report's
emphasis on structures rather than content of education, but at the time

she was extremely cautious, and did not press ahead with its plan to have 'licensed' student teachers in the classroom, an idea hated by the union because it would undermine their sense of their own professionalism if students were permitted to teach alone without being fully qualified.[72]

The Department began to feel at ease once more. The White Paper, provisionally entitled *Education – A Framework for Expansion* by Michael James (no relation of Lord James), the young official who drafted it, and preserving that name almost to the end of the process because 'No one gave a stuff what it was called,'[73] was really a Sir Humphrey's dream, creating new work for officials for years to come, and projecting not far short of a 50 per cent rise in expenditure over the coming decade (£2,162 million in 1971–2 to £3,120 million in 1981–2). In fact, because of the priority of nursery education, the plans included some economies about teacher numbers and restraining admission to universities in favour of polytechnics, which were cheaper, and, in her eyes, crucial to the expansion of higher education. But when the Cabinet considered the proposals on 30 November 1972 – virtually the only Cabinet discussion of education policy in Heath's entire administration – it was agreed to play economies down and, for propaganda reasons, to restore the title, *A Framework for Expansion*, which had been dropped in favour of 'A Framework for Advance'. Edward Heath declared to his Cabinet colleagues that it was 'the most important White Paper [on the subject] since 1944', but he also told them that the government should 'Make clear that the White Paper is concerned with the structure, not with the content of education'.[74] So Mrs Thatcher's urgings about content had got precisely nowhere. When it was published in December 1972, the White Paper identified five areas – nursery education, school building, staffing standards in schools, teacher training and higher education – where expenditure 'will continue to increase substantially in real terms over the coming decade' – and devoted most of the rest of the document to setting out the various projections. Although always following matters with her customary thoroughness, Mrs Thatcher did not inject many of her own ideas into the White Paper.[75] There was nothing about parental choice, little about standards, little that represented an ideology. The document was essentially a bureaucratic product, arising from a cross-government exercise invented by Heath called Programme Analysis and Review (PAR). It stated an official view of matters – quantitive, not qualitative, but one which, for political reasons, Mrs Thatcher was happy to endorse. Officials, by now appreciative of her energy and communicative talents,* were very pleased with the way she presented the

---

* Mrs Thatcher was always a 'quick study', and amazed people by how rapidly she made up

Framework to the world, but what she presented was not discernibly different from what any other secretary of state for education in those years would have offered. As she said at the press conference to launch the White Paper on 6 December, 'there is little that can be accomplished in education without money,' and really money was all that it was about. She won a great deal of it for education. At the press conference, Mrs Thatcher also said, 'Most of you . . . must have felt that over the last year or so I . . . have had very little hard news to put before you.' This quietism had been intentional, and it had succeeded, but it is doubtful if Mrs Thatcher enjoyed it very much. She found herself almost bored, and would have liked to move jobs.[76] Her emollient tactic had ensured her political survival, but the price – the loss of her distinctive voice – was high. Interviews and speeches of the period show her adopting a banal, goody-goody tone which does not suit her character. The *Guardian* was now praising her for being 'more than half-way towards a respectable socialist education policy', and she told the *Illustrated London News* how pleased she was that the atmosphere in primary schools was 'much better . . . much more progressive',[77] whereas in private she complained to inspectors that such education was 'all rag dolls and rolling on the floor'.[78] Floor speakers at the Conservative Party conference in October 1972 complained vociferously that not enough was being done to protect grammar schools and permit parental choice.

For the first and almost the only time in her political career, Mrs Thatcher started to face more attacks from the right than from the left. From time to time, she gave interviews and made speeches designed to show that her Tory heart remained in the right place over education. She expressed concerns about standards of reading, and commissioned a report from the historian and moderately left-wing Vice-Chancellor of Oxford, Sir Alan Bullock, on the subject. She worried that 'We are feeding doubts into our children not beliefs,'[79] she attacked 'levelling down',[80] and she maintained rhetorical, though not practical, support for parental choice. Privately, she felt that the school curriculum was 'going off the rails'.[81] But in public she became bland. Her period at Education after 1972 is the only time in her career when her contributions in the House of Commons largely lose their combative tone. She became the loyal, careful and on the whole strictly departmental spokesman of a government that found itself in more and

---

for her pre-existing ignorance of a subject like state education. Dame Kathleen Ollerenshaw, chairman of the Manchester Education Committee when Mrs Thatcher came into office, expounded the history and development of further education to her, and noticed how fast she picked it up: 'If she'd had to learn Hebrew from scratch by the end of the week to save the nation, she'd have done it and been word perfect' (letter from Dame Kathleen Ollerenshaw).

more trouble. As the economic prospect darkened, all spending plans came under closer scrutiny and in the course of 1973 it became clear the *Framework* ideas were a wish-list which could not be met. On 12 November the National Union of Mineworkers announced an overtime ban in pursuit of a pay claim, and the following day, worried about power supply, the government proclaimed a state of emergency. One of the consequent cuts planned was of heating in schools. Mrs Thatcher was not told about this, and the first she heard about it was on the BBC's *Today* programme. She went straight round in person to the Department of Trade and Industry to complain, and within twelve hours the order was stopped. Mrs Thatcher was at pains to reveal this decisive intervention to the world.[82] If the equivalent to the milk row was looming, she wanted this time to be on the right side of the fence.

The coming struggle that was to engulf the country and the Conservative Party made school milk seem a very small matter indeed.

10

Who Governs Britain?

'The extreme left is well in command'

In the general election campaign of May/June 1970, the Conservative manifesto had declared: 'We utterly reject the philosophy of compulsory wage control.' Although the manifesto had concentrated more on Heath's desire for a 'new style of government' than on an ideologically coherent programme, it was informed by a preference for free-market liberal economics, one which Heath himself, at that time at least, shared.* He believed, and the manifesto argued, that free collective bargaining in industry – as unregulated pay negotiation between management and trade unions was known – could exist happily, provided that there was 'a new context of labour law'.[1] This meant a curbing of the legal privileges of the trade unions, and the introduction of a new Industrial Relations Act. The manifesto was equally firm in its condemnation of inflation, which it attributed to 'Labour's damaging policies of high taxation and devaluation'. Government spending had risen from a 44 per cent share of Gross Domestic Product in 1964 to 50 per cent in 1969. That drift, the Tories had argued, had to stop and be replaced by a downward pressure and by a political direction which would be maintained. 'Nothing has done Britain more harm', said the manifesto, '. . . than the endless backing and filling we have seen in recent years.' The Conservatives who won in 1970 were committed to a smaller state, and a freer economy, and to the urgency of these matters. They failed, and their failure created the conditions for Margaret Thatcher to become their leader.

It is beyond the scope of this book to give a full account of the Heath government and its economic U-turn which culminated in the introduction of

---

* The phrase 'a new style of government' was taken from a Conservative pamphlet of that name by David Howell, later Mrs Thatcher's Energy Secretary, published shortly before the election with Heath's blessing. It was a very free-market document. It is thought to be the first British publication to use the word 'privatization', a policy that it advocated. See David Howell, *The Edge of Now*, Pan, 2000, pp. 341 ff.

an incomes policy in 1972. Numerous factors contributed. The early death of Iain Macleod meant that Heath had, in Anthony Barber, a politically weak Chancellor of the Exchequer, who did not bring important thinking of his own to economic policy and was therefore a prisoner of the Keynesian dominance of the age. Much more than later prime ministers, Heath was his own chancellor, and the men with whom he worked most closely – Robert Armstrong,* his principal private secretary, Sir Burke Trend, the Cabinet Secretary, and, above all, the head of the home Civil Service, Sir William Armstrong – were all opposed to liberal, free-market economics. Government-engineered increases in growth were seen as answering the problems of economic sluggishness. The fact that the most articulate Tory advocate of liberal economics was also Heath's most hated rival, Enoch Powell, meant that criticism of policy too quickly became connected with personal disloyalty. World conditions, including President Richard Nixon's adoption of emergency economic measures in August 1971, and the oil-price shocks which followed the Yom Kippur War of 1973, did not help. Nor did the Conservative fear of unemployment as electorally lethal to the party associated with privilege and with the sufferings of the 1930s: there was alarm when the figure passed 1 million in January 1972. But by far the biggest difficulty the government faced was that of industrial relations; pay and trade unions, particularly in the nationalized industries, dominated the scene from the beginning. Union leaders who had seen off Harold Wilson in his attempt to reform industrial relations in 1969 were not going to make it easier for a new prime minister who led the party to which they were opposed. From the start, they flexed their muscles.

Douglas Hurd,† who ran Heath's political office in Downing Street from the election until the winter of 1973, recorded that 'there is no doubt what swallowed up most of my working time. The government's handling of public sector disputes was the dominant theme.'[2] This was true from the first, not only in the later, darker days. As soon as the government came into office, there was a dock strike, requiring the declaration of a state of emergency. It was settled at a very high price. In November 1970,

* Robert Armstrong (1927–), educated Eton and Christ Church, Oxford; joined Treasury, 1950; private secretary to R. A. Butler (Chancellor of the Exchequer), 1954–5; joint principal private secretary to Roy Jenkins (Chancellor), 1968; principal private secretary to the Prime Minister, 1970–75; Permanent Under-Secretary, Home Office, 1977–9; Cabinet Secretary, 1979–87; created Lord Armstrong of Ilminster, 1988. The two Armstrongs were not related.
† Douglas Hurd (1930–), educated Eton and Trinity College, Cambridge; joined FCO, 1952; political secretary to the Prime Minister, 1970–74; Conservative MP for Mid Oxon, February 1974–83; for Witney, 1983–97; Secretary of State for Northern Ireland, 1984–5; Home Secretary, 1985–9; Foreign Secretary, 1989–95; contested Conservative leadership unsuccessfully, 1990; created Lord Hurd of Westwell, 1997.

arbitrators awarded what was seen as a shockingly large 14 per cent increase to local authority workers. In the following month, regular power cuts began, as power-station employees worked to rule.* In January 1971 there was a postal strike. In March there was a serious dispute at the Ford Motor Company.

A similar, related pattern emerged in government dealings with ailing industry, whether nationalized, private or – as was often, and complicatedly, the case – somewhere between the two. In February 1971 the aero-engine company Rolls-Royce informed the government that it could not afford to complete the RB211 engine and was insolvent. Heath rescued the company in the interest of national defence. On 14 June that year he announced to the Cabinet that Upper Clyde Shipbuilders, a partly government-backed conglomerate on which depended 15,000 jobs, mainly in Scotland, was going to apply for liquidation that day. There was no question of a bail-out, he said. But over the summer, as union militants began a 'work-in' at the Clydeside yard, refusing to leave the premises, and the police authorities warned that they might not be able to preserve order, Heath weakened. On 19 October the Cabinet agreed to rescue the consortium. And the following February the Secretary of State for Trade and Industry, John Davies,† used a parliamentary debate on unemployment to proclaim the final rescue package for the company, thus explicitly linking government rescues with jobless totals, an act which even Heath came to regard as a mistake.[3]

By this time, the government was already immersed in its most significant industrial dispute, and with its most symbolically important foe. In July 1971 the National Union of Mineworkers had made a demand for a wage increase of 45 per cent, which was rejected. In December the union revised its rules, reducing the percentage required to vote for a strike to 55 per cent. Fifty-nine per cent voted that way, and on 9 January 1972 the first national miners' strike for nearly fifty years began. The government considered that it had enough stocks of coal to weather the dispute. The problem lay in their distribution. Union picketing could prevent the movement of stocks from their depots and also the movement of oil to power stations. On 10 February a session of the Cabinet was interrupted by a message for Reginald Maudling, the Home Secretary, from the Chief Constable

---

* Working to rule is a union tactic of minutely following the office or factory rulebook so that normal service is disrupted.

† John Davies (1916–79), educated St Edward's School, Oxford; Conservative MP for Knutsford, 1970–78; director-general, CBI, 1965–9; Minister of Technology, July–Oct. 1970; Secretary of State for Trade and Industry, 1970–72; Chancellor of the Duchy of Lancaster, 1972–4; Shadow Foreign Secretary, 1976–8.

of Birmingham. The message stated that he had asked for the closure of the Saltley coke depot because lorry drivers there were being prevented from entering the depot by the huge pickets. The 500 police deployed were not in a position to restrain the violent threats of the 10,000 or so pickets, who were led by the rising star of the hard left in the NUM, Arthur Scargill.* Saltley was, remembered Heath, 'the most vivid, direct and terrifying challenge to the rule of law that I could ever recall emerging from within our own country',[4] and it came at a time when the shortage of power, which had already put much of industry on a three-day week,† threatened a total blackout. Mrs Thatcher later identified Saltley as the turning point for Heath: 'Until Saltley, Ted gave a strong lead and made up his mind. Then he made up his mind the other way.'[5] Heath's response to Saltley – and probably by then he had little choice – was to find a way of giving in. He invited the judge Lord Wilberforce to conduct a hurried inquiry into the dispute. Wilberforce recommended a punishingly generous settlement of more than 20 per cent, but even this the miners rejected. Heath intervened in person, inviting the miners' leaders to 10 Downing Street and negotiating with them into the small hours. In the end, they accepted the Wilberforce pay offer, but pocketed from Heath an additional improvement in their substantial fringe benefits, such as longer holidays, so extravagant as to be the equivalent of the extra wages they had sought.

Faced with this defeat, Heath concluded that there had, after all, to be an 'industrial strategy'. On 21 March 1972 Barber presented a reflationary Budget to Parliament. The following day, John Davies unveiled his White Paper, called *Industry and Regional Development*, which contained mechanisms by which ministers could, in the phrase of the time, use public money to 'back winners' in industry, with a bias in favour of depressed regions. The new policy, not previously disclosed to the Cabinet, had been prepared mainly by Heath and William Armstrong, with Davies as little more than its spokesman, and the Treasury in the dark. When it became the Industry Bill in May, Tony Benn greeted it warmly from the Labour benches as 'spadework for socialism'. In June, the pound was floated. Over the summer, Heath organized a series of tripartite meetings between government, the Confederation of British Industry (CBI) and the TUC to discuss the objectives of economic management. These discussions tried to

---

* Arthur Scargill (1938–), educated White Cross Secondary School and Leeds University; President, Yorkshire National Union of Mineworkers, 1973; President, NUM, 1981–2002; Honorary President from 2002.

† This was not *the* 'three-day week', a formal arrangement imposed by the government from 1 January 1974.

produce the basis for an agreed policy to control prices and wages. However, the TUC ultimately baulked at the wages part of the agreement, and
after a weekend discussion at Chequers on 28–29 October Heath decided
that the government would press ahead unilaterally with wage and price
control. On 6 November he announced to the House of Commons that he
would impose a ninety-day freeze on wages, prices, rents and dividends.
This was framed as an emergency measure – and probably the government
genuinely intended it as such – but the fact was that the government had
broken decisively with the principles of a free economy with which it had
entered office. There was no general revolt in the party, but, in a sign of
their growing dissatisfaction with their leader, Tory backbenchers elected
Edward Du Cann,* a long-standing opponent of Heath, as chairman of
the 1922 Committee† that autumn. The holder of that position, which at
that time commanded great prestige, was a counterbalance to the power
of the Prime Minister. On the whole, the crisis measures were well received
in the country, at first. But for the rest of Heath's time in office the emergency deepened, and the distance from the intentions of 1970 grew.

In after years, critics of Mrs Thatcher attacked her for her acquiescence
in changes which she later so decisively repudiated. She herself had a somewhat uneasy conscience in the matter. In her memoirs, she makes much of
the fact that she was not present at the Cabinet meeting of 20 March 1972
which considered the Budget and Davies's White Paper. However, at the
meetings which she did attend, she launched no frontal assault on the new
policy. 'Should I have resigned?' she wrote. 'Perhaps so. But those of us
who disliked what was happening had not yet either fully analysed the
situation or worked out an alternative approach. Nor, realistically speaking, would my resignation have made a great deal of difference. I was not
senior enough for it to be anything other than the littlest "local difficulty".'[6]
In fact, there is no evidence that she even considered resigning. If she did,
she kept it to herself.‡ And, as she rather self-contradictingly points out in

---

* Edward Du Cann (1924–), educated Woodbridge School and St John's College, Oxford;
Conservative MP for Taunton, 1956–87; Chairman, Conservative Party, 1965–7; Chairman,
1922 Committee, 1972–84. A leading figure in the City, he was ultimately discredited by his
controversial financial record.
† The 1922 Committee consists of all Conservative Members of Parliament. Its executive is
drawn from the back benches. Its private meetings provide a forum for backbenchers and the
chance to discuss matters with frontbenchers.
‡ It is true, however, that The Times reported that Mrs Thatcher was among those ministers
who objected to the Industry Bill when it was published in May (The Times, 17 May 1972).
The report is likely to have been correct, since David Wood, the paper's political correspondent,
was one of Mrs Thatcher's few journalistic contacts at that time. He had known her father in
Grantham.

the same paragraph, some of those who disliked what was happening *had* analysed it. Notable among them were Enoch Powell, Nicholas Ridley,* John Biffen† and Jock Bruce-Gardyne.‡

Partly because she was a woman in a man's world, and partly because she was a busy minister, Mrs Thatcher was not a member of any gang of like-minded people who debated these matters. The discontented, including the four named above and John Nott§ and Cecil Parkinson,¶ were part of the influential, free-market-oriented Economic Dining Club, which met once a month in one another's houses when Parliament was sitting: Mrs Thatcher was not a member, and was not invited to join until after the general election of February 1974. Indeed, earlier suggestions that she should join were blocked by those who thought her presence would reduce the jollity of the all-male proceedings and force them to start serious discussions even before dinner had begun.[7] Mrs Thatcher later alleged that she objected, in Cabinet, that the tripartite system of economic discussions was 'anti-parliamentary',[8] but Cabinet records contain no evidence of this. Heath himself took some pleasure, in later years, in pointing out that Mrs Thatcher 'didn't argue a great deal in Cabinet', and that, if she showed signs of 'being difficult', 'once she'd heard three taps on the Cabinet table, then she knew [that the debate was over].'[9] Other pro-Heath witnesses have also maintained that she voiced no dissent in his Cabinets.[10]

Some light on Mrs Thatcher's attitude to her own political career at this time, and to the government of which she was a part, is shed by an airgram

* Nicholas Ridley (1929–93), educated Eton and Balliol College, Oxford; Conservative MP for Cirencester and Tewkesbury, 1959–92; Minister of State, FCO, 1979–81; Financial Secretary to the Treasury, 1981–3; Secretary of State for Transport, 1983–7; for the Environment, 1987–9; for Trade and Industry, 1989–90; forced to resign after a frank interview criticizing Germany and the EEC in the *Spectator*, July 1990; created Lord Ridley of Liddesdale, 1992.

† John Biffen (1930–2007), educated Dr Morgan's School, Bridgwater and Jesus College, Cambridge; Conservative MP for Oswestry, 1961–83; for Shropshire North, 1983–97; Chief Secretary to the Treasury, 1979–81; Secretary of State for Trade, 1981–2; Lord President of the Council, 1982–3; Leader of the House of Commons, 1982–7; Lord Privy Seal, 1983–7; created Lord Biffen, 1997.

‡ Jock Bruce-Gardyne (1930–90), educated Winchester and Magdalen College, Oxford; Conservative MP for South Angus, 1964–74; for Knutsford, 1979–83; Minister of State, Treasury, 1981; Economic Secretary to the Treasury, 1981–3; created Lord Bruce-Gardyne, 1983.

§ John Nott (1932–), educated Bradfield and Trinity College, Cambridge; Conservative MP for Cornwall St Ives, 1966–83; Secretary of State for Trade, 1979–81; for Defence, 1981–3; knighted, 1983.

¶ Cecil Parkinson (1931–), Royal Lancaster Grammar School, Lancaster and Emmanuel College, Cambridge; Conservative MP for Enfield West, 1970–74; for Hertfordshire South, February 1974–83; for Hertsmere, 1983–92; Secretary of State for Trade and Industry, June–Oct. 1983; for Energy, 1987–9; for Transport, 1989–90; Chairman, Conservative Party, 1981–3 and 1997–8; created Lord Parkinson, 1992.

from the US Embassy in London to the State Department. It was sent by the Ambassador, Walter Annenberg* (much later one of her close American friends), on 25 June 1973, accompanying the memorandum of a conversation at lunch at the Connaught Hotel by Dirk Gleysteen of the Embassy staff.[11] Mrs Thatcher, Annenberg wrote, has put in a performance which is 'solid, respectable and unspectacular. She has not sought to introduce radical remedies to deal with Britain's problems in education and science.' 'She is a strong supporter of Heath,' he went on, and he poured cold water on the idea that she might become prime minister: 'it is most doubtful that she could, or does, realistically expect to lead her party . . . A well-educated, intelligent and even sophisticated woman herself, Mrs Thatcher shares with others in her party a certain anti-intellectual bias.'

Gleysteen's memo was more gossipy. His lunch the previous month had taken place the day after Anthony Barber had announced spending cuts from which education had been exempted. Mrs Thatcher told Gleysteen that she had persuaded colleagues not to cut education as planned: 'When the chips were down, education policy would not win an election and it was therefore important not to let this area be vulnerable to negative attacks.' Asked by Gleysteen what the next election would be about, she 'unhesitatingly said: "Food prices and housing"', and viewed these in what Gleysteen described as an 'ideological' light: 'She said she considered it a Tory duty to try to frame all government policy in such a fashion as to lessen the growing dependence of the citizen on the government.'

Becoming loquacious, she then passed comments on various colleagues in government: 'Geoffrey Howe. Mrs Thatcher obviously respects and thinks highly of him but said he is "too willing to compromise" and she wondered if he would get "over this weakness".' 'She said Michael Haseltine [sic] had everything it took in politics except brains.' And she reserved her highest praise for Keith Joseph: 'She has tremendous admiration for Joseph and considers him brilliant, versatile and full of further promise. She said that he could handle any ministry and she was confident that he has been marked for higher responsibility.' Bits of this report indicate that Mrs Thatcher is a woman of her own views ('slightly to the right-of-center' said Annenberg). Nothing suggests serious revolt against the direction of the government.

The records do show, however, that Mrs Thatcher maintained a fairly consistent position in Cabinet – though not an important one, because of

* Walter Annenberg (1908–2002), businessman and philanthropist; US Ambassador to Britain, 1969–74.

her non-economic brief and her lack of seniority. Seated on the same side of the table as Heath, but as far away from him as it was possible to sit, she sometimes found difficulty in getting attention, and on one occasion the Cabinet Secretary, Burke Trend, actually records her intervention as 'not heard' (though he heard it himself). Robin Butler,* later cabinet secretary and, from 1972, one of Heath's private secretaries, noted that Mrs Thatcher's interventions 'sounded rather shrill and fell on stony ground': they were delivered with 'more emphasis than confidence'.[12]

Almost all her interventions on topics outside her department, though, showed her opposed to corporatism, union power and wage and price control. In March 1971 she objected in Cabinet to the fact that supplementary benefits were paid to the families of strikers. In May of that year she complained about public sector pay outstripping that of the private sector and attacked the fashionable notion of 'comparability'. In July she opposed government purchase of shares in BP, saying, 'We are passing up the chance to tap the market.' In February 1972 she called for sources of power supply to be 'more widely diffused in smaller units'; and in December, when Heath proposed to pour more money into the coal industry, she argued for a policy of conserving more coal and extracting less. She had a strong sense of the political opportunity for Conservatives presented by strikes, and urged a readiness to make the argument against union power as wide and as public as possible. During the rail dispute of June 1972 she declared to her Cabinet colleagues, 'The real battle is – and should be presented [as being] – between unions and people, not between unions and government.' When the prices and incomes policy was introduced, she did not confront it head on, in general terms, but deployed practical, grocer's-daughter arguments against aspects of it. On 30 October 1972, for example, she explained that a freeze before Christmas would cause shortages, and she insisted that luxury items should remain exempt from the freeze, as this was 'essential if the basics are not to disappear'. When the Cabinet discussed how to 'de-escalate' the freeze in January 1973, Mrs Thatcher said that a 'clean break' with the policy might be 'psychologically wiser'.[13] Cecil Parkinson, who had entered Parliament in a by-election in 1970, remembered her taking him aside at some time in 1973 and saying, 'Look, I'm fighting all these incomes policies and statutory controls in Cabinet, but I need people outside Cabinet to speak up.'[14] She intensely disliked the idea that inflation was a price worth paying for economic growth and

---

* Robin Butler (1938–), educated Harrow and University College, Oxford; principal private secretary to the Prime Minister, 1982–5; Second Permanent Secretary, Public Expenditure, Treasury, 1985–7; Cabinet Secretary, 1988–98; created Lord Butler of Brockwell, 1998.

social peace. She always remembered a conversation in the rose garden at Chequers with Robin Butler, then (1971) a youngish member of Heath's so-called Think Tank, the Central Policy Review Staff (CPRS). He told her, she recalled, 'If we can't beat inflation, we've got to learn to live with it.' Mrs Thatcher replied emphatically, 'Robin. No. No!'[15] Ten years later, when she interviewed Butler for the post of principal private secretary, she reminded him of the incident: 'You said inflation was endemic. I've never heard a more shocking remark from a young man.'[16]

On non-economic subjects, too, Mrs Thatcher pursued lines which were to become recognizable in her subsequent career, putting her, for the most part, to the right of the majority of her Cabinet, though not her parliamentary colleagues. When it was explained by Barber that the introduction of Value Added Tax (VAT) was a necessary consequence of British entry into the EEC,* which finally took place on 1 January 1973, she nevertheless opposed the tax as 'dislocating and politically unpopular'. On Northern Ireland, a problem by then so great that Heath gave it a huge proportion of his mental energy, Mrs Thatcher wanted to threaten the Irish Republic with reprisals if it did not control the IRA, and opposed the prorogation of the devolved, Unionist-dominated Parliament at Stormont on the grounds that it would be to 'suspend democracy in part of the UK'. Heath rebuked her, saying that direct rule would merely put the province in the same category as Scotland and Wales. When the Yom Kippur War broke out with the Arab attack on Israel in October 1973, she allied herself in Cabinet with Keith Joseph (who was Jewish) and the Lord Chancellor, Lord Hailsham, against the prevailing, pro-Arab view of the Foreign Office and of Heath himself. On 18 October she burst out bitterly that the British policy of standing aside from the conflict had 'lost support of everyone, especially young. Must say no question of Israel being wiped off face of earth.' Heath immediately slapped her down, saying: 'Don't accept Educ's [in Cabinet, ministers are always referred to by department rather than by name] view of public opinion. It's a Jewish-inspired press campaign.'[17] She was perfectly capable of speaking her mind, and that mind was already of a distinct cast. What is also true, however, is that she did not think it her place to raise large issues of principle in direct form. On 1 July 1971, for example, the Cabinet discussed how much the question of loss of British sovereignty to the EEC should be dealt with explicitly in the White Paper making the case for entry, and how serious the loss of sovereignty involved really was. Mrs Thatcher was silent throughout. She said in later years,

---

* The European Treaty required a common form (though not amount) of indirect taxation to raise revenues for the Community.

with regret, that she had regarded the arguments that Powell and others put forward about sovereignty at the time as 'rhetorical devices'.[18]

It is not hard to understand why Mrs Thatcher, and any other colleagues who felt dissatisfaction with the trend of the Heath government, nevertheless went along with it. In addition to the natural desire of ministers to stick together for as long as possible, there was something subsequent generations have forgotten – the personal prestige of Ted Heath. Having won the 1970 election in defiance of the opinion polls and the pundits, Heath was highly successful in establishing himself in public respect, though not affection. The contrast between him and the 'slippery' Harold Wilson was marked, and worked, most of the time, in his favour. His commitment to British entry into the EEC and to power-sharing between Unionist and Nationalist in Northern Ireland assured him of the support of the establishment; his concern to tackle Britain's economic failure and industrial relations chaos was clearly sincere and energetic. In his conduct of government business, Heath was surprisingly good at forging a loyal team, and making traditional Cabinet government work. Mrs Thatcher later complained that his Cabinet was much reduced in importance after the first year in government,[19] and there is some truth in this, particularly over economic policy. But the records show many lively discussions, even towards the end of the administration. In private conversation years later, Mrs Thatcher paid Heath a backhanded compliment for his way of dealing with colleagues: 'I was impressed by the lead Ted gave in Cabinet. If I'd have done it, I'd have been called bossy.'[20] In truth, Heath maintained loyalty and unanimity to a great degree, until the end, and suffered very little from leaks to the press.

It followed from this that, when the skies darkened, the reaction of colleagues and, to some extent, of public opinion was to draw closer to Heath rather than to attack him. Although a prices and incomes policy defied the principles on which the Conservatives had come into office, the context for its introduction was widely seen as that of a crisis – an extreme situation demanding extreme, and temporary, measures. The danger for Tory critics of the policy was that they would find themselves in effective, though not ideological, alliance with trade union militants, both trying to undermine the Prime Minister. This is something that Margaret Thatcher would never for a moment have contemplated. She was as desperate as Heath to defeat trade union power, and so saw herself on the same side of the barricade. Besides, her instincts always inclined towards party loyalty, and Heath was the leader of her party.

It was also important that the drama of the industrial disputes which led to the U-turn was played out against a fast-changing background of labour law reform. In the first six months of its existence, the Heath government began a serious attempt to fulfil its election promise on industrial relations. It sought to accomplish what Harold Wilson had been forced to abandon, and change the state of the law on trade unions. The Industrial Relations Bill, which finally passed into law in August 1971, 'was the centrepiece of our long-term economic programme', wrote Heath, 'and we had a clear mandate to introduce it.'[21] The Bill established the right to join or not to join a trade union and provided that future collective agreements should be legally enforceable. It established a new National Industrial Relations Court to adjudicate the cases that the new law would create. The idea was to bring regularity and legal form to procedures which had become wild and uncontrollable. The political and economic prize of success was huge, and one which had eluded all British governments since the war. The new law did not come into force until March 1972, and its progenitors had high hopes of it. By early August, it had failed, and was seen to have failed.

The law foundered on the non-cooperation of the unions, and the contradictory workings of the courts. Unions refused to register under the Act or to recognize the new court. In the first month of the Act's operation, the new court declared that the blacking of container lorries by Liverpool dockers should cease. The dockers' union, the TGWU, was fined £5,000 for contempt because it would not recognize the court. Refusing to pay, it was fined a further £50,000 and threatened with the sequestration of its assets. It then paid the fine, but the unofficial blacking of container lorries continued, and spread. Meanwhile, during a dispute with the three rail unions, the Act was invoked by the government to enforce a so-called cooling-off period and then a compulsory ballot on a strike. The members voted by five to one in favour of industrial action, and so the new law had worked smoothly against the purpose of its framers.

Matters got worse for the government. The TGWU appealed against the Merseyside ruling by Sir John Donaldson in the National Industrial Relations Court (NIRC), which held that unions, rather than their individual members, were legally responsible for those members' actions and should be made to pay accordingly. In the Appeal Court, the Master of the Rolls, Lord Denning, took the opposite view, saying that individual trade unionists were legally liable. The new court thus had its authority cut away. Confusion then ensued as the NIRC tried to turn its attention from collective lawbreakers to individuals, many of whom were only too happy to be arrested in defence of their cause. In July five dockers who defied an order from the NIRC to stop obstructing container lorries in Hackney were arrested and detained in Pentonville prison, quickly becoming the

'Pentonville Five'. There were sympathy stoppages, including five days in which no national newspapers appeared, and also, because of the continuing dispute about containerization, a national dock strike. The TUC voted for a one-day general strike and broke off the tripartite talks which Heath had begun.

Coming to the rescue with a speed which looked more political than legal, the Law Lords, led by Lord Wilberforce, who had recently been in charge of the capitulation to the miners, overturned Denning, returning to Donaldson's original contention that the law did hold unions responsible for the actions of their members. The Pentonville Five were consequently cheated of martyrdom, and released. The government was saved from out-and-out confrontation, but not from the humiliation of its new legal procedures and of the entire Industrial Relations Act. Although the government refused to give in to the TUC demand to repeal its precious Act, its tripartite approach to economic management effectively meant putting the Act on one side. In August 1972, ACAS, the Advisory Conciliation and Arbitration Service, was set up by the TUC and the CBI as the approved mechanism for dealing with industrial disputes. The strategy behind the Industrial Relations Act had therefore collapsed. The attempt to give a legal frame to labour relations had not worked. Given the push of inflation and the power of the unions, another way had to be found to seek industrial sanity. By a logic which the Heath government did not like, but could no longer resist, the way that presented itself was a prices and incomes policy. Enoch Powell later noted that Sir Geoffrey Howe, the Solicitor-General, had told a backbench colleague in June 1972 that he was 'mad' to advocate an incomes policy, but by November, as minister for trade and consumer affairs, Howe was implementing one himself.[22] When Howe brought the Counter-Inflation (Temporary Measures) Bill before the House, Powell was the only Conservative to vote against it. The U-turn was complete.

Even more than she was worried by the change of economic policy, Mrs Thatcher was shocked by the unions' challenge to the rule of law. When Wilberforce had made his recommendations on the miners' pay, she had publicly regretted the damage done ('it is the people who have to pay'), but had declared that in future the Industrial Relations Act would come to the rescue: 'If we ever face a similar situation again, the law on picketing . . . will be quite different.'[23] It turned out that the 'quite different' law made no difference. In a speech in Devon on 29 July 1972, she linked, in terms of moral obliquity, the defiance of the Industrial Relations Act with the sectarian disorders in Northern Ireland which had led Heath to impose direct rule from Westminster in March. She deplored 'an industrial situation where the orders of the courts were being challenged'.[24] The lesson she learnt was that labour law had to be framed differently if it was to work: 'Never, never, never put a trade unionist in prison for going on strike' and 'Never go for the person; go for the funds.'[25] She also learnt from the mistakes of the supposedly more moderate Heath, 'not to try to do everything with the unions at once'.[26]

The psychological situation of the government after the U-turn was an odd one. It bought trade union acquiescence with a financial profligacy which undermined economic health, but at the same time prepared for confrontation, as if it sought both war and peace. Right up until the end, this split state of mind afflicted the government, and Heath in particular, producing a fundamental ambiguity in the election campaign of February 1974. Still in her post at Education, Mrs Thatcher was pretty well powerless to influence events, but she did not feel ambiguous. She expected conflict and almost welcomed it. She considered union co-operation with government to be bogus because the unions were using the threat of 'naked force', and she feared the growing power of Communists and others on the hard left within the union movement: 'It was very obvious to me that this was a power struggle.'[27]

The final conflict took some time to come. At first the prices and incomes policy, with its Stage 1 and Stage 2, was reasonably orderly, and the short-term economic growth caused by Barber's expansionary policies anaesthetized the wounds. But many saw that a battle could not be indefinitely delayed, and the mood soured. In a private diary that he began on 1 January 1973, the senior and disgruntled Conservative backbencher Airey Neave foresaw it. In his entry for 15 February he used a phrase which was soon to acquire public resonance. Stage 2 of the prices and incomes policy, he wrote, raised the question of 'Who governs Britain?'[28] He did not much enjoy the way Heath was governing his country. Three days later, Neave heard his leader speak at the Savoy Hotel: 'No recognition of backbenchers. He does not realise how unpopular he is. I also realise that while he is PM I shall never receive an honour.'[29]* Gradually, the tide of public opinion, which had moved back towards the Conservatives, turned against them once more. In July a surge of support for the Liberals gave them amazing by-election victories in Ripon and the Isle of Ely. Late in the same month the inflationary effects of monetary laxity forced Barber to raise the Minimum Lending Rate from 7.75 per cent, first to 9 per cent and then

---

* A knighthood for a Conservative backbencher after twenty years' service had been considered almost automatic, but Neave had not received one.

to 11.5 per cent. In late August the twenty-year-old Carol Thatcher wrote to her aunt Muriel succinctly summing up her mother's predicament: 'I think Education and the prospect of losing her seat to the Liberals at the next election is driving Mum round the bend ... don't write here [the Thatcher home in Flood Street, Chelsea, to which they had moved in 1972 after selling the house in Lamberhurst]* – everything goes to Dept Ed. for metal detecting and bomb checks – bloody Irish.'[30]

Stage 2 of the prices and incomes policy had given workers an increase of £1 per week plus 4 per cent, a formula designed to benefit the low-paid disproportionately. It had worked, in the sense that no group of workers had successfully defied it. Over the summer, Stage 3 was prepared. It involved formulae of considerable complication, and included the establishment of a study of 'relativities' by the Pay Board, so that the lot of different groups of workers could be compared and their grievances about these differences addressed in Stage 4. Mrs Thatcher was very little involved in any of this, but in her memoirs she records the moment when the absurdity of the processes was borne in upon her. As a member of the Cabinet Economic Sub-Committee which dealt with pay, she one day attended a meeting at which William Armstrong was also present. The main subject was the pay of senior civil servants, such as William Armstrong. 'What struck me ... was that no one doubted that this particular group needed a larger pay increase than pay policy allowed. And what was true for Under-Secretaries in the civil service was true for innumerable other groups throughout the economy. Our pay policy was not just absurd: far from being "fair", it was fundamentally unjust.'[31]

Shortly after the announcement of Stage 3 on 8 October 1973, the Yom Kippur War broke out with the Arab attack on Israel. The oil producers' cartel, OPEC, announced a price rise of 70 per cent in the price of crude oil, and also imposed cutbacks in supply. By the end of the year, the price was to double again. This sudden change of circumstances gave new power to the National Union of Mineworkers as it set out to press its latest pay claim. It became much harder for the government to burn oil in order to conserve coal stocks, and the dependency of British industrial production on coal was increased. Heath, however, believed that the miners had been squared. Over the summer, he had held a secret meeting in the garden of 10 Downing Street with Joe Gormley, the moderate miners' leader. Heath and William Armstrong, who was also present, had got the impression that the miners' 35 per cent pay claim could be transmogrified into an agreement about special payments for 'unsocial hours' which could be brought

---

* The Thatchers continued in Lamberhurst at weekends, renting a flat in Scotney Castle.

within the ambit of Stage 3. For reasons beyond Gormley's control, this turned out not to be the case. The NUM executive was more militant than he. An overtime ban, which, because of the nature of coal production, had an immediate effect on output, began on 12 November. The Trade and Industry Secretary, Peter Walker,* announced the fifth state of emergency in that Parliament. There were restrictions on heating in shops, offices and schools, and petrol ration coupons were printed, though not used. On 28 November, Heath, who had lost faith in the National Coal Board and taken personal charge of the negotiations, received the whole of the NUM executive at No. 10. At this meeting, there was an exchange between Heath and Mick McGahey, the Scottish miners' leader, who was a Communist. Its exact words are disputed, but it seems that Heath said: 'What is it you want, Mr McGahey?' and McGahey replied, 'I want to see the end of your government.'[32] The impression grew that the motive of the dispute was political. The natural conclusion was that the Last Battle approached.

Heath's reaction to the crisis, however, was strange. Though convinced of the political motivation of the miners and utterly committed to standing his ground on compliance with Stage 3, he also hated the idea of an electoral confrontation. He kept telling the miners that they stood to benefit from the relativities provisions of Stage 3, and kept looking for a deal. He was extremely reluctant to use the public rhetoric of confrontation. Seeing the strength of support for the government's position in the opinion polls, William Waldegrave,† who was just taking over from Douglas Hurd as head of Heath's political office, advised the Prime Minister to exploit the crisis and go for a 'Who governs Britain?' election. Senior Tories, such as Lord Carrington‡ and Ian Gilmour,§ were more doubtful. They feared

---

* Peter Walker (1932–2010), educated Latymer Upper School; Conservative MP for Worcester, 1961–92; Secretary of State for the Environment, 1970–72; for Trade and Industry, 1972–4; Minister of Agriculture, Fisheries and Food, 1979–83; Secretary of State for Energy, 1983–7; for Wales, 1987–90; created Lord Walker of Worcester, 1992.

† William Waldegrave (1946–), educated Eton, Corpus Christi College, Oxford and Harvard University; younger son of 12th Earl Waldegrave; Conservative MP for Bristol West, 1979–97; Secretary of State for Health, 1990–92; Chancellor of the Duchy of Lancaster, 1992–94; Minister of Agriculture, Fisheries and Food, 1994–5; Chief Secretary to the Treasury, 1995–7; created Lord Waldegrave of North Hill, 1999.

‡ Peter Carrington (6th Baron Carrington) (1919–), educated Eton and Royal Military College, Sandhurst; First Lord of the Admiralty, 1959–63; Leader of House of Lords, 1963–4 and 1974–9; Secretary of State for Defence, 1970–74; for Energy, 1974; for Foreign and Commonwealth Affairs, 1979–82; Secretary-General, NATO, 1984–8; created life peer, when hereditary peerages were partially abolished, 1999.

§ Ian Gilmour (1926–2007), 3rd baronet; educated Eton and Balliol College, Oxford; Conservative MP for Norfolk Central, 1962–74; for Chesham and Amersham, February 1974–92; owner (1954–67) and editor (1954–9) of the *Spectator*; Secretary of State for Defence,

'We'd have let the genie of social revenge out of the bottle.'[33] Heath shared this anxiety, and also hated the idea of an early election because he rightly feared that it would bring down the Sunningdale power-sharing agreement in Northern Ireland which he had only just achieved. He had not had a proper holiday that year, and was utterly exhausted, a condition which always makes decisions more difficult. On 13 December 1973 he broadcast to the nation, without really having decided what his line was. He called on the British people to 'close our ranks so that we can deal together with the difficulties'. Did he want a fight or not? Airey Neave wrote in his diary, 'we watched PM give a wooden appeal to the nation on television. Today I suggested to some Members that Whitelaw should be PM but they thought him "too emotional".'* Mrs Thatcher remembered going to a party of her Lamberhurst neighbours Kenneth and Patricia McAlpine shortly before Christmas, where all the steps were lit with candles. She erroneously recalled this as being because of power cuts, whereas in fact they were merely decorative. What she did remember clearly was that everyone at the party was urging the government to fight: 'Go on, you show 'em this time.'[34] Tory supporters were waiting for a lead.

None was yet forthcoming, although the atmosphere was heavy with doom. On 1 January 1974 Airey Neave wrote in his diary, 'The next few weeks may decide the future of the parliamentary system.' On the same day, a three-day week was introduced by the government to conserve fuel and avoid power cuts. Television closed down each night at 10.30. The measures worked quite well, and productivity rose, creating a political problem for the government: if the overtime ban could thus be circumvented, what was the need for the atmosphere of political crisis? Heath's indecision about an election continued, with Lord Carrington and Jim Prior, by now chairman and deputy chairman of the party, crying 'Forward!' and Willie Whitelaw crying 'Back!'† Carrington and Prior settled on the date of 7 February as the last polling day where the Tories would have the initiative, but Heath, still dithering, rejected it after Whitelaw took him out to dinner to dissuade him.‡ Heath held out for yet another

---

1974; chairman, Conservative Research Department, 1974–5; Lord Privy Seal, 1979–81; created Lord Gilmour, 1992.

* Willie Whitelaw, whom Heath had just recalled from his post as Northern Ireland secretary to help sort out the miners' dispute, was drinking very heavily at this time. The word 'emotional' is partly a code-word for drunk.

† Mrs Thatcher was among those who wanted an early election, and she told Heath this when he summoned his ministers in small groups to give him their views on the subject. Her voice would not have been persuasive to him.

‡ So great was the uncertainty about the election date, and the extent of rune-reading that preceded the choice, that Cabinet Office officials claimed to have seen a copy of the popular

meeting with the TUC to try to resolve the crisis. Mrs Thatcher's patience was wearing thin. In Cabinet she agreed to 'one last heave but with miners and not TUC. Can't go on being a puppet government.'[35] 'The opinion polls show us 4 percent ahead,' wrote Neave, 'but the delay is swinging opinion the other way.'[36] On 4 February the NUM ballot showed 81 per cent in favour of any action the executive chose to take. A strike was called for 9 February. On 7 February Heath announced a general election for the 28th of that month. At the Cabinet meeting which agreed the final decision, Mrs Thatcher told colleagues that it 'will be a bitter election but at the same time the most idealistic'. She also, in contrast to her later description of her attitudes at the time, argued that Heath should seek 'a doctor's mandate'* from the electorate, campaigning more on 'fairness' than on confrontation.[37] Willie Whitelaw said to Heath: 'If we lose we're all in this together and you will have preserved our honour.'[38]

Although the logic of his electoral decision dictated otherwise, Heath still disliked the idea of a fight about 'Who governs Britain?' He did not want a head-on collision with the miners. He announced, even as he launched his election campaign, that he would refer their claim to the relativities panel of the Pay Board and would abide by its view, making people ask why an election was needed at all. He persuaded himself that he needed a new mandate to deal with the new economic circumstances created by the oil price shock. Heath had made the bold, immoderate decision to go to the country over a great issue of principle in the middle of winter and almost a year and a half before an election was due by law, yet he insisted on conducting the campaign in terms so moderate that people wondered what the fuss was about. At a mass meeting in Gravesend shortly before the end of the campaign, a heckler called out to Heath: 'What can you do if you win that you can't do now?'[39] There was never a satisfactory answer to this question.

Various things went wrong for Heath in the course of the campaign. The relativities board found that it had used the wrong figures in determining the miners' claim and that miners' pay had been overstated by 8 per cent. This discovery, which a day later proved statistically false itself, was leaked, with damaging effect. In the middle of the campaign, the new retail price figures showed inflation running at 20 per cent per annum, which emphasized that the Conservatives had got less than nowhere with

---

astrological work *Old Moore's Almanack* at Heath's place at the Cabinet table (interview with Ralph Baxter).
* The phrase, indicating an appeal to voters on non-ideological grounds of professional competence, originated with Stanley Baldwin.

inflation. At the outset, Enoch Powell had declared that he would not stand again as a Conservative Party candidate because the government had betrayed the promises it made in 1970. Two weeks later, he intervened again, calling on his supporters to vote Labour because of its opposition to membership of the EEC. In Powell's stronghold of the West Midlands, enough of his followers duly did so. Given that the margin of defeat proved so small, it could fairly be said that it was Powell who turned Heath out.

The campaign was not, in fact, a particularly glorious one for the Labour Party. Harold Wilson, fighting his fourth election as leader, seemed jaded. His party avoided offering any answers to the economic crisis of the day and its proposed 'Social Contract' with the trade unions, concocted suddenly after the beginning of the campaign, had little content. But that did not matter much. It was Heath who had called the election when he did not have to, perhaps when he did not want to. It was Heath who had submitted an unsatisfactory record to the electorate, Heath who was causing all this bother. 'I'm like Baldwin,' Wilson said to Bernard Donoughue, who was to run his Policy Unit after the election. 'I'm here to give people a quiet life.'[40] And if Labour's quietist position seemed no more of an answer than the Tories' confrontational one, there were always the Liberals, capitalizing on popular disillusionment with both the parties who had so mismanaged things over the previous ten years.

Mrs Thatcher, like most of her party, believed that the Conservatives would win. Although she had grown more and more dissatisfied with Ted Heath, and privately critical of his tactics in handling the miners' dispute, particularly of his delay in election timing, she thought the fight was right: 'There was a feeling that we were being tough, and that that was a good thing.'[41] Although she played no prominent part in the national campaign, she fought it in Finchley on the rhetorical high ground. At her adoption meeting, she said that this was 'perhaps the most crucial' in her career, because it was a test of whether Britain was serious about fighting inflation (which, heretically for the future monetarist, she attributed to 'wage-push') and whether wage claims were to be decided by force or by reasonableness. Her own patch of Education was not a leading feature of the election. She focused, more uncompromisingly than Heath, on the problem with the miners:

> The coal industry is nationalised. You own it. One of the arguments put forward for nationalised industry was that people would not strike against the rest of the people of the country, but that has not worked out. All our problems are now coming from nationalised industries because they have created a monopoly. This election is a ballot of all the owners of the industry.[42]

Her campaigning style was combative. In her only national broadcast of the campaign, a BBC *Election Call* programme in which she shared a platform with Willie Whitelaw, Mrs Thatcher dismissed the idea of a nation-saving coalition of all the talents which was beginning to come up: 'I think it's a false assumption that if you get a government of all the best brains, the best brains will agree what to do.'[43] And in her only full press interview of the campaign, in the *Daily Express* three days later, she presented herself as doughty: ' "I get *very* wild with people who don't realise that underneath all this" – she taps a gold suit button – "there's a bit of tough steel that's me." '[44]

By mid-morning of polling day, Mrs Thatcher was worried. She didn't like the way so many people on normally apathetic non-Tory council estates in Finchley were turning up to vote.[45] Her fears were justified. Her own majority was almost halved.

Mrs Margaret Thatcher (Conservative)	18,180
Martin O'Connor (Labour)	12,202
Laurence Brass (Liberal)	11,221
Conservative majority	5,978

The national result gave the Conservatives a larger share of the vote than Labour, but four fewer seats. The Liberals, with an astonishing 6 million votes (almost 20 per cent of the whole), pulled the Tories down, although their gain of seats was tiny. Labour won 301 seats, the Conservatives 297, the Liberals 14. No party had an overall majority in the House of Commons.

Heath tried to cling to power. By convention, he was entitled to do this, as the Queen, breaking her visit to Australia and returning home because of the crisis, was advised. She let him try to form a new administration. But, although the rules permitted him, public opinion was more impatient. He had gambled, was the feeling in the country and even in much of the party, and he had failed. 'I thought from the start that E. Heath would have done better to resign,' wrote Airey Neave in his diary for 2 March 1974. A sense of doom hung over the few frantic days that followed. If Heath had not broken with the Ulster Unionists, many of whom, until his suspension of Stormont, had taken the Tory whip, he could have struggled on. Overtures were made from that direction, but came to nothing.[46] A more likely partner was the Liberal Party. On 1 March the Cabinet met to discuss the suggestion coming from Heath and those closest to him, such as Carrington and Prior (Willie Whitelaw was ill), that a deal should be sought. The idea was that 'moderates' should come together, and a coalition be mustered of the 'anti-socialist vote'. In words that suggest the weakness of the enthusiasm for this, Robert Armstrong, who was Heath's principal private secretary at the time, recorded that the Cabinet gave 'an indication of their inclination towards an attempt to come to an understanding with the Liberals'.[47] But even this tepidity was too much for Mrs Thatcher. For the first time in three and a half years in Cabinet, she let rip. She protested at the suggestion that the Liberals were a force that had to be accommodated: 'But 5 m. Lib. votes are non-Liberal. They are ours, and if we coalesce we lose them for ever. And don't sell constitution for a mess of pottage.'[48] Recorded by the Cabinet Secretary Sir John Hunt* as one voice speaking together, she and Keith Joseph said: 'We must keep our integrity.' 'What wd effect on parly party be of dabbling with electoral reform?' asked Mrs Thatcher. 'We must accept consequences of election and offer patriotic opposition to Labour,' said Joseph.

The Cabinet overruled its two rebels, however, and the following day Heath saw Jeremy Thorpe, the Liberal leader.† The following night, Sunday 3 March, after attending a dinner given in No. 11 by Anthony Barber, which Mrs Thatcher also attended, Heath saw Thorpe again and on the morning of Monday 4 March reported the conversations to the Cabinet. Neither side could give enough ground to satisfy the other. The Cabinet approved Heath's final letter to Thorpe, offering only a full coalition, rather than the loose arrangement he preferred, and no more than a Speaker's Conference on proportional representation. Thorpe duly rejected it later that day, and the Cabinet met once more to hear this before agreeing that the matter was at an end. Armstrong recorded the last moments of Heath's premiership: 'At 6.25 p.m., the Prime Minister left 10 Downing Street for Buckingham Palace. I went with him; on the drive neither of us said a word. There was so much, or nothing, left to say.'[49] The Queen asked Harold Wilson to form his third Labour administration.

Unusually for a secretary of state for education, the Department gave a farewell party for Mrs Thatcher: they had grown quite fond of her by the end. Her secretary, Alison Ward, noticed that, in accordance with her long-standing habit of taking nothing for granted, she was the only person on

---

* John Hunt (1919–2008), educated Downside and Magdalene College, Oxford; served RNVR, 1940–46; joined Home Civil Service, 1946; Cabinet Secretary, 1973–9; chairman, Prudential Corporation, 1985–90; created Lord Hunt of Tanworth, 1980.

† It is a reflection on the more gentlemanly mores of the time that throughout the campaign of February 1974 the Conservatives were in possession of information about the homosexual scandal involving Jeremy Thorpe which was later to bring him down. Lord Carrington, the party Chairman, ordered that it be locked away and not used in any form. It is hard to imagine such a policy being followed today. (Information from Lord Waldegrave.)

the ministerial corridor in the House of Commons who had cleared her desk before the government had fallen.[50] In a newspaper interview a few days after the defeat, Mrs Thatcher claimed that 'It is easier for a woman than a man to give up power because you are not so lost. I can fill the time by spring-cleaning the house.'[51] But her later memory of her reaction was almost the opposite: 'I can't tell you how lost I felt.'[52]

Tory disappointment at the election result was deep, and therefore discontent grew. Heath addressed the 1922 Committee the following day and Airey Neave spoke to him afterwards: 'he is much deflated. He was also, one remembers, a bad Leader of the Opposition.'[53] The plotting was pretty well instantaneous: 'Hugh Fraser* said I should be on the front bench,' said Neave. 'He is beginning to campaign against Heath.'[54] Even at the grandest level, there was feeling against Heath, or at least a sense that he could not just carry on regardless. On the night that Heath resigned as prime minister, Carrington gave him dinner at his house in Ovington Square, along with Tim Kitson,† Douglas Hurd and Charlie Morrison.‡ These men agreed that Heath should offer himself for re-election as party leader and deputed Morrison, after dinner, to say this to him. Morrison did so, but Heath simply replied, 'The rules don't allow it,' and that was that.[55] About a week later, Harold Wilson told Bernard Donoughue of a conversation he had just had with Lord Home, whom Heath had replaced in 1965. Lord Home, said Wilson, '(and especially Lady Home) wants Heath out from Tory leadership. He is like me. He wants revenge.'[56]

Possible successors to Heath began to be touted, though none found very widespread favour. On 13 March, Neave joined a dinner attended by Whitelaw who, he noted, was 'drinking a fair amount of whisky'. 'Willie wants Ted Heath's job but would not be my choice, though I thought so a few weeks ago.'[57] Other names thrown up in conversation among leading

---

* Hugh Fraser (1918–84), younger son of Lord Lovat; educated Ampleforth and Balliol College, Oxford; Conservative MP for Stafford, previously Stafford and Stone, previously Stone, 1945–84; Secretary of State for Air, 1962–4; at this time, married to Lady Antonia Fraser (née Pakenham), writer, beauty, diarist, who later married the Nobel Prize-winning playwright Harold Pinter. Fraser unsuccessfully contested the leadership of the Conservative Party against Heath and Mrs Thatcher in the first ballot in 1975.
† Timothy Kitson (1931–), educated Charterhouse and Royal Agricultural College, Cirencester; Conservative MP for Richmond, Yorkshire, 1959–83; PPS to Edward Heath, 1970–74; knighted, 1974.
‡ Charles Morrison (1932–2005), younger son of Lord Margadale; educated Eton; Conservative MP for Devizes, 1964–1992. His then wife, Sara, was probably the only woman politically and personally close to Heath. She was vice-chairman of the Conservative Party, 1971–5.

Tories at this time included Robert Carr,* Mrs Thatcher, Du Cann and Geoffrey Howe, though there were anti-feminist anxieties that Howe's wife Elspeth† would be too busy to help him. But on the whole these names did not excite enthusiasm.[58]

The first test of the new Opposition was over the Labour government's proposal to get rid of Stage 3 of the prices and incomes policy. The Conservative business managers put down an amendment opposing this. Tory backbenchers were furious. It was an issue on which the government might be defeated, provoking a second election in which the Tories could expect to do worse than before. Besides, more and more of them believed that prices and incomes policies had failed and should be ditched. Luckily for the Opposition front bench, the government indicated that it would stick to Stage 3 for the time being – while ending the miners' dispute by giving them their rise on the basis of the recommendations of the Pay Board. The Tories were therefore able to withdraw their amendment. But the backbenchers poured out their anger. 'His leadership is bad and he and his Cabinet have been wrong about everything for the last 3½ months,' wrote Neave.[59] Four days later he went on: 'the knives are really out for Heath . . . I believe the whole Shadow Cabinet should resign and submit themselves for re-election by party each session.'[60] The next day Neave noted, 'Tonight Du Cann is seen as the alternative candidate,' and recorded his own intention of standing for the Executive of the 1922 Committee.[61]

Heath was able to maintain his position through this perilous time, partly because of the disunity of his opponents, but more because of the electoral quandary. No one knew when the next general election would come, but all agreed that, because Labour lacked an overall majority, it could be at any moment. As Mrs Thatcher herself put it in a debate on the Housing Bill in Parliament: 'In this Parliament it is difficult to know what to do: if one is not cooperative, one is in trouble; if one is cooperative, one is in trouble.'[62] In the face of such uncertainty, Conservative backbenchers did not dare force a leadership contest, and indeed, under the rules, devised for the 1965 contest, there was no clear mechanism for doing so. Heath was not going to offer one. On 22 March Neave discovered that he, in common with many other malcontents, had been elected to the '22 Executive. On 25 March some of the rebels, including Du Cann and Nicholas

---

* Robert Carr (1916–2012), educated Westminster and Gonville and Caius College, Cambridge; MP for Mitcham, 1950–74; for Sutton, Carshalton, February 1974–6; Secretary of State for Employment, 1970–72; Home Secretary, 1972–4; created Lord Carr of Hadley, 1976.

† Elspeth Howe, née Elspeth Morton Shand (1932–), educated Bath High School, Wycombe Abbey and LSE; deputy chairman, Equal Opportunities Commission, 1975–9; chairman, Broadcasting Standards Commission, 1997–9; created Baroness Howe of Idlicote, 2001.

Ridley, dined at Hugh Fraser's house in Campden Hill Square. Airey Neave was present: they 'decided', he wrote, 'that Heath would not go'.[63]

The grumbling continued. In the following month Neave bumped into a fellow backbencher, Dr Gerard Vaughan,* who told him that the party was 'rudderless': 'He said new MPs liked Margaret Thatcher and thought the rest of the Front Bench technocrats.'[64] George Gardiner,† a new and, at that time, pro-European MP, in later years confirmed this unhappiness among the new boys, saying they all felt ignored by Heath.[65] Even the Chief Whip, Humphrey Atkins,‡ had by this time developed a low opinion of Heath himself.[66] Yet more irritation was created when it became clear that Heath was determined to carry over from his time as prime minister his unusually personal grip on economic policy. On 9 May the new, anti-Heath 1922 Executive met and discussed policy-making. 'It is said E. Heath is in charge of the important area of counter-inflation . . .' wrote Neave. 'The Executive is very opposed to this arrangement and will protest. I get the impression he is still an autocrat. The grumbling about him is still serious. He has to be made to understand that he will lose another election if he does not alter his curt attitude but how can he do it? He seems as afraid of everyone as they are of him.'[67]

By late May the unhappiness had almost reached breaking point, and the 1922 Executive seriously discussed a planned campaign of revolt. The problem was how to manage the succession. At a dinner given by David Renton, Hugh Fraser, Nicholas Ridley, Edward Du Cann, Neave and others discussed the matter: 'We agreed we might have to take action if things blew up. Edward would have to tell Heath the Party would not support him. People do not think we have yet reached this point but I think we soon shall. The difficulty is that Heath will fight.'[68] Faced with that difficulty, Heath's opponents stood back. A few days later, Neave saw Heath about nuclear reactors, on whose behalf he was a paid lobbyist: 'He was in a v. poor state, red faced, far too fat§ and depressed. I think he should stand down in favour of Whitelaw but he will need a lot of persuading.'[69]

---

* Gerard Vaughan (1923–2003), educated privately in East Africa; Conservative MP for Reading South, 1970–97; Minister of Health, 1979–82; knighted, 1984.
† George Gardiner (1935–2002), educated Harvey Grammar School, Folkestone and Balliol College, Oxford; Conservative MP for Reigate, February 1974–97; knighted, 1991; one of Mrs Thatcher's first biographers. He was a prominent right-winger, never holding office. He eventually left the party because of disagreements with John Major's policy on Europe in the 1990s.
‡ Humphrey Atkins (1922–96), educated Wellington; Conservative MP for Merton and Morden, 1955–70; for Spelthorne, 1970–87; Secretary of State for Northern Ireland, 1979–81; Lord Privy Seal, 1981–2; created Lord Colnbrook, 1987.
§ It was not known at the time that Heath had been suffering from a thyroid condition since 1973. This made him irritable, indecisive – and fat.

Neave did not dare attempt such persuasion in person. Faced with Heath's intransigence, the 1922 Executive 'decided to keep the leadership question "on ice" '.[70]

   In a tragi-comic attempt to create better relations with backbenchers, Heath's PPS, Kenneth Baker,* who had got wind of a small party the Neaves were giving for new Conservative MPs, asked Neave why the leader had not been asked. Taken aback, Neave pretended that he had been planning a second party to which Heath would be invited. This went ahead. Neave had thirty-eight acceptances and one and a half dozen bottles of champagne from Oddbins. His brief description of the occasion conveys the atmosphere: 'E. Heath arrived with many others at 7 p.m. and was very frosty for the first 10 mins. I had a job to get him to talk to anyone. I started with George Gardiner and his wife, Ivan Lawrence,† Patrick Mayhew . . .'‡ Winston Churchill,§ grandson of the late Prime Minister, was one of the few guests who was not of the new intake, so Heath asked him what he was doing there. In return, Churchill asked him the same question: 'Whereupon Heath replied, "I am the chief fornicator." ¶ This', said Neave, 'sounds a strange joke.'[71] It was also typical of Heath's bewildering conversational style. Neave felt he got nothing out of the party. His wife had received no flowers or card from the leader, he complained to his diary, and Heath 'gets fatter every day which gives a poor impression on TV'.[72] A week later, he recorded again: 'Heath has never thanked Diana for the party. I wonder very much whether it was worth it. I certainly have no hopes of patronage in his direction. My advice has never been sought on those policy areas in which I might have been useful.'[73] In later years, when asked why he had lost the leadership of his party, Heath used to say that it was simply because

---

* Kenneth Baker (1934–), educated St Paul's and Magdalen College, Oxford; Conservative MP for Acton, 1968–70; for St Marylebone, 1970–83; for Mole Valley, 1983–97; Secretary of State for the Environment, 1985–6; for Education and Science, 1986–9; Chancellor of the Duchy of Lancaster, 1989–90; Chairman, Conservative Party, 1989–90; Home Secretary, 1990–92; created Lord Baker of Dorking, 1997.

† Ivan Lawrence (1936–), educated Brighton, Hove and Sussex Grammar School and Christ Church, Oxford; Conservative MP for Burton, February 1974–97; chairman, Conservative Party legal committee, 1987–97; knighted, 1992.

‡ Patrick Mayhew (1929–), educated, Tonbridge and Balliol College, Oxford; Conservative MP for Royal Tunbridge Wells, 1974–83; for Tunbridge Wells, 1983–97. He was the Solicitor-General, 1983–7, whose letter lay at the heart of the Westland affair in 1985–6; Attorney-General, 1987–92; Secretary of State for Northern Ireland, 1992–7; knighted, 1983; created Lord Mayhew of Twysden, 1997.

§ Winston Churchill (1940–2010), educated Eton and Christ Church, Oxford; Conservative MP for Stretford, 1970–83; for Davyhulme, Manchester, 1983–97; Shadow Defence Secretary, 1976–8.

¶ Churchill had a much better claim than Heath to being called the 'chief fornicator'.

he had not handed out enough honours.[74] There were other, bigger reasons, but he was not completely wrong.*

Heath might have been more successful at maintaining his position if he had tried to incorporate critical voices into his new Shadow Cabinet. His instinct, though, was to surround himself with those closest to him, and he made the crucial decision to deny Keith Joseph his ambition to become shadow Chancellor and give the post instead to the likeable, loyal but unexciting Robert Carr. Joseph refused the substitute post of Industry and insisted instead on a position without portfolio, but with an emphasis on economic questions, leaving him free to range over the whole field of ideas. To prevent him leaving the Shadow Cabinet and so causing a public division, Heath granted Joseph his request. This was dangerous. There was an accompanying agreement that Joseph could approach Conservative donors to set up his own think tank to look at market-based solutions to the political and economic problems of the day. This was fatal. At the time, though, the idea seemed more worthy than threatening. The declared purpose of the think tank was to study the workings of the market economy, particularly abroad. Joseph wanted to use the term 'Social Market' – then an admired model from post-war Germany – in the title of his new organization, but was dissuaded by his more rigorist adviser Alfred Sherman. The Centre for Policy Studies was born.† Putting in Adam Ridley,‡ the deputy director of the Conservative Research Department, as his spy on the putative board, Heath thought that all was well. He was wrong. The CPS gave Joseph the platform and back-up he needed to launch a full intellectual critique of the Heath years. The Heathites did not pay enough attention. 'We were a bit one-eyed about what was going on in the party,' said Sara Morrison.[75] In May, Mrs Thatcher, the only potential rebel whom Heath had promoted, making her shadow environment secretary, joined the CPS as Joseph's vice-chairman.

It was largely through Joseph and the CPS that Mrs Thatcher's interest in the power of conservative ideas rekindled. Until February 1974 her career had been mentally conformist. Although her sex and her social

---

* Sara Morrison recommended to Heath that he shore up his position by dispensing honours 'out of a pepper pot'. He declined. (Interview with Sara Morrison.)

† There is some dispute about who first conceived the Centre for Policy Studies. In the view of Alfred Sherman, the original idea was Heath's own. But Simon Webley, also present at the birth of the CPS, remembered that Joseph persuaded Heath by emphasizing that the Centre wanted to study Continental European examples.

‡ Adam Ridley (1942–), educated Eton and Balliol College, Oxford; deputy director, Conservative Research Department, 1974–9; special adviser to the Chancellor of the Exchequer, 1979–84; knighted, 1985.

background made her something of an outsider in the Tories' higher circles, and although she had staked out her position as someone on the mainstream right of the party, she had never before felt cause to question the very basis of her party's policies. Now she did, and as she began to question, she began to think more boldly. Alfred Sherman, who assisted the process, described her, approvingly, as a person of 'beliefs, not of ideas'.[76] This was true. She never possessed the intellectual's spirit of free inquiry, impracticality or love of paradox. She was motivated always by moral earnestness and by her desire to achieve certain right results, rather than indulge in what she would have considered idle speculation. But ideas and the men – almost all of them were men – who purveyed them excited her. Apart from the mugging up that she did for her CPC Lecture in 1968, Mrs Thatcher had never before made time for much reading of political and economic thought. Now she got started – reading Keynes (whose *Economic Consequences of the Peace* she admired much more than the demand-management theories of the Keynesians which she so often attacked), Milton Friedman, Frédéric Bastiat, the mid-nineteenth-century French free-trader, Arthur Koestler and much more. The Institute of Economic Affairs (IEA), presided over by Ralph Harris* and Arthur Seldon,† provided an intellectual forum for the development of free-market ideas, then outside the mainstream of political discourse.‡ Mrs Thatcher devoured their pamphlets and others, including work by liberal economists such as Graham Hutton,§ Brian Griffiths¶ and Douglas Hague.‖ Sherman, who had a long memory for real and imagined slights, recalled that he lent her a great many books which she never returned.[77]

---

* Ralph Harris (1924–2006), educated Tottenham Grammar School and Queens' College, Cambridge; founder president, Institute of Economic Affairs, 1990–2006 (general director, 1957–87; chairman, 1987–9); chairman, Bruges Group, 1989–91; created Lord Harris of High Cross, 1979.

† Arthur Seldon (1916–2005), educated Raine's Foundation School and LSE; army service in Africa and Italy, 1942–5; founder editorial director of the Institute of Economic Affairs, 1957–88; author of numerous books and pamphlets, including *Capitalism* (1990).

‡ After she became prime minister, Mrs Thatcher wrote to thank the Directors of the IEA for their efforts: 'It was primarily your foundation work which enabled us to rebuild the philosophy upon which our Party succeeded in the past' (Margaret Thatcher to Harris, Seldon and Wood, 18 May 1979, THCR 2/4/1/8).

§ Graham Hutton (1904–88), educated Christ's Hospital, LSE and French and German universities; economist, author; research fellowship and teaching staff, LSE, 1929–33; assistant editor, *Economist*, 1933–8.

¶ Brian Griffiths (1941–), educated Dynevor Grammar School and LSE; Professor of Banking and International Finance, City University, 1977–85; head of Prime Minister's Policy Unit, 1985–90; vice-chairman, Goldman Sachs (Europe), from 1991; created Lord Griffiths of Fforestfach, 1991.

‖ Douglas Hague (1926–), educated King Edward VI High School, Birmingham and Birming-

The CPS gave Mrs Thatcher the context, the sense of direction and the camaraderie that she sought. She remembered its office in Wilfred Street as 'a very cosy place', and when it set up shop she went along to help, even assisting with wiring up the electric plugs.[78] Simon Webley, one of the CPS's moving spirits, remembered her holding up the wires and exclaiming, 'The brown one is supposed to be the live one. That is absolutely ridiculous. Brown is for earth.'[79] Her practicality and her ideological enthusiasm combined. For her, the CPS was the chance to 'get back to the north star', almost literally to find the words for what she knew she believed, but which the Heath years had suppressed. She did not contribute new ideas herself but drew them from Keith Joseph and from Alfred Sherman. From the beginning to the end of her career, Mrs Thatcher maintained an unbounded admiration and affection for Keith Joseph, although when she was prime minister she quite often found him exasperating and spoke rudely to him. His gentlemanly public-spiritedness, his sometimes tortured courtesy, his Jewishness, his enthusiasm for policy, his interest in the intersection of economic, social and welfare subjects which many Tory grandees considered beneath their notice, all these endeared him to her. So did the fact that, from her earliest days in Parliament, Joseph had helped her, encouraged her rise and often worked with her on subjects such as housing. In Heath's Cabinet, the two were drawn closer by a growing unease which neither fully articulated at the time. After the defeat of February 1974 their feelings burst out, like a forbidden love at last permitted to express itself. Mrs Thatcher considered Joseph 'the most sensitive human being I have ever met in forty years of politics'.[80] Lord Carrington, *au contraire*, described him as 'the gentlest, kindest, most insensitive man I've ever met'.[81] Yet in a way both meant the same thing – that Joseph cared so desperately, thought so deeply, meant so well, and yet somehow bungled things. All these qualities were to become even more apparent in the course of 1974, and all of them, the bungling included, were to help the cause of Margaret Thatcher.

Alfred Sherman was a very different character. A former Communist, and former machine-gunner for the anti-Franco Republicans in the Spanish Civil War, Sherman maintained a Marxist rigour of thought after his conversion to the right, and a Leninist capacity to identify virtually everyone else as the enemy. His style of argument was absolute. When arguing against public spending on railways, for example, he was not content to call for privatization or a reduction of subsidy: he argued that all rail track should be torn up and the lines converted into bus lanes. He was manifestly,

ham University; Professor of Managerial Economics, Manchester Business School, 1965–81; adviser to the Prime Minister's Policy Unit, 1979–83.

almost proudly, ill fitted to the compromises of party politics, but that did not, at first at least, undermine his importance. He took pride in 'thinking the unthinkable'. Having known Keith Joseph since advising him on aspects of Middle East policy in 1969,[82] he had persuaded him of the virtue of market solutions to problems at the time of the Selsdon conference. As the Heath government began to go wrong, Sherman returned to the charge, and by February 1974 he had found in Joseph a repentant sinner desperate to atone for his misdeeds. He told him how to do so. Mrs Thatcher, at this stage, liked Sherman. 'Alfred Sherman was a genius,' she remembered. She linked his Jewishness with that of Joseph as part of their combined virtue and declared: 'We owe them so much.'[83] She added, however, that Sherman was 'very difficult to get on with'. This was an understatement.

Partly as a means of raising money for the CPS, Joseph embarked on a series of setpiece speeches examining the basis of economic policy, in both its technical and its political aspects, and then ranging wider still. In his first, at Upminster on 22 June, he called for greater attention to 'a market economy within a framework of humane laws and institutions' and developed the international comparisons which were part of his brief:

> Compare our position today with that of our neighbours in Germany, Sweden, Holland, France. They are no more talented than we are. Yet, compared with them, we have the longest working hours, the lowest pay and the lowest production per head. We have the highest taxes and the lowest investment. We have the least prosperity, the most poor and the lowest pensions.

He said that Britain was becoming a socialist country, and that Conservative governments, including the one of which he had been a part, had not dared to repudiate socialism, but had 'tried to build on its very uncertain foundations instead'. The tone of Joseph's speech marked a clear break from that of the Heathites, and this division was made more apparent by the fact that the Conservative Research Department, with Ian Gilmour as its new chairman and Chris Patten* as its new director, was becoming more eloquently consensual and social democratic. In the previous month, Gil-

---

* Christopher Patten (1944–), educated St Benedict's School, Ealing and Balliol College, Oxford; director, Conservative Research Department, 1974–9; Conservative MP for Bath, 1979–92; Secretary of State for the Environment, 1989–90; Chancellor of the Duchy of Lancaster, 1990–92; Chairman, Conservative Party, 1990–92; Governor, Hong Kong, 1992–7; European Commissioner, 1999–2004; Chancellor of Oxford University, from 2003; chairman of the BBC Trust, from 2011; created Lord Patten of Barnes, 2005.

mour had published three articles in *The Times*, developing the theme of 'national unity'.[84]

As the long-expected general election approached in the early autumn, Joseph took greater risks. On the day after the Labour government had agreed the full terms of its new, pre-election Social Contract with the trade unions – a corporatist deal involving price controls, rent freezes and the repeal of Tory union legislation in return for moderate wage claims – Joseph offered something much less cosy. At Preston on 5 September 1974, he gave the fullest airing yet to the theory of monetarism, and its application to the political crisis. In his drafting, he was assisted not only by Sherman, but by Alan Walters* and by Samuel Brittan† of the *Financial Times*. Worried about what Joseph might say, but feeling too weak to forbid it, Heath asked Mrs Thatcher and Geoffrey Howe to inspect the text and prevent trouble. They duly inspected, but made no decisive alterations.

'Inflation is threatening to destroy our society,' was Joseph's opening sentence, and he warned of 'the processes of despair and disintegration which ultimately invite dictatorship'. He expounded the notion that inflation was caused not by wage rises or even by world commodity prices, but by excessive increases in the supply of money, a matter which governments had the means to control. Repudiating the suggestion that 'monetarism' was the answer to everything, he said rather that it was 'a pre-essential for everything else we need and want to do'. The most devastating and, for Heath, embarrassing part of the speech was Joseph's admission of collective and repeated error by Conservative as well as Labour governments in ignoring this pre-essential. 'For the past thirty years in this country governments have had unprecedented power over economic life,' Joseph said. 'It is only fair that we should accept correspondingly heightened responsibility for what has gone wrong.' The motive for the error had been honourable – a fear of a return to the unemployment of the early 1930s – but it was an error nonetheless. The weapons of the 1930s were being used to fight the battles of the 1970s. Governments had believed that a bit of inflation would help unemployment, economic growth and the funding of the social services: now it had turned out to be a 'mortal threat to all three'. The

---

* Alan Walters (1926–2009), educated Alderman Newton's School, Leicester, University College, Leicester and Nuffield College, Oxford; Professor of Economics, LSE, 1967–76; chief economic adviser to the Prime Minister, 1981–3 and (provoking the resignation of Nigel Lawson) 1989–90; knighted, 1983. He had resigned from Heath's CPRS in October 1971 because of the government's failure to pursue a tight monetary policy.

† Samuel Brittan (1933–), brother of Mrs Thatcher's future Home Secretary, Leon; educated Kilburn Grammar School and Jesus College, Cambridge; columnist at the *Financial Times*, from 1966; knighted, 1993.

'menacing tensions' created by inflation 'cannot be cured by incomes policy'. Incomes policy as a means of curbing inflation was 'like trying to stop water coming out of a leaky hose without turning off the tap; if you stop one hole it will find two others.' Joseph advocated that incomes policy be abandoned, and that governments sustain a clear, gradual policy of bearing down upon the excessive supply of money. Within three or four years, this would yield the right results, which would include, he emphasized, a more sustainable form of full employment than that provided by the current governmental attempts to manage demand.

Joseph flagellated himself harder than anyone else, but this did not conceal the fact that his argument undermined the economic basis on which Heath had governed the country, had fought and lost the previous election, and was about to fight the next. Joseph's words were neither unexpected nor, like some of Enoch Powell's interventions in the years of the Heath government, mischievous. The Preston speech was simply the full enunciation of arguments he had been making privately to colleagues since March and in several speeches, including one to the House of Commons on 8 July. Its effect, however, was to raise the standard of revolt for a battle which could be fought only after the next general election was out of the way.*

Within the Tory Party, only a small minority understood the precise nature of the monetarist arguments, but a much larger number were looking for a different approach to the economic problems which beset them. The respect in which Joseph was held meant that many gravitated towards his views. In the Shadow Cabinet, Margaret Thatcher, along with the much more low-key Geoffrey Howe, whose interest in the IEA's liberal economics predated her own, were the only two who supported Joseph's rethink. Contrary to her memory,[85] it was not true that Heath forbade all discussion of these matters, though he certainly did not welcome it. On three occasions, including one on 3 May when it met in the form of its manifesto group, the Shadow Cabinet did give some consideration to Joseph's views on the causes of inflation. But the case was presented in rather tentative form and Joseph himself did not argue flat out that a prices and incomes policy should be abandoned, only that it should be reassessed.† Even in the minds of the radicals, the growing belief that the control of the money

---

* Ever the practical politician as well as the true believer, Mrs Thatcher, though she agreed with every word of Joseph's Preston speech, said a few months afterwards that it had been a straightforward minus for the party in the October election (private information).

† This call for reassessment was too much for Heath, who took it personally. 'Your analysis of the Government's record has left me heart-broken,' he said to Joseph. See Philip Ziegler, *Edward Heath: The Authorised Biography* (Harper Press, 2010), p. 451.

supply was the key to beating inflation seemed to be at war with a feeling that union demands for wage rises had to be held back, and also that the rise for one group could not be too different from that of another. They were groping their way towards coherence. When Mrs Thatcher told the Shadow Cabinet of her support for Joseph, she did so quite cautiously. She said things like 'I think we should give careful attention to what Keith is saying'[86] rather than arguing for a complete break with the past.

Partly because they all expected an election at any time, Mrs Thatcher also kept her public expressions of dissent to a minimum. In May, in a radio interview with the right-wing former editor of the *Spectator* George Gale, she let her hair down enough to say, 'I do hope that we shall return to being the party which I believe can get the economy right,' and 'I think we shall finish up being the more radical party,' but, when Gale invited her to declare herself a Powellite, she easily deflected him by concentrating on Powell's wickedness in turning against the party at the election.[87] People began to point her out more often as a rising star. A newspaper interview in June described Mrs Thatcher as 'currently the person whose name is rustling along the corridors of power as someone who could supplant Ted Heath as Tory Party leader';[88] but she was careful not to promote herself excessively, and even in private gave no indication of any personal ambition for Heath's job. Between February and the election in October, there were only a handful of occasions when Mrs Thatcher spoke in public on anything beyond her shadow brief.

In giving Mrs Thatcher the subject of the environment, which included housing and local taxation, Heath put her at the centre of his strategy for the coming election, although he brought her no nearer to his inner circle. As Alison Ward, her secretary, remembered it, 'Ted piled more and more on her because he resented her, but she did better and better.'[89] Prompted by a discussion with Pierre Trudeau, the Prime Minister of Canada, Heath had become obsessed with the idea that he had lost the February election because he had been too honest and not given people enough of what they wanted.[90] In particular, he believed that it was the middle classes, denied the goodies which they expected from a Conservative government, who had defected to the Liberals. After the property boom of the early Heath years, house values had slumped, and the introduction of Peter Walker's unpopular reorganization of local government had produced large rises in the rates (as local property taxes were known). Heath therefore decided that a fairly shameless electoral pitch should be made for these votes, and that housing and rates were the ground on which to make it.

In one sense, Mrs Thatcher was happy to oblige. Housing was one of her interests, and she identified absolutely with the bourgeois aspiration to own one's own home. In another, she was chary of what Heath wanted. She was cautious about reform of the rates, because she had already seen the difficulties of the alternatives, and about government intervention in the housing market. One of her strongest criticisms of socialism was that its controls had damaged housing. It had taken rented housing off the market, and forced people to live in council tower blocks rather than the Victorian and Edwardian terraces which they preferred. Of such blocks, she complained that 'The architects who build them don't live in them.'[91] 'If we are anxious to have maximum housing standards it pays to have as many people as possible as owner-occupiers,' she told the House of Commons,[92] and in principle she favoured the idea, long current in Tory circles, that council house tenants should be free to buy their homes. In practice, however, she worried that such purchase, if put into law as a right and offered at too great a discount, would annoy 'our people' who were having to pay full prices on the open market. She later came to see her own objections as 'narrow and unimaginative'.[93]

Mrs Thatcher formed a housing policy group, on which sat, among others, a new MP and former editor of the *Spectator*, Nigel Lawson,* who had helped to draft the February manifesto. As an economist and free-marketeer, Lawson opposed government subsidy for mortgages. Mrs Thatcher worried about the size and effects of subsidy too, but, despite Lawson, her housing group worked on the assumption, politically encouraged by Heath, that there would be subsidy in some form.[94] Dispute was to come about how much the subsidy should be, and how specific the promises made about it. When the group presented its report to Heath towards the end of June, it recommended a reduction in the tax rate paid by building societies and, for first-time buyers, a lump sum to match the amount of savings they had accumulated in building societies. Another idea to which Mrs Thatcher gave encouragement was that of 'shared purchase', by which owners could acquire equity in stages.[95] She worried that a publicly stated commitment to hold mortgages to a particular rate would prove irresponsibly expensive. She preferred to speak only of keeping the rate within 'reasonable limits'.[96]

Similarly, on rates, Mrs Thatcher was cautious. At a Shadow Cabinet meeting in late June she unsuccessfully advocated an all-party study of rate reform rather than a Tory commitment to abolition.[97] And in a debate in

---

* Nigel Lawson (1932–), educated Westminster and Christ Church, Oxford; Conservative MP for Blaby, February 1974–92; Financial Secretary to the Treasury, 1979–81; Secretary of State for Energy, 1981–3; Chancellor of the Exchequer, 1983–9; created Lord Lawson, 1992.

the Commons on 27 June in which the Conservatives succeeded in defeating the government in two votes, she called for 'a fundamental reform of
the rating system',[98] but declined to say exactly what that would be. She
spoke of interim rate relief, a central government power to cap local council spending and an investigation of the possibility of local income tax, but
went no further than that. Her performance disappointed Airey Neave:
'Margaret Thatcher a little uncertain. We seem to be very coy in pressing
home our advantage about rates and Crosland* demolished most of her
arguments.'[99]

It was a fairly dismal summer. 'The weather continues cold and windy
and the Stock Exchange gets lower and lower,' wrote Neave.[100] Increasingly
desperate, Heath, urged on by Peter Walker, who was boldly populist on
the subject of housing, decided to toughen up the policies for the election.
Fed up with Mrs Thatcher's resistance to promising an exact figure for the
mortgage rate, he summoned her back from holiday in Lamberhurst for a
meeting on 1 August at his house in Wilton Street with Walker, Ian Gilmour
and Robert Carr. They prevailed on her to accept that a figure of 'below
10 per cent' could be promised. The next step came at the end of the
month.† Heath's purpose was to ensure that, rather than say 'below 10 per
cent', Mrs Thatcher be as specific, and set her rate as low, as possible. She
said she would accept 9.5 per cent, but would go no lower. Heath put on
similar pressure over the rates, again summoning Mrs Thatcher to Wilton
Street, again backed by senior colleagues, this time on 16 August, to make
her promise to abolish domestic rates in the next Parliament. This she
reluctantly did, even though none of them really knew what the replacement would be. Part of the rate burden, at her suggestion, would be
transferred to central government, which would pay directly for the salaries of teachers.

It is typical of Mrs Thatcher's political professionalism that, despite her
reluctance, and her resentment at being strong-armed, she seized the chance
and made the most of the policies which she had not wanted. At a press
conference on 28 August, she announced that a Conservative government
would reduce the mortgage rate from 11 to 9.5 per cent and make that
rate the future ceiling. She also drew attention to the 'real problem' of
domestic rates, seeking financial independence for local authorities 'in such

---

* Anthony Crosland was Labour Secretary of State for the Environment at this time.
† By her own account, Mrs Thatcher was en route from Lamberhurst to Tonbridge (a short
journey) to make a party political broadcast about housing when she received a message on
the 'bleeper' to telephone Heath (Margaret Thatcher, *The Path to Power*, HarperCollins, 1990,
p. 247). This seems unlikely, since bleepers did not exist at that time. But the call, in some form,
undoubtedly took place.

a way that they are responsible to those whom they tax. (Only a minority of electors are ratepayers.)' There were 9 million more income taxpayers than ratepayers, she pointed out,[101] and pledged to get rid of the rating system. On her party political broadcast that night with a voice-over that said, 'For the first time someone has gone back to basics,' Mrs Thatcher repeated her mortgage promise and attacked rates because they 'often have nothing to do with what you can afford to pay or with the services you receive'. Whatever new system the Tories brought in would be 'based on what you can afford'. Her performance made a strong impression, even among those who saw the policies (rightly) as electoral bribery. 'This almost gave Crosland apoplexy,' wrote Neave of the 9.5 per cent promise, 'and he said it was irresponsible.'[102]

Events rushed forward, most of them unhappy ones for Ted Heath. On 2 September his yacht, *Morning Cloud*, was capsized in a storm. Heath was not on board, but two of her crew, one of them his godson, died. On 8 September, while Heath was away in Washington, the Conservative manifesto for the expected general election was leaked to several newspapers. For it, Mrs Thatcher had made another concession in her area of policy. She had consented to the idea that the Conservatives would offer a 'right to buy' to all council house tenants, and that a third of the market price should be discounted. The manifesto said that the Tories would 'place a duty on every council to sell homes on these terms'. Variation of the 'composite rate' of tax on the building societies would allow the government to keep the mortgage rate at 9.5 per cent or below. Rates would be replaced by taxes 'more broadly based and related to people's ability to pay'. Unable to resolve the party's own internal confusion about the causes of inflation, the Conservative manifesto mentioned control of the money supply as one of the necessary tools, but also spoke of the need for a prices and incomes policy. It preferred a voluntary one, it said, but 'no government could honestly say that it would never be necessary to use the law in the national interest to support an effective policy for fighting inflation.'

On 18 September 1974, Harold Wilson called a general election for 10 October. He felt justified in doing so by the need to get an overall majority, and he had spent the summer making what he hoped would be electorally beneficial deals with the trade unions. Partly because the Conservatives were anxious to preserve a studied vagueness and moderation in their approach to the great economic and industrial questions of the moment, Mrs Thatcher's specific policy promises were almost the only important ones of the Tory campaign. She fought it with gusto, and without embarrassment, strongly promoting the middle-class interests which Heath criticized himself for having neglected when in office. It was the first campaign in which party strategists made her nationally prominent, and she profited from this, proving herself combative, persuasive and much better than people had expected on television. Home ownership, she argued, 'gives people independence and a stake in their country'[103] and 'provides the best possible protection for people's savings against inflation'.[104] 'A home, like food,' she told constituents in Finchley, 'is a basic need in our lives. All governments avoid taxing food for that reason ... And yet we single out the home for an extra tax.' At a Central Office election press conference devoted to her policies, on 27 September, she declared: 'The right to own the land on which your house stands is quite emotive in English history ... I do not propose to deny that right to people because they live in council houses'; she upped the excitement about her mortgage-rate offer by promising that it would come into effect before Christmas. And she even turned the inconsistency with her pure economic doctrines into a sort of virtue. 'I am dealing with a problem', she told the monetarist interviewer Peter Jay, 'in which the economics are probably different from the human answer.'[105] As election day approached, Mrs Thatcher was one of those chosen to present the culminating party political broadcast. The pledges on rates, she said, were 'firm, unshakeable, categorical'. She delivered such lines very well, and they rattled the Labour Party. Bernard Donoughue recorded in his diary: 'The only new issue is Thatcher's 9½ percent mortgage commitment, and everybody is frightened of that – and furious with Tony Crosland for failing to deal with it.'[106]

But there was another reason why Mrs Thatcher's were almost the only concrete Conservative promises of the campaign. It was because Heath had decided to push the notion of 'national unity', with its implicit suggestion of coalition. He therefore wanted as few policies as possible which would quarrel with this aim. The manifesto said that 'as a national party we will pursue a national policy in the interests of the nation as a whole. We will lead a national effort. In normal times, the party struggle is the safeguard of freedom. But the times are far from normal. In a crisis like this, it is the national interest that must prevail.' The atmosphere of doom was to be built up, the details of possible solutions to be played down: 'we see this as part of the Tory strategy', wrote Donoughue, 'to create a sense of cataclysmic crisis, like 1940, as the build-up to the necessary coalition.'[107]

'National unity' annoyed Mrs Thatcher very much. As in the aftermath of the February election, she was intensely suspicious of any deal with the Liberals. She instinctively preferred the public two-party battle to a world of private understandings and shifting alliances, and she believed that the answer to the national crisis was not the forging of a national consensus round the old, wrong policies, but a bold leap for new, right ones. To the extent that her own election campaign was allowed to differ from that of the party leadership, it indicated this preference, often echoing words from Keith Joseph's speeches. 'The central issue', she said at her adoption meeting in Finchley, 'is do we continue the free society with its emphasis on individual freedom and responsibility or do we become the most state-controlled society in the world outside the Iron Curtain,' warning that 'The extreme left is well in command.'[108] On the BBC's *Any Questions?* in the last week of the campaign, Mrs Thatcher maintained the party line that a government of national unity might be a good thing, but went out of her way to say that she 'could never sit in the same government with Michael Foot or Anthony Wedgwood Benn, because they believe in nationalizing the lot'.

It was unreasonable of Mrs Thatcher to complain, as she did in after years, that 'national unity' had been foisted upon her at the last minute. It had been agreed, if in rather nebulous form, in mid-July, and she herself had called for it in her election address: 'We are the only party pledged to work with all people of goodwill for national unity and therefore our main aim is to safeguard the existence of a free society.' But she had reason to be annoyed that, once again, Heath summoned her to a meeting and tried to bounce her into a change of policy, this time at the climax of the campaign. Behind her performance on *Any Questions?* lay her anger at what had happened in the two days before. On 2 October, Heath had floated the idea of a government 'of all the talents', thus pushing the idea of coalition more explicitly. The next day, he had summoned Mrs Thatcher to Wilton Street to brief her before her BBC appearance. He said he wanted to push for a 'government of national unity' and asked her to be ready to drop her housing and rates pledges on air. Having been marched up to the top of the hill on these subjects by Heath before the election, Mrs Thatcher was not going to be marched down again. 'I was absolutely fed up,' she remembered. 'I wasn't going to say: "I'm going to become half-socialist."'[109] On *Any Questions?* she stuck to her guns. Her Labour opponent, Roy Hattersley,* spotted and exploited the half-hidden disagreement between Heath and 'his principal spokesman on housing matters, who baldly announces this evening that her housing proposals are non-negotiable'.[110]

Besides, there was a fundamental incoherence about the 'government of national unity' idea. Who was going to lead it? Heath naturally thought

---

* Roy Hattersley (1932–), educated Sheffield City Grammar School and University of Hull; Labour MP for Birmingham, Sparkbrook, 1964–97; Deputy Leader of the Labour Party, 1983–92; created Lord Hattersley, 1997.

that he would, but polls showed that it was he, more than any other leading politician, whom the public regarded as divisive. Many of those close to Heath tried to persuade him to offer the 'supreme sacrifice', in which he would publicly suggest that he would be prepared to step down in the interests of unity. They argued that he had nothing to lose since, if he won, he would be in a strong position to lead any coalition he chose and, if he lost, he had no chance anyway. But Heath was made thoroughly suspicious by the idea, and rejected it. The Tory campaign therefore ended in incoherence. Wilson was able to present the 'national unity' idea as a 'Con trick'. The Labour Party increased its majority to forty-two over the Conservatives, though its overall majority in the Commons was only three. The final state of the parties was Labour 319, Conservatives 277, Liberals 13, SNP 11, Plaid Cymru 3, Ulster Unionists and others 12. In Finchley, Mrs Thatcher's majority fell by 2,000:

Mrs Margaret Thatcher (Conservative)	16,498
Martin O'Connor (Labour)	12,587
Laurence Brass (Liberal)	7,384
Mrs Janet Godfrey (National Front)-	
Conservative majority	3,911

'I was now in no doubt', Mrs Thatcher recalled, 'that Ted should go.'[111]

I I

The gelding and the filly

'Heath will murder you'

After the October defeat, it was not only the right of the Conservative Party that wanted Heath to go. Indeed, plans had been laid, or rather inconclusively debated, beforehand. On 7 August 1974, Sara Morrison, as loyal as anyone to Heath, had spoken privately to Airey Neave: 'She agreed that E. Heath has to go if we lose. She favours Ian Gilmour but accepts W. Whitelaw interim. She rules out Margaret. Robert Carr can't decide "whether he wants a boiled or a fried egg". Keith Joseph is played out.'[1] On the day of the result, Sara Morrison tried to get Heath to resign.[2] So did Lord Carrington and Jim Prior. Some complained that Heath's close friend Lord Aldington was a bad influence in helping him shield himself from the reality of defeat,[3] but really there was only one big reason why Heath still stayed, one object that proved immoveable. This was, as Lord Carrington put it succinctly, 'Ted'.[4] Despite a weight of opinion to the contrary, Heath continued to believe that he alone was fit to be national leader when, as he expected, the economic crisis would demand some sort of coalition government. He sat still therefore, and his unhappy close supporters stayed loyal, but the Tory Party began to move against him.

On Monday 14 October 1974 the Executive of the 1922 Committee met in Edward Du Cann's house in Lord North Street. Du Cann asked each in turn for his views. As Neave recorded it, 'All thought Heath should go, but varied when ... The only dissident was Du Cann himself who thought Heath should stay two years perhaps because he has thoughts of the job.'[5] The Executive agreed that Du Cann should go at once to Heath and tell him what they thought. They arranged to meet the next morning so that Du Cann could report the result of the conversation, and chose the offices of his bank, Keyser Ullmann in Milk Street, to avoid the scrutiny of the press. At the Milk Street gathering, a meeting of the full 1922 Committee (that is, all Tory backbenchers) was set for 31 October. 'A letter was then dictated', wrote Neave, '... saying it was in the best interests of the party that he [Heath] should state his intention. It was to be delivered by hand. I hope it has more success than the Du Cann interview yesterday evening with Heath when the latter made no comment as he told him our opinion that he should resign!! We are being snubbed as usual. It is Heath's attitude to Parliament of which I most disapprove. Du Cann said he was the only one at the meeting who "liked" Heath which is the most palpable nonsense.' Despite the precautions, the press were lurking outside. The Executive took evasive action: 'Du Cann led us to the back door and a key was found, with many jokes about Colditz.' Photographers popped up, though, and snapped Du Cann, Neave and others as they tried to sneak out. The pro-Heath *Evening Standard* ran the picture with the headline 'The Milk Street Mafia'. Heath gave a television broadcast that night in which he was more effective than usual. 'We have lost the first round,' wrote Neave.[6] Indeed, the Heath camp counterattacked. The Chief Whip, Humphrey Atkins, told the left-wing but anti-Heath MP Nigel Fisher* that the Executive of the '22 would be rejected *en bloc* in the coming elections. Heath said that he would not meet the Executive until after these elections on 7 November. He was taking his stand on the principle that until there was a new House of Commons in session, and therefore new elections to the Executive, he would not deal with the '22. For Neave, a period of anxiety and gloom ensued. Travelling on the Brighton train to stay with friends, he noted: 'I was rather disgusted by the vulgar, sleek, first-class passengers. I wonder if they realised that the country is on the verge of revolution.'[7]†

When the full 1922 Committee met on 31 October, however, Edward Du Cann was cheered, and only two speakers supported Heath: nineteen opposed him. One backbencher, Kenneth Lewis, struck home with his deadly phrase that the leadership was 'a leasehold, not a freehold'. 'Anyone but he [Heath] would resign after this meeting,' wrote Neave.[8] But when the Chief Whip telephoned Heath, who was in Wales, to report the mood of the meeting, Heath refused to give up. Willie Whitelaw told friends that Heath was being unbelievably arrogant,[9] but he and the other Tory grandees continued to shield him. On 7 November the entire, anti-Heath 1922

---

* Nigel Fisher (1913–96), father of Labour minister Mark Fisher; educated Eton and Trinity College, Cambridge; MC, 1945; Conservative MP for Hitchin, 1950–55; for Surbiton, 1955–83. His book *The Tory Leaders* (1977) includes a good account of the 1974–5 leadership contest.

† Neave's was not a partisan point of view. The sense of Britain on the verge of collapse was widespread. Bernard Donoughue spent August in France. On his return he wrote in his diary: 'From abroad I could see England a little clearer. It looked in a terrible mess. Falling apart socially as well as economically. Seems very frail compared to France, which is becoming a giant again' (*Downing Street Diary*, 2 vols, Jonathan Cape, 2005, 2008, vol. i: *With Harold Wilson in No. 10*, p. 174).

Executive was re-elected, despite the whips. Emboldened, its members drafted a letter to Heath calling for an early contest. Part of the difficulty surrounding all of this was that the 1965 rules for the election of the leader – the first balloted election in the party's history – made no provision for a challenge to a sitting leader. New rules were therefore needed and the 1922 Executive were intensely suspicious that Heath would find a way of spinning out – or suddenly rushing forward – rule changes, or of constructing all changes in his favour. They knew they could, eventually, force a contest, but they did not know when, or under what rules. On 14 November, however, Heath came to the '22 ('He was coldly but politely received,' wrote Neave in his diary of that day) and agreed to set up a review of the system for electing the leader. The man in charge of the changes was Lord Home, the leader whom Heath, though not by direct challenge, had displaced. It was now expected that there would be a leadership election in February 1975. Much less certain, though, was who, apart from Heath, would be a candidate. Neave, and most of the 1922 Executive, including Nigel Fisher, Charlie Morrison and Philip Goodhart,* wanted Heath out, but cast rather desperately around for an alternative. Neave's diary reveals his perplexity. In the course of 1974 he looked with favour often on Du Cann, quite often on Margaret Thatcher, sometimes on Whitelaw, sometimes on Joseph, occasionally on Gilmour. Like most Conservative MPs at the time, he was following no very strong ideological line. He was simply searching for a credible replacement for Heath, a response to what he saw as national and party failure. Just after the October defeat he noted that there was not much support for Whitelaw: 'This makes K. Joseph the favourite, though Jack Weatherill deputy chief whip† says he is liable to nervous breakdowns!'[10] At a dinner party the following evening, 'We could find nothing but objections to possible candidates e.g. Whitelaw, K. Joseph, Carr, Margaret Thatcher. K. Joseph most likely.' On the day before Heath finally agreed to review the leadership election rules, Nigel Fisher organized a meeting of MPs to consider the candidacy of Du Cann. Neave was interested in the idea, and attended the meeting, but recorded: 'It appears that he [Du Cann] is not yet willing to stand partly owing to his wife's dislike

---

* Philip Goodhart (1925–), educated Hotchkiss School, Lakeville, Connecticut and Trinity College, Cambridge; Conservative MP for Beckenham, 1957–92; Parliamentary Under-Secretary, Northern Ireland Office, and minister responsible for DOE (NI), 1979–81; Parliamentary Under-Secretary, MOD, 1981; knighted, 1981.

† Bernard 'Jack' Weatherill (1920–2007), educated Malvern; tailor; Conservative MP for Croydon North East, 1964–92; Deputy Government Chief Whip, 1973–74; Deputy Opposition Chief Whip, 1974–9; Speaker of the House of Commons, 1983–92; created Lord Weatherill, 1992.

of politics. We discussed how rumours about his reputation in the City can be countered as inquiries show nothing against him although Keyser Ullmann has a doubtful reputation . . . It is premature to start a campaign.'[11]

If Mrs Thatcher's own account is to be believed, she had no thought, in the wake of the October election, of challenging for the party leadership herself. She has recorded that she gave her wholehearted backing to Keith Joseph. While she is undoubtedly accurate, in her memoirs, about her loyalty towards Joseph, she is over-innocent about her attitude to her own fortunes at this time. In the course of 1974 more and more people had begun to notice her abilities, and some had told her so. One omen, auspicious at a time when the Morrison family was credited with preternatural powers of understanding the Tory psyche, was a visit paid her by Peter Morrison, brother of Charlie, and at that time a new MP, in August 1974.* He reported to her and endorsed the view of his father, Lord Margadale, who, as John Morrison, had been chairman of the 1922 Committee in the 1950s and 1960s: 'Mark my words, Mrs Thatcher is going to be the next Leader of the Conservative party.'[12]†

The press began to take notice. Everyone agreed that Mrs Thatcher had had a good campaign in October 1974, and on polling day the *Sun* singled her out as the only Tory to have done so. The next day, in reply to leadership speculation from the *Evening News*, she said, 'You can cross my name off the list.' The journalist John Clare, who met Mrs Thatcher for a piece he was writing about her in the *Observer* for 13 October, remembered that she was seeking press attention at the time, letting it be known that she would be at a particular place at a particular moment: 'She was testing the water.'[13] The following Sunday, in an artful interview in the *Sunday Express*, Mrs Thatcher insisted that 'my only wish is to further the Conservative Party and the philosophy upon which it is founded.' (References to Tory 'philosophy' were coded attacks on Heath, because he was thought to have abandoned it.) But she added that 'the prejudice against women is dropping faster than I expected,' and phrased her sympathy for Heath in a way that

---

* Peter Morrison (1944–95), youngest son of Lord Margadale; educated Eton and Keble College, Oxford; Conservative MP for Chester, February 1974–92; Minister of State, Department of Employment, 1983–5; of Energy, 1987–90; PPS to the Prime Minister, 1990; knighted, 1990. It was Peter Morrison who, as her PPS, was to preside over Mrs Thatcher's unsuccessful campaign to retain the leadership in 1990.

† Margadale had stated this view to a large lunch at his Scottish house on the island of Islay as early as 1972: 'Mrs Thatcher is going to be the next leader of the Conservative Party and so she should be.' When he made the remark all those present considered it 'very extraordinary'. (Unpublished interview with Peter Morrison (interviewer unknown), 1993.)

contrasted him unfavourably with herself: 'All this is so wretched for him . . . And unlike me he hasn't a family around him from whom to draw strength.'* She then answered, quite specifically, the question of whether she would stand: 'If that time comes and people thought I was that woman, I would accept the challenge and do the job – as I have tried to do everything in my life – to the utmost of my ability.'[14] Her family would support her, she said. These were not the remarks of a person who had not given the leadership a moment's thought.

In private, indeed, Mrs Thatcher was explicit on the point. On 15 October Fred Silvester, a disillusioned Heathite MP,† wrote to her asking her to allow herself to go forward for the party leadership. In her (undated) reply, she was frank: 'If the contest were to come immediately, I wouldn't stand a chance. If later, I may . . . At present the country contains too much prejudice to accept a woman but with the sort of discussion that is now taking place through the media, it may change.'[15]

Nevertheless, Mrs Thatcher's working assumption remained that Joseph would challenge Heath and that she would back him. She was spoken of, informally, as his campaign manager. But between her giving her *Sunday Express* interview on 17 October and its publication on 20 October, the scene changed. On 19 October, Keith Joseph made a speech at Edgbaston which stirred up a hornets' nest. Most of the speech was a thoughtful development of his earlier setpieces. He was trying to move the debate beyond the purely economic to 'the tone of national life', arguing, to adapt a phrase from a later row about Thatcherism, that there *is* such a thing as society. He called for a 'battle of ideas to be fought in every school, university, publication, committee, TV studio' to counter collectivism. And he developed his idea of the 'cycle of deprivation', deriving from work done by the left-wing Child Poverty Action Group (CPAG) which showed demographic trends that he found dismaying. 'The balance of our population,' Joseph said, 'our human stock, is threatened . . . A high and rising proportion of children are being born to mothers least fitted to bring children into the world . . . Some are of low intelligence, most of low educational

---

* It is possible that Mrs Thatcher was also ambitious enough to be dropping a hint, at a time when such things were considered a source of shame, that Heath was homosexual. Many at the time believed that he was. W. F. Deedes noted a private conversation with Mrs Thatcher in 1976: 'M. seems convinced TH is a homosexual. (Women have more accurate instincts than we.) I said charitably: "an instinct sublimated in boats!"' (W. F. Deedes, note, 28 July 1976, unpublished).

† Fred Silvester (1933–), educated Sir George Monoux Grammar School and Sidney Sussex College, Cambridge; Conservative MP for Walthamstow West, 1967–70; for Manchester, Withington, February 1974–87; Opposition whip, 1974–6; PPS to Secretary of State for Employment, 1979–81.

attainment . . . They are producing problem children . . . Yet these mothers, the under-twenties in many cases, single parents, from classes four and five, are now producing a third of all births . . .' Joseph appeared to argue that such young women should be much more vigorously encouraged to use contraceptives.

In after years, there was some dispute about how this passage of argument came about. Alfred Sherman suggested that he had warned Joseph against using the CPAG's material, because it was left wing, but said that he had indeed argued that we 'needed a sexually structured society [that is, stable marriage] for free enterprise to work'.[16] Most of the phrases that Joseph used, including his numerical classification of social classes, had a Shermanic ring to them. What is certain, however, is that Joseph had not followed his usual practice of running drafts past Mrs Thatcher and other colleagues. The first that Mrs Thatcher knew of the speech was when she picked up a copy of the *Evening Standard* (which then published on a Saturday) at Waterloo station on her return from an engagement in Bournemouth.[17] 'SIR KEITH IN "STOP BABIES" SENSATION' said the headline. She knew at once that this was trouble. Airey Neave's reaction was fairly typical. 'Keith Joseph made a speech in favour of the family yesterday,'* he wrote, 'and deplored the decline in morals. Unfortunately he recommended that family planning be particularly applied to one-parent families. He was very tactless and this has raised a storm and will affect his chances of replacing Heath. The latter seems to have recovered his position and I suppose we have to accept the worst.'[18]

Joseph might, perhaps, have survived the original mauling if he had been ready to rebut attack. His speech was, in fact, a thoughtful one which inaugurated an era of public agonizing about morality and the 'underclass' which has been with us ever since. But he had no back-up, and little inclination for a fight. Characteristically, he began to apologize for what he had said. He publicly admitted that he had damaged the cause he was trying to advance. Bernard Donoughue, head of Harold Wilson's No. 10 Policy Unit, sat opposite Joseph at an evening meeting four days after Edgbaston: 'we talked at length about various social problems . . . He was pleasant and interesting but obviously very jumpy about his recent speeches and current bid for the leadership. Later in the meeting he just sat with his head in his hands.'[19] If Joseph wouldn't defend his words, nor, fully, could anyone else. In an *Evening Standard* interview with Max Hastings, the bulk of which was conducted before Joseph's speech, Mrs Thatcher answered, to a question which Hastings must have inserted after Joseph's speech, that

---

* Actually, the day before that.

'Keith is perfectly right. This is the twilight of the middle class,' but she also admitted that his Edgbaston speech had done harm to the mission.[20] She was aware, however, that it did no harm to her. In an interview in the *Scottish Sunday Post* of 3 November, she acknowledged that she was receiving many letters from the public urging her to stand for the leadership. Joseph himself appears to have understood the way things were going. Shortly after the Edgbaston speech, he shared a cab with Cecil Parkinson. 'I think Margaret could become the standard-bearer,' he said.[21]

But a period of uncertainty ensued for almost a month. As Heath argued with the 1922 Committee about changes in the rules, opinion surveys of constituency chairmen showed that he still had their support. Even among Tory voters in general, just over half backed him to continue. The race had not quite started and Joseph, though wounded, had not yet withdrawn from it. The weakening of Joseph seemed to favour Willie Whitelaw. Airey Neave met Whitelaw at the Wessex Area Council. Whitelaw was confidential: 'He was afraid it could not go on much longer. I said Heath must go by Christmas and he (Whitelaw) must take the initiative. There were 40 or 50 hardliners who would bring Heath down. Willie said he might have to give up the Chairmanship [in which he had succeeded Lord Carrington after the election] as he would be in a strong position. Evidently he feels Keith Joseph has put himself out of the running.' Despite urging him on, however, Neave was not impressed: 'No one really trusts him and I suspect he is rather weak in character.'[22]

At this time the atmosphere was altered by what was happening in the House of Commons. In his reply to the Queen's Speech on 29 October 1974, Heath was heard in what Bernard Donoughue described as 'almost total silence from his own backbenchers ... Each party privately thinks that it is time for a change of leadership.'[23] Then, on 7 November, timed to weaken his opponents in the 1922 Executive elections, Heath announced changes to his Shadow Cabinet. The press had spoken of Mrs Thatcher as a possible shadow Chancellor, but in fact she was offered the almost humiliating post of number two Treasury spokesman (though with a seat in the Shadow Cabinet) under Robert Carr. Rather than grumbling, however, she set to work with a will. On 12 November, the Chancellor, Denis Healey,* introduced a full-scale Budget, which invented Capital Transfer Tax and imposed a new tax on North Sea oil. On 14 November, Mrs Thatcher

---

* Denis Healey (1917–), educated Bradford Grammar School and Balliol College, Oxford; Labour MP for Leeds South East, 1952–5; for Leeds East, 1955–92; Secretary of State for Defence, 1964–70; Chancellor of the Exchequer, 1974–79; Shadow Foreign Secretary, 1980–87; Deputy Leader of the Labour Party, 1980–83; created Lord Healey, 1992.

debated the Budget in the Commons. She teased Healey for 'trying not to reveal that if he was right now he was wrong in his March Budget'. The Public Sector Borrowing Requirement was up by £6 billion since then, though he had said at the time that he would try to get it down. Now he was opting for 'sacrifice by instalments' when the people would have accepted the full thing there and then: 'The people were ready. The Chancellor was not. He and they will regret it.'[24] She pointed out that the government had imposed no penalties on the trade unions for breaching the Social Contract. Airey Neave was delighted by her performance: 'I heard part of a brilliant speech by Margaret Thatcher on the Budget. She dealt very well with ... the Social Contract, was amusing and increased her reputation.'[25] Geoffrey Finsberg MP,* in the neighbouring constituency of Hampstead, urged her to stand, as, earlier, did Fergus Montgomery,† her PPS. But she told the latter: 'The party isn't ready for a woman and the press would crucify me.'[26]

On 20 November, the committee on the leadership election rules, agreed by Heath six days earlier, was set up. 'Talk of Margaret Thatcher standing and Du Cann more likely,' noted Neave. The following day, in the early evening, Keith Joseph telephoned Mrs Thatcher and asked if he could come and see her in her office in the Commons. She quoted her memory of the conversation in her memoirs: Joseph said, 'I am sorry, I just can't run. Ever since I made that speech the press have been outside the house. They have been merciless. Helen [his wife] can't take it and I have decided that I just can't stand.' 'His mind was quite made up,' Mrs Thatcher went on. 'I was on the edge of despair. We just could not abandon the Party and the country to Ted's brand of politics. I heard myself saying: "Look, Keith, if you're not going to stand, I will, because someone who represents our viewpoint *has* to stand."'[27] Joseph then said, 'I will give you all my support.'[28] Remembering the occasion, Mrs Thatcher used to say that she had been 'really rather shocked ... he [Joseph] really was the leader.' Characteristically, she shifted blame for Joseph's failure to grasp his opportunity on to his wife: 'I *was* surprised. I thought Helen would be 100 per cent behind him.'[29]

It may be doubted, however, whether Mrs Thatcher was either surprised or upset. What she 'heard myself saying' was what she had been ready to

---

* Geoffrey Finsberg (1926–96), educated City of London School; Conservative MP for Hampstead, 1970–83; for Hampstead and Highgate, 1983–92; Parliamentary Under-Secretary, DOE, 1979–81; DHSS, 1981–3; created Lord Finsberg, 1992.

† Fergus Montgomery (1927–2013), educated Jarrow Grammar School and Bede College, Durham; Conservative MP for Newcastle-upon-Tyne East, 1959–64; for Brierley Hill, 1967–February 74; for Altrincham and Sale, October 1974–97; PPS to the Leader of the Opposition, 1975–6; knighted, 1985.

say before the meeting began. On 19 November the Chief Whip had been told by the MP David Mitchell* that Joseph would not stand, but that he would propose and support Mrs Thatcher.[30] The following day Humphrey Atkins had a conversation with Mrs Thatcher on other matters, at the end of which she told him of Joseph's decision not to stand and of her decision that she should, indeed must.† Atkins, of course, preserved impartiality, but those close to him believed that he personally tended to support Mrs Thatcher.[31] There is no reason to doubt that Mrs Thatcher's meeting with Joseph took place as she records, and it was obviously important because it was face to face, rather than through intermediaries, but it was a formality: she had already decided to stand. She knew that she was better suited for the task than he. She genuinely loved and admired Joseph, both for his kindness to her and for the intellectual power he brought to the attack on socialism.‡ 'Socialism was like having a sheet of graph paper and putting a regulation on every square,' she said, whereas Joseph's conservatism was 'like building a house'. But she understood his character quite well enough to know that he was unsuitable for the highest command. Although she said it was 'a tragedy that he never became prime minister', she added, in the same breath, that he 'would have agonized over every decision'.[32] Besides, even without the embarrassment of Edgbaston, those who shared Joseph's and Mrs Thatcher's political views had never been wholly convinced that Joseph had what it took. As a result, there was no real Joseph campaign team.

One person who saw what was happening was Gordon Reece,§ the public relations guru who advised the Conservatives on their party political broadcasts. He had noticed, watching clips of unused party political broadcasts from the 1970 election, how Mrs Thatcher 'dominated the screen when she was on it'.[33] He came to know her better, and by December 1973

---

* David Mitchell (1928–), educated Aldenham; Conservative MP for Basingstoke 1964–83; for Hampshire North West, 1983–97; Parliamentary Under-Secretary, Department of Industry, 1979–81; Northern Ireland Office, 1981–3; Minister of State, Department of Transport, 1986–8; knighted, 1988.

† According to Fred Silvester, who had just been appointed a junior whip, Mrs Thatcher told him on the evening of 17 November that she had just informed the Chief Whip of her intention to stand (Correspondence with Fred Silvester).

‡ Mrs Thatcher dedicated the first volume of her memoirs, *The Path to Power*, to the memory of Keith Joseph.

§ Gordon Reece (1929–2001), educated Ratcliffe College and Downing College, Cambridge; newspaper journalist and, from 1960, independent television producer and director; joined EMI, 1970; worked for Mrs Thatcher on secondment, 1975; director of publicity, Conservative Central Office, 1978–80; returned to CCO for general election of 1983; director of public relations, Occidental Petroleum, 1980–84; knighted, 1986.

had decided that she was the answer for the Tories – 'It was the clearness with which she saw things.' After the October 1974 defeat, Reece told Mrs Thatcher that there was a 'unique opportunity for a woman leader'. She told him, however, that she was backing Joseph, and urged him to offer him his televisual skills. Reece went to interview Joseph the following day and asked the sort of penetrating personal questions (for example, the extent of family support for his candidacy) which he thought television interviewers might wish to pursue. Joseph displayed 'visible unease' with cameras, he thought. Reece told him that he could win the party leadership contest, but not a general election. Joseph said: 'I think I agree with you.' The essence of this conversation was known to Mrs Thatcher. There was never a definite Joseph campaign which was then aborted by his agonies over the reaction to Edgbaston. Rather, a Joseph candidacy had been a sort of working hypothesis for those, including Mrs Thatcher, who thought as he did. When that hypothesis collapsed, there was more relief than dismay.

Mrs Thatcher wrote that she went home to Flood Street that night and told Denis of her decision to stand. 'You must be out of your mind,' she says he said. 'You haven't got a hope.'[34] His own version of the moment is more coloured, but to the same effect: 'I did suck my teeth a bit. "Heath will murder you," I told her.'[35]

It did not at all follow from her brave decision to stand that Mrs Thatcher's way now lay clear. Many regarded her candidacy as nothing more than a chance to prepare the ground for a challenge by someone more serious, or merely for malcontents to let off steam. The *Economist*, jaunty in its erroneous confidence, described her as 'precisely the sort of candidate who ought to be able to stand, and lose, harmlessly'.[36] Paying one of his state visits to the Conservative Research Department which he had once run to such effect, R. A. Butler paused at the lift and said to Chris Patten, the director: 'We don't need to take this Thatcher business seriously, do we?'[37] Many Tory MPs looked on the contest almost with ribaldry. At the 1922 Committee on 28 November, one Member said that it was a two-horse race:

A MEMBER: You mean one filly.
ANOTHER MEMBER: And a gelding.[38]

Mrs Thatcher herself was extremely worried about her chances, by the exile she feared would follow if she failed, and also, of course, by the reaction of Heath himself. When Peter Morrison told her, before she had announced her candidacy, that he would support her, she said, 'You must understand, I have no chance.' She added that she welcomed his support, 'but I implore you not to announce it for your own sake [that is, for the sake of his career]'.[39]

Events moved quite fast. On 21 November 1974, the day of her conversation with Keith Joseph – a dramatic date because of the Birmingham IRA pub bombings in which twenty-eight people died* – Geoffrey Finsberg informed the Executive of the 1922 Committee that Mrs Thatcher would definitely stand.[40] On the following day, Airey Neave noted, 'I have arranged to have a private meeting with Margaret Thatcher on Tuesday at 7.30 to find out what she intends.'[41] Mrs Thatcher spent the weekend at Lamberhurst, but returned to Flood Street a little early, from what her interviewer, Gordon Greig, called 'the wilds of Kent', to speak to the *Daily Mail*. In doing so, she made clear that she had had strong support all along, before she had offered herself as a candidate: 'When I knew that Keith wasn't standing I knew I had to consider all the people who had been asking me day in and day out to put myself forward . . . The party has got to be given a choice.'

The *Mail* presented her as 'Thoroughly Modern Maggie', the 'candidate of change', and praised her 'guts and honesty' instead of the 'grotesque hypocrisy that [has] so far marked the fight to get rid of Edward Heath'. On the next day, Monday, taking the advice of Fergus Montgomery that she must speak to Heath in person, rather than write him a letter, to tell him formally that she was to challenge him, she called on her leader in his room in the Commons. Accounts vary as to what was said, but, whatever it was, the meeting was short. In her memoirs, Mrs Thatcher recounts that he told her, 'If you must,'[42] but on other occasions she remembered him saying, 'You'll lose,' to which she added, 'That remark gave a certain zest to my competitive spirit.'[43] In his own memoirs, Heath says, 'I thanked her.'[44] The atmosphere was not warm.

The day before this interview, Airey Neave had spent a good deal of time on the telephone to Edward Du Cann, 'who has still not decided whether to stand. I think he thinks he has much to lose by giving up the City. I told him I would see Margaret,' but, Neave added cautiously, '. . . it is going to be fairly hard to "sell" Margaret Thatcher.'[45] Two days later, Neave saw her in her room in the House:

> She said she was definitely a candidate to run in the Leadership stakes. She seemed rather apprehensive about the effect on her Shadow Cabinet

---

* The Birmingham bombings prompted the Shadow Cabinet to discuss the return of the death penalty. They rejected the idea, but the revival of the issue in relation to terrorism gave Mrs Thatcher the chance to reiterate her long-standing support for the rope which probably stood her in good stead in her campaign.

colleagues. She had told E. Heath she would stand against him and he said, 'If that's what you want to do, go ahead.' I told her I would see her again in a week. She has a good chance.[46]

Neave was becoming irritated by Du Cann's hesitation, and the worries about his chiaroscuro business career were growing. A day after seeing Mrs Thatcher, Neave recorded a conversation which gives the flavour of the intrigue, rumour and complication of the time: 'Cecil Parkinson told me that the Whips had heard via J. Selwyn Gummer* that Shirley Williams (of all people) had said the Labour Party had a "dossier" on Edward Du Cann and his City connections. They hoped he was going to stand so they could make use of it.'[47] The Heath camp rather hoped that Du Cann would be a challenger because they 'all knew that he had such a dubious financial record as to make him an easy target.'[48] The whips had heard a rumour that a forthcoming book about the fraudster Bernie Cornfeld would implicate Du Cann.[49]

It did not take long for the first dirty-tricks story of the campaign to break. On 28 November 1974 the newspapers were full of an interview which Mrs Thatcher had given on 18 September, before the general election and before she was a candidate for the leadership (a fact which the reports did not make clear), to an obscure magazine called *Pre-Retirement Choice*. Because of the long lead times of magazines in those days, the interview (or rather the first half of it – the second half appeared the following month) was published on 27 November. The article discussed how Mrs Thatcher was planning for her retirement – an odd topic in the light of subsequent events and the fact that she was not yet – when she gave the interview – forty-nine years old: the peg was that Denis was approaching sixty. It gave her the chance to talk about the effects of inflation on housekeeping. 'I, for the first time in my life,' she said, 'have started steadily buying things like tinned food,' and also things that will be needed in ten years' time, like sheets and towels. Following her mother's wartime example, she went on, she was collecting 'the expensive proteins: ham, tongue, salmon, mackerel, sardines. They will last for years,' and she explained that the 'sugar shortage will eventually work through to tinned fruit'. She noted that honey which was 30 pence the previous year now cost 40 pence: 'It's interesting to mark the prices on the jars as you buy it and you can see how the prices go up.' She expected inflation to persist,

---

* John Selwyn Gummer (1939–), educated King's School, Rochester and Selwyn College, Cambridge; Conservative MP for Lewisham West, 1970–74; for Eye, 1979–83; for Suffolk Coastal, 1983–2010; Chairman, Conservative Party, 1983–5; Minister of Agriculture, 1989–93; created Lord Deben, 2010.

she said, and so this policy would continue to make sense: '£2,000 a year might not be worth much, but a tin of ham is still a tin of ham.' Hoarding 'huge amounts' was wrong, but 'being prudent' was right.

The Heath team, probably through the agency of Peter Walker, seized on the story and drew it to the media's attention. Mrs Thatcher was accused of the unpatriotic vice of 'hoarding' (a resonant word because of the importance of the question during the war), and the attacks came thick and fast. An anonymous caller rang a phone-in on LBC radio to say that Mrs Thatcher had been spotted buying sugar in bulk in the Finchley High Road, though there was, in fact, no grocer there. Lord Redmayne, chairman of Harrods and a former Conservative chief whip, appeared on television to denounce her ('I bet he "hoards" wine in his cellar,' whispered one of her team). For a short time, it looked as though her whole campaign could be blown off course: 'Margaret Thatcher gave an interview to a magazine saying she laid in stocks of food,' wrote Neave, '. . . as a hedge against inflation. This has been written up as a "hoarding" in a destructive way especially by the *Daily Telegraph*. She has only a shelf of this it seems but it was very silly of her to talk to the press at this time. Feel disillusioned but must not take it too seriously.'[50] It was not until 3 December that Neave learnt that the interview had been given nearly three months previously and that the story was a plant by the Heathites.

Mrs Thatcher was extremely upset by the hoarding story. It brought back memories of her ordeal over school milk and it emphasized once again how women politicians were attacked more personally than male ones. It showed her 'the blackness of the official Tory Party'.[51] Precisely because she took an offence like hoarding much more seriously than would most men, she was mortified to be accused of it. She quickly rallied, however, saying, 'They [the press] are never going to do to me what they've just done to Keith.'[52] So she set about what in the next generation would become known as rapid rebuttal. She told Radio 1: 'Well, you call it stockpiling, but I call it being a prudent housewife.'[53] She invited the press in to look at her larder in Flood Street. The *Daily Express* printed a full inventory, worth quoting to illustrate the mores of a middle-class housewife of that time. Mrs Thatcher's larder contained:

Eight pounds of granulated sugar,
One pound of icing sugar ('for Christmas'),
Six jars of jam,
Six jars of marmalade,
Six jars of honey,

Six tins of salmon ('to make salmon mousse'),
Four 1lb cans of corned beef,
Four 1lb cans of ham,
Two 1lb cans of tongue,
One tin of mackerel,
Four tins of sardines,
Two 1lb jars of Bovril,
Twenty tins of various fruits,*
'One or two' tins of vegetables, 'but we don't really like them from
   a tin'.[54]

The domestic setting gave Mrs Thatcher the chance to impress the public with the extent to which she differed from the old Tory establishment. Neave felt reassured: 'Many housewives think she is taking a sensible precaution.'[55] When Denis Healey shouted a jibe about hoarding at her across the floor of the House of Commons during the debate on the Finance Bill, Mrs Thatcher was ready with her equally cheap but effective retort, referring to his comfortable properties: 'I am not as successful as the Chancellor at hoarding houses.'[56] Her 'housewife' economics had been used against her, but she had turned the attack to her advantage.

Meanwhile, Du Cann's indecision continued. Both at the time and in later years, Du Cann would cite his wife's reluctance and his position as chairman of the 1922 Committee as reasons why he did not stand. 'I never thought I should challenge, because I was the umpire,' he recalled. But if these were the real reasons, it is hard to see why the matter took so long to resolve, since they already existed before the contest began. It seems more likely that Du Cann was trying to work out whether the trouble at Keyser Ullmann would be too great for him to stand, and this was obviously not something he could discuss with others (at this time of extreme financial difficulties, most City institutions were suffering distress, so the exact degree of danger was hard to determine). On 6 December, Neave 'saw Margaret and arranged to have another talk on Wednesday. I shall back her if Edward Du Cann does not stand. The Party is depressed and leaderless.'[57] But less than a week later, when Neave had his further chat with Mrs Thatcher, 'She made it clear that if Edward Du Cann were to stand she would drop out. Much depends upon the form of election system which will be published next week.'[58]

Home's committee suggested two significant rule changes. Both, as it

---

* Mrs Thatcher often served tinned peaches, to the dismay of her staff. Playing on one of her favourite later phrases about peace, Alison Ward and Caroline Ryder used to joke about 'peach, with freedom and justice' (interview with Lady Wakeham and Lady Ryder of Wensum).

turned out, were to have notable effects on Mrs Thatcher's later career. The first was that it should be possible to challenge a sitting leader once a year. The second was that, to win on the first ballot, the leading candidate needed not an absolute majority plus a margin of 15 per cent over his nearest rival (as was provided for in the 1965 rules), but only a 15 per cent margin over his nearest rival, with that percentage being calculated as one of all those eligible to vote. In short, the barrier any challenger to Heath needed to jump had been lowered. This was 'Alec's revenge'. The committee's recommendations could not be voted on and implemented until the new year, so the exact date of the contest remained uncertain. On 19 December, Nigel Fisher organized a meeting of Du Cann supporters in which all present, including Neave, signed a letter urging him to stand. 'I said', recorded Neave, 'that if Du Cann did not stand ... we should all support Margaret but there is no unanimity. She has less chance at present. Heath's stock is rising again.'[59]

On Christmas Day itself, Neave was fretting: 'Not too happy about E. Du Cann since his bank, Keyser Ullmann, is clearly in difficulties. I plan to ring him in a week's time to discover whether he has decided to stand. If not, we must back Margaret.'[60] Three days later, he wrote to Mrs Thatcher suggesting a meeting in the New Year. Well before this took place, though, Du Cann himself had seen her. As he remembered the meeting, she came to his house accompanied by Denis. They sat on the sofa together, so that 'It was like interviewing a housekeeper and her husband.'[61] She had come to the meeting saying that she would back Du Cann as the leadership candidate if he would make her his shadow chancellor, but he told her that he would not stand. This account is probably not completely accurate. Mrs Thatcher, in her memoirs, considered that the conversation with Du Cann showed him 'undecided'.[62] On 5 January 1975, Neave and Du Cann talked on the telephone for forty minutes. Neave records Du Cann as saying that:

> He thought her naïve but admired her character. He still had not made up his mind whether to stand. He thought we should organise a 'head count' as soon as possible so that we knew what the probable figures were ... I said it was difficult to commit myself entirely to Margaret and he said I must do what was right for the country! But this does not help. Until we know how many will back Margaret Thatcher I do not think any decisions will be made.

It was time for lunch with Mrs Thatcher. The meeting took place on 9 January. Neave noted it in some detail:

> drove to 19 Flood Street where we [Neave went with his wife Diana] lunched alone with Margaret Thatcher. A very nice house, a bit too tidy, and everything

wrapped in cellophane. However M looked well, rather fatter and in good form. We discussed Historic Houses [their tax exemption was being debated] . . .

We then got on to the leadership. She said G. Howe and one or two other Shadow Cabinet members supported her. A change was essential. No real talks on policy and when in office it had never been a 'real Cabinet'. Ted never confided in anyone. She agreed that a headcounting must come first and that it was possible that she and E. Du Cann might get the same type of support. There was so far no campaign structure. I said this was not possible until a provisional assessment of the figures could be made. She had heard from the press that E. Heath would get 120. (He would have to get 159 to win on the first ballot.) I said 70 or 80 was more like it. The numbers for E. Du Cann and her could be close in which case they would have to settle whether both should stand. I find it difficult because having promised her support, I have also signed the letter to E Du Cann but we do not yet know if he will stand. We also discussed whether W. Whitelaw who is ambitious would stand. I did not fancy his chances but it was possible that Central Office would influence MPs on his behalf through their constituency associations.[63]

Three days later, Du Cann was still dithering. At his flat, Neave 'found a private note from Nigel Fisher saying Edward was still undecided. His wife did not want to give up their beautiful house in Somerset which they could not afford without the Bank.'[64] The next day, Neave rang Mrs Thatcher and told her he would give her a definite view of how to proceed by Thursday 16 January. On the Tuesday, he at last got a decision out of Du Cann: 'Du Cann told me he would definitely not stand: he could not "let down" his wife.'[65] The following evening, during a division on the committee stage of the Finance Bill, on which Mrs Thatcher was leading for the Conservatives, Neave 'agreed with Nigel Fisher that I should chair a new group to support Margaret Thatcher'.[66]

A meeting was held in Interview Room J to discuss aspects of organization, but even at this late stage 'Several "anti-women" voices' were raised. 'Afterwards I spoke to Fergus Montgomery who has been running Margaret Thatcher's "organisation" (which hardly exists) and arranged with W. Shelton* to hold a meeting to discuss "identification" of her supporters on Monday at 9 p.m.'[67] The next day, 16 January, the 1922 Committee approved the Home committee's recommended change of rules for the leadership elections.

---

* William Shelton (1929–2003), educated Radley, Tabor Academy, Marion, Massachusetts and Worcester College, Oxford; Conservative MP for Clapham, 1970–74; for Streatham, February 1974–92; knighted, 1989.

A further complication entered Neave's calculations: 'Having told me that he would not stand, Hugh Fraser has now changed his mind. He would certainly take votes off Margaret and Heath but what would it avail?'[68] Fraser, a charming, romantic man, and a long-standing critic of Heath, had been tempted to throw his hat in the ring by various favourable mentions in the press. His wife, Lady Antonia, described by Neave as 'beautiful, arrogant like Lady Glencora Palliser [heroine of Anthony Trollope's Palliser sequence of novels, which, at that time, was a hugely successful BBC television serialization with Susan Hampshire as Lady Glencora]', recorded in her own diary at this time her husband's 'argument for' standing: 'to call public attention to his continued existence in the world of politics. This needs not many votes but some. Programme: to call attention to the continued existence of another kind of Toryism, radical, right, patriotic, non-Socialist. Under Heath Toryism becoming extinct as did Liberals.'[69] Publicity made Hugh Fraser feel optimistic. 'Thinks he may get as many as 50 votes,' Lady Antonia wrote on 19 January. 'I think 35.' Two days later she recorded: 'Dinner with Hugh at the H of C . . . Norman St. J S [St John-Stevas]* (camply): "I'm voting for Hugh so that you can grace No. 10."'†

The Fraser intervention was not considered very serious, and Neave continued with his plans. On Sunday 19 January he spoke to Mrs Thatcher on the telephone and told her the names of the people in the group which had been backing Du Cann: 'She said I should consult Keith Joseph who would back her. This means that supporters of Joseph, Thatcher and Du Cann are now united. I told her to forget about it [that is, not worry about the leadership campaign] and stick to the Finance Bill.'[70] The following evening Neave and Shelton met to seal the pact and record the extent of her support. 'So the balloon has gone up,' wrote Neave. 'The Campaign group is formed of people of all shades of thought in the party.'[71]

Neave had not been exaggerating when he said that Mrs Thatcher's campaign team hardly existed. Before the Neave alliance, her only two known

---

* Norman St John-Stevas (1929–2012), educated Ratcliffe College, Fitzwilliam College, Cambridge and Christ Church, Oxford (he is thought to have been unique in holding office in both the Oxford and Cambridge Unions); barrister, author (editor of the complete works of Walter Bagehot); joined *Economist*, 1959; Conservative MP for Chelmsford, 1964–87; Parliamentary Under-Secretary, Department of Education and Science, and Minister for the Arts, 1973–4; Leader of the House of Commons and Minister for the Arts, 1979–81; created Lord St John of Fawsley, 1987.
† William Shelton's canvass returns suggest that St John-Stevas actually voted for Heath. The whips' list has him down as 'TH or MT'.

lieutenants had been William Shelton and Fergus Montgomery, neither of whom stood high in parliamentary seniority or reputation. Shelton was considered a lightweight and, by some, 'fond of the bottle',[72] and Montgomery, in an age when these things mattered much more than today, was thought effeminate. He had a 'mincing walk',[73] and looked like 'a pantomime drag queen'.[74] Montgomery himself was engagingly self-critical about his efforts – 'It was just Bill Shelton and me, and we were useless'[75] – and, in the climactic days of the campaign, he went off on a long-planned parliamentary jaunt to South Africa. The third man helping Mrs Thatcher from the start was not in the Commons at all – Gordon Reece. Reece believed that the MP who was most important in winning support for Mrs Thatcher was Peter Morrison: 'It was he and he alone who persuaded a significant section of the knights of the shires that she was an acceptable alternative to Ted Heath.'[76] Morrison was undoubtedly important. It is unlikely, though, that someone who had entered the House of Commons only in February of that year could have carried enough weight.

Where Reece was right was in his view that the 'Knights of the Shires' – the name traditionally given to the mainly rural, mainly gentry backbone of the Conservative parliamentary party – represented the key constituency Mrs Thatcher had to win. In later years, it was often written (particularly often by Julian Critchley,* who had voted for Mrs Thatcher but later became a full-time critic) that Mrs Thatcher's supporters were 'garagistes' taking on the landed gentry in the party, and that she won because of a 'peasants' revolt'. This is not the case. There was not really a class war in the Tory Party at this time and, to the extent that there was, 'Grocer' Heath (as the satirical magazine *Private Eye* christened him) was just as likely to be the victim of it as the grocer's daughter Margaret Thatcher. The Knights of the Shires were men who came mostly from public schools, very large numbers of whom had served in the Second World War. Some were aristocratic; some were 'petty gentry'; some were from the professions and some from business. What they tended to share was a rather regimental, officers'-mess attitude to the party and a strong, though vague, patriotism much more powerful than any definite ideology which could be called left or right.

This was a group of men (more than 90 per cent of them were men) for whom the habits of politics were those of a club. By the autumn of 1974, large numbers of them were coming to the conclusion that Heath had let

---

* Julian Critchley (1930–2000), educated Shrewsbury, Sorbonne and Pembroke College, Oxford; writer, broadcaster and journalist; Conservative MP for Rochester and Chatham, 1959–64; for Aldershot and North Hants, 1970–74; for Aldershot, 1974–97; knighted, 1995.

down the regiment, weakened the spirit of the club and offended their patriotism. They felt cross that he had so often overlooked their own talents and, through sheer bad manners, snubbed them, and they were bewildered at the way his policies had failed to prevent socialism taking a grip of the country they loved. As Sara Morrison put it, 'The men with double-barrelled names never really took to Ted.'[77] Mrs Thatcher admired the values of this club – she had more or less married into it – but was not herself part of it: 'I was conscious of being a woman and being of a different social background, although they never made me feel it . . . Airey had the contacts I didn't have.'[78] It would not have occurred to most of the Knights of the Shires, unprompted, that a woman could lead the Conservative Party, but when the proposition was brought to their attention they were surprisingly unworried by it. A significant minority of them were softened by Mrs Thatcher's sex appeal,[79] and a larger number rather took to her character. Her parliamentary performance and the manner of her challenge convinced them that she had the quality they admired above everything else – courage.

In the run-up to his own leadership bid in 1965, Ted Heath had distinguished himself in the role of debating the Finance Bill in committee. This had taken place as 'a committee of the whole House' (as opposed to a 'select' or 'standing' committee) and therefore gave MPs an opportunity to shine in the large forum of the Chamber, while deploying a mastery of detail. The same was true in 1974–5. Parliamentary proceedings were not televised at that time, or even broadcast on the radio: MPs felt they were addressing an intimate audience of their colleagues and performance on television was much less important than in the House of Commons, a view which, before the end of the twentieth century, was to be reversed. Taking the opportunity that Heath had inadvertently given her by making her the Treasury number two, Mrs Thatcher threw herself wholeheartedly into the assault on Denis Healey and his Chief Secretary to the Treasury, Joel Barnett (a man of whom, as so often with Jews, especially those with good economic brains, she was very fond). In the debate on the second reading, she railed against Healey's inflation and delighted her troops with her attack on his proposals for capital taxes: 'a capital transfer tax does not redistribute wealth, nor does a wealth tax. They concentrate wealth in the hands of the Government, which is the very opposite of distribution.'[80] From 15 January to 11 February 1975, including the days of both of the leadership ballots, Mrs Thatcher spoke in twelve Finance Bill Committee debates, often very late at night, and almost always to good effect. She combined an astonishing mastery of the technical facts with a sure sense of the emotions aroused among voters by tax, inflation and economic mismanagement. She kept pushing the idea, for example, that any policy of encouraging savings must welcome a vital motive to save – that of wanting to safeguard one's posterity. 'Fathers saved for them [their children] and then', she said sarcastically, 'did an awful thing – handing those savings to their children,' for which they were now to be penalized.[81] On 22 January, Mrs Thatcher reiterated her attacks on a grander scale. Healey responded to her criticisms by saying that her 'whole speech was a defiant reassertion of birth and privilege': 'she emerged in this debate as La Pasionaria [a reference to the eloquent Communist orator and broadcaster in the Spanish Civil War] of privilege. She showed that she has decided . . . to see her party tagged as the party of the rich few.' Mrs Thatcher was equal to this: 'I wish I could say that the Chancellor of the Exchequer had done himself less than justice. Unfortunately, I can only say that I believe he has done himself justice. Some Chancellors are macro-economic. Other Chancellors are fiscal. This one is just plain cheap.' She emphasized that she was born 'with no privilege at all'.[82] Her combativeness, particularly against the able and aggressive Healey, won her much admiration.

It was Airey Neave who knew how to turn all this to good electoral effect among his colleagues, not least because his own mindset was similar to that of the men he was trying to win over. Though much more intelligent than most of them, he shared the career disappointments, the grumpy solidarity of the cash-poor upper-middle class, the experience of war and the dismay at the country's steep decline. He also, despite his hesitancy in backing her candidacy, had always liked Margaret Thatcher. He had known her since they had been young candidates together and also at the Bar. In the 1970 Parliament, Neave had found her an ally, sharing an interest in science (which came within her departmental responsibilities) and in nuclear power. In 1972, Mrs Thatcher helped persuade him to stay on as chairman of the Select Committee on Science and Technology 'since the establishment would be only too keen to get rid of a "strong man"'.[83] In the course of that year, the Thatchers twice went to stay with the Neaves in the country, once to visit the nuclear power station at Harwell ('Margaret made a hit with the scientists').[84]* Neave found her physically attractive, provoking, according to their daughter, a small gleam of jealousy from his wife Diana.[85] He was less charmed by Denis – 'an awkward, complaining character very jealous of his wife – who is really beautiful and brilliant'.[86]

---

* The Harwell encounter was characteristic. According to W. F. Deedes, recording the conversation of Neave's wife, Diana, Mrs Thatcher had arrived at the power station 'in a flowery dress and a hat, looking most unsuitable for the day. But the instant she entered into conversation with the scientists their mood was seen to change. She knew what to ask; the change in their somewhat patronising air towards her was comical.' (W. F. Deedes note of conversation with Lady Neave, 26 March 1983, unpublished.)

Once he was her campaign manager, Neave saw it as his task to keep Mrs Thatcher out of the fray of intrigue. She should stick to her parliamentary guns, avoiding media interviews until the very late stages, seeing all MPs who wanted to see her, but not ingratiating herself with anyone or acting out of character. With Shelton as the keeper of what turned out to be highly accurate lists, Neave, who loved skulduggery and backstairs work, sidled up to people in the corridors and the Smoking Room, and told broken-down backbenchers that Mrs Thatcher admired them. One trick he used on John Farr,* a fairly typical example of the genre, was to say, 'Margaret assumes you must have turned down a job offer from Ted.' Farr: 'Why?' Neave: 'Oh, because you so obviously should have one if you want it.'[87] Since Mrs Thatcher had a reputation for naivety, it did her no harm that her campaign manager had a reputation for the opposite which was linked with rumours that he had worked, or even worked still, for the security services. According to Joan Hall,† who had been MP for Keighley until losing her seat in February 1974, and was roped in by Neave to help organize Mrs Thatcher's campaign, 'Airey would always clutch to the wall, never walk down the corridor straight,' whereas Mrs Thatcher was 'very practical and straightforward'.[88] Although Mrs Thatcher gained much of her impetus and her nucleus of support from Keith Joseph and members of the Economic Dining Club such as Nicholas Ridley and John Nott, Neave did not much concern himself with these. He concentrated on the men who sat in the Smoking Room and grumbled – men like Robin Cooke,‡ little known then and forgotten now, but men whose votes needed to be won. He also made the most of his acquaintance with Humphrey Atkins, the Chief Whip, supposedly neutral in the contest, but actually inclined towards Mrs Thatcher.[89] Atkins resisted pressure from Francis Pym§ to support Heath and almost campaign for him. Atkins privately believed that Heath should withdraw.[90]

The Thatcher campaign was greatly assisted by the tactics of the Heath camp. Heath himself was a hopeless campaigner, resenting the very idea

---

* John Farr (1922–97), educated Harrow; Conservative MP for Harborough, 1959–92; knighted, 1984. He never got a job from Mrs Thatcher either.

† Joan Hall (1935–), educated Queen Margaret's School, Escrick and Ashridge House of Citizenship; Conservative MP for Keighley, 1970–February 1974.

‡ Sir Robert Cooke (known as Robin) (1930–87), educated Harrow and Christ Church, Oxford; Conservative MP for Bristol West, 1957–79; knighted, 1979.

§ Francis Pym (1922–2008), educated Eton and Magdalene College, Cambridge; Conservative MP for Cambridgeshire, 1961–83; for Cambridgeshire South East, 1983–7; Secretary of State for Northern Ireland, 1973–4; for Defence, 1979–81; Chancellor of the Duchy of Lancaster and Leader of the House of Commons, 1981–2; Secretary of State for Foreign and Commonwealth Affairs, 1982–3; created Lord Pym, 1987.

and, even more than in the past, extremely bad at affecting an interest in other people. The Tory Party, he told Bernard Weatherill, consists of 'shits, bloody shits and fucking shits',[91] and he was not successful at concealing this belief from the colleagues whose votes he wanted. According to Tim Kitson, Heath would be persuaded by his team to go into the Smoking Room, but would then pick up the *Evening Standard*, drink some whisky and not talk to anyone.[92] His campaign managers made him give lunches and dinners to backbenchers, but these proved to be sepulchral occasions, only provoking those invited to ask themselves, 'Why haven't we been asked over the last five years?'[93] Those close to Heath believed that his natural awkwardness in situations of this kind was added to by his resentment of his opponent on grounds of her sex. 'It was all tied up with Ted's psychology about women,' according to his other PPS, Kenneth Baker.[94] Heath seldom seemed to enjoy the company of women. He was so surprised at the idea of being challenged by a woman, and found it so distasteful and disloyal, that he could not quite face it or work out how to deal with it. 'It's a matter of opinion', he told Sara Morrison, 'whether you think she's a woman or not,'[95] but if Mrs Thatcher had not been, he would have found it much easier.

Although the only electorate in the contest was parliamentary, the attitudes of MPs would obviously be affected by public opinion and the media. Gordon Reece attended to this aspect of the campaign. Since the aim was to pick up the widest range of the disaffected, he wanted a negative campaign in the first stage and 'nothing on policy at all'.[96] Mrs Thatcher needed to look like a winner and 'This was quite a tall order, particularly as she was not at this stage good at either communicating with people, or on television.'[97] There was no question, in the first ballot, of candidates debating with one another on television, because of the doctrine that 'Conservative must not appear against Conservative.' For two months Mrs Thatcher gave no press or broadcast interviews whatever, breaking her silence only a week before the first ballot. As the nominations closed, her managers felt it was time for her to go public. Speaking to ITN, she stayed off policy, saying merely that it was time for a contest, and noting that she was the same age as Heath had been when he became leader and that he, like herself now, had been distinguishing himself in the Finance Bill at that time. She compared herself to Mrs Gandhi, the Prime Minister of India ('a delightful person').[98]* Two days later, she appeared in an interview by

---

* On the same day, Heath went to a meeting with the Canadian High Commissioner, a lunch at the German Embassy and a reception at the French Embassy – all of these, from the point of view of his campaign, a complete waste of time.

Michael Cockerell on BBC's *Midweek*, and was filmed having her hair done. Antonia Fraser recorded, 'Margaret Thatcher awful – physically she is not good. Flutters her eyelashes in an unattractive way which is terrible!'[99] But these were the words, of course, of a rival's wife. Most thought that Mrs Thatcher seemed fresh compared with Heath, who was not interviewed, but was shown attacking the new leadership election rules.

On the same day, in the *Daily Telegraph*,* Mrs Thatcher offered the nearest thing to a manifesto in her campaign. Under the headline 'My Kind of Tory Party', the piece, which had been drafted chiefly by Angus Maude,† began with the premise that the Conservatives had 'failed the people'.[100] There were two lessons of this failure – that inflation was 'the worst enemy' and that the preoccupation with macro-economics should not 'blind us to the day-to-day problems of ordinary people'. 'International interest rates', she wrote, 'must be thought of in terms of the young couple's mortgage as well as of the balance of payments.' There was nothing wrong with defending what people called 'middle-class values': 'This is not a fight for "privilege"; it is a fight for freedom – freedom for *every* citizen.' She continued her attack on Capital Transfer Tax, and said that those who did not respect private property should 'become a socialist and have done with it'. She added, 'people believe too many Conservatives *have* become socialists already.' She argued that 'industrial democracy' and 'co-partnership', as currently promoted, were means of increasing union power, and she took the part of those workers who resented 'State subsidies to shirkers'. The

---

* The position of the *Daily Telegraph* at this time reflected that of the Conservative Party. Officially, the paper supported Ted Heath's continuation in office, a line maintained by the proprietor, Lord Hartwell, and strongly pushed by his wife, Pamela. But the majority of the staff who concerned themselves with these matters – the deputy editor Colin Welch and leader writers such as T. E. Utley, Frank Johnson and John O'Sullivan, as well as Alfred Sherman, who worked part-time at the paper – were fierce critics of Heath and had led the way in attacking the U-turn when he was in office. W. F. Deedes, who left Parliament at the October 1974 election, was made editor immediately after it, but not with immediate effect. The day before his appointment was announced, Deedes dined with Heath, who enlisted him in his plan to try to cling on to the leadership. In a private memo he sent to his predecessor, Maurice Green, the next day, Deedes set out Heath's reasoning, and his own view that 'Labour would be swift to exploit the appearance of Heath being Shanghai'd by an ungrateful party . . . Therefore he owes it to his own party . . . to take his time' (memo from W. F. Deedes to Maurice Green, 14 October 1974, unpublished). Deedes took up his position as editor at the beginning of 1975, shortly before the contest was held. He saw it as the paper's role to hold the ring in the Tory Party. The *Daily Telegraph* therefore endorsed Heath, but, pre-Deedes, it had prepared the intellectual ground for Mrs Thatcher.

† Angus Maude (1912–93), educated Rugby and Oriel College, Oxford; Conservative MP for Ealing South, 1950–58; for Stratford-upon-Avon, 1963–83; Deputy Chairman, Conservative Party, 1975–9; Paymaster-General, 1979–81; knighted, 1981; created Lord Maude of Stratford-upon-Avon, 1983.

message was reinforced in a speech to her constituents in Finchley the next day:

> In the desperate situation of Britain today, our party needs the support of all who value the traditional ideals of Toryism: compassion, and concern for the individual and his freedom; opposition to excessive State power; the right of the enterprising, the hard-working and the thrifty to succeed and to reap the rewards of success and pass some of them on to their children; encouragement of that infinite diversity of choice that is an essential of freedom; the defence of widely distributed private property against the Socialist State; the right of a man to work without oppression by either employer or trade union boss.
>
> There is a widespread feeling in the country that the Conservative Party has not defended these ideals explicitly and toughly enough, so that Britain is set on a course towards inevitable Socialist mediocrity.[101]

Reece remained worried that Mrs Thatcher might be trapped into over-exposure and too much public argument. He arranged for her to be filmed for Granada Television's *World in Action* because the programme was to be more personal. He had a row with Neave (Neave refers to him in his diary as 'one Rees') because he thought she should not appear on *Midweek* as well – a row which he lost. *World in Action*, though filmed the week before, did not appear until the eve of the first ballot. It showed Mrs Thatcher with her family discussing the Sunday papers, working in her constituency, meeting a council cleaner, chatting to colleagues and speaking at a public meeting. She spoke, as she had done so often before, about managing a home as well as a career. She said that her experience of the October election had led her to feel that she could cope with the leadership 'every bit as well as my colleagues' (thus accidentally confirming that she had entertained thoughts of the job when still backing Keith Joseph), and she once again dismissed the notion of herself as a defender of privilege. She emphasized her Grantham background and declared: 'All my ideas about [Britain] were formed before I was seventeen or eighteen.' She promised to offer Heath a post in her Shadow Cabinet, but not, 'for the present', Enoch Powell (now back in Parliament as an Ulster Unionist), since he had 'deserted his own people'.

The reason that Mrs Thatcher put herself more in the front line in the last week, and expressed her views more strongly, was a growing confidence within her team. Neave and Shelton kept poring over the figures on Shelton's sheet. As early as 21 January 1975, Neave noted: 'It became evident during the day that Margaret was in the lead and I told her so. She distinguished herself by a brilliant attack on the capital transfer tax late tonight.'[102] The next day, Neave decided to release the news that Mrs Thatcher was ahead on the first ballot by their count. On 23 January the BBC *Today* programme led with this story. 'This has caused a sensation,' wrote Neave, 'and sent the establishment into a flat spin. My birthday aged 59 today. I went to see Margaret. She does not want too much TV exposure.'[103] On Sunday 26 January, Neave spoke to George Clark of *The Times*: 'I said Margaret was in a "strong position" on the first ballot. I had agreed this line with Bill Shelton who went with me and Keith Joseph to see Margaret at 19 Flood Street at 6 p.m. ... She has 112 pledges and Heath less than 80 but this must be too optimistic. It is essential to give out no figures.'[104] In the Labour government, these developments were observed with interest, and provoked disagreement. In his diary for 24 January, Bernard Donoughue records a conversation between Harold Wilson and his press secretary, Joe Haines: 'Before he left Joe suggested to him [Wilson] that we should give a police escort to Mrs Thatcher – to help her subtly in the leadership contest with Heath because Joe said he wanted Heath beaten: "He is still the most dangerous." HW agreed at first and then wavered – he said he feared Thatcher as well, especially as a woman.'[105]

As the campaign entered its closing phase, the 'establishment' which Mrs Thatcher had decided to take on pulled out all the stops. Lord Home announced his support for Heath. The constituency chairmen, generally more supportive of the central power than the rank and file beneath them, declared heavily for Heath too. And even the battered rank and file, according to a poll in the *Daily Express* published on 3 February, backed Heath: 70 per cent of Conservative voters said they preferred him to any rival. Heath's campaign managers, believing their own counts of pledges, put it about that Ted was winning, hoping that this momentum would carry him through and frighten off opposition which would fear the repercussions that would follow a Heath victory. This in turn caused Neave to alter tactics. His earlier assertion that Mrs Thatcher was ahead had increased her support. In his last diary entry before he became too busy to keep it going – 28 January – he wrote: 'There are allegedly signs that Heath support is growing ... but our canvass does not support this.' But he saw that many of those inclining to Mrs Thatcher did so not because they actually wanted her to be leader, but because they sought a second ballot in which other candidates could stand. Neave wanted to make such people feel that a vote for Mrs Thatcher in the first ballot would make it easy for Willie Whitelaw or Jim Prior or another to enter the race, whereas a Heath victory would obviously kill everything dead.

On 1 February, *The Times*, edited by Mrs Thatcher's Oxford contemporary William Rees-Mogg,* endorsed Whitelaw, even though he was not yet a candidate. Neave decided to exploit all this and therefore put it about, though his numbers told him otherwise, that 'Margaret is doing well, but not quite well enough.' On the night before the ballot, Neave spoke to Robert Carvel, the political correspondent of the *Evening Standard*, and told him that Heath's figures were higher than he really thought they were. The paper's first edition duly ran with the story and Bill Shelton was instructed to buy extra copies for the Commons smoking and tea rooms for the supporters of alternative successors to Heath, such as Whitelaw or Prior, to peruse.[106] The tactic worked. Faced with the prospect of yet more Heath, several men with no time for Mrs Thatcher voted for her. Outside the Thatcher camp, information about support for Heath was tainted. On the day before the poll, Bernard Weatherill, worried that his chief, Atkins, was leaning too much to Mrs Thatcher, showed Tim Kitson the whips' office's own figures.[107] They reported twenty-five more votes than there were MPs. People were lying, and naturally they were lying more to the incumbent than to the challenger. For his part, Atkins told Heath that he ought to be confident of 129 votes.[108] At the heart of all this, the challenger herself remained calm, almost detached. Mrs Thatcher did as Neave told her and got on with the Finance Bill. Although always in a terrible state before making a public speech, she was much less nervous about a behind-the-scenes campaign. Those close to her at that time were impressed. Joan Hall thought that Mrs Thatcher understood that she was riding a tide: 'She was above all ordinary mortals,' waiting quietly for whatever fate held in store.[109]

On the day of the first ballot, Mrs Thatcher kept a lunch appointment at Rothschild's Bank to which she was taken by the young MP Norman Lamont,† who worked for them. On the way there, noticing an *Evening Standard* placard saying, 'Constituencies rally to Heath', Mrs Thatcher remarked: 'CCO [Conservative Central Office] has been working hard.'[110] Sir Evelyn de Rothschild was the only senior member of the family to attend the lunch. Lord (Victor) Rothschild, who had run Heath's Think Tank, refused to attend, as did his son Jacob. All through the lunch,

---

* William Rees-Mogg (1928–2012), educated Charterhouse and Balliol College, Oxford; editor, *The Times*, 1967–81; vice-chairman, Board of Governors, BBC, 1981–6; chairman, Arts Council of Great Britain, 1982–9; Broadcasting Standards Council, 1988–93; created Lord Rees-Mogg, 1988.

† Norman Lamont (1942–), educated Loretto School and Fitzwilliam College, Cambridge; Conservative MP for Kingston-upon-Thames, 1972–97; Financial Secretary to the Treasury, 1986–9; Chief Secretary to the Treasury, 1989–90; Chancellor of the Exchequer, 1990–93; created Lord Lamont, 1998.

Mrs Thatcher found herself attacked on all sides. On the way back, she said to Lamont: 'Never take me to that red bank again.'[111]* Lamont found himself drafting insincere thank-you letters from both the guest and the host.

The poll closed at 3.30, and the result did not take long in coming. Shelton's final canvass had suggested 124 votes for Mrs Thatcher and 122 for Heath. Standing as a 'teller' of the votes outside Committee Room 14, which had been set aside for the ballot, he publicly bet Kitson a pound that his candidate would win. In fact, the figures were better for Shelton's candidate than he himself had predicted. Among votes cast on the spot, the two leading candidates were neck and neck, but the postal votes pulled Mrs Thatcher ahead: she got 130 votes, Heath 119, Fraser 16. There were six abstentions and five spoiled ballot papers. Canvass records suggest, though he has never confirmed this, that one of these abstentions was Michael Heseltine.† Another was certainly Jim Prior, a Heath supporter, whose train arrived too late for him to vote.

It has often been reported that when Ted Heath heard the news of his defeat he said, 'We got it all wrong,'[112] implying a mismanaged campaign. William Waldegrave, who was present, remembered it differently. Heath said, 'So it's all gone wrong then,' by which he meant that something had fundamentally changed, and that the politics which Heath stood for had lost. 'He thought he'd lost the Apostolic Succession.'[113]

The Thatcher camp, which had retained discipline throughout, now suffered a lapse of taste. On the night of the result, Neave gave a party with champagne in his flat, and the television cameras were allowed in – a mistake since there was, as yet, no final winner. It looked as though they were rubbing Heath's nose in his defeat. Denis was filmed grinning toothily, and making one of his very few public utterances. Asked for his reaction, he said, 'Delighted! Terribly proud, naturally. Wouldn't you be?'[114] Due to the astonishing demands of her parliamentary timetable, Mrs Thatcher then returned, after dinner with the Neaves, to the Commons for further debate of the committee stage of the Finance Bill. She was not able to go home until 2.30 in the morning. When she tried to leave with Joan Hall, who

---

* When Mrs Thatcher was in office, Rothschild's was reconciled with her, through the diplomatic skills of Michael Richardson, who joined the bank from Cazenove's in 1981. Rothschild's became the leading institution in the history of privatization.

† Michael Heseltine (1933–), educated Shrewsbury and Pembroke College, Oxford; Conservative MP for Tavistock, 1966–74; for Henley, February 1974–2001; Secretary of State for the Environment, 1979–83; for Defence, 1983–6; for the Environment, 1990–92; President of the Board of Trade, 1992–5; First Secretary of State and Deputy Prime Minister, 1995–7; chairman, Haymarket Publishing Group, from 1999; created Baron Heseltine, 2001.

had been driving her all through the campaign, they found the gates of the House of Commons closed and Hall's car locked in.[115] The staff had to be found to unlock them and allow the two women to drive away in Miss Hall's MGB GT harvest-gold two-seater.

Under the rules, Mrs Thatcher had not won outright. There would be a second ballot, and her team expected that there would be a third. Heath at last faced the inevitable, and resigned, making Robert Carr interim leader until the ultimate result. With hindsight, it is easy to see that Mrs Thatcher's victory on the second ballot was almost assured. She had the momentum, the press excitement and the prestige which came from having had the courage to challenge. She had set the agenda, and proved that she could triumph over the establishment. But that was not how she saw things at the time. It seemed perfectly possible that the party, having screwed itself up to get rid of Heath, would turn ungratefully upon its chosen assassin.* Many agreed with Reggie Maudling, who bumped into Kenneth Baker in the hours after the result of the first ballot and told him: 'This is the darkest day in the history of the Tory Party: they've all gone absolutely mad.'[116] Willie Whitelaw declared his candidacy on the night of Heath's defeat and Mrs Thatcher always maintained in later years that she thought he would beat her.[117]† There was also talk of Julian Amery‡ and Maurice Macmillan, brothers-in-law, standing too. In fact, it was John Peyton,§ Jim Prior and Geoffrey Howe who entered the fray. The first was not a serious candidate, the second, more serious, would never have been an ally of Mrs Thatcher, but the third, Howe, perturbed her. She had told Neave¶ that Howe would be almost the only member of the Shadow Cabinet apart from Joseph to support her. In fact, he had voted for Heath in the first ballot. Supported by his old friend Ian Gow,** who was later to play such an important part

---

* Heath himself may have hoped for this effect: at a Buckingham Palace reception at this time he told the editor of the *Economist*, Andrew Knight: 'Gangsters! She's a gangster. They're all gangsters!' [interview with Andrew Knight]

† Whitelaw immediately picked up the support of the third candidate, Hugh Fraser. Lady Antonia recorded in her diary of 4 February that Hugh would have had twenty more votes 'if people had not been frightened of Ted's publicity and thought they should vote for Margaret to catch him'. On the Chief Whip's instructions, Fraser went off to see the defeated Heath: 'Ted was sitting behind his desk looking very fat. Like a pathetic whale,' said Hugh. 'I wanted to hug him. I did manage to get him in a sort of embrace.'

‡ Julian Amery (1919–96), educated Eton and Balliol College, Oxford; Conservative MP for Preston North, 1950–66; for Brighton Pavilion, 1969–92; Minister for Housing and Construction, DOE, 1970–72; Minister of State, FCO, 1972–4; created Lord Amery, 1992.

§ John Peyton (1919–2006), educated Eton and Trinity College, Oxford; Conservative MP for Yeovil, 1951–83; Minister of Transport, 1970; Minister for Transport Industries, DOE, 1970–74; created Lord Peyton, 1983. ¶ See p. 281.

** Ian Gow (1937–90), educated Winchester; Conservative MP for Eastbourne, February

in Mrs Thatcher's life, Howe put himself forward quite strongly. 'I didn't have the wit to realize it at the time,' Mrs Thatcher remembered, 'but he had far more naked ambition than I'd thought.'[118] Even at this stage, Howe was not as close to her as their shared economic views might have suggested.

Whitelaw quickly couched his appeal as one of unity and moderation, particularly reaching what the *Guardian* called 'the northern and working-class folks'.[119] Mrs Thatcher's campaign therefore moved towards the centre, denying that she was a monetarist or necessarily opposed to incomes policy. She spoke up, too, to quash rumours that she was anti-European: 'This torch [of pro-Europeanism] must be picked up ... by whoever is chosen ... Experience shows that our presence in the Community has helped ensure that it is outward-looking.'[120] To attract centrist votes, an approach was made to Prior, hinting that, if he dropped his candidacy, he could become Mrs Thatcher's deputy leader. He turned this down.[121]

Despite a fierce row, Gordon Reece managed to persuade Mrs Thatcher not to go on *Panorama* for a debate with the other four candidates. She had wanted to do so to prove that she was not frightened just because she was a woman, but, after much acrimony, Reece's argument that 'The dragon in shallow water is the sport of shrimps' prevailed.[122] The only setpiece public appearance before the second ballot was therefore the chance provided by the Young Conservatives conference in East-bourne that weekend. Mrs Thatcher and Whitelaw paraded together on the seafront for the cameras, and he offered her a public kiss with the unintentionally hilarious justification to the press that they had done it often before 'and it is perfectly genuine and normal and right to do so'.[123] Whitelaw's opportunity at the conference was confined to a question-and-answer session with the delegates on party organization and devolution at which his performance was considered lacklustre. Mrs Thatcher, by contrast, risked wrath by campaigning more obviously. In her platform speech, she told the delegates: 'I believe we should judge people on merit and not on background. I believe the person who is prepared to work hardest should get the greatest rewards and keep them after tax; that we should back the workers not the shirkers ... You would not have political liberty for long if all power and property went to the State.'[124] She

---

1974–90; PPS to the Prime Minister, 1979–83; Minister for Housing and Construction, 1983–5; Minister of State, Treasury, 1985; resigned from the government over the completion of the Anglo-Irish Agreement; murdered by the Provisional IRA who exploded a bomb under his car at his home in Sussex.

received sixty-seven seconds of applause. In the next morning's *Sunday Express*, Mrs Thatcher spoke of the nation's 'thousand years of history' and the 'challenge to [the] survival' of the British people. She spoke of a 'turning-point for Britain'. 'We may not have a Churchill now [subtly hinting that they might soon be getting one] – but the instincts and traditions on which Churchill founded his appeal to the nation to fight and to survive are very far from dead.' 'The party will unite itself,' she said. 'What *I* want to do is to unite the country.'[125] Against all this, Whitelaw's television stunt, in which he was filmed drying the dishes at home in his cardigan, was not powerful.

On Tuesday 11 February 1975, the second ballot took place. The result was 146 votes for Mrs Thatcher, 79 for Whitelaw, 19 apiece for Prior and Howe, 11 for Peyton and two spoilt papers. She had therefore won outright, without needing a third ballot. Shelton's count was again pretty accurate. He had underestimated Whitelaw's support by one, and Mrs Thatcher's by nine. She sat with Fergus Montgomery in Airey Neave's small room in an attic corridor of the Commons. She remembered Neave opening the door softly and saying, 'so quietly', 'I have to tell you you are the new Leader of the Opposition.'[126]

12

The Iron Lady

'It is a moral struggle'

Meeting the press in the Grand Committee Room immediately after her victory, Mrs Thatcher said: 'To me it is like a dream that the next name in the line* after Harold Macmillan, Sir Alec Douglas-Home, Edward Heath, is Margaret Thatcher.' There was a becoming modesty about her way of putting it, but the fact that her election did indeed seem like a dream was a large part of her problem.

It is hard to exaggerate the sheer strangeness, as it seemed at the time, of the event. Geoffrey Howe, whom Mrs Thatcher had just soundly beaten, described the scene when, two days after her election, she appeared in Committee Room 14 to address the regular meeting of the 1922 Committee: 'The new leader, escorted by the chairman Edward Du Cann, entered the room through a door opening on to the platform. She was flanked only by the all-male officers of the Committee. Suddenly she looked very beautiful and very frail as the half-dozen knights of the shires towered over her. It was a moving, almost feudal, occasion. Tears came to my eyes.'[1] The oldest, grandest, in many people's eyes the stuffiest political party in the world had chosen a leader whose combination of class, inexperience and sex would previously have ruled her out. And it was not obvious that it had really meant to do so, or that it was confident of its choice. 'As the Conservative Party now begins to take stock,' reported an official at the US Embassy in London, 'its mood is a curious mixture of relief, excitement, guilt, and misgivings.'[2] Apart from anything else, the instant change in verbal and visual style produced by a woman leader was bewildering. What was the issue on which she had won, the press asked Mrs Thatcher in Conservative Central Office on the day of her triumph? 'I like to think it was merit,' she answered. 'Could you expand on that?' they asked. 'No, it doesn't need expansion. You chaps don't like short answers, or direct

---

* In her memoirs, Mrs Thatcher quotes herself as saying 'lists', but contemporary reports, for example in *The Times*, say 'line'.

answers. Men like long, rambly, waffly answers.' Interviewed by Michael Cockerell on the BBC's *Midweek*, she described her reaction to the news of her victory. With an intense, almost sensual expression, she said, 'I almost wept when they told me. I *did* weep.' Such ways of speaking would have been unknown and unthought of in a Conservative leader twenty-four hours earlier. Would her 'dream' – which, for her establishment opponents, was a nightmare – turn out to be waking reality, or would it vanish in the cold light of normal politics?

Mrs Thatcher was at least as conscious of this problem as anyone else. On the day of her victory, she dined with the Chief Whip, Humphrey Atkins, in his room in the Commons, to discuss how to compose her Shadow Cabinet. In her memoirs, Mrs Thatcher says, 'I told Humphrey that although there were some people, like Keith Joseph and Airey Neave, to whom I felt a special obligation, I did not want to make a clean sweep of the existing team.'[3] But she also told Atkins that she was aware of Joseph's shortcomings and of Neave's unpopularity in some quarters. She toyed with the idea of keeping Neave running her office until such time as she could give him a peerage.[4]

The most urgent and delicate part of the discussions in the Chief Whip's room concerned Ted Heath. In the course of her campaign, Mrs Thatcher had promised to offer Heath a place in her Shadow Cabinet, but she naturally hoped that this offer would be refused. Seeking to appear correct and polite, and to settle the matter without delay, she conveyed a message to Heath that she would like to call on him at once and talk about what he was going to do. Heath was advised by his friends – Willie Whitelaw, Lord Carrington (who was in Australia) and Francis Pym – that it would be better to let her settle down in the job and for him to join the team six months later, so a message came back from Heath's people indicating that an offer at this stage was not a good idea.[5] Mrs Thatcher was determined, however, to be seen to fulfil her promise, and so told Heath's office that she would call on him in Wilton Street on the morning after her victory. Heath received her in his study off the hall, without getting up. 'He was like a bird who's broken its wing,' Mrs Thatcher remembered. 'He was hurt, and so would I have been. I offered him whichever post he wanted in the Shadow Cabinet. He just said "No."'[6] Heath's memory was different: 'She offered me nothing.'[7] Tim Kitson, who was present, and getting coffee, recalled: 'Ted made it quite clear that he wouldn't take a job, and therefore she didn't actually offer him one.'[8] The meeting was over so quickly that the coffee had not even arrived. Heath withdrew without ceremony. Mrs Thatcher felt she could not leave at once in case the press thought there had been a row: 'I really couldn't walk straight out, so I had a natter with

Tim in the kitchen. I've had no private conversation with Ted since then, which is sad.'[9]* She left the house and told Joan Hall, who was driving her: 'Ted won't come into my Shadow Cabinet. Well, that's that.'[10] Thus began Ted Heath's self-exclusion from contact with his successor which became known as 'the incredible sulk', and which lasted, with one or two tiny deviations, until his death in 2005.

Mrs Thatcher had more success, on the same day, with Willie Whitelaw. In accordance with his regimental attitude to his role, he had made clear his readiness to serve her as soon as his defeat had been announced, and she duly offered him the post of deputy leader. He accepted, reportedly on the condition that Keith Joseph not be made shadow Chancellor.[11] On 17 February 1975, however, Joseph told her that he wanted the shadow Chancellorship or nothing[12] – the same position, oddly enough, in which he had found himself with Ted Heath – but she dissuaded him skilfully and he was satisfied with being made her number three, in charge of policy and research. Geoffrey Howe became shadow Chancellor, though she had first dangled the post before Edward Du Cann, who preferred to remain chairman of the '22 and continue to earn money in the City. The prominent Heathites Robert Carr and Peter Walker were removed, but there was no general purge of the left of the party. Jim Prior took on employment. Francis Pym accepted agriculture, though he was to give up the post, following a nervous breakdown, a few weeks later. Ian Gilmour was promoted to shadow home secretary, and Mrs Thatcher brought back Reggie Maudling to the front bench as shadow foreign secretary. Airey Neave, at his request, was made shadow secretary for Northern Ireland. Keen to have the backing of the elder statesmen of the party, she kept Lord Hailsham and Lord Carrington in the team, the first without portfolio, and the second as leader of the Lords, and accepted Willie Whitelaw's suggestion that his cousin, Lord Thorneycroft, should become party chairman. Mrs Thatcher chose her Shadow Cabinet for their variety of opinion. Of the twenty-four who met round the table, perhaps four – Neave, Joseph, Angus Maude and Sally Oppenheim – had voted for her in the second ballot and only two of these – Neave and Joseph – had been her leading supporters. In a memo to Joseph in April, the founder-director of the Centre for Policy Studies, Nigel Vinson,† questioned the need for the CPS's continued existence 'now that the Tory Party is in the hands of true believers'.[13]

---

* It is not strictly correct that she had no subsequent private conversation with Heath. Mrs Thatcher did meet him privately, though not alone, in 1978; see p. 394.

† Nigel Vinson (1931–), educated Pangbourne Naval College; founder and chairman, Plastic Coatings Ltd, 1952–72; pioneer of the idea of portable pensions; created Lord Vinson, 1985.

But it wasn't, and Mrs Thatcher did not feel nearly strong enough yet to make sure that it would be.

Nor was her own entourage, at the beginning, a source of strength. Following his defeat, Willie Whitelaw replied to a message of commiseration from Robert Carr, saying, 'Of course it is now becoming clear that her cohorts have a. little talent and b. have no idea at all about running a party.'[14] Although she would not have phrased it thus, Mrs Thatcher did not really dissent. Thanking her old friend Edward Boyle for his letter of congratulation, she wrote that she had 'too few people of high calibre to spot what is important and to alert me in time'.[15] Few thought much of her PPSs William Shelton and Fergus Montgomery, and it quickly, though privately, became rumoured that Montgomery had been involved in the homosexual scandal involving the Soviet spy John Vassall in the early 1960s. His exposure was feared. Within a fortnight of the leadership election, Neave, whom Mrs Thatcher made titular head of her private office, had recruited Richard Ryder,* a journalist on the *Daily Telegraph*, to run the operation day to day. Ryder was highly intelligent and competent, but he was also only twenty-five years old and not, at first, vested with much authority by his new boss. In theory, Airey Neave ran the office, but in practice he attended to his Shadow Cabinet portfolio of Northern Ireland, and Ryder did all the work. Mrs Thatcher also recruited the 'very attractive, bright and sexy'[16] Caroline Stephens,† who had previously worked for Heath, as her private papers secretary. The only important member of her staff who had worked for her before her promotion was her secretary, Alison Ward. Among the existing staffs at Conservative Central Office in Smith Square and the Conservative Research Department, which at that time existed more or less independently in Old Queen Street, she had few friends. Ian Gilmour she quickly replaced as chairman of the CRD with Angus Maude, but Chris Patten stayed on as director.‡

In reshaping all these arrangements, Mrs Thatcher was cautious – partly because of the weakness of her political position, partly because of her lack of organizational experience, and partly because, for all her courage at critical moments, caution was always an important part of her character.

---

* Richard Ryder (1949–), educated Radley and Magdalene College, Cambridge; Conservative MP for Mid-Norfolk, 1983–97; Government Chief Whip, 1990–95; vice-chairman, BBC, 2002–4; created Lord Ryder of Wensum, 1997.

† Richard Ryder married Caroline Stephens in 1981.

‡ Patten was particularly loyal to Heathite views. On Heath's resignation he wrote to him saying, 'You stood for the sort of Conservatism we believe in. You are the reason for some of us being in – or staying in – politics.' See Philip Ziegler, *Edward Heath: The Authorised Biography* (Harper Press, 2010), p. 489.

There was yet another reason, too – a sense of social inferiority. Although she was to acquire a reputation as the scourge of the Tory grandees, and she certainly hated to be patronized by anyone, she was by nature deferential to social systems and respected the way that the Conservative Party had been run. In many ways, her *beau idéal* of a Tory leader was Alec Douglas-Home – 'Alec would still be there if he had learnt how to communicate his message,' she declared extravagantly in the late 1990s. 'He was a marvellous man.'[17] Her romantic sense of history and her dislike of dreary mediocrity drew her instinctively to aristocratic patterns of behaviour, though she had too much integrity and earnestness to try to imitate them. She wanted to observe the proprieties, and had no desire to turn everything upside down. Those who worked for her noticed how worried she always was by all matters of dress and protocol. Not long after becoming leader, for example, she was invited to dinner with the Carringtons at their house in Ovington Square. Since the dinner was formal, Mrs Thatcher became filled with anxiety about whether or not she should wear gloves for it, and would not rest until her office had telephoned Lady Carrington for guidance.[18] Writing to the Queen for the first time as leader, she got in a tizz about how to end the letter. Caroline Stephens advised her simply to write 'yours sincerely', an error which prompted Sir Martin Charteris, the Queen's private secretary, to tell Caroline ('very sweetly') the proper form, and ask her to convey it to her boss.[19]*

The party grandees were carefully watched by Mrs Thatcher's team for how well they treated her. Lord Carrington did pretty well. Willie Whitelaw 'behaved beautifully to her face though he would make snide comments behind her back'.[20] Ian Gilmour was favoured at first, but increasingly seen – he was very tall – as 'lofty'. Christopher Soames, at that time a European commissioner, but actively looking for a return to British politics, was considered 'top of the list of snobs'.[21] For their part, the old establishment watched the new Leader with a mixture of fascination, admiration, repugnance and bemusement. Some doubted whether she would last; others genuinely wanted to help her and to break down what they saw as her isolation, as they had once embraced the equally lower-middle-class Heath. Humphrey Atkins and other party managers well disposed to her sought ways to furnish her with a group of friends she could trust – people like Carrington, Whitelaw and Thorneycroft – but there was always the problem, compounded by her sex, class and personality, that she found it hard to relax in such company. They were struck by her extreme privacy, which went right down, they thought, to a reluctance

* The proper form is (with slight variants) 'I remain, Your Majesty's obedient servant'.

to have others assist her with matters like her clothes and domestic help.[22] There was a cultural gulf. Chris Patten, though himself of what the grandees would have considered humble birth, sided culturally and politically with them. He and his colleagues in the Conservative Research Department used to express their humorous exasperation with their Leader by referring to her by her starchy Victorian second name, 'Hilda',[23] or sometimes 'Milksnatcher'.[24]

But before the impression is collected that Margaret Thatcher as the new Leader was some little girl lost, it should be pointed out that she had something that compensated for all these disadvantages. In her speech to the 1922 Committee after her election, she had turned her weakness into a strength by telling her MPs that she was a frail little woman who needed the help of strong men such as they.[25] She was not as vulnerable as she wished to seem, however. She had a burning sense of mission. On the day of her election, she had told ITN News that 'You don't exist as a party unless you have a clear philosophy and a clear message.' She was confident from the first that she could supply both. The propagation of ideas was one of her greatest strengths.

In her speech on 20 February 1975 formally accepting the leadership from the wider party, Mrs Thatcher appealed to the nation's past. With a slight nod in the direction of Queen Elizabeth I's speech at Tilbury, she declared that the country would never have embarked on the Elizabethan expeditions, or enunciated great legal principles, or founded parliamentary democracy, or made sure that 'liberty did not perish', if it had lived only for the moment. There was a need for more forthright and visionary leadership, 'more emphasis on principle'. There was urgency too, because Britain now had the unpleasant experience of being treated 'as a poor nation whose only greatness lies in the past'.* If Labour won the next election, Britain would be 'irretrievably on the path to a socialist state'. It is notable that, from the start, Mrs Thatcher used party meetings as the occasions for enunciating her convictions, preferring a less missionary tone in Parliament. On 15 March she told the Conservative Central Council to resist 'those [the trade unions] who use their weight to push others around' and declared that 'the individual is the sun and the state is the moon which shines with borrowed light'. On 25 March, she enthused the Federation

---

* This phrase may have come from a chance conversation which, Mrs Thatcher told the present author, she had had with a builder in her house in Flood Street. He had told her that Britain just had to accept that it was now a second-rate nation. She remembered being 'deeply shocked'.

of Conservative Students by telling them that 'This Party of ours has been on the defensive for too long.' 'If we can win the battle of ideas, then the war will already be half won.' To her Heathite critics in the party, it was this language that proved her dangerous. Jim Prior privately opined that it was 'wrong to speak of winning an intellectual argument because that implied you had a body of doctrine'.[26] But it was her readiness for the battle of ideas which sustained her, directed her, won her support from outside her party and riveted public attention upon her.

Strictly speaking, Mrs Thatcher was ill equipped for intellectual battle. Despite the brisk efficiency for which she was renowned, she did not have an intellectually orderly mind; nor did she have an original one. Rather than developing ideas of her own, she was a sort of 'stage-door Johnny' for the ideas of others – admiring, overexcited. But this was not, in fact, a handicap. Alfred Sherman, who, at this period, supplied so much of the material, developed his theory about Mrs Thatcher's intellectual character. 'She wasn't a woman of ideas,' he said, 'she was a woman of beliefs, and beliefs are better than ideas.'[27] David Wolfson,* who was to become her chief of staff, described her as 'a prophet not a king. History remembers prophets long after kings are forgotten.'[28] John Hoskyns,† an independent businessman desperately casting around for ways of rescuing Britain from economic collapse, first met her in August 1976. She was so excited by their meeting that she cancelled her lunch so that they could go on talking. Hoskyns was struck by her belief that 'something simply had to be done'. 'I don't think she had any idea what to do, but she had a patriotic impulse and a sense of shame about what had happened to our country.' He was struck by her combination of 'insecurity, sense of destiny and reckless courage'.[29]

From the first, these qualities constituted a form and style of leadership, and they created the space for ideas to come forward. Keith Joseph and his Centre for Policy Studies were the means of production, distribution and exchange. As Alfred Sherman put it, characteristically: 'Early Thatcherism was pure Keith, which meant pure Sherman. She lacked coherence.'[30] And it was 'pure Keith' that the new Shadow Cabinet soon had to consider when Joseph submitted to them a document entitled (echoing T. S. Eliot) 'Notes Towards the Definition of Policy'.[31] It was thoroughgoing,

---

* David Wolfson (1935–), educated Clifton, Trinity College, Cambridge and Stanford University, California; Chief of Staff, Political Office, 10 Downing Street, 1979–85; chairman, Great Universal Stores, 1996–2000; created Lord Wolfson of Sunningdale, 1991.

† John Hoskyns (1927–), educated Winchester; head of Prime Minister's Policy Unit, 1979–82; director-general, Institute of Directors, 1984–9; knighted, 1982.

self-lacerating and explosive. Joseph sought to attack the post-war Conservative approach of which he had, he admitted frankly, been a keen supporter: 'We made things worse when, after the war, we chose the path of consensus. It seems to me that on a number of subjects we have reached the end of that road.' They had promised too much and been guilty of 'subordinating the rule of law to the avoidance of conflict'. 'In short, by ignoring history, instincts, human nature and common-sense, we have intensified the very evils which we believed, with the best of intentions, that we could wipe away.' There was a need for a strategy to put things right, one which fought shy of any national coalition and of efforts to solve the crisis with a siege economy ('there is no case for a siege economy when the enemy is within the gates'). This strategy should consider economic problems not in technical isolation but in the light of the threat to the nation which came from economic weakness, the threat of the Soviet Union from without and from Communist subversion within. 'If we lose independence, we lose all,' said Joseph, and 'already we are being disarmed by inflation.' If we want patriotism, he continued, 'we must define the *patria*', introducing better immigration controls. Both the money supply and public spending must be controlled and price increases must be permitted. Benefits should be removed from strikers' families and there should be 'sharply lower direct taxes on earnings and investment'. In a climate of such economic weakness and trade union power, 'Presumably we do not think that denationalisation is practicable,' but he did argue that a legal framework for trade union activity 'will come one day'. The Tories should get rid of regional subsidies, try to arrest the decline of the family because 'the family . . . is the sole reliable transmitter of attitudes and culture', consider education and health vouchers, and perhaps decriminalize drugs (a revolutionary suggestion for a Conservative at that time) and introduce a Bill of Rights.

With the exception of the last two suggestions and the eventual but at that time unimaginable triumph of privatization, this startling paper furnished the main elements of what came to be called Thatcherism, both in specific policy and in general psychological terms. Building on an atmosphere of crisis and doom, and appealing to a sense of national greatness that had been lost, it set out a straight and narrow path to recovery, deliberately at odds with prevailing views. There was one important respect, however, in which it reflected the difference of character between Keith Joseph and Margaret Thatcher. Joseph's tone was gloomy and dark. Her natural tone, though just as severe about what had gone wrong, was much more optimistic and energetic about how it could be put right. She knew how to inspire hope as well as fear. It was one of the qualities which made her a much better natural leader than Joseph.

The Joseph paper caused consternation in the Shadow Cabinet, though Mrs Thatcher supported it. The official minutes express the disagreements gently. There was 'some anxiety', they say, about Joseph's rejection of consensus, and 'it was generally felt that the Conservative Government of 1970–4 had, on the whole, tried to do the right things, but had failed to explain its intentions adequately.'[32] But Lord Hailsham kept his own private, less discreet record of some of the dialogue:

REGGIE [Maudling]: I do NOT agree with ONE little bit.

GILMOUR: Up to 1970 consensus was a *Conservative* consensus, not a Labour one.

HOWE: 1970 manifesto was a *departure* from consensus. It does not differ from the present document. What we failed to do was to explain it and present it properly.

MARGARET: Ian, do you believe in capitalism?

IAN: That is almost blasphemy.* I don't believe in Socialism.

KEITH: The hundred years of relative decline (since the Great Exhibition) is objectively demonstrable.

RAISON:† Too much misery in Keith's paper. There are matters on which we have *got* to operate a consensus e.g. We must persuade Healey to produce a sensible budget.

MAUDE: That is not on. The right of the Lab. Pty. will always let us down.

PYM: Society is moving more left. There must be continuity – which means a broad measure of agreement – The Keith paper is a recipe for disaster.

HESELTINE: On TV we don't look like anyone people know.

WW [Whitelaw]: The most fatal thing in politics is to try and look different from what we are. People always complain that I look very large on TV. What wd: they say if I appeared in a bathing dress?

Hailsham concluded, dead-pan, 'There was hardly a dull moment.'[33]

Joseph raised the spectre of 'Finlandization', as the West's quietism towards Soviet Communism was then known, and Mrs Thatcher presciently warned that 'a serious crisis could well occur were the Government forced to borrow from abroad on terms which were unacceptable to the

---

* Lord Gilmour later explained that what he meant was that 'belief' was a word best reserved for religion (interview with Lord Gilmour).

† Timothy Raison (1929–2011), educated Eton and Christ Church, Oxford; Conservative MP for Aylesbury, 1970–92; Minister of State, Home Office, 1979–83; FCO, and Minister for Overseas Development, 1983–6; knighted, 1991.

Left.'[34] But there was, to use the word she so disapproved of, no consensus within the senior ranks of the Conservatives about the analysis of the basic problems, and therefore no agreement about most of the possible solutions. In the coming few weeks, the Shadow Cabinet split, along similar lines, on the question of proportional representation (Mrs Thatcher adamantly opposed) and on that of a wages freeze (Jim Prior in favour). These splits persisted, and the latter was a very important one.

Part of Mrs Thatcher's difficulty was that the current political situation did not present obvious, immediate opportunities. The precariousness of the Labour majority meant that yet another election could be precipitated at any time, but this would be unlikely to work to the advantage of the Tories. The sense of crisis made party politics a hard game to play. At a time when wages and prices were shooting up (the retail price index for June 1975 recorded an annual inflation rate of 26 per cent), it could be made to seem unpatriotic and irresponsible to oppose a policy to keep them down. The urgent language of emergency weighed more heavily with the public than the seemingly abstract ideas of monetary control and free collective bargaining. Mrs Thatcher therefore showed an untypical desire to remain silent, and tried, unsuccessfully, to avoid making a speech in the big economic debate in the House of Commons on 22 May. By her own account, the speech she did make was 'not . . . able to provide a coherent alternative to the Government's policy'.[35] Public opinion strongly backed a prices and incomes policy, and so did her most outspoken opponents in her own party, Peter Walker and Ted Heath. When the Labour government came up with a proposal in July for maximum wage increases of £6 per week, backed by the threat of statute if necessary, Mrs Thatcher felt able to criticize the Chancellor, Denis Healey, for having only half a package,[36] but she agreed that her party should abstain rather than be tarred with opposing wage restraint. She could not get a purchase on events.

The first big political campaign of her leadership also offered her no very useful opportunities. This was the referendum on continuing Britain's membership of the European Economic Community, an idea of Harold Wilson's born out of his need to balance the divided factions on the subject within his own party. Like almost all senior Conservatives (Edward Du Cann turned out to be a last-minute exception), Mrs Thatcher supported a 'yes' vote, but she did not pretend to any great expertise in the subject and she therefore asked Ted Heath to lead the Conservative contribution to the 'yes' campaign for the referendum to be held on 5 June. From a party point of view, this was both a sensible and a generous thing for her to do, and although Heath technically refused her invitation, preferring an informal role, it was he who made the most prominent Tory speeches on the subject. At the campaign launch on 16 April 1975, Mrs Thatcher sat next to Heath on the platform and said that 'Naturally, it's with some temerity that the pupil speaks before the master.'[37] Heath did not respond with similar generosity.

In her speech that day Mrs Thatcher repeated rather uninterestingly the standard pro-European lines – 'Are the French any less French?' and so on – and it has been suggested by some supporters of her subsequent Euroscepticism that her heart was not in it. It is true that she never manifested great excitement in the European arguments of the period, and was mildly criticized for this at the time. Harold Wilson called her 'the reluctant debutante'. Those close to her remembered her sitting watching the rather amateurish 'no' campaign broadcast and saying 'Gosh, that was good,'[38] and when polling day came she told a member of her staff she wished she didn't have to vote at all.[39] It is also true that she never bought the more visionary version of Europeanism. In a television interview three days before the poll, she rejected the notion of a federal Europe, saying that 'The United States of America is a different thing from the United States of Europe' and that all she favoured was 'closer co-operation';[40] but she defended membership on the grounds that British loss of sovereignty was largely 'technical' and that the nation was 'getting far more than you're giving up'.[41] She strongly subscribed to the prevailing Tory view of the time that the EEC could be made to work as a bulwark against Communism and that a victory for the 'no' campaign would be, as she told the audience at the campaign launch, 'a victory for the tribunes of the Left'. The convincing endorsement of continuing membership by nearly two-thirds of those voting did her no harm politically, and no good. But the campaign helped to restore Ted Heath's reputation, reminded people that he was more of a statesman than she and rekindled in some minds the idea that he might yet return, or at least that she might go. Because the 'yes' campaign had been a cross-party coalition, secretly supported by the BBC and backed by most of the establishment, it provided a possible model for the way the country could be run if there were to be a coalition of national unity to deal with the economic crisis. Such a coalition would have been the end of Margaret Thatcher.

Faced with these difficulties in the high politics of her party and the position in the House of Commons, Mrs Thatcher worked out a way of getting round them. In May 1975, her friend Gordon Reece was seconded from EMI to work for her once more.

In an unpublished memoir which he wrote in the late 1990s, Reece explained how, in 1975, he approached the task of persuading more people to vote Conservative. The traditional political wisdom was that people voted on issues – tax, defence and so on:

> Mrs Thatcher was advised by me that this was not true. Ordinary people, she was told, voted on impressions. Issues . . . were just some of the strands which made up a voting intention.
>
> Another factor . . . would be an answer to the question: 'Do I like or admire or respect one of the candidates more than another?' Television, itself a medium of impressions, had revolutionised political campaigning, putting more emphasis on the presidential character, the leader being the face of the political party.

Reece believed that most floating voters, in particular, were not very interested in politics:

> Mrs Thatcher was advised by me that the majority of the electorate in the late 70s voted for what they perceived to be their own best interests, the party that would do best for them and their families . . . Mrs Thatcher saw that the middle class divide was breaking down, and she decided to concentrate upon the voters who had the greatest need or ambition to improve their lives. Priority was given to women in Labour-voting households, the people who actually spent the family budget, the people most at risk from economic mismanagement. Secondly priority was given to skilled and semi-skilled workers, those who had the best opportunity to benefit from increasing prosperity. And thirdly to first-time voters, people who would not just hope for a better life but vote for one.

In Reece's view, such people were not much to be found among the readers of broadsheet newspapers and the watchers of serious political programmes and the longer, night-time, news bulletins: 'The people we had to reach would read the *Mirror*, increasingly the *Sun*, the *Express*, the *Mail*, the *People*, the *News of the World*, they would watch *Coronation Street*, Jimmy Savile, *Top of the Pops*, they listened to Jimmy Young on the wireless. And any aspiring Prime Minister had better go to them, and not expect them to come to her.'[42]

Mrs Thatcher aspired passionately to be prime minister. She accepted this advice, and acted upon it, although much of it was resisted by Central Office, and the full flowering of the Reece strategy did not take place until the summer of 1978. She spoke to Jean Rook in the *Daily Express*, and to *Woman's Own*; she appeared on *Woman's Hour* on Radio 4 and *The*

Jimmy Young Show on Radio 2. After she appeared on Jimmy Savile's *Jim'll Fix It*, in December 1976, the two struck up a friendly acquaintance.*
Bearing in mind her target of women who actually managed the family budget, she frequently spoke as a woman who did just that, and related her own experience to that of the entire nation as it struggled with inflation. In some ways, she was not a natural with the media. She had an instinctive distrust of the press and a dislike of television. Because Parliament was still not televised, or even, until 1978, broadcast regularly on the radio, she had a limited experience of the medium, and was used to constructing her public utterances as formal speeches or sharp debates. She was also intensely serious and high-minded, and touchingly cut off from some of the coarser aspects of daily life. She was in West Germany – her first visit abroad as leader, and her first ever visit to Germany – on 26 June 1975 when the news came through that the Conservatives had gained Woolwich West in a by-election. Mrs Thatcher was naturally delighted, particularly as she felt that her decision to break the old custom by which leaders did not campaign in by-election constituencies had paid off. She expressed her pleasure by making a 'V for victory' sign to the cameras. To the dismay of Reece, she did the sign the wrong way round, turning it into the well-known obscene gesture. She had no idea of the mistake, and so great was her innocence that 'Even when we had explained it, she still didn't really understand what she had done.'[43]

But, for all her lack of vulgarity, Mrs Thatcher was not detached from other aspects of normal daily life. She was perfectly genuine in her housewifely attitudes and her interest in the prices in the shops. She always had the gift of very direct speech, free of jargon, and she had an instinct for placing herself on the side of the person without power, rather than the official or the union boss. The actressy side to her character made her extremely effective in walkabouts and factory visits; far from dreading these encounters, she found that they energized her. And she well understood how to play to the huge interest in her which resulted from

---

* Not only did Savile's audience include an important slice of the electorate rarely accessible to Mrs Thatcher, but she genuinely admired his charitable work. In early 1980, as he began fundraising for the construction of Stoke Mandeville Hospital, not far from Chequers, she invited him for lunch at Number 10. 'My girl patients pretended to be madly jealous + wanted to know what you wore and what you ate . . .' Savile wrote to her afterwards by way of thanks. 'They *all* love you. Me too!' (Savile to PM, undated, TNA: PRO PREM 19/878). Following multiple posthumous allegations against Savile of child sex abuse and other sexual offences, this correspondence feels distinctly macabre. At the time, however, Mrs Thatcher, like so many others, took Savile at face value.

the fact of her sex. A week after her victory, she kept an engagement inherited from Heath to visit Scotland. In later years, Scotland was to be the part of the United Kingdom where she was probably least popular, but on this occasion she was overwhelmed in Princes Street, Edinburgh, by a friendly crowd so large that she had to take refuge in a shop to escape the crush.

In her attitude to her image, and to communicating with the public, Mrs Thatcher showed a remarkable humility and professionalism. 'Gordon Reece taught me', she said later, 'that television is a conversation, not a lecture,'[44] though this was not a lesson she invariably remembered in front of the cameras. She was nervous of television, and Reece used to bring a microphone to rehearsals so that she could practise being at the right distance to it. He told her to get up close in order to sound more 'sexy, confidential and reasonable'.[45] 'Your voice goes slightly tight and high-pitched,' she recalled him saying, 'you must consciously keep it down.' She learnt that 'Every speech should tell a story or a fable' and that 'A speech is to be heard,' a living performance which the speaker must enact with hands, eyes and voice as well as verbal content.[46] For his part, though full of charm and good at flattery, Reece was frank with Mrs Thatcher about the changes that were required. He told her that her clothes were too fussy; her hats should go; she wore too much jewellery for television; her hair was too frizzy for a potential prime minister.[47] She must also flatter Fleet Street editors. To the end of her life, Mrs Thatcher remembered her lessons from Reece, and would repeat them enthusiastically as essential truths. She would say, 'You must wear plain, tailored clothes on television' rather in the same tone of voice as she would say, 'You must have liberty – and not just liberty, but law-based liberty.'

All leading politicians, of course, worry about their image, and it is a well-known criticism of spin-doctors (as they later came to be called) that they are not interested in presenting the truth or in what their principals' principles are. But one reason why the Reece treatment worked so well with Mrs Thatcher was that he himself was in accord with the moral and ideological thrust of what became known as Thatcherism and believed from the first in her character as the vehicle for advancing it. This meant that he warmly welcomed her openness to intellectuals, commentators and assorted policy mavericks, and had none of the instinctive hostility to such people that is bound to exist in party bureaucracies. Chris Patten, at the Conservative Research Department, saw the existence of the Centre for Policy Studies as a 'provocation'.[48] Reece saw the CPS as an ally. He did his best to help Mrs Thatcher make the eggheads feel at home with her.

When, for example, she received Robert Conquest,* the historian of Stalin's purges and critic of rapprochement with the Soviet Union, Reece had warned her in advance that her visitor liked plenty to drink. Reece had arranged for Conquest to arrive at nine-thirty in the morning, but Mrs Thatcher enjoyed the conversation so much that it was still going strong at noon: because of Reece's advice, she was able to go to the fridge and produce champagne.[49]†

Avoiding the delicate domestic political situation, Mrs Thatcher chose to make the first highly controversial speech of her leadership on the Cold War. She felt that, as the new leader, she should establish a position on 'Britain's role in the world'. This was a normal thing to do, but it was not at all normal to dive in so deep and swim so strongly against the tide. In 1975, the dominant mood of the Western elites towards the Soviet Union was one of rapprochement, against a background of weakness. The American disengagement from Vietnam, seen as dishonourable by some and overdue by others, had produced its logical conclusion in the fall of the South Vietnamese capital, Saigon, to the Communist forces in April. The buzz word for the policy was détente. The Western allies had committed themselves to the Helsinki process of talks which began in 1973 and were due for completion in a 'Final Act' in August 1975. Helsinki was designed to trade an acceptance of the Soviet domination of Eastern Europe for the improvement of human rights in the Soviet bloc. The process had been initiated by President Richard Nixon, and so support for it came from Republicans in the United States, and from Conservatives in Britain, as well as from the centre and the left. It was considered maverick right wing to question the whole thing.

Mrs Thatcher, however, chose to do so, and asked Conquest to draft her speech. She particularly wanted to know from him whether the Soviets had the long-term aim of getting rid of Western democracy – 'The answer was yes' – and whether the Soviet Union was, in the long term, viable – 'The answer was no.'[50] She also feared that the effect of Communism at home, chiefly through influence on students, media and trade unions, was to undermine the national will. The result of these discussions was her speech

---

* Robert Conquest (1917–), educated Winchester and Magdalen College, Oxford; author of *The Great Terror*, *The Harvest of Sorrow* and numerous other works mainly about the Soviet Union. Though British, Conquest lived for many years in California, where he was a Fellow of the Hoover Institution. Conquest was a great friend of the novelist Kingsley Amis, and introduced him to Mrs Thatcher.
† Conquest himself was always full of praise for Mrs Thatcher's ability to have alcohol at the ready: 'She seemed to know when it was six o'clock without having to look at her watch' (interview with Robert Conquest).

to Chelsea Conservative Association on 26 July 1975. She identified a threat to freedom all over the world. Communists were attempting to undermine the new democracy in Portugal, she said; Cambodia and Vietnam had been lost ('Where are the protest marchers now?'). Despite the fact that the Soviets had 'more nuclear submarines than the rest of the world's navies put together', the Labour government was pulling the Royal Navy out of the Mediterranean and ditching its base at Simonstown in South Africa. It was wrong to pretend, as the Helsinki Final Act approached, that there was 'peace and trust' between East and West: 'the fact remains that throughout this decade of détente, the armed forces of the Soviet Union have increased, are increasing and show no signs of diminishing.' The power of NATO, she said, was 'already at its lowest safe limit', and if the allies did not maintain enough conventional weapons, they would be confronted, in the face of Soviet aggression, with the appalling choice of either surrender or 'early use of nuclear weapons'. This language was strong enough, but what really separated Mrs Thatcher's approach was not so much its hawkishness about Soviet military intentions as its definition of the nature of the Soviet threat. She was not content to see this in traditional terms of the rivalry between global powers, and the consequent need to strike a deal and achieve a balance. She saw the Soviet Union as, by its nature, an attack on the West. The Soviets were 'arrayed against every principle for which we stand,' she declared, and she judged them not just by their arsenal, but by the sufferings they inflicted upon their own people:

> So when the Soviet leaders jail a writer, or a priest, or a doctor or a worker, for the crime of speaking freely, it is not only for humanitarian reasons that we should be concerned. For these acts reveal a regime that is afraid of truth and liberty; it dare not allow its people to enjoy the freedom we take for granted, and a nation that denies those freedoms to its own people will have few scruples in denying them to others.

She held up the recently exiled Soviet novelist Alexander Solzhenitsyn* as the model of truth-telling against Communist lies. Her test of whether peace was really coming closer was whether there was any advance in 'the free movement of people and of ideas'.

In her memoirs, Mrs Thatcher makes it a point almost of pride that she

---

* Alexander Solzhenitsyn (1918–2008), educated University of Rostov and Moscow Institute of History (correspondence course); author of many works, including *One Day in the Life of Ivan Denisovich*, *The First Circle* and *The Gulag Archipelago*; sentenced to eight years in the Gulag for anti-Soviet activities, 1945; released, 1953; exile in Siberia, 1953–6; officially rehabilitated, 1957; expelled from the Soviet Union, 1974; Soviet citizenship restored, 1990; Nobel Prize for Literature, 1970.

did not consult or inform Reggie Maudling, whom she had just appointed shadow foreign secretary, about what she was going to say in Chelsea. '. . . I knew that all I would receive were obstruction and warnings,' she writes sharply, and with a revealing lack of confidence in her own choice of spokesman, 'which would doubtless be leaked afterwards – particularly if things went wrong.'[51] But she may well have been emboldened against possible establishment criticism by the help she received (but does not mention in her memoirs) from Lord Home. Of all the Tory leaders between Churchill and Mrs Thatcher, Home was the most robust in his dislike of Soviet Communism. Before speaking at Chelsea, Mrs Thatcher had meetings with him on the subject, and invited his comments on the draft. After making the speech, she wrote to thank him 'first for providing the framework for the foreign affairs speech and then for going through it so carefully'.[52] Home wrote back to her that she had been 'absolutely right' to make the speech.[53] Chelsea was the first time in her career that Margaret Thatcher made a major public statement about the state of the world. It set a standard of clarity and controversy which she was to maintain.

It was natural that one of Mrs Thatcher's earliest decisions was to visit the United States. Her first foreign visit, out of deference to the recent EEC referendum, had been to West Germany (see above), where she had met and been impressed by the then Chancellor Helmut Schmidt,* and also met the Christian Democrat leader Helmut Kohl.† She decided at once that Kohl was 'the German equivalent of Ted Heath',[54] a view which was to have important and malign consequences.‡ But the visit to Bonn had not been intended as a big show. America was. There was a conscious desire, by putting her on the world stage in the United States, to establish her as somebody of substance in time for what promised to be a difficult first party conference as leader in early October. This was linked with her ideological interest in the language of freedom and liberty which she found very attractive in American politics and which she believed the English-speaking peoples shared. She wanted to relaunch such language into

---

* The feeling, however, was not mutual. Following a later meeting with Schmidt, one US official reported to the Secretary of State, Henry Kissinger, that the German Chancellor had a 'terrible view of Margaret Thatcher. He says that she is a bitch, she is tough, she lacks scope and cannot lead' (Memorandum of Conversation, 'British and Italian Economic Situations', 3 Nov. 1976, The Kissinger Transcripts, Item 02123, National Security Archive, Washington DC).
† Helmut Kohl (1930–), educated Heidelberg University; Minister-President, Rhineland Palatinate, 1969–76; leader, CDU/CSU, 1976–98; Chancellor of Federal Republic of Germany, 1983–90; of reunified Germany, 1990–8.
‡ Mrs Thatcher also found time to pay her respects to the by then very infirm Ludwig Erhard, author of West Germany's free-market economic recovery which she so much admired.

British political debate, and saw her American trip as providing the time and place to do so.[55] She also wanted to repair Conservative relations with American politicians, which had fallen on hard times during Ted Heath's time as leader. This *froideur* was partly attributable to Heath's single-minded devotion to Britain's entry into the EEC, which was seen by some Americans as unfriendly, and partly to his personal anti-Americanism, the strongest of any Tory leader in modern times.* Her own feelings were the opposite.

On 18 February 1975, shortly before announcing her Shadow Cabinet, Mrs Thatcher had breakfast with the American Secretary of State, Henry Kissinger,† at Claridge's. The two had met once before, when Mrs Thatcher was education secretary, a meeting which Ted Heath had discouraged,[56] and had got on well. The breakfast was also a success. Mrs Thatcher wrote to William Galloway, the US Embassy official who had arranged her 1967 US trip, to say that she had 'become one of his [Kissinger's] many fans'[57] and that she hoped to visit America soon. Kissinger remembered: 'I found her totally different from other politicians. Every other politician I knew said that in order to win elections you had to win the centre. Her position was that you have to articulate your position as clearly as you can and the centre will come over to you ... I was always very taken with her. You could say she seduced me ... But I thought she might never get elected with those views.'[58] That doubt is visible in the contemporary record. In a discussion about which European leaders President Gerald Ford should meet, Kissinger advised him: '... Soames may be a big Conservative leader sometime. I don't think Margaret Thatcher will last.'[59]

On 9 April 1975, Mrs Thatcher sat down with a visiting American dignitary in her office in the Commons. His name was Ronald Reagan.‡ Although this was their first tête-à-tête, Reagan had initially come to her attention some years earlier.§ Back in 1969, Denis had attended a meeting

---

* In a briefing document, prepared for Ford for his meeting with Edward Heath in September 1974, Henry Kissinger did not mince his words: 'Heath is a doctrinaire person, Gaullist in his outlook, and the only anti-American UK Prime Minister in many years. He is a complex, sensitive man who tends to sulk' (Meeting with Edward Heath, 10 Sept. 1974, Box 15, National Security Advisor, Presidential Country Files for Europe and Canada, Gerald R. Ford Library).

† Henry Kissinger (1923–), born in Germany; educated George Washington High School, New York City and Harvard University; US Secretary of State, 1973–7 (National Security Advisor, 1969–75); Member President's Foreign Intelligence Advisory Board, 1984–90; Hon. KCMG, 1995.

‡ Ronald Reagan (1911–2004), educated public schools in Tampico, Monmouth, Galesburg, and Dixon, Illinois and Eureka College, Illinois (AB); Governor, California, 1967–75; President of the United States, 1981–9.

§ There is the intriguing prospect that Mrs Thatcher may have seen Reagan, at the zenith of

at the Institute of Directors in London addressed by Reagan, then Governor of California, and had come home full of praise for him.[60] Three years later, on 17 July 1972, Mrs Thatcher attended a group luncheon at No. 10 in Reagan's honour, although there is no evidence that she and Reagan spoke. By early 1975, Reagan's second term as governor had expired and he was positioning himself to run for the Republican presidential nomination in 1976.* His visit to the UK, which included meetings with the Labour government and a setpiece speech to the Pilgrims Society, was designed to bolster his foreign policy credentials. The suggestion that Reagan also meet Mrs Thatcher came from a member of his kitchen cabinet, Justin Dart, whose Tupperware company had a strong presence in the UK. 'Ronnie, you've got to meet her,' Dart told Reagan, 'she's terrific.'[61] Reagan's meeting with Mrs Thatcher, planned for forty-five minutes, went on for an hour and a half. 'I was immediately won over by his charm, directness and sense of humour,' Mrs Thatcher later wrote.[62] Reagan recalled: 'It was evident from our first words that we were soul mates when it came to reducing government and expanding freedom.'[63] Reagan drew on his experiences in London in crafting one of the radio addresses that he delivered weekly during this period. 'This is the time of year when winter isn't quite ready to loosen its grip on London,' Reagan told his listeners, 'but still the daffodils are up over Hyde Park and even a few rays of sunshine are enough on a Sunday afternoon to bring out throngs of strollers . . .' Reagan went on to outline the debate in Britain over joining the EEC, highlighting the splits in the Labour Party:

> Failure by Labor to heal the breach in its ranks might lead to elections as early as this fall, some say. If so, Britain may get its first woman Prime Minister in its more-than-900-year history. Mrs. Margaret Thatcher, the new leader of the Conservative Party, is a woman of charm and poise and also strength. The British like their politicians to stand for something and she does. In a recent nationwide poll she was named as the country's most popular political figure.[64]

Reagan repeatedly sang Mrs Thatcher's praises in conversations with aides after the meeting.[65] 'That evening, Reagan was still going on and on about this wonderful woman he'd met.'[66] Writing to thank her, he invited

---

his acting career, on the big screen in Grantham in the 1940s. In later life she claimed to have done so, but could not name a single Reagan film (Correspondence with John O'Sullivan). There is no mention of these films in her letters to her sister Muriel, which regularly comment on her experiences at the cinema, so whether she actually saw any of them remains doubtful.
* Reagan failed to get the nomination, which went to the incumbent President, Gerald Ford, but succeeded when he tried again in 1980.

Mrs Thatcher to visit him in California. She replied warmly, but said she would not have the time to reach the West Coast during her planned visit in September. They were not to see one another again or indeed speak until 1978, but their staffs stayed in touch. Reagan's people would send over transcripts of his radio broadcasts and speeches, which would be filtered by Mrs Thatcher's office, the more interesting offerings ending up in her weekend box. One could scarcely talk of a relationship between Mrs Thatcher and Reagan at this stage, but the seeds of future friendship had been sown.

In mid-April Mrs Thatcher received a letter from the British Ambassador to the United States, Sir Peter Ramsbotham, who had heard that she was contemplating a visit, inviting her to stay with him at the residence in Washington. She also took advice from Sir Patrick Dean, one of Sir Peter's predecessors in Washington. Despite her enthusiasm for the trip and for America, she had few channels of her own which she could open. She did not exactly know what to do or whom she wanted to meet or which media outlets she should seek. As a result, although there was a strong ideological element in what she planned to say, there was little in her itinerary or range of contacts. She aimed only to be received at the highest levels. Her private office arranged her speaking engagements but asked the Foreign Office to put together the rest of her programme. She accepted most of the official suggestions, although she did reject the idea of a lunch at Brookings, the liberal-left think tank which, she suspected, represented the 'consensus' she disliked.[67] She sounded out Ramsbotham to check that she would not cause offence in America if she arrived without her Shadow Foreign Secretary, Maudling: she did not want her personal impact diluted and was keen to travel without any rival attraction.

As the plans for her visit developed, it became clear that the Foreign Office wanted Mrs Thatcher to give American audiences an upbeat account of the state of Britain. The American media were full of stories about British decline. An article in the *Wall Street Journal* entitled 'Goodbye, Great Britain, it was nice knowing you' attracted much notice and was quoted by Mrs Thatcher that summer. 'It is to Britain that journalists now come,' she read out from the piece to Scottish Conservatives on 13 May, 'following the scent of economic and political decay.' Private discussion was equally gloomy. In a conversation with President Gerald Ford in January, Henry Kissinger told him that 'Britain is a tragedy – it has sunk to begging, borrowing, stealing until North Sea oil comes in . . .'[68] And Britain's economic plight had become a cautionary tale for Americans. In April, Alan Greenspan, the future chairman of the Federal Reserve Board, at that time the chairman of the President's Council of Economic Advisors, noted to Ford:

'Observe that the British economy appears to be at the point where they must accelerate the amount of governmental fiscal stimulus just to stand still. This is clearly a very dangerous situation. The frightening parallels, with a lag, between the financial policies of the US and those of the UK should give us considerable pause.'[69]* A Foreign Office official wrote to Derek Howe, her press secretary: 'Mrs Thatcher's audiences will want to hear her affirm strongly that Britain is going to come through its current difficulties. The North American press has overdone the gloom. Mrs Thatcher will no doubt wish to underline the positive side of the picture (relatively low level of unemployment, improved balance of payments, firm action to grasp the nettle of inflation etc).'[70] Beside these suggestions, Mrs Thatcher wrote two large question marks. She certainly wanted to tell a good story about the potential of her country, but she had no desire to talk up the achievements of the Labour government.

Mrs Thatcher arrived in New York on 13 September 1975, and on the 15th delivered her first full speech, under the title 'Let Our Children Grow Tall'. This was a fierce and full expression of her belief that 'The pursuit of equality is itself a mirage.' Those who wanted yet more equality, she said, had an 'undistinguished combination of envy and what might be called "bourgeois guilt"'. It was essential to create wealth before giving so much attention to its distribution. In Britain in 1975, some 56 per cent of Gross Domestic Product was 'controlled and spent by the State'. In 1963, the man on average industrial earnings paid 5 per cent of them in tax; now he paid 25 per cent. There was a cycle of low profits, extra wages, more government spending, more taxes, and controls leading to loss of profits which meant that people no longer wanted to invest in equities. 'Let our children grow tall,' she declared, 'and some taller than others if they have the ability to do so.' 'You'll be the next PM,' shouted out one of the guests, to general applause.

Back in Britain, the speech nearly turned to disaster because Conservative Central Office – with, Gordon Reece believed, unfriendly intent – released an early draft which appeared to suggest that government spending on kidney machines should be limited. Central Office refused to withdraw what it had circulated, so it was left to Reece, who was with Mrs Thatcher in New York, to ring round Fleet Street, calling in his well-established friendships. 'The truth is', he told them, 'she's not going to say it.' His intervention was just in time: Larry Lamb, the editor of the *Sun*,

---

* These fiscal stimuluses were as nothing beside those which Greenspan, at the Fed, encouraged in the early twenty-first century. He was widely blamed for the severity of the resulting 'credit crunch'.

told him that he had prepared a front-page headline 'LET 'EM DIE, SAYS MAGGIE'.[71] Even without the kidney machines, her words caused controversy at home. Her attack on British socialism was interpreted by some as a violation of what Michael Brunson, reporting for ITN, called the 'so-called unwritten rule that visiting British politicians here don't discuss internal party politics'.[72] The Foreign Secretary, Jim Callaghan, criticized her for putting 'argumentative passages' into her speech. Ministers complained privately to the Foreign Office about what she had said, and a British Embassy official, Hamilton Whyte, who was close to Labour, briefed against her unattributably in Washington.[73] Mrs Thatcher was unrepentant, however: 'It's no part of my job', she told *The Times*, 'to be a propagandist for a socialist society.'[74] The speech's explicit support for inequality was extremely bold. She was careful to contrast her attacks on the poor state of her country with praise for its innate capacities. She told Barbara Walters on the *Today Show*, 'we are the same people that we always were. We have the same sense of adventure. We are inventive . . . We are an eleventh-hour nation. We tend to wait until the last minute until we act. Well, we are at the eleventh hour now and action is being taken.'[75] Overall, the general impression Mrs Thatcher created in New York was highly favourable, one of pleasant surprise. 'The most operative word is lady,' the *New York Times* quoted one luncheon guest as saying. 'Here is this little blonde, blue-eyed woman in this pale peach dress with baby blonde hair. She is a flower among thorns. But it's no little girl act either. She is just plain well-informed and extremely articulate.'[76]

Mrs Thatcher was much happier when the focus of attention was her views rather than her sex. When she arrived for the interview with Barbara Walters, Walters warned her beforehand that she 'might have to ask some questions about how it felt to be a woman in such a high post, much as she disliked that kind of question'. Mrs Thatcher shook her head. 'Isn't it too bad that there aren't more women around who feel as we do,' she said.[77]

On 17 September, Mrs Thatcher flew to Washington. Within twenty-four hours of arriving, she met Kissinger, the Defense Secretary James Schlesinger, the Treasury Secretary Bill Simon and President Ford, as well as members of both Houses of Congress. As far as the US administration was concerned, there was not much of an agenda to these meetings. Mrs Thatcher was largely unknown in Washington, but her surprise victory in the leadership election had made its own impression. 'Becoming leader of a party that has its fair share of male chauvinists was a remarkable achievement for Mrs. Thatcher, who has displayed courage, deftness and determination,' noted her internal State Department biography.[78] While Kissinger's briefing for the President was largely favourable to Mrs Thatcher personally, it also pointed out that she was not yet master in her own house. The Secretary of State gave a crisp summary of her main political problem at home:

> Themselves divided on inflation policy between the advocates of statutory wage controls and 'strict monetarists', the Tories clearly are waiting to see if Labor can make a voluntary incomes policy stick with the unions – where the Conservatives failed with a statutory policy ... The crucial test of individual unions' compliance with the wage increase ceiling will come later this winter when the next rounds of wage bargaining get underway in earnest. Mrs Thatcher has tried to occupy a middle ground, resulting in a lack of clear public understanding of what exactly Tory policy is on this vital issue.[79]

Mrs Thatcher's unorthodox views on détente did not appear in Kissinger's briefing, largely because the Americans had yet to recognize how deeply held these views were. The US Embassy in London, for example, chose to characterize her provocative speech to the Chelsea Conservative Association in July as offering 'little that is new on the topic of relations between the West and the Soviet Union'.[80] Kissinger was acutely aware of Mrs Thatcher's inexperience in foreign policy* and was thus disinclined to take the ideas she was beginning to expound seriously. She was known to be generally friendly to the United States and that, for the moment, was enough. On the other hand, the administration clearly did not treat the Thatcher visit perfunctorily. She met all the important people she wanted to meet.

Mrs Thatcher was also more concerned with 'face-time', friendly talks and the exchange of ideas than with any more definite discussions. Her meeting with President Ford on 18 September passed off successfully, but unremarkably. General Brent Scowcroft,† who was present at the meeting, remembered: 'She was very warm, very friendly, very composed. I remember almost nothing about the meeting and my overall impression was "nice lady" ... We felt she was nice, but we didn't see her as a heavyweight who was going to change the course of anything.'[81] Mrs Thatcher was similarly pleased, and similarly unexcited, by the conversation: 'Ford did not register very highly. She was pleased to have met Ford, but more due to his

---

* 'She is a great gal,' Kissinger told President Ford in late February, 'but she is not experienced at all in foreign policy' (Memorandum of Conversation, National Security Advisor, Box 9, 'February 27, 1975 – Ford, Kissinger, Richardson', Gerald R. Ford Library).

† Brent Scowcroft (1925–), educated US Military Academy, Columbia University, Lafayette College and Georgetown University; Lieutenant General, US Army; Deputy National Security Advisor, 1973–5; National Security Advisor, 1975–7 and 1989–93.

position than the substance of their discussions,'[82] recalled one of her entourage.

Other encounters, however, were more rapturous. Vast numbers turned up for her meeting with the House International Relations Committee. According to the British official present: 'The level of enthusiasm was extraordinarily high – partly due to her being a woman, but also she was already manifesting very strong convictions that appealed to American Congressmen.'[83] On the same day, Mrs Thatcher called on James Schlesinger, the Defense Secretary. His staff had not even informed him that she was party leader (they had billed her as a member of the Shadow Cabinet), and he expected a fifteen-minute meeting:

> To my great surprise, in came this striking woman singing the praises of what was then called the Schlesinger doctrine.* She didn't know much about it, but she was very eager to learn. We talked about our strategic nuclear forces for perhaps an hour and a half ... She was very interested in everything I had to say and shortly afterwards she went on the road in support of the ideas.[84]

Over at the Treasury, Bill Simon collected the same flattering impression of a soulmate cum disciple who was keen to learn. Writing to her later, the Secretary of the Treasury expressed himself with a warmth that went well beyond normal, official language: 'Your dedication and knowledge made a deep impression ... You face a very difficult task in restoring the equilibrium of your own economy. You are to be commended, Mrs Thatcher, for your courage in pursuing the policies necessary to bring inflation under control. I will follow with great interest and sympathy your progress in dealing with the problem.'[85]

The following night, Mrs Thatcher achieved another mark of Washington acceptability, a dinner given for her by Mrs Kay Graham, proprietor of the *Washington Post*. One of those present remembered: 'She spoke, largely off the cuff, and made a huge impression. She talked about free markets and liberty, using language that no previous British leader had done since the war. This speech was not false or designed to please. It came from the heart.'[86] It went well enough, but Mrs Graham was never much of a friend to Mrs Thatcher.† Beside her at the dinner was Alan Greenspan:

---

* The Schlesinger doctrine was an attempt to strengthen nuclear deterrence through laying out the level and scope of US nuclear retaliation in the event of acts of Soviet aggression of varying magnitudes.

† At a lunch given shortly afterwards in London by Lady Hartwell, wife of the owner of the *Daily Telegraph* (who was also no fan of Mrs Thatcher), Mrs Graham provoked fierce argument by declaring: 'I think she's just a vulgar fishwife' (interview with Lord Deedes).

I knew little about her . . . I wasn't quite sure what she knew. And the very first thing she said to me was 'So, Dr Greenspan, why is it that we in Britain don't have an M2?' She was referring to a monetary aggregate that was not then used in Britain for technical reasons. This, of course, was not the first question I was expecting her to ask me. And when I attempted an explanation I could see she was following me closely . . . I found our conversation startling. She had a level of understanding of the way the world worked that most people in the political realm are unable to acquire. And it was a view that I would agree with. She believed in free-market discipline . . . [87]

Every British politician visiting Washington makes a point of networking. The difference in Mrs Thatcher's case was not just that she did so successfully, but that she was searching for allies who would help validate the ideological and political change she sought at home.

During the rest of her trip, Mrs Thatcher made two more setpiece speeches. In the first, to the National Press Club in Washington the day after the dinner, she spoke darkly of Britain's plight, and put it in the context of political and cultural struggles across the world. Her country was facing not so much technical economic problems as 'one of the life and death of the human spirit'. Western allies should admit that 'our ways' were not winning: 'We represent a diminishing band of brothers and sisters.' If there was a thaw, producing détente, she worried that 'we are losing the thaw in a subtle and disturbing way. We are losing confidence in ourselves and in our case.' Marxism was 'the negation of human dignity', and it was the duty of the United States and Britain to 'revive belief in freedom under the law'. Though acknowledging America's current low spirits, she said, 'But as I look at America, if this is failure, what in Heaven's name is success?' And she explicitly linked her own life and beliefs with the story of America: 'I was not brought up to prosperity. Hard work was the only way . . . It is a moral struggle . . . the puritan morality of the founders of America.' The joint task involved political, moral and economic reinvigoration – 'The period of high spending and slack thinking is over' – but she believed her country could do it: 'We may suffer from a British sickness now, but we have a British constitution and it's still sound, and we have British hearts and a British will to win through.'

In Chicago, her last port of call before she flew to Canada for the final part of her trip, Mrs Thatcher gave a full-scale lecture[88] on economic problems and the virtues of 'political economy'. Linking Britain and America by pointing out that Adam Smith's *The Wealth of Nations* and the Declaration of Independence were of the same date (1776), she set out her case against government intervention in the economy, and her view of the

scale of the threat posed by inflation. 'Inflation', she declared, 'is a perni-
cious evil capable of destroying any society built on a value system where
freedom is paramount. No democracy has survived a rate of inflation
consistently higher than 20 per cent. When money can no longer be counted
on to act as a store of value, savings and investment are undermined, the
basis of contracts is distorted and the professional and middle-class citizen,
the backbone of all societies, is disaffected.' The free world needed to unite
against inflation: there should be a 'Declaration of Interdependence' which
would help 'to produce a just and enforceable international economic
order'.

On the day of Mrs Thatcher's Chicago lecture, a woman called Sara
Moore tried but failed to shoot President Ford in San Francisco. The attack
naturally limited American coverage of Mrs Thatcher's words, but in
Britain they were noticed. The *Guardian* pulled together everything she
had said in the United States to conclude: 'Mrs Thatcher's speeches ...
show that she has broken decisively with the Disraelian Tory tradition of
pragmatism ... the Conservative Party is now launched on a crusade in
the cause of reaction; the Tories have been taken over by the extremists.'[89]
Mrs Thatcher would not, of course, have agreed about the extremism, but
she was not sorry to have stirred up attention to her message. Her last
setpiece speech in North America, at the Empire Club in Toronto, Canada,
took to task the phrase, commonly associated with R. A. Butler, that was
most emblematic of post-war Tory centrism: 'It is often said that politics
is the art of the possible. The danger of such a phrase is that we may deem
impossible things which would be possible, indeed desirable, if only we
had more courage, more insight.' She was beginning to develop her unique
contribution to British politics – the art of the impossible.

In his private analysis of the US visit sent to a Foreign Office colleague, Derek Thomas on the North America desk summed up favourably:

> Mrs Thatcher certainly seemed to get what she wanted out of her visit. But
> it seems to me that it also served a useful non-partisan purpose in giving her
> American audiences a less pessimistic view of Britain than the one which
> they have been getting from their media in recent months. It was inevitable
> that Mrs Thatcher should ... make no bones about her political beliefs, but
> it does seem that what was more important for her American audiences was
> her manifest confidence in Britain's future.[90]

It was part of her achievement to link in American minds that confidence
in Britain with her own prospects of success.* Those close to her at the

* Mrs Thatcher actually turned in a small profit from her US visit because of the honorariums

time also noticed that her American trip helped to solidify her position before her party's conference in the following month, 'and how much it did for her confidence'.[91]

Between her election in February 1975 and her first party conference as leader in early October, Mrs Thatcher had gradually built up the sort of entourage she needed. To the rage of Jim Prior, she had quickly got rid of the Heathite director-general of Central Office, Michael Wolff, and abolished the post. She had also brought back Gordon Reece. In June, she chose Alistair McAlpine* as party treasurer, with the instruction, born of her wariness of the party machine: 'You work for me. You're my appointment.' She also told him to get rid of his Mercedes and get a British car.[92] McAlpine came through Airey Neave's contacts. His father, Edwin, ran the family building firm, Sir Robert McAlpine and Sons, and, as deputy chairman of British Nuclear Associates, was in charge of a lobby organization called the Nuclear Power Group which had hired Neave during the Heath government, as its parliamentary spokesman.† When he ran Mrs Thatcher's office, Neave continued to be paid, in part, by Edwin McAlpine. Alistair, who also worked for Robert McAlpine, had been born in the Dorchester Hotel, which his father owned, in 1942, and from this auspicious beginning had learnt how to acquire and enjoy the good things of life, being an expert on food, drink, clothes, restaurants, birds, gardens, art and many species of collecting. At that time an enthusiastic pro-European, McAlpine had been deputy treasurer for the 'yes' campaign in the referendum and had noted with alarm how the Heathites used it to push Mrs Thatcher to the margins. From the first, he was devoted to her personally and much less concerned for the Conservative Party. Young, hospitable, short, tubby and eccentric, McAlpine was extremely well connected, both with traditional sources of Tory funding and with more raffish and arty worlds of which Mrs Thatcher knew almost nothing. He saw it as his job to spread the right buzz about Mrs Thatcher while at the same time keeping her away from having to ingratiate herself with potential donors. With his guidance, she began to build up a group of powerful businessmen who were ready to

---

of £3,250 for her lectures. After expenses had been deducted, the surplus was paid to Conservative Central Office to boost its empty coffers (THCR 6/4/1/13).

* Alistair McAlpine (1942–2014), educated Stowe; director, Sir Robert McAlpine & Sons Ltd, 1963–95; Deputy Chairman, Conservative Party, 1979–83; created Lord McAlpine of West Green, 1984.

† It was partly in this capacity that Airey Neave invited Mrs Thatcher to Harwell (see p. 285). Neave was criticized by some for mixing political and commercial interests.

help, including Sir Frank McFadzean of Beechams, Michael Richardson,* at that time at the stockbrokers Cazenove's† and later to be important to her at Rothschild's, and Sir Marcus Sieff and Sir Derek Rayner‡ of Marks and Spencer. McAlpine immediately took to Gordon Reece, sharing his love of champagne and gossip, and when Reece's marriage broke down took him into his flat in London, provoking false rumours, on which McAlpine longed to sue, that the two were lovers. This odd couple were crucial in maintaining Mrs Thatcher's morale.

The vital, painful matter of speech-writing also needed attention. Mrs Thatcher was, in fact, well served by the party machine in the quality of drafting available. And she had the good grace to recognize that Chris Patten, and his assistant director at the Research Department, Adam Ridley, were skilled at this, even though neither, particularly Patten, was her ideological soulmate. Patten was noted for his turn of phrase, and Ridley was her main economic adviser from within the party (officially, to the whole Shadow Cabinet), providing much of the material for her Chicago speech that summer. She could also call on outsiders such as Alfred Sherman for more original and ideologically based contributions, but Mrs Thatcher understood from the first that she needed to be supplied with material in her own tone of voice for setpiece speeches – something of which she could say 'Yes, that's me.' Being by nature a scholarship girl, hating to say anything which was not carefully grounded in fact and tending to produce arguments in regimented, point-by-point form, she needed a speech-writer who could capture her essence and yet at the same time loosen her up. He should be someone without ideological or party baggage of his own. She told everyone that what she wanted was a 'wordsmith'. Enter Ronald Millar.§ Ronnie Millar, one of the many homosexuals who worked for and loved Mrs Thatcher without her having the least idea of their propensity, was a playwright and screenwriter. His stage adaptations of C. P. Snow's novels, his musical *Robert and Elizabeth* and his play *Abelard and Heloise* had been West End successes. He had helped Ted Heath with some of his speeches and so expected to be *persona non grata* with

---

* Michael Richardson (1925–2003), educated Harrow; partner, Cazenove & Co., 1971–81; managing director, N. M. Rothschild and Sons, 1981–90; knighted, 1990.

† Cazenove's used to give Mrs Thatcher an annual dinner, organized by Richardson, and contributed money to the party's general funds to help with the running of her office.

‡ Derek Rayner (1926–98), educated City College, Norwich and Selwyn College, Cambridge; chairman, Marks and Spencer, 1984–91; adviser to the Prime Minister on improving efficiency and eliminating waste in government, 1979–83; knighted, 1973; created Lord Rayner, 1983.

§ Ronald Millar (1919–98), educated Charterhouse and King's College, Cambridge; playwright and screenwriter; knighted, 1980.

Mrs Thatcher. He was therefore surprised to be ordered by her to contribute a script for her first television party political broadcast as leader, which
was to go out on 5 March 1975. For it, Millar chose some words which
he, like most others, attributed wrongly to Abraham Lincoln (the true
author was one William Boetcker, writing some seventy-five years later):
'You cannot strengthen the weak by weakening the strong. You cannot
bring about prosperity by discouraging thrift . . .' When he came to see
Mrs Thatcher with the draft, she asked him to read it aloud to her. After
he had done so, there was a silence which Millar attributed to her dissatisfaction. Then she reached slowly and dramatically for her handbag and
produced from it a piece of yellowing paper containing the same 'Lincoln'
lines. 'It goes wherever I go,' she told him.[93] The lines were duly delivered
in the broadcast, and forever afterwards Mrs Thatcher had faith in Millar.
Like many of her most trusted associates, Millar was an unlikely companion for her. Humorous, camp, silk-dressing-gowned, slightly seedy, he was
from the world of Noël Coward, not of Westminster. His stated recreations
in *Who's Who* were 'all kinds of music, all kinds of people'. He was not
highly political, although he certainly believed in Mrs Thatcher's call for the
revival of Britain. He lightened any gathering which he attended. It says a
good deal for the surprising broadmindedness of her taste that Mrs Thatcher
got on so well with people like Reece, McAlpine and Millar. It was part of
the sense in which, though extremely correct, she was never stuffy.* Richard
Ryder recalled: 'She was exceptional with every member of her staff, however junior. It was the happiest office in which I have ever worked.'[94]

Before long, Mrs Thatcher would use the word 'Ronniefied' to describe
a speech improved by Millar's hand, but as she approached her party conference speech for October 1975 she had not yet developed a pattern of
speech composition. As a result, the chaos and tension were frightful.
Always extremely nervous before any setpiece speech, Mrs Thatcher was
triply so before her performance at the party conference. Her first as leader,
she well knew, would be the most important single speech of her career so
far. Under the electoral system then obtaining, the rank-and-file members
of the Conservative Party had played no direct part in choosing her as
leader. They were known, in the majority, to have supported Heath. Would

---

* There were limits, however, to Mrs Thatcher's tolerance. Patrick Cosgrave, the political editor of the *Spectator*, had been one of the first to support her and tip her for the top. He also
wrote one of her early biographies. Cosgrave was brilliant, but seldom sober, and it was
rumoured that he had once been sick on Mrs Thatcher's shoes (with her inside them). In
any event, he ceased to be part of her inner circle, although he listed himself in *Who's Who* as
'Special Adviser to The Rt Hon. Margaret Thatcher 1975–9'. The verdict on Cosgrave of one
who remained in the inner circle was that 'The cocktails overcame him.'

they accept her now that she had overthrown him? If they did not, her support was certainly not so secure in Parliament, press or party hierarchy that her leadership could easily survive. By her own account, she was dissatisfied with the early drafts of her speech from Patten and others in the Research Department, and spent the weekend at home writing her own.[95] Throughout her time in Blackpool that week, Mrs Thatcher remained unhappy with the drafts, and numerous hands, including Angus Maude, as well as Ridley and Patten, and Richard Ryder to keep control of the material, slaved away. Alison Ward and Caroline Stephens retyped fifty-page drafts again and again on a manual typewriter, using six carbons and collating the copies on their hands and knees.[96] After many laborious hours of laying out endlessly retyped texts on the floor in front of her, however, Mrs Thatcher still did not believe that she had a proper speech, and at last agreed to Gordon Reece's suggestion that Ronnie Millar be called up to Blackpool (a painfully long train journey from London) to sort it out. It was not until 4.30 on the morning of Friday 10 October, the day of delivery, that her speech was ready and she went to bed.

Mrs Thatcher's nerves in Blackpool had not been improved by the conduct of Ted Heath. The Conservative National Union, the body responsible, among other things, for organizing the party conference, was known to be sympathetic to Heath. When one of her staff took her to the room of the chairman of the National Union in the Imperial Hotel, they could hear Heath's voice from inside, and rude remarks about her issuing through the closed door, so they hurried away. As they did so, Mrs Thatcher remarked: 'Some men are bitches.'[97] On the night before the speech, Willie Whitelaw telephoned to tell her that he thought he had effected reconciliation between her and Heath and that the two of them should meet in his room that night for a drink. She should await his call, he said. She did, for two hours, but no call came, so she telephoned Whitelaw who told her, crest-fallen, 'It won't work.' She was upset both by Whitelaw's carelessness or weakness in not ringing her as promised and by Heath's snub. 'Tears came regardless,' she remembered.[98]

Despite these tribulations, Mrs Thatcher looked well when she mounted the platform that Friday afternoon, three days before her fiftieth birthday. She wore a peacock-blue dress, tie collar and a slim-fitting turquoise coat. On the top of her script, she had written, as she often did with speeches at this time: 'Relax. Low Speaking Voice. Not too slow.' She addressed head-on the complaint that in the United States she had criticized Britain. She had criticized socialism, she said – 'Britain and Socialism are not the same thing.' She painted a gloomy picture of the economic situation – 'We've really got a three-day week now, only it takes five days to do it' – but, as so often, she gave it a moral rather than a technocratic context. There was a 'moral challenge' to the nations of the West, especially to Britain. 'What kind of people are we?' Mrs Thatcher asked. The British had invented or discovered 'the computer, refrigerator, electric motor, stethoscope, rayon, steam turbine, stainless steel, the tank, television, penicillin, radar, jet engine, hovercraft, float glass and carbon fibres. Oh, and the best half of Concorde.'* She advocated a freer economy, though not pure laissez-faire ('We Conservatives hate unemployment'), and she developed her defence of inequality that she had begun in America. 'We are all unequal,' she said, '. . . but to us every human being is equally important.' In appealing for a great change, she cast her eyes back to the traditions of her country:

> Let me give you my vision: a man's right to work as he will, to spend what he earns, to own property, to have the state as servant and not as master – these are the British inheritance . . . We must get private enterprise back on the road to recovery, not merely to give people more of their own money to spend as they choose, but to have more money to help the old and the sick and the handicapped . . . We are coming, I think, to yet another turning point in our long history. We can go on as we have been going and continue down. Or we can stop and – with a decisive act of will we can say 'Enough'.[99]

The ensuing standing ovation was much more than customary: it was genuine, the reaction of long-disheartened troops hearing their own innermost beliefs expressed with vigour and optimism. The idea that there was now a clear difference between one party and the other, and that a decision could and must be made about the country's destiny, was exhilarating. And the enthusiasm from the hall was echoed in the press and in the country. A Marplan poll after Mrs Thatcher's speech gave the Conservatives 54 per cent support, compared to 31 per cent for Labour. Speaking to the German *Stern* magazine, and therefore, in those pre-internet days, slightly less cautious than she would have been in the British press, Mrs Thatcher attributed the huge cheers at Blackpool to the fact that she had broken with Heath's tactics of staying close to Labour.[100] Certainly she had secured a grass-root loyalty which was to prove unparalleled – 'She cheered up the troops more than any party leader since Churchill,' remembered Chris Patten with reluctant admiration[101] – and was to last pretty much to the end. For the first time since winning, she felt secure in her leadership.

Changes took place at this time in the Thatcher family life. Denis, who had reached the age of sixty, retired from Burmah Oil in May 1975. At the

---

* The other half was French.

moment of retirement, he remembered, he was earning £12,000 per annum, plus a £1,500 bonus in that final year.[102] This he considered good money. (At that time, his wife's salary was £9,000.) Although he remained busy with non-executive directorships, Denis no longer had the daily reverse commute to Swindon. He therefore became more important than in the past in the counsel he gave his wife in political matters and was often present at the more informal meetings which took place in their house. Having sold The Mount in Lamberhurst, as too big and too little used, and later rented a flat in Court Lodge, the 'big house' of the village, the Thatchers moved into the old dower flat in Scotney Castle, also in Lamberhurst, that October. Over the dining-room table, they hung a large Arabic inscription presented to Mrs Thatcher by the Syrian Ambassador. Jonathan Aitken,* then a young MP who became Carol's boyfriend at about this time, used to visit Scotney and was surprised to see the inscription hanging there because, unknown to the Thatchers, it declared: 'There is one God, and Mohammed is his Prophet.'[103] Margaret and Denis enjoyed Scotney, but they had no domestic help there and the demands of the job meant that Margaret had even less time than before for country weekends. Besides, the twins did not want to spend much time in Lamberhurst. So most of life was lived in Flood Street, Chelsea, and it was not altogether easy. The twins, aged twenty-two, were based at home. Carol, dutifully but without enthusiasm, was completing her training as a solicitor. Mark, who had greatly upset his parents four years earlier by refusing a place at Keble College, Oxford,[104] in favour of having fun in South Africa, was failing to obtain his qualifications as an accountant. Short of time and always inclined to look indulgently on her son, Mrs Thatcher was considered by some who worked with her to be 'the ultimate chequebook mum'.[105]† In Carol's view, after her Grantham upbringing, 'which had control as its middle name', her mother erred on the side of not ordering her children about.[106] But Sue Mastriforte, whose back door in Flood Street abutted that of the Thatchers, was impressed by the efforts she made to preserve a proper home life.

Ms Mastriforte, whom Carol described as 'a very good neighbour',[107] had been deserted by her husband in the mid-1970s and left to bring up her children with very little money. Mrs Thatcher was, in turn, a good

---

* Jonathan Aitken (1942–), educated Eton and Christ Church, Oxford; Conservative MP for Thanet East, February 1974–83; for Thanet South, 1983–97; Chief Secretary to the Treasury, 1994–5; journalist and author; jailed in 1999 and served seven months of an eighteen-month sentence for perverting the course of justice.

† Denis used to exclaim, despairingly: 'The boy's a financial alcoholic!' (private information).

neighbour to her. Shocked that she could be left in this plight, she was kind and tactful in giving her food and other objects (often presented to her on her travels as leader), and sometimes slipped her small sums of money. She also arranged to pay her to do some of her shopping and look after her house. It was Sue Mastriforte, for example, who bought material in a Harrods sale out of which Mrs Thatcher had a dress made for her visit to America. Mrs Thatcher always arranged jaunts for the Mastriforte children in their holidays too. Under the strain of her marriage break-up, Ms Mastriforte had a heart attack in her flat one night and rang Carol, whom she had babysat when she was a teenager and who had become a close friend, to ask her to help. Carol's mother raced across with her daughter, and rang 999. Sue Mastriforte was struck by Mrs Thatcher's consideration as she spoke on the telephone to the ambulancemen: 'When you arrive, please don't ring the doorbell, because there are children asleep upstairs.'[108] There was no doubt in her mind that Carol did not enjoy her mother's eminence: 'I think Carol would have liked a suburban mother with a pinny ... baking cakes all day.'[109] Carol sometimes felt neglected, becoming overweight and suffering Mrs Thatcher's criticism for dressing frumpily (she particularly disliked a garment which Carol called her 'fireman's coat').[110] But, in Ms Mastriforte's view, 'Margaret was fairer than Carol gave her credit' and certainly cared for her welfare. She 'always knew what was happening with Carol'[111] and tried rather vainly to find better ways of communicating with her. For her part, Carol liked Flood Street less than their previous homes: it was too small for all the traffic which started to flow through the door once her mother had become leader of the Opposition, and 'not brilliant for four adults'.[112] Family life, in these conditions, was not ideal, but, to Sue Mastriforte, Denis and Margaret seemed 'a very close couple'; the fact that she was Conservative leader made him 'ten feet tall with pride'.[113]

Even after her leadership victory, Mrs Thatcher remained a careful and proud housewife. 'She always remembered that people had to eat.'[114] She 'made a big thing' of Sunday lunch at Flood Street or Scotney, producing large, unimaginative meals of Coronation chicken and tinned mandarin oranges in the style she had learnt in the 1950s.[115] She took a keen interest in her soft furnishings ('She never stopped saying, "When I first got married, I had to make my own curtains"'),[116] always knew how much was in her bank account, but never what was in Denis's, and amassed in the kitchen the Green Shield stamps (the equivalent of modern reward cards) that in those days many shops issued with purchases. She paid for all her clothes, and she and Denis split the household bills. Sue Mastriforte's impression was that the Thatchers were comfortably off, but not rich. The children's private education and subsequent training took their toll and Denis also helped support his divorced sister Joy. Theirs was the unostentatious life of the hard-working upper bourgeoisie in the age of inflation, never seriously feeling the pinch, but never luxurious.

In November 1975 the IRA murdered Ross McWhirter, a Thatcher supporter and a leading light in founding the National Association for Freedom, publicly launched very soon after his death, which tried to combat trade union power. His killing meant that, for the first time, Mrs Thatcher was given police protection, which was to remain with her for the rest of her life. This separated her more than before from anything that could be described as normality. But Bob Kingston, the Special Branch officer who came to guard her and stayed until the mid-1990s, was struck at once by how 'remarkably easy' Mrs Thatcher was and how friendly. She took a particular interest in Kingston's handicapped son and never, in his view, gave herself airs. 'She had difficulty with people who weren't correct,' he remembered, but to people who were presentable and efficient, she behaved impeccably: 'In twenty years, she never once raised her voice to me.'[117]

In the autumn of 1975, Mrs Thatcher tried to capitalize on her success at Blackpool. In the House of Commons, this was hard to do. Although disillusioned, often drunk, and in declining health after having fought five elections as Labour leader, Harold Wilson remained a cunning and attractive parliamentary performer. In their twice-weekly duels at Prime Minister's Questions, he found Mrs Thatcher 'more pointed and less ideological' than Heath had been, and decided that the best way not to build her up was not to attack her.[118] To the eyes of his senior policy adviser, Bernard Donoughue, Mrs Thatcher seemed 'petrified' when she had to face the Prime Minister in the Chamber, 'like a rabbit in front of a stoat'.[119] Her voice counted against her too.[120] To improve matters, Mrs Thatcher built up a group of young MPs, Nigel Lawson, Norman Tebbit,* Geoffrey Pattie† and George Gardiner, soon known, in echo of the Maoist clique in China at the time, as the 'Gang of Four', who would help her prepare for the

---

* Norman Tebbit (1931–), educated Edmonton County Grammar School; Conservative MP for Epping, 1970–74; for Chingford, February 1974–92; Parliamentary Under-Secretary, Department of Trade, 1979–81; Minister of State, Department of Industry, 1981; Secretary of State for Employment, 1981–3; for Trade and Industry, 1983–5; Chancellor of the Duchy of Lancaster, 1985–7; Chairman, Conservative Party, 1985–7; created Lord Tebbit, 1992.

† Geoffrey Pattie (1936–), educated Durham School and St Catharine's College, Cambridge; Conservative MP for Chertsey and Walton, February 1974–97; Minister of State for Defence Procurement, 1983–4; Department of Trade and Industry, 1984–7; knighted, 1987.

Questions. She learnt fast, Tebbit remembered, and improved her technique with the help of Gordon Reece, but 'she hadn't really focused on a lot of issues' and she felt inhibited from using some forms of expression because she was a woman.[121] In those pre-broadcast days, male MPs also felt no such inhibition in trying to mock Mrs Thatcher on the grounds of her sex. When she rose to speak, Labour backbenchers would often emit 'female-type whoops'[122] to try to make her look silly. Tebbit felt frustrated by her reaction to these difficulties, which was to be ultra-correct, concentrating on the issue rather than the man. For her part, Mrs Thatcher regarded Wilson as clever, nice, courteous and 'subtle',[123] which was, in part, her way of saying that she did not want to engage with him too closely.

Studying her parliamentary performances in her first year as leader, one cannot find any occasion on which she won control of the House. Always well prepared and always sharp in argument, she nevertheless failed to tip the parliamentary scales in her favour. She lacked, at this stage, the confident spontaneity required. This was bad for the morale of her parliamentary colleagues, particularly as Heath remained an effective and baleful presence in the Chamber. By the turn of the year, Mrs Thatcher had made serious attempts to improve her links with all shades of parliamentary opinion. William Shelton had gone in October, to be replaced as her PPS by Adam Butler,* son of RAB and therefore well connected. An attempt was made to appoint Peter Morrison as her other PPS, but this was rejected on the grounds that it would look bad if both men were 'Honourable' (that is, sons of peers) Old Etonians.[124]† After Christmas, poor Fergus Montgomery was replaced by the more able, though not more popular, John Stanley.‡ Her parliamentary position was improving incrementally, but she had no palpable hits in the Chamber of which she could boast.

Mrs Thatcher was much more successful in the public preaching role which she had designed for herself, with its accompanying projection of her combative personality. Her speeches, mainly those to Conservative audiences, continued to attack the global Communist threat and to link it, to use the phrase which would become famous in the 1980s, with 'the

---

* Adam Butler (1931–2007), educated Eton and Pembroke College, Cambridge; Conservative MP for Bosworth, 1970–92; Minister of State, Department of Industry, 1979–81; Northern Ireland Office, 1981–4; Defence Procurement, 1984–5; knighted, 1986.

† If this had happened, history might have been different, since Morrison would not have been available to become her PPS in 1990.

‡ John Stanley (1942–), educated Repton School and Lincoln College, Oxford; Conservative MP for Tonbridge and Malling, from February 1974; Minister for Housing and Construction, 1979–83; Minister of State for the Armed Forces, 1983–7; Northern Ireland Office, 1987–8; knighted, 1988.

enemy within'. She exposed left-wing subversion of local government, deploying one of her most famous phrases about the spending of 'other people's money',[125] and she proclaimed her vision of 'Every man, every woman a capitalist'.[126] In addition to the power of her general arguments on this subject, there was a specific one which guaranteed Mrs Thatcher the sympathetic attention of most of the press. This was the growing and disruptive power of trade unions within the newspaper industry. The print unions, entirely unreformed in their restrictive and often corrupt practices, were becoming more militant, stopping the production of the papers more frequently. Under the Trade Union and Labour Relations Bill proposed by the left-wing Employment Secretary, Michael Foot, the closed shop was to become easier to impose than ever before. Mrs Thatcher pointed out that this could mean that the National Union of Journalists would gain a monopoly in newspapers. This enabled her to draw comparisons with Communist China and the Soviet Union where 'the press is in chains'.[127] This had happened because one body had taken control of the entire press. 'Are we so sure', she asked, in a letter to the *Finchley Times*, 'our liberties are safe when extremists are so active on all sides?'[128] Newspapers feared that their freedom of expression and their right to manage themselves would be taken away: they naturally gravitated towards the woman who expressed their fears.

But it was to the subject which she had raised in Chelsea the previous July to which Mrs Thatcher returned with the most incendiary effect. In January 1976, following an investigation in the *Daily Mail* of the Soviet military build-up, and in the absence of Robert Conquest, who had returned to America, Richard Ryder contacted Robert Moss, a young expert on terrorism and subversion then working for the *Economist*. Moss was asked to write her a speech about the Soviet menace, and was given a pretty free hand. On this occasion, however, to avoid the previous criticism of failing to consult, Mrs Thatcher brought Reggie Maudling along to Flood Street late at night to study the draft with her. He did not like what he saw, complaining that it was wrong to describe Soviet society as 'sterile': 'Think of Tchaikovsky!'[129]* Maudling's objections were largely overruled, however. As in her Chelsea speech, Mrs Thatcher was entirely resistant to the idea that her major speeches on world affairs should go in a neat box marked 'foreign policy', still less 'diplomacy'. Her views on the state of the world were part of her account of life, the universe and everything. Moss understood that Mrs Thatcher was consciously harking back to Churchill's speech at Fulton, Missouri, in 1946, when he famously spoke of 'an iron

---

* He may have meant Shostakovich.

'curtain' descending on Europe. She sought just such a 'clarion effect', and he drafted accordingly.[130]

Speaking in Kensington town hall on 19 January 1976 after a visit to British armed forces in West Germany, she declared that 'The first duty of any Government is to safeguard its people against external aggression.' She then applied this test to the Labour government and found that it was 'dismantling our defences at a moment when the strategic threat to Britain and her allies from an expansionist power is graver than at any moment since the end of the last war' – 'Perhaps some people in the Labour Party think we are on the same side as the Russians!' The Russians, she said, were 'bent on world dominance', and, having no success of which to boast but their military might, were pursuing it through arms; the Politburo 'put guns before butter, while we put just about everything before guns'. In Central Europe, the Warsaw Pact forces outnumbered those of NATO by '150,000 men, nearly 10,000 tanks and 2,600 aircraft'. The Soviet Union produced one new nuclear submarine per month, threatening our sea routes. She had been right, she insisted, to warn about the illusions of Helsinki, and she called upon her audience to listen to Solzhenitsyn's claim that the West had been fighting the Third World War since 1945, and – as Vietnam, and now Portugal and Angola (in which, following Portuguese colonial collapse in 1975, Marxists struggled for supremacy), showed – losing ground. The remedy, said Mrs Thatcher, lay not only in rearming, but also, and here she quoted the American Democrat Daniel Patrick Moynihan (who would shortly be elected to the Senate), in 'a reasoned and vigorous defence of the Western concept of rights and liberties'. She asserted her Atlanticism: 'we believe that our foreign policy should continue to be based on a close understanding with our traditional ally, America. This is part of our Anglo-Saxon tradition as well as part of our NATO commitment.' She was more cautious about closer links within the EEC, saying that 'Any steps towards closer European union must be carefully considered.' Much of Britain's decline had been brought about by socialism – 'the Conservative Party has the vital task of shaking the British public out of a long sleep.' This, said Mrs Thatcher, was 'a moment when our choice will determine the life or death of our kind of society': 'Let's ensure that our children will have cause to rejoice that we did not forsake their freedom.'[131]

This was a powerful speech, combining a strong line of fresh arguments and facts with plenty of passion. But Mrs Thatcher could not have known how lucky she would be in the reaction to it. The excited, sometimes angry response at home was fanned by that of the Russians. The Red Army's newspaper *Red Star*, amplified by being reported on Moscow Radio, described Mrs Thatcher, intending an insulting comparison with Bismarck, the nineteenth-century 'Iron Chancellor' of Germany, as 'the Iron Lady'. She seized the opportunity. Speaking to her own Conservative Association in Finchley, she reintroduced herself to her admiring audience:

> I stand before you tonight in my Red Star chiffon evening gown, my face softly made up and my fair hair gently waved, the Iron Lady of the Western world. A Cold War warrior ... Yes, I *am* an iron lady, after all it wasn't a bad thing to be an iron duke; yes, if that's how they wish to interpret my defence of values and freedoms fundamental to our way of life.[132]

It is hard to think of a neater way of placing herself where she wanted to be – a wholly feminine but strong woman, a figure respected by her enemies, a patriotic leader in the tradition of the Duke of Wellington ('the Iron Duke'), a defender of the nation and its values. Thanks to her opponents, she had graduated to being a global figure with a sobriquet that marked her out – the Iron Lady.

Trapped in moderation

'She does not lead and manage her Shadow Cabinet'

On 16 March 1976, Mrs Thatcher delivered a substantial speech to the Bow Group, the home of more liberal-minded and intellectual Conservatives, for its twenty-fifth anniversary. Taking its inspiration from Alexander Solzhenitsyn's recent broadcast on the BBC, the address linked the fight against socialism to the need for the cultivation of excellence: 'For the greatest advances of the ordinary person are the products of the achievements of the extraordinary person.'[1] No one outside her immediate audience in the Café Royal paid the slightest attention, however, because Harold Wilson had chosen that morning to resign as prime minister.

To this day, no one knows for certain why Wilson resigned. There were rumours about approaching scandal and about illness. Given that he had led for so long, it was not surprising that he wanted to go, but the exact timing was a complete surprise. Mrs Thatcher's handling of the occasion won her little praise on either side of the House. Watching Prime Minister's Questions that afternoon, in which tributes to Wilson were paid, Bernard Donoughue recorded: 'Heath was superb. But Thatcher got it wrong again, graceless, with some snide petty points and a call for a general election, which clearly embarrassed many people on her own side.'[2] Barbara Castle watched her from the government front bench: 'He [Wilson] just played with Margaret Thatcher, who sat, as she usually does before a parliamentary effort, head down and with lips pursed, as if summoning up some superior wisdom of which we ordinary mortals do not know. Her intervention, when it came, was not . . . exactly masterly.'[3]

Mrs Thatcher seems to have been perfectly sincere in her ill-grounded belief that a general election was what constitutional propriety required. But the Labour Party had no such ideas, and proceeded to choose Wilson's successor. The government was, in fact, in deep trouble, having lost parliamentary votes the previous months on the first of its cuts to public expenditure plans for future years, and faced an ensuing crisis in the money markets when sterling fell below $2 on 2 March. But attention now transferred to the contest, and left Mrs Thatcher looking irrelevant and some-how uninteresting. It is a curious fact that although the Labour government of 1974–9 was largely unsuccessful, it contained an extraordinary abundance of talent. Those who stood to replace Wilson were Jim Callaghan, Roy Jenkins, Tony Benn, Anthony Crosland, Michael Foot and Denis Healey, all eloquent, experienced and charismatic figures, and all more substantial, at that time, than Mrs Thatcher. On 5 April 1976 the third ballot produced a victory for Jim Callaghan. Labour MPs had preferred the only candidate without an Oxford degree over Michael Foot, the main choice of the left.

This was not a good result for Mrs Thatcher. If Foot had won (he had amazed everyone by coming top in the first ballot), her excoriations of socialism would immediately have resonated with the voters. With Jim Callaghan, the Red wolf wore more effective sheep's clothing than ever before. Callaghan was thirteen years older than Mrs Thatcher, and had been an MP since 1945. He was an unquestionably patriotic product of the respectable working class and he embodied the idea, still persuasive to many voters, that only Labour could get on with the trade unions. A tall man, who deployed what Mrs Thatcher well described as 'avuncular flan-nel',[4] Callaghan treated her at the despatch box with a condescension which usually worked in the heavily male House of Commons. In one of their early exchanges at Prime Minister's Questions, Mrs Thatcher claimed that 'his only policy is to put Britain deeper in the red, to keep the red flag flying here.' Callaghan replied: 'I still have hopes that one day Question Time will be a serious period, without Members just thinking up clever phrases in advance and then shouting them across the Dispatch Box ... I am sure that one day the right honourable Lady will understand these things a little better.'[5] On another occasion, when Mrs Thatcher was trying to press Callaghan on the revolutionary opinions of one of his colleagues, he put her down: 'I could, of course, give the right honourable Lady my views on these matters, but unfortunately I do not seem able to endow her with a sense of humour.'[6] Mrs Thatcher remembered Callaghan as a more 'dominating' political figure than Wilson.[7] Throughout his time as Prime Minister, Callaghan had a higher personal popularity rating with the pub-lic than she did.

Two days after Callaghan became leader, Labour lost its overall major-ity in the Commons through the death of one of its Members and the resignation of the whip by the fraudster John Stonehouse.* This loss of

* John Stonehouse (1925–88), educated Tauntons School, Southampton and LSE; Labour MP for Wednesbury, 1957–74; for Walsall North, February 1974–6; Postmaster-General, 1968–9; Stonehouse was at the time an agent of the Czech security and intelligence service, the StB; he

control was not the blessing for the Tories which many of their supporters took it to be. Many now expected the Labour government to fall, but the Liberals and the minor parties could and did ensure that it stayed in office. Mrs Thatcher therefore found herself in the difficult position of having to keep her troops in permanent readiness for a war which might still be as much as three years away – the end of the legal life of the Parliament. With most Commons votes so finely balanced, parliamentary chaos became more frequent. At the end of May 1976, Labour's Bill to nationalize the shipbuild-ing and aircraft industry was pushed to the vote even though the Speaker had declared it 'hybrid' (that is, a Bill which, because it mixed general provi-sions with ones applying to specific businesses, required a special procedure in the House of Commons, which the government had failed to follow), and then was carried only, the Tories alleged, when the government whips induced one of their MPs to break his pair. Left-wing Labour MPs started to sing 'The Red Flag' in the Chamber of the House of Commons. Then Michael Heseltine, the Conservative industry spokesman, grabbed the Mace, which symbolizes the delegated authority of the Crown, and waved it aloft. Jim Prior and Willie Whitelaw restrained him, but not before everyone saw what had happened. Heseltine claimed ever afterwards that he was satirically offer-ing the Mace to the Labour left, not brandishing it,[8] but that is not how the matter was viewed. Mrs Thatcher seems quite to have enjoyed the kerfuffle, and did not reprimand Heseltine. The result of these dramas was that she suspended all parliamentary co-operation with the government until Calla-ghan agreed to hold the vote on the Shipbuilding Bill once more. This he did, four weeks later, but by that time he had made sure of the votes he needed.

Even the economic plight of the nation was not pure advantage to the Tories. The previous December, when the International Monetary Fund had agreed standby credit for the British government, the monetary disease which the Conservatives, starting with Keith Joseph, had identified had been confirmed by impartial medical opinion. In the debate on the Budget which came the day after Callaghan became prime minister, Mrs Thatcher turned in her most effective parliamentary performance yet as leader. She pointed out that when Healey had stood up to present his Budget a year before, the pound had been worth $2.37; now it was worth $1.87. The Public Sector Borrowing Requirement of £12 billion meant that 'the size of the deficit dominates everything the Chancellor can do.' The 'influenza' was recession: the 'cancer' was 'the underlying structural problem, that we

had faked his own death by leaving his clothes on a beach in Miami in 1974 in order to escape creditors and probable arrest in Britain. He resigned the whip to join the English National Party, and shortly afterwards went to prison for theft and fraud.

are living beyond our means'.[9] Two months later, as sterling came under pressure, a further standby credit, of $5,300 million available for three months, was offered by the Bank for International Settlements. And then, on 28 September, a new sterling crisis, in which the pound fell to $1.63, forced Healey to turn back at the airport minutes before he had been due to fly to a Commonwealth financial conference in Hong Kong. Britain applied to borrow $3.9 billion from the IMF. Although interest rates rose to 15 per cent, the pound fell still further in October 1976, reaching a low of $1.56. This time, the IMF loan came with strict conditions, and required a Letter of Intent about the next Budget, which was delivered by the British government in December. For the next fifteen years, the memory of Labour going 'cap in hand' – as it was always expressed – to the IMF became a standard feature of Tory propaganda.

Although these humiliations proved the Conservatives right, they also changed the political atmosphere. In such a crisis, there was talk once more of the need for national unity. A coalition government with such a purpose was touted by Harold Macmillan, who secretly imagined himself, aged eighty-two, at its head.* With rhetoric of belt-tightening and pulling together in the air, Mrs Thatcher's message that incomes policies could not work struck the wrong note with many. Shortly after Parliament had approved Stage 2 of the government's incomes policy in early May, she was interviewed by the journalist Peter Jay (who happened also to be Callaghan's son-in-law) on LWT's *Weekend World*. 'No pay deal will solve our problems at the moment, if pursued alone,' she told him. 'Is Britain to be thought of wholly in terms of restraint? Can't we advance?'[10] Her demand for public spending cuts to be 'immediate' and 'real'[11] combined with her preference for free collective bargaining to make many think that she would end up giving big wage settlements to overmighty unions and letting the weaker workers get worse deals. Senior Conservatives continued to disagree on this vital area of policy.

At the same time, the Labour government became more visibly responsible in its conduct. On 22 July, Healey announced public spending cuts of £1 billion. In response to the IMF crisis at the end of September, he produced the 'stern, decisive measures' which Mrs Thatcher had demanded. And although the Labour Party conference, which took place in the middle of that crisis, produced a show of strength from the left which helped sink the pound, it was also notable for the speech by Jim Callaghan (written

---

* Mrs Thatcher recalled visiting Macmillan for a talk about these matters at this time at the house of his son, Maurice. She said she heard the old man asking his son, 'Has the call come?' – meaning was there a move to ask him to lead a national government. (THCR 4/4.)

by Peter Jay) in which he declared that the option of borrowing and spending one's way out of economic trouble 'no longer exists'. The era of 'cuts', which Mrs Thatcher was later frequently accused of inaugurating, really began with this speech. As the man to lead the nation soberly through a crisis, Callaghan looked convincing, even if the crisis had been of his own government's making.

In her speech to her own party's conference, which took place in Brighton the following week, Mrs Thatcher was therefore, in her own words, 'almost neurotically cautious about the need for responsibility and caution'.[12] John Gummer, who often helped draft her party conference speeches, rather wearily recalled that 'What she liked best was being defiant, so it was one's job to find something for her to be defiant about.'[13] In October 1976 that something was not to be found. Mrs Thatcher had to be seen to support what Callaghan was doing without boosting him at the same time. Her line was to take a stand which appeared to eschew party advantage in the interests of 'the prosperity, the freedom – yes – and the honour of Britain'. 'Now half the Cabinet are beginning to tell half the truth,' she told the party faithful, but the chance of the government changing course was 'nil', because of the power of the left. She highlighted the document produced by the party's National Executive, *Labour's Programme* (which was not binding on the party leadership), as 'frankly and unashamedly Marxist', and said that the behaviour of the left in barracking poor Healey at Blackpool the week before had been 'a sight the country is unlikely ever to forget'.

Her proposed remedies were very cautious. As a form of thanks to Ted Heath for the (somewhat grudging) support he had offered for the general direction of policy in his Brighton speech, Mrs Thatcher praised him as 'a man who never sells the truth to serve the hour', and kept to an unspoken agreement with the left of the party not to damn all forms of incomes policy. She spoke of the virtues of 'a generally agreed basis for wage bargaining'. At the same time, she declared that she sought no confrontation with the unions: 'the confrontation that matters to us is confrontation with rising prices, with rising unemployment, with rising debts.'[14] As a piece of political positioning, the speech did its work. *The Times* tried to wrap her to its establishment heart: 'Mrs Thatcher has moved with characteristic caution on to the middle ground of politics ... the party has rallied on a set of policies and approaches that are markedly closer to Mr Heath than to Sir Keith Joseph.'[15] But the audience in the hall was much less excited than the previous year, and the speech fell rather flat. Frank Johnson,* the sketch-writer of the *Daily Telegraph*, and one of those

---

* Frank Johnson (1943–2006), educated Chartesey Secondary School, Shoreditch and

sympathetic to the change that Mrs Thatcher represented, noted how much better she spoke in an impromptu speech to an overflow meeting organized after her setpiece speech (because the main event had taken place, due to building works, in a small, temporary hall). The earlier performance, he wrote, 'was markedly inferior to her showing last year'.[16] In acknowledging its comparative failure in her memoirs, Mrs Thatcher is probably displaying a bad conscience: she had conceded more than she liked to the consensual wing of the party.

The text which bound Mrs Thatcher and Ted Heath in uneasy unity for the party conference of 1976 was a document called *The Right Approach*, which was published as the Conservatives convened in Brighton. Drafted chiefly by Chris Patten, the lengthy document was subtitled 'A Statement of Conservative Aims' in order to avoid having definite policies hung round the party's neck at too early a stage. It represented, as Patten himself put it, 'a treaty'[17] between the Heathite and Thatcherite strands of Conservatism and so, like all good treaties, sought to express itself in a way from which both sides could draw comfort. In rhetorical terms, the centrist voice, which was really Patten's own, dominated. *The Right Approach* talked repeatedly of 'a return to common sense', and warned against being 'too dogmatic'. 'A Philosophy of Balance' between man as an individual and as a social being was offered. The document sought a 'whole-hearted contribution to the development of the European Community' and it represented the Conservative approach as being 'in tune with the instincts and views of the overwhelming majority of our fellow citizens'. It praised the Heath era as one in which 'tough decisions' had been taken. In its substance, however, *The Right Approach* was almost Thatcherite enough for Mrs Thatcher. The key section entitled 'Bringing the Economy into Balance' ('balance' here being a word that appealed to Heathites as suggesting moderation and to Thatcherites as implying a balanced budget) spoke of 'a steady and disciplined monetary policy', a reduction in government borrowing and cash limits. Control of the money supply was 'a key feature of economic policy, though by no means the only one'. Public spending cuts were described as 'essential' and it was stated as 'probable . . . that reductions in the scale of some public services are inescapable'. Once borrowing had been successfully reined in, direct taxes would be cut and the tax burden 'as a whole' would be reduced. The Price Code, which sought to

Shoreditch Secondary School; parliamentary sketch-writer of the *Daily Telegraph*, 1972–9 and 1999–2006; staff of *The Times*, 1981–8; deputy editor, *Sunday Telegraph*, 1993–5; editor, *Spectator*, 1995–9.

control prices, should be relaxed, the National Enterprise Board, which had the power to take controlling stakes in strategic industries, should be abolished and clear financial objectives set for nationalized industries: there was no general proposal to sell them off. Tenants of more than three years' standing would be given a statutory right to buy their council house or flat. In only two areas was the caution arising from internal disagreement visible. The first concerned the reform of trade unions. This was approached under the heading of increasing 'the authority of Parliament'. Public money for union postal ballots would be provided and individual rights against the closed shop better protected, but the rest was vague: 'We do not intend to introduce a major round of new industrial relations legislation.' Although this certainly represented less than Thatcherites sought, there was agree-ment, right across the party, that discretion was the better part of valour: the wounds of the Heath Industrial Relations Act were still raw.

It was in the second, related area of incomes policy that *The Right Approach*'s need for compromise reduced it almost to nonsense. Restraint in pay bargaining, it said, did not necessarily mean a prices and incomes policy. 'Experience does not suggest that this [incomes policy] is the best way of finding a long-term solution to the problem. The same experi-ence demonstrates the unwisdom of flatly and permanently rejecting the idea.' Noises were made in the direction of German 'Concerted Action' by which unions and management agreed general financial outlines with-out producing a percentage guideline for wage increases. The internal Tory battle about incomes policy would have to be fought another day. On the whole, Mrs Thatcher was well pleased with the treaty-drafting. *The Right Approach* even produced a phrase which later came, falsely, to be attrib-uted to her: 'The facts of life invariably *do* turn out to be Conservative.'

Although she suffered from the political weakness discussed above, and a lack of kindred spirits at the top of the party, Mrs Thatcher had the great advantage that the battleground on which she wished to conduct most of her fight was economic. Her critics within the party were weak on eco-nomics. Most of the political heavyweights were economic lightweights (and vice versa). William Waldegrave, one of the few originating in the Heath camp who was interested in and sympathetic to liberal economics, remembered that the grandees paid very little attention to the subject: '"Didn't Keynes settle all this for ever?" they thought.'[18] And although they instinctively disliked the direction that Mrs Thatcher wanted to take, they did not have the knowledge to mount a resistance based on actual argu-ment. Even incomes policy, over which they fought the hardest, was something which its supporters tended to see as merely temporary – 'the economic equivalent of internment in Northern Ireland'[19] – and they therefore found it hard to resist the tide of objection which gradually eroded it. This economic ignorance of the men who later became known as the Wets was reflected in the portfolios which Mrs Thatcher assigned in her Shadow Cabinet. Of those who dealt with economic matters, only Jim Prior, at Employment, represented a block on the analysis of Keith Joseph and the passion of Margaret Thatcher, and he was the only man brave enough to raise serious objection to the direction of policy in Shadow Cabinet meetings. But since Prior objected on principle to ideas, he was ill equipped to have many of his own. Of her other critics in the Shadow Cabinet, the most economically literate was Reggie Maudling, who had been Chancellor of the exchequer. He did protest from time to time, but he did not exert himself and was on the downward slope of his career.* Her Shadow Cabinet critics took refuge in the general, pragmatic hope that 'events would modify her views.'[20]

On the Thatcher side of the argument were ranged an intellectually impressive group of mainly younger men, much less well known to the public than the old grandees. Rather like soldiers who have forged a camaraderie by fighting in the same campaigns, some of these were veterans of the resistance to the Heath U-turn, and all of them served at some point on the Finance Bill Standing Committee, the body on which Mrs Thatcher had so distinguished herself during her fight for the leadership. They included David Howell,† Nigel Lawson, Nicholas Ridley, John Nott, John Biffen, Ian Gow, Cecil Parkinson, Norman Lamont and Jock Bruce-Gardyne. All of these men possessed considerable brainpower and applied it in the years of opposition to develop new economic policy. There were important differences of emphasis – Biffen, for example, was much more cautious and Baldwinesque than Ridley or Lawson – but all pointed essentially in the same direction, towards greater freedom in the economy.

In addition to these politicians, those who advised Mrs Thatcher on economic matters were also economic liberals. With the partial exception of Adam Ridley, who, though no dirigiste, came from the Heath stable, none

---

* One of Mrs Thatcher's assistants met Maudling as he was leaving the Commons and asked him why he was not listening to Denis Healey's Budget statement. 'I practically went to sleep in my own Budget speeches,' Maudling told him. 'I'm f***ed if I'm going to sit through anyone else's.' (Private information.) On one occasion during the Heath government, the Prime Minister was out of the country and Maudling was deputizing for him. He returned to work at 4 p.m. after a convivial lunch: 'What's the sentence for being drunk in charge of a government?' he was heard to ask a secretary.

† David Howell (1936–), educated Eton and King's College, Cambridge; Conservative MP for Guildford, 1966–97; Secretary of State for Energy, 1979–81; for Transport, 1981–3; Minister of State for Foreign Affairs, 2010–; created Lord Howell, 1997.

of her economic advisers felt any need to justify anything that Heath had done. Indeed, they were raring for change, and shared her impatience with the formal policy processes of the Conservative Party. She complained that at the Conservative Research Department, supposedly the party's intellectual powerhouse, 'there was nobody in the room with a single idea that was worth having'.[21] As Chris Patten, of the Research Department, who tried to manage the policy process, remembered ruefully, Mrs Thatcher would study the work of the formal policy groups, but 'You'd know that she was also seeing a crazed Swiss professor.'[22] Through Keith Joseph, Alfred Sherman and the Centre for Policy Studies, and to a lesser but significant extent through Arthur Seldon, Ralph Harris and the Institute of Economic Affairs, Mrs Thatcher met a steady stream of economic and political thinkers, of whom Friedrich von Hayek* and Milton Friedman† were the most famous. She took as her watchword Solzhenitsyn's dictum that 'it is part of the business of the artist and the philosopher to light up the politician's path,'[23] and the path which she most wanted illuminated was that which led to greater freedom, under the rule of law. She instinctively disliked mere individualism: what she was searching for was liberty in a strong moral and social order. She had read Hayek's *Road to Serfdom* as an undergraduate at Oxford, and in the 1970s used to pull his *Constitution of Liberty* out of her handbag, declaring '*This* is what we believe.'[24] And she loved to invoke the authority of great thinkers as part of her campaign of public evangelizing. During the opposition years, Mrs Thatcher's speeches referred admiringly to, among many others, Karl Popper, Bastiat, Keynes, Burke, Schumpeter, Tocqueville, Alfred Marshall, C. S. Lewis, Adam Smith and Rudyard Kipling. Although she had often not read these authors before someone else drew her attention to them, their inclusion in her speeches was almost always an authentic representation of her interest and her views. On the recommendation of others, Mrs Thatcher would set herself homework. 'I have just embarked on holiday reading,' she wrote to Adam Butler to thank him for a Christmas present. 'But after Dostoevsky's *The Possessed* and Koestler's *Darkness at Noon* am none too cheerful!'[25]‡

---

* Friedrich von Hayek (1899–1992), educated University of Vienna; Tooke Professor of Economic Science and Statistics, University of London, 1931–50; Professor of Moral and Social Science, University of Chicago, 1950–62; Nobel Prize in Economic Sciences (jointly), 1974; Companion of Honour, 1984.

† Milton Friedman (1912–2006), educated Rutgers, Chicago and Columbia universities; economist and writer; Professor of Economics, University of Chicago, 1946–77; Professor Emeritus from 1982; economic columnist, *Newsweek*, 1966–84; Nobel Prize in Economic Sciences, 1976.

‡ In her memoirs Mrs Thatcher records that she read *The Possessed* on the recommendation of her country neighbour, the journalist Malcolm Muggeridge, who told her that it would give

She amazed the novelist and journalist Jilly Cooper by telling her that in the course of the broiling summer of 1976 she had read the entire 845 pages of Kipling's Collected Poems.[26] In the preparation of her more substantial speeches, particularly at weekends, Mrs Thatcher drew heavily on these authorities, and also on more current thinkers and commentators. Records of the preparation for a speech entitled 'The will-o-the-wisp of the classless society', delivered on 26 January 1977, are typical. She heavily underlines articles from current newspapers and magazines by Shirley Robin Letwin,* P. T. Bauer,† Milton Friedman, Samuel Brittan, Robert Skidelsky,‡ Hayek, Alan Walters and Paul Johnson.[27]

Mrs Thatcher had no less an appetite for drier economic reading. By the time she met Alan Walters in America in September 1977, she had read his *Money in Boom and Slump*.[28] According to Douglas Hague, who had first advised her when she was in Ted Heath's Shadow Cabinet in the late 1960s, she was a keen student, 'good on finance, very good on law, not very good on economics'. She settled down to read his *A Textbook of Economic Theory* and proved herself to have 'the best memory I've ever met in anybody'.[29] After becoming leader, she complained to him that 'This chap Adam Ridley writes the most appalling stuff about economics'[30] and asked Hague to be her economic adviser in 1975, but he was working for the Price Commission and could not give her his full attention until he left it in 1978. Hague and she shared a Methodist background and both had, at different times, attended the Wesley Memorial Church in Oxford. Hague reminded her of the famous advice of John Wesley – 'Get all you can; save all you can; give all you can' – and she deployed it in public argument. He would prove important later in persuading Mrs Thatcher to lift exchange controls. In addition to Hague's valued but intermittent help, she received more technical advice on the workings of money from Gordon

her an understanding of the Communist frame of mind (see *The Path to Power*, HarperCollins, 1995, pp. 309–10).

* Shirley Robin Letwin (1924–93), educated Chicago University and LSE; philosopher and historian of ideas; author of *The Anatomy of Thatcherism* (1992). Her husband Bill, Professor of Political Science, LSE, 1976–88, also contributed advice and help with speeches to Keith Joseph and Mrs Thatcher. Their son, Oliver, worked in Mrs Thatcher's Policy Unit, and, at the time of writing, is a member of the Coalition government.

† Peter Bauer (1915–2002), educated Scholae Piae, Budapest and Gonville and Caius College, Cambridge; Professor of Economics, LSE, 1960–83; best known for his work on international development and his scepticism about government aid to developing countries; created Lord Bauer, 1982.

‡ Robert Skidelsky (1939–), educated Brighton College, and Jesus College and Nuffield College, Oxford; Professor of Political Economy, Warwick University, 1990–2007; biographer of Oswald Mosley and of Keynes; created Lord Skidelsky, 1991.

Pepper,* a senior partner at Greenwell's, the stockbrokers. Pepper would spend two hours with her before each Budget and would sometimes go over to see her informally at Scotney because he lived close by. He said that her reputation for 'chewing people up' arose from what was really her 'thirst for knowledge' and he was struck by her unusual combination of an appetite for minutiae and a passionate conviction. He found that their technical discussions were usually preceded by ten minutes of diatribe from Mrs Thatcher in which she would express her 'moral hatred of inflation' and her associated belief in the importance of saving.[31] Pepper helped deepen her suspicion of the Bank of England and the doctrines prevailing there at that time. She did not take to Gordon Richardson,† the Governor, describing him as 'a peacock of a man'.[32]

For more practical, business-based advice, Mrs Thatcher roped in John Sparrow,‡ the head of the investment department at Morgan Grenfell, early in 1977. She wanted his views on 'the steps that need to be taken to turn us from a wealth-distributing to a wealth-creating country again'.[33] Seconded to her office from his bank, Sparrow quickly found that he was more help to her if he stayed in the City, rather than working in Parliament. From there, he sent her weekly reports about what was actually happening in the economy and business, which were followed up by weekly meetings. Sparrow considered that, in terms of economic and business knowledge, Mrs Thatcher had led 'a fairly cloistered life', but that she had a 'tremendously good intuition'.[34] He did much to buttress Mrs Thatcher's instinctive dislike of high interest rates, a view which was to prove a constant source of disagreement with her Chancellors when she reached office. He believed that the country was suffering from an excessive supply of money not an excessive demand, and argued that banks should have their credit limited, as in Germany, to a multiple of reserves. Like Douglas Hague, he consistently advocated a loosening of exchange controls. His task, in part, was to tell her what the City thought. This was sometimes depressing for her, but she listened. After the IMF package was put in place, he reported, 'The dominant theme in City minds was ... that ... for the time being, we are probably best off with an emasculated Labour government carrying out Conservative (or

---

* Gordon Pepper (1934–), educated Repton and Trinity College, Cambridge; partner, Greenwell's, 1962; chairman, Lombard Street Research, from 2000.

† Gordon Richardson (1915–2010), educated Nottingham High School and Gonville and Caius College, Cambridge; Governor, Bank of England, 1973–83; created Lord Richardson of Duntisbourne, 1983.

‡ John Sparrow (1933–), educated Stationers' Company's School and LSE; head of Central Policy Review Staff, 1982–3; chairman, Horserace Betting Levy Board, 1991–8; knighted, 1984.

IMF) policies.' Many people in the City, he added, actually wanted a pay policy.[35]

An important subsection of the movement which might be called Intellectuals for Margaret was composed of converts from socialism. It was sometimes easier for those who had come from the left to see the threat that socialism posed than it was for Tories who had never been tempted. Woodrow Wyatt,* for example, a journalist and former Labour MP, had been involved in the fight to resist Communist takeover of the Electricians Union in the early 1960s. Brian Walden,† considered the most eloquent of his generation of Labour MPs, but disillusioned by the rise of the left in the Labour Party, was more clear-sighted than most in seeing that Mrs Thatcher stood for real change. As a grammar school meritocrat who had originally looked for social progress from the Labour Party, Walden recognized her as offering what he sought. Soon after she won the leadership, Jim Prior told him, 'She is, of course, completely potty, Brian. She won't last six months,'[36] but Walden disagreed. In May 1975 he had lunch with Humphrey Atkins and offered to cross the floor and bring six Labour right-wingers with him.[37] Nothing came of this – although, in a separate development, Reg Prentice,‡ Labour's former Education Secretary, did defect to the Conservatives – and Walden left Parliament in 1977 to take up a career as a television interviewer. His interviews with Mrs Thatcher became famous for the rapport he established with her, and his perceptiveness about the elemental force of Thatcherism. 'The only way the Tories can lose the next election', he told the whip Bernard Weatherill early in 1978, 'is if they are not Conservative enough,'[38] exactly the opposite approach to that of many centrist Tories.

Alfred Sherman, himself originally from the extreme left, made it his business to cultivate defectors. He advocated a strategy of taking the initiative and saying, 'We are the heirs to the Social Democratic heritage.' This would outflank 'fainéant pseudo D'Israelians [sic], and give us a truly

---

* Woodrow Wyatt (1918–97), educated Eastbourne and Worcester College, Oxford; journalist; Labour MP for Aston Division of Birmingham, 1945–55; for Bosworth Division of Leicester, 1959–70; chairman, Horserace Totalisator Board, 1976–97; created Lord Wyatt of Weeford, 1987.

† Brian Walden (1932–), educated West Bromwich Grammar School and Queen's College and Nuffield College, Oxford; Labour MP for Birmingham All Saints, 1964–74; for Birmingham, Ladywood, 1974–7; presenter, *Weekend World*, 1977–86.

‡ Reg Prentice (1923–2001), educated Whitgift School and LSE; Labour MP for East Ham North, 1957–74; for Newham North East, 1974–7; Conservative MP for Newham North East, 1977–9; for Daventry, 1979–87; Secretary of State for Education and Science, 1974–5; Minister for Overseas Development, 1975–6; Minister of State for Social Security, DHSS, 1979–81; created Lord Prentice, 1992.

central position in British politics'.[39] Mrs Thatcher enthusiastically supported the idea, and made a great deal of time available to see the converts
and flatter them. One such was Hugh Thomas,* the historian of the Spanish Civil War, who had become a socialist while at university, and now
repented of his ways, partly because of his concern about the Communist
threat. Sherman kept Mrs Thatcher informed about Thomas's pilgrimage,
telling her in the summer of 1978 that he was lying low: 'Like the nightingale (*per* Horace) he sings most sweetly from the shade of the thicket.'[40]
In fact, Thomas, accompanied by Leon Brittan,† who was in charge of the
party's efforts to engage with academics, had lunched with Mrs Thatcher
in the spring of 1975, and again with her and Sherman in November of
that year. She used his materials on 'The Ideals of an Open Society' as the
basic text of her speech of that title to the Bow Group in May 1978, and
drew on him for advice on foreign policy, particularly the Communist
threat in southern Africa. Thomas was always a strong European, but this
did not trouble Mrs Thatcher at the time. She happily took up his call for
a European defence capability to share more of the burden of resisting the
Soviets with the Americans. As well as Thomas and Robert Conquest (see
above), Mrs Thatcher also roped in distinguished historians and thinkers
such as Leonard Schapiro,‡ Michael Howard§ and Isaiah Berlin¶ – all
three of whom also advised the Liberal Party at the time – to give her ideas
on subjects relating to the nature and danger of Soviet Communism. 'She
was interested to know how historians saw things, though she hadn't done
much background reading.'[41]

Hugh Thomas, in turn, was influential with his old friend Paul Johnson
(though Johnson claimed that the process worked more the other way).

---

* Hugh Thomas (1931–), educated Sherborne, Queens' College, Cambridge and Sorbonne,
Paris; Professor of History, University of Reading, 1966–76; chairman, Centre for Policy Stud-
ies, 1979–90; author of *The Spanish Civil War* (1961); created Lord Thomas of Swynnerton,
1981.
† Leon Brittan (1939–), brother of Samuel Brittan; educated Haberdashers' Aske's School,
Trinity College, Cambridge and Yale University; Conservative MP for Cleveland and Whitby,
February 1974–83; for Richmond, Yorkshire, 1983–8; Chief Secretary to the Treasury, 1981–3;
Home Secretary, 1983–5; Secretary of State for Trade and Industry, 1985–6; European
Commissioner, 1989–99; knighted, 1989; created Lord Brittan of Spennithorne, 2000.
‡ Leonard Schapiro (1908–83), educated St Paul's and University College London; Professor
of Political Science with special reference to Russia, LSE, 1963–75.
§ Michael Howard (1922–), educated Wellington and Christ Church, Oxford; Regius Professor
of Modern History, Oxford University, 1980–89; Professor Emeritus, from 1989; knighted, 1986.
¶ Isaiah Berlin (1909–97), educated St Paul's and Corpus Christi College, Oxford; Chichele
Professor of Social and Political Theory, Oxford, 1957–67; president, Wolfson College, Oxford,
1966–75; President of the British Academy, 1974–8; Fellow of All Souls College, Oxford;
knighted, 1971.

By the mid-1970s Johnson was increasingly disenchanted with the growing power of the left, particularly the trade unions, and in 1977 brought together his discontents in a book called *Enemies of Society*, a list of Britain's ills which accorded very closely with Mrs Thatcher's own analysis. By 1980, he felt happy enough with the way things were going to write a book called *The Recovery of Freedom*. From 1975 he talked to her sometimes about policy ('She was completely at sea'), and about history, ideas and what books she should read: 'I got her to read David Watkin's *Morality and Architecture*. She said she found it hard going.' Although a strong Thatcherite, Johnson looked down on Mrs Thatcher somewhat. He described her as 'the most ignorant politician of her level that I'd come across until I met Tony Blair', but she was touchingly aware of her ignorance, being 'the eternal scholarship girl'. He summed up by saying, 'I always liked her, but she always bored me a bit.'[42]

Johnson's support was valuable to Mrs Thatcher, however, as his prolific journalism, notably in the *Daily Mail* and the *Spectator*, made a great impact. He was one of many newspaper journalists whose support helped change the conversation of what later became known as the chattering classes. Others included John O'Sullivan,* Frank Johnson and T. E. Utley,† all of the *Daily Telegraph*, Andrew Alexander of the *Daily Mail*, George Gale of the *Daily Express* and, later in the process, Bernard Levin of *The Times*. Samuel Brittan, the main economic commentator of the *Financial Times*, though by no means a Thatcherite politically, was her chief economic guru in the press, and his weekly column was the only piece of journalism which she read without fail.[43] Collectively, these writers contributed to an exciting feeling that the tide of ideas was changing away from collectivism and that, at last, 'everything was possible'.[44] Mrs Thatcher celebrated some conversions in public. In her party conference speech in October 1977, she concluded with words by Paul Johnson, acclaiming his 'writer's clarity', about why he had deserted the left: 'I have come to appreciate . . . the overwhelming strength of my attachment to the individual spirit.'[45]

A similar excitement pervaded the proceedings of the Conservative Philosophy Group, an informal society, set up by Hugh Fraser and Jonathan

---

* John O'Sullivan (1942–), educated St Mary's College, Crosby and London University; special adviser to the Prime Minister, 1986–8. His journalistic positions have included: parliamentary sketch-writer, *Daily Telegraph*; associate editor, *The Times*; editor, *National Review*.

† T. E. (Peter) Utley (1921–88), educated privately and Corpus Christi College, Cambridge; journalist; leader writer, 1964–80, and chief assistant editor, 1980–87, *Daily Telegraph*; obituaries editor and columnist, *The Times*, 1987–8; contested (Unionist) North Antrim, February 1974.

Aitken, which mingled politicians and men of the world with writers and thinkers. Organized on the academic side by Roger Scruton* and John Casey,† the group would meet in Fraser's or, later, Aitken's house to hear papers read on a wide range of subjects from immigration, or religion, or the monarchy, to the money supply or nuclear weapons. Initially suspicious of the group, because of its link with her defeated rival, Fraser, Mrs Thatcher then asked to come to its meetings, and did so several times in opposition. Among other things, the group provided a place where she could meet Enoch Powell, now an Ulster Unionist MP, on neutral ground. Mrs Thatcher was particularly taken with a talk, which she heard on her only visit to the group as prime minister, by Edward Norman,‡ the Dean of Peterhouse, Cambridge, in which he predicted that the issue of nuclear weapons, which had fallen comparatively quiet since the early 1960s, would soon reappear as a great moral struggle in the West. Norman argued that the moral objections to nuclear weapons were not different in kind from those to any other weapons, and that it was a worthy object of policy for the West to resist the philosophical materialism of Soviet Communism.[46] Those present remembered Mrs Thatcher shouting out, in the discussion after the talk, 'I agree with Dr Norman: we must defend Christian values with the ATOM BOMB.'[47] As this shortly predated the great CND battles of the early 1980s, she was much impressed by Norman's powers of prediction, later referring to him as a 'prophet' and consulting him both on the ethics of the nuclear question and in her search for Christian justifications for capitalism. These last had long been active in her mind. In an almost philosophical speech to the Zurich Economic Society, Mrs Thatcher claimed the moral high ground for her economic beliefs. 'Choice is the essence of ethics,' she said, and 'The economic results [of the Western way of life] are better because the moral philosophy is superior.'[48]

It was this quest for the Christian roots of her beliefs, particularly of her economic doctrines, which gave depth and breadth to Mrs Thatcher's approach to the national crisis. She always had very strong personal

---

* Roger Scruton (1944–), educated Jesus College, Cambridge; lecturer in philosophy, Birkbeck College, London, 1971–9, reader, 1979–85, Professor of Aesthetics, 1985–92; Professor of Philosophy, Boston University, Massachusetts, 1992–5; editor, *Salisbury Review*, 1982–2000.
† John Casey (1939–), educated King's College, Cambridge; lecturer, Cambridge University, and Fellow of Gonville and Caius College; founder (with Roger Scruton) Conservative Philosophy Group (1975).
‡ Edward Norman (1938–), educated Chatham House School, Ramsgate and Selwyn College, Cambridge; priest in the Church of England, 1971; lecturer in history, University of Cambridge, 1965–88; Dean of Peterhouse, Cambridge, 1971–88; historian of Church and society in Victorian England, and of modern Ireland; Reith Lecturer (published as *Christianity and the World Order*, 1979), 1978; Chancellor, York Minster, 1999–2004.

Christian beliefs, in what Edward Norman called 'the English sense'.[49] In other words, she was not interested in spirituality, sacraments or questions of authority in the Church, but she was extremely interested in duty to God and in ethics, and had a particular, almost nostalgic idea of a life lived according to the teachings of the Gospel. She had, in Norman's words, 'a pre-existing sense of neatness and order in society' which she derived in large part from her childhood and her father. Alfred Roberts had believed in what Gladstone called 'effort, honest manful effort', and it was a combination of Gladstonian economic views of retrenchment and reform with Methodism which animated Mrs Thatcher. Denis Thatcher shared this analysis of her attitudes. He believed that some of what people thought of as his wife's 'right-wingery' actually came from her religious upbringing: 'She can't find a sustainable argument that people should be paid for not doing any work.'[50] 'It is noteworthy', she told the bankers of Zurich, 'that the Victorian era – the heyday of free enterprise in Britain – was also the era of the rise of selflessness and benefaction'.[51] Mrs Thatcher wanted, said Norman, to 'resuscitate a world we had lost', and she 'ransacked' Christian thought for intellectual backing.

As leader of the Opposition, she delivered two substantial public accounts along these lines. The first was the Iain Macleod Memorial Lecture in the summer of 1977. Although Jewish, Alfred Sherman, who did much of the drafting, always regarded the term 'Judaeo-Christian values' as a cop-out and believed that British Conservatism should be explicitly Christian.[52] In her Macleod Lecture, Mrs Thatcher sought the roots of Conservatism not in opposition to socialism, but in an earlier age. It is 'part of the living flesh of British life', she said, and it depended on the idea that man is individual and social and spiritual, all at once. Far from being the antithesis of care for others, self-interest worked with it because 'man is a social creature, born into family, clan, community, nation, brought up in mutual dependence . . . "Love your neighbour as yourself" expresses this.' This is what she always believed, and it is what she meant ten years later when she uttered a phrase constantly held against her: 'There is no such thing as society.' The full quotation makes this clear. Interviewed by *Woman's Own* in 1987, Mrs Thatcher criticized those who thought it was up to the government to solve all their problems: 'They're casting their problem on society. And you know, there's no such thing as society. There are individual men and women, and there are families. And no government can do things except through people . . . It's our duty to look after ourselves and then, also, to look after our neighbours.'[53] Her Macleod Lecture praised Adam Smith for his view that 'A moral being is one who exercises his own judgement in choice' and went on to argue that 'economic choices have a moral dimension.'[54]

In a speech, drafted by T. E. Utley and Simon Webley, from the pulpit of St Lawrence Jewry in the City of London the following year, Mrs Thatcher was more explicit about religion. She recalled her upbringing: 'What mattered fundamentally was Man's relationship to God, and in the last resort this depended on the response of the individual soul to God's Grace.' She went on, 'I never thought that Christianity equipped me with a political philosophy, but I thought it did equip me with standards to which political actions must, in the end, be referred.' She said that Christian teaching and worship should not be taken out of schools because 'To most ordinary people, heaven and hell, right and wrong, good and bad, matter.' The relief of poverty and suffering was a religious duty, but not one necessarily best performed by the state, she declared, taking her favourite example: 'I wonder whether the State services would have done as much for the man who fell among thieves as the Good Samaritan did for him?' The worst political doctrines, notably Marxism ('utterly inconsistent with the Gospel'), proclaimed the perfectibility of man through politics. She did not, but 'There is a well-known prayer which refers to God's service as "perfect freedom". My wish for the people of this country is that we shall be "free to serve".' There was an apparent contradiction, she said, between the idea of interdependence and individual responsibility, but not a real one: 'the whole of political wisdom consists in getting these two ideas in the right relationship to each other.'[55]

The reaction of the intellectuals to all of this was interesting to behold. Some of them fell in love with Mrs Thatcher. John Vaizey,* an educationalist who had moved from the left during her time at the Department of Education, wrote to her to tell her how interesting her voice was to listen to.[56] Most were flattered by her enthusiasm and, of course, by her praise for their writing. 'You just put things so marvellously: I wish I had your gift for words,' was one of her corny but effective lines. The historian David Dilks,† who met her through Leon Brittan, was struck by her 'directness, quickness on the point, anxiety to listen to a wide range of views, conscious exploitation of feminine charm, and a certain motherly quality.'[57] He was also impressed by her desire to recapture 'intellectual capital' from universities to rebuild Conservative ideas. Some, however, thought her naive. Edward Norman, though an admirer, recalled that she 'had all that ven-

---

* John Vaizey (1929–84), educated Colfe's Grammar School, Lewisham, Queen Mary's Hospital School, Carshalton and Queens' College, Cambridge; economist and educationalist; Professor of Economics, Brunel University, 1966–82; created Lord Vaizey of Greenwich, 1976.
† David Dilks (1938–), educated Royal Grammar School, Worcester, and Hertford College and St Antony's College, Oxford; Vice-Chancellor of Hull University, 1991–9; biographer of Neville Chamberlain.

eration for intellectual life which real intellectuals don't share'.[58] She had 'no real sense of intellectual inquiry' and 'an extraordinarily intelligent, but unformed mind'. Some simply doubted whether she was up to the task. After meeting her for the first time in 1978 – an occasion on which he told her to abolish exchange controls – Milton Friedman wrote to thank his host Ralph Harris: 'Rose and I both enjoyed our dinner with Margaret Thatcher . . . very much indeed. She is a very attractive and interesting lady. Whether she really has the capacities that Britain so badly needs at this time, I must confess, seems to me a very open question . . .'[59]

But all shared a certain wonderment at the phenomenon of a party leader in search of ideas. Almost all responded to her demands, and it quite quickly became noticed that no equivalent mental activity was forthcoming either from the left of the Conservative Party or from the social democratic elements of Labour. Mrs Thatcher was the most clamorous customer in the ideological market-place. As a result, she was able to stimulate a good supply, and buy up more than any rivals. Her energy in this area made her critics look dingy and negative. Chris Patten's memory of his own reaction can stand for many others:

> The most fundamental aspect of her leadership . . . was that she believed she
> was engaged in a battle of ideas. And that unless the Conservative Party won
> it, she wouldn't have the Opposition in office . . . Now that came as a particu-
> larly rude shock to many of us. Even though I was running the Conservative
> Party's Research Department, interested in ideas, I was much more used to
> an approach to politics that saw things in a less intellectually confrontational
> way. I happen to think she was right. But I remember the first time she said
> to me, 'We have to win the battle of ideas in British politics,' I thought, 'This
> is a bit rum.'[60]

Against all this intellectual firepower, some Heathite arguments began to crumble. 'Monetarism', by which was really only meant the control of inflation by attacking what Keith Joseph called 'monetary incontinence', was able to advance more or less unimpeded, so long as it was not too loudly proclaimed. It was to guard against this danger that Joseph entitled his Stockton Lecture of 1976 'Monetarism is Not Enough': he emphasized how an over-large public sector could play havoc with the best-designed monetary policy. Mrs Thatcher could still be slowed down by appeals to the political danger of what she was trying to do, but nothing could stand in the way of the general direction of travel.

None of this ferment of ideas would have been much use, however, without anyone to try to relate it to actual policies. Here the most important person was not Keith Joseph, who was more 'the licensed thinker scouting ahead in Indian country',[61] but Geoffrey Howe. According to Richard Ryder, Howe was the 'tapestry master of Thatcherism'.[62] He was slightly unusual in being to the left of the party and yet having a record of supporting free-market economics which went right back to the 1950s. It was he, much more than Mrs Thatcher, who had close and long-standing links with the Institute of Economic Affairs, and he had learnt bitter lessons from his close involvement in piloting Ted Heath's trade union reforms through the House of Commons and in implementing his incomes policies. Always a glutton for paperwork and one of the few senior politicians to be what is nowadays called a policy wonk, Howe spawned a vast amount of detailed policy rethinking. His informal group, meeting at his house in Fentiman Road, and including Keith Joseph, Nigel Lawson and the tax expert Arthur Cockfield,* tried to plot a free-market path for a future Conservative government. Naturally civil-servantish and emollient, Howe was better than any other leading party figure in establishing links between freelance advice from bodies like the Centre for Policy Studies and the policy work produced within the party and serviced by the Conservative Research Department. The policy group on taxation, for example, presided over by Cockfield, and assisted by Peter Cropper,† one of the few free-market men in the CRD, did detailed work on subjects like the reform of capital taxation in a way which prepared for government and gave Mrs Thatcher confidence. This was chiefly thanks to Howe. His approach was cautious, but also dogged. It was Howe who formulated the idea, embodied in *The Right Approach*, that the need for freedom was best expressed in the language of common sense rather than anything more ecstatic. Although he shared most of the aims of Keith Joseph, he was concerned about what he called 'too breakneck a pace': 'You know my own preference for not-so-benign neglect of harmful institutions rather than theatrical reform.'[63]

Unfortunately, from the very beginning of her leadership, Mrs Thatcher had certain reservations about Geoffrey Howe. She had been surprised and slightly unnerved when he stood against her in the second ballot, and she harboured a suspicion, which grew with time, that he was ambitious for

* Arthur Cockfield (1916-2007), educated Dover Grammar School and LSE; director of statistics and intelligence, Board of Inland Revenue, 1945-52; managing director, Boots, 1961-7; chairman, Price Commission, 1973-7; Minister of State, Treasury, 1979-82; Secretary of State for Trade, 1982-3; Chancellor of the Duchy of Lancaster, 1983-4; Vice-President, European Commission, 1985-8; created Lord Cockfield, 1978.
† Peter Cropper (1927-), educated Hitchin Grammar School and Gonville and Caius College, Cambridge; special adviser to Chief Secretary to the Treasury, 1979-82; to Chancellor of the Exchequer, 1984-8; Conservative Research Department, 1951-3, 1975-9, director, 1982-4.

her job.[64] She had uneasy relations with Howe's wife, Elspeth, who was too much of the bluestocking, too much on the left and perhaps, being of grander class origin, too socially confident a woman to appeal to Mrs Thatcher. Many years later, Denis Thatcher would refer to Elspeth Howe as 'that bitch of a wife'.[65] Things were nothing like so bad in the early days, but late in 1975 a problem arose which helped to sour relations ever after. Under the sex equality legislation of which Mrs Thatcher anyway disapproved, the Equal Opportunities Commission was established. According to Lady Howe, Mrs Thatcher was 'positively not interested' in women's issues and suffered from 'Queen Bee Syndrome – "I made it. Others can jolly well do the same"'.[66] Lady Howe was invited to serve as the deputy chairman of the EOC, and Mrs Thatcher learnt of this with displeasure, feeling it might compromise Conservative positions on the subject. Using the MP Peter Rees* as an intermediary, she raised the matter with Geoffrey Howe, who sent Rees a rather characteristically hangdog reply ('I understand your anxiety') which nevertheless defended his wife's appointment.[67] The matter was to rumble on into Mrs Thatcher's time in office, and it gave her the ineradicable impression that Howe was rather unmanly in the way he veered between two powerful women – his wife and her. Lady Howe had something of the same feeling, later suggesting that her husband was at fault in not complaining about his ill treatment. She liked to quote John Biffen's image, also from the insect world, that she and Mrs Thatcher were 'like two wasps in a jam-jar'.[68]

Mrs Thatcher was always irritated by Geoffrey Howe's quiet, almost inaudible voice, his tendency to be long-winded and his slightly pudgy, soft, bespectacled demeanour. He was never dashing, and she liked dash. Howe saw his own role as the patient antidote to her 'reluctance to think ahead', and it was partly his very patience which made her cross. She was intelligent, he believed, but there was 'an intellectual void which others had to fill'.[69] In Chris Patten's view, he was 'like a country solicitor with an increasingly demanding client'.[70] Howe acidly recalled that 'Unlike most men, she hadn't appeared to learn that you don't rebuke officers in front of other ranks.'[71] These temperamental differences led Mrs Thatcher to suspect, falsely, that Howe was not to be relied on in the fight for the economic change she wanted. He had not been her first choice as shadow Chancellor, and most of the period in opposition was punctuated by her half-hearted attempts to move him. In November 1975, she told Humphrey Atkins that she wanted

---

* Peter Rees (1926–2008), educated Stowe and Christ Church, Oxford; Conservative MP for Dover, 1970–74; for Dover and Deal, 1974–83; for Dover, 1983–7; Chief Secretary to the Treasury, 1983–5; created Lord Rees, 1988.

Howe to have the Home Office portfolio and Keith Joseph as shadow Chancellor,[72] though in the end she was dissuaded and relieved her frustration by sacking Reggie Maudling instead. Sixteen months later, when an election seemed imminent and Mrs Thatcher was wondering who should be her Chancellor of the Exchequer if she won, she again expressed anxiety about Howe, questioning his competence. But party managers, worried that she was bad at communicating with the left of the party, saw Howe as one of that wing. She was not good with him or with Jim Prior, they agreed, but she needed to make it clear that both men would keep their jobs if the Tories won.[73] Howe stuck it out, and did more than any other politician to prepare the Conservatives to rescue the British economy. Norman Strauss,* one of the most radical of those involved in the Thatcher project, remembered Howe with admiration: 'We all thought Geoffrey Howe was great. He seemed to have the greatest understanding of what we were about.'[74]

All the tensions, personal and ideological, tactical and strategic, which beset Mrs Thatcher's period in opposition were at their tautest on the question of incomes policy and of what to do about trade unions. The subject involved both high principle and low tactics, and it evoked bitter dispute about the recent history of the Conservatives and why the 1974 elections had been lost. No believer in a free economy could seriously suggest that the government should make itself permanently responsible for the level of wages employers paid their workers. On the other hand, the coming of inflation had thrown workers into fierce competition for wage increases and no government, many believed, could afford to stand aside from this. This was most obviously the case in the public sector, where the government produced the money. At a time when many of the 'commanding heights' of British industry were in the hands of the government, a pay policy, in fact if not in name, seemed inevitable. The idea that it was the government's job to control the supply of money in the economy and the employers' job to settle wages with employees at whatever both parties could agree seemed simultaneously too radical to understand and too old-fashioned to countenance.

Talking to Ted Heath in March 1977, the journalist Hugo Young recorded, 'The note of contempt for Thatcher and her team remains unabated. If they get in, Ted says, "They wouldn't know what to do" about the unions and economic policy. But they would be driven, he says, to a

---

* Norman Strauss (1936–), educated Kilburn Grammar School; worked for Unilever, 1961–81; part-time member, Prime Minister's Policy Unit, 1979–82; co-founder, Oxford Strategic Leadership Programme, 1982.

form of incomes policy. "But they would have wasted all this time ... Why won't people learn the lessons of the past?"[75] The feeling of the time is conveyed by an interview given to the *Observer* in the summer of 1975 by the Canadian-born guru of the economic left J. K. Galbraith. 'America's celebrated economist explains ... why pay and price curbs will be a permanent feature, both in Britain and in every other industrial nation,' said the paper, by way of introduction, 'and argues that the monetarists who oppose this view are romantics who should be "cherished only for their irrelevance".'[76] The Labour government's counter-inflation policy will 'last forever', said Galbraith, and monetarists 'should be treated as museum pieces'.[77] This was the orthodoxy of the age, and it required some intellectual self-confidence to resist it. By the end of the twentieth century, no Western country had price and pay curbs.

In moral though not in intellectual terms, the subject of incomes policy was even harder for Conservatives to handle than for Labour. The history of the 1930s had taught the Tories to fear unemployment above all things, and had linked them with high unemployment in the public mind. To people like Heath and Jim Prior, a pay policy was an earnest that government would not stand aside and let chill economic winds blow where they would. Drawing on the instincts of wartime solidarity that dominated peacetime rhetoric for more than thirty years after 1945, they promoted the idea of everyone pulling together, tightening their belts and making necessary sacrifices for the common good. Rather like the RAF commander in the *Beyond the Fringe* sketch sending a pilot up with the instruction not to return, they believed that 'We need a futile gesture at this stage.' For many voters, this had a strong emotional appeal, and there was constant indecision in the public mind, exemplified in both the general election results of 1974, about which party could better deal with these problems. Ted Heath somehow got the worst of both worlds, linked to a pay policy yet regarded as 'confrontational'. He had won a lot of support from people who wanted to 'take on the miners'. But a fairly marginal majority seemed to think that Labour was a better bet because it could 'get on with the unions'. To someone like Prior, it followed that the Conservatives risked permanent exclusion from power unless they could convince voters that they had a friendly working relationship with trade union bosses. To do this, agreement about pay and prices to 'control' inflation would have to be reached.

At root, Mrs Thatcher did not agree with this. Her nature revolted against the notion that trade union leaders should have anything to do with deciding economic policy, or even general levels of wages. She was in principle opposed to the idea that it was the business of government to negotiate pay, except for its direct employees. And since she did not believe that inflation was caused by wage rises – inflation being, in the monetarist phrase, 'a disease of money' – she was quite sure that prices and incomes policies could not cure anything, although she did think they could sometimes be justified on grounds of emergency. Nor did she share Prior's view that unemployment levels must be kept artificially low at all times. She wanted people to have jobs, of course, but they must be what she called 'real jobs', not those created or maintained just to make the figures look good. On the other hand, she shared Prior's political anxieties. She had seen how the Heath Industrial Relations Act had collapsed, and although she had no temperamental aversion to a fight with the trade union leaders, she had seen what had happened when the Tories picked one which they then lost. She therefore listened to Prior, and other cautious voices, notably Willie Whitelaw's, while trying all the time to push the argument on.

The process was necessary but painful. In the summer of 1976 Prior produced a paper on employment policy for the Shadow Cabinet. Mrs Thatcher's copy shows her leaving untouched the more general parts of the argument – 'we . . . must convince the public (and as far as possible the unions themselves) that we are not antipathetic towards trade unions and do not seek a major confrontation.' She becomes tetchy, however, whenever Prior starts to make specific recommendations. When he urges that under Labour's new employment law employees should be 'reassured' that it 'does *not* mean that they must either join a union or lose their jobs', Mrs Thatcher scribbles, 'But it does.' When Prior floats the idea of a 'deal' allowing some secondary picketing in return for limitations on the number of pickets, Mrs Thatcher writes, 'Why?'[78] She was instinctively more attracted to Keith Joseph's private suggestions, brought together later, at the beginning of 1977, that blame should be laid where blame was due: 'Trades unions and the Labour Party are the manifestations of the same purposes. Their common aim has become to usurp political and economic power.' Joseph advocated a programme of educating the public that the medicine required would take 'at least five years' and would involve confronting the unions.[79]

Hating confrontation, but wanting real reform, Geoffrey Howe searched for a middle way. In a paper called 'Our Attitude towards Pay Policy', which he submitted to the Leader's Steering Committee (a more directed and smaller version of the Shadow Cabinet) in the spring of 1977, he said that free collective bargaining, though desirable, was not enough. He warned against believing that rank-and-file trade unionists would oppose their leaders: 'is there not a great underlying sense of loyalty to the movement? . . . Clearly no government would wish to have such a powerful influence pitted against its entire economic policy.'[80] Howe's Economic Reconstruction Group duly came up with a paper, drafted by Adam Ridley, which advocated a version of German 'Concerted Action'. Using the word 'consensus', which was always a red rag to Mrs Thatcher, it sought a 'united national commitment to sensible policies'. Mrs Thatcher wrote on top of her copy: 'Please tell Geoffrey Howe and Adam Ridley that I <u>disagree most strongly</u> with this paper. We are trying to cut down advisory bodies and requests for statistics – not multiply them.'[81] Trying to explain, Howe sent her a learned paper by a German economist about how Concerted Action would work. This made matters much worse: 'This paper frightens me to death <u>even more</u>. We really must avoid some of this terrible jargon [for Mrs Thatcher, an attack on 'jargon' was often a disguised attack on substance]. Also we should recognise that this German talking shop <u>works</u> <u>because</u> it consists of Germans.'[82]

Mrs Thatcher became increasingly cross at the thought that 'talking shops' might be the answer to the problems of prices and wage bargaining, and this coloured her approach to *The Right Approach to the Economy*, the document intended to follow up *The Right Approach*, which appeared in time for the party conference of October 1977. Drafts of the document, chiefly from the pen of David Howell, tried to give a role to the National Economic Development Council (NEDC), a corporatist body of the kind Mrs Thatcher detested. It even envisaged a formal link between the NEDC and a parliamentary committee, adding that 'The West German experience offers some useful lessons.' Beside this, Mrs Thatcher wrote 'Why?', and her copy of the draft had question marks all over it.[83] With her support, Joseph tried to strengthen those sections which dealt with incomes policy. A few days later, a harassed Adam Ridley wrote to her to say that 'The process of drafting has, I suspect, proved almost impossible.'[84] In the end, the lack of final agreement was such a problem that Mrs Thatcher decided that the paper should be published not as a Shadow Cabinet document, but under the names of its authors – Joseph, Prior, Howe and Howell. Its conclusion on incomes policy reflected the agonies – arguing why an incomes policy was a bad thing, but then weakly concluding that 'some kind of forum is desirable, where the major participants in the economy can sit down calmly together to consider the implications ... of the Government's fiscal and monetary policies.' In fact, Mrs Thatcher more or less held the line in public, trying to take a stand against mandatory incomes policy, but speaking of not returning to free collective bargaining too suddenly. But she was impatient about the crablike progress of the whole enterprise. 'I never felt much affection for *The Right Approach to the Economy*,' she wrote in her memoirs.[85]

The difference between what Mrs Thatcher felt could be said in public and in private was marked. In her 1977 party conference speech, she avoided concentrating on incomes policy and sought to show how any confrontation with the unions under the Conservatives would be not unions versus government but unions versus people. In private, though, she was much more explicit. In a handwritten letter to Jack Peel, a right-wing trade unionist, two weeks earlier, she explained why even voluntary incomes policies did not work: 'Any voluntary guideline divorces employees' rewards from the success of the enterprise. That cannot be right.' She went on: 'We are constantly talking in terms of <u>restraint</u> – whereas all my correspondence refers to phrases as "make it worthwhile to work" . . . Sooner or later we must talk in terms of incentive.' She admitted the problem that those with the biggest industrial strength got the biggest increases: 'It has been aggravated in the nationalised industries because of their monopoly position. The irony is that "public ownership" has therefore resulted in sharply rising prices because of bargaining power. It is the power given <u>by</u> the people being used <u>against</u> the people.'[86]

The problem of union power also took particularly contentious form in the course of 1977 because of the dispute at Grunwick. The firm, a photographic processing plant in north-west London, had dismissed a number of workers in a dispute the previous year. Some of those dismissed had then joined the APEX trade union which demanded 'recognition' from Grunwick, and the reinstatement of the sacked workers. A court upheld the legality of the dismissals, and a secret ballot at Grunwick showed that 80 per cent of those working at the plant did not want to join any union. By the summer of 1977, the dispute had become a cause célèbre with the left, with huge pickets trying to prevent workers and mail going in and out of the plant. The pickets were briefly joined by two supposedly moderate Cabinet ministers, Shirley Williams and Fred Mulley, and the Labour government stood back from condemning the scenes of violence. Although the row was not strictly about union membership, it came to be seen as a battle about the closed shop which, it was expected, APEX would seek to impose on Grunwick if it prevailed. It also brought home to people the street-power of the left – the sense, as with the Saltley coke depot under Heath, that government and police did not have the power or the will to impose order in the face of industrial intimidation.

Mrs Thatcher was shocked by Grunwick, and everyone knew where her sympathies lay. She sent Adam Butler and Barney Hayhoe,* an MP close to Jim Prior, to accompany the workers to the plant so that they could accurately report the level of intimidation to her. But it was not in any way due to her that the plant kept in business. The National Association for

---

* Barney Hayhoe (1925–), educated state schools and Borough Polytechnic; Conservative MP for Heston and Isleworth, 1970–74; for Brentford and Isleworth, 1974–92; Minister of State, Treasury, 1981–5; Minister of State for Health, DHSS, 1985–6; created Lord Hayhoe, 1992.

Freedom, which the murdered Ross McWhirter had helped set up to counter what it saw as left-wing intimidation, managed to smuggle out Grunwick's mail which had been illegally blacked by the postmen's union. The Conservatives, while naturally condemning violence and lawlessness, kept their distance. In part this was because of doubts raised by other industrialists about George Ward, the owner of Grunwick. In his weekly letter to Mrs Thatcher, John Sparrow warned her of strong reaction to press stories that she was personally close to Ward: 'There would be quite a lot of unhappiness if it were felt that there was a close relationship between you and Mr Ward.'[87] Partly this was because Ward's personal business behaviour was criticized, but the wider reason was that a great many businessmen, particularly those in large companies, were in favour of the closed shop. They told the Conservatives that they found it simpler to negotiate with only one group of people.

This irritated Mrs Thatcher, who considered such people spineless, but it also inclined her to listen more to Jim Prior about the need to go slowly in trying to change trade union law. Indeed, objectively, though not emotionally, she moved closer to the Prior position than to that of Keith Joseph. While she was in the United States for her second visit there as party leader in early September 1977, Lord Scarman's inquiry into the Grunwick dispute recommended the reinstatement of the dismissed (now APEX) workers. This caused a public disagreement between Prior and Joseph. Joseph condemned Scarman and appeared to call for the outlawing of the closed shop. Mrs Thatcher, at a disadvantage because she was in Washington, was forced to pronounce. She felt she had little choice but to support Prior who was, after all, her party's spokesman on the subject. 'We do not like the closed shop,' she told a press conference hijacked by this subject when she wanted it to be about her meeting with President Jimmy Carter. 'We do not think it is right. We are against it . . . But because I do not like it, and think it is against the freedom of the individual, does not necessarily mean that I can pass legislation about it.'[88] Her interview on *Weekend World* the following Sunday, the first of many she was to have with Brian Walden, illustrated the delicacy of her situation. Walden began by saying that the Grunwick dispute raised the question 'If we vote Margaret Thatcher into No. 10 . . . will we be voting for a disastrous and futile confrontation between the government and the unions?' Asked about trade union legislation, Mrs Thatcher played it down, saying that it would be 'Not of the kind that Ted had . . . It didn't work.' The only legislation on the closed shop would be against its 'worst aspects'. Walden pursued her about what would happen if a Conservative government were again confronted by the miners as in February 1974. Without having squared this with colleagues in advance, Mrs Thatcher came up with the arresting idea that if – which she claimed was unlikely – agreement could not be reached, the issue could be put to a referendum, on the grounds that 'all of the people of this country are shareholders in miners'. She quoted her own remarks about the 1975 referendum on remaining in the EEC to argue that this was a legitimate way, for constitutional issues, of 'letting the people speak'.[89] Her line enabled her to reach over the heads of trade union leaders and claim that rank-and-file trade unionists would be on her side. It also enabled her to deflect press attention from the Joseph–Prior disagreements about union reform. But it was no solution to those disagreements and it was, in essence, a different way of asking the 'Who governs Britain?' question that had caused the Heath government so much grief. A working group looked into the referendum idea, and Mrs Thatcher later referred to it from time to time, but it never became, in her view or anyone else's, the answer.

Perhaps burnt by this experience of internal disagreement publicly displayed, Mrs Thatcher became increasingly protective of Jim Prior's exclusive right to pronounce on trade union matters. At the beginning of January 1978, Geoffrey Howe sent her a draft of a speech which he proposed to make about the unions. Her notes on it are almost the angriest she penned while leader of the Opposition. She disliked both what she saw as his weakness in being too nice to the unions and his unwisdom in trespassing into the subject at all. When Howe wrote, 'These questions do not involve any special criticism of trade unions,' Mrs Thatcher wrote, 'Ha, ha!' When he said that change should be made 'step by step', she wrote 'Why.' 'Too defensive,' she scrawled, '– If you can only be defensive – leave it alone!' 'Geoffrey – This is not your subject. Why go on with it – the press will crucify you for this … It would be better if Jim Prior said these things.'[90] Much frustration is contained in her notes – at the hesitations of policy, at the need for those hesitations, at Shadow Cabinet indiscipline, and at the personality of poor Geoffrey Howe himself. His text was not delivered.

The uncomfortableness of the whole subject of the trade unions in the period of opposition comes through very clearly in the diaries and memory of John Hoskyns. Hoskyns, who had no previous association with the Conservative Party, had sold his successful computer company to devote himself to finding some way of rescuing Britain from its economic malaise. He had come on the scene through the agency of Keith Joseph. After a successful first meeting, set up by Joseph, between Hoskyns and Norman Strauss, and Mrs Thatcher, in August 1976, a second, in which they were to offer her their thoughts for her party conference speech, was a disaster. Sitting, with Margaret and Denis, in what Hoskyns described in his diary as 'her rather boringly elegant drawing room' in Flood Street, they tried to give her a speech structure about how 'change and recovery were possible if people believed it enough to act on that assumption'. 'She nitpicked Norman's semantics ... defensively holding forth, lecturing us on things we were quite well aware of. I showed slight irritation once & Mr T looked at me, stunned that I shouldn't be party to the inevitable mild sycophancy which makes her feel she's so much more remarkable than she is. She is a limited, pedantic bore, with no lateral grasp, very little humour. I may be wrong but that was my view. God help the Tories ...'[91]* Hoskyns and Strauss persisted, however. Their aim was to get it into Tory heads that the unions had to be confronted in order to bring about the economic changes required. At the same time, they were as aware as anyone that the prospect of confrontation was electorally disastrous, and that a confrontation for which a Conservative government was not prepared would be even worse than no confrontation at all. In a letter to Joseph in June 1977, Hoskyns wrestled with the problem of how to implement the right economic policies. The 'key question', he said, was 'What political innovation is needed to remove the political constraints on government's freedom to pursue such policies?'[92]

The result was a process known as Stepping Stones designed to produce a plan for preparing the ground, campaigning and then governing. Hoskyns explained to Joseph that he was following the business concept of the 'critical path'. By mid-November 1977 the first report was ready. It said that the 'one major obstacle' to the national recovery which the Tories sought was 'the negative role of the trade unions' and that 'To compete with Labour in peaceful coexistence with an unchanged union movement will ensure continued economic decline.'[93] What Hoskyns called the 'secret garden' had a key marked 'trade union power'.[94] Stepping Stones tried to establish a project, both to unstitch the unions in public debate and to get the Tories to make explicit commitments to trade union reform which would give them an electoral mandate on which the Civil Service would have to work if they won office.[95] At a working supper in the Commons which Hoskyns regarded as the 'turning-point', Mrs Thatcher endorsed the report. On this occasion, Hoskyns saw her virtues more clearly, but some of his criticisms stood: 'Margaret's key contribution is guts and determination and a complete lack of the self-importance and pomposity which would make it so hard for many politicians to take advice of this kind. She

* The evening was not helped by the fact that, at one point, the cat stroked Norman Strauss's leg and then Mrs Thatcher's. She started, apparently thinking for a second that Strauss had been stroking her leg, and was then embarrassed. (Interview with Norman Strauss.)

is quite limited intellectually ... and philosophically. The problem intellectually ... is that she is unaware of the fact that other people's intelligence may be superior to her own.'[96] Emboldened, Stepping Stones then set up small groups to investigate details such as the payment of benefits to strikers' families, involving people like Nigel Lawson, David Howell and Norman Lamont.

A battle then ensued, along fairly predictable lines, with Jim Prior, Lord Thorneycroft, Ian Gilmour and Chris Patten most opposed. Their opposition was ideological, but also tactical. Patten saw Stepping Stones as the work of the CPS, which he greatly disliked. Many years later, he described the document as an 'inflexible strategy' which 'read as though it lay somewhere between a management consultant's brief and a plan of battle. It showed little political understanding or touch.'[97] In a paper called 'Further Thoughts on Strategy' written at the end of February 1978, he tried to push Stepping Stones to one side: 'The authors of "Stepping Stones" have described their political strategy in terms of painstakingly building a model of St Paul's with matchsticks. I would use a different metaphor. A successful strategy is like an artillery bombardment with half a dozen properly targeted heavy guns.' Stepping Stones should therefore be confined to an 'up-market campaign' 'without interfering with any of our other plans'.[98] Patten's 'heavy guns' would aim at tax, law and order, housing, education and other matters. On the subject of the unions, they were silent. Although Patten used the word 'strategy', his approach was not strategic, but tactical.

As the Patten paper approached, Hoskyns confided his fears to his diary:

> the breathtaking vision and innovation which the situation calls for is [sic] not going to come from Thatcher – of that I am almost certain. Alfred has been warning of a 'putsch' against her from Prior, Whitelaw, Gilmour – but this seems unlikely at such a time. Pym is seen as the successor ... it seems a preposterous fear. But there's no doubt she does not lead and manage her Shadow Cabinet. There is much press criticism (leaks by Patten, Alfred says) of this and of her failure to debate policy and philosophy.[99]

Had Hoskyns been allowed to attend the meeting of the Steering Committee on 30 January 1978, he would have been even more depressed. With a remarkable frankness which led Mrs Thatcher to write on them a note to Ryder saying 'Richard – please keep in safe,' the minutes recorded her as saying that there was 'too much detail in the "Stepping Stones" paper ... it was generally desirable for members to exercise self-discipline on the problem of the unions. Mrs Thatcher stressed that Mr Prior would lead the campaign and would speak where appropriate.' They went on: 'When Mr Davies [John Davies, who had replaced Reggie Maudling as shadow foreign secretary] argued that if we told the truth about the unions we should certainly lose the election, Mrs Thatcher acknowledged that this could not be the centrepiece of our strategy.'[100] In the end, bursting with frustration, Hoskyns and Strauss went to see Mrs Thatcher to tell her to get rid of Prior. She naturally refused and 'thought we were naive',[101] but 'She was not too put out by it. I think she sees Jim as a disaster in the context of any really intelligent and resolute plan for recovery ... Now he's in a very strong position and, with an election pending, she can do nothing.'[102]

It might have been a comfort to Hoskyns to have known that some people on the other side of this argument felt equally uneasy. In an interview given privately that summer, Chris Patten said that the moderates dominated the Shadow Cabinet and the draft of the manifesto, but 'had to lie low because of the impossible behaviour of Ted'. Patten set up Mrs Thatcher's future behaviour towards Adam Ridley as the litmus test of her own moderation.[103] As the election expected in October 1978 approached, the Tories fought themselves to a stalemate. Mrs Thatcher's heart was with Joseph, Stepping Stones and taking on the unions. She realized that Stepping Stones 'gave her a clear, practical and intellectual path which she didn't have before'.[104] But her head was with those – who included the ideologically supportive Gordon Reece – who argued that a fuzzier, more cautious approach was electorally necessary. As late as 22 August, Airey Neave told David Butler in a private interview that it had taken eighteen months' work to move Mrs Thatcher towards centre position on the trade unions and to accept the Prior approach.[105] She was trapped in moderation. But Jim Callaghan's decision about the date of the election was to make a huge difference to the type of campaign she eventually felt able to fight.

14

Labour Isn't Working

'I know what. You tell me how'

In the autumn of 1977, Arnold Ashdown, one of the joint treasurers of the Conservative Party, died, and a memorial service was held for him in north London, attended by all living Tory leaders. Ashdown was Jewish, and so all the men, as well as Mrs Thatcher, wore hats for the ceremony. In appearance, each leader fulfilled his popular caricature. Harold Macmillan wore an Edwardian silk top hat. Alec Home had on the more modest Homburg that had been customary in his youth. Ted Heath forgot that a hat was needed at all, and had to borrow a paper yarmulke from the Jewish organizers. Mrs Thatcher, in the view of those present, stole the show, looking striking all in black, with a hat with a very large brim.[1] The occasion was a small example of how she was successfully achieving a presence on the public stage.

For all her inexperience, nervousness and social insecurity, she had undoubted public impact. She displayed the conspicuousness and panache which are inseparable from leadership. This was partly because of the uniqueness of her sex in her chosen sphere, but also owed much to her physical presence and her force of character. There were others within her party who had enjoyed far longer and more distinguished careers than she, but there was none, with the partial exception of Heath, who could rival the hold on the popular imagination which she was beginning to exert. She liked being seen; she liked being noticed; she liked leading. Michael Portillo,* then a young employee of the Conservative Research Department, was detailed to help in the campaign for the Cambridge by-election of November 1976. He had to meet Mrs Thatcher and her team early in the morning outside a pub in Trumpington. As she got hurriedly out of the

---

* Michael Portillo (1953–), educated Harrow County Boys' School and Peterhouse, Cambridge; Conservative MP for Enfield, Southgate, 1984–97; for Kensington and Chelsea, 1999–2005; Secretary of State for Employment, 1994–5; for Defence, 1995–7; unsuccessful candidate for the leadership of the Conservative Party, 2001.

car, she flashed her eyes at him and said, 'Take me to the battle!' Although
it was a semi-comic moment, it also impressed him deeply: 'She had a thing
about needing to look and play the part of leader.'[2]

No leader can play the part of future prime minister without a presence
on the international stage. It was the beginnings of this that Mrs Thatcher
had sought – and achieved – with her visit as party leader to the United
States in 1975. She had complemented this, in policy terms, with her 'Iron
Lady' speech the following year. She needed to overcome the disadvantage
that when she became leader, as Lord Carrington unkindly put it, 'She
hardly knew where Calais was.'[3]* In the ensuing years, she visited European capitals, the Middle East, China† and Australasia. All these helped
to some extent to build her reputation, and certainly increased her knowledge, but none had great impact on the public. More important, though
not wholly successful, was her second visit to the United States. The victory
of the Democrat, Jimmy Carter, over Gerald Ford, in the US presidential
election of 1976, had been marginally unhelpful to Mrs Thatcher's cause.
Although she did not have a very high opinion of Ford, her links to
Republicans were better than those to Democrats. Besides, Carter, with his
rather starry-eyed belief that the hearts of dictators could be changed by
the expression of the West's sincere desire for peace, was emotionally at
odds with her alert suspicion of the Soviet Union. So she saw the need
for new work – to establish friendly relations with the President and to

---

* Early in Mrs Thatcher's leadership, Jonathan Aitken got into trouble for his joke at a dinner
in Beirut that Mrs Thatcher 'probably thinks Sinai is the plural of sinus'. This got back to Airey
Neave, who made Aitken apologize to her. (Interview with Jonathan Aitken.)

† Mrs Thatcher's first visit to Communist China, in April 1977, was not politically eventful,
but it made an impression. Because of extreme Chinese hostility to the Soviet Union at that
time, she was welcomed with some pomp by the party leadership. She gave a reception for
which the invitation read:

Margaret Thatcher
At Home
In the Great Hall of the People

But she did not feel at home at all. John Gerson, the official who accompanied her and briefed
her, recalled that 'To say she was open-minded would be an insult. She understood they *were*
Communist, and she hated Communism' (interview with John Gerson). In background conversation with journalists, she predicted that 'the spark of human spirit' would be the undoing
of China and would eventually make India a more successful country (*Sunday Times*, 12 April
1977). In public, she described the Chinese approach as 'wholly alien to us. They have a correct
view, and they hand down that correct view ... Fortunately, we don't have a correct view'
(BBC Television interview, 14 April 1977). She was accompanied by Douglas Hurd, who had
served as a diplomat in China before entering politics. After she had been up the Great Wall,
she asked him, 'Did I get to the top quicker than Ted?' (George Gale, *Spectator*, 23 April 1977.)

maintain a flattering profile in a United States whose policy elites were now more likely to be in sympathy with the right wing of the Labour Party than with her.

A September visit was planned in March 1977, but before this took place Mrs Thatcher met Carter for the first time during his visit to Britain in May. The courtesy call, at Winfield House, the American Ambassador's residence in London, lasted for twenty minutes. Carter was accompanied by Cyrus Vance, the Secretary of State, and Zbigniew Brzezinski, his National Security Advisor. Brzezinski's assistant Robert Hunter, who was taking notes, recalled: 'The most striking and memorable thing about this meeting was how vigorous and enthusiastic Mrs Thatcher was. Carter was very impressed by this. And she endeared herself to Brzezinski at the very beginning: "Oh yes, Dr Brzezinski," she purred, "I spent all afternoon reading your books." This left Zbig immensely pleased.'[4] Brzezinski's contemporary diary confirms these recollections: 'P[resident] met with Thatcher in the evening. She impressed me as a shrewd and forceful politician. She amused me by mentioning a number of times that she had read several of my books ... Perhaps she would have done better to have read Carter's book. She didn't mention this at all(!)' Then Brzezinski sounded one note of anxiety: 'The views on Africa expressed by Thatcher ... were not quite what we would have liked. She did not come right out and say it, but I formed the distinct impression that she was inclined to support the white position.'[5] For her part, Mrs Thatcher later remembered a successful meeting 'in spite of my growing doubts about his foreign policy'.[6] The *New York Times* reported: 'Brimming with self-confidence, she told Mr Carter that her party would win the election no matter when it came, with the size of the majority the only matter in doubt.'[7] It was this desire to convince people that she was the Prime Minister in waiting, more than any policy issue, which shaped Mrs Thatcher's second US trip as leader. 'I'm the next government,' she told a group of American journalists. 'I think I should meet your Cabinet.'[8]

As the visit approached, certain obstacles presented themselves. Mrs Thatcher found the cursory briefing produced for her by the Foreign Office inadequate. 'She thinks it's terrible,' Caroline Stephens told Rob Shepherd of the Conservative Research Department, who was tasked with rewriting the document to Mrs Thatcher's more exacting standards.[9] More worryingly, the White House was trying to impose a rule upon itself that the President would not normally meet leaders of foreign opposition parties. The administration had already rejected just such a request from François Mitterrand, the leader of the French Socialists (and future President of France). In a memo for Carter, Brzezinski suggested that in light of this precedent 'and at the risk of offending Mrs. Thatcher, it seems to me that the principle should be established that opposition leaders meet with the Vice President, not you.' He advised Carter to 'plead a heavy schedule' and pass Mrs Thatcher off to the Vice-President.[10] Carter's aides may also have had ideological objections to Mrs Thatcher* and they certainly did not want to upset Callaghan, to whom they were close. Faced with these concerns, Carter dithered. 'Leave possibility open,' he wrote on Brzezinski's memo. 'Tell them either VP or I will see them.'[11] A good deal of bureaucratic toing and froing followed. In the end, according to a White House aide, 'It was due to the general closeness of the UK/US relationship that we agreed to see her. Peter Jay also intervened on her behalf and said, in effect, you ought to get to know this lady.'[12] Mrs Thatcher actually benefited from the fact that Peter Jay, the new British Ambassador in Washington, was Jim Callaghan's son-in-law, and therefore, since he was also not a professional diplomat but a journalist, a controversial appointment. Given his 'unusual connections' with the Labour government, Jay felt he should 'lean over backwards' to help Mrs Thatcher, so much so that David Owen,† the Foreign Secretary, felt he was going 'a little too far'.[13] She got her meeting with the President.

Before the meeting, Mrs Thatcher flew first to New York City. Emphasizing her commitment to free enterprise, she travelled on the fledgling, cut-price Laker Airways rather than British Airways, which was then still in public ownership. In her main speech there, to the British American Chamber of Commerce, she took as her text President Theodore Roosevelt's words that 'In this life we get nothing save by effort' and won applause from her audience for her attack on statist economic fallacies and her declaration that the Western world was now moving into a post-socialist era,[14] but media interest in her was less than in 1975, and the speech was not extensively reported. At a dinner given by NBC, she nearly fainted because of a combination of heat, exhaustion and a lifelong tendency to low blood pressure. Caroline Stephens who was on the trip, discussed the problem with Adam Butler, her PPS, and recorded it at the time: 'She retires and ACB [Butler] and I discuss these bouts which are really quite serious

---

* According to the late John Carbaugh, at that time aide to the right-wing Senator Jesse Helms, there was a concerted effort by Carter's people to prevent senior staff in the administration seeing Mrs Thatcher. Helms threatened to put Senate approval for some appointments to the executive branch 'on hold' unless Carter and his Defense Secretary, Harold Brown, agreed to see Mrs Thatcher. No corroboration of this account has been found.

† David Owen (1938–), educated Bradfield and Sidney Sussex College, Cambridge; Labour MP for Plymouth Sutton, 1966–74; for Plymouth Devonport, 1974–81; SDP MP for Plymouth Devonport, 1981–92; Foreign Secretary, 1977–9; Leader, SDP, 1983–7; created Lord Owen, 1992.

and we decide that she should really play the grande dame more and demand to sit down if she feels faint. But she is too polite and socially insecure.'[15]

The next stop was Houston, Texas, because, Mrs Thatcher explained, 'Houston helped Britain enormously with North Sea Oil – it is nice to say thank you to friends.'[16] The English Speaking Union organized a dinner at the River Oaks Country Club, though organized is scarcely the right word. Caroline Stephens recorded:

> No hairdresser for MT (as ordered); no one to press her dress (as ordered) and just to crown it MT got locked in the bathroom. Since we only had 40 minutes in all before arriving at the River Oaks Country Club for dinner these setbacks did not amuse MT and she became distinctly irritated apart from being up-tight which she always is before a major speech ... Chaos reigned for the remainder of the evening. There was no one to greet us ... and 500 people all very overdressed mostly already sitting down at their tables drinking cocktails. We entered unannounced as nobody recognised MT! Eventually dinner started without any formal announcement – toast to the Queen – long pause – MT supposed to toast the President but no one had warned her. However, she made a brilliant speech and got a standing ovation.[17]

Her speech was the sort of preaching to the converted at which Mrs Thatcher always excelled. She identified the 'common heritage' of British and American ideas and declared it under attack. 'The Christian values, which rest on Hebrew and Hellenic foundations ... family life, the innocence of children, public decency, respect for the law, pride in good work, patriotism, democracy' would all be undermined without a properly functioning free economy. 'Keynes ... is reputed to have said: "In the long run, we are all dead." But in the long run, our children and their children will live; let it be in freedom.' She announced her wish for Britain, with its new oil, to become 'the Texas of Europe' earning the money which would enable it to meet its NATO commitments.[18] Roy Fox, the Consul-General in Houston, was struck by the speech's power: 'It was a glorious banquet with the new rising star in total control of her listeners for some 45–50 minutes – with hardly a note in front of her. She manifestly gained in confidence ... They loved her more and more as the minutes ticked away. Her message could have been a bible for the Republican Party.'[19] A slightly more equivocal form of compliment was given her by the man who introduced her at the dinner, one George H. W. Bush,* billed by the *Daily*

---

* George Bush (1924–), Vice-President of the United States of America, 1981–9; President, 1989–93.

Telegraph as 'the former head of the CIA'. He said Mrs Thatcher was 'a bright lady ... frighteningly bright'.[20] The impression he took away was of 'a woman with a very forceful personality'.[21] The future President's nervous praise foreshadowed some of their later interactions.

Mrs Thatcher then flew to Washington, and into an atmosphere of unease. She was met at the airport by Peter Jay and the television cameras, and taken to the Embassy, where she was staying. Caroline Stephens recorded: 'I got an explosion from MT while I was helping her to change; "This visit is going to be worse than I feared – P.J. doing everything for his own self-aggrandissment [sic]; cameras at the airport were for him not for me; pointless briefing; they told me nothing new; I have better contacts than they do; they are all socialist and hostile" (rather unjustified I thought as Lord Bridges [the relevant Foreign Office official] had given her an energy brief).'[22] These slights were more imagined than real, and in fact by the end of her stay she had become very appreciative of the efforts which the Jays made for her; but there was a grain of truth in her fears. 'There is no doubt about it but that the FO is hostile to MT,' Stephens wrote in her diary, '– there is an obvious reason for this in that almost all the ones I know vote Socialist.'[23]

As for the serious politics of her Washington visit, it was Rhodesia which gave her the greatest trouble. At the beginning of the month, David Owen and Andrew Young, Carter's Ambassador to the United Nations, had put forward a plan for transition from Ian Smith's white minority government in Rhodesia to majority rule (the government was illegal because it had unilaterally declared Rhodesia's independence from Britain in 1965). But the pitch for this plan had been queered by Carter's earlier announcement, at the beginning of August, that he had unilaterally agreed with President Julius Nyerere of Tanzania that the existing (largely white) Rhodesian security forces would need to be disbanded and the army of the new nation would be 'based on the liberation armies' that were fighting the guerrilla war against Smith. This threat strengthened Smith's position with his white tribe at home (he won every seat in Parliament in the elections of 31 August 1977) and upset the British. Mrs Thatcher told *Time* magazine that the disbanding of the Rhodesian security forces 'could introduce a destabilising factor',[24] and was ready to say the same to Carter in person. The Shadow Foreign Secretary John Davies, who accompanied her in Washington, did not share her robust views and they had a lengthy row over the issue before seeing Carter. Mrs Thatcher did not relent. 'Why did I ever ask him [Davies] to join me,' she later fumed to Caroline Stephens, 'he can't possibly take that view on Rhodesia; if he carries on like that I shall have to tell him to shut up etc.'[25] Meeting Cyrus Vance, the Secretary of State, the day before she saw Carter,

Mrs Thatcher made her views clear. 'She is strongly opposed to including any black "terrorists" in the Rhodesian Army – which she likened to the British Army accepting elements of the Irish Republican Army,' Vance reported to the President. 'I hope they are not giving support to Smith,' Carter wrote in the margin.[26] In his briefing for Carter before the meeting in the Oval Office, Vance struck a pessimistic note: 'We will be lucky if her US visit passes without further public acknowledgement on her part of strong opposition to key elements of the UK–US plan.'[27]

The meeting, though certainly friendly, was not wholly easy. Gregory Treverton of the National Security Council (NSC), who was present, remembered:

> Mrs Thatcher spoke very nicely but very aggressively when addressing President Carter. It soon appeared that she had launched into a campaign speech, rather as if she were addressing the Rotary Club. Carter was such a sweet man that he didn't seem to mind and just sat there listening. Walter Mondale [the Vice-President] however started to squirm. Finally Carter got a word in edgeways. Assuming she would be well versed in international issues he asked her: 'What would your view be on a CTB?' There was silence. You could see Mrs Thatcher frantically rifling through her mental card file but to no avail. Eventually John Davies tactfully prompted her, reminding her that Carter was talking about the Comprehensive Test Ban.[28]

Mondale himself recalled:

> Margaret Thatcher was very clear and instructive [that is, giving instructions] on how the US approach was all wrong. Rhodesia, she insisted, needed to be given a chance to work itself out. Carter didn't say anything, but I knew him well. There was a blood vessel in his neck that used to throb when he got irritated. And when Margaret Thatcher got onto the subject of Rhodesia it started to throb with a vengeance. It wasn't the fact that she disagreed with him, but it was the way she did it. She was imperious.[29]

A similar impression was collected by the Secretary of Defense, Harold Brown, who, at a separate meeting with Mrs Thatcher, got something close to a dressing-down on the Carter administration's soft attitude to arms control: 'A mutual friend had told me, "She's not the sort of person you would find very agreeable on a one-to-one dinner date," and I swiftly reached the same conclusion.'[30]

At the press conference after the meeting, Mrs Thatcher naturally avoided any impression of disagreement with Carter, although she did stress her anxiety about the disbanding of the Rhodesian security forces, but there was a slightly uncomfortable overall impression about her relations with the new administration. Friendly Americans felt it too. Henry Kissinger recalled that 'She came to Washington and foolishly the Carter people did not receive her so I gave dinner for her every night she was in Washington . . . it seemed to me she felt snubbed by the Carter adminis- tration but she did not show her frustration.'[31] In fact, Dr Kissinger's memory was mistaken – he gave only one dinner for Mrs Thatcher – but he was not wrong in remembering a rather frosty atmosphere at the White House. Mrs Thatcher consoled herself by meeting Jesse Helms and with what Caroline Stephens called 'private and disturbingly rightwing meet- ings',[32] including one with Major General George Keegan Jr who had recently retired as chief of USAF intelligence. Keegan had argued, after his retirement, that the Soviet Union had overtaken the US in military power and could now survive a nuclear war in its network of underground shel- ters, and win it.[33] Ronald Reagan had used Keegan's pronouncements in his own public utterances, and Mrs Thatcher was fascinated by his gloomy warnings.

A combination of this unspoken tension with Carter's people and the intrusion of party rows about the closed shop back home (see Chapter 13) proved too much for Mrs Thatcher. Before flying home on 14 September 1977, she gave an informal but on-the-record briefing to the press in the drawing room of the Ambassador's residence. It quickly went wrong. Peter Jay was witness:

> The journalists got on to the issue of the White House press spokesman on television as the voice of the administration. They regarded the US system as far superior to the British system, which was dominated by the lobby journalists [who have privileged access to the Houses of Parliament]. They raised this, thinking they would have a background chat, as Callaghan would have done. Mrs Thatcher took it differently. She considered it an attack on Britain. She got very angry. She gave a real hectoring speech – an O Level on the responsibilities of ministers and accountability to Parliament. This got worse and worse. And then suddenly, she stood up and walked out. I followed her as the dutiful host – we went all the way down the long marble corridors to the other end of the house and the library. And then I saw – she was in tears – tears of rage I think, partly. I had to give her several whiskies to restore equilibrium.[34]

When Mrs Thatcher reached London, she wanted to hide. The *Financial Times* reported: 'She was in no mood to receive the battery of reporters and photographers which met her at Heathrow Airport . . . A spokesman said: "Mrs Thatcher has absolutely nothing to say. She made a statement before leaving Washington, and I am afraid she has nothing to add."'[35]

Although the *Guardian* reported, following White House private briefing, that her attitude to Rhodesia had made the Carter administration 'uneasy',[36] there had been no public breach and the courtesies had been perfectly well maintained. She had gone down well in New York, and a storm in Houston, but she knew that her Washington visit had not been politically successful, and that, in a world naturally hostile to opposition leaders, she was if anything more friendless than she had been two years earlier. As she returned to her party's divisions about trade unions, she had reason to feel dispirited.

Because it is easy and, in many ways, accurate to portray Mrs Thatcher as a conviction politician, other vital aspects of her style of leadership are too readily neglected. One was the skills of the performer, which Michael Portillo had already noticed. Another was the skills of the party manager. It was said at the time, and throughout her career, that Mrs Thatcher was a poor manager of her Shadow Cabinets and Cabinets. This is true in the sense that she often affronted the *amour-propre* of colleagues, and could be surprisingly disorderly in the transaction of business. But, particularly in the 1970s, she was a skilled manager of her wider party, both in Parliament and in the country, and adept at preserving a working coalition of opinion at the top of the party. She knew she was on probation, and operating in a hung Parliament. She listened to the Chief Whip, Atkins, and to Willie Whitelaw, and was endlessly patient in attending to the party grassroots and to backbenchers. Once she had worked out those issues – chiefly economic – which she regarded as the key to national recovery, she was usually happy to treat everything else with an eye more to party unity than to doctrinal purity.

Rhodesia is a case in point. In March 1978, ignoring the 1977 initiative of the Callaghan and Carter administrations, the Rhodesian Prime Minister, Ian Smith, reached an 'internal settlement' for a form of majority rule with significant elements of the black population, led by Bishop Abel Muzorewa. The agreement was immediately denounced by Robert Mugabe* and Joshua Nkomo, the main black leaders fighting the civil war, and by most of the 'international community'. To many Conservatives, however, who had always been uncomfortable with what they saw as the persecution of 'our kith and kin' in Rhodesia, Smith's ability to make a deal seemed

---

* Robert Mugabe (1924–), educated Kutama Mission School, Rhodesia and Fort Hare University, South Africa; co-founded Zimbabwe African National Union (ZANU), 1963; detained in Rhodesia, 1964–74; led insurgency from Mozambique, 1975–9; Prime Minister, Zimbabwe, 1980–87; President 1988–.

laudable, and the party leadership came under pressure to support it. These sentiments, strongly backed by Denis, who knew the region well, were Mrs Thatcher's own. Echoing Lord Randolph Churchill's famous inflammatory comment about Ulster ninety years earlier, she told an *ad hoc* party policy meeting on the subject that if Marxist Mugabe were allowed to come to power, 'The whites will fight, and the whites will be right.'[37] An arrangement which kept whites in the country and united them with moderate blacks was really her ideal, and she was passionate in her dislike of the Soviet-backed Marxists who helped arm, train and inspire many of the guerrillas. She duly supported what had happened, but without committing herself to it in full. The fact that black and white in Rhodesia needed one another laid 'the foundations of a lasting settlement', she said.[38] But when the pressure increased for the Conservatives to nail their colours to the Smith–Muzorewa mast, Mrs Thatcher became very cautious.

As the Conservatives' annual party conference approached, an amendment was put down by party representatives to support the unilateral lifting of sanctions against Rhodesia as a positive response to the internal settlement. When the Shadow Cabinet discussed the matter the week before the conference, Mrs Thatcher asked for very full minutes to be kept to help those preparing for Blackpool. These show Lord Carrington, though he was not shadow foreign secretary, leading resistance to the amendment on the grounds that it would be a diplomatic disaster and would prevent a Tory government from being a 'bridge between the various parties'. They also show Mrs Thatcher looking for some way of calming matters down at the conference, rather than expressing any personal preference for or against sanctions: 'Mrs Thatcher suggested that the obvious response would be on the lines that we understood and sympathised with the powerful emotions of the floor, but could not accept that the motion would bind any future Conservative government.'[39] At the conference, the feared revolt duly took place and John Davies's weak speech on behalf of the Shadow Cabinet was savaged from the floor. (It later turned out that Davies had been suffering from an acute headache caused by the brain tumour which was to kill him a few months later.) In her memoirs, Mrs Thatcher describes Carrington's line as 'contorted and unpopular',[40] but she acquiesced in it at the time. When the renewal of sanctions came to the vote in the House of Commons, the frontbench decision to abstain caused the largest Tory rebellion since the Second World War, with 114 Conservatives disobeying the whip and two frontbenchers, John Biggs-Davison and Winston Churchill, resigning. Mrs Thatcher later claimed that she would rather have opposed the renewal, and explained her decision to back abstention purely in terms of party management: 'it was better to have a full-scale backbench revolt than to lose members of the Shadow Cabinet at this delicate juncture,'[41] the 'delicate juncture' being the fact that the general election, though delayed, was certain within a year, and that the party was faltering in the polls and continued to be publicly split on incomes policy. She used a technique which was to serve her well in many tight spots – to make clear her sympathy with grass-roots, usually right-wing, feeling while giving the party establishment most of what it wanted.

Rhodesia evoked particularly strong emotions in Tory breasts, but it was a much easier issue for Mrs Thatcher to manage than that of devolution for Scotland. Ever since Ted Heath's Declaration of Perth in 1968, the Conservative Party had maintained a theoretically devolutionist position, though Heath's government had not implemented its own proposals for a Scottish assembly. Scottish nationalism was growing fast, and the call for the North Sea oil, which was beginning to be extracted off the coast of Aberdeen, to be treated as 'Scotland's oil' became popular. For the election campaign of October 1974, the Conservatives promised a Scottish assembly, though its nature was not specified. In that election, the Scottish Nationalists returned triumphant with eleven seats in Scotland, and the Conservative Scottish representation fell to sixteen, its lowest since the introduction of universal suffrage. At first, under pressure from her leading Scottish MPs, Mrs Thatcher reluctantly renewed the commitment to an assembly, speaking to this effect in Perth in May 1975. It survived even into the text of *The Right Approach* in October 1976, which spoke of 'a directly elected Scottish assembly, acting as another chamber of the UK Parliament', a phrase which indicated disagreement with the Labour idea of a separate Scottish executive. But beneath the surface the policy began to shift, for several reasons.

The first was that the majority of English Tory MPs (and of Tory MPs in Wales, where Conservative opposition to devolution was much more nearly unanimous) felt increasingly uncomfortable with anything which might lead to the break-up of the Union. The second was that those Tories who did support devolution – Ian Gilmour, Francis Pym and Alick Buchanan-Smith,* the shadow Scottish Secretary, were among the most prominent – tended also to be those who were attracted by 'national' or coalition government. Many of them favoured proportional representation which, they believed, would contain Scottish separatism and make for

---

* Alick Buchanan-Smith (1932–91), educated Trinity College, Glenalmond, Pembroke College, Cambridge and Edinburgh University; Conservative MP for North Angus and Mearns, 1964–83; for Kincardine and Deeside, 1983–91; Minister of State, Ministry of Agriculture, Fisheries and Food, 1979–83; Department of Energy, 1983–7.

permanent moderate government across the United Kingdom. All this was anathema to Mrs Thatcher, and aroused her suspicion of the motives of those who promoted it. Besides, devolution began to emerge as Labour's problem. It was Labour which had more seats than any other party to lose in Scotland, Labour which had the most serious rebellions on the subject, and Labour which had the almost impossible task of preserving its House of Commons majority on such a controversial matter.

Mrs Thatcher contemplated the question with quite a cold eye. Although she was certainly an instinctive Unionist, it did not engage her passionate interest. As with Northern Ireland, which in opposition she delegated almost entirely to Airey Neave, she always hoped that the subject of devolution would go away. She was very conscious, however, that Scotland was an area of weakening Tory support, and when she became leader she immediately sought to remedy this with a series of Scottish visits, three in her first seven months, all of them considered successful. She needed to work out whether Conservative support for devolution was an electoral plus or minus north of the border. This was hard to do, because her Scottish party was divided into bitter factions, so bitter that, in one of their conferences, they actually starting scuffling with one another. Broadly speaking, the more upper-class and rural elements, which dominated the party hierarchy and produced two-thirds of the Scottish MPs, were pro-devolution, and the more urban and working-class elements were anti. A vote on the subject at a special conference in Edinburgh in January 1976 produced 103 for devolution, with 60 against and 40 abstentions. Given the efforts of the party establishment to control the voting, this result showed how powerful was the undertow of opposition.

These first Tory explosions on the subject were just about contained. Mrs Thatcher's Iron Lady speech in Kensington in January helped overshadow the party's muddles on devolution. But in the course of the year, the situation worsened. She felt irritated to be saddled with Heath's commitment, writing to Maurice Macmillan, an opponent of devolution in March 1976: 'The one clear lesson seems to be – never make major pronouncements in Opposition.'[42] The obvious solution for the party was to try to unite round opposing the Labour government's plans rather than tear itself apart on the principle. This was possible because the Tory position, formally expressed in Alec Home's report on the subject, was in favour of 'a directly elected assembly tied to the Westminster legislative system', whereas the Labour plan was for a separate Scottish parliament with its own executive. Willie Whitelaw, Scottish by birth, and sitting for a Border seat, moved from earlier support for devolution to this anti-Labour stance, thus shifting the balance of opinion. As Mrs Thatcher put it, the Conservatives wanted 'a diffusion of power and not a confusion of power'.[43] This stance was intended to make it possible for pro- and anti-devolution Tories to stay loyal. In this spirit, in her reshuffle of November 1976, Mrs Thatcher actually promoted Francis Pym, a devolutionist, to be party spokesman on the subject.

Almost as soon as Pym was appointed, however, the strain became intolerable. The Labour government now wanted to push forward with its Bill, and the Conservatives therefore had to decide whether or not to oppose it on second reading. A faction led by Buchanan-Smith was adamant that they should vote for the Bill, but the Shadow Cabinet went the other way. He and his juniors, including the young Malcolm Rifkind,* threatened to resign their frontbench posts. Mrs Thatcher did almost everything in her power to stop them. She asked all the troubled Scots, led by Buchanan-Smith and Rifkind, to come and see her. In a note written shortly after the meeting, Rifkind recorded:

> Margaret stated categorically that she was not prepared to contemplate our mass resignations and that some compromise must be found. First, our departure would destroy the party in Scotland. Secondly, she stressed that she felt committed to a directly-elected Scottish Assembly. If we went she would have to appoint antis like Teddy Taylor† as Scottish front-bench spokesman and this would be impossible ... She remarked, laughingly, that if we had to resign, she would appoint us again the following day if necessary!

She promised that a Tory government would put proposals for a Scottish assembly before Parliament. Rifkind concluded, 'After the meeting we felt we had lost the battle but won the war!'[44] In the event, Rifkind and Buchanan-Smith did resign, but others were dissuaded from doing so, and Mrs Thatcher showed maximum flexibility in keeping people on board. When Ian Gilmour threatened to resign, she persuaded him to absent himself from the vote instead with an excuse of attending to party business.[45] Faced with her losses, Mrs Thatcher approached three other MPs to be shadow Scottish secretary before turning, in desperation, to the man she had tried to avoid, Teddy Taylor, who was unaware of the manoeuvrings

---

* Malcolm Rifkind (1946–), educated George Watson's College and Edinburgh University; Conservative MP for Edinburgh Pentlands, February 1974–97; for Kensington and Chelsea, from 2005; Secretary of State for Scotland, 1986–9; for Transport, 1990–92; for Defence, 1992–5; for Foreign and Commonwealth Affairs, 1995–7; unsuccessful candidate for leadership of the Conservative Party, 2005; knighted, 1997.

† Teddy Taylor (1937–), educated Glasgow High School and Glasgow University; Conservative MP for Glasgow Cathcart, 1964–79; for Southend East, 1980–97; for Rochford and Southend East, 1997–2005; knighted, 1991. Despite his shadow role, Taylor never held office in any of Mrs Thatcher's administrations.

behind the scenes.[46] Taylor, a tough and eccentric working-class Glaswe-gian whose seat in that city depended on high Scottish Nationalist support taking Labour votes, remembered that Mrs Thatcher told him: 'I want you to destroy the SNP.' Taylor was more than willing to try, but replied: 'If we do that, I'll destroy my seat too.'[47]* In the parliamentary vote, twenty-seven Conservatives, including Heath, abstained, and five voted with the government. A comparable number of Labour MPs rebelled against their whip the other way.

The thing was a mess, but from it there emerged, from Mrs Thatcher's pragmatic point of view, a much more satisfactory state of affairs. Pro-devolution Tories felt that they had been politely treated in their desire to express their views; anti-devolutionists knew that things were going their way; all felt more able to unite against Labour. A further chance soon benefited the Tories. Anxious not to have its Bill talked out, the government tried to break the convention that constitutional matters should not be held to a fixed timetable, and put forward a motion to guillotine (that is, cut short debate on) the Bill. It duly lost its guillotine motion by twenty-seven votes. Callaghan then lost the Nationalist support which had given him a small working majority. Two weeks later, after ignominiously refus-ing to contest an adjournment motion on the subject of public expenditure, the government found itself confronted with a vote of no confidence which, if lost, would produce an immediate general election.

By 22 March 1977, however, it became clear that the Liberals had negotiated an agreement to sustain the government in office, the 'pact' which Mrs Thatcher had tended to discount. This was not wholly bad news for the Tories, since they did not feel confident of victory if a general elec-tion were called – but the Lib–Lab Pact naturally deflated them and produced in Mrs Thatcher's contribution to the now redundant no-confidence debate one of her worst parliamentary speeches. 'Thatcher was very poor,' Bernard Donoughue recorded, 'cliché after cliché . . . She made no adaptation to the fluid and turbulent mood of the House.'[48] Privately, Mrs Thatcher told friends that she was conscious of her own failure, and blamed herself. Tory victory in the Stechford by-election of 1 April with a 17.6 per cent swing lifted the gloom.

By the time the Labour government next felt ready to return to devolution, Mrs Thatcher was ready too, with her party in one piece. To pro-devolution MPs demanding a stronger line, she wrote, 'Our commitment to the principle

---

* Taylor's prediction was correct. The Conservatives gained seven Scottish seats from the SNP in the 1979 general election. The only one they lost was his, to Labour. So the Conservative net gain in Scotland was six.

of a directly elected assembly for Scotland ... stands. I have not retracted it and do not intend to do so,' but she added, 'I do not believe it would be sensible to put formal detailed proposals at this stage.'[49] In the autumn Francis Pym had another go, submitting to the Shadow Cabinet a paper called 'The Need to be More Positive', which argued for a directly elected assembly; but he did not prevail. On 2 November the Shadow Cabinet agreed that 'the best way forward was to set up a Constitutional Conference and put all the alternative proposals into it.'[50] As Teddy Taylor recalled, 'No decision was ever made in the Shadow Cabinet to reject devolution. It just quietly slipped away.'[51] Callaghan ploughed on, but he was hampered by an amendment carried by rebels in his own party which prescribed a threshold of 40 per cent of the electorate voting 'yes' in the referendums before devolution could be enacted. In the votes in Scotland and Wales on 1 March 1979, this threshold was not reached. Wales, indeed, voted 'no' outright. It was the resulting strains with the Nationalist parties which caused the government to fall later that month.

As for the Conservatives, they had been able to oppose the government's Bill without rejecting the principle of devolution, and to campaign, low-key, for a 'no' vote. Their manifesto for the general election of May 1979 confined itself to promising 'discussions about the future government of Scotland'. At that election, the Tories won a net gain of three seats in Wales and six in Scotland. There were many who would argue that, by edging away from devolution, Mrs Thatcher eventually brought about the collapse of Scottish Conservatism which led the Tories to lose every single seat in Scotland in 1997. But that is probably to impose later problems upon those of the period.* In terms of the calculations required by the strange parliamentary situation and the divisions within her own party between 1975 and 1979, Mrs Thatcher surely acted with qualities which her opponents claimed she lacked – tact, the ability to listen, and a good measure of cunning.

There was another matter, much less public at that time than devolution, but of far greater long-term significance, which called for Mrs Thatcher's political management. In the summer of 1978, Chancellor Helmut Schmidt of West Germany and President Valéry Giscard d'Estaing of France decided to push forward with the formal creation on 1 January 1979 of the European

---

* Some Tories had this worry at the time. The late R. A. Butler told the present author in 1978 that he had threatened to write 'Scotland' on Mrs Thatcher's breast with a piece of chalk. When she asked why, he said, 'Because a queen of England had "Calais" written on her heart, and you should have "Scotland" written on yours.' In another version of this story, also told by Lord Butler, he wrote 'Scotland' on the suit of his son Adam, Mrs Thatcher's PPS. The truth of either version has not been established. Adam had no memory of the incident.

Monetary System, which all EEC member states joined from the start. The most important element of the EMS, however, was the Exchange Rate Mechanism, and participation in that was voluntary. An earlier effort at European monetary co-ordination, known as the snake, had been joined by the Heath government for a brief and ignominious six weeks, but now the arrangement was to be institutionalized in the ERM, and so the governments of member states, including Britain, would have to decide whether to take part.

The Conservatives were relieved that the decision fell to Callaghan, whose party was beset by divisions on Europe, and not to them. But they nevertheless had to take up a position on the subject. The views of the party establishment were clear. The Heathites, who had got Britain into the EEC in the first place and carried the day in the 1975 referendum on whether or not to stay in, were still intent on developing their project. In the summer of 1978, Adam Ridley wrote a memo to Mrs Thatcher which, though raising technical difficulties, presented the choice as being between Britain playing a 'constructive and positive part' or 'increasing obscurity on the fringes'.[52] In the autumn, as the decision approached, Ridley wrote to her again emphasizing that the question was 95 per cent politics rather than economics, and advocating, rather boldly for an adviser whose chief purpose was technical and economic, that Britain should 'leap before you look'.[53]

Two days later, the shadow ministers chiefly concerned – Howe, Pym, Nigel Lawson and John Nott, with Lord Soames (as a senior Tory with relevant knowledge as a former European commissioner) and Adam Ridley in attendance – met to discuss the ERM. In the background was a recent speech by the consistently Powellite Eurosceptic John Biffen which attacked the ERM as a strengthening of the Franco-German axis in Europe. Lawson was extremely cautiously in favour of some sort of mechanism: 'We have to decide first whether it would work or not; then if terms were right, if we should join.'[54] Nott was worried about unpopular devaluations imposed from abroad. Soames and Pym were in favour of the ERM, as was Geoffrey Howe, a strong pro-European all his political life. Howe is recorded as saying: 'the answer to Biffen's original threat of a Franco-German axis was to put us on the other end and make a real triangle.'

Lawson and Howe then wrote separately to Mrs Thatcher. Lawson sought to steer a course between 'Eurofanatics and Europhobes' and advocated that 'we should avoid committing ourselves to any firm position on the EMS* for as long as possible . . . it is a hideously complex and awkward

---

* Politicians at the time often referred to joining the EMS when they meant the ERM.

issue, both economically and (more important) politically.' 'A case can be made', he went on, '. . . that no British Government will – in practice – feel able to maintain a sufficiently tight monetary and fiscal policy unless buttressed by the external constraint of a fixed exchange rate.' On the other hand, the ERM conditions might render the EEC 'so unpopular as to make support of continuing EEC membership political suicide'. He compared the situation with Britain's decision to go back on to the gold standard in 1925, and worried about an 'artificially high sterling parity'. But, by not joining, Britain would 'risk abdicating for good the leadership of Europe'. Lawson coolly added that the best hope was therefore a quick collapse of the system so that 'we could propose some alternative and more sensible framework for European economic convergence'. It would be better for the Tories, he thought, if Labour were to enter, but if they did not, the Conservatives could attack Callaghan 'for being afraid of the big bad Benn'. He concluded: 'we should not give any undertaking that . . . we will bring Britain into the EMS. To give such an undertaking would gratuitously split the party.'[55]

Geoffrey Howe, by contrast, was unequivocal. He supported the ERM both economically and politically: 'Fundamentally, we do believe in German principles of economic management and should be able to get ourselves alongside them.' The Tories, he said, should 'pronounce in favour' of the ERM for 'providing greater currency stability and encouraging convergence of economic policies'. He went on: 'The political case for this conclusion is a strong one: the alternative means surrendering the direction of the EEC . . . to the Franco-German high table.' In terms of tactics, Howe argued that it would be impossible to make Britain's ERM entry conditional on reform of the Common Agricultural Policy (CAP), which fixed agricultural subsidy systems throughout the EEC, and of Britain's contributions to the EEC budget because 'our bargaining position is far too weak.'[56]

As was usual with her correspondents on matters of policy, Mrs Thatcher wrote no reply, but her marginal notes on Howe's letter made her feelings clear. Against his claims about currency stability and economic convergence, she wrote 'Why?' Beside his view that budget and CAP concessions could not be used as a price for ERM entry, she wrote 'Can't do it afterwards.' Beside his proposition about the Franco-German high table, she wrote simply 'No.'[57] Thanking Sir George Bolton, a Bank of England director, who had given her his views on the subject, on 13 November 1978, she said: 'It's the most illuminating memorandum I have had on the practical problems of an EMS. They look well-nigh insuperable at the moment.'[58]

In practical terms, Jim Callaghan made the question easy for the

Conservatives. He decided against British entry into the ERM, reporting this to the House of Commons on 6 December 1978. It was simple enough for Mrs Thatcher to say that the failure to join was a sign of Britain's economic weakness and of Labour's divisions and 'a sad day for Europe',[59] and leave it at that. But the documents and letters quoted above perfectly foreshadow – in tone, in content, in personalities, even in the choice of words – the matter which was to cause such extreme bitterness and division in her Cabinets towards the end of the 1980s. Even before she became prime minister, Mrs Thatcher was suspicious of the project of European integration, but was surrounded by senior colleagues who disagreed with her.

The Tory argument about the ERM remained private at this stage, but these documents exhibit Mrs Thatcher's habit – one could almost call it a technique – of setting the terms of policy discussion by expressing opinions more trenchant than those of her colleagues. Often, she did this in public. The subject of immigration gave her a notable opportunity. Ever since Enoch Powell's 'Rivers of Blood' speech in 1968, the question had been toxic in Conservative politics, but public feeling against immigration (and continuing wide working-class support for Powell) was real enough. Indeed, it began to grow again because of Labour relaxation of the rules. For example, the permission given by the Home Secretary, Roy Jenkins, to fiancés of Asian women to enter the country quickly became a means of abusing the system. When Jenkins temporarily left British politics in 1977 to become president of the European Commission, the by-election campaign in his former constituency of Stechford was dominated by the question of immigration. The Conservative candidate, Andrew Mackay,* sent out 30,000 leaflets headlined 'Stop immigration'. The Tories dramatically gained the seat from Labour, but it was also notable that the virulently anti-immigration National Front, the forerunner of today's BNP, won 8.1 per cent of the vote.

By the end of 1977, with Labour's measures of economic restraint having some effect, the Conservative lead in the opinion polls had more or less vanished. This seems to have prompted Mrs Thatcher to pay more attention to non-economic issues where there was public discontent.

---

* Andrew Mackay (1949–), educated Solihull; Conservative MP for Birmingham, Stechford, 1977–9; for Berkshire East, 1983–97; for Bracknell, 1997–2010; Deputy Government Chief Whip, 1996–7; senior political and parliamentary adviser to the Leader of the Opposition, 2005–9. He was forced to resign his post in the expenses scandal which engulfed Parliament in 2009.

According to Richard Ryder, 'She felt hemmed in on incomes policy, so she thought she would take a free hit on immigration.'[60] In an interview for Granada's *World in Action* which was broadcast on 30 January 1978, she noted that there would probably be 4 million Pakistani and New Commonwealth immigrants in Britain by the end of the century. This was 'an awful lot', she said, and British people feared that they 'might be rather swamped by people with a different culture and, you know, the British character has done so much for democracy, for law, and done so much throughout the world that if there is any fear that it might be swamped people are going to react and be rather hostile to those coming in.' She added that she had been brought up in a small town of 25,000 people, and that about twice that number was entering the country every year. 'We are a British nation,' she said, 'with British characteristics.'[61]

There was widespread outrage in the broadsheet press and at Westminster, and widespread approval in the country. The person in the most difficult position was Willie Whitelaw. He was furious both at the tone of Mrs Thatcher's remarks and at the fact that she had made them without warning him. He would have liked her to qualify them, but he knew that the circumstances of the interview, which had not been recorded live, had given her the opportunity to erase her own remarks before she went on air; she had not done so. Characteristically, Whitelaw went round talking of resignation, but did not actually resign. He told Roy Jenkins 'how absolutely ghastly life was with that awful woman, how he was thinking of resigning',[62] but continued much as before. In private, Chris Patten, at the Conservative Research Department, expressed the perturbation felt by everyone on the more liberal wing of the party. 'Just imagine', he told Michael Portillo, 'if she'd said we were being swamped by Jewish people.'[63] In the House of Commons, the excitable Labour MP Andrew Faulds was ordered by the Speaker to 'control himself' in his attacks on Mrs Thatcher. Faulds shouted back: 'With that bloody woman in the House, how can you expect it?'[64] His phrase 'that bloody woman' was taken up by many who did not like Mrs Thatcher, often abbreviated to 'TBW'. Her remarks were significant not for any change in policy – most Tories agreed that immigration controls should be strengthened – but for her choice of language. The way a person talked about immigration was a touchstone of other attitudes then, as it remains today. As with her personal support for capital punishment – a conscience issue on which there could be no party policy – Mrs Thatcher knew this, and was happy to stand up against the chattering classes. There was a sense in which she enjoyed being 'TBW'. She considered herself to be saying what others sought to conceal.

Twenty-five years later, remembering the 'swamping' interview, she quoted Kipling's poem 'The Fabulists':

> When all the world would keep a matter hid
> Since Truth is seldom Friend to any crowd,
> Men write in fables, as old Aesop did.[65]*

Enoch Powell considered that Mrs Thatcher had quickly backed away from her own position on immigration under pressure from her party – because the Tory bosses were 'Athenian oligarchs who would always sacrifice culture for class'.[66] In fact, however, she stood by her words, and used the occasion to reiterate her belief that the National Front, far from being the authentic, or even the perverted, voice of the patriotic right, was 'a socialist front',[67] concerned to bring about a siege economy and state control. She was interested in the fact that the word 'Nazi' was short for National Socialist, and felt that the socialist aspect was dangerously ignored. She saw the issue of immigration as one where a politician must attend to people's legitimate fears, and where people were entitled to greater certainty about numbers and commitments. The Conservatives shot up in the opinion polls from neck and neck with Labour to an eleven-point lead and Callaghan, sensing political vulnerability, invited Mrs Thatcher to all-party talks on immigration which she, recognizing an attempt to smother the subject, rejected. The immigration issue helped the Tories win the Ilford North by-election in February 1978. From the whole 'swamping' controversy, she took away a growing belief, most annoying to her Shadow Cabinet, but undeniably validated by voters, that 'I must trust my own judgment in crucial matters, rather than necessarily hope to persuade my colleagues in advance; for I could expect that somewhere out in the country there would be a following and perhaps a majority for me.'[68]

The only way, of course, that Mrs Thatcher could prove that there was 'a majority for me' was in a general election. With this in mind, in the early

---

* An interesting example of Mrs Thatcher's personal attitude to immigrants was noted by the young Michael Portillo when, as a member of the Research Department, he attended part of a Shadow Cabinet meeting in the summer of 1976. In the middle of a discussion of immigration, the division bell rang. Mrs Thatcher asked what the vote was about and was told that it was about giving Sikhs special exemption from wearing crash helmets on their motorbikes, so that they could keep their turbans on. Carrington made some *sotto voce* remark about the piquancy of this vote at this precise moment. Mrs Thatcher said sharply, 'What did you say?' Carrington said, 'It was a joke, Margaret,' and explained. She replied, 'Well, it's not very funny. These people fought for us in the war.'

spring of 1978 the party made a bold decision in its choice of advertising agency. Three companies were invited to pitch for the account, but Gordon Reece, to whom the party Chairman Lord Thorneycroft, doubting the value of having an advertising agency at all, had delegated the work, did not like pitches. 'My experience in commercial advertising', Reece later wrote, 'had told me that agencies put their best efforts into the pitch when they should be putting it into the client's business.'[69] He made sure that Saatchi and Saatchi, the only one of the three to refuse to pitch, got the account. The Saatchi brothers, Maurice* and Charles,† who owned the company, were completely outside the world of the Conservative Party. Born into a family of Baghdad Jews, they had no previous political involvement. When Reece offered Maurice Saatchi the account, Saatchi rang his chairman, Tim Bell,‡ the only known Tory at the top of the company, who was on holiday in Barbados, to ask his opinion. Bell, who had worked with the Conservative Party in another agency in the Macmillan era, thought it was a bad idea. There was no money in it, he said, and a great deal of aggravation. He thought the Saatchi brothers were not Conservatives and felt socially uneasy with Tories because they feared they would be seen as 'upstart Jewboys'. Would they be able to put their heart into it?[70] Bell was overruled, however, and quickly became the link man with Reece. The Saatchis stayed in the background, Maurice meeting Mrs Thatcher only once before the election of May 1979, and Charles not at all. Alistair McAlpine, the treasurer, shocked Saatchis by saying to them: 'If we win the election, we'll pay you. Otherwise not.'[71] But he was actually one of the most enthusiastic for their work. When trying to drum up money from rich men for the election, he would go round to them with a sheaf of the best Saatchi suggestions for posters and ask, 'Which one of these would you like to pay for?'[72]

In effect, Reece, Bell and McAlpine formed a team within Conservative Central Office unconstrained by the normal organizational structures, rivalries and bureaucracies of party life. They offered a rather unusual combination of attitudes – a belief in the black arts of advertising and the most modern methods of image-management with a serious ideological commitment to radical Conservatism. Even more important, perhaps, they

* Maurice Saatchi (1946–), educated LSE; co-founder, Saatchi & Saatchi, 1970, chairman, 1985–94; partner, M&C Saatchi, from 1995; Co-Chairman, Conservative Party, 2003–5; created Lord Saatchi, 1996.

† Charles Saatchi (1943–), educated Christ's Hospital; co-founder, Saatchi & Saatchi, 1970; partner, M&C Saatchi, from 1995; noted collector of contemporary art.

‡ Tim Bell (1941–), educated Queen Elizabeth's Grammar School, Barnet; managing director, Saatchi & Saatchi, 1970–75; chairman and managing director, Saatchi & Saatchi Compton, 1975–85; chairman, Bell Pottinger, from 1987; created Lord Bell, 1998.

were all 'in love' (Tim Bell's words) with Margaret Thatcher. All three men, by now in early middle age, and none of them at that time married, liked drink and women and parties and fun. They also carried with them 'the knowledge that we were engaged in a great crusade'.[73] They saw in the apparently straitlaced Mrs Thatcher an indulgent mother or nanny, a patron saint and a unique opportunity. Their emotional loyalty was to her, not to the Tory Party, and this gave an edge to their work.

The Saatchi–Reece strategy, however, was not to focus public attention on their heroine. Bell told Thorneycroft that Mrs Thatcher was 'hard to sell' because she looked too like people's idea of a Tory wife, and the image of a Tory wife supporting her husband was incompatible with the image of a leader.[74] Reece was concerned that the radio broadcasting of Parliament, which began in April 1978, had made life even more difficult for a woman leader because the public could hear her shrieking to make herself audible over the hubbub.[75]* He also had a high opinion of Jim Callaghan's skills on radio and television. Although the tendency of ever more televised politics was to make election campaigns more presidential, Saatchis did not seek to encourage this. They thought that it was their task to present an optimistic philosophy of freedom and national recovery and the idea that it was time for a change. Their first party political broadcast, in May, was an upbeat message about the creation of wealth. But they quickly realized that the Tories should try to exploit the old saw that 'oppositions don't win elections; governments lose them', and should tap into growing popular discontent. People in general were saying how ghastly everything was, so the Conservatives should say so too. They advised that the Tories should not let Labour keep them at its mercy through its power of choosing the date of the contest, but should attack right away. They recommended that Conservative advertising should strike at what had traditionally been Labour's strongest points.

Unemployment, which had hit 1.5 million in 1977, was an obvious example. One of their creative staff, Andrew Rutherford, invented the slogan 'Labour isn't working'. A gaggle of Young Conservatives from Hendon, so small in number that the same people had to be repeated several times in the poster, formed an imitation of an old-fashioned dole queue snaking into the distance. Designed to cause trouble at a quiet time, and perhaps

---

* Bernard Donoughue, head of Callaghan's Policy Unit, noted Mrs Thatcher's first broadcast Prime Minister's Questions with satisfaction from a Labour point of view: 'She looked very pale and tense and sounded harsh. This was in some ways a trial run for the election, and we came away feeling very confident.' (Bernard Donoughue, *Downing Street Diary*, 2 vols, Jonathan Cape, 2005, 2008, vol. ii: *With James Callaghan in No. 10*, 4 April 1978, p. 305.)

to put Labour off their expected electoral timetable of the early autumn of 1978, the poster was put up in very few sites, but heavily trailed to selected newspapers, such as the *Daily Mail*. It was Labour, however, who gave it the attention it needed to take off. Denis Healey, whose undoubted cleverness and eloquence tended to be vitiated by bad temper, raged against the poster – partly for the rather odd reason that it insulted the unemployed by portraying 'actors' – and so ensured acres of free publicity. Jim Callaghan retired for a summer holiday at his farm in Ringmer in Sussex, accompanied by *The Times Guide to the House of Commons*,[76] and there he went through the statistics of all the marginal seats before making a decision about the date of the election. The Saatchi poster helped to make him nervous. It is a tribute to the power of the 'Labour isn't working' poster that the belief has grown up that it led the election campaign of May 1979. This is not the case, but it is a natural error for the memory to make, for the poster did mark the beginning of the Conservatives' rhetorical conquest of Labour. The poster found the right terms in which to mount the challenge. Variations on the theme followed later: 'Educashun isn't working' said a poster of a boy writing those misspelt words on a blackboard. 'Britain isn't getting any better' said another of pensioners queueing for miles under a sign marked 'Hospital'.

Faced with the Saatchi proposals that summer, Mrs Thatcher behaved in a very characteristic way. She had little natural feel for what made a good election poster or slogan, though she often made small, practical comments. 'The public don't know what 20 per cent means,' she would say, and she warned that it was dangerous to produce posters on which opponents could easily write graffiti because she remembered that in Dartford her opponent's poster 'Dodds again for Dartford' had quickly been defaced by her Young Conservatives to read 'Odds against Dodds for Dartford'.[77] She made commonsense objections on grounds of taste or comprehensibility – refusing to appear at all if they went ahead with a party political broadcast which would have shown a baby in nappies and boxing gloves,[78] and requiring every joke to be laboriously explained to her. Jeremy Sinclair, the creative director of Saatchis, remembered that 'When we wrote for her, she'd cross it all out, rewrite it, and end up pretty much where we'd started.'[79] She rejected Saatchis' first proposed photograph of her because the rings on her fingers were prominent, saying 'It makes me look rich.'[80] Her first reaction to the 'Labour isn't working' poster was to complain because 'the largest word on it is "Labour",'[81] but, Bell remembered, she was quickly won over 'because she saw it was hurtful [to Labour], and she liked that'.[82]

Although she could be pernickety, Mrs Thatcher was quite humble in areas of which she had little knowledge, and advertising was one of them. She trusted Reece, accepted his analysis of what needed doing and liked the people, notably Bell, whom he brought in. She was meekly obedient about what she should wear and how she should speak, and grateful to those who helped her improve. As early as 1972, when she was only a Cabinet minister, Reece had helped her with her voice. He had bumped into Laurence Olivier* on a train from Brighton and had asked the great actor's advice. Olivier had arranged to lend her the services of Kate Fleming, the National Theatre's voice coach, to make her sound less shrill.[83] Mrs Thatcher had submitted to this uncomplainingly, and she stuck by these lessons as leader. Conscious that she could sometimes be wooden in front of the camera, she asked Bell to sit just behind and below it whenever she did a broadcast so that she could address her words to a real and friendly person. She also accepted the Saatchi–Reece doctrine that no politician should appear continuously on a party political broadcast (which, in those days, had an enormous, statutory length of nine minutes and forty seconds) for more than thirty seconds. They wanted the broadcasts to be untraditional, stylish and funny. These were not natural Margaret Thatcher characteristics, but she endorsed them; and so the most serious-minded of Tory leaders found herself presiding over advertisements full of ingenious innovations like film running backwards (to show the direction in which Labour was taking Britain) and little dramas acted out (of people in a cinema queue complaining about inflation, for example), rather than old-fashioned films of MPs stiltedly delivering standard messages. She also agreed with Reece that the voters the Tories most needed to reach were those outside the tent of traditional party allegiance, often people without a strong interest in politics. So she warmly supported advertising campaigns that aimed directly at women shoppers. Advertisements were placed in women's magazines, which said: 'Do this quiz to find out if you're Labour or Conservative.' After a series of questions about policies, the quiz ended:

> Which of these people is more likely to know what it's like to do the family shopping?
> a. James Callaghan
> b. Your husband
> c. Mrs Thatcher.

Cultivation of the popular newspapers was part of the same strategy,

* Laurence Olivier (1907–89), actor and director; co-founder of the National Theatre, and its Director, 1973–4; knighted, 1947; created Lord Olivier, 1970.

as Reece had argued from the first, and Mrs Thatcher readily did her duty. As if to confirm Reece's analysis of the rising trends in society, the circulation of Rupert Murdoch's right-wing *Sun* overtook that of the Labour-supporting *Daily Mirror* for the first time in May 1978. Mrs Thatcher sent the *Sun* a message of congratulation. She flattered its editor, Larry Lamb, and placed great faith in the power of its leading articles. In those days, the leading articles appeared on page two, opposite the famous page-three girls. On one occasion, arguing with her advisers, Mrs Thatcher alighted on two leaders in that day's *Sun* which vigorously confirmed her prejudices. 'There,' she cried, spreading the paper before them. 'What do you think of those two?' The young aides found themselves staring at a large pair of breasts and almost suffocated with suppressed laughter. Mrs Thatcher, of course, failed to notice the source of their mirth.[84]* Gordon Reece had his own friendships with editors, including John Junor of the *Sunday Express* and David English of the *Daily Mail*. When the *Mail* got hold of the previously unknown story of Denis's first marriage, Reece exploited his friendship with English to ensure that the story was written in a friendly manner. Indeed, English wrote it himself.[85] It says something about the difference between Mrs Thatcher's successful management of her public image and her uneasy management of her children that the fact of the first marriage had been unknown to Mark and Carol. Carol was in Australia as the story broke and it fell to Alison Ward to inform her about it.[86] Mark remembered the incident as very distressing.[87] It was part of Reece's skill that he unlocked in such a correct and almost inhibited woman the showbiz, populist, communicative gifts which lurked within. Her ability to master the media in this way made life far more difficult for her potential opponents in the party.

Working on the assumption that there would be an election in the autumn of 1978, the Conservatives drew up their manifesto. All policy groups (there were no fewer than ninety-three of them) were told to wind up their work on 30 June. Most of the policy papers and manifesto drafts show the victory of the cautious over the bold. Michael Heseltine, who had been asked to look into the abolition of domestic rates which the party had promised

---

* Mrs Thatcher always had to have double entendres explained, and she came to dread uttering them by mistake. She saw them as a specifically male thing which would always remain a mystery to her. Once she wanted to use the word 'blackball' in a speech, and her advisers tried to prevent her without quite having the courage to tell her why. Eventually, Adam Butler solved the problem by saying, 'Doesn't it sound a bit too clubby, Margaret?' (Interview with Lord Dobbs.) Perhaps the best-known example was her statement in a 1984 television interview that she was 'always on the job' (*Aspel & Company*, LWT).

in October 1974, reported that all the possible replacements were fraught with difficulty. A poll tax, for example, was 'extremely regressive' for the poor. He recommended that the pledge stand but that the manifesto should state that it would take a 'lower priority' than income tax cuts. He also proposed a 'root-and-branch reappraisal of centralised decision-taking' and the granting of 'increased discretion to local authorities'.[88] Beside this passage, Mrs Thatcher put the wiggly line which was always the mark of her disapproval.

Even the radical Nicholas Ridley, charged with recommending a policy on the nationalized industries, wrote of denationalization (the word 'privatization' was not used in the documents) that 'The objective must be pursued cautiously and flexibly, recognising that major changes may well be out of the question in some industries such as the utilities.' As for telecommunications, which at that time were entirely controlled by the Post Office, they would be split into a separate enterprise, but 'The telephone network would remain nationalised but private telephone suppliers would be given a larger role.'[89] Ridley did, however, recommend that there could be a direct sale to the public of assets in the British Steel Corporation, British Rail, the National Freight Corporation, the British National Oil Corporation and the National Bus Company. On 10 July 1978 the Shadow Cabinet agreed that the ideas about denationalization would not be published.

The pulling together of the manifesto coincided with a row about Mrs Thatcher's entourage. Early in her leadership, she had been worried that her office was unable to deal properly with the vast number of letters (3,000 a week) pouring in. Matters came to a head in 1976 when the Duke of Rutland, the local Duke from her Grantham childhood, and not one to ignore *lèse-majesté*, received a reply, from a member of Mrs Thatcher's staff, to a letter he had written to Mrs Thatcher. The reply began 'Dear Mr Rutland'. When she heard about this, Mrs Thatcher exploded. Alistair McAlpine recruited David Wolfson, who was helping run his family business, Great Universal Stores, and therefore knew about direct mail, to advise on improvements. Soon Wolfson developed a role of improving communication between Central Office and the Leader's office. In the summer of 1978, when she thought the general election was imminent, Mrs Thatcher asked Wolfson to work for her full time, and made him secretary to the Shadow Cabinet. This caused a row because, by virtue of being director of the Research Department, Chris Patten was automatically secretary to the Shadow Cabinet. Patten was therefore upset by what he saw as a personal and ideological snub. Mrs Thatcher probably intended no offence. She seems not to have been aware that Patten held the post, a fact which, in itself, must have been galling to him. Wolfson's view was that it all started because there was nowhere for him to sit in the Leader's crowded offices, except in the Shadow Cabinet room. She therefore hit upon the title to go with the geography, and asked him to take the minutes. He never actually did so, and life went on very much as before.[90]* But the incident illustrated Mrs Thatcher's surprisingly vague attitude to position, hierarchy, job titles and so on, in some ways an attractive trait, but one which often caused affront. It also brought out her fondness for having people about her whose first loyalty was to her, not to the machine.

The process of manifesto-making made all factions anxious. While Chris Patten feared that he and what he saw as his enlightened liberal conservatism might be excluded, Thatcherites worried that sogginess would prevail. A fragment of Wolfson's comments to Mrs Thatcher on the manifesto's early draft survives. On the proposal that competition be promoted by 'Strengthening the Monopolies Commission', he writes, 'Help. Haven't we learnt anything?', and when it is suggested that the government should be 'enlarging' the Office of Fair Trading, he writes 'MORE UNPRODUCT-IVE CIVIL SERVANTS'.[91] For her part, Mrs Thatcher fretted that the energy and discipline of their policy-making were being dissipated in too many promises. The minutes for the Shadow Cabinet meeting of 31 July record, 'Mrs Thatcher pointed out that because a large number of nuggets were being inserted, we were in danger of losing our credibility on the reduction of expenditure. She proposed that the next manifesto draft put the main emphasis on a few central objectives on which everything else depended: (a) the cutting of taxes and (b) strengthening internal and external defence.'[92] But the same meeting went on to agree that 'We should not pick a fight with the unions on a minor issue by a crude commitment on strikers' benefits.'

Mrs Thatcher's feelings at the time reflected the conflict she harboured between prudence and conviction. In a private interview given to David Butler and Dennis Kavanagh on 9 August 1978, she said that she had tidied her desk and was ready for 10 Downing Street. She explained how a leader needed a 'total lack of fear', and that she had achieved 'a degree of intellectual and political freedom which came from not having a wife and kids' to support. She analysed the three main problems of the day as inflation, taxation and regulation, and said that all three were created by government. She had no time for any government of national unity, she said, or for proportional representation, the method of voting likely to bring such

---

* In fact, Patten did not normally take the minutes either. They were taken by David Nicholson.

a coalition about. In the Shadow Cabinet, she told Butler and Kavanagh, only Carrington, Prior and Ian Gilmour wanted PR, which just showed. Carrington, her interviewers reported her saying, 'was an old Whig, a superb tactician but who could not think long ... However he was always articulating his doubts and uncertainties and this made her impatient. She said to people like him: I know what. You tell me how.'[93] That last sentence could stand as a summary of her approach throughout her years of opposition.

Asked in the same interview what were the sources of her political strategy, she said, 'My beliefs,' but she squared these with political caution by arguing that the Tories should not make Hugh Gaitskell's mistake in 1959, in relation to tax cuts, of floating good ideas too early. It would take a huge amount of time to 'unscramble socialism': ten years were needed to change everything, so that, for example, the market would gradually infringe on welfare services and health insurance services would become 'things that trade unions were willing to negotiate about'. Privately defying those colleagues who still supported wage controls, Mrs Thatcher said that the worst thing about the Heath government's incomes policy had been that it 'undermined respect for the rule of law'. Foreshadowing the preoccupation with the environment which was to grow stronger in later years, she told the two dons that she had spent part of the morning defrosting her fridge and had noticed the energy waste: 'Wasn't it possible to use some of the heat that was generated from a refrigerator into house heating?'[94] In this private interview, more than in public utterances at the time, Mrs Thatcher articulated the robust views for which she would later become famous.

The full draft of the manifesto came together at the end of August 1978. The first version of the leader's foreword – all versions were written chiefly by Ian Gilmour – shows how tentative was the approach. 'This election', it convolutedly began, 'is not just about unemployment and inflation, important as these are to many people. It is about all the things that seem to have gone wrong in Britain in the last few years.'[95] This vagueness and negativity were improved for the full draft. The new opening sentence declared: 'The people of Britain have been suffering from too much government – but they have not been well served by government.'[96] But, although the new words enunciated a clearer theme, there was still no sense of urgency, and, despite 'Labour isn't working', the foreword failed to mention jobs as a priority until Mrs Thatcher wrote it in herself. The longing, felt so strongly by Butskellites,* to be seen to be 'striking a balance'

---

* The word, meaning moderates of all parties, was created by amalgamating the surnames of R. A. Butler and Hugh Gaitskell.

governed much of the document. 'We will be even-handed in our approach to industrial problems,' said the draft, and 'What we propose is neither revolutionary nor reactionary.' 'We shall not undertake any sweeping changes in the law on industrial relations,' it promised. Mrs Thatcher went to work on this document with her pen. She deleted the suggestion that union reforms must come from within the union movement, and where the draft said that the closed shop could be retained when a 'massive majority' voted for it, she wrote caustically, 'i.e. no rights for minorities'. 'Need for more emphasis on left wing drift of Labour,' she scrawled, and where the draft spoke of constitutional reform being based on 'as much cross-party agreement as possible', she crossed it out. Against the economic section, she complained, 'This is a goldmine of promises.' The paragraph on pay wandered around the subject of not having a single norm and spoke of the importance of 'informed discussion about the Government's economic objectives'. Mrs Thatcher wrote, 'This paragraph is pathetic.' Against some pious hopes about jobs for young people, she scribbled, 'There is absolutely no recognition in this paragraph that jobs come from satisfying the customer.'[97]

And although most of her interventions were on the main areas of economic and industrial policy, Mrs Thatcher peppered the document with other comments. On immigration, she added, 'but there can be no question of compulsory repatriation.' In the section which included Europe, the draft wanted Members of the European Parliament to 'have the authority to halt the flow of unnecessary legislation'. Mrs Thatcher, ever alert against increasing the EEC's constitutional powers, crossed out 'have the authority to halt' and substituted 'should deter'. She had no objection, however, to supporting 'the development of a concerted EEC foreign policy'.[98] At this time, she was anxious that the EEC act as a stronger and more united bloc against Soviet expansionism. In general, even with the Leader's injections of vim, the document which the Conservatives planned to offer the electorate that autumn was bland.

15

May 1979

'There's only one chance for a woman'

On 7 September 1978, Jim Callaghan announced in a television broadcast that there would not be an autumn election. It was a surprising decision that wrongfooted everyone, including, perhaps, himself. That summer, inflation, which had roared ahead before the intervention of the IMF, had fallen below 10 per cent. The July introduction of Stage 3 of the government's pay policy, a 5 per cent norm for pay increases, had seemed to promise an orderly management which public opinion contrasted favourably with Mrs Thatcher's apparent devotion to a 'free-for-all'. Yet Callaghan wobbled. His voting arithmetic made him doubtful of victory – he was very anxious not to have to struggle through another hung Parliament – and he knew there would be pay disputes in the autumn. He seems to have believed that his prices and incomes policies would have inflation beaten by the summer of 1979.[1] He thought the 5 per cent rule would be his salvation. In fact, it turned out to be his crucifixion. Bernard Donoughue who, like almost everyone close to Callaghan, had been kept in the dark by his boss about the postponement, recorded in his diary, 'I felt terribly disappointed,' and Tom McNally,* Callaghan's political adviser, told him: 'Either he [Callaghan] is a great political genius or he has just missed the boat.'[2]

On the day that Callaghan announced his postponement, Mrs Thatcher was touring the Midlands. Since Callaghan had chosen a broadcast to the nation as his means of announcing his decision, most had assumed that an election would be called and so a huge press-pack was following Mrs Thatcher. The news, which reached her by bush telegraph a few hours before the broadcast, surprised and deflated her, although she knew, rationally, that it did not damage her chances. She had been so girded for battle

---

* Tom McNally (1943–), educated College of St Joseph, Blackpool and University College London; Labour MP for Stockport South, 1979–81; SDP MP for Stockport South, 1981–3; created Lord McNally, 1995; Leader of Liberal Democrats in House of Lords, from 2004.

that it was difficult to lay her armour down again. Michael Dobbs,* who accompanied her, remembered her, conscientious as ever, spending far too much time late at night in the hotel talking to the travelling press, whom she did not want to let down. She was exhausted. At last Denis pushed his way into the crowded room, and said, 'Come on, woman. Bedtime.' She meekly followed.[3]

The news of delay was more enthusiastically received in the Conservative Research Department. Chris Patten was inspecting galley proofs of the Conservative manifesto with Angus Maude when it came through. Until then, he had been worrying that Callaghan was bound to win as a reassuring 'management of decline' figure. Postponement gave the Tories their chance: 'We danced on the table with joy.'[4]†

There were plenty of signs of coming industrial trouble that might invalidate Callaghan's decision to delay. On 22 September, for example, Ford workers walked out in protest at the 5 per cent pay limit, and at the Labour Party conference at the beginning of October the pay policy was rejected, thanks to union block votes,‡ by a big margin. But the short-term effect of Callaghan's decision was to help Labour and put pressure on the Conservatives. Callaghan's own speech at the conference was thought to have 'changed the atmosphere'[5] for the better, and the opinion polls shifted. Gallup, which had recorded a 7 per cent Tory lead in September, returned a 5 per cent Labour lead the next month. The Tories duly obliged their opponents with another public split about pay policy.

The immediate cause of the split was Ted Heath. At the beginning of the year, strenuous attempts had been made by Humphrey Atkins and Lord Carrington to improve Heath's relations with Mrs Thatcher. Atkins suggested that she meet Heath to get his advice following his recent trip to the Middle East. To his surprise, she agreed and the two met secretly in her house in Flood Street. This was not a success. Mrs Thatcher considered that Heath did not unbend.[6] Heath's version was the same, but the other way round. 'It turned into *her* views,' he recalled.[7] In February, Atkins took further

---

* Michael Dobbs (1948–), educated Christ Church, Oxford and Fletcher School of Law and Diplomacy, Tufts University; government special adviser, 1981–7; chief of staff, Conservative Party, 1986–7; deputy chairman, Saatchi & Saatchi, 1983–6, 1988–91; Joint Deputy Chairman, Conservative Party, 1994–5; author of *House of Cards* and other political novels; created Lord Dobbs, 2010.

† Michael Portillo, who was also present, was impressed with how quickly Patten scooped up the proofs of the manifesto and locked them away, as soon as it became clear that they would not be needed immediately (interview with Michael Portillo).

‡ In this era, the union leaderships could cast the votes of all their members without consulting them. Motions were often passed at Labour conferences by extraordinary margins, such as 6 million votes.

soundings from Heath's doctor and confidant, Brian Warren, about what role, if any, Heath would like in Conservative politics. Atkins then saw Heath and was dismayed to find that he had chosen to interpret this feeler from the Chief Whip as a job offer from Mrs Thatcher herself. Heath expressed his readiness to be in the Shadow Cabinet (which had not been mentioned).[8] Poor Atkins then had to write Heath a letter making clear that Mrs Thatcher had not known of his approach to Warren. The opportunity for wilful mis-interpretation was there, and Tim Kitson, still, out of kindness, looking after Heath in Parliament, suspected he would take it, because of his tendency to self-deception.[9] This proved to be the case. Heath resumed his 'incredible sulk' for the next six months, and at the party conference made a speech from the floor, described by *The Times* as 'stuffy and charmless'.[10] He referred to Mrs Thatcher's suggestion that the 5 per cent pay limit had already been broken and said that, if it had been, 'there is nothing for gloating, nothing for joy. We should grieve for our country.' On television that night, he said that 'free collective bargaining produces massive inflation' and that if Cal-laghan 'says he is going to the country and expresses the view that we cannot have another roaring inflation or another free-for-all, I would say I agree with that'. Heath supporters, notably Jim Prior, took their stand on the word-ing of *The Right Approach to the Economy*, which had said that 'the Government must come to *some* conclusions about the likely scope for pay increases,' but Keith Joseph caused further discord by saying on television that this sentence referred only to pay in the public sector.

In a weak internal political position, and with opinion polls showing that the public preferred the Heath–Callaghan view about pay to the free-for-all which she was thought to advocate, Mrs Thatcher was embarrassed. But she was also determined not to get trapped into committing to an incomes pol-icy. In a private conversation with Bill Deedes after the Labour Party conference and before her own, she revealed her anxieties about the idea that the country could be run by a pact between unions and government. 'Sover-eignty of Govt has to be reasserted,' Deedes's notes recorded her saying. 'Govt and Unions have roles to play – honourable roles, but must be clear what these roles are.' Deedes reminded her that 'TUs have done in 2 Govts and are about to do in a third.' 'No, she couldn't say that,' Mrs Thatcher told him cautiously. '– But ... they must revert to their proper job.' She complained to Deedes that Jim Prior had been 'behaving very oddly' and that it was 'not too clear what he would be saying at the Brighton Conf'.[11] At Brighton, Prior told his audience that a statutory incomes policy might have to happen 'under certain circumstances'. Mrs Thatcher publicly contradicted him on television: 'None of us could think of the circumstances.'[12] And in her party conference speech, which the dispirited rank and file considered slightly weak, she stuck to a formula which allowed scope for differences without conceding her position: 'We believe in realistic, responsible collective bargaining, free from government interference'.[13] Before the end of the month, Labour held the fairly marginal seat of Berwick and East Lothian at a by-election, its best by-election result in that Parliament. Heath had appeared on the hustings in the campaign and reiterated his support for an incomes policy. 'So it still looks open and interesting,' wrote Bernard Donoughue in his diary, 'and suggests we might have won an election now.'[14] Thatcherites were angry at what they saw as Heath's disloyalty. 'Receiving support from Ted Heath is like being measured for the undertaker,' said George Gardiner.[15] But an NOP poll in November showed a Tory lead of 3 per cent which rose to 14 per cent if Heath were once again leader of the party. The Tories felt stuck. For the only time in its history, the party had published its compendious election *Campaign Guide* in the wrong year, assuming a poll in the autumn of 1978. The mood was: 'There was nothing more we could do.'[16]

Luckily for Mrs Thatcher, both arms of the Labour movement – parliamentary and trade union – continued to try to cut their own and each other's throats. On 12 December, the public sector unions rejected Stage 3 of the pay policy. On 13 December, the government was defeated in Parliament on a vote on its sanctions against employers, most notably Ford, which had broken the policy's 5 per cent limit. This meant, Donoughue thought at the time, that the government was 'effectively finished'.[17] Yet in the debate on the vote of confidence the following day, which the government won, it was Callaghan who appeared in charge and Mrs Thatcher who failed to rise to the occasion. Donoughue recorded: 'She sped on as if nobody else was in the House, and very soon people were chatting on the back benches or leaving for tea – because she does not *involve* them.' Discussing the debate afterwards, Callaghan said to Donoughue that Mrs Thatcher didn't realize that a large part of success in Parliament came from treating it as a form of show business, but he added that 'she was good when provoked'.[18]*

On the last day of the old year, the Thatchers gave a lunch party at Scotney Castle. It was the first day of heavy snow, and roughly half the guests failed to appear. Mrs Thatcher told Bill Deedes, who had made it through the blizzard, that she had 'just endured the worst two months of her time as Leader'. 'By no means down – but low ebb,' Deedes commented.[19] But Britain's difficulties were to prove her opportunity. On 3 January 1979 a strike by lorry drivers began. Jim Callaghan, sitting in-

---

* Mrs Thatcher was aware of this tendency in herself. She told the *Observer* in an interview conducted nine days later, 'This animal, if attacked, defends itself' (*Observer*, 18 February 1979).

Downing Street with surprisingly little to do, ruminated. Things were 'all falling apart', he told Bernard Donoughue. 'We shall wake up in a few weeks' time and find that it is too late, everybody is settling for 20 per cent.'[20] The next morning's *Daily Mail* carried an NOP poll putting Labour 3 per cent ahead of the Conservatives, but Callaghan was nevertheless correct. He set off for the summit of the G7 – the main world economic powers – on the Caribbean island of Guadeloupe. It was far away, it seemed irrelevant to the crisis confronting the country, and it was hot and sunny at a time when the British winter was peculiarly beastly cold. Press photographs of Callaghan in shirtsleeves with other world leaders roused feeling against him, and when he returned to Britain on 10 January the upbeat briefing he had received on the aeroplane that the oil tanker drivers' dispute was settled (it had been, but disputes were under way in road haulage and railways, and approaching in coal, gas, electricity, local authorities and the Civil Service) caused him to appear complacent in his remarks to the press at the airport. 'Crisis? What Crisis?' was the splash headline in the *Sun*. Callaghan never uttered these words, but they expressed the attitude behind his remarks, and they stuck to him.

Even before Callaghan's return to Britain, Mrs Thatcher had already begun to change her tone. Interviewed by Brian Walden on *Weekend World* on 7 January, she turned more fiercely than before upon the union leaders. 'I am not in Parliament', she said, 'to enable anyone to have a licence to inflict harm, damage and injury on others and be immune from the law.'[21] She called for postal ballots before strikes, though she was 'reluctant' to impose them, and for a tax on benefits to strikers. In a letter to Hugh Thomas three days later, Mrs Thatcher wrote: 'If I have one resolution for the New Year it is that I should not depart from my convictions by one iota – nor should I fear the reaction of the so-called Liberal Establishment to what I have to say.'[22] In a Commons debate on the industrial situation on 16 January, she expressed outrage at what was happening. Donoughue recorded: 'Typical of her at her best, articulating popular resentment and prejudices . . . If she comes to power it will be wholly because of the trade unions . . . Moss Evans [General Secretary of the Transport and General Workers Union] and his T & G have acted as her stormtroopers.'[23]

But despite Donoughue's observation of her rhetorical fierceness, Mrs Thatcher's political stance in the debate was, in a way, conciliatory. She offered to support Callaghan if he introduced the necessary reforms, such as firmer action on picketing and the outlawing of secondary picketing.[24] This was part of a strategy culminating in her party political broadcast of the following evening, and involved departing by more than an iota from her convictions – that the Opposition should not seek to bargain with the government. As the 'Winter of Discontent', as people, invoking Shake-speare, were starting to call it, deepened, it had become obvious to a wide range of Mrs Thatcher's advisers – not just the centrist Chris Patten, but also the loyalist Gordon Reece, Tim Bell, T. E. Utley and Ronnie Millar – that an offer of conciliation would be much more electorally popular, and much more lethal to Callaghan, than a piece of partisan aggression. Mrs Thatcher was intensely suspicious. To Tim Bell, who literally went down on his knees to beg her to broadcast in such terms, Mrs Thatcher said: 'You're going to try to sell me a One Nation Tory message, aren't you?'[25] She feared she was being painted into a Macmillanite corner and made to endorse some sort of coalition government. Her advisers persuaded her, however, that the question was tactical and tonal, not one of principle: they were going to turn her into a statesman and make the government look like the party of opposition refusing to come together for the greater good of the country. Gordon Reece cunningly added the bait that, by speaking out now and in this way, she would put herself on the right side of the argument with public opinion and so force Jim Prior to endorse all the main trade union reforms she wanted and anticipate any attempt to block her that he might make.[26]

Mrs Thatcher was thoroughly grumpy about the whole idea, a fact which she partially conceals in her memoirs,[27] but, as always, once she had agreed to something she went into it with gusto and professionalism. Reece and Bell filled her room in the House of Commons, from which her broadcast took place, with flowers to make her feel that she had not lost the argument.[28] She began by saying that she intended to rise above partisanship: 'it is our country, the whole nation, that faces this crisis . . . This is no time to put party before country.' She wondered 'what has happened to our sense of common nationhood and even of common humanity' that the sick and disabled could be made to suffer in these disputes, and she attacked the state of the law on picketing which meant that 'almost any determined group can strangle the country.' This particular storm might pass, she said, but the same thing would happen again – 'What we face is a threat to our whole way of life.' There had to be changes in the law: 'there will be no solution to our difficulties which does not include some restriction on the power of the unions.' She offered parliamentary co-operation to the government if it would ban secondary picketing, make provision for postal and secret ballots in strike votes and union elections, and establish no-strike agreements in essential services such as the fire brigades. The broadcast was artfully constructed so that it reminded viewers of Labour's responsibility for the problem and yet reached out to Labour in the name of national unity. 'I recognise how hard this is for the Labour Party,' said

Mrs Thatcher, 'because of their close connection with the unions. Without the unions there would be no Labour Party. Without union money there would be no Labour funds.' But she hoped that it would take the chance in the interests of all, since for the past fifteen years both the parties had tried and failed to crack the problem of the unions. 'We have to learn again to be one nation,' she concluded, casting aside her earlier anxiety about the phrase, 'or one day we shall be no nation.'[29]

The broadcast was a success. Critics of the Thatcher administrations who allege that they promoted selfishness tend not to recall that it was a revulsion against selfishness – in the form of arbitrary union power – which brought Mrs Thatcher into office in the first place. The Winter of Discontent, after all, involved innumerable disputes in which the public were made to suffer. There was even a time, in Liverpool, when (as Tory propaganda in later years never failed to point out) the dead went unburied. In her broadcast, she articulated this revulsion powerfully. She also turned the pressure on to Callaghan. She knew that the precariousness of his parliamentary and trade union position made it impossible for him to grant what she asked, and yet that most voters would see her offer as reasonable. On the following day, the Cabinet met to discuss whether to call a state of emergency (they decided not to): 'Afterwards, the PM said to McCaffrey* with a straight face: "How do you announce that the Government's Pay Policy has completely collapsed?" He also said to McCaffrey, "Well it will all be over in 11 weeks."'[30] Suddenly, there was a sense that the main point of the Labour government – that it could combine with the unions to achieve industrial harmony – had vanished. The following day, Bernard Donoughue recorded, 'The end of the worst week . . . since I came to No. 10 . . . The atmosphere is one of quiet despair.'[31] All Callaghan could do in public was to talk of voluntary codes of practice and new union agreements about pay – he reached a 'Concordat' with the TUC on 23 February 1979 – and urge people to cross secondary picket lines. Even this got him into trouble in his own party.

At last, the Conservatives felt emboldened, having discovered, almost by accident, a way of sounding tough and yet non-partisan at the same time. The minutes of the Leader's Steering Committee for 22 January – the date chosen for a 'Day of Action'† by a million local authority workers – recorded the understated view that 'When we came to revise the Manifesto

---

* Tom McCaffrey (1922–), head of News Department, FCO, 1974–6; chief press officer to the Prime Minister, 1976–9; knighted, 1979.

† 'Action' at that time, in the parlance of industrial disputes, always meant striking, never working.

draft it would be necessary to give greater emphasis to the problem of union power ... than we had in the draft the previous autumn.'[32] Mrs Thatcher warmed to her themes. On *The Jimmy Young Show*, as rubbish accumulated in the streets and the power station workers and dockers were demanding 15 per cent pay rises, she spoke of the nation's 'spiritual crisis'. And she adopted the rhetoric of battle, against which, earlier, she had been cautioned: 'If someone is confronting our essential liberties, if someone is inflicting injury, harm and damage on the sick, my God, I will confront them.' She drove home her point that the rule of law was under threat, explicitly disagreeing with Arthur Scargill, not yet the leader of the National Union of Mineworkers but already its leading firebrand, who had appeared on the programme the day before: 'There can be no liberties unless the law is enforced. That is my great quarrel with Scargill.'[33] An opinion poll in the *Daily Express* on 6 February put the Conservatives 19 per cent ahead of Labour.

The last few weeks of the Labour government were dominated, even more than the previous five years had been, by parliamentary arithmetic. Until the devolution referendums on 1 March, Callaghan could hold on to his majority in the Commons. But once the Scottish 'yes' vote had failed to meet the required threshold of 40 per cent of those entitled to vote and the Welsh had voted 'no' outright, the government might fall at any time. Callaghan tried to string things out, but the Liberals, worried about the trial in May of their former leader, Jeremy Thorpe, for conspiracy to murder his ex-lover Norman Scott, were now anxious for an election. On 22 March, Callaghan offered the Scottish Nationalists further talks on devolution, to be settled by the end of April. This did not impress them. Seeing that they could now hope for Liberal, Nationalist and Unionist support (though Mrs Thatcher refused any binding deals), the Tories tabled a vote of confidence, designed to bring down the government.

Although Callaghan was curiously divided about whether or not he wanted an immediate election (the last permitted date for one was October), Labour still made frantic and comical efforts to secure this vote. Could the Liberal MP Cyril Smith, famous for his vast bulk, be persuaded to vote with the government by the offer of a peerage? Negotiations about this went on with his mother, who made all important decisions for him. Would the Northern Irish Social Democratic and Labour Party MP Gerry Fitt* vote with the government if offered a less pro-Unionist Northern Ireland

---

* Gerry Fitt (1926–2005), educated Christian Brothers' School, Belfast; Leader, SDLP, 1970–79; Irish Labour MP for Dock Division of Belfast, Parliament of Northern Ireland, 1962–72;

secretary than Roy Mason? Could the Labour MP Alfred 'Doc' Broughton be dragged from his sickbed to vote? The Independent Republican MP for Fermanagh and South Tyrone, Frank Maguire, who rarely attended the House, announced his intention of coming to 'abstain in person'. Maguire was often the worse for drink and had therefore, in the past, been told by his minders where and how to vote in the Lobby, but on this occasion his wife accompanied him in order to prevent this. In short, on the morning of the debate, 28 March, almost nothing was clear. To add to the almost far-cical nature of the proceedings, there was a strike of catering staff in the House of Commons. Two Tory whips went out and bought most of the contents of the Lower Belgrave Street delicatessen,* and plenty of alcohol.

Mrs Thatcher did not speak very well. Concerned only to win the vote, she did not want to give any hostages to fortune or start any new contro-versies. Britain, she said, was 'a nation on the sidelines' with 'far too much power in the hands of the centralised state', whose taxes and controls produced a 'pocket-money society policy'. Labour was in hock to the unions, and all substantive reform 'takes second place to the survival of the Government'.[34] 'She made a bad, flat speech,' said Bernard Donoughue, 'and sat down to a disappointed reception from her side.' Callaghan per-formed rather more effectively, but, having done so, he told Donoughue the bad news: 'They cannot get Doc Broughton. He is too ill. We will lose. Please go and get Audrey.'[35]† Michael Foot, the Leader of the House, wound up for the government in what was generally regarded as a brilliant speech of partisan denunciation. Denis Thatcher was 'under the Gallery' watching it, and got furious at Foot's jibes. He had had a drink or two, and kept saying 'Rubbish', until rebuked by an usher.[36]

Then there was the vote. As the counting came to an end, Bernard Donoughue noticed that 'The Tories looked down and seemed to expect to lose. One of them who is a friend signalled to me a thumbs down.'[37] Then Humphrey Atkins went over to Mrs Thatcher and Willie Whitelaw: 'They looked disappointed, even angry. Then our teller came in waving his paper gleefully. Our side began to cheer. But when the tellers all came in, it was clear from the grins on the Tory faces and the gloom on ours that we had lost – by one vote.'[38] The figures were 310 for the government and 311 against. Broughton had, indeed, not made it to the Chamber. Frank Maguire,

---

MP for West Belfast: Republican Labour, 1966–70; SDLP, 1970–79; Independent Socialist, 1979–83; created Lord Fitt, 1983.

* Not Fortnum's, as Mrs Thatcher erroneously states in her memoirs.

† Audrey was Callaghan's immensely supportive wife. He liked to have her near him on all difficult occasions, and when she died in 2005 he survived her by only eleven days.

who had tried to vote with the government at the last minute, had, despite his wife, been forbidden by Irish Republican heavies* who accompanied him, and was 'nearly in tears';[39] so it could be said that IRA supporters were the occasion of Mrs Thatcher's victory.

Ignoring Mrs Thatcher's plea for an early poll, Callaghan chose the last possible date for a general election now open to him – 3 May.† He hoped by doing so to allow plenty of time to turn the attention of the campaign away from Labour's problems and on to Mrs Thatcher herself, contrasting his own experience, moderation and reliability with what he thought were her shrillness and extremism. For better or worse, Callaghan believed, 'she is the dominant personality of the campaign. If we win, it will be because people cannot take her.'[40] It was for this reason that Callaghan broke the tradition that it is the incumbent who refuses the invitation to a television debate between the party leaders which is always offered but which never took place until the general election of 2010. Although he did not under-estimate Mrs Thatcher's debating skills, Callaghan calculated, surely correctly, that she had more to lose in a debate than he, and so indicated that he would accept the television invitation. Mrs Thatcher was very keen to accept it too. She was terrified of being considered terrified, particularly being terrified 'as a woman',[41] and wanted to be seen on equal terms with the Prime Minister. Chris Patten, too, advised her to have the debate. Those ranked on the other side of the argument, though, weighed more heavily. They included Willie Whitelaw, Lord Thorneycroft, Gordon Reece and everyone at Saatchis. All of them believed that the debate would be make-or-break for Mrs Thatcher, but not for Callaghan, who was a much better-known quantity, and that the possibility of 'break' when the Conservatives were ahead in the polls anyway was not worth the risk. There was also a view that, because of her sex, it would have been bad for Mrs Thatcher both if she had lost and if she had won. If she had lost, she would have demonstrated straightforward incompetence. If she had won, that would have been a woman humiliating a man, and this would have been unsettling for many male voters. As Thorneycroft put it to David Butler, 'many men would have resented it. They would have said, "That's my wife" and it wouldn't have been a good thing.'[42]

---

* Sinn Fein–IRA had turned against the Labour government because of the very strong security stand taken by Roy Mason.

† The general election was not due by law until October, but Callaghan could not continue any longer than six weeks, the maximum permitted notice period for a poll, without a working majority in Parliament.

Gordon Reece was so worried that Mrs Thatcher would accept the invitation to debate that he actually hid the first letter of invitation from her and refused it, hoping that it would somehow be swept aside by events.[43] A second letter arrived, however, and Mrs Thatcher challenged Reece about why she had not been shown the first. Reece remembered: 'All the moisture in my mouth dried up because the row was so terrible.'[44] Mrs Thatcher said, 'Gordon, you'd better go home.' In the early hours of the morning, Reece, by this time drunk, rang Tim Bell and said, 'It's all over. My career is finished,' but Bell advised him simply to return to work the next day and say nothing.[45] He did so, and, somehow or other, his view prevailed. Comforting herself with the excuse that the debate would give an unwarranted advantage to the Liberal leader, David Steel, because the television authorities would have to make some sort of provision for him in all this, Mrs Thatcher refused – writing, as if butter wouldn't melt in her mouth, 'Personally, I believe that issues and policies should decide elections, not personalities. We should stick to that approach. We are not electing a president, we are choosing a government.'[46] In 10 Downing Street, her decision was greeted with relief. Callaghan had felt he must be seen to be ready to debate, and Mrs Thatcher be seen to refuse, but he had been worried about it. Bernard Donoughue recorded: 'He [Callaghan] is very pleased that Thatcher has declined to go on television against him – a relief to us all, since I think she would have done well. She is much more effective than most of our people – or her advisers apparently – seem to realise.'[47] For Reece and his allies, though, this was an important victory, one that kept their strategy intact. As David Butler noted Reece saying just after the election, 'He [Reece] did not want the election to be about the election. He wanted it to be about what happened last winter.'[48]

In a sudden flurry, starting in early February, the Conservatives redrafted their manifesto. On 5 February, Angus Maude wrote to Mrs Thatcher telling her that the manifesto would be reworked. On this letter, she scribbled: 'I think the existing draft will have to be radically changed consequent on recent events and on much more robust union policy. But the general approach of limited objectives first (i.e. tax cuts etc. to encourage wealth creation) remains. In my view the average person and a lot of non-average as well, wants "tax cuts and order".'[49] When the second draft of the new version reached her in March, Mrs Thatcher wrote a note on the title page to Chris Patten, who was in charge of the drafting: 'Chris – have read through this with considerable dismay. See comments.' She set to work on the section entitled 'Our Five Main Tasks', slashing whatever she thought was too vague or feeble. Where the draft said, 'Our economic weakness has been partly caused by failure to accept that the interests of all classes within the nation are ultimately the same,' Mrs Thatcher put a line through it and wrote, 'No it hasn't – it isn't.' Where the draft said, 'It would be dishonest to pretend that substantial cuts can be made painlessly,' she wrote, 'It depends where you make them.' Beside the assertion, 'Nor can we go on, year after year, tearing ourselves apart in increasingly bitter and calamitous industrial disputes,' Mrs Thatcher wrote, 'The chances are we shall for quite a time.'

Mrs Thatcher was irritated by the consensual tone which still kept creeping in. On trade union reform, the draft declared, 'We have proposed a "moderates' charter" based on three changes . . .' She scrawled, 'Don't be "moderate" in the defence of liberty or the rule of law. It is the way to lose both.' On picketing, the draft stated, 'We will clarify the law to ensure that its provisions against such behaviour are enforceable.' She wrote, 'How. I haven't seen any proposals that will do this. This <u>must</u> be more specific.' And where the draft, on the subject of pay bargaining, meandered, 'those involved in pay bargaining . . . must understand properly the scope for total increase in pay and that unemployment is bound to rise if this figure is exceeded while monetary policy remains, as it must, under firm control,' Mrs Thatcher wrote, 'This is <u>awful</u>.' In all references to the EEC, she tried to excise anything which offered more power to Europe. When the draft spoke of 'common economic and industrial problems that lie beyond the scope of any national government', she cut the second half of the phrase. Where it suggested 'a more positive approach' to the Common Agricultural Policy and the Common Fisheries Policy, she added, 'This is not quite right. It looks as if we shall be more pliant.' Throughout, she sought to toughen everything up. Yet at the same time her natural caution showed through. Whenever a commitment seemed too specific, she wrote, 'Hostage!' or 'hostage to fortune'.[50]

Despite the ferocity of Mrs Thatcher's assault on the drafts, the final product was not at all rabid in tone. Indeed, the foreword which appeared under her name now began with a rejection of dogma: 'For me, the heart of politics is not political theory, it is people and how they want to live their lives.' Power was being tilted away from people and towards the state: 'This election may be the last chance we have to reverse that process.' She placed herself as the voice of the future – the leader who could achieve greatness for the country – but she saw this achievement as a restoration of the past. Some said that a once great nation could not recover: 'I don't accept that. I believe we not only can, we must.' Her party's manifesto was based 'above all on liberty of the people under the law'. She appealed to an almost wartime feeling of 'we're all in this together': 'The things we have in common as a nation far outnumber those that set us apart.'

The Conservatives proclaimed that they had five main tasks – economic and social health, the restoration of incentives, the upholding of Parliament and the rule of law (in part a coded phrase referring to trade union over-mightiness), support for family life (for example, council house sales, where a tenant's right to buy was promised) and parent power in schools, and the strengthening of defence. On trade unions, the sentence which Mrs Thatcher had questioned about 'tearing ourselves apart' stayed. There were three specific reforms proposed – the removal of immunities from second-ary picketing, a proper ballot about a closed shop and the right of individual appeal against membership, and secret and postal ballots, paid for out of public money, for union elections and strike votes. Pay policies were condemned, and the manifesto made no mention of the Pay Compa-rability Commission, chaired by Professor Hugh Clegg, whose findings, for electoral reasons and much against Mrs Thatcher's will, the Tories decided they must promise to honour. In a concession to her future Chan-cellor, Mrs Thatcher did allow Geoffrey Howe his beloved point about 'concerted action' by conceding the need for what the manifesto called 'more open and informed discussion of the Government's economic objec-tives (as happens, for example, in Germany and other countries)'.

On taxes, under the heading of 'A more prosperous country', the mani-festo declared, 'We shall cut income tax at all levels to reward hard work,' but offered no particular rate. There would be cuts in public spending, but the document was deliberately vague about where these would fall. *Sotto voce*, the manifesto explained that income tax cuts could not be paid for without a 'switch to some extent from taxes on earnings to taxes on spend-ing'. The five-year-old promise to abolish the domestic rating system was repeated only to be postponed: 'cutting income tax must take priority for the time being over abolition of the domestic rating system.' Nationaliza-tion was denounced, but denationalization was not strongly proclaimed. Only shipbuilding and aerospace were specifically marked for denation-alization; it was also promised that shares in the National Freight Corporation would be sold off. There would be better police pay, a new British Nationality Act and firmer immigration controls, and higher defence spending. On Europe, the manifesto called for a 'single voice' in foreign policy, but was in other respects rather cool. 'National payments into the budget should be more closely related to ability to pay,' it said, a low-key harbinger of a row to come.

By the admittedly low standards of the genre, the Conservative mani-festo reads well. It is clear and coherent, and sets out a scale of priorities. It was reticent, but not dishonest, about the need for spending cuts and for an increase in VAT. It expressed a sense of urgency without lapsing into extremism, and it offered a clear difference from Labour's message of reassurance. It also represented an enormous amount of policy work, fairly well digested. Adam Ridley, who by the time of publication had already had a transition meeting with Bernard Donoughue, the man he expected to succeed in the No. 10 Policy Unit, remembered: 'I was excited. We had prepared well.'[51] For three years, the Research Department had produced shadow spending White Papers which were ready to go to the Treasury after the election. Mrs Thatcher herself had seen Sir Ian Bancroft,* the head of the home Civil Service, to discuss her transition to prime minister, but had forbidden all her shadow ministers, except for Geoffrey Howe, to see the permanent secretaries of their putative departments, since she did not wish to commit herself in advance to choosing who would get what job. Kenneth Stowe,† who, as Callaghan's principal private secretary, would be hers for the transition, talked to Bernard Donoughue about the process; 'Ken says she gives the impression of wanting to run the whole show herself. It is clear that the Civil Service is viewing the prospect of her arriving with some dismay.'[52]

In modern, televisual election campaigns, which are always so tightly controlled, the press looks for what it calls a gaffe. Thanks to Gordon Reece's preoccupation with getting the right television images, the campaign of May 1979 was perhaps the first such election. The gaffe duly came, though not through television, even before the campaign had been officially launched. In 1978, Matthew Parris,‡ a young member of the Conservative Research Department, who dealt with much of the Leader's correspondence, had replied to a Mrs Evelyn Collingwood, of Erith (Mrs Thatcher's first electoral stamping ground), who had complained about the state of her council house, as follows:

> At Mrs Thatcher's request I am replying on her behalf to your recent letter. I hope you will not think me too blunt if I say that it may well be that your council accommodation is unsatisfactory, but considering the fact that you have been unable to buy your own accommodation you are lucky to have been given something, which the rest of us are paying for out of our taxes.[53]

---

* Ian Bancroft (1922–96), educated Coatham School and Balliol College, Oxford; head of the Home Civil Service and Permanent Secretary to the Civil Service Department, 1978–81; knighted, 1975; created Lord Bancroft, 1982.

† Kenneth Stowe (1927–), educated County High School, Dagenham and Exeter College, Oxford; principal private secretary to the Prime Minister, 1975–9; Permanent Under-Secretary, Northern Ireland Office, 1979–81; Permanent Secretary, DHSS, 1981–7; knighted, 1980.

‡ Matthew Parris (1949–), educated Waterford School, Swaziland and Clare College, Cambridge; Conservative MP for West Derbyshire, 1979–86; author, columnist for The Times, from 1987.

This was a freelance expression of Parris's own irritation with Mrs Collingwood's querulous tone, and had not been cleared with Mrs Thatcher.

The *Daily Mirror* had obtained a copy of this letter, and sat on it until the electoral moment judged most damaging to the Tory campaign. When the story broke on the *Mirror*'s front page on 30 March, including words of apology from Mrs Thatcher – 'It was offensive and lacked understanding' – the Labour Party printed three million copies for delivery to every council house of every marginal seat in the country. The story could be made big because it seemed to confirm the fear many voters had that Mrs Thatcher was a divisive figure, the fierce spokesman of her own class, the fierce opponent of those below her.

That morning, however, while Mrs Thatcher was attending a charity function in her constituency, a bomb went off under Airey Neave's car as he attempted to leave the House of Commons car park. He died that day. The bomb had been planted by the Irish National Liberation Army, an Irish Republican splinter group. Republicans were keen to murder Neave, chiefly because he was close to Mrs Thatcher, but also because his approach to the subject of Northern Ireland was closer to integrationist moderate Unionism than had been the policy under Heath. From their point of view, his murder was worth while, since from then on the anti-Unionist search for 'power-sharing' dominated Tory thinking, even though Mrs Thatcher herself never much cared for it. Republicans believed that power-sharing – the division of the spoils between Unionists and Nationalists – gave them more chance for ultimate success in Northern Ireland than did the integration of the province with the rest of the United Kingdom. In the period of opposition, Mrs Thatcher had devoted very little personal attention to the problem of Northern Ireland, trusting Neave to develop the right policies himself. His death brought out her strongest native feeling on the subject – her hatred of giving any sort of victory to terrorists. Outside her house in Flood Street later that day, Mrs Thatcher told the BBC: 'Some devils got him. They must never, never, never be allowed to triumph.'[54]

It sounds callous to say it, but Mrs Thatcher's campaign benefited from Neave's murder, not only because it removed attention from Matthew Parris's letter. Such terrible occasions brought out both her natural human warmth – all the Neave family were much touched by the attention and sympathy she gave them* – and her attachment to certain simple principles. On 2 April, paying tribute to the man who, more than any other MP, had won her the leadership, she said: 'Airey's death diminishes us, but it will enhance our resolve that the God-given freedoms in which he believed, and

---

* Neave's widow, Diana, was made Baroness Airey of Abingdon.

which are the foundation of our parliamentary democracy, will in the end triumph over the acts of evil men.'[55] Few in the House would have disagreed with these sentiments, but equally few would have expressed them with such fervent conviction. For the public, the death of Airey Neave sublimi-nally deepened the idea that Mrs Thatcher was serious, and stood for something important. This struck Alistair McAlpine when he attended Neave's funeral a few days later. He noted that the funeral had, strangely, 'quite a joyful atmosphere'. It gave the Tories an 'incentive to win'. There was a sense that 'This was definitely the moment, the feeling that this was her hour.'[56]

The campaign itself was slow to start. Reece, aware of Callaghan's tactic of trying to get Mrs Thatcher to make mistakes, kept her quiet. Chafing to be doing something, she made her staff's life a misery, and Ronnie Mil-lar tried to distract her by taking her off to a musical.[57] She explained the delay in a newspaper interview with one of her favourite aphorisms – 'Time spent on reconnaissance is seldom wasted'[58] – but she was not enjoying herself. When the manifesto was launched at Central Office in the opening press conference of the campaign on 11 April, the heat from 300 journal-ists trying to crowd in was almost unbearable, but Mrs Thatcher's message was quite cool. Flanked by Whitelaw, Howe, Joseph, Prior, Thorneycroft, Maude, Atkins, Carrington and Pym, she wished to give an impression of unity and calm. She was more concerned to avoid being trapped than to say anything new. She promised – though she hated it – to honour the Clegg Commission's pay findings; she said that there could be no sudden end to industrial subsidy, and she pushed aside arguments about the dis-tribution of the 'national cake' by saying that the point was to create more cake 'before we can decide how the extra shall be sliced up'.[59] Her more emotional speeches – disparaged by Chris Patten as 'hot-gospelling' – were confined to the ticket-only rallies which she addressed across the country.

At her adoption meeting in Finchley the same day, Mrs Thatcher spoke of the 'choice between good and evil'[60] for each person, and implied that such a choice now presented itself. At a rally in Cardiff five days later, she exclaimed: 'Now, Mr Chairman, because I hold some of these views, I am dubbed as a reactionary. "Maggie Thatcher, reactionary." Well, Mr Chair-man, there's a lot to react against!'[61] Then she delivered one of her classic self-descriptions: 'in politics I've learnt something that you in Wales are born knowing. It's this: if you've got a message, preach it! [applause] The Old Testament prophets didn't go out into the highways saying, "Brothers, I want consensus." They said, "This is my faith and my vision! This is what I passionately believe!" And they preached it.'[62] This refusal of consensus was something which Callaghan tried to exploit, but it also helped her dominate the debate. At the same time as she proclaimed her faith, though, Mrs Thatcher made raids into enemy territory. One of her most frequent themes was the half-hidden extremism of Labour, contrasted with the sturdy patriotism (which she had certainly not noticed in her youthful speeches at the time) of Clement Attlee's generation. At Cardiff, this was expressed in one of Ronnie Millar's dire puns, which nevertheless, to pursue his beery metaphor, went down nicely: 'Labour today is like a pub where the mild is running out. Soon all that's left will be bitter, and all that's bitter will be Left.' And in Birmingham, she took the example of the city's famous son, Joe Chamberlain, to show how a politician may change his party, but remain 'passionately true to his beliefs'.[63] She was trailing her coat for converts. In the course of the campaign, the press reported that Harold Wilson's wife, Mary, was thinking of voting for Mrs Thatcher. And behind the scenes Marcia Williams, Lady Falkender (Harold Wilson's former political secretary), was working with Reece and McAlpine. She had confided in McAlpine, who was a friend, that she admired Mrs Thatcher and would like to help her. At discreet meetings in the flat of the pro-Thatcher businessman James Hanson,* McAlpine effected the introductions to Reece and an aide of Lord Thorneycroft. The purpose of the meetings was for Lady Falkender to convey to the Tory campaigners her assessment of what the Labour Party was thinking.[64]

The Reece plan for the campaign was to get Mrs Thatcher shown in the right television pictures. Indeed, Reece wanted to do away with the London press conferences, which he saw only as traps, but was overruled by his boss because she felt it essential to be in London each day to control the campaign at Central Office. The most important coverage, in Reece's view, was the least political – the early-evening television news watched by women, the local papers reporting favourably the leader's visit to their area, rather than the national ones trying to take apart every word she said. He got her out of London, lockstitching clothes in Leicester, wiring herself and Denis up to a heart machine in Milton Keynes, joining tea-tasters in a factory and, famously, cuddling a calf on a farm in Suffolk for thirteen minutes to get the right camera angles. These techniques are now considered old hat, but then they were novelties, the more novel because they were being performed by the first woman to lead a British political party. She was blonde, 5 foot 5, size 14 and weighing 9½ stone:† she was

---

* James Hanson (1922–2004), educated Elland Grammar School and Merlegh; chairman, Hanson PLC, 1965–97; knighted, 1976; created Lord Hanson of Edgerton, 1983.

† Mrs Thatcher found it hard to keep her weight down, and for two weeks of the campaign she subjected herself to a diet, aimed at losing 20 lb, which she checked against a daily sheet

different, and she was bursting with energy. Frank Johnson, then parliamentary sketch-writer for the *Daily Telegraph*, accompanied Mrs Thatcher
to a Cadbury chocolate factory in the marginal constituency of Birmingham, Selly Oak. He described the visit as:

> the most picturesque which your correspondent has witnessed in a decade
> or so of observing politicians trying to become Prime Minister. Mrs Thatcher
> would descend on a chocolate woman . . . They would have a conversation.
> Because of the din, neither could hear the other . . . the leader of the Oppos-
> ition would inevitably be urged to try chocolate packing herself. The problem,
> of course, would be to stop her. Maniacally, she would raid the hazel crispy
> clusters and shove them in passing boxes . . . What a scene! The genius at
> Conservative Central Office who thought it up must get a knighthood.[65]

He did. Reece became Sir Gordon in 1986.*

An added reason for stunts of this sort was that Mrs Thatcher, as she
had proved at the start of her leadership, was very good at them. The
artificiality which she sometimes showed in the television studios melted
away when confronted with members of the public. Her actressy ability
combined with her practical streak and her genuine interest in shopping
and how things are made. She loved discoursing about how convenient
teabags were, or the best way of mending a garment, and loved hurtling
up and down streets, always rushing, always talking. Although Mrs
Thatcher was often accused of being humourless, and it was certainly the
case that she did not always 'get' jokes, she always had a sense of occasion
and of fun. She injected drama into these visits, and made the members of
the public caught up in them amused and excited to be there.

During the campaign, Michael Cockerell followed Mrs Thatcher round
for the BBC, compiling a documentary about what he saw as her campaign
made for the media – 'the most professionally organised ever'. He noted
two Margaret Thatchers, the 'crusading Iron Maiden', woman of principle,

---

of instructions. This began: 'Abstain from everything not included in the diet and be sure to
eat what is assigned rather than do without. NO EATING BETWEEN MEALS.' (Minute,
1 January 1979, THCR 6/1/1/31.) The diet involved eating twenty-eight eggs per week, grapefruit for breakfast (with 'black coffee or clear tea'), steak and salad. By the time she entered
No. 10, she did look more slender.

* Mrs Thatcher, however, was a little slow in realizing Reece's full importance. That was certainly his opinion. In 1981, she offered him the CBE. He wrote back, with icy anger: 'It is my
view that with the exception of yourself, no member of the Conservative Party contributed
more effectively to the result of the 1979 election than I did . . . Not that such services demand
a knighthood . . . But I respectfully suggest that that or nothing were the alternatives . . . I am
conscious of the honourable estate of the CBE. In the circumstances I would prefer not to
accept it.' (Letter from Gordon Reece to Margaret Thatcher, 25 May 1981, THCR 1/3/6.)

and 'Our Maggie', the normal housewife. Mrs Thatcher was interviewed for the programme. She said there were 'at least three' Margaret Thatchers – 'There is the logical one, there's the instinctive one and there's just one at home' – and she was surprisingly frank about how she played everything for the camera. In a passage in which her manner now seems almost comically flirtatious, she explained the incident with the calf: 'The press say, "Look, we don't want just another photograph of you, with a hundred, uh, bullocks looking in *superb* condition." There was a beautiful calf, and after all, we had 70 or 80 cameramen around with us. They have to do their job . . .'[66] It was important to consider, she said, 'what you're like in three dimensions'. She emphasized that she had to get everything right because 'There's only one chance for women. 'Tis the law of life.'[67] This determination to make the most of her one chance brought out her showman's flair, and contrasted with Callaghan, good performer though he was, who perhaps by this time (he was sixty-seven and had held all the main offices of state) had too little to prove. 'I am not eaten up with ambition to get here, like she is,' he told Bernard Donoughue in 10 Downing Street.[68]*

Nevertheless, Mrs Thatcher's campaign was not strikingly successful. It suffered from beginning so well in front. Opinion polls which began by giving the Conservatives a lead of 10 per cent or so narrowed quite sharply. There was some feeling that the Saatchi campaigns which had been so popular in the previous year were too frivolous and clever for the electorate. One, shown on 19 April, depicted the 'International Prosperity Race', an athletic contest turned by Labour into an obstacle course. The athletes were burdened with large weights of taxation, unemployment and so on. The crowd protested at the handicaps and Tory managers took over. Another showed a patient in a bed covered with the Union Jack, suffering from a cold and sneezing. Thanks to Labour, said the voiceover, 'That cold seems to have turned to double pneumonia.' Film of a stereotypical German in a Bavarian hat and with a cigar showed him doing much better than the British. These were amusing and innovative approaches to political broadcasting, but to some they all looked slightly silly. There seemed to be a disjunction between an election whose result could be momentous, and a campaign which did not want to emphasize this too much.

With the passage of time, the press got to work on those areas of tax and spending which the Conservatives did not much want to talk about. Would the Tories break the link between earnings and pensions? Yes, but

---

* Evidence of the lack of dynamism in Callaghan's camp is provided by the fact that there were no typists at weekends during the campaign to type the Prime Minister's speeches: such weekend working was against union rules.

they were reluctant to say so in so many words. Would there be new, or increased, health charges? Would they double VAT? Callaghan havered about driving this point home because he feared that if Labour won he too would have to increase VAT,[69] but towards the end of April Labour started to push much harder on tax and prices. Michael Portillo, whose job it was to brief Mrs Thatcher on the contents of the press every morning of the campaign, remembered drafting an answer which said: 'We won't double VAT, or anything like.' When Geoffrey Howe crossed out 'or anything like', he realized for the first time how big were the tax changes contemplated.[70]* In Central Office, to Mrs Thatcher's annoyance, Thorneycroft worried that the tone of the campaign might be too extreme.[71]

After two weeks, the Conservative campaign felt as if it was stalling. Polls on 25 April showed the gap between the parties down to 5 per cent (Gallup) and 6 per cent (MORI). That night, after a successful rally in Edinburgh, Mrs Thatcher was dining with colleagues in her hotel in Edinburgh, when Janet Young,† the deputy chairman of the party, returned to the room from a telephone conversation with Thorneycroft and conveyed to her his view that she now needed to share a platform with Ted Heath to show unity and rescue centrist votes. According to Michael Dobbs, who was present, Mrs Thatcher said, 'No, I won't have it.' There was a furious row and she stormed out in tears, being comforted by Carol. In Dobbs's view, they were tears of frustration at men telling her she wasn't good enough.[72] Her sense of upset persisted, exacerbated by her tiredness; and at the press conference back in London two days later Mrs Thatcher reacted with exaggerated fury to two unsympathetic journalists. She asked Geoffrey Goodman of the *Daily Mirror*, who asked a question about the effect on jobs of technological change, 'Why are you getting so *frightened*?' And to David Holmes of the BBC, she said, 'Where have you been this last fifty years?' Her manner and also her voice showed signs of strain, and her organizers cancelled a speech and walkabout in Fulham that day. A MORI poll in the *Daily Express* the following morning brought the Tory lead down to 3 per cent, and gave Callaghan his biggest lead yet as the 'best

---

* Agreement about the near-doubling of VAT if the Conservatives came into office had been secretly reached by Geoffrey Howe, Lord Cockfield and Nigel Lawson, the main people concerned with the policy. Mrs Thatcher herself was not privy to this at this stage. As a result of her distance from this process, she could say in an election broadcast that the VAT increase would be 'Not a lot, but a little' (27 April) without actually lying. (Interview with Lord Lawson.)

† Janet Young (1926–2002), née Baker, married Geoffrey Young, 1950; educated Headington School, Oxford, in America and St Anne's College, Oxford; Leader of House of Lords, 1981–3; Lord Privy Seal, 1982–3; Minister of State, FCO, 1983–7; Vice-Chairman, Conservative Party, 1975–83; Deputy Chairman, 1977–9; created Baroness Young, 1971. Lady Young was the only woman Mrs Thatcher ever chose to serve in her Cabinet.

PM' – 19 per cent ahead of Mrs Thatcher. Tory jitters were also increased, at least in the memory of some sources, by advance notice of an NOP poll which actually gave Labour a 0.7 per cent lead. This was not published in the *Daily Mail* until 30 April, so it is strange if the information it contained was already circulating the previous week. The reasons for this delayed publication, if such it was, are not clear. Certainly rumours about bad polls helped fray some nerves. Giving a hostile judgment shortly after the campaign ended, Chris Patten told David Butler that the Conservatives lost the campaign – though they won the election – 'because they had a leader who was unpopular, and they had no adequate economic spokesman'. He remembered the Tuesday nine days before the poll as a day of 'desperate panic',[73] though he may have been getting the date wrong – Mrs Thatcher's embarrassing performance at the press conference was on Friday 27 April.

Looking back, one can see that the Tory jitters of the penultimate week of the campaign failed to take into account the underlying situation. Famously, it was Jim Callaghan who was clear on the subject. Driving with Bernard Donoughue round Parliament Square about halfway through the campaign, he analysed the situation with detachment: 'It does not matter what you say or do. There is a shift in what the public wants and what it approves. I suspect there is now such a sea-change – and it is for Mrs Thatcher.'[74] In this sense, although she certainly made some tonal mistakes, Mrs Thatcher was right about the almost prophetic message of change in her campaign, and the more cautious centrists, such as Thorneycroft, were wrong. She displayed her great gift for getting to the simple heart of an often complicated public issue and conveying it urgently. She stood for something which she presented as necessary, and which she contrived to make seem attractively new and yet also reassuringly old fashioned. Perhaps the most telling television programme to convey this was *The Granada 500*, a forum offered to all three party leaders separately, in which each appeared before an audience in Bolton, chosen as a town whose seats were highly marginal. On his appearance on the programme, Callaghan scored badly, being seen by some to have bullied a nurse. Gavyn Davies,* who worked in Callaghan's Policy Unit, told David Butler after the election result that Mrs Thatcher's appearance on the programme had 'struck all the right notes'.[75]

The range of questions allowed Mrs Thatcher to convey her key points. On the 'woman' question, she inserted a comparison with Queen Elizabeth

---

* Gavyn Davies (1950–), educated St John's College, Cambridge and Balliol College, Oxford; economic adviser, Prime Minister's Policy Unit, 1974–9; chief UK economist, Goldman Sachs, 1986–93; chairman, BBC, 2001–4.

I, without pushing it too vaingloriously far. On the unions, she sided with the majority against 'the few destroyers' and declared, 'Someone's got to tackle this problem.' On the poverty trap, she argued that it should never pay people not to work. On capital punishment, she took advantage of the moment to reiterate her personal support for hanging, while explaining that it could not be party policy. On immigration, answering an immigrant worried about proposed tightening of the rules so that fiancés would not automatically be admitted, she maintained a tough position which made no concessions to the questioner and won big applause from the audience. No individual answer was strikingly new or unusual, but the overall impression was of a woman well in touch with the anxieties of 'lower-middle' England, and ready to do something about them. It was this England – the C2s whom Gordon Reece had cultivated so assiduously – that had really lost faith in Labour and was ready to turn. With them in mind, Mrs Thatcher published her last newspaper article of the campaign, entitled 'The Britain I want', in the *Sun*.[76] The *Sun* front-page headline on polling day was 'Vote Tory This Time – It's the Only Way to Stop the Rot'.

On the same day as *The Granada 500*, Mrs Thatcher gave the final Conservative election broadcast, the first in which she alone spoke. The hoarseness in her voice which was worrying her managers could be detected, but she looked fresh and elegant, indeed almost too immaculate, beside a bowl of daffodils. Her message was of a great country gone wrong, which it was not yet quite too late to put right. 'In recent years,' she said, 'we haven't been true to ourselves,' but with courage, and a rejection of the socialism which was unnatural to Britain and (she mentioned the Soviet threat) menaced the whole world, the nation could recover: 'What matters are your convictions.' As if the tune from the patriotic hymn 'I vow to thee, my country' was playing in the background, she said, 'there's another Britain which may not make the daily news' of 'thoughtful people, oh, tantalisingly slow to act yet marvellously determined when they do': 'may this land of ours, which we love so much, find dignity and greatness and peace again.'[77] In Downing Street, the broadcast seemed preposterous. 'It was extraordinary,' wrote Bernard Donoughue, 'completely artificial, all sugary, an attempt by Mrs Thatcher to imitate the Queen's Christmas broadcast.'[78] Certainly the broadcast was stagy. But what the criticism misses is the genuineness behind it. As Mrs Thatcher put it in a speech the following day, quoting Victor Hugo without attribution, 'there is one thing stronger than armies, and that is an idea whose time has come.'[79] She believed that she had an idea and that its time had come, and therefore, as she told the closing press conference, the Tory campaign had been 'all of a piece stemming . . . from our deep beliefs about society'.[80]

In the month after the election, Nigel Lawson gave a private interview. He said something so blindingly obvious that its importance tended to be neglected by many observers used to the politics of Harold Wilson: 'A key to understanding Mrs Thatcher was that she actually said what she believed.'[81]

At about the same time, the former Labour MP Brian Walden, by then a television interviewer and strong Thatcher admirer, offered his own private analysis of her campaign. He said that Gordon Reece had been right in his strategy 'not to expose [her] to journalism but to the cameras' because if the journalists had been more alert, they would, being mainly leftist, have done much more to oppose her. 'The editors', said Walden, 'have simply not kept pace with Thatcherism': 'Mrs Thatcher was saying something *quite* different, but didn't want to be seen to be *too* different . . . This election *was* about a woman who believes in inequality, passionately, who isn't Keynesian, who is *not* worried about dole queues.' In his view, if interviewers had wanted to find the truth, they should have asked her, 'Mrs Thatcher, do you believe in a more unequal society?'[82]

For the practitioners, British general elections always end up in their constituencies. Mrs Thatcher went to Finchley to speak in an eve-of-poll rally on 2 May 1979. As they approached the Woodhouse School, Michael Dobbs, who was in the entourage, saw a young man step out of the crowd and punch Denis Thatcher in the stomach. Dobbs watched Denis stop and consider retaliation. 'Then he braced his shoulders and went on. This showed amazing discipline. He knew that if he had hit back, he, not she, would have become the story.'[83] Inside, Mrs Thatcher roused the troops. 'The moral case', she said, 'is on the side of the free society'.[84]

The following day, Mrs Thatcher voted in Chelsea (for the extremely unThatcherite candidate, Nicholas Scott),* while Denis voted in Lamberhurst. Just before midnight, she and Denis arrived at Barnet town hall for the count. By this time, the early results made clear that she would be prime minister, but, with her usual combination of caution and a respect for form, she refused to claim victory until it had been arithmetically achieved, which meant 318 Conservative seats. Jim Callaghan was quicker to react: he telephoned No. 10 from his constituency in Cardiff at 3 a.m. and told his staff that Labour had lost and they should all vacate their offices by 3.30 that afternoon.[85]

---

* Nicholas Scott (1933–99), educated Clapham College; Conservative MP for Paddington South, 1966–February 1974; for Chelsea, October 1974–99; held various junior ministerial posts, notably Minister of State, DHSS, later DSS, 1987–94; knighted, 1995.

In Finchley, the result was:

Mrs Margaret Thatcher (Conservative)	20,918
Richard May (Labour)	13,040
Anthony Paterson (Liberal)	5,254
William Verity (National Front)	534
Mrs Elizabeth Lloyd (Independent Democrat)	86
Conservative majority	7,878

Her majority was nearly twice what it had been in October 1974.

The final national result gave the Conservatives 339 seats to Labour's 269; there were twelve Ulster seats, eleven Liberal ones, two Scottish and two Welsh Nationalists. The Conservative overall majority was forty-three. The swing to the Tories was 5.1 per cent, the biggest swing either way since 1945. It was bigger in the south and midlands than in the north and Scotland, and notably bigger among C2s. The Conservative share of the vote was just under 44 per cent (13,897,690 votes). Among Labour's losses was the seat of Shirley Williams, the party's leading and most appealing woman. The only Conservative disaster of the night was the loss of Teddy Taylor's seat in Glasgow Cathcart.

Mrs Thatcher drove to Central Office, arriving at about 4 a.m. She was still not admitting victory, but Michael Dobbs, who was in the car with her, noticed that, as they passed Buckingham Palace, the escort of two cars suddenly gained three more cars and a motorcycle escort. This, he considered, was 'the moment of power'.[86]

In Smith Square, Mrs Thatcher told the press, 'I feel a sense of change and an aura of calm,' but still refused to claim victory. This only became certain at 2.45 p.m. A few minutes later, Mrs Thatcher drove to Buckingham Palace to kiss hands* with the Queen. 'Good luck, Prime Minister,' Alistair McAlpine shouted after her, as she left. 'Don't call me that yet,' she said, with constitutional correctness.[87]

---

* Hands are not actually kissed.

PART THREE

Power, 1979–1982

16

Downing Street

'They thought she was a sort of right-wing baboon'

Margaret Thatcher arrived at Buckingham Palace shortly before 3 p.m. on 4 May 1979, accompanied by Denis. Jim Callaghan had left about an hour earlier. The first woman Prime Minister wore a blue outfit with a pleated skirt which Cynthia Crawford, her assistant who had helped her choose it, described as 'very dainty'.[1] Mrs Thatcher saw the Queen, and thus received the authority to take up office. Callaghan's principal private secretary, Kenneth Stowe, who automatically continued to do the same job for the new Prime Minister, was waiting for her at the Palace as she came down the steps after her audience. He advised her to sit in the official car immediately behind the driver, rather than, as is more usual, on the other side of the back seats. This was to ensure that she could get out of the car at the door of 10 Downing Street without the waiting press and photographers seeing her legs first.[2]

When the Thatchers arrived, to cheers from the huge crowd which, in those pre-security days, was allowed into Downing Street, a journalist asked her how she felt. Mrs Thatcher said that she was 'very excited, very aware of the responsibilities.' Emphasizing her idea of herself as a woman of conviction, she promised that she would 'strive unceasingly to try to fulfil the trust and confidence that the British people have placed in me and the things in which I believe'. Then she quoted 'some words of St Francis of Assisi which I think are really just particularly apt at the moment. "Where there is discord, may we bring harmony. Where there is error, may we bring truth. Where there is doubt, may we bring faith. And where there is despair, may we bring hope."' These words (not, in fact, by St Francis, but by a nineteenth-century follower) had been supplied to her, at the very last minute, and to the chagrin of her private office,[3] by Ronnie Millar. They were to be used against her in later years by those who accused her of sowing more discord than ever. Even at the time, they seemed a little pious. Michael Dobbs, who was listening from the hall of No. 10 said: 'I thought she'd gone mad.'[4] Mrs Thatcher half acknowledged the point in

her memoirs when she wrote that the overcoming of the forces of error,
doubt and despair was bound to produce 'some measure of discord'.[5] But
her choice reflected the fact that it was the divisions of the nation, exposed
by the Winter of Discontent, which caused the greatest public anguish. The
new Prime Minister had to address them. Although she knew a fight might
come, she was not spoiling for one.

Quoting Airey Neave, 'whom we had hoped to bring here with us', Mrs
Thatcher said, 'There is now work to be done,' and made to go inside. But
a reporter jumped in to ask whether she had any thoughts at this moment
about Mrs Pankhurst, the leader of the Votes for Women campaigns before
the First World War, and about her own father. Mrs Thatcher ignored Mrs
Pankhurst and invoked Alfred Roberts: 'I just owe almost everything to
my own father . . . He brought me up to believe all the things I do believe . . .
And it's passionately interesting for me that the things that I learned in a
small town, in a very modest home, are just the things that I believe have
won the election. Gentlemen, you are very kind, may I just go . . .' and with
that she pushed through the door to be greeted, as is customary, by the
assembled staff, roughly seventy strong. Among the tiny group of party
men accompanying her, expecting to take up political appointments, was
Michael Dobbs. Looking at the ranks of career civil servants in the hall,
he decided that 'it was an uneven contest'.[6]

The introductions completed, Ken Stowe led Mrs Thatcher to the Cabinet Room, where all the briefs, which he had compiled in his adjacent
office, awaited. At the door, she turned to Stowe and asked him: 'Ken, what
do I do now?' 'You might want to speak to John Hunt [the Cabinet Sec-
retary], Prime Minister,' said Stowe. 'You've got to form an administration.'[7]

This little exchange was heartening for Stowe and his colleagues in the
private office, and appeared to confirm Dobbs's fears. The officials were
relieved to find her turning to them for help. Mrs Thatcher had a temperamental and ideological suspicion of the Civil Service; her time at Education
had made her angry about how officialdom could frustrate what she believed
needed doing. In opposition, she had complained of the difficulty in 'finding
enough colleagues with the character and ability to stand up to the Civil
Service', and claimed that she had met with success only 'by nearly killing
herself to get on top of 3,000 [officials] at DES'.[8] Many expected that she
would make radical changes in the machinery of government. Besides, the
plots and dramas of the Lib–Lab Pact, involving a good deal of monkeying
with the business of the House of Commons, had made bad blood between
government and Opposition. Stowe, as the official charged with operating
the pact, half expected to be punished by Mrs Thatcher when she arrived.
In his first meeting with her the previous year, to brief her on the Civil List

(the system of parliamentary payments to support the cost of the monarchy), he thought that he had 'never encountered someone before who was such a bad listener', and yet when he sat in on the Opposition front-bench speech on the subject shortly afterwards in the House of Commons, 'My jaw dropped as I heard my briefing coming back ... She'd taken it all in.'[9] He knew she was formidable, and he did not expect her to be sympathetic.

The most junior private secretary, Michael Pattison,* had joined No. 10 in late March and immediately found himself sitting in the officials' box in the Commons watching the no-confidence debate. 'I wasn't at all sure about the lady in the blue rinse,'† he remembered.[10] Bryan Cartledge,‡ who was the private secretary assigned to foreign affairs, recalled that an atmosphere of 'Lib–Labbery' prevailed among No. 10 officials, and a fear of Mrs Thatcher's 'general stridency'.[11] At lunchtime on the day of the handover of power, Jim Callaghan had collected all his closest Downing Street assistants, including the private secretaries, for a modest and melancholy farewell meal of cottage pie before going to take leave of the Queen. The civil servants present had fully expected to be the victims of the fierce new broom which would begin sweeping that afternoon. That night, however, they found themselves sitting at a scratch supper in the State Dining Room with the new Prime Minister, huddled at the end of the table by the fireplace eating cottage pie for the second time in a day.§ Mrs Thatcher had no plans to get rid of anyone.

In fact, in this area, she had almost no plans at all. To the constant surprise and frustration of many advisers and supporters who were on what Denis called the 'Long March' with her, Mrs Thatcher never showed much interest in how to organize matters and control appointments to achieve the results she sought. No one in her office was in charge of co-ordinating the work of government. She did not believe that the bureaucracy should be reshaped from top to bottom, but rather that it should be regalvanized. 'It was not', according to Richard Ryder, 'the Maoists arriving at No. 10.'[12] She was very correct about the non-political structure of the Civil Service and considered it a sign of inadequacy for all but the most senior ministers to have political advisers. Before the election, she had asked Richard Ryder

---

* Michael Pattison (1946–), educated Sedbergh and University of Sussex; private secretary to successive Prime Ministers, 1979–82; director, Sainsbury Family Charitable Trusts, 1995–2006.
† Mrs Thatcher.
‡ Bryan Cartledge (1931–), educated Hurstpierpoint and St John's College, Cambridge; head of East European and Soviet Department, FCO, 1975–7; diplomatic private secretary to the Prime Minister, 1977–9; Ambassador to Hungary, 1980–83; to the Soviet Union, 1985–8; Principal of Linacre College, Oxford, 1988–96; knighted, 1985.
§ Caroline Stephens, later Lady Ryder of Wensum, who was present, remembers sandwiches, not cottage pie. Others mention shepherd's pie.

to be her political secretary in No. 10, and told him that only her personal secretaries, including his future wife Caroline Stephens, should come with her. For other appointments, she 'wished to keep her options open'.[13] She was obsessed by the need to keep entourages as small as possible. Although she disliked officials as a class, she loved individual examples of the breed and depended very heavily on them. The private office she inherited was touched and 'astonished that she accepted us without any question'.[14]* Nick Sanders,† another private secretary inherited from the Labour administration, recalled that Callaghan, though always courteous, had seemed to hold back from his officials what he was really thinking. Mrs Thatcher, on the other hand, 'told us exactly what she thought'.[15] John Hoskyns, who was the first head of her Policy Unit and therefore her leading non-career civil servant, remarked on 'a strange contradiction: her instinct when she's scared is to fight. But she was quite in awe of Whitehall mandarins.'[16] But it may not have been a contradiction at all: she understood the importance of the men who made the machine work, and would always support them so long as they made it work for her. After a few months of governing, she looked up from her desk at Clive Whitmore,‡ who had replaced Ken Stowe as her principal private secretary in June, and said: 'Clive, I'd be able to run this Government much better if I didn't have ministers, only permanent secretaries.'[17]

Mrs Thatcher's chief method of exerting her will over the machine was not institutional but personal. She used every remark, every memo, every meeting as an opportunity to challenge existing habits, criticize any sign of ignorance, confusion or waste and preach incessantly the main aims of her administration. Just five days after her election victory, for example, Mrs Thatcher directed her private secretary to inform the Foreign Office of her dissatisfaction with the briefing documents produced for her so far. 'She hopes that in future Departments will avoid wordy generalisations

---

* The officials were less enamoured of Mark Thatcher, who accompanied his mother as she entered No. 10 that day. Turning to one, he asked how many people were employed there. 'About seventy,' he was told. 'Hmm, would make a nice little business,' he said. (Private information.)

† Nicholas Sanders (1946–), educated King Edward's School, Birmingham and Magdalene College, Cambridge; principal private secretary to Secretary of State for Education, 1974–5 (also worked at the Department of Education when Mrs Thatcher was Secretary of State); private secretary to the Prime Minister, 1978–81; higher education adviser, Department for Education and Skills, 2004–5.

‡ Clive Whitmore (1935–), educated Sutton Grammar School, Surrey and Christ's College, Cambridge; principal private secretary to the Prime Minister, 1979–82; Permanent Under-Secretary, MOD, 1983–8; Home Office, 1988–94; director, N. M. Rothschild and Sons Ltd from 1994; knighted, 1983.

and the re-statement of facts or conclusions which are, or should be, well known to all those for whom the briefs are designed. The Prime Minister, who is a quick reader, is fully prepared to tackle long briefs when necessary: but she would like their content to be pithy and concisely expressed.'[18] Determined to work harder and know more than any other minister, she used the ritual of Prime Minister's Questions in Parliament every Tuesday and Thursday that the House was sitting as the means of familiarizing herself with the work of all departments. She would be briefed early in the morning about what was likely to be asked (though the device of the 'open question' meant that she could never know exactly), and then, over a light lunch which everyone ate holding plates on their knees, would rehearse possible answers with Nick Sanders, the relevant private secretary, Ian Gow, her parliamentary private secretary, and others.[19] Gow would tell her which questions he had been able to 'plant' with whichever loyal Tory MPs had been drawn in the ballot. She would then go over to the Commons, armed with a book of about forty 'subject notes' per question time, and take her place on the bench at 3.10 for the fifteen-minute contest. 'She had a virtually photographic memory and always knew more than the Opposition,' recalled William Rickett,* who served after Sanders as her private secretary for Questions.[20] She hardly ever made a factual error. On one occasion during the Falklands War, her civil servants told her immediately afterwards that she had given an incorrect answer to a question about the Labour government's sale of warships to Argentina. 'She went ballistic' at having been wrongly briefed, according to Rickett, but 'it then turned out she'd been right after all.'[21] From time to time, reforms attempting to make Prime Minister's Questions more rational would be suggested to her, but Mrs Thatcher always opposed them, saying, 'It would be seen as a sign of weakness if I proposed changes.'[22] She did very well out of the combination of the parliamentary political joust and the twice-weekly cramming of facts. Her strongest form of self-criticism, she herself recalled in old age, was provoked 'whenever I had not prepared thoroughly enough for something'.[23]

Her other method of control, used much more rarely, was to make visitations to different departments to see for herself what they were up to. These were memorably demanding occasions. In the case of the Department of Employment, with which, as the department closest to the trade unions, she was naturally out of sympathy, the outing was particularly

---

* William Rickett (1953–), educated Eton and Trinity College, Cambridge; private secretary to the Prime Minister, 1981–3; Director-General, Energy, Department of Trade and Industry, 2006–10.

painful for her hosts. Due to some confusion at the front desk, Mrs Thatcher went upstairs without being greeted by Jim Prior and his junior ministers, who came down in one lift just after she had gone up in another. Prior, red-faced at the best of times, went purple in his race to catch up with her. When his panting party arrived, he found the Prime Minister already in full flood.[24] At this meeting, Mrs Thatcher got into an argument with an able official called Donald Derx, who was so nettled by her hectoring that he said, 'Prime Minister, do you want to know the facts or not?' Derx had been lined up by the Civil Service for the highest posts. As a result of this incident, it was said, his career stalled.[25] Such scenes were unpleasant, and sometimes resulted in unfair judgments being made, but they were also useful in helping her search for talent and energy. At a better-starred visit to the Ministry of Defence, she marked out an official called Clive Whitmore (see above), whom the mandarins, hoping she would notice him, had pushed to the fore. She promptly made him her principal private secretary in succession to Ken Stowe. The visits also had a very important general effect. They meant that Mrs Thatcher was feared. From first to last, for eleven and a half years, she sent tremors through the whole of Whitehall.

But she did not necessarily show clarity about lines of command. Mrs Thatcher's rather unworldly vagueness, even weakness, about who should do which job caused immediate confusion. Adam Ridley, who had been giving her the main economic advice from the Conservative Research Department, fully expected to take charge in office, running the Policy Unit, perhaps with John Hoskyns in tow. Ten days before the election, Mrs Thatcher had, he had every reason to believe, offered him the job.[26] Without receiving her final confirmation, he arrived at No. 10 before she did, having recruited Michael Portillo, George Cardona* and Michael Dobbs as the team which she had initially agreed. Richard Ryder, who knew that she had wanted to avoid appointing people to jobs in advance, reported Ridley's precipitate arrival to Mrs Thatcher. She was not pleased.[27] She told Ridley that the officials were 'so marvellous' that his team was not needed after all. He and Hoskyns, she suggested, should share the Policy Unit between them with, in effect, no support from anyone other than Norman Strauss.[28] Piqued, Ridley refused, saying that such a unit would be too small. A place was found for him instead as special adviser to Geoffrey Howe, whom Mrs Thatcher had made Chancellor of the Exchequer, and his three juniors trickled down to other posts. John Hoskyns was put in

---

* George Cardona (1951–), educated King's School, Canterbury and Trinity College, Oxford; Conservative Research Department, 1974–9; special adviser to the Treasury, 1979–81; HSBC, 1985–2000.

charge of the Policy Unit. He was allowed to bring Norman Strauss with him on the condition that Mrs Thatcher, who found Strauss' eccentric manner and informal style of dressing alarming, never had to see him.[29] According to Hoskyns, she had already decided before the election that he, not Ridley, should advise her. One evening, at dinner with the Wolfsons in early March, Denis had taken Hoskyns aside and told him that he would get the appointment. 'You spark her,' he told Hoskyns, while Adam Ridley 'cannot see the wood for the trees'.[30] There was, in addition, an ideological question involved. Though not an out-and-out Heathite, Ridley was not a monetarist either. Despite Chris Patten's 'litmus test' approach to the appointment of Ridley,[31] Mrs Thatcher decided to defy the centrists and prefer the more radical Hoskyns. What she failed to do, however, was to sort this out directly with the people involved. In his diary for Tuesday 8 May, Hoskyns noted: 'I had to bring to a head a problem she would not face.' Even more surprising, she did not have much idea about what the Policy Unit should do, and never, in all Hoskyns's time there, tasked it with any particular job. It always had to generate its own momentum. Tim Lankester,* who was her first economic private secretary, noted that 'she wasn't very interested in strategy.'[32] From the other side of the official fence, Hoskyns thought exactly the same. The most missionary of all modern prime ministers never sat down to define her mission or to plan its implementation.

In such a hurry to get on with her task, as she saw it, of rebuilding the British economy, Mrs Thatcher tended to grab whatever tools lay to hand, rather than try to forge new ones. One such body was the Central Policy Review Staff, known as the Think Tank, which had been founded by Ted Heath. Under the Cabinet Office rather than directly answerable to the Prime Minister, its job was not political. Its purpose was to think, as people did not then put it, 'outside the box', and investigate policy issues too long term for the ordinary run of Civil Service life. Its head could attend any Cabinet committees on whose subject the Think Tank was working, and would produce useful briefing notes for these. But, because of its structure, floating free of any chain of departmental or prime ministerial command, the CPRS tended, despite its high intellectual calibre, to be ineffective. Its reports were both too controversial for comfort and too unimmediate to demand action.

---

* Tim Lankester (1942–), educated Monkton Combe School, St John's College, Cambridge and Yale University; private secretary to the Prime Minister, 1979–81; Deputy Secretary, Treasury, 1988–9; Permanent Secretary, Overseas Development Administration, 1989–94; Permanent Secretary, Department for Education, 1994–5; President, Corpus Christi College, Oxford, 2001–10; knighted, 1994.

In 1979, for instance, it was working on a report on the future of the motor industry and another on alcohol abuse. Mrs Thatcher could not at first see the point of it. She called in the Think Tank's head, Sir Kenneth Berrill,* and said, 'If I want to know about industry, I ask Keith Joseph. Why should I ask you?' Berrill's reply was 'You'll get independent input.'[33]

Dr John Ashworth,† the Chief Scientist, who worked within the CPRS, asked to see Mrs Thatcher shortly after she had arrived at No. 10. As he entered, the Prime Minister said: 'Who are you?' 'I am your Chief Scientist,' Ashworth replied. 'Oh,' said Mrs Thatcher, 'do I want one of those?' He explained his work, mentioning that he was completing a report about the then almost unstudied subject of climate change. Mrs Thatcher stared at him: 'Are you standing there and seriously telling me that my government should worry about the *weather*?'‡ She told Ashworth that she was not going to have a minister for science at all: 'I'm a scientist. I shall be my own Minister for Science.'[34] But, despite this typically, frighteningly challenging way of approaching the matter, Mrs Thatcher quickly realized that, her Policy Unit being so small and staffed by people without experience of the workings of government, she needed experts who could help with progress-chasing. After a bit, the two organizations found they could make common cause, as both, regardless of their precise political views, shared a desire to rescue Britain from the collapse of the Winter of Discontent. Both enjoyed working for Mrs Thatcher because, as Berrill remembered it: 'She's active, highly critical: you're on your toes. I didn't have to say what she'd like to hear ... I never found a subject on which you were wasting your time analysing something as deeply as you wanted.'[35] She communicated her passion for reform and for new ideas. But, at the Policy Unit, in the CPRS and in the regular Civil Service, officials quickly came to recognize that Mrs Thatcher was not, in the normal managerial sense, much good at running things, despite her appetite for official paper. As John Ashworth put it: 'She hated muddle, but she also caused it, because she did not really appreciate how bureaucracies need sharp lines.'[36] She did not know how the machine worked and, as Hoskyns put it, 'My worry was that she didn't know what she didn't know.'[37]

*

---

* Kenneth Berrill (1920–2009), educated LSE and Trinity College, Cambridge; chief economic adviser to the Treasury, 1973–4; head of Central Policy Review Staff, 1974–80; knighted, 1971.
† John Ashworth (1938–), educated West Buckland School, Devon and Exeter College, Oxford; chief scientist, Central Policy Review Staff, 1976–81; vice-chancellor, University of Salford, 1981–90; director, London School of Economics, 1990–96; knighted, 2008.
‡ Much later in her time as prime minister, however, Mrs Thatcher was the first head of government to make a major speech on the subject of climate change.

In forming her first Cabinet, as in her dealings with the Civil Service, Mrs Thatcher displayed a similar, slightly surprising tendency not to want to upset the institutional applecart. Her appointments sought political balance more than ideological affinity. She turned first to Willie Whitelaw, whom she immediately made Home Secretary and, in effect, though not in formal title, deputy prime minister. He had never disappointed her in the loyalty he had promised after she beat him for the leadership in 1975, and he possessed qualities and connections which she knew she lacked. Her friend Hector Laing* once praised Whitelaw to her for his 'low cunning and lovable dimness'. Mrs Thatcher laughed and said: 'I'm not very good at either.'[38] Cunning, lovability and at least the appearance of dimness were essential characteristics in the Tory tribe, so Whitelaw was indispensable. He did not arrive in London from his seat in the Borders until the Friday afternoon. When he had done so, he joined Mrs Thatcher and the Chief Whip, Humphrey Atkins, in No. 10 for the rest of the evening to advise her. Filling the hole left by the death of Neave, she offered Atkins the post of Northern Ireland secretary. When he had reluctantly accepted it, she rang Michael Jopling,† also in the fastness of his northern constituency, to ask him to succeed Atkins. Jopling drove to London through the Friday night to help handle the process of appointments the following day.

When he accepted the post of deputy leader in 1975, Whitelaw had told Mrs Thatcher: 'I shall give you my 100-per-cent loyalty on one condition: that you never make Keith Joseph Chancellor.'[39] For this reason, she had never made Joseph shadow Chancellor, and now she kept her promise. Mrs Thatcher had to stick with the man whom the past four years had made the only logical choice for the Chancellorship, Geoffrey Howe. Her relations with Howe were not very easy, and she tended to say, 'The trouble with people like Geoffrey – lawyers – is that they are too timid,'[40] conveniently forgetting she was a lawyer herself. But although in her heart she would have preferred Keith Joseph, she was not seriously reluctant to give Howe the job for which, she could not deny, he was now well qualified. Her love for Joseph, which was the strongest of all her affections for her senior colleagues, did not blind her to the fact that he would have been

* Hector Laing (1923–2010), educated Loretto and Jesus College, Cambridge; chairman, United Biscuits, 1972–90; created Lord Laing of Dunphail, 1991.

† Michael Jopling (1930–), educated Cheltenham and King's College, Newcastle-upon-Tyne; Conservative MP for Westmorland, 1964–83; for Westmorland and Lonsdale, 1983–97; Government Chief Whip, 1979–83; Minister of Agriculture, Fisheries and Food, 1983–7; created Lord Jopling, 1997.

unable to bear the heat and burden of the Treasury. She made him Secretary of State for Industry.

It was only in those portfolios which dealt with economic matters that Mrs Thatcher sought out men who were ideologically sympathetic to her. As well as Howe and Joseph, she appointed John Nott, who had been one of the most original free-market economists in opposition, making him Trade Secretary. To assist Howe, she made John Biffen Chief Secretary to the Treasury, in charge of the control of public spending. This appointment was based on a misunderstanding. Mrs Thatcher had a great respect for Biffen's intellect and what she called his 'ability to think laterally'[41] and believed, because of his opposition to the Heath U-turn, that he was at one with her. She also felt motherly towards him because he had suffered from depression and had to step down from the Shadow Cabinet for a year as a result. Biffen was grateful for her kindness over this episode. But he was a Powellite rather than a Thatcherite by belief, and a quietist by temperament. He was a lifelong Eurosceptic and he believed in balanced budgets and the control of inflation by monetary means, but he was not averse to high public spending in itself. Besides, he was not combative – 'I don't like the sound of breaking crockery'[42] – and he disliked policy detail. He was not as much 'on board' as Mrs Thatcher thought. In an attempt to co-ordinate the advancement of economic policy and steer it through the rest of the Cabinet as things grew gradually rougher, these ministers – Howe, Joseph, Nott and Biffen – eventually established a secret breakfast with Mrs Thatcher every Thursday morning. Its existence was unknown to colleagues until revealed in the press in November 1980.

As secretary of State for Employment, Jim Prior was the only exception, the only Heathite with an economic job. With those listed above, he joined the important E Committee of the Cabinet, which dealt with economic matters, but he was never part of the Thursday breakfast club. Although Mrs Thatcher did not personally dislike him from the start ('Jim's a jolly, red-faced Englishman'),[43] she had no doubt at all that he was wrong in his belief that trade unions should be appeased. She appointed him nevertheless because she felt she had to. Party unity demanded it, and she recognized that the arts of appeasement might well prove necessary in the short term. Although she expected that confrontation with the unions would one day come, she was not planning it or even, for the time being, wanting it. She believed that the immediate task was the steadying of the economy and the control of inflation. For the time being, Prior, who knew much more about the trade union leadership than any of her senior colleagues, and was trusted in this by large numbers of Conservative MPs, was the inevitable choice.

In most of her other appointments, Mrs Thatcher's chief concern was to construct a government which reflected the balance of power and experience in the party. Before the election she told the Cabinet Secretary, John Hunt, 'I'm going to have a very good Foreign Secretary and I shan't go on any foreign trips at all. My job is to turn the economy round.'[44] This was impossible, of course, since all prime ministers in modern times have to travel, but it was obvious that Lord Carrington was the man who fitted Mrs Thatcher's frame of mind. Extremely senior and yet, because he sat in the House of Lords, no threat to her job, he had the relevant experience, contacts and prestige. That Carrington was well regarded in Washington also pleased Mrs Thatcher. 'I view his appointment as Foreign Secretary as one of the most encouraging signals Mrs Thatcher could send us at the start of her stewardship,' Zbigniew Brzezinski noted in a memo to President Carter.[45] She was willing to accede to Carrington's request that Ian Gilmour join him as the Foreign Office spokesman in the Commons and in the Cabinet as Lord Privy Seal. Following similar principles, she appointed the veteran Lord Hailsham as Lord Chancellor, the same job he had done for Ted Heath, Francis Pym as Defence Secretary, and Christopher Soames as Leader of the Lords, Lord President of the Council and minister in charge of the Civil Service. Norman St John-Stevas was made Leader of the House of Commons and the rebellious Peter Walker was brought in from the cold in what was considered the unthreatening job of Agriculture. There were no women in Mrs Thatcher's first Cabinet, apart from herself. Of the six most senior men in the Cabinet, all were older than she, and only two (Howe and Joseph) agreed with her economic strategy. For most of the older men, who had fought in the Second World War – and, in the case of Whitelaw, Carrington and Pym, won the Military Cross – there was a difficulty in taking their new Prime Minister seriously. They did not conspire against her, but neither did they think it very likely that she would survive. She was conscious of being patronized and of being in a minority.

The process of appointment proceeded efficiently on the morning of Saturday 5 May. The only hitch came when Mrs Thatcher offered Michael Heseltine the Energy portfolio. 'No,' he said, 'I've been rehearsing Environment for three years. That's what I want to do.' Mrs Thatcher's handwritten list[46] of her planned appointments shows that she had planned to offer Environment to the Labour defector Reg Prentice, but she gave in on the spot, fobbing Prentice off with a post outside the Cabinet. After Heseltine had left, she said to Michael Pattison, who had been present at the interview, 'I don't like one-to-one confrontations with Michael.'[47] Even in opposition, she had felt wary about his ambition. One day, her protection officer, Barry Strevens, had told her that David Owen, as Foreign Secretary, had been so demanding in his dealings with staff that he had got through eight drivers and two personal protection teams. Mrs Thatcher's comment was: 'That's the mistake of promoting someone too early. We won't make the same mistake with Michael Heseltine.'[48] But, now that the time had come, Heseltine had forced her to do what she had wished to avoid. From the start, he proved both an awkward and a formidable customer. The Energy job was given instead to David Howell, one of the intellectual architects of the free-market ideas which had briefly appealed to Ted Heath when he was in opposition, and the man who claimed to have been the first to use the word 'privatization' in Conservative circles. When the Cabinet was complete, it was, in terms of party management, a successful balance of all the forces and talents available.

There was only one important deliberate omission – Ted Heath himself. Given the history between the two leaders, and the fact that her government's majority of forty-three made Mrs Thatcher fairly safe from immediate revolt, few expected that she would feel the need to offer Heath a Cabinet post. She herself believed that 'he would never have been able to take orders from a woman.'[49] But Heath had maintained hopes. These were dashed by a letter from the new Prime Minister which arrived by despatch-rider at the house of Sara Morrison, with whom Heath was staying, early on the Saturday morning after the election. In it, Mrs Thatcher informed him that she had offered the foreign secretaryship to Peter Carrington, not to him. Heath took great offence at the fact that she signed the letter 'Margaret Thatcher', rather than just 'Margaret', though in truth she did this out of her habitual correctness rather than out of coldness.[50] Heath was plunged into gloom. Matters were then made worse by the well-meaning suggestion of Carrington that Heath be offered the ambassadorship to Washington. 'I thought a little sop would be a good idea, but it was a thoroughly bad idea,' Carrington recalled.[51] Jopling took round a second letter from Mrs Thatcher to Heath, this time signed 'Margaret', offering the post. 'She's trying to get me out of the bloody House,' Heath complained,[52] and he wrote her a curt letter of rejection ('I am sure you will be able to find somebody to do the job').* The news of his refusal leaked from No. 10 to the press. From then on, throughout Mrs Thatcher's administrations, Heath's hostility would prove absolute.

Mrs Thatcher had left it to her new Chief Whip, Jopling, to draw up a list of the seventy or so proposed appointments to junior ministerial posts. He

---

* At this time Heath also rejected the idea that he might become NATO Secretary General. Later in 1980 Mrs Thatcher tried again, hoping to nominate Heath to replace Joseph Luns, who had served as Secretary General since 1971. Careful feelers went out from Number 10, but were once again firmly rebuffed. (Interviews with Sir Clive Whitmore and Lord Armstrong of Ilminster).

noticed that she was not looking for factional advantage in these choices; 'She named a few as "my people", but gave no impression of political bias; she saw it all in terms of talent.'[53] On Sunday, he joined her and Whitelaw for lunch in No. 10 to discuss the list. It was, he discovered, her first sight of the flat which she and Denis were to inhabit for more than eleven years.

The flat, which was at the top of the house, was small and almost poky. Cynthia Crawford, who helped sort it out, found its laundry room 'full of dead plants'.[54] Its kitchen was no more than a galley.* It suited Mrs Thatcher, however. She liked the idea of 'living over the shop', as in her Grantham childhood,[55] and the convenience of being so close to the work she loved. Security was greater, and she hoped that her children could come and see her easily.† Denis, retired since 1975, though with various non-executive directorships, was happy to throw himself into the life of No. 10. 'Margaret thought I helped at receptions,' he remembered. 'I thought I might as well enjoy it.'[56] The couple continued to live in Flood Street until early June, while the flat was being refurbished, and then moved in. Denis paid rent to the government of £3,000 per year for the flat; Mrs Thatcher paid for its redecoration and also, at her own request, for the redecoration of her first-floor study in No. 10, which looks over St James's Park, banishing the sage-green wallpaper which she disliked. Due to the remarkable strictness of government rules on such matters, the Thatchers were provided with no help of any kind in looking after their flat. They paid cleaning women themselves, and it fell to them, in practice to Mrs Thatcher herself, since Denis had old-fashioned views on these matters, to procure, generally with the help of Caroline Stephens and more junior secretaries, their own food and cook it. Denis was known to hurry home from drinks with chums after ringing No. 10 – 'She says if I don't come now dinner will be cold, and by that she means it will have *got* cold.'[57] Quite often, owing to the demands of office, he came home to nothing, but he did not mind unduly, being a man who preferred drinking to eating. He used to fear what he called 'cosmic obloquy from her' when he did not eat whatever food was put before him.[58] Mrs Thatcher's lack of time meant that

---

* Next door, in No. 11, where Geoffrey Howe was installed as Chancellor, Elspeth Howe spent £4,000 modernizing the kitchen. This annoyed Mrs Thatcher, who was always easily irritated by Lady Howe: 'I can make do. Why should No. 11 have a bigger kitchen?' (Interview with Amanda Ponsonby.)

† In practice, there were problems. Mark had to leave for the United States in 1984 when press criticism of him for exploiting his relationship with his mother for commercial gain became too great. Carol liked bringing friends to the flat at the weekend. One boyfriend, a journalist without security clearance, was brought along, after which the rules were tightened. (Interview with Derek Howe.)

the more wholesome sort of convenience foods – fish pie from Marks and
Spencers, for example – were consumed in large quantities. Sometimes she
would get Downing Street caterers to cook something for her freezer, at
her own expense. Sherry Warner, who worked there from March 1981,
used to sell her moussaka.[59] Mrs Thatcher herself usually ate quite heartily
but without much attention, treating food as fuel.[60] She drank plentiful
quantities of Famous Grouse whisky with ginger ale, 'but she was never
drunk'. Denis 'was on the Gordon's'.[61]

Living in the No. 10 flat also made it easier for the Thatchers to call on
the help they needed which the normal government machine did not provide. David Wolfson was the unpaid chief of staff of her political office.
Those in the professional Civil Service often wondered what purpose he
served, but Wolfson saw it as his job to 'be aware of the few things that
mattered and to make sure that she saw the right people at the right time'.[62]
Wolfson's links with the business world gave Mrs Thatcher comfort, and
so did his money. Cynthia Crawford, always known as 'Crawfie', a secretary who was to become more and more important in the smooth running
of Mrs Thatcher's life, and to serve her right up until her death, was paid
for by Wolfson. Mrs Thatcher also brought into No. 10 the highly trusted
personal staff she had used in opposition. Richard Ryder, in day-to-day
reality, though not in title, ran the political office. Caroline Stephens, who
was to marry Ryder in 1981, was the private papers secretary. Alison Ward,
the longest-serving Thatcher employee, came as constituency secretary.
Tessa Jardine-Paterson, who came as a political secretary after having
worked for Mrs Thatcher in Parliament, remembered that she and her
colleagues always saw it as part of their jobs to rustle up drinks and even
meals for Mrs Thatcher. They felt perfectly happy to do so because she
herself was so unsnooty in her readiness to help in such matters, often
plunging her hands into the sink to wash up with the words 'It's much
easier to do it yourself.'[63] She also brought with her her two trusted personal detectives, Barry Strevens and Bob Kingston. Despite the fact that
Mrs Thatcher was an egotist, she was also almost always extremely considerate towards staff and their families. 'It was a great mistake to tell the
Prime Minister that one of your children had got measles or something,
because she'd go on talking about it for some days afterwards . . . she could
carry this to really quite absurd lengths for a Prime Minister.' She would
send drivers home if they were not needed and check that those working
for her had eaten, which was often difficult to do in No. 10 because,
although it had vast state kitchens for banquets, it had no canteen: 'She
hated being a nuisance. She never, ever put herself first.'[64]

In 1979, there were no computers at all in Downing Street and Mrs

25. The new Member for Finchley arrives to take her seat in the House of Commons, 20 October 1959.

26. In October 1961, Mrs Thatcher was one of the first of her parliamentary intake to achieve ministerial office, as parliamentary secretary at the Ministry of Pensions and National Insurance. She is reading the parliamentary order paper.

27. Meeting the first Minister under whom she served, John Boyd-Carpenter. He noted her 'quick-trained barrister's brain'.

28. 'Women about the House': a *Sunday Times Magazine* cover, 21 June 1964, about female Members of Parliament. Mrs Thatcher is at the back, and at the top.

29. Mother in the Cabinet: Margaret plays to her family in their house, The Mount, Lamberhurst, after the Conservative election victory of June 1970.

30. The Secretary of State for Education. Despite being called 'milksnatcher', Mrs Thatcher was better than most politicians at talking to children. Here she is at the London American School in 1971.

31. Ted Heath called an emergency Cabinet to discuss President Nixon's anti-inflation economic measures in August 1971, hence Mrs Thatcher's almost holiday wear in Downing Street.

32. With a portrait of Ted Heath in 1973. Her part in his downfall was yet to come.

33. As environment spokesman offering a cap on mortgage rates, Mrs Thatcher played an unexpectedly large part in the general election campaign of October 1974. Beside her at an election press conference are Lord Carrington (party Chairman) and Ted Heath.

34. 'My cupboard is not a hoard in any sense of the word': 'Maggie' the housewife fends off accusations of hoarding by showing her larder to the cameras during the leadership challenge to Heath, December 1974.

35. A head start: Mrs Thatcher at the hairdresser Chalmers of Mayfair, 31 January 1975. Eleven days later, she became leader of the Conservative Party.

36. Round-one knock-out: Mrs Thatcher tries to calm the press after defeating Heath in the first ballot of the leadership election, 4 February 1975.

37. Wife, mother, Leader: the Thatchers celebrate her victory in the second ballot, 11 February 1975, outside the house of William Shelton, one of her campaign managers.

38. The victor on *The Jimmy Young Show* on BBC Radio 2. Young gave her just the right platform.

39. This is the only known example of Mrs Thatcher holding the torch for Europe. She is wearing a jersey carrying the flags of all the member states of the EEC during the campaign for a Yes vote in the referendum on whether Britain should stay in the Community, March 1975. Winston Churchill presides.

40. Friendship off the cuff. The first meeting between Mrs Thatcher and Ronald Reagan, April 1975. From their rapport when both were out of office much later success flowed.

41. 'Dad did hold a soft spot for Auntie Margaret': Willie and Muriel Cullen and their elder son, Morton, receive the Thatchers at their farm Foulton Hall, Essex, in the late 1970s.

42. Never off duty: Mrs Thatcher consults her watch while on holiday with the Morrison family on the isle of Islay in August 1978. Beside her is Peter Morrison, who would become her parliamentary private secretary at the end of her time in office. She is dressed more for work than for the Scottish islands: she could never see the point of holidays.

43. The famous Saatchi poster often supposed to have appeared during the election campaign of May 1979 was actually launched in the late summer of 1978. Here Mrs Thatcher speaks vehemently above it at a local government conference in March 1979.

44. The notes for Mrs Thatcher's St Francis of Assisi speech given on the steps of No. 10. The 'HM' referred to at the beginning is Her Majesty the Queen. The 'AN' at the bottom is Airey Neave.

45. 'Where there is despair, may we bring hope': Mrs Thatcher enters 10 Downing Street for the first time as prime minister, 4 May 1979. To the extreme left is the broadcaster Jon Snow.

46. The Prime Minister removes an offending piece of fluff from the collar of Norman St John-Stevas, leader of the House of Commons, before the State Opening of Parliament, May 1979. Early in 1981, she would remove him too.

47. On the front line: Mrs Thatcher in the uniform of the Ulster Defence Regiment, visits 'bandit county' in South Armagh, Northern Ireland, after the murders of Lord Mountbatten and of eighteen British soldiers at Warrenpoint, 19 August 1979. Her appearances in uniform had a great impact.

48. 'You turn if you like – the lady's not for turning': Mrs Thatcher holds to her course of economic austerity at the party conference, October 1980.

Thatcher drew heavily on the services of the career secretaries and typists, traditionally known as the 'Garden Room girls' because they worked in the two basement rooms which look on to the garden of No. 10. They took dictation, summoned by buzzers, in which a single buzz represented the principal private secretary and more buzzes represented more junior officials, and they generally made everything work. Each night they locked the carbons and ribbons for their electric typewriters in the safe, since these would bear the impression of secrets they had typed during the day.[65] Mrs Thatcher strongly approved of the traditional smallness of the No. 10 set-up. It meant, in the words of Jane Parsons, who ran the Garden Room when the Thatchers arrived and had worked for every prime minister since Attlee and Churchill, that the whole enterprise felt like 'a cosy family unit and the PM was head of the family'.[66] Some of the girls would enter No. 10 through the door in the garden wall, wheeling their bicycles.[67] A few prime ministers, notably Heath and Wilson, had been rather difficult or stand-offish about this ethos, but the Thatchers loved it. Denis, making himself available, said, 'I'll do whatever you want me to do so long as it doesn't coincide with rugger.'[68]* Mrs Thatcher would 'bounce' into the Garden Room to see what was going on. Sometimes, wandering round the various offices when she didn't have enough to do, she would riffle through in-trays and snatch up correspondence from the public. On one occasion, she came across a letter from a small florist in Wandsworth who said that his business was being undermined by the supermarket sale of flowers. From then on, she placed all her flower orders with him.[69] On another, shortly after she had arrived at No. 10, Mrs Thatcher was standing with the private secretaries, asking one of them how their telephone system worked.† Suddenly she grabbed the phone as the light flashed and said, 'No. 10 Downing Street.' On the other end was Stephen Wall,‡ a Foreign Office official. Alerted by the half-recognized voice, he said, 'Who am I

---

* If an occasion did clash with rugby matters, Denis was not pleased. In November, after Caroline Stephens had written to him to enlist him for the state banquet for the President of Indonesia, Denis replied, reluctantly agreeing to go: 'J.C. [Jesus Christ] What I do for the Party! . . . The same evening I was going to probably the best Rugby Football Dinner this year . . . All the chums will be there.' (Denis Thatcher to Caroline Stephens, undated, in response to her note of 17 October 1979, THCR 6/2/2/6.)

† The Downing Street switchboard was legendary for its ability to find anyone, anywhere in the world. The telephone system was very old fashioned, however. When Mrs Thatcher arrived in 1979, no one could make a direct call from his or her desk, but had to ask the switchboard to get the number and ring back. (Interview with Lady Ryder of Wensum.)

‡ Stephen Wall (1947–), educated Douai and Selwyn College, Cambridge; private secretary to the Prime Minister, 1991–3; Ambassador and UK Permanent Representative to EU, 1995–2000; head of European Secretariat, Cabinet Office, 2000–2004; knighted, 2004.

speaking to?' 'It's the Prime Minister,' said Mrs Thatcher. 'Oh good,' said Wall, with some presence of mind, 'then I'll get an answer quicker than usual.'[70] She liked to watch her own office in action. One private secretary was at his desk one day having a long argument with the Treasury on the telephone. He felt he had lost the battle, and as he put down the receiver, he said, 'S***! F***!' Then he noticed that the Prime Minister had come in and was sitting at the desk beside him. Her eyes were shining with pleasure. 'Temper! Temper!' she said.[71]

This cosiness extended to the Thatchers' life at Chequers, the large country house in Buckinghamshire bequeathed by Lord Lee of Fareham for all British prime ministers, and staffed by the armed services. Mrs Thatcher liked to be driven there on Friday evenings and return, usually in time for supper, on Sunday. At Chequers, as in London, Mrs Thatcher quickly established a mixture of formality – she and Denis always dressed neatly and smartly – with friendliness towards those working for her. The duty private secretary each weekend had to stay in a cottage on the estate. A nervous Michael Pattison, on his first weekend in the role, came with his young family. To his surprise, the Thatchers invited them all to drinks before Sunday lunch. His two-year-old daughter climbed over Mrs Thatcher on the sofa and removed one of her earrings.* 'She met with a very soft response,' he remembered.[72] For anyone who had experienced the Heath days, such a scene was unimaginable (even allowing for the fact that Heath would not have worn earrings).

The first woman Prime Minister had needs previously unknown in Downing Street. Frequent hairdressing was required and, once television cameras were introduced to the House of Commons in 1989, these appointments became twice weekly. As had happened when Mrs Thatcher was education secretary, the private office was uneasy about putting the word 'hairdresser' into the diary on the grounds that it detracted from the dignity of the office. It asked Caroline Stephens how to deal with this self-invented problem. After discussion, the phrase 'Carmen rollers' was agreed as a sort of code.[73] Mrs Thatcher's clothes were looked after, in the early days, chiefly by Lady (Guinevere) Tilney, wife of Sir John, who had befriended Margaret Thatcher when they were both looking for parliamentary seats in the late 1940s. Lady Tilney was known, slightly mockingly, as 'the Mistress of the Robes', and was also responsible for organizing Downing Street receptions. Crawfie later succeeded to the informal title.

---

* Mrs Thatcher's ears were never pierced. In her generation, it was often considered gypsyish to have pierced ears. According to John Ashworth, if she became excited while wearing earrings, her lobes would become engorged; occasionally, under the pressure, an earring would pop off.

Strict government rules prevented the acceptance of personal presents of any substantial value, but Mrs Thatcher was allowed to take such gifts on loan. She wore British clothes on these terms, and also the many jewels which Arab potentates tended to press upon her. With her seamstress's love of getting detail right and her wartime generation's devotion to 'make do and mend', she combined a very smart appearance with economy. Care was taken to record which dress she wore at which occasion, and dresses were given nicknames for easy recognition. One with red and white circles on it, for example, was called 'Balloons'.[74] Her attitude to her appearance and that of her surroundings combined two things which were potentially in conflict – her love of propriety and economy, and her love of attractive, high-quality objects which would enhance the dignity of the premiership and the prestige of Britain. One official noted that she had 'an almost Queen Mary-type' magpie desire for pretty things. One day early in her first administration, she discovered that one of the ministerial flats in Admiralty House, vacant at the time, had several good bits of government furniture. She procured the key and personally led a party of the No. 10 steward, her appointments secretary and her detective to the flat. She walked round, pointing at pictures, chairs and so on, and saying 'I'll have that and that.' The party of burglars, carrying their loot, then returned to No. 10 with the Prime Minister at their head.[75]

Although extremely conscious of her femininity, Mrs Thatcher had frequently to be reminded of the symbolic importance of her role as the leading elected representative of her sex. As part of her drive to reduce the number of quangos which received large sums of public money, Mrs Thatcher found herself confronted with the two such that were the direct responsibility of the Cabinet Office. John Hunt, assisted by John Ashworth, told her that she must choose between cutting the National Council for Women and a scientific body, the Advisory Council for Applied Research and Development (ACARD). Without hesitation, Mrs Thatcher, the scientist, said: 'Can't get rid of ACARD. Better get rid of the other one.' Ashworth pointed out to her that she was the first woman Prime Minister and it might look bad to get rid of the National Council for Women. Mrs Thatcher reluctantly agreed and the result, which the two officials in this *Yes, Prime Minister* game had intended, was that both quangos survived.[76]

Probably the most important member of Mrs Thatcher's personal entourage was her parliamentary private secretary. Adam Butler and John Stanley, the latter having become known in the Thatcher team as 'Flapper Jack' because of his tendency to panic, had left for junior ministerial positions. Now that she was Prime Minister, Mrs Thatcher chose as her PPS Ian Gow, the MP for Eastbourne. Because he had been a friend of his fellow

Wykehamist Geoffrey Howe since working as an assistant in Aberavon during the 1959 election, Gow had supported Howe's leadership bid in 1975 and was therefore not, at first, close to Mrs Thatcher. He was PPS to Airey Neave, however, until Neave's assassination, and so his move to Mrs Thatcher herself in 1979 came naturally. After the election, Gow's friendship with Howe became an advantage, since it helped good communication between No. 10 and the Treasury. Gow, bald, bespectacled, usually in a heavy three-piece suit, had the half-pompous, half-obsequious manner of a private doctor (his father's profession) or solicitor (his own) between the wars. This was part of an elaborate self-parody. Gow was a keenly intelligent and intensely diligent man. He was completely, chivalrously committed to Mrs Thatcher, whom he was the first to describe as 'The Lady'. 'I shall love her', he declared to the less enamoured Howe, 'till the day I die,'[77]* and he saw his job, normally considered only a useful step on the ladder to higher things, as the great task of his life. He was at his desk at seven every morning, having often stayed up into the small hours doing his boss's business in the House of Commons the night before.

Gow's commitment to Mrs Thatcher was ideological as well as personal. In the eyes of officials, who found his mode of operation 'difficult' because he would pretend that he had not seen official papers when he had, he was the closest upholder of her sense of purpose: 'She drew from him the spirit of what she was trying to achieve.'[78] For his part, Gow regarded bureaucrats collectively as 'Martians', and enjoyed battles with them. Self-consciously an old fogey, though only forty-two years old at the time of the 1979 election, he had an extreme reluctance to trust any official who had a beard, a prejudice shared by Mrs Thatcher who liked to declare that 'Only men with weak chins have beards.'[79] Gow was also a romantic who could quote entire speeches by General de Gaulle from memory. He was

---

* A significant factor in Mrs Thatcher's political success was that quite large numbers of men fell for her. The Scottish genealogist Sir Iain Moncreiffe of that Ilk was the only man known to have made an indecent suggestion to her while she was Prime Minister, but many harboured a romantic devotion which teetered on the edge of the sexual. Sir Hector (later Lord) Laing, the chairman of United Biscuits, would send her notes which he requested be placed under her pillow. Kingsley Amis, the novelist, described Mrs Thatcher as 'one of the best-looking women I had ever met ... The fact that it is not a sensual or sexy beauty does not make it a less sexual beauty, and that sexuality is still, I think, an underrated factor in her appeal (or repellence)' (Kingsley Amis, *Memoirs*, Hutchinson, 1991, p. 316). Brian Walden reported David Owen as saying to him: 'The whiff of that perfume, the sweet smell of whisky. By God, Brian, she's appealing beyond belief' (interview with Brian Walden). Alan Clark, when asked by the present author about the nature of his love for Mrs Thatcher, said: 'I don't want actual penetration – just a massive snog.'

particularly attracted to the more High Tory aspects of Thatcherism, and was a strong supporter of the Union with Northern Ireland. It was through Ian Gow that Mrs Thatcher was to have many meetings with Enoch Powell in the first years of her premiership, Gow smuggling Powell into No. 10 by the back door.

Gow's chief role as PPS was to keep open the links between the Prime Minister and her parliamentary party, links which had broken, with such disastrous results, in the days of Ted Heath. He did this by a huge amount of controlled but sustained drinking with Members of Parliament. 'Cars run on petrol,' he would say, 'I run on alcohol,' and he was particularly fond of White Ladies (two parts gin, one part Cointreau, one part lemon juice). When he arrived in No. 10, and found himself sharing a handsome ground-floor office next to the Cabinet Room with Richard Ryder, he immediately denounced the room as 'appalling' on the grounds that it did not have a fridge.[80] One was soon installed, and filled with the produce of El Vino's, the Fleet Street bar owned by David Mitchell, one of the new administration's junior ministers. Gow devoted endless hours to listening to the complaints of Members of Parliament. Finding discontent, he would approach the diary secretary and say, 'X is unhappy and needs to be loved. Please get him in to see Margaret.'[81] With the large intake of new Conservative MPs in 1979, roughly a third of the parliamentary party was more or less unknown to the leader. Gow remedied this, taking her regularly to the tea-room, and 'day by day getting her to connect'.[82] Known half-affectionately as 'Supergrass', he would attend the meetings of Conservative backbench committees in Parliament and report to Mrs Thatcher who had said what. Building on her own remarkable tendency to criticize 'the government' as if she, as Prime Minister, had nothing to do with it, Gow was not above concerting parliamentary resistance to proposals from Cabinet colleagues which she did not like. In this respect, he could sometimes cause unnecessary trouble. But he was the most useful sort of aide for a leader – the one who knows his principal's mind so completely that he does not need to ask her permission before he acts. Unfortunately for posterity, however, most of Ian Gow's operations and thoughts were not committed to paper, and, when he was murdered by the IRA in 1990, he left few written records. The testimony of his contemporaries is that no one was more important in helping Mrs Thatcher survive the potential political crises of her first years, and that his role, after he left the post in 1983, was never so successfully replicated by his successors.

This personal team, instantly loyal, cohesive and overworked, had to cope with the astonishing demands of their boss's routine. Mrs Thatcher would rise at about six in the morning, listening first to the news on the

BBC World Service and then to Radio 4's *Today* programme. In the course of the night she would have demolished two or sometimes three of the red boxes that her private office had handed to her the previous evening. At about eight, Caroline Stephens would meet the private secretaries in the study below and then take up urgent requests to see Mrs Thatcher to the flat where, though she had always been up for hours, she was sometimes dressing in her bedroom. Denis, who also rose early, was invariably out of the bedroom by this time, and at his desk in his own study in the flat.[83] After 8.30, the Prime Minister would descend from the flat to her study and begin a day of meetings, which would normally end up, during the parliamentary session, in the House of Commons. She took virtually no exercise, without any apparent ill effects, except for going up and down the stairs to the flat. These journeys were required, among other things, to use the lavatory, because there was none for her on the same floor as her study, though her staff noted her ability, like the Queen, never to seem to need to 'go'.

She allowed herself no leisure. She would work, or talk about work, until one or two in the morning, occasionally catnapping for fifteen minutes at about 11 p.m. In the evening, she would often take her shoes off, tuck her legs beneath her on the sofa, and chat – always shop – with a glass of weak whisky to help her. Sometimes, Denis would join her, with rather more to drink, but there were often occasions when she ignored him in the pressure of business. On one evening, her husband came in after dinner when she was engaged in composing a big speech about Rhodesia. He offered a few comments to which she paid no attention, and then went up to the flat. About half an hour later, the ceiling of the room in which Mrs Thatcher was sitting shook with a tremendous crash. 'Oh,' said Mrs Thatcher. 'That must be Denis. I think he must have fallen out of a broom cupboard.' She made no attempt to find out what had happened.[84] The hardest task for her entourage was to make her go to bed. Although she did, indeed, have immense stamina and a huge appetite for work, she was not as invincible as she believed. She got very tired, and when this happened, she talked more and achieved less.

The global impact of Margaret Thatcher was immediate and enormous, because she was, after Golda Meir of Israel, the first elected woman leader in the Western world. Yet despite the criticism she had already attracted for being image-conscious in opposition, Mrs Thatcher gave extraordinarily little thought to media relations. Charles Anson,* who was a No. 10

---

* Charles Anson (1944–), educated Lancing and Jesus College, Cambridge; seconded from

press officer when she arrived, noticed an 'absolutely instant' change in the level of outside interest. The press mêlée outside No. 10 on the day of her victory had been so great that his colleagues had found it hard to get the tape recorder near enough to record her St Francis of Assisi remarks. Journalists from all over the world wanted to know things like whether there was a women's lavatory near the Cabinet Room, and fashion editors seemed to telephone almost as much as members of the parliamentary press lobby. But it struck Anson that Mrs Thatcher showed 'very little interest in how she was projected'.[85] She was so irritated by questions about being a woman that the press office had to warn foreign journalists off the subject. She did not really read the newspapers herself, beyond a cursory glance at Denis's *Daily Telegraph*, and it was hard to persuade her to pay much attention to what they were saying. Unlike Harold Wilson, who was obsessed with press coverage, and all prime ministers who were to succeed her, Mrs Thatcher needed reminding that the media mattered. It did not occur to her to alter the existing structure of the Downing Street press operation. All those running it were career civil servants, and the man she first put in charge of it was Henry James, a former head of the Central Office of Information who was then working at Vickers, whom she appointed as a temporary measure. It is notable that she did not take the opportunity to appoint a press secretary from a party or ideological background. Indeed, she consciously reverted to a less political approach to the press job because of what was seen as the excessively political one of Callaghan's press secretary, Tom McCaffrey,[86] choosing James precisely because he was unpolitical. Her relations with James were good, but she did not see his work as central to hers. At the beginning of her time in office, the Prime Minister received no daily press digest. There was no separate daily meeting about the media, and she did not automatically see her press secretary every morning, often dealing with these matters through her private secretaries alone.

Although Thatcher supporters were adept at using sympathetic journalists to push their line, there was nothing like the modern, systematic management of coverage. The idea of planning an announcement round the hoped-for headline was unknown, and the word 'spin' had no currency in British politics. Mrs Thatcher was usually punctilious in observing the convention that announcements of new legislation, green papers and so on should be made first to Parliament, not on television, although there were occasions when she made important policy changes on the spur of the moment, under the heat of the television lights. Despite the intense

FCO to No. 10 Press Office, 1979–81; press secretary to the Queen, 1990–97.

interest in her, there was no twenty-four-hour news cycle such as exists today. Between her election in May 1979 and her first summer recess that August, Mrs Thatcher gave only four formal press conferences and no full-dress interviews. Once inside No. 10, she paid much less attention to people, such as Gordon Reece, who had handled her media appearances in opposition. She ignored Reece's advice to give more television interviews, and crossly stamped on his request that her image be used for merchandising in aid of the party: 'No permission to be given on any goods of any kind. Don't mind a straight photograph.'[87] Her main public communications were in the House of Commons and through setpiece speeches. In this, as in so much else, Mrs Thatcher conformed to existing rules.

From 1 November 1979, however, James was recalled to Vickers, and Mrs Thatcher appointed Bernard Ingham* as her press secretary. A former Labour supporter who had once stood unsuccessfully for Leeds City Council and had later been an information officer at the Departments of Employment and Energy, Ingham was a naturally combative man. Perhaps excessively proud of his Yorkshire common sense, he was strongly in sympathy with the changes Mrs Thatcher was trying to make in British society. As his power grew in later years – he was to stay with her until the very end – Ingham would be criticized for intriguing on her behalf against ministers who were out of favour. He was always, however, rigorous about following the rules which prevented him having any contact with the party (never attending party conferences, for example, but going on holiday instead). However much he bruised individual feelings, he did not violate the Civil Service structure.

After he had arrived at No. 10 in October, understudying James for a few weeks, Ingham took up his place in the bow window which surveys everyone who comes and goes in Downing Street. He soon decided that his most immediate problem was to make the Prime Minister pay any attention at all to how she was being reported. He therefore developed a daily press digest of about five foolscap pages and 'sat down with her while we read it to make sure she *did* read it' most mornings at 9 o'clock.[88] This briefing became her window on the world. Mrs Thatcher did pay attention to what the *Daily Telegraph* said, since it was the main line to her natural supporters, and also to the *Sun*, whose importance in winning working-class voters over from Labour she readily acknowledged. In October 1979,

---

* Bernard Ingham (1932–), educated Hebden Bridge Grammar School; reporter, *Yorkshire Post*, 1952–61; *Guardian*, 1961–5; director of information, Department of Employment, 1973; Department of Energy, 1973–7; chief press secretary to the Prime Minister, 1979–90; knighted, 1990.

the *Sun* asked her to send the paper a message of congratulation on the tenth anniversary of its Murdoch revamp. Ingham, who was still three days short of formally starting his job, recommended against, complaining of the 'somewhat flimsy basis'. Mrs Thatcher, however, scribbled: 'The *Sun* is a friend! Will do.'[89] But in general she was distant from the media, and from the tastes of mass readerships. It is clear from the occasional notes she scribbled on these digests that she was thinking about particular issues – economic crises, for example, or the fate of servicemen killed in terrorist attacks – rather than about how she was herself being portrayed or what the current conversation in pub or coffee break might be. 'The real problem', Ingham remembered, 'was that she was not in touch.' She knew nothing about pop music or popular television programmes. She might, in her early days, read the first two columns of the *Financial Times*, but 'they did not exactly keep her in touch with what Britain was thinking.' Sometimes, when he and Mrs Thatcher were sitting on the tarmac waiting for an aeroplane to take off, Ingham would say to her, 'You might usefully read the leader in X paper,' and then notice that she did not know where the leader page was.[90]

It was a strength of hers that she did not bother her head with the petty intrigues and black arts of newspapers – 'she didn't have a dirty barrow-boy's mind' – but Ingham thought 'she was unprofessional in not thinking about presentation enough.' Much though she trusted him, she was so 'naturally secretive' about the distribution of paper that he fought a constant battle to keep up with what she was doing. In 1980, for instance, the report of the Top Salaries Review Body, with its controversial recommendations for generous increases, reached Ingham only half an hour before he was supposed to see the lobby about it. He did not know what the government line on it would be. 'It's madness,' Ingham told her. What Ingham also noticed at once, however, was Mrs Thatcher's gifts as a public performer. She was very concerned about her physical appearance and, when going on television, 'indulged herself with the make-up girl'.[91] Charles Anson observed that she considered her right profile better than her left, and was at pains to be photographed from that angle.[92] As Ingham put it: 'She was an actress who could turn on a tremendous performance when it had to be turned on.'[93] She was not media-minded, but she was a media star.

The first foreign politician to ring Mrs Thatcher to congratulate her on her victory on Friday 4 May 1979 was Ronald Reagan. But at that stage the ex-Governor of California was, in the official mind, little more than the unsuccessful challenger for the Republican nomination of 1976.* The

---

* A report from the Embassy in Washington in April conceded that Reagan was currently the

Downing Street switchboard did not put him through. President Jimmy
Carter was advised by aides to call, in addition to sending the usual congratulatory cable, to 'help counter some of the distorted speculation we
saw during the campaign (to the effect that we were hoping for a Labor
win ...)'.[94] Carter made the call quite late in the day, and he and Mrs
Thatcher spoke for only two minutes.

Luckily for Mrs Thatcher, she and Reagan managed to speak a few days
later, and Reagan's enthusiasm was not deflected by the snub from No. 10.
He was confident in his relationship with Mrs Thatcher, having enjoyed a
second meeting with her in London back in November 1978. This meeting
had been arranged after Reagan, scheduled to visit Europe, 'expressed a
wish to call on Mrs Thatcher to renew their friendship'.[95] 'They sparked,'
said Richard Allen,* who witnessed the encounter.[96] Mrs Thatcher confided
in Reagan her rather unfavourable evaluation of President Carter, before
urging him to 'keep working for his goals. She told him that while it might
be too late to turn things around in her country, she hoped not and, in any
case, would do everything she could to make a success of it.'[97] In one of
his regular weekly radio broadcasts, Reagan, who by May 1979 was campaigning once again for the Republican nomination, now cheered her on
from the sidelines:

> I couldn't be happier than I am over England's new Prime Minister. It has
> been my privilege to meet and have two lengthy audiences with Margaret
> Thatcher and I've been rooting for her to become Prime Minister since our
> first meeting.
>
> If anyone can remind England of the greatness she knew during those
> dangerous days in WWII when alone and unafraid her people fought the
> Battle of Britain it will be the Prime Minister the English press has already
> nicknamed 'Maggie'.
>
> I think she'll do some moving and shaking of England's once-proud indus-
> trial capacity which under the Labor Party has been running downhill for a
> long time. Productivity levels in some industrial fields are lower than they
> were 40 years ago. Output per man hour in many trades is only a third of
> what it was in the 1930s. Bricklayers for example laid 1000 bricks a day in

---

front-runner for the 1980 Republican nomination, but noted a number of liabilities including
'his age ... a rather passé image ... and a reputation for laziness'. 'Although some astute
political observers tell us that they feel in their bones that his campaign is beyond redemption,
it is probably too soon to write him off' (Jonathan Davidson to Nicholas Jarrold, 'Republican
Contenders for President', 19 Apr. 1979, TNA: PRO FCO 82/973).

* Richard V. Allen (1931–), advised Ronald Reagan on foreign policy and worked on his
presidential campaigns, 1976, 1980; National Security Advisor, 1981–2; president, Richard V.
Allen Co., 1982–90; senior fellow, Hoover Institution, from 1983.

1937 – today they lay 300. I think 'Maggie' – bless her soul, will do something about that.[98]

There was no comparable rapture in the chancelleries of Europe, but there
was certainly keen interest. And the main European leaders, frustrated by
having had to suffer the Labour Party's internal divisions over the EEC,
were quite pleased to have a return of the Tories, who were regarded at that
time as definitely the more Europhile of the two parties. The attitude of
officialdom, always pro-EEC, was to welcome the Conservatives because
they seemed more united: 'We all felt "Thank God we've got rid of that very
weak government."'[99]

It chanced that, by arrangement with the previous government, the first
foreign leader scheduled for a visit to No. 10 was Helmut Schmidt, the Chancellor of West Germany.* This did not please Mrs Thatcher, though she knew
about it and had provisionally accepted it before coming into office. 'Why's
he coming?' she complained to John Hunt. 'I didn't ask for it.' But the visit,
which took place only a week after her victory, was a success. Schmidt was
staggered by Mrs Thatcher's mastery of her brief.[100] For her part, Mrs
Thatcher never expressed, even in private, the anti-German feeling that would
appear in later years.[101] In public, she was admiring of German achievements,
noting in her speech at the dinner that Germany's 'enviable example' of economic success had been mentioned in both the main parties' election
manifestos. She then launched into a statement of Britain's attitude to the
EEC which, while warm – 'Ours is not a grudging acquiescence in Community membership' – was also realistic rather than visionary. She complained
that Britain paid the 'lion's share' of the bill for wasteful agricultural surpluses,
and emphasized the 'variety of our distinct nation states'. The strongest link
between Germany and Britain, she said, was not the EEC but that 'First and
foremost, we are both members of the North Atlantic Alliance.'[102] At the
joint press conference the next day, Mrs Thatcher was asked, for the first of
scores of occasions in her administration, when Britain would join the
Exchange Rate Mechanism (ERM) of the European Monetary System
(EMS), which was something which Germany strongly urged. Also for the
first of scores of occasions, she played for time. The government would look
at the matter, she promised, when the system was reviewed in September.[103]

Her remarks on EEC subjects at this time were conditioned by the fact
that, eleven days after winning one election, she had to start fighting another.
For the first time, direct elections were held for the European Parliament,

---

* Jack Lynch, the Irish Taoiseach, however, slipped in an unscheduled meeting just before
Schmidt; see Chapter 21.

or Assembly as it was still properly called and as Mrs Thatcher, wary of its pretensions, preferred to call it. The Conservative manifesto, launched on 15 May, declared a vague aim of joining the ERM at an unspecified point. Apart from launching the manifesto, Mrs Thatcher made only one campaign speech, to a 'Youth for Europe' rally on 2 June. Here she maintained the party's pro-European orthodoxy, but expressed it in a way that fitted with her other preoccupations. The EEC, she argued, should promote freedom, both in economic terms and against Soviet tyranny: 'the Treaty of Rome says little about the ideal of freedom, but defines at length the economic structures necessary to sustain it.' European values would never be secure so long as there was a Berlin wall. And without beating an anti-Brussels drum, she signalled her strong dissatisfaction with the European budget: Britain's contribution was 'manifestly unjust'.[104] In the poll on 7 June 1979, the Conservatives won sixty seats against the Labour Party's seventeen.

The first European journey – indeed the first journey abroad – of Mrs Thatcher's premiership was to France, to meet President Giscard d'Estaing. In accordance with her desire to keep official parties to a minimum, only she, plus Carrington, two private secretaries and two detectives, arrived at Le Bourget in a tiny Hawker jet to be received by the vast panoply of the French state.[105] Although the two leaders were politicians of the centre-right, the meeting with Giscard was not a success. At the luncheon he gave for her at the Elysée Palace, he was served first, because, in terms of protocol, a head of state takes precedence over a head of government. She had not been forewarned of the rule. 'Her lips tightened as she noticed,' Bryan Cartledge observed. 'Giscard was insufferable towards her.'[106] She later, in private conversation, described Giscard as 'very [long, disdainful pause] *noble*'.[107] Giscard, who had met Mrs Thatcher briefly once before, when she was in opposition, recalled their Elysée encounter thus: 'When our children were young, my family, being rather snobbish, employed an English nanny. She was very correct, very tidy, with a very neat hairdo. She was efficient, religious, always opening the windows, especially when the children were ill; rather tiresome. When I met Mrs Thatcher, I thought "She is exactly the same, *exactly* the same!"' In his view, the rules of protocol were no sort of insult – 'The President is in the line of Sovereigns': he had not intended any slight.[108]

Official records of their talks suggest that Mrs Thatcher expressed herself with slightly unwelcome trenchancy. Discussing the forthcoming economic summit in Tokyo, she said that 'she had never attended an Economic Summit but she had studied their communiqués closely: they were always the same. Meanwhile, the world's economic problems continued, and so did the communiqués.' She also volunteered the first of many firm statements that the British government 'could not possibly contemplate sanctions against South Africa'.[109]

Because France held the six-month rotating presidency of the EEC at that time, the first EEC Council of Ministers attended by Mrs Thatcher was in Strasbourg. It was therefore Giscard who set the agenda and tone of the meeting and thus helped, because of his treatment of her in Paris, to prejudice her against it. The Council meeting, which took place on 21 and 22 June 1979, gave Mrs Thatcher her first formal chance to express her dissatisfaction with the British contribution to the European budget. Although only the seventh richest member state (per head of population) at that time, Britain paid, after Germany, the largest net contribution. This derived from the fact that Britain had higher levels of non-EEC trade than other member states, therefore attracting an EEC tariff, and an economy much less geared to agricultural subsidy than the Continental ones. The Common Agricultural Policy was designed to assist those economies which, after 1945, were emerging from peasant agriculture. For Britain, whose agriculture was much more modern, the cost was higher than the benefit. Mrs Thatcher sought to gain acceptance of the need for action from her partners, and to get proposals for long-lasting reform on to the agenda for the next summit, which was to be in Dublin in the autumn.

The conduct of the Strasbourg summit was, in the words of Clive Whitmore, who had joined as her new principal private secretary the week before, 'quite an eye-opener for her'.[110] Although, in private conversation, Giscard had indicated to Mrs Thatcher over lunch that he would grant her request for a proper discussion of the budgetary problem on the first day, so that it could be included properly in the communiqué, he then played what she considered to be a trick. He devoted the afternoon to other subjects, proposing, late in the day, that the budgetary question be reserved for the dinner that night. This would have made it vaguer, because no officials would have been present, and would have kept it out of the communiqué. Mrs Thatcher said 'no'. Giscard's account is different: 'I was irritated by her insistence that the budget problem be at the top of the agenda, because it was not a common topic: it was a British topic.'[111]

'She always wanted to nail things down; Giscard always wanted to leave them to the *fonctionnaires*,' recalled Bryan Cartledge. In this case, she was successful, to the extent that the communiqué mandated the European Commission to come up with proposals in time for the Dublin summit to solve the budget problem. But Mrs Thatcher was angry at the attempt to circumvent her, and was still so irritated that, as crowds gathered on the pavements to watch her go off to the dinner that night in the ambassadorial Rolls-Royce, she turned to Cartledge and asked: 'Do I really have to go through with this?'[112] Giscard, who had organized a special parade of the Garde Republicaine to greet the leaders before dinner at the Royal Palace, noted with amusement that Mrs Thatcher arrived last (which was very untypical of her and can only have been because of her reluctance to come at all) and was overdressed: 'She was in an evening gown; we were in normal suits. But all the others were captivated. She was a good-looking English lady.'[113] For her part, Mrs Thatcher immediately, and ever afterwards, disliked the process and style by which the EEC did its business. 'She was hostile to the European Community from the beginning,' Giscard considered.[114]

A good deal of the talk at Strasbourg had taken place in the light of the forthcoming summit of the G7 to be held from 27 to 29 June 1979 in Tokyo. The biggest subjects to be discussed were inflation and the growing energy crisis, caused in part by the effects of the Islamist revolution in Iran earlier in the year, which had reduced the world supply of oil. These were matters of keen interest to Mrs Thatcher. In her uncomfortable meeting with Giscard on 5 June, she had indicated the special difficulties which the British context raised:

> The Prime Minister said that the British Government was at present pursuing a policy of requiring power stations in the UK to substitute coal for oil: if continued, however, this policy could affect the UK's capacity to build up coal stocks, which would be needed against the possibility of further trouble from the miners during the coming winter. The Government might, therefore, have to reconsider.[115]

Coal might help because of the oil shortage, but, from a domestic political point of view, it was the most dangerous fuel for a Conservative government to rely on. It is not surprising that Mrs Thatcher looked more favourably on nuclear energy. She was also conscious that she was governing a country, which, unlike all its G7 partners (bar Canada) was moving fast, because of the North Sea, to being a net oil exporter.

Mrs Thatcher approached Tokyo with the native suspicion she brought to summitry. She told Bryan Cartledge, who accompanied her, to count the size of the respective national delegations, in the hope that Britain's would be the smallest, and was annoyed to discover that the Canadian was smaller still. She was particularly impatient of the Japanese fondness for platitudinous communiqués, and was very keen that the summit focus on energy problems and oppose any attempt to reflate the world economy.[116] For their part, the Japanese, to whom the idea of a woman prime minister was quite fascinatingly alien, devised a special security plan. Every other national leader at the summit was assigned twenty male karate experts to protect them. The

Japanese proposed twenty 'karate ladies' to guard Mrs Thatcher. The Cabinet Secretary had to intervene. The Foreign Office reported that John Hunt had told the Japanese that 'Mrs Thatcher will attend the Summit as Prime Minister and not as a woman *per se* and he was sure she would not want these ladies.' If it were the form for other leaders, the Prime Minister would have 'no objection' to being attended by twenty 'karate gentlemen'.[117]

At the last-minute invitation of the Kremlin, Mrs Thatcher broke her flight to Tokyo at Moscow airport, where she was given an impromptu supper by the Soviets. The decision to fly through Soviet air space reduced the journey time by two and a half hours and had been taken on purely logistical grounds. However, the Soviet Prime Minister, Alexei Kosygin, decided, late in the day, to host the occasion personally. By her own account, she gave Kosygin a talking-to about the plight of the Vietnamese Boat People – victims, she told him, of Communism.[118] 'It was very plain speaking from a prime minister, not wrapped up at all in diplomatic nicety,' recalled Whitmore, who was present, 'but to be fair, Kosygin was not knocked sideways but gave as good as he got.'[119] Mrs Thatcher had never encountered the Soviet leadership before, and they were very curious about the Iron Lady. 'Neither thought the other was as bad as each had expected,' noted Bryan Cartledge.[120] Although Mrs Thatcher felt no affection for her Soviet interlocutor, and vice versa, both leaders rather enjoyed their verbal joust.*

Despite her aversion to summitry, Mrs Thatcher was pleased with Tokyo, partly because she was the centre of vast media attention. 'She relished being the new girl,' said Cartledge.[121] It also offered her first big chance to try out her skills at these occasions. Although she was often the despair of officials because of her disdain for diplomatic niceties, in another way Mrs Thatcher was an excellent negotiator, because she was so well informed and so eager to get business properly transacted. Negotiation, said Cartledge, 'came entirely naturally to her. She read her briefs and she took them seriously.' Before a major meeting, she would conduct an inquisition of officials, asking them sharp questions that her legal training prompted. She had no self-doubt, but neither was she overconfident: 'If she didn't understand something, she just asked.'[122] She was also unafraid of cutting through the summit hierarchy if her purposes demanded it. Unlike other leaders, she would visit the 'sherpas' (the summit officials) and harangue them directly on points of detail. 'It was excellent, really smart lobbying,' recalled Bob Hormats, the US sherpa. 'I remember saying to Carter, "Well, if you want to get some of your stuff in, maybe you should come around . . ." He said, "Oh, I'll let Margaret do

* Further discussion of this meeting appears in Chapter 20.

that.'"[123] In her opening statement at the Tokyo conference Mrs Thatcher spoke succinctly and without notes. Declaring that 'pious platitudes' should be avoided, she painted a gloomy picture of a world economy declining month by month because of the oil price. She nevertheless pleaded with colleagues to 'let the price mechanism work in full' and also argued the need for more nuclear energy. One reason she advanced in favour of nuclear energy was an ecological one. People who were concerned about the environment, she said in a pre-summit interview, 'should also be worried about the effect of constantly burning more coal and oil because that can create a band of carbon dioxide round the earth which could itself have very damaging ecological effects'.[124] She also warned the G7 that the fight against inflation would mean that a decline in real income was 'unavoidable in the short term'.[125] She stuck to her opposition to reflation. While the Seven were gathered in Tokyo, the price of Saudi oil rose from $14.54 to $18 a barrel. Their collective impotence was emphasized.

In the margins of Tokyo, Mrs Thatcher met Jimmy Carter, for the first time as prime minister. Her election had led to a shift in the way she was perceived in the White House. 'King Brewster [Kingman Brewster, US Ambassador to Britain] believes the new PM to be a cooler, wiser, more pragmatic person now than the Opposition Leader you met in May, 1977 or the dogmatic lady who visited you in Washington that fall,' Zbigniew Brzezinski minuted Carter in May 1979. 'I agree,' Carter wrote in the margin. But despite her 'tempering', Brzezinski continued, 'I think it will take patience to deal with Mrs Thatcher's hard-driving nature and her tendency to hector.'[126] Although each saw something to admire in the seriousness of the other, the relationship was not warm. Carter recorded in his diary that she was 'highly opinionated, strong-willed, cannot admit that she doesn't know something'. He added, limply: 'However, I think she will be a good prime minister for Great Britain.'[127]* She regarded Carter's analysis, both economic and political, of the state of the world as 'badly flawed'.[128] Giscard d'Estaing, though not at ease with Mrs Thatcher, noted the difference between the two, in her favour: 'She knew what she wanted to do, and she tried to do it. Jimmy Carter didn't.'[129] The most pressing and most immediately difficult issue that the two had to discuss was Rhodesia.

---

* Carter cites this diary entry in *Keeping Faith*, his memoirs, published in 1982. However, in the fuller version of his diary, *White House Diary*, that appeared twenty-eight years later, he deleted the final sentence (suggesting that Mrs Thatcher would 'be a good prime minister') from the published text. Carter's refusal to admit that he had once harboured positive thoughts about her prospects indicates his own attitude to Mrs Thatcher in later life.

Under the internal settlement devised by the Rhodesian Prime Minister Ian Smith, multi-racial elections, albeit ones that entrenched disproportionate white power in Parliament, the police and the armed services, had taken place in April 1979. Rejecting the provisions favouring the white minority, the popular black radical parties, including Robert Mugabe's Patriotic Front, had boycotted the election. Consequently, on a 64 per cent turn-out, the voters had returned a government led by Bishop Muzorewa, the more accommodating black candidate favoured by Smith. Mrs Thatcher, who remained sympathetic towards the white minority, had taken the Conservatives into the general election saying that she would await the result of a report into the elections which she had commissioned from Lord Boyd, the former Colonial Secretary. The strong implication of her stance was that, if Boyd pronounced the election fair, she would recognize the legitimacy of the new government.* Such a policy went strongly against that of Jimmy Carter and of the previous British government, in which David Owen had been foreign secretary. Their approach, in line with much of world opinion, had been to reject the internal settlement because of the privileged position it entrenched for the white minority. They intended to keep Rhodesia isolated on the world stage until a more inclusive constitutional settlement, with participation from Mugabe's Patriotic Front and other black radical parties, was adopted. Driven by the power of the black caucus in Democratic politics, and by its own ideological beliefs, the Carter administration had been fearful of Mrs Thatcher's approach before she assumed office. According to Raymond Seitz,† who worked at the US Embassy in London at that time: 'If Mrs Thatcher was the victor, then the Anglo-American relationship was in for a rocky time. She made it pretty clear during the campaign that she would recognise the Muzorewa government if she won. And we made it just as clear that we wouldn't. And that more or less public disagreement hung over the election and of course excited the press even more.'[130] Even Lord Carrington, who was not sympathetic to the internal settlement, felt that the Carter administration were making life more difficult for themselves: 'They were rather against her. They were pretty unpleasant . . . they thought she was a sort of right-wing baboon, even after she had been elected. It was her reputation. They were

---

* The significance of this implication was not lost on Ian Smith, who was delighted by her election. 'All Rhodesians thank God for your magnificent victory,' he wrote to congratulate her (Ian Smith, *Bitter Harvest: The Great Betrayal and the Dreadful Aftermath*, Blake Publishing, 2001, p. 298). Smith's enthusiasm would prove short lived.

† Raymond Seitz (1940–), executive assistant to Secretary George Shultz, Washington DC, 1982–4; Minister and Deputy Chief of Mission, US Embassy, London, 1984–9; Ambassador to the UK, 1991–4.

pressing rather hard not to recognize Muzorewa, and I think that was rather counterproductive.'[131]

Lord Boyd's report, whose substance she knew by 14 May, declared that the elections in Rhodesia had been, allowing for the difficult conditions of civil war, as free and fair as possible. 'There was an election,' she told *Time* magazine, even before Boyd reported, 'one person, one vote for four different parties. Where else would you get that in Africa?'[132] 'The main question-mark at the moment', Brzezinski warned Carter shortly after her election victory, 'remains the extent to which Mrs. Thatcher may be serious in her expressed intention to recognize the Muzorewa government.'[133] Recognizing Muzorewa would, at a stroke, end Rhodesia's international isolation and rubberstamp Smith's internal settlement. Carter's people held their breath. 'I thought probably that the game was up,' said one.[134] Yet Mrs Thatcher held back. In her first political speech in Parliament as prime minister, in the debate on the Queen's Speech on 15 May, she spoke of the developments within Rhodesia as good, but added that she wanted 'a return to legality in conditions that secure wide international recognition'.[135] It was this which was not forthcoming.

Visiting London on 21 May, the American Secretary of State, Cyrus Vance, told Lord Carrington that Carter did not think the elections had been free and fair, and that US sanctions against Rhodesia (which the Senate had voted to lift) would stay. The United States administration wanted an all-party conference, an amended constitution and fresh elections. Carrington asked the Americans not to go public with their specific demands, to give him room for manoeuvre; and manoeuvre he did, sending Lord Harlech, the former British Ambassador to Washington, off to tour the 'front-line' African states and get their views. He succeeded in deflecting Mrs Thatcher from acceding to the internal settlement: 'The thing that really persuaded her was that no one was going to support her. No member of the Commonwealth. The Americans were against it and all the members of the EEC were against it. And there might have been sanctions against us. These were the things which persuaded her. Not love of black majority rule. Lord Harlech came back reporting all this. Which of course is why I sent him. She respected his conclusions.'[136]

Although she listened, however, Mrs Thatcher was not going to revert to the policy of the previous government either. She had to be convinced of a new course. Robin Renwick,* head of the Rhodesia department at the Foreign

---

* Robin Renwick (1937–), educated St Paul's and Jesus College, Cambridge; Rhodesia Department, FCO, 1978–80; Assistant Under-Secretary, FCO, 1984–7; Ambassador to South Africa, 1987–91; to the United States, 1991–5; created Lord Renwick of Clifton, 1997.

Office, devised a plan which he hoped would appeal to her: 'I managed ... to give her something really radical: we should seek to intervene directly ourselves in Rhodesia. This was point number one. Point number two was that instead of trying to reach agreement with Nkomo and Mugabe ... we should build on the internal settlement ... and try and turn [it] into something that was internationally respectable. Then we should offer everyone the chance to participate in elections that we would have to supervise ... Since it wasn't what she was expecting, she was impressed by it.'[137] But Mrs Thatcher did not hurry to make up her mind. She knew that she had to have a position in time for the Commonwealth Heads of Government Meeting (CHOGM) in Lusaka, the capital of Zambia, in August, but until then she veered back and forth. Visiting Australia after the Tokyo summit, she made what Carrington remembered as a 'ghastly speech'[138] in which she pushed for international recognition of the new government in Salisbury.

On 12 July 1979, in London, Mrs Thatcher met Kurt Waldheim, the United Nations Secretary-General. She told Waldheim that 'Rhodesia was closer to democracy than any other country in Africa,' that Muzorewa was 'a very wise man', and that the Western world should support him. 'Mrs Thatcher opined', said the UN minutes, 'that if the West were to follow a policy which preferred bullets to ballots, there was no hope ... When Lord Carrington interjected that some changes like a reduction of the white presence in parliament and Government should be achieved, the Prime Minister said: "Poor Peter always has to pick up the pieces when I have made my statements."'[139] This report vividly conveys Mrs Thatcher's perennial hostility to dealing with anyone she considered a terrorist* and her habit of expressing herself with what, for diplomats, was almost unbearable directness. But it also contains a hint of another of her characteristics – a readiness to give in, protesting, to people who knew more than she about a particular subject. She worried that she was 'being conned by aristos',[140] but she almost enjoyed the process. 'The critics were quite right,' remembered Carrington, 'it *was* devious,'[141] but it suited Mrs Thatcher to go along with a policy from which she kept a personal distance. 'She wasn't the only person who could say "There is no alternative,"' recalled Carrington – she accepted the argument of inevitability, but at the same time she gave herself a let-out. 'If it had gone wrong, she would have ratted.'

On 25 July, Mrs Thatcher finally made a statement to the House of Commons which contained, in slightly wrapped-up language, what the Foreign Office wanted. She promised that Britain would take charge and make firm

---

* At that time, roughly 500 people per week were being killed in the Rhodesian civil war; 1,000 whites per week were leaving the country.

proposals for broadly acceptable constitutional arrangements for Rhodesian independence. The key sentences were: 'We shall aim to make the proposals comparable to the basis on which we granted independence to other former British territories in Africa. They will be addressed to all the parties to the conflict.'[142] In other words, the internal settlement, as it stood, would not be enough, and the Patriotic Front would, if possible, be part of any agreement.

Then it was on to Lusaka, arriving on 30 July. Although it was not true, as Lord Carrington believed, that she had never been to sub-Saharan Africa before (she had visited South Africa when Education Secretary), Mrs Thatcher certainly knew little about the place. Cartledge believed that she had 'no strong personal views' on the issue of Rhodesia, but her general approach was strongly coloured by those of Denis, who had kin in South Africa and had travelled widely in the continent on business. He had an unreconstructed belief in the political and economic incompetence of black regimes, and a natural sympathy, based on ethnicity and sport, for the whites of southern Africa. One US official was present at a small dinner at the Ambassador's residence during Mrs Thatcher's period as leader of the Opposition: 'The Thatchers wanted to watch a BBC programme on South Africa, so we adjourned upstairs. The programme began, and I realized for the first time, from the conversation between Margaret and Denis, that she had no use at all for blacks.'[143] This is not a fair characterization of Mrs Thatcher's attitudes – she usually avoided racial generalizations, except about the Germans and (more jocular) the Irish and the French – but it does indicate something of the atmosphere at home. She was also 'physically frightened'[144] of what would happen to her in Lusaka. Carrington recorded that she carried dark glasses on the aeroplane there. He asked her why: 'Margaret answered very clearly, "I am absolutely certain that when I land at Lusaka they are going to throw acid in my face." There had been some reported hysterical outburst, using that sort of violent language. I laughed. "You totally misunderstand Africans! . . . They're more likely to cheer you." Margaret stared at me, "I don't believe you."'[145] It was on that flight that Cartledge particularly noticed, with pleasure and some surprise, how well Mrs Thatcher got on with Carrington. The Foreign Secretary had successfully developed the ability to tease her. He could 'make her throw her head right back with laughter'.[146] Since virtually everyone else was too terrified of Mrs Thatcher to attempt such a thing, Carrington gained a particular standing in her eyes, and a particular freedom to do what he wanted. Denis, who certainly did not agree with Carrington about Rhodesia, was nevertheless a keen admirer, always referring to him as 'a mighty man'.[147]*

---

* As for Carrington, he had a genuine respect and affection for Mrs Thatcher, but he was also

As well as her anxiety about her reception in Zambia, Mrs Thatcher was worried by something else – the presence of the Queen, in her capacity as the head of the Commonwealth. The Queen's duty towards and affection for the Commonwealth meant, at least in principle, that she might find herself at odds with her own, British government. Mrs Thatcher's attitude to the monarch was one compounded of constitutional correctness, old-fashioned deference and a certain unease, probably related to the fact that both were women, and neither had much experience of working with women at a high level.* Mrs Thatcher was 'nervous about how to comport herself with the Queen' and worried by a series of occasions in which she would either upstage the Queen by mistake or be overshadowed by her. There was a problem, though Mrs Thatcher would never have put it like this, of 'Who's the star?' Besides, 'The two', Clive Whitmore noted, 'were not exactly natural social partners.'[148] Caroline Stephens, who knew Mrs Thatcher as well as anyone at this time, used to remind new private secretaries, 'The first thing you have got to bear in mind is that Mrs Thatcher is a very ordinary woman.' It was a strange thing to say about someone so clearly *extra*ordinary, but it was also true. Mrs Thatcher was anxious about meeting the Queen in the way that most ordinary citizens would be, worrying about what to wear, when to curtsey and how to avoid being late.† She needed frequent reassurance.

In fact, the problem of proximity was overcome by the fact that the Queen left Lusaka after two days, the opening formalities having been completed. And her initial presence actually made life easier for Mrs Thatcher since the respect felt for the Queen by the Commonwealth leaders rubbed off on her. Once her individual meetings with African leaders began, matters improved sharply. Cartledge had discovered that the Zambian President, Kenneth Kaunda, was, like Mrs Thatcher, the parent of twins. It is auspicious, in African culture, to have twins. This helped. Mrs Thatcher was charmed by Kaunda, and also had a successful meeting with Julius Nyerere, the left-wing President of Tanzania. She told the conference, in closed session, that the white blocking mechanism in the new constitu-

driven mad by what he saw as her stubbornness and lack of realism. One day, climbing the stairs to her study, he turned to Clive Whitmore and said: 'Clive, if I have any more trouble from this f***ing stupid, petit-bourgeois woman, I'm going to go.' (Interview with Sir Clive Whitmore.)
* This was the view of the Queen's sister, Princess Margaret (conversation with Lady Penn).
† When she attended the first meeting of the new Privy Council at Buckingham Palace after her victory in 1979, Mrs Thatcher arrived without her own officials – as is customary for Privy Council gatherings – and was so worried by lateness that she was forty-five minutes early. A junior official had to make small talk to the nervous Prime Minister until the Queen was ready. (Interview with John Dauth.)

tion was not acceptable, and that the rules about some armed service appointments (which favoured whites) were also wrong, but she insisted as well that Rhodesia was a problem which it was Britain's responsibility to sort out through a constitutional conference. The Commonwealth gave its support. 'When she went to Lusaka,' Robin Renwick remembered, 'they were all expecting her to say, "Let's recognize Muzorewa," but she came up with a "Britain will take over" plan, which she loved, because it threw them all completely off balance.'[149] On the morning of Sunday 5 August, after agreement had been reached, Mrs Thatcher, despite suffering from a severe stomach upset, 'embarked on a perfectly dreadful evening presenting the Zambian press awards ... I thought she was going to faint at one moment, particularly as she had had nothing to eat for 24 hours, but she got through it OK and even started the dancing with Kaunda.'[150] Carrington was delighted by Mrs Thatcher's achievements: 'She did terribly well at Lusaka. She really was brilliant. She had never been to Africa [not true: see above] and I think she thought they were a lot of savages. When they turned up and Kaunda was a smooth old guy and they were all very agreeable, I think she thawed a bit.'[151]

Mrs Thatcher had a clear understanding of the nature of her success at Lusaka. Sir Anthony Parsons, the British Ambassador to the United Nations, congratulated her afterwards: 'I said to her, "Prime Minister, I don't want to sound like a sycophant, but you did very, very well in Lusaka." And she laughed and said, "Well, Tony you know how it is, you people convinced me, but when it came to doing it in public, I think I did it a great deal better than you could have done."'[152] A conference was called at Lancaster House in London for September. Although it included Joshua Nkomo and Robert Mugabe, whom she regarded as terrorists, Mrs Thatcher had achieved, in terms of diplomacy and reputation, an undoubted success. Worried about possible attacks within her own party, she had made sure to take her PPS, Ian Gow, with her to Lusaka, to have him be part of the deal and in a position to sell it to the party's right, with which he was sympathetic.* There were rumblings on the right at the party conference in October, but nothing unmanageable. For the first but by no means the last time, Mrs Thatcher was able to force something upon her party which they would have found unpalatable coming from almost anyone else.

---

* Gow's active participation in Lusaka was hampered by the fact that he took his sleeping pills, with alcohol, at lunchtime, thinking they were malaria pills. He passed out. (Private information.)

17
'Cuts'

'I asked for too little, didn't I?'

On her first day in office, Mrs Thatcher saw briefs from the Cabinet Secretary and the Think Tank (CPRS) about the state of the British economy. She also read a copy of the Treasury's briefing to the Chancellor on the same subject. These documents were relentlessly gloomy.

The Treasury predicted that the Retail Price Index (RPI) would rise to an annual rate of 10–11 per cent in the course of 1979 and that the Public Sector Borrowing Requirement (PSBR) would rise from £8.5 billion to £10 billion. This increase would result chiefly from the public sector pay settlements proposed by Professor Clegg's Comparability Commission which, during the campaign, she had promised to implement. John Hunt reminded her of the vast range of public employees – including the armed services, doctors and dentists, 'top people', local government non-manual workers, postmen and teachers – whose pay she would shortly have to settle. In a separate note on timing, Hunt told her that the priority was the Budget. Second, 'close behind in terms of time, and ahead in terms both of intrinsic importance and inherent difficulty, is the development . . . of a strategy for public expenditure.' The outgoing Labour government had been putting up spending by 3 per cent per year in real terms since the austerity of 1977–8, and had left plans in train for more of the same. Summarizing, Hunt wrote: 'the overall picture in the short term on present policies is a rising rate of inflation and slow growth, leading to continued uncertainty and instability.'[1]

The CPRS, as was its role, gave a broader context: 'our industrial performance has been so poor for so long that in Western industrial terms we have now become a low productivity, cheap labour, country.' It noted that unemployment was at present accepted 'with surprising equanimity', but foresaw that 'if unemployment were to increase sharply, the present equable acceptance might break down, especially in the Inner Cities, with large numbers of young coloureds unable to find jobs.' The world trade situation was bad, and 'The UK is now exposed to the "Dutch disease" – the tendency of oil and gas revenues to raise the exchange rate,' a tendency which would be reinforced, it said, by monetarist policies. It recommended leaving more oil in the ground, loosening exchange controls and joining the ERM. Income tax thresholds should rise, the high rates should be cut (though this could be delayed), and indirect taxes should be put up. Public spending should be cut, partly by means of 'staff cuts', and also by the 'contentious' means of indexing benefits to prices rather than earnings. There was 'consensus', said the Think Tank, which clearly did not yet know Mrs Thatcher's allergy to that word, that the main problems facing the nation were 'inflation, industrial performance, and unemployment, in that order'.[2] The paper did not mention trade union reform as a remedy for any of the above.

The dismal economic news was not unexpected for Mrs Thatcher, though Tim Lankester, who, as her economics private secretary, had to lay it before her, did note, slightly surprised, that 'she wasn't terribly well briefed on the macroeconomic problems when she arrived'.[3] In a way, it was helpful to Mrs Thatcher that things were so bad. Only disaster had led voters to reject the soothing approach of Jim Callaghan. Only disaster would incline them to accept the nasty medicine that the strict new nurse was offering. The Conservatives had fought the election on the need for economic change, and now had a decent mandate for bringing it about. Although the Tory old guard were known to be worried by monetarism, economic liberalism and public spending cuts, they had no alternative analysis or programme. The scope for radicalism seemed clear.

But there was an enormous gulf between the seriousness of the situation and the practical readiness of the new government to do something about it. There was a potentially fatal combination of the natural complacency of the Conservative Party and the ingrained pessimism of a bureaucracy that had managed decline for more than a generation. Mrs Thatcher was instinctively alert to this problem, and feared, from the moment that she first sat at her desk, that events might run away from her. She began immediately to scribble with frantic energy over the briefs she received. Civil servants quickly came to recognize that her repeated underscoring of a passage with straight lines signified approval. A wavy line meant the opposite. Virtually never writing separate memoranda of her own, she preferred the margins of the document she received from others. There she would express her feelings with some violence. 'No!!', or '<u>No</u>' (underlined three times), or even, as was much later to become famous in another context, 'No. No. No.' In his initial memo of 4 May 1979, John Hunt asked her to confirm that 'comparability (properly carried out) is the key to establishing public sector pay.'[4] 'No', she wrote, choosing to ignore the fact that she had committed her party to honour the findings of the Clegg Comparability Commission which were due in August. And when Hunt drafted her a memorandum for Cabinet discussion on pay and cash limits, setting out the options on the subject, she wrote on his covering note: 'Discussion on this paper in Cabinet would be <u>futile</u> – and on any other paper which raises such enormous questions and supplies so few answers! It would weaken our hand – not strengthen it. <u>Delete from Agenda</u>.'[5] From the very beginning, she dreaded using the Cabinet as a place where people, especially people who did not agree with her, could merely air opinions: she wanted it to focus on action.

Over the future of Clegg, in fact, Mrs Thatcher was determined to avoid further commitment. She saw the basic principle of comparability – the idea that wages could be determined by comparing them with those of other workers rather than being based on productivity and affordability – as wrong and financially ruinous. The institutional bias in favour of keeping the arrangement was very strong, however, and during the election campaign she had committed the Tories, despite Geoffrey Howe's opposition, to honouring Clegg's findings. A plan was in place to appoint a successor to Professor Clegg when he stepped down, and the expectation was that some sort of overall machinery for comparing and determining public sector pay would have to continue. On 16 May, Hunt wrote to Mrs Thatcher to say that 'arguments against dismantling the Commission at <u>this</u> stage look conclusive.'[6] But she was determined to avoid anything but a short-term commitment. She also wanted to alter the way Clegg did his work. She went through the biographies of the proposed new members of the Commission trying to suggest people more sympathetic to her stance. What about Professor Patrick Minford,* she asked, or the businessman Frank McFadzean 'or someone of similar <u>views</u> [underlined three times]?' And she tried to change Clegg's terms of reference to 'consider the economic consequences of any award'.[7] When she realized that such changes might serve only to entrench Clegg, she got the Cabinet to agree to a holding position in which no new members should be added since this might imply government support for an ongoing role for the Commission. Presented with a draft parliamentary answer to a question asking whether Clegg would be abolished, she struck out the word 'No', but left the rest about 'completing its existing work' to stand.[8] Clegg clung to life because

---

* Patrick Minford (1943–), educated Winchester, Balliol College, Oxford and LSE; adviser to HM Treasury, 1971–3; Professor of Applied Economics, University of Liverpool, 1976–1997; Professor of Economics, Cardiff Business School, from 1997; published books and articles on monetary and international economics.

of the fear of industrial disruption from winding it down too quickly. It was not until August 1980 that its abolition was announced.

Pursuing the subject of pay, Jim Prior submitted a memorandum recommending early talks between the government and the TUC and, separately, the government and the CBI, to consider 'objectives'. Beside this, Mrs Thatcher wrote, 'No.' Prior also urged that the Clegg Commission be allowed to continue its work after it had next reported. 'We simply cannot take the required decisions on a flimsy paper like this,' Mrs Thatcher scrawled.[9] At her request, it was taken off the Cabinet agenda. The main forum of discussion was moved from the full Cabinet to E Committee, with a memo from the Chancellor to be used as the basis for discussion. This memo, however, fared little better. In it, Geoffrey Howe recommended that the government should await the completion of the Clegg round in August and then 'take stock' before deciding how much Rate Support Grant (RSG) should be paid to the local authorities ('i.e. follow the settlements!' wrote Mrs Thatcher derisively). Once that decision had been made, he said, 'the local authorities would themselves be left to negotiate without interference.' 'This is a mistake,' Mrs Thatcher noted. 'He who pays the piper must have some say in calling the tune.'[10] As for comparability itself, Howe argued that the whole question of whether it should be a permanent feature of pay bargaining should be left open until after the end of the Clegg round.

Howe also canvassed the subject of some kind of economic and industrial forum after which he still hankered, and to which the Tories were, vaguely, committed. Although he rejected the idea that such a body should be used to set pay norms or limits, he went on, 'The question is whether it [a forum] would be useful in conveying better public understanding of the processes and prospects of the economy'.[11] The TUC must not be given a platform for formal confrontation, Howe argued, but there should be 'informal contacts' with union leaders. As time passed, the concept of the forum became weaker and weaker.* The Chancellor sought endorsement from Cabinet colleagues of the principles contained in his first three paragraphs. 'There aren't any principles in those paras,' wrote Mrs Thatcher crossly, and she covered the document with a note which said, 'This is a very poor paper and we can only charitably assume that the Treasury is "otherwise occupied" at the present ... we certainly cannot wait until

---

* In early July, Howe suggested, using language unlikely to endear itself to the anti-Sixties Mrs Thatcher, that the forum might be 'more of a "happening" than an institution in a formal sense', which might achieve 'broad agreement' on future economic policy. Mrs Thatcher wrote 'No' on his note. The 'happening' never happened.

Clegg has finished all his work.'[12] On 31 May 1979, having effectively
gatecrashed a meeting originally planned for Professor Clegg and Prior
alone, Mrs Thatcher told Clegg that he should add considerations of efficiency and overmanning to his remit. When he objected that this would be
impossible, 'The Prime Minister said that she was very disappointed to
hear what Professor Clegg had to say about efficiency. This only confirmed
her fears that the commission's first reports would produce inflationary
settlements. She asked Professor Clegg to consider the implications for the
future reputation of the Commission.'[13]

The matter in which the Treasury was 'otherwise occupied' was the Chancellor's first Budget. Mrs Thatcher was determined not to repeat the mistake
of the Heath government which, coming into office in June 1970, had
waited until the customary time the following spring before presenting its
first Budget. The same applied to public spending, which the government
was determined to cut even though the spending year had already begun.
The date of 12 June was chosen for the Budget, so there was great haste.

Before this, however, there had to be a Queen's Speech, with its announcement of the legislative programme. In preparing this programme, Mrs
Thatcher revealed how, despite having firm objectives and a clear philosophy to govern its approach, her government did not yet have an agreed
strategy. This was visible in the matter of the Price Commission, a statutory
body whose attempt to control prices artificially contradicted Thatcherite
principles. On his first day at work, the new Trade Secretary, John Nott,
wrote to Mrs Thatcher to urge immediate abolition. Mrs Thatcher, though
she did not put it in so many words, was worried about the sudden effect
on the RPI. She noted, on a letter from her private secretary:

> I must tell you at the outset that I favour metamorphosis rather than extinc-
> tion. The two main purposes of our strategy are
>   i. to restore incentives by direct tax cuts and consequently to tolerate
> indirect tax increases and
>   ii. to establish credibility and authority by the necessary amendments to
> trade union law. It would be unwise to jeopardise these objectives.
>   Finally decisions reached in haste tend to be repented later.[14]

This version of her own strategy was strangely partial, leaving out the
attack on inflation and on public spending. It was also, at least as she
applied it to the Price Commission, abandoned. Keith Joseph intervened
in support of Nott and immediate abolition was agreed at E Committee
on 14 May. In her memoirs, Mrs Thatcher writes: 'Perhaps the first time
our opponents truly realised that the Government's rhetorical commitment

to the market would be matched by practical action was the day we announced abolition.'[15] This is correct, but at the time her confusion about what to do in which order had come close to preventing it.

At the State Opening of Parliament, in which the Commons are summoned to wait upon the Queen in the House of Lords, Mrs Thatcher, in a white hat, set a new tone of smartness. She was seen, as MPs sat waiting for Black Rod to call them to the Upper House, brushing specks of scurf from Norman St John-Stevas's collar. On 15 May, she led the debate on the Loyal Address in the Commons. In political terms, her words were combative. This had been, she said, 'a watershed election',[16] in which a clear choice had been made in favour of the individual and against government. She gleefully quoted the right-wing Labour ex-minister Bill Rodgers* who had declared: 'Above all the Labour Party has let the idea of freedom be filched.' Commenting on the unhappy state of inner cities, she blamed municipal socialism: 'where one finds poverty in inner cities, there one finds that socialist government has operated for many years.'[17] Mrs Thatcher announced the quick abolition of the Price Commission. She ordered the National Enterprise Board to dispose of its holdings in profitable companies. Inter-city coach services were to be deregulated, immigration controls tightened. She promised a Bill to give tenants the right to buy their council house and the introduction of a new shorthold tenure to liberalize the private rented sector. And she foreshadowed what was later called the Assisted Places Scheme, which would pay for talented state school pupils to be educated in independent schools. There was the hint of compromise about the future of Rhodesia, and a hint of confrontation over the EEC budget. The increases in police and armed services pay, promised in the election campaign, were presented as the defence of 'freedom under the law' and justified because 'security is essential to our survival as a free nation'. Their implications for the public purse were not discussed.

Treating the subject of trade unions 'under the heading of the rule of law', Mrs Thatcher also introduced the most controversial measure of the speech – the Bill to reform some of their practices. It was not, in reality, very radical, continuing to reflect the compromise within the party between the conciliator Jim Prior and those who wanted a complete reordering of British industrial relations. Prior, being the minister responsible, got the

---

* Bill Rodgers (1928–), educated Quarry Bank High School, Liverpool and Magdalen College, Oxford; Labour MP for Stockton-on-Tees, 1962–74; for Teesside, Stockton, 1974–81; founder member of SDP, 1981; SDP MP for Teesside, Stockton, 1981–3; created Lord Rodgers of Quarry Bank, 1992.

better part of the bargain. The Bill tried to restrict picketing to the place of work (but did nothing about blacking – the boycotting of goods and firms breaking a strike), gave individuals the right of appeal against closed-shop membership (without undermining the institution of the closed shop itself) and made public funds available for postal ballots for union elections. In avoiding the criminal prescriptions that had undone Heath's approach to industrial relations, and in signalling a direction of travel, the Bill had some significance. But it would have little practical effect on the conduct of industrial disputes. It was not enough to establish the 'credibility and authority' which her strategy sought.

Except for the abolition of the Price Commission, key economic measures had to await the Budget. As the days of preparation passed, in addition to his weekly bilateral with the Prime Minister, Geoffrey Howe went more and more often through the door that connects No. 11, the Chancellor's residence, with No. 10. He had to bring Mrs Thatcher worse and worse news. The consequences of the Callaghan government's pre-election spree of borrowing and spending, including the cost of wage settlements, were playing havoc with monetary control. On 10 May 1979, Howe informed her that sterling M3, the measure of all coins, notes and bank deposits, now preferred by the Treasury as the best measure of money supply, was growing at an annual rate of 12.8 per cent, above its target range. Given that the government believed and publicly asserted that inflation was caused by excessive growth of the money supply, this was a clear warning of inflation ahead. On 6 June he warned of 'more bad news (to place alongside the trade figures) to show that our inheritance was much worse than we had appreciated'.[18] The money supply growth rate was now 13.1 per cent and would be higher still that month, the figures being 'right outside even Denis Healey's target range'. The government's own target was 7–11 per cent. Howe went on to say that Gordon Richardson, the Governor of the Bank of England, advised a 2 per cent increase in the Minimum Lending Rate (MLR) to 14 per cent. This was bound to put up mortgage rates to 13 per cent. The rise should take effect the following day, Howe insisted, to avoid it becoming involved in the Budget.

Mrs Thatcher was presented, for the first time, with a dilemma which was to trouble her again and again. In those days, before the independence of the Bank of England's Monetary Policy Committee decreed in 1997, control of interest rates rested, in effect, with the Chancellor, consulting with the Prime Minister. Decisions on putting rates up or down were therefore inevitably political, as well as economic. They were also more noticeable than most such decisions were to become by the end of the century: because of high inflation, it was hard to give a little touch to the tiller. The quarter-per-cent rate changes familiar in modern times would have been imperceptible then. Rises were often of two, once even of three, percentage points. They placed politicians in the middle of controversies which they disliked, but gave them a power that few at the time would have dreamt of giving up. Mrs Thatcher had an innate distrust of the Bank of England for what she saw as its Keynesian approach, and she was particularly suspicious of Gordon Richardson, the Governor. 'I just don't know how you can trust them,' she said to Adam Ridley.[19] And when, that November, a crisis in the funding of government debt in the gilts market precipitated a three-point rise in interest rates, Mrs Thatcher wrote in the margin of a memo about the Bank's conduct: 'I must put someone there I can rely on.'[20] Richardson was an intellectual who preferred expressing himself in indirect and apparently inconclusive ways which irritated her. He was also a handsome man, but one who did not treat her as if she were an attractive woman – a fatal combination in her eyes: 'He was feline; she was canine.'[21] In her frank way which both delighted and alarmed officials, she looked up one day as John Ashworth, the government's Chief Scientist, came into her office and said, 'What do you think of Gordon?' 'Gordon who?' said Ashworth. 'Oh, you know, that fool who runs the Bank of England.'[22] Even though monetarists such as Tim Congdon* and Hayek himself had already floated the idea of surrendering political control of interest rates, she did not contemplate passing authority to Richardson. Richardson had been Governor under Heath; even before Mrs Thatcher came into office, Gordon Pepper had persuaded her that Richardson had been as 'guilty as hell' over the Barber boom.[23]

Mrs Thatcher longed to make her role as First Lord of the Treasury real as well as titular. She saw interest rates as her main immediate weapon in her war against inflation, and would never cede political power over them. But although no one was stronger than she on the need to beat inflation, no one was more conscious of the effect of high interest rates on what she sometimes referred to as 'our people'. The most consistent of all threads in the economic history of Margaret Thatcher was her initial objection to interest rate rises whenever they were proposed. She hated the idea that young people on or approaching the housing ladder should be penalized by a Tory government. She was fierce, in theory, about the wickedness of a person or a nation borrowing more than he, she or it could afford, but she

* Tim Congdon (1951–), educated Oxford University; economist. On economics staff, *The Times*, 1973–6; economist, L. Messel and Co., 1976–86; founder, managing director, Lombard Street Research, 1989–2001, chief economist, 2001–5.

also knew that preventing people from borrowing was a sure way to crush the aspirations which she wished, for reasons of belief and of party politics, to foster.

In early June 1979, the Chancellor and Governor were summoned to her presence. 'The Prime Minister said she could not accept the Chancellor's argument on timing,' her private secretary minuted Howe's after the meeting, because it left out consideration of the European elections. She said that the increase would have to be on Tuesday (the day of the Budget), and 'she was doubtful whether a full 2 per cent was needed' and was worried about mortgage rates. She asked for a reconsideration over the weekend.[24]

Reverting to Mrs Thatcher on Monday, Howe held fast. He and Richardson took the view that the government must send the right signals. The most basic point of all was that the government had to be able to fund its borrowings in the market: it could not do this if its strategy was disbelieved. It was essential, said Howe, to avoid the 'subsequent feeling that the change [in interest rates] is insufficient'. He added, 'given our commitment to monetary targets, our first use of a monetary policy instrument should be effective and unequivocal.' Lankester wrote on Howe's note: 'PM seen and willing to abide by Chancellor's judgement, albeit very reluctantly.'[25] She made it clear that she thought the increase was mistaken, and would have preferred one of 1.5 per cent.

In doing so, Mrs Thatcher was perfecting a technique she was often to deploy – permitting a decision, but distancing herself from it. When, as night follows day, the rise in the Minimum Lending Rate which she had agreed led to a rise in mortgage rates, Mrs Thatcher decided to be so shocked that she broke her normal habit of writing in the margins of memos received and wrote a full memorandum to Geoffrey Howe herself: 'I am very worried about the reports in today's press that mortgage rates may have to go up within a few days. This must not happen. If necessary, there must be a temporary subsidy (as in 1973) from the contingency reserve to keep the rate where it is (11¾ per cent). That rate is already too high. Can you consult with Michael Heseltine and the Building Societies forthwith.'[26] This subsidy was not, in the end, forthcoming; but the intervention indicated Mrs Thatcher's unhappiness with the situation, and her readiness, for political reasons, to diverge from the market stringencies, on which, in principle, she insisted. Again and again, the Treasury and various free-market purists urged her to get rid of Mortgage Interest Relief at Source (MIRAS), the tax write-off of mortgage interest, but Mrs Thatcher refused. When rumours got out that MIRAS might be removed, Jim Callaghan challenged her at Prime Minister's Questions. She did not hesitate:

'I am delighted to deny it. One's advisers are not always right, and I often tell them so.'[27]

As the first Budget was prepared, Mrs Thatcher quickly came into conflict with the Treasury. At a full-dress meeting with all the Treasury ministers and senior officials she complained that 'The Treasury approach . . . was not nearly tough enough' on public expenditure. She wanted a PSBR of £7.5 billion, rather than the £8.5–10 billion projected. 'The Prime Minister said that it was essential to get the overall strategy right from the start. This must involve large public expenditure cuts this year leading on to more substantial reductions in later years; a lower growth in the money supply . . . and lower interest rates.'[28] The search for new cuts was agreed, including a reduction of the Rate Support Grant by a further £100 million, a cut in the contingency reserve and a target of £400 million in other savings. Asset sales would raise £1 billion. There would be no adjustment to cash limits,* and there would be a cutting of staff costs in the Civil Service.

Mrs Thatcher was less robust, however, about the tax plans: 'she was extremely perturbed at the prospect of having to increase VAT from 8 per cent to 15. This would mean a sudden jump in the RPI of at least 3 per cent. The result could be catastrophic for the next pay round.'[29] As Geoffrey Howe pointed out in his memoirs, Mrs Thatcher was displaying 'the ambivalence she often showed when the time came to move from the level of high principle and evangelism to practical politics'.[30] After considering matters further for a few days, Howe wrote back. His Budget, he knew, would be seen as 'contractionary', but that would not matter if it also gave 'really firm and convincing indications' of the government's long-term determination. He wanted to cut income tax from 33 to 30 per cent at the basic rate and from 83 per cent to 60 per cent at the top rate. This could be paid for only by a 15 per cent rate of VAT.

In the constant battle in her own breast between her cautious and radical instincts, Mrs Thatcher now edged towards caution. Was it really wise, she wondered, to try to cut income tax so much, so quickly? 'She referred in this context to the Budgets of 1952 and 1953. Mr Butler's first Budget had been a tough one, and it was only in his second Budget that he had introduced major reductions in income tax.'[31] But Howe maintained his

---

* Cash limits, though not invented by Thatcherites, were a key concept for their budgetary control. Rather than planning spending by volume, as had happened in the past – two aircraft carriers, for example, or a hundred new schools – they would work out how much cash should be allocated for projects. If that cash limit was exceeded, the agreed projects could not go forward.

position. The PSBR would go way over £8 billion without 15 per cent VAT. 'What matters', he wrote, 'is a comparison between take home pay and prices, and everyone would be securing substantial income tax cuts. Such a package would be presented as giving greater personal choice.' And he wanted the Budget to mark a decisive departure: 'this Budget provides our only opportunity to make a radical switch from direct to indirect taxation and thus honour the commitment on which our credibility depends.'[32] The two met the following day, and Mrs Thatcher gave her reluctant agreement to the increase in VAT, winning in exchange a decision, for the sake of the Retail Price Index, not to increase the duties on alcohol and tobacco. They also agreed that it was essential for the PSBR to be below £8.5 billion, a slippage from the originally desired £7.5 billion which they would quickly rue. In hindsight, many shared the view that Mrs Thatcher had advanced (though they did not know she had advanced it), criticizing Howe for tax cuts and changes too sudden for the precarious state of the public finances. There was much to be said for this criticism. Against this, though, was the importance of symbol. Howe could see, more clearly than Mrs Thatcher, that a new Conservative government had to signal a new view about what tax was for. It had to emphasize incentive and choice. It even, as Brian Walden had noted before the election, had to suggest the benefits that came from inequality. In a strong moral defence of her economic policies delivered not long after the Budget, Mrs Thatcher justified the cut in the top rate of tax in anti-egalitarian terms: 'Nations depend for their health, economically, culturally and psychologically, upon the achievements of a comparatively small number of talented and determined people.'[33] If her first Budget had not been bold about tax, her later ones would almost certainly have been more cautious still, and the impetus for change would have been lost.

The theme with which Howe introduced his Budget on 12 June 1979 was the decline of Britain. In 1954, he pointed out, Britain's share of world trade had been the same as that of France and Germany combined. In 1979, a quarter of a century later, the Franco-German share was three times larger than Britain's. Such a stark admission of decline was a prelude to reversing it. His measures included all the major tax changes that he had wanted. In addition, he changed the basis of calculation for the state pension. In the past, pension increases had been linked to the rise in prices or earnings, 'whichever is the greater'. Now they were to be linked to prices alone. Since one of the problems of the British economy was the tendency of wages to outstrip prices without compensating improvements in productivity, this change was huge in its long-term effect. So was the decision, announced in the Budget, to begin the staged lifting of exchange controls. For the first

time in a generation, large-scale foreign investment in the UK private sector became a serious proposition, as did new British investment abroad.

Everyone could see the radical change that Howe's first Budget
represented, and it was duly acclaimed or reviled depending on the commentator's attitude to that radicalism. Cheering news for the government
was the annual report by the International Monetary Fund which, since
the disaster of 1976, had been making health visits to the British economy
as the patient convalesced. Its report in early July praised the restraint
on public spending, the tight financial policies and 'the courageous
decision ... to act to improve the productivity performance of the UK
economy whatever the short-term cost'.[34] Less encouraging for Mrs
Thatcher was the reaction of Jim Prior. He found the Budget an 'enormous
shock'.[35] This may seem strange, given that the chief points of the Budget
had been foreshadowed in the election campaign, but Prior admitted in
later years that he had been 'working on the assumption that the rhetoric
of opposition would become softened by the experience of government'.[36]
Besides, because of Mrs Thatcher's extreme (and, as later events were to
show, justified) fear of leaks, there had been no Cabinet discussion of the
Budget. Ministers heard its contents only on the morning of the day when
it was delivered, by which time protest was too late. Prior, who had earlier
got wind of the possible increase in the rate of VAT to 15 per cent, had
been to see Mrs Thatcher to lobby against this, and she, who had her own
objections to the rise, 'heard me with sympathy'.[37] On the night before the
Budget, Prior gave dinner to Moss Evans, the head of the giant Transport
and General Workers Union, and told him that he doubted that the rate
would go as high as 15 per cent.[38] When it did so, Prior lost standing as
an interlocutor with the unions, and felt foolish, even misled. He vented
his anger by protesting privately at the increases in the RPI which the
Budget would cause, and at the policy of encouraging nationalized industries to increase their prices in order to restrain their 'external financing
limits' (the subsidy they received from central government). These rises, in
turn, would push wages higher. For an anti-monetarist like Prior who
believed that wage increases, not the quantity of money, caused inflation,
the Budget was indeed a great error. For anyone concerned with pay bargaining, it was certainly a high risk.

The real problem, however, was not the price increases, politically
uncomfortable though they were. Most of them, as Geoffrey Howe had
successfully persuaded Mrs Thatcher, would drop out of the RPI after a
year because they would not be repeated. They were not, in the proper sense,
inflationary. The much greater difficulty was whether the course charted by
the Chancellor could be sustained. Would the government really be able to

contain public spending enough to reduce taxes over time without having to borrow more and more money? Mrs Thatcher sensed at once that she had missed her first chance to be really tough on spending. At the party she gave to celebrate the Budget, she said to Robin Butler, then a Treasury civil servant charged with public spending, 'I asked for too little, didn't I?'[39] If the government did have to borrow more money, how could it possibly, according to its own theories, reduce inflation? If it did not reduce inflation, how could it bring down interest rates? How was inflation to come down faster if the government was spending and borrowing too much and if, as some were beginning to assert, the measurement of money supply was wrong anyway? The speed of events was such that the government had made a series of important decisions before it was able to think about them. There was a legislative programme; there was a Budget; there were good intentions. But was there a strategy, in the sense of something that linked everything to everything else in order to find a way through the maze?

John Hoskyns thought not. He remembered observing in Mrs Thatcher what General Sir Alan Brooke had observed in Winston Churchill: 'I despair of getting the Prime Minister to understand the connection between different theatres of war.' 'She *was* very remarkable, but like Churchill she had no strategic sense in the executive meaning of the word.'[40] He kept trying to get her and her colleagues to look at the situation in the round. On the day of the Budget he sent to Mrs Thatcher a paper entitled 'Government Strategy' which sought a 'coherent approach to the task of turning round the British economy' and declared: 'The problem is a single problem ... The expectations within the system tend to be self-fulfilling. Government therefore has to persuade people to think and feel differently before the behaviour of the system can change.' His first concept was what he called Stabilization, which would take up most of the first term. It meant getting the economy on an even keel of zero inflation, market pay systems, a stable exchange rate at a competitive level, and so on. It might even require, he doubtingly suggested, a pay freeze to deal with the fact that the public sector would not respond readily to market pressures. From Stabilization could come Rebuilding, a greater reduction of the government's percentage of GDP, a freeing up of the labour market, a switch of talent to the private sector ('What is really needed is 10 years of vulgarly pro-business and pro-industry policies'). Rebuilding without Stabilization would be 'like trying to pitch a tent in the middle of a landslide'. Perhaps the most important single thing, said Hoskyns, was to change the role of trade unions. He questioned whether the proposed reform of the union law would be enough. Reverting to what he had argued in the Stepping Stones papers written in opposition, Hoskyns urged that the 'union debate' be 'started properly: We need to force unions to address their members in the language of the real world.'[41]

Mrs Thatcher drew a large black arrow pointing to this last sentence, showing that she approved of it. But it is doubtful whether the paper succeeded in getting the focus Hoskyns sought. Mrs Thatcher used it as the basis for a strategy discussion with a special group of ministers, including Howe, Whitelaw, Heseltine, Joseph and Prior, on 18 June 1979, but it quickly became bogged down. As Hoskyns himself recorded at the time, his mention even of the possibility of a pay freeze 'got things off on a slightly wrong note'.[42] On her copy of Hoskyns's paper which she used at the meeting, the Prime Minister wrote 'Pay <u>freeze out</u>'.[43]* And she took his word 'stabilization' the wrong way, believing that it was 'a stagnation-type word'[44] condemning the country to no growth. She had a habit of seizing on a particular word in someone's argument and wrestling with it. Sometimes this was extremely effective. At other times, she got the wrong end of the stick. The latter was the problem with Hoskyns's 'stabilization'. Mrs Thatcher could not see that it was his word to describe the normalizing of a free economy which both of them wanted. In a third strategy paper submitted in December, Hoskyns explained the process of Stabilization further, but Mrs Thatcher scribbled in the margins, 'This description is not compatible with vigorous action.'[45] It was an unnecessary misunderstanding, but not an untypical one. Serious though she always was in pursuing her long-term aims and discussing how to pursue them, Mrs Thatcher never had the 'critical path' which people of Hoskyns's military and business background considered essential. In that sense, Hoskyns was right about her lack of strategy. She preferred to jump about, seizing one phrase, rejecting another, contradicting sometimes herself and, much more often, everyone else. Such methods sometimes drove those working with her to distraction, but in the view of others they showed the flexibility which is always necessary for political survival. Richard Ryder, her political secretary, saw it as evidence that 'she was a brilliant, intuitive, instinctive politician', rather than a doctrinaire one.[46] And even Hoskyns conceded that only she had the stomach needed for the fight, pursuing his analogy with the Second World War: 'Without Churchill i.e. her, we'd have surrendered in the first few months.'[47]

*

* It was typical of her political caution, however, that, when asked by the Liberal leader, David Steel, in the House of Commons the previous month why she would not rule out a comprehensive pay policy, Mrs Thatcher replied: 'Natural caution and good financial instinct' (Prime Minister's Questions, Hansard, HC Deb 24 May 1979).

There was only one area of political combat where the battle proved surprisingly easy – the sale of council houses. Back in the mid-1970s, despite initial reservations from Mrs Thatcher that such a scheme would disadvantage natural Tory voters who had received no assistance from the state, the Conservative Party had taken up the idea of turning the tenants of public housing into owners. Even in the 1960s, a party committee on which Mrs Thatcher herself sat had worked on schemes of encouraging this trend, but the policy developed in the 1970s was stronger. Recognizing that many Labour councils were adamantly opposed to allowing tenants to buy, it proposed to give the tenants the statutory right to do so. By the general election of 1979, this policy was undisputed within the party and extremely popular with voters. In the view of Michael Heseltine, the Cabinet minister whose department implemented the policy, the right to buy had been 'next to the "Winter of Discontent" itself ... the single most important contributory factor' in victory.[48] So much was the policy agreed that when Mrs Thatcher held her first meeting with Heseltine on the subject of housing, a few days after the May election, she did not specifically discuss the right to buy at all but ranged more widely over everything which needed to be done to spread home ownership. This included an attack on rates, the sale of vacant property and a concentration on allowing 'most young people to enter the market'. She 'emphasised the long-term objective of eliminating subsidies in housing for the great majority of people'.[49] In the debate on the Queen's Speech on 15 May, she told Parliament that the right to buy provided in the forthcoming Housing Bill would fulfil 'Anthony Eden's dream of a property-owning democracy' and 'give to more of our people that freedom and mobility and that prospect of handing something on to their children and grandchildren which owner-occupation provides'.[50]

There were, in fact, two main thoughts behind the policy. As well as the principal political and social purpose of bestowing the freedom of ownership on more people, it also helped the Treasury. As a Think Tank paper which Mrs Thatcher received two weeks after coming into office pointed out, housing had been quietly singled out by the Conservatives, in opposition, 'to produce proportionally greater savings than any other programme'.[51] As well as emancipating the buyers, therefore, council house sales would yield revenue, remove large numbers of people from future council housing provision and even make it politically easier to put up council house rents to more realistic levels. In short, the 'giveaway' was also, in some sense, a cut. Not surprisingly, therefore, the social and financial objectives were in partial conflict. Heseltine at Environment wanted the largest possible number of council house sales. The Treasury wanted the largest sums of money. The two things were not necessarily identical. The 1979 party manifesto had promised 'to ensure that 100 per cent mortgages are available for the purchase of council and new town* houses'. In the Treasury's view, such mortgages were a thorough nuisance if councils had to provide them, and were much better obtained from private providers. Nor should house sales lead to more council house building, it argued. Nigel Lawson, the Financial Secretary to the Treasury, wrote quickly to Heseltine to warn him: 'It will make no sort of economic sense if stock sold at a discount is replaced by new building.'[52]

For her part, Mrs Thatcher behaved as prime ministers are conventionally supposed to do, promoting the policy while trying to reconcile differing departments. She warmly supported the right to buy, and constantly deployed it as part of wider themes of freedom and opportunity. She also agitated for other measures which would spread private owner-occupation – 'shared ownership' which allowed people to gain the equity by degrees, 'homesteading' by which people could improve council properties in poor condition, and an end to the 'red-lining' by which building societies refused mortages completely in areas which they considered too run down. But she did not become heavily engaged in the detail of the legislation. The record shows a fairly small volume of traffic with her on the issues involved. According to John Stanley, who was her first Housing Minister, this was because the government's commitment to the policy was unquestioned. It was simply a matter of the 'huge technical undertaking'[53] involved in resolving matters like good title and price and dealing with those properties which were defective because they had been built in the 1950s and 1960s under 'industrialized building systems' which caused them to fall apart later. In this, the Prime Minister did not need to be deeply involved. The Housing Bill that established the right to buy also offered a discount, based on length of tenure, which began at 33 per cent of the market value and rose to 50 per cent at the maximum. It also empowered the government to intervene if, as was correctly predicted, councils hostile to the right to buy tried to find ways of impeding it.

As the Bill developed, Mrs Thatcher helped settle the continuing division between Environment and Treasury about 100 per cent mortgages, broadly in favour of Heseltine. 'Privately, I am with DoE on this,' she noted to her private secretary when matters came to a head in January 1980.[54] She feared that, without provision for such mortgages, councils opposed to the right to buy would be able to stop sales to poorer people. She also supported Heseltine's insistence that half the proceeds of the sales be remitted to

---

* Formally designated 'new towns' had a special planning and ownership status.

councils, to incentivize them, where the Treasury had sought much more for itself. As Labour councils later tried to block sales, she waited until enough evidence had built up for the legal advice to be securely in the government's favour, and then urged ministers to act. Successful court action against Norwich City Council in 1981 marked the turning point for the policy. After that it became clear that the right to buy was, indeed, a right, rather than dependent on the wish of each council. But Mrs Thatcher was always cautious. In April 1981, Heseltine, with the support of Geoffrey Howe, put forward suggestions for rent deregulation, since the private rented sector had become moribund because of controls. Mrs Thatcher favoured the idea in principle, but 'did not believe that this would be politically wise'.[55] She dreaded a 'fear campaign' from Labour about rising rents. Her attitude to housing policy was governed by her strong, instinctive sense about timing. Politically, her instincts paid off. By the time of the party conference of October 1982, John Stanley was able to tell the audience that the average mortgage paid by a council tenant was only 43 pence a week more than the average council rent. By the end of Mrs Thatcher's first administration, half a million families were living in council houses which they had bought, mainly under the right to buy. The policy had its disadvantages. The most notable were the gradual build-up of a housing shortage which, in 1979, had not existed, and the stoking, for the future, of a housing bubble. But it worked extraordinarily well in its stated aims. It also produced huge political loyalty to Mrs Thatcher, often from people who had never voted Conservative before. Tory canvassers reported that they could tell their supporters at a glance by the improvements they had carried out to their doors and windows as soon as they had bought their council house. By 1983, it would become commonplace for people, mainly from the upper working class, to declare 'Maggie got me my house.' It was one of the few areas in which her personal reward extracted was disproportionate to the amount of work she personally had put in.

The overall economic situation followed no such steady course. The biggest factor preventing the stabilization that John Hoskyns sought was public spending. In her memorandum for the first Cabinet meeting about the subject on 17 May, Mrs Thatcher had set out the main, related problems of pay, cash limits and spending. There were 'inherited promises' on pay, the Tories' own promises of increases in police and army pay, and their promise to exempt the National Health Service from cuts. Then there were the problems of the nationalized industries. How far could they be allowed to run themselves? How could the outflow of central government money to them be minimized? What about the National Coal Board, which was 'in a category of its own': 'Do we ask them to take the whole strain on prices, investment and pit closures?' Then there was local government. Local authorities should use their 'quite large cash balances' so that central government could 'trim the level of Rate Support Grant support we offer for the next and subsequent years'. In central government, the pay settlement for the non-industrial civil service, reached before the election, was only one-third covered by the cash limit. If there was now to be a 'resumed dialogue with both sides of industry' 'should we seek to hold them [the unions] to the target they accepted jointly with the last Government of reducing inflation below five per cent by 1982?'[56] When the Cabinet actually met, Mrs Thatcher told it that the high forecasts for the PSBR meant that cuts would have to be £500–600 million greater than already sketched out by John Biffen, the Chief Secretary. Therefore even defence and law and order would have to get rid of 'waste' to fund their promised expansion. Asset sales, though necessary, should not be used as a substitute for real cuts in expenditure, and the sales should be placed with British institutions to avoid foreign buyers.

Energy price increases were seen as a possible cover for price rises in the nationalized industries to recover the cost of broken cash limits. 'The right course', the Cabinet minutes recorded with frank dishonesty, 'might be to seek very large price increases immediately, and attribute this to the inefficiency of the industry.'[57] On 31 May the Cabinet agreed the spending reductions which John Biffen had proposed. It also agreed immediate large sales of public sector assets to balance the books, but stipulated that the assets be sold, said Geoffrey Howe, 'in a way which would secure the best possible spread of ownership, and pave the way to successful disposal of an equity interest in some of the nationalised industries in due course'.[58]

Immediately, however, the implications of the cuts became clearer and the demands greater. On 4 June, Biffen informed Mrs Thatcher that the squeeze on central government expenditure to keep within the agreed cash limits turned out to mean a 6–7 per cent cut in Labour's inherited plans, 2 per cent higher than expected. By July, Howe was looking gloomily at what would be needed to meet the agreed target of getting public spending back to the level for 1977–8 by 1982–3. Five and a half billion pounds would have to come off the last government's White Paper for 1980–81. 'Cuts of this size', said Howe, 'are larger than we envisaged when in Opposition,' but even then might not be enough to prevent tax rises 'if the proportion of the PSBR to GDP is to be reduced'. To avoid this, public expenditure cuts of £6.5 billion would be needed. The effects of Clegg, he went on, would be to push up public sector wages by 18.5 per cent in 1980–81, compared to 14 per cent in the private sector. What was Mrs Thatcher's preference, asked Howe – cuts of £5.5 billion or of £6.5 billion? Mrs

Thatcher noted that her answer was 'Given orally'. It was £6.5 billion.[59] In her zeal, she considered no economy too small to be worthy of her notice. Thinking that the Garden Room needed better equipment, Kenneth Stowe had ordered thirty-two new typewriters. One day, returning from Prime Minister's Questions, Mrs Thatcher entered the hall of No. 10 to find these objects in packing cases, just delivered. 'What's going on?' she cried. The situation was explained to her. After forty-eight hours, she issued Stowe with an order: 'You can keep three.' The other twenty-nine had to go back.[60]

At the very same time as the spending figures were proving that the situation was worse than had been thought, some Cabinet ministers, led by Jim Prior, were starting to say that the policy was already too tough. John Hunt summed it up in a note to Mrs Thatcher preparatory to the Cabinet of 12 July:

> Although it is true that Cabinet decided the Budget strategy only six weeks ago, some Ministers may argue that the climate has changed ... Your own view remains, I believe, that the Government should stick to the present PSBR target for this year, and to a lower target for next year, to leave room for further tax cuts. But some Ministers are becoming alarmed at the consequences of this policy (for example, Mr Prior's remarks about interest rates at E on Monday) and you may want to give them a brief opportunity to voice these worries. The immediate situation is worse, and the long haul rather longer, than ministers believed immediately after the election. Some may be tempted, therefore, to adopt a more gradual approach. I think you could bring this issue to a head yourself.[61]

Hunt recommended asking the Chancellor to say what the consequences of higher public spending would be for GDP and for interest rates. His proposed way of 'steering' the discussion was to push all individual spending arguments into bilateral meetings with the Chief Secretary and stick to general points in Cabinet. On the same day, Keith Joseph, the voice of her conscience, wrote to Mrs Thatcher to say: 'The fact of the matter is that public expenditure on pay is soaring without real restraint.'[62]

At Cabinet on 12 July, Mrs Thatcher blatantly employed the unorthodox style of chairmanship for which she was already known, and announced the conclusion of the meeting at its very beginning: 'Unless we go for this, we'll be taking a larger proportion of national revenue and have no scope for further tax reductions.'[63] Howe then told the assembled company that British economic performance was deteriorating and that all the economic indicators were pointing in the wrong direction, with everything made worse by the high oil price. 'Got to go through this vale of tears but is the last chance of restoring sanity,' Hunt noted Howe as saying.[64] There was a fierce debate in which, as the official minutes put it, 'it was suggested that the Government faced the most serious dilemma in economic policy of any post-war Government.'[65] Mrs Thatcher, haunted more by past Tory failure than by anything the previous Labour government had done, begged colleagues to support the Chancellor: 'Remember the Barber spending spree,' she cried.[66] Cuts, said Jim Prior, with some support, would lead to 'massive redundancies', and would be worse politically than putting up taxes. He warned of 'severe depression'.[67] Using the time-honoured official formula for expressing both sides of the case, the minutes added, 'Against this, it was argued strongly that no one had faulted the Chancellor's analysis of the economic prospects.'[68] At a meeting four days later, Prior had it out with Mrs Thatcher at No. 10. The official Note for the Record said:

> Mr Prior said that he was very worried that the Treasury were aiming for excessive public spending cuts. In his view, the Treasury forecasts for the PSBR were too pessimistic. It would be disastrous for industry if public expenditure was cut too much. The Prime Minister ... did not accept the premise that public expenditure cuts would damage industry: industry would only recover if resources were freed from the public sector to the private sector.[69]

Mrs Thatcher had no intention of trimming in Prior's direction, but debate raged both about the methods of public expenditure control and about its extent. The desire to avoid a public sector pay norm, with its tendency to unite unions in resistance and to make what was intended as a ceiling become a floor, remained, but on the other hand those paying salaries – local government, for example – had to have some idea of what the government could afford. This would imply a view about what the appropriate level of settlements was. The alternative, favoured by Prior and other 'moderates', was to set cash limits separately from pay, to reflect only the decisions on the volume of spending and on price changes. They would then be adjusted in the light of pay decisions. It was not until September, after the summer break, that the Treasury and No. 10 carried the point, in principle at least, that cash limits should include pay right from the start. The battle against spending increases was still not successful enough. When the public spending plans for 1980–81 were finally presented to the House of Commons by John Biffen on 1 November 1979, they were £500 million adrift from the reduction sought in July. The White Paper's striking first sentence was no more than the truth: 'Public expenditure is at the heart of Britain's present economic difficulties.'

The Treasury's tactic, therefore, was to try work out firmer, medium-term spending plans to compensate for what, it knew well before it announced its figures, would not be a good enough result. Cabinet ministers returned from holiday in September to a stern memo from Howe and John Biffen on spending plans after 1980–81; 'we cannot confidently take credit for any significant growth in the GDP over the next few years,' it said. 'So even with rising receipts from the North Sea, there will be little, if any, increase in total government revenue at unchanged tax rates.' Howe and Biffen continued:

> The conclusion is inescapable . . . it is only through substantial reductions in the inherited expenditure plans for the years after 1980–81 that we shall be able to implement our policies for the money supply and taxation – which form the core of an economic strategy. Our ability to face up to this issue will be seen as the crucial test of our determination to stick to our announced policies, and will thus play a vital part in affecting expectations.[70]

Howe's and Biffen's reference to inherited plans was intended to remind ministers that they were not being asked for actual, aggregate cuts, but this distinction between cuts in planned increases and genuine cuts in spending totals was one which the public never readily understood. The general view was that the Thatcher government was engaging in 'cuts', even when the real problem was that public expenditure was rising far more sharply than intended. The only two years since the Second World War when public spending actually fell were under the Labour administration of Jim Callaghan. In 1976–7 public expenditure fell by 2.5 per cent, and in 1977–8 by 6 per cent. There was to be no year in which it fell under Mrs Thatcher, although it did decrease as a proportion of GDP.

Political objections were not the only difficulty the government faced. As well as the question of how much to cut, there was also the problem of how to achieve it. In addition to the Clegg difficulties, an enormous amount of public spending, all of it contributing to the PSBR, was attributable to local government. Some of this was paid for by the local rates, but 61 per cent was contributed by central government through the Rate Support Grant (RSG). Labour local authorities, many of them then in the process of being taken over by the hard left, were more than happy to use their position to raise the standard of revolt, increase the rates – which fell mainly on Tory-voting homeowners and on businesses – and complain loudly about the effect of government meanness on the level of local services. A rigorous central government approach, reducing the percentage of RSG, could easily damage prudent local authorities as much as extravagant ones. From the beginning, Mrs Thatcher found this problem neuralgic. In a memo to her as early as 16 July 1979, John Hunt mentioned in passing 'your own view that it may be necessary to take powers directly to control rates'.[71]

Should the government control local government expenditure by a block grant, or by a mechanism which tried to allocate resources more precisely, penalizing the extravagant? The minutes of E Committee's discussion on 17 September of how cash limits could apply to local government record magisterial indecision: 'All these measures involved a degree of intervention with local government which might seem contrary to the Government's policy of giving the authorities greater freedom. But it was arguable that the greater freedom now being given to local authorities justified an over-all control on the level of their expenditure and rate demands.'[72] During October, it was agreed that the RSG should be controlled by a single over-all cash limit rather than cash limits on individual local authorities.

Michael Heseltine, the Environment Secretary, put forward his own interpretation on the government strategy, in order to avoid a reduction of the RSG. He wrote to Biffen describing the 1980–81 settlement as 'crit-ical' for the whole Parliament: 'It will set the key note for our relations with local authorities for the rest of this Parliament.' The aim should be to keep the domestic rate down, said Heseltine. 'This would fit in with our economic strategy and the attack on inflation and would be seen as not incompatible with our longer term intention to abolish domestic rating.'[73] Rates should not go up above inflation and therefore, he argued, the RSG should not change. He also tried to make space for himself about the announcement of council house rent increases, which he described at Cab-inet on 18 October as 'the single most explosive political issue which faced the Government'.[74] He caused irritation. On 24 October Hunt wrote to Mrs Thatcher, rather wearily complaining that 'At the very last minute' Heseltine was making trouble about the rent increase: he 'wants to announce it in his own way, at a time of his own choosing . . . Every Min-ister could deploy arguments like that, and the result would be no White Paper at all. You might like to support the Chief Secretary.'[75] She did. But she also gave in, in the last arguments before the deadline for the 1980–81 White Paper, to those who said that the RSG percentage must remain unchanged in order to protect Conservative shire counties.

Although she supported the Treasury in Cabinet discussions, Mrs Thatcher was also increasingly displeased with it as political pressure on her grew. So irritated was she by what she saw as John Biffen's feebleness under fire that Geoffrey Howe brought in Nigel Lawson, the Financial Secretary to the Treasury, to assist the beleaguered Chief Secre-tary. She felt that there was a lack of focus, and was perhaps irritated by Howe's prolixity (paper poured forth from him as from no other member of the government). 'This is not in suitable form for Cabinet discussion,' she wrote on a paper from him in mid-September about the handling of public sector pay. 'Send it back . . . We are getting far too many "woolly" papers from the Treasury.'[76]

In the very last days before the White Paper was unveiled, Biffen wrote to the Prime Minister, trying to overturn the Cabinet's agreement to delete unemployment assumptions from it. He wanted to include them in his speech, he said, because they would be helpful to Parliament. Conscious of the political embarrassment of making such assumptions known, Mrs Thatcher tried to avoid publication, and also to question the accuracy of the assumptions themselves, saying that 1.65 million projected unemployed for 1980–81 was 'unduly pessimistic'.* She wanted a lower figure mentioned 'if Ministers are pressed to reveal the assumptions'[77] and questioned whether it was essential to do so. Biffen, a strong parliamentarian, wrote back to her, rather bravely: 'To deny the House as a whole what I am prepared to give in due course to a Committee would set a damaging precedent for this Government's dealings with the House. I personally attach great importance to this.'[78] The Prime Minister gave in, but her enthusiasm for Biffen had now markedly diminished.

The public spending White Paper was not badly received in the Commons. Indeed, throughout the first Thatcher administration, it was Tory grandees far more often than rank-and-file Tory MPs who protested at the harsh economic measures which were put before them. But at Prime Minister's Questions on the same day, the veteran Labour MP Douglas Jay, father of the journalist Peter, asked Mrs Thatcher: 'As this Government have been in office for six months and as, according to the CBI, business confidence is falling, industrial production is falling, investment is falling and the pound is falling, does the Prime Minister feel that her policies are yielding results?' Mrs Thatcher seemed flummoxed by the question and replied, weakly, 'I was pleased to see what the CBI actually said after its survey came out and that it fully recorded its support for the Government.'[79] Jay's question pointed to an undoubted fact – that the government had little positive to show so far. Even the IMF, supportive of the government's overall stance, doubted its will. The day after the White Paper, a minute to the organization's managing director from the head of its European Department, Alan Whittome, reported:

Talking privately in the Treasury and the Bank, there is doubt and unease. There is a strong suspicion that some in the Government, including the Prime Minister, believe that the perceived stance of policy will by itself change

* The figure turned out to be 2.8 million by the end of 1980, so she was wildly over-optimistic.

expectations . . . many officials believe – as we would – that one may achieve a change in expectations and behaviour, but only after there has been a noticeable downturn in the economy. A consequence is that at the minister-ial level little if any advance thought is being given to the attitude to be taken to . . . well-organized and lengthy strikes in such key areas as coal and trans-port.

Whittome's outlook was not encouraging. It was 'unlikely but not entirely impossible that we may find the Fund lending to the UK again', he warned.[80] Mrs Thatcher had herself indicated awareness of the lack of progress in her first speech as prime minister to her party's annual conference in Black-pool three weeks earlier when she had explained to her enthusiastic audience that the Tory electoral mandate was to change four main things – inflation, public spending, industrial relations, income tax – but that results would come slowly. 'We have to think in terms of several Parliaments,' she declared.[81]

In fact, as well as the changes announced in the Budget and the Queen's Speech, a key decision had been made only a week before Jay's question. On 23 October 1979, Howe announced to the Commons the complete lifting of exchange controls. In the interests of market secrecy, this had not been put to an amazed, though, except for Michael Heseltine, supportive Cabinet until the last moment. Some restrictions had been lifted in the Budget in June and since then Nigel Lawson, the minister who had argued in print for the change during the election campaign, had pressed Howe to go further. He believed in the symbolic importance of removing exchange controls completely – a 'sign that we would now live and die in the real world economy'.[82] Howe, though more cautious than Lawson, was per-suaded, partly by a paper advocating going all the way by David Hancock* of the Treasury. Howe found it hard to persuade Mrs Thatcher, who was more cautious still about acting too fast. In a meeting on 24 September 1979, she told ministers and the Governor that 'it would be a mistake to relax the controls further until the Government's market philosophy was being seen to work. To move any further now could easily lead to a larger outflow of funds.'[83] In the end, she was persuaded that the controls had to be lifted before the sale of government-owned BP shares, but she remained dubious. When she eventually agreed, she said to Howe, 'On your own head be it, Geoffrey . . . if anything goes wrong,' a remark which Howe interpreted, surely wrongly, as a joke.[84] She used a very similar form of

---

* David Hancock (1934–), educated Whitgift School and Balliol College, Oxford; private secre-tary to the Chancellor of the Exchequer, 1968–70; Deputy Secretary, Cabinet Office, 1982–3; Permanent Secretary, Department of Education and Science, 1983–9; knighted, 1985.

words when she told Carrington that she would accept his Rhodesian proposals. It was her way of keeping a political escape route. As so often, her radicalism was tempered by her instinct for survival.

The lifting of controls was a very bold step. Ever since the war, British governments had believed that they had to control the movements of money in and out of the country in order to prevent a collapse of sterling. British tourists going on holiday had to register the currency they took with them: in the 1960s, the maximum was £50 per head. When the day of currency freedom dawned, there was no collapse but rather, if anything, the opposite problem. The British economy, and particularly the City of London, at last had the opportunity to compete globally. In her speech at the Lord Mayor's annual banquet on 12 November, Mrs Thatcher told the assembled financial grandees that sterling was no longer locked in the Bastille: 'the prison doors have been thrown open.'[85] In the Commons on the day of the announcement, Enoch Powell said: 'Is the Chancellor aware that I envy him the opportunity and privilege of announcing a step that will strengthen the economy of this country and help restore our national pride and confidence in our currency?' Although Powell's confidence in the change was to prove fully justified, its effects were not immediate enough to deflect the force of Jay's pointed question on 1 November. For the British economy, things might eventually get better, but, in the meantime, they could only get worse.

Less than a week after the White Paper's publication, the money supply target, by which the government set such store, was heavily exceeded. Sterling M3 was growing at an annual rate of 14 per cent in October, when the government's target remained within the range of 7–11 per cent. The spending targets in the White Paper were not tough enough to convince the markets that the future was going to be different: they were £2 billion, Howe quickly came to think, above where they should have been. At this rate of money growth, and with inflation running at an annual rate of 16 per cent, the purchasers of government debt 'went on strike'[86] and a funding crisis ensued. Internationally, the stage had been set for tougher action by the decision in October of Paul Volcker,* the new chairman of the Federal Reserve Board, to bear down on the money supply and accept the painfully high interest rates that resulted. Britain needed to show a comparable toughness. On 5 November, Howe came to see Mrs Thatcher, to warn her of the situation and the fact that, a further fiscal package being 'unthinkable', 'the only option for bringing the money supply back within

---

* Paul Volcker (1927–), president, New York Federal Reserve Bank, 1975–9; chairman, American Federal Reserve Board, 1979–87; chairman, President's Economic Recovery Advisory Board, from 2008.

the target seemed likely to be a further increase in MLR'.[87] Mrs Thatcher said she was 'most disturbed' by the news. Howe added that he doubted whether inflation would fall below 14 or 15 per cent by the end of 1980. She said she was 'most unhappy' and asked, 'How could this be so if the Government were pursuing a tight monetary policy?'[88] It was a question to which more and more people would demand an answer in the coming months.

Mrs Thatcher had little choice but to agree with her Chancellor, however. On 15 November interest rates went up by 3 per cent to 17 per cent, a punitive increase, and the highest nominal level in the whole of British history, before or since. The rise was designed to be so big as to brook no doubt in the markets. When Howe informed the Cabinet of his decision on the morning of 15 November, Jim Prior pronounced himself 'disappointed and shocked' by the increase and said that he did not 'know where it's going to stop'. But it was a vivid illustration of Howe's case that the low interest rates for which the more centrist members of the party particularly pined could come only if the strict policies he sought were genuinely pursued. Mrs Thatcher pointed out acidly to colleagues that 'It wouldn't be 17 per cent if we got our expenditure down.' In a characteristic formulation, Howe told the Cabinet that he was trying to keep things 'as un-unpleasant as possible'.[89] Events were proving him right that – the famous phrase was, in fact, his, not Mrs Thatcher's* – 'There is no alternative.' As he put it in a memo on the economic outlook despatched to relevant ministers early the following month, 'The general strategy remains the only feasible one but the difficulties we face are greater than we had any reason to expect.'[90] The worse things got, the stronger, by a strange logic, his case became.

The consequence was that two arguments about the government's economic policy were being conducted separately but at the same time. The first, by far the noisier, was that between Howe and Mrs Thatcher and their allies on the one hand and the Keynesians, Heathites, the Labour Party and the corporatists on the other. This concerned whether or not the policy, often characterized as cruel and 'doctrinaire', was destroying British jobs and prosperity. The second, by far the more important for the economic future, was between those who agreed about the essential thrust of the policy, but believed that the balance was wrong or that reform was not coming fast enough or that the methods chosen for controlling the money supply were having perverse effects. In terms of party management, Mrs

---

* The phrase first gained currency in the course of 1978. It was sometimes shortened to the acronym TINA, and became a nickname for Mrs Thatcher.

Thatcher had to deal with anxious colleagues, such as Jim Prior, who did not really understand the policy, and who certainly did not like it. She was absolutely confident that Prior and co. were wrong and had little to contribute to the debate, but it was they who had more political capacity to break her. In terms of the decisions she required to make the policy succeed, she was debating matters with those – Howe, Nott, Lawson, Joseph, as well as advisers like Hoskyns and civil servants like Peter Middleton* at the Treasury – who were of similar mind, but far from unanimous about the methods to be used. These were the people whose opinions made a real difference, yet whose weight in the eyes of politics and public opinion was much less. By this time, by the adaptation of a public school usage, Mrs Thatcher's opponents within the Conservative Party were coming to be known as 'Wets', which in turn required a new coinage to describe her supporters: they became 'Dries'. However beleaguered she was, Mrs Thatcher always knew that if she were forced to adopt a Wet position she would catch her political death of it. It was among the Dries, therefore, that real debate took place.

This helps to explain the testimony of so many people close to Mrs Thatcher in the early years that, however appalling were the political and economic pressures, there was never panic about the entire direction of economic policy. The world beyond Downing Street expected a U-turn, having seen one with Heath. Those within knew that this would not happen. What they feared was simply that events would overtake Mrs Thatcher and that electoral unpopularity or a party coup would bring her down. If people like John Hoskyns were right that recovery would take two full Parliaments, how could the Conservatives contrive a way to win the election which would have to be held halfway through? She said as much herself in an interview given to the *New York Times* on 9 November when she already knew, though the public did not, that the huge interest rate rise was on the way: 'Can we get far enough by the next election to show that it – our program – is working?'[91]

* Peter Middleton (1934–), private secretary to the Chancellor of the Exchequer, 1969–72; Permanent Secretary, Treasury, 1983–91; knighted, 1984.

18

Our doubts are traitors

'I cannot play Sister Bountiful'

Growing economic difficulties did not immediately damage Mrs Thatcher's public standing. This was partly because they seemed, in 1979 at least, to be proof of the arguments she was making. She told her party conference in October that she had 'the task of leading this country out of the shadows',[1] so she did not suffer, in the short term, if those shadows seemed dark indeed. It was also because the sense of courage in adversity, of one woman battling against heavy odds, was intrinsic to her style of leadership and to her popular appeal. This leadership was quickly evident not only in economic matters, but on many other fronts.

On 27 August 1979, Lord Mountbatten, the Queen's cousin and the last Viceroy of India, was murdered, with three others, while sailing near his home in the Irish Republic. The IRA were responsible. On the same day, eighteen British soldiers were blown up and killed in an IRA booby-trap at Warrenpoint in Northern Ireland, the result of a failure of intelligence so dire that it inspired the creation of a new security directorate under Maurice Oldfield, the recently retired head of the Secret Intelligence Service, better known as MI6,* whose existence, throughout Mrs Thatcher's time as prime minister, remained 'unavowed' in public by the government. Two days later, Mrs Thatcher flew to Northern Ireland. There she went on a lightly protected walkabout in Belfast. Then, against the advice of the Royal Ulster Constabulary and the Northern Ireland Office, but with the encouragement of the army, who wanted her to see just how bad things were, she flew to the so-called bandit country of County Armagh. In Crossmaglen, she put on the uniform of a 'Greenfinch', the female members of the Ulster Defence Regiment, the only regiment of the British army per-

---

* Mrs Thatcher had first struck up a friendship with Oldfield during her days in opposition. With Callaghan's approval Oldfield had met her on several occasions to offer seminars about the intelligence world and help 'preserve a politician from falling into pitholes' (Richard Deacon, 'C': *A Biography of Sir Maurice Oldfield*, Macdonald, 1985, p. 187).

manently serving in Northern Ireland. The UDR's members, many of them part-time and local, were the subject of endless terrorist attack. Brigadier David Thorne, who commanded the 3rd Infantry Brigade, produced an epaulette of the Queen's Own Highlanders, which had belonged to Colonel David Blair, the most senior soldier killed at Warrenpoint: 'This, Prime Minister, is all that is left of Colonel Blair.' Mrs Thatcher wept.[2] Her dash, courage and human sympathy were much admired, and her intuitive bond with the military was noted. Mrs Thatcher's views on the politics of Northern Ireland were sometimes confused and her attention intermittent, but her instinct of solidarity with the British security forces was strong, deep and always vividly expressed.*

The new Prime Minister also had to contend with a different sort of enemy of the country. She was faced with the unravelling of a fifteen-year cover-up. Ever since the defections of the Communist spies Guy Burgess and Donald Maclean to the Soviet Union in the 1950s and that of Kim Philby in 1963, there had been a hunt for 'the Fourth Man' of the original Cambridge spy ring. This was Anthony Blunt. Blunt, who had become a Communist in the late 1930s, spied for the Soviet Union from 1940 to 1945, while working for the British Security Service (MI5). A distinguished art historian, especially learned on Poussin, he later became director of the Courtauld Institute and Surveyor of the Queen's Pictures. In the autumn of 1979, Andrew Boyle published a book called *The Climate of Treason*, in which he dropped heavy hints about Blunt, referring to him as 'Maurice'. It had earlier got out that the Fourth Man was a don with a Cambridge background with a surname five letters long and beginning with B. *The Times* had run the story, wrongly identifying a blameless old Fellow of King's College called Donald Beves. As the *Observer* started to print extracts of Boyle's book in early November, *Private Eye* named Blunt. In interviews about his book, Boyle refused to identify Maurice, but challenged the government to do so.[3]

Inside Downing Street, the issue was hotly debated. Ever since the early 1950s, there had been strong official suspicions against Blunt, and he was interrogated on eleven occasions. In 1964, because of new evidence from the American traitor Michael Straight, the suspicions became certainties. The British authorities concluded, however, that Straight's evidence was not the sort which could be used in court. They believed, although this turned out to be mistaken, that there was a Fifth Man in the ring, and so they had not yet succeeded in identifying the 'Ring of Five' British traitors,

---

* For a full discussion of Northern Ireland, see Chapter 21.

and did not want to prejudice their hunt for the Fifth Man by going public.[4] They therefore decided to offer Blunt a deal – immunity from prosecution in return for a confession, and the information which that confession would supply. Blunt confessed. The embarrassment consisted in his royal connection. It would be damaging if it ever became known that the government and the Palace had agreed to cover up Blunt's treachery, and yet, successive governments felt, once the cover-up had happened, it must be preserved. Because of the secrecy involved, there was also a good deal of confusion about who had ever been told. Alec Douglas-Home, the Prime Minister at the time, had not known, though the Queen's then private secretary, Sir Michael Adeane, had.

Mrs Thatcher asked Sir Robert Armstrong, by now the Cabinet Secretary, to investigate. He found little on paper, and several politicians with apparently faulty memories. He concluded that the Queen had been informed, though this was never officially confirmed to him.[5]* Within Whitehall, there were differing views about how to proceed. The head of MI5, Michael Hanley, advised against any prime ministerial intervention, but the Attorney-General, Sir Michael Havers,† advised that if Blunt were not named by the government he would be free to sue for libel if others named him. This would create an intolerable position. Mrs Thatcher, who was new to all this, listened carefully to both sides, but was inclined to name him. Her straightforward instinct was that 'he had betrayed his country',[6] and there was no reason to protect him unless exposure would cause intolerable embarrassment to Crown or government. She was also worried that 'the finger was pointing at several innocent people',[7] and only the government had the power to tell the truth. Blunt's right to immunity from prosecution did not automatically guarantee him anonymity. It was decided to take advantage of a written security question put down by the Labour MP Ted Leadbitter and ask him to raise the issue of Blunt. Armstrong gave Blunt's lawyer twenty-four hours' notice.

Mrs Thatcher duly gave Leadbitter a written parliamentary answer naming Blunt, and later, on 21 November, a full statement to the Commons.

---

* In his official history of MI5, Professor Christopher Andrew records that the Queen had been informed in 'general terms' in 1963, and in greater detail by the Heath government in 1973, when Blunt seemed likely to die of cancer thus leaving the press free to expose him without fear of libel (Christopher Andrew, *The Defence of the Realm: The Authorized History of MI5*, Allen Lane, 2009, p. 706).

† Michael Havers (1923–92), educated Westminster and Corpus Christi College, Cambridge; lieutenant RNVR, 1941–6; called to Bar, 1948; Conservative MP for Wimbledon, 1970–87; Attorney-General, 1979–87; created Lord Havers, 1987; Lord Chancellor for three months in 1987 before having to retire because of ill health.

There was tremendous excitement about the story. Acting as the establishment person which, in one half of his mind, he was, Blunt gave his version of events exclusively to *The Times*, and was served white wine and smoked trout in the paper's offices by the deputy editor, Louis Heren, to the rage of the other newspapers. Meanwhile, in another dining room in the building, the editor, William Rees-Mogg, was giving lunch to Ted Heath, who was surprised and, until he realized what had happened, pleased to emerge from the building to a barrage of cameras.[8] The optics of the moment were very good for Mrs Thatcher. It looked as if she would have nothing to do with the corrupt and weak old ways of doing things. She had told the Commons that Blunt's behaviour had been 'contemptible and repugnant'.[9] In the lobby of the Commons, she saw Leadbitter and told him, 'And it damn well serves him [Blunt] right.'[10] Shortly after Mrs Thatcher's statement to the House, Buckingham Palace announced that Blunt would be stripped of his knighthood. Because she had insisted on openness in this case, many jumped to the conclusion that Mrs Thatcher would inaugurate a new era of transparency in the security services, but this was not her intention at all. As she also told the House, 'Our task now is to guard against their [the Communist traitors'] counterparts of today.'[11] She wanted the Blunt embarrassment out of the way, but she had no desire to shed light on secrecy which she thought was vital in the defence of the nation.

Nothing did more than the long row over the EEC budget to bring out the qualities which made Mrs Thatcher so impressive to her admirers and so irritating to her detractors. When Bryan Cartledge left his job as her foreign affairs private secretary in September 1979, she wrote him a thank-you letter which was remarkably frank about affairs of state. 'Rhodesia', she wrote, 'goes desperately slowly. Peter [Carrington] and Ian [Gilmour] are doing a superb job and are much more reconciled to a long stint than I am. I think it is time we forced the pace a bit . . .' Then she continued: 'I get more and more disillusioned with the EEC. We are going to have a real fight over the budget and by one means or another we have to get our way. We need the money.'[12] These few words summarize fully her approach to the question at the time. She wanted a fight; she wanted the money; and she found the whole EEC set-up uncongenial. She had not, as she was later to do, sat down and considered the constitutional implications of the whole European project. Since the disputes of the early 1970s and the 'yes' vote in 1975, European controversies had, to the relief of party managers, died down. There was a strong 'atmospheric pressure' to be pro-Europe and leave it at that. Mrs Thatcher half succumbed to this, but only half. She was not, in any general sense, anti-European, but she was frustrated and displeased, and jealous of encroachments upon British sovereignty. The attitudes of her main European counterparts brought out her combative instincts. And although she agreed with the general proposition advanced to her by officials when she came into office that the new government must show itself more friendly to Europe than Britain had been in the fraught Wilson–Callaghan years, she did not like most of the suggested ways of doing so.

One of these was joining, or promising soon to join, the Exchange Rate Mechanism (ERM). On the very day she reached No. 10, John Hunt had sent her a memo advocating 'an open-minded approach to the concept of a zone of monetary stability in Europe consistent with the mainstream of Community development'. She wrote beside this: 'I doubt whether this can be achieved by a currency system. Indeed it can't – unless all of the under-lying policies of each country are right.' (And for good measure, she added: 'Fish should <u>never</u> have been made a common resource.')[13] Lord Car-rington argued in a similar strain to Hunt's, and the Foreign Office's generally conciliatory attitude provoked her to write on one of their reports: 'I despair of FO memos . . . This is jabberwocky to me. What is it supposed to mean.'[14] Records of her discussion with Roy Jenkins, the Commission President, over the summer and autumn, show him pushing her to join the ERM, and her dragging her feet: 'she recognised the polit-ical advantages but was not prepared . . . to take the risk with the money supply that full membership would involve.'[15] In October the government privately decided that it was the wrong time for Britain to join the ERM.

Although her European attitudes gave ministers and officials in the For-eign Office the vapours, they were popular in the country. They also caused her little political difficulty in her own party. Bernard Ingham told the usual off-the-record lobby briefing, 'I personally voted to go in, admittedly more for political than economic reasons. But, I am sure like millions of others, I didn't vote to go in to be fleeced.' He was annoyed to find these words quoted in the papers and attributed to Mrs Thatcher herself,[16] but they probably reflected the prevailing mood among Tory supporters and did his boss no harm. Nor was Mrs Thatcher arraigned by the Opposition. The feeling in the rank and file of the Labour Party, though not of most of the leadership, remained anti-EEC. At Prime Minister's Questions, she was often pressed on the subject by Labour MPs, almost always from the point of view of those who wanted her to insist on an even larger rebate than that for which – the quantum varied as negotiation progressed – she was arguing. On her own side, a newly elected MP by the name of John Major*

---

* John Major (1943–), educated Rutlish; Conservative MP for Huntingdonshire, 1979–83; for

put down an early day motion in the Commons congratulating her on her tough negotiating stance.

In her first setpiece interview of the autumn, Mrs Thatcher took the budget row as the touchstone for whether people would regard Britain as being fairly treated in the EEC – 'it is about free people living together.'[17] And in her speech to the party conference at Blackpool she spoke of the 'appalling prospect' of paying out £1 billion net per annum to Brussels (the net contribution five years before had been £16 million). Even when asked to lift her sight to the far horizon for the Winston Churchill Memorial Lecture in Luxembourg later that October, Mrs Thatcher was frank and fierce about the 'manifest inequity' of the budget problem. 'Our friends may despair – I sometimes do myself –', she said, 'at the daily bickering over small matters,' and she warned: 'I cannot play Sister Bountiful to the Community while my own electorate are being asked to forgo improvements in the fields of health, education, welfare and the rest.'[18] The Thatcher vision of the EEC, even at this early stage in her premiership, was one that no other European leader would have advanced. It was to link the EEC and NATO so that 'The principle at the heart of our European institutions is the principle of liberty.' This principle needed to be advanced in the face of the fact that the West had nothing better than 'prolonged armed truce' with the Soviet Union. Away with 'grey uniformity', away with the 'unnecessary standardisation' which 'sits ill with liberty' – the point of the whole thing, she believed, was to advance in 'the struggle between liberty and tyranny'.[19] In an interview in Luxembourg the next day, she was asked about a United States of Europe. 'That has never, I believe, been the practical intention,' she said.[20]

In fact, for most of those at the heart of the project, that was indeed the intention. According to Sir Michael Jenkins, who at that time worked with Roy Jenkins, the President of the Commission, 'The Commission *was* trying to create a United States of Europe – with a common currency and a constitution,'[21] and most of the relevant people in the British Foreign Office were of a like mind. Michael Butler,* who was the United Kingdom's ambassador to the EEC (a position always known as UKREP) from 1979, and David Hannay,† who ran European Community affairs for the Foreign

Huntingdon, 1983–97; Foreign Secretary, 1989; Chancellor of the Exchequer, 1989–90; Prime Minister and Leader of the Conservative Party, 1990–97; Knight of the Garter, 2005.

* Michael Butler (1927–2013), educated Winchester and Trinity College, Oxford; Ambassador and UK Permanent Representative to EEC, 1979–85; Under-Secretary, FCO, 1976–79; knighted, 1980.

† David Hannay (1935–), educated Winchester and New College, Oxford; chef de cabinet to Sir Christopher Soames, European Commissioner, 1973–7; Ambassador and UK Permanent

Office at the same time, were lifelong, committed European integrationists. So was Sir Michael Palliser,* the Permanent Secretary at the Foreign Office. As Michael Jenkins put it, 'We were Ted's children.'[22] Many British ministers, though perhaps less Euro-visionary than the Commission, saw 'Europe' as an unquestionably 'good thing'. When they met at the councils of European foreign ministers, Roy Jenkins and Ian Gilmour, who were anyway great friends, would 'wring their hands' about Mrs Thatcher.[23]

Even before she entered into the battle of the budget, Mrs Thatcher lacked the instinctive sympathy with the European Continent and Community institutions which, for much of the British educated elite, was seen as a mark of being civilized. Michael Palliser first met her in 1975, when she had just become leader of the Opposition and he was the United Kingdom's ambassador to the Community. At dinner with him in Luxembourg, she told him what an unsatisfactory lot the European Commissioners were: 'She found them rather tiresomely foreign.'[24] He found her 'exceptionally ignorant, but with some deep-rooted prejudices' which did not alter over the years. One of these was that the French were preternaturally cunning, and therefore almost always had to be resisted in negotiation. 'They are cleverer than us,' she told him. 'They will run rings round us.'[25]† From the start, the mindset of those of all nations who were involved with the running of Europe was quite different from that of Mrs Thatcher. This difference probably only increased her determination. It was a very strong part of her character that she felt the need to fight if everyone else seemed to disagree with her: 'My father taught me to "dare to be a Daniel",' she told Bernard Ingham.[26] She felt isolated in Europe, and among her own officials and ministers. A few days before the Dublin summit at the end of November, she told Geoffrey Howe that 'she could not understand why Mr Ridley [Nicholas Ridley, the free-marketeer whom she had made a junior minister at the Foreign Office] was not working on economic issues. He was the only FCO minister who understood economics. She intended to take this up with Lord Carrington.'[27] For the European leaders con-

---

Representative to EC, 1985–90; UK Permanent Representative to UN, 1990–95; knighted, 1986; created Lord Hannay, 2001.

* Michael Palliser (1922–2012), educated Wellington and Merton College, Oxford; joined FCO, 1947; private secretary to the Prime Minister (Harold Wilson), 1966–9; Ambassador and Head of UK Delegation to European Communities, 1973–5; Permanent Under-Secretary and head of Diplomatic Service, 1975–82; knighted, 1973. Married to the daughter of the EEC founding father Paul-Henri Spaak, Palliser was a lifelong Europhile.

† It is interesting that the French believed the same thing, in reverse. 'It was dangerous for us. The British are more clever than we are, and what they wanted was not legitimate,' Giscard d'Estaing told the present author, speaking of the EEC budget negotiations.

fronted by Mrs Thatcher, her request for a rebate was more than a bruising battle about particular sums. It had a quasi-theological significance. Mrs Thatcher insisted on referring to the British payments involved as 'our money', sometimes as 'my money'. This offended against the European doctrine that 'own resources' – the percentage of VAT receipts voted to the Community by the member states – belonged absolutely to the EEC and so could not be broken down nationally or talked of in terms of a 'net contribution'.* Mrs Thatcher took refuge in the promise, made by the other member states during Britain's accession negotiations in the early 1970s, that, should an 'unacceptable situation' arise, 'the very survival of the Community would demand that the institutions find equitable solutions'.[28] At a joint press conference with Mrs Thatcher in Bonn at the end of October, in which she once more complained that Britain's payment was 'very unfair and inequitable', the German Chancellor, Helmut Schmidt, sharply questioned the principle on which she took her stand. If Germany were to take her view that there had to be a 'broad balance' between what a country put in and what it got out, he said, 'it would mean the end of the Community in a few weeks.'[29] European leaders feared that she was trying to revive the concept, beloved of General de Gaulle, of the 'juste retour', which, according to Euro-enthusiasts, had been destructively nationalistic. At a similar occasion in London three weeks later, President Giscard d'Estaing of France also attacked the 'broad balance' idea. Mrs Thatcher, determined not to be bamboozled by clever Frenchmen, was tart. The battle over the budget was not a matter of technicalities, she said, but of will: 'I trust I make myself clear.'[30]

At the European Council in Dublin on 29 November 1979, Mrs Thatcher made herself clearer still. In preparing for the summit, she had continued to come under pressure from her own officials who believed that only by signing up to grand European beliefs could she gain specific, detailed negotiating advantages. At the end of October, for example, when Sir Donald Maitland retired as UKREP, he sent the customary farewell despatch to the Foreign Secretary. It concluded with the idea that a common market and a customs union provided 'an inadequate basis on which to face the challenges of today', and he hailed the aspiration for an 'eventual political community'. Michael Alexander,† who had succeeded Bryan Cartledge as

---

* Though the ever-ingenious Michael Butler found an EEC policy document of 1978 which referred to the 'net contribution'. He brought this up against his counterparts in the negotiations. (Interview with Sir Michael Butler.)

† Michael Alexander (1936–2002), educated St Paul's and King's College, Cambridge; diplomatic private secretary to Mrs Thatcher, 1979–82; Ambassador to Austria, 1982–6; to NATO, 1986–90; knighted, 1988. Although she greatly respected his abilities, Mrs Thatcher sensed

Mrs Thatcher's foreign affairs private secretary, sent her Maitland's memo. He commended the conclusion and wrote on top: 'Selfish, wilful and short sighted though our partners are, they are so far as I can see, the only partners we have. I . . . believe that you personally could play a major role in pointing the Community in the right direction.'[31] Against Maitland's notion of a 'political community', however, Mrs Thatcher inscribed her customary wiggly line of disapproval.

But, contrary to some of the myths that grew up later, there was no great disagreement within the government about what to demand at Dublin. Although Mrs Thatcher and even, despite his lifelong Euro-enthusiasm, Geoffrey Howe, were more hawkish than Carrington and the Foreign Office, it became increasingly obvious to all that Britain was being set up by its partners. In the words of Maitland's successor, Sir Michael Butler, 'They certainly thought they'd score off her.'[32] Giscard gave no ground, and even Schmidt, the friendliest of the main players, warned her of isolation and that, if it came to a matter of take it or leave it in reference to budget reform, 'The other members might well say leave it.'[33] The government prepared its position. It would not hold out for a complete rebate – a reduction in Britain's net contribution of between three-quarters and two-thirds was privately agreed as the acceptable minimum so long as, in the favoured phrase, 'the solution was as long as the problem' rather than one-off – nor would it plan to break EEC law if it did not get its way. But it would accept isolation at Dublin and warn, in the words of a note from Howe to Mrs Thatcher, that, unless she got satisfaction, 'you would not thereafter be able to facilitate the operation of the Community'.[34] On 28 November the Cabinet agreed this approach. Even the Europhile Lord Soames, who could not attend the meeting, wrote to her before it: '. . . I hope that you will make the punishment fit the crime and you may ultimately need to withhold payments.'[35] Two days earlier, a rather agonized Roy Jenkins had called on Mrs Thatcher to try to calm matters down. He failed. Mrs Thatcher reiterated her positions, even regretting that she had not gone so far as to demand that Britain become a net beneficiary of the EEC budget. She bridled at criticisms by member states: 'The Prime Minister expressed impatience with the wish of other members of the Community to have more evidence that the Government was Community-minded.' In response to Jenkins's prediction that she would not get what she wanted at Dublin, she warned that there would be 'no movement in the Community' unless she prevailed.

---

that the strongly pro-European Alexander was not of similar mind to her: 'His father is Irish, and his wife is German,' she once warned Hugh Thomas (interview with Lord Thomas of Swynnerton).

Jenkins said she should avoid building up a 'head of steam' about the budget question. Mrs Thatcher 'said that there was already an uncontrollable head of steam'. The record of the meeting ended thus: 'Mr Jenkins commented that the Dublin Council promised to be an interesting one.'[36]

It *was* interesting. From the beginning, Mrs Thatcher went to war. She refused all prepared texts for her opening statement in Dublin Castle, preferring to extemporize and thus speak more vigorously. At the dinner of the heads of government, she kept them all at table for four hours, talking, as Roy Jenkins put it, 'without pause, but not without repetition'.[37] 'I want my money back,' she said again and again. Schmidt pretended to fall asleep and Giscard was alleged, though he denied this to the author, to have read a newspaper. 'I am not a night bird,' Giscard remembered. 'I hate discussions after dinner. It bores me.'[38] Mrs Thatcher's performance was, according to Carrington, 'a rant'.[39] Giscard agreed: 'It was unpleasant, because it wasn't a conversation. It was a repetition.'[40] Britain was offered £350 million in rebate. Mrs Thatcher, who was arguing in public that the full £1 billion contribution should be rebated, scornfully dismissed it as 'a third of a loaf' at the press conference afterwards. She felt she was being ganged up against, and resented it. Her own notes scribbled during the summit say, 'We thought we had joined an equitable system.'[41] She considered the Continental approach unBritish: 'What I would not accept was the attitude that fairness did not seem to enter into the equation at all.'[42] 'Equity, of course, is historically a British concept,' she said in reply to Alan Clark* when she reported on the summit to the House of Commons:[43] the EEC, in her view, had not displayed it. There was no basis for agreement, except, as Britain had planned, agreement to have another meeting. Mrs Thatcher amplified her anger at the press conference. The negotiations had been 'totally unsatisfactory': 'all we are doing is asking for our own money back.'[44]

There is no doubt that Mrs Thatcher's behaviour did annoy the other European leaders. In the days after the summit, Foreign Office telegrams keened with reports of upset from their Continental counterparts. But even Euro-enthusiasts like Michael Butler, who thought that it 'didn't do her any good' to talk about 'having my money back', believed that her stance was essentially correct. She set out the case with 'great aplomb', he considered, and the other heads of government 'were always pretending to be

---

* Alan Clark 1928–1999, educ. Eton, Christ Church Oxford; MP for Plymouth, Sutton, February 1974–92, and for Kensington and Chelsea 1997–99. Junior Minister at Employment, at Trade and Industry and at Defence, from 1983–92. Military historian. Clark published the first volume of his *Diaries* to great excitement. The diaries covered the Thatcher period and were scandalous.

outraged by what she said'.[45] The budget mechanism *was* inequitable, and the nations – the majority – which benefited from this tried very hard to avoid the issue. France, in particular, worried that a Common Agricultural Policy constructed from the start essentially for its benefit was threatened by Mrs Thatcher's approach, and so resisted fiercely. More than 70 per cent of the Community budget went on the CAP, strikingly little of it benefiting Britain. Given the state of public opinion at home, Mrs Thatcher had little choice but to fight, and her style of doing so did her more political good than harm. 'It was an uncomfortable manner of doing it,' recalled Carrington, but an uncomfortable manner was what was required, and Mrs Thatcher 'did her homework and the other heads of government didn't'.[46]

Returning home, she felt pleased with her stance, and redoubled her energy for combat. One compromise suggestion floating around was that Britain should make some concessions to the EEC about privileged access to North Sea oil, the resource which was doing so much to secure Britain's balance of payments at a time of wider economic difficulty. She hated the idea of 'linkage' between her budget position and other issues, and scrawled on a memo from Robert Armstrong: 'Energy – I am not prepared to bargain away our few resources. To suggest that we might be allowed to keep our own money in return for giving up some of our oil is ridiculous.'[47] In the New Year, the Foreign Office had another go, producing a draft statement on North Sea oil. Mrs Thatcher wrote on it: 'The idea that we should have to sacrifice our main asset to secure some of our own money back is one that may appeal to the Foreign Office but it doesn't to me. Wouldn't it have been courteous to have come to me first?'[48] Her blood was up.

As winter turned into spring, it gradually became clear to all sides that a settlement would have to be reached fairly soon. In Giscard's view, Mrs Thatcher 'with good judgment saw that she would get better from the Germans than from the French'.[49] Helmut Schmidt helped move things on by setting up an informal meeting between the personal representatives of all the heads of government. Giscard also observed that Mrs Thatcher 'thought that the male was weaker than she'.[50] This was true.* On the other hand, France had not only the high ground of European doctrine but also the low ground of doing very well out of the existing budget and the CAP, and so wanted to fight hard. Giscard told his close associate Prince Poniatowski that 'we must keep on bashing the British steak to make it tender.'[51] As the special summit in Luxembourg at the end of April 1980 approached, the whole thing turned into a blame game. Intensive British

---

* She was fond of quoting Kipling's line about 'the female of the species' being 'deadlier than the male'.

diplomacy round Europe revealed that the other partners were getting restive with France for its insistence on linkage between agreeing the budget and putting up agricultural prices. On 24 April, just days before the summit, Giscard telephoned Mrs Thatcher in some anxiety, in order to accuse her of 'perpetual postponement'. She replied that she was not qualified to negotiate agricultural prices at the summit. Echoing the language she had used publicly during Giscard's visit to London in November, she reminded him that the problem at issue was not a technical problem, but 'a question of the will'.[52] Without resorting to active illegality, Mrs Thatcher told the Cabinet on the same day, Britain stood ready to block progress on sheepmeat, agricultural prices and the entire Community budget for 1980.[53] At the Luxembourg summit, though improved offers for British rebates were made, the issues were not resolved, and there was no agreed communiqué.

Carrington, however, got wind of the general desire for a settlement, brokered by Italy, which held the incoming presidency, and started working on Mrs Thatcher with the idea that a three-year deal, pending a longer-term solution, could at last be achieved by the foreign ministers meeting together at the end of May. His first memo on this displeased her. She wrote on it: 'I am so horrified with this approach that I think it would be better if we didn't have the meeting [planned with Carrington to discuss the situation]. I feel as if the FCO is going to cancel out all my own efforts.'[54] Yet the meeting between Carrington and Mrs Thatcher took place, and Carrington pushed ahead, though not without much storming from Mrs Thatcher. Clive Whitmore recalled a meeting in the Cabinet Room shortly before the EEC Foreign Affairs Council, when Carrington, needing to leave, got up, still arguing, and walked to the door without looking where he was going. He knocked into one of the Doric pillars. 'My God,' he exclaimed, 'I've hit another immoveable obstacle.'[55]

On 30 May, in Brussels, Carrington and Ian Gilmour reached a provisional deal with their opposite numbers. Carrington immediately telegraphed Mrs Thatcher to give her the details, which included agreed amounts of refund for 1980 and 1981— a two-thirds reduction of the net contribution – and a repetition of the formula upon which the 1980 and 1981 refunds were based for 1982, so they had at last got a three-year deal. He had fought off, he said, any link between the 1981 refund and agreement on agricultural prices for that year. By 1981, a longer-term settlement would be agreed, within the 1 per cent VAT 'own-resources ceiling'. Carrington said: 'I am convinced that this is the limit of what we can negotiate.'[56] Luckily for Carrington's cause, the Continental press interpreted the deal as a victory for Mrs Thatcher ('British Europe' said the headline in Le Monde), and a great improvement on what had been offered at Luxembourg. Clive Whitmore improved the shining hour, writing on the telegram from the British Embassy in Paris, 'Michael Alexander has just telephoned me from Paris to say that all the French media are presenting the Brussels proposals as a great victory for you and a defeat for France.'[57] Mrs Thatcher was highly suspicious, however. When Carrington and Ian Gilmour flew straight to Chequers to see her, she gave them a hard time for which they were unprepared. She did not like the figures; possibly she did not like the feeling that the wind had been taken out of her sails. 'She didn't even offer us a drink,' remembered Carrington, who had been negotiating for eighteen hours continuously before flying back, and had not slept. '"I'll resign," she said. "No," I said, "I'll resign."'[58]

No one resigned. The Chequers meeting was uncomfortable but inconclusive. Gilmour returned to London and briefed the press that the deal was Mrs Thatcher's triumph. This was faithfully reflected in the next day's headlines. On Monday the Cabinet endorsed the deal, without demur, though also without enthusiasm, from the Prime Minister. It recorded, however, that the deal gave the United Kingdom 'less than would be ideally desirable'.[59] Lord Hailsham summed up the reasons for acceptance: 'We have no alternative but to accept. We shan't get better. The press have treated it as a victory. The alternative would be a complete leap in the dark, with the Community's future and our membership at stake.'[60]

In the ensuing weeks, everything went quiet. In early July, Robert Armstrong sent her a note headed 'Cabinet: Community Affairs' which read, in full: 'There have been no developments in the Community during the last week calling for discussion by the Cabinet. This is perhaps the shortest brief I shall ever submit to you.'[61] There would, indeed, be few other weeks when the EEC did not intrude upon Mrs Thatcher and her Cabinet.

Despite the complaints about Mrs Thatcher's stridency, her first big European battle, long though it was, was generally seen as successful. From the British point of view, the budget situation which she remedied was indeed unjust, and her determination to put it right won admirers at home and even, though they were more reluctant to say so, abroad. The Carrington–Gilmour deal held, and provided a good base for the negotiations on a longer-lasting settlement which were finally completed at Fontainebleau in 1984.

It is also true, however, that the budget row contained the seeds of most of the problems which were to become toxic by the end of the 1980s. The experience confirmed in Mrs Thatcher a constant irritation, even a deeper resentment, at the way the EEC worked. Again and again, on memos she received through the course of the negotiations, she would scribble exclamations of exasperation ('The more I read the more appalled I become')[62] or worse. On one from Geoffrey Howe about EEC rules on how refunds should be approved, she wrote: 'No – the procedure is ridiculous. Its whole purpose is to demean Britain.'[63] For her, the encounter with the EEC was a series of mostly unpleasant surprises in which she discovered that more powers had been ceded than she had realized. And she found it hard to resolve the conundrum of all negotiation in the EEC: how much should a matter of principle, such as national independence, be sacrificed for a specific, material advantage or for the Foreign Office concept of 'influence'?

In the relatively quiet months after the Brussels deal of 30 May, John Nott, the Trade Secretary, wrote her a thoughtful note about future strategy towards the Community. He said that the whole process had brought out 'deep but genuine differences of opinion about the Community among colleagues'. In his view, 'far too much power already resides in the institutions of the Community': 'own resources' should not be increased, and the CAP must be reduced. He added: 'One of the misfortunes for me of the Budget negotiations was that we had very nearly achieved this objective [reforming the CAP] as a result of French threats, but we lost the opportunity when we accepted a temporary settlement.'[64] Mrs Thatcher underlined these words twice and put three ticks beside them. Nott had identified what it was that she had not liked about Carrington's deal in Brussels – the sense that any victory, however good in its specifics, was always bought by the longer-term sacrifice of Britain's best interests.

No sooner had Mrs Thatcher confronted the leaders of Europe in Dublin in November 1979 than she began to prepare for her first visit to the United States as prime minister. Her instinctive sympathy with the United States was as ingrained as her instinctive distance from Continental Europe. She was already an object of considerable interest and admiration in America. But she nevertheless lacked a powerful ally among the political elite in Washington. Her cordial relationship with Ronald Reagan was something she hoped might bear fruit in the presidential contest due the following year, but at this stage it was not even clear that he would be the Republican candidate. Her relationship with President Jimmy Carter, though correct, was not close. Mrs Thatcher had originally wanted to visit in September, but Carter put her off, pleading a hectic schedule. When Zbigniew Brzezinski, the National Security Advisor, advised the President to call Mrs Thatcher to discuss the date change personally he demurred, telling Brzezinski to deliver a message via the State Department instead.[65] The two respected one another, but they did not particularly like one another, and they certainly did not agree on many of the key issues of the day, especially how to deal with the Soviet Union.* There was also a question

* An internal Foreign Office memo from late June warned of growing disagreement with

in the minds of both leaders about how much effort should be put into their relationship. In the United States administration, the idea was abroad that Britain no longer mattered very much. A CIA report sent to Carter in October noted the United Kingdom's 'now largely secondary political, economic, and military role' and declared that 'The "special relationship" between the United States and the United Kingdom, finally, has lost much of its meaning.' The report added, unpresciently, 'Insofar as the Thatcher government is interested in expanding that role, it apparently intends to do so in an EC more than an Atlantic framework.'[66] For her part, Mrs Thatcher was conscious of the weakness of the Carter presidency. On 4 November, the US Embassy in Teheran was occupied by Islamic extremists, described as 'students', and the Embassy staff taken hostage. There then began a long, carefully calibrated humiliation of the American presidency by Iran. This, combined with economic weakness and the energy crisis – the spot price of Saudi oil was three times higher at the end of 1979 than it had been at the beginning of 1978 – drained the Carter administration's will and occupied its every waking moment. 'The Oval Office had become a black hole from which the President rarely escaped,' recalled Jim Rentschler, a National Security Council staffer. 'Everything was set aside to focus on the hostage crisis, so the Anglo-American relationship was not exactly "on hold", but it was largely left to the bureaucracy to manage.'[67]

The briefing to the President from the Secretary of State, Cyrus Vance, in advance of Mrs Thatcher's visit reveals a mild unease, both about the personal rapport between the leaders and about the issues they might discuss. Among the principal objectives of the meeting, Vance noted, would be to 'Enhance . . . your personal relationship with its strong-minded Prime Minister' and to 'Get a reaffirmation of British support for SALT II [Strategic Arms Limitation Treaty] ratification.' By way of 'setting', Vance explained that 'The British economic situation will get worse before it gets better,' but described the Thatcher government as being 'well-placed to ride out the storm, since it has a 43 seat majority in the House of Commons . . . The Labor Party is in disarray.' He also pointed out that there were some Tory suspicions because of the closeness of Carter to Jim Callaghan: 'the Thatcher government has shown its willingness to make decisions on matters of interest to the US more independently than the Callaghan government.'[68]

Washington in the aftermath of Mrs Thatcher's election victory. There are 'more bones of contention now than, say, a year ago between the Americans and ourselves', commented one official; '. . . the general tone of our relations at present is perhaps less good than it was' (John Leahy's note on Ramsay Melhuish's memo, 'Anglo-US Relations', 26 June 1979, TNA: PRO FCO 82/980).

For her part, Mrs Thatcher was concerned above all to make a favourable general impact during her visit. In this regard she was unimpressed by the first schedule of events proposed by the Foreign Office. 'She does not regard the day's programme as a whole as sufficiently interesting,' noted a memo from Downing Street.[69] Extra meetings at the Pentagon and with British businessmen were duly added. Breaking with her usual determination to travel with a minimal entourage, for this visit Mrs Thatcher had a range of expertise on tap. As well as her No. 10 staff and Foreign Secretary, she brought with her not only the Cabinet Secretary but also the permanent secretaries from both the Foreign Office and the Ministry of Defence. There were important issues to discuss, such as American support for the modernization of the British nuclear deterrent and progress in the Rhodesian negotiations, but none, at this point, was critical. What the still new Prime Minister needed to do was to establish herself as a player on the Washington stage. At the British Embassy on the night of her arrival, 16 December, the Ambassador, Sir Nicholas Henderson (commonly known as 'Nicko'),* noted with surprise and pleasure how much she listened to her Foreign Secretary, Lord Carrington. The party discussed whether or not Britain should support the United States in its plan to seek Chapter Seven powers (which could include sanctions or even the use of military force) from the United Nations Security Council over the hostage-taking in Iran. Mrs Thatcher, influenced by pressure at home about British interests in Iran, was doubtful. It was Carrington who took the strong line: 'Leaning forward on the sofa, Peter Carrington said, "Margaret, you have got to say, yes. You have got to do so."'[70] Mrs Thatcher did not clearly indicate then and there which way her mind would go on this subject.

The next morning, the Prime Minister was received in solitary splendour by the President and First Lady on the White House lawn, with military honours. At the arrival ceremony, she immediately praised Carter for the way he was dealing with the 'agonizing problem' of the hostages, and went on: 'At times like this you are entitled to look to your friends for support. We are your friends. We do support you. And we shall support you. Let there be no doubt about that.'[71]† The ceremony had been a 'great emotional experience', she told Carter privately, stressing that when it came to Iran

---

* Nicholas Henderson (1919–2009), educated Stowe and Hertford College, Oxford; Ambassador to Poland, 1969–72; to West Germany, 1972–5; to France, 1975–9; to the United States, 1979–82; knighted, 1991.

† This warm, humanizing reference to 'friendship' had been written into the speech by Mrs Thatcher personally, replacing the cooler and rather wooden language provided by the Foreign Office ('Speech of [sic] the White House Lawn – 17 December 1979', TNA: PRO PREM 19/127).

'everything the British Government could do to help they would do'. If Carter wanted action under Chapter Seven, she would support him: 'No other course of action was thinkable.'[72] Afterwards, she expanded on this to the waiting press, confirming that she would back a Chapter Seven resolution.[73] Although there was really no new policy involved, the force of her words had an immediate effect. 'Warm Words on a Wintry Day; Thatcher Vows to Back Iran Sanctions' was the *Washington Post* headline the next morning. The *Daily Telegraph* reported her 'tremendous personal success with President Carter and the American public'.[74] Zbigniew Brzezinski looked at the matter more realistically: 'There was an arrival ceremony for Mrs Thatcher at the White House. She made quite an impression as a tough-minded lady. She had a good meeting with the President, but in my view the President was not sufficiently forceful in pressing her over economic sanctions against Iran. I followed this up with her myself, but felt that the President was not particularly pleased that I had intervened and pressed her for a commitment.'[75] Carter's aides were acutely aware of the need for tangible British support. 'If it is perceived that we cannot get full British cooperation on voluntary steps with Prime Minister Thatcher in Washington, the credibility of allied support will collapse,' warned Jody Powell, Carter's Press Secretary, privately.[76] Brzezinski was thus eager for Britain to implement some sanctions against Iran even before going to the UN under Chapter Seven. Mrs Thatcher did not want to take this step, nor was she ready to give America anything very specific. But as she had set such a supportive tone, this mattered less than the Americans might have feared.

At lunch at the British Embassy that day, Mrs Thatcher was able to announce, impromptu, that a constitutional settlement for Rhodesia had just been initialled at Lancaster House. The *New York Times* the next day noted that she had been considered 'a tyro in diplomacy' when she first reached No. 10, but 'The Margaret Thatcher who arrived yesterday for her first American visit as Prime Minister is being received as the most effective British statesman (she would scorn "stateswoman") since Harold Macmillan, the fabled Supermac.'[77] That afternoon, Mrs Thatcher went to Capitol Hill, where her reception was almost rapturous. Henderson recorded that one senior Senator told him three times how marvellous she had been and said: '"I do not recall any visitor to the USA who has made such an impact." I asked whether he was referring to visitors to Congress. "No," he replied, "I mean any visitor anywhere to the United States."'[78] At the White House dinner which he gave for her that night, Carter applied a quotation from *Pickwick Papers* to Mrs Thatcher: 'She knows what's what, she does.' There was a faint feeling that the President found this quality in her irritating.

The following morning, Mrs Thatcher flew to New York where she was freer to indulge in the 'hot-gospelling' at which she excelled. She told a lunch at the Foreign Policy Association that 'Self-questioning is essential to the health of any society. But we perhaps have carried it too far and carried to extremes of course it causes paralysis. The time has come when the West – above all Europe and the United States – must begin to substitute action for introspection.' She reminded her audience that her enemies had called her the Iron Lady and said, 'They're quite right – I am.'[79] Without being guilty of any diplomatic incorrectness, Mrs Thatcher was supplying a gap in the rhetoric and attitude of the West which many Americans felt had been created by Carter's vacillation. At a dinner that night given by David Rockefeller and attended by grandees like Averell Harriman, Alexander Haig* and Henry Kissinger, Mrs Thatcher cast aside her notes and spoke extempore. Brian Urquhart, an Englishman who was then the UN Under-Secretary-General for Special Political Affairs, wrote: 'she evoked an almost revivalist atmosphere with a ringing assault on socialism and on generally unsatisfactory behaviour throughout the world. When she was done, ancient bankers staggered to their feet to foreswear 1776 and suggest that she ought to be the President of the United States. She was urged to tell the United States, then in the throes of the hostage crisis, where it had gone wrong. Along with the other Brits present, I was acutely embarrassed.'[80] Urquhart's snooty reaction was typical of the majority of the British official classes throughout Mrs Thatcher's time as prime minister, but his account gives an accurate picture of the emotions stirred among the American audience. Even within the administration, Mrs Thatcher appealed to people who felt that their own country's leadership was lacking. Jim Rentschler recalled: 'Carter did not loom large in personal strength. Bob Blackwill [a colleague on the National Security Council staff handling European issues] came out of a meeting that included both Carter and Thatcher: "In that room there was one giant and one pigmy," he said, "and the giant was female."'[81]

The conclusion of the Lancaster House Agreement over Rhodesia was by and large not Mrs Thatcher's doing. She felt little natural warmth towards the process, indeed a fierce distaste towards Joshua Nkomo and even more towards Robert Mugabe. But, having decided to leave the entire negotiation to Carrington, and to put her confidence in him, she behaved, almost always, correctly. Robin Renwick, the head of the Rhodesia desk, remembered, 'She

* Alexander Haig (1924–2010), Assistant to the President and White House Chief of Staff, 1973–4; Supreme Allied Commander Europe, NATO, 1974–9; US Secretary of State, 1981–2.

was excellent at Lancaster House, because she refused to intervene at all. We explained to her that she mustn't act as a court of appeal for disgruntled participants ... She said, Carrington and the FCO are going to do this and no one should go behind Carrington's back.'[82] At the party conference in October, when rebellion threatened, she led a standing ovation for Carrington. As the talks progressed, she left the daily negotiations entirely to her Foreign Secretary, who briefed her each night on progress. Within the privacy of No. 10, these briefings often led to vigorous exchanges, as Michael Alexander recalled: 'Her role was to be rather extreme, to criticize all the participants all the time. (So much so that I did not keep a record of these nocturnal discussions. They would not have done her reputation much good!) "I won't have it; I won't do it" and "Absolutely not!" "Why not propose this new approach, or that, to Muzorewa or Nkomo?" Peter would then go back to Lancaster House and say that the Prime Minister was giving him a hard time and that the participants had better agree to whatever he proposed "for fear of something worse".'[83] After one such evening session, faced with intransigence from Ian Smith, Renwick briefed the US Embassy that Mrs Thatcher had been in a 'feisty, militant mood'. She was determined to move the conference forward, the Embassy reported to Washington. 'If Carrington does not succeed, Prime Minister Thatcher is prepared to take Smith on herself.'[84] Mrs Thatcher also sent regular updates to President Carter. The Americans remained suspicious of British intentions, fearing that a fully democratic solution would somehow be avoided. Carter, coming from a Southern state, always felt the pressure from black activists in the Democratic Party for whom the issue of Rhodesia seemed not unlike the issue of slavery itself: such people were impatient with the compromises which might be required to achieve a peaceful transition, and unfriendly towards the British.

There were one or two matters, however, on which American co-operation was required, and here Mrs Thatcher dealt with Carter, sometimes on the telephone. The first was in October 1979, when negotiations at Lancaster House threatened to break down over the issue of land reform. Here she successfully persuaded the United States to offer money to help (though, as it turned out, little ever appeared). The second arose when Carrington decided to send out Lord Soames, the designated Governor of Rhodesia for the transitional period to independence, to Salisbury (modern Harare) before a ceasefire had been agreed. To do this successfully, Britain wanted the signal of international support which would be given by lifting international sanctions immediately. The Americans were reluctant. When the State Department dug its heels in, wanting to wait until the electoral process was in motion, the Foreign Office asked Mrs Thatcher to intercede with the White House. On 14 December, two days before her visit to the United States, she wrote to Carter claiming that the Patriotic Front were deliberately spinning out the talks, and asked Carter to announce that he would lift sanctions as soon as Soames arrived in Rhodesia as governor. He agreed at once, and made the announcement the next day.

Although Mrs Thatcher was prudent and, where Carter was concerned, persuasive in advancing the Lancaster House process, there is evidence that her scepticism continued. From her time in opposition, she had maintained links with Jesse Helms, the right-wing Senator from North Carolina whose unbending anti-Communism and segregationalism led him to support Ian Smith's white government in Rhodesia and, when that could no longer be sustained, the internal settlement which gave power to Muzorewa. On 4 July 1979, Helms had visited her in No. 10. In September, two of Helms's staff, John Carbaugh and James Lucier, came to London to try to persuade Smith, who, they felt, was being outmanoeuvred at Lancaster House, to refuse to make any concessions and thus break up the conference.[85] They also tried, unsuccessfully, to raise the standard of revolt within the Conservative Party, visiting the main rebel, Julian Amery. Mrs Thatcher agreed to see Carbaugh. Carbaugh recalled their exchange:

> I said to her, 'You're going to get one man, one vote, I promise you that, one time.' It's true she was going along with the negotiations but she was extremely uncomfortable. I said, 'Mrs Thatcher, Peter Carrington is not serving you well.' She said, 'That is not for you to decide.' I said, 'Of course it's not. I'm a stupid American. I'm here by your grace, but he's not serving you well. Somebody's got to tell you about the new clothes they've been trying to put on you.' She said, 'You shouldn't have done this.' I said, 'Yes ma'am. But thank God it's a free world this side of the Iron Curtain.'[86]

If Carbaugh's account is correct, it shows that Mrs Thatcher was not seriously tempted to follow the Helms way, but the fact that she saw Carbaugh at all is evidence of her alertness to the right-wing threat to Lancaster House and perhaps of her sympathy for it. When the visit by Helms's aides became known in America there were condemnations on Capitol Hill, and Vance, the Secretary of State, asked Carrington to issue a written complaint about the intervention. This Carrington refused to do 'for domestic political reasons'.[87] For Carrington to criticize Helms's men would have amounted to an indirect criticism of Mrs Thatcher. When Vance claimed to Helms's office that London had made a 'démarche' saying that Lucier and Carbaugh had broken the law, Carbaugh arranged a telephone call between Helms and Mrs Thatcher: 'Mrs Thatcher came on the line and I put Helms on the phone. There was silence [after Helms had explained the position] and then she said, "There has been no such démarche." [88] Thus she protected Helms. Probably, she was trying to have it both ways. Looking back, Carrington summed up her attitude to the whole thing:

> I don't think that Margaret, in her heart of hearts, was ever convinced about the process – in the sense that if it had gone wrong . . . [here Carrington made a throat-slitting gesture and laughed], which I can understand and I don't particularly blame her for it, she wouldn't have taken the can. It would have been me that was responsible, which in a way was true. She was supportive, but it was rather reluctant support: 'My mind tells me that this is the right thing to do, but my instinct tells me you're a pig.' She did become more supportive as the process looked more and more likely to succeed because I think she realized there was some credit going. And fair enough. [89]

What happened much later in Zimbabwe, when Robert Mugabe, from the mid-1990s, began the complete repression and impoverishment of his country, was to confirm Mrs Thatcher's pessimism about the whole enterprise. The once prosperous country conformed to the sad pattern of so many African former colonies and squandered its great initial advantages. On the other hand, her task, on coming into office, was essentially to find an agreed way out to a problem which had consumed vast amounts of British government time for no clear benefit. With such enormous problems at home, and with Britain's economic and diplomatic reputation at a low ebb, Mrs Thatcher was naturally inclined to seek a quick settlement. The one she chose, under Carrington's direction, was, given the circumstances, bold. It involved casting aside plans for UN involvement and risking the displeasure of Britain's closest ally, the United States, which had planned to be part of the solution. It was also threatened by violence. When he went out as governor to supervise the elections and the transfer of power, Lord Soames said privately that he expected 50 per cent casualties among the 350 servicemen who went with him. [90] In the event, although there was some factional violence during the election campaign, Soames and his troops were largely unmolested. By the standards which it set itself, the Lancaster House Agreement was an astonishing success, and Mrs Thatcher showed the flexibility and opportunism that leadership requires by letting it happen. David Owen, the former Labour Foreign Secretary who had watched her overturn his own policy towards Rhodesia, noted how closely she resembled Barbara Castle, once his boss at the Department of Health and Social Security, who had warned him, when Mrs Thatcher was first made Tory leader, not to underestimate her: 'She was very like Barbara – the same hair, dress sense, good ankles, a very similar intelligence. Both would resist right to the end, and then cave in.'[91] By adopting the policy which she instinctively disliked, Mrs Thatcher won an international reputation and gained a standing which was to prove crucial as, later in the 1980s, the problems of South Africa came to a climax.

But the Rhodesian settlement never made her happy. As she stood in the hall of No. 10 on 21 December 1979, to leave to put her initials, as Carrington had requested, to the Lancaster House Agreement, Mrs Thatcher had a last-minute attack of anger. She turned to Clive Whitmore and said, 'I am not going to shake the hands of terrorists.' Whitmore held out her coat and said, 'Put this on, Prime Minister. We're going to Lancaster House.' She did so, but with an ill grace.[92]

As 1979 drew to a close, Mrs Thatcher was in an odd position. She was known as a conviction politician, and admired or reviled accordingly. Her critics said she was rigid, dogmatic, unfeeling. This was a political danger for her. But a much greater problem, for her economic policy, was the suspicion that she was infirm of purpose.

The idea known as 'monetarism' was not, in itself, an innovation of Mrs Thatcher's government. When she came into office, Mrs Thatcher inherited the approach that the Labour government had developed after the intervention of the IMF in 1976. Denis Healey, the Labour Chancellor, had turned to policies of monetary control, not because of any personal monetarist commitment, but out of a political calculation that inflation, for the time being at least, was even more unpopular than unemployment. As early as June 1976 he had announced a money supply growth target (of 12 per cent) for the coming year. This was the first time such a target had been used by a British government. In 1978, after various disasters with trying to achieve a particular sterling exchange rate, Healey more explicitly moved away from Keynesian demand management. The government, he said, was 'determined to control the growth of public expenditure so that its fiscal policy is consistent with its monetary stance'.[93] Mrs Thatcher's new administration wished to do the same, and Mrs Thatcher, unlike Healey, saw this as a matter of principle as well as of expedience. But according to Peter Middleton, who was the Treasury under-secretary in charge of monetary policy at the time and the official there most sympathetic to monetarism, Geoffrey Howe was 'more like Denis Healey than you might think'. Unlike the still relatively junior Nigel Lawson, who was 'a real enthusiast',[94] Howe was more a politician making use of convenient tools than a man with a particular economic vision. Given that the Labour government had demonstrably failed in its objectives during the winter of 1978–9, and given that the idea of British decline was now an accepted fact in political and economic discourse, people were sceptical about whether a new Conservative government could do any better. Markets did not believe the government. What would happen, people wondered, when it reached what Treasury officials privately called 'sod-off point' in 1980, and ceased to be under the supervision of the IMF? As Middleton put it, 'You must make the point that you are serious before you can get relaxed and sophisticated.'[95]

To make this point, it was not enough to increase interest rates by fearsome amounts, as happened in November 1979. It was a key part of monetarist theory, as set out, for example, by Karl Brunner,* that governments and central banks adhere strictly to monetary rules, rather than merely acting on their own discretion. In the phrase of Nigel Lawson, who was the keenest advocate of the approach and had argued for it publicly in opposition, 'Rules rule, OK?'[96] Instead of the 'letters of intent' which the IMF had extracted, under virtual coercion, from the previous government, there should be free-will declarations of financial objectives, with dates. There was a world of difference between temporarily curbing inflation for electoral advantage and a longer-term commitment to squeezing it out of the system. People needed to know not only the current target, but also the intended path in the coming years. Rules would also, Lawson and Howe believed, have a hortatory effect within government, driving doubters in the right direction, and making it harder to backslide. The idea, which had intellectual support from Milton Friedman, was gradualist, avoiding the shock which other intellectuals, notably Friedrich von Hayek, preferred. Its emphasis on direction was important in the internal workings of the Treasury, where Terry Burns,† a supporter, arrived as chief economic adviser early in 1980. Doubters were led by the more Keynesian Permanent Secretary, Sir Douglas Wass,‡ who was considered by Thatcherites a wet blanket on innovation. As well as rules producing economic benefits, their supporters argued that they would produce political ones, because they could help to explain the absence of jam today by reference to jam tomorrow. They could show how, if public borrowing fell, there would be room

---

* Karl Brunner (1916–89), Gowen Professor of Economics, University of Rochester, New York, 1979–89.

† Terry Burns (1944–), educated Houghton-le-Spring Grammar School and Manchester University; Professor of Economics, London Business School, 1979; chief economic adviser to the Treasury and head of Government Economics Service, 1980–91; Permanent Secretary, Treasury, 1991–8; created Lord Burns, 1998.

‡ Douglas Wass (1923–), educated Nottingham High School and St John's College, Cambridge; Permanent Secretary, Treasury, 1974–83, and joint head of the Home Civil Service, 1981–3; knighted, 1975.

for tax cuts, and, just as important, how if it didn't, there wouldn't. The name devised for the set of rules was the Medium-Term Financial Strategy (MTFS).

Although she does not mention this in her memoirs, Mrs Thatcher was nervous of the MTFS. She referred to plans of this sort disparagingly as 'graph-paper economics'[97] and 'numbers marching across the page'.[98] She feared that the MTFS would leave no room for political flexibility. Her doubts were encouraged by John Biffen, who was opposed to the MTFS because he believed governments should never impale themselves on hooks. In the minds of Lawson and Howe, however, this was precisely the advantage: the MTFS would prevent faint-hearted ministers from finding what is nowadays called wiggle-room.[99] Mrs Thatcher gradually came round to the idea as Howe cleverly exploited her obsessive desire to bring down interest rates. The MTFS would bear down on rates, he argued, and put a straitjacket on big-spending ministers.[100] He also told her that the presentation of the 1980 Budget would be 'greatly enhanced' by the context that an MTFS would give: 'This will offer the prospect of more substantial tax reductions when we have surmounted the next two tight years.'[101] In the end, the MTFS was agreed by the pre-Budget Cabinet in March 1980 without much fuss, although Prior, Gilmour, Michael Heseltine and others did all express 'doubts' about the wisdom of producing figures against which the government in future years would be judged.[102] It was a remarkable fact, and one which provoked untypically caustic comment from Howe after his retirement, that the Wet critics within the Cabinet did not take a stand against the MTFS at the time. After all, it directly defied their desire to improve demand in the economy and it set a course to which they were opposed. Perhaps they continued to believe that such plans had little meaning. Perhaps they hoped that, for Mrs Thatcher – to reverse Mr Micawber's remark – something would turn down.

Howe well knew, however, because he had been part of her plot himself, that Mrs Thatcher had gone to some lengths to avoid a general economic debate in Cabinet of the sort which would have given potential rebels an opportunity. Although she agreed in principle that such general discussion should take place, she decided, at the beginning of November 1979, to prepare the ground by creating an 'Inner Group', which included Howe, Joseph, John Nott, Biffen, David Howell, Patrick Jenkin and, as Tim Lankester put it to her, 'Mr Whitelaw and possibly Lord Soames (the latter two might be counted upon to raise some of the arguments of those who are less sympathetic to the strategy) . . .'.[103] In the event, Soames was not made a member. Robert Armstrong, the Cabinet Secretary, reported to Mrs Thatcher that 'it is already clear that Mr Prior feels he has been outflanked ... He has told the Chancellor ... that he disagrees with the whole approach.' Francis Pym, the Defence Secretary, had also been kept in the dark – 'The papers have not been copied to him' – and Howe, Armstrong explained, wanted to leave room open for defence cuts: 'His paper deliberately does not mention this.'[104] The workings of the Inner Group should be linked, Armstrong advised, to the announcement of the MTFS. He warned Mrs Thatcher to beware of the Cabinet claiming a right to make decisions on monetary policy,[105] because it would be a usurpation of the Chancellor's traditional freedom of action. As Howe circulated his paper on the economic outlook and further public spending cuts only to the Inner Group, Robert Armstrong was moved to protest to the Prime Minister: 'I think it is wrong that Ministers should be asked to take far-reaching policy decisions, involving major political issues, on the basis of two or three lines in the Chancellor's annual Public Expenditure paper.' The word 'wrong' was a big one for a civil servant to use, even a Cabinet Secretary. Mrs Thatcher scribbled: 'They don't. They ought to know their departments and what is going on.'[106] By one means or another, a general economic discussion in Cabinet was postponed until after the Budget. And even then, thanks to some cunning handling of the agenda, Mrs Thatcher's officials managed to decouple Cabinet debate of public expenditure plans from a general discussion of the economy. They broke them into two gatherings in July and thus got rid of the setpiece meeting, originally planned for later in the month, where critics had hoped for a showdown. As Clive Whitmore wrote silkily to Armstrong: 'If we proceeded in this way, there would be no need for the special meeting of the Cabinet on Wednesday 16 July, though nothing need be said for the time being about cancelling the meeting.'[107]

Just before Cabinet approval of the MTFS, John Hoskyns sent a note to Mrs Thatcher about the Budget. He recalled the objection by the Governor of the Bank of England, at a meeting the previous week, to the introduction of the MTFS, and attributed it to the 'subconscious desire to avoid announcing that you're going to do something difficult, in case you fail'. Hoskyns supported the MTFS because it helped with what he thought should be the 'main message' of the Budget – 'the commitment, over time, to ending inflation' – but he complained that 'Our scope here is limited by our failure to de-index [that is, to remove the automatic upward adjustment of wages and benefits to keep pace with inflation] on an adequate scale in public expenditure.' This weakness on public expenditure had decelerated the private sector but not the government sector: 'we have tackled it completely the wrong way round.' He warned, not for the first time, that the government would have to do 'something else on more Hayekian lines some time in the next year (i.e. along the lines of the "shock package" I suggested in January)'.[108]

Geoffrey Howe, by contrast, was rather more optimistic than his Eeyor-ish countenance, or the facts, suggested. Prompted by Nigel Lawson, who was very suspicious of what he called 'nonsensical forecasts',[109] he told Mrs Thatcher privately that he thought the Treasury's forecast which pre-dicted 'a larger drop in output in 1980 than any other forecasting body is expecting' was too gloomy. He thought, too, that the PSBR would be smaller than expected, but promised not to publish an 'unduly optimistic' forecast.[110] Perhaps subconsciously, he was using the idea of the MTFS as a way of postponing one or two tough decisions. He warned her that his range for the growth of sterling M3 could not come below 7–11 per cent: 'I know that this will be a disappointment to you,' but otherwise interest rates would have to be so high as to be 'out of the question'.[111] The MTFS, which Howe announced in the Budget, set out a path by which the range would fall by 1 per cent annually, reaching a growth rate of 4–8 per cent for sterling M3 in 1983–4. The PSBR would fall from 4 per cent of GDP in 1980–81 to 1.5 per cent in 1983–4. The Treasury published a green paper entitled *Monetary Control* in March, and later, in June, its *Memo-randum on Monetary Policy*. The MTFS did not, in itself, change the policy already being pursued, but it did formalize the position and hold the government to its course. The monetarist government now had a mon-etarist strategy.

But, as Keith Joseph had long before said, 'Monetarism is not enough.' Sound money was a necessary but not a sufficient condition of recovery. The successful control of inflation would be a cold comfort unless it was accompanied by a transformation of economic and industrial attitudes and opportunities. As John Hoskyns kept complaining, Clegg's awards, and the failure to contain public spending at a time when interest rates and the sterling exchange rate were soaring, attacked the private sector fero-ciously. In June 1980, he backed up his view with a paper submitted to Mrs Thatcher by Douglas Hague, called 'The Central Problem of Public Expenditure'. Hague wrote: 'Even if we hold the proportion of output coming from the public sector constant, if private sector productivity rises faster than public, then any "comparability" means that tax rates will rise exponentially ... We have designed an arrangement for destroying the British economy.'[112] Hoskyns saw the process of economic recovery as having three legs – the attack on inflation, the ending of indexing and other privileges of the state sector, and the curbing of the power of the trade unions. The MTFS had been introduced, but little else had happened. The stool had only one leg to stand on.

The sharpest internal disagreement was about the trade union leg. When the Conservatives had come into office in May 1979, Jim Prior had found it relatively easy to carry the day for his cautious Employment Bill. On 14 May he wrote to Mrs Thatcher, saying that 'it is absolutely crucial to our whole Administration to get this right,' and continued, 'it would be fatal to follow the 1970 pattern and rush things too much. We must live up to our promises to consult.'[113] Despite the promise in the Conservative manifesto to review the legal immunities of trade unions to 'ensure that the protection of the law is available to those not concerned in the dispute but who at present can suffer severely from secondary action (picketing, blacking and blockading)', Prior was firmly opposed to doing anything which would 'put at risk the support we must seek to win from moderate opinion in the trade union movement itself and more generally'.[114] In the view of Lord Gowrie,* one of Prior's junior ministers at this time, 'The civil servants [in the Department of Employment] were counting the days until a return to incomes policy.'[115] Prior had no objection in principle to such a return. To make it easier if it did come, he wanted relations with union leaders to be on a friendly footing.

Although tetchy about Prior's slowness, Mrs Thatcher was conscious both of the need to carry her Cabinet and of the threat of strikes in the first winter of her government which she was not yet prepared to resist. She therefore let him have most of his way in his first Employment Bill. By the end of 1979, however, the picture of industrial relations had become more desperate. In a court case (McShane v Express Newspapers Ltd) about the extent of permitted trade union action, the Court of Appeal found on 13 December that anything could be considered to be 'in furtherance of a trade dispute' if the person doing the disputing thought it was. In other words, the law afforded no protection to firms dragged into a dispute with which they were not concerned. Then, on 2 January 1980, a steel strike began. Against the background of a plan for 52,000 redundancies in the hugely loss-making British Steel Corporation, the steelworkers' union, the ISTC, called a strike over its pay claim. On 16 January, the union spread the strike to private sector steel producers who were not part

---

* Alexander Patrick Greysteil Hore-Ruthven, 2nd Earl of Gowrie (1939–), educated Eton and Balliol College, Oxford; Opposition spokesman on Economic Affairs, 1974–9; Minister of State, Department of Employment, 1979–1981, Northern Ireland Office, 1981–3; Minister for the Arts, 1983–5; Chancellor of the Duchy of Lancaster, 1984–5.

of the dispute. Those already dissatisfied by Prior's foot-dragging became extremely anxious. On 28 January, Hoskyns sent a note to Mrs Thatcher about a conversation he had held with Keith Joseph, David Wolfson and Leon Brittan, at that time the Minister of State at the Home Office.* 'The only way to penalise unions', it said, 'is to attack their funds. Never go after the individual . . . The only thing the union leaders really care about is their funds.' Unions were 'financial enterprises which operate on a no-risk basis'. The law on immunities must therefore change because it is 'a matter of power': 'If we don't act Frank Chapple [the moderate and robust leader of the Electricians Union] will in due course be replaced by militants, and then the switches could be turned off. Similarly, Scargill will eventually succeed Gormley [as leader of the miners].'[116] The government must stand firm in the steel strike, insisted Hoskyns, and act immediately against immunities.

Hoskyns followed this up by reminding Mrs Thatcher that the situation was not unlike that of the previous winter ('of Discontent') when, in opposition, colleagues had been divided about whether or not to accept the union status quo. His suggestion, unspoken, was that she should act as she had then, and go public in defiance of Prior's wishes. On 1 February, Prior wrote to Mrs Thatcher telling her that it would be a terrible mistake to remove the immunities of unions. The immunities, he said, had 'immense symbolic significance'. He counselled against 'over-hasty action'. Mrs Thatcher wrote her wiggly line of disapproval under the word 'over-hasty'.[117] On 3 February, Prior got his retaliation in first by telling the BBC's *World This Weekend* that he would not rush through changes to immunities: if the government got it wrong on industrial relations, 'the outlook for our country, and I mean *our* country, is very bleak indeed.'[118] With a fierceness of which, despite his 'dead sheep' reputation, he was sometimes capable, Geoffrey Howe wrote to Mrs Thatcher the following day, demanding action on immunities. Unless the Conservatives acted, he wrote, 'we might as well not have fought (and won) the last General Election.' He agreed with the principle of 'step by step', but added that there would be massive union trouble whatever the government did, and so there was no point

---

* What Hoskyns's note did not mention was that Brian Walden, the former Labour MP, was part of the conversation he reported. Despite his theoretical impartiality as a television interviewer, Walden was passionately concerned that union power should be broken, and feared that the government, as in 1974, would paralyse itself on the issue. At this time, he met Mrs Thatcher to tell her that 'the trade unions have become an estate of the realm', above the law. 'She said, "Tell me something I don't know."' (Interview with Brian Walden.) The next week, Walden's programme concentrated on the need for laws against secondary action, with hostile reaction from Arthur Scargill and others.

trying to avoid it. The union question, said Howe, was 'the most important issue in the life not just of this Government but of the nation'.[119]

By now, almost everyone wanted to pitch in. Lord Thorneycroft circulated a hawkish paper to the Cabinet. John Nott inveighed against the union blacking of international shipping. Hoskyns, the Centre for Policy Studies and sympathetic businessmen worked tirelessly against Prior. The *Daily Express* began to refer derisively to 'Pussyfoot Prior'. John Methven, the head of the CBI, confused everyone by calling for 'profound changes' while also backing Prior. Sir Hector Laing, the chairman of United Biscuits, was a fervent admirer of Mrs Thatcher. 'I thought she was very attractive a. physically and b. for her command of language,' he said years later.[120] But he was also a friend of Jim Prior, whom he later put on his board. Laing wrote to the Prime Minister thus: 'You will know what Elizabeth I said to William Cecil: that "without respect of my private will you will give me that counsel you think best."'[121] What he thought best was Jim Prior's step-by-step approach; otherwise confrontation would be 'insupportable'. Mrs Thatcher rang Laing at home that weekend. 'How are you?' he asked. 'I was fine until I got your letter,' she replied.[122] In a private letter answering Laing the following week, Mrs Thatcher put her own position very frankly. If the government did not change the law, she said, 'we should be telling the law-abiding citizen that we prefer to strengthen the powers of those who inflict injury rather than to help those who suffer from it. That course is not open to anyone who fought the last election on the Conservative manifesto, and it is therefore not open to me.' Immunity, she said, should be confined to the primary action, and common law remedies should be restored to those who suffered from secondary action. She thought that now was the time:

> If we flinch from this task now, when we have public and massive trade union opinion with us, they are not likely to have much faith in us to do it next winter.
>
> For obvious reasons I have not been able to put this view publicly yet. Judging from my correspondence, a lot of industrialists share it and would go much further. Some want a new criminal offence of 'unlawful picketing'. I would prefer to see what we can do through the civil law.
>
> You quoted a saying to me. Let me counter with another famous quotation: 'Our doubts are traitors / And make us lose the good we oft might win / By fearing to attempt.' *Measure for Measure*.[123]

Even as she wrote, however, Mrs Thatcher knew that the practicalities, not to mention Cabinet nervousness, were such that new material on immunities could not be included in Prior's Bill. On 13 February 1980,

E Committee agreed that the Bill should not be amended, but that 'trade union immunities should eventually be considered' and a green paper prepared.[124]

Prior was in no hurry for this document to be completed, so what Mrs Thatcher had feared was likely to come to pass – another winter without the necessary legislation in place. Although the conventional wisdom has it that Jim Prior was right in his tactics, and that 'step by step' was indeed the way to deal with union reform, the difference between him and Mrs Thatcher was not only about pace. Prior believed that the point of the whole exercise was not to undermine the structure of union power but to bring about more moderate attitudes which would produce a new era of co-operation. In his daily press digest for the Prime Minister for 11 March, Bernard Ingham reported: 'Mr Prior on TV stakes his political future on Employment Bill; admits he is on trial politically. No question of attacking union funds while he is Minister.'[125] Prior's ambition at this stage was to be secretary of state for industry[126] and he saw establishing a good relationship with the unions as the flip side of doing the same with business, an essentially corporatist approach. Mrs Thatcher, on the other hand, believed that it was only by fundamentally changing the legal rights of trade unions and bringing them under the law which applied to everyone else that progress could be made. Rather than wanting to establish a good relationship with the unions, she wanted to bring about conditions in which government had virtually no need for a relationship with the unions at all. In later years, Prior said, 'It was really an argument about pace,' but then added, 'though perhaps it was more fundamental.' But he also argued, in retrospect, that the politics of the conflict between himself and Mrs Thatcher worked quite well for the government: 'It was quite a good position, in government, for her to be pushing Jim Prior and him to be resisting.'[127]

Mrs Thatcher was now clearly frustrated by slow progress and felt ready to explode. On the weekend of 17 February 1980, she did so. Staying at Chequers that Sunday, she confronted the news that a mass picket at Hadfields, the private steelworks in Sheffield, organized by Arthur Scargill, the militant hero of the Saltley coke depot incident under the Heath government, had succeeded. She took a telephone call that morning from Keith Joseph in which he told her that the picket had been 'a massive breach of common law'.[128] No, she said, it had surely not been a criminal matter, but a civil one. Angry at her government's impotence, Mrs Thatcher rang Willie Whitelaw, the Home Secretary. 'The Government could not sit aside and do nothing,' she told him: there should be a one-clause Bill that week to prevent such picketing.

For the rest of the day, telephone calls ricocheted back and forth. Joseph rang back with the Lord Chancellor Lord Hailsham's suggestion that a charge of unlawful affray be brought against Scargill. To this Mrs Thatcher replied that 'It might suit Mr Scargill very well to be charged.' The new picketing clause she sought would follow the better route of allowing injunctions to be taken out. Joseph then said that what the record calls 'the other man' – a reference to Prior – would be putting in his proposals in the coming week. Mrs Thatcher 'said she feared that Mr Prior was trying to push the Government into a Court of Inquiry' over the steel strike. Increasingly heated, she rang the Attorney-General, Michael Havers. At 9.30 p.m., Whitelaw rang her and she told him that 'the *People* leader was right. The Hadfields situation had not been a matter of mass picketing but of mass intimidation . . . The Prime Minister said that the Chief Constables should meet the Law Officers. The Home Secretary said that this would have to be treated with great care, as the Chief Constables could not take direction from the Law Officers.' Mrs Thatcher then demanded a Cabinet or Cabinet committee the next day because it was too urgent to wait till Tuesday. At 10.45, Whitelaw rang her again to tell her about the state of the Sheerness steelworks, also threatened with mass picketing. The Chief Constable of Kent was 'quite determined to keep Sheerness working: he hoped that Ministers would support him though he feared they would not.' Mrs Thatcher repeated her desire for a civil law remedy: 'The Sheerness steelworks had at present no basis on which to seek an injunction. The proposed new law would provide this. She had just received a telegram from Sheerness wives.'

The record of this hectic, semi-coherent day suggests that Mrs Thatcher was really alarmed. The fact that Arthur Scargill, who appeared for five minutes on the scene at Hadfields, had successfully organized the picket made her fear that she was suffering her own Saltley. Here was the defeat by the unions which she dreaded. Here was the fate of Ted Heath staring her in the face, and here, thanks to Prior, was a government which had not provided itself or employers or, she feared, the police with the necessary legal powers. That was why she was casting about so desperately for last-minute remedies. A special meeting of E the next day agreed that the Attorney-General would remind the Commons of the criminal law about picketing, but that a separate Bill about picketing would not be brought forward. In an additional shaft of rage, announced at Prime Minister's Questions the next day without consulting Prior, Mrs Thatcher said that the rules would be changed so that strikers claiming benefit would be deemed to have been paid by their union. In an interview with Robin Day on *Panorama* a few days later, Mrs Thatcher was asked about comments by Prior critical of British Steel's management which had leaked from an off-the-record lunch. 'I think it was a mistake,' she said, 'and Jim Prior was very, very sorry indeed for it, and very apologetic. But you don't just sack a chap for one mistake.'[129] Perhaps not, but the fact that she spoke about sacking him at all subconsciously reflected her state of mind.

As it turned out, though, the militants' victory at Hadfields did not signal a wider war between government and unions. The failure to achieve a similar success at Sheerness was very important. The essentially moderate steel union was looking for a deal, not a bloodbath, and British business found ways of getting enough steel to keep going. The government's policy of not intervening in nationalized industry disputes, but leaving it to management and unions to sort them out, paid off. The expectation had built up over many years of Labour and Conservative government that the secretary of state would come forward with 'new money'. This did not happen. Keith Joseph stayed out of the negotiations, and the ISTC began to look for a way out. A penalty for the government's non-intervention was that there was little it could do when the British Steel Corporation wanted a court of inquiry into the dispute. This resulted in a pay award greater than the government would have liked. But although the financial costs of the settlement were too high, the political winner, on points, was the government. The huge internal tension about trade union reform, though the issue was still completely unresolved, eased for a few months. A TUC Day of Action in May 1980 against government policies proved a damp squib. The steel dispute had failed to reverse government policy; indeed, it probably accelerated change. The BSC losses were so bad that the government had a freer hand than before in reorganization. In April a Scottish American businessman called Ian Macgregor* was appointed, at Jim Prior's recommendation, to succeed the outgoing Sir Charles Villiers as BSC chairman. Mrs Thatcher referred to him in public as a 'mighty man', a favourite phrase of Denis about anyone he admired.[130] Macgregor had the opportunity and the ability to turn BSC into a functioning business.

Even bigger, and therefore even more disastrous, than British Steel was the car-manufacturer British Leyland. The unhappy product of an amalgamation by the Labour government in 1968, the company employed 160,000 people when Mrs Thatcher came into office. About the same number of jobs again were directly dependent on the company's existence. Leyland's

---

* Ian Macgregor (1912–98), educated George Watson's College, Edinburgh, Hillhead High School, Glasgow and Glasgow University; chairman and chief executive, British Steel Corporation, 1980–83; chairman, National Coal Board, 1983–6; knighted, 1986.

UK market share, which had been 33 per cent in 1974, had fallen to 20 per cent by 1979. It was not technically a nationalized industry, but the government owned the controlling share, and paid ever more for the privilege. Although it contained promising bits, such as Land Rover and Jaguar, Leyland was chiefly an unsuccessful volume car maker, with such low levels of productivity, caused mainly by terrible trade union problems, that it could not compete with the likes of Vauxhall and Ford or foreign manufacturers. It was operating under the Ryder Plan for expansion, devised in 1975 to inject £1.7 billion of government money over seven years, and opposed by the Conservatives at the time. Mrs Thatcher was not well disposed to the company. Its dynamic chairman, Sir Michael Edwardes,* who had taken over in 1977, had her to lunch with his board in early 1979, when she was still leader of the Opposition: 'I put her opposite me so that I could get a dialogue going, but I didn't have to wait long. She said, "Well, why should I give you any money?"'[131] Once she became prime minister, this was essentially the question which Mrs Thatcher kept asking, and she never felt that she received a wholly satisfactory answer. Nevertheless, she did give the money – more than once and in large quantities.

All Mrs Thatcher's inclinations, and those of her economic advisers, were that BL should close, or be broken up and its workable bits sold off. Robin Ibbs,† who advised her on the subject from the CPRS, remembered that BL offended her beliefs: 'She had a practical mind, and she had Denis.' Denis was good at reading company documents, and telling her what they really meant. In BL's case, they meant disaster. Ibbs and, in more lurid terms, Alfred Sherman told her that BL was 'just a sink', but it was also 'an appalling problem which no one knew what to do with'.[132] The political difficulty confronting Mrs Thatcher in relation to BL was twofold. How could she introduce economic reality without job losses which would cause the Conservatives to lose every seat in the west midlands where people were dependent on the company for their living? How, also, could she support the tough and necessary things which Michael Edwardes was doing to bring about sane industrial relations and at the same time pull the plug?

In September 1979, a new BL 'Recovery Plan' sought more money

* Michael Edwardes (1930–), educated St Andrew's College, Grahamstown, South Africa and Rhodes University, Grahamstown; chairman, BL (formerly British Leyland), 1977–82, 1984–5; knighted, 1979.
† Robin Ibbs (1926–), educated Gresham's School, University of Toronto and Trinity College, Cambridge; on secondment from ICI as head, Central Policy Review Staff, 1980–82; adviser (part-time) to Prime Minister on efficiency and effectiveness in government, 1983–8; knighted, 1982.

(eventually, an extra £300 million for 1980) on top of what Ryder had promised. John Hoskyns wrote Mrs Thatcher a briefing note setting out the dilemmas. 'Refusal to rescue' would produce a wave of industrial unrest, job losses and the loss, short term, of foreign exchange earnings. 'Rescue', on the other hand, would weaken the government's credibility, have a bad impact on the PSBR and mean that 'we can be 95 per cent certain that the whole problem will come round again.' Hoskyns considered that there was a third way – a form of rescue which 'buys us other advantages in terms of <u>more responsible union behaviour</u>' (words which Mrs Thatcher underlined), and would put pressure on unions in other industries to change. If the company were later to collapse, blame would then lie at the door of the unions, not the government. Hoskyns acknowledged that this strategy would conflict with that of Edwardes: 'His objectives and ours would be quite different. He has nailed his flag to BL's mast, where we would be using BL simply as a lever for a much larger strategy.'[133]

In October, Edwardes called a ballot on the plan. '<u>Please – no hostages to fortune</u>,' Mrs Thatcher begged Keith Joseph as he planned his response to the ballot result,[134] but of course the government could not ignore the ballot result: 87.2 per cent voted to accept Edwardes's plan. As Hoskyns put it:

> The main difficulty about closing BL now is a psychological one and related really to Edwardes's own personality and image . . . In a sense he symbolises the possible renaissance of British management . . . The BL ballot was seen as the workers putting their faith in good managers instead of politically motivated union activists. To reward Edwardes's efforts and his work-force backing with closure would seem to be a deliberate blow against everything the Government is trying to encourage.[135]

Edwardes strengthened his position by firing Derek 'Red Robbo' Robinson, the hard-left convenor of the shop stewards at the Longbridge plant and master of much of the union disruption.* Mrs Thatcher was pleased, but continued to object to suggestions for saving BL. She wrote 'Why?' on documents advocating rescue and put heavy underscorings of approval against suggestions of sell-off. But, shortly before Christmas, she followed political logic and accepted Joseph's recommendation. The £300 million

---

* The Security Service, MI5, had conducted an operation against Robinson, leaking to Edwardes and others the minutes of a secret meeting Robinson held with the Midland District Committee of the Communist Party of Great Britain in September 1979 to plan the subversion of the BL Recovery Plan (see Andrew, *The Defence of the Realm*, p. 672).

extra was promised. The condition was that Edwardes sign a letter agreeing that the Plan would be abandoned – resulting in total closure – if thrown off course by strikes.

By February 1980 a strike over Robinson threatened and the car market was continuing to fall. Ministers began to consider aborting the Plan, but did not do so. Just as Mrs Thatcher wanted to get away from 'beer and sandwiches at No. 10', by which trade unions took part in the making of government policy, so she wanted an almost equally arm's-length relationship with the heads of nationalized industries. She therefore had no substantive meeting with Edwardes at all until, at Keith Joseph's prompting, she gave dinner to the BL board on 21 May. By this time, Edwardes had successfully faced down the strike threat, but the dinner was still combative. In advance, Hoskyns had advocated 'deliberate brinkmanship', seeing the dinner as the moment 'To increase, through Edwardes's understanding and cooperation, our chances of . . . "Sell or Merge"'.[136] At the dinner, Edwardes told her that the planned Mini Metro, to be launched in the autumn, would be the saving of the company. He was working on a collaborative deal with a German company which he would not name (it was BMW), but even so cash flow would fall well short of the plan. The exchange rate was very damaging. The company would need up to £500 million extra over the next three or four years. This 'immediately established a frosty atmosphere'.[137]

Mrs Thatcher's manner was 'somewhat reminiscent of the Spanish Inquisition'.[138] She told him she was 'very disturbed'.[139] There could be 'no presumption' that extra funds would be provided. 'What worried her', Edwardes recalled, 'was that I wasn't presenting a budget . . . We weren't ready because of the changes in the exchange rate . . . and that annoyed her. We had to talk in generalities whereas she wanted hard figures.'[140] She appeared unhelpful. After dinner, the party moved to the drawing room:

> Suddenly she turned everything on its head . . . She turned to Geoffrey Howe and said, 'Geoffrey, how much have we got in the contingency fund?' Geoffrey said, 'Do you think it is proper for them to know?' 'Get on with it. Tell Michael how much is in there,' she said. There was actually two or three billion in it . . . I walked out of there knowing that I had had an indication . . . I was confident that the battle was won and confident that we would get the money.[141]

It is probably true that Mrs Thatcher found Edwardes persuasive enough to want to go on giving BL a chance, but in fact things got very much worse. In December 1980, Joseph reported to colleagues that BL's demand for 1981-3, which had been £130 million in the 1980 Corporate Plan, was now £1,140 million. For each car produced, BL was losing £600. Mrs Thatcher peppered Joseph's document with exclamation marks and wrote, in reference to Jaguar and Land Rover, 'Sell off.'[142] 'I seem to remember he [Edwardes] told us he would come to govt if he could not carry out the previous corporate plan. He never came.'[143]

Cabinet ministers disagreed among themselves. John Nott, at Trade, told Mrs Thatcher that if the government paid out the extra sum demanded 'we would be ridiculed, and rightly so, since such an investment will be seen to be wholly contrary to the industrial and economic policy which we have been promoting for the past five years.'[144] Keith Joseph, agonized, went back, somewhat half-heartedly, on his pre-Christmas belief that more money should be advanced, and argued that it should not be. At the beginning of the year, Mrs Thatcher had brought her rising ally, Norman Tebbit, into the Department of Industry to be Joseph's minister of state. 'Norman,' she told Tebbit, 'I want you to look after Keith – dear Keith, they are so unkind to him, and he needs someone to protect him.'[145] Observers noted that, much as she loved Joseph, Mrs Thatcher was not above being unkind to him herself, as he groaned and hesitated and tried to reconcile his beliefs in economic necessity with his personal humanity. But at a meeting on 12 January 1981 Geoffrey Howe argued that further subsidy would be no worse for the PSBR than closure and Mrs Thatcher, using a phrase not often associated with her, sought the 'middle way' in which, in return for support, Edwardes would agree to sell or merge the company. The meeting thought that 'closures in the steel and shipbuilding industries should have higher priority; and it was not politically possible to achieve all at once.'[146]

Still no final decision emerged, however, and Mrs Thatcher started once more to harden against extra subsidy. Norman Tebbit recalled one meeting at this time when she had summoned Joseph and him to express her concern about the Corporate Plan. 'Is there anything else you need, Secretary of State?' asked Joseph's private secretary as the pair set out for Downing Street. 'Yes,' said Joseph, 'ambulances at three-thirty.'[147] The dispute about what to do had dragged on so long that Edwardes wrote to complain that he could not run a business if he did not know whether or not it would exist in two weeks' time.[148] Before E Committee met to decide, Robert Armstrong, conscious of Mrs Thatcher's politically precarious position, counselled caution: 'I think it is very important that you should not show your hand in the discussion. I believe that serious consequences would ensue if the decision was to continue financial support . . . and it then came out (as I fear it might) that that decision had been taken against your advice.'[149] He was warning her about the leaky habits of far from loyal Cabinet colleagues.

In the end, the extra money was agreed, but Mrs Thatcher was not pleased. On the draft of the statement to Parliament, she jibbed at the sentence 'The Government wishes the BL Board and the companies' employees well in their difficult task.' She crossed out the word 'difficult' and wrote, 'Not difficult compared with those who haven't got a government subsidy of £1 billion.'[150] In fact, the 'middle way' did begin to set the company on a path towards winding down what was unsustainable and selling off what was not. In the course of 1981, the word 'privatization' would start to feature strongly in government discussion of British Leyland. But at the time the capitulation to BL's demands was seen by many Thatcherites as a tremendous disaster. It had been advised against by Alan Walters, who had only just taken up his post as economic adviser to the Prime Minister. At the Centre for Policy Studies, Alfred Sherman turned the framed photograph of Keith Joseph to the wall.[151]

19

Not for turning

'They are all against me, Robert. I can feel it'

The pay-out to British Leyland in January 1981 was only one of a series of grave embarrassments which had accumulated for Mrs Thatcher's government in her second year of office. On 19 June 1980, John Hoskyns sent the Prime Minister a note covering a long paper about the next pay round. It said: 'Experience of past Governments suggests a tendency to drift into what the historians later recognise as the crucial period with little or no idea of what they are doing. We are now moving into what could be the first, and critical, six months of a make-or-break year. The thinking must be done before the uproar begins.'[1]

Mrs Thatcher made no record of her reaction to this note, but it probably combined irritation with recognition. If there was drift in her government, it was, by implication, she that was being criticized: the note expressed a hint of the exasperation Hoskyns often felt at her lack of strategy. But, at the same time, she felt exasperated herself.

Her feelings had come to a head in the previous month. As soon as she had entered No. 10 a year earlier, Mrs Thatcher had set up a mechanism for investigating waste in government. She appointed Derek Rayner, formerly of Marks and Spencer, as her adviser on efficiency and waste. The Rayner Scrutiny, as it was known, was based in the Cabinet Office. It not only searched out particular examples of waste and the pointless generation of paper, but also worked to change the culture of Whitehall. It sought to alter the belief at the top of the Civil Service that brains alone mattered, and encourage the idea that results mattered too. It wished to import notions of management from the private sector, including reviews of performance so that people who worked well were rewarded and people who worked badly were punished. This was the sort of thing in which very few prime ministers in the past had shown any interest, but it was a continuing preoccupation of Mrs Thatcher's. It fitted, said Clive Priestley, who was the deputy at the Efficiency Unit – the Scrutiny's formal title – with her 'womanly theme of good household management',[2] and also with her suspicion that the Civil Service conspired to frustrate the aims of elected governments. When she came into office, the Civil Service, whose numbers, structure and conditions had once been run by the Treasury, was under the charge of a separate Civil Service Department. This tended, in the view of Rayner and of Mrs Thatcher herself, to make it even more resistant to reform because it was cut off from the realities of cost and power. From the start, relations between her and the Permanent Secretary, Ian Bancroft, were uneasy.

At first, colleagues and senior officials were uncomprehending. When the Rayner scrutineers came to see Willie Whitelaw to discuss their task, he said, 'I don't know why she wants to do this, but she does, so we must help her.'[3] Mrs Thatcher wanted to carry the permanent secretaries with her, however, and in discussion with Whitelaw, Bancroft, Lord Soames, the minister for the Civil Service, and Robert Armstrong, early in 1980, she proposed a meeting with all of them so that she might enthuse them with the task. Perhaps sensing trouble, Whitelaw argued that a dinner would be more congenial than a meeting, and this was duly arranged at No. 10 for 6 May.

Six days before the dinner, Iranian Arab terrorists, Iraqi-trained, stormed the Iranian Embassy in Princes Gate, took the occupants hostage and made a series of demands, including the release of political prisoners in Iran. At first, negotiations were attempted, both by telephone and by Muslim inter-mediary, but with no result. Other plans were made. On the Monday Bank Holiday afternoon,* Whitelaw, who, as Home Secretary, was the minister in charge, telephoned Mrs Thatcher as she was driving back to London from Chequers and explained that a dead body had been thrown out of the Embassy building on to the street.† He asked for her agreement to support the Metropolitan Police Commissioner's request for the Special Air Service (SAS) to be mobilized 'in aid of the civil power' and to rescue the hostages. 'Yes, go in,' she said.[4] In the course of this crisis, Mrs Thatcher paid three visits to the Cabinet 'war room' from which operations were being conducted. On the first two, according to John Chilcot, ‡ Whitelaw's private secretary, she was 'frankly dreadful', trying to dominate the occa-

---

* In her memoirs, Mrs Thatcher erroneously attributes this call to the day before, perhaps forgetting that the Monday was a Bank Holiday.
† It later turned out that the body was of a hostage (the press attaché Abbas Lavasani) killed earlier, but at the time it looked as if it was the first of many, designed to ratchet up the crisis.
‡ John Chilcot (1939–), educated Brighton College and Pembroke College, Cambridge; prin-cipal private secretary to the Home Secretary, 1978–80; Deputy Under-Secretary, Home Office, 1987–90; Permanent Under-Secretary, 1990–97; chairman, Iraq War Inquiry, 2009–13; knighted, 1994.

sion without really being on top of the detail. On the third, however, when she saw the seriousness of what was required, she was 'cheerful, resolute' and happy to place her full confidence in Whitelaw.[5] 'She was very good,' judged Sir Peter de la Billière, the Director of SAS, also based in the Cabinet 'war room'. 'She simply set the overall direction of policy and delegated it to Whitelaw to execute.'[6] That afternoon, the world watched as cameras trained on the building picked up hooded gunmen leaping in through the windows of the Embassy which they had blown open. In the operation, all the hostages still alive at the moment of attack were rescued. One terrorist was captured, and the other four were killed. It was the first time that the SAS had been authorized to use force to resolve a crisis on the British mainland. The public reaction was immensely favourable. The SAS, previously relatively little known, became a household word for heroism. Although the person in charge was Whitelaw, not Mrs Thatcher, the incident added to her reputation for dash and decisiveness. Ever afterwards, the fantasy of Mrs Thatcher dressed in black combat kit and swinging into buildings with a gun in her hands became a staple of newspaper cartoonists.

The very next day, Mrs Thatcher gave her dinner for the permanent secretaries. Elated by the success of the Princes Gate siege, she was painfully conscious of what Clive Priestley remembered as the contrast between 'the boys in black and the men in grey'.[7] Although no one present can remember exactly what was said, all agree that the evening was a failure. 'Her speech was, "You and I can beat the system." They effectively replied, "We *are* the system." '[8] At one point, Sir Frank Cooper,* from the Ministry of Defence, left the room. 'Where's Frank gone?' someone asked. 'He's gone to get the SAS,' was the *sotto voce* reply.[9] Mrs Thatcher remembered only 'a menu of complaints and negative attitudes'.[10] Robin Ibbs, who had just arrived to take charge of the CPRS, noted that 'They were speaking opposite languages to each other.'[11] Mrs Thatcher whispered to Armstrong: 'They are all against me, Robert. I can *feel* it.'[12] Eventually she said icily, 'Gentlemen [there were no women present], your cars are waiting for you.'[13] As the man theoretically in charge of civil servants, Ian Bancroft attracted her blame for this fiasco, and he never recovered his standing with her.

In later years, Mrs Thatcher liked to say, 'That meeting is etched on my soul.'[14] Not only did she feel discouraged in her attempts to get more efficient administration. She felt more generally beleaguered and – which she

* Frank Cooper (1922–2002), educated Manchester Grammar School and Pembroke College, Oxford; Permanent Under-Secretary, Northern Ireland Office, 1973–76; MOD, 1976–82; knighted, 1974.

disliked even more – patronized and whinged at. It made her wonder whether she would ever be able to wrench the country round to face reality.

Although there was not yet the 'uproar' of which John Hoskyns had warned, the early months of 1980 had seen much louder grumbling than before. In February, Ian Gilmour made a speech in Cambridge which set out with remarkable frankness (though not, of course, mentioning Mrs Thatcher by name) the basic Wet disagreement with her approach. 'Lectures on the ultimate beneficence of competition and the dangers of interfering with market forces will not satisfy people who are in trouble,' he said, and he declared that 'In the Conservative view, economic liberalism à la Professor Hayek, because of its starkness and its failure to create a sense of community, is not a safeguard to political freedom but a threat to it.' He warned, in effect, of defeat: 'While I agree that we are embarked on a programme that could well take the best part of two Parliaments to carry through, I also note that between the first Parliament and the second, the electorate will have its chance of a say.' Such words spoken in public sailed very close to breaching the doctrine of collective Cabinet responsibility. In his critique of the Thatcher era, *Dancing with Dogma*, published twelve years later, Gilmour admitted this, but argued that it was justified because Mrs Thatcher herself had departed from a collective approach, making economic policy through a 'secretive monetarist clique'.[15] His other reason for speaking as he did, he wrote, was: 'Ridiculous as it now seems, like many colleagues I still had lingering if fading hopes that common sense . . . would soon be introduced into the conduct of economic policy.'[16] This was, perhaps, an oblique and retrospective way of saying that, at the time, Gilmour and his allies felt emboldened to criticize because they believed that Mrs Thatcher was almost bound to fail.

Mrs Thatcher's reaction to Gilmour's speech probably emboldened him further. In the same television interview in which she explained that Jim Prior was 'very, very sorry' for his remarks about the British Steel chairman, she denied that there was any disagreement over strategy within her Cabinet. 'We only have arguments about the timing,' she said. Asked specifically about Gilmour's speech, she said that all Gilmour's speeches were 'very scintillating' and that there was 'something in it for everybody'.[17] She made no public attempt to rebut the criticism or to put down the man, although, within the (imperfect) privacy of Cabinet, Robert Armstrong recorded, 'The Prime Minister drew attention to the importance of maintaining collective responsibility, and the trust and confidence among colleagues on which it depends.'[18] The conclusion of the Wets, possibly correct at that moment, was that she did not have the power to slap them down. Although they made little complaint in Cabinet when the MTFS was announced the following month, they began to increase their resistance to measures – union reforms, pay stringencies and above all spending cuts – which would give practical effect to Mrs Thatcher's intentions.

At the same time, people essentially sympathetic to her aims were also becoming more alarmed. In a speech in April of uncomfortable frankness, John Biffen warned of 'three years of unparalleled austerity'. Mrs Thatcher rebuked him with apparent affection on *The Jimmy Young Show*: 'I think he was not quite right. It was a Biffenism, you know.'[19] Less than two months earlier, Milton Friedman had called on Mrs Thatcher at No. 10. His arrival had been preceded by a briefing note from Nigel Lawson, explaining that, although Friedman was strongly supportive of the central thrust of the government's policies, he was worried that the government's chosen method of controlling the money supply was wrong. 'He has been concerned recently', Lawson went on, 'lest the Bank of England should be intervening too heavily on the foreign exchange markets. He has always stressed the incompatibility between pursuing targets for the money supply and the exchange rate.'[20] (This incompatibility would, years later, be the chief criticism aimed at Lawson himself.) Mrs Thatcher gathered a small, senior group, including Lawson, Geoffrey Howe, Ian Gilmour and Gordon Richardson, to meet Friedman, and matters were discussed in broad, almost philosophical terms. At one point, after Friedman had uttered a piece of wisdom, Mrs Thatcher swept the gathering with her finger, saying, 'Now, we all believe that, don't we?' Her finger stopped when it reached Gilmour, and lingered, accusingly.[21] At the beginning of July, Friedman sent a submission to the Treasury Select Committee of the House of Commons, a body which, despite its in-built Conservative majority, was critical of the government's economic approach. Friedman told the committee: 'I strongly approve of the general outlines of the monetary strategy' published as the MTFS, but he went on to take issue with a key sentence in the green paper on *Monetary Control* which said that 'The principal means [of controlling the money supply] must be fiscal policy ... and interest rates.' That sentence, said Friedman, 'is simply wrong. Only a Rip Van Winkle could possibly have written it.'[22] At issue here was a complex yet important dispute over which measure of money supply a government should target. Under both Labour and the Conservatives, the favoured measure of money supply was the sterling M3 aggregate, a broad measure that included cash and bank deposits. The MTFS stipulated M3 as the preferred measure. It was the choice of such a broad measure of money supply that had led the Treasury to propose both fiscal policy and interest rates as necessary instruments of control. Friedman's critique was based on two points: first, fiscal policy affects money supply only indirectly and imprecisely through its effect on the supply of credit. At best, it has a blunt, second-order effect on inflation. And second, it was backward to suggest that interest rates control the money supply. Instead, interest rates reflect the prevailing supply and demand for money. To avoid these difficulties, Friedman advocated control of the monetary base (also known as M0), a far narrower measure of money supply than M3. Rather than relying on interest rates or fiscal policy, this approach called for a central bank to take direct measures to alter the amount of currency in circulation such as printing less money. In Friedman's view, M0 was not only easier to control but also more directly correlated with inflation than M3.

This argument had been rumbling along throughout Mrs Thatcher's time in No. 10. Gordon Pepper, on whom she had relied heavily in opposition, had seen her on 18 May 1979, and advised switching to monetary base control then. She had told him cautiously that she sympathized with his suggestion, but was worried about the extreme swings it might produce in the figures.[23] This was, on one level, a technical argument, and some close to Mrs Thatcher criticized her for bothering her head with a matter which she did not fully understand. Its political importance, however, which grew in 1980, was that, just as the government was being attacked for its harsh 'monetarism' and just as Britain moved into sharp recession, at the same time its chosen measure of money supply, M3, took off. Interest rates were punitive. So were exchange rates. The value of the pound to the dollar moved from $1.63 in October 1976 to $2.42 in October 1980. At the end of March 1980, two weeks after approval of the MTFS, Howe told the Cabinet, when he unveiled the Budget to them, that 'The money supply seems to be coming under control.'[24] It did not appear to be so, at least according to the government's preferred measure. The growth of M3 turned out at 19.4 per cent in the target period of 1980 to 1981.

Part of the reason for this apparent disaster was the enthusiastic reaction of the financial sector to the government's reforms. As the economist Brian Griffiths put it, 'People decided she means what she says, so let's buy pounds.'[25] In the Budget of March 1980, Geoffrey Howe announced the removal of the 'corset', the system of penalizing the banks for allowing their deposits to expand too rapidly which had now been rendered obsolete by the ending of exchange controls. When the corset was removed in July, sterling M3 immediately jumped by 4-5 per cent. The government also got rid of the old restrictions on mortgage lending by the banks, and this, too, made room for an explosion in the growth of credit. At the same time, high interest rates made people readier than before to hold deposits, in turn adding to the growth of

M3. None of these was necessarily a bad thing – all were natural short-term reactions to the lifting of constraints – but none had been fully foreseen, and so the figures looked alarming. When she was informed by an official briefing that 'The removal of the corset will raise the growth of M3 for a month or two; its underlying trend may be difficult to estimate,' Mrs Thatcher was rendered, unusually, wordless. Beside this sentence she wrote, '!!!'.[26]

Through the summer of 1980, Mrs Thatcher and her Treasury ministers began to fight a fiercer but still inconclusive battle with the ministers of the spending departments. Finding it very hard to get her way in private, Mrs Thatcher increased, if anything, the passion of her public rhetoric. It was one of her unusual and effective political techniques that she almost always ignored Denis Healey's 'First Law of Holes': 'If you are in a hole, stop digging.' She dug furiously. In a speech to the Press Association on 11 June, she declared that 'The day that I am not causing controversy, I shall not be doing very much.' She said that she was attacking equality and the economic primacy of government, and returning to 'old values'. 'Ministers, Treasury knights, and civil servants', she said provocatively, 'can never understand budgeting by cash' (as opposed to volume), but cash limits were 'something which every woman knows'. 'There will be no U-turns along this road,' she added.[27] Two weeks earlier, the government had announced a plan to reduce the number of civil servants from 705,000 to 630,000 over four years. In private discussion within government, the records show a series of occasions on which both sides, though anxious not to give ground, were also reluctant to have a fight so open that one or the other would have to lose. John Hoskyns's diary for 28 May recorded the mood: 'David [Wolfson] v. despairing about Margaret at present. Reads papers superficially, treats colleagues very badly, still overexcited by being PM, will not sit down and think about key issues. Prior and Co. simply registering their reservations for the record, but biding their time for a forced U-turn when she will have to resign.'[28]

At E Committee on 17 June, Mrs Thatcher began the meeting with a little speech indicative of her state of mind at that moment and of her idea of chairmanship in general. As Robert Armstrong noted it, she said:

Indicators of output down, earnings up.

We have nothing to distribute.

If we go on like this in the public sector, we shall be redistributing wealth from the private sector to the public sector.

Resentment against public sector wage increases enormous.

Devaluing savings to give public sector increases.[29]

This prelude was by way of supporting Geoffrey Howe in his attempt to impose a cash limit on Civil Service wages which would drive their rate of increase down below the private sector rate. Howe wanted comparability, still in operation, 'dethroned but not defenestrated'. He provoked Christopher Soames to declare: 'If we do this, we shall have major industrial strife in the public sector.'[30]

Not long after this, a last-minute and unsuccessful attempt was made to toughen up Jim Prior's Employment Bill provisions against secondary blacking. Various right-wing peers introduced an amendment to the Bill, and Mrs Thatcher, even though they were acting against her own Secretary of State's wishes, encouraged them. She asked Prior and his deputy Patrick Mayhew to come and meet the rebel peers in her room in the Commons. There was a heated argument in which, on one clause, she attacked Mayhew, saying, 'The clause doesn't do what you say it does. You're only saying it to frustrate the idea.' 'I won't take being accused of dishonesty,' said Mayhew. 'I'm going home,' said Prior.[31] When the rebellion, which took place in the Commons as well as the Lords, was being organized by Conservative backbench MPs, Mayhew entered the Chamber one night and was surprised to hear Ian Gow calling out to Tory MPs, 'This way for the PM's amendment,'[32] as he provocatively described it, in support of the rebels against Prior. In fact, the amendment failed. According to Mayhew, Prior, who hated everything about the detail of legislation, was inclined to 'a bit of "allakeefik" [shrugging of the shoulders to indicate resignation to fate]' and did not want a full-scale battle, but it was obvious that the relationship between Prime Minister and Employment Secretary was worsening all the time.

In order to deal with the problem of how best for the Cabinet to discuss the vital economic questions on which they were so divided, Mrs Thatcher agreed to a presentation by Terry Burns, still fairly new as the Treasury's chief economic adviser, with a supporting talk by Robin Ibbs, of the CPRS, about the dangers of indexation. There was a jostling among officials about attendance at this meeting which revealed the tensions. At an early stage of its planning, Robert Armstrong wrote to a presumably irritated Douglas Wass at the Treasury, 'I have little doubt that, if the Chancellor were to take the view that you should come as well as – or even instead of – Terry, the Prime Minister would be perfectly content.'[33] She was not content at all. Beside Armstrong's suggestion a few days later that Wass should attend the meeting, Mrs Thatcher wrote, 'No.'[34] As was usual in such matters, Armstrong, in the role of Sir Humphrey, prevailed, and Wass accompanied Burns to the meeting, but it was Burns, not Wass, who did the talking. The purpose of his 'talk-in', which took place in the state dining room on 3

July 1980 and was illustrated by acetate slides, was to give an expert view of the financial situation, illustrating both the gravity of the crisis and the necessity of the government's monetary policies. Burns pointed out early signs that the inflation rate was beginning to fall. He impressed Hoskyns: 'Terry's presentation did the trick, made colleagues realise just how much historical evidence was on the side of monetarism and how little alternative there was to our policies.'[35] But, to the more hierarchically minded members of the Cabinet and the mandarinate, there was something irritating about being made to sit down and take instruction from a man still in his thirties. Wass recalled that Burns gave 'a child's guide to the economy . . . I don't know what good it did.'[36] Robert Armstrong began his record of the day in his Cabinet notebook with the mocking headline: 'Burns – his lecture'. Burns remembered the discussion after his talk as 'quite a rough event'.[37]

In that discussion, political anxiety centred on the unemployment figures, and where they might end up. Prior, fearing 2.6 million unemployed in the course of 1982,* argued for more measures to help the young unemployed. Burns predicted (wrongly, as it turned out) that unemployment 'should do better than that'. Peter Walker warned that there would be 'no British industry to recover', and Nicholas Edwards,† the Welsh Secretary, who was by no means a paid-up Wet, worried that the downturn was more sustained than the MTFS allowed for and called for more flexibility over interest rates. This gave Howe his cue to tell the meeting that he would announce a 1 per cent cut in interest rates that day. There was so little reaction to the news that Mrs Thatcher said: 'Did everyone hear that?' Someone, probably Prior, said: 'It's a mistake. People will think it's just because of this meeting.'[38] Howe acknowledged the severity of the situation: 'Of course we are facing a dangerous spectacle. The alternatives don't make it any less dangerous . . . If we relax, it validates high pay and diminishes the return to competitiveness.' He said that it was not the government's policies which were doing 'fundamental damage to the industrial base', but 'unchanged attitudes'. He hoped these attitudes would change because of the shock that the policies were administering. Mrs Thatcher came in after him: 'One thing, and it's in our control: public spending. If we don't, interest rates [will go] back up.'[39]

---

* The figure hit two million at the end of August 1980, and reached Prior's prediction for 1982 in June 1981. It hit three million in January 1982.

† Nicholas Edwards (1934–), educated Westminster and Trinity College, Cambridge; Conservative MP for Pembrokeshire, 1970–87; Opposition spokesman on Welsh affairs, 1975–9; Secretary of State for Wales, 1979–87; created Lord Crickhowell, 1987.

For Mrs Thatcher and her supporters, the teach-in set the scene for a sterner meeting about public spending the following week. On 10 July, Howe waved in front of colleagues the *Financial Times* report that 40 per cent of the year's PSBR had already been used up in three months. Against that background, John Biffen, the Chief Secretary, announced that he wished to maintain the spending total, but with a larger contingency reserve within it to deal with the spending overruns of nationalized industries such as coal, steel and rail. This meant further cuts in spending departments. Jim Prior reacted angrily. 'Is this right in a recession?' he asked. 'Nationalised industries can't meet their targets in a recession. If we make cuts to compensate, we deepen recession.' 'An increase in PSBR', he added heretically, 'will not necessarily put up [interest] rates.' Michael Heseltine attacked from a rather different direction, hankering, as always, for a more coherent strategy for industry. 'I can't go on hacking my department to ribbons to finance consumption elsewhere,' he complained. This provoked Mrs Thatcher to the sort of bluntness which did not endear her to colleagues: 'We never get the reductions in consumption ... People, including you, won't make the cuts.' She said that there was, in fact, 'lots of money for investment. The reason why it does not happen is attitudes of those who use it.' Tiring of the discussion, she snapped: 'We must have decisions on [spending] totals this morning. Or no credibility,' and referred to the *Financial Times* story about the PSBR. Prior snapped back, in Armstrong's rendering: 'Fed up with having Cabinets set up by the press.'[40] Prior, however, was not above some hostile briefing of his own. Just five days later he vented his frustration with Mrs Thatcher – unattributably, of course – to Hugo Young of the *Sunday Times*. 'She hasn't really got a friend left in the whole Cabinet,' Prior said, rather unfairly. 'One reason she has no friend is that she subjects everyone to the most emotionally exhausting arguments; the other is that she still interrupts everyone all the time. It makes us all absolutely furious.'[41] This ill-tempered meeting was the last full discussion of economics and public spending before the House rose for the summer recess. At Chequers in early August, Mrs Thatcher gathered an end-of-term dinner for close advisers, including Hoskyns, Douglas Hague and Norman Strauss. 'It was', said Terry Burns, who attended, 'a very curious event ... There was a sense of her against the world' – the pre-dinner discussion was very 'gossipy', with Mrs Thatcher 'extraordinarily frank' in her criticism of Jim Prior. Burns remembered being 'quite shocked'.[42]

As a parting shot before she went on holiday in August, Mrs Thatcher deployed a phrase for which, in another context, she would become famous. Would she relax the squeeze, asked her interviewer Hugo Young in the *Sunday Times*? 'No, no, no!' she cried. And she went on: 'Deep in their instincts ... they [the British people] find what I am saying and doing right ... if I give up, we will lose.'[43] In a comparison which risked vainglory, she told an American interviewer: 'If we had ever looked at Dunkirk as a kind of balance sheet, as sometimes I am asked to look economically at this country, well I don't think we would have gone on at that time. If you looked at it as a matter of the spirit of the people then it is totally different.'[44] Her belief that she naturally intuited 'the spirit of the people' was taken by some as a sign almost of insanity, but it sustained her when mere statistics, headlines and opinion polls offered gloom.

One who wanted her to give up her policies was the first Prime Minister under whom she had served, Harold Macmillan. At her invitation, he had visited her at Chequers early in August, and he followed up their conversations there with a memorandum. Because of the world oil situation, he told her, 'All the circumstances ... would demand ... not restriction and deflation, but powerful reflationary measures.' He went on: 'The so-called "money supply" policy may be useful as a guide to what is happening just as a speedometer is in a car; but like the speedometer it cannot make the machine go faster or slower.'* Macmillan's remedy, if a wages policy were ruled out, was a productivity drive, possibly through an 'industrial parliament' of the sort for which, he said, Churchill had once argued. If everyone discussed productivity, he said, 'we may hope to obtain a return to "consensus" politics, sneered at by some, but the essence of Tory democracy. Devisive [sic] politics in a democratic system are not likely to be applied for sufficient length of time to become effective even if such methods were desirable.'[45] Although courteous in tone, Macmillan's memo said, in essence, that Mrs Thatcher was completely wrong. It also contained the implication, which was keeping the Wets going through what they saw as the dark night of Thatcherism, that her policies were bound to fail. There is no record that she replied to it.

Mrs Thatcher always disliked holidays. She found their break with what she called 'rhythm' unsettling, and she did not know what to do with them. Once, when she was Education Secretary, she and Denis went on holiday to Corsica for ten days. After four days, her secretary Alison Ward was surprised to receive a telephone call from her: 'Hello, dear. We're at Heathrow.'

---

* Macmillan liked comparisons between Mrs Thatcher and driving. Once a visitor to his country house, Birch Grove, said, 'I've got a new kind of car. It says things to me like "Now fasten your seatbelt" in a Japanese voice.' 'Ah yes,' said Macmillan, 'a Mrs Thatcher type of car.' (Correspondence with Professor David Dilks.)

'Oh,' said Alison, 'has something dreadful happened?' 'Oh no, dear. We've done Corsica.'[46] In her first summer as Prime Minister, Mrs Thatcher had joined the Morrison clan for her second stay with them on the Hebridean island of Islay. Ted Heath had also stayed there as party leader and had even shot a stag. Mrs Thatcher was a more popular guest than Heath, joining in activities with gusto, but it was 'not easy to get her into a pair of walking shoes' and she went for her first walk in patent leather.[47] In the summer of 1980, she went to stay, as she had done in 1978 and was to do on several subsequent occasions, with Sir Douglas and Lady Glover at Schloss Freudenberg in the Zug canton of Switzerland. Douglas Glover had been a long-standing backbench Conservative MP, and was now retired. His wife, Eleanor, was the rich and clever widow of a Swiss industrialist. Lady Glover was an active-minded woman who liked to advise Mrs Thatcher on how to look her best and tried to bring interesting people to meet her. She provided her with a lady's maid and a hairdresser and, for five days in August, would scour Switzerland and neighbouring countries for people of sufficient brainpower and eminence to come to the daily lunches and dinners given for the Thatchers. According to Lord Gowrie, who was sometimes a fellow guest with the Thatchers, these meals could be 'slightly nightmaric'.[48] Otherwise, there was not much to do at Schloss Freudenberg except admire the magnificent views and walk, which Mrs Thatcher always did in a skirt, up the nearest little mountain.[49] On one of these occasions in 1980, Mrs Thatcher met Karl Brunner, the Swiss-born, American-based monetarist economist (Yehudi Menuhin added artistic tone to the luncheon), and, on another, Fritz Leutwiler, the President of the Swiss National Bank. They told her, as Friedman was arguing, that her government's reliance on sterling M3 was undermining its attempt to conquer inflation and suggested that the Bank of England was mishandling the management of the money supply.

Mrs Thatcher came steaming back from the Alps to London, even less relaxed than she had been when she left. She was furious at what she had heard. Wishing to arraign the Bank of England, she called for the Governor and his deputy, only to find that both were on holiday. This did not improve her temper. Instead she had to make do with two more junior officials, one of whom was Eddie George, who was subsequently to become the Governor of the Bank.* When Gordon Richardson finally returned from his break, he was summoned too, and carpeted. The Prime Minister was in an ill temper with the Bank, regarding Richardson as being vain and indecisive, and

---

* Eddie George (1938–2009), educated Dulwich College and Emmanuel College, Cambridge; Deputy Governor of the Bank of England, 1990–93; Governor, 1993–2003; knighted, 2000; created Lord George, 2004.

saying of his deputy, Kit McMahon, 'He'll never be Governor of the Bank of England while I'm Prime Minister.'[50]*

Mrs Thatcher became ever more convinced of the need to move away from targeting the broad M3 monetary aggregate in favour of some form of monetary base control. Although officially both the Bank of England and the Treasury opposed this move, she found a sympathizer within the Treasury machine. On 2 September 1980, Michael Pattison, her private secretary, sent her a document with a covering note which said: 'Here is an anonymous (i.e. Peter Middleton) agenda for tomorrow's meeting on monetary policy. Peter Middleton would be most grateful if you could avoid waving this piece of paper around. He has not admitted to the Chancellor or Treasury colleagues that he has produced it.'[51] Middleton's covert role as Thatcher spy was itself a symptom of the uneasiness between the Treasury and No. 10. None of the most senior Treasury officials – Douglas Wass, Anthony Rawlinson, Bill Ryrie and Kenneth Couzens – really believed in Mrs Thatcher's approach. Middleton, more junior, but in charge of the detail of monetary policy, was the main defender of the monetarist approach within the Treasury as well as a skilled and ambitious operator. The Middleton document asked whether it was time to try monetary base control. Terry Burns, who attended the meetings with Mrs Thatcher and Geoffrey Howe which followed, remembered being treated to 'a bit of a rant',[52] with Mrs Thatcher, as was her wont when on the warpath, 'making the same few points over and over again'. Banks were being allowed to lend as freely as they liked, she complained, with disastrous consequences for interest rates. She sought other methods of control: 'She had in her head what she had learnt in an early phase of life about reserve asset ratios'[53] and did not fully recognize that the internationalization to which her own measures had contributed so much meant that money could no longer be physically controlled in the way that had once been the case. Nevertheless, she was not trying to repudiate Geoffrey Howe – 'They were still together in the same, small tent'[54] – but to find better ways of controlling spending, public borrowing and inflation within the agreed framework.

From across the Atlantic, Professor Alan Walters, with whom Mrs Thatcher had stayed in touch since their conversations in opposition, also favoured monetary base control. In September, she persuaded him to come to Downing Street from 1 January 1981 as her economic adviser. But, speaking to John Hoskyns on the telephone having read his various papers on the current situation, Walters told him: 'These things still haven't been done? I keep wondering whether it's already too late.'[55]

---

* She was as good as her word: McMahon never was Governor.

Perhaps it would have been too late if Mrs Thatcher had lost the support of her backbenchers or of the party in the country, but this had not happened. Ian Gow's assiduity with Conservative MPs reaped rewards, and there were, proportionally, far more rebels in the Cabinet than on the back benches.* It was obviously vital, however, for Mrs Thatcher to work to retain the support of the party grass-roots, and so she prepared for the party's annual conference at Brighton in the second week of October 1980 with even greater care than usual.

The strain of composing her most important party conference speech yet put Mrs Thatcher into a frenzy. John Hoskyns, who deeply resented what he called 'the waste of time on this bloody speech',[56] was, with Ronnie Millar, the main draftsman. His diary describes Mrs Thatcher as being 'obviously in a panic' on 6 October, having herself written what Hoskyns called 'some dross on economics' for the speech, as having 'a shouting match at dinner' with Millar on 7 October, and as needing a draft or she 'would never sleep a wink' on 8 October.[57] On Thursday 9 October, the day before the speech was to be delivered, she calmed down a little:

> Ian [Gow] and Clive [Whitmore] beginning to handle Margaret more firmly, Denis showing a more robust impatience – 'Honestly, love, we're not trying to write the Old Testament.' Clive and Tim [Lankester] frequently convulsed with concealed giggles . . . We had a laugh about something while Margaret was still in the bedroom, changing. Sure enough, Clive told us this went down badly and she said to Caroline [Stephens], 'Make sure they keep their noses to the grindstone.'[58]

When she spoke the following day, Mrs Thatcher took advantage of what had happened at the Labour conference in Blackpool the week before, where the left, led by Tony Benn, had showed itself stronger than ever, convulsing the party with a row about how to elect the next leader and carrying a motion in favour of unilateral nuclear disarmament. At home, she said, there were practices like the intimidation of those wanting to work which offended against 'the deepest instincts of our people'. Abroad, in the aftermath of the Soviet invasion of Afghanistan at Christmas 1979, there were 'darkening horizons'. Unemployment was a 'human tragedy', but

* At the meeting of the backbench Conservative Finance Committee on 11 November, seven of the eighteen speakers pooh-poohed the idea that unemployment was as serious as the figures suggested, whereas only two explicitly took the opposite view. Alan Clark went so far as to say that 'the level of unemployment was what was holding the Party activists steadfastly together in many constituencies. For better or for worse it was seen as giving the Trade Unions their deserts.' (Minutes of Finance Committee, 11 Nov. 1980, noted by Peter Cropper, THCR 2/6/2/48.)

it could never be successfully addressed until the fight against inflation had been won. Then she addressed the unspoken fear – or, depending on point of view, hope – that the government would change course, as it had done under Ted Heath: 'To those waiting with bated breath for that favourite media catchphrase, the "U" turn, I have only one thing to say, "You turn if you want to. The lady's not for turning."'[59] The phrase, which stuck, was a characteristic Ronnie Millar word-play, adapting the title of the by then unfashionable play *The Lady's Not for Burning* by Christopher Fry. In the view of Hoskyns, as he listened, it did the trick: 'The punchline worked perfectly and she delivered it just right ... Prolonged laughter and applause.'[60]

Mrs Thatcher closed by pointing up the political division in the country: 'Let Labour's Orwellian nightmare of the left be the spur for us to dedicate with a new urgency our every ounce of energy and moral strength to rebuild the fortunes of this free nation.'[61] She won a six-minute, heartfelt standing ovation from the hall and extreme hostility from left-wing demonstrators outside. Five days later, Jim Callaghan resigned as Labour leader. On 10 November, he was replaced by Michael Foot, the most left-wing of the candidates, rather than the original favourite, Denis Healey. It was as if the Labour Party was determined to realize Mrs Thatcher's binary, divided picture of British politics. Its choice of Foot benefited her enormously. The leaders of Labour's social democratic right – Shirley Williams, David Owen and Bill Rodgers – had, in the summer, begun to look for a future outside the Labour Party, and to enlist Roy Jenkins, across the water in Brussels. Now there could be little doubt that Labour would split.

Within the government, though, the pounding got ever harder. In October 1980, the latest figures for earnings that month showed that central government pay had risen by 34.5 per cent in a year, as opposed to 20.5 per cent for the private sector. Jim Prior wanted these figures to be played down, by putting them in what he called a 'proper perspective', but John Hoskyns minuted Mrs Thatcher with the opposite suggestion: 'Better to say that we've all behaved like greedy idiots and are now paying the price.'[62] Mrs Thatcher picked up this point, scribbling to Tim Lankester, 'You cannot talk down the figures ... So use their message – no Government has given the public sector a better deal than this one. This cannot continue unless and until the private sector recovers its trade.'[63]

At a meeting on 12 November, preparing for the Chancellor's Autumn Statement, Howe and Mrs Thatcher agreed to cut interest rates by 2 per cent to 14 per cent, and contemplated gloomy facts and gloomy prospects: 'The Prime Minister said the most disappointing feature of the current PESC [Public Expenditure Survey Committee] review was the deteriorating financial position of the nationalised industries. They had undermined the Government's whole public expenditure strategy.'[64] Howe commented that 'the Government's experience with the nationalised industries over the last 18 months reinforced the arguments for denationalisation.'[65] Nothing, for the present, came of this point, since the government still felt too financially beleaguered and politically weak to launch large nationalized industries upon an uncertain market. What was becoming clear was that, to maintain course, the government might have to get tougher still. As the official note put it, 'questions would be raised as to whether the Government was doing enough to get the fiscal balance right, and this might mean that the next budget would have to be even more restrictive.'[66]

The Cabinet was not agreeable to further stringency. The Wets still believed that, ultimately, Mrs Thatcher would be forced to reverse course: 'she is mad to cut off so many possibilities,' Francis Pym told Hugo Young in confidence. 'Why the hell does she keep on saying that she's not for turning, etc. etc.?'[67] In her memoirs, Mrs Thatcher says that the Cabinet agreed in principle to further cuts in public spending for 1981–2, on 30 October 1980, when Howe told the assembled company that the expected PSBR of £11.75 billion was intolerable and that 'If we are to have a chance of success, we have to face questions from which most Cabinets have run away.'[68] Rebellious and, in her view, cowardly ministers chose instead to fight about most of the specifics. It is true that the Wets preferred not to confront Mrs Thatcher and her ideas directly, Prior being the only exception. As Hoskyns remembered, with exasperated affection, 'Jim was the only person with the guts. God, he was a stupid man.'[69] But in fact the 'agreement' reached on 30 October, though formally recorded, was not really given. Sir Robert Armstrong's Cabinet notebook shows several ministers, notably Prior, Walker, Pym and Soames, jibbing at agreement, proposed by Willie Whitelaw, to a 2 per cent cut across the board. 'I don't think we are agreeing the same thing,' protested Prior.[70] The Wets felt supported by the leadership of the CBI, meeting for their annual conference. On 11 November, the conference backed Prior's 'softly, softly' approach to union reform, and the CBI's director-general, Sir Terence Beckett, promised a 'bare-knuckle fight' with the government over interest rates. Michael Edwardes, the chairman of British Leyland, told the conference that since North Sea oil was having such a punitive effect on the exchange rate it would really be better to 'leave the bloody stuff in the ground'.

On 13 November 1980, Howe told colleagues in Cabinet that they should save money by breaking the indexing of benefits to inflation. Prior warned of social unrest and said, 'If we believe in One Nation, we can't do it.'[71] Even the loyal Willie Whitelaw said, 'We should be putting a noose round the neck of the Conservative Party for a long time.'[72] Benefit de-indexation was rejected, but the Cabinet agreed to increase employees' National Insurance contributions by 1 per cent. Some of these arguments leaked, and newspapers began to run articles about division and loss of confidence. Peter Jenkins, in the *Guardian*, wrote of the 'dawning of dis-belief' in Thatcherism and also claimed that Mrs Thatcher had lost confidence in her Chancellor.[73] As Howe ruefully admitted in his memoirs, his Autumn Statement had turned 'despite all our protestations to the con-trary' into one of the mini-Budgets which, in the era of Denis Healey, the Tories had excoriated.[74] The statement was a poor piece of presentation, and this was made worse by the fact that Howe omitted to mention the automatic increases in National Insurance payments caused by the rise of wage levels. There was general outrage – about direction, about handling, about honesty. The Treasury Select Committee, chaired by the fair-weather friend Edward Du Cann, duly attacked the Chancellor's approach. The government had reached a low point. In her memoirs, Mrs Thatcher recalled that 'By the end of 1980, I began to feel that we risked forfeiting the public's confidence in our economic strategy.'[75] Just before Christmas, Bill Deedes, the editor of the *Daily Telegraph*, noted a conversation with Brian Griffiths, who had just been to see Mrs Thatcher at No. 10. Griffiths was:

> met by G Howe who hustled into adjoining room – begged BG not to be too critical – 'She's in a very odd mood . . .' Hour with PM. Twice, says BG, near to tears. What had gone wrong? Speechless on the Governor of the Bank of England . . . BG much depressed by the experience. Clearly feels that Chancellor has lost grip. (Remind him how far PM & C o E are tied together. Shades of Macmillan/Selwyn Lloyd in 1962.) [Griffiths] left unclear as to purpose of summons, save that we agree January 1981 may prove decisive . . .[76]

Mrs Thatcher was very badly rattled, and doubtful of her lieutenants.

It was Geoffrey Howe, though, who gave the fairest assessment of the situation. At the turn of the year, he wrote to Mrs Thatcher to comment on the latest caustic and pessimistic strategy paper from John Hoskyns. 'You will be disconcerted, as I was,' he told the Prime Minister, 'to find the transatlantic commentators referring to "Thatcherisation" as a condition to be avoided, if possible!', but he went on to say, with a touch of flattery, that there was an underlying strength in the government's position: 'the Thatcher factor. People <u>do</u> have a sense that this Government – more par-ticularly you . . . is possessed of a tenacity, which might just work, if only its [sic] sustained.' 'More than a few people think we're quite mad!' he continued. 'Yet <u>very</u> few are able ... to proffer ... a coherent alternative solution.'[77] Bernard Ingham minuted the Prime Minister with the prediction from the latest edition of the venerable soothsaying publication *Old Moore's Almanack*: 'There are rare moments in history,' it said, 'when one man or woman can, almost alone, shape the future of the nation. Now is such a moment. Margaret Thatcher is such a woman. The compelling pattern of her fate is so intimately interwoven with the present destiny of the UK that it is impossible to imagine that she will pass from power before her mission to heal and reinvigorate Britain is complete.'[78] Howe, Ingham and Old Moore were on to something. 'Thatcherism' was never a philosophy, but a disposition of mind and character embodied in a highly unusual woman.

Brooding over Christmas, Mrs Thatcher planned a reshuffle. Given her irritation with several in her Cabinet, the smallness of the changes shows that she did not feel in a strong position. No one seemed to have noticed a wide-ranging and remarkably frank interview that she had given to the American magazine *People Weekly* at the end of July. There she was asked what she thought of being called the 'Leaderene', a satirical coinage of the Leader of the House, Norman St John-Stevas. She replied ominously that the author was usually a witty person and should have shown 'a bit more style'.[79] St John-Stevas was the notable casualty of her reshuffle, which was announced on 5 January 1981. Francis Pym, whose stout and largely successful resistance to defence cuts had annoyed her, was moved to replace Stevas. He was also put in charge of policy presentation, an extraordinary choice given his own scepticism about the direction of policy and his melancholy, nervous disposition. John Nott replaced him at Defence. John Biffen, who had not been strong enough in the spending negotiations, replaced Nott at Trade, and was in turn replaced by Leon Brittan, a close friend and ally of Geoffrey Howe. Mrs Thatcher had shifted the centre of gravity only very slightly in her favour.

Bernard Ingham, her press secretary, wrote a blunt note to the newly installed Pym, copied to the Prime Minister. The government, he said, 'is prone to operate on the basis of that well-known hymn: you in your small corner and I in mine ... The Government is divided and seen to be divided; nothing has done more damage than the 1981–82 public expenditure review. This was taken as a licence to hold the Cabinet in public ... It is to be hoped that the reshuffle marks the point of departure.' The government was also getting the worst of both worlds, said Ingham: 'it is criticised at once for unfeeling monetarism, while at the same time money supply, on one definition at least, is soaring along with the PSBR.'[80]

*

In their attempt to bring the nationalized industries under proper financial control, Mrs Thatcher and Geoffrey Howe did not intend to spare the coal industry. As soon as she had come into office in May 1979, Mrs Thatcher had demanded action to prepare for battle with the National Union of Mineworkers. She summoned Willie Whitelaw and Sir Robert Wade-Gery, the Deputy Secretary to the Cabinet, and announced: 'The last Conservative Government was destroyed by the miners' strike. We'll have another one, and we'll win. And you, Willie, will do it.'[81] Whitelaw chaired the Civil Contingencies Unit, which tried to draw up the strategic principles and practical measures. It realized, for example, that if there was to be a strike it should begin in the spring and it should be over pit closures, which tended to divide miners, rather than over pay, which tended to unite them. It also sought to persuade the Treasury of the need for the 'dual firing' of power stations by oil and coal, and above all to plan the accumulation of coal stocks, not only at pitheads but at power stations. The immediate problem the unit encountered, however, was to get any department to listen. As Wade-Gery remembered it, people said, 'The woman's mad. You can't win miners' strikes. All you can do is buy them off.'[82] Besides, there was as yet no co-ordination in government between civil contingencies – the thinking that had emerged in reaction to the General Strike of 1926, which was essentially a military task – and the management of tactics about pay and closures.

There was a further problem. While it might make political sense to pile up the coal, it made no immediate financial sense. From the first, the Treasury sought to run down coal production and cut where it could in order to help bring the industry's atrocious overspending under control. The lack of overall strategy meant that this conflict was not, for a long time, resolved. The Treasury itself recognized this. In April 1980, Howe's private secretary wrote to Clive Whitmore about the need to co-ordinate policy, giving as his example 'the cost to electricity including of coal stocks versus the risk of a miners' strike. We tried to raise this whole question with the Prime Minister in the context of the miners' pay award last autumn, but it was not at the time sufficiently near the top of everybody's list.'[83]

Forty per cent of the energy requirements of nationalized industries, including two-thirds of electricity production, were met by coal. And international pressure to keep down the consumption of oil encouraged – in the absence of more nuclear power stations – greater dependence on coal in the future. Although high wage increases (setting a bad example to other nationalized industry workers) had restrained industrial militancy among the miners, the National Coal Board was being told by the government to meet its severe financial targets. In June, a briefing to E Committee from the relevant officials predicted that, by the turn of the year, stocks of five to six weeks would have been built up. They added, though, that the 'survival period depends on the extent of picketing outside the industry itself and, if there is secondary picketing, the extent of stockholdings that are vulnerable to picketing'.[84] The state of the law on the subject did not inspire confidence. As for contingencies, 'No plan involving servicemen is now considered practicable.'[85]

In September 1980 the Energy Secretary, David Howell, presented his Strategy for Coal to E Committee. He saw a growth of coal production 'as supplies of other fossil fuels decline', but believed this could come from low-cost pits and that many existing, high-cost pits should be closed. He warned that 'There could be an explosion over closures,' and recommended that the coming winter pay claim be got out of the way before closure plans were presented to the miners.[86] On her copy of the document, Mrs Thatcher wrote: 'Thin – what I don't find in these papers is any attempt to cut the costs of production. That is what private industry would have to do.' She did not, at this point, indicate any anxiety about industrial unrest. Closure plans pressed ahead.

In November, the miners' annual pay claim was settled. In his daily press digest, Bernard Ingham reported to the Prime Minister thus: 'Miners settle for 9.8 per cent . . . for 10 months. Generally portrayed as 13 per cent but as a triumph for government policy . . .'[87] The details of pit closure plans continued to be developed in secret, although the news of a coming, comprehensive closure plan attracted press criticism ('The Great Pit Blunder', said the *Daily Mail* of 17 January) for making it easy for the union to co-ordinate resistance. On 29 January, three days after Keith Joseph had announced his rescue package of £990 million for British Leyland, in a meeting with Sir Derek Ezra, the chairman of the Coal Board, Mrs Thatcher backed the closure plans on the grounds that there was 'no alternative'.[88] Twenty-three pits were to be closed, though rumour quickly raised this number to fifty. At its meeting with the National Union of Mineworkers on 11 February, the NCB still refused to give the precise list of proposed closures, and did not mention the improved redundancy terms which it would offer. It also tried to join the union in pressing the government for more subsidy and more protection from coal imports. The famed 'triple alliance' between railwaymen, steelworkers and miners appeared to be in place. Suddenly, a national strike against closures seemed possible.

At this point, because of his background in the Department of Energy, Bernard Ingham stepped briefly outside his normal tasks and sent Mrs Thatcher a note. He counselled that the NCB was doing too much, too quickly, and that Joe Gormley, the moderate miners' leader, would be forced to act toughly 'to protect his flank against Scargill'. The public would like the idea of 'defending one's livelihood', he thought, and would therefore be sympathetic to the miners, and he said that 'behind the scenes we need a much more extensive and vigorous examination of the situation than is implied by an E Committee discussion of coal industry redundancy terms.'[89] On 16 and 18 February, Mrs Thatcher had meetings with David Howell at which it became clear that the government was not ready for a strike, and that coal stocks could not withstand one. As Howell remembered the first meeting, Mrs Thatcher held up a copy of the *Evening Standard* which Bernard Ingham brought in with the words 'That's that, then, isn't it.' The headline proclaimed, 'Government dithers.' Mrs Thatcher said, 'Bring it to an end, David. Make the necessary concessions.'[90] Without Cabinet discussion, she decided to give in. In Howell's view, though he resented her anger with him for his handling of the matter and for bringing on the crisis 'out of the blue', 'she *was* right to cut and run' because 'we just weren't ready.'[91]

After the government's complete capitulation on 18 February, Ingham minuted Mrs Thatcher on the reaction of the lobby to his briefing. The press, he reported, tried to establish first 'a massive U-turn', second whether Howell had been authorized to give in without knowing the cost (he had, in effect), third that there would be 'profound consequences for the Government's economic strategy and pay negotiations' and fourth that there would be 'an entirely different approach to nationalised industries with flexibility the order of the day'. As Ingham described it, his reply had been that 'no Government ever gets from A to B in a straight line'.[92] With grim relish, Ingham's press digest that day departed from its usual practice and quoted virtually every headline about the U-turn – '"Surrender to King Coal". *Express*. "You've won, lads". *D. Star*' and so on. And he informed his boss of the *Sun*'s judgment: 'for the first time since you came to power your credibility at stake.'[93] At a further meeting with Howell on 19 February, Mrs Thatcher expressed her lack of confidence in Derek Ezra, and said frankly that the government's policy was 'to go along, to a large extent, with whatever Mr Gormley proposed in order to ensure that the militants did not regain the ascendancy'.[94] The government lost £400–500 million by its concessions, and contributed to the myth that the miners were invincible. It seemed to be following the pattern of the Heath government, which gave in to the miners in 1972. By the same logic, people believed, the next confrontation would result in the fall of the Tory government (as in February 1974). Even the loyal *Daily Telegraph* said that the recent reverses in the handling of the nationalized industries, 'taken together, have been a disaster'.[95]

It was a timely distraction from the government's woes that on 24 February 1981 the engagement was announced between the Prince of Wales and Lady Diana Spencer.

The next day, Mrs Thatcher flew to the United States as the guest of the new President, Ronald Reagan. Her previous meetings with Reagan, in 1975 and 1978, provided a firm foundation on which to build a close relationship now that he had been elected. During his election campaign, he had even arranged for his aides Bill Casey* and Richard Allen to visit Mrs Thatcher secretly and brief her on his election strategy and foreign policy stance. 'It was almost exclusively East–West and NATO-orientated,' Allen recalled of the meeting, held in July 1980, adding, 'I think she was quite enthused.'[96]† Allen was right. The day after his inauguration, on 20 January 1981, President Reagan took a call from Mrs Thatcher. She told him that she was 'thrilled' by his inauguration speech, and by the release of the American hostages, timed by Iran to deliver maximum humiliation to poor Jimmy Carter. She went on, 'The newspapers are saying mostly that President Reagan must avoid Mrs Thatcher's mistakes [about economic policy] so I must brief you on the mistakes.' Reagan replied genially, 'I don't think I have to worry about that,' and commiserated with her on the 'uphill battle' she was fighting in her own country:

MRS THATCHER: Well you know it makes it worth it because you are fighting for the things we are fighting for . . .
REAGAN: We'll lend strength to each other.
MRS THATCHER: We will.[97]

A few days later, Hugh Thomas had reported to Mrs Thatcher on a private conversation with Edward Luttwak,‡ then consulting for the new administration. Luttwak summed up the President neatly: he 'knows much less than he seems to' but 'is personally and socially secure', and is '<u>genuinely</u>

---

* William J. Casey (1913–87), served in Office of Strategic Services (OSS) during the Second World War; chairman, Securities and Exchange Commission, 1971–3; campaign manager, Ronald Reagan's presidential campaign, 1980; Director, CIA, 1981–87.
† Via Hugh Thomas, Allen supplied her with lists of all Reagan's policy groups and who his advisers were. Michael Alexander asked her if these could be sent on to the Foreign Office. 'No,' Mrs Thatcher replied sharply, '– they will go round the F.O. Keep the names here. <u>Strictly private</u> means what it says.' (Thomas to Alexander, 9 June 1980, Prime Minister's Papers, USA: Call on the PM by Mr Richard Allen and Mr Casey; document consulted in the Cabinet Office.)
‡ Edward Luttwak (1942–), principal, Edward N. Luttwak Inc. International Consultants, from 1981; consultant to Policy Planning Council, State Department, 1981; National Security Council, 1987; Department of Defense, 1987.

morally brave'. Mrs Thatcher underlined these last words. Luttwak thought that Britain and America could now have 'a period of very close friendship if this opportunity were to be seized properly'.[98] Mrs Thatcher was determined to seize it.

Months earlier, in July 1980, Reagan's aides had been talking secretly to British officials about an early meeting with Mrs Thatcher, should Reagan be elected president.[99] Contingency planning had been under way well in advance of the election. Mrs Thatcher thus easily fought off an attempt by Helmut Schmidt to become the first to meet Reagan after his inauguration. As she told the Pilgrims' Dinner at the end of January, 'next month I shall be visiting the United States at the invitation of President Reagan and as the first European Head of Government to visit him. Perhaps, though it's for others to say, that too is not altogether a coincidence. I believe that that visit will underline the closeness of the friendship between our two countries but it will also, I am certain, mark the opening of a period of particularly close understanding between the two Heads of Government.'[100] Three days later, Reagan cabled to thank her, 'You are indeed right that we share a very special concern for democracy and for liberty,'[101] and he instructed his aides to 'make the visit special'.[102] The aim, as Secretary of State Al Haig put it, was to 'Demonstrate publicly and privately that Thatcher is the major Western leader most attuned to your views on East–West and security issues. The Prime Minister wants, above all, to build upon her relationship with you and to have her visit perceived as a very strong reaffirmation of the "Special Relationship".'[103] The challenge, in the words of the National Security Advisor Richard Allen, would be to 'dramatize' the 'meeting of minds' between the two leaders.[104] But in reality the situation was more difficult for Mrs Thatcher than these warm words made it sound. Many Americans, even among those who supported Reagan, were coming to the view that Thatcherism was going wrong and had begun to distance themselves from the British approach. Earlier in January, Charles Anson, press officer at No. 10, had written to Mrs Thatcher's private office noting that 'There has been a good deal of editorial writing lately in American papers about "the failure of the Thatcher economic experiment" and advising Ronald Reagan not to follow down the same road.'[105] The Treasury duly briefed her on these views.

Critics came from different camps. Supply-siders, who believed that tax cuts would bring automatic benefits, disliked Mrs Thatcher's failure to cut the overall burden of taxes. They preferred what the economist Herbert Stein called 'the economics of joy'.[106] With her greater insistence on prudence and her anxiety about the size of the government deficit, Mrs

Thatcher stood, at this time, for the economics of misery. 'I'm not sure she was as committed as Ronald Reagan was to the idea that if you get taxes low enough you are going to generate increased tax revenues by virtue of increased economic growth,' recalled James Baker,* then Reagan's Chief of Staff.[107] As she herself wrote, 'We feared that the new administration's plans for tax cuts might widen the deficit – though at this stage we were still hopeful that the President would succeed in achieving the large expenditure cuts he had put before Congress.'[108] Bernard Ingham remembered a fundamental difference with Reagan about economic matters, almost one of temperament:

> I think she probably felt that Reagan was never more wayward than over economic management. She used to worry intensely about the huge propensity for spending and refusal to tax. She felt this was altogether too lax. She said that he believed that it would all come right in the end. That was the sunny disposition, the optimistic outlook on life to which she was not entitled, being a British politician who'd seen 35 years of post-war mismanagement. She was constantly worried about the budget deficit.[109]

But even those sympathetic to monetarism were highly critical. Paul Volcker, who was chairman of the Federal Reserve Board at the time, recalled: 'My impression of the UK was that nothing was working very well';[110] his own development of monetary policy owed little to the British example. In advance of Mrs Thatcher's visit, Reagan's Treasury Secretary, Don Regan,† requested a last-minute paper from the arch-monetarist Beryl Sprinkel, then his under-secretary for monetary affairs, comparing and contrasting the Thatcher and Reagan plans. Sprinkel pointed out Mrs Thatcher's tax increases 'as a percent of national income', her failure to cut government spending and the apparent 'soaring' of the money supply, in the form of M3, by a government committed to its tight control.

Sprinkel went on, however, to report on a conversation with 'Messrs Allen [sic] Walters and Terry Burns' after which he was 'convinced that in fact the UK has been through a period of severe monetary restraint'. He concluded, 'I should add that Mrs Thatcher's government has the same overriding objectives that we have, namely reducing the public sector while

---

* James A. Baker III (1930–), White House Chief of Staff, 1981–5; US Secretary of the Treasury, 1985–8; US Secretary of State, 1989–92; White House Chief of Staff and senior counsellor, 1992–3.
† Donald Regan (1918–2003), chairman and CEO, Merrill Lynch, 1971–80; US Secretary of the Treasury, 1981–5; White House Chief of Staff, 1985–7.

increasing the private sector, cutting government spending, cutting taxes and reducing inflation by reducing monetary growth. So far results have been mixed but I am confident that the lady will not turn, and that if she can hang on politically somewhat longer as I believe is the probable case, she will make further progress.'[111]

The State Department's briefing for Mrs Thatcher's visit was more ambivalent still: 'so far she has failed to implement effectively her tactical policy goals of reducing the budget deficit, government consumption and the growth in the money supply, but it is too early to say whether or not she will eventually succeed.' A core objective for the visit, the briefing continued, would be to 'Exchange views with Thatcher on her experience, in part to learn from British mistakes.'[112]*

It was the new President himself who ignored all these difficulties. He liked Mrs Thatcher, and he knew that he and she were essentially on the same side. 'You know what I want to do in the United States is what Margaret Thatcher has started to do in the United Kingdom,' Reagan had told one of Mrs Thatcher's associates during his election campaign, 'to get the government off the backs of the people.'[113] He was not interested in second-order or technical disagreements. To the question, 'Where did the President stand in the debate over how to implement economic policy?' Paul Volcker answered, 'I think the President stood nowhere in all this. He had a few basic convictions. Fortunately one of these convictions was that inflation was a bad thing.'[114] This worked to Mrs Thatcher's advantage. Briefing Reagan in advance of his meeting with the Prime Minister on 26 February 1981, Richard Allen began with an exordium about the relationship between the two leaders which could read equally well as its epitaph:

> Your reunion with British Prime Minister Margaret Thatcher – whom Nico [sic] Henderson, her old-pro Ambassador here, calls a 'committed monetarist' – will dramatise something rare in the exchanges between US and West European leaders these past few years: a meeting of minds which encompasses not only philosophical affinities, similar economic outlooks, and a common allegiance to the idea of revitalized defense efforts, but also a tough, pragmatic determination to do something about them.

---

* When Helmut Schmidt visited Washington later that year he lectured Reagan on economic policy and the dangers of 'political destabilization'. 'You don't read much about stability in Thatcher's government,' the West German Chancellor asserted, 'but I can assure you that it is not all that stable.' Reagan made no comment. (Memorandum of Conversation: Reagan and Schmidt, 21 May 1981, Exec Sec, NSC: Subject File, MemCons, President Reagan (May 1981), Box 48, Reagan Library.)

In Allen's view,

> Mrs Thatcher's problems [he listed her economic and trade union woes]
> merely accentuate what I feel should be the major theme, both public and
> private, of your meeting with her. The image which could most usefully
> emerge from these talks is of two like-minded leaders who have taken the
> measure of the difficulties their nations confront, who underestimate none
> of the situation's gravity, but who are neither daunted by such problems nor
> doubtful of our ultimate success in dealing with them. Sleeves-rolled-up,
> sobriety-with-optimism is the main message you should be getting across
> with this visit; politically it can prove an especially effective chord both at
> home and abroad.[115]

The woman Prime Minister who flew into what *The Times* called a
'lavish, colourful ceremony of the kind not seen in the American capital
for the past four years'[116] had a packed schedule, but was also careful to
make the right impression.* Her office set aside forty minutes each day for
hairdressing (with rollers), and submitted her personal details in preparation for receiving an honorary degree at Georgetown University: 'Height
5′4″;† Weight 10.5 stone; Coat 14 English; Hat size 7'. In the White House,
Reagan welcomed her, declaring, 'we share laws and literature, blood, and
moral fibre',[117] and she responded, 'The message I have brought across the
Atlantic is that we, in Britain, stand with you. America's successes will be
our successes. Your problems will be our problems, and when you look
for friends we will be there.'[118] The private reception was equally warm,
which encouraged Mrs Thatcher to be frank. In his diary, Reagan recorded:
'We had a private meeting in Oval office. she [sic] is as firm as ever re the
Soviets and for reduction of govt. Expressed regret that she tried to reduce
govt. spending a step at a time & was defeated in each attempt. Said she
should have done it our way – an entire package – all or nothing.'[119]

But not everyone in the Reagan administration was willing to be as
supportive as the President. On the same day, Don Regan testified before
a Congressional committee. Mrs Thatcher, Regan said, had failed to control

---

* Mrs Thatcher's nervousness before the ceremony is indicated by the row she began at Blair
House, the official guest house where she and her party were staying. She fiercely attacked Lord
Carrington for what she called 'your policy in the Middle East', which she considered dangerous in its attempt at a rapprochement with the Palestine Liberation Organization, adding, 'I'll
lose my seat at Finchley.' By his own account, her Foreign Secretary said, 'And I'll lose my
temper,' and went out, slamming the door (interview with Lord Carrington). Clive Whitmore
hurriedly scribbled a note to Mrs Thatcher which said, 'This place is bugged.' She then drew a
circle in the air with her finger to indicate bugging. (Interview with Sir Clive Whitmore.)
† Mrs Thatcher sometimes gave her height as 5 foot 4 inches, and sometimes as 5 foot 5 inches.

the money supply, produced 'an explosive inflationary surge' by her pay increases to public employees and kept taxes too high, which 'provides little incentive to get the economy started again'. 'She failed', he added, 'in the effort to control the foreign exchange market and the pound is so high in value that it ruined their export trade.'[120] Here was a clear effort to distance the administration's policy from the perceived mistakes associated with Margaret Thatcher. Such perceptions were commonplace in US media reports throughout the visit.* Regan then left Capitol Hill to hurry over to the British Embassy for lunch with Mrs Thatcher.

She did not react unfavourably, but publicly praised President Reagan, giving a sanitized version of what she had told him privately: his attack on expenditure was 'the one thing which I could have wished that we had been even more successful at'.[121] Reagan recorded in his diary that Mrs Thatcher 'Went up to the hill [Capitol Hill] and was literally an advocate for our ec. program. Some of the Sen's. tried to give her a bad time. She put them down firmly & with typical British courtesy.'[122]

As far as issues of substance went, the visit was fairly thin. Mrs Thatcher was a little worried by the administration's obsession with Central America, when she felt more attention should be paid to the East–West relationship. She and Reagan did, however, discuss the Soviet President Leonid Brezhnev's speech of 23 February in which he had called for an international summit and a moratorium on Intermediate Nuclear Forces (INF) in Europe, and they agreed on a cautious response (see Chapter 20).

More important, for both sides, was the need for éclat, for the dramatization of the 'meeting of minds' of which Dick Allen had written. The state dinner for Mrs Thatcher at the White House gave Reagan's people the chance to show the difference their President made:

> The Reaganauts were determined to throw off the grungy, downtrodden look of the Carter Administration ... Some of the Carter people used to walk about the White House in bare feet. As soon as Reagan came in, out went the memos banning jeans, banning sandals and requiring everyone to wear a suit. 'Glamour' was a word often used, and 'class' too. The Reagan people thus planned the Thatcher dinner as a white tie affair. It was going to be infused with Hollywood glamour and would show the world how classy the Reagan people were.[123]

---

* 'A new verb has entered the Washington lexicon,' declared the *New York Times*. 'It is said to be possible to "Thatcherize" an economy. The verb is not precisely defined, but many see it as a bad thing to do. Since "Thatcherization" bears a conservative label, some people fear that our new conservative President will lead us down the same disagreeable path.' (*New York Times*, 1 Mar. 1981.)

Mrs Thatcher, however, asked the White House if the dinner could be black tie, since 'some of her people would not have the requisite clothing'. She had another concern too: 'she was the grocer's daughter. She didn't want to come over here dressed up like that. It was an impoverished time in Britain after all.'[124] Black tie was agreed, but the dinner was still grand enough in all conscience.

Then there was the return match. Taking advantage of the Reagan team's inexperience, Nicko Henderson had got Dick Allen to promise that the President would come to the customary reciprocal dinner at the British Embassy the following night. This was in violation of the existing convention that only the Vice-President attended these return dinners, but the Reagan team did not know this. By the time they had realized their mistake and tried to get out of it, Henderson had sent out the invitations.[125] Reagan came with a good grace.*

In her speech that night, Mrs Thatcher added her own passage to Henderson's draft, words about the 'two o'clock in the morning courage' which leaders have to have when faced with lonely decisions.[126] This greatly pleased Reagan, who replied that she herself had already shown such courage 'on too many occasions to name'.[127] 'Truly a warm & beautiful occasion,' Reagan wrote in his diary.[128] The only disappointment for Mrs Thatcher was that the Reagans left without dancing to the band. After they had departed, Henderson invited her on to the floor: 'Mrs T accepted my offer without complication or inhibition, and, once we were well launched on the floor, confessed to me that that was what she had been wanting to do all evening. She loved dancing, something, so I found out, she did extremely well.'[129] She was most reluctant to go to bed, threatening a different sort of 'two o'clock courage' by going off to see the floodlit Washington monuments, 'but Denis put his foot down, crying, "bed".'[130] On her last night in America, after a rapturous reception for a speech in New York, Mrs Thatcher gathered with Denis, Henderson and aides in her suite in the Waldorf before taking the plane home. 'Mrs T was still in a state of euphoria from the applause she had received which was indeed very loud and genuine and burst out: "You know we all ought to go dancing again" . . . Denis' foot came down heavily.'[131]

---

* Although Henderson's manoeuvring annoyed the sticklers for protocol, Allen and others realized that the President's attendance at this return dinner (and others) could have its advantages. This would be one way, suggested an NSC memo, to 'underscore the substantive importance' Reagan placed on US relations with key allies, and signal a break with the discord in the transatlantic alliance seen in the recent past. (Rentschler to Tyson, 'Thatcher Visit and Related Thoughts', 26 Jan. 1981, 5. Official Working Visit of Prime Minister Thatcher of United Kingdom 02/26/1981 (1 of 8), Box 4, Charles Tyson Files, Reagan Library.)

Both sides rejoiced at the visit. 'It was a great success,' Henderson remembered. 'They saw completely eye to eye.'[132] 'We needed a crowbar to pull them apart,' remarked Reagan's press secretary, Jim Brady.[133] 'I believe a real friendship exists between the P.M. her family & us,' Reagan commented.[134] The essence of this friendship was simple and effective. They believed the same things, and they both wanted to work actively to bring them about. 'I have full confidence in the President,' Mrs Thatcher scribbled at the bottom of a thank-you note to Henderson. 'I believe he will do things he wants to do – and he won't give up.'[135] They also had compatible, though utterly different, temperaments – he the relaxed, almost lazy generalist who charmed everyone with his easygoing ways, she the hyperactive, zealous, intensely knowledgeable leader, who injected energy into all her doings but also displayed what Reagan considered to be the elegance of a typical, gracious English lady. They shared a moral outlook on the world and also, in their emphasis on formality, dressing smartly and being what Americans call classy, a sort of aesthetic. The personal chemistry was undeniable. 'He treated her in a very courteous and sort of slightly flirtatious way, to which she responded,' recalled Robin Butler.[136] It turned out that they would often disagree about tactics, and that his more optimistic and her less sunny view of the possibilities of a non-nuclear future would lead to problems, but their basic personal trust and sense of common purpose never failed.

Yet, for all her enthusiasm and affection for the leader of the free world, Mrs Thatcher was not blind to his limitations. Lord Carrington recalled their meeting on the first day:

> After the arrival ceremony we went into the Oval Office and I remember Reagan saying: 'Well of course, the South Africans are whites and they fought for us during the war. The blacks are black and are Communists.' I think even Margaret thought this was rather a simplification . . . She came out and she turned to me and, pointing at her head, she said, 'Peter, there's nothing there.' That wasn't exactly true, because there was something there and she no doubt didn't really mean that.[137]

Mrs Thatcher came to realize that Reagan's strengths and mental abilities were very different from her own, but she never lost her underlying admiration for him. To the typed letter of thanks she sent him, she added, in her own hand: 'We shall never have a happier visit.'[138] She felt she had a powerful friend. She knew that he would help in the economic and political struggles ahead. Her pleasure and gratitude were genuine.

*

In November 1980, John Hoskyns had minuted Mrs Thatcher reminding her that she had herself spoken of the need for a 'shock package'. 'The UK economy', he wrote, 'is simply unmanageable until the underlying structure of trade union power, public spending, and public sector indexing commitments, and nationalised industry/union monopoly power, is changed. That is why Governments fall.' Her administration kept underestimating the scale of the problem, he went on, and therefore 'We have 18 months' leeway to make up and the 1981 Budget/PEWP [Public Expenditure White Paper] are our last chance to start doing so.'[139] Sending her a copy of Peter Jenkins's article about the 'dawning of disbelief' in Thatcherism, nine days later, Hoskyns pushed his argument about the 1981 Budget further: 'On the one side, we can start to move increasingly towards what is "politically possible" but simply inadequate for solving the problem. On the other, we will have to find ways of doing things which appear to be "politically impossible" but which are essential if we are to have the slightest chance of getting back onto our strategic course.'[140]

Events in the ensuing months appeared to drive the government ever further from that strategic course. The capitulations to the miners, to BL and to other nationalized industries, the rows about how to measure the money supply, the growing mutterings from the Wets, the damp squib of Prior's January green paper on trade union immunities, which seemed to offer no solutions, and of course the continuing rise both in public spending and in unemployment, all seemed to force the government in the direction of the increasingly narrow path of what was 'politically possible' against which Hoskyns had warned.

In reality, however, there were two reasons why the situation was not quite as bad for Mrs Thatcher as most people believed. The first was political. At the end of January 1981, at a special conference in Wembley, the Labour Party confirmed new rules for electing the leader of the party which finally drove away its rebellious moderates. The 'Gang of Four' proclaimed a Council for Social Democracy. On 25 January, Roy Jenkins, Shirley Williams, David Owen and Bill Rodgers produced their Limehouse Declaration, which announced that 'the need for a realignment of British politics must now be faced.' A new political party, though not explicitly promised, was expected by the summer. *The Times* published a mock death notice: 'In Memoriam: Labour ... after a long illness'.[141]* The immediate result was

---

* In the same month, Labour produced a policy document entitled 'The People and the Media', calling for legal controls on what newspapers could publish. Such threats, combined with the damage done to newspapers by trade union practices, made the press far more hostile to Labour than it would otherwise have been, and more keen to lead the charge for Mrs Thatcher. In

a collapse in Labour's opinion poll lead, which fell from 16 per cent over the Conservatives to 2 per cent. On 1 February, a poll in the *Observer* said that 45 per cent would support a new centre party if it emerged. Although these developments seemed to make it more likely that the Tories would be squeezed out by the new entity in the centre, they also took some of the heat off the government. The Social Democrats, as they were formally to become at the end of March, were almost all refugees from Labour* and it was with Labour that they had their quarrel. Public attention focused on Labour extremism and Labour divisions and the weakness of Michael Foot's leadership.

The truth was that the Gang of Four did not give very much thought to Mrs Thatcher. With the partial exception of David Owen, who, under the influence of Jim Callaghan and Peter Jay, had been impressed by the importance of monetarism, they more or less ignored her. 'Roy and Shirley and Bill thought Mrs Thatcher was an aberration and they were looking ahead to the next bit. They assumed that they would come through the middle when Thatcherism failed.'[142] Jenkins, who was in charge of economic affairs, looked forward to the return of a prices and incomes policy. Owen could not remember 'any specific discussion of her' as they made their plans.[143] At a time, therefore, when Mrs Thatcher and her government were extremely unpopular, they were also, to some extent, ignored. None of her political opponents in the other parties had any strategy for undermining her: they blindly assumed that she would fall. This catastrophic misjudgment of the most formidable politician of the age afforded her some space.

The second factor which helped Mrs Thatcher to survive was that the key members of her team did not have serious doubts about their direction

---

February 1981, Rupert Murdoch, who already owned the *Sun* and the *News of the World*, bid to buy *The Times* and the *Sunday Times*, a takeover which John Biffen, the minister responsible, eventually approved. Until that time, *The Times* and the *Sunday Times* had become increasingly disenchanted with Mrs Thatcher. But once Murdoch gained full control, until almost the end of her time in office, she was supported by his papers, as well as by Rothermere's Associated Newspapers, the Telegraph group and Express Newspapers. This assisted her enormously. Comment in later years has suggested that it was controversial or underhand of Biffen not to refer the purchase to the Monopolies and Mergers Commission. This is not the case, because *The Times* was loss-making, and the vendors and senior editorial staff welcomed the sale to Murdoch. What is true, however, is that Mrs Thatcher entertained Murdoch to lunch at Chequers on 4 January 1981 to discuss the bid. The official record (B. Ingham, Note for the Record, 4 Jan. 1981, Margaret Thatcher Foundation) does not indicate that she formally agreed to support him, but it is fair to assume that, informally, she did. As Murdoch put it, 'Probably because of the political stance of the *Sun*, she knew where I stood. I'm sure Biffen must have got instructions or just read the tea-leaves' (interview with Rupert Murdoch).

* Only one Conservative MP, Christopher Brocklebank-Fowler, actually joined them.

of travel. Although Hoskyns and others complained, with some justification, about the lack of strategy, and although there were fierce arguments
about questions such as how best to measure and control the money supply, the main people – above all, Geoffrey Howe and Mrs Thatcher
herself – did not consider that they could or should abandon the path they
had chosen. Beleaguered though they were, they retained more intellectual
confidence than their critics, especially the critics within their own party.
There was even, despite all the strains, a good esprit de corps. In the memory of Robin Ibbs, men such as Hoskyns, Tim Lankester and Clive
Whitmore were 'a joy to work with', and 'we did not believe that her
experiment would collapse.'[144] There was, despite everything, a belief in
the leader. Mrs Thatcher drove everything on. As Andrew Duguid, in the
Policy Unit, recalled: 'Force of personality was the most striking thing
about her – almost too powerful for easy rational discussion to take
place.'[145] The very impossibility of some of Mrs Thatcher's demands and
moods – her veering between excessive caution and dangerous boldness –
fostered a camaraderie among those who worked closely with her. Some
of her womanly qualities inspired a loyal affection. When times were particularly rough, and people felt at the end of their tether, Ian Gow would
say, 'Our girl's tired this evening,' and the inner circle would feel the urge
to protect her and help even more. Ronnie Millar would protest, 'Beware
pity!', but succumb to it himself.[146]

In a government losing its way, Nigel Lawson's speech in Zurich on 14
January 1981 would have been impossible. As Financial Secretary to the
Treasury (and someone who, ten days earlier, had been baulked, for the
time being, of his expected promotion to the Cabinet), Lawson, though
important, was not senior. Yet he made himself the first government minister, he claimed, to use the word 'Thatcherism' in public, giving his speech
the title 'Thatcherism in practice'. He chose the moment of greatest perturbation to give what he saw as 'the first detailed and coherent account
of the Government's economic policy'.[147] This self-description was unlikely
to appeal very much to Howe, from whom Lawson withheld the speech
until the very last moment. He might have seen such an account as his
business. But it pleased Mrs Thatcher, and impressed observers who felt in
need of guidance.

Lawson sought to explain to people how Thatcherism contained not
only 'monetarism' but also, accompanying the battle against inflation, the
attempt to create what Lawson was eventually to christen the 'enterprise
culture'. He did this, he later explained, because 'a necessary precondition
of economic success is a fundamental business optimism based on self-
belief and the will to succeed. Defeatism, the characteristic of pre-Thatcher

Britain, is invariably self-fulfilling.'[148] More narrowly, he tried to prepare opinion for the toughness of the coming Budget. He said that the problem with government borrowing had so far been greater than expected and admitted that the government had 'so far, on balance, *increased* the real burden of taxation overall'.[149]

Yet for all Lawson's articulation of a common purpose, even of sunlit uplands, the immediate problems were desperately serious. That weekend, at a Chequers seminar on 17 January to discuss Hoskyns's latest strategy paper, Geoffrey Howe changed the subject with a warning. To the assembled company – Mrs Thatcher, Keith Joseph, Alan Walters (who had by now arrived as her economic adviser), Terry Burns, Robin Ibbs, David Young,* Norman Strauss and Hoskyns – he explained, as Hoskyns recorded it at the time, that 'all the latest forecasts said that public expenditure is continuing to "run away from us" and we can't see any end to it. So, in Keith's words, we "face a cliff edge in two or three years" . . . As we spoke, Margaret said, "We should really have taken some of these measures a year ago."'[150] 'It now looked as if we were heading,' Hoskyns later recalled, 'for a replay of the sort of crisis that had overwhelmed Denis Healey and the Labour Government in 1976' – a funding crisis caused by a loss of confidence in the government's ability to control the public finances. 'With the Budget due on 10 March we had less than eight weeks to break out of the box. If we failed, we were finished.'[151]

---

* David Young (1932–), educated Christ's College, Finchley and University College London; director, Centre for Policy Studies, 1979–82; special adviser, Department of Industry, 1980–82; chairman, Manpower Services Commission, 1982–4; Secretary of State for Employment, 1985–7; for Trade and Industry, 1987–9; Deputy Chairman, Conservative Party, 1989–90; created Lord Young of Graffham, 1984.

20

Russia ... and Reagan

'The only European leader I know with balls'

While economic policy necessarily took centre stage during Mrs Thatcher's early years as prime minister, it was only part of what she saw as the struggle to restore the strength and freedom of the Western way of life. The global backdrop to all her efforts was the weakness of the West. The Cold War dominated everything. She wanted to make sure that Britain was in a position to fight it properly.

Within days of becoming prime minister, Mrs Thatcher received a recommendation from the Foreign Secretary, Lord Carrington. President Leonid Brezhnev* had been 're-elected' (the post was not, needless to say, contested) as chairman of the Praesidium of the Supreme Soviet, and Carrington wanted the Queen to send a message of congratulation, since other European leaders were doing so. On the margin of the letter, Mrs Thatcher wrote: 'Please not. Some election. Let the Foreign Secretary write or send a message through our Ambassador. Not the Queen.'¹ Under this pressure from No. 10, Carrington eventually decided to send no message at all.

As was often her way, Mrs Thatcher was using a small thing to make a bigger point. She had arrived in office at a delicate moment in the progress of the Cold War. She had shown with her 'Iron Lady' speech at the beginning of 1976 that she was extremely suspicious of détente, because she did not believe in the good faith of the Soviet Union. The ensuing years had only strengthened her view. She believed that the Soviets were working hard, both politically and militarily, to achieve world mastery, and that the West should not bargain with them unless it could bargain from strength. On the other hand, she also believed that the disunity of the NATO alliance was the prize which the Soviet Union sought most. So, while she was worried by what she saw as the weakness of NATO leadership, she decided to bite her lip in public. Besides, although she intended to fulfil her mani-

---

* Leonid Brezhnev (1906–82), General Secretary of the Communist Party of the Soviet Union, 1964–82.

festo commitment to increasing Britain's spending on NATO defence by 3 per cent per year in real terms, she was prime minister of a country that was broke. Britain was not in a position to set as strong an example as she would have liked.

In refining her ideas, Mrs Thatcher drew on two, often opposing sources. The first were her 'irregulars'. As Carrington put it, 'her problem with Russia was that she didn't really trust the Foreign Office. When she started off, she had her own gurus, who were never really part of the FCO.'[2] Of these the most important was Robert Conquest. When she moved into Downing Street, she took the unusual step of shifting the file of her correspondence with Conquest into No. 10, whereas most files from opposition were sent off to Conservative Central Office for storage. In June 1979, she wrote to Conquest thanking him for his advice and adding: 'Now that the battle has begun I shall need your encouragement more than ever before.'[3] For a major speech on foreign policy she made in Brussels as Opposition leader in June 1978, she had drawn extensively on an advance manuscript of a new book Conquest was working on. Writing to thank him later, she told Conquest that 'your book and draft provided the meat of the text in the places where it really mattered.'[4] Conquest published the book, entitled *Present Danger*,[5] in 1979 and dedicated it to Mrs Thatcher. Its message, as summarized by the author, was 'There's nothing the Russians can do so long as we keep our level of arms right.'[6] This was the essence of her own approach.

In Conquest's view, the coming years would be the 'period of enormous danger'. What worried him even more than Soviet behaviour was 'the erosion of Western sense and nerve',[7] especially because of what he considered to be the weak character of President Jimmy Carter. 'I feel the real urgency', he wrote to her in late August 1979, 'to stiffen up Washington', a sentiment which Mrs Thatcher underlined in green ink. Conquest feared, in particular, that the Soviet army might contrive military 'incidents' in West Germany which would then lead to a ceasefire of which the Russians could take advantage – 'And the Soviet armies are now [that is, would be if this happened] on the Rhine.'[8] He believed that the American official understanding of the problem was poor, and that Mrs Thatcher could make matters better: 'The way you keep alerting the West to reality is splendid, and inspiriting.'[9] He thought that Mrs Thatcher's warnings were more likely to strike home with the US administration than anything from inside the Washington machine.

Mrs Thatcher also drew on Hugh Thomas. Thomas was less of an expert on the Soviet Union than Conquest, but was better connected in British academic and literary life. He played an important role in bringing together other experts, such as the military historian Michael Howard, Elie Kedourie* and Leonard Schapiro, and in introducing Mrs Thatcher to a wide range of thinkers. He also furnished her with a historian's justification for taking the advice of outsiders. He sent her a note on the use of 'irregulars' (Churchill's word) by past prime ministers, and their role in countering official advice: 'Churchill, for example, as recorded by Sir John Colville, "had no love for the Foreign Office [since] he suspected them of pursuing their own policy irrespective of what the Government might wish, and he mistrusted their judgment" ... naturally it is desirable to avoid drawing general conclusions from mere chance remarks. But a historical reflection may here, too, yield a useful contemporary judgment.'[10] Part of Mrs Thatcher's hold over the intellectuals, as had been the case in opposition, was her female allure. Conquest wrote to Ian Gow in 1983, mentioning a 'party Hugh Thomas gave last November for the Prime Minister to meet a dozen or so writers. Several have written me about it and I think you may like Anthony Powell's† comment. He says that afterwards "I did some market research as to whether people find her as attractive as I do and all, including Vidia [Naipaul],‡ were in complete agreement."'[11] Philip Larkin,§ the poet, was similarly smitten: 'Very few people are both right and beautiful.'[12]

In the run-up to the 1979 election, Conquest floated the idea that Mrs Thatcher agree to appoint him ambassador to the UN once she became prime minister. This she declined to do and her native caution weighed in against offering him any other job. 'I wish we could use him,' she scribbled on a memo from Richard Ryder, 'but I think it would have to be through the Centre for Policy Studies & that is mostly unpaid!'[13] Despite her affection for the irregulars, she maintained her view that the paid Civil Service should not be formally supplanted at the public expense. Conquest left Britain for a better-paid living than he could find in England, ending up at the Hoover Institution at Stanford University in California. Their correspondence continued and remained important to her, but Conquest was obviously not in a position to advise her on every twist and turn of policy. This advice was provided by the regular Civil Service.

It would be wrong to suggest that Mrs Thatcher was dissatisfied by the

---

* Elie Kedourie (1926–92), educated Baghdad, LSE and St Antony's College, Oxford; lecturer, then Professor of Politics, LSE, 1953–90; author of *The Chatham House Version* (1970).

† Anthony Powell (1905–2000), novelist, author of the *Dance to the Music of Time* sequence; Companion of Honour, 1988.

‡ V. S. Naipaul (1932–), novelist; knighted 1990; Nobel Prize for Literature, 2001.

§ Philip Larkin (1922–85), poet and novelist; Companion of Honour, 1985.

officials with whom she dealt most intensely over Soviet policy. She reposed trust in Bryan Cartledge, her first foreign affairs private secretary, whom she inherited from Jim Callaghan, although his attitudes were different from hers. When Cartledge left the job to become ambassador to Hungary in September 1979, he was replaced by Michael Alexander, one of the Foreign Office's greatest experts on East–West relations, and a man of formidable intellect. From time to time, his views would hew too closely to Foreign Office orthodoxy for her taste, but she respected him. According to Clive Whitmore, her principal private secretary, 'Having seen the Russians at close quarters, Michael was under no illusions about how tough they were. She relied very much on his advice. He wasn't at all soft. But as a good member of the diplomatic corps he realized that we had to live with the Soviets, which was her approach too.'[14] Alexander's opinion of Mrs Thatcher was also respectful, but he thought that she was 'inclined to oversimplify and overdramatize the issues'.[15]

With Alexander's help, Foreign Office views were conveyed to Mrs Thatcher in ways which minimized friction, but there were differences. When Carrington invited her to come and meet 'the Foreign Office gurus', including Rodric Braithwaite* and Christopher Mallaby,† so that she could compare them with 'your own gurus', she said, 'Oh, they don't know anything about Russia at all.' When she came, however, she was impressed by the knowledge displayed.[16] Mallaby gave a detailed presentation of the difficulties the Soviet Union faced on a range of economic, technological, social and political fronts. 'Well,' Mrs Thatcher replied, 'if it's like that, the Soviet Union can't survive, can it?'[17] The officials politely demurred. 'The germs of change are at work inside Soviet society. The system may eventually become more democratic and less expansionist. But it will not easily happen while the Soviet Communist Party and its apparatus of repression are still intact'.[18]‡ The disagreement centred not on knowledge, but on attitude. How should Britain deal with a hostile Soviet Union whose global influence and military might were beyond question, but whose long-term

---

* Rodric Braithwaite (1932–), educated Bedales and Christ's College, Cambridge; head of Planning Staff, FCO, 1979–80; Minister, Washington Embassy, 1981–4; Deputy Under-Secretary, FCO, 1984–8; Ambassador to Soviet Union, 1988–92; knighted, 1988.

† Christopher Mallaby (1936–), educated Eton and King's College, Cambridge; head of Arms Control, Soviet and Eastern European Planning Departments, FCO, 1977–82; Deputy Secretary to the Cabinet, 1985–8; Ambassador to West Germany, 1988–92; to France, 1993–6; knighted, 1988.

‡ Mrs Thatcher held two further discussions on the Soviet Union with the FCO gurus in 1980. In February, over lunch at Chequers, she had them argue directly against the 'irregulars', represented by Hugh Thomas, Michael Howard and Elie Kedourie. Rodric Braithwaite was later told that she felt the FCO team had 'come out on top' (interview with Sir Rodric Braithwaite).

future was uncertain? The Foreign Office had put its eggs in the basket of détente several years earlier, and many officials were 'deeply hostile to the speeches she had made on Helsinki and détente'.[19] They considered her rhetoric overly provocative and undiplomatic. Foreign Office officials were sensitive to Soviet criticism in this regard, so much so that, on one occasion, when Moscow objected to the West's oft-stated desire to negotiate from a 'position of strength', Mallaby penned an internal memo urging that Britain oblige. It might be 'preferable', he suggested to a colleague, 'if Ministers said that we wish to negotiate on equal terms or that we are ensuring that we shall not negotiate from a position of weakness'.[20] This was just the sort of Foreign Office timidity that infuriated Mrs Thatcher. Whenever such requests reached her, she took very little notice.

Mrs Thatcher was always far more willing than the Foreign Office to draw attention to the Soviet Union's failure to live up to its promises. The continued suppression of Soviet dissidents, in defiance of the Helsinki Accord, provided an important example. Like all bureaucracies, the Foreign Office was instinctively suspicious of contacts which were not government to government. It therefore regarded dissidents as a bit of a nuisance, and diplomats in Moscow reported that they were highly unpopular within their own country. Here was another role for the irregulars, notably the Conservative MEP Lord Bethell.* Mrs Thatcher always encouraged them to bring dissidents who had managed to get out of the Soviet Union to come and call on her, so that she could hear their stories and draw attention to their plight.† She regarded human rights abuses as indicative of the disease of Soviet totalitarianism, and, of course, as evidence of bad faith over the détente agreed at Helsinki, and wished to publicize them. The Foreign Office disliked this, and tended to regard the subject as an irritating distraction.

Whatever the long-term prognosis for the Soviet Union, Mrs Thatcher was determined to challenge Moscow from the start of her premiership. The Foreign Office was uncomfortable with the idea that confrontation might be more effective than quiet diplomacy. As John Coles,‡ who succeeded Michael Alexander in her private office, put it: 'The FCO never

---

* Nicholas, 4th Lord Bethell (1938–2007), educated Harrow and Pembroke College, Cambridge; MEP for London North West, 1975–94; for London Central, 1999–2003.

† In January 1980, at the suggestion of Lord Bethell, she saw the dissident Alexander Ginzburg in Downing Street.

‡ John Coles (1937–), educated Magdalen College School, Brackley and Magdalen College, Oxford; private secretary to the Prime Minister, 1981–4; Ambassador to Jordan, 1984–8; High Commissioner to Australia, 1988–91; Deputy Under-Secretary, FCO, 1991–4; Permanent Under-Secretary and head of Diplomatic Service, 1994–7; knighted, 1989.

really shared her attitude towards the Soviet Union. They were used to dealing with the Soviets and thought it was better dealing with them than not. I think they were often frustrated that she was not supportive of having a relationship with the Soviet Union.'[21] Some officials believed this approach stemmed from her limited experience. John Hunt, the Cabinet Secretary, spoke discreetly with US Embassy officials to counsel 'patience with the Thatcher government, which he said had a "learning curve" and an ingrained "emotional" resistance toward negotiations with the USSR'.[22] Carrington was less willing to put her views down to inexperience: 'I don't think she thought there was any point in negotiations. The aim was to win the Cold War really. I don't think she saw an end to it at all, but that we had to go on with it because they were dangerous wicked people.'[23] The very title of the analytical paper which the Foreign Office presented to Mrs Thatcher in her first autumn in office illustrated the problem. It was called 'Managing Russia'. Mrs Thatcher did not want to 'manage' the Soviet Union she faced in the early 1980s, but to defeat it.

The Carter administration was under no illusion about the change Mrs Thatcher would bring to East–West relations. 'Tories are far less convinced than Labor that detente works to the West's advantage,' Brzezinski warned Carter shortly after Mrs Thatcher came to office.[24] In his first letter to the new Prime Minister, congratulating her on her election victory, Carter stressed the overwhelming importance he attached to the ratification of his Strategic Arms Limitation Treaty (SALT II). Under this treaty, both sides agreed to broad and equal limits on strategic offensive nuclear weapons systems. Mrs Thatcher, who had no love for SALT II, scribbled, 'We shall have to send quite a long and frank reply.'[25] Her concerns about the agreement were twofold. She worried that the deal could see Britain's own nuclear capacity bargained away. She was also concerned that this public focus on limiting nuclear weapons would make it more difficult to achieve the increase in Western nuclear capacity that she believed essential. In her view, the recent Soviet build-up of SS-20 missiles threatened the system of nuclear deterrence that had kept the peace in Europe since the Second World War.* The SS-20 was an intermediate-range missile designed to reach European targets, but not the United States. Nuclear deterrence was effective only so long as a potential aggressor believed that a nuclear strike would result in nuclear retaliation. Many questioned whether, faced with a Soviet nuclear strike limited to the European theatre, the US would

---

* This was a concern she had discussed at length with Ronald Reagan during their meeting in November 1978 (interview with Peter Hannaford).

unleash its long-range, US-based ballistic missiles, thus risking a Soviet attack on the continental US. Europe-based nuclear forces were largely outdated and ineffective, so, for nuclear deterrence to retain credibility, Mrs Thatcher believed that it was crucial for NATO to station new US Intermediate Nuclear Forces (INF),* consisting of Pershing II missiles and ground-launched Cruise missiles (GLCMs), on European soil. 'What she was acutely aware of, relatively quickly after coming into office, was that the alliance had to develop a credible and coherent policy on INF,' recalled Clive Whitmore. 'There was a sense that if the alliance did not produce a credible policy we would be seriously outmanoeuvred by the Soviets.'[26]

When Mrs Thatcher's reply to Carter's letter was finally sent, more than a month later, she urged him to 'strike the right balance' between SALT II ratification and making sure that public opinion grasped NATO's need to 'maintain and modernise its nuclear forces'. There had to be 'concrete decisions' on INF modernization and deployment by the end of the year.[27] Receiving the West German Chancellor, Helmut Schmidt, in Downing Street a week after coming into office, Mrs Thatcher discussed INF with him. He told her that West Germany would accept the new nuclear weapons on its soil – the first ever intermediate-range missiles with the capacity to hit Moscow – but only if other non-nuclear European powers would also agree to do so. She was encouraged by his desire to help, and held forth to him about the need for the West to reverse the psychological defeat inflicted on it by Brezhnev outwitting Carter over his attempt to develop the neutron bomb in 1978. She felt the mood had strengthened since then: 'The full extent of the Soviet military build-up was now much more widely recognised in the UK,'[28] and so the government was authorized by public opinion to spend more on defence. NATO had to counter the SS-20s. Schmidt agreed, but warned her of the Soviet propaganda campaign against INF deployment which would now commence.

A month later, Mrs Thatcher also received General Alexander Haig. At the beginning of 1981, he would re-enter Mrs Thatcher's life when he became Ronald Reagan's Secretary of State, but the occasion for his call in June 1979 was his retirement as NATO's Supreme Allied Commander, Europe. Mrs Thatcher told him that the West had allowed its military position to fall from superiority over the Soviet Union to equivalence 'without, apparently, noticing it'.[29]

Her belief that American leadership was absolutely vital to the health of the alliance stood in contrast to the views of President Giscard d'Estaing

---

* INF were often also referred to as Theatre Nuclear Forces (TNF), or more properly Long-Range Theatre Nuclear Forces (LRTNF).

of France. When he called on Mrs Thatcher in Downing Street in November, Giscard told her that 'The period of American strategic supremacy was over' and that he sought some 'European grouping' to defend the West.[30] She was not tempted in Giscard's direction; but so long as Carter, with his indecision and naivety, was at the White House, she could never hope for a relationship with the US President which was more than correct, and the alliance would be leaderless.

At the end of July 1979, Mrs Thatcher saw Haig's successor, General Bernard Rogers, who suggested that, with the death of the ailing Brezhnev which was expected soon, the new Soviet leadership would face 'the temptation to test the West'. He predicted that 1982 would be 'the critical year for the West', and told Mrs Thatcher that NATO must reach an INF decision by Christmas.[31] Three days later, she wrote to Carter to agree that the INF decision must come before the end of the year: 'You can count on our support.'[32] In September, the Cabinet agreed that Britain should accept 144 of the 464 GLCMs planned for Europe. (A further sixteen were later accepted, at West Germany's request.)

In purely domestic political terms, Mrs Thatcher's decision did not prove difficult; nor was she at odds with political colleagues. What was important, both at home and abroad, was her tone, very different from the conciliatory one of the Labour years. She injected a sense of urgency and danger into all the discussions. 'We in Europe have unrivalled freedom,' she told her first party conference as prime minister in October. 'But we must never take it for granted. The dangers to it are greater now than they have ever been since 1945. The threat of the Soviet Union is ever present. It is growing continually.'[33] She spread the same word on the Continent, making the Soviet threat a leading theme of her Winston Churchill Memorial Lecture in Luxembourg later that month: 'The Russians have equipped themselves with military forces whose capabilities and philosophy are better matched to the demands of an offensive than of a defensive policy and whose ambitions are global in scale. Nor is the Russian challenge only military. It is also political and ideological.'[34]

She was frank when meeting the enemy. In May 1979, Cecil Parkinson, then a trade minister, took his Soviet counterpart, who was in London to launch the Soviet National Exhibition at Earls Court, to call on her:

> He had been the Trade Minister for some twenty-one years and he had only one joke, which was 'Every time I come here, you have a new agriculture/ trade etc. minister.' When I took him to see the PM he said, 'Every time I come here, you have a new prime minister.' She said, 'I can't promise to serve for as long as Mr Brezhnev, but I'm not without ambition.'

And then she said, 'You know my views about Russia and Communism, but we are the hosts of this exhibition and I will be coming to it.' He looked surprised. She said, 'I don't say these things for effect. I mean what I say and if I say I'll come, I'll come. And if you say you'll do something I'll expect you to do it. And if we both keep our word, we'll get on famously.'[35]

She duly attended the show, telling the press, as she walked round the exhibits, that, despite her presence, she was still the Iron Lady.*

At Mrs Thatcher's supper with the Soviet Prime Minister Kosygin at Moscow airport on her way to the Tokyo summit in June, the record shows a similar tough playfulness: 'Mr Kosygin told the Prime Minister that . . . the Soviet Union was a peace-loving country which did not produce all the massive armaments which the Prime Minister attributed to them . . . The Prime Minister told Mr Kosygin that he should not be so modest. Nobody who had seen the Soviet tanks and missiles which were paraded through Red Square would underestimate the Soviet Union's capacity.' She also tackled Kosygin about problems for the Soviet Union in the Islamic world: 'When the Prime Minister referred to current unrest in Afghanistan and Pakistan, Mr Kosygin made no comment.'[36]

Mrs Thatcher had more than held her own with Kosygin, but she remained extremely sensitive over her relationship with the Soviet Union. Shortly after this encounter, the *Daily Telegraph* reported that Kosygin had invited Mrs Thatcher to visit Moscow again and that she had responded positively.[37] Kosygin had indeed made a very informal, passing reference to the Prime Minister returning to Moscow and Mrs Thatcher, equally informally, had replied that she would be glad to. She had intended this reply to be more polite than substantive and certainly not for public consumption. 'The Prime Minister was much angered by the leak,' wrote Stephen Band, a Foreign Office official, to a colleague in the Embassy in Moscow, 'and the FCO were asked to state formally that they were not responsible for it . . . The incident has not helped FCO/No 10 relations, which are already not good.'[38] Reflecting a common Foreign Office frustration, Band later noted that 'Ministers, and the Prime Minister in particular, are extremely conscious of the platform on which they won the election and of the right-wing interest groups both inside and outside Parliament to which they feel they owe allegiance. They are therefore

---

* The Foreign Office had earlier advised her to refuse to attend the exhibition and to plead a prior engagement. She had replied, with her strict Methodist honesty: 'Please do not give prior engagement as a reason unless it is <u>wholly true</u>.' (Visit by the Soviet Minister of Foreign Trade Mr Patolichev, 23 May 1979, Prime Minister's Papers; document consulted in the Cabinet Office.)

determined not to be seen <u>publicly</u> to be getting too close to the Russians too fast.'[39] In fact, Mrs Thatcher's suspicions of the Soviets went far beyond any allegiance to right-wing groups. She considered them untrustworthy and intrinsically hostile, a view that would soon be borne out by events.

Almost exactly six months after Mrs Thatcher's meeting with Kosygin, the Soviets invaded Afghanistan, on Christmas Day 1979. The existing Communist leader, whose regime showed signs of falling apart, was murdered, and a new puppet ruler, Babrak Karmal, was installed. Soviet tanks soon occupied the streets of Kabul.

When Mrs Thatcher had visited President Carter in Washington before Christmas, he had told her privately that Soviet troop numbers were building up on the Afghan border.[40] On 20 December, the Foreign Office had summoned a Soviet diplomat to express British concern, but had been told that no interference was planned. Once the invasion had taken place, Mrs Thatcher wrote a formal letter of protest to Brezhnev, beginning, 'I have been profoundly disturbed at recent developments in Afghanistan . . .'[41] But although her anger was real enough, 'disturbed' was not really the right word. The invasion fitted with her expectations of Soviet behaviour. Robert Conquest wrote to her office: 'For anyone with an ounce of sense, there is no lesson to be learnt from the Afghan events: <u>they merely confirm, in dramatic fashion, what was known to many and should have been known to all of those concerned with Western</u> policy. For the time being, those who have been dangerously in error about Soviet motivations and intentions <u>have been shocked into facing reality</u>' (Mrs Thatcher's underlinings).[42] This was her view too. She summoned the Soviet Ambassador and told him that the invasion of Afghanistan was even worse than that of Czechoslovakia in 1968, because Afghanistan had not been a Soviet satellite.[43] Michael Alexander, who was with her as the details of the invasion came through, noted her reaction to the news, and recorded that his own was different: 'she interpreted the invasion as an exercise in Russian expansionism . . . I must confess that I argued with her that night that the invasion was if anything an act of desperation on the part of the Russians – rather out of keeping with their usual caution. The Russians were going in because they could not control the situation in any other way. That struck me as something over which we should not lose too much sleep.'[44]

The disinclination to lose sleep over something always irritated the hyperactive Mrs Thatcher. To her, the enemy was now in plain view. She felt vindicated, and her blood was up. Her arguments were now listened to more carefully, and the case for deploying GLCMs and Pershing IIs in Europe became easier to make. President Carter was one of those whom

Conquest described as 'shocked into facing reality'. He suspended efforts
to ratify SALT II, imposed an embargo on grain sales to the Soviet Union
and used his State of the Union address at the end of January 1980 to say
that the Afghan invasion 'could pose the most serious threat to peace since
the Second World War'. Mrs Thatcher was keen to help him wake up the
West. When Carrington wrote to her about the Western reaction to the
invasion, to say, rather languidly, that 'It may of course take time to work
out the most appropriate positive steps to take, ' she wrote a wordless '!'
on his letter.[45] But she herself did not have a very clear idea of how best to
react. Her immediate response was to see if the news might enable the West
to bring Iran, which, two months earlier, had occupied the US Embassy in
Teheran, holding fifty-two diplomats hostage, back into the fold. Partly
motivated by the British commercial interest in avoiding the trade sanctions
against Iran which President Carter sought, she argued that Afghanistan
made the UN sanctions resolution against Iran inappropriate. She told the
Foreign Office to make sure that the 'enormity of the act' of invasion 'was
not lost to sight', but without suggesting how.[46]

The most obvious way of ostracizing the Soviet Union was to try to
boycott the Olympic Games which were due to be held in Moscow that
summer, an idea encouraged by the United States. When she and Carrington met to discuss this, Mrs Thatcher urged a boycott, but also said
that the government could not forbid athletes to take part if they wanted.
With magnificent world-weariness, Carrington commented that 'perhaps
the best outcome would be if the Government recommended against participation but the various committees, and the participants themselves,
decided to go to Moscow none the less.'[47]

This, in fact, is what happened. Carter forbade American athletes to
take part, but was not followed by other countries. Mrs Thatcher lobbied
Helmut Schmidt and others to hunt for an alternative Olympic venue, and
unsuccessful efforts were made to see if the Games could move to Mon-
treal. Mrs Thatcher was partly motivated by the need to console potential
American hurt feelings about Iran. She told OD Committee* that because
Britain was opposed to sanctions on Iran it should be extra-supportive of
the United States over the Olympic boycott.[48]† Initially the President was

---

* OD was the Overseas and Defence Committee of the Cabinet. It was there, rather than at
full Cabinet, that most business relating to the Cold War was transacted.
† In fact, in April Mrs Thatcher gave her rather reluctant blessing to a European-wide effort
to impose sanctions on Iran in sympathy with the United States. An agreement was reached,
but when it came to a vote in the Commons on 20 May a backbench rebellion forced the
government to back down. This failure to enact the EEC-agreed sanctions earned Britain considerable resentment in Washington, DC.

unimpressed by the response in London and elsewhere to the Soviet invasion. 'UK and other Europeans reaction to SU/Afghan situation are <u>very</u>
weak,' he wrote on a memo from the National Security Advisor, Zbigniew
Brzezinski.[49] But, as Brzezinski later explained, Carter's view towards Mrs
Thatcher's government soon shifted: 'all things considered we were very
happy with their actions. Far more so than most European nations.'[50] A
speech Mrs Thatcher delivered in the Commons at the end of January,
condemning Soviet aggression and calling for Europe to stand behind the
United States, was particularly welcome in the White House.[51] 'Frankly, I
consider it to be the best statement on this subject,' Brzezinski wrote to the
British Ambassador, Nicko Henderson. 'I say this with heavy heart, having
made some myself.'[52] While Americans were generally dismayed by the
European reaction, Mrs Thatcher, reported *Time* magazine, was 'one outstanding exception'.[53]

A series of letters were exchanged between the Prime Minister and Sir
Denis Follows, the President of the British Olympic Committee. But no
amount of rhetoric from Mrs Thatcher about the example of the Berlin
Games helping Nazi propaganda in 1936 or the fact that, by going to
Moscow, athletes 'would seem to condone an international crime'[54] had
any effect. The Olympic Committee ignored the parliamentary vote in
favour of a boycott and went ahead with its plans for the Games. Further
embarrassment was caused because the Queen's husband, Prince Philip,
was president of the International Equestrian Federation, and therefore
had originally expected to go to Moscow. At the end of April, he signed a
statement by the International Olympic Sports Federation condemning the
boycott. It is understood that he wrote privately to Mrs Thatcher to apologize and explain that he had tried to tone down the statement. Mrs Thatcher,
who by this time knew the form about writing to royalty ('With my humble duty, I am, Sir, your Royal Highness's obedient servant . . .'), was
nevertheless quite tart in her reaction to the idea that politics could be kept
out of the matter: 'Alas, everything in connection with the USSR has a
political flavour. That unfortunately is the problem.'[55] In the end, the Olympic boycott went off at half-cock. Some British athletes, encouraged by
their official bodies, went to Moscow. Others, following Mrs Thatcher's
urging, decided to stay at home. The Games were no great success, but nor
was the boycott.

Much the same no-score draw was achieved by short-term Western
reaction to the invasion in general. On the one hand, the Russians had
made a mistake, in both propaganda and military terms, from which Soviet
Communism never fully recovered. On the other hand, the West's response
was largely ineffective. Certain decisions with huge and controversial

consequences were made – the arming of Afghan mujahidin resistance to the Soviets, and a much greater Western support for increasing the military power of President Zia's Islamist regime in Pakistan (about which Mrs Thatcher professed herself 'a little unhappy')[56] – but the more immediate acts were inconsequential, and often showed the West divided.

As she tried to encourage a robust and co-ordinated alliance response, Mrs Thatcher was dismayed by much of what she found. Against her copy of the communiqué on Afghanistan from the Franco-German summit at the beginning of February, she wrote: '!!! All <u>words</u>' (underlined three times). When she met Helmut Schmidt later in the month, she expressed herself 'bitterly disappointed' by the failure of the EEC to support Carter and his Olympic boycott. Schmidt told her that he thought 'There is now a clear and present danger of a Third World War.'[57] She failed in her attempt to implement Carter's request for an emergency NATO summit on Afghanistan, and the truth was that, although she supported Carter's desire to be strong, she doubted his tactics and skill. When she discussed the proposed NATO meeting with Schmidt, she admitted that she questioned 'the wisdom of the proposal but felt it necessary to support President Carter'.[58] She feared the summit would highlight disunity. In June, President Giscard decided to take the withdrawal of some Soviet military units from Afghanistan as 'un element nouveau et positif', and to make France the intermediary in possible discussions between the West and the Soviet Foreign Minister Gromyko. Passing this on to Mrs Thatcher, Michael Alexander wrote: 'Giscard was very prompt in circulating this message.' Mrs Thatcher scribbled: 'Yes – he is – half way to Neville Chamberlain.'[59]

She felt quite sure, after Afghanistan, that the argument was coming her way. Addressing her party conference that autumn, she made the point explicitly:

Long before we came into office, and therefore long before the invasion of Afghanistan, I was pointing to the threat from the East. I was accused of scaremongering. But events have more than justified my words. Soviet Marxism is ideologically, politically and morally bankrupt. But militarily the Soviet Union is a powerful and growing threat . . . The British Government are not indifferent to the occupation of Afghanistan. We shall not allow it to be forgotten. Unless and until the Soviet troops are withdrawn, other nations are bound to wonder which of them may be next. Of course there are those who say that by speaking out we are complicating East–West relations, that we are endangering détente. But the real danger would lie in keeping silent. Détente is indivisible and it is a two-way process.[60]

What she still lacked in her battle with Soviet Marxism was a powerful ally who shared her worldview. This was about to change. As she spoke to her party conference, the American presidential campaign was in full swing, and Jimmy Carter was fighting to survive. That July, on a flight to the Republican convention in Detroit which nominated him as the party's presidential candidate, Ronald Reagan had chatted with his political guru, Stuart Spencer: 'Spencer asked the question all political pros learn to ask their candidates early on. "Why are you doing this, Ron? Why do you want to be President?" Without a moment's hesitation Reagan answered, "To end the Cold War."'[61]

While Reagan's election in November thrilled Mrs Thatcher, it alarmed British officials. 'I think we were concerned', recalled Christopher Mallaby, 'that it might turn out to be a very hard-line, perhaps a crude, policy towards the Soviet Union,'[62] but it was this 'crude' or, as she would have said, principled approach which attracted Mrs Thatcher. Carrington summed it up: 'I think that in many ways Reagan and Thatcher were exactly the same. She was basically extremely hostile towards the Soviets. Talk about evil empire . . . she believed it really was an evil empire. They had the same kind of values. The difference between them was that while he had gut feelings, she had an intelligence that he did not have.'[63]

The 'evil empire' was, of course, Reagan's own phrase, first used later, in March 1983. The slogan, calculated to make diplomats blanch, reflected the moral tone which both Reagan and Mrs Thatcher employed in describing the Soviet Union. 'Reagan believed it was essential to take on the Soviets on the moral plane: aggression and oppressing their own people and others was not something that would be countenanced,' said Edwin Meese,* a Reagan confidant and counsellor to the President.[64] In his very first press conference as President, Reagan declared that 'the only morality [the Soviets] recognise is what will further their cause, meaning they reserve unto themselves the right to commit any crime, to lie, to cheat . . .'[65] On the same day, 29 January 1981, in London, Mrs Thatcher attacked the dishonesty with which the Soviets conducted détente, in terms which prompted a personal letter of thanks from Reagan; and in a press conference a couple of weeks later for American journalists in London, she focused on how the lack of genuine détente produced the oppression of the Soviet Union's own people: 'You will have seen that

* Edwin Meese (1931–), campaign chief of staff for Ronald Reagan, 1980; counsellor to President Reagan, 1981–5; US Attorney-General, 1985–8.

Sakharov* was sent to Gorky, you have seen Yuri Orlov,† after all he was there to monitor Helsinki ... Détente should be two-way ...'[66] All this registered strongly with Reagan, who referred to Mrs Thatcher privately at this time as 'the only European leader I know with balls'.[67]

Hoping to capitalize on Reagan's inexperience, Brezhnev issued a surprise invitation to the President after he had been in office for just a month. He offered to meet him at a superpower summit to discuss whatever he wanted. The idea was to present Moscow as eager to defuse tensions through dialogue. In fact by this stage Brezhnev was no longer well enough to discuss international issues coherently, so the invitation was issued in the knowledge that the meeting would never take place. Publicly, Reagan gave it a cautious welcome, but discussed it with Mrs Thatcher in private, when she paid her first visit to him as president, in Washington three days later.

> Prime Minister Thatcher asked the President if he had considered what kind of fundamental response [was] to be given to Brezhnev's proposal for a meeting ... It is recognized, of course, that one simply cannot say 'no, we will never talk'. In the back of everyone's mind there is the idea of 'yes, of course, we must talk', but we cannot talk until every problem, every possible pitfall is carefully examined. The Soviets are skilled negotiators. We can expect them to play on the peace-loving sympathies of people. She was struck, for example, by the reference [in Brezhnev's invitation] to a moratorium on Theatre Nuclear Forces. The Prime Minister said that her attitude is that when you sup with the devil you must have a long spoon. In fact you had better have a whole lot of long spoons.[68]

She proposed that the answer should be 'yes, in due course'. Reagan 'replied that this is the position we've taken; not a no, not a yes – we are considering it very carefully.'[69]

Mrs Thatcher developed this line in a speech in New York two days later. Her criticisms of the Soviet Union – 'what is there in the Soviet system to admire? Material prosperity? It does not produce it. Spiritual satisfaction? It denies it'[70] – were so harsh as to drive Carrington out of town to avoid attending. 'She gave a very very very right-wing address' he recalled, 'quite a lot of which I disapproved of.'[71] But in fact she restated the position which she and Reagan shared, which was that dialogue should be explored when

---

* Andrei Sakharov, the Nobel Prize-winning physicist, internally exiled shortly after the invasion of Afghanistan.

† Yuri Orlov, the Soviet nuclear physicist turned dissident who, after pressing for Soviet adherence to the Helsinki Accords, was arrested in 1977 and consigned to a gulag in Siberia.

the time was right: 'In this perilous world, negotiation between governments must continue, particularly in the field of arms control – or better
still of arms reduction. We need to establish a military balance between
East and West and to ensure that that balance holds.'[72]

Early in March 1981, the Soviet Ambassador in London presented a
letter from Brezhnev to her (and to all alliance leaders) offering an international summit and an INF moratorium in the hope of heading off INF
deployment. Mrs Thatcher told him that Britain would reduce arms only
from a position of security. Détente could be pursued if the Russians withdrew from Afghanistan: otherwise, 'it gave rise to the question, "Who
next?"' 'The conflict seemed to encircle the globe,' she said, citing the adven-
turism of Cuba in Africa and the Caribbean (a subject on which Robert
Conquest had briefed her). There should be a summit only if it were fully
prepared, with 'genuine' discussions. She attacked the Ambassador for the
treatment of Yuri Orlov, and added, 'Ours was an open society, while that
in the Soviet Union was not.'[73]

To her irritation, the Foreign Office was pursuing a rather different line.
At the end of January she was informed that Carrington intended to negotiate a new Cultural Agreement with the Soviet Union. 'I am very sorry
that we are negotiating a new cultural agreement,' she noted. '. . . They will
gain from it – we shall lose. So much for Afghanistan.'[74] And shortly after
her meeting with the Ambassador, Carrington went against her confrontational stance by suggesting he should go to Moscow in person to
establish better Soviet contacts. 'I am very worried indeed,' she wrote. 'We
should have to consult with the US. Can we not keep contacts to meetings
in the margins of international fora.'[75]* One dark evening, she was standing at the door of No. 10, staring up at the bulk of the Foreign Office
opposite. 'Look at that,' she said to an official, 'the place that keeps the
light out of Downing Street.'[76]

It was to restoring the military balance which she had emphasized in New
York that Mrs Thatcher devoted her main energies. In her mind, INF
deployment was the key. Although she had not liked the idea of negotiations with the Soviets over INF, she had come to the view that the best
way of persuading European allies to accept INF missiles was the strategy
of 'dual track', by which deployment was linked to a US commitment to
pursue such negotiations. Mrs Thatcher was convinced that a willingness

---

* In the end Carrington managed a trip to Moscow in July 1981 on behalf of the EEC during
the British presidency. 'I don't think she was terribly pleased,' he recalled, 'but I think I got
away with it' (interview with Lord Carrington).

to negotiate was essential if the allies were to win public support for the arrival of new American missiles. With the arrival of the Reagan administration, she found herself in the surprising situation of having to uphold the plan agreed with Carter in the face of criticism from her new friends in Washington. Those in the administration, such as Al Haig, the new Secretary of State, who knew Europe well, agreed with Mrs Thatcher and argued forcefully in favour of dual track. Other, more hawkish members of the administration resisted the idea of any negotiation with the Soviets. One or two, notably Richard Perle,* then an assistant secretary of defense, were against INF deployment altogether, on the grounds that European public opinion would never allow the American missiles to be moved around the country in a crisis, and so the weapons would prove useless.[77] According to Richard Allen, President Reagan himself favoured the dual-track approach,[78] but at this stage he made no effort to redress the sceptical tone being set by many in his administration.

The difference between Mrs Thatcher and the Reaganites really arose from the difference of their respective situations. The new Republican administration, longing to make up for the Carter years of drift, wanted to change the whole approach towards the Soviet Union. So did Mrs Thatcher. But, being, geographically if not mentally, a European, she was very conscious of the danger of the alliance splitting, and the strong desire of the Russians to bring this about. Her experience in the autumn of 1979 of European anxieties over INF, especially those in the Netherlands, Belgium and Germany, had made her sensitive to the danger of rupture. She could see how Britain, in particular, could be made vulnerable by Continental weakness or American unilateral action, or both. She was playing – and playing surprisingly well – the unaccustomed role of bridge-builder. As a State Department briefing paper put it:

> Prime Minister Thatcher's government approaches East–West issues with a combination of vocal anti-communism and a pragmatic desire to harmonize Western interests in responding to Soviet adventurism … the British fear being whipsawed between contradictory US and 'European' approaches to the Soviets. Accordingly, while they favour greater linkage† in general, they

---

* Richard Perle (1941–), Assistant Secretary, International Security Policy, Department of Defense, 1981–8; member, Defense Policy Board, 2001–4.

† 'Linkage' required Soviet actions in one sphere to be rewarded or punished by Western actions in another. As neighbours to the Soviet bloc, Western European nations favoured the development of a working relationship with the Soviets in areas such as trade and arms control. They felt that disagreements, such as those over human rights, should not be allowed to spoil the more positive spheres of the relationship. Hardliners in Washington, by contrast, argued that

are conscious of the greater constraints operating on the Europeans (particularly the FRG [Federal Republic of Germany]) and favour examining linkages closely on a case by case basis. This makes the UK a strong proponent of Allied consultation and harmony.[79]

Reagan supporter though she was, Mrs Thatcher thus stood in opposition to the administration's most ardent hawks, who at this moment were making the running. As Al Haig remembered, 'The Pentagon was, oddly enough, "don't waste the money." You can see what kind of trouble that gets you in. Margaret Thatcher was always steady, "Deploy." There was no question about her position. It was an invaluable help to me within the Administration.'[80]

In advance of her visit to Washington in February 1981, British officials lobbied the administration strongly in favour of sticking with dual track. As the State Department briefed:

> The UK will seek reassurance that we are not embarking on a major policy change on TNF and will welcome confirmation of continued US support for NATO's two track approach ... Provided they are persuaded that we do not underestimate the strength of arms control pressures in Europe, the British can also be helpful with other Allies in buying time for us to develop our policies.[81]

Haig's Department duly provided the White House with language reiterating the US commitment to the dual-track approach, which the NSC staff incorporated into a public statement delivered by the President at the conclusion of Mrs Thatcher's visit.[82] Those drafting these remarks considered the language unremarkable, 'total boilerplate',[83] but the words were significant in that they put the President's support for dual track on the record.* The hawks, whose opposition to negotiations remained undiminished, refused to accept defeat and now sought to avoid, or at least delay, the policy's implementation. At the end of April, Haig returned from a visit

---

it was wrong to try to work with the Soviets in one sphere when their actions in another were unacceptable.

* A theory has grown up that adopting this language was the culmination of a State Department ploy to outmanoeuvre the Pentagon, in which Mrs Thatcher was complicit (see Richard Aldous, *Reagan and Thatcher: The Difficult Relationship*, W. W. Norton, 2012, p. 41, and Geoffrey Smith, *Reagan and Thatcher*, Bodley Head, 1990, p. 48). This does not seem to have been the case. Both Richard Allen and the NSC staffer involved, James Rentschler, denied it outright. British officials have no memory of the incident, Mrs Thatcher never made this claim and the official papers do not support it. Mrs Thatcher's view was known, but there is no evidence that she colluded with the State Department to shift Reagan's position.

to Europe and urged Reagan to move ahead with dual track and set a date
to begin negotiations. He prayed in aid all the main European players:

> The British remain our most reliable ally, the French by far the most robust.
> However, both Mrs Thatcher and Giscard are deeply concerned that we take
> into account the situation in the FRG. Mrs Thatcher almost pleaded with
> me in London that we take care not to isolate Chancellor Schmidt, whom
> she described as 'a really good friend of the US'. As I reported to you, they
> deeply fear the consequences of misunderstanding between a resurgent US
> and an exposed FRG.[84]

History does not usually write down Mrs Thatcher as a healer of wounds
between alliance members but so, at this stage, she was. Reagan decided
to proceed with both aspects of dual track.

If negotiations were to take place, however, what was to be their aim?
Against the wishes of Haig's State Department, Reagan approved a stance,
championed by Richard Perle, known as the zero option.* Under this
approach, the US would consider only an agreement that led to the complete withdrawal of all existing Soviet intermediate forces from the
European theatre in return for NATO agreement not to deploy American
INF in Europe. Proposals for lower levels of intermediate missiles on both
sides were off the table unless the level in question was zero. Perle explained:
'I certainly believed that it was a lot less likely that we would get the agreement than the easier-to-reach agreements that would favour the Soviets.
But, if we got it, it would be very useful. And since I wasn't all that eager
for an agreement and certainly an agreement for agreement's sake, it made
perfect sense to go for the harder but more useful.'[85] When the zero option
was publicly announced in November 1981, Mrs Thatcher commended it
to the Commons because it proposed 'not merely a limitation of nuclear
arms but an actual reduction both in nuclear arms and conventional forces.
I believe that he [Reagan] has seized the initiative.'[86] Michael Foot claimed
that the zero option was something which Labour would welcome more
than she because his party's defence policy also favoured a zero option.
The difference of course was that Reagan was proposing to negotiate zero
missiles on both sides, whereas Foot advocated a unilateral Western zero.
Mrs Thatcher soon pointed this out: 'it takes two to agree to a zero option,'
she insisted.[87]

---

* The concept of a 'zero option' originated with Helmut Schmidt's Social Democratic Party,
but the version worked up by Perle and adopted by Reagan led to a tougher posture than the
West Germans had ever envisaged.

It was true, however, that Mrs Thatcher welcomed the zero option only on the calculation that it would not be taken up. 'I had always disliked the original INF "zero option",' Mrs Thatcher wrote in her memoirs, 'because I felt that these weapons made up for Western Europe's unpreparedness to face a sudden, massive attack by the Warsaw Pact; I had gone along with it in the hope that the Soviets would never accept.'[88] She wanted INF deployment not only to counter Soviet SS-20s, but to deter a conventional attack. The zero option, if accepted, would, she believed, leave the Western allies exposed, and risk uncoupling the US strategic nuclear force from Europe's defence.

Inside her thinking was a real difference with Reagan, not important at the time but highly significant later on. As Ken Adelman,* who became director of the Arms Control and Disarmament Agency, put it: 'Thatcher was always very good on zero INF, as long as the zero proposal wasn't going to go anywhere. She was less excited about it going anywhere than Reagan was. He, however, was thrilled.'[89] The truth is that Mrs Thatcher was a firm supporter of nuclear weapons, because she believed in the doctrine of deterrence. She considered that world war was prevented by the capacity of the West to frighten the East with its nuclear arsenal. It was therefore important for world peace that the arsenal be large and credible. Reagan, although he wanted just as much to defeat Soviet totalitarianism and believed in peace through strength, actually wanted to abolish nuclear weapons. He considered them immoral, and a cause of instability more than of peace. He thought the world could be free of them. Like Mrs Thatcher, Reagan wanted to build up Western military strength, but his purpose was different. 'Reagan's basic aim, always, was arming in order to disarm,' said Richard Allen.[90] This was to bulk large in his efforts during the Gorbachev era. In his memoirs, Reagan describes the zero option as 'the first step to the elimination of all nuclear weapons from the earth'.[91] He did not say this to Mrs Thatcher at the time, and if he had, she would have been horrified – as she later was. In the early 1980s, however, President and Prime Minister were at one in wishing to reassert the power of the West against the Soviet Union, and the zero option, as a tactic, helped.

When she came into office in 1979, Mrs Thatcher immediately set about finding a replacement for Britain's ageing Polaris submarine-based nuclear missiles which the Callaghan government had planned but had not dared to enact. This was to be the third generation of British nuclear weapons.

---

* Kenneth Adelman (1946–), US Ambassador and Deputy Permanent Representative to UN, 1981–3; Director, Arms Control and Disarmament Agency, 1983–8.

Mrs Thatcher followed up where Callaghan left off by formally requesting President Carter's permission to procure the US Trident system. Carter, however, dragged his feet well into 1980. Partly, he was obsessed with the Senate ratification of SALT II, but more fundamentally Carter was 'allergic to a lot of nuclear things' and viewed the idea of providing missiles to Britain 'rather sceptically'.[92] According to Mrs Thatcher, he even used the excuse that announcing the Trident decision 'could be seen as an overreaction to events in Afghanistan'[93] to delay acceding to the British request. Others, such as Carrington and Michael Palliser,[94] denied that this was a serious problem, but there was certainly haggling over price. In the end, and contrary to what Mrs Thatcher states in her memoirs, a deal was struck by which Carter agreed to waive the bulk of pro-rata research and development costs of the missiles in return for Britain allowing greater US use of the British Indian Ocean island of Diego Garcia for military purposes.[95] The details of the deal were settled at a meeting between Mrs Thatcher and Harold Brown, Carter's Defense Secretary, on 2 June 1980, in Downing Street, on terms fairly expensive to Britain.*

With Reagan's arrival in the White House, the situation changed. The new administration was keen to let Britain have Trident, but was considering upgrading the existing C-4 version, which Carter had agreed to supply to Britain, to the more powerful and more expensive D-5 version. In March 1981, Caspar Weinberger,† Reagan's appointment as Defense Secretary, met the British Defence Secretary John Nott and 'reaffirmed our commitment' that the US would provide 'Whatever TRIDENT missile (C-4 or D-5) that we decided to pursue on completion of our review'.[96] In August, he informed Britain that the US had resolved to upgrade to the D-5 and that it would be available to Britain. Nott recalled: 'I was very much in favour of going to D-5. The difficulty was money.'[97]

There was a certain irony in the fact that the US could bestow or withhold what was supposed to be Britain's independent nuclear deterrent: 'It wasn't entirely satisfactory to [Mrs Thatcher] that we had to be so dependent. We were always just a little worried about if we ever actually needed the thing whether the Americans would allow us to make it work. But it was the best we could do.'[98] This concern, the significant cost involved and the fear of an escalation in the arms race made the acquisition of Trident

---

* In addition to the Diego Garcia deal, Britain also agreed to pay a nominal $100 million towards R & D costs and to cover the cost of manning air defence systems at US bases in the UK. In later years, the ceding of Diego Garcia became extremely controversial because of the effective expulsion of the local population.

† Caspar Weinberger (1917–2006), born in California; lawyer; Director of Finance, California, 1968–9; counsellor to the President, 1973; US Defense Secretary, 1981–7; Hon. GBE, 1988.

controversial, even within Conservative ranks. In early 1981, Nott warned Mrs Thatcher that 'two-thirds of the Party and two-thirds of the Cabinet were opposed.'[99] But for Mrs Thatcher, as for Nott and Carrington, securing the future of Britain's deterrent was essential. As Carrington noted: 'Failure to acquire TRIDENT would have left the French as the only nuclear power in Europe. This would be intolerable.'[100] With a strong lead from the Prime Minister and her senior colleagues the Cabinet agreed in principle to accept D-5.* The remaining issue was price. Mrs Thatcher wrote to Reagan on 1 February 1982 offering to send officials over to settle the deal. Although she did not know this at the time, the US administration wanted to help as much as possible. In October 1981, Richard Perle and Weinberger had exchanged correspondence about waiving Trident's R & D costs for Britain.[101] The deal, designed to observe the legal requirement that development costs could be waived only if this was in the national interest, agreed that it was in the US national interest for Britain to maintain a stronger naval capability than was proposed by Nott's forthcoming defence cuts. In exchange for a waiver of the Trident R & D costs, therefore, Britain promised to keep more of its surface ships. 'So one could say', recalled Richard Perle, 'that we ended up subsidizing the Royal Navy.'[102]

Reagan wanted agreement, on terms favourable to Britain: 'The President and I gave the bureaucracy the sense that we wanted the Trident deal to be struck. It was one more arrow in the quiver. Britain was the lynchpin to NATO and more important than any other single power.'[103] The deal was pushed through quickly, being formally agreed on 11 March 1982. Mrs Thatcher was delighted by the speed and by the terms, both of which she contrasted favourably with the Carter era.[104] In a brief personal note to Reagan she expressed her gratitude for his help: 'I can think of no way in which our two countries could more powerfully have illustrated our common resolution in defence of freedom and our unique ability to reinforce each others [sic] efforts.'[105]

In May 1980, Mrs Thatcher had a frank discussion with the UN Secretary-General, Kurt Waldheim. Lord Carrington, she told him, believed that the Russians were looking for a way out of Afghanistan, but 'She took the more cynical view that the Russians would remain for a very long time.'

---

* In his biography of Mrs Thatcher, John Campbell asserts that in an effort to win over the doubters the Cabinet were treated to a two-hour presentation on the merits of D-5 by the MOD official Michael Quinlan (John Campbell, *Margaret Thatcher*, 2 vols, Jonathan Cape, 2000, 2003, vol. ii: *The Iron Lady*, p. 187). This is not the case. According to the late Sir Michael Quinlan this presentation did not take place. He had, in fact, left the MOD earlier. (Interview with Sir Michael Quinlan.)

The Russians liked to annex states: 'it was only a matter of time before they marched into another.'[106]

In fact, the next Russian aggression did not take the form of actual invasion. It was concentrated on Poland, a country, unlike Afghanistan, internationally recognized as being in the Soviet sphere, but one which was showing stirring signs of change. Ever since the election of Karol Wojtyła* as Pope John Paul II in 1978, any moral authority still clinging to Communism in Eastern Europe had withered away. When the Polish Pope returned to visit his own country the following year, millions of people attended his speeches and Masses, with the authorities powerless to prevent them. The Polish spiritual rebellion also took a more political form. The trade union Solidarity, under the leadership of Lech Wałęsa,† organized the mass of industrial (and later agricultural) workers to resist the Communist government, notably through strikes in the Gdańsk shipyards.

Mrs Thatcher was naturally thrilled by these developments. At first, the Polish government seemed to respond to them almost sympathetically. In December 1980, she received Henryk Kisiel, the Deputy Prime Minister of Poland. He told her that democratization was 'the right of the people', and that a new generation of workers 'believed that they owned the means of production and they wanted a say in how they were used'. He quoted favourably Wałęsa's dictum that 'A Pole with a Pole will always find a solution.' He wanted Solidarity to be confident that there would not be a crackdown. Mrs Thatcher replied warmly and urgently: she had 'witnessed change of a kind that had not occurred in a socialist state in the last 60 years ... the present developments were very exciting for someone who believed, as she did, in liberty.'[107]‡ Kisiel told her that 'The fundamental desire was the desire to govern one's own future.' He reported that, after the Polish leadership had visited Moscow the previous week, they had returned 'in a more relaxed frame of mind'. He was not expecting trouble

---

* Karol Wojtyła (1920–2005), Pope John Paul II, Archbishop of Kraków, 1964–78; elected pope, 1978.

† Lech Wałęsa (1943–), co-founder and chair, Solidarity trade union, 1980–90; President of Polish Republic, 1990–95.

‡ Mrs Thatcher's personal affection for the Polish cause was strong. When she came into office, a dispute arose about ministerial attendance in London at the annual commemoration of the Katyń massacre in 1940 in which Soviet troops had massacred 4,000 Polish officers. Fearing the wrath of the Soviet bloc, and arguing that it was not certain whether the Russians or – as the Soviets claimed – the Nazis had murdered the officers, the Foreign Office counselled against representation. Mrs Thatcher, who had sent Airey Neave on her behalf to the ceremony before she came into office, replied: 'I do not agree ... that is why Airey Neave attended last year.' (Lever to Alexander, 10 Sept. 1979, Prime Minister's Papers, Defence: The Katyn memorial; document consulted in the Cabinet Office.)

from the Soviets. Mrs Thatcher was less optimistic: 'The Prime Minister urged Mr Kisiel not to relax and to remember Czechoslovakia.'[108] She had a specific reason for her warning. The day before, she had received her second message from President Carter that intelligence showed Soviet military preparations and that the decision had been made to intervene in Poland. She had replied that 'This goes further than our own judgment,'[109] but she was obviously alarmed.

In the course of 1981, jitters recurred, though the Carter prediction about Poland was proved wrong. The NATO allies made rather ineffective plans for counter-measures. 'There is precious little in this whole list,' wrote Mrs Thatcher on one set of ideas. Mrs Thatcher showed some signs of changeability in her own views, as if she were, on this occasion, accepting a Foreign Office line. When she saw Al Haig in April, she told him that 'There were signs that Solidarity was seeking political power for its own sake,' and she warned Haig not to go so hard against the Soviet Union as to isolate Germany: 'Germany was divided and in the front line. This was one of the reasons why the European Community was so important and had to be kept in being.' As always, her Europeanism depended on her anti-Communism. She worried that NATO was 'in a very fragile state'.[110]

The Polish 'Renewal' was not snuffed out, but the atmosphere became more menacing. The Soviet Union launched public attacks on Solidarity and private ones on the weak response of the Polish government. In October, General Jaruzelski, Poland's Prime Minister since February, also took over as first secretary of the Polish Communist Party. On 13 December 1981, he imposed martial law on Poland, swooping on the Solidarity headquarters and appointing a military council to run the country.

Even as late as November, the British government had taken a reasonably optimistic view. Carrington wrote to Mrs Thatcher advising that she accept the Polish government's invitation to visit their country in 1982 because this 'could be a timely demonstration of our interest in the Polish "Renewal"'.[111] Once martial law had been imposed, she was not exactly surprised but, in common with her European allies, she was not quite sure how to react.

It was President Reagan who took the most forceful view. 'Dear Maggie,'* he wrote, on 19 December 1981, in a message warning her of the possibility

---

* In early correspondence Reagan had addressed Mrs Thatcher as 'Madam Prime Minister', graduating to 'Dear Margaret' in early August 1981. The attempt to reach an even greater level of intimacy through moving to 'Maggie' (first seen in October 1981) no doubt led to wry smiles in No. 10, as no one close to Mrs Thatcher ever called her by that name. Realizing the error, Reagan reverted to 'Dear Margaret' for his next letter and retained this salutation for almost all of their subsequent correspondence.

of direct Soviet intervention, 'This may well be a watershed in the political
history of mankind – a challenge to tyranny from within.' He wanted a
strong, shared allied reaction: 'The time has come to avert this tragedy.'[112]
The following morning Mrs Thatcher, who was at Chequers, discussed his
message with Carrington over the telephone. The Foreign Secretary was
dismissive. He said that Reagan's message seemed 'so vague I didn't think
it was worth reading last night'. More surprisingly, Mrs Thatcher was also
critical. She said, 'it's simply an internal situation,' and when Carrington
opined that Reagan wanted to take it out on the Russians, she answered,
'it seems a bit absurd if the Russians aren't actually in the front line to take
it out on them when they're not,' though she did attack them for 'crushing
the first signs of freedom'. 'When one sits down and thinks about it,' said
Carrington, 'I mean what is there we can do?'[113] He was cross with the US
administration for announcing publicly a secret meeting of the foreign
ministers of the four main NATO powers: 'The Americans have once again
gone and made a mess of it.' 'Well this of course', said Mrs Thatcher, 'is
appalling.' She replied in uncharacteristically weak terms to Reagan, saying
that this was a 'complex and difficult situation', avoiding commitments.[114]

Before the end of the year, the US administration produced a list of
measures against the Soviet Union which were enacted without agreement
with NATO allies. These included the suspension of Aeroflot flights, the
halting of negotiations on a long-term grain agreement with the Soviets
and sanctions preventing the export of oil and gas equipment to the USSR.
In this last measure were contained the seeds of a huge controversy.

There was an important strand within the early Reagan credo that the
Soviet Union could and should be beaten into economic submission. The
Reaganites had been horrified by President Carter's acquiescence, in 1978,
in the agreement between West Germany and the Soviet Union to build a
gas pipeline across western Siberia. The pipeline would supply natural gas
to ten European countries, including West Germany, France, Italy and the
Netherlands. In Reagan's view, this allowed the Russians to make energy
an instrument of their foreign policy. It would also earn them hard currency. In July 1981, the administration decided to do what it could to
prevent the construction of the pipeline. 'The Soviets have spoken as plainly
as Hitler did in "Mein Kampf",' Reagan told an NSC meeting. 'They have
spoken world domination – at what point do we dig in our heels?'[115]
Caspar Weinberger led the charge. Weinberger hoped that Britain, which
was not buying Soviet gas, would feel free to co-operate; but, as some
White House aides warned, Britain did have commercial interests in the
pipeline because of contracts to help build it and was unlikely to want to
drop them. Hundreds of jobs were at stake with John Brown Engineering,

a Scottish company, supplying turbines. Between July and December, American attempts to persuade Europeans, including Britain, got nowhere.

In his decision to go ahead with the sanctions, Reagan was intolerant of what he called 'those "Chicken Littles" in Europe'.[116] The 'Chicken Littles' were duly furious, partly because they wanted the pipeline, partly because they disliked the unilateralism and partly because they felt that America was imposing hardship on them which it was not applying to itself. Europeans were particularly angry that Reagan lifted the grain embargo against the Soviet Union, to help farmers in the Midwest, while pushing for sanctions on the pipeline.

Mrs Thatcher had more sympathy with Reagan's aims than did most of the Europeans.* To the draft of a letter to Reagan written early in the new year, she added, '... I am less than happy with the European reaction so far'[117] – a line which Carrington persuaded her to remove before the letter was sent. But, faced with constantly rising unemployment, she was seriously worried about British jobs, and she was alarmed at the prospect of alliance disunity. The draft which she actually despatched argued that 'We must ensure that the focus of attention is directed where it belongs – at a blatant example of the failure of the Soviet system and Soviet ideas – and not at differences between Alliance partners whose aims are identical.'[118]

At the end of January 1982, she saw Haig, who, of all the senior figures in the Reagan administration, was closest to agreeing with her fears about alliance unity. The French and Germans, she said, would not agree to what America wanted. 'We should not do the Russians' job for them' by causing a split, she told Haig. The United States had abandoned a grain embargo because of the effect on them: she noted drily 'a certain lack of symmetry'. When Haig told her that there might be further measures still, she replied, 'in that case there would be nothing left ... The Russians might conclude that they had nothing further to lose by invading.' Actions taken by the West would not reverse the situation in Poland. 'She regarded the new freedom in Poland as a gangrene in the Soviet system. She wanted it to spread.' Haig encouraged her to write personally to the President on the subject because he (Reagan) had a 'great respect' for her. Mrs Thatcher said that she 'reciprocated that respect. She also regarded Helmut Schmidt as a great friend. He was a most loyal member of the Western Alliance,

---

* Mrs Thatcher was familiar with the idea of defeating the Soviet Union by economic means. At the end of 1980, Hugh Thomas and Leonard Schapiro had furnished her with a paper called 'A Western policy towards the Soviet economy', which advocated 'economic warfare' to exploit Soviet weakness. She told Thomas that she was attracted to the idea but did not feel in a position to accept it ('A Western policy towards the Soviet economy', 31 Dec. 1980, THCR 1/10/17; interview with Lord Thomas of Swynnerton.)

despite his difficulties with his Party.'[119] As over the dual-track decision, she did not want Schmidt put in an impossible position. Haig reported to Reagan that Mrs Thatcher had shown 'unusual vehemence'.[120]

On the same day, Mrs Thatcher despatched her letter to Reagan. 'We risk losing the prize if we act hastily or out of step,' she told him, and she pointed out that France and Germany 'cannot and will not give up the gas pipeline project'. She urged Reagan to relent on sanctions against existing contracts. In return, the Europeans could 'reach agreement on measures comparable to yours. We should look resolute and united.'[121] Behind her talk of the 'prize' was always, and above all, her belief in the overriding need to deploy INF weapons, for which alliance unity had to be at the maximum. Her words seemed to have some effect. Reagan noted in his diary the following day, 'Our choice – to go it alone with harsher steps against Poland and risk split in the alliance or meet with European alliance on things we can do together. The latter is my choice. The plain truth is that we can't – alone – hurt the Soviets that much. The Soviets will however be disturbed at evidence their attempts to split us off from the allies have failed.'[122] 'I must take the blame for having been careless,' the President conceded at an NSC meeting in February. Reagan explained that he had assumed that the construction of the pipeline depended predominantly on firms based in the United States, rather than in Europe. 'Now', he continued, 'Maggie Thatcher has made me realise that I have been wrong.'[123]

On 2 April 1982, Argentina invaded the British colony of the Falkland Islands.* Mrs Thatcher, fighting for national honour and political survival, had very little time for anything else. Her approach to Anglo-American relations was suddenly governed by the imperative of winning US military and diplomatic assistance against Argentina, and for the course of the war she was much too preoccupied to take part in Washington's debates about how to deal with the Soviet Union. While the Falklands War was in progress, these debates took, from her point of view, a turn for the worse.

With the arrival of Judge William Clark† as national security advisor at the beginning of the year, the 'Reagan doctrine', by which Soviet Communism had to be defeated rather than contained, and anti-communist liberation movements should be actively supported, had begun to gain firmer shape. Reagan reverted to his idea of economic aggression against

---

* See Chapters 23 and 24.
† William Clark (1931–), Chief of Staff to Governor Reagan, Sacramento, 1966–9; Justice, Supreme Court of California, 1973–81; US Deputy Secretary of State, 1981; National Security Advisor, 1982–3; US Secretary of Interior, 1983–5.

the Russians. 'Why can't we just lean on the Soviets until they go broke?' he asked at an NSC meeting in March, and he answered his own question by saying, 'That's the direction we're going to go.'[124] In May, he signed a top-secret policy document – NSDD 32 – which sought to 'contain and reverse the expansion of Soviet control and military presence throughout the world . . . and weaken the Soviet alliance system by forcing the USSR to bear the brunt of its economic shortcomings'.[125] It was in this spirit that the administration now approached the pipeline. While US officials would have preferred to see the pipeline cancelled altogether, they realized that the lack of international support made this unrealistic. Instead, they resolved to use the sanctions to delay construction for as long as possible, thus making the process more costly for the Soviets and providing time for alternative European gas reserves to be developed. They also hoped to block Soviet plans to add a second strand to the pipeline in the future. As Roger Robinson, NSC senior director of international economic affairs, put it, 'We needed to take on the Siberian gas pipeline project because it would have made Europe inordinately dependent on Soviet gas and cata-pulted Moscow into a new echelon of hard currency earnings – some $10–15 billion annually per strand.'[126]

Luckily for Mrs Thatcher, all this – and the Falklands – coincided with the formal visit (for technical reasons, not a state visit) by President Reagan to Britain. With Reagan due to attend the Versailles G7 in June 1982, Mrs Thatcher had proposed, back in 1981, that the President also visit Britain. In December, it had also been suggested that the Reagans stay with the Queen at Windsor. There was tremendous toing and froing about the visit. Would security permit the President to ride in an open-topped carriage? Given the importance of courting West Germany in his visit to Europe, would he take time to come to Britain at all? Would the President, if he came, make a speech? In February, the view from the White House was that he would not speak. This greatly disappointed Mrs Thatcher. Report-ing the White House view to her, her private secretary, John Coles, pointed out that 'One of the main reasons' for Reagan's coming was to 'help lessen the impact of the unilateralists'.[127] 'I really think we should press for a speech,' Mrs Thatcher scribbled, and not only the one at the banquet with the Queen, because that 'couldn't contain anything controversial and would ∴ not meet the need'.[128] The idea of a speech to both Houses of Parliament in Westminster Hall was eventually agreed, but was then leaked to the American press by Michael Deaver, the President's Deputy Chief of Staff.*

* Michael Deaver (1938–2007), Assistant to Governor Reagan during 1960s; Deputy Chief of Staff to the President, 1981–5.

A huge row ensued. With widespread discontent on the Opposition benches, Michael Foot complained that the invitation to give such a speech was the prerogative of Parliament, which had not been consulted, not of the executive.* This was constitutionally correct. The suggested compromise was that Reagan speak in the Royal Gallery in the Palace of Westminster instead. This was less grand than Westminster Hall, in which, among foreign leaders, only General de Gaulle had previously spoken. Mrs Thatcher was angry, both with the White House gaffe and with Foot and co., particularly when, in the wake of the controversy, the White House suggested again that it might be better if the President did not deliver a speech at all. She reminded staff that the US was 'our staunchest ally' and 'President Reagan should be accorded the same treatment as General De Gaulle.'[129] On a list of previous addresses to Parliament supplied to her by officials, she added, to emphasize her views: 'Reagan – a strong and good friend of Britain and a defender of the free world.'[130] Parliamentary feelings, however, ran so high that she had no choice but to accept the Royal Gallery compromise. The White House was informed that Mrs Thatcher 'personally would be very disappointed' if the President decided not to speak after all.[131] Reagan bowed to her wishes.

After these initial hesitations, the White House became enchanted with the whole idea of the visit. Reagan was particularly excited by the suggestion that he would go riding with the Queen in Windsor Great Park. Judge Clark, a rancher and horseman, let it be known that, if anyone else besides the two heads of state would be in the mounted posse, he would like to be one of them.[132] There was discussion about what gift should be presented to Reagan, and Judge Clark opined that the President could 'always use more leather'. An English saddle and bridle were duly agreed.

This expectation of pleasure and amity was helpful to Mrs Thatcher in winning Reagan's support for the Falklands operation. He did not like the idea of visiting Britain in an atmosphere of unpopularity. Even less did he want to cancel the visit. It was also generally assumed that pressure from the allies at the Versailles G7 would deliver another boon for Mrs Thatcher in encouraging Reagan to bring sanctions on the pipeline to an end. This was not the case. In fact, urged on by the hardliners, Reagan had been considering extending his sanctions, particularly if the allies would not agree to tough limits on credits for the Soviet Union. 'There was a lot of talk about not having a set to with our allies,' Reagan noted in his diary.

---

* The Reagans were also mortified lest the great trip be compromised: 'Nancy was very unhappy with me because I had blown that,' said Deaver (interview with Michael Deaver). Reagan wrote to Mrs Thatcher to apologize for the leak.

'I finally said to h—l with it. It's time we tell them this is our chance to bring the Soviets into the real world and for them to take a stand with us – shut off credit etc.'[133] No agreement was reached at Versailles. Reagan was particularly disappointed that his attempt to win tougher credit constraints had got nowhere.

After the summit, Reagan began his visit to Britain on 7 June 1982. Mrs Thatcher was delighted by his presence and by the help which America, after some hesitations, had given so munificently over the Falklands. When the President addressed MPs and peers in the Royal Gallery, how he would appear on television was all important. For the first time in Britain, a transparent Perspex autocue system was used, making it look as if Reagan were speaking off the cuff or reciting from memory. Much thought had been given to each detail. Jim Hooley, part of the President's advance team, recalled: 'We wanted the guys in the really cool uniforms [that is, Beefeaters] in the photo when Reagan was speaking. Our counterparts were looking bemused, but we kept saying "couldn't they be just a little closer?"'[134] But the speech was not merely image-peddling. It was full of serious content. With a phrase that consciously echoed Winston Churchill's 'Iron Curtain' speech at Fulton, Missouri – 'From Stettin on the Baltic to Varna on the Black Sea', Reagan said, there had been no free elections in thirty years – it set out in classic form Reagan's governing idea. Poland was 'at the centre of European civilization' and the Berlin wall was 'the dreadful grey gash across the city'. The Soviet state, inspired by that 'barbarous assault on the human spirit called Marxism-Leninism', was collapsing under the weight of its own contradictions. He called for a 'crusade for freedom', an attempt to establish 'the infrastructure of democracy' and to subvert Soviet tyranny just as the Soviets tried to subvert Western freedom. He invited people to consign Marxism-Leninism to the 'ash-heap of history'. In a passage on which he had personally insisted, Reagan linked British troops in the Falklands with his wider cause: they had been fighting for 'the belief that armed aggression must not be allowed to succeed'.[135]

Mrs Thatcher was thrilled. In her private speech for Reagan, given at the lunch at No. 10 which followed his address to the Royal Gallery, she told him that, for his help over the Falklands, 'We are grateful from the depth of our national being.'[136] Into her text, she inserted, in her own hand, words from General Eisenhower: 'One truth must rule all we think and all we do. The unity of all who dwell in freedom is their only sure defence.'[137] The Royal Gallery speech, and the visit, were extremely important in making manifest the unity with America which Mrs Thatcher sought, and the more positive and vigorous advancement of Western values which she espoused. The speech also complemented the attitude to peace which, bolstered by the Falklands, she was developing. She saw peace not as a rather abject posture, merely avoiding war, but as a more tough and durable thing – 'peace with freedom and justice'.

Nothing, however, did the trick on the pipeline. At Versailles, Mrs Thatcher had badgered Reagan on the subject, but he had conceded nothing. Aware that it, and particularly the turbine jobs at John Brown, would come up again in London, Haig counselled delay: 'I suggest that you tell Mrs Thatcher that . . . you will need to consider this issue after your return to Washington.'[138] For her part, Mrs Thatcher raised John Brown with Reagan during his visit, but without success.

Reagan returned to Washington to find his administration's conservatives angry with the failure of the Versailles summit to get results, and his White House staff intriguing against Haig, who, they believed, was trying to bypass the President and run his own foreign policy. On 18 June 1982, with Haig away in New York City, Reagan decided at an NSC meeting to extend sanctions extraterritorially, increasing the headache for many non-US firms trying to honour their contracts with the Soviets. This was publicly announced without consultation with the allies.

The decision was 'a bolt from the blue', said Mrs Thatcher,[139] and it made her 'very, very angry'.[140] During his visit to Europe, she had been absolutely clear with Reagan that she wanted to see the sanctions lifted. Instead, the President had actually extended them. Due in New York to make a speech about disarmament, she was invited to Washington to meet with Reagan, originally at the behest of Al Haig, and arrived there on 23 June.* Despite the excellent relations between President and Prime Minister, the meeting was strained. As State Department officials reported to the US Embassy in London, Mrs Thatcher contrasted the US decision to continue grain sales to the Soviet Union with the decision on the pipeline: 'She pointed out that the United States was getting a bad name internationally as a country which will not live up to its commitments.'[141] Usually, to preserve her relationship with Reagan, Mrs Thatcher would avoid direct confrontation with him, picking instead on his advisers. 'She would turn to the relevant Secretary or official and say "Bill, how could you ever go in that direction?"' recalled Judge Clark. 'The President would sit there

---

* After Haig had offered the invitation via Nicko Henderson, Judge Clark sought, unsuccessfully, to withdraw it (Nicholas Henderson, *Mandarin: The Diaries of an Ambassador, 1969–1982*, Weidenfeld & Nicolson, 1995, pp. 477–9). Clark cited scheduling difficulties, but having just persuaded Reagan to extend the sanctions he may have been disinclined to expose the President to Mrs Thatcher's objections. Haig, of course, had the opposite motive.

with a catbird smile and roll his eyes as if to say, "Yes, Bill, how *could* you ever have done such a thing?"[142] This time, however, her ire reached beyond Reagan's aides. Thomas Niles, of the State Department, who attended the meeting, remembered it vividly:

> The PM was in a bad mood. She was unhappy . . . She laid it all out. 'This is just unacceptable . . . our companies cannot be put under US law.'
>
> The real key moment during the meeting came when, unbeknownst to us, the NSC staff had prepared some material for the President. It essentially had him saying, 'Look Margaret, we've talked to your company John Brown and they told us that this doesn't bother them. They don't really care.' That was the point at which she really went ballistic. She told us to stop taking notes. 'Put down your pencils,' she said, and banged the table. I'll never forget it. And she said to the President, 'Ron, you talk to your companies and I'll talk to mine.' It was rough. It was not a very wise thing for the President to have said.

Reagan's reaction was interesting: 'The President was chagrined. Deeply. But I couldn't say that he hesitated. He was gracious to a fault . . . but this was a matter of East–West relations. It really was one of those lines in the sand: you do not provide money to the Soviet Union.'[143] 'The Prime Minister's opposition was a source of puzzlement to the President,' recalled Bud McFarlane, who at that time was Deputy National Security Advisor.* 'She was strong in her convictions about containing the Soviet Union and ultimately rolling it back. So the President was struck by the inconsistency of her position . . . It was always in sorrow, not anger, but he never wavered.'[144]

For Mrs Thatcher, the episode was a shock, because it brought her up against the limits of her relationship with Reagan just at the moment when it seemed to be going so well. According to Clive Whitmore: 'He had made up his mind . . . and having made up his mind on the main issues there wasn't really very much concern about the repercussions for other people. I think this really did come as a bit of a blow for her. She was unable to make the good old personal relationship work in such a way that she could enlighten him.' She also learnt something about Reagan himself that alarmed her.

> I think she was really rather dismayed at how little understanding Reagan seemed to have of the issues. She had a remarkably detailed grasp of every aspect of this big policy question and it was quite plain that the President

---

* Robert 'Bud' McFarlane (1937–), counsellor, Department of State, 1981–2; Deputy National Security Advisor, 1982–3; National Security Advisor, 1983–5.

didn't . . . I think she for the first time was unhappy that he was unable to respond to her concerns . . . And so she began to take the view that well, maybe he wasn't quite as intelligent as she had always held him out to be . . . He was a bear of very little brain. It was disappointing for her. You felt a significant change in her mood after the visit.

Her officials were faintly pleased. They had been telling her 'for months and months' that Reagan did not understand a great deal. Now, felt Whitmore, 'The scales fell from her eyes.'[145]

The bickering continued through the summer. Mrs Thatcher wrote to Reagan to say that John Brown would indeed suffer severely following the US sanctions. He wrote back, maintaining his position that it would not. The disagreement was publicly known, with Mrs Thatcher characteristically taking her stand not on the rights and wrongs of the pipeline itself (she did not much like it), but on a rule-of-law argument that there could be no American jurisdiction over British companies.[146] At the end of July, Mrs Thatcher wrote to Reagan to say that she would forbid four companies, including John Brown, from complying with American law. She did so, however, in a conciliatory tone: 'I should like to stress that we are taking . . . no more than the absolute minimum action. I am very anxious that this matter should not be allowed to escalate and thus become a serious irritant in our relations . . . I would very much hope that your administration would respond in the same spirit.' On his copy of this telegram, Reagan wrote, 'We must keep our relationship on the level it is as exemplified by this message,'[147] and he replied formally in similar vein. By September, the Pentagon had started to increase its own purchases from John Brown, as a sort of covert compensation.

There is no doubt that Mrs Thatcher's displeasure did weigh with Reagan. Roger Robinson recalled: 'The President felt the pressure of his relationship with Mrs Thatcher on this matter. He would ask us periodically about progress towards our goals. "Can we lift these damn things yet?" he would say.'[148] But what really broke the impasse was Reagan's decision to replace Secretary of State Al Haig with George Shultz* at the end of June. Shultz recalled, 'I said to President Reagan, "This is a wasting asset. As time goes on, our companies are all being engineered out of this project anyway. We should try to get what we can out of this."' Shultz understood the wider context which worried Mrs Thatcher so much: 'I had it very much in mind that the following year was going to be the year of

---

* George Shultz (1920–), educated Princeton University; US Secretary of Labor, 1969–70; Director, Office of Management and Budget, 1970–72; Secretary of the Treasury, 1972–4; Secretary of State, 1982–9.

missile deployment in Europe. We couldn't afford to go into that year with this dispute in the air, so we got it settled.'[149] This was the case that Haig had put too, but Shultz, personally closer to Reagan and with new authority, was able to get a better hearing.

At the NATO foreign ministers' meeting in October, Shultz won agreement. In return for the lifting of American sanctions, the allies would develop a series of security-minded East–West economic policies. There would be a review of energy alternatives for Western Europe and no new Soviet gas-supply contracts signed. 'I worked out a deal whereby we got a beefed-up agreement among the like-minded countries not to sell things to the Russians. Margaret was very co-operative with that. The proposed settlement was something that she agreed with and so she was an ally in that sense, although she was opposed to the sanctions.'[150] Many hawks opposed Shultz's agreement. 'I don't know that this is enough to give up the pipeline sanctions,' said Cap Weinberger,[151] but Shultz prevailed. Face was saved.* On 13 November 1982, Reagan announced that the sanctions would be lifted. The hawks stressed the delay they had caused to the pipeline and the additional costs imposed on the Soviets. They also noted that construction of a proposed second strand to the pipeline had been suspended indefinitely. The view in the British Embassy, however, was that the Americans had suffered a great defeat, although officials were given strict instructions not to say so.[152] John Brown would now be permitted to sell its equipment to Moscow after all and pipeline construction would proceed. Mrs Thatcher sent a telegram to Reagan. The lifting of sanctions was 'very good news', she said, 'I am pleased that we have all been able to reach agreement on a common approach to the handling of East/West relations, particularly at a time when we must be seen to be standing together.'[153]

The pipeline episode proved the untruth of the accusation that Mrs Thatcher was ever the poodle of the United States. She argued her case with a frankness and tenacity which caused shock in Washington. And she did, after ten months of wrangling, prevail. The alliance stayed intact, and ready for the much more important business of INF deployment in Europe

---

* Unknown to Mrs Thatcher and indeed to everyone else involved with the pipeline outside a tiny circle of Reagan advisers, the CIA had managed to insert a bug into the software the Soviets had acquired to operate the pipeline. According to Thomas Reed, then an NSC staffer, when this faulty software eventually came online US satellites detected 'the most monumental non-nuclear explosion and fire ever seen from space' deep within the Soviet Union. (Thomas C. Reed, *At the Abyss: An Insider's History of the Cold War*, Presidio Press, 2004, p. 269.) Knowledge of this capability may also have played some role in Reagan's decision to lift the sanctions.

the following year. But the row forced Mrs Thatcher to be more realistic about her greatest ally, and to be aware that, even with her prestige as high as it was at the end of the Falklands War, she could not expect an easy ride.

Three days before Reagan announced the lifting of sanctions, Leonid Brezhnev, the President of the Soviet Union, died. The Foreign Office sent Mrs Thatcher a draft of the proforma letter of condolence that she was to send. In her own hand, she deleted anything suggestive of grief, and added the sentence, 'The consequences of his death will be felt far beyond the frontiers of his own country.'[154] It was intended as an optimistic prophecy, not a funerary platitude. She was looking to the future, and hoping for change.

Hunger in Ireland

'The lady behind the veil'

By the time Mrs Thatcher became prime minister, she did not have a policy towards Northern Ireland. It had died with Airey Neave just as the election campaign began. As well as the loss of a friend and ally, Neave's death was, she recalled, 'a terrible blow, because I'd never thought of anyone else for Northern Ireland ... He understood the "Irish factor". He'd studied it.'[1] She considered Humphrey Atkins, whom she made secretary of state, 'a very nice person'[2] and was even said by some to have a *tendresse* for him, but he did not want the job,[3] and knew nothing about the subject. Mrs Thatcher, and not Atkins, would therefore be the one to give a lead on Northern Ireland, but she herself did not know very much either.

More important, she had little feel for the problem. She did not go so far as Denis, who had an English, saloon-bar impatience with the whole thing: 'If the Irish want to kill each other that does seem to me to be their business.'[4] Indeed, Mrs Thatcher was, in principle, a strong Unionist, but she nevertheless possessed what Robert Armstrong, whose part in the Irish drama was to prove central, called 'a very English Englishness',[5] and little natural rapport with the people whose cause she believed she favoured. She admired what she regarded as the thrifty attitudes of Ulster people, and, as Secretary of State for Education (although schools were a matter devolved to the Northern Ireland government at Stormont), she had been impressed by what little she had seen of the province's educational standards.[6] But she was an outsider looking in. In private conversation, she had a rather revealing way of expressing her attitude: 'Airey was a convinced Unionist and, in a way, so was I, because they had been jolly loyal to us.'[7] She always thought of the people of Northern Ireland, even the Unionist population, as 'they', quite separate from 'us'.

In addition, she found the Irish, on both sides, irritating – their preference for cultural politics over the more clear-cut economic debates at Westminster, their prolixity and what she believed to be their unreliability. 'You don't expect anything decent to come from an Irishman,' she said in private,[8] and she was only half in jest. She also found it extremely hard to take in the idea that citizens of her own country might feel that they owed allegiance to another. In private conversation in retirement, she once said that Nationalists in the North were 'traitors' because of their wish for British withdrawal and a united Ireland. Then she stopped herself: 'No, no. I shouldn't say that. That is not the right word.'[9] But she never worked out what the right word was. The whole business upset her. In her memoirs, it is this tone of crossness and exasperation which dominates when she writes about Northern Ireland. As with all important questions of policy, she treated it with care and attention, and worked hard at it. She was invariably brave in the face of threats of violence, and felt a strong rapport with all those, especially soldiers and policemen, who had to deal with terrorism. Almost her first intervention on the subject of Northern Ireland after coming into office was to take up a letter from a member of the public who complained that British troops in the province were ill equipped ('we must take this <u>very seriously indeed</u>').[10] But, unlike economic matters, or East–West relations, Northern Ireland was a subject which, though she would not have put it so, she wished would go away.

Airey Neave was a famously secretive man, and his attitude to Northern Ireland will forever be disputed. Some believed that he had become a convinced integrationist, arguing that the province should be administered in the same way as other parts of the United Kingdom. If this was his position, it would have been momentous, had he had the chance to act on it. It would have reversed the policy, pursued in one way or another since the partition of Ireland in 1921, by which Northern Ireland was treated as a place apart. Even after British troops arrived to restore order in the province in 1969, and the Unionist-dominated Stormont Parliament was replaced by direct rule from London in 1972, the prevailing British orthodoxy was that Northern Ireland should be governed, though still under the Crown, by different rules from those prevailing in Westminster. Devolution and 'power-sharing', which ensured places in government for both sides of the community, were considered sacred, even if, because of conflict, they were usually suspended in favour of direct rule. Others thought, however, that Neave was more pragmatic, and, seeing how the power-sharing devolution established by the Sunningdale Agreement of 1973 had collapsed, was simply taking things very slowly and cautiously.* The wording of the Conservative election manifesto of 1979 captured Neave's deliberate

---

* In a speech to the Ulster Unionist Council in 1978, Neave had argued for a regional council or councils, but said these 'should not be regarded as a substitute for eventual devolved government'. This seems to indicate gradualism rather than pure integrationism.

ambiguity: 'In the absence of devolved government, we will seek to establish one or more elected regional councils with a wide range of powers over local services.' These actually quite non-committal words gave heart to Unionists in Ulster and within the Tory Party, because they appeared to encourage the idea that the province could return to governing itself, at least in local matters, without the imposition of power-sharing or the intervention of the Irish Republic. But they did not constitute a veto on devolution.

When she came into office, Mrs Thatcher found no expectation among her civil servants that much attention should be paid to the manifesto policy. The memo from the Cabinet Secretary, John Hunt, which awaited her on her first day, told her that a 'new initiative' was widely expected, and that 'Expectations are also high in Dublin and the United States.' Mrs Thatcher put her wiggly line of doubt under the words 'new initiative' (the phrase invariably referred to some form of power-sharing devolution and/ or an 'Irish dimension') and 'Dublin'.[11]

'Dublin', though, was worried by the manifesto's regional-councils commitment. Although history has officially recorded that the first foreign head of government to visit Mrs Thatcher as prime minister was Helmut Schmidt of Germany, it was actually Jack Lynch, the Taoiseach (prime minister),* who got in first with a 'courtesy call' just before she met Schmidt on 10 May. The discussion, at least on Lynch's side, went beyond courtesies. The note of the meeting shows that Mrs Thatcher voiced no opinions beyond saying that Northern Ireland presented a problem 'which did not yield to instant solutions'. Lynch, though, had come with an agenda: 'Mr Lynch referred to the late Airey Neave's ideas on Regional Councils.' These, he said, would lead to 'discrimination in housing matters ... This process could quickly break down the goodwill which had slowly been created.'[12] The nationalist SDLP, whom Dublin was trying to encourage, regarded power-sharing as the sine qua non for their participation in Northern Ireland politics.

In the United States, President Jimmy Carter came under pressure from the Irish-American lobby. 'I am sure that a personal expression of interest by you to Mrs. Thatcher will encourage the new Government to pursue a political solution more vigorously,' Tip O'Neill, the Speaker of the House of Representatives, wrote to Carter.[13] The President promptly called Mrs Thatcher personally and asked her for a paper setting out the situation in

---

* John (Jack) Lynch (1917–99), educated Christian Brothers' Schools, North Monastery, Cork, University College, Cork and King's Inns, Dublin; Fianna Fáil TD (Member of Dáil), 1948–81; Leader of Fianna Fáil, 1966–79; Taoiseach, 1966–73, 1977–9.

Northern Ireland. Contrary to O'Neill's hopes, Mrs Thatcher made the document as cautious on politics and as tough on security as possible. Carter's administration acquiesced in Congressional efforts to prevent the supply of US Ruger personal-protection weapons to the Royal Ulster Constabulary despite a personal appeal from Mrs Thatcher. Meeting with Carter in December 1979 she told the President that 'She herself had handled both the gun which the RUC at present used' and the new gun being requested: 'There was no doubt that the American Ruger was much better.' 'It had never occurred to her that there would be a problem about completing the order,' she continued, demanding to know whether the President's difficulty was one of 'principle or timing'. Carter pleaded the latter, limply ceding leadership to the Congress: 'The President said that he himself would like to approve the sale but did not wish to be defeated in Congress or to have a major altercation with them.'[14] Governor Hugh Carey of New York tried to drag Humphrey Atkins and the Irish Foreign Minister together to meet him to discuss a plan for the future of the province. Mrs Thatcher intervened to prevent this, telling Atkins that he should not see Carey, because 'Northern Ireland was part of the United Kingdom and she herself would not think of discussing with President Carter, for example, US policy towards his black population.'[15]

Looking at the matter from a very different point of view, Ian Paisley's* sectarian Democratic Unionists also opposed integration with the rest of the United Kingdom. They had adopted various positions on this matter in the past, but after 'the Big Man's' success in topping the poll in the European elections in Northern Ireland in June 1979 Paisley now saw himself as more powerful. Integration would destroy Paisley's dream of becoming, in constitutional fact, what he wrote to tell Mrs Thatcher he already was – 'the leader of Ulster'.[16] The right sort of devolution could assist it. As for her senior Cabinet colleagues, all those with any experience in the field, with the partial exception of the Lord Chancellor, Lord Hailsham, were personally committed to some version of power-sharing and a greater role for the Irish Republic. The Home Secretary, Willie Whitelaw, was chairman of the ministerial group on policy in Northern Ireland. As one of the architects of the Sunningdale Agreement, which, under Ted Heath, had imposed power-sharing upon Northern Ireland in 1973 (and

---

* Ian Paisley (1926–), educated Ballymena Model School, Ballymena Technical High School, South Wales Bible College and Reformed Presbyterian Theological College, Belfast; ordained, 1946; moderator, Free Presbyterian Church of Ulster, 1951–2008; Protestant Unionist MP for Antrim North, 1970–74; Democratic Unionist MP for Antrim North, 1974–2010; Leader of Democratic Unionist Party, 1972–2008; Member of Northern Ireland Assembly, 1998–2011; First Minister of Northern Ireland, 2007–8; created Lord Bannside, 2010.

had failed because of the Ulster Workers' Strike the following year), he was never going to depart from that mental model. His usual answer to all the ills of Northern Ireland was: 'When things get bad, have a conference.'[17]

In short, almost all the players in the drama were against anything resembling the policy orphaned by the death of Neave. The only exceptions to this were the 'Official' Unionists, the largest political party in Northern Ireland, formally called the Ulster Unionist Party, led by Jim Molyneaux* and provided with intellectual rigour by Enoch Powell. They had allies in the Tory Party, of whom by far the most important was Ian Gow. The only other exception was Mrs Thatcher herself, and although she knew what she did not like, she did not really have a coherent policy of her own.

Northern Ireland therefore lacked direction for the first few months of Mrs Thatcher's time in office. She and the whole government were busy with other things. What changed matters was the assassination on 27 August 1979 of Lord Mountbatten and, on the same day, the murder of eighteen British soldiers at Warrenpoint, both carried out by the IRA. One obvious effect of these atrocities was to strengthen Mrs Thatcher in her conviction of the need for strong security measures and much greater pressure on the Republic to prevent terrorism. The Republic was 'harbouring known murderers',[18] she angrily told a meeting of senior ministers the following day, and she wanted to use 'leverage against the Republic', including 'administrative action against Irish immigrants',[19] to get the extradition of suspects to Britain. Fired up by the success of her morale-boosting visit to the province in the wake of the outrages, Mrs Thatcher was full of eagerness to sort out the lack of co-ordination between the army and the Royal Ulster Constabulary and to make cross-border security co-operation a reality. With typically energetic sympathy, she wrote letters to the families of each of the eighteen murdered soldiers, each one different, and all in her own hand. No prime minister had ever thought of doing this before. It was a custom which she was to maintain. As well as giving comfort to the families, it served to remind Mrs Thatcher, after each death, of the human cost of Ulster's tragedy.†

---

* James Molyneaux (1920–), educated Aldergrove School, Co. Antrim; Ulster Unionist MP for Antrim South, 1970–83; for Lagan Valley, 1983–97; Leader, Ulster Unionist Party in House of Commons, 1974–9, and Leader of the party, 1979–95; created Lord Molyneaux of Killead, 1997.

† Mrs Thatcher never ceased to pay close attention to the victims of terrorism and to be strongly affected by their suffering. In October 1981, the IRA blew up the dismounting Tower of London Guard near Chelsea Barracks, wounding twenty-three Irish Guardsmen and killing two civilians. The commanding officer, Robert Corbett, recounted Mrs Thatcher's visit to the injured

A second meeting with Jack Lynch was arranged to coincide with his visit to London for Lord Mountbatten's funeral. Humphrey Atkins asked Mrs Thatcher to promise the Taoiseach 'political progress'. 'I see no possibility of opening up in this way with Mr Lynch,' she replied.'. . . The most we can contemplate going to is preparation for <u>effective local government</u>. The rest sounds too much as if we are treating them [Northern Ireland] as a colony – not as part of the UK.'[20] Instead, at the meeting, Mrs Thatcher pressed Lynch to do more about security. Lynch's reaction was to say that everything was very difficult. He preferred a political solution, agreed between the two governments. Mrs Thatcher, in her turn, was cautious: 'It would help enormously if people would stop talking about the total unity of Ireland.'[21] At a plenary meeting on the same day, matters became heated. Backed by an unusually hawkish Carrington, Mrs Thatcher warned Lynch that 'she would be unable to restrain public opinion in this country if . . . she and Mr Lynch were unable to point to anything new [on security] that would be done.' She 'asked whether the Irish side were prepared to get down to brass tacks'.[22] The Irish delegation were taken aback by her vehemence, and Lynch was slow to reply. George Colley, the Tánaiste (deputy prime minister), tried to argue back. According to Dermot Nally,* then Deputy Secretary to the Department of the Taoiseach, who was present as part of the Irish delegation, 'One of the ministers made the remark that "You may not like the idea but some people have a quantity of sympathy with the men of violence." That made her furious. "Are you condoning murder?" She nearly had to be held back. The meeting with Lynch was not a success.'[23]

Yet the very thing which made Mrs Thatcher so angry – the feebleness of the Irish Republic towards terrorists operating from within its borders – was the factor used to push forward the idea of a political initiative: without more political conciliation, it was argued, there could not be better security. In October, Atkins announced an initiative which involved talks with all the parties in Northern Ireland about possible ways of bringing devolution about. At the same time, senior ministers and officials, privately sceptical of Atkins and his rather half-baked plan, pushed for

---

the following day: 'When she saw how terribly injured many of them were she turned to one side so deeply affected that I had to take her out of the ward for a brief moment. She was in tears.' Weeks later, she invited Corbett and his wife to No. 10. 'The most striking thing about her was that she knew precisely the state of health and progress of each of those injured soldiers.' (Correspondence with Major-General Sir Robert Corbett.)

* Dermot Nally (1927–2009), Deputy Secretary to the Department of the Taoiseach, and head of Northern Ireland Affairs, 1973–80; Secretary-General to the Department of the Taoiseach (and Cabinet Secretary), 1980–93.

something more. Following the favourable publicity given to Pope John Paul II's appeal, during his acclaimed visit to the Republic at the end of September 1979, for an end to violence and an effort to fill the political vacuum, they sought a bigger political initiative. John Hunt suggested to Mrs Thatcher that Atkins should be bypassed by a working group which would produce a consultation document.[24] Within the British administrative machine, there were signs that matters would be settled – chiefly by a combination of the Foreign Office and the Cabinet Office – at a higher level. Less attention should be paid to what parties in Northern Ireland wanted, and more to a deal with the Republic.

Atkins's initiative then confronted Mrs Thatcher with an awkward surprise. The Official Unionists, the more moderate of the Unionist parties, declined to take part in the Atkins discussions, because the Atkins plan was anti-integrationist. This was not, in itself, unexpected, but the precise trigger for their non-cooperation was. Following a meeting with the Unionists' leader, Ian Gow, always the conduit between the government and the UUP, wrote to Mrs Thatcher:

> Earlier this month, Jim Molyneaux told me that when he agreed to deliver the Official Unionist Members of Parliament on our side in the crucial vote at 10 p.m. on Wednesday 28th of March 1979, it was on the understanding that if our party was elected in the General Election which followed, we would set up one or more elected regional councils. If Airey had not given a clear indication that this would be our policy, there is some doubt (to put it at its lowest) whether Jim Molyneaux could have delivered the Ulster Unionist votes . . . Airey told me nothing of any undertaking which had been given to Molyneaux . . . and of course Airey was murdered two days later. Nevertheless, it is, of course, correct to say that the policy on which you and Airey had agreed for Ulster had been [given] the broad assent of the Official Unionists.[25]

Gow then improved the shining hour by enclosing a memo by T. E. Utley arguing that the Atkins strategy was 'disastrously wrong' and would fail, and that the retreat from Neave's policy was a 'serious mistake'. 'A devolved Parliament in Ulster . . . is likely to be dominated by hardline Protestants far more nervous and bitter than Craigavon or Brookeborough [the first and third (Unionist) prime ministers of Northern Ireland], feeling no special link with any British party and determined to rule the Province itself.'[26] Mrs Thatcher underlined this sentence approvingly.

Mrs Thatcher – who kept Gow and her civil servants carefully separate in all dealings about Northern Ireland – seems to have sat on this suggestion of a promise from Neave to the Unionists and done nothing about it.

Months later, it came to the notice of officialdom. Kenneth Stowe, who had moved on from being the Prime Minister's principal private secretary to become permanent under-secretary at the Northern Ireland Office, had fairly frequent, approved private conversations with Enoch Powell. At the end of March 1980, Powell raised the matter of the Neave promise with him. Stowe was 'absolutely appalled by this', since he and Atkins had explicitly denied in Northern Ireland that such a promise had been made.[27] He made an official record of this talk, which was immediately taken by Atkins and him to Mrs Thatcher. In the note, marked 'secret and personal', Stowe said that Powell had asked to see the Prime Minister herself about the breaking of the alleged promise, which, he said, had been made to him personally: 'I was struck by the stark clarity and precise terms in which Mr Powell referred to his agreement with Mr Neave. I was also struck by the fact that he seemed not to assume that the secretary of state was a party to, or even aware of this agreement, but plainly indicated that the PM was, hence his decision that he must go to see her.'[28] Stowe and Atkins then went to see Mrs Thatcher and Gow, and she declared that she had known nothing about it at the time.[29] Gow, too, had not known of it. Willie Whitelaw was also consulted. He likewise denied all knowledge of the 'deal' by anyone in his ministerial group, and warned that any attempt to act upon it would have terrible consequences 'if the minority were totally disillusioned at apparent British duplicity'.[30] Apparent British duplicity towards the *majority* seems to have been regarded less seriously.

In any event, Mrs Thatcher herself then met Enoch Powell, with Ian Gow, on 1 May. Powell advanced his criticisms of the Atkins proposals, because they were a step towards devolution, but, oddly, made no mention of the Neave promise. In the absence of Neave himself, and therefore of any proof, Mrs Thatcher and her colleagues decided that there was nothing to be done and that they should press on with the Atkins plan regardless. They were inclined to do so not only by the general institutional push for devolution, but by the belief in some official circles that Ian Paisley might, after all, prove to be a constructive force from their point of view, and more inclined to a deal than his granite rhetoric suggested. Much damage was done to the relationship between Official Unionism and Mrs Thatcher's government. From then on, trust was undermined, and Unionists tended to conclude either that Mrs Thatcher herself was deceiving them or – more often, because many of them admired her personally for her robust attitude to terrorism – that she was not fully master in her own house. Traditional conspiracy theories about the Foreign Office sprang up again. As Utley had predicted, moderate Unionism was sidelined, and Paisleyism, which prospered whenever 'sell-out' and 'betrayal' were suspected, continued to grow. From the point of view of those who wanted an 'Irish dimension' to the problem of Northern Ireland, the fact that Mrs Thatcher seemed to have had no knowledge of the Neave 'promise' was crucial. If she had done so, they believed, she would never have authorized the conversations between British officials and the Taoiseach's office which, in the long run, were to prove so important.[31]

In the first six months of 1980, as the Atkins initiative stuttered on, the British government – though not Mrs Thatcher herself – became still more interested in dealing directly with Dublin. The Prime Minister came under official pressure to take up the suggestion of Charles Haughey,* who had become Taoiseach in December 1979, for a meeting. She resisted requests from Haughey and from Carrington, Atkins and Stowe for a meeting to discuss Northern Ireland in the margins of the European Council in Brussels ('It would be easier to meet him first in the company of others,' she wrote, almost bashfully),[32] but eventually succumbed to the idea that she should give Haughey lunch at No. 10. This took place on 21 May and, in human terms, went well. Haughey presented Mrs Thatcher with a Georgian silver teapot. It came with a silver tea-strainer on which were inscribed the words from the prayer attributed to St Francis of Assisi which she had declaimed on her first day in Downing Street: 'Where there is disharmony, let there be peace.'[33] It was intended to prick her conscience. 'That will set her back a bit,' Haughey had predicted.[34] There is no known official record of the lunch, but Haughey was 'cock-a-hoop' after it[35] and came away with a 'great admiration' for Mrs Thatcher, whom he considered to be 'a woman of her word'.[36] He told the British Ambassador in Dublin, Robin Haydon, that he had no religious prejudices, and, in a choice of phrase not best calculated to appeal to Mrs Thatcher's serious temperament, did not mind if someone wanted 'to worship Ali Baba and the Seven [sic] Thieves'.[37]† For her part, Mrs Thatcher had been quite charmed at the lunch, but this did not lead her to concede anything of importance. As one official put it later: 'The PM liked being led up the garden path by Haughey, but didn't like the garden when she got there.'[38] She resisted Haughey's flattery of her settlement in Rhodesia in order to make it a template for what might happen in Northern Ireland ('I said the circumstances were totally different'),

* Charles Haughey (1925–2006), educated St Joseph's Christian Brothers' School, Fairview, Dublin, University College, Dublin and King's Inns, Dublin; Fianna Fáil TD, 1957–92; Leader, Fianna Fáil, 1979–92; Taoiseach, 1979–81, March–December 1982 and 1987–92.
† In view of Haughey's subsequent exposure for corruption, he may, in this phrase, have been thinking of himself.

but she was interested by his suggestion that, if Northern Ireland were 'solved', the Republic might re-examine its neutrality and be ready to join NATO.[39]* The idea of joining NATO was being floated more widely at the time, however. It helped fuel Enoch Powell's paranoia about American motives in Ireland. There is little evidence that the United States, or anyone else, pushed it hard. Mrs Thatcher was content that the communiqué afterwards spoke of the 'unique relationship' between the 'peoples' of Ireland and the United Kingdom. She did not give thought to the danger that this idea of a unique relationship might be built on by those with more visionary ideas about political co-operation – and what were known as 'parallel' developments – than her own.

During the next month, drafts of Atkins's proposals circulated. Sure enough, they included ideas arising from the Haughey encounter, including 'parallel talks'. The draft reformulated the British 'guarantee' to Northern Ireland, which Haughey so much disliked, as 'Northern Ireland will not cease to be part of the United Kingdom without the consent of the majority of the people.' Mrs Thatcher noted: 'Wholly written in the negative i.e. as if it is truly wanting Ulster to go.'[40] She roped in Ian Gow to help her with the drafts. He fastened on a phrase about developing 'the special relationship with the Republic of Ireland', writing, 'WE MUST NOT HAVE THIS,' to which she added, by way of agreement, 'Oath of allegiance.' Gow went on, '. . . WE MUST NOT FRAME OUR PROPOSALS TO PLEASE THE REPUBLIC.' When the draft stated that the extension of local government 'would encounter much opposition', she scrawled 'So will this [plan].' She was sensitive, too, to possible ramifications for other parts of the Kingdom. In response to the suggestion that there should be an advisory council of Northern Ireland, she wrote, 'leading to a Council of Scotland?', and protested that the secretary of state should be accountable to Parliament and nobody else. And she ridiculed some of the ideas by applying them to an English context: 'Are we going to have power-sharing in permanently Socialist counties? Or in permanently Tory counties?'[41] In short, she was not pleased. Finding some allies in the Cabinet, she insisted on substantial redrafting, reducing hostages to fortune in relation to Scotland and, as OD minutes put it, removing the draft's 'negative features [to] avoid the impression that the Government's longer-term policy was to give Northern Ireland away'.[42]

Despite Mrs Thatcher's unwillingness to make too many concessions to

---

* Mrs Thatcher refused to mention this tentative offer in her memoirs because she considered that by relaying it she would be breaking the privacy that Haughey had demanded (THCR 4/3).

Irish opinion, her relationship with Haughey had already produced the unintended effect of undermining Atkins's plans. The SDLP had taken heart from the fact of Thatcher and Haughey meeting and were less minded to support a purely British settlement. Atkins's revised proposals were nevertheless published on 2 July 1980. Just before everyone went away on holiday, a worried Northern Ireland Office made contact with No. 10, with word of some Chinese, or rather Irish, whispers. John Hume* had reported that Haughey had told him that, at the European Council in Venice on 12–13 June, Mrs Thatcher had told him (Haughey) that 'she did not expect the Government's initiative to get anywhere.' Beside this report, Mrs Thatcher wrote '!!!' and 'I'm sure I said no such thing.' She protested, slightly guiltily, that she had meant only that it would not get anywhere before the recess. Her private secretary, Michael Alexander, noted that a record-taker should always be present whenever she met Haughey. 'I agree,' wrote the Prime Minister.[43]

Ever conscientious, Mrs Thatcher asked for a reading list about Ireland for her holiday, and went off, at the suggestion of the Northern Ireland Office, with several books, none from a Unionist perspective, including *Ireland since the Famine* by F. S. L. Lyons, *A Place Apart* by Dervla Murphy and *Peace by Ordeal* by Lord Longford.[44] When politics resumed in the autumn, no agreement was reached between the parties which would have allowed the Atkins plan to go forward. Political initiatives were pushed aside by dramatic events.

It was part of the IRA's belief in itself as an army that its men, if convicted and imprisoned, should be treated like prisoners of war. For this very reason, it was important for British governments to resist this demand. In 1976, the Labour government had righted a grave political error of the Heath government and removed 'special-category status' from all new terrorist prisoners, putting them, at least in principle, on a par with common criminals. This had provoked both the 'blanket' protest, in which prisoners had dressed only in their bedclothes and refused to wear prison uniform, and the 'dirty' protest, in which they had smeared their cells with excrement.† In the course of 1980, aware that these protests were not succeeding, and angry that restrictions on special-category status had been further tightened, the Republican inmates in the Maze prison decided to

---

* John Hume (1937–), educated St Columb's College, Derry and St Patrick's College, Maynooth; Leader of SDLP, 1979–2001; MEP, Northern Ireland, 1979–2004; SDLP MP for Foyle, 1983–2005; joint winner of Nobel Peace Prize, 1998.
† The dirty protest always provoked in Mrs Thatcher a reaction of extreme disgust.

go further. On 10 October, they announced a hunger strike, which started on 27 October. If the strike held, Mrs Thatcher was warned, deaths could be expected by Christmas.

Pressure quickly came on her to make concessions. Rather surprisingly, she did so, before the strike began. On 23 October, a secret message from Charles Haughey warned her of 'serious repercussions for the security situation in Ireland' if the strikes went ahead.[45] On the same day, the Cabinet decided that the prisoners should, after all, be allowed to wear 'civilian-type clothes', rather than the existing prison uniform.* Mrs Thatcher explained her thinking on this to Cabinet colleagues: 'I am concerned to get us into the most reasonable position before the start, and stick to it.'[46] She also stated that she did not want to lose Haughey's security co-operation. As so often, her own preoccupation with security was used against her to weaken her political determination. Concerned to prevent Cardinal Tomas O'Fiaich, the Irish primate, claiming the credit for this concession, which he had advocated, and thereby enraging Protestants, she made sure it was rushed out. Even so, Unionists were angry, and so were Tory backbenchers, who also attacked Atkins for trying to push forward his initiative in these unpropitious circumstances.

The strikes went ahead all the same, with seven prisoners taking part. Once this had happened, Mrs Thatcher toughened up. When Robert Armstrong wrote to her to say that it was important 'to find a way of getting the strikers and PIRA off the hook',[47]† Michael Alexander, her foreign affairs private secretary, noted that it was not the government's business to get the IRA off any hook: 'Our aim should be to break the strike.' Mrs Thatcher agreed. 'We cannot make <u>any concessions</u>,' she scribbled, but then, referring mentally to the concessions already made, added: 'When will the new issue clothing be ready?'[48]‡

Pope John Paul II sent a private message to the Irish bishops urging them to persuade the hunger strikers to stop, and when Mrs Thatcher visited the Pope in Rome on 24 November 1980 she was informed that there was a good chance of the strike being called off.[49] But compromise proposals put forward by two Catholic prison chaplains asked for concessions too big for the gov-

---

* 'Civilian-type' clothes were different from 'civilian' clothes, because the former, though not uniform in style, were issued by the prison authorities rather than the personal property of the prisoners. This point, it was argued, allowed control to be maintained.

† The Provisional IRA was formed out of the split in the IRA in 1969. The Official IRA effectively foreswore violence. PIRA supported it.

‡ Shortly after this, Armstrong drew Alexander into détente with the Republic by using him as the conduit for messages from Haughey's office about the hunger strike, thus making him a party in the process of concession.

ernment to make. When Haughey met Mrs Thatcher in the margins of the
European Council in Luxembourg at the beginning of December, he pressed
her to take an initiative on the hunger strike before the summit which was
due in Dublin the following week. Mrs Thatcher said she would not make
any new concessions but would be prepared to 'dress up' what was already
on offer.[50] In early December, Atkins put out a statement to this effect. At the
Dublin summit, Haughey told Mrs Thatcher privately that he thought Britain
should talk 'quietly and unobtrusively' to the strikers through the prison
chaplains. He believed that they were looking for a way out, and could decide
for themselves rather than at the command of the PIRA leadership outside
the prison.[51]

   This was dangerous territory for Mrs Thatcher, who was fearful of linking the sort of political movement which the Republic wanted with any
concessions to terrorists. But British officialdom was, in fact, moving even
more 'quietly and unobtrusively' than Haughey was demanding. In the mid-
1970s, an SIS officer, working for his service in Northern Ireland, had
established contact with the IRA through a Londonderry businessman
called Brendan Duddy.[52] Duddy operated from a flat above his fish and chip
shop in Londonderry. His close contact was the commander of the IRA
Brigade in Londonderry, Martin McGuinness.* A link, unauthorized by
MI6, was maintained, and, at the beginning of December 1980, Duddy
reactivated it. He told the officer[53] that Gerry Adams† and Martin McGuinness, who, by this time, had gained ascendancy in the Provisionals, wanted
the hunger strike stopped. They needed a formula for this to happen, involving apparent concessions which would save Republican face. In the officer's
mind, it was not a deal, but a matter of Britain making reasonably visible
gestures. He decided to take the idea to Frank Cooper at the Ministry of
Defence (who was formerly the head of the Northern Ireland Office), and,
on Cooper's advice, to Ken Stowe at the Northern Ireland Office, who
thought that it should be pursued. Stowe drew up a paper of what the
necessary gestures might be.

   · It was considered necessary for the officer, whom Stowe regarded as 'a
very entrepreneurial spy',[54] to take this at once to Northern Ireland to hand

---

* Martin McGuinness (1950–), educated Christian Brothers' Technical College, Londonderry;
Vice-President, Sinn Fein, from 1983; Sinn Fein MP for Mid-Ulster 1997–2013; Member,
Northern Ireland Assembly, from 1998; Minister of Education, 1999–2002; Deputy First
Minister from 2007; Sinn Fein candidate in Irish presidential election, 2011.
† Gerard (Gerry) Adams (1948–), educated St Mary's Christian Brothers' School, Belfast;
Vice-President, Sinn Fein, 1978–83, and President from 1983; Sinn Fein MP for Belfast West,
1983–92 and 1997–2011; Member, Northern Ireland Assembly, 1998–2010; TD for Louth
from 2011.

the paper to his IRA contacts there. Because of the political danger and the risk of kidnapping, Stowe decided that this should not be done without Mrs Thatcher's permission, so he arranged an urgent meeting with her in the House of Commons, also attended by Atkins. He told the Prime Minister what had occurred and what was proposed. While this was in progress, the officer sat in Stowe's official car, waiting to be rushed to Heathrow. Mrs Thatcher agreed to the mission. According to Stowe, she specifically endorsed the plan, 'fully aware that it involved dealing with Sinn Fein [the political arm of the IRA]'.[55] In Mrs Thatcher's view, this was a very different thing from direct talks between herself or other ministers and Sinn Fein–IRA. She was simply inheriting a contact, and allowing officials to make use of it. 'I didn't deal directly with the PIRA leadership,' she recalled, 'I've never, never in my life. I wouldn't deal with these people – they kill left, right and centre.' But, she added, 'What Security did was approach people to try to get a message through.'[56] She was being disingenuous.

Stowe considered that what the SIS officer was offering was 'a façade of concessions about the treatment of prisoners which gave them a ladder to climb down'.[57] The concessions were presented as 'humanitarian', and therefore applicable to all prisoners in Northern Ireland, not just terrorist ones – civilian clothing from their families to be worn during visits and recreation to be permitted as quickly as possible, 'civilian-type' clothing during the working day, free association at weekends, the prospect of restored remission. The central issue on which the government said it would not move was control and authority. On 18 December 1980, the prisoners climbed down the ladder available and ended their strike. Atkins duly announced the 'humanitarian' concessions and had to fend off charges that the government had made a deal with the strikers. Nevertheless, the strike's collapse was a victory for Mrs Thatcher. But the very fact that the government insisted that these limited concessions were not connected to the strike contained the seeds of future trouble. The prisoners naturally wanted to believe that they had won real concessions and were quick to seek evidence of bad faith. The IRA had also learnt something vital, which they had known in the past but doubted in the case of Mrs Thatcher – the British government, including the Prime Minister herself, were prepared to take part in what was, in effect, negotiation.[58] After a strike which they had not really wanted, they pocketed this knowledge to help them plan better next time.

In later years, Mrs Thatcher recalled the moment when she heard of the end of the strike. She was presiding over the office Christmas party at No. 10 when Michael Alexander came up the stairs to give her the good news. 'I remember thinking that we had ended for all time the method of the hunger strike.'[59] It was not to be.

Mrs Thatcher was fortunate that the failure of the hunger strike burnished her reputation for toughness, because her summit with Charles Haughey ten days earlier had caused outrage among Unionists. As so often in Irish matters, occasions which she regarded as minimal and practical were seen by the Republic as mightily symbolic. This was the first prime-minister-led bilateral delegation of British ministers to Dublin since Partition, and it took place on the Feast of the Immaculate Conception. The venue, Dublin Castle, was the old seat of British power. Due to a last-minute decision for Mrs Thatcher to land on the lawn there, rather than arriving at Baldonnell aerodrome, she was early, and the only people present to greet her were junior officials and electricians making final preparations for the visit. One official took her on an impromptu tour of the Castle. He recalled:

> She was going about in her usual bossy fashion saying 'What's that?' . . . She walked into a room and saw a big plaque on the wall in the Irish language, and she said in her usual fashion, 'What does that say?' An official was starting to stammer out what it was when a worker, who was fixing a light switch, turned and said, 'I'll tell you what it is, ma'am. That's the sign that says this is where youse took James Connolly [the socialist Republican trade union leader and commander of the Dublin Brigade in the 1916 Rising] before youse took him out and shot him.' She said, 'Oh, very interesting,' and they marched on. It was the best possible introduction to a meeting with Charlie Haughey because Charlie would have to explain that in Ireland the wounds of history were still very open, and it would take work to move things on.[60]

Mrs Thatcher arrived with a high-powered delegation, including Carrington and Geoffrey Howe. In her mind, this was to emphasize the fact that a wide range of business, especially relating to the EEC – rather than merely Northern Ireland – was being transacted; but in Irish eyes it added to the historical significance of the occasion. She had been briefed that the Irish were looking for an intergovernmental way of making progress. Whenever this had been suggested, she had put a wavy line against it. Her briefing paper about the UK's objectives for the meeting was expressed with almost comically agonized care – the pressure from officialdom for movement in a 'green' (that is, Irish Nationalist) direction reined in by the knowledge that she was intensely suspicious: 'Cautiously to explore the extent to which it may be possible, in the United Kingdom's interest, to devise arrangements under which the Northern Ireland problem can be considered by the two governments in the context of an evolving "unique relationship". But to avoid any commitment which would risk provoking a loyalist backlash in Northern Ireland.'[61]

The meeting itself went well enough. Haughey told Mrs Thatcher that he wanted a conference in 1981 which could end the violence and review 'in a fundamental way the totality of our relationship'. Mrs Thatcher primly replied that it was 'too soon for such a conference',[62] but agreed to the idea of 'joint studies' which might develop 'new structures' of co-operation. She declared herself pleased with security co-operation. Before lunch, Haughey had shown Mrs Thatcher the throne room in Dublin Castle and invited her to sit on the throne once occupied by Queen Victoria. She 'firmly' declined, but suggested Haughey should do so if he wished. 'Both laughed.'[63] After Mrs Thatcher had left the Castle, Haughey returned to the throne room. One of his officials turned to him and told him he could now sit on the throne with impunity: 'Sure after today aren't you the King of Ireland?'[64] Leonard Figg, the new British Ambassador to Dublin, reported to Michael Alexander that Haughey sat on the throne, 'his feet not quite touching the floor, and told the company they should now all kneel. He has a good sense of fun, and we might take comfort from the fact that he clearly thought the day had gone well.'[65]

One must doubt whether Mrs Thatcher was pleased with this image of a clowning pseudo-king of Ireland occupying the former seat of British royalty. She was certainly not happy that Haughey felt the day had gone so well, because his success, she believed, had been bought at her expense. The trouble lay in the communiqué. It announced that the leaders' next meeting, in 1981, would be devoted to 'the totality of relationships within these islands', and that the Joint Studies had been commissioned 'for this purpose'. There was uproar from Unionists, who thought that Dublin would now have a role in deciding the future of the province. Enoch Powell described the summit as a 'mini-Munich'. Ian Paisley raged, and insulted Mrs Thatcher at a meeting which he had with her before Christmas. The following month, he began a 'Carson trail' of rallies of men, sometimes holding up shotgun licences to show their readiness to fight, in imitation of Edward Carson, the great leader of early twentieth-century Unionism.

Mrs Thatcher afterwards blamed herself for not having given her usual minute attention to the drafting of the communiqué. She had not understood the incendiary implication of the phrase 'the totality of relationships'. Her officials, such as Stowe, who had drafted it, almost certainly did, but, perhaps because they supported the idea, had not warned her. 'Ever after that,' Mrs Thatcher recalled, 'I was wary.'[66]

The situation was then made much worse by the Irish Foreign Minister, Brian Lenihan,* who told BBC Radio Ulster: 'As far as we are concerned,

---

* Brian Lenihan (1930–95), educated St Mary's College (Marist Brothers), Athlone and Uni-

everything is on the table. This attitude had been the consistent attitude of the Taoiseach and, as far as new institutional structures are concerned, we regard them as new political ways of resolving the problem that exists between North and South, within Northern Ireland itself and between the two parts of Ireland and Britain.'[67] In March of the following year, Lenihan made further public remarks, this time about how he envisaged that a federal structure for the whole of Ireland might emerge from Anglo-Irish discussions. Haughey and Mrs Thatcher met in the margins of the European Council at Maastricht. She told Haughey that Lenihan's outbursts 'might well have "undone" everything'.[68] Haughey admitted that the whole thing was a 'mess'. Dermot Nally, who was present at the conversation, remembered Mrs Thatcher's anger: '"I said nothing about the constitution, nothing whatsoever was said." She went on and on and on. She was so vitriolic in her criticism. This destroyed her belief in the idea that she could reach agreement with Haughey. It destroyed her faith in him.'[69]

The process, however, was not destroyed. The Joint Studies gave British and Irish officials what bureaucrats always need in order to advance their processes – a framework of regular contact. After the row about the communiqué, British officials were nervous. They feared Mrs Thatcher's displeasure about how they would proceed. In a masterly piece of mandarin handling, Robert Armstrong wrote to her to explain that the Foreign Office, which would normally be in charge of discussions with a foreign country, wished to stay out of the Joint Studies. Lord Carrington, he told her, was worried about 'possible suggestions that he and his Department are associated with "sell-out" e.g. over Rhodesia or the Falklands* and are preparing to play a similar role in the Irish question.'[70] Carrington also thought that the Taoiseach's office, run by Nally, and not the Irish Foreign Ministry, should handle the matter in Dublin. Prudence and symmetry therefore demanded, suggested Armstrong, that the Joint Studies should be handled by the Cabinet Office, run, of course, by Armstrong himself. The Cabinet Secretary added that, for the same reasons relating to 'sell-out' accusations, the potentially relevant Wet (not, of course, the word he used) ministers did not want to chair the group in charge of the studies. Willie Whitelaw felt 'slightly tarred with the Sunningdale brush'.[71] The unstated implication was that Mrs Thatcher herself should preside. She did not want to take the hint. 'I am very unhappy with these proposals,' she wrote. 'FO

---

versity College, Dublin; Fianna Fáil TD, 1961–73, 1977–95; Minister of Foreign Affairs, January–March 1973, 1979–81 and 1987–89; Tanaiste, 1987–90.

* An issue which had just returned to public view because of MPs' angry reception of the idea of 'leaseback', by which sovereignty of the islands would be ceded to Argentina – see Chapter 23.

<u>must</u> take the lead – otherwise the relationship with the Republic will be being treated in a wholly different way from other EEC bilaterals.'[72] She also wished to avoid being personally associated with an enterprise of which she was so suspicious. But she gave Armstrong the Cabinet Office control which he sought.

Robert Armstrong was also, in his phrase about Whitelaw, 'tarred with the Sunningdale brush', having played an important role as Ted Heath's principal private secretary at the time of the agreement. He knew, of course, her attitude to Heath and so 'didn't remind her of Sunningdale too much . . . but it went back to that'.[73] Armstrong had long had a personal interest in the Irish question, and his mental model was always that of Sunningdale – power-sharing and some sort of Irish dimension, such as the Council of Ireland which Sunningdale had proposed. From the Sunningdale era, he had established a good relationship with Dermot Nally, who, from 1980, was his equivalent in Dublin. To a man of Armstrong's elite, administrative mind, it was far more attractive to turn arrangements about the future of Northern Ireland into an intergovernmental affair, rather than let them be a matter to be decided chiefly by the inhabitants of the province. This was an additional reason, as well as his sympathy for a united Ireland, for putting his own Cabinet Office in the lead. He wanted the Unionists kept at bay; and although he was close to Kenneth Stowe at the Northern Ireland Office, after Stowe had departed in 1981 he worked quietly to exclude the NIO from major decisions. As Stowe put it, 'Robert would never have dreamed of going behind my back, but after me, he did.'[74] As a loyal, able and professional civil servant, Armstrong was always careful to protect Mrs Thatcher's position and give her his best advice, but there can be no doubt that he was also trying to push her towards a view of Ireland which she did not like.

Once the Joint Studies were agreed at Dublin, it was all but inevitable that they would progress in a way which Mrs Thatcher found unwelcome. Armstrong was able to exploit his liaison with Dublin over the Joint Studies to find out what Dublin thought and move the political situation forward. As well as travelling to Dublin himself, he sent his deputy, Robert Wade-Gery, there for secret meetings with officials in the Taioseach's office. Wade-Gery recalled that they were 'very gingerly' beginning to talk about what would eventually, in 1985, become the Anglo-Irish Agreement.[75] Some of these meetings took place even before the Joint Studies were under way. Because of the need for security, Wade-Gery did not go near the British Embassy in Dublin for these encounters, but travelled under a concealed identity. He would walk past the Taioseach's office at a prearranged time and 'a door in the wall would open'. Such contacts were not forbidden –

'Mrs Thatcher would have had to OK them' – but their full content was not known to the Prime Minister. In Wade-Gery's view, Mrs Thatcher was anti-Irish and 'not at all reasonable. It was a long process of persuading her that it was worth doing.'[76] In addition to his more informal activities, Wade-Gery was also in charge of drafting the reports of the Joint Studies. So he, too, had the right cover.

As the plans for the Joint Studies developed, Mrs Thatcher did what she could to modify their work and challenge their assumptions. In January 1981, she handed the terms of reference over to Ian Gow and asked him for his suggestions. He added extradition from the Republic under the heading of 'citizenship rights' and said that one task of the Studies should be 'to review the claim of Irish Constitution [expressed in Articles Two and Three] to part of the territory of the United Kingdom'.[77] His ideas were not followed through. Mrs Thatcher herself was nervous of pressing the Republic on its constitutional claim to Northern Ireland because, she told Enoch Powell, she wanted the Joint Studies to discuss 'only institutional and not constitutional matters. If the Prime Minister were to seek to raise the constitutional issue with the Irish Government, it would then seek to raise the constitutional position of Northern Ireland within the United Kingdom, and that was something which the Prime Minister would never agree to discuss.'[78]* The one issue which Unionists were prepared to discuss with the Republic was thus ruled out of order by Mrs Thatcher. For some time, the precise format of the Joint Studies remained vague, and the secrecy surrounding them added to Unionist concerns. The original communiqué had explained that the Studies concerned 'possible new institutional structures, citizenship rights, security matters, economic cooperation and measures to encourage mutual understanding'. The wide-ranging nature of the agenda allowed the officials to discuss anything they wanted. Although the phrase had caused Mrs Thatcher so much trouble, the Joint Studies did, in fact, cover the 'totality of relationships within these islands', and this formula reappeared when the reports were published almost a year later. The main purpose of the whole thing was to lay the ground for a more formal relationship between the two governments, while making the idea seem as inoffensive as possible.

---

* Powell took a different view: 'He said that if he was contemplating lending his lawn mower to his next door neighbour, when his next door neighbour was claiming that the lawn mower was his, and not Mr Powell's, he, Mr Powell, would find it difficult to continue discussions as to whether he, Mr Powell, should lend the lawn mower to his neighbour.' (Gow note of Powell meeting with Thatcher, 10 Feb. 1981, THCR 2/6/2/116.) The analogy is, untypically for Powell, inexact. The dispute was over the ownership not of the lawn mower but, as it were, of the lawn.

In March 1981, Wade-Gery reported to Armstrong that the Irish government was looking for an Anglo-Irish Council to emerge from the Joint Studies, and a joint parliamentary forum too. Their 'eventual objective was a federal Ireland'.[79] Mrs Thatcher was perturbed and called a meeting of the key figures – Whitelaw, Carrington, Ian Gilmour, who now chaired the Joint Studies work, Atkins, Armstrong and Wade-Gery (all of whom, with the partial exception of Atkins, privately disagreed with her). She complained that 'The talks were moving faster than she had originally contemplated' and said she particularly disliked the word 'Council': '. . . Mr Haughey would certainly exaggerate `the significance of whatever was achieved.'[80] When the full set of Joint Studies papers were presented at the end of April, she finally exploded:

> This is the most alarming set of papers on the UK/Irish situation I have read. They reveal starkly a total difference of approach. We are trying to achieve increasing cooperation and reconciliation between our two countries . . . They are using every study as a step towards takeover. If these papers go ahead to publication even on an agree to differ basis, I am not prepared to go along with the studies. The Irish view would incur such mistrust, hostility and downright anger in the North that it would set Anglo-Irish relations back for years and do untold harm to many innocent people if the Protestant paramilitary groups reacted. It is no longer a question of changing the wording of a few sentences. We are at the heart of the matter.

All over the studies, sometimes as often as four times on the same page, she wrote 'NO', and, *in extremis*, 'NO!' When British officials suggested that the word 'Council' should be conceded in order to keep Irish goodwill, she wrote, 'What about our good will?' To the Irish suggestion that their citizens should sit on juries and hold elected office in the North, she wrote: 'This is monstrous.'[81] Her argument and her indignation were classic encapsulations of Mrs Thatcher's approach to the project. She strongly disliked the whole vision while not having any very clear idea of what she wanted to do instead. The consequence of her fury, assisted by the calling of another general election in the Republic for June, was a pause for reflection and redrafting.

It is remarkable, given everything else that was happening, that Mrs Thatcher devoted such close attention to this large and often tedious bundle of documents. The Joint Studies process coincided with the economic and political crisis which followed the 1981 Budget and the Brixton riots in April.* And in Northern Ireland itself a second and much more formid-able hunger strike was by now in progress. On the day Mrs Thatcher wrote her angry note on the Joint Studies, she knew that the first hunger striker, Bobby Sands, was on the point of death.

Early in January 1981, Mrs Thatcher had been informed that the hard men in the Maze were trying to engineer a second hunger strike. Allegations were made that the British had failed to implement the concessions offered via the earlier contact, but it seems likely that these grievances, though genuinely felt, were a pretext. From the point of view of the IRA prisoners, the fact that the first strike had failed meant that, for reasons of pride, there had to be a second one which would succeed. Atkins informed Mrs Thatcher that the strike was essentially about political status and that the prisoners sought at least one death.[82] Sands, who was leader of the IRA prisoners in the Maze until he went on hunger strike, was a romantic, vio-lent, poetry-loving young man, in prison for trying to blow up a furniture showroom. His wife had left him because he beat her up.[83] He felt he had little to lose by dying. On 1 March, Sands began the strike himself. On 5 March, speaking in Belfast, Mrs Thatcher reiterated her simple position: 'There is no such thing as political murder, political bombing or political violence. There is only criminal murder, criminal bombing and criminal violence. We will not compromise on this. There will be no political sta-tus.'[84] On the same day, Frank Maguire, the Republican MP for Fermanagh and South Tyrone, died. Sands, from his prison bed, became a candidate for his seat. It was thought by Republicans that if Sands were elected to Parliament the case for political status would become unanswerable. A decision by the SDLP not to contest the election made Sands the only candidate of the Nationalist side and, on 9 April, he was elected. Riots ensued. Until then, Provisional Sinn Fein–IRA had shunned the electoral process, but now the fact that an IRA man could win a popular contest in the United Kingdom gave them a huge propaganda boost.

Mrs Thatcher came under immense pressure. At home on mainland Britain, and among Unionists in the province, there was almost complete support for resistance to the hunger strike; she was much more aware than most of her colleagues that it was essential not to break this trust with the majority. In the rest of the world, the opposite was the case. In the Repub-lic, the United States and the EEC, calls for a way out grew louder.† On

* See Chapter 22.
† While there was plenty of criticism for Mrs Thatcher's stance in the US Congress, President Reagan and his close advisers never joined this chorus. 'We do not wish to place any pressure on Britain regarding the situation there,' the National Security Advisor Richard Allen wrote to

22 April, Armstrong wrote to Mrs Thatcher about the Republic's attitude. With an almost guilty punctiliousness, he explained the exact reason why Dermot Nally had telephoned him that morning: 'The first purpose of the call was to discuss the date for the next meeting of the steering Group of the Anglo-Irish joint studies.'[85] But the real purport of the call, and of Armstrong's note, was to convey Haughey's anxiety about the hunger strike. The Taoiseach was worried, said Nally, as reported by Armstrong, that, if Sands died soon, 'The whole areas [sic] would go up in flames.'[86] How about getting the European Commission for Human Rights involved in some solution, Haughey suggested? He wanted the Commissioners to go into the Maze as, in effect, mediators, which would then allow him to call for the strikers to give up. Mrs Thatcher resisted mediation, though not absolutely, by the Human Rights Commission. A record of a telephone conversation with Humphrey Atkins at this time shows that she was pre-pared for Sands's death and that of the others who had followed him into a hunger strike:

THE PRIME MINISTER: But there are two or three others behind him [Sands] aren't there Humphrey?
SECRETARY OF STATE FOR NORTHERN IRELAND: Yes . . . I think there is bound to be a weak link later.
THE PRIME MINISTER: Yes I think they will be getting worried after all if one died and then a second one died then a third one died and nothing happened.
SECRETARY OF STATE FOR NORTHERN IRELAND: Yes it doesn't look very attractive.[87]

The situation was not, in Atkins's inadequate phrase, very attractive to either side. On 5 May 1981, Sands died. Thirty thousand people – 100,000 in the estimation of the organizers – attended his funeral in Belfast. In death, Sands became a world figure. Streets were named after him in Paris and Teheran. Haughey urged Mrs Thatcher to give ground, fearing the political rise of Sinn Fein in the Republic as well as in the province. John Hume of the SDLP called on her at No. 10 and begged her to make con-cessions on clothing and free association, lest he be 'swept away' politically by the disturbances. Mrs Thatcher dismissed his anxieties: 'The people who had been killed by the PIRA had had no choice. The hunger strikers had a choice . . . Any wavering on the issue of political status would be a licence

Reagan during this period. 'It is up to Mrs Thatcher's government to work with its own citizens in Northern Ireland and with the government of the Irish Republic.' (Allen to the President, 26 May 1981, UK: Prime Minister Thatcher, Box 35, Exec Sec, NSC: Head of State File, Reagan Library.)

to kill.'[88] Michael Foot came to see her later the same day, asking for an 'escape-route' over the hunger strike. Mrs Thatcher rebuked him: 'The Prime Minister said that Mr Foot's message had been exactly the same as that of Mr Hume. Her answer was "No". Foot was giving notice that he was "a push-over".'[89]

On 12 May, the second hunger striker, Francis Hughes, had died. On 19 May Mrs Thatcher was given chilling evidence of the attitude of some of those involved. Raymond McCreesh, a hunger striker who had given some indications that he wanted to end his fast, was visited by his brother Brian, a Catholic priest. Father McCreesh was overheard telling Raymond: 'Your brother and I were proud to carry the coffins of Bobby Sands and Frank Hughes. They are in heaven waiting for you.'[90]*

Throughout this tense time, Robert Armstrong was firm against concessions to the prisoners. Disagreeing with Robert Wade-Gery, who was more anxious to appease, he had held to a line similar to Mrs Thatcher's.[91] But he continued to push his belief that there had to be 'long-term political development',[92] and he warned the Prime Minister of the dangers of another Bloody Sunday (the rioting in Londonderry in 1972 when thirteen people were killed by British soldiers). His anxieties about the Catholic reaction were shared by what the IRA liked to call the 'securocrats'. At Chequers on 27 May the General Officer Commanding Northern Ireland, General Sir Richard Lawson, and the Chief Constable of the RUC, Jack Hermon, joined Kenneth Stowe to tell Mrs Thatcher that the alienation of the Catholic population was now a greater challenge than the security problem. The government should 'dispel the impression of inflexibility' and make a gesture towards Catholics by setting up an inquiry into prison conditions.[93] A clearly windy Humphrey Atkins warned Mrs Thatcher that 'I now feel strongly that a continuing, apparently endless, series of deaths from hunger strikes will cumulatively lose us both the Catholic population of Northern Ireland and the sympathy of world opinion,' and recommended more 'political development in the North' to match the policy of 'continuing to pursue – as we are committed to doing – the development of relations with Dublin'.[94] Armstrong, however, was silkily dismissive of any Atkins initiative as he prepared his chief for the OD meeting to discuss these matters: 'You will also wish to have at the back of your mind the possibility that you may wish to appoint a new Secretary of State before long.'[95] He knew that a Cabinet reshuffle was imminent.

---

* Following the release of the state papers in 2011, the McCreesh family said that 'the statements attributed to family members in the recently released report of a prison officer are untrue, inaccurate and falsified' and that the claims had been made as part of an attempt by the British state to 'vilify' the family. (*Irish Times*, 31 December 2011.)

The international clamour intensified. Tip O'Neill, always vocal on behalf of the Irish lobby, called on President Reagan to intervene with Mrs Thatcher privately to help break the impasse. Reagan studiously avoided any commitment and went on holiday. At the beginning of June, the members of the Irish Commission for Justice and Peace (ICJP), a body set up by the Irish Catholic hierarchy primarily concerned with aid to Third World countries, suggested that they might be able to play a role in bringing the hunger strike to an end. Beginning on 23 June, Michael Alison,* the Minister of State at the NIO responsible for prisons, had a series of meetings with the members of the ICJP. On 29 June, Humphrey Atkins released a statement which the ICJP took to be positive but which emphasized the government's 'bottom line' – that there could be no concessions or reforms until the hunger strike had ended. In their secret communications, smuggled out of the prison by mouth, the IRA leader in the Maze, Brendan 'Bik' McFarlane, told Gerry Adams that he was worried by the opinion of the strikers' families: 'If Brits don't meet with Commission and forward a very watery offer, can we cope with the families i.e. prevent their disintegration if we refuse ... It appears that they [the British] are not interested in simply undermining us, but completely annihilating us ... They are insane – at least Maggie is anyway.'[96] But 'Maggie' was not insane, nor bent on annihilation. She was perplexed, even confused, about tactics.

What happened next is a story so tangled with the needs of the different parties to justify themselves that no wholly accurate account seems possible, and even after the release of state papers under the thirty-year rule the actions and motivations of those involved are greatly disputed.[97]

From Mrs Thatcher's point of view the aim was to make no concessions 'in any way', and yet to entertain the suggestion of the new Taoiseach, Garret FitzGerald,† who had come into office on 30 June 1981, that the ICJP should be allowed to play a greater role. The Commissioners, it was suggested, would be allowed into the Maze to repeat the government's message to the prisoners and, without negotiating, would return with the prisoners' reply.[98] Mrs Thatcher discussed this idea with Alison and senior colleagues. Although she thought that it was 'unlikely' to work, she was persuaded by colleagues such as Carrington and Whitelaw to allow it to

---

* Michael Alison (1926–2004), educated Eton and Wadham College, Oxford; Conservative MP for Barkston Ash, 1964–83; for Selby, 1983–97; Minister of State, Northern Ireland Office, 1979–81; Department of Employment, 1981–3; PPS to the Prime Minister, 1983–7.

† Garret FitzGerald (1926–2011), educated Coláiste na Rinne, Waterford, Belvedere College, University College and King's Inns, Dublin; PhD; Irish Senator, 1965–9; Fine Gael TD, 1969–92; Minister for Foreign Affairs, 1973–7; Leader of Fine Gael, 1977–87; Taoiseach, June 1981–March 1982, December 1982–March 1987.

go ahead. At least there might be some value in the scheme, she believed, if it could 'demonstrate that the blame for the hunger strikers lay with the strikers themselves'.[99] In his meetings with the ICJP, Alison referred to 'the lady behind the veil' as the final, exacting arbiter of his position. The Commission understood him to be referring to Mrs Thatcher in person, but Alison later claimed that this was only a symbolic way of telling the Commission that he was not the ultimate authority.[100] On 4 July, Mrs Thatcher spoke to Alison twice on the telephone about his discussions with the ICJP, indicating the seriousness with which she considered the proposals. She instructed him that the ICJP could go into the prison so long as they accepted that 'control and security remain with HMG [Her Majesty's Government]'. She agreed with Alison that the Commission would tell the prisoners that they must end the strike unconditionally, but in the knowledge that the government was under a moral 'obligation to move forward' on the areas of clothing, free association and prison work.[101] The ICJP thought this was an 'about-face' on clothing which might bring a result.

On 4 and 5 July 1981, as the death of the next hunger striker, Joe McDonnell, seemed imminent, the ICJP went into the Maze. The proposals which they brought appeared that they might satisfy the strikers. It was clear to the ICJP that the prisoners' families were at odds with Brendan McFarlane, making it more difficult to obtain a settlement.[102] At this point, however, the ICJP's efforts crossed wires with the once-more active British secret contact with the IRA. Through this contact, it was made clear to the government that the IRA were concerned about the role of the ICJP. From this point the secret channel became the primary means of communication. An associate of the IRA, codenamed Soon, was the interlocutor. Many years later, Brendan Duddy confirmed[103] that he had once again been involved in discussions at this time. The contact asked the British to allow a Provisional Sinn Fein representative secretly into the prison. They refused to permit Adams or McGuinness, whom the IRA suggested, but allowed Danny Morrison.* In the course of conversations with the contact, some of them probably with McGuinness in the room,† the PIRA requirements were set out. As well as the substantive concessions about clothing and so on (which fell short of the prisoners' five demands, but which they were inclined to accept), the IRA were very concerned about the danger of what they called 'panic', by which they meant the fear within their own ranks

---

* Danny Morrison (1953–), director of publicity for Sinn Fein during the hunger strikes; Member, Northern Ireland Assembly, 1982–6. He was a prisoner between 1990 and 1995.
† In 2009, Martin McGuinness confirmed that he had been in contact with Duddy, though not that the British had made any concessions (*Irish News*, 28 Sept. 2009).

of the appearance of sell-out or of double-crossing by the British. They therefore wanted parcels of clothes to be ready for wear immediately after the end of the strike and for the statement which the British would make after the end to be agreed by them in advance.[104] Mrs Thatcher herself was shown the draft of the message which would be sent through the channel, and altered it, toughening it up a little on points about work and association. She also approved the following: 'If the reply we receive is unsatisfactory and there is subsequently any public reference to this exchange we shall deny it took place.'[105] There can be no doubt, therefore, that Mrs Thatcher went against her public protestations about not negotiating with terrorists, and actively did so, though at a remove. 'The lady behind the veil' had weakened.

On 7 July, a meeting took place between Mrs Thatcher, Atkins, Whitelaw, Gilmour and others. It was agreed that the proposed Atkins statement should be shown to PIRA in advance, with its terms revised at the order of Mrs Thatcher.[106] The message was sent. Shortly after midnight Atkins met Mrs Thatcher to explain that PIRA had objected to the message received, and that the government had therefore responded that discussions were now at an end. The IRA then ('a very rapid reaction') said that what they did not like was the tone rather than the content of the statement.[107] The government therefore decided to 'elaborate' on the draft statement to PIRA overnight, presumably in the hope of getting agreement. At 5.40 that morning, however, Joe McDonnell, the next hunger striker in the queue, died, and it was too late for any means of ending the strike.

In the endgame, Adams and his associates had mishandled matters. As McFarlane had written to Adams at 10 p.m. the night before: 'I've been thinking that if we don't pull this off and Joe dies then RA [IRA] are going to come under some bad stick from all quarters.'[108] The problem for Adams and McGuinness was that the political success caused by the hunger strike seemed too great to take the risk of ending it unless they could claim an unambiguous victory: hence their preoccupation with the 'tone' of the British statement more than the content.[109] It may also be that Gerry Adams was nervous that those of his senior colleagues who did not know about the back-channel would suspect double-dealing on his part. As the hunger strike unfolded, it became clear that the IRA had missed a big chance to deal and had 'shot their bolt'.[110]*

---

* In 2005 the former prisoner Richard O'Rawe published a controversial memoir of the hunger strike, *Blanketmen: An Untold Story of the H-Block Hunger Strike*, New Island Books, 2005. In this account O'Rawe revealed that the prison leadership, including McFarlane, had wanted to accept the British offer but that their decision had been overruled by the Republican

The British were also blamed, of course. In the propaganda war, Britain was made to look intransigent for not reaching agreement when the prisoners, it was alleged, had withdrawn their demands for political status. The ICJP accused the government of bad faith. Garret FitzGerald also blamed British intransigence for the failure to find a solution. In an angry letter to Mrs Thatcher, conveying these thoughts, he called future cross-border co-operation into question. She was beset with reports from embassies, notably in Dublin and Washington, about unfavourable foreign reaction, and was persuaded by Carrington, worried that relations with the Republic and the United States 'were now at serious risk', to allow the International Committee of the Red Cross into the Maze.[111] But she refused his suggestion that the prisoners should be surreptitiously fed intravenously with glucose in their drips. Force-feeding, she believed, 'was almost a violence against the person', and if people wanted to kill themselves, they should be discouraged but not prevented.[112] In Britain, public opinion remained solidly behind her.

The dilemmas besetting Mrs Thatcher in her handling of the hunger strike are well illustrated by a further attempt, later in July, to use the channel to the IRA. On 18 July, Philip Woodfield,* who had succeeded Stowe as permanent under-secretary at the NIO, came to her to report that PIRA had just asked that a British official go to meet the hunger strikers. Would this be a good idea, he asked, so that the official could clarify the government's position, in effect offering a little bit more? As Woodfield put it, coldly, there was, in Northern Ireland terms, 'a good deal to be said for letting the hunger strike continue',[113] but the opposite applied to the Republic and the United States. Mrs Thatcher said that she was 'less concerned about the situation in Dublin than in North America'. She decided that the channel should be activated that night and the official should go in the next day. But she rang Atkins first. Probably stung by what had happened a fortnight earlier, he counselled against this course, saying that the thing was bound to leak. So Mrs Thatcher went back on her earlier decision, comforting herself over her change of mind by saying that she was 'more

---

leadership outside the prison, specifically by a committee which included Gerry Adams. O'Rawe alleged that the Sinn Fein leadership wanted to delay the ending of the hunger strike for political gain. This account is neither corroborated nor repudiated by the evidence contained in the state papers, but there is a bitter debate within the Republican movement about where responsibility lay for the decision to continue the strike. See also Richard O'Rawe, *Afterlives: The Hunger Strike and the Secret Offer that Changed Irish History*, Lilliput Press, 2011. Danny Morrison disputes O'Rawe's account of events; see the *Andersonstown News*, 12 January 2012.
* Philip Woodfield (1923–2000), educated Alleyn's School, Dulwich and King's College London; Deputy Secretary, Northern Ireland Office, 1972–4; Home Office, 1974–81; Permanent Under-Secretary, Northern Ireland Office, 1981–3; knighted, 1983.

concerned to do the right thing by Northern Ireland than to try to satisfy international critics'.[114] The following morning, however, it emerged that the channel had, in fact, been activated without waiting for Mrs Thatcher's final approval. Since this had happened, Atkins decided to use it to send a message to the Provisionals that more might be done on prison clothes. No useful reply came from PIRA, and Atkins ordered the channel closed on the evening of 20 July. Farce and tragedy were near allied.

Brendan McFarlane had made it clear that the prisoners 'have no power to give up'.[115] He meant that the decisions on their life and death were for the IRA alone, and therefore it was the IRA alone with whom the government should deal. But in fact the IRA's grip on the prisoners, most of whose families naturally did not want them to die, was weakening. On 31 July, the family of Paddy Quinn, who had been on hunger strike for forty-seven days, intervened to save his life. By the middle of August, three more hunger strikers had died. On 20 August, Owen Carron, who had been Bobby Sands's agent in the first Fermanagh by-election, was victorious in the second. The tenth hunger striker died on polling day. With each death, there were protests and renewed rioting, but each time the public attention was less. Mrs Thatcher's government was winning, at least in the sense that no one now believed that she would give in to the IRA. Garret FitzGerald, who had been so loud against her in July, quietened down over the summer. He realized that his public criticisms of the British government undermined the possibility of further progress on the political side. He may also have realized that the Republic was on weak ground in suggesting any concessions to hunger strikers when its own history was one of robust refusal. Dermot Nally remembered FitzGerald quoting Eamon de Valera, arguably the most nationalist of Irish prime ministers: 'No government which I have led has given in to this sort of blackmail.'[116] FitzGerald reverted to his aspirations for a change in the relationship between the Republic and the United Kingdom, and publicly floated his idea that the Irish constitution's claim to Northern Ireland should be amended.

On 14 September 1981, Mrs Thatcher reshuffled her Cabinet. She replaced Humphrey Atkins, as Secretary of State for Northern Ireland, with Jim Prior. Prior had fought hard against the move* and his reluctance to go to the province made him immediately unpopular with the Unionist population. Nor were Unionists pleased that, as part of the deal by which, in return for 'exile', he could have his own people round him, he chose junior ministers – notably Lord Gowrie and Nicholas Scott – whose views were well known to be green.† But the fact that Mrs Thatcher gave Prior

---

* See Chapter 22.
† Lord Gowrie recalled that he asked to go to Northern Ireland with Prior because he, Gowrie,

quite a free hand in his new job did at least clarify the decision-making process. He had more scope than Atkins. In relation to the hunger strike, he used it. 'He came in saying to himself and to us that he was going to get things moving. To get the SDLP on board he would want to make progress with the hunger strikers. So there was a linkage with political progress.'[117] On 17 September, he visited the Maze prison to see for himself.

On 24 and 25 September two hunger strikers gave up their fast. The mother of one of them, Liam McCloskey, had written personally to Mrs Thatcher asking her to see her and to intervene to save her son's life. Although Mrs Thatcher refused this meeting, referring Mrs McCloskey, in a highly sympathetic letter, to officials, this unpolitical and sincere approach from a mother showed the way things were going. At this time one of the prison chaplains, Father Denis Faul, stepped up his efforts to bring the strike to an end by meeting the relatives. In public, the prison leadership were critical of this and Faul was attacked by the prisoners' spokesman as 'a treacherous, conniving man'. It is probable that he privately agreed to be scapegoated in this way by the IRA, who were looking for a way out but could not say so, in order to prevent further deaths.[118]

Jim Prior himself believed that 'The hunger strike was beginning to lose its impact' before he took up his post, but he still saw ending it as 'of absolute paramount importance'.[119] He agreed to have meetings with the Catholic primate, Cardinal Tomas O'Fiaich (who had crossed swords with Mrs Thatcher at a meeting in early July), and Father Faul: 'The quid pro quo for ending the hunger strike was to allow prisoners to wear their own dress and I thought on balance this was a small price to pay, particularly as some of the prisoners did not wear anything [a reference to the blanket protest]. The Cardinal and Father Faul came to see me and they said that if you are prepared to do something about dress then I think we can bring it to an end.'[120] The minutes of their meeting on 30 September show that Father Faul also told Prior that the prisoners should be allowed to retain their 'military structure' (that is, freedom of association) and that they should have their lost remission restored. Such concessions, Faul believed, would help 'take the sting out of defeat' for the prisoners.[121]

An understanding was at hand. On 2 October, Prior promised a statement on 'the development of the prison system'. The next day, the hunger strike ended. A statement from the prisoners complaining that they had been 'robbed of the hunger strike as an effective protest weapon' by the 'successful campaign waged against our distressed relatives by the Irish

had been born in Ireland and was becoming increasingly concerned about the hunger strike (interview with Lord Gowrie).

Catholic hierarchy' showed the anger of the IRA, but was also a cover for their own capitulation. Prior's statement on 6 October made clear that prisoners would now have more freedom of association, in choice of work and in what clothes they wore, and better recovery of remission. These changes were similar to those which had been recommended by Father Faul. They went slightly further than the concessions which had been the subject of negotiation in July, but they did not differ in principle from the terms that Mrs Thatcher had been prepared to offer. No changes were implemented before the hunger strike had ended.

Talk of concessions, even *post hoc* concessions, did worry Ian Gow, who was probably unaware of the secret attempts to bring an end to the strike earlier in the summer. Realizing what Prior was about to do, Gow belatedly wrote to Mrs Thatcher commending to her 'the advice which you received from a Privy Councillor [he probably meant Enoch Powell] . . . that there should be a decent interval over the hunger strikers and what some will perceive to be their partial victory over "the authorities"'.[122] Writing later in the day, on the same note, Gow added: 'It is clear that Jim's proposed Statement has been leaked already . . . This may mean, whatever reservations you may have about Jim's Statement, it is too late to alter it.'[123] It was. The private secretary added: 'The Prime Minister agreed that this statement could be issued on the understanding that what was being done about clothing was no more than was already the practice in women's prisons in Great Britain and Northern Ireland.'[124] What had happened, in essence, was that Mrs Thatcher had allowed Prior to make his own decisions. Asked in retirement whether she had been aware of what he was doing, Prior replied: 'To be honest, I am not sure whether she was or not. I think she probably was . . . aware, but she didn't raise any objections.'[125]

Who won the hunger strike? Mrs Thatcher certainly emerged from it with her reputation for determination and courage enhanced. This helped her greatly with Unionist opinion, and made her politically much more formidable. If she had capitulated to the strikers, her Iron Lady reputation might never have recovered. The IRA had expected that Mrs Thatcher would be forced to make concessions, perhaps because she was a woman,[126] but they had been proved wrong. Moreover, the '1916 syndrome' for which they had hoped – a tide of unstoppable anger rising with each death – failed to materialize from the sixth death onwards. Their discipline over their prisoners, terrifyingly strong though it was, did not prove absolute.

On the other hand, the temporary electoral success that accrued to Sinn Fein because of the strike led to their strategy, articulated by Danny Morrison at their Ard Fheis (annual conference) at the end of October, of 'a ballot box in one hand and an Armalite in the other'. It can also be argued that the prisoners did, in fact, succeed, in substance though not in form, in gaining a more favourable prison regime which ensured that the IRA could do more or less what they liked within the Maze. It is also true that, as a sort of trade-off for her toughness, Mrs Thatcher came under even greater pressure to move towards political developments which she would have preferred to avoid. Most damaging to her reputation, had it been known, and to her own conscience was that she did, in effect, negotiate with terrorists. She never quite admitted this, even privately, but it was so.

Mrs Thatcher herself felt sad about the hunger strike. She admired the strikers' courage – 'You have to hand it to some of these IRA boys' – and described them as 'poor devils' who knew that 'if they didn't go on strike they'd be shot . . . What a waste! What a terrible waste of human life!' And, she added, to emphasize the pointlessness of it all, 'I don't even remember their names.'[127] She also, of course, noted the effect on herself. As a result of the hunger strike, though she did not immediately know this, she went to the top of the IRA's death list: 'This is why I will forever have to be protected.'[128] In public, she never complained about the inevitable fear, but she did feel it, both for herself and for her family. In private, she said: 'After that [the death threat], you walk into a crowd – it's always absolutely terrifying. Or if someone hands you something – look at Rajiv Gandhi – hidden in flowers.'[129]

Despite all the difficulties caused by the hunger strike, contacts between London and Dublin had been maintained, with Nally and Armstrong working quietly together. A summit between Mrs Thatcher and Garret FitzGerald went ahead in London on 6 November 1981, the ground for it laid by Armstrong, who took the procedurally unusual step of seeing Fitz-Gerald alone to plan it. In the run-up to the meeting, Mrs Thatcher had continued to make difficulties. She still protested about the name of an Anglo-Irish Council, which the Joint Studies had proposed, and conceded it only if it were to be called the Anglo-Irish Intergovernmental Council. She was alert to anything which might imply any jurisdiction by the Republic in the affairs of Northern Ireland, and particularly resisted FitzGerald's desire for a rephrasing of the British guarantee to Northern Ireland in what he called a 'more positive' – by which he meant a more Nationalist – form. Armstrong wrote to the Prime Minister to try to win her over on this point. He made the mistake of invoking the Sunningdale Communiqué which had pledged Britain 'To support any future wish by the majority in Northern Ireland to become part of a united Ireland'. 'We have never withdrawn that pledge,' he added.[130] Mrs Thatcher, seldom impressed by any action of Ted Heath, scribbled: 'It never had any lasting status.' Rather desperate,

Michael Alexander felt the need to remind her that friendly Anglo-Irish summitry was supposed to be something she was keen on: 'The improved relationship between London and Dublin is an achievement of yours which you want to preserve and build upon.'[131] In fact, she never internalized this thought, and constantly resented what she had herself agreed. At a meeting with FitzGerald in 1983, she read out the phrase 'the Anglo-Irish Inter-governmental Council' 'in tones of contempt'. 'What's that?' she asked. 'Margaret, you invented it,' said FitzGerald.[132]

The summit itself, however, laid the foundations for a good working relationship between Mrs Thatcher and Garret FitzGerald. Although she was rather sour about FitzGerald in her memoirs, possibly retaliating for his criticisms of her in his, she did, at this time, like him, inclining to Nigel Lawson's view that he was 'the only completely honest Taoiseach the Republic have ever had'.[133] At the top of the draft communiqué, she wrote out the adjectives she would use to describe the meeting: 'Friendly, con-structive, practical'. But, after her experience at Dublin, she was extremely anxious about the precise wording of the communiqué, and asked for the advice of Ian Gow (Gow reminded her: 'We both remember what the For-eign Office did to us last time!').[134] Gow's wholly Unionist suggestions, many contributed by Enoch Powell, did not carry the day, but Mrs Thatcher did succeed in rejecting a draft which said that the British government would 'support' movement to a United Ireland if the majority in the North so wished, and replaced it with the word 'accept'.[135] In the House of Commons, defending the communiqué, she made much of the fact that FitzGerald had publicly accepted the principle of consent in relation to the North. But she was assailed by Unionists who feared the implications of the new Council and the Joint Studies. One asked her if she still stood 'rock firm' for the Union, as she had said in Belfast three years previously. 'Northern Ireland is part of the United Kingdom,' she replied, 'as much as my constituency is.'[136] This was altered, in mythology, to a claim that Ulster was 'as British as Finchley', but this was not quite what she was saying. She was not assert-ing, and did not believe, that Northern Ireland and north London were culturally the same. Rather, she was defending the constitutional position, and the rights of the people protected by it.

On 11 November 1981, four of the five Joint Studies were published, the report on security matters being excluded. The first report on the 'pos-sible new institutional structures' proposed the formation of the Anglo-Irish Intergovernmental Council. Although the precise nature and powers of the Council remained vague, the two countries agreed to set up a secretariat to run the Council. It was this idea of a permanent secretariat which made Unionists uneasy, then and later. Events quickly distracted attention from

my life easy.'[144] In the event, twenty-six Conservative backbenchers voted against the guillotine motion. Mrs Thatcher probably had it in her power to prevent the passage of the Bill, but she chose not to do so. It was enough for her purposes to indicate her displeasure, and then let it pass.

The Falklands also had the effect of freezing Anglo-Irish relations. Charles Haughey, who continued to believe that Mrs Thatcher's behaviour during the hunger strikes had lost him the election in the summer of 1981, had returned to power on 9 March 1982. He saw the Falklands as the chance for revenge. In the EEC and at the United Nations, Ireland became by far the most awkward Western European country, voting against sanctions on Argentina and for UN resolutions advancing an Argentine agenda.* Already opposed to the Prior proposals because his government had had no involvement in them, Haughey did what he could to throw a spanner in the works. Sean Aylward, his private secretary at the time, explained: 'Now I don't think it was his finest hour . . . but it did pose policy difficulties . . . because quite simply the Falklands/Malvinas was a classic piece of colonial history [and therefore problematic in Irish politics] . . . it was a combination of substantial sympathy in Ireland for the Argentinian position and the smouldering resentment of the way in which the Thatcher government had influenced the hunger strikes that influenced our foreign policy at the time. Retrospectively, there is no question that it was a mistake because it simply wasn't understood in England and we lost a lot of friends too.'[145] At the end of May, Figg, the British Ambassador in Dublin, had an uncomfortable meeting with Haughey. The Taoiseach told him that the 'spirit of the Anglo-Irish Initiative' was 'quite dead' because of the failure to consult Dublin.[146]

Unlike her officials, Mrs Thatcher did not mind that the Irish government had withdrawn from political partnership. In answer to a question from Enoch Powell, she told the House of Commons, almost with glee, that 'no commitment exists for Her Majesty's Government to consult the Irish Government on matters affecting Northern Ireland. That has always been our position. We reiterate and emphasise it, so that everyone is clear about it.'[147]† But she minded very much indeed that the Irish had tried to impede British victory in the Falklands. In a discussion about improving

---

* For full details of this see Chapter 24.

† This reply led to an unfortunate misunderstanding on the part of Enoch Powell, who believed that Mrs Thatcher was 'putting on ice' her administration's discussions with the Irish government. He spoke of a 'real prospect' of bringing the Official Unionists into communion with the Conservative Party. Ian Gow, noting Powell's 'passion for logic', was well aware that Mrs Thatcher's answer 'does not have the implication Enoch thinks it does'. (Gow to PM, 2 Aug. 1982, THCR 2/6/2/117.)

reciprocal voting rights that had been rumbling on for some time, Armstrong wrote to her, implicitly rebuking her for her reluctance to press forward and reminding her that reform was a British commitment. Mrs Thatcher's pen scribbled back: 'I am aware of this – but events have changed matters since then. Certainly I have no intention of having further bilateral meetings with the Taoiseach.'[148] Her patience with the whole subject of Ireland, and particularly with the Republic, was temporarily exhausted. When the elections for Prior's Assembly were held on 20 October 1982, her fears about the process were confirmed. Sinn Fein shot up to 10 per cent of the first-preference votes, a third, in other words, of the votes on the Nationalist side.

Ian Gow hoped to turn Mrs Thatcher's frustration with Northern Ireland to the advantage of his Unionist allies. Writing to the Prime Minister in mid-November, he told her, 'After the next General Election, I hope that you might find it possible to make a really fresh start with our policy in the Province.' The 'present combination of Prior and Gowrie', he continued, 'is doing great damage to Ulster'.[149] Mrs Thatcher, however, was soon exposed to other influences. Early in December 1982 she gave a dinner for Lord Shackleton, to thank him for his work on restoring the economy of the Falkland Islands. Afterwards, she invited a couple of officials up for a drink. One of them, David Goodall,* Deputy Secretary to the Cabinet, and a Roman Catholic of Irish descent with a long-standing commitment to Anglo-Irish rapprochement, turned the conversation to Ireland. Rather boldly, he told her that it was a 'scandal' that British troops, though triumphant in the Falklands, were still being lost in anger within the United Kingdom, in Northern Ireland. The Prime Minister and he talked about Irishness. 'I am completely English,' said Mrs Thatcher, stoutly. 'I'm not,' said Goodall; 'both my grandfathers were Irish.' 'Actually,' said the Prime Minister, reflectively, 'my great-grandmother was a Sullivan,† so I'm one-sixteenth Irish.' She mused a little. 'If we get back [after the next general election],' she said, 'I should like to do something about Ireland.'[150]

---

* David Goodall (1931–), educated Ampleforth and Trinity College, Oxford; diplomat; head of Western European Department, FCO, 1975–9; Cabinet Office, 1982–4; Deputy Under-Secretary, FCO, 1984–7; High Commissioner to India (1987–1991); knighted, 1987.

† In fact, she was an O'Sullivan. The descent was on her father's side. She is believed to have been descended from Colonel Sir John William O'Sullivan, Quarter-Master General to Prince Charles Edward Stuart (Bonnie Prince Charlie) in the rising of 1745. (Correspondence with Iain Thornber.)

rejected.[141]* She knew, too, that the majority of the Cabinet tended to side with Prior. Even after further revisions, the White Paper alarmed her, and in Cabinet on 1 April 1982 she continued to tone down phrases, which she called 'devastating', about the co-operation of the British and Irish Parliaments.[142] But she felt she had to let the Bill go ahead. Somehow, perhaps by a few kind words, perhaps by quietly authorizing him to foment rebellion, she had squared Ian Gow. On 2 April, he wrote to her: 'The die is now cast, but you understand, and <u>thank</u> you for understanding, how difficult my position is. I cannot forget Airey.'[143]

The day after the Cabinet had agreed the Prior Bill, Argentina invaded the Falkland Islands.† The crisis enabled Mrs Thatcher to order the postponement of the Bill, though not the publication of the White Paper, until after Easter. The delay helped Gow, now more essential than ever to Mrs Thatcher because of his skill at shoring up her position in the House of Commons. But there was a sense in which it helped Prior too. Faced with a battle for the very survival of her government, of national honour, of her whole career, she had little time for anything else. True, Gow had Mrs Thatcher's licence to cause trouble for Prior.‡ Leading Unionist Tories such as Nick Budgen,§ who resigned as a whip, and Lord Cranborne,¶ who resigned as a PPS, protested against the Bill. To quell revolt, the whips decided to guillotine the Bill. Jim Prior recalled his chief's reaction: 'I always remember when I told the Cabinet that we were going to have to guillotine it. She turned to me and said, "Thank God I am going to be in the United States and am not going to have to vote for it." I mean, she didn't make

---

* Armstrong himself was not enthusiastic about the Prior proposals because they pressed forward without consultation with the Republic (from February, governed once again by Charlie Haughey). He did not mind if they eventually failed, but he did not want them replaced in government by more Unionist policies.

† See Chapter 23.

‡ Along with the correspondence from Gow there is a note in Mrs Thatcher's hand listing those Cabinet Ministers 'against us' and 'for us'. There were ten in the 'against' column, including Geoffrey Howe, Francis Pym, and Lord Hailsham. The five in the 'for us' column included Keith Joseph, Nigel Lawson and Cecil Parkinson. The list related only to the Northern Ireland Bill, and was not a reflection on wider divisions within the Cabinet. ('MT Note' ((Northern Ireland Bill Guillotine Motion)), 17 June 1982, THCR 2/6/2/117.)

§ Nicholas Budgen (1937–98), educated St Edward's School, Oxford and Corpus Christi College, Cambridge; Conservative MP for Wolverhampton South West, February 1974–97; resigned as government whip in 1982 over devolution to Northern Ireland; a leading Eurosceptic and, in the 1990s, rebel against the Maastricht Treaty.

¶ Robert Cecil, later 7th Marquess of Salisbury (1946–), educated Eton and Christ Church, Oxford; Conservative MP (as Viscount Cranborne) for Dorset South, 1979–87; Under-Secretary of State for Defence, MOD, 1992–4; Lord Privy Seal and Leader of House of Lords, 1994–7; Leader of the Opposition, House of Lords, 1997–8.

the Joint Studies. Three days later, an Official Unionist MP, the Revd Robert Bradford, was assassinated by the IRA. Gow reported to Mrs Thatcher
the view of leading Unionists that 'The whole place is a tinderbox'[137] and
that, to the majority, talk of a 'political solution' sounded like incorpora-
tion in the Irish Republic. At Bradford's funeral, Jim Prior was jostled by
angry mourners. His remedy for the situation was to pursue devolution
once more, and he tried to sell the idea to Mrs Thatcher. She remained
unconvinced, and read across from Northern Ireland to the mainland: 'My
main worry about devolved government is the effect it would have on
Scotland. Further I see little prospect of sufficient agreement to secure an
effective devolution.'[138] Although Prior devised what he called 'rolling
devolution' by which powers would be devolved by agreed stages, the
problems were very much the same as they had been with Atkins – that
the Nationalists insisted on power-sharing and the Unionists on the rights
of the majority. He presented his ideas to OD in February 1982. Mrs
Thatcher covered his draft with wiggly lines, and Gow wrote to her in
passionate terms, reminding her of the government's manifesto pledge and
the legacy of Airey Neave. He ridiculed power-sharing: 'To seek to combine
Republicans and Unionists in the same power-sharing Executive is as
absurd as asking Petain and De Gaulle to sit in the same Cabinet in 1940.'
Prior's plans were 'moving in fundamentally the wrong direction' and were
'doomed to failure'. With a frankness which showed that he knew his boss
would not be horrified at the idea of undermining the proposals, Gow
wrote: 'I fear that the Government, which is on the whole disinterested in
Northern Ireland, will back Jim's proposals. It may be that the best way
of preventing this initiative is the absence of Parliamentary time this
Session . . .'[139]

The Prior proposals were much disputed within the government, and
OD Committee failed to reach agreement on them. When they came back,
revised, towards the end of March, the White Paper proposed, under the
heading of 'Bilateral Arrangements', a role for the Republic, via the Council and its inter-parliamentary arm, in the affairs of Northern Ireland. Gow
then told Mrs Thatcher, in effect, that he would have to resign if Prior's
plans were to become law: 'I well understand what the consequences would
be; but I do not see how I can vote for the Second Reading of a Bill which
I consider would be gravely damaging to Northern Ireland and to the unity
of this Kingdom.'[140] Mrs Thatcher was in a quandary. She more or less
agreed with Gow, and was worried about dissension within her party.
Equally, she had put Prior in Northern Ireland so that each could leave the
other alone; and she was warned by Armstrong, probably correctly, that
Prior's 'personal position' would be 'very difficult' if his proposals were

The 1981 Budget and beyond

'We've got to move fast to save her'

Because 'success has many fathers and failure is an orphan', the paternity, or indeed maternity, of the 1981 Budget is hotly disputed. The politicians, including Mrs Thatcher, who were trying to agree the Budget were in the middle of a crisis, wrestling with figures that seemed to get worse every day. They were so worried by the possible result that they strove for a situation in which disaster could not be pinned on them. It was only after-wards, when the Budget came to look like a triumph, that they began to claim authorship. As it approached, it threatened to be the climactic disaster of her premiership.

At the Chequers meeting of 17 January 1981, the desperate state of the economy had become clear to Mrs Thatcher and her closest advisers. To date, the government had failed to stem the relentless rise in public expenditure, and a funding crisis, with the potential to bring down the government, seemed a real possibility. Following this meeting, therefore, debate turned urgently to the need for a severe Budget to bring the PSBR under control. 'In the early stages of talk about a tough Budget,' Terry Burns remembered, 'Mrs Thatcher was quite nervous about it.'[1]

John Hoskyns, Alan Walters and David Wolfson felt that they could not make Mrs Thatcher focus on the problems. She seemed tired and cross: when she appeared, the next day, not to remember a late-night meeting, Hoskyns noted in his diary: 'Oh dear! I think she'd had one or two drinks on an empty stomach.'[2] On 10 February, after a meeting with Mrs Thatcher and Howe at which the PSBR was now forecast at £13 billion, Walters sent the Prime Minister a note warning what would happen if the Budget were not tough enough: 'The trend of the forecasts of PSBR is upwards – and, by the nature of extrapolative forecasts, they are unlikely to undershoot . . . We are likely therefore to budget for too low a reduction in PSBR (as we did in 1980/81).' Walters went on: 'This will lead either to an additional late summer or autumn budget (which is to be avoided) or to putting great strain on funding. This last <u>may</u> lead to a funding crisis, but it certainly will lead to high interest rates, retaining high exchange rates and yet another squeeze on the private sector. This outcome must be avoided – it would be a quite impossible scenario for the approach to an election.' He called for 'painful decisions now'.[3]

Hoskyns's memo to Mrs Thatcher agreed with Walters and was more apocalyptic in expression. He said the Budget offered a choice between 'underkill' and 'overkill'. Overkill would require tax increases. Underkill, aimed at better growth and lower unemployment, would be politically popular, but 'If we underkill we will face a mid-summer funding crisis, with a desperate attempt at further cuts, splits in Cabinet, trivial savings to show for it, and finally a further rise in MLR and then the exchange rate. This will lead to yet lower activity, higher unemployment and PSBR, which will no longer be reversible before the election. The credibility of MTFS and of Geoffrey himself will be destroyed and our own position undermined.'[4]

He added to Mrs Thatcher's anxieties – and bolstered his own arguments – by enlisting detached, expert help about the damage done by the high exchange rate. On 5 February Hoskyns sent Mrs Thatcher summaries of the work done by the Swiss economist Jurg Niehans to try to answer the question 'Why is sterling so high?' Niehans maintained the view that monetary control was the only way to beat inflation, but argued that the shock administered by the government's monetary squeeze had been too great and too abrupt. Sterling M3 figures gave a misleading picture of what had happened to money: money supply targets would be better expressed in terms of the monetary base, which had been ruthlessly held down. The unpleasing conclusion was that the government's policy was in danger of undermining its own aims. The Treasury, with its MTFS, had been pursuing the 'gradualist' approach advocated by Milton Friedman. But the markets' perception of what was happening had produced a high exchange rate, thus precipitating the crisis advocated as a necessary shock by Friedrich von Hayek. David Willetts,* then private secretary to Nigel Lawson, remembered: 'Though we were trying to do Friedman, we were actually doing Hayek.'[5] In conversation with Hoskyns, Niehans put his point of view bluntly: 'If the Government goes on with its present monetary squeeze, you won't just have a recession; you'll have a slump.'[6] What Douglas Wass called an 'impeccable outside source'[7] was predicting disaster.

---

* David Willetts (1956–), educated King Edward's School, Birmingham and Christ Church, Oxford; Prime Minister's Policy Unit, 1984–6; director of studies, Centre for Policy Studies, 1987–92; Conservative MP for Havant from 1992; Parliamentary Secretary, Office of Public Service, Cabinet Office, 1995–6; Paymaster-General, 1996; Shadow Secretary of State for Education and Skills, 2005–7; for Innovation, Universities and Skills, 2007–10; Minister of State for Universities and Science from 2010.

"GOOD MORNING GENTLEMEN!"

49. In the Princes Gate siege in May 1980, the SAS successfully rescued hostages held by terrorists in the Iranian Embassy in London, killing their captors. This bold action became a favoured metaphor for the Thatcher style of government.

50. The Patterson family look a little nervous as Mrs Thatcher has tea in their council house, August 1980. The Pattersons were the 12,000th tenants of the Greater London Council to exercise their 'right to buy' – one of the most popular, though controversial, of all Mrs Thatcher's measures.

51. The Brixton riots, April 1981. Mrs Thatcher's critics said her policies caused them. She sympathised with the looted shopkeepers.

52. Mrs Thatcher listens with displeasure as Ted Heath furiously attacks government politics at the party conference of October 1981. The vehemence of his attack probably made ministerial rebellion against her more difficult.

53. In January 1982, Mark Thatcher was briefly lost in the North African desert. It was the only time when officials found Mrs Thatcher too upset to do her work properly. Leaving a meeting in the Imperial Hotel, London, she shed a tear.

54. Margaret and Denis at Chequers. 'I am glad that Chequers played quite a part in the Falklands story,' she wrote. 'Winston had used it quite a lot during World War II.'

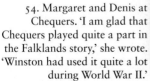

55. 'Rejoice' – Mrs Thatcher celebrates the recapture of South Georgia, the first victory of the Falklands War, with John Nott, Secretary of State for Defence, at her side, on 25 April 1982.

56. This famous picture of Royal Marine commandos captured the improvised courage of the Falklands campaign. British troops 'yomped' to victory – and saved Mrs Thatcher's premiership.

57. At the Falklands Commemoration Service at St Paul's Cathedral, October 1982, Mrs Thatcher is standing with Admiral Lord Lewin, Chief of the Defence Staff, whom she trusted and admired. She was outraged at attempts by the St Paul's clergy to avoid giving thanks for the Falklands victory.

58. Mrs Thatcher tours the streets of Strasbourg with President Valéry Giscard d'Estaing and Chancellor Helmut Schmidt for her first European summit, June 1979. She hated it.

59. Arriving at the first session of the Tokyo G7 summit in June 1979, with the US President Jimmy Carter. Their relationship was polite but not warm.

60. En route to Tokyo, Mrs Thatcher stopped at Moscow airport and had her first meeting with the Soviet leadership, in this case the Prime Minister Alexei Kosygin. Both leaders enjoyed their verbal joust.

61. With the Queen at the Commonwealth Heads of Government Meeting in Lusaka, October 1979. There was a problem of 'Who's the star?'

62. Mrs Thatcher thought she would be physically attacked when she arrived in Lusaka. Instead she was charmed. This picture of her dancing with the Zambian President Kenneth Kaunda enraged the Tory right.

63 and 64. The Thatchers visited India in April 1981. It suited Margaret better than Denis.

65. Welcoming Indira Gandhi to Downing Street, 1982. The two prime ministers enjoyed the chance to talk about problems with their children.

66. The Queen Mother, the greatest royal Thatcher fan, greets the Prime Minister at a Lancaster House reception congratulating Her Majesty on her eightieth birthday. Mrs Thatcher was notable for curtsying very low to royalty. Lord Soames, like many of the establishment, found this funny.

67. Ronald Reagan ensured that Mrs Thatcher was the first European to visit him in the White House after he became president in January 1981. 'She's the only one with balls.'

68. With Airey Neave, soldier, man of secrets, queenmaker, assassination victim.

69. Bernard Ingham, Mrs Thatcher's blunt but wily press spokesman. He sometimes seemed to know her thoughts before she did.

70. Gordon Reece, the PR and political strategist who, despite admiring her, was determined to keep her out of any television debate.

71. With Ian Gow, her Parliamentary Private Secretary, and perhaps her most faithful servant. 'Whatever the future holds in store', he told her, she had given him 'the privilege of trying to help the finest chief … and the kindest and most considerate friend that any man could hope to serve'.

72. The 'Gang of Four':
David Owen, Bill Rodgers,
Shirley Williams and Roy
Jenkins spent so much time
breaking the Labour left
that they did not take Mrs
Thatcher seriously enough,
which helped her.

73. At the feet of Harold Macmillan.
But he had no time for her economic
policies, and she knew it.

74. Jim Prior was the only 'Wet'
brave enough to take on Mrs
Thatcher about economic policy.
She successfully exiled him, to
Northern Ireland.

75. Mrs Thatcher and Michael
Foot in his 'donkey jacket' at the
Cenotaph Remembrance Day
ceremony, November 1981. 'He was
a little uncertain about what to do,'
she wrote charitably.

76. With Geoffrey Howe, her Chancellor of the Exchequer (1979–1983). The relationship was never really warm but he was the 'tapestry master of Thatcherism'.

77. Keith Joseph, Mrs Thatcher's dearest political friend and the man who made way for her to be leader. She loved him, but could be rude to him for his lack of political sense.

78. Norman Tebbit, Employment Secretary from 1981, the 'bovver boy' of Thatcherism. Of Mrs Thatcher's colleagues on the right, only he could match her passion, and he exceeded her in wit.

79. Willie Whitelaw – first her opponent then her loyal deputy (and Home Secretary). 'Everyone needs a Willie,' she said, not seeing why others might laugh. Whitelaw was really one of the 'Wets', but he let them down, not her.

David Wolfson noted that at each meeting he attended with Chancellor and Prime Minister in these weeks the PSBR kept expanding: 'If you're a retailer [which he was], you know that if you see a trend it is likely to continue. Walters, Hoskyns and I said to her: "If we let this continue we will no longer be economically credible."' In Wolfson's account, Mrs Thatcher picked up on their implied recommendation that the PSBR must be reined in by all means, including further cuts and tax rises, and replied, 'Are you sure you're right, because if not, my prime ministerial term is going to be pretty short.'[8] At a meeting on 13 February attended by, among others, Mrs Thatcher, Howe, Burns, Walters, Hoskyns and Wolfson, Walters advocated that the PSBR be held back to £10 billion and that the basic rate of income tax be raised. Howe argued that a PSBR of £11.5 billion would do, and he and Mrs Thatcher united against a tax rise. In her memoirs, Mrs Thatcher reported the discussion thus:

> Alan was the economist. But Geoffrey and I were politicians. Geoffrey rightly observed that introducing what would be represented as a deflationary budget at the time of the deepest recession since the 1930s would be difficult enough; doing so via an increase in the basic rate would be a political nightmare. I went along with Geoffrey's judgement about the problems of raising income tax, but I did so without much conviction and as the days went by my unease grew.[9]

Those present did not notice Mrs Thatcher's lack of conviction on the subject of tax rises at the time. Alan Walters recalled that 'she screamed at me: "You're just an academic and you don't know what the political implications are."'[10] He replied that she would be politically ruined by the collapse of financial markets and referred (knowing this would sting her) to how this had produced the fiasco of Edward Heath's 'dash for growth'.[11] Hoskyns and co. found that, unusually, she had not read their paper on the subject. Afterwards, Hoskyns recorded in his diary, he and Walters talked 'and I was pleased to find that Alan had been wondering whether he ought to leave, whether the whole thing wasn't a waste of time.'[12] Walters, Hoskyns and Wolfson began to speak of resigning en masse if their Budget advice was not taken.

In the course of the following week, further meetings did not seem to be winning Mrs Thatcher round. Walters kept telling her that she could not have the lower interest rates for which she longed unless there was lower government borrowing. This reduction in borrowing, if it could not come from spending cuts, *had* to come from higher taxes. He thought he had failed to convince her. Throughout the week, she was distracted by the disaster over pit closures. On 20 February, two days after the coal climbdown,

Hoskyns sent her another note, saying that the PSBR would now get bigger yet, and reiterating that the 'overkill' Budget would be the 'turning-point'. She wrote 'sharp comments' on it, and Hoskyns felt 'We were now close to the point at which the relationship between advisers and the advised begins to break down, and the advisers themselves are seen as part of the problem.'[13] But, just when all seemed dark, Hoskyns's diary for 24 February then recorded: 'In the afternoon we heard ... of an amazing volte-face by Margaret. She started swinging back, in a budget bilateral with Geoffrey and Douglas Wass, to the need for a smaller PSBR and perhaps to raise income tax ... Then she says that it is their problem (because Geoffrey and Douglas Wass have said it's politically impossible), it's up to them. Then, as they start to leave, she says words to the effect, "if there's a funding crisis then you (Geoffrey) are for the chop." '[14] The official record confirms some of this, sanitized. A note from Tim Lankester to Howe's private secretary of 24 February reported: 'The Prime Minister said she was dismayed at the prospect of a PSBR for 1981/82 of £11.25 billion [which Howe was advocating]. She doubted whether it would be possible to justify a reduction in MLR unless the PSBR was reduced to around £10.5 billion. From a political standpoint, she thought it might now be possible to justify a 1p increase in the basic income tax rate on account of the increased spending on the NCB and BSC.' Howe continued to argue that an increase in the basic rate 'would be extremely difficult politically and would be very bad for business morale', and Mrs Thatcher eventually said that she was 'prepared to accept his political judgement', but her point about the lower PSBR figure stood.[15]

Alan Walters called on Mrs Thatcher the next morning. She was packing her hats for her visit to the United States the following day. She told him she had said to Howe that he must take £3.5 billion off the PSBR. Walters said, 'Are you sure?' Mrs Thatcher replied: 'Of course I'm sure. That's what you want, isn't it?'[16]*

Perhaps because Mrs Thatcher then left for America, perhaps because of the intensity and confusion of the proceedings, it was not immediately clear to all that a decision had been made. In a sense, it had not, since Howe's astute solution to the tax-raising problem, which was eventually

---

* On this important and busy day, Mrs Thatcher also delivered a speech to the Parliamentary and Scientific Committee, for which she had prepared very extensively. Her private secretary, Nick Sanders, drew her attention, in the preparation, to an essay by Sir Peter Medawar in which he quoted Hilaire Belloc on the fate (electrocution) of the peer who did not recognize 'the duty of the wealthy man / To give employment to the artisan'. Medawar wrongly named the peer as Lord Norwich. Mrs Thatcher was attentive and knowledgeable enough to alter it, correctly, to Lord Finchley. (Interview with Nick Sanders.)

accepted, was that the money should come not from a rise in the basic rate, but by failing to raise the tax thresholds in line with inflation. Still not sure what was happening, Walters sent a note to Howe advocating an even bigger cut in the PSBR. Hoskyns, Walters and Wolfson prepared a note of resignation for when, as they still expected, their Budget advice was not taken ('The opportunity to turn the UK economy round ... has passed ...').[17] But in fact Mrs Thatcher had come round to their way of thinking and found ways of getting Howe to accept it.

The Treasury account of the Budget preparations disputes the 'myth' that the 1981 Budget was 'made in Downing Street'. Douglas Wass maintained that the Treasury mandarins had prepared a 'broadly neutral' Budget intended to be consistent with the MTFS. When Mrs Thatcher told them that 'I want a lower PSBR so that we can have lower interest rates,' they were perfectly ready to co-operate: 'Geoffrey didn't fight very hard. If this was the objective, it was the objective.'[18] In his memoirs, Howe fairly points out that he and Walters were more or less on the same side.[19] He made sure that a close relationship existed between Walters and Peter Middleton, co-ordinating between No. 10 and the Treasury. Howe's special adviser, Adam Ridley, remembered that 'we all realized in advance this was it.' The threat of a crisis in the gilts market dominated everything. The Treasury and No. 10 both wanted to bring about a situation in which people would say, 'This Government is for real: we can buy lots of gilts.'[20] To the extent that there was competition between the two institutions, it was that 'each side thought the other might crack'.[21] Peter Middleton recalled that he and Walters were not at odds: 'There was a growing feeling that it [the entire anti-inflation policy] might just slip out of our hands.' In the course of all the pre-Budget discussions between the Treasury and No. 10, 'Geoffrey never spoke about anything that sounded like a row.'[22]

Nor was it unusual that Mrs Thatcher changed her mind in the course of the Budget discussions: she was often at her most apparently confused and difficult when she was in the middle of trying to persuade herself of something. It would have spoken ill of her political judgment if she had rushed into a contractionary Budget without protest. Nevertheless, there can be little doubt that the orchestration in favour of a tough Budget by her Downing Street advisers did make a great deal of difference. So did the advice and character of Walters himself. In the view of Terry Burns, who watched proceedings from the Treasury side, 'At some stage [in February], she swung and overtook us.'[23] 'It was Walters she really listened to,' Burns believed, drawing comfort from the clarity of what he said. Walters had a 'disarming way of being absolutely sure he was right'.[24] She, in turn, 'did strengthen the backbone of the Treasury', which was weakened by division between the old guard, such as Wass and Ryrie, and the younger set, including Middleton and Burns himself.[25] She also emboldened Nigel Lawson, the most radical minister in the Treasury, in resisting the more consensual inclinations of Geoffrey Howe.[26] In Clive Whitmore's view, Mrs Thatcher suspected Howe of being over-influenced by the old Keynesians at the Treasury, and this made Walters all the more important.[27] It was galling for a senior elected politician such as Howe that a personal adviser to the Prime Minister should have so much influence – this influence would later become intolerable to his successor, Lawson – but it was also a fact. In the weeks coming up to the 1981 Budget, so fraught with disaster and promises of even greater disaster to come, Mrs Thatcher was forced to confront the possibility that she might actually fail, and fail, at that, dishonourably, by abandoning what she believed. Walters, and other advisers close to her, helped to keep her on the straight and narrow.

Geoffrey Howe presented his Budget to Parliament on 10 March 1981. By then, the Treasury forecast for the PSBR had risen to £14.5 billion (6 per cent of GDP).* Howe's tax increases were designed to reduce it to £10.5 billion. Child benefit and one-parent-family benefit were indexed, but the decision not to index tax thresholds brought £2 billion. There was double indexation of the levies on alcohol, tobacco and car and petrol duties. There was a once-for-all levy on the non-interest-bearing deposits of the banks, which brought £400 million. Interest rates were to come down by 2 per cent to 12 per cent. Howe also announced that in future public spending would be controlled in cash rather than volume terms.†Although this last measure made the controls on spending tougher than in the past, it also made them more predictable and therefore easier to handle. If departments knew their cash limits in advance, they were less likely to find themselves confronted with the 'in-year' cuts that they hated so much.

It was and is a convention that the Chancellor has sovereignty over the Budget. It is the product of his judgment, in consultation with the Prime Minister, rather than the collective decision of the Cabinet. Knowing, however, that this Budget was more controversial than usual, Howe took the precaution of exposing it privately the day before to the most senior figures in the government – Whitelaw, Carrington, Prior and Pym – seeing them

---

* To illustrate how bad the situation was, it should be borne in mind that, for the next thirty years, a deficit of 3 per cent of GDP was considered the maximum desirable. Towards the end of Gordon Brown's administration in 2010, however, it was more than 11 per cent.

† In other words, departments would no longer agree the need for x number of helicopters, hospitals or whatever, and then find the money needed. Instead, they would negotiate the amount of money needed and then buy only as much as they could afford.

individually. Although none was thrilled, only Prior expressed clear hostility, telling Howe that it was 'pretty disastrous'.[28] The following morning, before the full Cabinet was presented with the Budget in advance of the Chancellor's statement in Parliament, Prior had breakfast with Peter Walker and Ian Gilmour, the other most dissident ministers. They debated whether they should resign. According to Peter Walker, they continued this debate outside the Cabinet room just after they had heard the full details of the Budget, but concluded that they should not do so 'because of the effect on sterling'.[29] Gilmour remembered that he, in particular, had wanted to resign, but was talked out of it by the others on the grounds of the need to 'fight the good fight'.[30] Prior, in retrospect, considered their decision, or rather indecision, feeble: 'We were wet in the true sense of the word.'[31]

In the full Cabinet, Howe, who, unlike Mrs Thatcher, had always sought to include Wets in his discussions and was frustrated by their reluctance to engage, focused on their main worry – unemployment. It depended, he said, on inflation. 'We are all at the eye of the storm.' The reaction, apart from strong support from Keith Joseph, was gloomy. Gilmour spoke of a 'political disaster'; Walker said he was 'very concerned'; Pym warned that industry would be 'depressed and disappointed'. Prior expressed his 'immense disappointment and deep concern'. Even Willie Whitelaw, his criticism shaded by loyalty, said there was an 'enormous need for hope'. Lord Carrington said, 'We've been doing this for two years, and it doesn't seem to be working.' He then opened up the line of argument which was to be the Wets' chosen weapon: the whole future of the government was at stake and yet, he complained, they had had no opportunity to discuss the content of the Budget.[32] All that Mrs Thatcher felt able to say was that they should unite behind the Chancellor.

'The Budget is not well received,' began Bernard Ingham's daily press digest for the Prime Minister the following day. The *Sun*, with the headline 'Howe It Hurts', said that the government had 'failed to deliver the goods'. The *Financial Times* spoke of 'an admission of general defeat apart from inflation', and offered the headline 'The Strategy's Last Chance'. There was praise – the *Daily Mail* spoke of 'an act of stubborn political courage' – but not much, and the press reported unhappiness from at least six Cabinet ministers. Changing the subject, the digest also reported: 'Mark Thatcher to advertise Scotch on Japanese TV'.[33] At the presentation of the *Guardian*'s Young Businessman of the Year Award, Mrs Thatcher departed from her prepared text to speak angrily about her critics: what 'gets me', she said, was that 'those who are most critical of the extra tax are those who were most vociferous in demanding the extra expenditure.'[34] The next day, telling tales out of school, Ingham sent Mrs Thatcher a secret memo about

Francis Pym's behaviour in his briefing of the parliamentary press lobby: 'I think you should know that Mr Pym this afternoon ... rather deftly applied public pressure for a pre-Budget discussion in Cabinet of economic strategy.' Ingham went on: 'How typical was his view in Cabinet? Probably typical, he said ... he did not think that a tough line by the Treasury during the next public expenditure review in the autumn would be particularly well received.' Ingham said he had subsequently discovered from a journalist that ministers were concerting for an economic strategy discussion, perhaps during a weekend at Chequers. The idea 'is not merely being nursed by a few Ministers; it is beginning to take off.'[35] Sure enough, the next day's papers were full of stories about the group of ministers who were now demanding a say in Budget strategy: 'Never again', Ingham's digest reported, 'will they put up with the shock of learning its secrets on the morning before delivery. All this is characterised by words like "mutiny" ... with Messrs Whitelaw, Pym, Prior, Walker, Gilmour and Carrington named ... *Guardian* says many Ministers and backbenchers are openly discussing possibility of Palace revolution in summer when Government is told to change policies.'[36]

Luckily for Mrs Thatcher, the mood on the back benches, though hardly rapturous, was not as mutinous as the *Guardian* reported. They relieved their feelings by focusing on a side-issue of particular relevance to rural constituencies, the increases in the duty on DERV (diesel), and Howe was able to make a concession at no net cost to the Budget by cutting the DERV duty and making up for it with yet higher imposts on tobacco. But there could be no mistaking the emergence of a clear and semi-concerted opposition within Mrs Thatcher's Cabinet. There might not be a proper plot to get rid of her – there was certainly a want of boldness among the dissidents – but there was now a move, clothed in demands for changes in process, to isolate her, or create a situation in which her lack of majority among her own ministers could be made to work against her. This coincided with a time when the ranks of her trusted associates had thinned out. About a week after the Budget, John Hoskyns noted in his diary that:

> Ronnie [Millar] was very worried indeed about the way Margaret had lost or allowed the departure of so many supporters – Richard Ryder* [leaving No. 10 to prepare to become an MP at the next election], Gordon Reece [who was working for Armand Hammer in the United States] ... Alistair

---

* Mrs Thatcher was conscious of some of these losses. At the beginning of 1982, she sought unsuccessfully to persuade Richard Ryder to return. She told him that she was worried by Alan Walters's lack of political feel and wanted Ryder to 'ride shotgun' for him. (Interview with Lord Ryder of Wensum.)

McAlpine [who had been temporarily pushed off his Treasurer's perch in Central Office by Lord Thorneycroft], and so on. He said that Gordon had heard in the US that Kissinger says his friends in the Cabinet (Carrington?) say she'll be out within a year. He feels we've got to move fast to save her.[37]

It was probably helpful that, at this moment, to use Ingham's words, '364 economists cook up round-robin to condemn your economic policies'.[38] The letter, published in *The Times*, was signed by five former chief economic advisers to the government, including Terry Burns's immediate predecessor, Fred Atkinson. It was also signed by Kenneth Berrill, the former head of the CPRS, and by Mervyn King, who much later became the Governor of the Bank of England. It read:

> There is no basis in economic theory or supporting evidence for the Government's belief that by deflating demand they will bring inflation permanently under control and thereby introduce an automatic recovery in output and employment;
>   Present policies will deepen the depression, erode the industrial base of our economy and threaten its social and political stability;
>   There are alternative policies;
>   The time has come to reject monetarist policies and consider which alternative offers the best hope of sustained recovery.

Whatever its distaste for the government's policies, the public was not particularly likely to be impressed by the views of economists, nor to think that 364 of them were better than one. On the same day as the letter, Ingham's digest also reported: 'Sam Brittan, FT, says this could be a favourable leading indicator for economic recovery.'[39] Peter Middleton remembered that, as soon as the 364 had spoken, 'Everything began to look up.'[40]

As Nigel Lawson put it in his memoirs, 'The timing was exquisite.'[41] Output touched its lowest point in the quarter that ended on the day when the 364 economists' letter was published. In the eight years from 1981 to 1989, real GDP growth averaged 3.2 per cent, whereas there were sixteen months of negative growth during 1980 and 1981. From the first quarter of 1983, the number of people employed began to rise, and from the third quarter of 1986 the number of unemployed began to fall. Alan Walters's prediction that the inflation rate would fall to 5 per cent in 1982 was over-optimistic, but the rate for 1983 was 4.6 per cent. As for the PSBR, its eventual outturn was £8.5 billion, £2 billion better than budgeted for. Neither the 364 nor their opponents were, of course, to know this at the time, but it was significant that, beyond stating that alternative policies existed, the *Times* letter did not say anything about them. As with internal critiques by the Wets, the letter was clear in its revulsion at what the government was doing, but much less confident about what to do instead. What the critics failed to recognize was that the old remedies of fiscal expansion did not work if confidence was low. The Budget, as Peter Middleton described it, was 'all about the *demonstration* effect of what was happening'.[42] As Alan Walters argued, fiscal expansion became, in such circumstances, a symptom of trouble and therefore the actual effect of a deficit intended to be 'expansionary' was to contract the economy. The 'toughest peacetime Budget in memory' was therefore, perversely, the one to inspire the confidence required.[43] As Douglas Wass, no monetarist, recalled: 'The 1981 Budget did enable us to have lower interest rates and therefore did lower exchange rates.'[44]

Not that confidence and calm returned quickly. There was some good economic news – a stock market high, for example – but there was also trouble. At the end of March, the Civil Service unions began a 'selective' strike, which soon impeded the flow of government revenue and therefore worsened the public finances still further. It was typical of the situation in which Mrs Thatcher's government found itself that the day when industrial production turned up for the first time in ten months was also the day when serious rioting broke out in the streets of London. Anti-police riots by mainly black youths in Brixton, south London, on 13 April 1981 injured 150 police, produced more than 200 arrests and gave rise to widespread looting. Four days earlier, the IRA hunger striker Bobby Sands, in prison and still on hunger strike, had been elected to Parliament in the Fermanagh and South Tyrone by-election. Extremists were involved in stirring up trouble in Brixton; against a report, in Ingham's digest, that the 'riot started when supporters of IRA H block prisoners [in the Maze] announced stabbed black youth had died', Mrs Thatcher wrote a strong squiggle of excited disapproval.[45] She came out strongly, saying there was 'no excuse' for the riots, and that public money had already been 'poured into' Lambeth to little effect.[46] She probably benefited politically from the fact that the left wing of the Labour Party, including the controversial Labour Leader of Lambeth Council, 'Red Ted' Knight, were involved in anti-police agitation. The public were deeply shocked by the scale of the violence, and were disposed, unlike the metropolitan elites, to blame it on the people who had rioted. On the other hand, Mrs Thatcher did not appear to offer any practical 'Thatcherite' answer to the problems of rioting, and she allowed Willie Whitelaw, the Home Secretary, to appoint a left-liberal judge, Lord Scarman, to conduct the inquiry into the riots. It was natural that her critics should allege that the disturbances were a response to the unemployment she was creating: Wets could claim that their prophecies of tears in the social fabric had come true.

The month of May was no merrier. On 4 May, Bobby Sands died of his hunger strike, his death provoking violence in Northern Ireland and worldwide protests. On 7 May, Labour took control of the Greater London Council and the very next day, in an internal coup predicted before the polls, replaced their moderate leader with the rising star of what the tabloids called the 'loony left', Ken Livingstone.* On 10 May, François Mitterrand† was elected the first Socialist president of France's Fifth Republic, on a programme which included the nationalization of the banks. On 13 May, Pope John Paul II was shot and nearly killed in St Peter's Square in Rome by a professional assassin who, it much later emerged, probably had links with the Bulgarian secret services and ultimately the Soviet KGB. On 18 May, Mrs Thatcher felt compelled to sack her Navy Minister, Keith Speed, for resisting the unpopular cuts which John Nott, with her encouragement, was imposing. At this time, she was exhausted by the pressure of events and by trouble with her teeth which was a recurrent intrusion upon her generally very good health. As a result, her staff had to cancel a session with Wolfson, Hoskyns and others at Chequers, planned as part of the great fight over public spending which, after the Budget, was the next area of Cabinet conflict.[47]

Mrs Thatcher was extremely wary of her colleagues' demand for discussions of economic strategy. Unlike the ever conciliatory Geoffrey Howe, who reasoned with her that 'If we cannot convince colleagues that we are right, then we shall find it difficult to convince the country,'[48] she had an obsession, based on painful experience, with the danger of leaks; she also feared, again with reason, being ambushed and outnumbered. She did eventually accept, however, that some discussion must take place, in the context of the control of public expenditure, and she decided that, unlike the Burns 'lecture' of the previous year, this should be based on a paper by Howe himself. Howe's paper was circulated, and ministers had the chance before the meeting to give notice of questions they might raise. Howe set out the extent of the growth in public spending since 1979 and concluded that, unless the policy changed, 'we shall enter the election with

* Ken Livingstone (1945–), educated Tulse Hill Comprehensive School and Philippa Fawcett College of Education; Greater London Council, Member for Norwood, 1973–7; for Hackney North, 1977–81; for Paddington, 1981–6; Leader of Council and of Labour Group, 1981–6; Labour MP for Brent East, 1987–2001; Mayor of London, 2000–2008.

† François Mitterrand (1916–96), Interior Minister of France, 1954–5; Justice Minister, 1956–7; candidate of the left in presidential elections of 1965 and 1974; President of the French Republic, 1981–95.

the overall tax burden much heavier than the one we inherited. Not only politically, but also economically, that is not tolerable.' On his draft, Mrs Thatcher added the one area of proposed reform which was common ground between her and the Wets. 'Plans to train and occupy young people,' she wrote.[49] In advance of the meeting, Robert Armstrong warned Mrs Thatcher that Prior would call for a debate on whether 3 million unemployed was politically acceptable and that Michael Heseltine would demand higher capital expenditure financed by savings on current account. In best mandarin style, he added, 'You may also want to agree in the Cabinet the line to be taken with the press – and to invite them to resist the temptation to embroider it.'[50]

At the meeting, on 17 June 1981, Prior led the charge. 'Don't know how we shall get through the coming year,' Armstrong recorded him as saying. 'I see solution not in cutting public expenditure but in getting growth.' Walker, Carrington, Pym and others also expressed unhappiness. Even Willie Whitelaw allowed himself to say, 'I fear the effects of unemployment on crime are very serious,' and warned of the risks of 'future Brixtons'.[51] The next day's press carried excited accounts of how Mrs Thatcher had seen off the rebels ('Maggie Crushes Jobs Revolt by Wets – Lonely Prior's Jobs Plea is Rejected'), which rather suggested that Ingham had done some embroidering of his own. There followed a fierce row at the regular Cabinet that day about the morning's leaks, and an additional row about the proposed defence cuts. Mrs Thatcher began to be written up in the papers as a successfully ruthless politician. On the following day, the rate of inflation reached a two-year low and the *Financial Times* reported that profits of UK firms had recovered sharply in the first quarter of the year. In a debate on unemployment on 24 June, following the publication of the monthly figure of 2,680,977 unemployed, Mrs Thatcher was generally agreed to have trounced Michael Foot, whose rambling and facetiousness were reported by *The Times* to have 'totally misjudged the House'. She was probably assisted, as usual, by the tone of an attack from Ted Heath, who said that the government's economic policies were 'incomprehensible'. He warned of severe social and racial strife.

But the sense of conflict and crisis grew. New riots, which began in Southall, west London, on 4 July 1981, spread to many other parts of the country, including Moss Side in Manchester, where a mob besieged a police station shouting 'kill, kill', and, most notably, in the Toxteth area of Liverpool. There were attacks, previously almost unknown in mainland Britain, on firemen and ambulance crews. Using a party political broadcast which was mainly a defence of policy on unemployment, Mrs Thatcher inserted a preamble about the riots. She was tough. She emphasized that 200 police had been injured in Liverpool alone. 'The law must be upheld,' she said. 'People must be protected.' She denied the link between unemployment and rioting.[52] But the fact that she settled for the uncomfortable mixture of subjects rather than devoting an entire broadcast to the shocking events showed that she was not sure how best to handle the crisis. It was alleged that Mrs Thatcher's private reaction to seeing the news of the rioting was to exclaim, 'Those poor shopkeepers!' The phrase made a chapter title in Hugo Young's largely hostile biography *One of Us*,[53] and it was considered laughable, almost contemptible, that she should have reacted in this way. In fact, the quotation has not been verified, and may be apocryphal, but, as often in matters concerning social order, Mrs Thatcher's sentiments may have been closer to those of the general population than were those of her critics. The problem was not that her feelings were at odds with the voters, but that she did not seem to have the situation in hand. Her rhetoric was strong, yet she seemed impotent. On 10 July there was rioting in twelve cities, the most extensive yet.

In the middle of this, Bernard Ingham wrote to Francis Pym in his (Pym's) capacity as head of government presentation. 'I held a meeting yesterday,' he explained, with the heads of information in the economic departments. 'The consensus can be summarised in two words: deeply worried.' July was always a dangerous time, and now there were riots, the Warrington by-election with its first test of the new SDP approaching, bad unemployment figures expected, and the possibility for the royal wedding at the end of the month of a 'national atmosphere soured'. The Tories, he said, would go into the parliamentary recess 'in a state of profound agitation'.[54]

At Cabinet on 9 July, Whitelaw reported from the riot zone. 'The area is shattering,' he said. 'The damage is worse than Belfast in 1972.' He called for better headgear for the police. Mrs Thatcher asked for the return of the Riot Act, which, once read out at the scene of a disturbance, had given extensive powers to the police to arrest, disperse and even open fire. She wanted summary courts too. Whitelaw murmured that these would have 'little real effect'. Michael Heseltine reported how much damage left-wing penetration of the Labour Party and of councils was doing in the riot areas, and called for 'ways of giving Government support for job creation and wealth creation'. There were several calls for intervention, on the model of Harold Macmillan, who had sent Lord Hailsham as special minister for the depressed north-east in the early 1960s. Mrs Thatcher was unconvinced: 'We have poured money into big employments in Merseyside; a failure,' Labour authorities had created problems with 'horrible housing, high rise etc' and 'We have a whole generation brought up on 5 hours a day of TV.' 'Perhaps,' she ended rather lamely, 'we must call some of the media together.' Heseltine returned to the charge, demanding a Hailsham-style minister, with the unspoken implication that he was the man for the job. Mrs Thatcher asked for time to think.[55]

On 13 July she visited Liverpool herself where, as Ingham's press digest put it, she was 'pelted with tomatoes and toilet rolls; most [newspapers] feature your 10 most worrying days since you took office.'[56] By the time the Cabinet met a week after its previous meeting, she had decided to send Heseltine to Liverpool for a fortnight to see what could be done, though she emphasized cautiously that this was not 'a special, ministerial appointment' but a 'pilot, prototype scheme'.[57]* This was the day of the Warrington by-election. Although the Conservatives did badly, losing their deposit, this fact was overshadowed by the damage to Labour. Challenged, with huge publicity, by the SDP candidate, Roy Jenkins, in the previously rock-solid Labour seat, Labour clung on with a majority of only 1,759 and a swing against it of 13.3 per cent. On polling day, the inflation rate was announced as 11.3 per cent, the lowest since Mrs Thatcher took office.

The Cabinet met on 23 July to discuss the public expenditure survey for 1981. Mrs Thatcher had just returned from the summit of the G7 in Ottawa. There, the final communiqué had pleased her by its emphasis on the role of the market and on the need 'urgently to reduce public borrowing'. In private, Mrs Thatcher had told President Reagan how worried she was about high US interest rates because of their effect on Britain: 'It would be difficult to get it [inflation] down any further now that the pound had fallen against the dollar because of US interest rates. We were, in effect, importing inflation.'[58] But in the sessions of the summit she had resisted French and German attempts (Helmut Schmidt spoke of the highest interest rates 'since the birth of Jesus Christ') to gang up on Reagan about this. She felt protective towards the President, who had only recently appeared on the public stage after having been shot and badly wounded by a lone, crazed gunman on 30 March. Her view was that Reagan, facing his first summit of this kind, needed support in his attempt to persuade Congress to cut taxes and spending. 'President Reagan was the new kid on the block, and most of the Europeans thought he was a Hollywood character without a brain,' recalled Reagan's close aide Mike Deaver. 'Margaret Thatcher not only helped Reagan to learn the ropes, but was the right flank.'[59] As the summit began, it was Reagan, and Reagan alone, who received a very public kiss on the cheek from Mrs Thatcher.[60] Over dinner with his fellow

---

* Eventually, and reluctantly, Mrs Thatcher gave Heseltine a more lasting role, earning him the moniker 'Minister for Merseyside'. His visits there, calling for more intervention, made a great splash.

world leaders, the President tried to explain his own economic approach, but was criticized, if not ridiculed, from all sides. As Reagan later recalled it, the only person who came to his defence was Margaret Thatcher. After dinner, he caught up with her to express his thanks. As he told the story, 'she leaned over to me and patted my elbow and said, "Don't worry about it, Ronnie, it's just boys being boys."'[61] She stored up much goodwill. On his way home from the summit, Reagan expressed his due gratitude in an interview: 'There were times in those meetings when Margaret Thatcher spoke up and put her finger on the thing we were trying to resolve.'[62] In his diary, he wrote: 'It was a successful summit – not divisive although it could have been with regard to our interest rates . . . Margaret Thatcher is a tower of strength and a solid friend of the U.S.'[63] Mrs Thatcher told the Cabinet that it had been 'quite the best economic conference the Government could have had'.*

The Cabinet, however, was not placated. It wanted a showdown. Fresh from his Liverpudlian experience, Michael Heseltine took up the charge, previously led by the Wets, against Geoffrey Howe's plans for cuts of £5 billion. 'Reducing taxes', he said, 'has nothing to do with problem of Merseyside. Colleagues don't understand how bad it is . . . We have a society which is close to much more violence.' He described Howe's paper on public spending as 'deeply disappointing' and said that the government should 'get a grip on the national economy' by going for a pay freeze and thus having '£5 billion at our disposal'. What was he proposing, cried Mrs Thatcher, a pay freeze, a pensions freeze, a social security freeze? 'I want the maximum of that package I can get,' said Heseltine, whose use of the first person singular was not calculated to make Mrs Thatcher comfortable about his motives. Ever conscious of the terrible Heath example, she said, 'it must not get out of this room that a pay freeze is being talked about'.[64]

All the Cabinet critics pitched in. The problem was 'desperate', said Peter Walker. Unemployment was much more of a worry than inflation, said Francis Pym. 'This paper points to the decline and fall of the Tory Party,' said Ian Gilmour. Jim Prior warned that the problem might 'overwhelm us, and destroy what we stand for as a party and as a country'. Carrington said that support was melting away. John Nott and John Biffen, intellectually committed to 'monetarism' though they were, sided with the Wets. Only Joseph backed the Treasury team. Willie Whitelaw played for time

---

* Mrs Thatcher was sufficiently impressed, and perhaps intrigued, by President Reagan that, when she noticed he had left an assortment of doodled heads and faces at the summit table, she took them home as a souvenir. Today they survive among her personal papers (THCR 1/3/6 f101, http://www.margaretthatcher.org/document/114249).

by pointing out that July was always a bad time to make any final decision, but he did tell Mrs Thatcher that 'There comes a moment in politics when you have pushed the tolerance of a society too far. We aren't there, but we aren't far from it.' He thought that 'We just aren't going to make these cuts.' It was the Lord Chancellor, Lord Hailsham, always mercurial, but also respected for his intelligence and experience, who made the most wounding intervention. He drew a comparison with the America of the 1930s, and the President at the beginning of the Great Depression, Herbert Hoover. 'Hoover succeeded in destroying the Republican Party,' said Hailsham; 'we are in danger of destroying our own. Almost all Roosevelt's policies were wrong, but political economics is applied psychology, and they worked.' Geoffrey Howe hit back that the 1980s were not like the 1930s, because inflation was 'still rampant'. Mrs Thatcher responded with her own historical example: 'We have been here before. We reflated in 1972/3 – it led to Barber boom, property market boom and collapse, 6 years of socialism.' Interest rates were on the way up again and yet people were speaking of increasing public expenditure. 'The most frightening thing I've heard is that we should abandon policy of keeping inflation down. OK for people with muscle . . . The rest would see savings being confiscated.' She concluded, 'Let's get a paper with both sides of the balance sheet. We must not get to a pocket money society [her phrase for a socialist, high-tax economy]. That's the end of us.'[65]

On the same day, Mrs Thatcher gave her end-of-term talk to the 1922 Committee, of which the message, according to Ingham's digest of the next day's press, was 'Now or never for Government's economic policies; stick to our guns; we can do it; no phoney boom.'[66] But, although she was combative as ever, she was also 'very upset' by the Cabinet arguments, and especially by Hailsham's comparison with Hoover.[67] She minded the disagreement with her policies less than the suggestion that she was destroying her party. The press duly reported the split in the public spending Cabinet, and some mentioned Francis Pym as an alternative leader to Mrs Thatcher. A reshuffle was expected in the autumn, they said. Discontent was public. The US Ambassador, John Louis, reported home under the title 'Britain drifts'. 'The problems begin with Thatcher and her government. It has visibly lost its grip on the rudder in recent weeks . . . the recent riots were a sharp shock. All along, the moderates in the party have insisted Thatcher was sacrificing too much to the fight against inflation. Last week, these moderates won a hard cabinet fight to achieve a youth employment package. Now they feel vindicated, but they're also frustrated: the moderates themselves have no better prescriptions than creeping reflation and more soothing rhetoric . . .'[68]

And yet, at this grim time, the atmosphere changed. On 27 July it became clear that the Civil Service dispute which had been running since March would be called off, a return to work presented as a defeat for the unions. On 29 July the Prince of Wales married Lady Diana Spencer, amid scenes of general happiness not witnessed since the Coronation. For Mrs Thatcher's amusement, Ingham included in his digest Soviet TV's reaction to the occasion: 'People of London hope the sound of wedding bells will drown out the rioting in Ulster and the shouts of young people being beaten mercilessly in Liverpool.' In the same day's report, Mrs Thatcher put a large arrow of approval beside the news that the House of Representatives had voted for Reagan's tax cut.[69] Ingham himself, who had written so gloomily to Francis Pym at the beginning of the month, wrote again at the end of it. He reported the conclusion of a meeting with his colleagues that 'we had emerged from a most difficult month . . . in far better shape than we might have reasonably expected, considering.' Warrington had been worse for Labour than for the government. Inflation, unemployment and industrial disputes had 'all turned out better than expected', and the Royal Wedding had been a 'national tonic'.[70]

No sooner were the words out of Ingham's typewriter than the row restarted. Geoffrey Howe's public announcement on the same day that the recession was now over was too much for some of the critics. Francis Pym denied that this was the case and called for remedial measures. The party chairman, Lord Thorneycroft, said in an interview that a 'survival package' was needed and played on the Wet/Dry division: he felt in himself 'a little rising damp'.[71] These were damaging criticisms from the two men charged with the public presentation of policy, but for that very reason they rebounded upon them. It looked as if they were plotting, and as if they had a vested interest in bad news. Tory supporters were outraged. The *Sun* said that a reshuffle was planned, which would include the sacking of Thorneycroft.[72] An opinion poll gave an SDP–Liberal Alliance 45 per cent, Labour 29 per cent and the Conservatives 25 per cent. It was time for the recess, which would work to Mrs Thatcher's advantage.

At the public spending Cabinet in July, Mrs Thatcher had said that the recess would allow time for 'fresh examination'. But, as Jim Prior put it, 'It wasn't fresh examination: it was fresh faces.'[73] The summer had shown her that it had become impossible to govern with her existing team. She railed against the Wets in private, calling them 'dumb bunnies'.[74] The impossibility of the existing Cabinet was even more visible to some of those advising her than it was to her. Willie Whitelaw and Michael Jopling, the Chief Whip, had been particularly 'outraged' by the challenge to her authority in the Cabinet of 23 July. Despite the fact that both men leant to the 'moderate' tendency in the party, they urged her that a Cabinet that did not support her was 'intolerable'.[75] Some of her supporters thought she was too passive in the face of insurrection. Charles Douglas-Home,* the deputy editor of *The Times*, wrote to her privately to tell her that he had been talking to her senior colleagues – Prior, Pym, Nott and Whitelaw himself – and had found their tone 'pretty depressing'. 'You cannot let them go on like this,' he said. 'The whole thrust of the government is crippled . . . by your ministers parading their consciences, frustrations, hysteria, snobberies, masculinities or ambitions before an audience.'[76] He recommended that she confront each critic individually and ask him to state his case. She did not follow his advice. The woman who had the reputation of being too dictatorial was really suffering from the opposite problem. With a shudder, she envisaged her own political mortality. 'I could always scrub floors,' she told her private secretary.[77]

Although Mrs Thatcher saw the process of the reshuffle in retrospect as a straightforward matter of weeding out dissidents and waverers and promoting true believers, it was rather more wayward than that. At first, she was sufficiently shaken by what had happened in the course of the summer to think seriously of getting rid of Geoffrey Howe. 'She came quite close to accepting this in private discussion,' remembered Clive Whitmore. Implicitly rebuking her for her tendency to see 'the government' as an entity from which she was somehow separate, Whitmore told her that she could not distance herself from her Chancellor's economic decisions: 'If Geoffrey Howe goes, you've got to go.'[78] 'She frequently behaved when in government as if she was still leading the Opposition,' he said. This was partly because she was 'shrewd politically and she always wanted to be in an "I told you so" position.'[79] But the strength of her position, such as it was, came from the fact that no one could drive a wedge between her and her Chancellor: it would have been fatal for her to have done the work of destruction herself. Howe himself got wind of the threat to his position, and warned his new private secretary, John Kerr,† that he might be gone by the party conference that October.[80] In the view of the Chief Whip, Michael Jopling, she was never serious about getting rid of Howe, but she did harbour suspicions about him because he was 'instinctively on the moderate side'.[81] She was

* Charles Douglas-Home (1937–85), educated Eton; defence correspondent, *The Times*, 1965–70; foreign editor, 1978–81; deputy editor, 1981–2; editor, 1982–5.
† John Kerr (1942–), educated Glasgow Academy and Pembroke College, Oxford; principal private secretary to Chancellor of the Exchequer, 1981–4; Assistant Under-Secretary, FCO, 1987–90; Ambassador and UK Permanent Representative to the EU, 1990–95; Ambassador to the United States, 1995–7; Permanent Under-Secretary, FCO, 1997–2002; created Lord Kerr of Kinlochard, 2004.

right in sensing this, but unwise to consider getting rid of Howe. Although Howe did not disagree with her, at this stage, about the main policies, his attitude was very different. He believed that his Welsh background gave him a stronger understanding than Mrs Thatcher of the pain of unemployment.

Her doubts about Howe were part of a wider problem, produced by the stress of the year, that she was almost as irritated with her allies as with her opponents, and they with her. In the first week of August, Hoskyns settled down to what he called a 'blockbuster' memo to his boss. To avoid her dismissing it as 'just me being disagreeable', he got David Wolfson and Ronnie Millar to add their names to his (though, since the paper mentions the merits of Millar by name, the pretence that he was one of its authors cannot have fooled Mrs Thatcher). The rather surprising involvement of Millar, who never saw government papers and was in no way a policy-maker, was sought by Hoskyns because Millar was, for Mrs Thatcher, 'that rare thing, a trusted friend who wanted her to succeed and was therefore prepared to tell her things she did not want to hear'.[82] Millar was extremely fond of Mrs Thatcher and used to say, 'Bless her little cotton socks!' when he spoke of her,[83] but he felt desperate at the idea that, partly through her own fault, her great enterprise might founder. The fact that Wolfson, so close an associate, was prepared to help Hoskyns is also striking. The frankness of the paper showed how bad they all felt the situation was. The paper was put into the Prime Minister's red box as she went on holiday on 20 August. It was entitled 'Your Political Survival'.[84]

The 'blockbuster' was quite possibly the bluntest official document ever seen in Downing Street. Although it recognized that 'your Government has achieved the beginnings of a near-revolution in the private sector and espe-cially in Industry,' and 'things in the economy are better than people realise,' the note warned that 'it is exactly at this moment that colleagues' nerves begin to crack and internal revolt (now clearly recognised in all the newspapers), threatens your own position.' Hoskyns told her that 'Your own credibility and prestige are draining away very fast.' The most likely outcome was 'you as another failed Tory prime minister sitting with Heath', but it was a serious possibility that she would be simply thrown out before the next election. He then listed her faults. 'You lack management competence' was the headline of one paragraph. 'Your own leadership style is wrong' was another. He warmed to his theme: 'You break every rule of good man-management. You bully your weaker colleagues. You criticise col-leagues in front of each other and in front of their officials. They can't answer back without appearing disrespectful, in front of others, to a woman and to a Prime Minister. You abuse that situation. You give little praise or credit, and you are too ready to blame others when things go wrong.' '<u>The result</u>', the next paragraph was headed, '<u>is an unhappy ship</u>': 'This demoralisation is hidden only from you. People are beginning to feel that everything is a waste of time, another Government is on its way to footnotes of history. And people are starting to speculate as to who might reunite the Party, as Macmillan did after Suez, if you go. But no-one tells you what is happening, just as no-one told Ted.' To survive, 'you have an absolute duty to change the way you operate.'

The Hoskyns memo called for Mrs Thatcher to '<u>Lead by Encouragement, not by Criticism</u>': 'Churchill provided the element of will and courage, as you do, without which nothing could have been achieved. But when the Battle of Britain was over, he gave <u>all</u> the credit to others. You must make the members of your team feel ten feet tall, not add to their own human fears and self-doubts. Say "we" and not "I".'* Hoskyns wanted a new party chairman, a thoroughgoing reshuffle and a 'Cabinet steering group' to provide direction, and movement towards 'a Radical Cabinet for the next Parliament'. Mrs Thatcher should restore her public image, taking more advice from Ronnie Millar and cut her diary commitments: 'To be frank, I believe you fill your diary because it's a good way to avoid having to do the unpleasant strategic thinking, involving unknowns and uncertainties, which you don't enjoy and which is not your forte.' He concluded: 'There is no other Politician ... who is likely even to attempt to lead the country in the right direction. But it will be no comfort to you, to us, or to the Country as a whole if you go into the history books with the prize for the "Best Loser".' He begged for the chance to 'talk through this paper calmly and carefully'.

In Hoskyns's view, the 'blockbuster' failed: 'Two or three weeks later she hissed at me, out of the corner of her mouth as we sat down to start a meeting in her study: "I got your letter. No one has ever written like that to a prime minister before" ... She had clearly never experienced advice of this kind before, and our working relationship, often uneasy at the best of times, was undoubtedly damaged ... Only if we had talked it through together could the letter have been helpful to her. But we never did. I suspect that it marked the point at which she decided she had had enough of me.'[85] Hoskyns continued ever afterwards to believe that 1981 was the time when Mrs Thatcher first began to suffer the isolation of high office: 'however it happened, the seeds of her downfall were being sown.'[86] This analysis may be right, but he surely underplayed the simple fact that almost no human

---

* It is possible that Mrs Thatcher followed this advice too closely. She became notoriously shy of using the word 'I', sometimes slipping into a 'royal we', as, famously, when she said, speaking in public after the birth of her first grandchild: 'We have become a grandmother.'

being, particularly one, like Mrs Thatcher, under intense strain, can be expected to take such brutal criticism easily. In his frustration at the inadequate use she made of the Policy Unit, Hoskyns made personal criticisms that were so negative that it was hardly possible for Mrs Thatcher to discuss them 'calmly and carefully'.

But Hoskyns's anger did reflect widespread views among people sympathetic to Mrs Thatcher. As well as being, in their eyes, inspiring, admirable, brave and, to many, surprisingly loveable, she was also intensely annoying. Hoskyns's criticisms of her overwork, lack of consideration for Cabinet colleagues, dislike of long-term thinking and poor management were essentially true, though he never made enough allowance for her remarkable political gift for seeing when the time was ripe and when it was not. His 'blockbuster' is testimony to how very trying she could be, even – perhaps particularly – to her friends. It is evidence, too, of the sense of crisis that prevailed in her administration that summer.

Although she never acknowledged the justice of criticism directly, Mrs Thatcher did have ways of listening to it. The sort of changes for which Hoskyns, Millar and Wolfson argued did take place. Mrs Thatcher deputed Ian Gow to fly to Venice, where Thorneycroft was on holiday, to ask him to resign as party chairman. It was a frosty encounter. Following it, on 25 August, Thorneycroft wrote to Mrs Thatcher offering his resignation. His letter included carefully phrased praise for 'the determined, undogmatic and caring party which we have always been'.[87] The next day, Mrs Thatcher, already back from a brief respite at the flat in Scotney Castle (she had earlier in the month spent a few days with the Wolfsons in Cornwall, where, Wolfson told Hoskyns, she had 'seemed like a zombie' because of the strain and tiredness),[88] revealed the main parts of her proposed Cabinet reshuffle to a meeting of Hoskyns, Wolfson and Ian Gow. The most important thing was that Jim Prior would be replaced at Employment by Norman Tebbit, and would be offered Northern Ireland instead. Cecil Parkinson would succeed Thorneycroft as chairman. At his own request, Keith Joseph would move from Industry to Education. Christopher Soames would be out. Ian Gilmour would go from his position as number two at the Foreign Office, and be replaced by Douglas Hurd. David Howell would move to Transport and Nigel Lawson would take his job at Energy.[89] This preview was fulfilled in all particulars, except that it was not Douglas Hurd, but Humphrey Atkins, moving from Northern Ireland, who displaced Gilmour.

Jim Prior heard what was afoot, however, and decided to resist. His determination was sharpened when he heard the rumour that he was to be succeeded by Tebbit, whom the Wets considered particularly rough and socially inferior. The next day's *Daily Mail* carried a big interview with

Prior under the headline 'I'll fight like hell'.[90] On 2 September, Mrs Thatcher, Prior and others met to discuss the reform of trade union immunities now that the consultation period for his green paper had ended. The meeting was ill-tempered. Prior dug his heels in, saying that 'History showed that the unions could defeat legislation if they wanted to.' Mrs Thatcher said his ideas, such as the ending of union-only agreements, were 'far too modest'. Thinking of the SDP, she warned that 'The field should not be left open to others to put proposals which would secure electoral support.'[91] There was impasse. It was widely believed that Mrs Thatcher was not in a strong enough position to move Prior. As the reshuffle approached, however, Prior's camp overplayed their hand. Richard Needham,* one of his young supporters in Parliament, told the press that Prior would resign if he were offered Northern Ireland. This gave the damaging impression that he regarded the job as unimportant, even perhaps that he was frightened of its dangers. A television interview that he gave sitting on his combine harvester at his Suffolk farm added to the feeling that he was presenting such a direct challenge to Mrs Thatcher's authority that she had to move him. Besides, for the first time since the general election, the politics of confronting the trade unions were starting to shift. The emergence of the SDP, which was vigorously anti-trade union political power, meant that the Tories could no longer assume that they had the monopoly of anti-union votes. Prior's caution on the subject might lead his party to be outflanked: his position was not as strong as he had believed.

The reshuffle took place on 14 September 1981. Prior accepted Northern Ireland, with the sop that he could remain on E Committee, and take the ultra-Wet junior minister Nicholas Scott with him to the province. Christopher Soames reportedly complained to friends that he would have sacked his gamekeeper with more courtesy than Mrs Thatcher had shown him (though why one should expect gamekeepers to be shown less courtesy than Lord Soames in matters of employment was not clear). Soames was replaced as leader in the Lords by Janet Young, an old friend of Mrs Thatcher with a background in Oxford city politics, the first and last woman ever appointed to her Cabinet. Gilmour wrote to Mrs Thatcher, in the normally courteous exchange of letters customarily published when a minister departs: 'You asked for my resignation . . . this was, in view of our disagreements, neither surprising nor unwelcome.'[92] But of course it *was* unwelcome: the Wets looked much less dignified sacked than they would

---

* Richard Needham (6th Earl of Kilmorey) (1942–), educated Eton; Conservative MP for Chippenham, 1979–83; for Wiltshire North, 1983–97; Parliamentary Under-Secretary, Northern Ireland Office, 1985–92; Minister of State, DTI, 1992–5.

have looked if they had resigned on principle; and there was something in their sense of affront at being sacked by a woman which was haughty. They had not bargained for this. Reporting the press reaction to the reshuffle to Mrs Thatcher, Bernard Ingham noted 'A good welcome (apart from *Mirror* and a v. sourpuss *Guardian*)'.[93] In the *Daily Mail*, Paul Johnson called it the 'most magisterial demonstration of a prime minister's authority since the Night of the Long Knives [Harold Macmillan's dismissal of a third of his Cabinet in July 1962]'. Mrs Thatcher still did not have a majority of true believers in her Cabinet, but by the addition of Tebbit, Parkinson and Lawson she had installed a new generation of active, clever, enthusiastic supporters. Equally important, she had proved that she could sack the grandees without the heavens falling.

There was no obvious or immediate improvement, however, in Mrs Thatcher's fortunes. On the same day as the reshuffle, interest rates, lowered with a fanfare at the time of the Budget, went up by 2 per cent to protect sterling. A combination of rising world interest rates, the great expansion of private domestic credit because of the relaxation of controls and worries about the gilts market forced the government to act. On 23 September the stock market index fell to its lowest level for seventeen years. On 1 October interest rates rose by 2 points yet again to 16 per cent, which was agonizingly high.* A Gallup poll privately conducted for the Conservatives showed that if a Social Democratic Alliance were to come into being, 40 per cent of voters would support it, and only 16 per cent would support the Conservatives.[94] In a decision which probably saved the party from complete collapse, Labour voted narrowly for the moderate Denis Healey as its deputy leader, rather than Tony Benn.

Ted Heath chose the run-up to the party conference to launch his fiercest and most direct attack on the government's economic policy: 'If more than three million unemployed are needed to get inflation down to a level higher than it was 2½ years ago, how many more millions of unemployed will be required to bring it down to ... to what level? – to a level that has never been revealed?' He said that 'The time has come to speak out.' He wanted

---

* At the time of the second interest rate rise on 1 October, Geoffrey and Elspeth Howe were staying with the Hendersons at the British Embassy in Washington. By chance, at the same time Roy Jenkins, an old friend of Nicko Henderson, and Ian Gilmour, were staying too. Henderson gave dinner to Jenkins and Gilmour himself, while arranging for the Howes and their entourage to have dinner in their room, an untypically gauche decision which indicated a bet about who was likely to be in, who out. Elspeth Howe said to the company: 'Insurrection is being plotted downstairs.' (Interview with Lord Kerr of Kinlochard. A sanitized version of this story appears in Geoffrey Howe's memoirs: *Conflict of Loyalty*, Macmillan, 1994, p. 228.)

'a return to consensus politics', membership of the ERM and the reintroduction of exchange controls, as well as much more capital investment and a 'massive' retraining programme.[95] Angrily, he exclaimed, 'How dare those who have run the biggest budget deficit in history reproach others with the heinous crime of printing money?'

Heath's advance text reached Mrs Thatcher, who was in Australia. She interpolated her repudiation of it into the Sir Robert Menzies Lecture about the virtues of choice which she was giving in Melbourne. Consensus, she said, was 'the process of abandoning all beliefs, principles, values and policies in search of something in which no one believes, but to which no one objects'.[96] In fact, as was almost always the case, Heath's intervention was useful to Mrs Thatcher. It made the dispute look personal, and as soon as that happened the party faithful naturally rallied to the leader.

In the same week, representatives of the younger generation of Conservative MPs produced a pamphlet called *Changing Gear*, which politely but definitely put down a marker against the trend of Mrs Thatcher's policies. The pamphlet issued from an informal group known as the Blue Chips, which included most of the brightest and best connected of the 1979 intake. Led by Chris Patten and William Waldegrave, the group also included Lord Cranborne, John Patten,* Tristan Garel-Jones† and Richard Needham. Soon afterwards, it was joined by John Major. It was seen by its own members as a rather grand network,[97] and even had its group portrait painted by Lord Cranborne's sister, Lady Rose Cecil. Most members of the group eventually attained ministerial and often Cabinet rank, and many people came, in later years, to see the Blue Chips as conspirators. In 1981, they were clearly ambitious young men, and the fact that, in Chris Patten's phrase, 'we asked one question too many',[98] was an ill omen for Mrs Thatcher. By the time the pamphlet was published, Waldegrave had actually taken a junior post in the government.

Full of the spirit of the Macmillan era and published, indeed, by Macmillan's firm, the pamphlet used as its epigraph two-edged words from the old man himself: 'We have at least the most important thing of all at the head of our Government, a Prime Minister of courage, who I hope will not be

---

* John Patten (1945–), educated Wimbledon College and Sidney Sussex College, Cambridge; Conservative MP for City of Oxford, 1979–83; for Oxford West and Abingdon, 1983–97; Parliamentary Under-Secretary, Northern Ireland Office, 1981–3; Minister of State, Home Office, 1987–92; Secretary of State for Education, 1992–4; created Lord Patten, 1997.

† Tristan Garel-Jones (1941–), educated King's School, Canterbury; principal, language school, Madrid, Spain, 1960–70; Conservative MP for Watford, 1979–97; government whip, 1982–9; Deputy Chief Whip, 1989–90; Minister of State, FCO, 1990–93; created Lord Garel-Jones, 1997.

led away from the old tradition of consensus.' The pamphlet called for greater capital expenditure in return for organized wage restraint, and included mildly heretical notions like elections to the House of Lords using proportional representation. After 'arm-wrestling' between Waldegrave and Chris Patten,[99] the document reflected the economically Drier views of Waldegrave, rather than the Heathite Keynesianism of Patten, but it was nevertheless a criticism of the social effects of Thatcherism by people who believed that the Conservatives would lose the next election. It declared that 'a political strategy based on economic theory is a house built on sand.' Geoffrey Howe wrote to Mrs Thatcher about it at once. The pamphlet's launch had been overshadowed by Heath's attacks, he said, but 'in the longer run I suspect that their relative importance could switch, Ted's outbursts being so much more immoderate in both tone and content, and much less well-written too'. He went on: 'in some cases the proposals offered are unrealistic . . . e.g. a Heseltine-like trade-off of lower pay for higher investment', but the arguments were chiefly about tone and flexibility and 'we must heed them.'[100]

At the party conference itself, Heath said, in the hall, what he had recently said in rather more explicit terms outside it. Almost every leading Wet, both inside and out of the government, made speeches of what the press called 'coded' criticism, though in truth the code was so easy to crack as hardly to deserve the name. The rank and file, however, were more worried that Mrs Thatcher might not be allowed to succeed than they were critical of her policies: revolt did not take off. The most notable platform speech of the week was by the new Employment Secretary, Norman Tebbit. Playing on the tough times he had known as a child in the 1930s, and speaking in the tone of slight menace which made him compelling to listen to, he said that he had grown up with an unemployed father: 'He didn't riot. He got on his bike and looked for work.' This was forever afterwards known as the 'on your bike' speech, and it became an object of hatred to the left and an encapsulation of the Thatcherite approach to work. It was particularly popular with its audience, both because of its way of dealing with the summer riots which they had so detested and because it was a message of defiance to the very angry and numerous 'Right to Work' protesters who were besieging the Blackpool Winter Gardens and shouting insults at Tory representatives as they went in and out. From then on, although his political course was in reality much more subtle, even changeable, Norman Tebbit was always considered as the bootboy of Thatcherism.

For her own speech to the conference, Mrs Thatcher's advisers pushed for what John Hoskyns called 'a serious effort to convey the historic significance of what was being attempted', but got instead what he thought was 'the most boring and anti-climactic speech I ever heard her make'.[101] The drafts by Hoskyns and Millar were full of rallying calls reasserting the difference between right and wrong. They quoted Mrs Thatcher's favourite chorus from T. S. Eliot's *The Rock* about 'dreaming of systems so perfect that no one will need to be good' and exalted the moral value of choice, and therefore of capitalism, above such dreams.[102] But the drafts were more or less superseded by 'large chunks of "wallpaper" from Jock [Bruce-Gardyne], and even worse stuff from [John Selwyn] Gummer' which, Hoskyns moaned in his diary, 'commend themselves to Margaret, who has no taste or judgment whatsoever'.[103] What the speech tried to do was to mix a conciliatory tone with the tough message of persistence in the face of economic difficulty. It welcomed 'strenuous discussion and dissent', and said of Ted Heath: 'We may have different ideas on how best to navigate but we sail the same ocean and in the same ship.' There were acknowledgments of the pain of unemployment, and of 'the dignity which comes from work'. The argument against any U-turn was presented pragmatically: 'It is sheer common sense,' she said. Outlining moves towards greater denationalization (the word 'privatization' was still avoided), Mrs Thatcher said, 'if this is dogmatism then it is the dogmatism of Mr Marks and Mr Spencer, and I'll plead guilty to that any day of the week.' She sought 'the common consent of the people of Britain to work together for the prosperity that has eluded us for so long'.[104] Without resiling from anything, the speech was fairly unspecific, declining to lead its audience into new areas of reasoning. Reform of the trade unions, for example, though so high on the agenda of the reshuffled Cabinet, was not discussed. Bernard Ingham's press digest to Mrs Thatcher the following day reported the newspaper view – 'shortest standing ovation any leader has received for years'.[105] The audience in Blackpool felt somewhat reassured, but not inspired. The press confidently predicted a leadership challenge.

On 20 October 1981 the Cabinet reconvened to discuss the proposed public spending savings of £3.5 billion. Despite the reshuffle, there was still very little agreement. Geoffrey Howe tried to reassure everyone that this was 'Not a matter of dogma, but of judgment based on practical experience. Markets decide how much we pay for our borrowing.'[106] Between the middle of August and September, the government had failed to sell any debt at all. The annual interest charges on government debt were now £15 billion, having been £8.5 billion in 1978–9. That was more than was spent on health, or defence, or education. There was no other route, Howe argued, but cuts in plans because of the danger of going beyond what the government could sensibly borrow. Many colleagues were unsympathetic. Michael Heseltine, whose paper on Liverpool, *It Took a Riot*, had been sidelined by Mrs Thatcher, complained: 'I have failed to persuade colleagues to take the right choices . . . I can't see my way through.' He said he would rather increase the PSBR than make the cuts proposed. John Biffen, who had been wavering since the Budget, argued for higher taxes because of the 'requirements of political survival'. Prior, of course, said the same. Lord Carrington said: 'I don't think this package is saleable . . . Some of your proposals are bashing the poor. If you are going to leave the rich unscathed and hit the poor, you are going to be very divisive.' Peter Walker declared that 'there is no possibility of getting out of the slump' with current policies, and Francis Pym warned: 'We haven't produced a ray of light; and we are asking people to make sacrifices without hope.'[107]

This time, however, some voices as well as that of Keith Joseph hit back in support of the Chancellor. Patrick Jenkin, now at Industry, and the new boys, Parkinson, Lawson and Tebbit, all backed Howe. Tebbit, seeing the way the external financing limits of the nationalized industries played havoc with the PSBR, argued for a 'fudging' to get investment in them off the figures. This came the day after privatization had been announced in relation to the British National Oil Corporation (BNOC) and gas showrooms, as well as the sale of the National Freight Corporation to its employees. Nigel Lawson, as Energy Secretary in charge of BNOC, proudly described it as the biggest programme of denationalization ever put before Parliament. The logjam of excessive caution was gradually breaking.

The Cabinet agreed to set up a small *ad hoc* group (MISC 62) under Willie Whitelaw to try to work through the options for cuts. But, as had happened so often before, the press were leaked details of disagreements: 'Headlines claim you are opposed by most of Cabinet and that MTFS is in ruins,' said Ingham in his press digest.[108] Mrs Thatcher angrily told the Cabinet that 'If anyone here is doing things which result in leaks to the press, the honourable course is to resign.' If it happened again, she said, Cabinet government would have to be differently conducted in future.[109] Ill feeling persisted.

But the spirit of innovation also strengthened. With Prior gone to Northern Ireland, the way at last lay open for trade union reform. Towards the end of October, Norman Tebbit presented his proposed changes to Cabinet colleagues in E Committee. In doing so, he adhered to the 'step-by-step' approach of Prior, but included the step which Prior had refused to take – an end to the immunity of trade union funds from claims for damages. His proposals revoked Section 14 of Labour's Trade Union and Industrial

Relations Act 1974, which had given unions immunity even if their action was not taken in furtherance of a trade dispute. The privileges of unions were to be reduced to those of individuals in the same situation. The definition of a lawful trade dispute was to be more strictly limited, and various changes, including periodic ballots, were offered to weaken, though not to abolish, the closed shop. The measures were explicitly presented by Tebbit to colleagues as, among other things, a means of outflanking the SDP, then gearing up for the Crosby by-election in late November with their candidate, Shirley Williams. The essence of the proposals managed to reach the statute book by December 1982. The end of the unique legal privileges of trade unions was eventually to prove decisive. In later years, Jim Prior magnanimously conceded this, saying simply: 'Tebbit was right rather than me.'[110]

As autumn turned into winter, there was no dramatic improvement in the economy or in Mrs Thatcher's political position. The small signs of recovery which had appeared in the summer, though genuinely present, now seemed, to most people, invisible. At the end of November, Shirley Williams won the Crosby by-election for the SDP with a majority of over 5,000, taking the seat from the Conservatives. A Gallup poll the following month gave 50.5 per cent to the SDP and Liberals in alliance, 23.5 per cent to Labour and 23 per cent to the Tories. Unemployment, as had long been expected, hit 3 million for the first time in the figures announced at the end of January 1982. Despite the failure of critics to mount the leadership challenge which, under the rules, had to happen in November, Mrs Thatcher did not feel secure. On the night before the Chancellor's Autumn Statement on public spending on 2 December 1981, fretting that Howe might be mishandling the preparations, she burst in, unannounced, on the late-night meeting he was holding with officials. John Kerr, Howe's private secretary, remembered her as 'quite full of whisky'.[111] In front of everyone, she berated Howe for his proposed speech and indeed rejected it completely (though this was forgotten in the morning). Howe records that at one point she shouted, 'If this is the best you can do, then I'd better send you to hospital and deliver the statement myself.'[112] This outburst was probably a sort of revenge. A couple of weeks earlier, she had given her annual speech at the Lord Mayor's Banquet, hailing 'some first signs of recovery'.[113] The Treasury had tried to make three changes to the draft and pressed her new economic private secretary, Michael Scholar,* very hard that these should be done. When Scholar put the points to her, 'She absolutely bristled: "Look

---

* Michael Scholar (1942–), educated St Olave's Grammar School, Bermondsey, St John's College, Cambridge and University of California at Berkeley; private secretary to the Prime

here, young man, you're here to do my bidding." I thought I was finished.'[114]*
The precariousness of her position, as had been the case all year, kept her
in a state of tension which made her very difficult to work with. But when
she got back to No. 10 from the Guildhall banquet she waited at the door
until Scholar entered, and invited him and his wife upstairs for a conciliatory glass of whisky.[115]

Nevertheless, Mrs Thatcher was not wrong about the trend which she
mentioned at the Lord Mayor's Banquet. It was true, as she told the Guildhall audience, that the trough of the recession had been passed in the
middle of the year. Small signs – a rising stock market, housing starts
increasing by 20 per cent over the previous year, exports at their second
highest ever (all these in November) – began to compose a picture of
improvement. Howe's Autumn Statement was unpopular: MISC 62 had
achieved compromises which meant that spending would not be cut as the
Treasury had wished, but neither would the Treasury give way on the need
to raise more revenue. More than £5 billion extra had to be found. Employees' National Insurance contributions rose by a further 1 per cent, council
house rents and prescription charges rose, and most social security benefits
went up by less than the rate of inflation. At the Cabinet meeting to thrash
it out beforehand, Francis Pym said gloomily: 'It is a very grave position we
have reached. The central plank of our strategy has gone ... Yes, we are
spending more money, but all the talk is about reductions.'[116] A group of
Tory backbenchers, known as the Gang of Twenty-Five, wrote a letter
expressing anxiety, and there was talk of Conservative defectors to the
SDP. It was, the Chief Whip told Mrs Thatcher, 'a very serious situation'.[117] And yet the revolt against the measures – fourteen Conservative
MPs abstained in the vote – was half-hearted compared with the anger and
division of the summer. 'A brief obituary of Thatcherism is now in order,'
pronounced Peter Jenkins in the *Guardian*,[118] but in fact the fight was going
out of the Tory rebels. In November, Mrs Thatcher finally got rid of the
Civil Service Department, which had been a thorn in the side of her efficiency drive in Whitehall. Ian Bancroft retired, and responsibility for the
Civil Service was split between Robert Armstrong, the Cabinet Secretary,
and Douglas Wass, Permanent Secretary at the Treasury. After Wass retired

---

Minister, 1981–3; Permanent Secretary, DTI, 1996–2001; President, St John's College, Oxford,
from 2001; knighted, 1999.
* In both these cases of anger, Mrs Thatcher, characteristically, felt remorse, and, equally
characteristically, expressed it indirectly. To Geoffrey Howe, she wrote a note congratulating
him on his Autumn Statement and its delivery (see Howe, *Conflict of Loyalty*, p. 233).

in 1983, the Cabinet Secretary assumed full responsibility. This reorganization could not have happened – indeed Mrs Thatcher had publicly declined to do it – when Christopher Soames had been the minister responsible, just as the trade unions' immunities could not have been removed so long as Jim Prior stayed at Employment. Now weakened in Cabinet, the Wets began to realize that it was too late to change course before the next election. All sides, including the Dries, knew that some sort of truce was needed for the party to survive: '*Telegraph* says the Chancellor is determined last week's announcement will be the last unpalatable one before the Election,' Bernard Ingham reported to Mrs Thatcher.[119] That was about the sum of it.

Besides, the political situation was calculated to make Tories stick together. Poor Michael Foot was becoming ever more a figure of fun. At the Cenotaph Remembrance Day ceremony, he appeared wearing a mouldy-looking donkey jacket* and laid his wreath with, as the *Daily Telegraph* put it, 'all the reverent dignity of a tramp inspecting a cigarette end'.[120] This moment seemed to confirm for all time in the public mind the idea that Foot could never conceivably be prime minister. He then embarked on a long, shambolic and ultimately unsuccessful attempt to force Peter Tatchell,† the hard-left Labour candidate for the expected Bermondsey by-election, to stand down, while all the time losing recruits to the SDP. In early December 1981, Arthur Scargill was elected president of the National Union of Mineworkers, and his victory was hailed publicly by Tony Benn as giving 'fresh hopes for battles inside and outside of Parliament'.[121] The miners rejected an improved pay offer of 9.3 per cent, and for several weeks people believed that the cosmic clash between Tories and miners, last seen in early 1974, was about to be replayed. In the same month, martial law was declared in Poland, with the house arrest of the Solidarity leader, Lech Wałęsa, and dozens of demonstrators being killed. The world watched anxiously to see if the Soviet Union would actually invade to back up the repression it had ordered. Not for the first time, the sense of threat helped Mrs Thatcher rally people to her side.

At the turn of the year, Ian Gow wrote her a thank-you letter for a

---

* Foot's wife, Jill, protested that it was, in fact, a smart new blue-green coat which she had bought for him. It was also reported that the Queen Mother had praised his coat. Mrs Thatcher herself was very polite about Foot's appearance. In a short private account of the ceremony, she noted, 'It was Michael Foot's first attendance and he was a little uncertain what to do.' (MT private account, 8 Nov. 1981, Margaret Thatcher Foundation.)
† Peter Tatchell (1952–), educated Mount Waverley High School, Melbourne and Polytechnic of North London; activist/organizer, Gay Liberation Front London, 1971–3; UK AIDS Vigil Organization, 1987–9; Green and Socialist Conferences, 1987–9.

Christmas present ('The Crown Derby coffee cups and saucers are really superb'), which sought to strengthen her. 'You have been a giant among pygmies,' he wrote. 'Your diagnosis of our national malaise and your prescription for national recovery are both more perceptive and more far-sighted than any of your contemporaries,' and he went on, 'I was so pleased when you said in September that you would like me to "see you through to the end".'[122] The letter expressed at the same time a sort of bunker mentality – what was 'the end' to be? – and a firm hope.

Early in 1982, Mrs Thatcher also revealed, which people had been inclined to forget, that she was a human being after all. Taking part in the Paris–Dakar motor rally, Mark Thatcher got stuck in the Sahara desert in Algeria. 'The car was buggered,' Mark remembered. 'I just had to sit still in it,' which he did, reading *The Dogs of War* by Frederick Forsyth.[123] Although he was not lost, nobody knew where he was for four days after he was noticed to be missing. '. . . Algerian report suggests kidnap,' said Bernard Ingham in his press digest, with rather brutal directness.[124] Mrs Thatcher was distraught. Very unusually for her, she cancelled some of her business, including a meeting with the Hungarian Foreign Minister, which would have been a possibly eye-opening venture for a prime minister who to date had largely avoided contact with Communist leaders. But she kept an appointment at a lunch for the National Federation of the Self-employed. Emerging from it, she was besieged by reporters and photographers, and could not keep back tears when the press asked her about her son's disappearance. This was the only time that anyone working with Mrs Thatcher could remember when private events made normal work impossible.[125] And although those around her were disgusted with the press intrusion, the resulting coverage helped her. The popular papers said how she touched 'the hearts and compassion of the people'[126] and that people now warmed to her 'as a woman and a mother'.[127]

With prompt and adroit courtesy which Mrs Thatcher never forgot, President Mitterrand offered her any military service that might help her find her son, although the Algerians inevitably took the lead. Denis flew out to Algeria on a plane provided by Hector Laing, to oversee the effort.[128] Thanks to the local knowledge of Colonel Khalil of the Algerian armed forces, father and son were reunited after thirty-one hours of searching from the air. Mark was flown home safe and well. Mrs Thatcher's private secretaries, genuinely moved by the maternal feeling they had seen, bought her a huge bunch of flowers.[129] After the generosity of the Algerian government and others had been taken into account, the remaining tab for Mark's adventure stood at £1,191, the cost of phone calls and telegrams. Considering these legitimate 'diplomatic costs', the Foreign Office intended to pick up the bill, but Mrs Thatcher demurred. 'I must pay the £1,191,' she scribbled. 'We can therefore say that *no* extra cost has fallen on the British taxpayer. To who [sic] do I make out the cheque?'[130]* It was left to Carol to provide a slightly critical note. In interviews in the tabloids, Ingham reported, she 'says she hopes Mark stops racing because the Prime Minister could do without this additional hassle'.[131]

On 21 January 1982, the miners' strike ballot came out against a strike, with only Scotland and Scargill's home patch, Yorkshire, voting in favour. The moderate outgoing president, Joe Gormley, had intervened to influence the vote against Scargill. The widespread view was that 'mortgage power' had got the better of militancy. Increasingly bourgeois workers did not seek political confrontation. This was good news for Mrs Thatcher. It seems to have taught Arthur Scargill that he should never again expose himself to the dangers of a ballot.

When the Cabinet met for its first discussion of Budget ideas on 28 January, contention had mysteriously vanished. Howe was able to tell colleagues that a PSBR within the range of £7.5 billion to £9 billion was achievable, and that exports were in a better state. He canvassed basic rate income tax reductions, or the raising of thresholds. Even Jim Prior, though asking for a PSBR of £11 billion and for British entry into the ERM, declared: 'I think we are just about out of recession.' Nigel Lawson encapsulated the Dry narrative of economic recovery: 'This Budget should be different from last year's Budget; because of last year's Budget, it can be.' Mrs Thatcher closed proceedings by saying that the discussion had been 'very interesting and harmonious'.[132] When the Budget came, on 9 March, Howe could boast that, for the first time in his chancellorship, the PSBR had come in below the figure forecast, as a result of which interest rates had already dropped 3 percentage points from their high of 16 per cent the previous autumn. He increased income tax thresholds above inflation and cut the National Insurance surcharge by 1.5 per cent. Addressing the dispute between supporters of sterling M3 as a measure of the growth of money supply and those who advocated monetary base control (Mo), Howe produced a compromise in which a 'diversity of targets' was to be aimed at. He also launched the Community Programme, by which the long-term unemployed could be paid to work in community schemes. This was the fruit of work by Norman Tebbit and David Young, whom Tebbit had put in to supplant the Priorite Sir Richard O'Brien as head of the Manpower Services Commission, the government body charged with addressing unemployment.

---

* In the end, Mrs Thatcher actually paid £1,799.96, which included extra miscellaneous travel costs.

The press reaction to the 1982 Budget was favourable, as was that of Conservative MPs. Although tremendous economic difficulties remained, the sting of the controversy which had been so poisonous in 1981 was drawn. A Thatcherite recovery – or at any rate a recovery with Mrs Thatcher firmly in charge – had begun, weeks before the news from the South Atlantic which was to convulse British politics.

The Falklands invasion

'The worst moment of my life'

Early in the morning of Friday 2 April 1982, Argentine forces invaded the Falkland Islands, a British colony in the South Atlantic. The prospect of imminent invasion had become clear only on 31 March, and as late as 5 p.m., London time, the following day Cabinet Office officials had been saying that the intelligence reports received 'did not necessarily provide definitive evidence that an invasion was about to take place'.[1] A week earlier, Argentina had not yet taken the decision to invade. A month earlier, there had been no obvious crisis at all. At 9.25 a.m., Falklands time (12.25 p.m. in London), on the day of the invasion, the British Governor ordered the small contingent of Royal Marines defending Government House in the capital, Port Stanley, to surrender. Argentine troops made them lie on the ground to be photographed. The Argentine flag flew over Port Stanley. The humiliation of Britain was sudden, and complete. Unless it could be reversed, Mrs Thatcher could not expect to survive as prime minister.

How could such a thing have happened? The final act of invasion was sudden, but the passions which gave rise to it were deep rooted. The origins of the dispute over the Falkland Islands dated almost as far back as their discovery by Europeans. An English captain in the Royal Navy was the first person to land on the islands, in 1690, and named them after Lord Falkland, then the First Lord of the Admiralty. The name for the islands always preferred by Argentina – Las Malvinas – was a Spanish version of the name Les Malouines (because of a supposed resemblance to St Malo in Brittany), reflecting the fact that France had occupied them in the middle of the eighteenth century. Having bought France out, Spain pressed her long-standing claim, which was always contested by Britain and nearly produced a war in 1770.* When Argentina became independent of Spain

---

* Emotions ran high. The Earl of Chatham (Pitt the Elder) challenged the government, 'Will you so shamefully betray the king's honour so to make it a matter of negotiation whether His

in 1816, it considered itself the heir to all Spanish claims. Britain, which had left the islands, though still claiming them, in 1774, renewed its interest in them after Argentina appointed a political and military governor there in 1829. In January 1833, the British reoccupied the islands, and have been there ever since.

The original British legal title to the Falkland Islands was not considered absolutely secure by the British government,* but government legal experts reposed greater confidence in the right of 'prescription' – the fact that, from 1833, British rule and occupation were continuous, and that the inhabitants were almost all of British stock and enthusiastically loyal to the Crown. Argentina, on the other hand, was quite uninterested in the opinions of the inhabitants of the islands. It regarded the Malvinas as part of the title deeds of the nation. In a country whose internal politics were often fraught and which, in 1982, was ruled by an unstable and unpopular military oligarchy, this was the only issue guaranteed to produce emotional unity. As the 150th anniversary of what Argentina saw as unjust occupation approached, the junta grabbed a symbolic moment to right the seeming wrong.

This coincided with a particularly weak British position. In modern times, the British government had increasingly come to regard the Falkland Islands as a nuisance. With only 1,800 inhabitants, 8,000 miles from Britain, and little apparent strategic significance, the islands needed economic development to have a future, and this was difficult without the help of Argentina, which is around 300 miles away at the nearest point. To the British Foreign Office, the Falklands got in the way of good relations with Latin America. For many years, attempts had been made to steer a course between the absolutism of Argentine claims of sovereignty on the one hand and the Falklanders' deep suspicion of Argentina on the other. Not long after Mrs Thatcher came into office in 1979, the Foreign Secretary, Lord Carrington, offered a solution. He resisted the idea, arising from Lord Shackleton's report on the subject,† that a 'Fortress Falklands' policy of economic development regardless of Argentina could be pursued. Carrington told

---

Majesty's possession shall be restored to him or not?' During the Falklands War, the historian Hugh Thomas (Lord Thomas of Swynnerton) sent Mrs Thatcher a paper about the future development of the Falklands, using this quotation to support her resolve against the less robust position of her Foreign Secretary, Francis Pym.

* For a discussion of these matters, see Sir Lawrence Freedman's *The Official History of the Falklands Campaign*, 2 vols, Routledge, 2005, vol. i: *The Origins of the Falklands War*, pp. 8–12.

† Lord Shackleton, son of the Antarctic explorer Ernest Shackleton, was asked by Harold Wilson's government to produce a comprehensive survey of the Falklands. His report, published in 1977, called for major new investment and development of the islands.

the Overseas and Defence Committee of the Cabinet (OD) that Fortress Falklands would produce 'a serious threat of Argentine invasion, which would require the long-term commitment of substantial British forces'.[2] In a letter to Mrs Thatcher on 20 September 1979, he told her that a form of leaseback, by which sovereignty was ceded to Argentina in return for continuing British administration and way of life, was the answer.

Mrs Thatcher's immediate and instinctive reaction to leaseback was hostile. In the notes she scribbled on Carrington's letter, and on John Hunt's covering memo about it, she expressed all the main objections which were to bulk so large later. Against a passage which spoke about the need to respect the wishes of the islanders, she wrote: 'And they must not be pressured into agreeing.' Commenting on the idea of leaseback itself, she wrote: 'As in Hong Kong – the 99 yr lease comes to an end & causes problems.' On top of Carrington's letter, she summed up: 'I cannot possibly agree to the line the Foreign Secretary is proposing. Nor would it get through the H of C – let alone the Parliamentary Party.'[3] When the Foreign Office brought the whole thing to OD the following month, in a much more detailed memo, Mrs Thatcher was even more suspicious. She thought that she was being almost double-crossed. 'I don't like this paper,' she wrote on its first page, '– the definition of the Options is designed not to enumerate the Options but to achieve the desired conclusion.' Alongside the memo's statement that 'the Argentine claim is not just a matter of law but of national honour and machismo,' she commented: 'According to the Foreign Office our national honour doesn't seem to matter!?'[4] 'Please don't deal with this before the Rhodesian issue is finished,' she added, fearing not only the pressure of time, but also of rebellion from the Tory right. This last request was followed, and the matter did not come back to OD until 30 January 1980. By this time, Carrington had managed to push his case. The minutes record that the Prime Minister, in her summing up, said that there was a 'danger that any resumption of talks might appear to foreshadow a surrender of sovereignty . . . There was no legal basis for such a surrender'; but they also record that she and the committee saw 'force' in the Foreign Secretary's argument that there should be 'general and exploratory' talks with Argentina 'particularly since it reflected the views of the Islanders themselves'. Nicholas Ridley, the relevant junior minister at the Foreign Office, was charged with seeing if leaseback could be made to work.

Although a close political ally of Mrs Thatcher's on economic matters (the only such ally in her Foreign Office team), Ridley had a lack of affection for British overseas possessions quite at odds with her own attitudes. He also had a dangerously flip turn of phrase. The record of his talks in

New York with Commodore Cavandoli, his Argentine opposite number, shows Ridley in best dismissive vein: 'We had given up a third of the world's surface and found it on the whole beneficial to do so. The only claim Britain had which he felt strongly about was our long-standing claim to Bordeaux, his motive being wine. He found it hard to see the motive towards the islands where there was no wine.'[5] At secret talks between Ridley and Cavandoli near Geneva in August, the principle of leaseback, with ninety-nine years as the probable extent of the lease, was hypothetically agreed.

At a meeting of OD on 7 November 1980, Mrs Thatcher expressed her doubts. 'This would be very difficult: surrender of sovereignty,' Robert Armstrong noted her saying.[6] According to her own memory, she reacted angrily to Ridley's claim that Britain could not defend the Falklands: 'We could bomb Buenos Aires if nothing else.' 'It was just an instinctive reaction,' she added. 'It was not recorded.'[7] What *was* recorded, by Armstrong, was her view that 'We can't afford to defend them. We are yielding to threats.' Carrington said that leaseback was the 'only idea that has any future'. Mrs Thatcher urged Ridley to work on backbenchers, and said: 'Our fallback is that we do nothing without consent of the islanders.'

This consent was not forthcoming. Towards the end of November, Ridley visited the islands, talking to as many of the inhabitants as he could. In one public meeting, an islander said: 'I don't think we should give them sovereignty. We're giving up our birthright.' To this Ridley replied, 'Well then you take the consequences [of not giving up sovereignty], not me.'[8] Although he added that Britain would defend the islands from Argentine attack, the phrase about taking the consequences was not a happy one. It stuck in the islanders' minds. He left the islands without carrying his point, though without a formal rejection of his proposals. On 2 December 1980, he made a statement to Parliament in which, as Mrs Thatcher had originally predicted, the idea of leaseback was fiercely attacked by MPs on all sides for betraying the Falklanders. At OD a month earlier, Mrs Thatcher had repeated her anxiety: 'My fear is an awful row from our backbenchers.'[9] She had been proved right.

Meeting the day after the 'awful row', ministers in OD cogitated inconclusively. Referring to the exclusion of Falklanders from the automatic right to emigrate to Britain under the forthcoming British Nationality Act, Mrs Thatcher mused: 'We shall have to give an undertaking that they should come here.'[10] But this was not followed through, because of the precedent it would set for all other citizens of British Dependent Territories (as colonies were now formally known). On 7 January 1981, the Falklands Councillors – the islands' elected representatives – gave a hostile view of leaseback and advocated a freeze to the sovereignty dispute. The Foreign Office did not attempt to develop a new policy to give some positive effect to the islanders' wishes, but treated them with borderline contempt. The islanders were 'simple people and they clung to simple ideas', declared Sir Michael Palliser that June.[11] If they would not agree to put leaseback on the table, the Foreign Office felt that negotiations would prove futile. The result was impasse, and rising Argentine impatience. In July 1981, in what turned out to be its last assessment of the problem before the crisis of the following March, the Joint Intelligence Committee (JIC),* while not predicting the worst, did say that if Argentina came to believe that it would not get a peaceful transfer of sovereignty 'a full-scale invasion cannot be discounted.'[12]

This uneasy situation coincided with the pressures on public spending at home. Exasperated by the resistance of the Defence Secretary, Francis Pym, to her demands for economies, Mrs Thatcher had moved him to Leader of the House at the beginning of January. The task of Pym's successor, John Nott, was to cut. And because Britain had made promises to NATO about increasing its alliance commitment, cuts could not come in Europe but had to be found elsewhere in the defence budget. Nott advanced the idea that surface ships were no longer as necessary to the navy as in the past. At an OD Committee to discuss the matter, the Chief of the General Staff, General Sir Edwin Bramall,† recalled Mrs Thatcher asking Carrington his opinion of this new doctrine. 'I've never heard anything so ridiculous,' said the Foreign Secretary, 'but the Defence Secretary has no other option because we'd never get the cuts through NATO.'[13] Because non-NATO cuts were easier to make in the navy than in the other services, this is what happened. The resistance from Admiral Sir Henry Leach,‡ the Chief of the Naval Staff, was so fierce that it may even have been counterproductive. According to David Omand,§ Nott's private secretary, the navy failed to make a 'modern case' for its surface ships, falling back on 'Atlantic convoy stuff', but was, in essence, in the right: the internal battle was

---

* The JIC is the Whitehall body responsible for directing the national intelligence organizations on behalf of the Cabinet.

† Edwin Bramall (1923–), educated Eton; Commander-in-Chief, UK Land Forces, 1976–8, 1978–9; Chief of the General Staff, 1979–82; field marshal, 1982; created Lord Bramall, 1987; Knight of the Garter, 1990.

‡ Henry Leach (1923–2011), educated Royal Naval College, Dartmouth; Commander-in-Chief Fleet, and Allied Commander-in-Chief, Channel and Eastern Atlantic, 1977–9; Chief of Naval Staff and First Sea Lord, 1979–82; admiral of the Fleet, 1982; knighted, 1977.

§ David Omand (1947–), educated Glasgow Academy and Corpus Christi College, Cambridge; private secretary to Secretary of State for Defence, 1981–2; Deputy Under-Secretary (Policy), MOD, 1992–6; Director, GCHQ, 1996–7; Permanent Under-Secretary, Home Office, 1998–2001; Security and Intelligence Co-ordinator, Cabinet Office, from 2006; knighted, 2000.

so intense that 'We'd taken our eye off the ball about what defence forces were really there for.'[14]

One of the victims of this process was the ice patrol ship HMS *Endurance*, the only Royal Navy vessel regularly in service in the South Atlantic. Its withdrawal, following the 1981–2 season, was announced in June 1981. The Foreign Office objected, because of the signals withdrawal would send to Argentina, but did not press its case to the utterance. Mrs Thatcher herself was not convinced of the importance of *Endurance*. As late as early March 1982, she chatted about the issue to Richard Luce,* who by then had replaced Nicholas Ridley at the Foreign Office. When Luce tried to tell her that *Endurance* mattered, 'She said that *Endurance* was no good; it just went "pop, pop, pop".'[15]

So Britain had failed to get a deal with Argentina, and failed to pursue the alternative of much stronger support for the regeneration of the Falklands. By sentencing *Endurance* to death, it had signalled a lack of will to defend the islands. As Rex Hunt, the Governor of the Falklands, noted in his annual review of 1981, 'by the end of the year even our most loyal friends were beginning to doubt the good faith of HMG.'[16] He expected the next set of talks with Argentina to break down and recommended 'contingency plans now' in case this happened.

Early in December 1981 a new junta grabbed power in Argentina, led by General Leopoldo Galtieri, the commander of the army. It quickly decided that a resolution of the Malvinas question was the priority for 1982. In mid-January, a secret National Strategy Directive was circulated, stating that the Military Committee had 'resolved to analyse the possibility of the use of military power to obtain the political objective'.[17] None of this reached British intelligence, nor was it relayed diplomatically. Richard Luce later wrote that Anthony Williams, the British Ambassador in Buenos Aires, 'never gave me any impression of a sense of urgency about the new Government's attitude to the Falklands'.[18] Britain, represented by Luce, went forward to talks with Argentina in New York at the end of February. Though not agreeing anything of substance, these talks seemed to set up a process which would go forward. The joint communiqué spoke of 'a cordial and positive spirit'.

On 3 March, however, the news appeared in the British press that Argentina had refused to publish the joint communiqué. Instead, the junta forced

---

* Richard Luce (1936–), educated Wellington and Christ's College, Cambridge; Conservative MP for Arundel and Shoreham, 1971–4; for Shoreham, 1974–92; Minister of State, FCO, 1981–2, 1983–5; Minister for the Arts, 1985–90; Governor of Gibraltar, 1997–2000; Lord Chamberlain, 2000–2006; created Lord Luce, 2000.

the Ministry of Foreign Affairs to put out a unilateral statement. This revealed the content of the New York discussions, although they had been confidential, and insisted that British recognition of Argentine sovereignty must be made within a period which 'will necessarily have to be short'. If this did not happen, Argentina would 'choose freely the procedure which best accords with her interests'.[19] At the same time, bellicose articles began to appear in the Argentine press, calling for direct military action in a few months' time, if Britain did not agree. On Williams's report from Buenos Aires about the threatening communiqué, Mrs Thatcher wrote, 'We must make contingency plans.' As Sir Lawrence Freedman puts it in his official history of the Falklands War, Mrs Thatcher's request 'does not appear to have reached any part of the intelligence community'.[20]

The prevailing view remained that Argentina would not actually attack the Falklands. The Reagan administration in Washington had established better relations with Argentina – a fact which itself emboldened the junta. Thomas Enders, the Assistant Secretary of State for Inter-American Affairs, had been visiting Buenos Aires on the day the junta had issued its aggressive communiqué on the New York talks. His telegram back to Washington suggested that the statement 'may have been no more than to satisfy domestic public opinion, but we cannot be certain. Clearly, a resolution of this ancient dispute is as far off as ever and the local jingos are speculating again about an armed Argentine landing in the islands.'[21] But on 12 March Enders told the British that in his view Argentina was not contemplating 'anything drastic'.[22]* On 19 March, Ambassador Williams wrote to Luce dismissing the idea of the use of force by Argentina: 'we know the current team to be much too intelligent to do anything so silly.' As soon as they received the letter, however, the Foreign Office wrote on it, 'overtaken by events'.[23] These events soon prompted Argentina's 'current team' to do something very silly indeed.

On 18 March 1982, Argentine scrap metal dealers had landed on the British dependency of South Georgia, which was governed from the Falklands

---

* There is no evidence that Enders or anyone else associated with the Reagan administration had any advance knowledge of the Argentine invasion, but some close to Mrs Thatcher saw connections nonetheless. 'It is hard not to believe that some Argentinean Generals let their US counterpart have some inkling as to what was being planned in March,' Hugh Thomas wrote to Mrs Thatcher later in April. 'Surely Dr Costa Mendez must have winked, at least, at Assistant Secretary of State Enders, after the latter's recent visit to Buenos Aires.' Reviewing the letter with felt pen in hand, Mrs Thatcher scored no fewer than four lines under 'Enders'. (Thomas to PM, 'British foreign policy towards the Falklands in the light of Argentinean psychology', 23 Apr. 1982, THCR 1/13/26.)

Islands. They were fulfilling a legitimate contract which originated with a British company, but they did not have permission to land, and they were taken to South Georgia by the Argentine navy. Once landed, they damaged and robbed property of the British Antarctic Survey and ran up the Argentine flag. Rex Hunt, the Governor, ordered them to leave. On 21 March the condemned but still functioning *Endurance* was despatched from the Falklands to make for South Georgia, with the strong agreement of Mrs Thatcher. The Foreign Office now tied itself in knots. Would the arrival of *Endurance* in South Georgia only make Argentina more intransigent? Was Britain wise to adopt a high tone when it was not in a position to enforce its will? Back home, the House of Commons sought answers. A statement by Richard Luce, promising 'firm action', was not really believed. The numerous Tory backbenchers who felt strongly on the subject were suspicious, not only of the Foreign Office, but even of Mrs Thatcher. When Alan Clark, discussing the situation with colleagues, suggested that Mrs Thatcher would surely sympathize with those, including himself, who 'think Imperially', Nick Budgen replied: 'Don't bet on that, Alan. She is governed only by what the Americans want. At heart she is just a vulgar, middle-class Reaganite.'[24]

There is no evidence that Argentina had contrived the original incident, but it certainly took advantage of it. On 23 March, the day of Luce's statement to the Commons, the junta decided to send Marines to Leith in South Georgia. These landed on the night of 24 March. On the same day, the junta secretly brought forward its plans for the invasion of the Falkland Islands. Two days later – again, of course, secretly – it ordered the invasion to proceed. Poor Ambassador Williams in Buenos Aires, uneasily conscious that he was being kept in the dark, wailed to the Foreign Office about the Argentine Foreign Minister, 'I have the growing impression that Costa Mendez has been less than honest with me.'[25]

On 25 March, the Cabinet discussed the matter unproductively. Carrington told his colleagues that the situation was 'escalating into something which may be very difficult politically and diplomatically'.[26] Mrs Thatcher said that she simply did not know what *Endurance* could do. The Lord Chancellor, Lord Hailsham, pressed for robust action: 'We said we're going to remove them.' But Carrington shied away: 'No – that they must go.' An Argentine invasion of the Falklands was discussed. The Cabinet minutes record the conclusion that 'if the Argentines thereafter threatened military action, Britain would face an almost impossible task in seeking to defend the Islands at such long range.'[27] The scrapping of *Endurance* 'might now need to be reconsidered'. But even now the government machine and No. 10 itself were not geared to a full-blown crisis. On the same day,

Richard Luce interceded with No. 10 to make an announcement that *Endurance* would be retained, but Clive Whitmore told him to plead his case with defence ministers, not with the Prime Minister.[28] The next day, the Ministry of Defence presented Mrs Thatcher with some hastily prepared contingency plans. Deterring any Argentine aggression, the Prime Minister was informed, would require a substantial Royal Navy flotilla, led by either *Hermes* or *Invincible*. Once it had arrived in the South Atlantic, the experts judged this force would be sufficient to ward off any invasion, but 'if faced with Argentine occupation on arrival there would be no certainty that such a force would be able to *retake* the dependency'. 'You can imagine that turned a knife in my heart,' Mrs Thatcher later recalled.[29] Her great concern was that to take such action would provoke the very thing that she was trying to forestall, i.e. an invasion. If this took place before the flotilla arrived, it would not be possible to undo it. 'That would have been the greatest humiliation for Britain,' Mrs Thatcher concluded.[30] She duly rejected the plan. On 29 March, Carrington and Mrs Thatcher flew to Brussels together for an EEC summit, and discussed the situation on the plane. Instead of a flotilla, they agreed to send a submarine* to the South Atlantic and order a second to be prepared. But despite the crisis, and the fact that Carrington had already written to the US Secretary of State, Al Haig, asking him to intercede with Argentina, they agreed that Carrington's planned visit to Israel should go ahead. According to John Coles, who travelled with Mrs Thatcher that day as her overseas private secretary, there was as yet no belief in her mind or that of Carrington that Argentina was about to invade.[31]

That day, the Foreign Office received the first indication of Argentine ships sailing, but 'no intelligence warning of an invasion'.[32] In a statement to the Commons the following day, Luce said that Britain would defend the Falklands 'to the best of our ability': 'I knew deep down how dangerously empty these words had become.'[33] The government was embarrassed, in the questions on Luce's statement, when Jim Callaghan revealed to the House that in 1977, when there had been some trouble with Argentina, he had ordered British ships to stand 400 miles off the Falklands, ready to protect them if necessary. It has subsequently emerged that Argentina did not know of this action at the time,[34] so Callaghan's revelation actually held no lessons about deterrence, but the House did not know this.

*

* This has sometimes been referred to as a 'nuclear' submarine. The description is misleading. The vessel was nuclear-powered, but not carrying nuclear weapons.

At 11 in the morning on Wednesday 31 March 1982, the Joint Intelligence Committee produced its first immediate assessment of the Falklands since the previous July. Although it hedged a bit, it did not assert that Argentina was about to invade, preferring the view that 'the Argentine Government does not wish to be the first to adopt forcible measures.'[35] An air of uncertainty prevailed in Whitehall.

Early that evening, however, everything changed. An intercept provided London with 'the first clear indication' that Argentina would invade the Falklands on Friday.[36] This news broke with Whitehall surprisingly empty. Lord Carrington was in Israel. Sir Michael Palliser, the Permanent Under-Secretary of the Foreign Office, was retiring that week. The Chief of the Defence Staff (CDS), Admiral Sir Terence Lewin,* was in New Zealand and the Chief of the General Staff, General Sir Edwin Bramall, was in Northern Ireland. The Commander-in-Chief Fleet, Admiral Sir John Fieldhouse,† was in Gibraltar. These absences may have added to the confusion of the day, but from Mrs Thatcher's vantage point they may also have made a positive difference to the outcome of the whole drama.

The first intelligence report of the invasion was brought to Mrs Thatcher by John Nott, the only relevant Cabinet minister in London that day. They met in her room in the Commons in the early evening. Nott was accompanied by his Permanent Secretary, Sir Frank Cooper. Sir Antony Acland,‡ Sir Michael Palliser's successor, was present, as was Richard Luce. Mrs Thatcher was attended by Clive Whitmore and John Coles. Ian Gow kept coming in and out. Mrs Thatcher later described Nott's announcement of the impending invasion as 'the worst . . . moment of my life'.[37] All those in the room remembered the atmosphere as gloomy and confused. The priority was drafting an urgent message to President Reagan, warning him of the impending invasion and asking him to intervene. Henderson was also told to see Haig and plead the British case. However, as was her wont when under stress, Mrs Thatcher soon hurried off down the byways of minutiae. Even worse for her than the appalling fact of invasion, however, was the attitude of those at the meeting about what could be done. Nott recalled that the

---

* Terence Lewin (1920–99), educated the Judd School, Tonbridge; Royal Navy, 1939; served in Second World War (DSC 1942); Chief of Naval Staff and First Sea Lord, 1977–9; Chief of Defence Staff, 1979–82; created Lord Lewin of Greenwich, 1982; Knight of the Garter, 1983.

† John Fieldhouse (1928–92), educated Royal Naval College, Dartmouth; Royal Navy, 1945; submariner from 1948; Controller of the Navy, 1979–81; Commander-in-Chief Fleet, 1981–2; knighted, 1980; created Lord Fieldhouse, 1990.

‡ Antony Acland (1930–), educated Eton and Christ Church, Oxford; joined FCO, 1953; head of Arabian Department, 1970–72; Ambassador to Spain, 1977–9; Permanent Under-Secretary and head of Diplomatic Service, 1982–6; Ambassador to the United States, 1986–91; Provost of Eton, 1991–2000; Knight of the Garter, 2001.

meeting was 'heavily weighted in favour of the Foreign Office search for a diplomatic solution',[38] but Luce noted almost the opposite, recording that there was much too little focus on how to try to head off the invasion by diplomatic means.[39] In fact it was Nott himself, in the absence of the other principals, who was the only person in a position to have given the Prime Minister a strong positive view of his own. This he did not do. Backed up by Cooper, he said he thought that recapture was all but impossible. According to John Coles, Mrs Thatcher was aware that doubts about the chance of recapture were also held by some of the service chiefs, notably Bramall, so the balance of expert knowledge was against her. Coles recalled the exchange between Defence Secretary and Prime Minister, which he noted: 'Mrs Thatcher: "You'll have to take them back." Nott: "We can't." Mrs Thatcher: "You'll have to."'[40] She had the will, but not yet the way.

Another man who had received the intelligence report was Henry Leach, the First Sea Lord. He had just got back to his office from a day of naval inspections near Portsmouth. On his desk, as well as the intelligence report of the impending invasion, was the navy's brief on the situation, saying, in effect, 'Don't touch it.'[41] He was struck by the incompatibility of the two documents. If the invasion was happening, he reasoned, the navy should be doing everything possible to respond. Still wearing his admiral's day uniform,* Leach went straight to Nott's office in the Ministry of Defence (MOD). Being told that he was already with the Prime Minister in Parliament, Leach hurried to the Commons. Despite his uniform, the ushers in the Central Lobby were reluctant to let him through and made him wait for a quarter of an hour, until he was rescued, fuming, by a whip who gave him whisky. When at last he reached the Prime Minister's office, he found 'an aura of complete gloom. No one was talking. They were patently floundering.' For Leach, it was 'a stroke of luck' that Mrs Thatcher was present, because if, as he had first expected, his meeting had been with Nott alone, 'Nott wouldn't have moved.'[42] Leach thoroughly despised Nott for what he believed – unfairly – was his attempt to break the navy. Inspired by the importance and drama of the situation, the presence of the Prime Minister and possibly by the urge to get his own back, he was fired up. 'I seriously believed that there was no point in having a navy if you couldn't use it.'[43]

Both Leach and Mrs Thatcher, who was always impressed by a uniform, were conscious that he was the only serviceman in the room. It was the admiral, not the Prime Minister, who took the initiative in the conversation.

---

* Accounts of this meeting usually describe Leach as wearing 'full-dress uniform'. In her memoirs, Mrs Thatcher says that he was 'in civilian dress'. Neither is correct.

Leach asked for her political clearance to assemble a task force. As Leach remembered it, 'No one uttered a word.' 'What does that mean?' she asked eventually.[44] He explained, and she asked further questions about naval capacity, such as aircraft carriers and helicopters. Leach pointed out that everything was in short supply, but not impossibly so. According to Coles, there was no direct reference to the defence cuts which she and Nott had been pushing through, but the consciousness of these was palpable.[45] This gave Leach the moral advantage. 'How long will it take to assemble the Task Force?' asked Mrs Thatcher. 'Three days,' said Leach.* 'How long to get there?' 'Three weeks.' 'Three weeks!' exclaimed the Prime Minister, innocent of geography and of the sea. 'Surely you mean three days.' 'No, I don't.'[46]

'Can we do it?' asked Mrs Thatcher with piercing urgency. 'We can, Prime Minister,' said Leach, 'and, though it is not my place to say this, we must.' 'Why do you say that?' 'Because if we don't do it, if we pussyfoot . . . we'll be living in a totally different country whose word will count for little.' At this, Leach remembered, Mrs Thatcher gave a sort of half-smile, as if this was what she had wanted to hear.[47] By the time he left the meeting several hours later, Leach had full authority to assemble the Task Force, though not to sail.

The meeting of 31 March has acquired mythical status in the history of the Falklands War, rightly so. For the rest of her life, Mrs Thatcher would often revert to this meeting in conversation, always making Leach the hero of the drama. He gave her 'tremendous heart', according to Clive Whitmore,[48] and it was heart, at that moment, that she needed most of all. Diplomacy was in ruins; defeat, in the imminent invasion, was certain. Her country's honour, her government and her career might all be lost in a matter of days. Her instincts told her to fight, but she could not do so in defiance of all expert advice. Leach gave her the necessary countervailing expertise. Nott, more generous to Leach than vice versa, admitted in later years that he had not been briefed about how the Task Force could be put together.[49] He was pushed to one side. His private secretary, David Omand, who was at the meeting, noted that Mrs Thatcher's very inexperience emboldened her; 'She was placing the entire trust of the government in the navy.'[50]

The next morning, Thursday, April Fools' Day, the Cabinet met, and wrung its hands. Humphrey Atkins, Carrington's number two at the Foreign

---

* Mrs Thatcher remembered him saying forty-eight hours (see *The Downing Street Years*, HarperCollins, 1993, p. 179), but this is almost certainly wrong.

Office, told colleagues that 'we are trying to solve the problem by diplomatic means.'[51] Mrs Thatcher added that 'The US [is] the most powerful
thing available to us.'[52] Disappointed by Haig's 'very flabby reply'[53] to Carrington's earlier request for help, Mrs Thatcher now awaited the results of
her own appeal to Reagan. Difficulties with America were soon to become
a recurring theme. They caused neuralgia in Whitehall because of the collective memory of the disaster in 1956 when the United States had decided
not to support the Anglo-French occupation of the Suez Canal. The result
had been the fall of Anthony Eden, the Prime Minister, and the end of
Britain's standing as an imperial power. On this day, however, President
Reagan did his best. Because he was in hospital undergoing tests on his
urinary tract, he was not able to ring President Galtieri until 6.30 p.m.
Eastern Standard Time. To the amazement of White House staff, Galtieri
refused to take the call. Dennis Blair of the National Security Council
(NSC) staff, quickly realized why: 'I said "No, wait a minute. They're
invading, but he hasn't worked out yet what to tell our President."' Blair
then rang Robin Renwick at the British Embassy to tell him that the invasion must be going ahead.[54] About two hours later, Galtieri agreed to speak
to Reagan. 'Galtieri had obviously been drinking,' recalled William Clark,
the National Security Advisor, 'and this habit may have influenced his
actions.'[55] The conversation lasted a tortured fifty minutes, with Galtieri
dancing around Reagan's questions before rejecting the President's good
offices for finding an agreement. When Reagan asked for his assurance that
there would be no landing the next day, 'Galtieri responded with a por-
tentous silence.'[56] According to Jim Rentschler, Blair's colleague on the
NSC staff, Reagan warned Galtieri that 'if armed force is involved we will
not be able to side with you ... you will be the guilty party.'[57] He also
warned the General that Mrs Thatcher would retake the islands by force
and that, if she did so, the US would back her.[58] Nicko Henderson, the
British Ambassador in Washington, was swiftly informed of this unsuccessful
conversation. According to Renwick, Henderson then telephoned the Prime
Minister direct to tell her the news. Waking her up at four in the morning*
he found her 'not at all in a bellicose mood, but in a very sombre one, understanding full well the dangers that lay ahead.' Renwick, meanwhile, 'asked
the Ministry of Defence to warn the Governor that he was going to have
Argentine marines on his doorstep next morning'.[59]

    In fact, Henderson told Mrs Thatcher little she did not already know.
Not long before midnight, she had received Carrington at No. 10. He had
come straight off the plane from Israel, and was exhausted. Also present

---

* Renwick inaccurately records the time as 2 a.m.

were Leach, Nott, Luce and various private secretaries. Luce was surprised, as he had been the previous day at the long meeting in Mrs Thatcher's room in Parliament, that 'no proper notes were taken by the private secretaries'.[60]* The meeting was frequently interrupted by calls from Haig to Carrington. Haig eventually reported that the President's conversation with Galtieri had been 'to no avail'.[61] It was decided to put British troops on immediate notice of deployment to the South Atlantic. Early the next day, Leach issued the directive: 'The task force is to be made ready and sailed.'

'The next day [2 April] was a nightmare,' Luce wrote later. 'I knew the invasion was coming and there was nothing we could do.'[62] The Cabinet met at 9.45 a.m., and was told that the invasion was imminent and was bound to succeed. Mrs Thatcher explained the plans for the Task Force, and said that the government could announce in public that 'we have put people on immediate notice to sail for operations.' Francis Pym was more robust: 'Why not instruct to sail?' 'I don't wish to close options,' Mrs Thatcher replied.[63] Geoffrey Howe thought even this announcement was a bad idea because it would 'give impression that we are in a position to reverse or reconquer. We ought to convey the opposite impression.' Nigel Lawson, however, thought that people would be passionately engaged: 'Public opinion won't regard this as a faraway island.'[64] Mrs Thatcher wanted to avoid a parliamentary debate, preferring a simple statement to the House. She also announced that the situation would be handled by a small group of ministers – Whitelaw, Carrington, Nott and Pym. This, rather than the full membership of the Cabinet's OD Committee, was the germ of what later became known as the War Cabinet. 'If your four main ministers get together quickly,' she explained later, 'you can carry OD or anything else with you.'[65]

At 11 a.m., Humphrey Atkins made a statement to the Commons on the latest situation. He was not able to confirm the invasion but reported, inaccurately, that the Governor had been able to communicate with the Foreign Office. Just as ministers were leaving the Commons, John Nott went to Mrs Thatcher's room there to tell her, on the strength of a message from the Marines, that the invasion had taken place; this was not fully confirmed till 6 p.m. Luce gave himself some grim amusement by reading the very last intelligence report which said there was 'no incontrovertible evidence of invasion'. Mrs Thatcher was deeply disturbed by the performance of the intelligence community. Patrick Wright,† newly appointed chairman of the

---

* Coles and Whitmore both say notes were taken. They do not survive in the archives, however.
† Patrick Wright (1931–), educated Marlborough and Merton College, Oxford; Ambassador to Luxembourg, 1977–9; to Syria, 1979–81; Deputy Under-Secretary, FCO, 1982–4; Ambassador

JIC, was summoned to Chequers following the invasion to be dressed down at considerable length for failing to predict the attack. Wright had only been in the job for a couple of weeks, but this made no difference to Mrs Thatcher. The encounter ended with Clive Whitmore coming into the room and Mrs Thatcher saying, 'Clive, I think Mr Wright needs a very strong drink.'[66]

Once the invasion was a known fact, the Cabinet met for a second time. The most important decision before colleagues, said the Prime Minister, was whether or not to put the fleet to sea. By doing so, it was not automatically committing to operations: 'It keeps open options.' Ministers asked Leach, who had been summoned to attend the meeting, about the military difficulties. He said the services were 'never confident in the face of air threat [which would be a particular problem when landing on the Falklands], but with anti-air capability we could provide, I would feel confident of success.' Lord Hailsham, the Lord Chancellor, summed it up: 'Do we hit back, or cringe?' But Mrs Thatcher preferred to revert to the immediate: 'We have to decide whether to tell the fleet to sail, and say so in the House tomorrow.' (It had been agreed that, as had not happened since the Suez crisis of 1956, the House should sit on a Saturday, and debate in full, rather than settle for the statement which Mrs Thatcher would have preferred.) Carrington said: 'I rather doubt whether our speeches are credible if we don't tell the force to sail.' 'We should lose a vote of confidence if we don't sail,' said Michael Heseltine, 'but we don't know where we are going.'[67] Mrs Thatcher asked the opinion of each Cabinet minister in turn. Only one, John Biffen – 'a little runt of a man' in the view of Henry Leach[68] – was brave enough to say that he was against the despatch of the Task Force.*

'It was a very bad day for the Foreign Office,' Luce admitted, 'and the machine appeared to collapse.'[69] The Foreign Office had provided the Prime Minister with a memorandum, written by John Weston† of its defence department, which enraged her. The memo was bleak. It claimed that Britain would not be supported in the Security Council if it used heavy force, the European allies could not be depended on, and it could not be assumed that

---

to Saudi Arabia, 1984–6; Permanent Under-Secretary and head of Diplomatic Service, 1986–91; created Lord Wright, 1994.

* Lord Biffen later told the author that Lord Hailsham had agreed with him, but had not said so in Cabinet. There is no other evidence for this, and it sounds surprising, but it is true that Hailsham, who was often bellicose, was also mercurial.

† John Weston (1938–), educated Sherborne and Worcester College, Oxford; Director of International Security Policy, FCO, 1981–5; UK Permanent Representative to NATO, 1992–5; UK Permanent Representative to UN, 1995–8; knighted, 1992.

the US would 'remain unambivalent . . . They did not support Anglo-French military action in 1956.' If Britain got the islands back, they would be difficult to hold, the paper went on, and anyway, 'Unless the 1,800 islanders were manifestly being subjected to inhumane treatment by Argentine occupying forces, it would be hard to persuade people that the game was worth the candle.'[70] This was the document Mrs Thatcher was referring to when she wrote in her memoirs that the Foreign Office advice received that day 'summed up the flexibility of principle characteristic of that department'.[71] King Charles Street also sent her a draft for her speech the following day which she considered inadequate. It did not mention the despatch of the Task Force. At 9.30 p.m., Mrs Thatcher rang Luce to tell him it was 'appalling' and to discuss various points. He offered to come round to her, 'but she preferred to rewrite it herself in the night.'[72] In fact, the drafting was done by Whitmore and Coles who simply, for lack of time, divided the work in half. Whitmore drafted the key words about the aims of the Task Force – the repossession of the islands, the removal of the Argentines and the fulfilment of the wishes of the islanders. 'The words were considered very carefully.'[73] At first they thought of aiming at the 'restoration of British sovereignty', but decided that it was safer and more accurate (since sovereignty had not been removed by the invasion) to use the phrase 'British administration'. Mrs Thatcher was under great strain. At one point during the speech preparation, she realized that all the GMT hours she had been working with in the draft had been wrongly computed against Argentine time. 'She almost visibly collapsed,' remembered John Coles. 'Whitmore calmed her down beautifully.'[74]*

But she remained capable of the tart expression which was her version of wit. That day, the Cabinet had decided to freeze Argentine assets in Britain. Late at night, John Kerr, Geoffrey Howe's private secretary, realized that there were not enough Lords of the Treasury around to sign the Order in Council required to act fast, so he took the necessary paper to the Prime Minister herself, because of her formal title of First Lord of the Treasury, for signature. 'Thank God someone in Whitehall still knows what to do,' Mrs Thatcher told him. Kerr pointed out that if Britain took Argentine money, Argentina would take British. 'I don't think this is the time for points like that, do you, John?' said Mrs Thatcher.[75]

In a broadcast to the Argentine people that night, General Galtieri explained that the British 'lack of goodwill' in negotiations had made the

---

* Throughout the Falklands War, the Task Force kept Greenwich Mean Time, 'Zulu' in military shorthand. This meant that the British services' working day in the South Atlantic began much earlier than the Argentine, which was generally considered an advantage.

invasion of the Malvinas necessary. The South Georgia incident had finally proved this. 'With Christian faith I pray', he said, that Britain would now understand its error. He invoked 'the protection of God and his holy Mother' and exclaimed, 'Glory to the great Argentine people. May this be God's will.' For all the vainglory, aggression and machismo of Argentine behaviour, Galtieri's position was not completely incomprehensible. It must indeed have seemed to Buenos Aires that negotiations in which the British always happily held out the possibility of conceding sovereignty and yet never did so were a dishonest game. And the junta could have been forgiven for concluding, from Britain's economic weakness and actions like the planned withdrawal of *Endurance*, that the will to resist Argentina was absent. In letting the invasion build up, Britain had failed to understand the mentality of a military dictatorship and had taken too little care for the Falkland Islanders. But Argentina had made a greater error: it did not understand the powerful interaction between the sympathy due to the plight of the islanders, who saw themselves as British, and the power of the British Parliament when roused.

Parliament met on Saturday 3 April 1982 in a state of high emotion, stirred up by a furious press. It was widely believed that the Royal Marines at Port Stanley had been ordered to surrender without a fight. This was not the case but the government did not have clear information at that point.* It had frighteningly little that it could say with confidence. Carrington and others were right that the government could not survive the wrath of MPs if it were not able to announce that the fleet would be ready to sail on Monday. Given the scale of the disaster, some clear and immediate military response was the minimum required. Mrs Thatcher opened the debate. Alan Clark recorded that she spoke at first 'very slowly but didactically' but later, when being barracked, 'She changed gear and gabbled.'[76] She was not derailed by the interruptions, but she failed to rouse her own benches. The Prime Minister related the series of events that had led to disaster and set out the position: 'I must tell the House that the Falkland Islands and their dependencies remain British territory. No aggression and no invasion can alter that simple fact. It is the Government's objective to see that the islands are freed from occupation and are returned to British administration at the earliest possible moment.'[77] These words bound her from the

---

* In fact, the lightly armed Marines resisted fiercely. The Argentine casualty figures are disputed. Freedman records 1 Argentine death and 3 wounded but others put the death toll as high as 5 (Freedman, *The Official History of the Falklands Campaign*, vol. ii: *War and Diplomacy*, p. 7; 'Sir Rex Hunt', *Daily Telegraph* obituary, 12 Nov. 2012). The Marines suffered no casualties.

beginning, as she intended they should. They set an irreducible minimum. Mrs Thatcher ended her speech with sentences which reflected the feeling on both sides of the House and brought the matter home: 'The people of the Falkland Islands, like the people of the United Kingdom, are an island race. Their way of life is British; their allegiance is to the Crown.' They had the right to choose and preserve their British way of life and Britain must 'do everything that we can to uphold that right'.[78]

Luckily for Mrs Thatcher, Argentina's junta was, in the eyes of the Labour leader Michael Foot, a semi-fascist regime, and so he found it much easier to expend his contempt on it than if it had been left wing. The attack on the islands had been a 'foul and brutal aggression', Foot told the Commons, and he dismissed the idea that Britain's position was in any way imperialist. He attacked the government's unpreparedness, but refrained from a personal assault on ministers, and accepted the sending of the Task Force. It was Enoch Powell, understanding Mrs Thatcher's mentality, who issued her with the most arresting challenge. She was known as 'the Iron Lady', he said. 'In the next week or two this House, the nation and the right honourable Lady herself will learn of what metal she is made.'[79] Alan Clark noted in his diary, when reflecting later on the debate, 'how low she held her head, how *knotted* with pain and apprehension she seemed as he [Powell] pronounced his famous judgment'.[80] It was this sense of being put to the test, by Parliament, nation and her own conscience, which Mrs Thatcher carried away from the debate. John Coles noticed that it was Powell's remark which stuck: 'She came back to her room afterwards, and that was what was in her mind.'[81]

John Nott, who wound up the debate for the government, was frequently absent from the Chamber before his speech, accumulating the latest fragments of information, and this was held against him by the MPs who crowded into it. When he came to speak, he was, in the words of Alan Clark, 'a disaster. He stammered and stuttered and garbled . . . He refused to give way; he gave way; he changed his mind; he stood up again; he sat down again. All this against a constant roaring of disapproval and contempt.'[82] Mrs Thatcher's speech had not been a triumph of oratory, but she had held the line and refrained from partisan politics. Nott made the 'terrible error'[83] of attacking Labour in the course of his self-justification. It was, Mrs Thatcher privately remembered, 'a lousy speech',[84] and he lost the House. As early as December the previous year, Nott had privately decided to leave politics, feeling that his career had been damaged by his behaviour in resisting and then accepting defence cuts, including that of the carrier *Invincible*, but Mrs Thatcher had refused to let him go.[85] Perhaps he felt that he was getting his comeuppance: certainly his heart was not in it any longer, and he was 'unnerved'.[86]

Nott, with Carrington, whose speech in the House of Lords had, as is customary in the Upper House, been courteously received, then had to appear before an impromptu meeting of the 1922 Committee (and Conservative peers), proposed by the Chief Whip, Michael Jopling. They were assailed. Jopling remembered the backbenchers 'baying for blood'.[87] Ian Gow attended, and scribbled Mrs Thatcher a note of proceedings, with each MP's contribution recorded and attributed. He came round to her room in the Commons immediately after the meeting, telling her how bad things had been, particularly for Carrington. His written record, of which what follows is a small part, slips into capital letters at moments of high stress.

PACKED MEETING.
<u>Buck</u>. MOST DISTURBING. MOST WORRYING ... <u>Griffiths</u>. Best loyalty we can show is frankness. Credibility of Conservative Government here – APPLAUSE ... <u>Hogg</u>. MUST RECOVER SOVEREIGNTY. Unless we do Party will not hold loyalty ... <u>Stokes</u>. Working men appalled at what has happened ... smell of appeasement about the FO ... <u>Waller</u>. They should resign. <u>Colvin</u>. NO RESIGNATIONS NOW ... <u>Lord Onslow</u>. SINK THE WHOLE FLEET. <u>Aitken</u>. <u>DECLARE WAR AS FLEET SAILS</u>. <u>Lloyd</u>. WHY THE HELL WERE WE NEGOTIATING.

Against these assaults, Gow records the rather murmured responses – 'accept political situation for our party is bad', 'we have no money', 'geography is difficult', 'misunderstandings' – of Nott and Carrington.* Carrington, who had never been elected to anything and had never had a good relationship with the parliamentary party, was badly shaken. So was Nott. Both edged towards resignation, Carrington indicating as much to Mrs Thatcher in her room after the meeting. Worried about Carrington's state of mind, Jopling got Whitelaw to invite him for lunch at his official residence, Dorneywood, the following day, and they thought they had persuaded him to stay.[88] Carrington also went to call on Lord Home for advice. Face to face, Home tried to persuade him that he should stay, but when Carrington left the drawing room to go to the lavatory, Lady Home met him in the passage and told him: 'Alec says if he were in your position,

---

* By no means all Conservative MPs were as robust as those who spoke up at the 1922 meeting. Three days later, Jopling drew up a report of backbenchers' attitudes. It mentioned several, including Julian Critchley and Chris Patten, who felt that an attempt at recapture was too dangerous ('the military difficulties are insurmountable'), Ian Gilmour, who said, 'It will make Suez look like common sense,' and Kenneth Clarke, whose view was summarized as 'Hopes nobody thinks we are going to fight the Argentinians. We should blow up a few ships but nothing more.' (Report by Michael Jopling to Francis Pym, 6 Apr. 1982, THCR 1/20/3/2, fascicule no. 4.)

he wouldn't have any hesitation about going.'[89] The Foreign Office had failed either to foresee or to avert the invasion of British soil. Rumours spread of a very hostile leading article which would appear in *The Times* the following morning. There was a sense that Carrington must now fall on his sword and assume responsibility. Although advised by Cecil Parkinson that the departure of Carrington was unfortunately necessary,[90] Mrs Thatcher was most reluctant to see him go. Apart from anything else, she felt exposed.*

But by Sunday night Carrington's mind was pretty much made up, and the leading article in *The Times* on Monday morning, just as tough as rumoured, finally decided him. 'How can I stay', he asked a protesting Michael Palliser, 'when I cannot defend my policy in the Commons?'[91] Luce followed Carrington's suit, and resigned as soon as he could; so did Humphrey Atkins. John Nott was furious that no one had told him in advance that Carrington was to resign. He felt himself in an impossible position and begged Mrs Thatcher that he be allowed to go too. She refused, saying, by her own account, that she 'could not possibly accept when the Task Force was on the ocean'.[92] The true reason for Mrs Thatcher's determination to keep him was political: she feared that the departure of the only other Cabinet minister apart from herself who had been involved in the debacle would leave her own position vulnerable. Even without Nott leaving, the departure of Carrington and his colleagues emphasized her isolation in her own mind. 'I felt totally bereft, I felt deserted, very lonely,' she told Richard Luce years later.[93]

When Carrington saw Mrs Thatcher to tell her his decision, she 'behaved with the greatest possible kindness'. Then she told him that she proposed to replace him with Francis Pym. By his own account, Carrington said to her, 'Margaret, you mustn't do that. You hate him. It'll all end in tears.' 'I know,' replied Mrs Thatcher, 'but he's the only one with the experience.'[94] Her stated reason for choosing Pym was a true one. Like Carrington, and Willie Whitelaw, Pym had won the MC in the Second World War. ('Don't forget, he was a brave soldier,' Mrs Thatcher was wont to say, when feeling guilty about criticizing him.)[95] He had been Northern Ireland Secretary (very briefly) for Ted Heath, and Defence Secretary for Mrs Thatcher. As leader of the House, until he became Foreign Secretary, and a former chief

---

* These dynamics were lost on the US Secretary of State, Al Haig. Haig initially refused to believe that Carrington had resigned on principle. Instead he pleaded with Nicko Henderson (and later with his wife Mary) for the 'real reason' that had led Mrs Thatcher to sack him. (Interview with Stanley Orman.)

whip, he could bring to the job a deep knowledge of the Commons from which Carrington had been absolutely disqualified.

The additional – and most unwelcome – reason why Mrs Thatcher felt she had to promote Pym was that he was now the favourite to succeed her as leader. In retrospect, it seems improbable that this somewhat nervous and hesitant man, whose public performances never excited the general public, could have been seen as Mrs Thatcher's most likely replacement, but this is to forget the precariousness of her position. Even before the Falklands crisis, she was on probation with the party, and had never been properly accepted by many in its higher echelons. Pym positioned himself in case 'anything should happen to her'. Brian Fall, who was Carrington's private secretary, and so became Pym's on 5 April, felt that 'Francis didn't vigorously enough deny the ambitions which others attributed to him.'[96] He could not be overlooked for promotion: he was in a strong position, but one of which Mrs Thatcher was bound to be suspicious. Besides, Carrington was right in his estimation of the personal relationship between the two. With his rather hunched, anxious demeanour, Pym was not her sort of man. He had suffered a minor nervous breakdown in the 1970s. Officials considered that he was 'actually very courageous',[97] but they were frustrated by his manner at meetings, particularly meetings with the Prime Minister: 'he can seem to be a branch bending in the wind . . . he gets red in the face and can't put his case very well.'[98] Pym was probably one of those men, quite common in his generation, who hated arguing with a woman, and found Mrs Thatcher intimidating. He quailed when she came at him 'with her hair glued up and her eyes flashing'.[99] According to Antony Acland, their encounters were 'slightly like the Mad Hatter's tea party. There she was opposite and Francis was the dormouse, who had snuck into the tea party and was getting smaller and smaller and smaller.'[100]*

That afternoon, the leaders of the Tory tribe, including Mrs Thatcher and Carrington, who read the lesson, attended the memorial service of R. A. Butler in St Margaret's, Westminster. Coming on the same day as Carrington's resignation, it provided the funeral rites for a certain sort of whiggish Conservatism. Bill Deedes, who attended the service, noted: 'View of PM – in black, composed . . . Carrington reads 1st lesson in clear tones, as if nothing had happened. She watches with distant eyes . . . Only sudden movement by the PM when Archbishop leads prayer for those who govern. She drops her head into her hands.'[101] Butler had always spoken of politics

---

* In the original, the dormouse does not, in fact, get smaller. He simply gets put into the teapot.

as 'the art of the possible', using that phrase for the title for his memoirs. Mrs Thatcher had criticized the phrase in the past. Now, both in her economic policies and in the Falklands crisis, she was truly attempting the art of the impossible.*

In the course of the day, and of the next, with bands playing and families weeping, the initial Task Force set sail from Portsmouth, led by the aircraft carriers *Invincible* and *Hermes*, accompanied by the assault ship *Fearless* and eleven frigates and destroyers. Among those on board *Invincible* was the Queen's second son, Prince Andrew, a helicopter pilot. In her memoirs, Mrs Thatcher says that the Queen had made clear that 'there could be no question of a member of the royal family being treated differently from other servicemen.'[102] What she does not add is that she herself opposed the sending of Prince Andrew, because she was frightened of hostage-taking and of political problems, but 'the Palace dug their toes in in a big way'.[103] It was to an earlier queen that Mrs Thatcher turned for inspiration as the fleet sailed. Interviewed on television, she was asked whether she would resign if the enterprise failed. 'Failure?' she replied. 'Do you remember what Queen Victoria once said? "Failure – the possibilities do not exist."'[104] In her manuscript memoir of the war, written a year later (see below), Mrs Thatcher summed up the day, including a comic slip of the pen: the Task Force, she wrote, left 'with a speed and inefficiency [sic] which astounded the world and made us feel very proud and <u>very</u> British.'[105]† In his diary, François Mitterrand's adviser Jacques Attali recorded: 'A large part of the British fleet begins its 14,000 km journey to South America. About Margaret Thatcher, François Mitterrand wonders: "Do I admire her . . . or envy her?"'[106]

That evening, Michael Palliser cancelled what would have been his farewell party in the Foreign Office and it became instead the wake for Carrington. But although the Foreign Office had probably never been at such a low ebb in modern times, one of its number had already secured the most lasting diplomatic success of the war. As soon as the Argentine

---

* Bill Deedes, who was temperamentally of a Butlerish disposition, recorded a conversation with his proprietor, Lord Hartwell, when he returned to the offices of the *Daily Telegraph* after the service: 'Tell him (a) PM at risk. (b) Expedition is a farce.' (Lord Deedes, diary (unpublished), 5 Apr. 1982.)

† As the Fleet departed, the Deputy Secretary to the Cabinet, Robert Wade-Gery, came in by ship by Portsmouth Head from a continental holiday. He had been out of touch with all news and had no idea what was happening. The next day, he found himself made secretary to the War Cabinet. (Interview with Sir Robert Wade-Gery.)

invasion of the Falklands had become imminent, Anthony Parsons,* Britain's Permanent Representative at the United Nations, had seen that the faster Britain acted at the UN, the greater the likelihood of success. He knew there was no prospect of getting UN support for the British claim to the Falkland Islands – existing General Assembly resolutions made clear that this was regarded with disfavour as colonial – but he believed that a straightforward condemnation of the Argentine use of force was obtainable. He called an emergency meeting of the Security Council, on which Britain has a permanent place, for the evening of Saturday 3 April, the day of the debate in Parliament. He sought to pass a resolution condemning Argentina, even though it seemed unlikely that Britain could muster the nine votes required. At the Foreign Office, Luce overruled cautious officials and authorized Parsons's action.

Early in the evening of that fraught Saturday, Mrs Thatcher had already had a most encouraging telephone call from President Mitterrand of France, who told her: 'I quite realise that Britain is quite big enough to find its own solutions to this problem. But it's important you should realise that others share your opposition to this kind of aggression.'[107]† His message was an important one. It showed the solidarity of one nation with far-flung possessions for another, and gave her reason to hope that there might be strong support for Britain from the EEC. It also showed that Mitterrand shared Mrs Thatcher's view, born, in both cases, from the experience of the 1930s, that 'you must never accept the modification of frontiers by force.'[108] It gave her a personal bond with the socialist French President that transcended their considerable ideological divide‡ and, at that precise moment, it added to her confidence about the Security Council resolution, in which France offered support and helped swing countries within its sphere of influence Britain's way. A message from Parsons quickly made clear, however, that Britain was still a vote short, and begged that Mrs Thatcher intervene personally with King Hussein of Jordan. Luce rang her in her flat at No. 10 and passed on the message, explaining that there were only twenty-five minutes left.[109] Mrs Thatcher rang the King. He promised

---

* Anthony Parsons (1922–96), educated King's School, Canterbury and Balliol College, Oxford; Ambassador to Iran, 1974–9; UK Permanent Representative to UN, 1979–82; special adviser to the Prime Minister on foreign affairs, 1982–3; knighted, 1975.

† Not everyone in the French diplomatic corps shared Mitterrand's sense of solidarity. In a memo dated 7 April the French Ambassador to the UK, Emmanuel de Margerie, described Mrs Thatcher as 'Victorian, imperialist and obstinate', with a 'tendency to get carried away by combative instincts' (*Document*, BBC Radio 4, 5 Mar. 2012).

‡ Jacques Attali, who acted as interpreter for the conversation, recalled that whenever Mrs Thatcher was reminded of the call in later times, tears would come into her eyes (interview with Jacques Attali).

to order Jordan to vote for the resolution, saying, 'I hope I will be in time.'
'You're a very kind and wonderful ally,' Mrs Thatcher replied.[110] Security
Council Resolution 502 was duly carried, with the Soviet Union, despite
Argentina pleading with it to use its veto, abstaining. It called for the
'immediate withdrawal' of Argentine forces and instructed the governments to seek 'a diplomatic solution to their differences and to respect fully
the purposes and principles of the Charter of the United Nations'. These
purposes and principles included Article 51, the right of self-defence, on
which Britain could now rest to justify armed response. It was a triumph
which, Parsons knew from the first, could not be improved upon, and Mrs
Thatcher brandished it from then onwards, to the greatest effect. Parsons
was, in a sense, the Henry Leach of diplomacy, hurrying forward with a
clear solution while others dithered. As in the case of Leach, Mrs Thatcher
loved him for it.

At Easter 1983, roughly a year after the crisis began, Mrs Thatcher composed her own private account, writing with the 'War Cabinet' minutes
beside her, of the Falklands War. She kept this so secret that it seems that
no one, not even her private secretaries, knew about it at the time. Her
motive, she said many years later, was the thought 'I'll damn well write
some of this down for posterity,'[111] and it was probably prompted in her
mind by the first anniversary of the war.* Mrs Thatcher gave her private
record the dry title 'Notes on the Emergency Cabinet Committee'. Rather
than starting 'at the beginning', she began with the question of how to fight
the war in Whitehall. Following legal advice, which showed that a declaration of war would make other countries neutral and thus forbidden to
assist Britain, it was decided early on that no war should formally be
declared. The word 'conflict' was preferred. There was no doubt, however,
that, in practical terms, this was war. The Cabinet, therefore, was much
too large and cumbersome a body to make any but the most important
decisions of principle, and even these would, in effect, be pre-cooked elsewhere. Mrs Thatcher was advised by Frank Cooper, who saw her about it
at lunch on Sunday 4 April,[112] that the trick was to avoid a situation in
which the Chancellor of the Exchequer could pull the plug on proceedings –
as Harold Macmillan, then the Chancellor, had done to Eden over Suez,

---

* She put the manuscript to good use in her memoirs. Most of her autobiography was ghosted,
though with her extensive co-operation and complete approval. The Falklands account, almost
uniquely in the book, is essentially in her own words, which are vivid and often emotional. As
will be seen, however, the published version toned down or omitted some of her private obser-
vations, as well as her frequent emphatic underlinings.

getting himself made prime minister in the process – by cutting off the money or warning of a loss of confidence in the currency. She should replicate the successful arrangements instituted by Winston Churchill during the Second World War. On Tuesday 6 April, Harold Macmillan himself came to see Mrs Thatcher in her room in the Commons. His first question was 'Have they got the [atomic] bomb?' (They hadn't.) His second contribution was: 'You will need a Pug Ismay.'[113] General Sir Hastings Ismay had been Churchill's chief of staff and deputy secretary to the War Cabinet. His job was to make sure that everything was smooth in the conduct of war between generals and politicians. He was known as 'the man with the oil can'. Some attempts were made to find such a person. Lord Carver, the former CDS, was considered, but rejected as being too maverick and left wing.[114] But in the event no such appointment was made, partly because it turned out that the job could be best done by the Chief of the Defence Staff himself, Admiral Sir Terence Lewin, and partly because Mrs Thatcher, unlike Churchill, had no inclination to try to tell the generals how to run a war.*

Knowing whereof he spoke, Macmillan told her that it would be 'fatal' to mix any 'economic committee' for the conduct of the war with the 'campaign committee'.[115] This was not displeasing news to Mrs Thatcher, who had already noticed at Cabinet and OD that Geoffrey Howe was inclined to harp more than she liked on the need for peace. She duly excluded him from the War Cabinet. He always maintained that he accepted this decision happily, but according to his private secretary, John Kerr, 'he *was* upset.'[116] Howe 'sulked', said John Coles.[117]

The bureaucratic solution to the problem was Robert Armstrong's creation of a South Atlantic sub-committee to OD. So OD(SA) (pronounced Odza) became the official name of the War Cabinet. It met daily, usually at 9.30 each morning, sometimes twice in a day, and held a total of sixty-seven meetings before being disbanded on 12 August 1982. It was chaired by the Prime Minister and its members were Whitelaw, Pym, Nott and Cecil Parkinson, who was brought in partly to handle press relations, but also to balance what was feared might prove to be a defeatist axis of Whitelaw and Pym.[118] When she summoned Parkinson to ask him to serve in the War Cabinet, Mrs Thatcher told him that there would be 'no room

---

* Two days later, having called in Michael Palliser to thank him on his retirement, Mrs Thatcher asked him to serve as her 'chief of staff for the Falklands' (interview with Sir Michael Palliser). But his job was not Ismay's. It turned out to be more a matter of long-term planning of Falklands issues, and besides, Mrs Thatcher, who associated him with Foreign Office 'wetness', did not really listen to his advice.

for fainthearts' in it.[119] The words echoed one of her father's sermons, 'God wants no fainthearts for His ambassadors.' The War Cabinet was serviced by Armstrong and Wade-Gery, and also attended by Lewin, the Chief of the Defence Staff, and by the Attorney-General, Sir Michael Havers. Others frequently present were Antony Acland, Frank Cooper and Michael Palliser, and the Foreign Office legal adviser, Sir Ian Sinclair. From time to time, the other service chiefs, in addition to Lewin, and also Admiral Sir John Fieldhouse, the Commander-in-Chief Fleet, would attend. Of the twenty or so most important people involved in the Falklands War politically, officially or militarily, about three-quarters had served in the armed forces (almost all of them, including all the service chiefs, in the Second World War). The exceptions were Acland, who was too young, Armstrong and Henderson, who had not served for medical reasons, and, most notably, the Prime Minister herself.

It was an important compensation to Mrs Thatcher for her own ignorance that Denis had served in the Second World War. He had loved his time in the army, and he followed military affairs closely ever afterwards, reading widely in the subject. She was to turn to him in the most difficult moments and he, for the course of the Falklands War, sometimes broke his self-imposed general rule and 'offered advice without being asked'.[120] His wife was obviously at a disadvantage in knowing nothing about war. On the few occasions when she made military suggestions to colleagues, they were usually wide of the mark. 'Couldn't we put up a smokescreen?' she suggested one day to the War Cabinet as a remedy for Argentine air attack. 'There were titters round the Cabinet Room,' John Coles recalled.[121] There were also a few 'Churchill moments' when she would suddenly propose something dramatic and impractical like the occupation of Tierra del Fuego.[122] But there was a less obvious sense in which her lack of knowledge helped. It gave her the humility which she was often, in other matters, accused of lacking, and encouraged her to listen to colleagues such as Whitelaw, who had military experience.* It also kept her mind clear for the political task and made her uncomplicatedly anxious to do everything possible for the Task Force. Ministry of Defence officials felt that 'It was clear from Day One that the military would get what they wanted.'[123] Her inexperience may also have given her the optimism necessary to carry

---

* Mrs Thatcher's lack of knowledge in the field meant that she was almost incapable of reading naval charts. Michael Havers, who had served in the RNVR, understood these charts well. He and she would spread them out on the floor and she would firmly point out the Falkland Islands in quite the wrong place. He would then find them for her. (Interview with Philip Havers QC.)

through the task without compromise. According to Philip Goodhart, a defence minister just before the Falklands crisis and himself a former soldier, 'She wouldn't have done it if she'd been a man and if she'd been in the armed forces during the war. Then she'd have been aware how dreadfully wrong everything was likely to go.'[124]

The War Cabinet met for the first time on Wednesday 7 April 1982, once in the morning and once at seven in the evening. It was working with the timetable that the first submarine could be on station near the Falklands by 11 April and the first surface ships by 24 April. There was pressure for it to decide on a Maritime Exclusion Zone (MEZ) round the Falkland Islands within which Britain would have authorized itself to attack all Argentine shipping. This was resisted by Francis Pym lest it prejudice the imminent visit of the US Secretary of State, Al Haig, who had announced his intention of coming to London to see, as an ally, what could be done to secure peace. By Mrs Thatcher's private account, there was a 'long argument' and 'eventually through patient persistence the rest of us managed to overcome Francis' objections. It was a pattern to be repeated many times.'[125] Haig had asked to come that day, but Mrs Thatcher had put him off for twenty-four hours because of a debate in the House of Commons that afternoon, the first setpiece since the drama of the previous Saturday.

The debate was notable for a skilful attack on Mrs Thatcher by her predecessor, Jim Callaghan, who wished to make clear how well he had handled the previous Falklands crisis, contrasting this with her performance. Bitingly, he said: 'we are sending an aircraft carrier that has already been sold to meet cash limits, from a port that is to be closed, and with 500 sailors holding redundancy notices in their pockets,'[126] and he held the Prime Minister personally responsible. When preparing her memoirs, Mrs Thatcher remembered the uncomfortableness of this, describing Callaghan as 'a very nasty, spiteful person'.[127] The debate was Francis Pym's first outing as Foreign Secretary and Mrs Thatcher did not speak in it, to let him make his mark and to allow Nott, who also spoke, the chance to recover ground. In his speech, Nott announced the 200-nautical-mile MEZ, to be imposed from midnight on 11 April, this being the first time that the first submarine would be ready. 'It was worth noting', wrote Mrs Thatcher the following year, 'that at <u>no time</u> during the Falklands operation did we say we would take action <u>until</u> we were in a position to do it . . . I was determined that we should never put ourselves in a position where "bluff could be called". And we never did.'[128] For the first time, the House noticed possible differences between Prime Minister and Foreign Secretary. It was Eric Ogden, a Labour backbencher with close family links to the Falklands, who said, 'I smell a sell-out.' Tony Benn, who positioned himself as the most extreme and prominent opponent of the war, declared: 'The Prime Minister must have an astonishing view of her power if she thinks that she can bring 1,800 hostages out of the Falkland Islands with the British Fleet, operating 8,000 miles from home, when Carter had the humiliation of seeing the inauguration of his successor before the Ayatollah Khomeini would release the hostages.' For his part, the Shadow Foreign Secretary, Denis Healey, started to qualify Labour support for the use of force, warning of the dangers of an opposed landing. It was becoming easier to see how the Opposition would undermine the government as soon as things started to go wrong. In Prime Minister's Questions the following day, David Owen called for an official inquiry into the causes of the Falklands disaster. Mrs Thatcher immediately conceded that such an inquiry should take place.

The biggest immediate problem, however, was America. As by far Britain's most important ally, the United States was essential in securing international backing for the British response. The Americans were also vital logistically, partly because, under the 1956 Bahamas Agreement, they used the British colony of Ascension Island in the middle of the Atlantic as a military base, and Ascension was the only stopping point from which the Task Force could operate effectively. The Americans had the power to deny or supply Britain with the satellite information, intelligence, technology and military hardware which were needed. Active American support was all but a necessity, and active American opposition would certainly be fatal.

Given her friendship with Ronald Reagan, her attitude to the United States in general, and her uncomplicated belief that the injustice of the invasion was obvious to all, Mrs Thatcher had assumed that American support would be wholehearted. 'I think she just felt that this was such an act of naked aggression – unprovoked and unnecessary – that there could not be any question that the Americans would take our view,' recalled Clive Whitmore.[129] As John Coles put it, 'She found it hard to understand how, given the issues, there could be any talk of "balance" from Washington.'[130] In terms of American public opinion, her instinct was immediately proved right: US public support for Britain easily overwhelmed that for Argentina. But in terms of the reaction of the US administration, Mrs Thatcher was quickly disappointed. On the evening of the invasion, Jeane Kirkpatrick,*

---

* Jeane Kirkpatrick (1926–2006), served as Ronald Reagan's foreign policy adviser in his 1980 campaign and later in his Cabinet; first woman to hold the post of US permanent representative to the UN.

the US Ambassador at the United Nations, had kept an appointment for a dinner given in her honour by the Argentine Embassy. The author of the distinction between 'totalitarian states' (bad) and 'authoritarian states' (sometimes tolerable), Mrs Kirkpatrick was the most ardent and articulate believer in the Reagan administration's strategy of getting close to Latin America in order to fight off the Communist threat there. She was furious at Anthony Parsons's quick move to get Security Council Resolution 502 passed, and when she saw that it would be impossible for the United States to veto it or abstain, she pointedly absented herself from the vote, sending her deputy. With Enders, and other Latin American experts at the State Department who were preoccupied with the danger of the Sandinista regime in Nicaragua and related subversion in El Salvador, she was ahead of the pack on a subject of which most of the administration was ignorant. On the other hand, at the Pentagon, whose worldview was built around the importance of the NATO alliance and the confrontation with the Soviet Union in Europe, the main players were firmly pro-British. John Lehman, the Secretary of the Navy, and his boss, Caspar Weinberger, the Defense Secretary, did everything they could for Britain, from the first: 'Weinberger believed very, very strongly in the Anglo-American alliance. It was clear that to him this was the bedrock of how to deal with the Soviets and ensure that the West eventually won the Cold War. He had a very strong sense of the importance of alliances generally, but the relationship really was special. It wasn't just Weinberger who was an anglophile, but John Lehman was an anglophile. He had studied at Cambridge and was the most powerful Secretary of the Navy in decades. He had a direct line to the White House. He was totally, totally committed to helping Britain.'[131] Weinberger also acted in the belief that, if there were a fight, Britain would probably win,* although at first he thought more in terms of a naval blockade than a successful landing. It was often said by British journalists that the Reagan administration, dominated by Californians, took a 'West Coast' view of things, keeping Britain at a greater distance than was traditional. Yet Jeane Kirkpatrick, the least sympathetic to the British of the main figures, was 'East Coast', and the anglophile Weinberger was a Californian, who was extremely close to the President.

As for the State Department, it was divided between its Latin American and European departments. In terms of personal sympathy, Al Haig, the former NATO Supreme Allied Commander in Europe, was pro-British. To a colleague in the European department, he said: 'How can we be

---

* In this view, he disagreed with much of the early advice he received from the Pentagon (interview with Lord Renwick).

neutral? This is our closest ally and territory under their control has just
been invaded.'[132] The pro-British faction further argued that, should Mrs
Thatcher not prevail, her government would fall and US plans to deploy
INF missiles on British soil would be in jeopardy. On the other hand, Haig
was conscious of the danger to the United States' position in Latin America, and he liked the idea that he could be an 'honest broker' between the
two countries. A further complication was Haig's mercurial and somewhat self-aggrandizing personality. Since his appointment as secretary of
State he had been regarded with disfavour by many in the White House,
particularly after his clumsy attempt to take charge after the shooting of
President Reagan the year before. According to Bud McFarlane, 'There
were suspicions among the senior White House staff of Secretary Haig's
actions being motivated in part by his political ambitions or perceived
ambitions that weren't uniquely relevant to the Falklands.'[133]

In the middle of all of this, President Reagan hesitated. Questioned by
reporters on Monday 5 April, he said: 'It's a very difficult situation for the
United States, because we're friends with both of the countries engaged in
this dispute, and we stand ready to do anything we can to help them. And
what we hope for and would like to help in doing is have a peaceful resolution of this with no forceful action or no bloodshed.'[134] At Cabinet the
following day, Mrs Thatcher characterized Reagan's remarks as 'unhelpful'
and contrasted them with the support of President Mitterrand.[135] Nicko
Henderson cabled London two days later, speaking of the 'habitual degree
of incoherence which characterises the US administration'.[136] On 7 April
the President attended a meeting of the National Security Planning Group,
chaired by his National Security Advisor, Judge William Clark. All the
principals, including Haig, Weinberger and Jeane Kirkpatrick, were present. According to Jim Rentschler, who took minutes during the meeting,
Haig declared that the US had a fortnight to work out a diplomatic solution, and felt he could do so. He proposed to go first to London to 'find
out what the British bottom line is' and then do the same with Argentina:
'I'll take along [General] Dick Walters.* He'll talk to some of those generals
down there in their native Spanish and scare the hell out of them.'[137]
According to Roger Fontaine, of the NSC staff, Haig declared, 'There will
not be a war in the South Atlantic.'[138] 'Then [as Rentschler recalls it] the
President came into the discussion. He said, "It seems to me that we have
an opportunity to do some good here. The main thing we have to do is to

---

* Vernon Anthony 'Dick' Walters (1917–2002), lieutenant general, US Army; Deputy Director,
CIA, 1972–6; Roving US Ambassador for Special Missions, 1981–5; US Permanent Representative to UN, 1985–9; US Ambassador to Germany, 1989–91.

get these two brawlers out of the bar room." [139] Supported by Weinberger, the President authorized Haig to try his mission. The President, dressed in blue blazer and polo shirt and about to take off for his Easter holiday in Barbados, felt he had made his decision, but then Jeane Kirkpatrick cut in: 'I hope you are determined, Mr President, to really keep our neutrality in this and not be seen to be favouring the British.' [140] This provoked an impassioned intervention from Bobby Ray Inman, the Deputy Director of the CIA. America had to stick with 'the links of language, law, culture, mother country', insisted Inman in his Southern drawl, not to mention 'the extremely serious, unparalleled co-operation we have with them [the British] in every military and intelligence chapter that's of interest to us'. If they let the Argentines get away with their aggression, he went on, they would believe they could get away with developing nuclear weapons themselves. [141] At this point, Reagan was visibly eager to go on holiday, and people were getting up to leave: 'Reagan then looked at Kirkpatrick and said, "Look, I would love to stay friends with Argentina, but I think our first loyalty, our first order of business if worst comes to worst, is to side with the Brits."' [142] It was with this mandate to seek a deal, and this understanding that, if no deal could be reached, the United States would have to back Britain, that Haig set off for London.

Before Haig reached London, Mrs Thatcher wrote, 'we made it clear [in public] that he was coming as a friend and not as a mediator,' [143] but this was not how Haig saw matters, and indeed it was not long before Foreign Office documents started to refer, unselfconsciously, to the Secretary of State's 'mediation'. The US Embassy in London had reported that 'Tory moderates and the Foreign Office are concerned that Prime Minister Thatcher has been listening largely to the Ministry of Defense, especially senior naval officers, and may not adequately be considering non-military options.' [144] Haig saw it as his job to ensure that such options were firmly on the table. He had already told Henderson, before leaving Washington, that there should be a 'mixed administration' to run the Falkland Islands. He suggested that an international commission to get Argentina out of the Falklands should be set up by the Organization of American States (OAS). Henderson objected immediately. The idea, he said, was 'totally deplorable'. [145] Haig protested that Galtieri could not survive if Argentina were to leave the Falklands with nothing. Henderson replied that 'It was not our purpose to help Galtieri survive.' [146] He emphasized the huge strength of British feeling on the subject, comparing it to American feeling about the fifty-two US hostages in Iran during the Carter presidency.

Arriving in London on Thursday 8 April, Haig was met at the airport by Edward Streator, the Chargé d'Affaires at the US Embassy in London.* Haig told Streator that, while ultimately the US would back Britain over the Falklands, now was the time for a display of even-handedness in the interests of fruitful negotiations. Streator warned that the Prime Minister was in no mood for compromise. 'If you think you can sway her you're dead wrong,' he told Haig.[147] Undeterred, Haig and an entourage that included General Walters and Enders, met Mrs Thatcher at 10 Downing Street later that afternoon.

Mrs Thatcher fielded Pym, Nott, Lewin and officials. Although Haig was friendly and polite, and Mrs Thatcher tried to be the same, the encounters were blunt. Jim Rentschler, who accompanied Haig, set the scene: 'And here's Maggie, appearing in a flower-decorated salon adjoining the small dining room ... La Thatcher is really quite fetching in a dark velvet two-piece ensemble with gros-grain piping and a soft hairdo that heightens her blond English coloring. "Listen, I want to show you guys something very appropriate considering the subject on our minds!" – and she pointedly leads us to a pair of recently hung oil portraits, one of Nelson and the other of Wellington!'[148] In conversation before dinner, Mrs Thatcher told Haig that she had been 'rather disturbed' by Reagan's public proclamation of friendship with both countries. 'Mr Haig said that the Prime Minister would well know where the President really stood' but he 'had to be cautious' about 'profile'.[149] Haig tried to show Mrs Thatcher some of the problems which might lie ahead, including military difficulties and the possibility that US public opinion, at that moment very pro-British, might swing the other way. He wanted a means of getting the Argentines off the islands without total loss of face: it was 'important to avoid a priori judgments about sovereignty'. Couldn't there be some sort of interim administration, perhaps involving the Canadians? But Mrs Thatcher would not accept that Argentina could gain anything by force that it could not have got by proper negotiation. Conflict was inevitable, said Haig, if Britain insisted on this. 'The implication of this', said Mrs Thatcher, 'was that the Russians could move into Berlin.'[150] She was determined not to lose sight of what she saw as the large principles at stake. Rentschler recorded the scene at dinner later:

> High color is in her cheeks, a note of rising indignation in her voice, she leans across the polished table and flatly rejects what she calls the 'wooliness' of our second-stage formulation, conceived in our view as a traditional face-

---

* The Ambassador, John Louis, was on leave in Florida when the invasion took place and was initially advised by the Embassy that he need not return. This changed with the onset of Haig's shuttle, but Louis was unable to reach London until Haig had already left.

saving ploy for Galtieri: 'I am pledged . . . to restore British administration. I did not dispatch a fleet to install some nebulous arrangement which would have no authority whatsoever. Interim authority! – to do *what*? I beg you, I beg you to remember that in 1938 Neville Chamberlain sat at this same table discussing an arrangement which sounds very much like the one you are asking me to accept; and were I to do so, I would be censured in the House of Commons – and properly so! We in Britain simply refuse to reward aggression – that is the lesson we have learned from 1938.'[151]

Poor Haig was rather battered. His advocacy of 'certain constructive ambiguities' did not find favour, but he did maintain his position about the need for an interim administration. He also picked up an important impression: 'When I got to London I learnt something that surprised me. She didn't have a unified Cabinet. The two guys that were totally unquestionably behind her were Terry Lewin and John Nott. The rest were not behind her. Poor old Pym. Dick Walters was sitting next to me and I said: "He's not long for this world."'[152] At one point Pym urged Mrs Thatcher to hear Haig out: 'The Good Lord did not put me on this planet so that I could allow British citizens to be placed under the heel of Argentine dictators,' she said, glaring at Pym.[153] But for all her bluster, Haig detected a deeper truth: 'I then realized that Mrs Thatcher needed this. We – the US and Britain – needed it, to be perceived to be trying to get a peaceful solution.'[154] Despite her irritation with Haig, Mrs Thatcher did not really dissent from this last point: 'She knew in her heart of hearts that one had to be seen as trying to arrive at a diplomatic outcome. This was necessary for the management of our relations with other countries – including the Americans . . . It was necessary too for the management of the government's position vis-à-vis the British public.'[155] As was often her way, Mrs Thatcher secretly registered the need for certain concessions while arguing flat out against them in conversation. On 11 April she was presented with the draft 'line to take' for government spokesmen. It said, 'There can be no negotiation about the future status of the Falkland Islands until the Argentine forces have withdrawn and British administration has been restored.' Despite all her toughness with Haig, she took her pen to the draft and crossed out 'and British administration has been restored'.[156]

On leaving London for Buenos Aires, Haig cabled to Reagan: 'The Prime Minister has the bit in her teeth, owing to the politics of a unified nation and an angry parliament, as well as her own convictions about the principles at stake. She is clearly prepared to use force, though she admits a preference for a diplomatic solution. She is rigid in her insistence on a return to the status quo ante, and indeed seemingly determined that any solution involve some retribution.'[157] Although he stated in his memoirs that he was not trying to urge any 'compromise of principle' upon Mrs Thatcher,[158] Haig thought somewhat differently at the time. The talking points for his meeting with Galtieri in Buenos Aires had Haig reviewing Mrs Thatcher's insistence that Argentina withdraw its forces before any negotiations began. 'I told her I was sure you could not accept this,' Haig's points continued, 'and frankly, I don't believe you should.'[159] He told Reagan: 'If the Argentines give me something to work with, I plan to return to London over the weekend. It may then be necessary for me to ask you to apply unusual pressure on Thatcher. If the Argentines offer very little, I would plan to return and confer with you. In this case, it may be necessary to apply even greater pressure on the British if we are to head off hostilities.'[160] As was often the case with Haig, however, his line was not entirely clear.* In a second cable to the President on the same day, he first declared that Mrs Thatcher's principle that aggression should not pay was vital for the US as well as for Britain: 'it is virtually as important to us that she have that success, for the principle at stake is central to your vision of international order, in addition to being in our strategic interests.' But he added that 'The consequences of hostilities would be devastating. Our interests through Latin America would be damaged, and the Soviets might even establish a foothold in the southern cone.' So Mrs Thatcher must get her way, and yet fighting must be avoided at all costs: it did not reflect reality: 'Just as Mrs Thatcher must be able to show that Galtieri got nothing for his use of force, he must be able to show that she got nothing.'[161]

Reagan himself was ambivalent. On the one hand, his instinctive sympathy with Mrs Thatcher was genuine. He was very anxious that her government should not fall, a concern that had been stoked by Rupert Murdoch, among others. Murdoch had earlier asked Vice-President Bush to warn Reagan that 'anything less than Argentina's pulling out of the Falklands will cost Mrs Thatcher her job', adding that he was 'very worried as to what will follow should Margaret Thatcher fall'. Bush reassured Murdoch that 'all concerned here would not want to see the fall of the Thatcher government.'[162] According to Judge Clark, for Reagan 'there was no question as to where the blade would have to lie,' and, from early on, the President authorized the trusted Weinberger 'to give smart weapons

---

* Brian Fall, Pym's private secretary, had experience in taking notes of what Haig had said at meetings, and recalled that his words had often seemed 'completely meaningless' (interview with Sir Brian Fall).

out the back door' to Britain.[163] But although he was consistent with his line of seeking a peaceful solution while in the end favouring Mrs Thatcher, Reagan was detached, almost cynical, in his approach. On 16 April the journalist Jack Anderson published the illicit tape of a call the President had made to Haig while the latter was flying to Buenos Aires. In it, Reagan asked about a possible British attack: 'That submarine of theirs, do you think it's apt to go ahead with retribution and sink anything within the 200 miles, and would that be enough to vindicate them?'[164] This report, which Mrs Thatcher was informed by Nicko Henderson was authentic, distressed her. When she came to write her memoirs, she decided not to mention it because of the sour taste it left:[165] she wanted to give a more positive account of her relations with Reagan.

Fortunately for Mrs Thatcher, the Haig party had a miserable time in Buenos Aires. Their treatment contrasted sharply with their experiences in London: 'The Argentinians completely misjudged how to handle the US delegation,' recalled Whitmore. 'They did not even give them decent office accommodation nor let them put in all the communications they needed. They even failed to supply them adequately with food, drink etc. . . . Small things, but at a time of intense activity, it's the type of thing that actually hits home. So they came back. It is fair to say that Haig's attitude had softened considerably. They were pretty fed up with the Argentinians. There was a clear leaning to us, more sympathetic.'[166] Haig experienced the greatest difficulty in persuading the junta that they should take the Task Force seriously and threatened to call off the negotiations. In the end, however, he cabled President Reagan that, after 'nearly twelve hours of gruelling and emotion-filled talks' with Galtieri and the Foreign Minister, Nicanor Costa Méndez, he had got from them 'a formula that would involve transitional US–UK–Argentine tripartite supervision of local administration, and we have blurred the question of whether the negotiations would result in Argentine sovereignty.'[167] This, he thought, was worth taking to London. As he left Buenos Aires on Easter Sunday, however, Haig was handed a paper by Costa Méndez which effectively retreated from the concessions made. He put this on one side, because Costa Méndez had described it to him as his 'personal thoughts', and continued to London, sending a message in advance that there were 'tentative cracks in the Argentine stone wall' and that the situation 'will need the highest statesmanship of both our governments'.[168]

The Haig team reached London on the morning of 12 April. Although Downing Street was in some disarray because of repainting, Haig and his men were given offices there. They were perched in the room of the patronage secretary responsible for ecclesiastical appointments in the Church of England. On the wall was a map of England divided according to its dioceses. Where Haig might have expected to see charts of the South Atlantic, with places like Southern Thule or Punta Arenas on them, he saw names like 'Bath and Wells' and 'Sodor and Man'. This exerted an odd fascination on Haig, who said to Robert Wade-Gery, 'Tell me about this C of E thing,' and 'went on and on about it'. As a result, the American party were late for their meeting with Mrs Thatcher. 'Robert, why were you so long?' asked Mrs Thatcher. 'If I told you, Prime Minister,' he replied, 'you wouldn't believe me.'[169] Pushing the bewildering world of Anthony Trollope from his mind, Haig gave the Prime Minister his account of what had happened in Buenos Aires: 'The Navy was looking for a fight. The Air Force did not want a war. The Army was somewhere in between.' He said that Galtieri had warned him that Cuba had offered Argentina all possible help 'with the full support of the Soviet Union' and that the Soviets were prepared to sink British vessels. Haig warned Mrs Thatcher that, without a settlement, Argentina might become a 'Soviet outpost'.[170] He then served up what was to be the first of many versions of essentially the same dish. His seven points included mutual withdrawal of troops, the US–UK–Argentine 'commission' and the restoration of 'traditional local administration', but with Argentine representation and no return of the British Governor; a final settlement of the problem would have to be achieved by 31 December that year.

When it discussed these proposals that afternoon, the War Cabinet was not disposed to reject them out of hand. In the early evening, Mrs Thatcher, Haig and their respective teams met to go over the draft from Buenos Aires more carefully. 'It soon became clear', wrote Mrs Thatcher in her private account, 'that we had <u>not</u> got the full story. Galtieri wanted the Task Force to <u>turn back</u> the moment an agreement was signed.'[171] She explained that she 'would not survive in the House of Commons if the Task Force stopped before the Argentine withdrawal had been completed', but she offered a bit more than she mentioned in her later accounts: it might be possible for the Task Force to move more slowly, she conceded.[172] Mrs Thatcher even agreed to drop the word 'interim' when referring to the proposed joint administration, seeing the point of some of the vagueness to which she was constitutionally averse. She accepted that 'it might be worth making big concessions if Argentine withdrawal could be guaranteed.'[173]

That morning's *New York Times*, however, had carried an article based on the 'personal thoughts' that Costa Méndez had pressed into Haig's hand, showing them to be the official Argentine position. In the evening, Haig, who had not previously mentioned these points to Mrs Thatcher, rang her to say that he had now spoken to Costa Méndez and this was indeed the case: his demands were 'absolute'. 'What a sad thing!' she exclaimed.[174] He telephoned her again at 1.20 in the morning after further talk with Costa Méndez. He said that Argentina still insisted absolutely on sovereignty, an unacceptable ultimatum. As she later recalled: 'It seemed as if our previous day [by which she meant earlier the same day] had been wasted – and yet – wasn't this really what we expected of a junta.* The condition for withdrawal was that they keep the spoils of invasion.'[175] She told him that the Argentine back-tracking meant that he could not now return to Buenos Aires, and that he should say so publicly, explaining why.[176]

Al Haig was, Mrs Thatcher said, 'very depressed'.[177] In the Foreign Office too, there was 'a terrible sinking feeling' as the advance towards hostilities began to feel to some like 'an unstoppable process'.[178] As Jim Rentschler noted in his diary, the next morning, 13 April, was perhaps 'the lowest point of the whole project': 'The first part of the day is mired in extreme pessimism; Haig's phone discussion with his Argentine opposite number late last night left very little room for maneuver.'[179] It was at this point that Mrs Thatcher could have pressed home her case that there was nothing left to talk about, and all negotiations should therefore end. She did not do so. Haig told her that he 'could say publicly that he was suspending his own efforts, making it clear that this was due to Argentine intransigence. But if he did so other less helpful people might try to intervene,' Mrs Thatcher later wrote. 'I was keenly aware of that and I also felt that public opinion here required us not to give up on negotiations yet.'[180] Haig agreed to continue his efforts and promptly returned to Washington before taking his latest proposals to Buenos Aires. At Chequers the previous weekend Anthony Parsons had impressed upon Mrs Thatcher how important it was to fill any diplomatic vacuum at the UN which might otherwise be occupied by a growing 'anti-colonial' coalition against Britain, spinning matters out so that the position adopted by Resolution 502 was maintained.†

Mrs Thatcher was also impressed by the level of international support that had accumulated since the Argentine invasion. First, covertly, had come Chile, whose own dispute with Argentina over the Beagle Channel had made it hypersensitive to Argentine aggression. Even before the

---

* As was often the case in her manuscript writings, Mrs Thatcher left out the question mark.
† Parsons liked to relate that Mrs Thatcher, maddened by him setting out his case with the phrases 'On the one hand' and 'On the other hand', said to him, 'Tony, I am so glad I don't belong to your class.' 'Which class is that, Prime Minister?' 'The class that cannot make up its mind.' (Private information.) But in fact she greatly admired his handling of the situation and the telegrams he sent her about it. He became her favourite Foreign Office person.

invasion was complete, Chile had offered Britain the use of its ports. From then on, intelligence and logistical co-operation was constant. By 6 April, it had offered the services of its air force and navy, authorized by the dictator, General Augusto Pinochet.* Most Commonwealth countries, notably the countries of the Old Commonwealth, also fell in quickly behind Britain. New Zealand's Prime Minister, Robert Muldoon, had offered his enthusiastic support on the first Saturday, as had Malcolm Fraser of Australia. Then, after the call from Mitterrand, had come real, though rather more cautious support from Helmut Schmidt and, to Mrs Thatcher's pleased surprise, an EEC vote, on 10 April, to impose a total ban on Argentine imports for four weeks from 17 April. She was conscious that this goodwill should not be presumed upon. At home, she came to understand that continuing the diplomatic process until the Task Force reached its destination was essential. Even though this process was very unlikely to produce a result she could accept, it would serve to placate the 'wetter' members of her party, and disable the Opposition, without enraging her natural supporters. John Nott summed up the role of Haig as it was emerging: he was 'polite, charming, a frightful nuisance, but he filled this great long vacuum'.[181]

The very next day, 14 April, provided an example of just how annoying, from the British point of view, Haig could be. The *Washington Post*, under the front-page headline 'US Aiding British Fleet in Atlantic', reported US satellite and intelligence assistance for Britain and the offer of fuel tanks in Ascension Island. Argentina immediately used this as an excuse for refusing further negotiations, and Haig rang Mrs Thatcher. He said he proposed to put out a statement denying the story and saying that there would be no help to Britain 'beyond the customary patterns of co-operation ... British use of facilities on the UK island of Ascension has been restricted accordingly.' 'Oh, now that's a bit devastating,' said Mrs Thatcher. 'The House of Commons', she went on, would be disappointed that 'the full difference between democracy and dictatorship is not appreciated and that we are both treated the same.'[182] In a later conversation with him the same day, she pointed out that his proposed statement was self-contradictory –

---

* Augusto Pinochet (1915–2006), Commander-in-Chief, Chilean armed forces, 1973; led coup against President Salvador Allende, September 1973; President of Chile, 1974–90; reviled by many for his human rights record, Pinochet was also, however, credited with restoring order and prosperity to his country. In 1988, he inaugurated a gradual restoration of democracy. In 1998, he was detained in London as a result of an attempt by a Spanish judge to have him extradited to face charges for crimes such as torture and murder. Lady Thatcher protested vehemently against his treatment. He was eventually released on grounds of being unfit to stand trial, and returned to Chile, where he died, under house arrest, several years later.

if there was no special co-operation, why was he withdrawing it? She summed up brusquely: 'What I'm saying, Al, is for Pete's sake, get that use of Ascension Island out of your statement, because it's our island and we can't exactly invade our island.' 'Of course not,' said Haig meekly, 'I will take that out.'[183]

Mrs Thatcher herself was only partially aware of how true the story in the *Washington Post* was. Almost from the first day, through the good offices of the Pentagon, the United States had been providing secret assistance to Britain.* Weinberger, confident in the support of his boss, acted at first without telling the President directly. When, days into the crisis, British requests became far more significant he met Reagan privately. The President's response was clear and simple: 'Give Maggie everything she needs to get on with it.'[184] The Americans had cracked Argentine military codes: 'The NSA [National Security Agency] had broken the code for Argentina's military communication. They were able to pass the data to the British in real time, so they got it even before those in the Falklands. It then leaked out that this was happening so the Argentines changed the code. But the NSA broke it again in just twenty-four hours.'[185]† The same co-operation extended to kit. According to Dov Zakheim, the point man on the subject in the Pentagon: 'Weinberger wanted to ensure that Britain had whatever it needed ... He wanted to know what had happened to each request. Had we met it? If not, why not?'[186] In acting thus, without formal authority, Weinberger probably broke the law, but no one was disposed to arraign him for it. Even before Haig's diplomacy had come to an end, US military help for Britain began to move on to a more formal footing. By 19 April, for example, presidential authority had been obtained to provide Britain with six surface-to-air missile launchers and twelve missiles.[187] As a result of his behaviour in the Falklands War, Weinberger was to become one of Mrs Thatcher's lifelong heroes.

On 14 April, Mrs Thatcher exposed the Haig proposals to the full Cabinet. She explained that Haig himself did not know whether his proposals would 'stick' in Buenos Aires. Argentina was holding out for an Argentine governor flying the Argentine flag and negotiations which must end in Argentine sovereignty (this was Mrs Thatcher's interpretation of

---

* The military-to-military relationship between the two countries was so close that, from the beginning of the conflict, US officials would grant many British requests without seeking permission from their superiors. Those closer to the top of the chain of command, on both sides, often failed to realize just how much help the US was providing.

† To Mrs Thatcher's fury, the former Labour minister Ted Rowlands had revealed past British readings of Argentine telegrams to Parliament in the first debate on 3 April.

Costa Méndez's five demands). These things were 'totally unacceptable', she said, according to Robert Armstrong's notes, but 'if we secure withdrawal and restoration of Ex and Leg Co [the Executive and Legislative Councils], a great prize'. 'Absolute sticking-point is paramountcy of wishes of islanders,' she added. In the discussion which followed, Pym and Geoffrey Howe argued that concessions had to be made and that there would be no return to the status quo ante. Nigel Lawson and Lord Hailsham took the opposite view, arguing that the sort of settlement Haig wanted would show that aggression had paid. Mrs Thatcher, for all her bellicosity with Haig, found herself sitting in the middle. 'All they are getting for withdrawal', she said in reply to Hailsham, 'is one-third of a Commission.'[188] At this time, her mind moved constantly back and forth between natural outrage at conceding anything and a reluctant sense of what might be politic. The fact was that the War Cabinet, with her approval, *had* made some concessions which Haig was authorized to use. In Parliament that day, she explained, as frankly as she could, the progress of the Haig mission, and said that Britain was negotiating. She emphasized the importance of the wishes of the islanders, using the word 'paramount'.[189]

On 15 April, Al Haig left Washington and again set off for Buenos Aires. Pessimistic about Argentine attitudes, he cabled the President, warning him that 'we should begin to prepare ourselves for the worst' and inviting him to consider whether Reagan himself should 'push Mrs Thatcher to come forth with a significant concession' or whether the whole mission should be broken off: 'Whether you should, or could, push Mrs Thatcher to this bitter conclusion – that they cannot in any event resist the course of history and that they are now paying the price for previous UK vacillation on the sovereignty question – with all that would mean for her, for our relationship, and our own principles, will require very careful thought.'[190] On that same day, Reagan had a civil but not very substantive telephone conversation with General Galtieri. 'I agree that a war in this hemisphere between two Western nations, both friendly to the United States, is unthinkable,' Reagan told Galtieri, who stressed repeatedly his anxiety at the approach of the British fleet.[191] He then sent Mrs Thatcher a message reporting the Galtieri conversation, neither approving nor disapproving of what the general had said. She replied fiercely the next day that the suggestion (from Galtieri) that the aggressor can be left in possession of his spoils was 'gravely misplaced . . . The fundamental principles for which the free world stands would be shattered.'[192] Reagan rang her the following day, offering some reassurance. As he put it in his diary: 'Al Haig is there [in Buenos

Aires] and as of noon the situation looked hopeless. I called Margaret Thatcher to tell her I'd cabled him to return home if there was no break in the Argentine position.'[193] Mrs Thatcher's version was: 'I said we could go <u>no further</u> and President Reagan <u>agreed</u> that it would not be reasonable to ask us to move further.'[194]*

Haig did, in fact, manage to extract some sort of text from Argentina before he left, but when he was at Buenos Aires airport the same thing happened as on his previous trip. Costa Méndez handed him an envelope going back on the modest concessions made and insisting that recognition of Argentine sovereignty over the islands by 31 December 1982 was a *sine qua non* of all negotiation. In the circumstances, it did not seem worth returning to London. Haig cabled Pym. He did not tell him about the Costa Méndez ambush, but he gave him the Argentine text, and did not try very hard to sell it: 'My own disappoint [sic] with this text prevents me from attempting to influence you in any way . . . Francis, I do not know whether more can be wrung out of the Argentines. It is not clear who is in charge here, as many as 50 people, including corps commanders, may be exercising vetos [sic]. Certianly [sic], I can do no better at this point.'[195] The War Cabinet, realizing Britain could not be blamed, happily and swiftly rejected the text, believing that this long game was now at an end.

There was less agreement, though, about the best way to handle the collapse of the Haig mission. Francis Pym suggested an idea for a new UN Security Council resolution that Britain might put forward itself. Mrs Thatcher was intensely suspicious, fearing that another country would introduce an amendment which would prevent the use of force. She rang Anthony Parsons in New York about it. It was 'utterly appalling', she said, and would show Britain 'washing our hands' of the islanders. 'I took one look at it and said well I suppose this is Foreign Office,' but the Foreign Office had assured her it was Parsons's idea, hence the call. Parsons managed to reassure her that he was very much against a new resolution, but that Britain should be ready with one if necessary to prevent a worse draft coming from the United States and Jeane Kirkpatrick. As they wound up the call on friendly terms, Mrs Thatcher added with a touch of pathos, 'I have no department here and I'm jolly well realising that I need a

* One factor that strengthened Mrs Thatcher's hand in resisting American conciliatory suggestions was that the United States itself was reluctant to guarantee the settlement which it sought. Britain kept asking America to be ready to provide forces to supervise any interim agreement that might be negotiated, but America, fearing the difficulty of getting Congressional approval, would never make a clear commitment.

department. I have no department and therefore I have to rely on third-hand hearsay and I don't like it.'[196]

These words are reminders of the astonishing extent of her isolation during the Falklands War. In all her long-running economic battles with the spending departments and the Wets, she was able to work closely with the Treasury team, but for the Falklands crisis she was not close to any other minister or department. With Carrington gone and Pym replacing him, she had little faith in her Foreign Secretary. She had been shaken by John Nott's performance in the first debate in the Commons and had noticed that he was 'often in a pretty febrile state'.[197] Although she did not regard him as politically hostile, Nott became, according to Clive Whitmore, 'rather suspect in the PM's eyes'.[198] When it came to the progress of the conflict, 'The PM wanted to hear from Terry Lewin, not from him,' admitted Nott's own private secretary, David Omand.[199] Willie Whitelaw, though useful for his political feel and his own experience of war, was not deeply engaged in the running of the crisis. Nor was the other member of the War Cabinet, Cecil Parkinson. He was politically loyal to Mrs Thatcher and performed well on television, but he was the most junior of the five ministers, and his experience of the armed forces was limited to a brief spell of national service in the RAF. Michael Havers, the Attorney-General, with his combination of wartime naval experience, political attitude and important legal advice on matters like Rules of Engagement, was a congenial spirit to the Prime Minister, but he was not a man with his own political standing. Perhaps her closest political companion was Ian Gow. He was passionately loyal, and seized of the romance of the situation.[200] Shortly after the Task Force had sailed, he sent Mrs Thatcher a handwritten letter about the 'loneliness of your task'. There were 'many of us', he said, 'who, whatever the future holds in store, will be forever thankful for having had the privilege of trying to help the finest chief, the most resolute and far sighted leader and the kindest and most considerate friend that any man could hope to serve'.[201] Gow worked tirelessly to secure her position in the House of Commons, and gave her great comfort; but he was not, of course, in any position of command, or of policy-making.

Mrs Thatcher was also served by able private secretaries in Clive Whitmore and John Coles, and turned to Whitmore, who had a Ministry of Defence background, for advice, but she certainly did not run policy through them as she was later to do with Coles's successor, Charles Powell. So, in a crisis that had seemed to come out of nowhere, on a subject about which, she admitted to Whitmore, she knew very little,[202] she was more or less on her own. It was not surprising that she turned not only for expertise but also for moral support to the naval and military commanders. She particularly admired John Fieldhouse, the Commander-in-Chief Fleet, and, above all, Lewin himself. According to John Coles, Lewin 'exuded calm, confidence, experience and a charm to which she was not immune'.[203] 'She had the wisdom to realize that she had a great deal to learn,' said Whitmore,[204] and Lewin was her ideal teacher, both because he was a sailor,* whose service was, until the actual landing on the Falklands, in the lead, and because of his own character. Seeing him every day at the War Cabinet, she came to rely on his judgment more than on anyone else's. The result was that, although Mrs Thatcher had to spend more of her time with diplomatic decisions than with military ones, in her eyes the needs of the armed services came first. The key to success, as Denis advised her, was 'Get the Chiefs, give them clear objectives and then get out of the way.'[205]

Exhausted though he was, Haig did not allow the collapse of his discussions with Argentina to bring the whole business to an end. Indeed, he did not sit back and analyse the situation very clearly. Robin Renwick assessed him thus: 'Haig, whose intentions were honourable, but who had none of Kissinger's intellectual power, had difficulty understanding that he was trying to bridge an unbridgeable gap. Temperamentally hyperactive, he also seemed to be operating under serious personal strain . . . it was disconcerting to find ourselves dealing with a US Secretary of State who, under the strain, had developed facial tics reminiscent of Dr Strangelove.'[206] When he saw Reagan on 20 April, Haig had a new suggestion. Instead of using his good offices any further, he would throw away earlier drafts and come up with his own proposal for presentation to both sides. 'I don't think Margaret Thatcher should be asked to concede any more,' Reagan had written in his diary the day before, but he now assented to Haig's request to revisit the issue.[207] Haig invited Pym to visit him in Washington on 22–23 April for a final round of discussion. Mrs Thatcher had her doubts about Haig even before this suggestion. Speaking on the telephone to Pym from Chequers on 18 April, she said: 'I have an awful suspicion that compromise is going to be everything to him [Haig],'[208] but she did not feel that she could refuse the request. The War Cabinet agreed that Pym should go, bearing counter-proposals to those last offered by Argentina, which Britain had already rejected.

*

* This was chance: the Chief of the Defence Staff is drawn, on a usual but not invariable rotation, from each of the three services. The Falklands War saw the first time when the CDS was definitely above the other service chiefs. Under the old system, the three Chiefs had been equals, though with the CDS primus inter pares, and all would have been represented in war cabinets. The new system simplified matters, though it might have worked badly, causing the RAF and the army to feel left out, if Lewin had not been so good at his job.

While Haig flew back and forth, the Task Force moved steadily onward. Meetings of the War Cabinet concerned themselves more and more with the military reality. On 15 April, at a meeting which took place in the Ministry of Defence, it was given a very full account, by the top brass, of the likely course of the war. There had been suggestions of blockading the Falklands if negotiations failed; now, 'anyone who had harboured such ideas was soon disabused of them.'[209] The politicians were warned of the possible loss of aircraft and the difficulty of maintenance of equipment in stormy seas. The 'window' of two to three weeks in May, when a landing 'without terrible casualties' would be possible, was emphasized. There was also a great need for more equipment and men: 'There was to be no respite at all' – 'The original Task Force seemed big but a veritable Armada was to follow.'[210] Mrs Thatcher recalled the scene when the full situation had been expounded to her political colleagues: 'I looked from the Chiefs of Staff to the committee. It was a lot for them to take and I realised that they were somewhat stunned . . . I remember saying everyone must look confident as they left.'[211]* The following day, the War Cabinet debated whether Britain should bomb enemy aircraft on the Argentine mainland. The OD(SA) minutes record: 'Although there was in reality no intention of attacking the Argentine mainland, there might be some military advantage in the Argentinians being afraid of that.'[212] It was also asked to agree the repossession of South Georgia and the Rules of Engagement (ROE) which would apply. Mrs Thatcher recalled that this was 'the first time any of us had had the awesome responsibility of ensuring that our Armed Forces had the right instructions'.[213] The recapture of South Georgia was not a military necessity, but it was seen as a political one. Mrs Thatcher pushed the idea, against the objections of Fieldhouse, though not of Lewin.[214] It would right the wrong of the first Argentine aggression which had begun the conflict and would show, much earlier than was logistically possible on the Falkland Islands themselves, that Britain really was prepared to land and fight to regain territory. On 19 April the War Cabinet decided that, regardless of the uncertain state of the Haig process, the attack on South Georgia should proceed.

Although this plan for military action was, of course, secret, it was

---

* There is some dispute whether this occasion, which Mrs Thatcher describes in her memoirs and in her private manuscript, took place on the date – 15 April, not 16 April as Freedman has it – she identified. Freedman concludes that she was actually referring to the War Cabinet meeting at Chequers on Sunday 25 April (see Freedman, *The Official History of the Falklands Campaign*, vol. ii: *War and Diplomacy*, p. 206, n. 7), but this does not accord with Mrs Thatcher's memory that the meeting took place at the MOD. Her engagement diary records a 9.30 meeting at the MOD.

decided that Haig should be informed. Nicko Henderson conveyed the information to the Secretary of State and then cabled London in some dismay. Haig had first of all tried to delay the operation until he and Pym and Costa Méndez, who would be in Washington, had met. 'I said', Henderson wrote, '. . . that I thought this was quite out of the question.'[215] After further discussion, Henderson cabled again. Haig had told him that he thought the attack on South Georgia would be seen by Argentina as US–UK collusion, and that he should therefore 'give the Argentine junta advance notice of our intended operation'.[216] Henderson said he had registered 'strong objection' to this, and Haig had backed off, saying, which was hardly better, that instead he would publicly criticize Britain for using force.[217] Henderson told him that this would cause great resentment in Britain. In the House of Commons on the same day, Francis Pym, when answering questions about possible military action against Argentina, said, 'I will exclude it so long as negotiations are in play.'[218] This was a departure from agreed policy, and so Pym was then forced to reappear in the Chamber immediately to correct what he had just said. It was against this uneasy background of rising tension – because of the secret yet imminent plans to attack South Georgia – that Francis Pym flew into Washington.

On the morning of Saturday 24 April, Pym returned blearily to London. In her own account composed the following year, Mrs Thatcher wrote: 'This was one of the most crucial days in the Falklands story and a critical one for me personally.'[219] Pym went straight to see her. He was accompanied by Sir Julian Bullard,* the Deputy Under-Secretary at the Foreign Office whom Mrs Thatcher had passed over for promotion in favour of Antony Acland. Although Pym admitted that he had not got several of the things that Britain wanted, he believed he had a deal he could recommend. Mrs Thatcher thought otherwise: 'The document he brought back was a complete sell-out. It differed infinitesimally from the Buenos Aires text.'[220] It would, she wrote on the master copy of the American draft, create 'Merger [of the Falklands] with Argentina' and, by mentioning only 'due regard for the rights of the islanders' rather than the paramountcy of their wishes, it would have 'signed away all possibility of [their] staying with us'.[221] Mrs Thatcher's analysis was correct. 'Our proposals, in fact, are a camouflaged transfer of sovereignty,' Haig later admitted to his American colleagues.[222] The US records reveal that Pym was well aware of the deficiencies of the

---

* Julian Bullard (1928–2006), educated Rugby and Magdalen College, Oxford; Fellow of All Souls College, Oxford, 1950–57; joined FCO, 1953; Deputy Under-Secretary, 1979–84 (also Political Director, 1982–4); Ambassador to West Germany, 1984–8; knighted, 1982.

draft. At the end of the negotiations he had told Haig starkly that the text they had agreed on 'rewarded Argentine aggression'.[223] Pym appeared resigned to this. Mrs Thatcher was certainly not. She considered that Pym had been weak: 'Haig had obviously played upon the closeness of hostilities . . . He is a powerful persuader and anyone the other side of the table <u>must</u> stand up to him and <u>not give ground</u>.'[224] Haig had 'got at him', she thought, and had threatened him that if we did not agree the text he (Haig) would put his own text to Argentina and 'then we might be on our own.' According to Mrs Thatcher, the conversation ended: 'I repeated to Francis that we could <u>not</u> accept them [Haig's terms]. He said he thought we should accept them. We were at loggerheads.'[225] 'If you wanted to avoid a war,' Pym later recalled, 'that's the price you would have to pay.'[226] Bravely, Bullard said to her: 'I thought the job of diplomacy was to try to bring peace.' To this, Mrs Thatcher made no reply.[227] In her memoirs, she describes what Pym proposed as 'conditional surrender'.[228]

The War Cabinet was due to meet to discuss the Haig–Pym document at 6.15 that night. With typical thoroughness, Mrs Thatcher prepared for the meeting and the expected battle: 'The rest of the day I spent comparing the <u>four texts</u> that we had considered over the whole of the negotiations demonstrating how far our position had deteriorated and how the Falkland Islanders were being betrayed.' She called in Michael Havers for his view, which served 'only to confirm my worst fears'. Despite her objections, 'Francis had put in a paper to the committee [that is, the War Cabinet] recommending <u>acceptance</u> of the Haig terms . . . A former <u>Defence Secretary</u> and present Foreign Secretary of Britain recommended peace at that price. Had it gone through the committee I could not have stayed.' She decided to try to head Pym off before the meeting began: 'Shortly before 6 p.m. people were assembling outside the Cabinet Room. And Francis was trying to get their support. I asked Willie Whitelaw to come and see me [in her study] and told him I could not accept these terms and gave him my reasons. As always, he backed my judgement.'[229] At the meeting, Pym presented his case, but Mrs Thatcher went through the draft 'clause by clause' comparing draft with draft. She got the support of most of those in the room, but there was no need to outvote Pym directly. 'John Nott found the procedural way through . . . His proposal was that we should make no comment on the [latest Haig] draft but tell Haig to put it to the Argentinians.' The War Cabinet recognized this as risky, but considered it 'virtually impossible' that Argentina would agree to withdraw.[230] Once Buenos Aires rejected the Haig proposal, the United States would have to come down on Britain's side. The minutes of the War Cabinet simply record agreement that the view of Argentina on the Haig–Pym proposals should be sought first. They gloss over this crucial, emotional disagreement between Prime Minister and Foreign Secretary, and of course she did not make any resignation threat at the meeting. As Mrs Thatcher put it in her private memoir – in a phrase she expunged when she adapted it for her published autobiography: 'So the crisis passed, the crisis of Britain's honour.'[231]*

Why, exactly, was Mrs Thatcher so beside herself about the text which Francis Pym brought back from Washington? In her memoirs, she makes much of various differences between it and earlier plans – for example, that the provision for British naval forces to stand 200 miles off the Falkland Islands within seven days of signature of the proposed agreement and before more than half the Argentine troops would have left the islands was worse than anything previously proposed. It is true that Pym had failed to get the American security guarantee of the proposed arrangements which the War Cabinet sought. This reinforced Mrs Thatcher's basic fear about most agreements: as Denis Thatcher characterized it, 'Let 'em off the hook and it's going to happen again.'[232] More importantly, the language Pym had accepted on long-term negotiations effectively ruled out a return to the *status quo ante*, while giving the Argentines the opportunity to alter the character of the islands before a final settlement. Mrs Thatcher was bound to be dissatisfied. But she had proved that she understood the need for concessions in the past and – as will be seen – in future negotiations she would be prepared to countenance further concessions just as damaging as those now proposed by Pym. The contents of the Haig–Pym plan do not fully explain the intensity of her reaction, which provides the most blazing passages in her private memoir.

Part of the explanation surely lies in the fact that the agreement was concluded by the Foreign Secretary alone, and abroad. As we have seen, Mrs Thatcher chafed at the lack of a proper Prime Minister's department. She hated not having full information, and she sometimes suspected she was being double-crossed. In general, as had been the case with the negotiations over the EEC budget, she tended to become very nervous when a minister went abroad on his own on an important mission. When Pym, whom, of all her senior ministers, she trusted the least, left the country

---

* It was typical of Mrs Thatcher's caution that, when writing her memoirs, she needed a good deal of persuasion to include an explicit account of this dramatic day. She worried that she might be unfair to Pym, even that she might be libelling him. She was also in a constant state of anxiety about revealing private conversations such as these. (THCR 4/3.)

and started to deal with the – as she saw him – unreliable Haig, all her fears were aroused. Although she would never have said it in so many words, she was frightened that a political rival would return with a 'peace' deal which would ditch her, lose the Falklands and put him in the best position to succeed her. As Brian Fall, Pym's private secretary, judged it, she had a picture in her mind of Pym returning to Britain with a false triumph: 'She didn't want a Munich-like piece of paper to be produced.'[233]

But there was an even stronger reason why Mrs Thatcher was in a state of such high emotion. On Thursday 22 April, while Pym was in Washington, she was presented with 'another matter which had made the decision on the Saturday evening one of very deep feeling'.[234] Lewin and Nott came to see her. British Special Forces had landed on a glacier in South Georgia for reconnaissance: 'There was a cruel wind which blew all the snow from the glacier and there was no way they could dig in and keep warm.'[235] They therefore sent a message to be rescued. Two helicopters came in and, in the appalling weather, crashed. 'We didn't know whether all lives had been lost or not. It was a terrible start to the campaign. Was the weather going to beat our courage and bravery.'[236] When they brought the news, Lewin and Nott did not know whether lives – as many as seventeen were at stake – had been lost. John Coles witnessed the intensity of this experience in Mrs Thatcher's mind. When Nott brought her the news of the crash, she wept. Clive Whitmore said to her quietly, 'There's going to be a lot more of this.'[237] 'My heart was heavy', remembered Mrs Thatcher, 'as I changed to go to a dinner at the Mansion House . . . I wondered how I could conceal my feelings, whether this was an omen and was there worse to come. Was the task that we had set ourselves impossible.' She went on: 'Just as I reached the bottom of the staircase Clive came rushing out of the office.' He told her that a third helicopter had managed to save all the men: 'I went out walking on air. Nothing else in the world mattered – the men <u>were safe</u>.'[238]

Years later, Mrs Thatcher described the day of the South Georgia rescue as 'one of the most terrifying I can remember'.[239] Because it was the first military adventure of the war, it was her first experience of what it was like to send men into situations in which they might die. Her natural, maternal human sympathy and her ardour for British servicemen's welfare made her even more sensitive to this than the average male political leader would have been. She was also acutely conscious of political danger: if the first bold strike, urged on by her, had ended in fiasco and tragedy – as, for a few hours, she feared had happened – how long would public support last? Two days later, with this risk overcome, but the retaking of South Georgia not yet effected, Mrs Thatcher was naturally even less patient than usual with the demands of diplomacy. The idea that the government might nullify the efforts of British troops even as they were going in to recapture a British possession took on a peculiar horror in her mind. She had given instructions that the War Cabinet should not be fully informed of the near-disaster in South Georgia, so while these emotions seethed within her their cause was unknown to Francis Pym.

The next day, Sunday 25 April, the War Cabinet met at Chequers as the attempt to retake South Georgia was in progress. Later in the afternoon, Mrs Thatcher was brought the news from South Georgia. British forces had recaptured the island. At Grytviken, they had spotted the Argentine submarine *Santa Fe*, on the surface of the water, and captured it too. In her memoirs, Mrs Thatcher wrote, 'An audience was arranged with the Queen that evening at Windsor. I was glad to be able personally to give her the news that one of her islands had been recovered.'[240] Her private memoir conveys her joy more strongly: 'I . . . went over to see the Queen at Windsor. It was so wonderful to be able personally to give her the news that one of her islands had been restored to her.'[241] She then returned to Downing Street and worked out how best to release the news of success. 'I felt that John Nott should have the privilege of announcing it so got him along to No. 10.'[242] Prime Minister and Defence Secretary emerged together from the front door and Nott made a statement. He read out the message from the victorious HMS *Antrim*: 'Be pleased to inform Her Majesty that the White Ensign flies alongside the Union Flag in Grytviken South Georgia. God Save The Queen.' The press then tried to get reaction from Nott. Mrs Thatcher intervened: 'Just rejoice at that news and congratulate our forces and the Marines.' Then the reporters turned to her, and one called out: 'Are we going to war with Argentina, Mrs Thatcher?' By this time, she and Nott were turning back towards the front door. 'Rejoice,' she said again,[243] and passed through the door. Her words were later reorganized by myth so that she was quoted as saying 'Rejoice! Rejoice!' and were represented as being triumphalist. In the 1983 general election campaign, Denis Healey referred to this moment and described Mrs Thatcher as 'glorying in slaughter'. In fact, South Georgia had been recaptured without loss of life on either side, and this, Mrs Thatcher considered, was worth rejoicing about. Besides, fortune, which on Thursday had seemed so doubtful, had now favoured the British cause: 'It had indeed been an eventful weekend. One went from near despair to confident reassurance.'[244]

Victory

'I don't think anyone else but you could have done it'

The retaking of South Georgia naturally strengthened Mrs Thatcher's position. She herself had championed this idea, against some military doubts. Now, through courage, skill and a good deal of luck, British forces had prevailed, captured 180 prisoners and shown the world that they meant business. An opinion poll for the *Economist* showed that public satisfaction with the government's handling of the situation had increased from 60 per cent to 76 per cent in two weeks. A Harris poll in the United States published on 28 April 1982 showed that 60 per cent of Americans supported Britain, compared to 18 per cent for Argentina. Nicko Henderson sent John Nott a cheery cable: 'Cap' Weinberger, whom he had just seen, was 'delighted' by South Georgia, and was already thinking about how to help Britain more 'when the talks broke down': 'Weinberger had just breakfasted with two Congressmen who were wearing "I Back Britain" badges.'[1]* The military impetus now became ever harder to stop. The War Cabinet of 26 April, the day after the victory in South Georgia, agreed a Total Exclusion Zone round the Falklands, including aircraft as well as ships, to be announced at the end of the week. The aim was to legitimize all attacks which British forces might wish to carry out in the area and to impose, by another name, a blockade. The TEZ was intended, among other things, to close the airport at Port Stanley.

But military advance also made the handling of negotiations even more delicate. It was at this time that Mrs Thatcher noted 'a feeling of discomfort among our own backbenchers that we might be giving up too much in negotiations'.[2] On *Panorama* that night, she pointed out that the timing of negotiations was tight because 'I have to keep in mind the interests of our

---

* Henderson himself deserved a good deal of the credit for the popularity of the British cause in America. He appeared constantly and successfully on American television. One commentator remarked affectionately that the slightly Bohemian-looking Henderson resembled 'a broken-down old English country house'.

boys.'[3] This controversy about timing had surfaced in the War Cabinet the previous week. John Nott had argued that the Fleet should wait at Ascension Island and not press on to the Falklands until after Pym had returned from his discussions with Haig in Washington. By taking this view, Nott had lost much of his standing with the Chiefs of Staff, which he never fully recovered. Such behaviour led Mrs Thatcher to say: 'He's either pure gold, or pure dross.'[4] Nott later admitted, disarmingly, 'I was completely wrong.'[5] But the argument was not just particular to that moment: it was recurrent. How could negotiations ever succeed if they could be blown out of the water by military engagements? Why, on the other hand, should military needs and servicemen's lives ever be prejudiced by the requirements of diplomacy?

After South Georgia, the Opposition became more inclined to favour negotiations. Picking up on the Prime Minister's statement in Parliament on 26 April that the Haig mission was in trouble, Michael Foot started to make great play with the possible peacemaking intervention of the new United Nations Secretary-General, Javier Pérez de Cuéllar. Foot told her that she should take no further military steps for the time being and that if she did not give a 'proper response' to Pérez de Cuéllar, she would 'inflict a grievous blow to our country's cause'.[6] Mrs Thatcher's leaning was ever more clearly the other way: 'I had to say in the House over and over again that no military steps were being held up because of negotiations. And they never were.'[7] As we shall see, this was not always strictly true,* but it is certainly the case that, as battle approached, Mrs Thatcher saw negotiation more and more as a delaying tactic contrary to Britain's interests, and less as a process with genuine content.

Besides, in her opinion, the recapture of South Georgia gave Britain more negotiating power. On 26 April she cabled Al Haig to suggest a 'simpler approach'.[8] Why not get Argentina to agree to the first two points of Resolution 502 – the cessation of hostilities and immediate withdrawal – and then settle down to discuss the third point – a diplomatic solution? The United States could give a military guarantee, and then, Mrs Thatcher promised, she would halt the advance of the Task Force. There was no chance of this happening. The recapture of South Georgia had, of course, enraged the Argentines. In particular, it had brought down upon the United States the Latin American anger that Haig and others had always feared.

---

* There were also earlier examples of actions not taken because of the pressure of diplomacy. According to Admiral Sir Henry Leach, a request to sink the Argentine carrier, the 25 *de Mayo*, was refused because it would have interfered with the progress of the Haig shuttle (interview with Admiral Sir Henry Leach).

Indeed, in many Latin American countries, irritation with the United States now trumped resentment towards Britain. Argentina suspected collusion between Britain and America over South Georgia and cancelled the planned meeting between Costa Méndez and Haig. When Haig addressed the Organization of American States in Washington on 27 April, he was icily received.* This meant that he did not fly to Buenos Aires as planned, which was probably lucky from the British point of view. He finally presented his proposals to Argentina via the US Ambassador on the morning of 27 April, demanding a definitive answer by midnight, Buenos Aires time. This was not forthcoming. Nor was there an answer the following day. The British government now became extremely nervous. Even Francis Pym, who wanted a settlement, warned Haig, via a cable to Henderson, that if the Argentines accepted, 'the political situation here will be extremely difficult to handle and we will need time . . .'[9] When the full Cabinet met on the morning of 29 April, Haig was still permitting Argentine delay. The mood of the Cabinet was very unhappy. Pym told colleagues: 'It is disturbing that his [Haig's] resolution to come off the fence on our side seems to be ambivalent.'[10] Without an American 'tilt' or an Argentine answer, would Britain be forced to state its unfavourable view of the document itself? Havers warned that paragraph 7 of the Haig document contained 'deadly words' which removed the Falklands' status as British self-governing territories. Lord Hailsham relayed some gossip: 'Lady Avon [the widow of Anthony Eden, Prime Minister during the Suez crisis] said that [Henry] Kissinger said to her that British were not aware of danger of Socialist Govt in Arg.' Hailsham argued that 'US have to understand that they are in danger of undermining US–UK relationship . . . this has demonstrated that they are playing along just as they did at Suez.' Nott urged the Cabinet not to reject the proposals but to continue, as he had suggested before, to leave the ball in Argentina's court – it would reject them. The Cabinet agreed that the Prime Minister, without formally or publicly rejecting the proposals, should tell the President that they were unacceptable, and that Argentina's failure to reply by the deadline meant that it had, in effect, rejected them.

Mrs Thatcher wrote to Reagan accordingly. She also reminded the President of his administration's promise of public support for Britain and went on: 'I cannot conceal from you how deeply let down I and my colleagues

* For Britain, however, the OAS meeting was not all bad news. Only two countries, Nicaragua and Guatemala, supported the Argentine invasion of the Falklands, and General Pinochet ordered Chile to abstain on any motion because of 'a conviction that Galtieri's days are numbered'. (John Heath, British Ambassador, telegram to Foreign Office from Santiago, 28 Apr. 1982, Prime Minister's Papers, Argentina: Position of the Falkland Islands; document consulted in the Cabinet Office.)

would feel if under these circumstances the US were not now to give us its full support . . . the US and Britain should be seen to be unequivocally on the same side, staunchly upholding those values on which the Western way of life depends.'[11]

In the US administration there was by now broad agreement that the Haig process had to end. There was also overwhelming support for Britain in the Senate, which, on the same day, passed by 79 votes to 1 (the one being Jesse Helms) a resolution calling for the implementation of Resolution 502 'to achieve full withdrawal of Argentine forces from the Falkland Islands'. President Reagan knew how opinion stood, and was worried about growing hostility to the United States in Britain, particularly as he was due to pay an official visit there in June. It was time to keep his promise to Britain. Before replying to Mrs Thatcher's letter, he at last received the Argentine rejection, predicted by Nott, of the Haig terms. He wrote to Mrs Thatcher to tell her this, and said:

> I am sure you agree that it is essential now to make clear to the world that every effort was made to achieve a fair and peaceful solution, and that the Argentine Government was offered a choice between a solution and further hostilities. We will therefore make public a general account of the efforts we have made. While we will describe the US proposal in broad terms, we will not release it because of the difficulty that might cause you. I recognise that while you see fundamental difficulties in the proposal, you have not rejected it. We will leave no doubt that Her Majesty's Government worked with us in good faith and was left with no choice but to proceed with military action based on the right of self-defence.[12]

Mrs Thatcher quotes this passage in her memoirs, and in her manuscript account she wrote: 'The President, Al Haig and we believe Mr Weinberger were magnificent . . . From then on he, Haig and Weinberger couldn't do enough for us.'[13] Neither of her accounts quoted the rest of Reagan's letter: 'it is as important as ever that we preserve the ground for a negotiated solution. While it may be possible forcibly to remove Argentine forces, the future will be fraught with instability, animosity, and insecurity if a mutually acceptable framework for peace is not found. Therefore, we should continue to work for a just peace. For our part, we will make clear that we stand ready to assist the parties toward this end . . .'[14] It was a clear signal that negotiation was not necessarily finished and that American support for Britain did not mean the automatic endorsement of British use of force. This was not a welcome message for Mrs Thatcher, and so she tried to exclude it from her mind at the time and, later, from her memory.

On 30 April, the day after Reagan's letter, the NSC met to consider just how far the US would tilt in Britain's favour and how this would be presented publicly. The discussion was a cautious one. Argentina's intransigence notwithstanding, Haig insisted that 'we do not want to close the door on diplomacy.'[15] The dilemma, as he saw it, was to respond to growing pressure to support Britain, without alienating Argentina altogether. He feared the rise of a left-wing, Peronist regime and was concerned about reprisals against Americans living in Argentina. 'Therefore, the Secretary said, we need to be careful in how we raise our tilt.'[16] Mrs Thatcher 'wants more than we can give', he warned, before adding with misplaced optimism, 'but she does understand the need for a negotiated solution.'[17]*

Reagan said little during the NSC meeting, but approved the cautious tilt proposed. Later that day Haig presented this publicly, announcing *matériel* support for Britain and economic measures against Argentina, such as the suspension of all military exports. Haig did not mention that officials had also been instructed to issue 'a private warning to Argentina that the measures announced do not encompass the full range of economic sanctions which the US has at its disposal and which could be applied depending on circumstances'.[18] US sanctions were considerably less harsh than those imposed on Argentina by the EEC. 'We should recognize that while these actions are necessary elements of our position of support for the UK none of them will have significant material effect on Argentina,' noted an NSC briefing paper.[19] Reagan also went public in support of the tilt, but in doing so used a phrase which hinted at a certain disdain for the whole business: 'we must remember that the aggression was on the part of Argentina', the President told reporters, 'in this dispute over the sovereignty of that little ice-cold bunch of land down there.'[20] He was so concerned not to lose his Latin American friendships that on 2 May he sent a message to many OAS leaders which appeared sympathetic to the Argentine claim to sovereignty over the Falklands and 'its frustration of long years of fruitless negotiations'. He said that 'no American believes that colonisation by any European power is to be accepted in this hemisphere'.[21] This made Mrs Thatcher so angry that when she had the American Ambassador to lunch at Chequers the following weekend, she tore out the relevant section of the telegram she had received on the subject and thrust it into his hand.[22]

Mrs Thatcher was immensely relieved by the Argentine rejection and the consequent American shift. Cecil Parkinson remembered: 'I had a chat

---

* In another example of misplaced optimism Jeane Kirkpatrick predicted that the 'Argentines will find a way to avoid war through a face-saving device in some forum perhaps by the weekend' (National Security Council Minutes, 30 Apr. 1982, NSC 00048, Box 91284, Exec Sec, NSC: NSC Meeting Files, Reagan Library, Simi Valley CA).

with Margaret after the Haig proposals were rejected by Argentina. She said, "I will never, ever, ever take a chance like that again. Those proposals were completely unacceptable to us and if the Argentinians had said yes we would have been in one hell of a mess." It was a gamble and it worked.'[23] As it turned out, Mrs Thatcher would take some other, equally big chances in the weeks ahead.

Mrs Thatcher had been planning to spend the weekend which began on 30 April 1982 at Milton Hall, the enormous Fitzwilliam family house on the edge of Peterborough which belonged to Lady Hastings, wife of one of her strongest supporters, Stephen, MP for Mid Bedfordshire. The Falklands crisis prevented her from staying the whole weekend, but she was always punctilious about keeping appointments, and so she still addressed the planned rally in Hastings's constituency, and then stayed the night at Milton. With the Argentine rejection and the American tilt known, Mrs Thatcher felt liberated. Her speech to the huge crowd of supporters ('The largest marquee I have ever seen')[24] was imperial in tone. She invoked her beloved Kipling, recalling an essay she wrote at school to mark his death in 1936. She spoke of 'might, right and majesty'. She praised the British monarchy, and declared, 'We still have the right, and we're not half bad when it comes to the might either.' The Falklands proved that 'the unexpected always happens' and this included the reappearance of 'a fantastic pride of country'. She traced a great tradition back through Churchill, Disraeli and Peel – 'the way the thread of history runs' – and came up with an answer to Dean Acheson's endlessly repeated quotation that Britain had lost an empire and not found a role: 'I believe Britain has now found a role. It is in upholding international law and teaching the nations of the world how to live.'[25] These were large, almost hubristic claims to make,* but they fitted the mood of her audience and her own inner feelings: 'I was given a rousing reception – but <u>more</u> than that. It was a very emotional time – Britain was being tested and the odds of weather and distance were difficult to overcome. And yet no one had any doubt we could and would win through. The responsibilities on one's shoulders were enormous.'[26] Mrs Thatcher knew, as she spoke, that the next military venture was under way. When she wrote of the 'odds of . . . distance', she was thinking in particular of the problems of flying from Ascension Island to the Falklands. The RAF had decided to overcome these by the dangerous procedure of

---

* Perhaps sensing this, General Galtieri broadcast to his nation the following day, speaking of 'the British empire', and, paying an unintended compliment, complaining of 'the unspeakable boldness of the invader'.

mid-air refuelling. On the night of the 30 April, it sent two Vulcan bombers, one of which had to turn back, supported by five mid-air refuellings, to bomb the runway at Port Stanley, the first British attack on the Falkland Islands themselves. The Royal Navy despatched nine Sea Harriers to attack other targets. Argentina also launched a major attack on British ships that day. Mrs Thatcher dined and slept at Milton, her romantic spirit revelling in 'that most beautiful ancestral home'.[27]* At the large formal breakfast the next morning, she was summoned from the table to the telephone. 'Everything all right, Prime Minister?' asked Lady Hastings somewhat tactlessly when she returned.[28] 'The Vulcans had bombed Stanley,' Mrs Thatcher recalled. '. . . I could not tell my hosts.'[29] After breakfast, she drove to Chequers, and in the early afternoon was informed that the Vulcans had returned safely to Ascension. The Sea Harriers, too, came back from their mission intact. In a broadcast which became an emblem both of accurate war reporting and of good news, the BBC's Brian Hanrahan reported: 'I counted them all out and I counted them all back.' As it turned out, the first was the most successful of all the raids that the RAF carried out on the airfield at Port Stanley. Later raids failed to inflict serious damage.† But the knowledge that British aircraft could reach the Falklands and return from them successfully was of immense propaganda and military importance.

During the night of 1 to 2 May, intercepts picked up Argentine naval plans. An intelligence summary was sent to the Task Force: 'it is believed that a major Argentine attack is planned for 2 May. *BELGRANO* is deploying to a position 54.00S 060.00W to attack targets of opportunity S of the Falkland Islands.'[30] The Task Force Commander, Rear Admiral John 'Sandy' Woodward, on board the carrier *Hermes*, was alarmed. He knew that an Argentine group led by Argentina's only aircraft carrier, the *25 de Mayo*, was seeking to attack the British fleet, perhaps in a dawn strike, and he feared that the *Belgrano*, a cruiser, accompanied by destroyers carrying Exocet missiles, supplied by France, was leading a pincer movement to help effect this: 'In exercises the previous year Woodward had shown that it was possible to get a destroyer close enough to a fully prepared American carrier to fire four Exocets. He did not want his own carrier to suffer

---

* Denis, who accompanied his wife to Milton, was less ecstatic. On being shown a painting by Stubbs of leopard cubs, his only comment was: 'Looks like it needs cleaning.' (Conversation with Sir Philip Naylor-Leyland.)

† Mrs Thatcher had been warned by Enoch Powell, whom she saw privately during the conflict, that bombing raids were rarely as successful as reported. She wanted to hear what he had to say and, of course, had no fear that he would take her job. 'You're the only person I can talk to,' she told him. (Interview with Mrs Pam Powell.)

the same fate.'[31] It was a given of the conflict, accepted by all the main British players, that the loss of their two carriers before the assault – perhaps the loss of only one of them – would deprive the Task Force of the necessary air-cover, and so be fatal to the British cause.[32] Nothing, therefore, was more important than to prevent such an attack. Following a War Cabinet decision made on 30 April, the Rules of Engagement had already been changed to allow the Task Force to attack the Argentine carrier even if it was outside the TEZ: the carrier could move 500 miles a day and her aircraft 500 more. Her escorts were carrying Exocets. The danger to the Task Force was considered such that the British were planning to attack the 25 de Mayo as early as possible, under cover of Article 51 of the UN Charter, the article justifying self-defence. To date, however, the carrier had evaded detection. The *Belgrano*, on the other hand, was being successfully shadowed by the submarine *Conqueror*. The problem for Woodward was that the changes made to the ROE for the carrier did not apply to the *Belgrano*. While the cruiser stayed just outside the TEZ, she would remain safe from attack. Frustrated that he could do no more to thwart the impending Argentine pincer movement, Woodward purposely ignored the ROE and, early in the morning of Sunday 2 May, he ordered *Conqueror* to sink the *Belgrano*. Woodward had no authority to do this, and so, as he knew would happen, the order was rescinded at the Joint Headquarters at Northwood. But the effect of his action was to bring the issue immediately before the Chiefs of Staff. As Woodward wished, the Chiefs quickly agreed to ask the War Cabinet to extend the altered ROE to all Argentine ships, submarines and auxiliaries outside the TEZ.

Mrs Thatcher was at Chequers that morning. Lewin and Fieldhouse arrived to see her with this urgent request. The War Cabinet was not due to meet until the afternoon and so Mrs Thatcher quickly assembled all those members of it who had already arrived – including Whitelaw, Nott, Parkinson, Havers and Antony Acland (Francis Pym was in Washington), as well as the two admirals – in the small white drawing room.* Although this was 'a very charged day' because of the dangers that seemed to be accumulating,[33] it was not one fraught with indecision or dispute. Clive Whitmore, who attended the key meeting, remembered a fairly brief discussion in which 'the issues were presented in stark and simple terms.'[34] Mrs Thatcher showed no desire to gainsay her admirals. She thought the intelligence showed 'there was no doubt she [the *Belgrano*] was a threat.'[35]

---

* Henry Leach was present at Chequers but, not being a member of the War Cabinet, was not invited to the meeting, to his irritation. He had to stay in the main drawing room drinking with Carol Thatcher. (Interview with Sir Henry Leach.)

Even the Foreign Office view, as advanced by Acland, was that 'If it hadn't wanted to be sunk, it shouldn't have been there.'[36] There was no disagreement. As always, Mrs Thatcher was very careful about legality. Havers assured her that the extension of the ROE was legal, though he successfully proposed that they should not be extended to auxiliaries and also pointed out that attacks became harder to justify the further away from the TEZ they got.[37] Within twenty minutes or so, matters were settled: the ROE should be extended, with the general purpose of allowing the British fleet the freedom of action in self-defence which the Argentines had given themselves, and the specific and immediate purpose of allowing *Conqueror* to attack the *Belgrano*. As Mrs Thatcher put it in conversation years later, 'You don't wait for them to get to your ships.'[38] At the formal meeting in the afternoon, more information was given about the threat to the Task Force. As Mrs Thatcher remembered it, 'We broke up desperately worried that we hadn't got or found the aircraft carrier again. We believed the navy had been <u>reserved</u> for a major attack on the Task Force.'[39]

That night, *Conqueror* torpedoed the *Belgrano*. At 0811Z (the 'Z' denotes GMT), the *Belgrano* had turned west because the Argentine Commander Allara had concluded that a lack of wind meant that his carrier could not launch Skyhawks against the British. The Argentines had also lost the positions of the British carriers. To protect his ships from submarine attack, Allara considered it safer for them to retreat to shallow water. Woodward guessed that this change of plan was taking place, but was not sure. In any event, no change of course would have affected his intentions, since a ship moving away from him one day could be expected to try to return the next. At 1857Z, *Conqueror* attacked, scoring two hits, and withdrew quickly, evading counter-attacks. About 200 men were killed by one of the two explosions. Another 850 took to the life-rafts. No immediate attempt by Argentine vessels was made to rescue them. In her private memoir, Mrs Thatcher remarked that even though *Conqueror* withdrew, deliberately leaving the Argentine destroyers unmolested,* they were 'slow to pick up survivors'.[40] She was implying that they did not care enough for their own men. This seems unlikely. The probable explanation is that it was not until after midnight that they realized the *Belgrano* had sunk.[41] In total, 321 men of the *Belgrano* died.

---

* The British decision not to attack the Argentine destroyers after hitting the *Belgrano* annoyed Admiral Woodward; 'each of them is likely to return with four Exocet,' he cabled to Fieldhouse. '. . . I request early political recognition that there is a war going on down here.' (Lawrence Freedman, *The Official History of the Falklands Campaign*, 2 vols, Routledge, 2005, vol. ii: *War and Diplomacy*, p. 302.)

'Gotcha' roared the *Sun* headline of the following day, and although this was later used as an example of callousness and jingoism, it did reflect widespread popular reaction. Public opinion was acutely conscious of the danger to the lives of British servicemen and was correspondingly relieved when any threat was removed. At the time the headline was composed, only the successful torpedo strike, rather than the large loss of Argentine life, was known. There was very little popular feeling that this had been an excessive action. It was only the following evening, when John Nott was in the middle of making a statement to the press on the subject, that the news of the sinking, and of the loss of life, came through. In the Commons the next day, Nott said that the *Belgrano* had been close to the Total Exclusion Zone 'and was closing on elements of our Task Force, which was only hours away'.[42] When it emerged that this had been an error, and that the *Belgrano* had actually been moving away from the TEZ, opponents began to suspect a cover-up.

The events surrounding the sinking of the *Belgrano* would later become a cause célèbre, even a 'King Charles's head', among those opposed to war. It was claimed that the ship had been sunk in order to destroy the US–Peruvian 'peace process', but this has been disproved, notably by Freedman:[43] at the time of its decision to allow the sinking of the *Belgrano*, the War Cabinet did not know of the Peruvian proposals. The military effect of the sinking was to prevent the Argentine fleet daring to engage the Task Force or break through the TEZ for the rest of the war. But its immediate political effect was to alter international opinion. Ireland pronounced itself 'appalled' and called for an end to the EEC sanctions against Argentina and a meeting of the UN Security Council to call for a ceasefire. There was highly unfavourable reaction even from more supportive EEC states, including Germany, Holland and France. Argentina immediately assumed (mistakenly) that the British had been able to hit the *Belgrano* because of US satellite intelligence, and so was furious with America. To a world which until then had regarded the Falklands crisis as almost a comic opera, the scale of the loss of life was horrifying. 'We're all trying to bring peace,' Ronald Reagan wrote in his diary, 'but the bleeding has started.'[44] It was the third anniversary of Mrs Thatcher's general election victory.*

---

* In that week's *Spectator*, the political columnist Ferdinand Mount wrote that the sinking of the *Belgrano* made it essential to call a ceasefire. This was a courageous thing for him to say in the circumstances, since he had already accepted an offer to succeed John Hoskyns as head of the No. 10 Policy Unit. Mrs Thatcher raised no protest at Mount's article, and he took up his new job as agreed.

No one reacted with more frenzied activity than Al Haig. On the day that the decision to sink the *Belgrano* was made (but before either man knew about it), he and Pym had met in Washington. Haig had told Pym that he thought the imposition of the TEZ obviated the need for a major assault, and had outlined his latest ideas 'which had originated in a Peruvian initiative'.[45] Pym had told a press conference in Washington that 'there is no other military action at present other than making the zone secure.'[46] Beside her transcript of this, Mrs Thatcher scrawled her wiggly line of disfavour. When the news of the *Belgrano* reached Haig, he pushed his seven proposals even harder, using President Belaúnde of Peru as the link with Argentina and the means of not making the plans look too much like his own. He spoke to Henderson in what the British Ambassador called 'an extremely active frame of mind'.[47] Henderson cabled home: 'He thought there was nothing to stop us sinking the whole Argentine fleet.' Then there would be collapse in Buenos Aires and the alienation of Latin America. The British, Haig said, should propose a ceasefire. 'I told him', wrote Henderson, 'that after waiting three weeks while the Argentines reinforced the islands we were not in a mood to rush to an Armistice just because the Argentines were losing hands down.'[48] In the course of the day, Haig rang Henderson three times, reporting that Belaúnde 'complained bitterly that British action had torpedoed the chances of peace',[49] and urging swift settlement on the basis of his proposals. Haig remained very sensitive in later life about this period: 'There wasn't any pressure from me. At all. You'd better look at Mr Pym there. He was a very active guy. I certainly wasn't putting any pressure on Britain. Margaret knew that.'[50] Mrs Thatcher's memoirs speak differently: 'Once again, Mr Haig was bringing diplomatic pressure to bear.'[51]* In private, she was more caustic: 'The devil! Al Haig!': she resented his talk of 'diplomatic magnanimity'.[52] Magnanimity is something offered by the victors: Britain had not yet won. The divisions within the American administration are well illustrated by the fact that Caspar Weinberger chose 3 May as the moment to make the British an offer so generous as to be actually embarrassing: he proposed to make an aircraft carrier available to the Task Force to provide a mobile runway.[53]† Despite its gratitude, Britain refused.

---

* This gave the blusterous Haig little pause for thought. He believed that everything she wrote about him in her memoirs was wrong: 'I assume that she was just so busy that it was ghostwritten and guided by a couple of turkeys around her.' (Interview with Alexander Haig.)
† US contingency planning for the loan of a carrier had begun earlier at the request of the Royal Navy. With the USS *Iwo Jima* in mind, the Americans proposed to provide a team of contractors and retired US Navy personnel to train the incoming British crew. (Interview with John Lehman.)

In the House of Commons on 4 May, Denis Healey, for the Labour Opposition, became more aggressive in calling for a peace deal. In words not likely to please Mrs Thatcher, Francis Pym replied: 'I agree . . . that in the end, whenever that is, there must be a negotiated settlement. The sooner that it comes, the better it will be.'[54]

Just before 11 o'clock that evening, John Nott had to come to the House. He informed MPs that the Type 42 destroyer HMS *Sheffield* had been hit by an Exocet missile earlier in the day. *Sheffield* was part of an 'Air Defence Screen' to protect the Task Force from Exocet attack, a little more than 50 miles south-east of Port Stanley, so, in taking the hit, she had, in a tragic way, been performing her function. Fires had broken out and spread fast. Eventually, the captain gave the order to abandon ship. Of a crew of 281, it later emerged that twenty had died and twenty-six had been wounded. 'We were indeed shocked at the fierceness of the fire . . . so many suffered such bad burns,' Mrs Thatcher recorded in her private memoir, and she was upset that 'We never learned how best to announce such grievous news.'[55] In this case, the decision was made to tell the world about the loss of *Sheffield* before the next of kin had been informed about casualties. She hated this, but thought it better than keeping people in doubt about which ship had been hit, particularly as Argentina often put out false statements which caused even more alarm uncorrected. The Prime Minister took the news very hard. After Nott's statement in the House, she sat in her Commons room, with Willie Whitelaw, in tears. Whitelaw emerged and said to her detective Barry Strevens, who was guarding the door: 'Don't let anyone in. She wants to be alone.'[56]

The loss of *Sheffield* exposed a gap in attitude between those who had served in the Second World War and the younger generation. The former more readily understood that such things were unavoidable in war. They realized that the effect of such losses would tend to harden British public opinion in support of the Task Force. Younger people, especially in the media, were more shocked and more inclined to think that such a blow would see the whole thing called off. Throughout the crisis, Clive Whitmore had made it his business to remind Mrs Thatcher that she needed to make some sort of private calculation, grim though it was, of how many British deaths the government could sustain. She refused to put a figure on it, but was interested in his answer. He told her a maximum of a thousand.[57] When the news of *Sheffield* broke, Mrs Thatcher understood very well that the public would need all the reassurance that could be offered. Lord Lewin later recalled:

Cecil Parkinson said he would go on lunchtime television to explain that casualties were necessary in war, but Mrs Thatcher said, 'No no, they'll never believe a politician, CDS must do it.' So I was sent out to Northwood on what was ostensibly a routine visit to discuss matters with John Fieldhouse. We emerged from the headquarters to be surrounded by television reporters and I said my little piece. It was the only time during the Falklands that I appeared on TV.[58]

*

The crisis had progressed, noted the CIA, from its 'comic opera stage into the grim business of killing'.[59] This led Washington to plumb new depths of desperation. Mrs Thatcher soon found herself under the greatest American pressure of the entire conflict as the so-called Peruvian Plan came to the fore. 'Will they all now give peace a chance?' wrote Ronald Reagan privately.[60] In his diary Jim Rentschler recorded the perspective from the NSC in graphic terms:

> The stance of these two disputants increasingly resembles that of a couple of staggering streetfighters, spastically-swinging at each other while blinded into fury by the flow of their own blood. Alarmed by the mounting ferocity, my Latin American counterpart Roger Fontaine and I co-author a quick memo for [Judge William] Clark ... 'The sinkings of the *Belgrano* and the *Sheffield* bring the South Atlantic conflict to an alarmingly new and perhaps desperate stage, one which throws into sharper relief the negative strategic factors which the US will increasingly confront as the hostilities persist ...'[61]

The memo proposed that Britain should now 'declare victory on the military level', and the US should launch a new peace initiative via the OAS. 'Now that we have come down on the British side,' the Rentschler–Fontaine memo continued, 'our leverage with Mrs Thatcher is greatly increased; we are a de facto partner in the enterprise and can use that position to push our own interests in ways denied to us in our previous "honest broker" role.'[62]

Haig pushed as hard as he could. He wrote almost desperately to Francis Pym, who had listed British sticking points with the Peruvian Plan that Haig had outlined to him in Washington: 'I must tell you with a candour possible only between closest allies that the ideas you have conveyed can lead only to one outcome: Argentine rejection ...'[63] But, as the US Embassy in London recognized, Pym was not the pivotal player. A cable sent back to Washington on 4 May reported that a 'well-informed FCO source' had told Embassy officials that 'the FCO is more than conscious of the pitfalls of winning military battles and losing political wars, and sensitive as well to a shift in allied opinion in recent days. The problem now, he said, was to convince Thatcher.'[64]

In light of all this, President Reagan was persuaded that it was time for him to intervene personally with Mrs Thatcher. Rather than using the telephone, where her greater grasp of detail tended to put him at a disadvantage, he approved the following letter:

Dear Margaret

The decisions I made last Friday [the tilt] were aimed at putting you in the strongest possible position to achieve a peaceful settlement in line with the basic principles and values to which we are both committed. I believe there is now a chance to realize that aim, and that we must seize it before more lives are lost.

Reiterating that Pym's answers to Haig's 'formulations' would not work with Buenos Aires, Reagan went on:

I urge you to agree to have these ideas proposed by us and Peru as soon as possible, recognizing that it will be difficult to get Peruvian agreement to join us in this initiative and more difficult still to gain Argentine acceptance. This, I am convinced, is now our best hope.

Sincerely,

Ron[65]

Mrs Thatcher summoned an emergency meeting of the full Cabinet, the first such since 2 April, for the morning of 5 May. She circulated the US–Peruvian proposals to colleagues. Pym gave the Cabinet his view that Argentina probably would not accept but it 'would be acceptable to us' if it did. He admitted that there was 'an area of controversy' about the nature of the local administration permitted under the plan: 'I acknowledge it's a fudge.'[66] Ministers then began a long debate. Nigel Lawson feared that, once enmeshed in talks, Britain would find it difficult to break them off and start fighting again. Patrick Jenkin, on the other hand, said that 'what happened yesterday' (the sinking of *Sheffield*) meant that Britain had to offer a ceasefire. Several others disagreed. Keith Joseph said that *Sheffield* should not make the government alter course, and the Chief Whip, Michael Jopling, warned that Conservative MPs would see British efforts to negotiate as a climbdown after the loss of *Sheffield*. Norman Fowler, the Secretary of State for Social Services,* said, 'we are giving up a great deal: e.g. on self-determination,' and Michael Heseltine declared, 'I regard terms

---

* Norman Fowler (1938–), educated King Edward VI School, Chelmsford, and Trinity Hall, Cambridge; Conservative MP for Nottingham South, 1970–74; for Sutton Coldfield, February 1974–2001; Minister of Transport, 1979–81; Secretary of State for Social Services, 1981–7; for Employment, 1987–90; Chairman, Conservative Party, 1992–4; created Baron Fowler, 2001.

in front of us as abandoning the things we set out to achieve.' Willie Whitelaw, on the other hand, argued that the Cabinet should not refuse the proposals because, if it did so, 'We'll lose [the] Americans,' and might lose in the House of Commons. He recommended acceptance, sticking in a few 'unfundamental changes' which would improve Britain's position.

It was the Prime Minister herself who pushed colleagues towards acceptance. She agreed that the Peruvian Plan 'compromises principles', but Britain simply would not be able to get everything it wanted into the plan: 'I fear we can't get wishes of people and self-determination . . . If we can get something different on local administration, exclusion of South Georgia [the government was anxious to establish that the 'dependent territories' such as the reoccupied South Georgia were not necessarily to be covered by the same agreement as the Falkland Islands], guarantee from US, then worth it.' Pym then told Mrs Thatcher that she would not get the 'consultation with the elected representatives of the people' that she wished to insist on. The discussion prompted Jopling to warn of the danger of leaks about a divided Cabinet. No, said Mrs Thatcher, supported by Geoffrey Howe, it was 'not a basically divided Cabinet', and – to counter the undercurrent which most worried her – she added, '*Sheffield* not a fatal moment'.[67] The official minutes of the Cabinet recorded the collective view that acceptance of the plan was required for presentational reasons: 'If Britain were seen to reject [it], she would be severely criticised by international opinion, which was already moving against her.'[68] Far from scuppering the US–Peruvian proposals, the sinking of the *Belgrano* had the opposite effect. Followed by the loss of *Sheffield*, it forced Mrs Thatcher to be seen to accept them.

After Cabinet, the Prime Minister replied to the US President. Unlike Reagan's slightly chilly letter, hers was more personal: 'I am writing to you separately because I think you are the only person who will understand the significance of what I am saying.' She had, she said, always tried 'to stay loyal to the United States'; the friendship between the two countries 'matters very much to the future of the free world'. Argentina, on the other hand, did not respect basic principles. She feared that, under US suggestions, 'we shall find that in the process of negotiation democracy and freedom for the Falklanders will have been compromised.' The settlement proposed 'did not provide unambiguously for the right of self-determination', and Haig had rejected any self-determination provision because Argentina would turn it down. Therefore, 'I have tried to temper Al Haig's latest proposals a little by suggesting that the interim administration must at least consult with the locally elected representatives. It is not too much

to ask – and I do not think you will turn it down.'[69] In short, she was following the Willie Whitelaw recommendation: although complaining as she
did so, she was making only 'unfundamental changes', while acceding to
Reagan's request. In the commentary for the President which he attached
to Mrs Thatcher's reply, Judge Clark wrote: 'In a word, Maggie accepts the
proposal.'[70]

In her memoirs, Mrs Thatcher says that she was 'deeply unhappy about
the US/Peruvian proposals' and implies that Pym was weaker on the subject than she was, 'but we had to make some response.' She makes much
of the modifications to the proposals which the Cabinet agreed and which
she communicated to Reagan. She records that her original letter to Reagan
had to be redrafted because it 'revealed perhaps too much of my frustration'.[71] This is true, but grossly understates the facts. The phrase about
Reagan being 'the only person who will understand the significance of what
I am saying' survived into the final draft, but had more or less lost the
powerful meaning it possessed in the first. That first draft, written in her
own hand, was a personal letter from Margaret to Ron, half begging, half
defiant – a cry of wounded friendship. In it, she bluntly rejected Reagan's
claim that his suggestions were 'faithful to the basic principles we must
protect' – 'alas they are not.' Haig was telling Pym, she said, that Argentina
would not accept the Falklanders' right of self-determination: 'So our principles are no longer what we believe, nor those we were elected to serve,
but what the dictator will accept.' And the proposals for interim administration gave Argentina more power than before it invaded – 'what then is
to stop another invasion to achieve the rest?' 'Before this aggression,' Mrs
Thatcher went on, 'the Falklands were a democratic country, with liberty
and a just law. After the proposed settlement, the one thing they <u>cannot
have</u> is the only way of life they want. Perhaps you will now see why I feel
so deeply about this. That our traditional friendship, to which I still loyally
adhere, should have brought me and those I represent into conflict with
fundamental democratic principles sounds impossible while you are at the
White House and I am at No. 10.'[72] Her message was that Reagan's proposed deal with Argentina betrayed both their common beliefs and their
friendship. If she had sent it, she would have forced the President to choose
one side or the other. In the end, she did not dare.

Mrs Thatcher hints at some of this in her memoirs, but she cannot quite
bring herself to say that she did, though with qualifications, approve the
plan which she so much disliked. She accepted what she had avoided
accepting with Haig's original set of ideas in April, and what, at that time,
she had so excoriated Francis Pym for advocating. In her memoirs, the
actual decision of the Cabinet to accept and the full purport of her letter

to Reagan are glossed over. In her private account, the days from 5 to 12 May are simply not described. This suggests that she had a bad conscience on the subject. After all, she had regarded Pym's attempt to get the April Haig proposals accepted as 'the crisis of Britain's honour'. The 'Peruvian' proposals, by her own admission, would have removed the self-governing and self-determining rights of the Falkland Islanders and removed the islands from British administration. Was this, after British blood had been shed, honourable?

Most of those close to Mrs Thatcher in the process have tended to explain her conduct away. Antony Acland considered that 'Reluctantly, she thought the Peruvian proposals *would* satisfy the wishes of the islanders.'[73] Both John Coles and Clive Whitmore believed that she accepted in perfect confidence that Argentina would refuse: it was 'inconceivable' to her that Argentina would ever accept any plan which made its troops leave the Falklands,[74] but the US–Peruvian plan was something that 'had to be explored' to sustain the presentation of the British case.[75] For Cecil Parkinson, the risk involved in accepting the plan gained no more than her 'glancing attention' because it was so clear that Argentina would reject it.[76] This evidence by people close to the scene needs to be carefully weighed. They are certainly correct when they state that Mrs Thatcher was always highly doubtful that Argentina would ever make a genuine deal, and this made it easier for her to offer apparent concessions. However, it is also clear that she did accept reductions of the rights of the Falklanders and, indeed, of Britain, against which she had always publicly set her face, and that she did so not only out of calculation, but out of desperation. The international sympathy for Britain after the sinking of the *Belgrano* and even of *Sheffield* became dramatically less favourable and the mood at home became more febrile. Above all, the pressure from the United States suddenly increased. The interventions of Haig and, which weighed more strongly with her, of Reagan convinced her that she could no longer rely on their support unless she gave them some concessions. So she conceded. And in her letter to Reagan, she did clearly acknowledge and plan for the possibility of Argentine acceptance. The letter ended: 'Assuming that they [the Haig proposals] are accepted by Argentines, then during the negotiation period that will follow we shall have to fight fiercely for the rights of the Falklanders who have been so loyal to everything in which you and we believe.'[77] Perhaps there was a complicity between Reagan and herself implied in the letter she eventually sent – I will pretend to accept, and you will pretend to accept my acceptance, and will make sure that I am not held to it. That is the implication of her tone, but there is no evidence that she had any assurances from Reagan on any of this. On 6 May, Ingham told her that the press reported a 'Big new diplomatic drive with UK apparently shifting its position over withdrawal as a precondition for ceasefire'.[78] She put her disapproving wiggly line beside this, but it was not an inaccurate picture. The truth is that she was in a tight corner, and gave away much more than she wanted. She may have been tactically correct to do what she did, but she had troubled her own conscience.

As before, it was General Galtieri who got Mrs Thatcher out of her immediate difficulty. It had been reported that Argentina would accept the Haig–Belaúnde ideas, but on the night of Wednesday 5 May Galtieri told Belaúnde that Argentina had rejected the proposals. It would go, instead, to the United Nations, where it believed that world opinion was now turning in its favour. Haig told Henderson that 'they were a gang of bandits down there [in Buenos Aires]'.[79] He said that, after a UN pantomime, the issue would eventually return to America to sort out, so it was important that Britain and the United States remained in close touch about UN tactics. The trouble for Britain, however, was that the US was represented at the UN by the person Henderson referred to as 'the ineffable Kirkpatrick'.[80] Argentina claimed that it had accepted all the suggestions of the UN Secretary-General Javier Pérez de Cuéllar – though this was not the case – and sought a UN motion for ceasefire without withdrawal. Attention now focused on the efforts of Pérez de Cuéllar.

The resourceful Anthony Parsons was ready. As early as 3 May, he had revised his view that the involvement of the Secretary-General was unwelcome to Britain, though it was undoubtedly unwelcome to Haig, who did not want anyone else to get credit for peace-making. Expecting the breakdown of Haig's US–Peruvian initiative, Parsons cabled Pym to say that there would soon be a need to 'fill the diplomatic vacuum'. He proposed to reply to Pérez de Cuéllar's aide-memoire of the previous week, inviting him to 'refine his ideas'.[81] Sure enough, offers of help, mostly unwelcome, poured in after the sinking of the *Belgrano* and then after the Argentine rejection of Haig's seven points. The King of Spain called for a ceasefire and proposed his good offices to the Secretary-General. The President of Mexico suggested to Mrs Thatcher that he set up a meeting between her and General Galtieri. Back at home, Cardinals Hume and Gray, the leaders of the Roman Catholic Church in England and Scotland respectively, sent Mrs Thatcher a letter questioning whether there was any longer a due proportion between ends and means in the Falklands conflict.[82] This caused Mrs Thatcher more anxiety than it might normally have done, because the cardinals were just off to Rome to discuss the proposed visit of Pope John Paul II to Britain, the first by any pope in history, which was planned for the end of the month, but now hung in the balance because of the war. Mrs Thatcher was very keen on the visit, and was dismayed by the potential propaganda effect of its cancellation. The handling of Britain's cause was not becoming any easier. *

As Parsons had correctly calculated, British readiness to deal with Pérez de Cuéllar enabled the Secretary-General to persuade the Irish not to press their case for a ceasefire resolution. Pérez de Cuéllar was 'behaving extremely well', he cabled,[83] by which Parsons meant that the Secretary-General was telling him what Argentina was up to. It was trying to force Britain to break off UN negotiations, so the best response was to spin them out. Possible texts flew back and forth. As she had done before when under stress about complicated negotiations, Mrs Thatcher telephoned Anthony Parsons in New York. 'I feel a little bit remote,' she told him. She sought Parsons's advice about whether she should ask Pérez de Cuéllar, whom she regarded as having 'tremendous integrity', to see her. Referring to the sinking of the *Belgrano*, she felt that 'perhaps ... we did not make the best impression last weekend'; now she wanted to appear as willing as possible. 'I realise', she said, 'that he [Pérez de Cuéllar] would also have to go to Buenos Aires. But in the back of my mind is that he is probably the only person who can sort something out between us. Are you with me?'[84] In other words, she was still contemplating the possibility of a deal with Argentina. Parsons slightly deflected the idea of a meeting, playing the gentle part of confessor or therapist to the Prime Minister. Mrs Thatcher continued: 'In the end you know we might have to go in ... I just feel deeply ... first that our people there were living in self-determination and freedom before this started and one can't hand them over to anything less. But secondly that it is going to be the most awful waste of young life if we really do have to go and take those islands.' In a rather mangled sentence which crammed in her concerns, she asked Parsons to tell Pérez de Cuéllar that 'I will do everything ... to see if we can upholding the rule of international law and the liberty and justice in which I believe passionately for our people to see if we can stop a final battle.'[85] When writing her memoirs ten years later, Mrs Thatcher argued with her assistants that her phrase about the 'awful waste of young life' should be taken out, lest it upset the families of those who had died.[86] But in fact her words indicate that she

---

* One unwelcome solution to the Falklands problem was proposed at this time by Mrs Thatcher's economic adviser, Alan Walters. He sent her a memo suggesting a plebiscite on the islands which would offer £50,000 per head in return for Argentine sovereignty, or continuing British sovereignty and no money. Mrs Thatcher remembered it as 'a rat's way out' (THCR 4/3).

did constantly feel the human concern which her opponents often accused her of lacking. In the end, she backed down, and the words appeared.

On 9 May the Argentine Foreign Minister, Costa Méndez, announced on CBS News that recognizing Argentine sovereignty over the Falklands was not, after all, a precondition of negotiations. This shift would prove short lived: just a week later the Argentines dropped this new language from their position. But, at least for a few days, Argentina appeared to be making the running. In the war of headlines, Britain now risked looking intransigent. As Parsons put it, 'it is rapidly becoming a game of who wrongfoots whom when the negotiations break down.'[87] Mrs Kirkpatrick was keen that President Reagan be made aware of the apparent shift on sovereignty, which she believed was a crucial Argentine concession. Through her contacts with Judge Clark and by asking Pérez de Cuéllar to intervene directly with the President, she pushed for Reagan to call Mrs Thatcher and urge compromise. At the same time, President Figueiredo of Brazil came to Washington and alarmed Reagan by telling him that he thought the British were on the verge of striking mainland Argentina.[88] This combination of pressures persuaded Reagan to telephone Mrs Thatcher.

The call came at a time when Mrs Thatcher was feeling particularly unreceptive. The previous day she had rejected the Foreign Office draft of a proposed message from her to the President seeking the elusive US military guarantee of the Falklands during Argentine withdrawal and interim administration. She had not liked its tone. 'It is not the kind of letter that would appeal to him,' she scribbled on the draft, 'and not the kind of letter I am prepared to write. It is based on the view that I would be prepared to settle for a less than satisfactory agreement. If anything, my views are <u>hardening</u> because I think much of the compromise texts will be totally unacceptable to our people.'[89] She felt vindicated in her tough line by the favourable results of the local elections on 6 May. In his press digest, Bernard Ingham had reported to her the newspaper view: 'Tories seen to have achieved major victory in the local elections – much better than they dared to hope.'[90] By the time she took Reagan's call on Thursday 13 May, Mrs Thatcher had digested a morning's press which was getting more and more anxious that Britain was conceding too much. 'Some "populars" . . . feel there is a smell of Munich in the air,' Ingham told her.[91] The leading article in the *Daily Telegraph* was headed 'A Dangerous Moment'. It attacked the suggestions coming from Pym and the Foreign Office: 'The idea that men went to the bottom of the ocean so that diplomats could go peacefully to their beds would provoke fury.'[92] The House of Commons was uneasy that day, too. Pym had dismayed many by speaking of 'genuine Argentine willingness' to negotiate, and when he said that the British government had an 'open mind' on sovereignty,[93] Enoch Powell, who had seen Mrs Thatcher privately a few days earlier to discuss the war, denounced him. Mrs Thatcher answered Prime Minister's Questions in more robust style. As she remembered it, 'There was a noticeable difference in approach ... between Francis and myself. His weaker line was not liked.'[94]

So Reagan's conciliatory opening lines on the telephone did not placate Mrs Thatcher: 'The President said that he understood that the Prime Minister had been answering questions in Parliament. He thought she might like to hear a friendly voice. The Prime Minister said that Parliament was rather restless.' She said there had now been six peace plans, and she was sick of Argentine game-playing. It was not true that the two sides were now close: there was no agreement about the interim administration or about whether South Georgia should, as Britain insisted, be treated as separate from the Falkland Islands. The President relayed to Mrs Thatcher his conversation with his Brazilian counterpart who, he said, would now talk to Galtieri and then report to him. Reagan would then talk again to Mrs Thatcher. In the meantime, would she 'hold off military action'? Reagan was trying to set up informal backdoor negotiation. Mrs Thatcher would have none of it. She said that Britain would not delay, because time was running out. Reagan replied that he worried that Britain looked to the world like Goliath against the Argentine David. But Britain was 8,000 miles away, Mrs Thatcher exclaimed, and besides: 'The President would not want his people to live under a similar regime.' Reagan then told her, without identifying Jeane Kirkpatrick as his source, that he 'had been under the impression that the Argentines had conceded the main points'. Mrs Thatcher said tartly that this was 'not the case'. Argentine rule was 'too much to ask the Islanders to accept'. 'They were a loyal, true and thrifty people' who wanted to 'live their own lives ... The two greatest democracies must surely protect that wish.' The President replied that he 'could not quarrel with these arguments'.[95] He retired hurt. 'I talked to Margaret,' he recorded in his diary, 'but don't think I persuaded her against further military action.'[96] Mrs Thatcher felt that she knew where to place the blame: 'Mrs Kirkpatrick's behaviour had been very vexing and thoroughly anti-British.'[97]

Mrs Thatcher was very aware of what Admiral Woodward called 'the tyranny of our timetable',[98] the fact that the South Atlantic winter would make action by the Royal Navy impossible by late June. Bearing in mind that the Task Force would be ready to try to land on the Falkland Islands from 16 May, Mrs Thatcher now had to balance these needs against those of anxious world opinion. Parsons represented to her that a British refusal to engage with the UN would lead to uncongenial proposals being tabled in New York. Against her instincts, she was persuaded to try to put together one final compromise negotiating package in a process which would not impede the Task Force but would convince the world of British reasonableness. Partly as a device to delay the British response to Pérez de Cuéllar on the various drafts, Mrs Thatcher recalled Parsons, and also Henderson, for discussions.

On Saturday 15 May, British Special Forces mounted a successful raid on Pebble Island in the Falklands, disabling eleven Argentine aircraft and an ammunition dump. On the next day the War Cabinet met at Chequers, with Parsons and Henderson in attendance. Proceedings went on from 10 in the morning until 4.30 p.m., and verged on the acrimonious. Although she was wholly complicit in the process – working out Britain's final negotiating position for presentation to Argentina on a take-or-leave-it basis – Mrs Thatcher was also resentful of having to go through it at all. She therefore took it out on her colleagues. Nicko Henderson recorded in his diary: 'The problem was that the PM veered the whole time towards being uncompromising, so that the rest of us, and in particular the FCO participants, constantly found themselves under attack for being wet, ready to sell out, unsupportive of British interests, etc.'[99] Parsons, being the diplomat at the UN, bore the brunt of her attacks. His self-confidence and sense of humour, however, won the Prime Minister over: 'He curled his feet under the chair, saying to her "I'm getting out of the way because you're going to kick me."'[100]*

He, Henderson and Mrs Thatcher led the drafting, as the entire party sat round the oblong table in the Great Parlour. The two Foreign Office men were 'absolutely superb at persuading her to have one more try for a settlement because "We've got to look reasonable in the eyes of the world"'.[101] Looking back on the day a year later, Mrs Thatcher did not recall undue friction: the meeting agreed that 'Anthony Parsons should hand over the text as our <u>final</u> negotiating position and ask [Pérez de Cuéllar] to put it to the Argentines. We required an answer by <u>Wednesday</u> evening [19 May].'[102] Wednesday was picked because that would allow just enough time for the expected rejection by Argentina to come before any British landing on the islands – the attack would therefore come after

---

* Parsons was one of very few officials who would stand up to Mrs Thatcher. On one occasion during the conflict the Prime Minister asked Parsons for his view but then interrupted him almost immediately. 'First, you have to shut up,' Parsons responded, 'then you have to listen to me and then you have to give what I say some consideration.' (Unpublished diary of Henry Brandon, 26 Mar. 1983, Box 11, Papers of Henry Brandon, Library of Congress, Washington DC.)

talks had failed and could not be accused of torpedoing them. Francis Pym proposed that, if the Argentines rejected the document, Britain should publish it, to display its moderation: 'The idea was a good one.'[103]

The text agreed several compromises of the British position, or, as Mrs Thatcher preferred to think of it, put forward 'a very reasonable offer'.[104] Although keeping South Georgia and the other dependencies out of the deal in a side-letter, it abandoned the British commitment to resumed British administration of the Falklands proper in favour of a UN administrator supervising a mutual withdrawal. The administrator would then govern in consultation with the representative institutions of the islands, which would include Argentines (even though hardly any Argentines lived on the Falklands). Self-determination was not mentioned, although references were included to Article 73 of the UN Charter which mentions 'developing self-government'. Under the British plan, the UN would conduct the ensuing negotiations about sovereignty which, given Argentine intransigence, were not likely to go Britain's way. When the meeting ended, Parsons felt that so much had been conceded that he needed to be doubly sure that Mrs Thatcher understood what had happened:

> I took the Prime Minister aside . . . Just the two of us. And I said to her . . . 'Look, we've been through this for hours now and we've been through it in such detail that maybe, in examining each tree with such microscopic intensity, we've lost sight of the wood. Do you realize what the whole thing amounts to, in terms of concessions, which take us a long way from our original negotiating position? You, you are content with what I'm taking back to New York?' And she said, 'Yes, I am content. I understand the full implications of it. You go ahead and do your stuff.'[105]

In her own private account, Mrs Thatcher effectively confirmed this version of how she saw the matter: she did not expect (or want) a deal, 'But we thought it possible that the Argentines might accept it. It would after all be very wise for them to do so. The world would then congratulate them on an act of statesmanship and the pressure would be on us to negotiate with them on sovereignty.'[106] The War Cabinet had gone as far as it felt it should, perhaps further.* As Parsons said to Pérez de Cuéllar when he sold him the package the following day, there could be no substantive alteration of the offer because 'The existing draft would already be

---

* It is significant, however, that David Goodall, the official succeeding Robert Wade-Gery as secretary to the War Cabinet, whose first day's work was on 17 May, immediately gathered the impression that 'We did not expect to have to make the concessions we had offered' (interview with Sir David Goodall).

extremely difficult to defend in Parliament.'[107] It certainly did not feel like it to the participants at the time, but the day at Chequers proved a successful, and for the Prime Minister a rare, exercise in compromise and consensus. Mrs Thatcher may have been right when she later wrote: 'I am glad that Chequers played quite a part in the Falklands story. Winston had used it quite a lot during World War II and its atmosphere helped to get us all together. It was a wonderful example of how odds can be overcome with singleness of purpose and total cooperation between the political and military aspects.'[108]

While the British package went back to Pérez de Cuéllar the following day, the War Cabinet had to consider yet another threat to the moral high ground. The onset of full-scale (albeit undeclared) war would, it was said, prevent the Pope's visit to Britain. The idea upset Mrs Thatcher very much indeed: 'After all the eager and detailed preparation of our Roman Catholics and the keen anticipation of many other people to see this good man who was such a courageous leader, I very much wanted the visit to go ahead.'[109] Her solution, derived from what had been reported to her about the attitude of the Vatican, was to take politics out of the visit: 'I suggested that all Cabinet Ministers should refrain from being involved' and that the visit should be purely pastoral. This solution was eventually accepted, and the Pope, as was his custom whenever he arrived in a new country, kissed English soil on 28 May 1982.

Britain's show of willingness certainly helped the diplomacy. The EEC voted to extend its sanctions, though allowing dissenters such as Ireland to opt out. Pérez de Cuéllar professed himself delighted with how far Britain was prepared to move in its final offer, and presented it to Argentina. In the hiatus before the response from Buenos Aires, the War Cabinet met on the morning of 18 May to make the key decision – whether or not to authorize the military repossession of the Falkland Islands. 'It was perhaps the crucial moment,' Mrs Thatcher recalled.[110] 'If this is not authorised,' said her preparatory briefing document, 'part of the narrow window of opportunity will be lost.'[111] She was advised to nail down the positions of each and all of the Chiefs of Staff, and of ministers. It was particularly important to get the clear views of the Chiefs because they had not been present on Friday 14 May when the War Cabinet had been presented by Admiral Fieldhouse with the plan of landing. Besides, only they could speak with authority for their respective services. Unusually for Cabinet or Cabinet committee minutes, therefore, she was urged to record the individual replies. If the casualties turned out to be 'controversially high or if the operation fails', her Cabinet Office briefing advised her, 'no one should be able to argue that the Chiefs were bullied by the politicians into undertaking it against their better judgment, or that they were forced to accept political restrictions of a militarily dangerous nature.'[112] Her briefing also recommended that she get estimates from the Chiefs of the likely number of casualties. She 'got rather ratty' at being asked to do this, since 'they could only guess.'[113]

At the meeting, the Force Commander's plan for landing was recapitulated by Admiral Lewin, and views were invited. There were shades of difference between the Chiefs. Leach, always the most set on battle, said that although there was a significant threat from the air, the troops must get on because of the danger of attrition and because of 'the erosion of her [Britain's] national standing'. Bramall, the Chief of the General Staff, and always the least optimistic of the group, warned that air superiority was 'one of the modern principles of war; and it had not yet been achieved.'[114] He was 'really very worried that it might not work'.[115] However, he endorsed the plan. The anxieties were clear, and common to all present: 'we should be <u>vulnerable on landing</u>, had we <u>enough air cover</u> [no question mark], British ships would be in range and their positions known.'[116] It was agreed that the danger from the air should be fully exposed to the full Cabinet at its meeting two days later. It was also agreed that the purpose of the landing, if it did not produce an immediate Argentine collapse, was not just to sit still, but to achieve the complete repossession of the islands. There would be tremendous pressure for a ceasefire once the troops had landed, and so there would be an urgent need for them to hurry to secure the whole of the Falklands before they could be held hostage to politics and diplomacy. The attack would take place by night, and 'we could stop it until late Thursday.'[117] The precise timing was for the Force Commander.

Mrs Thatcher went to bed at 2 a.m. on the night of 18/19 May and rose at 6.30. The daily Foreign Office 'sitrep' (situation report) produced at 7.30 informed her that 'The differing units of the Task Force have now joined up.' A telegram from Parsons reported that Argentina had in effect rejected the British final offer and that Pérez de Cuéllar accepted this as a fact.* At 8.30, Mrs Thatcher had an appointment with her doctor, John Henderson. She attended the War Cabinet at 9.30, which agreed that she

---

* The negative Argentine reply to the British proposals had reached Parsons late in the evening of 18 May. 'It didn't even address our proposals, it was just a kind of gush of rhetoric,' Parsons later recalled. 'I remember saying to Pérez de Cuéllar that as a result of their response a lot of young men who were alive today, in a few weeks' time were going to be dead, on both sides.' (Interview with Anthony Parsons, *The Downing Street Years* (BBC), 1993.)

should place the British draft before Parliament the following day. Then she appeared on *The Jimmy Young Show* on Radio 2, had drinks with Lord and Lady Carrington, and then lunch with Robert Mugabe, who by this point had become the internationally accepted and apparently respectable President of Zimbabwe. In the afternoon, she made a statement in Parliament about the EEC's vote on farm prices, which had taken advantage of the awkward moment to isolate Britain on the subject. In her room in Parliament, she received the Liberal leader David Steel and David Owen of the SDP to discuss the Falklands situation on Privy Council terms.* She then went back to Downing Street, but returned to Parliament to vote at seven. In the evening she saw Robert Muldoon, the extremely supportive Prime Minister of New Zealand, and gave a large dinner for him and the Duke and Duchess of Kent, at which she spoke.† She then spent five hours preparing her speech for the Commons debate the following day. Mrs Thatcher's PPS, Ian Gow, was interviewed on television that day about her work habits. 'Well,' he said, 'I don't know whether she *needs* less sleep. She certainly *gets* less sleep. But I think it's really a triumph of the spirit over the flesh.'[118]

In the course of Wednesday 19 May, Mrs Thatcher also spoke to Pérez de Cuéllar. Following the earlier Argentine rejection the Secretary-General had rung Galtieri, whom he found to be drunk,[119] but who now expressed a general willingness to continue negotiations. When the Secretary-General reported this to Mrs Thatcher she told him that nothing final would ever be forthcoming from Argentina, and so the process was pointless. Unfortunately, by way of courtesy in thanking Pérez de Cuéllar, Mrs Thatcher allowed herself to say that she would look at any 'totally fresh proposals'.[120] Parsons cabled later in the day: 'the Secretary-General has dropped an extremely embarrassing bombshell.' Over-interpreting Mrs Thatcher's readiness to talk, he had produced a new paper of his own and had even hinted publicly at its existence.[121] Pérez de Cuéllar's intervention, though made in good faith, risked throwing the British government into confusion in the debate in the Commons the following day and wrecking the military timetable.‡

---

* Members of the Privy Council, who are drawn from all parties, are bound by conditions of secrecy when discussing matters 'on Privy Council terms'.

† Bill Deedes, the editor of the *Daily Telegraph*, who was present at the dinner for Muldoon, sat with him and Mrs Thatcher. Muldoon, Deedes noted, told Mrs Thatcher how Charles Haughey, the Irish Prime Minister, had not wanted to vote to end sanctions against Argentina but '"his people" had wanted it.' 'PM's scorn irreproducable [sic],' Deedes commented. (Lord Deedes, diary (unpublished), 19 May 1982.)

‡ In her memoirs, Mrs Thatcher does not mention her unintended part in encouraging Pérez de Cuéllar to try to keep negotiation alive.

Sure enough, Haig told Nicko Henderson that this was a plan Britain could live with. Francis Pym thought the same, and recommended acceptance in order to improve Britain's chances of getting an American guarantee of the islands.[122] But the War Cabinet, meeting on the morning of 20 May, decided that the military operation would go ahead as planned. Notice that Argentina had rejected the British offer would be published at lunchtime, once Parsons had informed Pérez de Cuéllar that, while Britain did not reject the Secretary-General's ideas, it did not want to get into further textual discussions at this stage. The faltering UN effort alarmed Argentina's friends within the US administration, who argued that the President should now call publicly for a ceasefire. 'There is now an immediate and urgent need for a dramatic new effort on the part of the United States in order to prevent huge losses on both sides with grave consequences for the entire free world' read one internal memo, which suggested that Judge Clark personally launch a last-minute peace initiative.[123] Fortunately for Mrs Thatcher, these ideas went nowhere. Meeting after the War Cabinet, the full Cabinet heard from her that Argentina's response to the final British offer had been 'tantamount to total rejection of our proposals',[124] and that the authority for landing had been given two days before. By her own account, she told colleagues that the Secretary-General's proposals were 'sketchy and obscure and we would have been right back at the beginning again ... there could be no question of holding up the military timetable. It would be fatal for our forces.'[125] All agreed that Britain had been strung along enough, and no one jibbed at the idea of landing. Lord Hailsham captured the situation by saying: 'We are where we always expected to be. Now it's military.' Armstrong noted Mrs Thatcher's summing up: 'All agreed. This is the most difficult time we have ever faced. Our job to stick together, and keep up morale. Total confidence in Task Force and every good wish.'[126]

In Parliament that afternoon, Mrs Thatcher set out the British proposals which Argentina had rejected, explaining that, as a consequence of rejection, they were no longer on the table. This had been the seventh set of proposals, she said, and Argentina clearly was not serious about any of them. The Falklands crisis had entered a 'new and even more serious phase'. She played down Pérez de Cuéllar's aide-memoire as merely 'a number of formulations and suggestions'. The tactic of publishing the British proposals paid off. Those who had been arguing for a negotiated settlement were forced to admit that the British suggestions were reasonable, and those who had not wanted Britain to make concessions now felt relieved because they had been rejected by Argentina and removed from the table. Michael Foot pressed Mrs Thatcher to keep negotiating through Pérez de Cuéllar, and the anti-war Tam Dalyell warned of 'a military defeat of the first magnitude', but she had no difficulty in carrying the House. She did not say that a British landing was imminent, but this was understood. She avoided detail. All she would say was that 'Difficult days lie ahead,' but 'our cause is just.'[127]

By the end of the day, having received no response from Argentina to his aide-memoire, Pérez de Cuéllar decided to tell the President of the Security Council that his peace efforts were at an end. Even Jeane Kirkpatrick, looking back, believed that Argentina was to blame: 'I think the fault was almost entirely Argentine from start to finish. I tried to persuade them as they went into the quicksand and as they sunk in it. All they did was sink in it. They dug themselves deeper and deeper.'[128]

On 21 May 1982, British troops began to land at San Carlos Bay.

The location for landing was, in some ways, an odd choice. Although on the main island of East Falkland, San Carlos Bay was rather far – 50 miles – from Port Stanley, which was therefore very hard to reach over the wet and roadless terrain. In the view of some, notably General Bramall,[129] this was a major drawback. But the site was rightly chosen, despite this disadvantage, because of the danger of adverse winds and much higher casualties if a landing near Port Stanley were attempted, and because of the overriding need to prevent Argentine naval attack and minimize Argentine air attack. As well as being too remote for the 10,000 or so Argentine land forces to defend in any numbers, San Carlos Bay was considered to offer the best protection from both these threats. Once within its high surrounding cover, ships could be well protected: submarine attack was very difficult and Exocet attack impossible. Enemy aircraft would have only a very short time to take aim. Nevertheless, as senior officers kept warning one another and ministers, air superiority would not be achieved in advance. Brigadier Julian Thompson, the Commander of the Landing Force, had emphasized early on (and repeated later) that 'the politicians should be quite clear that if we are ordered to land without air and naval superiority, we risk very heavy casualties, possibly even before any landing takes place. Indeed if, for example, *Canberra* [a large, white, civilian vessel adapted as a troopship, carrying more than 1,500 men] is sunk, any landing is out of the question.'[130] There were also the elaborate problems of 'cross-decking' – the transferring of men and equipment from ship to ship in order to enable them to land. 'I suppose I knew', wrote Admiral Woodward, 'that on the morning of 21 May 1982 the Royal Navy would be required to fight its first major action since the end of the Second World War.'[131]

Mrs Thatcher was as clear as Thompson could have wanted about the risk, and in agony about it. As with the recapture of South Georgia, the start of actual operations left her superfluous to requirements and extremely anxious. On the day of the landing, a Friday, she kept a series of engagements in her Finchley constituency. Twelve hundred people and a military band gathered to watch her open an extension of Gersons storage company, and a speech was expected:

> What could I say but that 8,000 miles was really only a heartbeat away – And it <u>was</u> for <u>all</u> our people . . . It was a matter of pride, respect, conviction and <u>being free</u> that meant we must restore the Falklands . . . Somehow I inspected everything, rode on a forklift truck had lunch in an enormous warehouse and then fled to the office to see if there was any news – <u>Not yet</u>. Of course there was more to do than let us know what was happening.[132]

At her constituency office she learnt 'in concealed language' that 'events had happened but no more news . . . Then it was given on <u>TV</u> and the emotion at a reception at Woodhouse School that night was <u>overwhelming</u>. The Union Jack was flying in San Carlos Bay. We had returned to the Falklands. My heart was full but desperately anxious about casualties. We had landed on a hostile coast on a winter's night with a fleet of ships full of men and equipment. Was it possible we had not been detected.'[133] She returned to Downing Street, where cheering crowds had gathered. There John Nott informed her that there had been no casualties on landing, but the situation had grown worse in daylight. HMS *Argonaut* and HMS *Brilliant* had been badly damaged by air attack, and the frigate HMS *Ardent* had been lost, with twenty-two men dead. At that rate of attrition, Woodward calculated, his destroyer and frigate force would have been wiped out in two more days. Fortunately, he also calculated, the Argentine air force could not stand their rate of loss either.[134] At 2025Z hours, Nott issued a statement saying, 'British forces have now established a firm bridgehead on the Falklands.' Five thousand men had landed. It was, wrote Admiral Woodward, 'one of the most successful landings in military history'.[135]

This was true, but the protracted business of unloading gave many more opportunities for Argentina to attack. Mrs Thatcher was in a fever of impotent anxiety. She had very little to do and, on Bernard Ingham's advice, had decided not to make any media appearances until events were clearer. With Thompson's warning in mind, she worried particularly about the fate of the *Canberra*. While the ship was being unloaded, the Prime Minister could hardly bear it: 'You couldn't find me some decisions to take, could you?' she asked Wade-Gery. 'I find all this waiting around very difficult.'[136]

On the Saturday, 22 May, she visited Northwood to see what was going on. This did not please Admiral Fieldhouse, despite his excellent relations with the Prime Minister. 'Keep that woman away,' he said to Wade-Gery. 'I've got a war to fight.'[137] When she was at Northwood, Mrs Thatcher was sufficiently worried by the Argentine air attacks to ask Fieldhouse, 'Can we still win?'[138] In writing her memoirs, she did not want such a strong expression of doubt recorded. Instead, she quoted herself as saying, 'How long can we go on taking this sort of punishment?'[139]

Favoured by clear weather, the brave and skilful Argentine pilots began numerous daring attacks on the British forces, reaching maximum intensity on 24 and 25 May. The Rapier missiles, on which Admiral Woodward had set much store, had been shaken up in transit, and could not, for the most part, be fired. The burden of repelling Argentine air attack fell heavily on the Sea Harriers. The Harriers exploited their manoeuvrability with great skill, and enjoyed the decisive bonus of Sidewinder missiles, supplied, thanks to Weinberger, by the United States.* Without the Sidewinders, Mrs Thatcher wrote, 'we could not have retaken the Falklands.'[140]

Argentina's Independence Day falls on 25 May,† and the Argentine air force chose it to launch their most successful and audacious attacks of the war. The Prime Minister was working in her office in the House of Commons that evening when John Nott came to tell her that the destroyer HMS *Coventry* had been bombed by Argentine aircraft and was sinking. It later turned out that nineteen men had died. Because the details were so uncertain, it was decided not to release the name of the ship until the following day, but the fact that a ship, unnamed, had been hit, was announced that night: 'Whether the decision was right or wrong I do not know – the effect was that <u>every navy</u> family was anxious,' Mrs Thatcher remembered.[141] Later that evening, the duty clerk at No. 10 reported to Mrs Thatcher that the *Atlantic Conveyor*, which was carrying nineteen Harriers and the helicopters intended to transport troops across the Falklands terrain to Port Stanley, had been hit. There was even a false report from Argentina that *Invincible* had been struck. Denis Thatcher walked into the bedroom that

---

* After the official US tilt towards Britain on 30 April, the supply of US arms and *matériel* increased considerably. It included not just the Sidewinders, but also helicopter engines, thousands of tons of airstrip matting, Stinger ground-to-air missiles, assistance in ship repair and much else besides. 'I think the full extent of our assistance has never been fully documented,' recalled Richard Perle. 'There was *matériel* support on a massive scale.' (Interview with Richard Perle.) Deliveries were made both to Ascension Island and to the UK mainland, and the British transported them thence to the South Atlantic.

† In a vain attempt to maintain friendly relations with Argentina, President Reagan sent Galtieri a congratulatory telegram to mark Independence Day. This displeased him, since it seemed hypocritical, and enraged Mrs Thatcher.

night to find his wife sitting on the end of the bed, weeping: 'Oh no, oh no! Another ship! All my young men!' He sat down beside her and said, 'That's what war's like, love. I've been in one. I know.'[142] Early the next morning, Mrs Thatcher was informed that most of the crews of both the stricken vessels had been rescued, that the Harriers – though not the helicopters, eight of which were lost – had earlier been transferred to *Hermes* and *Invincible*, and that the report about the strike against *Invincible* was false, but she went to bed that night not knowing any of these things, and worrying, too, that 'somewhere east of the Falklands was the QEII* carrying 3,500 troops': 'Perhaps this was the worst night of all ... we learned the deep sorrows of war.'[143]

In Mrs Thatcher's mind, deep sorrow only strengthened her resolve to fight. Indeed, she was once again fired up by the idea that Britain should attack Argentine ships within their own waters – on the grounds that they were attacking British ones within theirs – and even launch raids on the Argentine mainland. Although 'visibly uncomfortable at having to disagree with her',[144] the Attorney-General, Michael Havers, told her that this would be contrary to international law, and the idea was not pursued. 'Our submarine commanders', Mrs Thatcher wrote, 'were left prowling up and down the line, very frustrated.'[145]

World opinion reacted adversely to the onset of the land war. From the UN in New York, Anthony Parsons reported that 'The elastic of our support, even from our close friends (with the exception of the Old Commonwealth) is stretching very thin.'[146] As soon as the British had landed on the islands, Pope John Paul II, whose visit to Britain the following week still remained in the balance, sent a message to Britain and to Argentina, beginning 'In deep anguish' and calling for a ceasefire and the 'magnanimous acceptance of reasonable renunciations'.[147] Mrs Thatcher replied the same day, saying that his anguish 'finds immediate echo here in London', but that the conflict was Argentina's fault.[148]† Chancellor Schmidt of Germany started to criticize Britain publicly.‡ On 24 May, Al Haig called in Henderson and Robin Renwick. He was fretting about the opportunities for Soviet and Cuban influence and pushing for 'magnanimity'. But Renwick had been briefed on Haig's line in advance so the two Britons came

---

* In what was a controversial decision at the time, the *Queen Elizabeth II*, the country's largest cruise ship, had been requisitioned to send reinforcements.

† On 27 May, the Vatican finally decided to go ahead with the visit to Britain.

‡ New Zealand, on the other hand, offered the use of its frigate HMNZS *Canterbury*, which was accepted.

prepared. 'Churchill was talking about magnanimity once victory had been achieved,' Henderson told Haig; '... with his [Haig's] military record he surely must understand that we couldn't ask servicemen to risk their lives fighting their way across the islands and then tell them at the moment of victory that they had to stop.'[149] Henderson also deployed a sensitive argument: 'I reminded Haig how often he had assured me that this would not be another Suez. If the US Government now took action which would have the effect of trying to bring our forces to a halt before their mission was accomplished, the charge of another Suez would be raised. How would it be if the Cubans occupied Puerto Rico and we then said that as part of any settlement the Americans must withdraw as well as the Cubans?'[150] These objections did not silence Haig, however. On 25 May, he telegraphed Pym, asking him to persuade the Cabinet to put forward terms for a just and reasonable settlement, and offered, for the first time, a US battalion-sized force (with Brazilian help) to guarantee the integrity of an interim administration on the islands.

Haig's latest ideas included an international peacekeeping force and a contact group of Britain, the United States, Brazil and Argentina. For Francis Pym and the Foreign Office, who still clung to the idea that there could not be 'simply a return to the *status quo ante*',[151] the Haig ideas contained some merit: they also assumed, as Haig did, that Argentina, once thrown off the islands, would go on fighting, or seek some form of revenge. Mrs Thatcher felt compelled to look at the American ideas politely, but, with British troops landed, she was no longer willing to concede anything substantial. According to Robert Armstrong, she was 'absolutely determined to see it through. She was not going to give in to pressure from Washington or anywhere else which implied any dilution or diminution of British sovereignty in the Falklands.'[152] Henderson was worried by her reaction, lest it provoke the Americans, and rang round private secretaries frequently to keep abreast of her mood.[153] On the various pieces of paper which, via Henderson, put forward Haig's proposals, Mrs Thatcher repeatedly scribbled 'No.' He wrote in his diary: 'Mrs T has not yet consigned me to the Tower; but I am told that her voice drops two dangerous decibels when she goes through my telegrams during inner Cabinet meetings. How much lower would it sink in patient but intolerant wrath if I included in my messages all Haig's pleas that she should ... even before we have overcome the Argentinian garrison, show magnanimity.'[154]

On 26 May, Pym informed Haig that with troops on the ground there had been a 'major change in parliamentary and public opinion' in Britain. The ideas he and Haig had discussed previously, of an interim administration or mutual withdrawal, were no longer realistic: 'They were just not political starters now.'[155] Bowing to reality, Haig began to back away from his efforts to force a deal. He realized that Britain was not going to agree to negotiations while hostilities were under way, and that same day he reported as much to the President. 'It would be a major error for us to pressure the British at all at this point,' he wrote to Reagan. 'Given the mood in London, American pressure would be in vain; we should conserve our leverage with Mrs. Thatcher until it can be used to produce results, i.e., when the islands are effectively in British hands.'[156] But not everyone in the US administration was ready to accept an Argentine defeat as a *fait accompli*. Jeane Kirkpatrick, who dismissed the British determination to deliver victory on the battlefield as 'part of the temperament of Mrs Thatcher',[157] kept up her pressure at the UN and with the White House.* Those around President Reagan were also anxious about the effect of the fighting on his forthcoming visit to Britain. The American press started to raise this concern, and Mike Deaver, Reagan's Deputy Chief of Staff, told Henderson that if there was still serious fighting during the visit, 'the banquet might not be televised and the President's ride [on horseback] with the Queen might have to be cancelled.'[158] It would look bad if the President were touring Britain and Europe during a bloodbath: 'The mid-term Congressional elections were coming up. One of the things that Deaver's crowd had been interested in was in showing Ronald Reagan the peacemaker.'[159] Kirkpatrick, with support from Clark and Reagan's staff, urged that the President should call Mrs Thatcher in the name of peace. He did so at 11 p.m. UK time on Monday 31 May.

The President began with flattery to make his point: 'Your impressive military advance could maybe change the diplomatic options . . .',[160] but Mrs Thatcher did not give him much of a chance. She said that British troops were only 'a third of the way' to reconquest. She would not countenance Reagan's Brazilian-based peace plan, or any idea of a premature settlement: 'This is democracy and our island, and the very worst thing for democracy would be if we failed now . . . I didn't lose some of my finest ships and some of my finest lives to leave quietly under a ceasefire.' Reagan was interrupted repeatedly by Mrs Thatcher's flow and found himself reduced to the occasional 'yes', 'Well . . .' or 'Margaret, I . . .'. How would the President feel, she asked, 'supposing Alaska were invaded'? Reagan

---

* For all Haig's earlier calls for magnanimity, Kirkpatrick had always believed that he was far too supportive of the British. His suggestion that the US should ease the pressure on Mrs Thatcher as the fighting intensified infuriated her. *Newsweek* reported that she considered Haig and his aides as '"Brits in American clothes . . . totally insensitive to [Latin] cultures" . . . Kirkpatrick is said to view Haig's support of Britain as a "Boys' Club" vision of gang loyalty – why not just disband the State Department and have the British Foreign Office make our policy?' (*Newsweek*, 7 June 1982.)

suggested that such a situation might not be entirely analogous. 'More or less so', she snapped. 'Ron, I am not handing over . . . I'm not handing over the island now . . . I can't lose the lives and blood of our soldiers to hand over the islands to a contact [group] . . . after we've lost some of our finest young men, your [sic] surely not saying, that after the Argentinian withdrawal that our forces and our administration become immediately idle? I had to go immense distances and mobilise half my country.' Mrs Thatcher insisted that Britain had fought unaided, and therefore had full rights about what happened next. Given the scale of American material and intelligence assistance, Reagan might well have jibbed at this 1940 notion of Britain standing alone, but he did not. 'Well, Margaret, I know that I've intruded,' he said, 'and I know how . . .' Mrs Thatcher cut him short yet again: 'You haven't intruded at all, and I'm glad you telephoned,' she said.[161]

In the White House, though, there was dismay. Jim Rentschler of the NSC staff listened in on the call. A 'disastrous phone exchange with the PM', he noted in his diary. No one had checked with the NSC to make sure that the President was properly briefed and so he 'came off sounding like even more of wimp than Jimmy Carter'.[162] Rentschler recalled: 'Here is the strongest US leader since Theodore Roosevelt on this telephone exchange with the British PM. And he tries to put his talking points across and she would just come back and say "Listen, Ron. They were the aggressors. They asked for this. We gave them every chance to pull back. They didn't pull back. I'm sorry. We're not going to stop this military campaign when we're at the point of total victory." Reagan would try to get in and would say, "Yes Margaret. Ah . . . er, er, er . . . yes, yes, yeah . . ."' Thatcher was just telling him what's for.'[163] Haig, too, was in a great agitation about the call. Opposed to further pressure on London just days earlier, he now reverted to prior form and rang Henderson warning of 'great difficulties ahead in our relations . . . you must help the Argentines to find a way out, short of total humiliation.'[164] Judge Clark saw Henderson and said that Reagan had been disturbed by Mrs Thatcher's claim that Britain had acted on its own.

Mrs Thatcher also chose to be angry about Reagan's intervention, complaining that the White House had not given warning of the President's concerns in advance of the call. For this reason, she wrote in her memoirs, 'I was perhaps more forceful than friendly.'[165] She rang Henderson on an open line soon after the call and said that she was 'dismayed' by Reagan's attitude and 'most upset' and she wanted Henderson to tell the President so. 'It is pure Haigism,' she said. 'This phrase', Henderson noted, 'was uttered in the most withering tone, the speaker no doubt aware of the openness of the line.' 'We've lost a lot of blood,' she went on, 'and it's the best blood.'[166] It seems likely that Mrs Thatcher was deploying her indig-

nation in a calculated way. The call had not seriously altered her attitude
to the President: 'I don't recall her being all that angry with Reagan personally over this,' said Whitmore. 'She understood that he was basically
personally sympathetic . . . but that he was straddling still an administration that was pulling in different directions.'[167] In an interview with the
Washington Post which appeared three days after her telephone conversation with Reagan, she declared that the President had been 'absolutely
marvellous' in his view that aggression should not pay.[168] In private she
drew confidence from her belief that, so long as she held her ground, 'the
administration was very largely behind the British position and she could
count on their support in the final analysis.'[169] In a sense she was right, but
the Americans did not give up their quest for some last-minute saving of
Argentine face. The diplomatic stage now moved to the UN and to Versailles, where the G7 leaders were due to gather on 4 June.

Given the course of the fighting in the ten days after the Task Force landed,
it was scarcely surprising that Mrs Thatcher hardened her attitude to any
deal with Argentina. The combination of painful losses and military success
fired up her passions. She worked in the spirit of Sir Francis Drake's prayer
that it is the pursuing of 'any great matter' until it be 'thoroughly finished'
which 'yieldeth the true glory'. She felt 'an element of guilt'[170] about the
entire Falklands operation, both because of her ultimate responsibility for
the policy failure which had made the Argentine invasion possible and
because of the direct danger to the men. 'At No. 10,' she wrote in her private memoir, 'one was protected and safe – one felt so guilty at the
comfort.'[171] Mrs Thatcher believed ever more strongly that would-be peace-
makers must be made to understand that nothing should prejudice the
success of the Task Force or unnecessarily endanger servicemen's lives. She
applied this not only to diplomats and foreign leaders, but also to the
media. As the landing at San Carlos approached, there was outrage among
the Task Force that the BBC External Services had broadcast that the Battle Group and the Amphibious Group had joined up. And when, later,
British troops were preparing to attack the Argentine forces at Goose
Green, the BBC broadcast the fact that the 2nd Battalion the Parachute
Regiment were within 5 miles of Darwin near by. Lieutenant Colonel 'H'
Jones, the officer commanding the attack on Goose Green, told comrades
that he wanted to sue the BBC for this. 'There was talk among the men
that the Director-General of the BBC should be charged with treason.'[172]
All Mrs Thatcher's sympathies were with the Task Force and against the
media. 'Many of the public (including us)', she wrote, 'did not like the
attitude [of the media] particularly of the BBC . . . My concern was always

the safety of our forces. Theirs was news.'[173] The BBC, in particular, seemed neutral between Britain and Argentina, and this she more than once criticized in the House of Commons. Of the Darwin report, she wrote, 'Can there ever have been an army which had to fight its battles against media reporting like that?'[174] Although Mrs Thatcher always had a good understanding of how to use the press and television to project herself in the Falklands crisis, her dislike of the media's behaviour probably made the task of running information during the war harder for the government. Bernard Ingham complained that the role of PR was being neglected.[175] There were times when the understandable desire to withhold information which might be of use to the enemy led to the withholding of information which the public needed to know, and created unnecessary anxiety about potential losses. Luckily for Mrs Thatcher, most of Fleet Street, though not the broadcast media, was extremely sympathetic to her cause.

Once the Task Force was landed, Mrs Thatcher felt she could return to the public sphere and strengthen her broad moral and political arguments for what it was doing. Speaking to the Conservative Women's Conference on the day after the Argentine Independence Day attacks, she deployed the phrase of Harry Truman which she was later repeatedly to apply to the conflicts of the Cold War – that she wanted not mere peace, but 'peace with freedom and justice'.[176] She emphasized the old imperial ties by quoting the New Zealand Prime Minister, Robert Muldoon, 'With the Falkland Islanders, it is family,' and she invoked Shakespeare (*King John*): 'Nought shall make us rue, If England to herself do rest but true.'* In her *Washington Post* interview a few days later, she took from the Falklands experience a renewed idea of the British character: 'If you ask a person here what he would associate with Britain, it's not this talk about the welfare state or any sort of benefits or jargon . . . he would say "We are a free country." '[177]

In her address to the Conservative Women's Conference, Mrs Thatcher also used a phrase which betrayed the problem on her mind. There was, she said, 'no question of pressing the Force Commander to move forward prematurely'.[178] But, in a sense, there was just such pressure. Two things had happened. The first was that the requirements of politics now diverged from immediate military needs. The greatest fear for the British government was no longer a negotiated settlement but irresistible international pressure for a ceasefire. It would have been intolerable for Britain to have had to stop fighting with only a toehold on the islands. Because of this, it was

---

* This reference to England rather than Britain aroused the ire in Parliament of a Scottish Nationalist MP, Gordon Wilson. Mrs Thatcher replied to him with false sweetness: 'I am sorry if by quoting Shakespeare I have caused offence.' (Hansard, HC Deb 27 May 1982.)

vital for the Task Force to recapture so much ground so quickly that all talk of a ceasefire would be superseded by the restoration of British administration in Port Stanley. Unfortunately, while the planning of the landing had been so careful and intense, the plan for moving on to repossess Port Stanley was surprisingly vague. The second consideration was the home front. The War Cabinet believed that any sense that the British forces were hanging around at San Carlos or unable to break out would dismay domestic opinion. It therefore urgently wanted a move forward, and if it was not possible immediately to close on Stanley, it wanted a visible victory. An attack on the Argentine garrison at Goose Green seemed to fit the bill.

On Wednesday 26 May, the day of Mrs Thatcher's speech to the Women's Conference, Fieldhouse sent Brigadier Thompson a signal making the political dimension of the risk of a ceasefire explicit and ordering that 'With this in mind you should do all you can to bring the Darwin/Goose Green operation to a successful conclusion with Union Jack seen to be flying in Darwin.'[179] In a radio telephone conversation with Thompson, Fieldhouse made it pretty clear that, if Thompson would not attack Goose Green, he would put in a commander who would.[180] On the ground, though, Thompson naturally did not want to do anything premature. Because of the loss of the helicopters in the *Atlantic Conveyor*, British troops would have to advance towards Port Stanley on foot. Thompson wanted to be in a position to do this properly: 'I didn't want to charge forward with just a packet of sandwiches in my pocket.'[181] He worried about moving outside the air defence umbrella now established at the beachhead and felt his logistical difficulties were not understood at Northwood. Thompson had always to bear in mind that the Task Force had only 'one shot'. It was not like Normandy in 1944, where reinforcements could correct a big setback. If his troops took a terrible hammering, that would be that.

There was also a confusion of communication and command. Thompson, though respected, was, as a brigadier, relatively junior. His senior, General Jeremy Moore, had been with Fieldhouse at Northwood, contributing the 'joint' element in an operation which was heavily balanced in favour of the navy. Late in the day, Moore moved down to the Falklands to take over from Thompson; for much of the time he was on the *QEII*, proper, secure communications proved impossible to maintain. Moore was therefore not in a position to take full control of the land battle until 1 June, and by the time he had done so, the top brass back home, worried by this delay, did not have great confidence in him. Nor did Northwood feel wholly happy about Sandy Woodward, who was regarded as holding such a heavily naval view of his job that he did not take the land war seriously. There was no overall in-theatre commander. Poor Thompson had a great deal to bear. 'He was left alone there, and he really felt rather bitter,' Mrs Thatcher remembered.[182] This was not a classic row between politicians demanding a propaganda victory and generals sticking to military priorities. Cecil Parkinson recalled that 'There was a feeling that Julian Thompson "had better get a bloody move on", but it wasn't the politicians who said this, it was the Chiefs.'[183] Thompson, receiving the difficult orders from Northwood, confirmed this, never feeling that Mrs Thatcher was trying to give the Chiefs military direction.[184] It was more to do with the difference between being on the spot and being in London. Mrs Thatcher did not get involved in the growing asperities between the generals and admirals, but she was desperate to push on, and she put her faith in Lewin and Fieldhouse. David Goodall, by this time taking the minutes of the War Cabinet, watched her: 'I greatly admired the way she contained herself. There were delays, and Lewin explained them to us each morning. She was obviously itching to get on, but she never forced him to do so . . . I never saw any evidence of political reasons for her military actions.'[185] When later pressed, on American television, about why the British were not yet attacking Port Stanley, Mrs Thatcher replied: 'You can't fight a battle around a Cabinet table.'[186] Perhaps her ignorance of war gave her the necessary humility. The War Cabinet minutes of 27 May 1982 record Mrs Thatcher expressing the general proposition that 'it was most important to make the earliest possible progress with the operations on land.'[187] It was the top brass, translating her inclination into specific action, who decided upon Goose Green.

Colonel 'H' Jones, commanding 2 Para, discovered on approach that the task was more formidable than expected, but decided to attack all the same. The battle of Goose Green, which went through the night of 27 May, was fierce, requiring the capture of a narrow isthmus under heavy fire. Jones had requested from Thompson, but been refused, four of the eight light-armoured tanks available, which would have speeded the battle up. As dawn, which would give advantage to the Argentines, approached, Jones decided to try to break through by leading the assault in person. He was killed. After fighting for much longer than the British had expected, the Argentines surrendered. They had lost forty-five dead, to the British loss, including Jones, of sixteen. The British took 961 prisoners, and released 112 Falklanders who had been locked up in the local community hall for nearly a month. In later analyses, the battle of Goose Green could never escape the question of whether it had been necessary. Denis Thatcher, for example, believed that '"H" Jones should never have been killed.'[188] Mrs Thatcher was deeply troubled by the death of Jones, more so, thought Robert Armstrong, than by any other disaster of the war except the loss of *Sheffield*.[189] She comforted herself by thinking, though Freedman's account suggests that this is not strictly correct, that 'His life was lost but his bravery was the turning point in the battle.'[190] In fact, Goose Green was not a battle on which the defeat of Argentina directly depended. On the other hand, it produced a victory with which no one could quarrel, and an example of astonishing heroism in 'H' Jones, who was posthumously awarded the Victoria Cross. In his message of congratulation to Major Chris Keeble, Jones's replacement as the commanding officer, Fieldhouse said: 'you have kindled a flame in land operations which will lead to the raising of the Union Jack in Port Stanley.'[191] This was correct. There was now no real doubt that Britain would win the war.

One last diplomatic minuet remained – the G7 economic summit in Versailles. It coincided with the United Nations Security Council debate over a resolution for a ceasefire. At President Reagan's request, Mrs Thatcher met him alone at the American Embassy in Paris before the summit began. Al Haig regarded Reagan's desire to meet without officials as 'a terrible mistake', but Judge Clark retorted – Whitelawesque – that 'It's the President's call, and maybe it is a mistake, but if it is, he's got every right to make it!'[192] Certainly the fact that only the two leaders were present made it easier for Mrs Thatcher, who always understood the detail of any situation much better than Reagan. But it may also have relieved Reagan of a burden. Before leaving Washington, he had refused to send a message to Mrs Thatcher, drafted by the State Department, calling for a ceasefire short of complete surrender and abridging the rights of the islanders to decide their own future.[193]* He may have preferred not to have officials witnessing his reluctance to tackle Mrs Thatcher head-on.

The President was, however, armed with talking points. In his diary,

---

* One prominent person trying to bring about a last-minute deal was Dr Henry Kissinger. He had already annoyed Mrs Thatcher earlier during the conflict when he called on her and asked her which of the existing ideas for a negotiated settlement she favoured: 'Luckily for Pym, she thought that I had had these ideas. And she exploded: "How can you, my old friend, when we have been talking for nearly ten years?" . . . I didn't have the heart to tell her they weren't really my ideas, but her Foreign Secretary's.' (Interview with Dr Henry Kissinger.) On 2 June, Kissinger sent Judge Clark a memo detailing a conversation he had had with General Miret, the Argentine Plenipotentiary at the UN. It proposed variations on the themes of four-nation administration, ceasefire and mutual withdrawal of troops. Kissinger recommended it to Reagan on the grounds that, though the US had an interest in British resistance to Argentine force, 'We do not have an equal interest in humiliating Argentina in its political objective and to bring about a cataclysmic reversal of its domestic policies and the disruption of the inter-American system, both of which we are now in severe danger of having happen.' (Kissinger to Clark, 2 June 1982, Falklands War (UN/Kirkpatrick/Haig) (05/13/82–06/04/1982), Box 3, William Clark Files, Reagan Library.)

Rentschler, who helped draft them, prefaced his copy of the points with the words: 'The trick now is to make the Iron Maiden realize that we will *not* be signing in for a permanent state of war in the South Atlantic.'[194] The points congratulated Mrs Thatcher warmly on her own 'courage and determination' and on Britain's military success. But they also said that the presence of American and other elements in the Falklands could help secure a negotiated settlement instead of permanent war: 'The inescapable fact is that the US has risked a great deal in the Hemisphere and is likely to risk a great deal more.' Therefore long-term 'military occupation' should be avoided. In their discussions, Mrs Thatcher did not concede this point, but she was no longer under great pressure to do so. The President had offered Britain public support before arriving in Paris, and suggested that the next step depended on Buenos Aires. Henderson believed that Reagan's imminent official visit to the UK had a role here: 'Always at the back of the mind was that he shouldn't say anything which would jeopardize or impair the visit.'[195] In their tête-à-tête, Mrs Thatcher asked the President for his support at the UN Security Council: there is no suggestion that he did not give it. The truth was that, whatever his government's feelings, Reagan no longer had any stomach for challenging Mrs Thatcher over the Falklands. He sympathized with Britain's position and he wanted to avoid the sharp end of her tongue. Mulling Versailles over with Henderson early the following week, Haig 'said that we were rapidly losing international support'. Henderson came back at him: 'I asked him whether the President had made this clear to Mrs Thatcher in their private talk in Paris last Friday. He regretted that he did not think that he had done so. I said it was hopeless my telling Mrs Thatcher that the US government felt strongly the need for Britain to show magnanimity towards the Argentinians . . . if the President himself said nothing about it in prolonged private conversation with the Prime Minister.'[196]*

Reagan's acceptance of Britain's position encouraged the same at Versailles. President Mitterrand, the host of the G7 summit, had, apart from the Old Commonwealth prime ministers, been the most consistently supportive foreign leader. He issued a declaration at the end of the summit: 'But we wished to make a point of affirming our full solidarity with Great

---

* On 8 June, Robert Armstrong wrote to John Coles with information that American support, especially that of President Reagan personally, was not as absolute as Mrs Thatcher, at her Versailles debriefing, had conveyed to her officials. It extended only to the complete cessation of hostilities and did not necessarily endorse what Britain intended to do next. Whitmore wrote on it: 'Sir Robert Armstrong and I were inclined not to show this to the Prime Minister.' (Armstrong to Coles, 8 June 1982, Prime Minister's Papers, Argentina: Position of the Falkland Islands; document consulted in the Cabinet Office.)

Britain whose national interests and national pride have been violated, such solidarity being natural. Great Britain's rights must be preserved, it being understood that we shall do all we can to ensure that, while these rights are recognized, peace proves stronger than war.'[197] In other words, there was no longer any attempt to persuade Britain to make a deal and stop short of Port Stanley. Mitterrand had been, to use one of Mrs Thatcher's favourite words, very staunch. Early in the conflict, according to Hubert Vedrine, his diplomatic adviser at the time, Mitterrand had personally insisted on providing Britain with the means to counter the threat from the Exocet missiles which France had sold to Argentina.[198] Britain was able to jam the missiles. Later, when Argentina was scouring the world for more Exocets, he had ensured that spurious 'technical problems' would delay the supply of new missiles to Peru, which was suspected of wanting to sell them on to Argentina.* Mitterrand's tone and manner had also pleased her: 'He treated her as a great leader of a great country.'[199] Mrs Thatcher considered that 'He was most understanding and splendid throughout.'[200]†

The atmosphere at the UN was less friendly than at the summit. As Anthony Parsons had warned, there was no chance of Britain winning the vote against the ceasefire resolution, so it would be forced to use the veto available to all permanent members of the Security Council. The question was whether the United States would veto too. The vote came on 4 June, the first day of the Versailles summit. Resisting pressure from Jeane Kirkpatrick and Enders for abstention, Haig had left instructions for the United States to support Britain in a veto. At the last minute, however, he changed his mind, and ordered abstention. This change came too late for Mrs Kirkpatrick, who had just, on behalf of her country, joined Parsons in vetoing the resolution. But then, as Parsons recorded, she 'astonishingly stated that she had been asked by her government to say that if it were possible to change a vote once cast the US would like to change its vote from a veto to an abstention'.[201] She read out a poem by the Argentine writer Jorge Luis Borges about the horrors of war. Kirkpatrick believed that the delay in Haig's instructions had been deliberate, part of a clumsy ploy to show

---

* Despite Mitterrand's staunch line, one French defence company, majority-owned by the French government, maintained a 'technical team' in Argentina throughout the conflict. This team helped repair at least three otherwise inoperable Exocets for use against British forces. (*Document*, BBC Radio 4, 5 Mar. 2012.)

† On a personal level there was often an element of flirtation in the relationship, which Mrs Thatcher recognized and enjoyed. 'Well, Prime Minister, that went rather well,' suggested Robert Armstrong after Mitterrand's first presidential visit to the UK in September 1981. 'Yes, I suppose it did,' she replied. And then she paused. 'He likes women, you know.' (Interview with Lord Armstrong of Ilminster.)

support for both Britain and Argentina and humiliate her in the process. In the excitement, Parsons was able to slip out almost unnoticed from the Council, avoiding the media. Britain was furious at American behaviour and yet benefited from its sheer oddness; as Pym cabled to Mrs Thatcher and her team at Versailles the following day: 'Her [Mrs Kirkpatrick's] performance therefore excited much more media attention than our veto.'[202]

At Versailles the next day, there was a luncheon for the leaders in the Palace and the television cameras came in before it. A reporter asked Reagan about the UN vote. Mrs Thatcher was watching: 'Poor Ron – he knew nothing about it to my amazement – he just said "I'm afraid you've got me there …"' The interviewer then asked Mrs Thatcher for her reaction: 'I wasn't going to have a row on the media so merely said I didn't give interviews over lunch! But alas it all went out over the world's TV sets and created a bad impression.'[203]* At a press conference after the summit, Mrs Thatcher made light of the American switch of vote: 'If that's the only thing I have to worry about,' she said tactfully, 'then I shall be a very lucky woman.'[204] Mrs Thatcher left the summit early, before the opera and fireworks: 'it would not have been right to stay for such revelry. All my thoughts were of what was happening in the South Atlantic. By this time General Moore was in charge from his headquarters in San Carlos and his problem was to get enough equipment and ammunition forwards before the final assault on Port Stanley.'[205]

The Reagan visit to Britain began on Monday 7 June. There was no whisper of disagreement over the Falklands. The following day, the President addressed MPs and peers in the Royal Gallery of the Houses of Parliament. It was a major setpiece speech making much more explicit, in the context of the Soviet repression of Poland where martial law had been declared the previous December, his belief that the West could and should win the Cold War. Freedom, he declared, was bound to triumph. In a passage which he wrote into the speech himself, against the advice of the State Department, Reagan made the Falklands part of his wider theme:

> On distant islands in the South Atlantic young men are fighting for Britain. And yes, voices have been raised protesting their sacrifice for lumps of rock and earth so far away. But those young men aren't fighting for mere real estate. They fight for a cause – for the belief that armed aggression must not be allowed to succeed, that the people must participate in the decisions of government – the decisions of government under the rule of law. If there had

---

* The blame for Reagan's ignorance lies with Haig, who had kept knowledge of the UN vote from both the President and Judge Clark to maximize his own room for manoeuvre (see Allan Gerson, *The Kirkpatrick Mission: Diplomacy without Apology*, Free Press, 1991, p. 131).

been firmer support for that principle some 45 years ago, perhaps our generation wouldn't have suffered the bloodletting of World War II.[206]

This was the only part of his speech which attracted applause. As British
troops prepared for the final assault, Mrs Thatcher could not have asked
for clearer public support.

On the day of Reagan's speech, Mrs Thatcher was receiving grim news.
The necessary reinforcement provided by 5 Infantry Brigade had to land,
and there was some dispute about how, when and where. General Moore
wanted to move as quickly as possible. Admiral Fieldhouse, who had previously been so keen, for political reasons, to press on, now felt confident
enough to move more slowly: 'PM has held out resolutely for victory not
ceasefire.'[207] He did not think delay in taking Stanley would any longer be
politically disastrous, and he did fear that the one thing which would
undermine the operation now in the eyes of public opinion would be 'catas-
trophe at sea with large loss of life'.[208] He therefore asked Moore to drop
the plan to land the troops at Bluff Cove and Fitzroy. In the end, however,
a revised version of the plan was agreed. On 8 June the Welsh Guards
arrived at Fitzroy in two ships, *Sir Galahad* and *Sir Tristram*. Due to various confusions and disagreements about command, the ships did not
unload quickly. When Argentine planes attacked later in the day, they hit
both ships. In all, forty-nine men were killed, including thirty-nine Welsh
Guards. 'There are "if onlys" throughout life,' Mrs Thatcher wrote, 'and
if only the men had been taken off and dispersed first – the casualties would
never have been suffered to that extent. General Moore was grief-stricken.
I was up at Northwood a day later – we all felt – <u>how</u> many more.'[209] The
government took the hard-headed decision to hold up the details of casualties from the public, though informing the next of kin, in order to make
Argentina believe that the losses had been greater than they really were
and that the assault on Port Stanley would now be seriously hampered.
There was a fierce row about the matter between John Nott and Admiral
Fieldhouse – 'the argument became an issue of confidence between the two
men'[210] – but Mrs Thatcher reluctantly sided with the admiral and sup-
ported the concealment, despite the anxieties of the No. 10 press operation.
She felt that 'Surprise was vital' for the attack on Mount Longden, Two
Sisters and Wireless Ridge, the hills round Stanley.[211]

As British troops conducted their remarkable 'yomp' on foot across East
Falkland in order to recapture Port Stanley, there was once again very little
left for Mrs Thatcher to do. Characteristically, she busied herself with the
details of the Sovereign's Birthday Parade (Trooping the Colour), which

included personally preparing the food she served after the ceremony for her private guests.* There was a debate beforehand about whether Last Post and Reveille should be sounded for those lost in the Falklands, but the Queen thought this 'might encourage "hysteria"'. She proposed a moment of silence at the beginning of the proceedings and to this Mrs Thatcher agreed.[212] Early in the morning of Saturday 12 June, the day of Trooping the Colour, Mrs Thatcher was brought a note by the duty clerk at No. 10. 'I almost seized it from him expecting news that the attack had begun,'[213] but in fact it was the bad news that HMS *Glamorgan* had been hit by a land-based Exocet. Thirteen men were killed. Memory of this last serious setback of the war prompted Mrs Thatcher to sum up all these experiences: 'It is impossible to describe the depth of feeling at these times. It is quite unlike anything else I have ever experienced. In fights for liberty – we lose our bravest and best. How unjust and heartbreaking. Now we know the sacrifices that previous generations made for us . . . That day the Colour was trooped for the Queen's birthday. It poured with rain and somehow that seemed fitting although unpleasant for the Guards. I wore <u>black</u> – there was so much to mourn.' Shortly before one o'clock, coming indoors, 'we heard that all the objectives had been achieved.'[214]

It took two more days for the reconquest to be complete. The last skirmish of the battle for Port Stanley began at 1545Z on 14 June, and just before 5 p.m., Sapper Hill, the last obstacle before Stanley, was secured. Luckily the collapse of Argentine resistance meant that there would be no need to attack the capital itself. Because final surrender negotiations were by then in progress, Thompson ordered 2 Para, who were in front, to halt at the racecourse. The journalist Max Hastings† walked on alone and into the Upland Goose pub, the first of the Task Force to enter Stanley. Large numbers of Argentines threw down their weapons. Surrender, however, was not immediate. President Galtieri, speaking to the Argentine officer commanding in the Falklands, General Menéndez, on the telephone, told him to 'use all the means at your disposal and continue fighting with all the intensity with which you are capable'. Menéndez replied that he had

---

* One example of Mrs Thatcher's attention to personal matters, even at the height of the Falklands crisis, was remembered with gratitude by Antony Acland. Learning that his wife was gravely ill with cancer, Mrs Thatcher sent a large bunch of roses from Chequers to her in hospital, with a handwritten note offering 'the scent of flowers from an English country garden for you'. (Interview with Sir Antony Acland.)

† Max Hastings (1945–), educated Charterhouse and University College, Oxford; journalist, war correspondent and historian; editor, *Daily Telegraph*, 1986–95; editor, *Evening Standard*, 1995–2002; author *The Battle for the Falklands* (with Simon Jenkins, 1983), *Bomber Command* (1979), *Overlord* (1984), *Armageddon* (2004) and many other works; knighted, 2002.

'no means at his disposal, no troops, no high ground, no ammunition'.[215] Galtieri gave him permission to begin negotiations and these were conducted by Lieutenant Colonel Michael Rose,* the commanding officer of 22 SAS, who was, in Mrs Thatcher's view, 'a much better negotiator than General Moore',[216] to whom he was answering. In saying this, she was probably expressing her dissatisfaction at Moore's decision, after he personally reached Menéndez, to cut himself off from any communication with Northwood and do the deal himself. Moore was worried that, if Argentina could not salvage any honour at all, it would continue pointless fighting which would incur civilian casualties, so, at Menéndez's request, he took out the word 'unconditional' from the surrender document. Nevertheless, the surrender was complete. At 0200Z on 15 June, Moore signalled to London: 'Major General Menendez surrendered to me all the Argentine armed forces in East and West Falkland together with their impedimenta ... The Falkland Islands are once more under the government desired by their inhabitants. God Save the Queen.'[217] Britain now had to deal with more than 11,000 captured Argentine troops. In the course of the war, 255 British servicemen had died, 649 Argentines† and three Falkland Islanders.

After the Marines had reoccupied Government House that night, Michael Rose found them among scenes of some disorder after they had raided the drinks store. In the chaos, he noticed the trophy given and inscribed by Galtieri to Menéndez for his original capture of the Falklands lying on the floor. He walked off with it and presented it to the Officers' Mess, 22 SAS. Later, Argentina demanded it back, but Mrs Thatcher refused.[218]

Given her natural caution, Mrs Thatcher's normal reaction would have been to wait for the formal act of surrender before making any public statement. The news that the Argentine resistance had collapsed, however, was all over the media, and the excitement was intense. Crowds were gathering in Downing Street. Punctilious, as she had usually been throughout the crisis, in informing Parliament of news before appearing on television about it, the Prime Minister went across to the House of Commons and used the rather irregular device of a point of order to address the Chamber at 10.14 p.m. 'After successful attacks last night,' she said, 'General Moore decided to press forward. The Argentines retreated. Our forces reached the

---

* Michael Rose (1940–), educated Cheltenham and St Edmund Hall, Oxford; Staff College; Royal College of Defence Staff; served with Coldstream Guards in Germany, Aden and Northern Ireland; Commanding Officer, 22 Special Air Service Regiment, 1979–82; Director, Special Forces, 1988–9; Commander, UN Protection Force, Bosnia-Herzegovina, 1994–5; knighted, 1994.

† There is some dispute about the exact figure for Argentine deaths.

outskirts of Port Stanley. Large numbers of Argentine soldiers threw down their weapons. They are reported to be flying white flags over Port Stanley.'[219]* She explained that the surrender negotiations were in progress and promised to report to the House the next day: 'it was important in that she used the phrase, " ... negotiate a *surrender*" (not a ceasefire)', wrote Alan Clark, who was present in the Chamber. 'Trust her. She has led from the front all the way.'[220]† 'The House <u>cheered</u>,' Mrs Thatcher recalled.[221] In her room in the Commons afterwards, colleagues gathered, and Willie Whitelaw proposed a toast to her. 'I don't think anyone else but you could have done it,' he said. Antony Acland, who was present, remembered, 'And she wept, out of sheer relief. Denis put his arm round her, and said: "Well done. Have a drink." '[222] At midnight, she went home, among crowds singing 'Rule, Britannia', with whom she mingled:

> Downing Street was full of people, young people. It was their generation who had done it. Today's heroes. Britain still breeds them ... As I went to sleep very late that night I felt an enormous burden had been lifted from my shoulders and future worries would be small compared with those of life or death which had been with us constantly for 11 weeks. It was a miracle wrought by ordinary men and women with extraordinary qualities. Forever bold, forever brave, forever remembered.[223]

*

The following day, with the surrender signed, the Cabinet met. The Lord Chancellor, Lord Hailsham, congratulated Mrs Thatcher on her 'courage and leadership ... which has added new lustre to our arms and the spirit of our people,'[224] and he quoted what Henry V had said after his victory at Agincourt: 'Non nobis, Domine, Non nobis ...' ('Not unto us, Lord, not unto us,' the full quotation continuing, 'but to Thy name be the glory'). Mrs Thatcher did not quite understand the Latin and looked a little baffled.[225]

At Prime Minister's Questions two days later, Enoch Powell rose to offer his answer to the question he had raised at the beginning of the crisis about the metal of which Mrs Thatcher was made: 'Is the right hon. Lady aware that the report has now been received from the public analyst on a certain substance recently subjected to analysis and that I have obtained a copy

---

* It seems unlikely that Argentine flags of surrender were, in fact, flying, though Sir Michael Rose thought that he remembered seeing them. (Interview with Sir Michael Rose.) The only known example of a white flag that day was flown by a civilian anxious to indicate that there was no longer any need for a British attack. (See Freedman, *The Official History of the Falklands Campaign*, vol. ii, p. 650.)

† In his broadcast to the nation the following day, vowing eventual victory for Argentina, General Galtieri did not mention the word 'surrender'.

of the report? It showed that the substance under test consisted of ferrous matter of the highest quality, that it is of exceptional tensile strength, is highly resistant to wear and tear and to stress, and may be used with advantage for all national purposes.'[226] The joke was laboured, but the compliment gave Mrs Thatcher great pleasure. Ian Gow had the Hansard of Powell's 'before' and 'after' interventions framed and hung in No. 10. Powell's conclusion seemed to most people to fit the facts. She had indeed proved herself to be the Iron Lady.

Because of the wholeness of the victory and, as she saw it, the rightness of the cause, Mrs Thatcher now felt no need to entertain any more ideas for a new constitutional status for the Falklands. As late as the Cabinet meeting of 9 June 1982, she had been happy to discuss these, including the suggestion, then being touted by the United States, of complete self-government. But, once Stanley had fallen, she lost all interest. 'There was no prospect of negotiating anything for the moment,' she told Pérez de Cuéllar on 14 June, 'nor did she think there would be for some time.'[227] The Foreign Office, particularly Michael Palliser, who had been charged with looking at the long term, continued to push for some sort of settlement which would be acceptable to the Argentine government. On 21 June, he sent her a paper – 'the last I shall inflict upon you' – in which he suggested making proposals to Argentina and submitting the British case for sovereignty of the Falklands to the International Court. His essential case was that the islands would always be insecure if Britain could not come to terms with Argentina. On Palliser's paper Mrs Thatcher wrote: 'I disagree profoundly with the underlying approach to the problem – but circulate.'[228] Her approach was to implement the spirit of the Shackleton report, without seeking international assistance. The Falklands garrison eventually settled down at 3,000-strong and the new runway was built. The 'Fortress Falklands' policy which the Foreign Office had always sought to avoid came into being. Argentina never abandoned its claims to sovereignty, but nor did it make much trouble, at least until the twenty-first century when oil exploration became a source of dispute. As a result of the Malvinas debacle, Galtieri's government fell, and Argentina eventually returned to democratic rule.

On 6 July, Mrs Thatcher announced that the inquiry into the build-up to the Falklands invasion, which she had promised early in the crisis, would be conducted by Lord Franks, the greatest of 'the Great and the Good'.

The consequences of Mrs Thatcher's victory in the Falklands were many. The most obvious was the transformation of political fortune. Although she had already come through the worst of her unpopularity before Argentina invaded, only a few far-sighted supporters had imagined that she was likely to win the next general election. Economic news was still grim and unemployment was rising. A new political party, the SDP, looked as if it was indeed 'breaking the mould' of British politics. Within Mrs Thatcher's own party, her opponents, though mostly pushed to the fringes of power, had continued to assume that she would not survive. Many, such as Ian Gilmour and Christopher Soames, had believed that the Falklands, like a rerun of Suez, would bring her down. The opposite happened. The Falklands War established Mrs Thatcher's personal mastery of the political scene, and convinced people of her special gifts of leadership.* The loneliness of command in those eleven weeks made her all the more unassailable in the time to come.

It was not mere flattery to say that only she could have done it – it was widely believed, and it is probably true. Within the armed services, for instance, there had been a feeling almost from the start that, despite a catalogue of post-war affronts to declining British power, things would be diffferent this time. Julian Thompson, who had seen the whole of his military career up to that point overshadowed by politicians who had 'been less than robust in confronting the Queen's enemies', had sensed 'that she was a different kettle of fish. I therefore always thought [once Argentina had invaded] that the war would happen.'[229] John Coles, who had come into her private office with the usual somewhat anti-Thatcher prejudices of the Civil Service, especially of the Foreign Office, 'became a very great admirer because of her extraordinary courage and clarity'.[230] In this, he was typical of most of those who worked with her. The cool-headed Clive Whitmore, who was never much in political sympathy with his boss, considered that she 'behaved with balance and a clear view and the good sense to listen to advice. She led as well as could possibly be expected.'[231]

The Falklands War brought out Mrs Thatcher's best qualities – not only the well-known ones of courage, conviction and resolution, but also her less advertised ones of caution and careful study. She did not allow her desire to fight all the way overwhelm the need to be pragmatic and diplomatic. She was always careful to prepare the ground and pick the right moment. Because she knew nothing about war before the crisis broke, she approached the subject modestly. Those who worked closely with Mrs Thatcher at that time noted that she was remarkably free of the long-

---

* As the war progressed, the producers of *Anyone for Denis?*, the satirical West End revue based on *Private Eye*'s fictitious 'Dear Bill' letters supposedly written by Denis, brought the show to an end.

winded digressions and tendency to lecture which were common at other
times. She felt the greatest possible respect and affection for the armed
forces, both officers and men, and had the good sense to trust them to do
their job. Even in the case of the Foreign Office, with whom she had much
less natural sympathy, she recognized the talents of individuals such as
Nicko Henderson and Anthony Parsons, and relied on them heavily.
Throughout, she understood that the crisis was a matter of her own political survival, and of national pride, and that only victory could ensure
both. The war also proved her to be utterly genuine. In private and in public, as her speeches, writing and private conversation reveal, she cared
passionately for the cause and for the people involved. In this, her sex was
important. She was the first female war leader with executive power in the
British Isles since Elizabeth I, and the first ever in a democratic age. She
felt a maternal, almost a romantic, identification with the men whom she
was sending into battle, and they responded with a chivalrous devotion, a
desire to protect her as a woman and as an embodiment of national spirit.
The Falklands was a great occasion, and she rose to it.

Mrs Thatcher was aware of this, though she was always very cautious
about analysing herself, even in private. As Robert Armstrong put it, the
Falklands crisis was 'the single part of her time in which she lived most
intensely'.[232] From it, she derived the self-confidence which, in some ways,
she had previously lacked. Rather as Britain standing alone in 1940 had
been the sustaining myth for Winston Churchill, Mrs Thatcher's solitary
leadership in the face of the sudden disaster of the Falklands became for
her the talisman of what she could do. In her mind, it helped to create the
dangerous idea that she acted best when she acted alone. But it also renewed
her belief that her efforts to transform her country were in accord with the
underlying desires and character of the British people. 'The public were as
resolute as ever' is a typical sentence from her private memoir of the war,
and opinion polls seemed to bear her judgment out. Writing to the New
Zealand Prime Minister, Robert Muldoon, who had passed her an admiring
letter from the Legion of Frontiersmen of the Commonwealth just before
the end of the fighting, she said: 'The response of the people of this country,
and of the Commonwealth, especially in New Zealand, has convinced me
that patriotism is a strong plant . . . and that its flowers will indeed bloom
even when peace is restored.'[233] When she spoke to a Conservative rally in
early July about what had been achieved, she was both expressing her real
beliefs about her country and, forgivably perhaps, boasting:

> We have ceased to be a nation in retreat. We have instead a new-found
> confidence – born in the economic battles at home and tested and found true

8,000 miles away ... And so today, we can rejoice at our success in the Falklands and take pride in the achievement of the men and women of our Task Force. But we do so, not as at some last flickering of a flame which must soon be dead. No, we rejoice that Britain has rekindled that spirit which has fired her for generations past and which today has begun to burn as brightly as before. Britain found herself again in the South Atlantic and will not look back from the victory she has won.[234]

Mrs Thatcher's idea of what had been achieved fitted her unusual mindset, which was both conservative and revolutionary. She saw herself as restoring an inherent British greatness which had unfortunately been lost because of imperial decline. At the same time, she saw herself as bringing about enormous change.

The Falklands set the standard by which she judged individuals. Anyone who had been 'staunch' in the war was in her good books for ever more. As well as the armed services, her list of heroes included – despite the wobbles – Ronald Reagan as well as Caspar Weinberger, President Mitterrand and President Pinochet, Robert Muldoon of New Zealand, King Hussein of Jordan, Rex Hunt, the Governor of the Falklands, and David Owen of the SDP. The British Antarctic Survey, who had advised her on the terrain, became such favourites that not only did she ensure they received more government money, she also listened to them when, years later, they warned of the damage to the ozone layer caused by pollution.[235] Mrs Thatcher even had a soft spot for Michael Foot who, she considered, had been basically patriotic. Her villains of the war included the Irish, the United Nations (though not Pérez de Cuéllar personally), Francis Pym, Jeane Kirkpatrick and Denis Healey.

The world, in turn, revised its estimation of her. For all their often justified anxieties about how the Falklands conflict would affect their own standing in Latin America, the Americans were deeply impressed by Mrs Thatcher's achievement. 'When the Argentines surrendered in Port Stanley the NSC staff and others were in the situation room in the White House and they all started cheering.'[236] In the middle of the Cold War, her Falklands rhetoric about free people standing up to aggression resonated with the American people. Her achievement in successfully projecting force halfway across the world also caused the Soviet Union to revise its estimation of the will and capacity of the West.[237]

In the attitude of the US administration, there was a mixture of irritation and admiration. When Mrs Thatcher went to Washington on 23 June 1982, fresh from her victory, Reagan was urged by his staff to press for some sort of compromise with Argentina over the long-term future of the islands. Mrs Thatcher, however, had got wind of this plan before arriving in Washington and was ready to thwart it. 'He wants me to be magnanimous in victory,' she told one of her officials, 'and I'm not going to be.'[238] The draft of Reagan's remarks to be delivered after his meeting with her said: 'I expressed my view that a just war requires a just peace and that we should bend our efforts toward a settlement in the South Atlantic that will bring lasting reconciliation and stability.'[239] But it was not to be. '<u>Thatcher blasted this position to smithereens on 2 networks this am</u>,' a frantic staffer scribbled on this draft just hours before the meeting.* Sure enough, when Reagan and Thatcher sat down together the Prime Minister had no intention of allowing the discussion to verge towards talk of compromise. 'The President had just started to say something about the Falklands when Mrs T interrupted him to say that she wanted to give him an account of the present position,' Nicko Henderson recorded in his diary. 'She described the state of the Argentinian prisoners: malnutrition, trench-foot, diarrhoea. We were spared nothing.' Mrs Thatcher also appealed for Reagan's help in clearing the thousands of mines left behind by Argentina. Reagan noted that, in the past, mules had been let loose in minefields, but had usually proved too 'canny' to detonate the mines. 'Mrs Thatcher laughingly suggested that she would use the Falkland sheep for that purpose.'[240] As Mrs Thatcher raised issue after issue, Reagan had little chance to insert the serious words of warning pressed on him by his staff. 'As a result, when, at the subsequent press conference, Mrs T was asked whether the President had urged her to adopt a more flexible attitude on sovereignty for the Falkland Islands, she was able to answer, No, with complete honesty.'[241]

All over the world, Margaret Thatcher now became a figure of legend, the embodiment of strong leadership, more famous, perhaps, than any other political leader of the time.

On the day of victory, Alan Clark bumped into Ian Gow in the Commons, 'looking like the cat that has swallowed all the cream': '"the Prime Minister has complete freedom of action now," I said, "no other Leader has enjoyed such freedom since Churchill, and even with him it did not last very long." I suppose he may have thought that I was referring to freedom of choice in making appointments, but I was not, really, I meant freedom in imposing domestic, foreign and defence policies.'[242] Clark was right. No transformation in modern British history had been swifter, or more complete. She now had command of the whole field.

It fitted Mrs Thatcher's deep gratitude to the armed services and also her sense of reverence and romance that there should be a service of thanksgiving

---

* Reagan's call for a 'just peace' was sent to Mrs Thatcher only as a private letter.

for victory, and other forms of public celebration. In this she faced two difficulties. The first was that some, particularly the Church authorities, were opposed on political/religious grounds to giving thanks for victory in a war which they believed should never have been fought. The second was that Mrs Thatcher feared she might be accused of triumphalism or hubris.

On the latter point, she was extremely sensitive and – despite her pride in her own achievements – genuinely reluctant to push herself forward. She was quite happy to lord it over political rivals, but hated the idea of upstaging the military or the monarchy. When, for example, it was debated who should read the lesson at the proposed service, Mrs Thatcher wrote to John Coles: 'It would be much more appropriate for CDS or CinC Fleet to read the lesson. If I did, it would be misinterpreted and leave a <u>bad taste</u>. <u>No</u> politician in my view!'[243] It was also suggested that, when the Queen left St Paul's cathedral at the end of the service, Mrs Thatcher should say a formal farewell to her at the west door. Mrs Thatcher queried this: 'Am I the right person to do it? I shouldn't like to intrude any political element into this service.'[244]*

The discussion of the service itself was fraught. As Mrs Thatcher recorded: 'This [the service] had its difficulties because of its ecumenical nature. No parade was allowed to the cathedral, no colours to the Altar <u>and</u> it was as much as we could do to persuade the Church authorities to allow anyone who had taken part in the Falklands campaign to take part in the service . . .'[245]

All this was true. Cardinal Basil Hume, for the Roman Catholics, objected to the service being for the 'liberation' of the Falklands and did not want combatants to read any lessons. Dr Kenneth Greet, for the Free Churches Federal Council, was entirely opposed to the war and therefore to any form of celebration. The left-wing Dean of St Paul's, Dr Alan Webster, objected to the idea of a 'thanksgiving' service at all and wanted one of 'reconciliation', suggesting that the Lord's Prayer be said in Spanish. All this dismayed the Ministry of Defence, who naturally wanted the armed forces prominently represented. At one stage some clerics suggested they would not take part in the service if members of the armed forces read the lessons. Furious, Mrs Thatcher 'threatened to make this known in parliament and therefore publicly'.[246] The conservative Bishop of London, Dr Graham Leonard, told her privately that 'even when the form of Service had been agreed, there was no guarantee that the Dean of St Paul's would

---

* When her behaviour is compared with Tony Blair's readiness to read the lesson at the funeral of Diana, Princess of Wales in September 1997 (an act entirely without precedent for a Prime Minister on a royal occasion), it will be seen that Mrs Thatcher was scrupulous about the proprieties.

follow it. On past form, he might well insert changes and additions at the last moment.'[247] Dr Leonard advised her to seek the help of the Archbishop of Canterbury ('or even the Queen') to prevent this.

Mrs Thatcher was infuriated by these clerical attitudes. When it was reported to her that the Dean wanted the Lord's Prayer in Spanish 'her eyes widened in absolute horror,'[248] and at the suggestion that it should be a service of reconciliation rather than thanksgiving she struck the table a tremendous blow and exclaimed scornfully 'A service of reconciliation!' 'All Christians stay away,' whispered Clive Whitmore to David Goodall, who was trying to co-ordinate matters with the Roman Catholics.[249] She was so angry that at the relevant meeting of OD(SA) she ordered her threat to publicize the attitudes of the clergy to be put into the official minutes. Going through the proposed text, she put her wiggly line against a prayer which asked God for the will to build defences against poverty, hunger and disease 'instead of against each other'.[250] In the end, the necessary compromises were reached and servicemen read various biblical sentences. But there was such a lack of trust between Downing Street and the clergy that when, on the proof of the service sheet, a printer's error had reduced the word 'thanksgiving' (which now headed a section, rather than appearing as part of the title of the service) to rather small type, the MOD official co-ordinating the arrangements had to obtain a 'personal assurance' from the Dean that this would be corrected.[251]

At the service, which took place at the end of July, Mrs Thatcher arrived 'looking absolutely like a thundercloud'[252] and was seated, as she had requested, in a fairly humble place. It was widely reported the next day that she had been enraged by the sermon of the Archbishop of Canterbury, Dr Runcie, which had called for reconciliation. But this was not the case. 'She gripped my hand,' he remembered, 'and said "Well done."'[253] What upset her was the fear that the armed services might be denied proper thanks and the spiritual comfort that these would provide. It was the Queen, in fact, who put her finger on the problem with the service. 'I don't think you should ever leave a Christian service feeling sad,' she said to the Archbishop. 'The service was not well arranged for that reason.'[254] Mrs Thatcher herself summed it up: 'The Thanksgiving part was virtually dropped from the Service. But because of the presence of the Queen and all the Royal Family – the superb pageantry of the military band – trumpeters, the service was a great comfort to the bereaved and that mattered more than anything else.'[255]

The secular celebrations were less awkward. On 12 October, 1,250 representatives of the Task Force marched to Guildhall, with a fly-past of helicopters and aircraft. Then there was lunch inside. The top brass sat with the Prime Minister and the Lord Mayor at the high table, the officers and other ranks at the lower tables. When Mrs Thatcher rose to speak, 'Suddenly, before she could say anything, there was a standing ovation from the floor, started by the boys. The other politicians couldn't believe what was happening. When Mrs Thatcher had quietened everyone down, she said "It is I who should be down there, thanking you."'[256] The night before, at No. 10, Mrs Thatcher gave dinner for the Lord Mayor and about 120 of those most involved in the Falklands victory. In her speech after dinner, she quoted the Duke of Wellington: 'There is no such thing as a little war for a great nation.' She spoke of 'the spirit of the Falklands' and went on, 'Or is it the spirit of Britain which throughout history has never failed us in difficult days?'[257] 'She spoke like Queen Elizabeth I,' remembered David Goodall. 'She *looked* like Queen Elizabeth I!'[258]

So many people had been invited to the dinner that there was no room for spouses at table: instead they were invited for post-dinner drinks in the drawing rooms. Because all the main players in the Falklands crisis had been men, Mrs Thatcher was the only woman at dinner. After the toasts which followed her speech, and the reply from Lord Lewin, the Prime Minister rose in her seat again and said, 'Gentlemen, shall we join the ladies?'[259] It may well have been the happiest moment of her life.

Notes

CHAPTER 1: GRANTHAM

1. Interview with Muriel Cullen (née Roberts).   2. Sermon notes prepared by Alfred Roberts, The Thatcher Papers, Churchill College, Cambridge, THCR 1/9/8.   3. Ibid.   4. Interview with Mary Grylls (née Wallace).   5. Margaret Thatcher, *The Path to Power*, HarperCollins, 1995, p. 5.   6. *Maggie: The First Lady* (Brook Lapping Productions for ITV and PBS, 2003).   7. Interview with Lady Thatcher.   8. Interview by Miriam Stoppard, *Woman to Woman* (Yorkshire Television), 19 Nov. 1985 (http://www.margaretthatcher.org/document/105830).   9. Interview with Lady Thatcher.   10. Interview with Muriel Cullen.   11. Ibid.   12. *Woman to Woman*.   13. Ibid.   14. Interview with Carol Thatcher.   15. Ibid.   16. Interview with Muriel Cullen.   17. Interview with Lady Thatcher.   18. Ibid.   19. Thatcher, *The Path to Power*, p. 9.   20. Ibid.   21. Interview with Lady Thatcher.   22. THCR 1/9/8.   23. Patricia Murray, *Margaret Thatcher*, W. H. Allen, 1980, p. 22.   24. THCR 1/9/8.   25. Interview with Lady Thatcher.   26. Ibid.   27. *Woman to Woman*.   28. Murray, *Margaret Thatcher*, p. 22.   29. Interview with Jean Dean (née Farmer).   30. Interview with Muriel Cullen.   31. Ibid. (see also Chapter 5).   32. Ibid.   33. Interview with Margaret Wickstead (née Goodrich).   34. Interview with Pamela Thomas.   35. Interview with Muriel Cullen.   36. Interview with Margaret Wickstead.   37. Interview with Lady Thatcher.   38. *Woman to Woman*.   39. Letter to Muriel, 30 July 1944.   40. Letter to Muriel, 20 Aug. 1944.   41. Interview with Jean Dean.   42. Private information.   43. Interview with Carol Thatcher.   44. Interview with Pamela Thomas.   45. Interview with Lady Thatcher.   46. Interview with Margaret Wickstead.   47. Interview with Rita Wright (née Hind).   48. Interview with Shirley Ellis (née Walsh).   49. *Maggie: The First Lady*.   50. Several conversations with Lady Thatcher.   51. *Maggie: The First Lady*.   52. Interview with Kenneth Wallace.   53. Interview with Mary Grylls.   54. Interview with Kenneth Wallace.   55. Interview with Mary Grylls.   56. Interview with Kenneth Wallace.   57. Interview with Madeline Hellaby (née Edwards).   58. *Maggie: The First Lady*.   59. Interview with Jean Dean.   60. Conversation with Lady Thatcher, as reported by David Heathcoat-Amory.   61. Letter to Muriel, 30 July 1944.   62. Thatcher, *The Path to Power*.   63. Interview with Nellie Towers, *Maggie: The First Lady*.   64. Thatcher, *The Path to Power*, p. 3.   65. *Maggie: The First Lady*.   66. *Woman to Woman*.   67. Interview with Muriel

Cullen. 68. *Grantham Journal*, 11 July 1936. 69. Thatcher, *The Path to Power*, p. 21. 70. Ibid., p. 25. 71. Interview with Lady Thatcher. 72. Ibid. 73. Ibid. 74. Ibid. 75. *Grantham Journal*, 28 Jan. 1939. 76. Ibid. 77. Interview with Lady Thatcher. 78. Ibid. 79. Ibid. 80. Letter from Edith Mühlbauer to Alfred Roberts, 21 Jan. 1939. 81. Letter from Edith Mühlbauer to Alfred Roberts, 23 Mar. 1939. 82. Interview with Lady Thatcher. 83. Interview with Muriel Cullen. 84. Ibid. 85. Interview with Madeline Hellaby. 86. Interview with Mary Grylls. 87. Ibid. 88. Interview with Kenneth Wallace. 89. Ibid. 90. Interview with Muriel Cullen. 91. Interview with Lady Thatcher.

CHAPTER 2: SCHOLARSHIP GIRL

1. Letter to Muriel, 25 July 1941. 2. Letter to Muriel, 20 Sept. 1941. 3. Ibid. 4. Margaret Thatcher, *The Path to Power*, HarperCollins, 1995, p. 21. In her memoirs, Lady Thatcher mistakenly attributes these festivities to the Silver Jubilee of King George V, which also took place in 1935. 5. Interview with Jean Dean (née Farmer). 6. Letter from Lorna Smith, 2003. 7. George Gardiner, *Margaret Thatcher: From Childhood to Leadership*, William Kimber, 1975, p. 20. 8. All above quotations from interview with Jean Dean. 9. Letter to Mr and Mrs Jack Farmer, 7 Mar. 1974. 10. Interview with Shirley Ellis (née Walsh). 11. Letter to Muriel, Dec. 1941. 12. Letter to Muriel, 20 Sept. 1941. 13. Letter to Muriel, Oct. 1941. 14. *Grantham Journal*, obituary of Lady Thatcher, 9 April 2013. 15. All these quotations are from Thatcher, *The Path to Power*, pp. 9–10. 16. Letter to Muriel, 30 July 1944. 17. Letter to Muriel, Oct. 1941. 18. Ibid. 19. Letter from Lorna Smith, 2003. 20. *Grantham Journal*, obituary of Lady Thatcher, 9 April 2013. 21. Interviews with Amy Ormond (née Wootten), Pauline Harrison (née Cowan) and Betty Robbins (née Spice). 22. Interview with Lady Thatcher. 23. Ibid. 24. Ibid. 25. Ibid. 26. Interview with Rita Wright (née Hind). 27. Interview with Lady Thatcher. 28. Interview with Rita Wright. 29. Letter from Lorna Smith, 2003. 30. Ibid. 31. Interview with Rita Wright. 32. Interview with Lorna Smith. 33. Interviews with Madeline Hellaby (née Edwards) and Margaret Wickstead (née Goodrich). 34. Letter to Muriel, Dec. 1941 (undated). 35. All quotations from Margaret's school reports come from copies in the possession of KGGS library. The author is grateful for the school's permission to see and publish them. 36. Patricia Murray, *Margaret Thatcher*, W. H. Allen, 1980. 37. *Grantham Journal*, obituary of Lady Thatcher, 9 April 2013. 38. KGGS archives. 39. Letter to Shirley Ellis, 6 July 1990. 40. Thatcher, *The Path to Power*, p. 18. 41. Ibid. 42. Letter to Muriel, Oct. 1941. 43. Interview with Jean Dean. 44. Interview with Rita Wright. 45. Ibid. 46. *The History of Kesteven and Grantham Girls' School, 1910–87*, pamphlet, 1987. 47. Interview with Lady Thatcher. 48. Letter to Muriel, Oct. 1941. 49. Russell Lewis, *Margaret Thatcher: A Personal and Political Biography*, Routledge & Kegan Paul, 1975, p. 12. 50. Interview with Muriel Cullen. 51. Thatcher, *The Path to Power*, p. 34. 52. Letter from Lorna Smith. 53. Interview with Madeline Hellaby. She says the aim of getting higher education was understood and accepted. 54. Interview with Mary Grylls (née Wallace). 55. Interview with Lady Thatcher.

CHAPTER 3: LOVE AND WAR AT OXFORD

1. Interview with Mary Grylls (née Wallace).   2. Interview with Margaret Wickstead (née Goodrich).   3. Margaret Thatcher, *The Path to Power*, HarperCollins, 1995, p. 37.   4. Papers relating to the compilation of Lady Thatcher's memoirs, The Thatcher Papers, Churchill College, Cambridge, THCR 4/4.   5. Thatcher, *The Path to Power*, p. 38.   6. Ibid.   7. See interview with Pamela Mason (née Rhodes), a fellow Somervillian, who says that Margaret 'gave a brown impression', *Maggie: The First Lady* (Brook Lapping Productions for ITV and PBS, 2003).   8. Interview with Rachel Kinchin-Smith.   9. Interview with Mary Grylls.   10. Letter to Muriel, Sept. 1944.   11. Interview with Lady Thatcher.   12. Letter to Muriel, Sept. 1944.   13. Interview with Betty Robbins (née Spice).   14. Letter from Joan Bridgman (née Parker); Letter from Jean Darmon (née Southerst).   15. Interview with Amy Ormond (née Wootten).   16. Letter from Mary Williamson (née Mallinson).   17. Interview with Pauline Harrison (née Cowan).   18. Interview with Betty Robbins.   19. *Maggie: The First Lady*.   20. Letter from Jean Darmon.   21. Letter from Mary Williamson.   22. Letter to Muriel, June 1946.   23. Letter from Mary Williamson.   24. Information provided by Lady Oppenheimer (née Helen Lucas Tooth).   25. Interview with Betty Robbins.   26. Private information.   27. Nicholas Wapshott and George Brock, *Thatcher*, Macdonald, 1983, p. 46.   28. Interview with Pauline Harrison.   29. THCR 4/4.   30. Interview with Lady Thatcher.   31. Letter to Muriel, 19 Apr. 1945.   32. THCR 4/4.   33. Interview with Betty Robbins.   34. Interview with Pauline Harrison.   35. Letter from Dorothy Hodgkin to Tony Epstein, 23 Aug. 1988, Bodleian Library, Oxford.   36. Interview with Betty Robbins.   37. Hugo Young and Anne Sloman, *The Thatcher Phenomenon*, BBC Books, 1986, p. 17.   38. Ibid.   39. Interview with Lady Thatcher.   40. Wapshott and Brock, *Thatcher*.   41. Interview with Betty Robbins.   42. Thatcher, *The Path to Power*, pp. 78–9.   43. Ibid.   44. Letter to Muriel from Walton Street, Oxford, 1947 (undated).   45. Conversation with Romilly, Lady McAlpine.   46. Letter from Jean Darmon.   47. THCR 4/4.   48. Ibid.   49. Interview with Amy Ormond.   50. Ibid.   51. Interview with Pauline Harrison.   52. Interview with Mary Grylls.   53. THCR 4/4.   54. Thatcher, *The Path to Power*, pp. 50–51.   55. Ibid.   56. THCR 4/4.   57. Ibid.   58. Interview with Lady Thatcher.   59. Ibid.   60. Ibid.   61. THCR 4/4.   62. Ibid.   63. Ibid.   64. Letter to Muriel, 25 Mar. 1945.   65. Speech in Sleaford, 25 June 1945, reported in *Sleaford Gazette*, 29 June 1945 (http://www.margaretthatcher.org/document/100817).   66. Letter from Liz Barrington to Muriel, 17 July 1945.   67. Thatcher, *The Path to Power*, p. 46.   68. THCR 4/4.   69. Thatcher, *The Path to Power*, p. 46.   70. THCR 4/4.   71. Ibid.   72. Oxford University Conservative Association Policy Sub-Committee report, Michaelmas Term 1945, kindly lent to the author by Michael Kinchin-Smith.   73. THCR 4/4.   74. Speech at Federation of University Conservative and Unionist Associations Conference, 28 Mar. 1946, reported in *Isis*, 1 May 1946 (http://www.margaretthatcher.org/document/100818).   75. THCR 4/4.   76. Thatcher, *The Path to Power*, p. 48.   77. Ibid.   78. Conversation with Lord Rees-Mogg.   79. Interview with Sir Michael Oppenheimer.

80. Private information. 81. Interview with Lady Thatcher. 82. THCR 4/4. 83. Conversation with the late Duke of Buccleuch. 84. THCR 4/4. 85. Letter to Muriel, Oct. 1946. 86. Letter to Muriel, May 1947. 87. Letter to Muriel, Jan. 1947. 88. Conversation with Max Findlay. 89. Ibid. 90. Letter to Muriel, May 1947. 91. Letter to Muriel from Galley Hill, Darenth Road, Dartford, probably late 1949. 92. Conversation with Max Findlay. 93. Letter to Muriel, 15 May 1947. 94. Interview with Kenneth Wallace. 95. Letter to Muriel, 20 Aug. 1944. 96. Letter to Muriel, 3 Jan. 1945. 97. Interview with Margaret Wickstead. 98. Ibid. 99. Interview with Tony Bray. 100. Ibid. 101. Ibid. 102. Letter to Muriel, 25 Mar. 1945. 103. Interview with Tony Bray. 104. Letter to Muriel, 25 Mar. 1945. 105. Ibid. 106. Interview with Tony Bray. 107. Letter to Muriel, 19 Apr. 1945. 108. Interview with Tony Bray. 109. Ibid. 110. Interview with Muriel Cullen. 111. Interview with Tony Bray.

CHAPTER 4: ESSEX GIRL

1. Papers relating to the compilation of Lady Thatcher's memoirs, The Thatcher Papers, Churchill College, Cambridge, THCR 4/4. 2. Margaret Thatcher, *The Path to Power*, HarperCollins, 1995, p. 62. 3. Letter to Muriel, 17 Nov. 1947. 4. Letter to Muriel, 17 Feb. 1948. 5. Letter to Muriel, probably early Nov. 1947 (undated). 6. Letter to Muriel, 21 Oct. 1947. 7. Letter to Muriel, probably June 1948 (undated). 8. Ibid. 9. Letter to Muriel, 3 Mar. 1948. 10. Letter to Muriel, 18 Aug. 1948. 11. Letter to Muriel, 28 Sept. 1947. 12. Letter to Muriel, probably Oct. 1947 (undated). 13. Letter to Muriel, 28 Sept. 1947. 14. Interview with Brian Harrison. 15. Letter to Muriel, probably Oct. 1947 (undated). 16. Letter to Muriel, 27 Apr. 1948. 17. Ibid. 18. Letter to Muriel, 17 Nov. 1947. 19. Letter to Muriel, 11 May 1948. 20. Letter to Muriel, probably Apr. 1948 (undated). 21. Letter to Muriel, probably June 1948 (undated). 22. Letter to Muriel, 17 Feb. 1948. 23. Interview with Tony Bray. 24. All above quotations from letter to Muriel, 18 May 1948. 25. All above quotations from letter to Muriel, early Sept. 1948 (undated). 26. Letter to Muriel, 8 Dec. 1948. 27. Letter to Muriel, 4 Jan. 1949. 28. Letter to Muriel, 16 Feb. 1949. 29. Interview with Tony Bray. 30. Ibid. 31. Letter to Muriel, 23 Nov. 1948. 32. Letter to Muriel, 19 Jan. 1949. 33. Interview with Brian Harrison. 34. Interview with Tony Bray. 35. Letter to Muriel, probably Sept. 1948 (undated). 36. Letter to Muriel, 18 Aug. 1948. 37. Letter to Muriel, 11 Oct. 1948. 38. Ibid. 39. Thatcher, *The Path to Power*, p. 63. 40. Ibid. 41. Interview with Ken Tisdell. 42. Interview with Shirley and Alan Wells, and June Wood. 43. TCHR 4/4. 44. Letter from Beryl Cook to J. P. L. Thomas, Vice-Chairman of the Conservative Party, 1 Feb. 1949, THCR 1/1/1. 45. Letter from Marjorie Maxse to J. P. L. Thomas, 1 Feb. 1949, THCR 1/1/1. 46. This, and all ensuing quotations from Margaret Roberts's references come from the Conservative Central Office files, copies at THCR 1/1/1. 47. Letter to Muriel, 22 Sept. 1948. 48. Ibid. 49. Letter to Muriel, 14 Nov. 1948. 50. Ibid. 51. Letter to Muriel, 4 Jan. 1949. 52. Letter to Muriel, 18 Jan. 1949. 53. Letter to Muriel, 16 Feb. 1949. 54. Ibid. 55. Letter to Muriel, 23 Feb. 1949. 56. Ibid.

57. Ibid.   58. Speech at adoption meeting, 28 Feb. 1949, reported in *Erith Observer*, 4 Mar. 1949 (http://www.margaretthatcher.org/document/100821).   59. Ibid. 60. Letter to Muriel, 17 Mar. 1949.   61. Interview with Sir Denis Thatcher. 62. Ibid.   63. Letter to Muriel, 17 Mar. 1949.   64. Letter to Muriel, 13 Mar. 1949.

CHAPTER 5: DARTFORD AND ROMANCE

1. Interview with Patricia Greenough (née Luker).   2. Interview with Lady Thatcher.   3. Interview with Patricia Greenough.   4. Ibid.   5. All the above quotations come from conversations with former Dartford Young Conservatives Shirley and Alan Wells, June Wood, Ken Tisdell and Gwen Morgan.   6. Ibid.   7. Interview with Patricia Greenough.   8. Letter to Muriel, 20 May 1950.   9. Letter to Muriel, 29 Sept. 1949.   10. Papers relating to the compilation of Lady Thatcher's memoirs, The Thatcher Papers, Churchill College, Cambridge, THCR 4/4.   11. Interview with Lady Thatcher.   12. Letter to Muriel, 29 Sept. 1949.   13. See *Dartford Chronicle*, 7 Oct. 1949.   14. Speech debating with Labour candidate (Norman Dodds), 25 Nov. 1949, reported in *Erith Observer*, 2 Dec. 1949 (http://www.margaretthatcher.org/document/100845).   15. Interview with Shirley Wells.   16. Speech to Belvedere Conservatives, 23 Apr. 1949, reported in *Erith Observer*, 29 Apr. 1949 (http://www.margaretthatcher.org/document/100824).   17. Speech to Dartford Young Conservatives, 13 Aug. 1949, reported in *Dartford Chronicle*, 19 Aug. 1949 (http://www.margaretthatcher.org/document/100831).   18. Speech to Bexley Conservative Women, 15 Sept. 1949, reported in *Kentish Independent*, 23 Sept. 1949 (http://www.margaretthatcher.org/document/100836).   19. Speech to Erith Conservative Women, 9 June 1949, reported in *Kentish Independent*, 17 June 1949 (http://www.margaretthatcher.org/document/100828).   20. Speech to Dartford Conservatives, 31 Mar. 1949, reported in *Dartford Chronicle*, 8 Apr. 1949 (http://www.margaretthatcher.org/document/100822).   21. Speech to Erith Conservative Women, 9 June 1949, reported in *Kentish Independent*, 17 June 1949 (http://www.margaretthatcher.org/document/100828).   22. Article in *Evening Post*, 27 Jan. 1950 (http://www.margaretthatcher.org/document/100855).   23. Speech to Dartford Young Conservatives, 13 Aug. 1949, reported in *Dartford Chronicle*, 19 Aug. 1949 (http://www.margaretthatcher.org/document/100831).   24. Letter to Muriel, probably early May 1949 (undated).   25. Speech to Dartford Rotarians, 3 Jan. 1950, reported in *Dartford Chronicle*, 6 Jan. 1950 (http://www.margaretthatcher.org/document/100851).   26. Information from Margaret Phillimore (née Pottle).   27. Letter to Muriel, 13 Mar. 1949.   28. Ibid.   29. Letter to Muriel, 23 Mar. 1949.   30. Ibid.   31. Letter to Muriel, May 1949 (undated).   32. Ibid.   33. Letter to Muriel, 23 May 1949.   34. Letter to Muriel, probably Apr. 1949 (undated).   35. Ibid.   36. Letter to Muriel, 23 May 1949.   37. Letter to Muriel, probably June 1949 (undated).   38. Letter to Muriel, 1949 (undated).   39. Letter to Muriel, mid-July 1949 (undated).   40. Letter to Muriel, 21 July 1949.   41. Ibid.   42. Letter to Muriel, early July 1949 (undated).   43. Letter to Muriel, Oct. 1949 (undated).   44. Ibid.   45. Letter to Muriel, probably early Jan. 1950 (undated).   46. Ibid.   47. Letter to Muriel, probably mid-Jan. 1950

(undated). **48.** Letter to Muriel, 14 Feb. 1950. **49.** Interview with Muriel Cullen. **50.** Letter to Muriel, 10 Mar. 1950. **51.** Ibid. **52.** Ibid. **53.** Interview with Muriel Cullen. **54.** Interview with Andrew Cullen. **55.** Interview with Muriel Cullen. **56.** Interview with Jane Mayes (née Cullen). **57.** Interview with Josie Henderson. **58.** Interview with Judy, Lady Percival. **59.** Interview with Josie Henderson. **60.** Letter to Muriel, probably early Jan. 1950 (undated). **61.** Letter to Muriel, probably mid-Jan. 1950 (undated). **62.** Letter to Muriel, 14 Feb. 1950. **63.** Letter from Anthony Hancox. **64.** General election address, 3 Feb. 1950 (http://margaretthatcher.org/document/100858). **65.** All above quotations from *Gravesend and Dartford Reporter*, 28 Jan. 1950 (http://www.margaretthatcher.org/document/100856). **66.** The train times are marginally different from those furnished by Mrs Phillimore (see note 26 above). **67.** *Dartford Chronicle*, 10 Feb. 1950. **68.** THCR 4/4. **69.** Ibid. **70.** Ibid. **71.** *Dartford Chronicle*, 3 Mar. 1950 (http://www.margaretthatcher.org/document/100874). Mick Jagger was a pupil at the school shortly afterwards. **72.** Speech on first anniversary as Conservative candidate for Dartford, 9 Mar. 1950, reported in *Erith Observer*, 17 Mar. 1950 (http://www.margaretthatcher.org/document/100875). **73.** Letter to Muriel, probably May 1950 (undated). **74.** Interview with Lord Renton. **75.** Letter to Muriel, probably early July 1950 (undated). **76.** Letter to Muriel, probably Sept. 1950 (undated). **77.** Letter to Muriel, 1950 (undated). **78.** Letter to Muriel, Mar. 1950 (undated). **79.** Letter to Muriel, probably spring 1951 (undated). **80.** Letter to Muriel, 20 May 1950. **81.** Letter to Muriel, probably May 1950 (undated). **82.** Letter to Muriel, 20 June 1950. **83.** Letter to Muriel, late Aug. or early Sept. 1950 (undated). **84.** Letter to Muriel, probably May 1950 (undated). **85.** Letter to Muriel, probably early July 1950 (undated). **86.** Quotations and information from letter to Muriel, 20 June 1950. **87.** Ibid. **88.** Quotations from letter to Muriel, 28 Feb. 1951. **89.** Interview with Lady Thatcher. **90.** Letter to Muriel, May 1951 (undated). **91.** Ibid. **92.** Letter to Muriel, 28 May 1951. **93.** Letter to Muriel, May 1951 (undated). **94.** Letter to Muriel, 23 May 1951. **95.** Letter to Muriel (undated). **96.** Ibid. **97.** Letter to Muriel, 23 May 1951. **98.** Letter from Alfred Roberts to Muriel, 28 Jan. 1951. **99.** Letter from Alfred Roberts to Muriel, 7 May 1951. **100.** Interview with Muriel Cullen. **101.** Letter from Alfred Roberts to Muriel, 8 Aug. 1951. **102.** Interview with Lady Thatcher. **103.** Interview with Muriel Cullen. **104.** Letter to Muriel, 28 Feb. 1951. **105.** Letter to Muriel, 28 May 1951. **106.** Letter to Muriel, probably May 1951 (undated). **107.** Letter from Alfred Roberts to Muriel, 25 Sept. 1951. **108.** Letter to Muriel, probably Oct. 1950 (undated). **109.** *Daily Express*, 11 Oct. 1985. **110.** Interview with Mrs Josie Henderson. **111.** Interview with Muriel Cullen. **112.** Conversation with Lady Thatcher. **113.** Letter to Muriel, 20 Jan. 1954. **114.** Interview with Mrs Josie Henderson. **115.** Letter to Mrs Josie Henderson from Margaret Thatcher, 20 Mar. 2000. **116.** Interview with Sir Denis Thatcher. **117.** Interview with Lady Thatcher. **118.** Interview with Sir Denis Thatcher. **119.** Interview with Lady Thatcher. **120.** See Margaret Thatcher, *The Path to Power*, HarperCollins, 1995, p. 66. **121.** Ibid. **122.** Interview with Lady Thatcher. **123.** Ibid. **124.** Ibid. **125.** Quotations from interview with Sir Denis Thatcher. **126.** Ibid. **127.** Ibid.

128. See Carol Thatcher, *Below the Parapet: The Biography of Denis Thatcher*, HarperCollins, 1996, p. 51. **129.** Ibid. **130.** Conversation with Lady Thatcher. **131.** Interview with Cynthia Crawford. **132.** Speech in Belvedere, 15 Oct. 1951, reported in *Erith Observer*, 19 Oct. 1951 (http://www.margaretthatcher. org/document/100917). **133.** Interview with Patricia Greenough. **134.** THCR 4/4. **135.** Interview with Sir Clive Bossom. **136.** Interview with Lord Deedes. **137.** Letter to Muriel, probably Sept. 1950 (undated). **138.** Interview with Sir Clive Bossom. **139.** Letter to Muriel, 23 May 1951. **140.** Letter to Muriel, 20 May 1950. **141.** Speech to Dartford Conservatives, 10 July 1950, reported in *Dartford Chronicle*, 14 July 1950 (http://www.margaretthatcher.org/ document/100885). **142.** Speech to Chislehurst Young Conservatives, 25 Sept. 1950, reported in *Dartford Chronicle*, 29 Sept. 1950 (http://www.margaretthatcher. org/document/100890). **143.** *Dartford Chronicle*, 29 Dec. 1950 (http://www. margaretthatcher.org/document/100896). **144.** Speech to Dartford Free Church Council, 30 May 1951, reported in *Dartford Chronicle*, 8 June 1951 (http://www. margaretthatcher.org/document/100905). **145.** Speech at adoption meeting, 8 Oct. 1951, reported in *Erith Observer*, 12 Oct. 1951 (http://www.margaretthatcher.org/ document/100911). **146.** Letter to Muriel, 28 Feb. 1951. **147.** Thatcher, *The Path to Power*, p. 69. **148.** THCR 4/4. **149.** Speech in Crayford, 22 Oct. 1951, reported in *Dartford Chronicle*, 26 Oct. 1951 (http://www.margaretthatcher.org/ document/100924).

CHAPTER 6: MARRIAGE, THE LAW AND FINCHLEY

1. Letter to Muriel, mid-Feb. 1952 (undated). **2.** Margaret Thatcher, *The Path to Power*, HarperCollins, 1995, p. 76. **3.** Carol Thatcher, *Below the Parapet: The Biography of Denis Thatcher*, HarperCollins, 1996, p. 65. **4.** Letter to Muriel, 19 Dec. 1951. **5.** Ibid. **6.** Carol Thatcher, *Below the Parapet*, p. 65. **7.** Postcard to Muriel, Dec. 1951 (undated). **8.** Letter to Muriel, 28 Jan. 1952. **9.** Thatcher, *The Path to Power*, p. 77. **10.** *Sunday Graphic*, 17 Feb. 1952 (http://www.margaretthatcher. org/document/100936). **11.** Letter from Alfred Roberts to Muriel, 1 Apr. 1952. **12.** Letter to Muriel, 21 Apr. 1952. **13.** Carol Thatcher, *Below the Parapet*, p. 69. **14.** Ibid., p. 71. **15.** Thatcher, *The Path to Power*, pp. 80–81. **16.** The Thatcher Papers, Churchill College, Cambridge, THCR 1/1/1. **17.** Ibid. **18.** Carol Thatcher, *Below the Parapet*, p. 71. **19.** Letter to Muriel, 20 Sep. 1953. **20.** Interview with Sir Denis Thatcher. **21.** Letter to Muriel, 20 Jan. 1954. **22.** Letter to Muriel, probably mid-Jan. 1955 (undated). **23.** Letter to Muriel, 10 July 1958. **24.** Letter to Muriel, 3 July 1958. **25.** Letter to Muriel, probably early 1960s (undated). **26.** Letter to Muriel, 18 Nov. 1963. **27.** Letter to Muriel, Sept. 1960 (undated). **28.** Letter to Muriel, probably Oct. 1957 (undated). **29.** Letter to Muriel, probably Jan. 1955 (undated). **30.** Carol Thatcher, *Below the Parapet*, p. 72. **31.** Letter to Muriel, early 1960s (undated). **32.** Interview with Carol Thatcher. **33.** Ibid. **34.** *Onward*, Apr. 1954 (http://www.margaretthatcher.org/document/100939). **35.** Letter to Muriel, probably June 1955 (undated). **36.** Interview with Carol Thatcher.

37. Interviews with Andrew Cullen and Jane Mayes (née Cullen). 38. Interview with Andrew Cullen. 39. Interview with Carol Thatcher. 40. Letter to Muriel, early 1960s (undated). 41. Letter to Muriel, Jan. or Feb. 1955 (undated). 42. Letter to Muriel, 20 Jan. 1954. 43. Letter to Muriel, 3 July 1958. 44. Letter to Muriel, 16 Feb. 1954. 45. Letter to Muriel, probably Oct. 1957 (undated). 46. Ibid. 47. Carol Thatcher, *Below the Parapet*, p. 77. 48. Letter to Muriel, probably Oct. 1957 (undated). 49. Letter to Muriel, 31 Dec. 1957. 50. Interview with Carol Thatcher. 51. Letter to Muriel, 20 Jan. 1954. 52. Interview with Pamela Thomas. 53. Interview with Sir Frederick Lawton. 54. Ibid. 55. Ibid. 56. Ibid. 57. Ibid. 58. See Thatcher, *The Path to Power*, p. 84. 59. Ibid. 60. Interview with Sir Frederick Lawton. 61. Ibid. 62. Interview with Sir Denis Thatcher. 63. Letter to Muriel, probably Jan. 1955 (undated). 64. Interview with Lord and Lady Brightman. 65. Ibid. 66. Information from John Stevenson. 67. Quoted in Patricia Murray, *Margaret Thatcher*, W. H. Allen, 1980, p. 54. 68. Interview with Pamela Thomas. 69. Ibid. 70. Thatcher, *The Path to Power*, p. 88. 71. Interview with Lord Jenkin. 72. Interview with Pamela Thomas. 73. Copy at THCR 1/1/1. 74. Ibid. 75. Interview with Muriel Cullen (née Roberts). 76. *Grantham Journal*, 23 May 1952. 77. Ibid., 13 Feb. 1970. 78. *Woman to Woman* (Yorkshire Television), 19 Nov. 1985 (http://www.margaretthatcher.org/document/105830). 79. *Grantham Journal*, draft obituary of Lady Thatcher. 80. See letter from John Hare to Margaret Thatcher, 15 Dec. 1954, copy at THCR 1/1/1. 81. Letter to John Hare, 3 Jan. 1955, copy at THCR 1/1/1. 82. Letter to John Hare, wrongly dated 1954, copy at THCR 1/1/1. 83. Letter to Donald Kaberry, 28 Feb. 1956, copy at THCR 1/1/1. 84. Letter to Donald Kaberry, 15 Mar. 1956, copy at THCR 1/1/1. 85. Letter to Donald Kaberry, 2 Dec. 1957, copy at THCR 1/1/1. 86. Letter to Muriel, probably Oct. 1957 (undated). 87. Copy at THCR 1/1/1. 88. Letter to Muriel, 3 July 1958. 89. Interview with Derek Phillips. 90. Interview with John Tiplady. 91. Letter to Donald Kaberry, 18 Aug. 1958, copy at THCR 1/1/1. 92. Thatcher, *The Path to Power*, p. 95. 93. Interview with John Tiplady. 94. Interview with Derek Phillips. 95. Interview with Haden Blatch. 96. Carol Thatcher, *Below the Parapet*, p. 78. 97. *Evening Standard*, 15 July 1958. 98. Copy at THCR 1/1/1. 99. Thatcher, *The Path to Power*, p. 97. 100. See Conservative Party Archive, Bodleian Library, Oxford, CCO 1/12/375. 101. Copy at THCR 1/1/1. 102. Speech at Finchley adoption meeting, 31 July 1958, reported in *Finchley Press*, 8 Aug. 1958 (http://www.margaretthatcher.org/document/100941). 103. Ibid., reported in *Finchley Times*, 1 Aug. 1958 (http://www.margaretthatcher.org/document/100941). 104. Ibid. 105. Interview with John Tiplady. 106. Letter to Miss Burgess, 17 Sept. 1958, CCO 1/12/375. 107. Interview with Lady Thatcher. 108. Ibid. 109. Thatcher, *The Path to Power*, p. 98. 110. David Kynaston, *Family Britain, 1951–57* (in the series *Tales of a New Jerusalem*), Bloomsbury, 2009, p. 697. 111. Quoted in Alistair Horne, *Macmillan*, vol. ii: *1957–86*, Macmillan, 1989, p. 62. 112. Ibid., p. 143. 113. *Finchley Press*, 26 Mar. 1959. 114. All above quotations from speech in Friern Barnet, 3 Apr. 1959, reported in *Finchley Press*, 10 Apr. 1959 (http://www.margaretthatcher.org/document/101016). 115. Speech at adoption meeting, 21 Sept. 1959, reported in *Finchley Borough News*, 26 Sept. 1959

(http://www.margaretthatcher.org/document/100944). 116. Interview with *Evening News*, 5 Oct. 1959 (Christopher Collins, ed., *Complete Public Statements of Margaret Thatcher 1945–90 on CD-ROM*, Oxford University Press, 1998/2000). 117. Ibid.

CHAPTER 7: MEMBER, MINISTER

1. Interview with Paddi Lilley. 2. Ibid. 3. Letter to Muriel, 15 Oct. 1959. 4. Letter from Alfred Roberts to Muriel, 18 Oct. 1959. 5. Conversation with Lady Thatcher. 6. *Any Questions?* (BBC Light Programme), 8 Jan. 1960 (Christopher Collins, ed., *Complete Public Statements of Margaret Thatcher 1945–90 on CD-ROM*, Oxford University Press, 1998/2000). 7. *Evening News*, 22 Jan. 1960 (http://www.margaretthatcher.org/document/101053). 8. Papers relating to the compilation of Lady Thatcher's memoirs, The Thatcher Papers, Churchill College, Cambridge, THCR 4/4. 9. Interview with Paddi Lilley. 10. See Margaret Thatcher, *The Path to Power*, HarperCollins, 1995, pp. 109 ff. 11. Ibid., p. 111. 12. John Campbell, *Margaret Thatcher*, 2 vols, Jonathan Cape, 2000, 2003, vol. i: *The Grocer's Daughter*. 13. Hansard, SC Deb (C) 6 Apr. 1960. 14. Interview with Lord Simon of Glaisdale. 15. The National Archives (TNA): Public Record Office (PRO) HLG 29/490 XC10776. 16. TNA: PRO HLG 29/490 XC10776, HA (59) 153. 17. TNA: PRO HLG 29/490 XC10776. 18. Ibid. 19. Ibid. 20. Ibid. 21. Interview with Lord Deedes. 22. Thatcher, *The Path to Power*, p. 112. 23. All above quotations from Hansard, HC Deb 5 Feb. 1960 (http://www. margaretthatcher.org/document/101055). 24. *Sunday Dispatch*, 7 Feb. 1960 (Collins, ed., *Complete Public Statements*). 25. *Evening News*, 25 Feb. 1960 (Collins, ed., *Complete Public Statements*). 26. All above quotations from *Daily Express*, 4 Mar. 1960 (http://www.margaretthatcher.org/document/100948). 27. Hansard, HC Deb 13 May 1960 (http://www.margaretthatcher.org/document/101069). 28. *Any Questions?* (BBC Light Programme), 4 Nov. 1960. 29. Letter from Alfred Roberts to Muriel Cullen, 13 Apr. 1961. 30. All quotations from Hansard, SC Deb (B) 14 Feb. 1961 (http://www.margaretthatcher.org/document/101088). 31. Ibid. 32. Letter from Alfred Roberts to Muriel Cullen, 26 Aug. 1960. 33. Letter from Alfred Roberts to Muriel Cullen, 16 Sept. 1960. 34. Letter from Alfred Roberts to Muriel Cullen, 27 Sept. 1960. 35. *Liverpool Daily Post*, 6 Dec. 1960 (http://www.margaretthatcher.org/document/100954). 36. Letter from Alfred Roberts to Muriel Cullen, 23 Dec. 1961. 37. Letter to Muriel, late 1960 (undated). 38. Letter from Alfred Roberts to Muriel Cullen, 27 Apr. 1961. 39. Letter from Alfred Roberts to Muriel Cullen, 24 June 1961. 40. Letter from Margaret Thatcher to Alfred Roberts, 4 Sept. 1961. 41. Letter from Margaret Thatcher to Alfred Roberts, probably June 1962 (undated). 42. Interview with Carol Thatcher. 43. Letter from Alfred Roberts to Muriel Cullen, 17 Apr. 1962. 44. *Daily Express*, 17 Apr. 1961 (Collins, ed., *Complete Public Statements*). 45. Ibid. 46. Peter Catterall (ed), *The Macmillan Diaries*, vol. ii: *Prime Minister and After, 1957–1966*, Macmillan, 2011, p. 417. 47. *Sheffield Telegraph*, 11 Oct. 1961 (Collins, ed., *Complete Public Statements*). 48. Cutting from unidentified newspaper, 10 Oct. 1961 (http://www.margaretthatcher.org/document/101112). 49. Thatcher,

The Path to Power, p. 119. 50. Ibid. 51. Ibid., pp. 118–19. 52. Interview with Lady Thatcher. 53. John Boyd-Carpenter, *Way of Life*, Sidgwick & Jackson, 1980, p. 133. 54. Ibid. 55. Interview with Sir Michael Partridge. 56. MPNI Annual Report 1962. 57. Hansard, SC Deb (B) 5 Dec. 1961 (http://www.margaretthatcher. org/document/101121). 58. Hansard, HC Deb 13 Dec. 1961 (http://www.margaret thatcher.org/document/101123). 59. Ibid., 13 Mar. 1962 (http://www.margarett hatcher.org/document/101134). 60. Ibid., 22 Jan. 1964 (http://www.margarett hatcher.org/document/101222). 61. Ibid., 6 Feb. 1963 (http://www.margaretthatcher. org/document/101172). 62. Ibid., 13 Mar. 1962. 63. Ibid., 6 Feb. 1963 (http://www. margaretthatcher.org/document/101173). 64. Ibid., 13 July 1962 (http://www.mar garetthatcher.org/document/101153). 65. Boyd-Carpenter, *Way of Life*, pp. 257– 8. 66. Richard Crossman, *The Diaries of a Cabinet Minister*, vol. iii: *Secretary of State for Social Services 1968–70*, ed. Janet Morgan, Hamish Hamilton/Jonathan Cape, 1977, 26 Oct. 1969. 67. Thatcher, *The Path to Power*, p. 120. 68. THCR 4/4. 69. Ibid. 70. Ibid. 71. Thatcher, *The Path to Power*, p. 121. 72. Interview with Sir Clive Bossom. 73. Speech to Finchley Conservatives, 14 Aug. 1961, reported in *Finchley Press*, 18 Aug. 1961 (http://www.margaretthatcher.org/ document/101105). 74. Remarks at Conservative Association meeting, 10 Aug. 1962, reported in *Finchley Press*, 17 Aug. 1962 (http://www.margaretthatcher.org/ document/101156). 75. Speech at Finchley Conservative Fair, 22 June 1963, reported in *Finchley Press*, 28 June 1963 (http://www.margaretthatcher.org/ document/101191). 76. Hansard, HC Deb 19 Apr. 1961 (http://www.margarett hatcher.org/document/101095). 77. Speech to Finchley Conservative Women, 15 Mar. 1962, reported in *Finchley Press*, 23 Mar. 1962 (http://www.margaretthatcher. org/document/101135). 78. Remarks at Conservative Association meeting, 10 Aug. 1962, reported in *Finchley Press*, 17 Aug. 1962 (http://www.margaretthatcher.org/ document/101156). 79. Ibid. 80. Letter from Margaret Thatcher to Alfred Roberts (undated). 81. Interview with Lady Thatcher. 82. Speech to Finchley Conservative Women, 11 July 1963, reported in *Finchley Press*, 19 July 1963 (http://www.margaret thatcher.org/document/101195). 83. See Alistair Horne, *Macmillan*, vol. ii: *1957–86*, Macmillan, 1989. 84. Interview with Lady Thatcher. 85. Thatcher, *The Path to Power*, p. 129. 86. Interview with Lady Thatcher. 87. Ibid. 88. Letter from Margaret Thatcher to Alfred Roberts, 18 Nov. 1963. 89. THCR 4/4. 90. Thatcher, *The Path to Power*, p. 128. 91. Ibid., p. 129. 92. Interview with Lady Thatcher. 93. Speech to Finchley Conservatives (Whetstone Ward dinner), 19 Oct. 1963, reported in *Finchley Press*, 25 Oct. 1963 (http://www.margaretthatcher.org/ document/101200). 94. See article by Margaret Thatcher in *Conservative Viewpoint*, 31 Dec. 1963 (http://www.margaretthatcher.org/document/101219). 95. Speech to Finchley Conservative Women, 16 Apr. 1964, reported in *Finchley Press*, 24 Apr. 1964 (http://www.margaretthatcher.org/document/101233). 96. Remarks visiting Golders Green (Brains Trust), 13 Feb. 1964, reported in *Finchley Times*, 21 Feb. 1964 (http:// www.margaretthatcher.org/document/100962). 97. THCR 4/4. 98. D. E. Butler and Anthony King, *The British General Election of 1964*, Macmillan, 1965. 99. Interview with Lord Donoughue. 100. *Daily Telegraph*, 5 Oct. 1964 (Collins, ed., *Complete Public Statements*).

CHAPTER 8: OPPOSITION, 1964–1970

1. Papers relating to the compilation of Lady Thatcher's memoirs, The Thatcher Papers, Churchill College, Cambridge, THCR 4/4. 2. Carol Thatcher, *Below the Parapet: The Biography of Denis Thatcher* HarperCollins, 1996, p. 91. 3. Interview with Sir Denis Thatcher. 4. Carol Thatcher, *Below the Parapet*, p. 92. 5. Interview with Carol Thatcher. 6. Ibid. 7. Ibid. 8. Interview with Sir Denis Thatcher. 9. Interview with Lady Thatcher. 10. Hansard, HC Deb 3 Dec. 1964 (http://www.margaretthatcher.org/document/101285). 11. Ibid. 12. Carol Thatcher, *Below the Parapet*, p. 93. 13. *Finchley Press*, 29 Jan. 1965 (http://www.margaret thatcher.org/document/101308). 14. Conversation with Sir Denis Thatcher. 15. Information from THCR 4/4. 16. Ibid. 17. Margaret Thatcher, *The Path to Power*, HarperCollins, 1995, p. 136. 18. Ibid., p. 135. 19. THCR 4/4. 20. *Finchley Press*, 13 Aug. 1965 (http://www.margaretthatcher.org/document/101346). 21. THCR 4/4. 22. See Hansard, HC Deb 6 Dec. 1965 (http://www.margaretthatcher.org/document/101366). 23. *Daily Mail*, 10 May 1966. 24. Speech to Reading Conservative Women, 21 May 1965, reported in *Reading Chronicle*, 28 May 1965 (http://www.margaretthatcher.org/document/101330). 25. *News of the World*, 5 May 1968 (http://www.margaret hatcher.org/document/101617). 26. Speech to Motor Agents' Association, 21 Oct. 1969 (http://www.margaretthatcher.org/document/101693). 27. THCR 4/4. 28. Hansard, HC Deb 31 Jan. 1966 (http://www.margaretthatcher.org/document/101442). 29. THCR 4/4. 30. Hansard, HC Deb 28 July 1966 (http://www.margaretthatcher.org/document/101513). 31. Ibid., 5 May 1966 (http://www.margaretthatcher.org/document/101481). 32. Ibid. 33. Ibid. 34. See Hansard, HC Deb 27 June 1966 (http://www.margaretthatcher.org/document/101497). 35. Ibid., 12 July 1966 (http://www.margaretthatcher.org/document/101505). 36. Ibid., 20 July 1966 (http://www.margaretthatcher.org/document/101511). 37. Ibid., 25 Oct. 1966 (http://www.margaretthatcher.org/document/101523). 38. James Prior, *A Balance of Power*, Hamish Hamilton, 1986, p. 42. 39. *Any Questions?* (BBC Light Programme), Culdrose, 10 June 1966, BBC Written Archives. 40. Ibid. (BBC Radio 1 and 2), Leeds, 5 Apr. 1968 (Christopher Collins, ed., *Complete Public Statements of Margaret Thatcher 1945–90 on CD-ROM*, Oxford University Press, 1998/2000). 41. Ibid., Northampton, 30 Jan. 1970 (Collins, ed., *Complete Public Statements*). 42. Ibid., Plymouth, 4 Oct. 1968 (Collins, ed., *Complete Public Statements*). 43. THCR 4/4. 44. Ibid. 45. *Woman's Hour* (BBC Radio 4), 9 Apr. 1970 (http://www.margaretthatcher.org/document/101845). 46. Speech to Conservative Party Conference, 10 Oct. 1969 (http://www.margaretthatcher.org/document/101687). 47. Letter to Muriel, 18 Oct. 1966. 48. Speech to Finchley Conservatives, 10 Mar. 1966, reported in *Finchley Press*, 18 Mar. 1966 (http://www.margaretthatcher.org/document/101458). 49. *Finchley Press*, 25 Mar. 1966 (http://www.margaretthatcher.org/document/101472). 50. Ibid. 51. *Daily Telegraph Magazine*, 18 Mar. 1966 (http://www.margaretthatcher.org/document/101465). 52. Speech in Finchley, 18 Mar.

1966, reported in *Finchley Press*, 25 Mar. 1966 (http://www.margaretthatcher.org/document/101466). **53.** Speech in Finchley, 14 Mar. 1966, reported in *Finchley Press*, 18 Mar. 1966 (http://www.margaretthatcher.org/document/101460). **54.** Hansard, HC Deb 26 July 1966 (http://www.margaretthatcher.org/document/101512). **55.** Hansard, HC Deb 28 July 1966 (http://www.margaretthatcher.org/document/101513). **56.** *Finchley Press*, 2 Sept. 1966 (http://www.margaretthatcher.org/document/101516). **57.** Hansard, HC Deb 27 June 1966 (http://www.margaretthatcher.org/document/101497). **58.** See Hansard, HC Deb 25 Oct. 1966 (http://www.margaretthatcher.org/document/101523). **59.** Hansard, HC Deb 31 Jan 1967 (http://www.margaretthatcher.org/document/101539). **60.** *Any Questions?* (BBC Light Programme), Paignton, 18 Nov. 1966 (Collins, ed., *Complete Public Statements*). **61.** Hansard, HC Deb 30 Nov. 1966 (http://www.margaretthatcher.org/document/101530). **62.** Ibid., 17 Apr. 1967 (http://www.margaretthatcher.org/document/101551). **63.** Ibid. **64.** Ibid., 6 June 1967 (http://www.margaretthatcher.org/document/101564). **65.** *Building Societies Gazette*, 9 Oct. 1967 (Collins, ed., *Complete Public Statements*). **66.** Speech to Conservative Party Conference, 20 Oct. 1967 (http://www.margaretthatcher.org/document/101586). **67.** *Sunday Times*, 5 Mar. 1967. **68.** Hansard, HC Deb 26 Oct. 1967 (http://www.margaretthatcher.org/document/101587). **69.** *Any Questions?* (BBC Radio 1 and 2), Llandaff, 3 Nov. 1967 (Collins, ed., *Complete Public Statements*). **70.** All above quotations from Hansard, HC Deb 28 Nov. 1967 (http://www.margaretthatcher.org/document/101594). **71.** Hansard, HC Deb 1 May 1968 (http://www.margaretthatcher.org/document/101616). **72.** THCR 4/4. **73.** Ibid. **74.** *Daily Mirror*, 10 Oct. 1968 (Collins, ed., *Complete Public Statements*). **75.** THCR 4/4. **76.** Ibid. **77.** Ibid. **78.** Ibid. **79.** John Campbell, *Margaret Thatcher*, 2 vols, Jonathan Cape, 2000, 2003, vol. i: *The Grocer's Daughter*, p. 205. **80.** Speech to Finchley Conservatives (Association AGM), 3 Mar. 1970, reported in *Finchley Press*, 6 Mar. 1970 (http://www.margaretthatcher.org/document/101721). **81.** Interview with Andrew Alexander. **82.** *Daily Telegraph*, 17 Mar. and 26 Apr. 1969 (http://www.margaretthatcher.org/document/101650; http://www.margaretthatcher.org/document/101651). **83.** Speech to Finchley Anglo-Israel Friendship League, 24 June 1965, reported in *Finchley Press*, 2 July 1965 (http://www.margaretthatcher.org/document/101293). **84.** Ibid., reported in *Finchley Times*, 2 July 1965 (http://www.margaretthatcher.org/document/101293). **85.** Ibid., reported in *Finchley Press*, 2 July 1965 (http://www.margaretthatcher.org/document/101293). **86.** See article by Giles Scott-Smith, '"Her Rather Ambitious Washington Program": Margaret Thatcher's International Visitor Program Visit to the United States in 1967', *British Contemporary History*, vol. XVII, no. 4, Winter 2003. **87.** THCR 1/10/1. **88.** See the Appointment Books of Walt Rostow, 2 Mar. 1967, Lyndon B. Johnson Presidential Library, Austin TX. **89.** Campbell, *Margaret Thatcher*, vol. i, p. 176. **90.** Jean Lashly to Natalie Greening, 29 Mar. 1967, Bureau of Educational and Cultural Affairs Collection (CU), Box 155, Folder 26. Special Collections Department, University of Arkansas Libraries Fayetteville. **91.** Main source for Mrs Thatcher's recollections of the visit: THCR 4/4. **92.** CU archives, University of Arkansas Libraries. **93.** *Houston Post*, 9 Mar. 1967. **94.** CU archives, University of Arkansas Libraries. **95.** THCR 4/4. **96.** Thatcher, *The Path to Power*, pp. 154–5. **97.** Hansard, HC Deb 2 May 1967 (http://www.margaretthatcher.org/document/101558). **98.** *Any Questions?* (BBC Radio 1 and 2), Llandaff, 3 Nov. 1967 (Collins, ed., *Complete Public Statements*). **99.** Hansard, HC Deb 6 June 1967, http://www.margaretthatcher.org/document/101564). **100.** Katharine Winn to Frances McPheeters, 19 Feb. 1969, English-Speaking Union (ESU) Archive, London. **101.** Katharine Winn to Frances McPheeters, 14 Feb. 1969, ESU Archive. **102.** Ibid. **103.** Mary Taggart to Frances McPheeters, 19 Mar. 1969, ESU Archive. **104.** All ensuing quotations from THCR 4/4. **105.** Ibid. **106.** Ibid. **107.** Conservative Party Archive, Bodleian Library, Oxford, LCC 1/2/6. **108.** Ibid., LCC 1/2/8. **109.** Speech to Finchley Conservatives (Association AGM), 4 Mar. 1965, reported in *Finchley Press*, 12 Mar. 1965 (http://www.margaretthatcher.org/document/101312). **110.** Speech to Friern Barnet Young Conservatives, 15 Sept. 1967, reported in *Finchley Press*, 22 Sept. 1967 (http://www.margaretthatcher.org/document/101584). **111.** Conservative Party Archive, CRD 3/8/8. **112.** BBC Radio News, 21 Oct. 1969 (Collins, ed., *Complete Public Statements*). **113.** Hansard, HC Deb 31 Oct. 1969 (http://www.margaretthatcher.org/document/101702). **114.** Conservative Party Archive, LCC 1/2/18. **115.** Hansard, SC (A) 5 May 1970 (http://www.margaretthatcher.org/document/101744). **116.** Letter to Muriel, 3 Nov. 1969. **117.** Letter to Muriel, 4 Dec. 1969. **118.** THCR 4/4. **119.** Interview with Carol Thatcher. **120.** *Daily Telegraph*, 11 Feb. 1970. **121.** Interview with Muriel Cullen. **122.** Ibid. **123.** Ibid. **124.** Edward Heath, *The Course of my Life*, Hodder & °Stoughton, 1998, p. 301. **125.** Ibid., p. 302. **126.** Conservative Party Archive, CRD 3/9/93. **127.** Ibid. **128.** See Campbell, *Margaret Thatcher*, vol. i, pp. 206–7. **129.** General election address, 28 May 1970 (http://www.margaretthatcher.org/document/101754). **130.** Interview with John Izbicki. **131.** See Carol Thatcher, *Below the Parapet*, p. 97.

CHAPTER 9: MILKSNATCHER

1. Letter to Muriel, 20 Aug. 1944. **2.** Letter to Muriel, 30 July 1944. **3.** Ibid. **4.** Letter to Muriel, 20 Aug. 1944. **5.** Letter to Muriel, Sept. 1944 (undated). **6.** Ibid. **7.** *Maggie: The First Lady* (Brook Lapping productions for ITV and PBS, 2003). **8.** Interview with Carol Thatcher. **9.** Interview with Michael James. **10.** Ibid. **11.** Papers relating to the compilation of Lady Thatcher's memoirs, The Thatcher Papers, Churchill College, Cambridge, THCR 4/4. **12.** Interview with Nicholas Stuart. **13.** Margaret Thatcher, *The Path to Power*, HarperCollins, 1995, p. 5. **14.** Cabinet Secretary's notebooks, 23 June 1970. **15.** Interview with John Hedger. **16.** THCR 4/4. **17.** *Daily Telegraph*, 22 June 1970 (Christopher Collins, ed., *Complete Public Statements of Margaret Thatcher 1945–90 on CD-ROM*, Oxford University Press, 1998/2000). **18.** *Times*, 11 Nov. 1970 (http://www.margaretthatcher.org/document/101813). **19.** See *Woman's Hour* (BBC Radio 2), 23 July 1970 (Collins, ed., *Complete Public Statements*) and *Sunday Times*, 15 Nov. 1970 (http://www.margaretthatcher.org/document/101814). **20.** Hansard, HC Deb 19 Oct.

1972 (http://www.margaretthatcher.org/document/102224). 21. THCR 4/4. 22. Interview with Max Morris. 23. *Finchley Press*, 25 June 1971 (http://www.margaretthatcher.org/document/102126). 24. Interview with Nicholas Stuart. 25. Ibid. 26. *Times Educational Supplement*, 2 July 1971. 27. Thatcher, *The Path to Power*, p. 166. 28. Interview with John Hedger. 29. Private information. 30. THCR 4/4. 31. Interview with Lord Belstead. 32. Interview with Nicholas Stuart. 33. Interviews with John Banks, John Hedger and Anthony Chamier. 34. Private information. 35. Interview with Anthony Chamier. 36. Interview with Carol Thatcher. 37. Interview with John Banks. 38. Interview with John Hedger. 39. The National Archives (TNA): Public Record Office (PRO) ED 207/103, 24 June 1970. 40. THCR 4/4. 41. Interview with Nicholas Stuart. 42. Interview with Lord Belstead. 43. Peter Hennessy, *Whitehall*, Secker & Warburg, 1989, p. 626. 44. TNA: PRO T 227/3146. 45. Ibid., 11 Aug. 1970. 46. TNA: PRO T 227/3147, 1 Sept. 1970. 47. THCR 4/4. 48. Cabinet Secretary's notebooks, 30 July 1970. 49. *Guardian*, 28 Oct. 1970. 50. TNA: PRO ED 269/1, memo from J. A. Hudson to Sir William Pile, 7 Jan. 1971. 51. TNA: PRO ED 269/1, letter from Edward Short to Mrs Thatcher, 20 May 1971. 52. Hansard, HC Deb 14 June 1971 (http://www.margaretthatcher.org/document/102119). 53. *Sun*, 9 July 1971. 54. *Observer*, 7 Feb. 1971 (Collins, ed., *Complete Public Statements*). 55. See *A Chance to Meet* (BBC1), 21 Mar. 1971 (Collins, ed., *Complete Public Statements*). 56. Interview with Anthony Chamier. 57. *Sun*, 25 Nov. 1971. 58. *Guardian*, 2 Nov. 1971. 59. *Daily Mail*, 15 Dec. 1971. 60. See Carol Thatcher's discussion of this in *Below the Parapet: The Biography of Denis Thatcher*, HarperCollins, 1996, p. 98. 61. Interview with Lady Thatcher. 62. Interview with Kenneth Clarke. 63. TNA: PRO ED 269/13. 64. Interview with Anthony Chamier. 65. Interview with Sir Edward Heath. 66. TNA: PRO PREM 15/1482, 13 Jan. 1972. 67. Interview with Lord Belstead. 68. *Sunday Express*, 16 Jan. 1972 (Collins, ed., *Complete Public Statements*). 69. *Daily Mail*, 8 Feb. 1972 (Collins, ed., *Complete Public Statements*). 70. *Liverpool Daily Post*, 21 Feb. 1972 (http://www.margaretthatcher.org/document/102180). 71. Interview with Nicholas Stuart. 72. Interview with Max Morris. 73. Interview with Michael James. 74. Cabinet Secretary's notebooks, 30 Nov. 1972. 75. Interview with Michael James. 76. Interview with Lord Belstead. 77. *Illustrated London News*, Nov. 1973 (Collins, ed., *Complete Public Statements*). 78. Interview with Eric Bolton. 79. *Daily Mail*, 9 June 1972. 80. *Sunday Times*, 8 Apr. 1973 (http://www.margaretthatcher.org/document/101823). 81. Interview with Anthony Chamier. 82. See *Evening Standard*, 17 Nov. 1973 (Collins, ed., *Complete Public Statements*).

CHAPTER 10: WHO GOVERNS BRITAIN?

1. Edward Heath, *The Course of my Life*, Hodder & Stoughton, 1998, p. 327. 2. Douglas Hurd, *An End to Promises*, Collins, 1979, p. 95. 3. Heath, *The Course of my Life*, p. 348. 4. Ibid. 5. Papers relating to the compilation of Lady Thatcher's memoirs, The Thatcher Papers, Churchill College, Cambridge,

THCR 4/4. **6.** Margaret Thatcher, *The Path to Power*, HarperCollins, 1995, p. 221. **7.** Interview with Lord Parkinson. **8.** THCR 4/4. **9.** Interview with Sir Edward Heath. **10.** For example, interviews with Lord Walker and Lord Prior. **11.** 059 State 1970–73 Central File, US National Archives and Records Administration (NARA). **12.** Interview with Lord Butler of Brockwell. **13.** All above quotations from the Cabinet Secretary's notebooks. **14.** Interview with Lord Parkinson. **15.** THCR 4/4. **16.** Interview with Lord Butler of Brockwell. **17.** All above quotations are from the Cabinet Secretary's notebooks. Sir John Hunt succeeded Sir Burke Trend in September 1973. The abbreviations of reported speech are his. **18.** THCR 4/4. **19.** See Thatcher, *The Path to Power*, p. 195. **20.** THCR 4/4. **21.** Heath, *The Course of my Life*, p. 334. **22.** Private information. **23.** Speech to Finchley Conservatives (Association AGM), 2 Mar. 1972, reported in *Finchley Times*, 10 Mar. 1972 (http://www.margaretthatcher.org/document/102186). **24.** Speech to Devon Conservatives, 29 July 1972, reported in *Exeter Express and Echo*, 31 July 1972 (Christopher Collins, ed., *Complete Public Statements of Margaret Thatcher 1945–90 on CD-ROM*, Oxford University Press, 1998/2000). **25.** THCR 4/4. **26.** Ibid. **27.** Ibid. **28.** Airey Neave, diary (unpublished). **29.** Ibid. **30.** Letter from Carol Thatcher to Muriel Cullen, 30 Aug. 1973. **31.** Thatcher, *The Path to Power*, p. 228. **32.** For a discussion of this incident, see John Campbell, *Edward Heath: A Biography*, Jonathan Cape, 1993, pp. 566–7. **33.** Interview with Lord Waldegrave of North Hill. **34.** THCR 4/4. **35.** Cabinet Secretary's notebooks, 17 Jan. 1974. **36.** Neave, diary, 17 Jan. 1974. **37.** Cabinet Secretary's notebooks, 5 Feb. 1974. **38.** Ibid. **39.** Interview with Lord Waldegrave of North Hill. **40.** Interview with Lord Donoughue. **41.** THCR 4/4. **42.** *Finchley Times*, 15 Feb. 1974 (http://www.margaretthatcher.org/document/102337). **43.** *Election Call* (BBC Radio 4), 19 Feb. 1974 (Collins, ed., *Complete Public Statements*). **44.** *Daily Express*, 22 Feb. 1974. **45.** Interview with Lady Thatcher. **46.** For a full account of all the negotiations of 1–4 Mar., see Robert Armstrong, Note for the Record, 16 March 1974, The National Archives (TNA): Public Record Office (PRO) PREM 15/2069. **47.** Ibid. **48.** Cabinet Secretary's notebooks, 1 Mar. 1974. **49.** Robert Armstrong, Note for the Record, TNA: PRO PREM 15/2069. **50.** Interview with Lady Wakeham. **51.** *Daily Mail*, 9 Mar. 1974 (Collins, ed., *Complete Public Statements*). **52.** THCR 4/4. **53.** Neave, diary, 5 Mar. 1974. **54.** Ibid., 7 Mar. 1974. **55.** Interview with Sir Charles Morrison. **56.** Bernard Donoughue, *Downing Street Diary*, 2 vols, Jonathan Cape, 2005, 2008, vol. i: *With Harold Wilson in No. 10*, 15 Mar. 1974, p. 71. **57.** Ibid., 13 Mar. 1974. **58.** Private information. **59.** Neave, diary, 14 Mar. 1974. **60.** Ibid., 18 Mar. 1974. **61.** Ibid., 19 Mar. 1974. **62.** Hansard, HC Deb 6 May 1974 (http://www.margaretthatcher.org/document/102360). **63.** Neave, diary, 25 Mar. 1974. **64.** Ibid., 24 Apr. 1974. **65.** THCR 4/4. **66.** Private information. **67.** Neave, diary, 9 May 1974. **68.** Ibid., 13 June 1974. **69.** Ibid., 17 June 1974. **70.** Ibid., 27 June 1974. **71.** Ibid., 2 July 1974. **72.** Ibid., 8 July 1974. **73.** Ibid., 14 July 1974. **74.** Interview with Sir Edward Heath. **75.** Interview with Sara Morrison. **76.** Interview with Sir Alfred Sherman. **77.** Ibid. **78.** Interview with Simon Webley. **79.** Ibid. **80.** Interview with

Lady Thatcher. 81. Interview with Lord Carrington. 82. For a full account see Alfred Sherman, *Paradoxes of Power*, Imprint Academic, 2005. 83. Interview with Lady Thatcher. 84. *The Times*, 2, 3 and 4 May 1974. 85. THCR 4/4. 86. Interview with Lord Walker. 87. Radio interview for *Feedback* (LBC), 17 May 1974 (http://www.margaretthatcher.org/document/102366). 88. *Liverpool Daily Post*, 17 June 1974 (http://www.margaretthatcher.org/document/102369). 89. Interview with Lady Wakeham. 90. Interview with Lord Patten of Barnes. 91. *Daily Telegraph*, 1 July 1974 (http://www.margaretthatcher.org/document/102377). 92. Hansard, HC Deb 29 Apr. 1974 (http://www.margaretthatcher.org/document/102358). 93. Thatcher, *The Path to Power*, p. 246. 94. THCR 4/4. 95. Interview with Sir John Stanley. 96. THCR 4/4. 97. Thatcher, *The Path to Power*, p. 247. 98. Hansard, HC Deb 27 June 1974 (http://www.margaretthatcher.org/document/102375). 99. Neave, diary, 27 June 1974. 100. Ibid., 14 Aug. 1974. 101. ITN interview, 28 Aug. 1974 (http://www.margaretthatcher.org/document/102390). 102. Neave, diary, 28 Aug. 1974. 103. *Daily Mail*, 18 Sept. 1974 (http://www.margaretthatcher.org/document/102397). 104. *News of the World*, 22 Sept. 1974 (http://www.margaretthatcher.org/document/102398). 105. *Weekend World* (LWT), 29 Sept. 1974 (http://www.margaretthatcher.org/document/101829). 106. Donoughue, *Downing Street Diary*, vol. i, 30 Sept. 1974, p. 204. 107. Ibid., 29 Sept. 1974. 108. Speech at adoption meeting, 23 Sept. 1974, reported in *Finchley Press*, 27 Sept. 1974 (http://www.margaretthatcher.org/document/102399). 109. THCR 4/4. 110. *Any Questions?* (BBC Radio 4), Southampton, 4 Oct. 1974 (Collins, ed., *Complete Public Statements*). 111. THCR 4/4.

CHAPTER 11: THE GELDING AND THE FILLY

1. Airey Neave, diary (unpublished), 7 Aug. 1974. 2. Ibid., 12 Oct. 1974. 3. See John Campbell, *Edward Heath: A Biography*, Jonathan Cape, 1993, pp. 654–6. 4. Conversation with Lord Carrington. 5. Neave, diary, 14 Oct. 1974. 6. All above quotations from Neave, diary, 15 Oct. 1974. 7. Ibid., 22 Oct. 1974. 8. Ibid., 31 Oct. 1974. 9. Private information. 10. Neave, diary, 13 Oct. 1974. 11. Ibid., 13 Nov. 1974. 12. Papers relating to the compilation of Lady Thatcher's memoirs, The Thatcher Papers, Churchill College, Cambridge, THCR 4/4. 13. Interview with John Clare. 14. *Sunday Express*, 20 Oct. 1974 (Christopher Collins, ed., *Complete Public Statements of Margaret Thatcher 1945–90 on CD-ROM*, Oxford University Press, 1998/2000). 15. Fred Silvester to Margaret Thatcher, 15 Oct. 1974; Margaret Thatcher to Fred Silvester, undated. Letters in the possession of Mr Silvester. 16. Interview with Sir Alfred Sherman. 17. THCR 4/4. 18. Neave, diary, 21 Oct. 1974. 19. Bernard Donoughue, *Downing Street Diary*, 2 vols, Jonathan Cape, 2005, 2008, vol. i: *With Harold Wilson in No. 10*, 24 Oct. 1974, p. 230. 20. *Evening Standard*, 24 Oct. 1974 (Collins, ed., *Complete Public Statements*). 21. Interview with Lord Parkinson. 22. Neave, diary, 26 Oct. 1974. 23. Donoughue, *Downing Street Diary*, vol. i, 29 Oct. 1974, p. 234. 24. Hansard, HC Deb 14 Nov. 1974 (http://www.margaretthatcher.org/document/102436).

25. Neave, diary, 14 Nov. 1974.   26. Interview with Sir Fergus Montgomery. 27. Margaret Thatcher, *The Path to Power*, HarperCollins, 1995, p. 266.   28. Interview with Lady Thatcher.   29. THCR 4/4.   30. Private information.   31. Private information.   32. Interview with Lady Thatcher.   33. This, and ensuing quotations from Sir Gordon Reece, are from the author's interview with him, and from an unpublished memoir that Sir Gordon wrote shortly before his death in 2001 (in the possession of his family).   34. Thatcher, *The Path to Power*, p. 266.   35. Interview with Sir Denis Thatcher.   36. *The Economist*, 30 Nov. 1974.   37. Interview with Lord Patten of Barnes.   38. Neave, diary, 28 Nov. 1974.   39. Unpublished interview with Sir Peter Morrison (interviewer unknown), 1993. (Manuscript in the possession of Dame Mary Morrison.)   40. Neave, diary, 21 Nov. 1974.   41. Ibid., 22 Nov. 1974.   42. Thatcher, *The Path to Power*, p. 267.   43. Interview with Paul Johnson.   44. Edward Heath, *The Course of my Life*, Hodder & Stoughton, 1998, p. 530.   45. Neave, diary, 24 Nov. 1974.   46. Ibid., 26 Nov. 1974.   47. Ibid., 27 Nov. 1974.   48. Interview with Lord Waldegrave of North Hill.   49. Private information.   50. Neave, diary, 28 Nov. 1974.   51. THCR 4/4.   52. Ibid.   53. BBC Radio interview, 28 Nov. 1974 (Collins, ed., *Complete Public Statements*). 54. *Daily Express*, 29 Nov. 1974 (Collins, ed., *Complete Public Statements*).   55. Neave, diary, 1 Dec. 1974.   56. Hansard, HC Deb 17 Dec. 1974 (http://www.margarett hatcher.org/document/102448).   57. Neave, diary, 6 Dec. 1974.   58. Ibid., 12 Dec. 1974.   59. Ibid., 19 Dec. 1974.   60. Ibid., 25 Dec. 1974.   61. Interview with Sir Edward Du Cann.   62. Thatcher, *The Path to Power*, p. 271.   63. Neave, diary, 9 Jan. 1975.   64. Ibid., 12 Jan. 1975.   65. Ibid., 14 Jan. 1975.   66. Ibid., 15 Jan. 1975.   67. Ibid.   68. Ibid., 16 Jan. 1975.   69. Lady Antonia Fraser, diary (unpublished), 10 Jan. 1975.   70. Neave, diary, 19 Jan. 1975.   71. Ibid., 20 Jan. 1975. 72. Interview with Lord Weatherill.   73. Interview with Sir Edward Du Cann. 74. Interview with Jonathan Aitken.   75. Interview with Sir Fergus Montgomery.   76. Reece, memoir.   77. Interview with Sara Morrison.   78. Interview with Lady Thatcher.   79. Interview with Lord Prior.   80. Hansard, HC Deb 17 Dec. 1974 (http://www.margaretthatcher.org/document/102448).   81. Hansard, HC Deb 15 Jan. 1975 (http://www.margaretthatcher.org/document/102588). 82. Hansard, HC Deb 22 Jan. 1975 (http://www.margaretthatcher.org/ document/102591).   83. Neave, diary, opening note for 1973.   84. Ibid., 21 Sept. 1972.   85. Interview with Marigold Webb (née Neave).   86. Neave, diary, 6 July 1972.   87. Interview with Sir Tim Kitson.   88. Interview with Joan Hall. 89. Interview with Lord Weatherill.   90. Private information.   91. Interview with Lord Weatherill.   92. Interview with Sir Tim Kitson.   93. Ibid.   94. Interview with Lord Baker of Dorking.   95. Interview with Sara Morrison.   96. Reece, memoir.   97. Ibid.   98. *First Report* (ITN), 28 Jan. 1975 (http://www.margaretthatcher. org/document/102597).   99. Fraser, diary, 30 Jan. 1975.   100. *Daily Telegraph*, 30 Jan. 1975 (http://www.margaretthatcher.org/document/102600).   101. Speech in Finchley, 31 Jan. 1975 (http://www.margaretthatcher.org/document/102605). 102. Neave, diary, 21 Jan. 1975.   103. Ibid., 23 Jan. 1975.   104. Ibid., 26 Jan. 1975.   105. Donoughue, *Downing Street Diary*, 24 Jan. 1975, p. 294.   106. Interview with Lord Ryder of Wensum.   107. Interview with Sir Tim Kitson.

108. Private information. 109. Interview with Joan Hall. 110. Interview with Lord Lamont. 111. Ibid. 112. See John Campbell, *Margaret Thatcher*, 2 vols, Jonathan Cape, 2000, 2003, vol. i: *The Grocer's Daughter*, p. 301. 113. Interview with Lord Waldegrave of North Hill. 114. *News at Ten* (ITN), 4 Feb. 1975 (http://www.margaretthatcher.org/document/102607). 115. Interview with Joan Hall. 116. Interview with Lord Baker of Dorking. 117. THCR 4/4. 118. THCR 4/4. 119. *Guardian*, 8 Feb. 1975. 120. Ibid. 121. Interview with Lord Prior. 122. Interview with Sir Gordon Reece. 123. Speech at Young Conservative Conference, 8 Feb. 1975, reported in *Observer*, 9 Feb. 1975 (Collins, ed., *Complete Public Statements*). 124. Ibid. 125. *Sunday Express*, 9 Feb. 1975 (http://www.margaretthatcher.org/document/102614). 126. THCR 4/4.

CHAPTER 12: THE IRON LADY

1. Geoffrey Howe, *Conflict of Loyalty*, Macmillan, 1994, p. 94. 2. 'Tories rally behind new leader', 12 Feb. 1975, 121546z Feb 75, Electronic Telegrams 1/1/1975–12/31/1975, US National Archives and Records Administration (NARA). 3. Margaret Thatcher, *The Path to Power*, HarperCollins, 1995, p. 282. 4. Private information. 5. Interview with Sir Timothy Kitson. 6. Interview with Lady Thatcher. 7. Interview with Sir Edward Heath. 8. Interview with Sir Timothy Kitson. 9. Interview with Lady Thatcher. 10. Interview with Joan Hall. 11. Interview with Lord Jopling. 12. Private information. 13. Memo from Nigel Vinson to Sir Keith Joseph, in Lord Vinson's possession, 14 Apr. 1975. 14. Letter to Robert Carr, 19 Feb. 1975, quoted in Mark Garnett and Ian Aitken, *Splendid! Splendid!: The Authorized Biography of Willie Whitelaw*, Jonathan Cape, 2002, p. 218. 15. Letter to Edward Boyle, 2 Apr. 1975, in the possession of Ann Gold. 16. Bernard Donoughue, *Downing Street Diary*, 2 vols, Jonathan Cape, 2005, 2008, vol. i: *With Harold Wilson in No. 10*, 17 Apr. 1975, p. 357. 17. Interview with Lady Thatcher. 18. Interview with Lady Wakeham. 19. Interview with Lady Ryder of Wensum. 20. Ibid. 21. Ibid. 22. Private information. 23. Interview with David Nicholson. 24. Interview with Michael Portillo. 25. Interview with Lord Weatherill. 26. David Butler interview with James Prior, 1978, David Butler Archive, Nuffield College, Oxford. 27. Interview with Sir Alfred Sherman. 28. Interview with Lord Wolfson of Sunningdale. 29. Interview with Sir John Hoskyns. 30. Interview with Sir Alfred Sherman. 31. Sir Keith Joseph, Notes Towards the Definition of Policy, 4 Apr. 1975, The Thatcher Papers, Churchill College, Cambridge, THCR 2/6/1/156. 32. Minutes of 57th meeting, 11 Apr. 1975, Conservative Party Archive, Bodleian Library, Oxford, LCC 1/3/6 . 33. Lord Hailsham, diary, 11 Apr. 1975, Hailsham Papers, Churchill College, Cambridge, HLSM 1/1/10. 34. LCC 1/3/6. 35. Thatcher, *The Path to Power*, p. 302. 36. See Hansard, HC Deb 21 July 1975 (http://www.margaretthatcher.org/document/102746). 37. Speech to Conservative Group for Europe, 16 Apr. 1975 (http://www.margaretthatcher.org/document/102675). 38. Interview with Lord Ryder of Wensum. 39. Ibid. 40. *Guardian*, 3 June 1975. 41. *Talk-in with Robin Day* (BBC1), 15 May 1975 (Christopher

Collins, ed., *Complete Public Statements of Margaret Thatcher 1945–90 on CD-ROM*, Oxford University Press, 1998/2000). 42. The above quotations all come from Gordon Reece's unpublished memoir. 43. Interview with Lady Ryder of Wensum. 44. Interview with Lady Thatcher. 45. Interview with Sir Gordon Reece. 46. Interview with Lady Thatcher. 47. Interview with Sir Gordon Reece. 48. Interview with Lord Patten of Barnes. 49. Interview with Sir Gordon Reece. 50. Interview with Robert Conquest. 51. Thatcher, *The Path to Power*, p. 351. 52. Letter from Margaret Thatcher to Lord Home, July 1975 (undated), Hirsel Archive. 53. See D. R. Thorpe, *Alec Douglas-Home*, Sinclair-Stevenson, 1996, p. 451. 54. Private Information. 55. Interview with Lord Ryder of Wensum. 56. Interview with Henry Kissinger. 57. Margaret Thatcher to William Galloway, 27 Feb. 1975. Cited in interview with William Galloway, Foreign Affairs Oral History Project, Association for Diplomatic Studies and Training, Arlington VA. 58. Interview with Henry Kissinger. 59. Memorandum of conversation, 'May 9, 1975, Ford, Kissinger', National Security Advisor, Box 11, Gerald R. Ford Library, Ann Arbor MI. 60. Interview with Sir Denis Thatcher. 61. Interview with Peter Hannaford. 62. Thatcher, *The Path to Power*, p. 372. 63. Ronald Reagan, *An American Life: The Autobiography*, Simon & Schuster, 1990, p. 204. 64. *Viewpoint*, Ronald Reagan Pre-Presidential Radio Broadcast, Apr. 1975; Disc 75–08, Box 39, SubSeries C, Reagan Library, Simi Valley CA. 65. Correspondence with Peter Hannaford. 66. Michael Deaver, cited in Peter Robinson, 'Ron and Margaret', unpublished paper; correspondence with Peter Hannaford. 67. Private information. 68. Memorandum of Conversation, 'January 8, 1975 Ford, Kissinger', National Security Advisor, Box 8, Gerald R. Ford Library. 69. Greenspan to Ford, 23 Apr. 1975, CO 160, Box 56, White House Central Files, Gerald R. Ford Library. 70. G. N. Smith to D. Howe, 21 July 1975, THCR 6/4/1/5. 71. Interview with Sir Gordon Reece. 72. *News at Ten* (ITN), 18 Sept. 1975. 73. Interview with Lord Ryder of Wensum. 74. *The Times*, 19 Sept. 1975 (http://www.margaret thatcher.org/document/102464). 75. Quoted in *Evening Standard*, 16 Sept. 1975 (http://www.margaretthatcher.org/document/102565). 76. *New York Times*, 18 Sept. 1975. 77. Ibid. 78. 'Margaret Roberts Thatcher', 24 July 1975, Box 56, CO 160, White House Country Files, Gerald R. Ford Library. 79. State Department Briefing Paper for the President, 30 July 1975, Box 11, National Security Advisor, Trip Briefing Books and Cables for Ford 1974–6, Gerald R. Ford Library. 80. 'A Tory view of the Helsinki Summit', 28 July 1975, 281801z Jul 75, Electronic Telegrams 1/1/1975–12/31/1975, NARA. 81. Interview with General Brent Scowcroft. 82. Interview with Lord Ryder of Wensum. 83. Interview with Jonathan Davidson. 84. Interview with James Schlesinger. 85. William Simon to Margaret Thatcher, 14 Oct. 1975, THCR 6/4/1/15. 86. Private information. 87. Interview with Alan Greenspan. 88. The Walter Heller International Finance Lecture, Roosevelt University, 22 Sept. 1975 (http://www.margaretthatcher.org/document/102465). 89. *Guardian*, 27 Sept. 1975. 90. Derek Thomas to R. M. Russell, 30 Sept. 1975, The National Archives (TNA): Public Record Office (PRO) FCO 82/491. 91. Interview with Lord Ryder of Wensum. 92. Interview with Lord McAlpine of West Green. 93. See Ronald Millar, *A View from the Wings*, Weidenfeld

& Nicolson, 1989, pp. 225–7.   **94.** Interview with Lord Ryder of Wensum.   **95.** See Thatcher, *The Path to Power*, pp. 305 ff.   **96.** Interview with Lady Wakeham and Lady Ryder of Wensum.   **97.** Interview with Lord Ryder of Wensum.   **98.** Interview with Lady Thatcher.   **99.** Speech to Conservative Party conference, 10 Oct. 1975 (http://www.margaretthatcher.org/document/102777).   **100.** *Stern*, 24 Oct. 1975 (Collins, ed., *Complete Public Statements*).   **101.** Interview with Lord Patten of Barnes.   **102.** Interview with Sir Denis Thatcher.   **103.** Interview with Jonathan Aitken.   **104.** Interview with Lady Wakeham.   **105.** Interview with Derek Howe.   **106.** Interview with Carol Thatcher.   **107.** Ibid.   **108.** Interview with Sue Mastriforte.   **109.** Ibid.   **110.** Interview with Carol Thatcher.   **111.** Interview with Sue Mastriforte.   **112.** Interview with Carol Thatcher.   **113.** Interview with Sue Mastriforte.   **114.** Interview with Lady Ryder of Wensum.   **115.** Ibid.   **116.** Ibid. **117.** Interview with Bob Kingston.   **118.** David Butler interview with Sir Harold Wilson, 18 July 1978, David Butler Archive.   **119.** Donoughue, *Downing Street Diary*, vol. i, 17 Apr. 1975, p. 357.   **120.** Ibid.   **121.** Interview with Lord Tebbit. **122.** Interview with Frank Johnson.   **123.** Interview with Lady Thatcher.   **124.** Private information.   **125.** Speech to Crisis in London Conference, 6 Dec. 1975 (http://www.margaretthatcher.org/document/102822).   **126.** *Nottingham Evening Post*, 2 Dec. 1975 (http://www.margaretthatcher.org/document/102467).   **127.** Speech to Norfolk Conservatives, 7 Nov. 1975 (http://www.margaretthatcher.org/document/102798).   **128.** Letter in *Finchley Times*, 21 Nov. 1975 (http://www.margaretthatcher.org/document/102806).   **129.** Interview with Robert Moss. **130.** Ibid.   **131.** Speech at Kensington Town Hall, 19 Jan. 1976 (http://www.margaretthatcher.org/document/102939).   **132.** Speech to Finchley Conservatives, 31 Jan. 1976 (http://www.margaretthatcher.org/document/102947).

CHAPTER 13: TRAPPED IN MODERATION

1. Speech to Bow Group, 16 Mar. 1976 (http://www.margaretthatcher.org/document/102984).   **2.** Bernard Donoughue, *Downing Street Diary*, 2 vols, Jonathan Cape, 2005, 2008, vol. i: *With Harold Wilson in No. 10*, 16 Mar. 1976, p. 700. **3.** Barbara Castle, *The Castle Diaries, 1974–76*, Weidenfeld & Nicolson, 1980, p. 692.   **4.** Hansard, HC Deb 29 June 1976 (http://www.margaretthatcher.org/document/103065).   **5.** Hansard, HC Deb 8 June 1976 (http://www.margaretthatcher.org/document/103045).   **6.** Hansard, HC Deb 5 July 1977 (http://www.margaretthatcher.org/document/103412).   **7.** Interview with Lady Thatcher. **8.** Interview with Lord Heseltine.   **9.** Hansard, HC Deb 6 Apr. 1976 (http://www.margaretthatcher.org/document/103000).   **10.** *Weekend World* (LWT), 9 May 1976 (http://www.margaretthatcher.org/document/102836).   **11.** Speech to Melton Conservatives, 22 May 1976 (http://www.margaretthatcher.org/document/103032).   **12.** Margaret Thatcher, *The Path to Power*, HarperCollins, 1995, p. 316.   **13.** Interview with Lord Deben.   **14.** Speech to Conservative Party conference, 8 Oct. 1976 (http://www.margaretthatcher.org/document/103105).   **15.** *The Times*, 9 Oct. 1976.   **16.** *Daily Telegraph*, 9 Oct. 1976.   **17.** Interview with Lord

Patten of Barnes. **18.** Interview with Lord Waldegrave of North Hill. **19.** Ibid.
20. Interview with Lord Gilmour of Craigmillar. **21.** Correspondence with Professor
David Dilks. **22.** Interview with Lord Patten of Barnes. **23.** Quoted by Mrs
Thatcher, speech to Bow Group, 16 Mar. 1976 (http://www.margaretthatcher.org/
document/102984). **24.** Richard Cockett, *Thinking the Unthinkable*, Harper-
Collins, 1994, p. 174. **25.** Letter from Margaret Thatcher to Adam Butler, late Dec.,
probably 1975 (undated). **26.** Interview in *Sunday Times*, 12 Sept. 1976, conducted
on 5 Aug. (Christopher Collins, ed., *Complete Public Statements of Margaret
Thatcher 1945–90 on CD-ROM*, Oxford University Press, 1998/2000). **27.** The
Thatcher Papers, Churchill College, Cambridge, THCR 2/6/1/173. **28.** Interview
with Sir Alan Walters. **29.** Interview with Sir Douglas Hague. **30.** Ibid.
31. Interview with Gordon Pepper. **32.** Ibid. **33.** Letter from Margaret Thatcher to
John Sparrow, 27 Jan. 1977. **34.** Interview with Sir John Sparrow. **35.** Letter from
John Sparrow to Margaret Thatcher, 25 Mar. 1977, THCR 2/6/1/226. **36.** Interview with Brian Walden. **37.** Ibid. **38.** Interview with Lord Weatherill. **39.** Letter
from Alfred Sherman to Margaret Thatcher, 25 Oct. 1977, THCR 2/6/1/226.
40. Aide-memoire from Alfred Sherman to Margaret Thatcher, 26 June 1978, THCR
2/6/1/226. **41.** Interview with Lord Thomas of Swynnerton. **42.** Interview with
Paul Johnson. **43.** Interview with Lord Ryder of Wensum. **44.** Interview with
Lord Thomas of Swynnerton. **45.** Speech to Conservative Party conference, Blackpool, 14 Oct. 1977 (http://www.margaretthatcher.org/document/103443).
46. Interview with Revd Edward Norman. **47.** Interview with John Casey. **48.** Speech
to Zurich Economic Society, 14 Mar. 1977 (http://www.margaretthatcher.org/
document/103336). **49.** Interview with Revd Edward Norman. **50.** Interview
with Sir Denis Thatcher. **51.** Speech to Zurich Economic Society, 14 Mar. 1977
(http://www.margaretthatcher.org/document/103336). **52.** Interview with Sir
Alfred Sherman. **53.** Interview with *Woman's Own*, 31 Oct. 1987 (the unedited
typescript of the interview, which differs from the published version, can be seen at
http://www.margaretthatcher.org/document/106689). **54.** All quotations from
Speech to Greater London Young Conservatives (Iain Macleod Memorial Lecture),
4 July 1977 (http://www.margaretthatcher.org/document/103411). **55.** All above
quotations from speech at St Lawrence Jewry, 30 Mar. 1978 (http://www.margaret
thatcher.org/document/103522). **56.** John Vaizey to Margaret Thatcher, 17 Feb.
1975, Folder 8, Box 14, papers of John Vaizey, Hoover Institution Archives, Stanford
CA. **57.** Letter from Professor David Dilks. **58.** Interview with Revd Edward
Norman. **59.** Letter from Milton Friedman to Ralph Harris, 4 Dec. 1978, Folder
12, Box 296, Papers of the Institute of Economic Affairs, Hoover Institution
Archives. **60.** Interview for *The Downing Street Years* (BBC 1), 1993. **61.** Interview with Lord Patten of Barnes. **62.** Interview with Lord Ryder of Wensum.
63. Sir Geoffrey Howe to Sir Keith Joseph, THCR 2/1/3/9. **64.** Interview with Lady
Thatcher. **65.** Interview with Sir Denis Thatcher. **66.** Interview with Lady Howe
of Idlicote. **67.** Letter from Sir Geoffrey Howe to Peter Rees, 12 Dec. 1975, THCR
2/1/1/30. **68.** Interview with Lady Howe. **69.** Interview with Lord Howe of
Aberavon. **70.** Interview with Lord Patten of Barnes. **71.** Interview with Lord Howe
of Aberavon. **72.** Private information. **73.** Interview with Sir Adam Butler.

74. Interview with Norman Strauss. 75. Hugo Young, *The Hugo Young Papers: Thirty Years of British Politics – Off the Record*, Allen Lane, 2008, p. 109. 76. *Observer*, 27 July 1975. 77. Ibid. 78. THCR 2/6/1/159. 79. Sir Keith Joseph, 'Our Tone of Voice and our Tasks', 7 Dec. 1976, THCR 2/6/1/160. 80. THCR 2/6/1/245. 81. 'Concerted Action' paper, 16 May 1977, THCR 2/6/1/96. 82. Sir Geoffrey Howe to Margaret Thatcher (including her comment scribbled on it), 26 May 1977, THCR 2/1/3/9. 83. 'The Right Approach to the Economy', draft, THCR 2/6/1/161. 84. Note from Adam Ridley to Margaret Thatcher, 22 Aug. 1977, THCR 2/6/1/161. 85. Thatcher, *The Path to Power*, p. 404. 86. Margaret Thatcher to Jack Peel, 1 Oct. 1977, THCR 2/2/1/25. 87. John Sparrow to Margaret Thatcher, 15 Dec. 1977, THCR 2/6/1/142. 88. *Daily Telegraph*, 14 Sept. 1977 (Collins, ed., *Complete Public Statements*). 89. *Weekend World* (LWT), 18 Sept. 1977 (http://www.margaretthatcher.org/document/103191). 90. Howe, draft speech, 12 Jan. 1978, THCR 2/1/3/9. 91. Sir John Hoskyns, diary (unpublished), 25 Nov. 1976. An edited version of parts of the diary appears in John Hoskyns, *Just in Time: Inside the Thatcher Revolution*, Aurum Press, 2000. This is the best detailed account of the early years of the Thatcher leadership. 92. Hoskyns, *Just in Time*, p. 26. 93. Ibid., p. 45. 94. Interview with Sir John Hoskyns. 95. Ibid. 96. Hoskyns, diary, 24 Nov. 1977. 97. Alistair Cooke, ed., *Tory Policy Making*, CRD, 2009, pp. 85–6. 98. 'Further Thoughts on Strategy', 23 Feb. 1978, THCR 2/6/1/233. 99. Hoskyns, diary, 19 Feb. 1978. 100. THCR 2/6/1/233. 101. Interview with Sir John Hoskyns. 102. Hoskyns, diary, 22 May 1978. See *Just in Time*, p. 67. 103. David Butler interview with Chris Patten, 1978, David Butler Archive, Nuffield College, Oxford. 104. Interview with Lord Ryder of Wensum. 105. David Butler interview with Airey Neave, 22 Aug. 1978, David Butler Archive.

CHAPTER 14: LABOUR ISN'T WORKING

1. Private information. 2. Interview with Michael Portillo. 3. Interview with Lord Carrington. 4. Interview with Robert Hunter. 5. Zbigniew Brzezinski, diary (unpublished), 8 May 1977; interview with Zbigniew Brzezinski. It seems likely that Brzezinski was referring to *A Government as Good as its People* (Simon & Schuster, 1977), a collection of Carter's speeches published the week before Mrs Thatcher met with the President. Alternatively he might have been thinking of Carter's campaign biography: *Why not the Best?* (Bantam Books, 1976). 6. Margaret Thatcher, *The Path to Power*, HarperCollins, 1995, p. 367. 7. *New York Times*, 9 May 1977. 8. Ibid., 6 Sept. 1977. 9. Interview with Rob Shepherd. 10. Brzezinski to Carter, 'Meeting with Mrs Thatcher', 6 June 1977, RAC NLC-126-8-4-1-8, Carter Library, Atlanta GA. 11. Ibid. 12. Interview with David Aaron, Deputy National Security Advisor to President Carter in 1977. 13. Interview with Peter Jay. 14. Speech to British American Chamber of Commerce, 8 Sept. 1977 (http://www.margaretthatcher.org/document/103436). 15. Caroline Stephens, note (unpublished), 7 Sept. 1977. 16. *Daily Telegraph*, 15 Sept. 1977 (Christopher Collins, ed., *Complete Public Statements of Margaret Thatcher 1945–90 on CD-ROM*, Oxford

University Press, 1998/2000).   17. Stephens, note, 9 Sept. 1977.   18. Speech to the English Speaking Union in Houston, 9 Sept. 1977 (http://www.margaretthatcher. org/document/103268).   19. Correspondence with Roy Fox.   20. *Daily Telegraph*, 12 Sept. 1977 (Collins, ed., *Complete Public Statements*).   21. Correspondence with President George H. W. Bush.   22. Stephens, note, 11 Sept. 1977.   23. Stephens, note, 12 Sept. 1977.   24. *Time*, 19 Sept. 1977.   25. Stephens, note, 11 Sept. 1977.   26. Cyrus Vance to the President, 12 Sept. 1977, RAC NLC-128-12-12-7-6, Carter Library.   27. Vance to the President, 'Meeting with UK Opposition Leader Mrs. Margaret Thatcher, 10:30am. Tuesday, September 13', US State Department Archives, released under FOIA Case #200502415.   28. Interview with Gregory Treverton.   29. Interview with Walter Mondale.   30. Interview with Harold Brown.   31. Interview with Henry Kissinger.   32. Stephens, note, 12 Sept. 1977. 33. See *National Review*, 21 Jan. 1977.   34. Interview with Peter Jay.   35. *Financial Times*, 16 Sept. 1977.   36. *Guardian*, 15 Sept. 1977 (Collins, ed., *Complete Public Statements*).   37. Private information.   38. Speech to Les Grandes Conferences Catholiques, Brussels, 23 June 1978 (http://www.margaretthatcher.org/ document/103720).   39. Leaders Consultative Committee meeting minutes 4 Oct. 1978, The Thatcher Papers, Churchill College, Cambridge, THCR 2/6/1/213.   40. Thatcher, *The Path to Power*, p. 418.   41. Ibid.   42. Margaret Thatcher to Maurice Macmillan MP, 29 Mar. 1976, THCR 2/6/1/87.   43. Hansard, HC Deb 13 Jan. 1976 (http://www.margaretthatcher.org/document/102935).   44. Malcolm Rifkind, note (unpublished), 3 Dec. 1976.   45. Interview with Lord Gilmour of Craigmillar.   46. Private information.   47. Interview with Sir Teddy Taylor.   48. Bernard Donoughue, *Downing Street Diary*, 2 vols, Jonathan Cape, 2005, 2008, vol. ii: *With James Callaghan in No. 10*, 23 Mar. 1977, p. 171.   49. Margaret Thatcher to Alick Buchanan-Smith and others, 5 Apr. 1977, THCR 2/6/1/86.   50. Leader's Consultative Committee meeting minutes, 2 Nov. 1977, THCR 2/6/1/161.   51. Interview with Sir Teddy Taylor.   52. Adam Ridley memo to Margaret Thatcher, 18 July 1978, THCR 2/12/2/4.   53. Adam Ridley to Margaret Thatcher, 23 Oct. 1978, THCR 2/12/2/4.   54. Minutes of meeting of 25 Oct. 1978, THCR 2/1/1/32.   55. Nigel Lawson memo to Margaret Thatcher, 30 Oct. 1978, THCR 2/1/2/12.   56. Sir Geoffrey Howe to Margaret Thatcher, 31 Oct. 1978, THCR 2/1/1/32.   57. Ibid.   58. Margaret Thatcher to Sir George Bolton, 13 Nov. 1978, THCR 2/2/1/5.   59. Hansard, HC Deb 6 Dec. 1978 (http://www.margaretthatcher.org/document/103794).   60. Interview with Lord Ryder of Wensum.   61. *World in Action* (Granada), 30 Jan. 1978 (http://www.margaretthatcher.org/document/103485).   62. Roy Jenkins, *European Diary 1977–81*, Collins, 1989, p. 215.   63. Interview with Michael Portillo.   64. Hansard, HC Deb 31 Jan. 1978 (http://www.margaretthatcher.org/ document/103605).   65. Interview with Lady Thatcher.   66. David Butler interview with Enoch Powell, 1978, David Butler Archive, Nuffield College, Oxford.   67. *The Jimmy Young Programme* (BBC Radio 2), 31 Jan. 1978 (Collins, ed., *Complete Public Statements*).   68. Thatcher, *The Path to Power*, p. 409.   69. Sir Gordon Reece, memoir (unpublished).   70. Interview with Lord Bell.   71. Interview with Lord McAlpine of West Green.   72. Interview with Lord Bell.   73. Reece, memoir. 74. David Butler interview with Tim Bell, 22 May 1979, David Butler Archive.

75. David Butler interview with Gordon Reece, 12 June 1978, David Butler Archive. 76. Private information. 77. Interview with Lord Bell. 78. Interview with Lord McAlpine of West Green. 79. Interview with Jeremy Sinclair. 80. Interview with Lord Bell. 81. Interview with Jeremy Sinclair. 82. Ibid. 83. Interview with Sir Gordon Reece. 84. Interview with Lord Dobbs. 85. Interview with Lord Ryder of Wensum. 86. Interview with Lady Wakeham. 87. Interview with Sir Mark Thatcher. 88. THCR 2/6/1/163. 89. Ibid. 90. Interview with Lord Wolfson of Sunningdale. 91. THCR 2/6/1/163. 92. Ibid. 93. Margaret Thatcher interview by David Butler and Dennis Kavanagh, 9 Aug. 1978, David Butler Archive. 94. Ibid. 95. Undated foreword draft, THCR 2/7/1/5. 96. Draft manifesto, 30 Aug. 1978, THCR 2/6/1/163. 97. Ibid. 98. Ibid.

CHAPTER 15: MAY 1979

1. David Butler interview with Gavyn Davies, 31 May 1979, David Butler Archive, Nuffield College, Oxford. 2. Bernard Donoughue, *Downing Street Diary*, 2 vols, Jonathan Cape, 2005, 2008, vol. ii: *With James Callaghan in No. 10*, 7 Sept. 1978, p. 359. 3. Interview with Lord Dobbs. 4. Interview with Lord Patten of Barnes. 5. Donoughue, *Downing Street Diary*, vol. ii, 3 Oct. 1978, p. 370. 6. Private information. 7. Interview with Sir Edward Heath. 8. Private information. 9. Ibid. 10. *The Times*, 23 Oct. 1978. 11. Lord Deedes, diary (unpublished), 4 Oct. 1978. 12. *Tonight* (BBC1), 10 Oct. 1978. 13. Speech to Conservative Party conference, 13 Oct. 1978 (http://www.margaretthatcher.org/document/103764). 14. Donoughue, *Downing Street Diary*, vol. ii, 27 Oct. 1978, p. 381. 15. *Evening Standard*, 27 Oct. 1978. 16. Interview with Lord Ryder of Wensum. 17. Donoughue, *Downing Street Diary*, vol. ii, 14 Dec. 1978, p. 402. 18. Ibid., p. 403. 19. Lord Deedes, notes (unpublished), 31 May 1979. 20. Donoughue, *Downing Street Diary*, vol. ii, 3 Jan. 1979, p. 413. 21. *Weekend World* (LWT), 7 Jan. 1979 (http://www.margaretthatcher.org/document/103807). 22. Letter to Hugh Thomas, 10 Jan. 1979, The Thatcher Papers, Churchill College, Cambridge, THCR 2/6/1/230. 23. Donoughue, *Downing Street Diary*, vol. ii, 16 Jan. 1979, p. 424. 24. See Hansard, HC Deb 16 Jan. 1979 (http://www.margaretthatcher.org/document/103924). 25. Interview with Lord Bell. 26. Interview with Sir Gordon Reece. 27. See Margaret Thatcher, *The Path to Power*, HarperCollins, 1995, pp. 427–30. 28. Interview with Lord Bell. 29. Party political broadcast, 17 Jan. 1979 (http://www.margaretthatcher.org/document/103926). 30. Donoughue, *Downing Street Diary*, vol. ii, 18 Jan. 1979, p. 425. 31. Ibid., 19 Jan. 1979, p. 427. 32. THCR 2/6/1/233. 33. *The Jimmy Young Programme* (BBC Radio 2), 31 Jan. 1979 (Christopher Collins, ed., *Complete Public Statements of Margaret Thatcher 1945–90 on CD-ROM*, Oxford University Press, 1998/2000). 34. Hansard, HC Deb 28 Mar. 1979 (http://www.margaretthatcher.org/document/103983). 35. Donoughue, *Downing Street Diary*, vol. ii, 28 Mar. 1979, p. 471. 36. Private information. 37. Donoughue, *Downing Street Diary*, vol. ii, 28 Mar. 1979, p. 471. 38. Ibid., p. 472. 39. Ibid. 40. Ibid., 8 Apr. 1979,

p. 480. **41.** Interview with Sir Gordon Reece. **42.** David Butler interview with Lord Thorneycroft, 31 May 1979, David Butler Archive. **43.** Interviews with Lord Bell and Sir Gordon Reece. **44.** Interview with Sir Gordon Reece. **45.** Interview with Lord Bell. **46.** Letter to David Cox, London Weekend Television, 3 Apr. 1979, THCR 2/7/1/32. **47.** Donoughue, *Downing Street Diary*, vol. ii, 4 Apr. 1979, p. 477. **48.** David Butler interview with Gordon Reece, 8 May 1979, David Butler Archive. **49.** THCR 2/7/1/5. **50.** Ibid. **51.** Interview with Sir Adam Ridley. **52.** Donoughue, *Downing Street Diary*, vol. ii, 5 Apr. 1979, p. 478. **53.** For a full account of this incident, see Matthew Parris, *Chance Witness: An Outsider's Life in Politics*, Viking, 2002, pp. 199–200 and 223–8. **54.** BBC News, 30 Mar. 1979 (http://www.margaretthatcher.org/document/103837). **55.** Hansard, HC Deb 2 Apr. 1979 (http://www.margaretthatcher.org/document/103992). **56.** Interview with Lord McAlpine of West Green. **57.** See Ronald Millar, *A View from the Wings*, Weidenfeld & Nicolson, 1989, pp. 247–8. **58.** *Daily Express*, 12 Apr. 1979 (Collins, ed., *Complete Public Statements*). **59.** General election press conference, 11 Apr. 1979 (http://www.margaretthatcher.org/document/104000). **60.** Speech at Finchley adoption meeting, 11 Apr. 1979 (http://www.margaretthatcher.org/document/104002). **61.** Speech to Conservative Party rally, Cardiff, 16 Apr. 1979 (http://www.margaretthatcher.org/document/104011). **62.** Ibid. **63.** Speech to Conservative Party rally, Birmingham, 19 Apr. 1979 (http://www.margaretthatcher.org/document/104026). **64.** Interview with Lord McAlpine of West Green. **65.** *Daily Telegraph*, 20 Apr. 1979. **66.** *Campaign '79* (BBC1), 2 May 1979 (Collins, ed., *Complete Public Statements*). **67.** Ibid. **68.** Donoughue, *Downing Street Diary*, vol. ii, 8 Apr. 1979, p. 480. **69.** Ibid., 11 Apr. 1979, p. 843. **70.** Interview with Michael Portillo. **71.** See Thatcher, *The Path to Power*, p. 451. **72.** Interview with Lord Dobbs. **73.** David Butler interview with Chris Patten, 24 May 1979, David Butler Archive. **74.** Bernard Donoughue, *Prime Minister: The Conduct of Policy under James Callaghan and Harold Wilson*, Jonathan Cape, 1987, p. 191. **75.** David Butler interview with Gavyn Davies, 31 May 1979, David Butler Archive. **76.** *Sun*, 2 May 1979 (http://www.margaretthatcher.org/document/104066). **77.** Party election broadcast, 30 Apr. 1979 (http://www.margaretthatcher.org/document/104055). **78.** Donoughue, *Downing Street Diary*, vol. ii, 30 Apr. 1979, p. 495. **79.** Speech to Conservative Party rally, Bolton, 1 May 1979 (http://www.margaretthatcher.org/document/104065). **80.** General election press conference, 2 May 1979 (http://www.margaretthatcher.org/document/104069). **81.** David Butler interview with Nigel Lawson, 13 June 1979, David Butler Archive. **82.** David Butler interview with Brian Walden, 6 June 1979, David Butler Archive. **83.** Interview with Lord Dobbs. **84.** Speech at eve-of-poll rally, Finchley, 2 May 1979 (http://www.margaretthatcher.org/document/104072). **85.** Donoughue, *Downing Street Diary*, vol. ii, 3 May 1979, p. 499. **86.** Interview with Lord Dobbs. **87.** Interview with Lord McAlpine of West Green.

CHAPTER 16: DOWNING STREET

1. Interview with Cynthia Crawford.   2. Interview with Sir Kenneth Stowe.
3. Interview with Lord Ryder of Wensum.   4. Interview with Lord Dobbs.   5. Margaret Thatcher, *The Downing Street Years*, HarperCollins, 1993, p. 19.   6. Interview with Lord Dobbs.   7. Interview with Sir Kenneth Stowe.   8. Lord Deedes, diary (unpublished), 17 Oct. 1977.   9. Interview with Sir Kenneth Stowe.   10. Interview with Michael Pattison.   11. Interview with Sir Bryan Cartledge.   12. Interview with Lord Ryder of Wensum.   13. Ibid.   14. Interview with Sir Tim Lankester.   15. Interview with Nick Sanders.   16. Interview with Sir John Hoskyns.   17. Interview with Sir Clive Whitmore.   18. Cartledge to Walden, 'Chancellor Schmidt's Visit, 10/11 May: Briefs', 8 May 1979, The National Archives (TNA): Public Record Office (PRO) FCO 28/3677.   19. Interview with Nick Sanders.   20. Interview with William Rickett.   21. Ibid.   22. Ibid.   23. Conversation with Lady Thatcher.   24. Interview with Lord Mayhew.   25. Interviews with Lord Prior and Nick Sanders.   26. Interview with Sir Adam Ridley.   27. Interview with Lord Ryder of Wensum.   28. Interview with Sir Adam Ridley.   29. Private information.   30. Interview with Sir John Hoskyns.   31. See David Butler's election interview with Chris Patten, 22 July 1978, David Butler Archive, Nuffield College, Oxford.   32. Interview with Sir Tim Lankester.   33. Interview with Sir Kenneth Berrill.   34. Interview with Sir John Ashworth.   35. Interview with Sir Kenneth Berrill.   36. Interview with Sir John Ashworth.   37. Letter from Sir John Hoskyns.   38. Interview with Lord Laing of Dunphail.   39. Interview with Lord Jopling, who was told this by Lord Whitelaw.   40. Interview with Sir Adam Ridley.   41. Interview with Sir Clive Whitmore.   42. Interview with Lord Biffen.   43. Interview with Lady Thatcher.   44. Interview with Lord Hunt of Tanworth.   45. Brzezinski to Carter, 'Thoughts on Thatcher: Foreign Policy Implications of the Tory Triumph', RAC NLC-6-77-2-8-1, Carter Library, Atlanta GA.   46. The Thatcher Papers, Churchill College, Cambridge, THCR 2/6/2/118.   47. Interview with Michael Pattison.   48. Interview with Barry Strevens.   49. Interview with Lady Thatcher.   50. For an account of this episode, see John Campbell, *Edward Heath: A Biography*, Jonathan Cape, 1993, pp. 713–15.   51. Interview with Lord Carrington.   52. Interview with Sir Timothy Kitson.   53. Interview with Lord Jopling.   54. Interview with Cynthia Crawford.   55. See Thatcher, *The Downing Street Years*, p. 21.   56. Interview with Sir Denis Thatcher.   57. Conversation with T. E. Utley.   58. Conversation with Sir Denis Thatcher.   59. Interview with Sherry Warner.   60. Interview with Lady Ryder of Wensum.   61. Interview with Sherry Warner.   62. Interview with Lord Wolfson of Sunningdale.   63. Interview with Tessa Gaisman.   64. Interview with Sir John Coles, British Diplomatic Oral History Programme, Churchill College, Cambridge.   65. Interview with Lady Ryder of Wensum.   66. Interview with Jane Parsons.   67. Interview with Lady Ryder of Wensum.   68. Ibid.   69. Interview with Tessa Gaisman.   70. Interview with Sir Bryan Cartledge.   71. Private information.   72. Interview with Michael Pattison.   73. Interview with Lady Ryder of Wensum.   74. Interview with Tessa Gaisman.   75. Interview with Colin Peterson.   76. Interview with Sir John Ashworth.   77. Interview with Lord Howe of

Aberavon. 78. Interview with Sir Michael Scholar. 79. Interview with Nick Sanders. 80. Interview with Lord Ryder of Wensum. 81. Interview with Tessa Gaisman. 82. Interview with Michael Pattison. 83. Interview with Lady Ryder of Wensum. 84. Interview with Sir Clive Whitmore. 85. Interview with Charles Anson. 86. Interview with Lord Ryder of Wensum. 87. Reece to Ryder, 9 May 1979, THCR 2/6/2/134. 88. Interview with Sir Bernard Ingham. 89. Ingham to PM, 29 October 1979, THCR 2/6/2/2. 90. Ibid. 91. Ibid. 92. Interview with Charles Anson. 93. Interview with Sir Bernard Ingham. 94. Rentschler to Brzezinski, 4 May 1979, CO167, WHCF-Subject file, Carter Library. 95. Hannaford to Howe, 178, Folder 6, Box 5, Papers of Deaver and Hannaford, Hoover Institution archives, Stanford CA. 96. Interview with Richard Allen. 97. Peter Hannaford, *The Reagans: A Political Portrait*, Coward-McCann, 1983, p. 188. 98. 'Miscellaneous II', Reagan Radio Address, 29 May 1979, Kiron K. Skinner, Annelise Anderson and Martin Anderson, eds, *Reagan, in his Own Hand: The Writings of Ronald Reagan that Reveal his Revolutionary Vision for America*, Touchstone, 2002, p. 47. 99. Interview with Lord Hannay of Chiswick. 100. Interview with Lord Hunt of Tanworth. This impression echoes the view picked up by the CIA. See *National Intelligence Daily*, 17 May 1979, CREST database, US National Archives and Records Administration (NARA). 101. Interview with Sir Bryan Cartledge. 102. Speech at dinner for West German Chancellor, 10 May 1979 (http://www.margaretthatcher.org/document/104080). 103. Joint press conference with West German Chancellor, 11 May 1979 (http://www.margaretthatcher.org/document/104081). 104. Speech to Youth for Europe rally, NEC Birmingham, 2 June 1979 (http://www.margaretthatcher.org/document/104088). 105. Interview with Sir Bryan Cartledge. 106. Ibid. 107. Conversation with Lady Thatcher. 108. Interview with Valéry Giscard d'Estaing. 109. Note of meeting with President Giscard, 5 June 1979, TNA: PRO PREM 19/27. 110. Interview with Sir Clive Whitmore. 111. Interview with Valéry Giscard d'Estaing. 112. Interview with Sir Bryan Cartledge. 113. Interview with Valéry Giscard d'Estaing. 114. Ibid. 115. Note of meeting with President Giscard, 5 June 1979, TNA: PRO PREM 19/27. 116. Interview with Sir Bryan Cartledge. 117. Miss E. A. Deeves to private secretary of Lord Privy Seal, 21 May 1979, TNA: PRO PREM 19/27. 118. Thatcher, *The Downing Street Years*, p. 66. 119. Interview with Sir Clive Whitmore. 120. Interview with Sir Bryan Cartledge. 121. Ibid. 122. Ibid. 123. Interview with Bob Hormats. 124. Interview, BBC World Service, 25 June 1979 (Christopher Collins, ed., *Complete Public Statements of Margaret Thatcher 1945–90 on CD-ROM*, Oxford University Press, 1998/2000). 125. Record of the Opening Statements, Akasaka Palace, 28/29 June 1979, TNA: PRO PREM 19/28. 126. Brzezinski to Carter, 'NSC Weekly Report, #96', 12 May 1979, Brzezinski Donated Papers, Carter Library. 127. See Jimmy Carter, *Keeping Faith: Memoirs of a President*, Bantam, 1982, p. 113. 128. Thatcher, *The Downing Street Years*, p. 68. 129. Interview with Valéry Giscard d'Estaing. 130. Correspondence with Raymond Seitz. 131. Interview with Lord Carrington. 132. *Time*, 14 May 1979 (Collins, ed., *Complete Public Statements*). 133. Brzezinski to Carter, 'Thoughts on Thatcher: Foreign Policy Implications of the Tory Triumph', RAC

NLC-6-77-2-8-1, Carter Library. **134.** Interview with Dick Moose. **135.** Hansard, HC Deb 15 May 1979 (http://www.margaretthatcher.org/document/104083). **136.** Interview with Lord Carrington. **137.** Interview with Lord Renwick. **138.** Conversation with Lord Carrington. **139.** Note of meeting with Prime Minister Thatcher at 10 Downing Street, 12 July 1979, file 13, Box 8, S-0987, UN Archives. **140.** Interview with Sir Bryan Cartledge. **141.** Interview with Lord Carrington. **142.** Hansard, HC Deb July 25 1979 (http://www.margaretthatcher.org/document/104122). **143.** Private information. **144.** Interview with Sir Bryan Cartledge. **145.** Lord Carrington, *Reflect on Things Past: The Memoirs of Lord Carrington*, Collins, 1988, p. 277. **146.** Interview with Sir Bryan Cartledge. **147.** Interview with Sir Denis Thatcher. **148.** Interview with Sir Clive Whitmore. **149.** Interview with Lord Renwick of Clifton. **150.** Unpublished notes of Caroline Stephens (Lady Ryder), written 7 August 1979. **151.** Interview with Lord Carrington. **152.** Interview with Sir Anthony Parsons for *The Downing Street Years* (BBC1), 1993.

CHAPTER 17: 'CUTS'

At the time of going to press, some of the government documents quoted had been transferred to the National Archives under the thirty-year rule, and others had not been. Where possible, the National Archives filing has been followed. Where the documents had not yet been released, the Cabinet Office filing is used. In a few cases, documents consulted in the Cabinet Office have either been destroyed in the move to the National Archives or placed in files which have not been traced. This is indicated in the Notes to Chapters 17 to 24 wherever relevant.

1. Hunt to PM, 4 May 1979, The National Archives (TNA): Public Record Office (PRO) PREM 19/24. **2.** CPRS Paper, 1–8 May 1979, TNA: PRO PREM 19/37. **3.** Interview with Sir Tim Lankester. **4.** Hunt to PM, 4 May 1979, TNA: PRO PREM 19/24. **5.** Note on Hunt to PM, 4 May 1979, TNA: PRO PREM 19/24. **6.** Hunt to PM, 16 May 1979, TNA: PRO PREM 19/186. **7.** Notes on Hunt paper on Clegg Commission, 9 May 1979, TNA: PRO PREM 19/186. **8.** Note on draft parliamentary answer, 23 May 1979, TNA: PRO PREM 19/186. **9.** Memo by Secretary of State for Employment, 'The Way Forward on Pay', 15 May 1979, Prime Minister's Papers, Economic Policy: Economic Strategy: Pay and Prices (document consulted in the Cabinet Office). **10.** Draft of Chancellor for E Committee, 24 May 1979, Prime Minister's Papers, Economic Policy: Economic Strategy: Pay and Prices (document consulted in the Cabinet Office). **11.** Ibid. **12.** Note, 25 May 1979, TNA: PRO PREM 19/24. **13.** Lankester to Fair, 1 June 1979, Prime Minister's Papers, Economic Policy: Economic Strategy: Pay and Prices (document consulted in the Cabinet Office). **14.** Note, 8 May 1979, TNA: PRO PREM 19/35. **15.** Margaret Thatcher, *The Downing Street Years*, HarperCollins, 1993, pp. 40–41. **16.** Hansard, HC Deb 15 May 1979 (http://www.margaretthatcher.org/document/104083). **17.** Ibid. **18.** Howe to PM, 6 June

1979, TNA: PRO PREM 19/33. **19.** Interview with Sir Adam Ridley. **20.** Note on Lankester to PM, 22 Nov. 1979, TNA: PRO PREM 19/34. **21.** Interview with Lord Laing of Dunphail. **22.** Interview with Sir John Ashworth. **23.** Interview with Gordon Pepper. **24.** Lankester to Battishill, 7 June 1979, TNA: PRO PREM 19/33. **25.** Howe to PM, 11 June 1979, TNA: PRO PREM 19/33. **26.** PM to Howe, 24 June 1979, TNA: PRO PREM 19/33. **27.** Hansard, HC Deb 24 July 1979 (http://www.margaretthatcher.org/document/104121). **28.** Note for the record, 16 May 1979, TNA: PRO PREM 19/29. **29.** Ibid. **30.** Geoffrey Howe, *Conflict of Loyalty*, Macmillan, 1994, p. 130. **31.** Lankester to Battishill, 22 May 1979, TNA: PRO PREM 19/29. **32.** Howe to PM, 23 May 1979, TNA: PRO PREM 19/29. **33.** Speech to CPC Summer School, Cambridge, 6 July 1979 (http://www.margaretthatcher.org/document/104107). **34.** Hall to Lankester, 10 July 1979, Prime Minister's Papers, Economic Policy: Consultations with the IMF (document consulted in the Cabinet Office). **35.** James Prior, *A Balance of Power*, Hamish Hamilton, 1986, p. 119. **36.** Interview with Lord Prior. **37.** Prior, *A Balance of Power*, p. 120. **38.** Ibid. **39.** Interview with Lord Butler of Brockwell. **40.** Interview with Sir John Hoskyns. **41.** Hoskyns paper on Government Strategy, 12 June 1979, TNA: PRO PREM 19/24. **42.** John Hoskyns, *Just in Time: Inside the Thatcher Revolution*, Aurum Press, 2000, p. 111. **43.** John Hoskyns paper on Government Strategy, 12 June 1979, Prime Minister's Papers, Economic Policy: Economic Strategy: Pay and Prices (document consulted in the Cabinet Office). **44.** Ibid. **45.** John Hoskyns 'Long Campaign' paper, 14 Dec. 1979, TNA: PRO PREM 19/171. **46.** Interview with Lord Ryder of Wensum. **47.** Interview with Sir John Hoskyns. **48.** Michael Heseltine, *Life in the Jungle: My Autobiography*, Hodder & Stoughton, 2000, p. 182. **49.** Note for the record, 25 May 1979, Prime Minister's Papers, Housing Policy: Housing Bill (document consulted in the Cabinet Office). **50.** Hansard, HC Deb 15 May 1979 (http://www.margaretthatcher.org/document/104083). **51.** CPRS paper, 22 May 1979, Prime Minister's Papers, Housing Policy: Housing Bill (document consulted in the Cabinet Office). **52.** Lawson to Heseltine, 17 May 1979, Prime Minister's Papers, Housing Policy: Sale of Council Houses (document consulted in the Cabinet Office). **53.** Interview with Sir John Stanley. **54.** Note to Pattison, 7 Jan. 1980, Prime Minister's Papers, Housing Policy: Housing Bill (document consulted in the Cabinet Office). **55.** Lankester to Wiggins, 18 June 1981, Prime Minister's Papers, Housing Policy: Housing Bill (document consulted in the Cabinet Office). **56.** Thatcher memorandum, 11 May 1979, TNA: PRO PREM 19/18. **57.** Cabinet minutes, 17 May 1979, TNA: PRO CAB 128/66/2. **58.** Cabinet minutes, 31 May 1979, TNA: PRO CAB 128/66/4. **59.** Howe to PM, 5 July 1979, TNA: PRO PREM 19/19. **60.** Interview with Colin Peterson. **61.** Hunt to PM, 11 July 1979, TNA: PRO PREM 19/19. **62.** Joseph to PM, 11 July 1979, TNA: PRO PREM 19/19. **63.** Sir John Hunt, Cabinet Secretary's notebooks, 12 July 1979. **64.** Ibid. **65.** Cabinet minutes, 12 July 1979, TNA: PRO CAB 128/66/9. **66.** Sir John Hunt, Cabinet Secretary's notebooks, 12 July 1979. **67.** Ibid. **68.** Cabinet minutes, 12 July 1979, TNA: PRO CAB 128/66/9. **69.** Note for the record, 16 July 1979, TNA: PRO PREM 19/19. **70.** Howe and Biffen memo to Cabinet, 7 Sep. 1979, TNA: PRO PREM

129/207/5.   71. Hunt memorandum, 16 July 1979, TNA: PRO PREM 19/19.
72. E Committee minutes, 17 Sept. 1979, Prime Minister's Papers, Economic Policy:
Public Expenditure and Cash Limits (document consulted in the Cabinet Office).
73. Heseltine to Biffen, 6 Sept. 1979, TNA: PRO PREM 19/21.   74. Cabinet
minutes, 18 Oct. 1979, TNA: PRO CAB 128/66/17.   75. Hunt to PM, 24 Oct.
1979, TNA: PRO PREM 19/23.   76. Note on Howe note for E Committee, 14
Sept. 1979, TNA: PRO PREM 19/21.   77. Lankester to Pirie, 26 Oct. 1979, TNA:
PRO PREM 19/23.   78. Biffen to PM, 30 Oct. 1979, TNA: PRO PREM
19/23.   79. Hansard, HC Deb 1 Nov. 1979 (http://www.margaretthatcher.org/
document/104161).   80. Whittome to Managing Director, 2 Nov. 1979, UK Country file, Box 17, IMF Archives.   81. Speech to Conservative Party conference, 12
Oct. 1979 (http://www.margaretthatcher.org/document/104147).   82. Interview
with Sir Peter Middleton.   83. Lankester to Hall, 24 Sept. 1979, Prime Minister's
Papers, Economic Policy: The Exchange Rate: Exchange Control Policy, part 1,
TNA: PRO PREM 19/437.   84. Howe, *Conflict of Loyalty*, p. 142.   85. Speech
at Lord Mayor's Banquet, 12 Nov. 1979 (http://www.margaretthatcher.org/
document/104167).   86. Howe, *Conflict of Loyalty*, p. 151.   87. Lankester, Note
for the Record, 5 Nov. 1979, TNA: PRO PREM 19/171.   88. Ibid.   89. Sir Robert
Armstrong, Cabinet Secretary's notebooks, 23 Oct. 1979–13 Dec. 1979.   90. Howe
memorandum, 6 Dec. 1979, TNA: PRO PREM 19/171.   91. Interview with R. W.
Apple, *New York Times*, conducted 9 Nov. 1979; published 12 Nov. 1979 (Christopher Collins, ed., *Complete Public Statements of Margaret Thatcher 1945–90 on
CD-ROM*, Oxford University Press, 1998/2000).

CHAPTER 18: OUR DOUBTS ARE TRAITORS

1. Speech to Conservative Party conference, Blackpool, 12 Oct. 1979 (http://www.
margaretthatcher.org/document/104147).   2. Interview with Sir Michael Rose.
3. For a full account of the sequence of events, see Miranda Carter, *Anthony Blunt:
His Lives*, Macmillan, 2001, chapter 18.   4. Christopher Andrew, *The Defence of
the Realm: The Authorized History of MI5*, Allen Lane, 2009, p. 438.   5. Interview
with Lord Armstrong of Ilminster.   6. Ibid.   7. Interview with Lady Thatcher.
8. Interview with Lord Rees-Mogg.   9. Hansard, HC Deb 21 Nov. 1979 (http://
www.margaretthatcher.org/document/104175).   10. Carter, *Anthony Blunt*,
p. 473.   11. Hansard, HC Deb 21 Nov. 1979 (http://www.margaretthatcher.org/
document/104175).   12. Letter to Bryan Cartledge, 23 Sept. 1979.   13. Hunt to
PM, 4 May 1979, The National Archives (TNA): Public Record Office (PRO)
PREM 19/53.   14. Note on Carrington to PM, 8 June 1979, TNA: PRO PREM
19/53.   15. Extract of record of meeting between Jenkins and Thatcher, 22 Oct.
1979, TNA: PRO PREM 19/54.   16. Ingham to Saunders, 26 Nov. 1979, TNA:
PRO PREM 19/52.   17. Interview in *Now!*, 30 Sept. 1979 (Christopher Collins,
ed., *Complete Public Statements of Margaret Thatcher 1945–90 on CD-ROM*,
Oxford University Press, 1998/2000).   18. Winston Churchill Memorial Lecture,
Luxembourg, 18 Oct. 1979 (http://www.margaretthatcher.org/document/

104149). **19.** Ibid. **20.** Interview with Television-radio Luxembourg, 19 Oct. 1979 (Collins, ed., *Complete Public Statements*). **21.** Interview with Sir Michael Jenkins. **22.** Ibid. **23.** Ibid. **24.** Interview with Sir Michael Palliser. **25.** Ibid. **26.** Interview with Sir Bernard Ingham. **27.** Lankester note of Howe and PM meeting, 22 Nov. 1979, TNA: PRO PREM 19/171. **28.** See Michael Butler, *Europe: More than a Continent*, Heinemann, 1986, pp. 92–3. **29.** Joint press conference with West German Chancellor, Bonn, 31 Oct. 1979 (http://www.margaretthatcher. org/document/104159). **30.** Joint press conference with Valéry Giscard d'Estaing, London, 20 Nov. 1979 (http://www.margaretthatcher.org/document/104174). **31.** Note on Maitland to Carrington, 31 Oct. 1979, TNA: PRO PREM 19/55. **32.** Interview with Sir Michael Butler. **33.** Record of discussion between Thatcher and Schmidt, 31 Oct. 1979, TNA: PRO PREM 19/55. **34.** Howe to PM, 21 Nov. 1979, TNA: PRO PREM 19/55. **35.** Soames to PM, 28 Nov. 1979, TNA: PRO PREM 19/52. **36.** Record of meeting between Thatcher and Jenkins, 26 Nov. 1979, TNA: PRO PREM 19/55. **37.** Roy Jenkins, *A Life at the Centre*, Macmillan, 1993, p. 498. **38.** Interview with Valéry Giscard d'Estaing. **39.** Interview with Lord Carrington. **40.** Interview with Valéry Giscard d'Estaing. **41.** MS note, Nov. 1979, TNA: PRO PREM 19/52. **42.** Margaret Thatcher, *The Downing Street Years*, HarperCollins, 1993, p. 81. **43.** Hansard, HC Deb 3 Dec. 1979 (http://www. margaretthatcher.org/document/104183). **44.** Press conference at end of Dublin Summit, 30 Nov. 1979 (http://www.margaretthatcher.org/document/104180). **45.** Interview with Sir Michael Butler. **46.** Interview with Lord Carrington. **47.** Armstrong to PM, 7 Dec. 1979, TNA: PRO PREM 19/222. **48.** Note on draft statement, 14 Feb. 1980, TNA: PRO PREM 19/223. **49.** Interview with Valéry Giscard d'Estaing. **50.** Ibid. **51.** Warner to Gilmour, 17 Apr. 1980, TNA: PRO PREM 19/225. **52.** Record of telephone conversation between Giscard d'Estaing and Thatcher, 24 April 1980, TNA: PRO PREM 19/225. **53.** Cabinet conclusions, 24 Apr. 1980, TNA: PRO CAB 128/67/17. **54.** Carrington to PM, 1 May 1980, TNA: PRO PREM 19/226. **55.** Interview with Sir Clive Whitmore. **56.** Carrington to PM telegram, 30 May 1980, TNA: PRO PREM 19/226. **57.** Hibbert to FCO telegram, 30 May 1980, TNA: PRO PREM 19/226. **58.** Interview with Lord Carrington. **59.** Cabinet conclusions, 2 June 1980, TNA: PRO CAB 128/67/21. **60.** Sir Robert Armstrong, Cabinet Secretary's notebooks, 2 June 1980. **61.** Armstrong to PM, 9 July 1980, TNA: PRO PREM 19/227. **62.** Note on Wiggins to Alexander, 15 July 1980, TNA: PRO PREM 19/227. **63.** Howe to PM, 12 Sept. 1980, TNA: PRO PREM 19/227. **64.** Nott to PM, 10 Oct. 1980, Prime Minister's Papers: European Policy: Future Policy towards the EEC, Community Budget (document consulted in the Cabinet Office). **65.** Brzezinski to President, 'Visit by Mrs. Thatcher', 31 July 1979, '8/2/79', Box 141, Files of the Staff Secretary, Carter Library, Atlanta GA. **66.** 'Changing power relations among OECD states', CIA: National Foreign Assessment Center, 22 Oct. 1979, RAC NLC-7-16-10-14-1, Carter Library. **67.** Interview with Jim Rentschler. **68.** Vance to Carter, 'Visit of U.K. Prime Minister Thatcher', 8 Dec. 1979, released by the US State Department under FOIA Case #200502415. **69.** Alexander to Lever, 'Prime Minister's Visit to the USA', 24 Oct. 1979, TNA: PRO FCO 82/989. **70.** Nicholas

Henderson, *Mandarin: The Diaries of an Ambassador 1969–1982*, Weidenfeld & Nicolson, 1994, p. 316. 71. Speech at White House arrival ceremony, 17 Dec. 1979 (http://www.margaretthatcher.org/document/104194). 72. Alexander to Walden, 'Prime Minister's Visit to the United States', 19 Dec. 1979, TNA: PRO FCO 82/991. 73. Remarks after meeting President Carter (http://www.margaretthatcher. org/document/104195). 74. *Daily Telegraph*, 18 Dec. 1979. 75. Interview with Zbigniew Brzezinski. 76. SCC Meeting Minutes, 18 Dec. 1979, NLC-25-98-20-4-1, Carter Library. 77. *New York Times*, 18 Dec. 1979. 78. Henderson, *Mandarin*, p. 320. 79. Speech to the Foreign Policy Association, 18 Dec. 1979 (http://www.margaretthatcher.org/document/104199). 80. Sir Brian Urquhart, *A Life in Peace and War*, Weidenfeld & Nicolson, 1987, p. 307. 81. Interview with Jim Rentschler. 82. Interview with Lord Renwick. 83. Interview with Sir Michael Alexander, 25 Nov. 1998, British Diplomatic Oral History Programme, Churchill College, Cambridge. 84. 141435z Sept 79, 'Lancaster House Conference', 14 Sept. 1979, released by the US State Department under FOIA Case #200502415. 85. Interview with John Carbaugh. 86. Ibid. 87. Cyrus Vance, *Hard Choices: Critical Years in America's Foreign Policy*, Simon & Schuster, 1983, p. 300. 88. Interview with John Carbaugh. 89. Interview with Lord Carrington. 90. Interview with Charles de Chassiron. 91. Interview with Lord Owen. 92. Interview with Sir Clive Whitmore. 93. Denis Healey, Mansion House speech, 19 Oct. 1978, reported in *The Times*, 20 Oct. 1978. 94. Interview with Sir Peter Middleton. 95. Ibid. 96. *The Times*, 14 Sept. 1978. 97. Interview with Lord Howe of Aberavon. 98. Interview with Lord Burns. 99. See Nigel Lawson, *The View from No. 11*, Bantam, 1992, p. 67. 100. Geoffrey Howe, *Conflict of Loyalty*, Macmillan, 1994, p. 171. 101. Howe to PM, 29 Feb. 1980, TNA: PRO PREM 19/176. 102. Sir Robert Armstrong, Cabinet Secretary's notebooks, 13 Mar. 1980. 103. Lankester to PM, 2 Nov. 1979, TNA: PRO PREM 19/171. 104. Armstrong to PM, 6 Dec. 1979, TNA: PRO PREM 19/164. 105. Ibid. 106. Armstrong to PM, 4 Mar. 1980, TNA: PRO PREM 19/166. 107. Whitmore to Armstrong, 11 June 1980, TNA: PRO PREM 19/166. 108. Hoskyns to PM, 12 Mar. 1980, TNA: PRO PREM 19/166. 109. Lawson, *The View from No. 11*, p. 50. 110. Howe to PM, 29 Feb. 1980, TNA: PRO PREM 19/165. 111. Ibid. 112. Hague paper, 6 June 1980, TNA: PRO PREM 19/166. 113. Prior to PM, 14 May 1979, TNA: PRO PREM 19/70. 114. Prior, 'The Approach to Industrial Relations', Paper for E Committee, 15 June 1979, Prime Minister's Papers, Industrial Policy: Industrial Relations Legislation (document consulted in the Cabinet Office). 115. Interview with Lord Gowrie. 116. Hoskyns to PM, 28 Jan. 1980, TNA: PRO PREM 19/261. 117. Prior to PM, 1 Feb. 1980, TNA: PRO PREM 19/261. 118. *The World This Weekend* (BBC Radio 4), 3 Feb. 1980. 119. Howe to PM, 4 Feb. 1980, TNA: PRO PREM 19/262. Denis Healey said (Hansard, HC Deb 14 June 1978) that being attacked by Geoffrey Howe was like being 'savaged by a dead sheep'. 120. Interview with Lord Laing of Dunphail. 121. Laing to PM, 6 Feb. 1980, TNA: PRO PREM 19/262. 122. Interview with Lord Laing of Dunphail. 123. PM to Laing, 11 Feb. 1980, TNA: PRO PREM 19/262. 124. Minutes of E Committee, 13 Feb. 1980, Prime Minister's Papers, Industrial Policy: Industrial Relations Legislation (document consulted in the Cabinet Office). **125.** Ingham digest, 11 Mar. 1980, The Thatcher Papers, Churchill College, Cambridge, THCR 3/5/1. **126.** Interview with Lord Prior. **127.** Ibid. **128.** This and all quotations in this and the following paragraphs from summary of telephone conversations, 17 Feb. 1980, TNA: PRO PREM 19/263. **129.** *Panorama* (BBC1), 25 Feb. 1980 (Collins, ed., *Complete Public Statements*). **130.** Interview in *Daily Mail*, conducted 1 May 1980; published 3 May 1980 (Collins, ed., *Complete Public Statements*). **131.** Interview with Sir Michael Edwardes. **132.** Interview with Sir Robin Ibbs. **133.** Hoskyns to PM, 18 Sept. 1979, THCR 1/15/2. **134.** Note, 26 Oct. 1979, TNA: PRO PREM 19/71. **135.** Hoskyns to Joseph, 15 Nov. 1979, TNA: PRO PREM 19/71. **136.** Hoskyns, briefing for PM, 20 May 1980, THCR 1/15/2. **137.** Interview with Sir Michael Edwardes. **138.** See Michael Edwardes, *Back from the Brink*, William Collins, 1983, p. 227. **139.** This and subsequent quotation from Lankester to Ellison, 22 May 1980, Prime Minister's Papers, Industrial Policy: The Future of British Leyland (document consulted in the Cabinet Office). **140.** Interview with Sir Michael Edwardes. **141.** Ibid. **142.** Joseph to E Committee, 15 Dec. 1980, Prime Minister's Papers, Industrial Policy: The Future of British Leyland (document consulted in the Cabinet Office). **143.** Joseph to PM, 10 Dec. 1980, Prime Minister's Papers, Industrial Policy: The Future of British Leyland (document consulted in the Cabinet Office). **144.** Nott to PM, 4 Jan. 1981, Prime Minister's Papers, Industrial Policy: The Future of British Leyland (document consulted in the Cabinet Office). **145.** Interview with Lord Tebbit. **146.** Lankester to Ellison, 13 Jan. 1981, Prime Minister's Papers, Industrial Policy: The Future of British Leyland (document consulted in the Cabinet Office). **147.** Interview with Lord Tebbit. **148.** Edwardes to Joseph, 21 Jan. 1981, Prime Minister's Papers, Industrial Policy: The Future of British Leyland (document consulted in the Cabinet Office). **149.** Armstrong to PM, 21 Jan. 1981, Prime Minister's Papers, Industrial Policy: The Future of British Leyland (document consulted in the Cabinet Office). **150.** Joseph draft statement, 22 Jan. 1981, Prime Minister's Papers, Industrial Policy: The Future of British Leyland (document consulted in the Cabinet Office). **151.** Interview with Sir Alfred Sherman.

CHAPTER 19: NOT FOR TURNING

1. Hoskyns to PM, 19 June 1980, The National Archives (TNA): Public Record Office (PRO) PREM 19/172. **2.** Interview with Clive Priestley. **3.** Ibid. **4.** See Margaret Thatcher, *The Downing Street Years*, HarperCollins, 1993, p. 90. **5.** Interview with Sir John Chilcot. **6.** Interview with Sir Peter de la Billière. **7.** Interview with Clive Priestley. **8.** Ibid. **9.** Private information. **10.** Thatcher, *The Downing Street Years*, p. 48. **11.** Interview with Sir Robin Ibbs. **12.** Interview with Lord Armstrong of Ilminster. **13.** Interview with Clive Priestley. **14.** Ibid. **15.** Ian Gilmour, *Dancing with Dogma: Britain under Thatcherism*, Simon & Schuster, 1992, p. 21. **16.** Ibid. **17.** Interview with Robin Day, *Panorama* (BBC1), 25 Feb. 1980 (Christopher Collins, ed., *Complete Public Statements of Margaret Thatcher 1945–90 on CD-ROM*, Oxford University Press, 1998/2000). **18.** Sir

Robert Armstrong, Cabinet Secretary's notebooks, 13 Mar. 1980. 19. Interview,
The Jimmy Young Programme (BBC Radio 2), 30 Apr. 1980 (Collins, ed., *Complete
Public Statements*). 20. Lawson to PM, 22 Feb. 1980, Prime Minister's Papers, The
Prime Minister's Meeting with Professor Milton Friedman on 27 February 1980
(document consulted in the Cabinet Office). 21. Private information. 22. Text of
Milton Friedman's evidence to the Treasury Select Committee, as reprinted in the
Observer, 6 July 1980. 23. Memo of meeting between PM and Gordon Pepper, 18
May 1979, TNA: PRO PREM 19/33. 24. Sir Robert Armstrong, Cabinet Secretary's
notebooks, 26 Mar. 1980. 25. Interview with Lord Griffiths of Fforestfach.
26. Monthly Economic Brief CSO, 31 July 1980, TNA: PRO PREM 19/173.
27. Speech to Press Association annual luncheon, 11 June 1980 (http://www.marga-
retthatcher.org/document/104377). 28. John Hoskyns, *Just in Time: Inside the
Thatcher Revolution*, Aurum Press, 2000, p. 187. 29. Sir Robert Armstrong,
Cabinet Secretary's notebooks, 17 June 1980. 30. Ibid. 31. Interview with Lord
Mayhew. 32. Ibid. 33. Armstrong to Wass, 25 Apr. 1980, TNA: PRO PREM
19/172. 34. Armstrong to PM, 2 May 1980, TNA: PRO PREM 19/172.
35. Hoskyns, *Just in Time*, p. 200. 36. Interview with Sir Douglas Wass. 37. Inter-
view with Lord Burns. 38. Ibid. 39. All quotations from Sir Robert Armstrong,
Cabinet Secretary's notebooks, 3 July 1980. 40. Ibid., 10 July 1980. 41. Hugo
Young, *The Hugo Young Papers: Thirty Years of British Politics – Off the Record*,
Allen Lane, 2008, p. 152. 42. Interview with Lord Burns. 43. *Sunday Times*, 1
Aug. 1980 (http://www.margaretthatcher.org/document/104214). 44. Interview
with *People Weekly*, 30 July 1980. 45. Macmillan to PM, 20 Aug. 1980, TNA:
PRO PREM 19/173. 46. Interview with Lady Wakeham. 47. Interview with
Dame Mary Morrison. 48. Interview with Lord Gowrie. 49. Interview with Rich-
ard and Veronique Bowdler-Raynar. 50. Private information. 51. Pattison to PM,
2 Sept. 1980, TNA: PRO PREM 19/173. 52. Interview with Lord Burns.
53. Ibid. 54. Ibid. 55. Hoskyns, *Just in Time*, p. 228. 56. Ibid., p. 230.
57. Ibid. 58. Ibid., p. 231. 59. Speech to Conservative Party conference, Brighton,
10 Oct. 1980 (http://www.margaretthatcher.org/document/104431). 60. Hoskyns,
Just in Time, p. 231. 61. Speech to Conservative Party conference, Brighton, 10
Oct. 1980 (http://www.margaretthatcher.org/document/104431). 62. Hoskyns to
PM, 24 Oct. 1980, TNA: PRO PREM 19/174. 63. PM to Lankester, 24 Oct.
1980, TNA: PRO PREM 19/174. 64. Lankester to Chancellor's private office, 13
Nov. 1980, TNA: PRO PREM 19/174. 65. Ibid. 66. Ibid. 67. Young, *The Hugo
Young Papers*, p. 157. 68. Sir Robert Armstrong, Cabinet Secretary's notebooks,
30 Oct. 1980. 69. Interview with Sir John Hoskyns. 70. Sir Robert Armstrong,
Cabinet Secretary's notebooks, 13 Nov. 1980. 71. Ibid. 72. Ibid. 73. *Guardian*,
19 Nov. 1980. 74. Geoffrey Howe, *A Conflict of Loyalty*, Macmillan, 1994, p.
190. 75. Thatcher, *The Downing Street Years*, p. 129. 76. W. F. Deedes, diary
(unpublished), 23 Dec. 1980. 77. Howe to PM, 31 Dec. 1980, TNA: PRO PREM
19/174. 78. Ingham digest, 29 Dec. 1980, The Thatcher Papers, Churchill College,
Cambridge, THCR 3/5/2. 79. Interview with *People Weekly*, 30 July 1980 (Collins,
ed., *Complete Public Statements*). 80. Ingham to Pym, 26 Jan. 1981, Prime
Minister's Papers, Economic Policy: Economic Strategy: Pay and Prices (document

consulted in the Cabinet Office). **81.** Interview with Sir Robert Wade-Gery. **82.** Ibid. **83.** Wiggins to Whitmore, 25 Apr. 1980, TNA: PRO PREM 19/181 (document consulted in the Cabinet Office). **84.** Note by Secretaries to E Committee, 12 June 1980, TNA: PRO PREM 19/181 (document consulted in the Cabinet Office). **85.** Ibid. **86.** Howell, Strategy for Coal for E Committee, 10 Sept, 1980, Prime Minister's Papers, Financial Position of the Coal Industry: Mineworkers' Pay (document consulted in the Cabinet Office). **87.** Ingham digest, 13 Nov. 1980, THCR 3/5/2. **88.** Note of Meeting with PM and Ezra, 29 Jan. 1981, Prime Minister's Papers, Financial Position of the Coal Industry: Mineworkers' Pay (document consulted in the Cabinet Office). **89.** Ingham to PM, 13 Feb. 1981, Prime Minister's Papers, Financial Position of the Coal Industry: Mineworkers' Pay (document consulted in the Cabinet Office). **90.** Interviews with Lord Howell of Guildford and Michael Portillo. **91.** Interview with Lord Howell of Guildford. **92.** Ingham to PM, 19 Feb. 1981, Financial Position of the Coal Industry: Mineworkers' Pay (document consulted in the Cabinet Office). **93.** Ingham digest, 19 Feb. 1981, THCR 3/5/3. **94.** Lankester to West, 20 Feb. 1981, Prime Minister's Papers, Financial Position of the Coal Industry: Mineworkers' Pay (document consulted in the Cabinet Office). **95.** *Daily Telegraph*, 20 Feb. 1981. **96.** Interview with Richard Allen. **97.** Reagan and Thatcher telephone conversation, 21 Jan. 1981, Prime Minister's Papers, USA: UK/USA Relations (document consulted in the Cabinet Office). **98.** Thomas to PM, 26 Jan. 1981, Prime Minister's Papers, USA: UK/USA Relations (document consulted in the Cabinet Office). **99.** Thomas to Berthoud, 24 July 1980, TNA: PRO FCO 82/1017. **100.** Speech at the Pilgrims' Dinner, London, 29 Jan. 1981 (http://www.margaretthatcher.org/document/104557). **101.** Reagan to Thatcher, 2 Feb. 1981, UK: Prime Minister Thatcher Cables [1], Box 34, Exec Sec, NSC: Head of State File, Reagan Library, Simi Valley CA. **102.** Interview with Richard Allen. **103.** Haig to President, 'Visit of Prime Minister Thatcher', 5. Official Working Visit of Prime Minister Thatcher of United Kingdom 02/26/1981 (6 of 8), Box 4, Charles Tyson Files, Reagan Library. **104.** Allen to Reagan, 'Your meeting with Prime Minister Thatcher (Thursday, 26 February)', Papers of Jim Rentschler. **105.** Anson to Lankester, 21 Jan. 1981, Prime Minister's Papers, USA: UK/USA Relations (document consulted in the Cabinet Office). **106.** Herbert Stein, *Presidential Economics: The Making of Economic Policy from Roosevelt to Clinton*, 3rd rev. edn, AEI Press, 1994, p. 233. **107.** Interview with James Baker. **108.** Thatcher, *The Downing Street Years*, p. 158. **109.** Interview with Sir Bernard Ingham. **110.** Interview with Paul Volcker. **111.** Sprinkel to Regan, 24 Feb. 1981, Box 185, Papers of Don Regan, Library of Congress, Washington DC. **112.** 'UK Domestic Economic Policy', Department of State Briefing Paper, 17 Feb. 1981, released by the US State Department Archive under FOIA Case #200505131. **113.** Interview with Harvey Thomas. **114.** Interview with Paul Volcker. **115.** Memo for the President from Richard V. Allen, 24 Feb. 1981, Papers of Jim Rentschler. **116.** *The Times*, 26 Feb. 1981. **117.** *New York Times*, 27 Feb. 1981. **118.** Remarks on arriving at the White House, 26 Feb. 1981 (http://www.margaretthatcher.org/document/104576). **119.** Ronald Reagan, *The Reagan Diaries*, HarperCollins, 2007, 26 Feb. 1981, p. 5. **120.** *Financial Times*, 27 Feb. 1981. **121.** Conference for

Washington Press Club, 26 Feb. 1981 (http://www.margaretthatcher.org/document/104578). **122.** Reagan, *The Reagan Diaries*, 27 Feb. 1981, p. 5. **123.** Interview with Jim Rentschler. **124.** Ibid. **125.** See Nicholas Henderson, *Mandarin: The Diaries of an Ambassador 1969–1982*, Weidenfeld & Nicolson, 1994, p. 383. **126.** Speech at British embassy dinner for President Reagan, 27 Feb. 1981 (http://www.margaretthatcher.org/document/104581). **127.** Ibid., Reagan's reply. **128.** Reagan, *The Reagan Diaries*, 27 Feb. 1981, p. 5. **129.** Henderson, *Mandarin*, p. 388. **130.** Ibid. **131.** Ibid. **132.** Interview with Sir Nicholas Henderson. **133.** Interview with Kenneth Adelman. **134.** Reagan, *The Reagan Diaries*, 27 Feb. 1981, p. 5. **135.** PM to Henderson, 5 Mar. 1981, TNA: PRO PREM 19/600. **136.** Interview with Lord Butler of Brockwell. **137.** Interview with Lord Carrington. **138.** Thatcher to Reagan, 5 Mar. 1981, UK: Prime Minister Thatcher, Box 35, Exec Sec, NSC: Head of State File, Reagan Library. **139.** Hoskyns to PM, 11 Nov. 1980, TNA: PRO PREM 19/174. **140.** Hoskyns to PM, 20 Nov. 1980, TNA: PRO PREM 19/174. **141.** *The Times*, 26 Jan. 1981. **142.** Interview with Lord Owen. **143.** Ibid. **144.** Interview with Sir Robin Ibbs. **145.** Interview with Andrew Duguid. **146.** Interview with Sir John Hoskyns. **147.** Nigel Lawson, *The View from No. 11*, Bantam, 1992, p. 64. **148.** Ibid., p. 65. **149.** Nigel Lawson, speech to the Zurich Society of Economics, 14 Jan. 1981. **150.** Hoskyns, *Just in Time*, p. 260. **151.** Ibid.

CHAPTER 20: RUSSIA . . . AND REAGAN

1. Lever to Cartledge, 8 May 1979, Prime Minister's Papers, Soviet Union: Misc (document consulted in the Cabinet Office). **2.** Interview with Lord Carrington. **3.** PM to Conquest, 6 June 1979, The Thatcher Papers, Churchill College, Cambridge, THCR 2/6/2/38. **4.** PM to Conquest, 26 June 1978, THCR 2/6/2/38. **5.** Robert Conquest, *Present Danger: Towards a Foreign Policy*, Hoover Institution Press, 1979. **6.** Interview with Robert Conquest. **7.** Conquest to PM, 30 July 1979, THCR 2/6/2/38. **8.** Conquest to PM, 28 Aug. 1979, THCR 2/6/2/38. **9.** Conquest to PM, 12 Dec. 1979, THCR 2/6/2/38. **10.** Thomas to PM, 'The Office of Prime Minister: a historical note', Oct. 1980, THCR 2/6/1/254. **11.** Conquest to Gow, 12 Apr. 1983, THCR 2/6/2/38. **12.** Interview with Robert Conquest. **13.** Ryder to PM, 3 Oct. 1979, THCR 2/6/2/38. **14.** Interview with Sir Clive Whitmore. **15.** Interview with Sir Michael Alexander, 25 Nov. 1998, British Diplomatic Oral History Programme, Churchill College, Cambridge. **16.** Interview with Lord Carrington. **17.** Interview with Sir Rodric Braithwaite. **18.** Rodric Braithwaite, *Across the Moscow River: The World Turned Upside Down*, Yale University Press, 2002, pp. 51–2. **19.** Interview with Lord Ryder of Wensum. **20.** Mallaby to Gillmore, 'Positions of Strength in Arms Control Negotiations', 6 Dec. 1979, TNA: PRO FCO 28/3865. **21.** Interview with Sir John Coles. **22.** 181220z Jul 79, RAC NLC-31-145-7-2-8, Carter Library, Atlanta GA. **23.** Interview with Lord Carrington. **24.** Brzezinski to President, 'Thoughts on Thatcher: Foreign Policy Implications of the Tory Triumph', RAC NLC-6-77-2-8-1,

Carter Library. **25.** Carter to Thatcher, 11 May 1979, The National Archives (TNA): Public Record Office (PRO) FCO 82/978-980. **26.** Interview with Sir Clive Whitmore. **27.** Thatcher to Carter, 15 June 1979, TNA: PRO FCO 82/978-980. **28.** Partial record of Thatcher Discussion with Schmidt, 11 May 1979, TNA: PRO PREM 19/15. **29.** Cartledge to Lever, 13 June 1979, TNA: PRO PREM 19/15. **30.** Note of Giscard d'Estaing/Thatcher meeting, 19 Nov. 1979, TNA: PRO PREM 19/15. **31.** Cartledge to Lever, 25 July 1979, TNA: PRO PREM 19/15. **32.** Thatcher to Carter, 28 July 1979, TNA: PRO PREM 19/15. **33.** Speech to Conservative Party conference, 12 Oct. 1979 (http://www.margaretthatcher.org/document/104147). **34.** Winston Churchill Memorial Lecture, Luxembourg, 18 Oct. 1979 (http://www.margaretthatcher.org/document/104149). **35.** Interview with Lord Parkinson. **36.** Cartledge to FCO, 27 June 1979, TNA: PRO PREM 19/124. **37.** *Daily Telegraph*, 4 July 1979. **38.** Band to Fall, 'Kosygin's Invitation to the Prime Minister', 6 July 1979, TNA: PRO FCO 28/3880. **39.** Band to Fall, 'Invitation to the Prime Minister', 3 Aug. 1979, TNA: PRO FCO 28/3865. **40.** Extract from record of meeting of Carter and Thatcher, 17 Dec. 1979, TNA: PRO PREM 19/134. **41.** Thatcher to Brezhnev, 29 Dec. 1979, TNA: PRO PREM 19/134. **42.** Conquest to Ryder, 4 Jan. 1980, THCR 2/6/2/35. **43.** Note for the Record, meeting with Lunkov, 3 Jan. 1980, TNA: PRO PREM 19/134. **44.** Interview with Sir Michael Alexander, 25 Nov. 1998, British Diplomatic Oral History Programme, Churchill College, Cambridge. **45.** Carrington to PM, 2 Jan. 1980, TNA: PRO PREM 19/134. **46.** Alexander to Walden, 3 Jan. 1980, TNA: PRO PREM 19/134. **47.** Alexander to Lyne, 8 Jan. 1980, TNA: PRO PREM 19/135. **48.** OD Minutes, 22 Jan. 1980, Prime Minister's Papers, Afghanistan: Internal Situation: Soviet Military Intervention (document consulted in the Cabinet Office). **49.** Brzezinski to Carter, 29 Jan. 1980, Plains File Box 2, Carter Library. **50.** Interview with Zbigniew Brzezinski. **51.** Hansard, HC Deb 28 Jan. 1980 (http://www.margaretthatcher.org/document/104298). **52.** Brzezinski to Henderson, 11 Feb. 1980, CO65, CO167, WHCF-Subject File, Carter Library. **53.** *Time*, 4 Jan. 1980. **54.** PM to Follows, 19 Feb. 1980, TNA: PRO PREM 19/374. **55.** PM to Duke of Edinburgh, 30 Apr. 1980, TNA: PRO PREM 19/375. **56.** Note on Carrington report on journey to Turkey, Pakistan etc., 19 Jan. 1980, TNA: PRO PREM 19/135. **57.** Record of conversation between Thatcher and Schmidt, 25 Feb. 1980, TNA: PRO PREM 19/136. **58.** Record of discussion between Thatcher and Schmidt, 8 March 1980, TNA: PRO PREM 19/137. **59.** Giscard d'Estaing to Thatcher, 26 June 1980, Prime Minister's Papers, Afghanistan: Internal Situation: Soviet Military Intervention (document consulted in the Cabinet Office). **60.** Speech to party conference, 10 Oct. 1980 (http://www.margaretthatcher.org/document/104431). **61.** Thomas C. Reed, *At the Abyss: An Insider's History of the Cold War*, Presidio Press, 2004, pp. 234-5. **62.** Interview with Sir Christopher Mallaby. **63.** Interview with Lord Carrington. **64.** Interview with Edwin Meese. **65.** Ronald Reagan, 29 Jan. 1981, The President's News Conference, Public Papers of the Presidents, The American Presidency Project, University of California. **66.** Press conference for Association of American Correspondents in London, 16 Feb. 1981 (http://www.margaretthatcher.org/document/104570). **67.** James Rentschler,

'A Reason to Get Up in the Morning: A Cold Warrior Remembers', unpublished memoir, p. 578. 68. Summary of President's meeting with Prime Minister Thatcher, 26 Feb. 1981, Reagan Memcons (2), Box 48, Exec sec, NSC: Subject File, Reagan Library. 69. Ibid. 70. Speech accepting the Donovan Award, New York, 28 Feb. 1981 (http://www.margaretthatcher.org/document/104584). 71. Interview with Lord Carrington. 72. Speech accepting the Donovan Award, 28 Feb. 1981 (http://www.margaretthatcher.org/document/104584). 73. Alexander to Walden, 9 Mar. 1981, Prime Minister's Papers: Soviet Union: UK/Soviet Relations (document consulted in the Cabinet Office). 74. Walden to Alexander, 30 Jan. 1981, Prime Minister's Papers: Soviet Union: UK/Soviet Relations (document consulted in the Cabinet Office). 75. Walden to Alexander, 18 Mar. 1981, Prime Minister's Papers: Soviet Union: UK/Soviet Relations (document consulted in the Cabinet Office). 76. Interview with Sir Murdo Maclean. 77. Interview with Richard Perle. 78. Interview with Richard Allen. 79. 'East–West Relations', 11 Feb. 1981, Department of State Briefing Paper, Released by the US State Department under FOIA Case #200505131. 80. Interview with General Alexander Haig 81. 'Security/Arms Control Issues', 17 Feb. 1981, Department of State Briefing Paper, released by the US State Department under FOIA Case #200505131. 82. Interview with Jim Rentschler. See also Rentschler to Allen, 'Thatcher Visit: Talking Points for the Press', 20 Feb. 1981, UK: Prime Minister Thatcher Visit, 02/25/1981–02/28/1981 (1), RAC Box 1, Exec Sec, NSC: VIP Visits, Reagan Library, Simi Valley CA. 83. Interview with Jim Rentschler. 84. Haig to Reagan, 'The Atlantic Alliance', 29 Apr. 1981, NSC 00008 30 April 81 (3/3), Exec Sec, NSC: NSC Meeting Files, Box 91282, Reagan Library. 85. Interview with Richard Perle. 86. Hansard, HC Deb 19 Nov. 1981 (http://www.margaretthatcher.org/document/104745). 87. Ibid., 18 Mar. 1982 (http://www.margaretthatcher.org/document/104896). 88. Margaret Thatcher, *The Downing Street Years*, HarperCollins, 1993, p. 472. 89. Interview with Ken Adelman. 90. Interview with Richard Allen. 91. Ronald Reagan, *An American Life: The Autobiography*, Simon & Schuster, 1990, p. 550. 92. Interview with David Aaron. 93. Thatcher, *The Downing Street Years*, pp. 245–6. 94. Interviews with Lord Carrington and Sir Michael Palliser. 95. Interview with Jim Thomson. 96. Sec. Def. Meeting with UK MOD John Nott, 11 Mar. 1981, 20 Mar. 1981, 1981 UK 1, Box 666, Papers of Caspar Weinberger, Library of Congress. 97. Interview with Sir John Nott. 98. Interview with Lord Butler of Brockwell. 99. 'Extract from Record, PM + S/S Defence', 10 Feb. 1981, TNA: PRO PREM 19/417. 100. Ibid. 101. Perle to Weinberger, Joint US/UK Review of Defense Program, 13 Oct. 1981, 1981 UK 7, Box 666, Papers of Caspar Weinberger. 102. Interview with Richard Perle. 103. Interview with Richard Allen. 104. Thatcher, *The Downing Street Years*, p. 248. 105. 110900z Mar 82, 'Message from the Prime Minister to President Reagan', 11 Mar. 1982, UK: Prime Minister Thatcher, Box 36, Exec Sec, NSC: Head of State File, Reagan Library. 106. Record of a conversation between PM and Waldheim, 20 May 1980, Prime Minister's Papers, Afghanistan: Internal Situation: Soviet Military Intervention (document consulted in the Cabinet Office). 107. Record of conversation between Thatcher and Kisiel, 9 Dec. 1980, Prime Minister's Papers, Poland: Situation and Relations (document consulted in the

Cabinet Office). 108. Ibid. 109. Thatcher to Carter, 8 Dec. 1980, Prime Minister's Papers, Poland: Situation and Relations (document consulted in the Cabinet Office). 110. Record of conversation between Thatcher and Haig, 10 Apr. 1981, Prime Minister's Papers, USA: UK/US Relations (document consulted in the Cabinet Office). 111. Richards to Alexander, 13 Nov. 1981, Prime Minister's Papers, PM's Tours: Suggestion that PM might visit Poland in 1982 (document consulted in the Cabinet Office). 112. Reagan to Thatcher, 19 Dec. 1981, Prime Minister's Papers, Poland: Situation and Relations (document consulted in the Cabinet Office). 113. Record of conversation between Carrington and PM, 20 Dec. 1981, Prime Minister's Papers, Poland: Situation and Relations (document consulted in the Cabinet Office). 114. Thatcher to Reagan, 22 Dec. 1981, UK: Prime Minister Thatcher, Box 35, Exec Sec, NSC: Head of State File, Reagan Library. 115. National Security Council Minutes, 6 July 1981, NSC 00016, Exec Sec, NSC: NSC Meeting Files, Box 91282, Reagan Library. 116. National Security Council Minutes, 22 Dec. 1981, NSC 00034, Exec Sec, NSC: NSC Meeting Files, Box 91283, Reagan Library. 117. Thatcher draft reply to Reagan letter of 24 Dec. 1981, Prime Minister's Papers, Poland: Situation and Relations (document consulted in the Cabinet Office). 118. Thatcher to Reagan, 8 Jan. 1982, Prime Minister's Papers, Poland: Situation and Relations (document consulted in the Cabinet Office). 119. Record of conversation between Thatcher and Haig, 29 Jan. 1982, Prime Minister's Papers, Poland: Situation and Relations (document consulted in the Cabinet Office). 120. Haig to Reagan, 29 Jan. 1982, UK: Prime Minister Thatcher, Box 35, Exec Sec, NSC: Head of State File, Reagan Library. 121. Thatcher to Reagan, 29 Jan. 1982, Prime Minister's Papers, Poland: Situation and Relations (document consulted in the Cabinet Office). 122. Ronald Reagan, *The Reagan Diaries*, HarperCollins, 2007, 30 Jan. 1982, p. 66. 123. 'Terms of Reference for High-Level USG Mission to Europe on Soviet Sanctions', 26 Feb. 1982, NSC 00043 02/26/83, Box 91283, Exec Sec, NSC: NSC Meeting Files, Reagan Library. 124. Reed, *At the Abyss*, p. 227. 125. NSDD 32, 20 May 1982, cited in Peter Schweizer, *Reagan's War: The Epic Story of his Forty-Year Struggle and Final Triumph over Communism*, Doubleday, 2002, pp. 154–5. 126. Interview with Roger Robinson. 127. Coles to PM, 12 Feb. 1982, Prime Minister's Papers, USA: Visits to UK by Presidents of the US (document consulted in the Cabinet Office). 128. Ibid. 129. Whitmore to Fall, 11 Mar. 1982, Prime Minister's Papers, USA: Visits to UK by Presidents of the US (document consulted in the Cabinet Office). 130. Whitmore to Halliday, 15 Mar. 1982, Prime Minister's Papers, USA: Visits to UK by Presidents of the US (document consulted in the Cabinet Office). 131. 221706z Mar 82, 'Presidential Visit to London: Thatcher decision on venue for speech', 22 Mar. 1982, UK (09/01/1981–03/31/1982) [4], Box 20, Exec Sec, NSC: Country File, Reagan Library. 132. Henderson telegram no. 948, 18 Mar. 1982, Prime Minister's Papers, USA: Visits to UK by Presidents of the US (document consulted in the Cabinet Office). 133. Reagan, *The Reagan Diaries*, 24 May 1982, p. 86. 134. Interview with Jim Hooley. 135. Ronald Reagan: Address to Members of the British Parliament, 8 June 1982, The Public Papers of the Presidents, The American Presidency Project, University of California. 136. Speech at lunch for US President, 8 June

1982 (http://www.margaretthatcher.org/document/104957). **137.** Text of speech at lunch for US President, 8 June 1982, Prime Minister's Papers, USA: Visits to UK by Presidents of the US (document consulted in the Cabinet Office). **138.** Haig to Reagan, 8 June 1982, UK (04/01/1982–07/31/1982) [6], Box 20, Exec Sec, NSC: Country File, Reagan Library. **139.** Thatcher, *The Downing Street Years*, p. 244. **140.** Interview with Sir Clive Whitmore. **141.** 250049z Jun 82, 'Official-Informal: Thatcher Visit', 25 June 1982, released by the US State Department under FOIA Case #200600789. **142.** Interview with Judge William Clark. **143.** Interview with Thomas Niles. **144.** Interview with Bud McFarlane. **145.** Interview with Sir Clive Whitmore. **146.** See Hansard, HC Deb 1 July 1982 (http://www.margaretthatcher.org/document/104986). **147.** Thatcher to Reagan, 30 July 1982, UK: Prime Minister Thatcher, Box 35, Exec Sec, NSC: Head of State File, Reagan Library. **148.** Interview with Roger Robinson. **149.** Interview with George Shultz. **150.** Ibid. **151.** George Shultz, *Turmoil and Triumph: My Years as Secretary of State*, Charles Scribner's Sons, 1993, p. 141. **152.** Interview with Sir Rodric Braithwaite. **153.** Thatcher to Reagan, 12 Nov. 1982, THCR 3/1/26. **154.** Draft condolence letter, 10 Nov. 1982, Prime Minister's Papers, Deaths: The Death of President Brezhnev (document consulted in the Cabinet Office).

CHAPTER 21: HUNGER IN IRELAND

1. Papers relating to the compilation of Lady Thatcher's memoirs, The Thatcher Papers, Churchill College, Cambridge, THCR 4/3. **2.** Ibid. **3.** Interview with Lady Colnbrook. **4.** Interview with Lord Gowrie. **5.** Interview with Lord Armstrong of Ilminster. **6.** THCR 4/3. **7.** Ibid. **8.** Ibid. **9.** Private information. **10.** Note, 8 June 1979, The National Archives (TNA): Public Record Office (PRO) PREM 19/80. **11.** Hunt to PM, 4 May 1979, TNA: PRO PREM 19/80. **12.** Cartledge to Lever, 10 May 1979, TNA: PRO PREM 19/79. **13.** O'Neill to Carter, 22 June 1979, UK 3–7/79, Box 77, NSA: Country File UK, Carter Library, Atlanta GA. **14.** Alexander to Walden, 'Prime Minister's Visit to the United States', 19 Dec. 1979, TNA: PRO FCO 82/991. **15.** Note of conversation between Atkins and PM, 23 Aug. 1979, TNA: PRO PREM 19/80. **16.** Paisley to PM, 11 June 1979, TNA: PRO PREM 19/80. **17.** Interview with Sir Kenneth Stowe. **18.** Note of discussion, 28 Aug. 1979, TNA: PRO PREM 19/81. **19.** Pattison to Pilling, 28 Aug. 1979, TNA: PRO PREM 19/79. **20.** Atkins to PM, 31 Aug. 1979, TNA: PRO PREM 19/79. **21.** Note of meeting between Thatcher and Lynch, 5 Sept. 1979, TNA: PRO PREM 19/79. **22.** Note of plenary meeting, 5 Sept. 1979, TNA: PRO PREM 19/79. **23.** Interview with Dermot Nally. **24.** Hunt to PM, 16 Oct. 1979, TNA: PRO PREM 19/82. **25.** Gow to PM, 27 Nov. 1979, TNA: PRO PREM 19/83. **26.** Ian Gow, note on Utley note, Nov. 1979 (undated), THCR 2/6/2/116. **27.** Interview with Sir Kenneth Stowe. **28.** Stowe record of meeting with Powell, 15 Apr. 1980, TNA: PRO PREM 19/280. **29.** Interview with Sir Kenneth Stowe. **30.** Whitelaw to PM, 30 Apr. 1980, TNA: PRO PREM 19/280. **31.** Interview with Sir Kenneth Stowe. **32.** Lever to Alexander, 1 Apr. 1980, TNA: PRO PREM

19/283. 33. Interview with Sean Aylward. 34. Frank Dunlop, *Yes, Taoiseach*, Penguin, 2004, p. 209. 35. Interview with Noel Dorr. 36. Interview with Dermot Nally. 37. Haydon telegram, 27 May 1980, TNA: PRO PREM 19/283. 38. Interview with Lord Gowrie. 39. THCR 4/3. 40. Whitelaw to PM memo, 5 June 1980, TNA: PRO PREM 19/280. 41. Ibid. 42. OD minutes, 10 June 1980, Prime Minister's Papers, Ireland: The Situation in Northern Ireland (document consulted in the Cabinet Office). 43. Ibid. 44. Stowe to Sanders, 12 Aug. 1980, Prime Minister's Papers, Ireland: The Situation in Northern Ireland (document consulted in the Cabinet Office). 45. Haughey to PM, 23 Oct. 1980, Prime Minister's Papers, Ireland: Hunger Strike at the Maze Prison (document consulted in the Cabinet Office). 46. Sir Robert Armstrong, Cabinet Secretary's notebooks, 23 Oct. 1980. 47. Amstrong to PM, 7 Nov. 1980, TNA: PRO PREM 19/282. 48. Ibid. 49. Armstrong to Alexander, 24 Nov. 1980, TNA: PRO PREM 19/282. 50. Haughey meeting with Thatcher, 1 Dec. 1980, Prime Minister's Papers, Ireland: Meetings with the Taoiseach (document consulted in the Cabinet Office). 51. Record of conversation between Haughey and Thatcher, 8 Dec. 1980, Prime Minister's Papers, Ireland: Meetings with the Taoiseach (document consulted in the Cabinet Office). 52. Duddy's role as 'the contact' was revealed by the journalist Peter Taylor in a 2008 documentary, *The Secret Peacemaker* (BBC2), 26 March 2008. For an account of the 1980 Hunger Strikes, see Taylor's *Brits: The War Against the IRA*, Bloomsbury Publishing PLC, new edition, pp. 233–6. 53. The account that follows, unless otherwise stated, is based on private information. 54. Interview with Sir Kenneth Stowe. 55. Ibid. 56. THCR 4/3. 57. Interview with Sir Kenneth Stowe. 58. Interview with Sean O'Callaghan. 59. THCR 4/3. 60. Interview with Sean Aylward. 61. Briefing paper on UK objectives, 25 Nov. 1980, Prime Minister's Papers, Ireland: Meetings with the Taoiseach (document consulted in the Cabinet Office). 62. Record of conversation between Haughey and Thatcher, 8 Dec. 1980, Prime Minister's Papers, Ireland: Meetings with the Taoiseach (document consulted in the Cabinet Office). 63. Figg to Alexander, 9 Dec. 1980, Prime Minister's Papers, Ireland: Meetings with the Taoiseach (document consulted in the Cabinet Office). 64. Dunlop, *Yes, Taoiseach*, p. 216. 65. Figg to Alexander, 9 Dec. 1980, Prime Minister's Papers, Ireland: Meetings with the Taoiseach (document consulted in the Cabinet Office). 66. THCR 4/3. 67. *Irish Times*, 13 Dec. 1980. 68. Alexander to Lyne, Mar. 1981, Prime Minister's Papers, Ireland: Meetings with the Taoiseach (document consulted in the Cabinet Office). 69. Interview with Dermot Nally. 70. Armstrong to PM, 18 Dec. 1980, Prime Minister's Papers, Ireland: Meetings with the Taoiseach (document consulted in the Cabinet Office). 71. Ibid. 72. Whitmore to PM, 19 Dec. 1980, Prime Minister's Papers, Ireland: Meetings with the Taoiseach (document consulted in the Cabinet Office). 73. Interview with Lord Armstrong of Ilminster. 74. Interview with Sir Kenneth Stowe. 75. Interview with Sir Robert Wade-Gery. 76. Ibid. 77. Joint Study Terms of Reference, 27 Jan. 1981, Prime Minister's Papers, Ireland: Meetings with the Taoiseach (document consulted in the Cabinet Office). 78. Gow note of Powell meeting with PM, 10 Feb. 1981, THCR 2/6/2/116. 79. Wade-Gery to Armstrong, 12 Mar. 1981, Prime Minister's Papers, Ireland: Hunger Strike at the Maze Prison (document consulted in the Cabinet Office). 80. Alexander to Walden, 19

Mar. 1981, Prime Minister's Papers, Ireland: Hunger Strike at the Maze Prison (document consulted in the Cabinet Office). **81.** PM note, 3 May 1981, attached to Joint Studies drafts of 28 April 1981, Prime Minister's Papers, Ireland: Hunger Strike at the Maze Prison (document consulted in the Cabinet Office). **82.** Atkins to PM, 23 Feb. 1981, Prime Minister's Papers, Ireland: Hunger Strike in the Maze Prison (document consulted in the Cabinet Office). **83.** Interview with Sean O'Callaghan. **84.** Speech in Belfast, 5 Mar. 1981 (http://www.margaretthatcher.org/document/104589). **85.** Armstrong to Sanders, 22 Apr. 1981, Prime Minister's Papers, Ireland: Hunger Strike in the Maze Prison (document consulted in the Cabinet Office). **86.** Ibid. **87.** Atkins telephone conversation with PM, 25 April 1981, Prime Minister's Papers, Ireland: Hunger Strike in the Maze Prison (document consulted in the Cabinet Office). **88.** Record of meeting between Hume and PM, 13 May 1981, Prime Minister's Papers, Ireland: Hunger Strike in the Maze Prison (document consulted in the Cabinet Office). **89.** Record of meeting with Foot and PM, 14 May 1981, Prime Minister's Papers, Ireland: Hunger Strike in the Maze Prison (document consulted in the Cabinet Office). **90.** B. Ingham to C. Whitmore, 19 May 1981, Prime Minister's Papers, Ireland: Hunger Strike in the Maze Prison (document consulted in the Cabinet Office). **91.** Interview with Sir Robert Wade-Gery. **92.** Armstrong to PM, 19 May 1981, Prime Minister's Papers, Ireland: Hunger Strike in the Maze Prison (document consulted in the Cabinet Office). **93.** Alexander to Boys Smith, 27 May 1981, Prime Minister's Papers, Ireland: Hunger Strike in the Maze Prison (document consulted in the Cabinet Office). **94.** Atkins, 'Northern Ireland: The Need for Movement', 12 June 1981, Prime Minister's Papers, Ireland: The Situation in Northern Ireland (document consulted in the Cabinet Office). **95.** Armstrong to PM, 17 June 1981, Prime Minister's Papers, Ireland: Hunger Strike in the Maze Prison (document consulted in the Cabinet Office). **96.** Comm. Brownie [Adams] from Bik, 29 June 1981, quoted in David Beresford, *Ten Men Dead: The Story of the 1981 Irish Hunger Strike*, HarperCollins, 1987, pp. 272–3. **97.** The most bitter disputes in this respect have taken place between Republicans themselves: see *Irish Times*, 31 December 2011, and *Belfast Telegraph*, 3 January 2012. **98.** Rickett to Boys Smith, 3 July 1981, Prime Minister's Papers, Ireland: Hunger Strike in the Maze Prison (document consulted in the Cabinet Office). **99.** Ibid. **100.** For a full account of this see Padraig O'Malley, *Biting at the Grave: The Irish Hunger Strike and the Politics of Despair*, Beacon Press, 1990, pp. 90–91. **101.** Record of telephone conversation between Alison and PM, 4 July 1981, Prime Minister's Papers, Ireland: Hunger Strike in the Maze Prison (document consulted in the Cabinet Office). **102.** O'Malley, *Biting at the Grave*, p. 93. **103.** *Sunday Times*, 5 Apr. 2009. **104.** Record of telephone conversation, 6 July 1981, Prime Minister's Papers, Ireland: Hunger Strike in the Maze Prison (document consulted in the Cabinet Office). **105.** Message to be sent through the Channel, 6 July 1981, Prime Minister's Papers, Ireland: Hunger Strike in the Maze Prison (document consulted in the Cabinet Office). **106.** Rickett to Boys Smith, 7 July 1981, Prime Minister's Papers, Ireland: Hunger Strike in the Maze Prison (document consulted in the Cabinet Office). **107.** Whitmore to Boys Smith, 8 July 1981, Prime Minister's Papers, Ireland: Hunger Strike in the Maze Prison (document consulted in the Cabinet Office). **108.** Brownie from Bik, 7 July 1981, see Beresford, *Ten Men Dead*, pp. 295–6. **109.** Interview with Sean O'Callaghan. **110.** Ibid. **111.** Alexander to Boys Smith, 14 July 1981, Prime Minister's Papers, Ireland: Hunger Strike in the Maze Prison (document consulted in the Cabinet Office). **112.** THCR 4/3. **113.** Note for the record, 18 July 1981, Prime Minister's Papers, Ireland: Hunger Strike in the Maze Prison (document consulted in the Cabinet Office). **114.** Ibid. **115.** Boys Smith to Alexander, 21 July 1981, Prime Minister's Papers, Ireland: Hunger Strike in the Maze Prison (document consulted in the Cabinet Office). **116.** Interview with Dermot Nally. **117.** Interview with Stephen Boys Smith. **118.** Interview with Sean O'Callaghan. **119.** Interview with Lord Prior. **120.** Ibid. **121.** *Irish Times*, 30 December 2011. **122.** Gow to PM, 6 Oct. 1981, Prime Minister's Papers, Ireland: Hunger Strike in the Maze Prison (document consulted in the Cabinet Office). **123.** Ibid. **124.** Ibid. **125.** Interview with Lord Prior. **126.** Interview with Sean O'Callaghan. **127.** THCR 4/3. **128.** Ibid. **129.** Ibid. **130.** Armstrong to Alexander, 4 Nov. 1981, Prime Minister's Papers, Ireland: Meetings with the Taoiseach (document consulted in the Cabinet Office). **131.** Alexander to PM, 4 Nov. 1981, Prime Minister's Papers, Ireland: Meetings with the Taoiseach (document consulted in the Cabinet Office). **132.** Interview with Sir David Goodall. **133.** Interview with Lord Lawson of Blaby. **134.** Gow to PM, 29 Oct. 1981, THCR 2/6/2/115. **135.** See Garret FitzGerald, *All in a Life*, Macmillan, 1991, p. 382. **136.** Hansard, HC Deb 10 Nov. 1981 (http://hansard.millbanksystems.com/commons/1981/nov/10/anglo-irish-bilateral-talks). **137.** Gow to PM, 16 Nov. 1981, Prime Minister's Papers, Ireland: The Situation in Northern Ireland (document consulted in the Cabinet Office). **138.** Prior to PM, 21 Dec. 1981, Prime Minister's Papers, Ireland: The Situation in Northern Ireland (document consulted in the Cabinet Office). **139.** Gow to PM, 15 Feb. 1982, Prime Minister's Papers, Ireland: The Situation in Northern Ireland (document consulted in the Cabinet Office). **140.** Gow to PM, 23 Mar. 1982, Prime Minister's Papers, Ireland: The Situation in Northern Ireland (document consulted in the Cabinet Office). **141.** Armstrong to PM, 24 Mar. 1982, Prime Minister's Papers, Ireland: The Situation in Northern Ireland (document consulted in the Cabinet Office). **142.** Sir Robert Armstrong, Cabinet Secretary's notebooks, 1 Apr. 1982. **143.** Gow to PM, 2 April 1982, THCR 2/6/2/117. **144.** Interview with Lord Prior. **145.** Interview with Sean Aylward. **146.** Aylward, 26 May 1982, Prime Minister's Papers, Ireland: Meetings with the Taoiseach (document consulted in the Cabinet Office). **147.** Hansard, HC Deb 29 July 1982 (http://www.margaretthatcher.org/document/105009). **148.** Armstrong to Coles, 6 Aug. 1982, Prime Minister's Papers, Ireland: Meetings with the Taioseach (document consulted in the Cabinet Office). **149.** Gow to PM, 15 Nov. 1982, THCR 2/6/2/117. **150.** Interview with Sir David Goodall.

CHAPTER 22: THE 1981 BUDGET AND BEYOND

1. Interview with Lord Burns. **2.** John Hoskyns, *Just in Time: Inside the Thatcher Revolution*, Aurum Press, 2000, p. 270. **3.** Walters to PM, 10 Feb. 1981, The Thatcher Papers, Churchill College, Cambridge, THCR 1/5/13. **4.** Hoskyns, *Just in Time*, p. 272. **5.** Interview with David Willetts. **6.** Hoskyns, *Just in Time*,

p. 269.   7. Interview with Sir Douglas Wass.   8. Interview with Lord Wolfson of
Sunningdale.   9. Margaret Thatcher, *The Downing Street Years*, HarperCollins,
1993, p. 135.   10. Interview with Sir Alan Walters.   11. Ibid.   12. Hoskyns, *Just
in Time*, p. 273.   13. Ibid., p. 276.   14. Ibid., pp. 276–7.   15. HM Treasury papers,
PDF file 51: drafts of the Budget speech c, 24 Feb. 1981 (http://hm-treasury.gov.
uk/d/foi_51draftsbudgetspeech_c.pdf).   16. Interview with Sir Alan Walters.
17. Hoskyns, *Just in Time*, p. 279.   18. Interview with Sir Douglas Wass.   19. See
Geoffrey Howe, *Conflict of Loyalty*, Macmillan, 1994, p. 202.   20. Interview with
Sir Adam Ridley.   21. Ibid.   22. Interview with Sir Peter Middleton.   23. Interview
with Lord Burns.   24. Interview with Andrew Duguid.   25. Interview with Lord
Burns.   26. Interview with David Willetts.   27. Interview with Sir Clive
Whitmore.   28. Interview with Lord Prior.   29. Interview with Lord Walker.   30. Interview with Lord Gilmour of Craigmillar.   31. Interview with Lord Prior.   32. All
quotations from Sir Robert Armstrong, Cabinet Secretary's notebooks, 10 Mar.
1981.   33. Ingham digest, 11 Mar. 1981, THCR 3/5/4.   34. Speech to *Guardian*
Young Businessman of the Year, 11 Mar. 1981 (http://www.margaretthatcher.org/
document/104594).   35. Ingham digest, 12 Mar. 1981, THCR 3/5/4.   36. Ingham
digest, 13 Mar. 1981, THCR 3/5/4.   37. Hoskyns, *Just in Time*, p. 288.   38. Ingham digest, 30 Mar. 1981, THCR 3/5/4.   39. Ibid.   40. Interview with Sir Peter
Middleton.   41. Nigel Lawson, *The View from No. 11*, Bantam, 1992, p. 98.
42. Interview with Sir Peter Middleton.   43. See Alan Walters, *Britain's Economic
Renaissance*, Oxford University Press, 1986, p. 157.   44. Interview with Sir Douglas Wass.   45. Ingham digest, 14 Apr. 1981, THCR 3/5/5.   46. Interview for ITN,
13 Apr. 1981 (http://www.margaretthatcher.org/document/104617).   47. John
Hoskyns, diary (unpublished), entry for 18 May 1981.   48. Howe to PM, 8 Apr.
1981, Prime Minister's Papers, Economic Policy: Economic Strategy: Pay and Prices
(document consulted in the Cabinet Office).   49. Howe note on Economic Strategy,
12 June 1981, Prime Minister's Papers, Economic Policy: Economic Strategy: Pay
and Prices (document consulted in the Cabinet Office).   50. Armstrong to PM, 16
June 1981, Prime Minister's Papers, Economic Policy: Economic Strategy: Pay and Prices
(document consulted in the Cabinet Office).   51. Sir Robert Armstrong, Cabinet Secretary's notebooks, 17 June 1981.   52. Party political broadcast, 8 July 1981 (http://
www.margaretthatcher.org/document/104679).   53. Hugo Young, *One of Us*, Macmillan, 1989.   54. Ingham to Pym, 8 July 1981, Prime Minister's Papers: Economic
Policy: Economic Strategy: Pay and Prices (document consulted in the Cabinet
Office).   55. All quotations from Sir Robert Armstrong, Cabinet Secretary's notebooks,
9 July 1981.   56. Ingham digest, 14 July 1981, THCR 3/5/8.   57. Ingham digest,
16 July 1981, THCR 3/5/8.   58. Note of meeting between Reagan and Thatcher,
20 July 1981, Prime Minister's Papers, Economic Policy: Ottawa Economic Summit
(document consulted in the Cabinet Office).   59. Interview with Mike Deaver.   60.
Richard Aldous, *Reagan and Thatcher: The Difficult Relationship*, W. W. Norton,
2012, p. 50.   61. Interview with Kenneth Duberstein.   62. *New York Times*, 23
July 1981.   63. Ronald Reagan, *The Reagan Diaries*, HarperCollins, 2007, 20–21
July 1981, p. 32.   64. All quotations from Sir Robert Armstrong, Cabinet Secretary's
notebooks, 23 July 1981.   65. Ibid.   66. Ingham digest, 24 July 1981, THCR 3/5/8.

67. Interview with Sir Tim Lankester. 68. Louis to Secretary of State, 31 July 1981, UK (01/20/1981–08/13/1981) [5], Box 20, Exec Sec, NSC: Country File, Reagan Library, Simi Valley CA. 69. Ingham digest, 30 July 1981, THCR 3/5/8. 70. Ingham to Pym, 31 July 1981, Prime Minister's Papers, Economic Policy: Economic Strategy: Pay and Prices (document consulted in the Cabinet Office). 71. *The Times*, 3 Aug. 1981. 72. *Sun*, 6 Aug. 1981. 73. James Prior, *A Balance of Power*, Hamish Hamilton, 1986, p. 132. 74. Interview with Sir Michael Scholar. 75. Interview with Lord Jopling. 76. Charles Douglas-Home to PM, 18 Aug. 1981, THCR 1/3/6. 77. Interview with Sir Michael Scholar. 78. Interview with Sir Clive Whitmore. 79. Ibid. 80. Interview with Lord Kerr of Kinlochard. 81. Interview with Lord Jopling. 82. Correspondence between Sir John Hoskyns and the author. 83. Ibid. 84. All quotations from 'Your Political Survival', Hoskyns to PM, 20 Aug. 1981, document in the possession of Sir John Hoskyns. 85. Hoskyns, *Just in Time*, pp. 327–8. 86. Ibid., p. 327. 87. See Stanley Crooks, *Peter Thorneycroft*, George Mann, 2007, p. 277. 88. Correspondence with Sir John Hoskyns. 89. See Hoskyns, *Just in Time*, pp. 332–3. 90. *Daily Mail*, 27 Aug. 1981. 91. Note for the record, 2 Sept. 1981, Prime Minister's Papers, Economic Policy: Industrial Relations Legislation (document consulted in the Cabinet Office). 92. Gilmour to PM, 14 Sept. 1981 (http://www.margaretthatcher. org/document/104704). 93. Ingham digest, 15 Sept. 1981, THCR 3/5/9. 94. D. K. Britto to D. Howe, 1 Oct. 1981, THCR 2/6/2/135 part 1. 95. Heath speech to Federation of Conservative Students, Manchester, *The Times*, 7 Oct. 1981. 96. Speech at Monash University, Melbourne, 6 Oct. 1981 (http://www.margarett hatcher.org/document/104712). 97. Interview with Lord Patten of Barnes. 98. Ibid. 99. Interview with Lord Waldegrave of North Hill. 100. Howe to PM, 9 Oct. 1981, Prime Minister's Papers, Economic Policy: Economic Strategy: Pay and Prices (document consulted in the Cabinet Office). 101. Hoskyns, *Just in Time*, p. 338. 102. Notes for conference speech, 16 Oct. 1981, THCR 5/1/4/24. 103. Hoskyns, p. 339. 104. Speech to Conservative Party conference, 16 Oct. 1981 (http://www.margaretthatcher.org/document/104717). 105. Ingham digest, 17 Oct. 1981, THCR 3/5/9. 106. Sir Robert Armstrong, Cabinet Secretary's notebooks, 20 Oct. 1981. 107. Ibid. 108. Ingham digest, 29 Oct. 1981, THCR 3/5/9. 109. Sir Robert Armstrong, Cabinet Secretary's notebooks, 29 Oct. 1981. 110. Interview with Lord Prior. 111. Interview with Lord Kerr of Kinlochard. 112. Howe, *Conflict of Loyalty*, p. 233. 113. Speech to Lord Mayor's Banquet, 16 Nov. 1981 (http:// www.margaretthatcher.org/document/104741). 114. Interview with Sir Michael Scholar. 115. Ibid. 116. Sir Robert Armstrong, Cabinet Secretary's notebooks, 26 Nov. 1981. 117. M. Jopling to PM, 4 Dec. 1981, THCR 2/6/2/49. 118. *Guardian*, 3 Dec. 1981. 119. Ingham digest, 6 Dec. 1981, THCR 3/5/11. 120. *Daily Telegraph*, 9 Nov. 1981. 121. See Ingham digest, 9 Dec. 1981, THCR 3/5/11. 122. Ian Gow to PM, 29 Dec. 1981, THCR 1/3/6. 123. Interview with Sir Mark Thatcher. 124. Ingham's digest, 14 Jan. 1982, THCR 3/5/12. 125. Interview with Sir Michael Scholar. 126. *Sun*, 14 Jan. 1982. 127. *Daily Express*, 14 Jan. 1982. 128. Interview with Lord Laing of Dunphail. 129. Interview with Sir Michael Scholar. 130. Coles to Thatcher, 12 Feb. 1982, TNA: PRO PREM

19/893.   131. Ingham digest, 15 Jan. 1982, THCR 3/5/12.   132. Sir Robert Armstrong, Cabinet Secretary's notebooks, 28 Jan. 1982.

CHAPTER 23: THE FALKLANDS INVASION

1. Lord Luce, private memoir. Lord Luce has also published a memoir, *Ringing the Changes* (Michael Russell, 2007), which gives an account of his Falklands experience. Since his earlier manuscript memoir is fuller at most points, however, it is the source for quotations here.   2. Carrington to OD, 12 Oct. 1979, Prime Minister's Papers, Argentina: Position of the Falkland Islands (document consulted in the Cabinet Office).   3. Carrington to PM, 20 Sept. 1979, Prime Minister's Papers, Argentina: Argentine Relations (papers seen by the Prime Minister that may be required during the Falkland Islands inquiry).   4. OD memo by Carrington, 12 Oct. 1979, Prime Minister's Papers, Argentina: Position of the Falkland Islands (document consulted in the Cabinet Office).   5. Record of Anglo-Argentine talks on the Falklands, New York, 28–29 Apr. 1980, Prime Minister's Papers, Argentina: Position of the Falkland Islands (document consulted in the Cabinet Office).   6. This and subsequent quotations are from Sir Robert Armstrong, Cabinet Secretary's notebooks, 7 Nov. 1980.   7. Papers relating to the compilation of Lady Thatcher's memoirs, The Thatcher Papers, Churchill College, Cambridge, THCR 4/3.   8. See Lawrence Freedman, *The Official History of the Falklands Campaign*, 2 vols, Routledge, 2005, vol. i: *The Origins of the Falklands War*, p. 127.   9. Sir Robert Armstrong, Cabinet Secretary's notebooks, 7 Nov. 1980.   10. Ibid., 3 Dec. 1980.   11. 'Record of a meeting held in 1 Carlton Gardens', 30 June 1981, FCO Archives (http://www.margaretthatcher. org/document/118468).   12. Joint Intelligence Committee, July 1981, JIC (81) (N) 34, Prime Minister's Papers, Argentina: Position of the Falkland Islands (document consulted in the Cabinet Office).   13. Interview with Lord Bramall.   14. Interview with Sir David Omand.   15. Luce, private memoir.   16. Hunt to Carrington, 19 Jan. 1982, Prime Minister's Papers, Argentina: Position of the Falkland Islands (document consulted in the Cabinet Office).   17. See Freedman, *The Official History of the Falklands Campaign*, vol. i, p. 154.   18. Luce, private memoir.   19. See Freedman, *The Official History of the Falklands Campaign*, vol. i, p. 158.   20. Ibid., p. 160.   21. Cable, 'Travel of Assistant Secretary Enders', 3 Mar. 1982, FOI Electronic Reading Room, US State Department (http://foia.state.gov/documents/ argentina/0000AF2F.pdf).   22. Luce, private memoir.   23. See Freedman, *The Official History of the Falklands Campaign*, vol. i, p. 167.   24. Alan Clark, *Diaries: Into Politics*, Weidenfeld & Nicolson, 2000, 22 Mar. 1982, p. 305.   25. Williams to Foreign Office, 27 Mar. 1982, Prime Minister's Papers, Argentina: Position of the Falkland Islands (document consulted in the Cabinet Office).   26. All quotations from Sir Robert Armstrong, Cabinet Secretary's notebooks, 25 Mar. 1982.   27. Prime Minister's Papers, Cabinet Conclusions, 25 Mar. 1982 (document consulted in the Cabinet Office).   28. Luce, private memoir.   29. Falkland Islands Review Committee: transcript of oral evidence by the Prime Minister, 25 Oct. 1982, TNA: PRO CAB 292/47.   30. Ibid.   31. Interview with Sir John Coles.   32. Luce,

private memoir. 33. Ibid. 34. See Freedman, *The Official History of the Falklands Campaign*, vol. i, pp. 84 ff. 35. Ibid., p. 206. 36. Luce, private memoir; 'Sir Rex Hunt', *Daily Telegraph* obituary, 12 Nov. 2012. 37. Freedman, *The Official History of the Falklands Campaign*, vol. i, p. 207. 38. Interview with Sir John Nott. 39. Luce, private memoir. 40. Interview with Sir John Coles. 41. Interview with Sir Henry Leach. 42. Ibid. 43. Ibid. 44. Ibid. 45. Interview with Sir John Coles. 46. Interview with Sir Henry Leach. 47. Ibid. 48. Interview with Sir Clive Whitmore. 49. Interview with Sir John Nott. 50. Interview with Sir David Omand. 51. Sir Robert Armstrong, Cabinet Secretary's notebooks, 1 Apr. 1982. 52. Ibid. 53. Luce, private memoir. 54. Interview with Dennis Blair. 55. Interview with Judge William Clark. 56. Alexander Haig, *Caveat: Realism, Reagan, and Foreign Policy*, Macmillan, 1984, pp. 264–5. 57. Interview with Jim Rentschler. 58. Interview with Roger Fontaine. 59. Lord Renwick of Clifton, unpublished manuscript. 60. Luce, private memoir. 61. Ibid. 62. Ibid. 63. Sir Robert Armstrong, Cabinet Secretary's notebooks, 2 Apr. 1982. 64. Ibid. 65. Falkland Islands Review Committee: transcript of oral evidence by the Prime Minister, 25 Oct. 1982, TNA: PRO CAB 292/47. 66. Private information. 67. Sir Robert Armstrong, Cabinet Secretary's notebooks, 2 Apr. 1982. 68. Interview with Sir Henry Leach. 69. Luce, private memoir. 70. Weston to Coles, 2 Apr. 1982, Prime Minister's Papers, Argentina: Position of the Falkland Islands (document consulted in the Cabinet Office). 71. Margaret Thatcher, *The Downing Street Years*, HarperCollins, 1993, p. 181. 72. Luce, private memoir. 73. Interview with Sir Clive Whitmore. 74. Interview with Sir John Coles. 75. Interview with Lord Kerr of Kinlochard. 76. Clark, *Diaries: Into Politics*, 3 Apr. 1982, p. 312. 77. Hansard, HC Deb 3 Apr. 1982 (http://www.margaretthatcher.org/document/104910). 78. Ibid. 79. Hansard, HC Deb 3 Apr. 1982. 80. Clark, *Diaries: Into Politics*, 15 June 1982, p. 333. 81. Interview with Sir John Coles. 82. Clark, *Diaries: Into Politics*, 3 Apr. 1982, p. 313. 83. Interview with Sir David Omand. 84. THCR 4/3. 85. See John Nott, *Here Today, Gone Tomorrow*, Politico's, 2002, ch. 8. 86. Interview with Sir Clive Whitmore. 87. Interview with Lord Jopling. 88. Ibid. 89. Interview with Sir Antony Acland. 90. Interview with Lord Parkinson. 91. Interview with Sir Michael Palliser. 92. Margaret Thatcher's manuscript account, THCR 1/20/3/1. 93. Interview with Lord Luce. 94. Interview with Lord Carrington. 95. THCR 4/3. 96. Interview with Sir Brian Fall. 97. Interview with Sir Michael Palliser. 98. Ibid. 99. Interview with Sir Antony Acland. 100. Ibid. 101. Lord Deedes, diary (unpublished), 5 Apr. 1982. 102. Thatcher, *The Downing Street Years*, p. 181. 103. Interview with Lord Jopling. 104. ITN News, 5 Apr. 1982 (http://www.margaretthatcher.org/document/104913). 105. THCR 1/20/3/1. 106. Jacques Attali, *Verbatim*, vol. i: *1981–1986*, Fayard, 1993, 5 Apr. 1982, p. 201. 107. Pattison to Coles, 3 Apr. 1982, Prime Minister's Papers, Argentina: Position of the Falkland Islands (document consulted in the Cabinet Office). 108. Interview with Hubert Vedrine. 109. Luce, private memoir. 110. Telephone conversation with King Hussein, 3 Apr. 1982, Prime Minister's Papers, Argentina: Position of the Falkland Islands (document consulted in the Cabinet Office). 111. THCR 4/3. 112. See Freedman, *The Official History of the*

Falklands Campaign, vol. ii: *War and Diplomacy*, p. 21. **113.** Interview with Sir John Coles. **114.** Ibid. **115.** THCR 1/20/3/1. **116.** Interview with Lord Kerr of Kinlochard. **117.** Interview with Sir John Coles. **118.** Interview with Sir John Nott. **119.** See John Campbell, *Margaret Thatcher*, 2 vols, Jonathan Cape, 2000, 2003, vol. ii: *The Iron Lady*, p. 141, n. 38. **120.** Interview with Sir Denis Thatcher. **121.** Interview with Sir John Coles. **122.** Interview with Sir David Omand. **123.** Ibid. **124.** Interview with Sir Philip Goodhart. **125.** THCR 1/20/3/1. **126.** Hansard, HC Deb 7 Apr. 1982 (http://www.margaretthatcher.org/document/104916). **127.** THCR 4/3. **128.** THCR 1/20/3/1. **129.** Interview with Sir Clive Whitmore. **130.** Interview with Sir John Coles. **131.** Interview with Dov Zakheim. **132.** Interview with David Gompert. **133.** Interview with Bud McFarlane. **134.** Ronald Reagan, 'Question and answer session with reporters on domestic and foreign policy', 5 Apr. 1982, The Public Papers of the Presidents, The American Presidency Project, University of California. **135.** Sir Robert Armstrong, Cabinet Secretary's notebooks, 6 Apr. 1982. **136.** Henderson to FO telegram, 7 Apr. 1982, Prime Minister's Papers, Argentina: Position of the Falkland Islands (document consulted in the Cabinet Office). **137.** Interview with Jim Rentschler. **138.** Interview with Roger Fontaine. **139.** Interview with Jim Rentschler. **140.** Ibid. **141.** Ibid. **142.** Ibid. **143.** THCR 1/20/3/1. **144.** 'The Falkland Islands Crisis', 7 Apr. 1982, Electronic Briefing Book #375, National Security Archive, Washington DC. **145.** Henderson to FO telegram, 6 Apr. 1982, Prime Minister's Papers, Argentina: Position of the Falkland Islands (document consulted in the Cabinet Office). **146.** Ibid. **147.** Interview with Edward Streator. **148.** Jim Rentschler, diary (unpublished), 8 Apr. 1982. **149.** Record of conversation with Haig, 8 Apr. 1982, Prime Minister's Papers, Argentina: Position of the Falkland Islands (document consulted in the Cabinet Office). **150.** Ibid. **151.** Rentschler, diary, 8 Apr. 1982. **152.** Interview with Alexander Haig. **153.** Interview with David Gompert. **154.** Interview with Alexander Haig. **155.** Interview with Sir Clive Whitmore. **156.** 'Draft Line To Take', 11 Apr. 1982, Prime Minister's Papers, Argentina: Position of the Falkland Islands (document consulted in the Cabinet Office). **157.** Haig to Reagan, 'Discussions in London', 9 Apr. 1982, Falklands War (04/09/1982–04/15/1982), Box 30, Exec Sec, NSC: Country File, Reagan Library, Simi Valley CA. **158.** See Haig, *Caveat*, p. 273. **159.** 'Talking Points: Galtieri', 9 Apr. 1982, United Kingdom – 1982 (03/01/1982–04/30/1982), Box 90233, Dennis Blair Files, Reagan Library. **160.** Haig to Reagan, 'Discussions in London', 9 Apr. 1982, Falklands War (04/09/1982–04/15/1982), Box 30, Exec Sec, NSC: Country File, Reagan Library. **161.** Haig to Reagan, 091120z Apr 82, 'Memorandum for the President', 9 Apr. 1982, released by the US State Department under FOIA Case #200600788. **162.** George Bush to Judge Clark, 7 Apr. 1982, UK (1982), Donald Gregg Files, Office of National Security Affairs, Vice-Presidential Records, Bush Library, College Station TX. **163.** Interview with Judge William Clark. **164.** *Los Angeles Times*, 16 Apr. 1982. The full transcript of the call, intercepted by an amateur radio operator and passed on to Anderson, can be found among Anderson's archived papers: 'Falkland Islands crisis', Folder 7, Box 293, Subseries 1, Series 4, Jack Anderson Papers, Special Collections Research Center, George Washington

University, Washington DC. **165.** THCR 4/3. **166.** Interview with Sir Clive Whitmore. **167.** Haig to Reagan, quoted in Rentschler, diary, 11 Apr. 1982. **168.** See Freedman, *The Official History of the Falklands Campaign*, vol. ii, p. 146. **169.** Interview with Sir Robert Wade-Gery. **170.** Note of meeting between Haig and Thatcher, 12 Apr. 1982, Prime Minister's Papers, Argentina: Position of the Falkland Islands (document consulted in the Cabinet Office). **171.** THCR 1/20/3/1. **172.** Note of meeting to discuss US draft agreement, 12 Apr. 1982, Prime Minister's Papers, Argentina: Position of the Falkland Islands (document consulted in the Cabinet Office). **173.** THCR 1/20/3/1. **174.** Telecon with Prime Minister Thatcher, Tuesday 13 Apr. 1982, 1.20–1.24am, released by the US State Department under FOIA Case #200600788. **175.** THCR 1/20/3/1. **176.** See Thatcher, *The Downing Street Years*, p. 198. **177.** THCR 1/20/3/1. **178.** Interview with Sir John Weston. **179.** Rentschler, diary, 13 Apr. 1982. **180.** Thatcher, *The Downing Street Years*, p. 198. **181.** Interview with Sir John Nott. **182.** Memcon Haig telephone call to Thatcher, 14 Apr. 1982, Prime Minister's Papers, Argentina: The Position of the Falkland Islands (document consulted in the Cabinet Office). **183.** Memcon Haig telephone call to Thatcher, second conversation, 2000 hours, 14 Apr. 1982, Prime Minister's Papers, Argentina: The Position of the Falkland Islands (document consulted in the Cabinet Office). **184.** John Lehman, Keynote Address, 'The Falklands War Thirty Years On', 19–20 May 2012, National Museum of the Royal Navy, Portsmouth. See also Weinberger's contribution to Falklands Roundtable, 5 May 2003, Miller Center, University of Virginia. **185.** Interview with Jim Rentschler. **186.** Interview with Dov Zakheim. **187.** See Freedman, *The Official History of the Falklands Campaign*, vol. ii, p. 380. **188.** Sir Robert Armstrong, Cabinet Secretary's notebooks, 14 Apr. 1982. **189.** Hansard, HC Deb 14 Apr. 1982 (http://www.margaretthatcher.org/document/104918). **190.** Haig to Reagan, cited in Rentschler, diary, 15 Apr. 1982. **191.** 160512z Apr 82, 'Memcon for Secretary Haig on President's phone call to President Galtieri', 16 Apr. 1982, Falklands Crisis 1982, Box 90224, Dennis Blair Files, Reagan Library. **192.** Thatcher to Reagan, 16 Apr. 1982, Prime Minister's Papers, Argentina: Position of the Falkland Islands (document consulted in the Cabinet Office). **193.** Ronald Reagan, *The Reagan Diaries*, HarperCollins, 2007, 17 Apr. 1982, p. 80. **194.** THCR 1/20/3/1. **195.** Haig to Pym, 19 Apr. 1982, Falklands War (04/19/1982–04/21/1982), Box 30, Exec Sec, NSC: Country File, Reagan Library. **196.** Memcon of PM and Parsons, 18 Apr. 1982, Prime Minister's Papers, Argentina: Position of the Falkland Islands (document consulted in the Cabinet Office). **197.** Interview with Sir Clive Whitmore. **198.** Ibid. **199.** Interview with Sir David Omand. **200.** Interview with Sir John Coles. **201.** Gow to PM, 8 Apr. 1982, THCR 1/20/3/5. **202.** Interview with Sir Clive Whitmore. **203.** Interview with Sir John Coles. **204.** Interview with Sir Clive Whitmore. **205.** Interview with Sir Mark Thatcher. **206.** Renwick, manuscript. **207.** Reagan, *The Reagan Diaries*, 19 Apr. 1982, p. 80. **208.** Telephone conversation between PM and Pym, 18 Apr. 1982, Prime Minister's Papers, Argentina: Position of the Falkland Islands (document consulted in the Cabinet Office). **209.** THCR 1/20/3/1. **210.** Ibid. **211.** Ibid. **212.** OD(SA) minutes, 16 Apr. 1982, Prime Minister's Papers, Argentina: Handling of the Falklands Invasion (document consulted in the Cabinet Office).   213. THCR 1/20/3/1.   214. Interview with Sir Henry Leach.   215. Henderson to FO telegram 1376, 21 Apr. 1982, Prime Minister's Papers, Argentina: Position of the Falkland Islands (document consulted in the Cabinet Office).   216. Henderson to FO telegram 1381, 21 Apr. 1982, Prime Minister's Papers, Argentina: Position of the Falkland Islands (document consulted in the Cabinet Office).   217. Ibid.   218. Hansard, HC Deb 21 Apr. 1982. 219. THCR 1/20/3/1.   220. Ibid.   221. Master copy of American draft, 23 Apr. 1982, Prime Minister's Papers, Argentina: Position of the Falkland Islands (document consulted in the Cabinet Office).   222. National Security Council Minutes, 30 Apr. 1982, NSC 00048, Box 91284, Exec Sec, NSC: NSC Meeting Files, Reagan Library.   223. Memcon, 'Falkland Islands Framework', 23 Apr. 1982, released by US State Department under FOIA Case #200600788.   224. THCR 1/20/3/1. 225. Ibid.   226. Interview with Francis Pym, *The Downing Street Years* (BBC), 1993.   227. Interview with Sir John Coles.   228. Thatcher, *The Downing Street Years*, p. 205.   229. THCR 1/20/3/1.   230. Ibid.   231. Ibid.   232. Interview with Sir Denis Thatcher.   233. Interview with Sir Brian Fall.   234. THCR 1/20/3/1. 235. Ibid.   236. Ibid.   237. Interview with Sir John Coles.   238. THCR 1/20/3/1.   239. THCR 4/3.   240. Thatcher, *The Downing Street Years*, p. 208. 241. THCR 1/20/3/1.   242. Ibid.   243. BBC Radio News, 25 Apr. 1982 (http:// www.margaretthatcher.org/document/104923).   244. THCR 1/20/3/1.

CHAPTER 24: VICTORY

1. Henderson to Haig telegram, 27 Apr. 1982, Prime Minister's Papers, Argentina: Position of the Falkland Islands (document consulted in the Cabinet Office). 2. Margaret Thatcher's manuscript account, The Thatcher Papers, Churchill College, Cambridge, THCR 1/20/3/1.   3. *Panorama* (BBC1), 26 Apr. 1982 (Christopher Collins, ed., *Complete Public Statements of Margaret Thatcher 1945–90 on CD-ROM*, Oxford University Press, 1998/2000).   4. Interview with Lord Parkinson.   5. Interview with Sir John Nott.   6. Hansard, HC Deb 27 Apr. 1982 (http:// www.margaretthatcher.org/document/104925).   7. THCR 1/20/3/1.   8. Thatcher to Haig, 26 Apr. 1982, Prime Minister's Papers, Argentina: Position of the Falkland Islands (document consulted in the Cabinet Office).   9. Pym to Henderson, 28 Apr. 1982, Prime Minister's Papers, Argentina: Position of the Falkland Islands (document consulted in the Cabinet Office).   10. All quotations from Sir Robert Armstrong, Cabinet Secretary's notebooks, 29 Apr. 1982.   11. Thatcher to Reagan, 29 Apr. 1982, Prime Minister's Papers, Argentina: Position of the Falkland Islands (document consulted in the Cabinet Office).   12. Reagan to Thatcher, 29 Apr. 1982, Prime Minister's Papers, Argentina: Position of the Falkland Islands (document consulted in the Cabinet Office).   13. THCR 1/20/3/1.   14. Reagan to Thatcher, 29 Apr. 1982, Prime Minister's Papers, Argentina: Position of the Falkland Islands (document consulted in the Cabinet Office).   15. National Security Council Minutes, 30 Apr. 1982, NSC 00048, Box 91284, Exec Sec, NSC: NSC Meeting Files, Reagan Library, Simi Valley CA.   16. Ibid.   17. Ibid.   18. NSDD 34, 14 May 1982, Exec Sec,

NSC: NSDDs, Reagan Library.   19. 'Next Steps on Falklands', 29 Apr. 1982, NSC 00048 04/30/1982 [Falkland Islands], Exec Sec, NSC: NSC Meeting Files, Box 91284, Reagan Library.   20. Reagan, Remarks and a Question-and-answer session with Editors and Broadcasters from Midwestern States, 30 Apr. 1982, The Public Papers of the Presidents, The American Presidency Project, University of California.   21. See Lawrence Freedman, *The Official History of the Falklands Campaign*, 2 vols, Routledge, 2005, vol. ii: *War and Diplomacy*, p. 359.   22. Ibid.   23. Interview with Lord Parkinson.   24. THCR 1/20/3/1.   25. Speech to Mid-Bedfordshire Conservatives, Shuttleworth Agricultural College, 30 Apr. 1982 (http://www.margaretthatcher.org/document/104929).   26.   THCR   1/20/3/1.   27.   Ibid. 28. Ibid.   29. Ibid.   30. Quoted in Freedman, *The Official History of the Falklands Campaign*, vol. ii, p. 285. Chapter 21 of this book contains the fullest account of the *Belgrano* incident yet written, benefiting from official papers.   31. Ibid., p. 287. 32. Interviews with Lord Bramall and Sir Henry Leach.   33. Interview with Sir John Coles.   34. Interview with Sir Clive Whitmore.   35. THCR 1/20/3/1.   36. Interview with Sir Antony Acland.   37. See Freedman, *The Official History of the Falklands Campaign*, vol. ii, p. 288.   38. Papers relating to the compilation of Lady Thatcher's memoirs, THCR 4/3.   39. THCR 1/20/3/1.   40. Ibid.   41. See Freedman, *The Official History of the Falklands Campaign*, vol. ii, p. 293.   42. Hansard, HC Deb 4 May 1982.   43. See Freedman, *The Official History of the Falklands Campaign*, vol. ii, ch. 21.   44. Ronald Reagan, *The Reagan Diaries Unabridged*, 2 vols, HarperCollins, 2009, vol. i: *January 1981–October 1985*, p. 129.   45. Henderson to FO telegram, 2 May 1982, Prime Minister's Papers, Argentina: Position of the Falkland Islands (document consulted in the Cabinet Office).   46. Transcript of Pym press conference in Washington, 2 May 1982, Prime Minister's Papers, Argentina: Position of the Falkland Islands (document consulted in the Cabinet Office). 47. Henderson to Pym telegram 1575, 3 May 1982, Prime Minister's Papers, Argentina: Position of the Falkland Islands (document consulted in the Cabinet Office). 48. Ibid.   49. Henderson to Pym telegram 1574, 3 May 1982, Prime Minister's Papers, Argentina: Position of the Falkland Islands (document consulted in the Cabinet Office).   50. Interview with Alexander Haig.   51. Margaret Thatcher, *The Downing Street Years*, HarperCollins, 1993, p. 216.   52. THCR 4/3.   53. Henderson to Pym telegram 1572, 3 May 1982, Prime Minister's Papers, Argentina: Position of the Falkland Islands (document consulted in the Cabinet Office).   54. Hansard, HC Deb 4 May 1982.   55. THCR 1/20/3/1.   56. Interview with Barry Strevens.   57. Interview with Sir Clive Whitmore.   58. Lord Lewin, quoted in Richard Hill, *Lewin of Greenwich*, Cassell, 2000, p. 370.   59. Atkeson to DCI, 'What's Next in the Falklands?', 7 May 1982, CREST database, US National Archives and Records Administration (NARA).   60. Reagan, *The Reagan Diaries Unabridged*, vol. i, p. 129. 61. Jim Rentschler, diary (unpublished), 4 May 1982.   62. Ibid.   63. Quoted in Freedman, *The Official History of the Falklands Campaign*, vol. ii, p. 326.   64. 041130Z May 82, 'Falklands Dispute: Rules of Engagement unchanged as British ponder next move', 4 May 1982, UK (04/01/1982–07/31/1982) [6], Box 20, Exec Sec, NSC: Country File, Reagan Library.   65. Reagan to Thatcher, 5 May 1982, THCR 3/1/21.   66. All quotations from Sir Robert Armstrong, Cabinet Secretary's notebooks,

5 May 1982. 67. Ibid. 68. Prime Minister's Papers, Cabinet minutes, 5 May 1982 (document consulted in the Cabinet Office). 69. Thatcher to Reagan, 5 May 1982, Prime Minister's Papers, Argentina: Position of the Falkland Islands (document consulted in the Cabinet Office). 70. Clark to Reagan, 'PM Thatcher's Reply on your Falklands Demarche', 5 May 1982, 'Falklands War (UN/Kirkpatrick/Haig) 05/13/1982–06/04/1982', Box 3, William Clark Files, Reagan Library. 71. Thatcher, *The Downing Street Years*, p. 217. 72. Draft Thatcher letter to Reagan, 5 May 1982, THCR 1/20/3/11. 73. Interview with Sir Antony Acland. 74. Interview with Sir John Coles. 75. Interview with Sir Clive Whitmore. 76. Interview with Lord Parkinson. 77. Thatcher to Reagan, 5 May 1982, Prime Minister's Papers, Argentina: Position of the Falkland Islands (document consulted in the Cabinet Office). 78. Ingham digest, 6 May 1982, THCR 3/5/14. 79. Henderson to Pym telegram, 6 May 1982, Prime Minister's Papers, Argentina: Position of the Falkland Islands (document consulted in the Cabinet Office). 80. Henderson to Pym telegram, 8 May 1982, Prime Minister's Papers, Argentina: Position of the Falkland Islands (document consulted in the Cabinet Office). 81. Parsons to Pym telegram, 3 May 1982, Prime Minister's Papers, Argentina: Position of the Falkland Islands (document consulted in the Cabinet Office). 82. Letter to PM from Cardinals Hume and Gray, 8 May 1982, Prime Minister's Papers, Argentina: Position of the Falkland Islands (document consulted in the Cabinet Office). 83. Parsons to Pym, telegram 686, 8 May 1982, Prime Minister's Papers, Argentina: Position of the Falkland Islands (document consulted in the Cabinet Office). 84. Telephone conversation between PM and Parsons, 8 May 1982, Prime Minister's Papers, Argentina: Position of the Falkland Islands (document consulted in the Cabinet Office). 85. Ibid. 86. THCR 4/3. 87. Parsons to Pym telegram, 10 May 1982, Prime Minister's Papers, Argentina: Position of the Falkland Islands (document consulted in the Cabinet Office). 88. Ronald Reagan, *The Reagan Diaries*, HarperCollins, 2007, 12 May 1982, p. 84. 89. Draft message from Thatcher to Reagan, 12 May 1982, Prime Minister's Papers, Argentina: Position of the Falkland Islands (document consulted in the Cabinet Office). 90. Ingham digest, 8 May 1982, THCR 3/5/14. 91. Ibid., 13 May 1982. 92. *Daily Telegraph*, 13 May 1982. 93. Hansard, HC Deb 13 May 1982. 94. THCR 1/20/3/1. 95. Telephone conversation between Thatcher and Reagan, 13 May 1982, Prime Minister's Papers, Argentina: Position of the Falkland Islands (document consulted in the Cabinet Office). 96. Reagan, *The Reagan Diaries*, 13 May 1982, p. 84. 97. THCR 1/20/3/1. 98. Admiral Sandy Woodward, *One Hundred Days*, HarperCollins, 1992, p. 230. 99. Nicholas Henderson, *Mandarin: The Diaries of an Ambassador 1969–1982*, Weidenfeld & Nicolson, 1994, 17 May 1982, pp. 461–2. 100. Interview with Sir Robert Wade-Gery. 101. Ibid. 102. THCR 1/20/3/1. 103. Ibid. 104. Thatcher, *The Downing Street Years*, p. 222. 105. Interview with Sir Anthony Parsons, *The Downing Street Years* (BBC), 1993. 106. THCR 1/20/3/1. 107. Parsons to Pym telegram, 17 May 1982, Prime Minister's Papers, Argentina: Position of the Falkland Islands (document consulted in the Cabinet Office). 108. THCR 1/20/3/1. 109. Ibid. 110. Thatcher, *The Downing Street Years*, p. 223. 111. Wade-Gery to PM, 17 May 1982, Prime Minister's Papers, Argentina: The Handling of the Falklands

Invasion (document consulted in the Cabinet Office). **112.** Ibid. **113.** THCR 4/3. **114.** OD(SA) minutes, 18 May 1982, Prime Minister's Papers, Argentina: The Handling of the Falklands Invasion (document consulted in the Cabinet Office). **115.** Interview with Sir Michael Palliser. **116.** THCR 1/20/3/1. **117.** Ibid. **118.** ITN News, 19 May 1982. **119.** See Freedman, *The Official History of the Falklands Campaign*, vol. ii, p. 372. **120.** Ibid. **121.** Parsons telegram, 19 May 1982, Prime Minister's Papers, Argentina: Position of the Falkland Islands (document consulted in the Cabinet Office). **122.** See Freedman, *The Official History of the Falklands Campaign*, vol. ii, pp. 373–4. **123.** 'UK–Argentine War', United Kingdom – 1982 (05/01/1982–07/31/1982), Box 90223, Dennis Blair Files, Reagan Library. **124.** Sir Robert Armstrong, Cabinet Secretary's notebooks, 20 May 1982. **125.** THCR 1/20/3/1. **126.** Ibid. **127.** Hansard, HC Deb 20 May 1982 (http://www.margaretthatcher.org/document/104943). **128.** Interview with Jeane Kirkpatrick. **129.** Interview with Lord Bramall. **130.** Quoted in Freedman, *The Official History of the Falklands Campaign*, vol. ii, p. 429. **131.** Woodward, *One Hundred Days*, p. 250. **132.** THCR 1/20/3/1. **133.** Ibid. **134.** See Woodward, *One Hundred Days*, pp. 269–70. **135.** Ibid., p. 263. **136.** Interview with Sir Robert Wade-Gery. **137.** Ibid. **138.** THCR 4/3. **139.** Thatcher, *The Downing Street Years*, p. 226. **140.** Ibid. **141.** THCR 1/20/3/1. **142.** Interview with Sir Denis Thatcher. **143.** THCR 1/20/3/1. **144.** Interview with Sir David Goodall. **145.** THCR 1/20/3/1. **146.** FO Sitrep, 24 May 1982, Prime Minister's Papers, Argentina: Position of the Falkland Islands (document consulted in the Cabinet Office). **147.** Pope John Paul II to Thatcher telegram, 22 May 1982, Prime Minister's Papers, Argentina: Position of the Falkland Islands (document consulted in the Cabinet Office). **148.** Thatcher to Pope John Paul II, 22 May 1982, Prime Minister's Papers, Argentina: Position of the Falkland Islands (document consulted in the Cabinet Office). **149.** Interview with Lord Renwick of Clifton. **150.** Henderson telegram, 24 May 1982, Prime Minister's Papers, Argentina: Position of the Falkland Islands (document consulted in the Cabinet Office). **151.** Pym to PM, 25 May 1982, Prime Minister's Papers, Argentina: Position of the Falkland Islands (document consulted in the Cabinet Office). **152.** Interview with Lord Armstrong of Ilminster. **153.** Interview with Sir Brian Fall. **154.** Henderson, *Mandarin*, 30–31 May 1982, pp. 465–6. **155.** Pym to Haig, 26 May 1982, released by the US State Department under FOIA Case #200600788. **156.** Haig to President, 'Falklands Crisis', 26 May 1982, Falklands Crisis 1982, Box 90224, Dennis Blair Files, Reagan Library. **157.** Interview with Jeane Kirkpatrick. **158.** Henderson telegram, 24 May 1982, Prime Minister's Papers, Argentina: Position of the Falkland Islands (document consulted in the Cabinet Office). **159.** Interview with Jim Rentschler. **160.** Records of this conversation were leaked years later and the gist appeared in the *Sunday Times* on 8 Mar. 1992. This account, however, draws on the official US transcript now available at the Reagan Library (Telephone Conversation, Reagan/Thatcher, 31 May 1982, UK (04/26/1982–09/29/1982), Box 20, Exec Sec, NSC: Country File, Reagan Library). **161.** Ibid. **162.** Rentschler, diary, 3 June 1982. **163.** Interview with Jim Rentschler. **164.** Henderson, *Mandarin*, 31 May 1982, pp. 467–8. **165.** Thatcher, *The Downing Street Years*, p. 230. **166.** Henderson, *Mandarin*,

31 May 1982, pp. 466–7. **167.** Interview with Sir Clive Whitmore. **168.** *Washington Post*, 3 June 1982. This was the first of two instalments published by the paper of an interview conducted on 2 June. **169.** Interview with Sir Clive Whitmore. **170.** Ibid. **171.** THCR 1/20/3/1. **172.** Woodward, *One Hundred Days*, p. 239. **173.** THCR 1/20/3/1. **174.** Ibid. **175.** Prime Minister's Papers, Argentina: Position of the Falkland Islands, 10 May 1982 (document consulted in the Cabinet Office). **176.** Speech to Conservative Women's Conference, London, 26 May 1982 (http://www.margaretthatcher.org/document/104948). **177.** *Washington Post*, 4 June 1982. **178.** Speech to Conservative Women's Conference, 26 May 1982 (http://www.margaretthatcher.org/document/104948). **179.** See Freedman, *The Official History of the Falklands Campaign*, vol. ii, p. 557. **180.** Interview with Lord Bramall. **181.** Interview with Major General Julian Thompson. **182.** THCR 4/3. **183.** Interview with Lord Parkinson. **184.** Interview with Major General Julian Thompson. **185.** Interview with Sir David Goodall. **186.** Interview with Tom Brokaw, NBC News, 9 June 1982 (Collins, ed., *Complete Public Statements*). **187.** OD(SA) minutes, 45th meeting, 27 May 1982, Prime Minister's Papers, Argentina: Handling of the Falklands Invasion (document consulted in the Cabinet Office). **188.** Interview with Sir Denis Thatcher. **189.** Interview with Lord Armstrong of Ilminster. **190.** THCR 1/20/3/1. **191.** See Freedman, *The Official History of the Falklands Campaign*, vol. ii, p. 576. **192.** Rentschler, diary, 4 June 1982. **193.** Draft message, Reagan to Thatcher, 2 June 1982, Trip: President's European: June 1982 (2), Box 7, William Clark Files, Reagan Library. **194.** Rentschler, diary, 3 June 1982. **195.** Interview with Sir Nicholas Henderson. **196.** Henderson, *Mandarin*, 8 June 1982, pp. 471–2. **197.** President Mitterrand's statement to the press at the conclusion of the Versailles summit (http://www.g7.utoronto.ca/summit/1982versailles/statement_english.html). **198.** Interview with Hubert Vedrine. **199.** Ibid. **200.** THCR 1/20/3/1. **201.** Parsons telegram, 4 June 1982, Prime Minister's Papers, Argentina: Position of the Falkland Islands (document consulted in the Cabinet Office). **202.** Pym to UK delegation at Versailles, 5 June 1982, Prime Minister's Papers, Argentina: Position of the Falkland Islands (document consulted in the Cabinet Office). **203.** THCR 1/20/3/1. **204.** Press conference after Versailles summit, 6 June 1982 (http://www.margaretthatcher.org/document/104955). **205.** THCR 1/20/3/1. **206.** Ronald Reagan, address to members of the British Parliament, 8 July 1982, The Public Papers of the Presidents, The American Presidency Project, University of California. **207.** Freedman, *The Official History of the Falklands Campaign*, vol. ii, p. 597. **208.** Ibid. **209.** THCR 1/20/3/1. In fact, Mrs Thatcher visited Northwood over the weekend of 12–13 rather than on the Wednesday immediately following the attacks. **210.** Pattison to PM, 10 June 1982, Prime Minister's Papers, Argentina: Position of the Falkland Islands (document consulted in the Cabinet Office). **211.** Scholar to Whitmore, 19 June 1982, Prime Minister's Papers, Argentina: Position of the Falkland Islands (document consulted in the Cabinet Office). **212.** THCR 1/20/3/1. **213.** Ibid. **214.** Ibid. **215.** Freedman, *The Official History of the Falklands Campaign*, vol. ii, p. 650. **216.** THCR 4/3. **217.** Freedman, *The Official History of the Falklands Campaign*, vol. ii, p. 652. **218.** Interview with General Sir Michael Rose.

219. Hansard, HC Deb 14 June 1982 (http://www.margaretthatcher.org/document/104967). **220.** Alan Clark, *Diaries: Into Politics*, Weidenfeld & Nicolson, 2000, 15 June 1982, p. 332. **221.** THCR 1/20/3/1. **222.** Interview with Sir Antony Acland. **223.** THCR 1/20/3/1. **224.** Sir Robert Armstrong, Cabinet Secretary's notebooks, 15 June 1982. **225.** Interview with Sir David Goodall. **226.** Hansard, HC Deb 17 June 1982 (http://www.margaretthatcher.org/document/104970). **227.** Notes on a meeting between the Secretary-General and Prime Minister Thatcher, 14 June 1982, S-1043-0002-05, UN Archives. **228.** Palliser to PM, 'The Falklands Repossessed', 21 June 1982, Prime Minister's Papers, Argentina: Position of the Falkland Islands (document consulted in the Cabinet Office). **229.** Interview with Major General Julian Thompson. **230.** Interview with Sir John Coles. **231.** Interview with Sir Clive Whitmore. **232.** Interview with Lord Armstrong of Ilminster. **233.** Thatcher to Muldoon, 11 June 1982, Prime Minister's Papers, Argentina: Position of the Falkland Islands (document consulted in the Cabinet Office). **234.** Speech to Conservative Party rally in Cheltenham, 3 July 1982 (http://www.margaretthatcher.org/document/104989). **235.** THCR 4/3. **236.** Interview with Lord Renwick of Clifton. **237.** See Thatcher, *The Downing Street Years*, pp. 173–4. **238.** Interview with Sir David Gillmore, 17 Mar. 1996, British Diplomatic Oral History Project, Churchill College, Cambridge. **239.** Draft Presidential remarks at the end of his 23 June 1982 meeting with UK Prime Minister Thatcher; papers of Jim Rentschler. **240.** 'President's Meeting with UK Prime Minister Margaret Thatcher', 23 June 1982, UK (04/26/1982–09/29/1982), Box 20, Exec Sec, NSC: Country File, Reagan Library. **241.** Henderson, *Mandarin*, 20–27 June 1982, p. 480. **242.** Clark, *Diaries: Into Politics*, 15 June 1982, p. 336. **243.** Coles to Whitmore, 2 July 1982, Prime Minister's Papers, Argentina: Falkland Islands Thanksgiving Service (document consulted in the Cabinet Office). **244.** Ridley to Stephens, 15 July 1982, Prime Minister's Papers, Argentina: Falkland Islands Thanksgiving Service (document consulted in the Cabinet Office). **245.** THCR 1/20/3/1. **246.** Ibid. **247.** Coles to Whitmore, 14 July 1982, Prime Minister's Papers, Argentina: Falkland Islands Thanksgiving Service (document consulted in the Cabinet Office). **248.** Interview with Sir David Goodall. **249.** Ibid. **250.** OD(SA), note by the Secretaries, 9 July 1982, Prime Minister's Papers, Argentina: Falkland Islands Thanksgiving Service (document consulted in the Cabinet Office). **251.** Ridley to Coles, 16 July 1982, Prime Minister's Papers, Argentina: Falkland Islands Thanksgiving Service (document consulted in the Cabinet Office). **252.** Interview with Sir David Goodall. **253.** Interview with Lord Runcie of Cuddesdon. **254.** Ibid. **255.** THCR 1/20/3/1. **256.** Interview with Major General Julian Thompson. **257.** Text of Falklands dinner speech, 11 Oct. 1982, THCR 1/20/3/29B. **258.** Interview with Sir David Goodall. **259.** Interview with Lord Bramall.

Bibliography

BOOKS

Aldous, Richard, *Reagan and Thatcher: The Difficult Relationship*, W. W. Norton, 2012

Alexander, Michael, *Managing the Cold War: A View from the Front Line*, RUSI, 2005

Amis, Kingsley, *Memoirs*, Hutchinson, 1991

Anderson, Jack, *Peace, War and Politics: An Eyewitness Account*, Tom Doherty, 1999

Anderson, Martin and Anderson, Annelise, *Reagan's Secret War: The Untold Story of his Fight to Save the World from Nuclear Disaster*, Crown Publishing, 2009

Andrew, Christopher, *The Defence of the Realm: The Authorized History of MI5*, Allen Lane, 2009

Attali, Jacques, *Verbatim*, vol. i: *1981–1986*, Fayard, 1993

Barrett, Laurence, *Gambling with History: Ronald Reagan in the White House*, Doubleday, 1983

Beresford, David, *Ten Men Dead: The Story of the 1981 Irish Hunger Strike*, HarperCollins, 1987

Berlinski, Claire, *There Is No Alternative: Why Margaret Thatcher Matters*, Basic Civitas, 2011

Boyd-Carpenter, John, *Way of Life*, Sidgwick & Jackson, 1980

Braithwaite, Rodric, *Across the Moscow River: The World Turned Upside Down*, Yale University Press, 2002

Brzezinski, Zbigniew, *Power and Principle: Memoirs of the National Security Advisor, 1977–1981*, Farrar, Straus & Giroux, 1983

Butler, David and Butler, Gareth, *Twentieth-Century British Political Facts, 1900–2000*, Macmillan, 2000

Butler, D. E. and King, Anthony, *The British General Election of 1964*, Macmillan, 1965

Butler, Michael, *Europe: More than a Continent*, Heinemann, 1986

Campbell, John, *Edward Heath: A Biography*, Jonathan Cape, 1993

Campbell, John, *Margaret Thatcher*, 2 vols, Jonathan Cape, 2000, 2003

Cannon, Lou, *Governor Reagan: His Rise to Power*, Public Affairs, 2003

Cannon, Lou, *President Reagan: The Role of a Lifetime*, Simon & Schuster, 1991

Carrington, Peter, *Reflect on Things Past: The Memoirs of Lord Carrington*, Collins, 1988

Carter, Jimmy, *Keeping Faith: Memoirs of a President*, Bantam, 1982

Carter, Jimmy, *White House Diary*, Farrar, Straus & Giroux, 2010

Carter, Miranda, *Anthony Blunt: His Lives*, Macmillan, 2001

Castle, Barbara, *The Castle Diaries, 1974–76*, Weidenfeld & Nicolson, 1980

Catterall, Peter, ed., *The Macmillan Diaries Vol.II: Prime Minister and After 1957–1966*, Macmillan, 2011

Charlton, Michael, *The Little Platoon: Diplomacy and the Falklands Dispute*, Basil Blackwell, 1989

Christopher, Warren, *Chances of a Lifetime*, Scribner, 2001

Clark, Alan, *Diaries: Into Politics*, Weidenfeld & Nicolson, 2000

Cockett, Richard, *Thinking the Unthinkable*, HarperCollins, 1994

Colacello, Bob, *Ronnie and Nancy: Their Path to the White House*, Warner Books, 2004

Coles, John, *Making Foreign Policy: A Certain Idea of Britain*, John Murray, 2000

Collins, Christopher, ed., *Complete Public Statements of Margaret Thatcher 1945–90 on CD-ROM* (Oxford University Press, 1998/2000)

Conquest, Robert, *Present Danger: Towards a Foreign Policy*, Hoover Institution Press, 1979

Cooke, Alistair, ed., *Tory Policy Making*, CRD, 2009

Cosgrave, Patrick, *Margaret Thatcher: A Tory and her Party*, Hutchinson, 1978

Croft, Stuart, ed., *British Security Policy: The Thatcher Years and the End of the Cold War*, HarperCollins, 1991

Crooks, Stanley, *Peter Thorneycroft*, George Mann, 2007

Crossman, Richard, *The Diaries of a Cabinet Minister*, vol. iii: *Secretary of State for Social Services 1968–70*, ed. Janet Morgan, Hamish Hamilton/Jonathan Cape, 1977

Crozier, Brian, *Free Agent: The Unseen War 1941–1991*, HarperCollins, 1993

Davidow, Jeffrey, *A Peace in Southern Africa: The Lancaster House Conference on Rhodesia, 1979*, Westview Press, 1984

Deacon, Richard, *'C': A Biography of Sir Maurice Oldfield*, Macdonald, 1985

Deaver, Michael, *A Different Drummer: My Thirty Years with Ronald Reagan*, HarperCollins, 2001

Dobrynin, Anatoly, *In Confidence: Moscow's Ambassador to America's Six Cold War Presidents*, Random House, 1995

Donoughue, Bernard, *Downing Street Diary*, 2 vols, Jonathan Cape, 2005, 2008

Donoughue, Bernard, *Prime Minister: The Conduct of Policy under James Callaghan and Harold Wilson*, Jonathan Cape, 1987

Dorman, Andrew, *Defence under Thatcher*, Palgrave, 2002

Dumbrell, John, *A Special Relationship: Anglo-American Relations in the Cold War and After*, St Martin's Press, 2001

Dunlop, Frank, *Yes, Taoiseach*, Penguin, 2004

Edwardes, Michael, *Back from the Brink*, Collins, 1983

FitzGerald, Garret, *All in a Life*, Macmillan, 1991

Freedman, Lawrence, *The Official History of the Falklands Campaign*, 2 vols, Routledge, 2005

Freedman, Lawrence and Gamba-Stonehouse, Virginia, *Signals of War: The Falklands Conflict of 1982*, Princeton University Press, 1991

Gardiner, George, *Margaret Thatcher: From Childhood to Leadership*, William Kimber, 1975

Garnett, Mark and Aitken, Ian, *Splendid! Splendid!: The Authorized Biography of Willie Whitelaw*, Jonathan Cape, 2002

Gavshon, Arthur and Rice, Desmond, *The Sinking of the Belgrano*, Secker & Warburg, 1984

Gerson, Allan, *The Kirkpatrick Mission: Diplomacy without Apology*, Free Press, 1991

Gilmour, Ian, *Dancing with Dogma: Britain under Thatcherism*, Simon & Schuster, 1992

Grasselli, Gabriella, *British and American Responses to the Soviet Invasion of Afghanistan*, Dartmouth Publishing, 1996

Greenwood, Sean, *Britain and the Cold War*, St Martin's Press, 2000

Haig, Alexander, *Caveat: Realism, Reagan, and Foreign Policy*, Macmillan, 1984

Hannaford, Peter, *The Reagans: A Political Portrait*, Coward-McCann, 1983

Hastings, Max and Jenkins, Simon, *Battle for the Falklands*, Norton, 1983

Hayward, Steven, *The Age of Reagan: the Conservative Counterrevolution 1980–1989*, Crown Forum, 2009

Heath, Edward, *The Course of my Life*, Hodder & Stoughton, 1998

Heffer, Simon, *Like The Roman: The Life of Enoch Powell*, Weidenfeld and Nicolson, 1998

Henderson, Nicholas, *Mandarin: The Diaries of an Ambassador 1969–1982*, Weidenfeld & Nicolson, 1994

Hennessy, Peter, *Whitehall*, Secker & Warburg, 1989

Hennessy, Peter, *The Prime Minister*, Allen Lane, 2000

Heseltine, Michael, *Life in the Jungle: My Autobiography*, Hodder & Stoughton, 2000.

Hill, Richard, *Lewin of Greenwich*, Cassell, 2000

Horne, Alistair, *Macmillan*, vol. ii: *1957–1986*, Macmillan, 1989

Hoskyns, John, *Just in Time: Inside the Thatcher Revolution*, Aurum Press, 2000

Howe, Geoffrey, *Conflict of Loyalty*, Macmillan, 1994

Howell, David, *The Edge of Now*, Pan, 2000

Hurd, Douglas, *An End to Promises*, Collins, 1979

Hurd, Douglas, *Memoirs*, Abacus, 2003

Ingham, Bernard, *Kill the Messenger*, Fontana, 1991

Jenkins, Roy, *European Diary 1977–81*, Collins, 1989

Jenkins, Roy, *A Life at the Centre*, Macmillan, 1993

Kavanagh, Dennis and Seldon, Anthony, eds., *The Thatcher Effect: A Decade of Change*, Clarendon Press, 1989

Keegan, William, *Mrs Thatcher's Economic Experiment*, Viking, 1984

Keeble, Curtis, *Britain, the Soviet Union and Russia*, St Martin's Press, 2000

Kengor, Paul and Clark Doerner, Patricia, *The Judge: William P. Clark, Reagan's Top Hand*, Ignatius Press, 2007

Kissinger, Henry, *Years of Renewal*, Simon & Schuster, 1999

Kissinger, Henry, *Years of Upheaval*, Little, Brown, 1982

Kogan, Maurice, *The Politics of Education: Edward Boyle and Anthony Crosland in Conversation with Maurice Kogan*, Penguin, 1971

Kynaston, David, *Family Britain, 1951–1957* (in the series *Tales of a New Jerusalem*), Bloomsbury, 2009

Lawson, Nigel, *The View from No. 11*, Bantam, 1992

Lettow, Paul, *Ronald Reagan and his Quest to Abolish Nuclear Weapons*, Random House, 2005

Letwin, Shirley Robin, *The Anatomy of Thatcherism*, Fontana, 1992.

Lewis, Russell, *Margaret Thatcher: A Personal and Political Biography*, Routledge & Kegan Paul, 1975

Luce, Richard, *Ringing the Changes: A Memoir*, Michael Russell, 2007

Mann, James, *The Rebellion of Ronald Reagan: A History of the End of the Cold War*, Viking, 2009

Matlock, Jack, *Reagan and Gorbachev: How the Cold War Ended*, Random House, 2004

Meese, Edwin, *With Reagan: The Inside Story*, Regnery Gateway, 1992

Millar, Ronald, *A View from the Wings*, Weidenfeld & Nicolson, 1989

Morris, Edmund, *Dutch: A Memoir of Ronald Reagan*, Random House, 1999

Mount, Ferdinand, *Cold Cream*, Bloomsbury, 2008

Murray, Patricia, *Margaret Thatcher*, W. H. Allen, 1980

Nau, Henry, *The Myth of America's Decline: Leading the World Economy into the 1990s*, Oxford University Press, 1990

Nott, John, *Here Today, Gone Tomorrow*, Politico's, 2002

O'Malley, Padraig, *Biting at the Grave: The Irish Hunger Strike and the Politics of Despair*, Beacon Press, 1990

O'Rawe, Richard, *Blanketmen: An Untold Story of the H-Block Hunger Strike*, New Island Books, 2005

O'Rawe, Richard, *Afterlives: The Hunger Strike and the Secret Offer That Changed Irish History*, Liliput Press Ltd; reprint edition 2010

O'Sullivan, John, *The President, the Pope, and the Prime Minister: Three Who Changed the World*, Regnery Publishing, 2006

Parris, Matthew, *Chance Witness: An Outsider's Life in Politics*, Viking, 2002

Pepper, Gordon, *Inside Thatcher's Monetarist Revolution*, IEA, 1998

Pérez de Cuéllar, Javier, *Pilgrimage for Peace: A Secretary-General's Memoir*, St Martin's Press, 1997

Pipes, Richard, *Vixi: Memoirs of a Non-Belonger*, Yale University Press, 2003

Pravda, Alex and Duncan, Peter, eds, *Soviet–British Relations since the 1970s*, Cambridge University Press, 1990

Prior, James, *A Balance of Power*, Hamish Hamilton, 1986

Pym, Francis, *The Politics of Consent*, Hamish Hamilton, 1984

Reagan, Nancy, *My Turn: The Memoirs of Nancy Reagan*, Random House, 1989

Reagan, Ronald, *An American Life: The Autobiography*, Simon & Schuster, 1990

Reagan, Ronald, *The Reagan Diaries*, HarperCollins, 2007

Reagan, Ronald, *The Reagan Diaries Unabridged*, 2 vols, HarperCollins, 2009

Reed, Thomas C., *At the Abyss: An Insider's History of the Cold War*, Presidio Press, 2004

Richardson, Louise, *When Allies Differ: Anglo-American Relations during the Suez and Falklands Crises*, St Martin's Press, 1996

Roberts, Paul Craig, *The Supply-Side Revolution: An Insider's Account of Policy-making in Washington*, Harvard University Press, 1984

Saltoun-Ebin, Jason, ed., *The Reagan Files: The Untold Story of Reagan's Top-Secret Efforts to Win the Cold War*, CreateSpace, 2010

Sandbrook, Dominic, *Seasons in the Sun*, Allen Lane, 2012

Schweizer, Peter, *Reagan's War: The Epic Story of his Forty-Year Struggle and Final Triumph over Communism*, Doubleday, 2002

Seldon, Anthony and Collings, Daniel, *Britain under Thatcher*, Pearson Education, 2000

Shepherd, Gillian, *The Real Iron Lady: Working with Margaret Thatcher*, Biteback Publishing, 2013

Sherman, Alfred, *Paradoxes of Power*, Imprint Academic, 2005

Shultz, George, *Turmoil and Triumph: My Years as Secretary of State*, Charles Scribner's Sons, 1993

Simon, William, *A Time for Truth*, Reader's Digest Press, 1978

Skinner, Kiron K., Anderson, Annelise and Anderson, Martin, eds, *Reagan: A Life in Letters*, Free Press, 2003

Skinner, Kiron K., Anderson, Annelise and Anderson, Martin, eds, *Reagan, in his Own Hand: The Writings of Ronald Reagan that Reveal his Revolutionary Vision for America*, Touchstone, 2002

Skinner, Kiron K., Anderson, Annelise and Anderson, Martin, eds, *Reagan, in his Own Voice*, Simon & Schuster Audio, 2002

Smith, Geoffrey, *Reagan and Thatcher*, Bodley Head, 1990

Smith, Ian, *Bitter Harvest: The Great Betrayal and the Dreadful Aftermath*, Blake Publishing, 2001

Stein, Herbert, *Presidential Economics: The Making of Economic Policy from Roosevelt to Clinton*, 3rd rev. edn, AEI Press, 1994

Sunday Times Insight Team, *The Falklands War: The Full Story*, Sphere Books, 1982

Talbott, Strobe, *Deadly Gambits: The Reagan Administration and the Stalemate in Nuclear Arms Control*, Alfred A. Knopf, 1984

Taylor, Peter, *Brits: The War Against the IRA*, Bloomsbury Publishing PLC, new edition, 2002

Tebbit, Norman, *Upwardly Mobile*, Weidenfeld and Nicolson, 1988

Thatcher, Carol, *Below the Parapet: The Biography of Denis Thatcher*, Harper-Collins, 1996

Thatcher, Margaret, *The Downing Street Years*, HarperCollins, 1993

Thatcher, Margaret, *The Path to Power*, HarperCollins, 1995

Thatcher, Margaret, *Statecraft: Strategies for a Changing World*, HarperCollins, 2002

Thorpe, D. R., *Alec Douglas-Home*, Sinclair-Stevenson, 1996

Thorpe, D. R., *Supermac*, Chatto and Windus, 2010

Urban, George, *Diplomacy and Disillusion at the Court of Margaret Thatcher: An Insider's View*, I. B. Tauris, 1996

Urquhart, Brian, *A Life in Peace and War*, Weidenfeld & Nicolson, 1987

Vance, Cyrus, *Hard Choices: Critical Years in America's Foreign Policy*, Simon & Schuster, 1983

Verrier, Anthony, *The Road to Zimbabwe, 1890–1980*, Jonathan Cape, 1986

Walden, George, *Lucky George: Memoirs of an Anti-Politician*, Allen Lane, 1999

Wall, Stephen, *A Stranger in Europe*, Oxford University Press, 2008

Walters, Alan, *Britain's Economic Renaissance*, Oxford University Press, 1986

Walters, Dennis, *Not Always with the Pack*, Constable, 1989

Wapshott, Nicholas, *Ronald Reagan and Margaret Thatcher: A Political Marriage*, Penguin, 2007

Wapshott, Nicholas and Brock, George, *Thatcher*, Macdonald, 1983

Weinberger, Caspar, *Fighting for Peace: Seven Critical Years in the Pentagon*, Warner Books, 1990

Weinberger, Caspar, *In the Arena: A Memoir of the 20th Century*, Regnery Publishing, 2003

White, Brian, *Britain, Détente, and Changing East–West Relations*, Routledge, 1992

Woodward, Sandy, *One Hundred Days*, HarperCollins, 1992

Young, Hugo, *The Hugo Young Papers: Thirty Years of British Politics – Off the Record*, Allen Lane, 2008

Young, Hugo, *One of Us*, Macmillan, 1989

Young, Hugo and Sloman, Anne, *The Thatcher Phenomenon*, BBC Books, 1986

Young, Hugo, *This Blessed Plot*, Macmillan, 1998

Ziegler, Philip, *Edward Heath: The Authorised Biography*, Harper Press, 2010

UNPUBLISHED MANUSCRIPTS

Brzezinski, Zbigniew, private diary

Deedes, W. F., private diary

Fraser, Lady Antonia, private diary

Hoskyns, Sir John, private diary

Luce, Richard, private memoir

Neave, Airey, private diary

Rentschler, James, private diary

Rentschler, James, 'A Reason to Get Up in the Morning', self-published using Lulu, 2008

Renwick, Robin, untitled manuscript on Anglo-American relations

Stephens, Caroline, private papers

Thatcher, Margaret, private appointment diary

ARTICLES

Bailey, Matthew and Cowley, Philip, 'Choosing the Lady: Another Look at the Leadership Contest of 1975', *Conservative History Journal*, issue 1, Summer 2003

Blundell, John, 'Margaret Thatcher's Revolution: How it Happened and What it Meant', *Economic Affairs*, vol. 26, no. 1, 2006

Cooper, James, 'The Foreign Politics of Opposition: Margaret Thatcher and the Transatlantic Relationship before Power', *Contemporary British History*, vol. 24, no. 1, 2010

Evans, Stephen, 'The Not So Odd Couple: Margaret Thatcher and One Nation Conservatism', *Contemporary British History*, vol. 23, no. 1, 2009

Jefferys, Kevin, 'Britain and the Boycott of the 1980s Moscow Olympics', *Sport in History*, Vol. 32, No. 2, 2012

King, Anthony, 'The Outsider as Political Leader: The Case of Margaret Thatcher', *British Journal of Political Science*, vol. 32, no. 3, 2002

Lehman, John, 'The Falklands War: Reflections on the Special Relationship', *RUSI Journal*, Vol. 157, No. 6, 2012

Scott-Smith, Giles, '"Her Rather Ambitious Washington Program": Margaret Thatcher's International Visitor Program Visit to the United States in 1967', *British Contemporary History*, vol. 17, no. 4, Winter 2003

Index

ALLEN LANE

an imprint of

PENGUIN BOOKS

Recently Published

James Lovelock, *A Rough Ride to the Future*

Michael Lewis, *Flash Boys*

Hans Ulrich Obrist, *Ways of Curating*

Mai Jia, *Decoded: A Novel*

Richard Mabey, *Dreams of the Good Life: The Life of Flora Thompson and the Creation of* Lark Rise to Candleford

Danny Dorling, *All That is Solid: The Great Housing Disaster*

Leonard Susskind and Art Friedman, *Quantum Mechanics: The Theoretical Minimum*

Michio Kaku, *The Future of the Mind: The Scientific Quest to Understand, Enhance and Empower the Mind*

Nicholas Epley, *Mindwise: How we Understand what others Think, Believe, Feel and Want*

Geoff Dyer, *Contest of the Century: The New Era of Competition with China*

Yaron Matras, *I Met Lucky People: The Story of the Romani Gypsies*

Larry Siedentop, *Inventing the Individual: The Origins of Western Liberalism*

Dick Swaab, *We Are Our Brains: A Neurobiography of the Brain, from the Womb to Alzheimer's*

Max Tegmark, *Our Mathematical Universe: My Quest for the Ultimate Nature of Reality*

David Pilling, *Bending Adversity: Japan and the Art of Survival*

Hooman Majd, *The Ministry of Guidance Invites You to Not Stay: An American Family in Iran*

Roger Knight, *Britain Against Napoleon: The Organisation of Victory, 1793-1815*

Alan Greenspan, *The Map and the Territory: Risk, Human Nature and the Future of Forecasting*

Daniel Lieberman, *Story of the Human Body: Evolution, Health and Disease*

Malcolm Gladwell, *David and Goliath: Underdogs, Misfits and the Art of Battling Giants*

Paul Collier, *Exodus: Immigration and Multiculturalism in the 21st Century*

John Eliot Gardiner, *Music in the Castle of Heaven: Immigration and Multiculturalism in the 21st Century*

Catherine Merridale, *Red Fortress: The Secret Heart of Russia's History*

Ramachandra Guha, *Gandhi Before India*

Vic Gatrell, *The First Bohemians: Life and Art in London's Golden Age*

Richard Overy, *The Bombing War: Europe 1939-1945*

Charles Townshend, *The Republic: The Fight for Irish Independence, 1918-1923*

Eric Schlosser, *Command and Control*

Sudhir Venkatesh, *Floating City: Hustlers, Strivers, Dealers, Call Girls and Other Lives in Illicit New York*

Sendhil Mullainathan & Eldar Shafir, *Scarcity: Why Having Too Little Means So Much*

John Drury, *Music at Midnight: The Life and Poetry of George Herbert*

Philip Coggan, *The Last Vote: The Threats to Western Democracy*

Richard Barber, *Edward III and the Triumph of England*

Daniel M Davis, *The Compatibility Gene*

John Bradshaw, *Cat Sense: The Feline Enigma Revealed*

Roger Knight, *Britain Against Napoleon: The Organisation of Victory, 1793-1815*

Thurston Clarke, *JFK's Last Hundred Days: An Intimate Portrait of a Great President*

Jean Drèze and Amartya Sen, *An Uncertain Glory: India and its Contradictions*

Rana Mitter, *China's War with Japan, 1937-1945: The Struggle for Survival*

Tom Burns, *Our Necessary Shadow: The Nature and Meaning of Psychiatry*

Sylvain Tesson, *Consolations of the Forest: Alone in a Cabin in the Middle Taiga*

George Monbiot, *Feral: Searching for Enchantment on the Frontiers of Rewilding*

Ken Robinson and Lou Aronica, *Finding Your Element: How to Discover Your Talents and Passions and Transform Your Life*

David Stuckler and Sanjay Basu, *The Body Economic: Why Austerity Kills*

Suzanne Corkin, *Permanent Present Tense: The Man with No Memory, and What He Taught the World*

Daniel C. Dennett, *Intuition Pumps and Other Tools for Thinking*

Adrian Raine, *The Anatomy of Violence: The Biological Roots of Crime*

Eduardo Galeano, *Children of the Days: A Calendar of Human History*

Lee Smolin, *Time Reborn: From the Crisis of Physics to the Future of the Universe*

Michael Pollan, *Cooked: A Natural History of Transformation*

David Graeber, *The Democracy Project: A History, a Crisis, a Movement*

Brendan Simms, *Europe: The Struggle for Supremacy, 1453 to the Present*

Oliver Bullough, *The Last Man in Russia and the Struggle to Save a Dying Nation*

Diarmaid MacCulloch, *Silence: A Christian History*

Evgeny Morozov, *To Save Everything, Click Here: Technology, Solutionism, and the Urge to Fix Problems that Don't Exist*

David Cannadine, *The Undivided Past: History Beyond Our Differences*

Michael Axworthy, *Revolutionary Iran: A History of the Islamic Republic*

Jaron Lanier, *Who Owns the Future?*

John Gray, *The Silence of Animals: On Progress and Other Modern Myths*

Paul Kildea, *Benjamin Britten: A Life in the Twentieth Century*

Jared Diamond, *The World Until Yesterday: What Can We Learn from Traditional Societies?*

Nassim Nicholas Taleb, *Antifragile: How to Live in a World We Don't Understand*

Alan Ryan, *On Politics: A History of Political Thought from Herodotus to the Present*